Schroeder's Collectible
TOYS
Antique to Modern
Price Guide

Third Edition

Edited by Sharon and Bob Huxford

COLLECTOR BOOKS
A Division of Schroeder Publishing Co., Inc.

The current values in this book should be used only as a guide. They are not intended to set prices, which vary from one section of the country to another. Auction prices as well as dealer prices vary greatly and are affected by condition as well as demand. Neither the Editors nor the Publisher assumes responsibility for any losses that might be incurred as a result of consulting this guide.

Searching For A Publisher?

We are always looking for knowledgeable people considered to be experts within their fields. If you feel that there is a real need for a book on your collectible subject and have a large comprehensive collection, contact us.

On The Cover:
Star Wars plastic model kit, boxed, $25.00; Mechanical bank, Indian shooting (brown) bear, J & E Stevens, NM, $3,500.00; Battery operated locomotive, Marx, MIB, $60.00; Ken doll, straight leg, flocked hair, 1961, MIB, $250.00; Midge doll, straight leg, 1963, MIB, $225.00; Mickey Mouse baseball pillow, M, $250.00; Dukes of Hazzard lunchbox with thermos, 1980, NM, $20.00.

Editorial Staff:
Editors: Sharon and Bob Huxford
Research and Editorial Assistants: Michael Drollinger, Nancy Drollinger, Linda Holycross, Donna Newnum, Loretta Woodrow
Cover Design: Beth Summers
Layout: Terri Stalions, Beth Ray, Joyce Cherry

Introduction

It seems that every decade will have an area of concentrated excitement when it comes to the antiques and collectibles market place. What Depression Glass was to the late sixties, Fiesta to the seventies, and cookie jars were to the eighties, toys are to the nineties. No one even vaguely involved in the field could have missed all the excitement toys have stirred up among many, many collectors. There are huge toy shows nationwide; scores of newsletters, magazines, and trade papers that deal exclusively with toys; cataloged toy auctions with wonderful color photographs and several hundred lots each; and more and more toy collector's guides are appearing in the book stores each week.

If you've been using *Schroeder's Antiques Price Guide*, you know that we try very hard not to omit categories where we find even a minor amount of market activity — being collectors ourselves, we know how frustrating it can be when you are unable to find any information on an item in question. But that book is limited to a specific number of pages, and as we watched the toy market explosion taking place, we realized that if we were to do it justice, we would have to publish a companion guide devoted entirely to toys. And following the same convictions, we decided that rather than to try to zero in on only the larger, more active fields, we'd try to represent toys of all kinds, from the nineteenth century up to today. This is the format we chose to pursue.

Our concept is unique in the collectibles field. Though we designed the book first and foremost to be a price guide, we wanted to make it a buying/selling guide as well. So we took many of our descriptions and values from the 'toys for sale' lists of dealers and collectors around the country. In each of those listings we included a dealer's code, so that if you were looking for the particular model kit (or whatever) that (S5) had to offer, you'd be able to match his code with his name and address in the 'Dealer's Codes' section and simply drop him a line or call him to see if it were still available. Our experiment has been very successful. Feedback indicates that many of our sellers do very well, making productive contacts with collectors who not only purchase items from them on their initial call but leave requests for other merchandise they are looking for as well.

Each edition contains about 24,000 listings, but even at that we realize that when it comes to the toy market, that only begins to scratch the surface. Our intent is to provide our readers with fresh information, issue after issue. The few categories that are repeated in their entirety in succeeding editions generally are those that were already complete or as nearly complete as we or our advisors could make them. But even those are checked to make sure that values are still current and our information up to date.

When we initially began to plan our layout, we soon discovered that organizing toys is mind boggling. Collectors were quick to tell us that toys generally can't be sorted by manufacturer, as we were accustomed to doing in our other price guides. So we had to devise a sort that would not only be easy to use but one that our staff could work with. With this in mind, we kept our categories very broad and general. On the whole this worked very well, but we found that the character section was so large (4,000 lines) it was overwhelming to our advisors. So even though our original approach was probably the most user-friendly, we have broken the character collectibles down into several groups of collectibles and genres and created specific categories for them. But you'll find 'See Alsos' in bold, cross-references within the description lines, and a detailed index to help you locate the items you're looking for with ease.

What we want to stress is that our values are not meant to set prices. Some of them are prices realized at auction; you'll be able to recognize these by the 'A' at the end of the description line. The listings that have neither the 'A' code or the dealer code mentioned above were either sent to us for publication by very knowledgeable collectors who specialize in those specific types of toys or were originally dealer coded but altered at the suggestion of an advisor who felt that the stated price might be far enough outside the average market price range to be misleading (in which case, the dealer's code was removed). There are so many factors that bear on the market that for us to attempt to set prices is not only presumptuous, it's ludicrous. The foremost of these factors is the attitude of the individual collector — his personal view of the hobby. We've interviewed several by telephone; everyone has his own opinion. While some view auction prices as useless, others regard them as actual selling prices and prefer them to asking prices. And the dealer who needs to keep turning his merchandise over to be able to replenish and freshen his stock will of necessity sell at lower prices than a collector who will buy an item and wait for the most opportune time to turn it over for maximum profit. Where you buy affects prices as well. One of our advisors used this simple analogy: while a soda might cost you $2.50 at the ball park, you can buy the same thing for 39¢ at the corner Seven-11. So all we (or anyone) can offer is whatever facts and information we can compile, and ask simply that you arrive at your own evaluations based on the data we've provided, adapted to your personal buying/selling arena, desire to own, and need to sell.

We hope you enjoy our book and that you'll be able to learn by using it. We don't presume to present it as the last word on toys or their values — there are many specialized books by authors who are able to devote an entire publication to one subject, covering it from 'A' to 'Z,' and when we're aware that such a text book exists, we'll recommend it in our narratives. If you have suggestions that you think will improve our format, let us hear from you — we value your input. Until next time — happy hunting! May you find that mint-in-the box #1 Barbie or if you prefer that rare mechanical bank that has managed to so far elude you. But even if you never do, we hope that you'll find a generous measure of happiness and success, a treasure now and then, and new friends along the way.

The Editors

Advisory Board

The editors and staff take this opportunity to express our sincere gratitude and appreciation to each person who has contributed their time and knowledge to help us. We've found toys to be by far the largest, most involved field of collecting we've ever tried to analyze, but we will have to admit, it's great fun! We've been editing general price guides for fifteen years now, and before ever attempting the first one, we realized there was only one way we would presume to publish such a guide. And that would be to first enlist the help of knowledgeable collectors around the country who specialize in specific areas. We now have more than 120, and we're still looking for help in several areas. Generally, the advisors are listed following each category's narrative, so if we have mentioned no one and you feel that you are qualified to advise us, have the time and would be willing to help us out with that subject, please contact us. We'd love to have you on our advisory board. (We want to stress that even if an advisor is credited in a category narrative, that person is in no way responsible for errors. Errors are our responsibility.) Even if we currently list an advisor for your subject, contact us so that we'll have your name on file should that person need to be replaced. This of course happens from time to time due to changing interests or because they find they no longer have the time.

While some advisors sent us listings and prices, others provided background information and photographs, checked printouts or simply answered our questions. All are listed below. Each name is followed by their code, see the section called Dealer and Collector Codes for an explanation of how these are used in the listings.

Matt and Lisa Adams (A7)
Geneva Addy (A5)
Diane Albert (T6)
Sally and Stan Alekna (A1)
Jane Anderson (A2)
Pamela E. Apkarian-Russell (H9)
Bob Armstrong (A4)
Richard Belyski (B1)
Bill and Jeanne Bertoia
Larry Blodget (B2)
Bojo (B3)
Dick Borgerding (B4)
Bromer Booksellers, Inc. (B12)
Sue and Marty Bunis (B11)
Jim Buskirk (B6)
Danny Bynum (B7)

Bill Campbell (C10)
Candelaine (Candace Gunther) (G16)
Casey's Collectible Corner (C1)
Brad Cassidy (C13)
Mark Chase and Michael Kelly (C2)
Ken Clee (C3)
Arlan Coffman (C4)
Joel Cohen (C12)
Cotswold Collectibles (C6)
Marilyn Cooper (C9)
Cynthia's Country Store (C14)
Rosalind Cranor (C15)
Allen Day (D1)
Marl Davidson (D2)
Larry DeAngelo (D3)
Doug Dezso (D6)

Donna and Ron Donnelly (D7)
George Downes (D8)
Larry Doucet (D11)
Allan Edwards (E3)
Paul Fink (F3)
Steve Fisch (F7)
Mike and Kurt Fredericks (F4)
Fun House Toy Co. (F5)
Lee Garmon
Carol Karbowiak Gilbert (G6)
Mark Giles (G2)
Bill Hamburg (H1)
Don Hamm (H10)
George Hardy (H3)
Ellen and Jerry Harnish (H4)
Tim Hunter (H13)
Dan Iannotti (I3)
Roger Inouye (I1)
Kerry and Judy Irwin (K5)
Terri Ivers (I2)
Keith and Donna Kaonis (K6)
Ilene Kayne (K3)
David Kolodny-Nagy (K2)
Trina and Randy Kubeck (K1)
Tom Lastrapes (L4)
Kathy and Don Lewis (L6)
Val and Mark Macaluso (M1)
Helen L. McCale (M13)
John McKenna (M2)
Nancy McMichael (M18)
Michael and Polly McQuillen (M11)
Lucky Meisenheimer (M3)
Bill Mekalian (M4)
Steven Meltzer (M9)
Bruce Middleton (M20)
Gary Mosholder (G1)
Judith Mosholder (M7)
Peter Muldavin (M21)

Natural Way (N1)
Roger Nazeley (N4)
Dawn Parrish (P2)
Diane Patalano (P8)
Sheri and John Pavone (P3)
The Phoenix Toy Soldier Co. (P11)
Pat and Bill Poe (P10)
Gary Pollastro (P5)
Judy Posner (P6)
Lorraine Punchard (P13)
Hank Quant
John Rammacher (S5)
Jim Rash (R3)
Robert Reeves (R4)
Craig Reid (R9)
Charlie Reynolds (R5)
David E. Richter (R1)
David Riddle (R6)
Cindy Sabulis (S14)
Steve Santi (S8)
Jim and Nancy Schaut (S15)
Scott Smiles (S10)
Carole and Richard Smythe (S22)
Irwin Stern (S3)
Steve Stephenson (S25)
Bill Stillman (S6)
Nate Stoller (S7)
Mark and Lynda Suozzi (S24)
Jon Thurmond (T1)
Richard Trautwein (T3)
Marcie and Bob Tubbs (T5)
Judy and Art Turner (H8)
Marci Van Ausdall (V2)
Norm Vigue (V1)
Randy Welch (W4)
Dan Wells (W1)
Mary Young (Y2)
Henri Yunes (Y1)

How to Use This Book

Concept. Our design for this book is two-fold. Primarily it is a market report compiled from many sources, meant to be studied and digested by our readers, who can then better arrive at their own conclusion regarding prices. Were you to ask ten active toy dealers for their opinion as to the value of a specific toy, you would no doubt get ten different answers, and who's to say which is correct? Quite simply, there are too many variables to consider. Where you buy is critical. Condition is certainly subjective, prices vary from one area of the country to another, and probably the most important factor is how badly you want to add the item in question to your collection or at what price you're willing to sell. So use this as a guide along with your observations at toy shows, flea markets, toy auctions and elsewhere to arrive at an evaluation that satisfies you personally.

The second function of this book is to put buyers in touch with sellers who deal in the type of toys they want to purchase. We contact dealers all over the country, asking them to send us their 'for sale' lists and permission to use them as sources for some of our listings, which we code so as to identify the dealer from whose inventory list the price and description are taken. Even though by publication much of their merchandise will have been sold since we entered our data in early spring, many of them tell us that they often get similar or even the same items in over and over, so if you see something listed you're interested in buying, don't hesitate to call any of them. Remember, though, they're not tied down to the price quoted in the book, since their asking price is many times influenced by what they've had to pay to restock their shelves. Let us know how well this concept works for you.

Toys are listed by name. Every effort has been made to list a toy by the name as it appears on the original box. There have been very few exceptions made, and then only if the collector-given name is more recognizable. For instance, if we listed 'To-Night Amos 'n' Andy in Person' (as the name appears on the box lid), very few would recognize the toy as the Amos 'n' Andy Walkers. But these exceptions are few.

Descriptions and sizes may vary. When we were entering data, we often found the same toy had sold through more than one auction gallery or was listed in several dealer lists. So the same toy will often be described in various ways, but we left descriptions just as we found them, since there is usually something to be gleaned from each variation. We chose to leave duplicate lines in when various conditions were represented so that you could better understand the impact of condition on value. Depending on the source and who was doing the measuring, we found that the size of a given toy might vary by an inch or more. Not having the toy to measure ourselves, we had to leave dimensions just as they were given in auction catalogs or dealer lists.

Lines are coded as to source. Each line that represents an auction-realized price will be coded 'A' at the end, just before the price. Other letter/number codes identify the dealer who sent us that information. These codes are explained later on. Additional sources of like merchandise will be noted under the narratives. These are dealers whose lists arrived at our office too late to be included in the lines themselves.

As we said before, collectors have various viewpoints regarding auction results. You will have to decide for yourself. Some feel they're too high to be used to establish prices while others prefer them to 'asking' prices that can sometimes be speculative. We must have entered about 8,000 auction values, and here is what we found to be true: the really volatile area is in the realm of character collectibles from the '40s, '50s, and '60s — exactly where there is most interest, most collector activity, and hot competition when the bidding starts. But for the most part, auction prices were not far out of line with accepted values. Many times, compared to the general market place, toys in less-than-excellent condition actually sold under 'book.' Because the average auction-consigned toy is in especially good condition and many times even retains its original box, it will naturally bring higher prices than the norm. And auctions often offer the harder-to-find, more unusual items. Unless you take these factors into consideration, prices may seem high, when in reality, they may not be at all. Prices may be driven up by high reserves, but not all galleries have reserves. Whatever your view, you'll be able to recognize and consider the source of the values we quote and factor that into your personal evaluation.

Categories that have priority. Obviously there are thousands of toys that would work as well in one category as they would in another, depending on the preference of the collector. For instance, a Mary Poppins game would appeal to a games collector just as readily as it would to someone who bought character-related toys of all kinds. The same would be true of many other types of toys. We tried to make our decisions sensibly and keep our sorts simple. But to avoid sending our character advisors such huge printouts, we felt that it would be best to pull out specific items and genres to create specific categories, thereby reducing the size of the character category itself. We'll guide you to those specialized categories with cross-references and 'See Alsos.' If all else fails, refer to the index. It's as detailed as we know how to make it.

These categories have precedence over Character:

Action Figures
Battery-Operated Toys (also specific manufacturers)
Books
Bubble Bath Containers
Celebrity Dolls (see Dolls)
Character and Promotional Drinking Glasses
Character Clocks and Watches
Character Bobbin' Heads
Chein
Coloring, Activity and Paint Books
Corgi
Dakins
Disney
Fisher-Price
Games
Guns
Halloween Costumes
Lunch Boxes
Marx
Model Kits

Nodders
Paper Dolls
Pez Dispensers
Pin-Back Buttons
Plastic Figures
Playsets
Puppets
Puzzles
Radios
Records
Rock 'N Roll
Snow Domes
Sports Collectibles
Telephones
Trading Cards
Toothbrush Holders
View-Master
Western
Windups, Friction and Other Mechanicals

Price Ranges. Once in awhile, you'll find a listing that gives a price range. These result from our having found varying prices for the same item. We've taken a mid-range — less than the highest, a little over the lowest — if the original range was too wide to really be helpful. If the range is still coded 'A' for auction, all that were averaged were auction-realized prices.

Condition, how it affects value, how to judge it. The importance of condition can't be stressed enough. Unless a toy is exceptionally rare, it must be very good or better to really have much collector value. But here's where the problem comes in: though each step downward on the grading scale drastically decreases a toy's value, as the old saying goes, 'beauty is in the eye of the beholder.' What is acceptable wear and damage to one individual may be regarded by another as entirely too degrading. Criteria used to judge condition even varies from one auction company to the next, so we had to attempt to sort them all out and arrive at some sort of standardization. Please be sure to read and comprehend what the description is telling you about condition; otherwise you can easily be mislead. Auction galleries often describe missing parts, repairs and paint touch-ups, summing up overall appearance in the condition code. When losses and repairs were noted in the catalog, we noted them as well. Remember that a toy even in mint restored condition is never worth as much as one in mint original condition. And even though a toy may be rated 'otherwise EX' after losses and repairs are noted, it won't be worth as much as one with original paint and parts in excellent condition. Keep this in mind when you use our listings to evaluate your holdings.

These are the condition codes we have used throughout the book and their definitions as we have applied them:

M — mint. Unplayed with, brand new, flawless.
NM — near mint. Appears brand new except on very close inspection.
EX — excellent. Has minimal wear, very minor chips and rubs, a few light scratches.
VG — very good. Played with, loss of gloss, noticeable problems, several scratches.
G — good. Some rust, considerable wear and paint loss, well used.
P — poor. Generally unacceptable except for a filler.

Because we do not use a three-level pricing structure as many of you are used to and may prefer, we offer this table to help you arrive at values for toys in conditions other than those that we give you. If you know the value of a toy in excellent condition and would like to find an approximate value for it in near mint condition, for instance, just run your finger down the column under 'EX' until you find the approximate price we've listed (or one that easily factors into it), then over to the column headed 'NM.' We'll just go to $100.00, but other values will be easy to figure by addition or multiplication. Even though at auction a toy in very good to excellent condition sometimes brings only half as much as a mint condition toy, the collectors we interviewed told us that this was not true of the general market place. Our percentages are simply an average based on their suggestions.

G	VG	EX	NM	M
40/50%	55/65%	70/80%	85/90%	100%
5.00	6.00	7.50	9.00	10.00
7.50	9.00	11.00	12.50	15.00
10.00	12.00	15.00	18.00	20.00
12.00	15.00	18.00	22.00	25.00
14.00	18.00	22.50	26.00	30.00
18.00	25.00	30.00	35.00	40.00
22.50	30.00	37.50	45.00	50.00
27.00	35.00	45.00	52.00	60.00
32.00	42.00	52.00	62.00	70.00
34.00	45.00	55.00	65.00	75.00
35.00	48.00	60.00	70.00	80.00
40.00	55.00	68.00	80.00	90.00
45.00	60.00	75.00	90.00	100.00

Condition and value of original boxes and packaging. When no box or packaging is referred to in the line or in the narrative, assume that the quoted price is for the toy only. Please read the narratives! In some categories (Corgi, for instance), all values are given for items mint and in original boxes. Conditions for boxes (etc.) are in parentheses immediately following the condition code for the toy itself. In fact, any information within parenthesis at that point in the line will refer to packaging. Collector interest in boxes began several years ago, and today many people will pay very high prices for them, depending on scarcity, desirability and condition. The more colorful, graphically pleasing boxes are favored, and those with images of well-known characters are especially sought-after. Just how valuable is a box? Again, this is very subjective to the individual. We asked this question to several top collectors around the country, and the answers they gave us ranged from 20% to 100% above mint-no-box prices.

Advertising. You'll notice display ads throughout the book. We hope you will contact these advertisers if they deal in the type of merchandise you're looking for. If you'd like your ad to appear in our next edition, please refer to the advertising rate chart in the back of the book for information.

Listing of Standard Abbreviations

These abbreviations have been used throughout this book in order to provide you with the most detailed descriptions possible in the limited space available. No periods are used after initials or abbreviations. When two dimensions are given, height is noted first. When only one measurement is given, it will be the greater — height if the toy is vertical, length if it is horizontal. (Remember that in the case of duplicate listings representing various conditions, we found that sizes often varied as much as an inch or more.)

Am	American	MIP	mint in package
att	attributed to	mk	marked
bl	blue	MOC	mint on card
blk	black	MOT	mint on tree
brn	brown	NM	near mint
bsk	bisque	NP	nickel plated
c	copyright	NRFB	never removed from box
ca	circa	NRFP	never removed from package
cb	cardboard	orig	original
CI	cast iron	o/w	otherwise
compo	composition	P	poor
dbl	double	Pat	patented
dia	diameter	pc	piece
dk	dark	pg, pgs	page, pages
dtd	dated	pk	pink
ea	each	pkg	package
emb	embossed	pnt	paint, painted
EX	excellent	pr	pair
F	fine	prof	professional
fr	frame, framed	rfn	refinished
ft, ftd	feet, foot, footed	rnd	round
G	good	rpl	replaced
gr	green	rpr	repaired
hdl	handle, handled	rpt	repainted
hdw	hardware	rstr	restored
illus	illustrated, illustration	sq	square
inscr	inscribed	sz	size
jtd	jointed	turq	turquoise
L	long, length	unmk	unmarked
litho	lithographed	VG	very good
lt	light, lightly	W	width, wingspan
M	mint	wht	white
MBP	mint in bubble pack	w/	with
mc	multicolored	w/up	windup
MIB	mint in box	yel	yellow

Action Figures

Back in 1964, Barbie dolls had taken the feminine side of the toy market by storm. Hasbro took a risky step in an attempt to target the male side. Their answer to the Barbie craze was GI Joe. Since no self-respecting boy would admit to playing with dolls, Hasbro called their boy dolls 'action figures,' and to the surprise of many, they were phenomenally successful. Both Barbie and GI Joe were realistically modeled (at least GI Joe was) posable 12" vinyl dolls that their makers clothed and accessorized to the hilt. Their unprecedented successes spawned a giant industry with scores of manufacturers issuing one 'action figure' after another, many in series. Other sizes were eventually made in addition to the 12" dolls. Some are 8" to 9", others 6", and many are the 3¾" figures that have been favored in recent years.

This is one of the fastest-growing areas of toy collecting today. Manufacturers of action figures are now targeting the collector market as well as the kids themselves, simply because the adult market is so active. You will find a wide range of asking prices from dealer to dealer; most of our listings are coded and represent only a sampling. Naturally, *where* you buy will also affect values. Be critical of condition! Original packaging is extremely important. In fact, when it comes to the recent issues, loose, played-with examples are seldom worth more than a few dollars. Remember, if no box is mentioned, values are for loose (unpackaged) dolls. When no size is given, assume figures are 3¾" or standard size for the line in question.

For more information we recommend *Collectible Action Figures* by Paris and Susan Manos, *Collector's Guide to Dolls in Uniform* by Joseph Bourgeois, and *Mego Toys* by Wallace M. Crouch (all published by Collector Books).

Advisors: George Downs (D8); Robert Reeves (R3), Best of the West.

Other Sources: B3, F1, I2, J2, J7, M15, M17, O1, P3, S17, T1, T2

See also Barbie Dolls; Character Collectibles; Dolls, Celebrity; GI Joe; Star Trek; Star Wars.

Action Jackson, figure, Action Jackson, Mego, 8", M (NM box), C1...$32.00
Action Jackson, outfit, Western #1108, Mego, NMIB, H4.$8.00
Advanced Dungeons & Dragons, figure, BowMarc, Grimsword or Morthlord, LJN, NM, D8, ea $25.00
Advanced Dungeons & Dragons, figure, Elkhorn, Kelek, Mericon, Strongheart, Warduke or Zarak, LJN, NM, D8, ea $18.00
Advanced Dungeons & Dragons, figure, Stalwart Men-At-Arms, LJN, MOC, D8 ....$25.00
Adventures of Indiana Jones, accessory, Map Room Playset, Kenner, NRFB (minor wear), H4............................$35.00
Adventures of Indiana Jones, accessory, Streets of Cairo Adventure Set, Kenner, MIB, J6...$65.00
Adventures of Indiana Jones, figure, Belloq in Ceremonial Robe or Cairo Swordsman, Kenner, complete, NM, H4, ea .$7.00
Adventures of Indiana Jones, figure, Cairo Swordsman, Kenner, MOC, H4...$15.00

Adventures of Indiana Jones, figure, German Mechanic, Kenner, MOC, H4...$24.00

Adventures of Indiana Jones, figure, Indiana Jones, Kenner, 3¾", MOC, $125.00.

Adventures of Indiana Jones, figure, Toht, Kenner, MOC, H4 ....$14.00
Adventures of Indiana Jones, horse, Arabian, Kenner, MOC, J6...$95.00
Aliens, figure, Colossus Rex, Colorforms, complete, EX, H4.$190.00
Aliens, figure, Commander Comet, Colorforms, complete, VG, H4 ....$160.00

Aliens, figure set, Space Marine Atax with Alien, Kenner, MOC, $12.00.

American West, figure, Cochise, Mego, 8", M (NM+ box), B3 ....$55.00

American West, figure, Wild Bill Hickok, Mego, 8", M (NM+ box), B3 ....$55.00

Archies, figure set, Marx, 9", M (EX/NM cards), H4, 4 for .$160.00

Batman, accessory, Batmobile, Toy Biz, NRFB, H4..........$50.00

Batman, accessory, Batmobile, Toy Biz, 8", remote control, D4 ....$20.00

Batman, accessory, Batwing, Toy Biz, NRFB, H4 ....$45.00

Batman, figure, Batman, Kid Biz (Australia), MOC, H4..$60.00

Batman, figure, Batman, Magnetic; Mego, 12", M, from $100 to $125.00

Photo courtesy of Mike's General Store.

Best of the West, dogs, Flick and Flack, Marx, NMIB, from $85.00 to $90.00 each.

Best of the West, figure, Captain Maddox, Marx, missing 3 pcs o/w EX, H4....................................$50.00

Best of the West, figure, Captain Maddox, Marx #1865, missing 2 pcs o/w complete, M (EX+ Fort Apache box dtd 1967), F5 ....$130.00

Best of the West, figure, Chief Cherokee, Marx, missing 3 pcs o/w EX (NM box), H4.......................$70.00

Best of the West, figure, Chief Cherokee, Marx #2063, w/accessories & instructions, M (NM box dtd 1967), F5 ....$160.00

Best of the West, figure, Daniel Boone, Marx #2060, complete, NM+ (EX box), F5 ....$270.00

Best of the West, figure, Fighting Eagle, Marx, 1st issue, w/accessories, NM+, F5 ....$140.00

Best of the West, figure, Fighting Eagle, Marx #1864, complete w/instructions, NM+ (VG+ Best of the West box), F5.$190.00

Best of the West, figure, General Custer, Marx, missing 3 pcs o/w EX, H4/O1 ....$40.00

Best of the West, figure, General Custer, Marx #1866, complete w/instructions, NM+ (EX+ Fort Apache box dtd 1970), F5 ....$150.00

Batman, figure, Man-Bat, Kenner, MOC, $22.00.

Batman, see also World's Greatest Super Heroes

Battlestar Galactica, figure, Commander Adams, Mattel, no weapon o/w EX, H4 ....$10.00

Battlestar Galactica, figure, Cylon Centurian, Mattel, 12", cloth jacket, EX, H4..........................$24.00

Battlestar Galactica, figure, Cylon Warrior, Mattel, silver, w/weapon, EX, H4 ....$14.00

Battlestar Galactica, figure, Daggit, Mattel, EX, H4.........$15.00

Battlestar Galactica, figure, Imperious Leader, Mattel, M (EX unpunched card), H5................................$15.00

Best of the West, accessory, Circle X Ranch, Marx, MIB, V1 ....$175.00

Best of the West, accessory, Jeep & Horsetrailer, Marx, MIB, V1 ....$145.00

Best of the West, accessory, Johnny West Travel Case, Marx, to carry figures & accessories, VG+, H4..........$22.00

Best of the West, buffalo, Marx, pnt plastic, NM, F5 ....$95.00

Best of the West, figure, Bill Buck, M (NM Fort Apache box), minimum value..............................$300.00

Best of the West, figure, Jane West, Marx, NMIB, $70.00.

Best of the West, figure, Geronimo, Marx, missing 2 pcs o/w EX (EX Best of the West box), H4..................................$75.00

Best of the West, figure, Geronimo, Marx, rare orange body, w/accessories, NM (NM Johnny West Adventure box), F5..$100.00

Best of the West, figure, Geronimo, Marx #1863, w/37 accessories in orig bag & instructions, NM (NM box dtd 1970), F5 ....$130.00

Best of the West, figure, Jaimie West, Marx, MIB............$75.00

Best of the West, figure, Jaimie West, Marx, missing tether o/w EX, H4 ....$34.00

Best of the West, figure, Janice West, Marx, complete, EX, H4...$38.00

Best of the West, figure, Janice West, Marx #1067-A, w/13 accessories, NM (EX+ box dtd 1967), F5...................$75.00

Best of the West, figure, Jay West, Marx, MIB $75.00

Best of the West, figure, Jay West, Marx, missing tether o/w EX, H4 ....$34.00

Best of the West, figure, Jed Gibson, Marx, M, $125.00.

Best of the West, figure, Jed Gibson, Marx, M (NM box).$325.00

Best of the West, figure, Johnny West, Marx, missing pistol o/w NM, H4...$65.00

Best of the West, figure, Johnny West, Marx, NMIB, from $110 to...$125.00

Best of the West, figure, Josie West, Marx, blond hair, 5 (of 13) accessories, NM+, F5..................................$30.00

Best of the West, figure, Josie West, Marx, MIB..............$75.00

Best of the West, figure, Princess Wildflower, Marx, w/13 (of 23) accessories, NM, F5.................................$85.00

Best of the West, figure, Princess Wildflower, Marx #2097, missing 2 accessories o/w complete, NM (VG+ box), F5 ....$140.00

Best of the West, figure, Sam Cobra, Marx, w/2 accessory pcs, EX+, F5...$30.00

Best of the West, figure, Sheriff Garrett, Marx, royal bl plastic, VG+, F5 ....$20.00

Best of the West, figure, Sheriff Garrett, Marx, steel bl plastic, w/4 (of 26) accessory pcs, NM, F5.....................$60.00

Best of the West, figure, Zeb Zachary, M (M Fort Apache box), minimum value..$150.00

Best of the West, figure set, Geronimo & Pinto, Marx, complete, in box, B3 ....$130.00

Best of the West, figure set, Sheriff Garrett w/Thunderbolt, M (M illus box)..$125.00

Best of the West, horse, Buckskin, Marx, complete, VG, H4 .$50.00

Best of the West, horse, Comanche, Marx, complete, EX (NM+ Fort Apache Fighter's box), H4 ....$125.00

Best of the West, horse, Comanche, Marx, dk brn w/brn tack, 15 accessory pcs, EX+, F5.....................................$45.00

Best of the West, horse, Flame, Marx, w/saddle, blanket & strap & bridle, missing bit & reins o/w EX, H4 ....$35.00

Best of the West, horse, Pancho, Marx, bay w/blk tack, 8 accessory pcs, NM, F5...$35.00

Best of the West, horse, Pancho, Marx, palomino, EX+, F5.$18.50

Best of the West, horse, Storm Cloud, Marx, w/blanket & strap, missing hackamore o/w EX, H4.................................$40.00

Best of the West, horse, Thunderbolt, Marx, cream colored, complete, VG, H4 ....$35.00

Best of the West, horse, Thunderbolt, Marx, rare blk version w/saddle, blanket, strap, bit & bridle, EX, H4............$45.00

Big Jim, accessory, Corvette, Mattel, Secret Agent Series, remote control, NRFB, H4 ....$70.00

Big Jim, figure, Dr Alec, Mattel, MIB, $90.00.

Big Jim, accessory, Gyrocopter, Mattel, Secret Agent Series, NRFB, H4 ....$14.00

Big Jim, accessory, talking backpack, Mattel, working, EX, H4 ....$5.00

Big Jim, figure, Capt Laser, Mattel, Space Series, European, NRFB, H4 ....$80.00

Big Jim, figure, Josh, Mattel, nude o/w VG, H4 ....$18.00

Big Jim, figure, Vector, Mattel, Team Command & Team Condor Force, European, NRFB, H4 ....$40.00

Big Jim, figure, Zorak the Enemy, Mattel, Big Jim's PACK, EX, H4 ....$22.00

Big Jim, outfit, Skin Diving #8855, Mattel, Action Adventure Series, MOC, H4 ....$10.00

Black Hole, figure, Booth, Durant, Holland, McCrae or Reinhardt, Mego, MOC, D8, ea..................$18.00

Black Hole, figure, Capt Holland, Charles Pizer, Dr Alex Durant or Dr Hans Reinhardt, Mego, 12½", MIB, H12, ea $38.00

Black Hole, figure, Dr Kate McCray, Mego, 12½", M (EX+ box), B3 ....$58.00

Black Hole, figure, Harry Booth, Mego, 12½", unused, M (poor box), D9 ....$15.00

Black Hole, figure, Sentry Robot, Mego, M (EX+ card), B3 .$48.00

Bonanza, coyote, Am Character, EX $15.00

Bonanza, figure, Ben Cartwright, Am Character, 8", w/horse & accessories, NM, C1 ....$180.00

Bonanza, figure set, Hoss w/horse, Am Character, 8", deluxe set, MIB (stables in background), H4 ....$200.00

Bonanza, horse, Am Character, brn, no accessories, H4...$12.00

Bonanza, mountain lion, Am Character, EX, H4 ....$15.00

Buck Rogers in the 25th Century, accessory, Laserscope Fighter, (for sm figures), Mego, M (EX+ box), B3..................$45.00

Buck Rogers in the 25th Century, figure, Ardella, Draco, Killer Kane or Tigerman, Mego, MOC, D8, ea..................$28.00

Buck Rogers in the 25th Century, figure, Buck, Twiki, Wilma or Vincent, Mego, NM, D8, ea..................$25.00

Buck Rogers in the 25th Century, figure, Buck Rogers, Mego, 12", MIB, from $35 to..................$50.00

Buck Rogers in the 25th Century, figure, Dr Huer, Mego, 12", M (EX+ box), B3..................$65.00

Buck Rogers in the 25th Century, figure, Draco, Draconian Guard, Kane or Tigerman, Mego, NM, D8, ea $15.00

Buck Rogers in the 25th Century, figure, Draco, Mego, 12", M (EX+ box), B3..................$60.00

Buck Rogers in the 25th Century, figure, Draconian Guard, Mego, 12", M (EX box), B3..................$60.00

Buck Rogers in the 25th Century, figure, Killer Kane, Mego, 12", MIB, from $40 to..................$55.00

Buck Rogers in the 25th Century, figure, Tiger Man, Mego, 12", M (EX+ box), B3..................$60.00

Buck Rogers in the 25th Century, figure, Walking Twiki, Mego, 7½", M (EX box), B3..................$50.00

Captain Action, accessory, Batman, boots, Ideal, NM, H4 .$10.00

Captain Action, accessory, Buck Rogers, gloves, Ideal, EX, H4..................$25.00

Captain Action, accessory, Captain Action, jet pack helmet w/strap, Ideal, EX, H4..................$10.00

Captain Action, accessory, Flash Gordon, belt w/holster, Ideal, EX, H4..................$10.00

Captain Action, accessory, Green Hornet, gas mask, NM, H4..................$75.00

Captain Action, accessory, jet mortar, Ideal, NM, M5...$115.00

Captain Action, accessory, Phantom, rifle, Ideal, EX, H4 ....$15.00

Captain Action, accessory, Sgt Fury, mask w/beard, Ideal, NM, H4..................$15.00

Captain Action, accessory, Spider-Man, belt, Ideal, NM, H4 .....$40.00

Captain Action, accessory, Steve Canyon, helmet w/oxygen mask, Ideal, NM, H4..................$20.00

Captain Action, accessory, Superman, Kryptonite, Ideal, NM, H4..................$14.00

Captain Action, accessory, Survival Vest, Ideal, complete, NM, M5..................$135.00

Captain Action, accessory, Tonto, shirt, Ideal, NM, H4..$25.00

Captain Action, accessory, Weapons Arsenal, Ideal, NM, M5..................$170.00

Captain Action, figure, Action Boy, Ideal, w/accessories, EX, H4..................$325.00

Captain Action, figure, Dr Evil, Ideal, orig shirt & pants, VG, H4..................$190.00

Captain Action, outfit, Aquaman, Ideal, w/accessories, EX, H4..................$95.00

Captain Action, outfit, Captain America, Ideal, w/accessories, EX, H4..................$120.00

Captain Action, outfit, Captain America, jumpsuit w/emblem, Ideal, VG, H4..................$15.00

Captain Action, outfit, Phantom, Ideal, complete, EX, H4 .$130.00

Captain Action, outfit, Superman, Ideal, complete, on orig mannequin, EX, H4..................$130.00

Captain Action, outfit, Superman, Ideal, on orig mannequin, missing 2 accessories o/w EX, H4..................$100.00

CHiPs, figure, Jimmy Squeaks, Ponch or Wheels Willy, Mego, 3¾", M (VG card), B3, ea..................$10.00

CHiPs, figure, Jon, Mego, 8", MOC, from $30 to $35.00

CHiPs, figure, Ponch, Mego, 8", MOC $25.00

Photo courtesy of Mego Toys, Wallace Crouch.

Buck Rogers in the 25th Century, figures, Drako and Killer Kane, Mego, MOC, $28.00 each.

CHiPs, figure, Sarge, Mego, 8", MOC, C1 ....$40.00

Clash of the Titans, figure, Charon, Mattel, NM, D8 ......$25.00

Clash of the Titans, figure, Kraken, Mattel, EX, J6 ....$95.00

Clash of the Titans, figure, Thallo, Mattel, complete w/accessories & orig backing cards, H4 ....$20.00

Combat Man, accessory, carrying case for 12" figure, Jeep pictures, clear windows, EX, H4 ....$9.00

Comic Action Heroes, figure, Batman, Hulk or Spider-Man, Mego, no accessories o/w EX, ea...................................$15.00

Crash Dummies, figure, Larry or Vince, MOC, D8, ea $12.00

Dark Knight, figure, Bruce Wayne, Kenner, 1990, MOC.$14.00

Dark Knight, figure, Iron-Winch Batman or Shadow-Wing Batman, Kenner, MOC, D4, ea $14.00

DC Comics Super Heroes, figure, Aquaman, Toy Biz, gr arm variation, MOC, D4 ....$20.00

DC Comics Super Heroes, figure, Flash, Toy Biz, turbo platform, MOC, D4 ....$10.00

DC Comics Super Heroes, figure, Green Lantern, Toy Biz, MOC, D4 ....$25.00

Defender, figure, Defender, Hasbro, 12", M (EX card), H4 .....$70.00

Dick Tracy, figure, Al 'Big Boy' Caprice, Dick, Itchy, Lips Manlis, Pruneface or Sam Catchem, Playmates, MOC, D8, ea.....$12.00

Dukes of Hazzard, figure, Bo or Luke, Mego, 3¾", MOC, C1, ea, from $18 to...$25.00

Dukes of Hazzard, figure, Bo or Luke, Mego, 8", MOC, ea, from $22 to...$30.00

Dukes of Hazzard, figure, Boss Hogg, Mego, 8", M (EX+ card), from $15 to...$25.00

Dukes of Hazzard, figure, Daisy, Mego, gr shirt, 3¾", MOC, C1...$24.00

Dukes of Hazzard, figure, Daisy, Mego, 8", MOC, from $35 to......$45.00

Dune, accessory, Dune Spice Scout, LJN, plastic, MIB, P4.$25.00

Dune, accessory, Fremen Tarpel Gun, LJN, M (EX box), B3.....$40.00

Dune, accessory, Sand Scout, LJN, NM (VG card), D9 ...$15.00

Dune, figure, Baron Harkonnen, Feyd, Rubban or Sardaukan Warrior, LJN, no accessories o/w EX, H4, ea $8.00

Dune, figure, Feyd (Sting), LJN, complete, EX.................$14.00

ET, figure, ET, LJN, M (VG card)......................................$12.00

Evel Knievel, accessory, Scramble Van, Ideal, VG (VG box)...$25.00

Flash Gordon, accessory, Ming's Space Shuttle, Mattel, EX (VG box), H4...$30.00

Flash Gordon, figure, Dr Zarkov, Mego, 9", M (EX+ box), B3...$80.00

Flash Gordon, figure, Flash Gordon or Ming, Mattel, MOC, H4, ea...$25.00

Flash Gordon, figure, Ming the Merciless, Mego, 9", M (EX box), B3...$60.00

Flash Gordon, figure set, Flash, Dr Zarkov & Thun, Mattel, M (illus mailer box), H4, set of 3 ....$40.00

Flash Gordon, figure set, Mattel, EX, H4, set of 8............$80.00

Freddy Kruger, see Maxx Fx

Grizzly Adams, figure, Grizzly Adams, Mattel, 9", NRFB (minor wear), H4...$45.00

Grizzly Adams, figure, Nakoma, Mattel, 9", M (EX box w/no insert), H4...$35.00

Happy Days, accessory, diecut restaurant, figures, '57 Chevy & motorcycle, MIB (sealed), M15.................................$35.00

Happy Days, figure, Fonzie, Mego, 8", MIB, M15 ....$50.00

Happy Days, figure, Potsie, Mego, 8", MOC, J6...............$60.00

Happy Days, figure, Ralph, Mego, 8", MOC, J6...............$45.00

Happy Days, figure, Richie, Mego, 8", NMOC (unpunched), H4, ea...$50.00

Hardy Boys, figure, Joe Hardy, Kenner, 12", NMIB, C1 ...$65.00

Honey West, accessories: lipstick whistle, handcuff bracelet, etc, for 12" doll, Gilbert, MOC (sealed), B3....................$30.00

Honey West, accessory, wardrobe, Gilbert, unused, MIB, J2.$85.00

Hook, figure, Peter Pan, Swashbuckling or Air Attack, Mattel, MOC, ea...$12.00

How the West Was Won, figure, Lone Wolf, Mattel, M (VG box w/no insert), H4...$45.00

How the West Was Won, figure, Zeb Macahan, Mattel, 9", MIB, H4/H12...$45.00

James Bond, accessory, scuba outfit, Gilbert, for 12" figure, MIB...$135.00

James Bond, figure, Domino, Gilbert, 3½", M (EX card).....$12.00

James Bond, figure, Gilbert, set of 10 movie characters, unused, NMIB, J2...$160.00

James Bond, figure, Goldfinger, Gilbert, NMOC, C1.......$15.00

James Bond, figure, James Bond, Gilbert, 3½", NMOC ...$25.00

James Bond, figure, Largo, Gilbert, 3½", NMOC $18.00

James Bond, figure, Moneypenny, Gilbert, 3½", NMOC $15.00

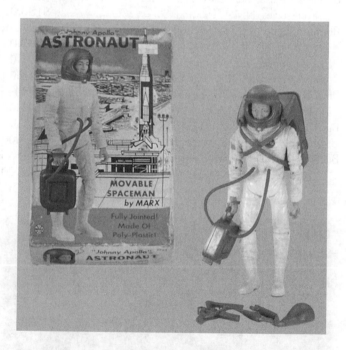

Johnny Apollo, figure, Johnny Apollo Astronaut, Marx, missing some accessories, NM (G box), $75.00.

Johnny Apollo, figure, Johnny Apollo Astronaut, Marx #1724, complete accessories in sealed pkg, NM+ (EX box) $100.00

Karate Commandos, figure, Chuck Norris, 8-pc set, MOC, H12...$45.00

Legend of the Lone Ranger, accessory, Western Town, Gabriel, mail order, for 1980s line of smaller figures, MIB, H4 ....$40.00

Legends of the Lone Ranger, Tonto, Gabriel, 3¾", M (NM card), B3...$15.00

Lone Ranger Rides Again, accessory, Apache Buffalo Hunt, Gabriel, VG, H4................$12.00

Lone Ranger Rides Again, accessory, Blizzard Adventure, Gabriel, NRFB (window cracked), H4................$35.00

Lone Ranger Rides Again, accessory, Hidden Rattler Adventure, Gabriel, NRFB, H4................$35.00

Lone Ranger Rides Again, accessory, Hidden Silver Mine, Gabriel, NRFB, H4................$40.00

Lone Ranger Rides Again, accessory, Landslide Adventure, Gabriel, NRFB, H4................$35.00

Lone Ranger Rides Again, accessory, 4-in-1 Prairie Wagon, Gabriel, EX (EX box), H4................$35.00

Lone Ranger Rides Again, figure, Butch Cavendish or Little Bear, Gabriel, 9", NRFB, H4, ea................$50.00

Lone Ranger Rides Again, figure, Lone Ranger or Tonto, Gabriel, 9", VG+, H4, ea................$18.00

Lone Ranger Rides Again, horse, Scout, Gabriel, M (EX box), B3................$40.00

Lone Ranger Rides Again, horse, Smoke, Gabriel, M (VG+ box), H4................$35.00

Love Boat, figures, Mego, M (NM cards), H4, complete series of 6 for................$110.00

M*A*S*H, accessory, jeep, Tri-Star International, w/figure, NM (EX box), C1................$36.00

M*A*S*H, figure, Hawkeye, Klinger, Makcahy or Winchester, Tri-Star International, sm, MOC, D8, ea................$18.00

Mad Monsters, figure, Dracula, Mego, 8", complete, EX, H4.....$60.00

Mad Monsters, figure, Frankenstein or Wolfman, Mego, 8", comlete, EX, H4, ea................$35.00

Mad Monsters, figure, Mummy, Mego, 8", MIB, H4.........$55.00

Major Matt Mason, accessory, Cat Trak, Mattel, red or wht, EX, H4, ea................$10.00

Major Matt Mason, accessory, communicator, Mattel, EX, H4................$6.00

Major Matt Mason, accessory, decontamination rifle w/tanks, Mattel, EX, H4................$10.00

Major Matt Mason, accessory, Firebolt Space Cannon, Mattel, complete w/paperwork, EX (EX box), H4................$70.00

Major Matt Mason, accessory, Gamma Ray Guard Gun, Mattel, EX, H4................$20.00

Major Matt Mason, accessory, Gamma Ray Guard Pack, Mattel, MIB, D8................$95.00

Major Matt Mason, accessory, Jet Pack, Mattel, EX, H4..$12.00

Major Matt Mason, accessory, knife, movie camera, wrench, binoculars, hammer, etc, Mattel, EX, H4, ea, from $5 to..........$8.00

Major Matt Mason, accessory, laser rifle, Mattel, EX, H4....$10.00

Major Matt Mason, accessory, Recono Jet Pack, Mattel, complete, EX, H4................$25.00

Major Matt Mason, accessory, Rocket Launch Pack, Mattel, complete, EX, H4................$22.00

Major Matt Mason, accessory, Satellite Launch Pack, Mattel, complete, EX, H4................$25.00

Major Matt Mason, accessory, Space Crawler, Mattel, VG (EX box), H4................$50.00

Major Matt Mason, accessory, Space Glider, Mattel, complete, VG, H4................$60.00

Major Matt Mason, accessory, Space Power Suit, Mattel, EX, H4................$24.00

Major Matt Mason, accessory, Space Probe Pack, Mattel, complete, EX, H4................$22.00

Major Matt Mason, accessory, Space Seeker, Mattel, w/instructions & cb planets, working, EX, H4................$45.00

Major Matt Mason, accessory, Space Shelter Pack, Mattel, complete, EX, H4................$25.00

Major Matt Mason, accessory, Space Shelter Pack, MIB, D8.$95.00

Major Matt Mason, accessory, Space Sled, Mattel, EX, H4 ...$15.00

Major Matt Mason, accessory, Space Station, Mattel, EX (VG box), H4................$125.00

Major Matt Mason, accessory, Space Travel Pack, Mattel, MIB, D8................$95.00

Major Matt Mason, accessory, Supernaut Power Limbs Pack, Mattel, MIB, D8................$95.00

Major Matt Mason, accessory, Supernaut Power Limbs Pack, Mattel, EX, H4................$24.00

Major Matt Mason, accessory, Talking Command Console, Mattel, mute o/w VG, H4................$70.00

Major Matt Mason, accessory, Uni-Tred Space Hauler, Mattel, w/instructions, EX+ (EX+ box), H4................$50.00

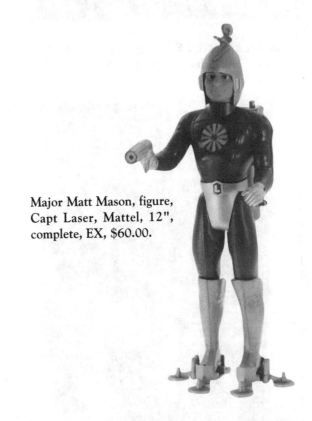

Major Matt Mason, figure, Capt Laser, Mattel, 12", complete, EX, $60.00.

Major Matt Mason, figure, Doug Davis, Mattel, w/helmet, EX, H4................$60.00

Major Matt Mason, figure, Matt Mason, Mattel, EX, H4.$45.00

Major Matt Mason, figure, Sgt Storm, Mattel, VG, D8....$28.00

Major Matt Mason, figure, Sgt Storm, Mattel, w/helmet, minor pnt touch-up, EX, H4................$55.00

Mario Bros, figure, Boomba, Koopa or Luigi, MOC, D8, ea....$12.00

Marvel Super Heroes Secret Wars, accessory, Secret Message Decoder, Mattel, MOC, H4................$5.00

Marvel Super Heroes Secret Wars, accessory, Tower of Doom Playset, Mattel, M (EX+ sealed box), D9................$36.00

Man From UNCLE, accessory, Cap-Firing Tommy Gun, Gilbert, MIP, $65.00.

Photo courtesy of June Moon.

Man From UNCLE, figure, Illya Kuryakin, Gilbert, 12", M (EX box), J6, $185.00.

Marvel Super Heroes Secret Wars, figure, Baron Zemo, Mattel, w/shield, no flasher o/w VG, H4 ....$12.00

Marvel Super Heroes Secret Wars, figure, Dr Octopus, Kang or Magneto, Mattel, MOC, D4, ea $15.00

Marvel Super Heroes Secret Wars, figure, Baron Zemo, Mattel, MOC, $25.00.

Marvel Super Heroes Secret Wars, figure, Wolverine, Mattel, MOC, H4 ....$50.00

Masters of the Universe, accessory, Castle GreySkull, Dragon Walker or Munstroid, Mattel, NM, D8, ea $25.00

Masters of the Universe, figure, Skeletor (battle armor), Stratus or Terror Claw Skeletor, Mattel, MOC, D8, ea $12.00

Maxx FX, figure, Freddy Kruger, Matchbox, NRFB, H4 ...$40.00

Micronauts, accessory, Rocket Tubes, Mego, MIB, D8 .....$95.00

Micronauts, figure, Giant Acroyear, Mego, MIB, D8 ....$45.00

Mike Hazard, accessory, trench coat, Marx, complete w/belt, NM+, F5 ....$12.50

Mike Hazard, figure, Mike Hazard Double Agent, Marx #2090, lacks 6 pcs o/w complete, orig instructions, NM+ (EX box), F5 ....$300.00

Mini Monsters, accessory, playcase, M (sealed, cellophane torn), H4 ....$18.00

Moonraker, figure, Drax, Mego, 12", NMIB, B3 ....$130.00

Moonraker, figure, Holly, Mego, 12", M (EX+ box), B3 ....$135.00

Moonraker, figure, James Bond, Mego, 12", M (NM+ box), B3 ....$90.00

Mork & Mindy, figure, Mork or Mindy, Mattel, 9", MIB, ea, from $25 to..$35.00

Muhammad Ali, figure, Opponent, Mego, 9", M (EX card), H4 ....$50.00

Noble Knights, figure, Eric the Viking, Marx, no accessories o/w EX, H4 ....$30.00

Noble Knights, figure, Sir Gordon the Gold Knight, Marx, full armor, 40 (of 45 accessories) o/w NM+, F5 ....$135.00

Noble Knights, figure, Sir Gordon the Gold Knight, Marx #5366, w/accessories, NM (EX+ box dtd 1968), F5 ....$180.00

Noble Knights, figure, Sir Stuart the Silver Knight, Marx, w/most accessories & most armor, G, H4 ....$50.00

Noble Knights, figure, Sir Stuart the Silver Knight, Marx #5364, accessories & instructions, MIB, from $220 to $270.00

Noble Knights, horse, Bravo the Gold-Armored Horse, Marx, complete, NM+ w/G wheels, F5.................................$70.00

Noble Knights, horse, Bravo the Gold-Armored Horse, Marx #5371, complete w/accessories, NM+ (VG+ box), F5/H4 ....$110.00

Noble Knights, horse, Valor, Marx, never used, MIB, H4 .....$135.00

Noble Knights, horse, Valor, Marx #5361, complete w/accessories, NM+ (VG box), F5 ....$110.00

Official Scout High Adventure, accessory, Avalanche at Blizzard Ridge, Kenner, EX, H4 ....$18.00

Official Scout High Adventure, accessory, Balloon Race to Devil's Canyon, Kenner, M (EX box), H4.................$22.00

Official Scout High Adventure, accessory, Danger at Snake River Set, EX, H4 ....$12.00

Official Scout High Adventure, accessory, Lost in the High Country, Kenner, EX, H4 ....$12.00

Official Scout High Adventure, accessory, Pathfinder Jeep & Trailer Adventure Set, Kenner, EX (VG box), H4 ...$30.00

Official Scout High Adventure, accessory, Search for the Spanish Galleon Set, Kenner, complete, EX, H4 ....$18.00

Official Scout High Adventure, figure, Craig Cub Scout, Kenner, NRFB (EX box), H4..$30.00

Official Scout High Adventure, figure, Steve Scout, Kenner, complete, EX, H4...$20.00

Official Scout High Adventure, figure, Steve Scout, Kenner, NRFB, H4..$30.00

Official World's Greatest Super Heroes, accessory, Batmobile, Mego, for 8" figures, M (NM box), H4.....................$95.00

Official World's Greatest Super Heroes, accessory, Captain America Car, Mego, for 8" figure, EX (VG box), H4 .$80.00

Official World's Greatest Super Heroes, figure, Batman, Mego, 8", MIB, $175.00.

Official World's Greatest Super Heroes, accessory, Mobile Bat Lab Van, Mego, for 8" figures, complete, EX, H4 ......$70.00

Official World's Greatest Super Heroes, accessory, Spider-Car, Mego, for 8" figures, VG (EX box), H4 ....$70.00

Official World's Greatest Super Heroes, accessory, Spider-Man Super Vader Super Action Flyby, Mego, for 8" figure, EX, H4 ....$40.00

Official World's Greatest Super Heroes, figure, Aqualad, Mego, 8", complete, EX, H4..$140.00

Official World's Greatest Super Heroes, figure, Aquaman, Mego, 8", complete, EX, from $42 to $49.00

Official World's Greatest Super Heroes, figure, Batgirl, Mego, 8", no purse o/w complete & EX, H4...............................$110.00

Official World's Greatest Super Heroes, figure, Batman, Mego, 12", MIB, D4...$75.00

Official World's Greatest Super Heroes, figure, Batman, Mego, 8", removable cowl, no gloves or emblem o/w VG, H4 ..$100.00

Official World's Greatest Super Heroes, figure, Bruce Wayne, Mego, 8", secret identity, nude, EX $65.00

Official World's Greatest Super Heroes, figure, Capt America, Mego, 8", M (VG box), H4.....................................$40.00

Official World's Greatest Super Heroes, figure, Catwoman, Mego, 8", no gloves o/w M, D8 ....$85.00

Official World's Greatest Super Heroes, figure, Conan, Mego, 8", M, complete, from $150 to $160.00

Official World's Greatest Super Heroes, figure, Conan, Mego, 8", M (EX+ box)..$250.00

Official World's Greatest Super Heroes, figure, Falcon, Mego, 8", EX (EX box)...$115.00

Official World's Greatest Super Heroes, figure, Falcon, Mego, 8", complete, EX, H4..$40.00

Official World's Greatest Super Heroes, figure, Green Arrow, 8", no accessories o/w G, D8 ....$25.00

Official World's Greatest Super Heroes, figure, Green Arrow, Mego, 8", NM (EX box) $175.00

Official World's Greatest Super Heroes, figure, Green Goblin, Mego, 8", M, complete, from $115 to $125.00

Official World's Greatest Super Heroes, figure, Hulk, Mego, 8", M, complete, from $25 to $35.00

Official World's Greatest Super Heroes, figure, Hulk, Mego, 8", M (EX- box w/no insert), H4 ....$50.00

Official World's Greatest Super Heroes, figure, Human Torch, Mego, 8", M, complete, D8..............................$30.00

Official World's Greatest Super Heroes, figure, Human Torch, Mego, 8", MOC, D8 ....$50.00

Official World's Greatest Super Heroes, figure, Human Torch, 8", NMIB, D8 ....$150.00

Official World's Greatest Super Heroes, figure, Invisible Girl, Mego, 8", VG+ (VG box), H4 ....$80.00

Official World's Greatest Super Heroes, figure, Ironman, Mego, 8", M (EX box), H4 ....$79.00

Official World's Greatest Super Heroes, figure, Joker, Mego, 8", M, complete, D8 ....$55.00

Official World's Greatest Super Heroes, figure, Joker, Mego, 8", MIB, H4...$175.00

Official World's Greatest Super Heroes, figure, La Torche Humaine (Human Torch), made for French trade, MIB, H12 ....$40.00

Official World's Greatest Super Heroes, figure, Mr Mxyzptlk, Mego, 8", EX, from $30 to $38.00

Official World's Greatest Super Heroes, figure, Mr Mxyzptlk, Mego, 8", smirk face, M (EX Kresge card), H4 ....$100.00

Official World's Greatest Super Heroes, figure, Penguin, Mego, 8", EX (EX box), D8/H4, from $70 to $85.00

Official World's Greatest Super Heroes, figure, Penguin, Mego, 8", M (EX card), H4 ....$60.00

Official World's Greatest Super Heroes, figure, Riddler, Fist-Fighting; Mego, 8", M, complete, D8 ....$150.00

Official World's Greatest Super Heroes, figure, Riddler, Mego, 8", NM, complete, D8...$95.00

Official World's Greatest Super Heroes, figure, Spider-Man, Mego, 8", MOC $35.00

Official World's Greatest Super Heroes, figure, Supergirl, Mego, 8", no emblem o/w EX, H4.......................................$140.00

Official World's Greatest Super Heroes, figure, Superman, Mego, 8", VG (VG- box), D8 ....$125.00

Official World's Greatest Super Heroes, figure, Tarzan, Mego, 8", M (NM box), H4......................................$70.00

Official World's Greatest Super Heroes, figure, Tarzan, Mego, 8", complete, EX, H4 ....$35.00

Official World's Greatest Super Heroes, figure, Thor, Mego, 8", M (NM box)...$240.00

Official World's Greatest Super Heroes, figure, Thor, Mego, 8", complete, EX, H4 ....$110.00

Photo courtesy of June Moon.

Official World's Greatest Super Heroes, figure, Robin, Mego, 8", M (French card), J6, $75.00.

Photo courtesy of June Moon.

Official World's Greatest Super Heroes, figure, Wonder Woman, Mego, 8", NM, J6, $125.00.

Official World's Greatest Super Heroes, figure, Robin, Fist-Fighting; Mego, 8", M, complete, D8.....................$125.00

Official World's Greatest Super Heroes, figure, Robin, Mego, 8", EX (EX- box), D8...$125.00

Official World's Greatest Super Heroes, figure, Shazam, Mego, 8", EX (EX- box), D8...$120.00

Official World's Greatest Super Heroes, figure, Speedy, Mego, 8", missing bow o/w complete & EX, H4 ....$140.00

Official World's Greatest Super Heroes, figure, Spider-Man, Mego, 8", EX (VG+ box), D8.................................$75.00

Official World's Greatest Super Heroes, figure, Spider-Man, Mego, 12", M, complete, D8.................................$35.00

Official World's Greatest Super Heroes, figure, Spider-Man, Mego, 12", NRFB, H4...$80.00

Official World's Greatest Super Heroes, figure, Wonder Woman, Mego, 8", MIB, H4...$225.00

Official World's Greatest Super Heroes, figure, Wonder Woman, Mego, 8", early, pnt-on boots, complete, EX, H4 ......$65.00

One Million BC, figure, Grok, Orm or Trag, Mego, 8", MOC, H4, ea...$40.00

Our Gang, figure, Mickey, Mego, 6", M (EX card), J5......$65.00

Pee-Wee's Playhouse, accessory, Magic Screen, Matchbox, w/up, MOC, B10..$7.00

Pee-Wee's Playhouse, figure, Pee-Wee, Matchbox, MOC, D8..$15.00

Pee-Wee's Playhouse, figure, Reba or Ricardo, Matchbox, 6", posable, MOC, H4, ea...$20.00

Planet of the Apes, accessory, Battering Ram, M (VG box), H4 ....$35.00

Planet of the Apes, accessory, Village, Mego, unused, M (EX box), D9 ....$50.00

Planet of the Apes, figure, Alan Verdon, Mego, 8", MOC .$85.00

Planet of the Apes, figure, Cornelius or Zira, Mego, 8", complete, EX, H4, ea...$30.00

Planet of the Apes, figure, Galen, Mego, 8", MOC $80.00

Planet of the Apes, figure, Gen Urko, Mego, 8", M (NM unpunched card), H4...$95.00

Planet of the Apes, figure, Gen Ursus or Soldier Ape, Mego, 8", complete, EX, H4, ea.................................$55.00

Planet of the Apes, figure, Peter Burke, Mego, 8", complete, EX, H4 ....$40.00

Planet of the Apes, figure, Soldier Ape, Mego, 8", rare all-brn version w/gloves, EX, H4...............................$70.00

Police Woman, accessory, Sabotage Under the Sea, Horsman, MOC, J6, $24.00.

Real Ghostbusters, figure, Ecto-Plasm, Nasty Neck, Terrible Teeth or Terror Tongue, Kenner, MOC, ea $18.00

Real Ghostbusters, figure, Stay Puft Man, Kenner, MOC, D8 ....$28.00

Robin Hood, Prince of Thieves, figure, Friar Tuck, Kenner, MOC, D8 ....$15.00

RoboCop & the Ultra Police, figure, Anne Lewis, Kenner, MOC, D8 ....$12.00

RoboCop & the Ultra Police, figure, Chainsaw, Dr McNamara, Headhunter or Nitro, Kenner, MOC, D8, ea $9.00

Robotech, accessory, Mac II Destroid Cannon, diecast, Harmony Gold, MOC, D4...$25.00

Robotech, figure, Dana Sterling, Lisa Hayes or Lynn Minmei, Matchbox, 12", MIP, D4, ea.....................................$25.00

Robotech, figure, Dana Sterling or Scott Bernard, Harmony Gold, MOC, D4, ea $10.00

Robotech, figure, Lunk, Matchbox, hard to find, MOC, D4 .$20.00

Robotech, figure, Lynn Minmei, Harmony Gold, MOC, D4 ....$30.00

Robotech, figure, Rand, Robotech Master, Roy Fokker, Zentraedi Warrior or Zor Prime, Matchbox, MOC, D8, ea.........$10.00

Robotech, figure, Rook Bartley, Harmony Gold, MOC, D4.$20.00

Robotech, figure, Rook Bartley, Matchbox, MOC, D8 ....$25.00

Rocky, figure, Apollo Creed, Phoenix Toys, 8", MOC, H4.$40.00

Rocky, figure, Clubber Lang, Phoenix Toys, 8", MOC, H4.$40.00

Rookies, accessory, City Patrol Set, MOC, J6..................$18.00

Rookies, accessory, Official Police Car, Fleetwood, 1975, MOC, C1 ....$36.00

Shogun Warriors, figure, Damios, Dragun, Gaiking, Great Mazinga or Raydeen, Mattel, 23½", EX, J6, ea ....:$75.00

Shogun Warriors, figure, Godzilla, Mattel, lg, firing hands, flashing tongue, EX, J6 ....$85.00

Planet of the Apes, horse, Stallion, Mego, M, J6, $85.00.

Pocket Super Heroes, figure, Batman, Mego, MOC $40.00

Pocket Super Heroes, figure, Hulk, Mego, EX, H4 ....$20.00

Pocket Super Heroes, figure, Lex Luther, Mego, EX, H4 ....$8.00

Police Academy, figure, Larvelle Jones or Zed, Kenner, MOC, D8, ea...$12.00

Power Rangers, figure, Billy (Blue Ranger), Zach (Black Ranger) or Jason (Red Ranger), Bandai, MOC, H4, ea, from $13 to...$19.00

Power Rangers, figure, Kimberly (Pink Ranger) or Trini (Yellow Ranger), Bandai, 1st issue, MOC (triangular), H4, ea........$35.00

Pulsar, accessory, Pulsar Life Systems Center, Mattel, EX (EX box), H4...$22.00

Pulsar, figure, Pulsar, Mattel, 13", NMIB, H4 ....$30.00

Rambo, figure, Rambo, Coleco, w/accessories, 7", MOC, C1 .$20.00

Rat Patrol, figure, Sgt Sam Troy, Marx, 1967, 7½", w/4 accessory pcs, EX+, F5 ....$98.00

Six Million Dollar Man, accessory, Transport & Repair Station, Kenner, MIB, M15..........................$20.00

Space: 1999, figure, Commander Koenig, Mattel, 9", M (VG+ card), B3...$50.00

Space: 1999, figure, Dr Russel, Mattel, 9", M (EX card), H4 .$45.00

Space: 1999, figure, Professor Bergman, Mattel, 9", NM (VG+ ard), B3 ....$45.00

Spawn, accessory, Violator Monster Rig, Todd Toys, MIB, J6.$32.00

Spawn, figure, Badrock, Todd Toys, MOC, D8 ....$12.00

Spawn, figure, Clown, MOC, D8 ....$18.00

Spawn, figure, Overkill, MOC............................$12.00

Starsky & Hutch, figure, Chopper, Mego, 8", M (EX card), B3 ....$35.00

Starsky & Hutch, figure, Huggy Bear, Mego, 8", MOC, $45.00.

Starsky & Hutch, figure, Hutch or Starsky, Mego, 8", M (NM card), B3, ea................................$27.00

Steve Canyon, accessory, Glider Bomb Truck, Ideal, plastic & metal w/decals, 17", missing glider bomb o/w NM, C1.$82.00

Steve Scout, see Official Scout High Adventure

Stony Smith, accessory, weapon, Marx, 16-pc set, MIP, F5..$30.00

Stony Smith, figure set, Paratrooper, Marx, missing 4 pcs o/w VG (VG box), H4................................$100.00

Super Powers, accessory, carrying case for figures, NM.....$25.00

Super Powers, accessory, Darkseid Destroyer, Kenner, MIB, from $35 to..$45.00

Super Powers, accessory, Delta Probe 1, Kenner, MIB, from $20 to..$30.00

Super Powers, accessory, Hall of Justice, Kenner, MIB.....$90.00

Super Powers, accessory, Supermobile, Kenner, M (VG box) .$15.00

Super Powers, figure, Batman, Kenner, complete, NM.....$35.00

Super Powers, figure, Batman, Kenner, M (NM unpunched card), H4..$55.00

Super Powers, figure, Brainiac, Kenner, no ID o/w complete & NM, H4...$10.00

Super Powers, figure, Clark Kent, Kenner, mail-in, no ID or comic o/w complete, NM, H4 ....$55.00

Super Powers, figure, Cyclotron, Kenner, M (EX card), H4 .$50.00

Super Powers, figure, Darkseid, Kenner, M (VG card), H4/D4..$14.00

Super Powers, figure, Darkseid or Lex Luther, complete, NM, H4, ea..$10.00

Super Powers, figure, Fire Storm or Mantis, Kenner, complete, NM, H4, ea..$18.00

Super Powers, figure, Flash, Kenner, M (Kenner bag), D4..$5.00

Super Powers, figure, Flash or Kalibak, Kenner, MOC, H4, ea..$10.00

Super Powers, figure, Golden Pharaoh, Kenner, complete, NM, H4 ....$50.00

Super Powers, figure, Green Arrow, Kenner, complete, NM, H4 ....$35.00

Super Powers, figure, Hawkman, Kenner, complete, NM, H4 .....$40.00

Super Powers, figure, Joker, Kenner, complete, NM.........$20.00

Super Powers, figure, Mr Freeze, MOC (unpunched), H4.....$80.00

Super Powers, figure, Mr Miracle, Kenner, no cape or ID o/w complete, NM..$22.00

Super Powers, figure, Orion, Kenner, MOC...............$28.00

Super Powers, figure, Penguin or Robin, Kenner, complete, NM, ea..$18.00

Super Powers, figure, Plastic Man, Kenner, M (NM card), H4 ....$130.00

Teenage Mutant Ninja Turtles, figure, April O'Neil, no stripe, Playmates, MOC, $175.00.

Super Powers, figure, Robin, Kenner, MOC (unpunched), H4.............................$55.00

Super Powers, figure, Samurai, Kenner, M (NM card), H4 ..$90.00

Super Powers, figure, Steppenwolf, Kenner, complete, NM, H4.............................$30.00

Super Powers, figure, Superman, Kenner, complete, NM, H4.............................$20.00

Super Powers, figure, Tyr, Kenner, MOC, H4 ....$60.00

Super Powers, figure, Wonder Woman, Kenner, M (NM card), H4.............................$30.00

Super Powers, figure, Wonder Woman, Kenner, M (sm card), D4.............................$15.00

Teenage Mutant Ninja Turtles, figure, April O'Neil, Playmates, bl stripe, MOC, D9.............................$15.00

Terminator II, figure, Blaster T1000, Damage Repair, Power Arm, Secret Weapon or Techno Punch, Kenner, MOC, D8, ea.............................$15.00

Terminator II, figure, China, jtd vinyl, NRFB (w/Arnold on cycle), H4.............................$50.00

Terminator II, figure, John Conner, Kenner, MOC, D8...$20.00

Terminator II, figure, Terminator, posable vinyl, limited video offer w/release of 1st movie, 11", EX, H4 ....$20.00

Thundercats, accessory, Luna-Lasher, LJN, MIB, H4 ....$18.00

Thundercats, accessory, Mutant Skycutter, LJN, M (NM box), H4.............................$22.00

Thundercats, figure, Berbil Bell or Berbil Bert, LJN, M (EX+ card), H4, ea.............................$35.00

Thundercats, figure, Capt Cracker, Safari Joe or Snowman of Hook Mountian, LJN, M (EX+ card), H4, ea............$25.00

Thundercats, figure, Capt Shiner, Jackalman or Tusca Warrior, LJN, MOC, D8, ea.............................$25.00

Thundercats, figure, Cheetara & Willykat, LJN, NMOC $45.00

Thundercats, figure, Hachiman, Jackalman or Monkian, LJN, M (EX+ card), H4, ea.............................$22.00

Thundercats, figure, Lion-O, LJN, MOC, D8 ....$35.00

Thundercats, figure, Mumm-Ra, MOC, D8 ....$25.00

Thundercats Miniatures, figure, Grime, Hutchiman, Lion, Monkian, Ratar-O or Tuska, LJN, 2½", MOC, H4, ea...$8.00

Ultraman, figure, Utraman, Dreamworks, 8", w/3" secret identity figure, MIB, J6.............................$24.00

Universal Monsters, figure, Creature From the Black Lagoon, Remco, MOC, D8.............................$25.00

Universal Monsters, figure, Dracula, Remco, NM, D8 .....$12.00

Universal Monsters, figure, Frankenstein, Dracula or Phantom, Remco, MOC, D8, ea.............................$18.00

Viking Warriors, figure, Brave Erik, Marx #5430, w/accessories, NM (G box), F5.............................$165.00

Viking Warriors, figure, Erik the Viking & horse, Marx #5434, w/8 accessories, NM (EX+ mailer), F5 ....$195.00

Waltons, figure, any, Mego, 8", complete & EX, H4 ....$18.00

Waltons, figure set, Mamma & Daddy, John Boy & Mary Ellen, or Grandma & Grandpa, NM (VG+ box), H4, ea pr .$45.00

Warlords & Warrior Beasts, figure, Remco, set of 12, MIB, H12.............................$125.00

Welcome Back Kotter, figure, Horshack, Mattel, 8", M (VG+ card), C1.............................$32.00

Welcome Back Kotter, figure, Mr Kotter, Mattel, 9½", M (VG resealed card), B3.............................$36.00

Who Framed Roger Rabbit, figure, Baby Herman, LJN, MOC, J6.............................$16.00

Who Framed Roger Rabbit, figure, Eddie Valiant or Judge Doom, LJN, MOC, J6, ea.............................$8.00

Who Framed Roger Rabbit, figure, Jessica, LJN, MOC, J6.$22.00

Wizard of Oz, accessory, Munchkinland Playset, Mego, complete, VG, H4.............................$150.00

Wizard of Oz, figure, Cowardly Lion, Mego, 8", M, D8 ....$25.00

Wizard of Oz, figure, Dorothy w/Toto, Mego, 8", MIB, from $22 to.............................$28.00

Wizard of Oz, figure, Flying Monkey, Multi-Toy, MOC, H4.$30.00

Wizard of Oz, figure, Scarecrow, Mego, 8", MIB, $65.00.

Wizard of Oz, figure, Scarecrow, Mego, 8", M, D8............$25.00

Wizard of Oz, figure, Tin Woodsman, Mego, 8", MIB, H12 .$35.00

Wizard of Oz, figure, Wicked Witch, Mego, 8", MIB, rare, H12/H4.............................$65.00

Wizard of Oz, figure, Wizard, Mego, 8", M (brn mailer box) .$14.00

Wizard of Oz, figure, Wizard, Multi-Toy, 12", MIB, H4 ...$30.00

Wonder Woman, figure, Steve Trevor, Mego, 12", MIB (cellophane cracked), H4.............................$70.00

World's Greatest Super Knights, figure, King Arthur or Sir Lancelot, Mego, 8", 1 pc missing o/w EX, H4, ea.......$45.00

WWF, World Wrestling Federation, figure, Bret Hitman Hart #2 (Series 5), Hasbro, M.............................$18.00

WWF, World Wrestling Federation, figure, British Bulldog (Series 3), Hasbro, MOC.............................$35.00

WWF, World Wrestling Federation, figure, Crush (Series 4), Hasbro, MOC.............................$25.00

WWF, World Wrestling Federation, figure, El Matador (Series 4), Hasbro, MOC.............................$10.00

WWF, World Wrestling Federation, figure, Elizabeth, LJN, MOC.............................$50.00

WWF, World Wrestling Federation, figure, Hulk Hogan (Series 1), Hasbro, MOC...$45.00

WWF, World Wrestling Federation, figure, Randy Savage (Series 1), orange, MOC $40.00

WWF, World Wrestling Federation, figure, Ricky the Dragon, LJN, MOC...$45.00

WWF, World Wrestling Federation, figure, Roddy Piper, LJN, MOC...$40.00

WWF, World Wrestling Federation, figure, Skinner, Hasbro, M $10.00

WWF, World Wrestling Federation, figure, Texas Tornado (Series 2), Hasbro, MOC.................................$25.00

WWF, World Wrestling Federation, figure, Ultimate Warrior (Series 2), Hasbro, M.................................$15.00

WWF, World Wrestling Federation, figure, 1-2-3 Kid, MOC .$75.00

WWF, World Wrestling Federation, figures, Nasty Boys (Tag Team), Hasbro, MOC $45.00

WWF, World Wrestling Federation, figures, The Rockers (Tag Team), Hasbro, M $20.00

Zeroid, accessory, Action Set, Ideal, w/rockets, launching pad & figure, EX (EX box), H4 ....$150.00

Zeroid, accessory, Robot Zogg Commander Set, Ideal, complete, EX, H4 ....$90.00

Zeroid, figure, Robot from Star Raiders, Ideal, M, H4 ......$45.00

Zeroid, figure, Zerak Robot, Ideal, EX, H4 ....$50.00

Zeroid, figure, Zintar Robot, Ideal, gray, EX, H4 ....$65.00

Zorro, figure, Amigo, Capt Ramon, Sgt Gonzales, Zorro, horse (Tempest or Picaro), MOC, H4, ea.................$20.00

90210, figure, Brandon, Brenda, Donna or Dylan, Mattel, 11½", NRFB, M15, ea.................................$30.00

Activity Sets

Activity sets that were once enjoyed by so many as children — the Silly Putty, the Creepy Crawlers, and those Mr. Potato Heads — are finding their way back to some of those same kids, now grown up, more or less, and especially the earlier editions are carrying pretty respectable price tags when they can be found complete or reasonably so. The first Thingmaker/Creepy Crawler (Mattel, 1964) in excellent but played-with condition will sell for about $65.00 to $75.00. For more information about Tinker Toys see *Collector's Guide to Tinker Toys* by Craig Strange.

Advisor: Jon Thurmond (T1).

See also Character, TV and Movie Collectibles; Coloring, Activity and Paint Books; Disney; Playsets; Western.

Boy's World Thingmaker, Mattel, EX+ (EX box), T1....$150.00

Casting Set, Rapco, 1969, EX (orig box), T1....................$25.00

Chemistry Set, 1930s, 14 vials w/orig contents, test tubes & droppers, 15-pc set w/papers, M (3-tiered wood box) $150.00

Come Into Miss Cookie's Kitchen, Colorforms, 1962, appears complete, NM (EX+ box), T2.................................$20.00

Conjurer Trick Set, Germany, ca 1875, complete w/wood & paper magic props, w/instruction sheet, 6x7", EX (EX box), A.................................$1,100.00

Creeple Peeple Thingmaker, Mattel, 1965, w/heater, NMIB .$65.00

Creeple Peeple Thingmaker Pak, VG+, T1 ....$45.00

Creepy Crawlers Thingmaker, Mattel, 1964, EX (EX box), from $65 to $75.00

Creepy Crawlers Thingmaker Molds, Mattel, 1964, set of 8, EX, F8.................................$15.00

Creepy Crawlers Thingmaker Pak #2, Mattel, 1965, missing 4 bottles of goop, EX+, T2.................................$50.00

DC Comics Super Hero Plaster Molding Set, complete, orig box, B10.................................$20.00

Eeeeks! Thingmaker Play-Pak, Mattel, 1968, unused, NMIB.$85.00

Electronic Transmitter Set, Science Electronics, 1956, NM (EX+ box), T2.................................$20.00

Etch-A-Sketch Magic Screen, Ohio Art, EX (NM+ box), F5.$20.00

Farm Animals Play-Doh Forge Press, Rainbow Crafts, 1962, EX+ (EX box), D9.................................$25.00

Fighting Men Mold Set, Ideal, NMIB, T1 ....$60.00

Fist Faces, Remco, 1966, MIB, J6, $14.00.

Fright Factory, Mattel, 1966, w/molds, cooling tray, safety hdl & accessories, EX (EX box) $60.00

Fright Factory Thingmaker Pak, Mattel, VG+, T1 ....$50.00

Frosty the Sno-Cone Machine, Hasbro, ca 1974, snowman-shaped ice shaver, missing flavor pkgs, EX (VG+ box), from $30 to $35.00

Fun Flowers Thingmaker Play-Pak, Mattel, 1966, 7 molds, 4 goop bottles (nearly empty) & instructions, EX (EX box) ...$30.00

Great Foodini Magic Set, Pressman, EX (EX box), J2 ......$85.00

Johnny Toymaker, Topper Toys, makes vehicles, EX (EX box), from $40 to.................................$55.00

Julius Sumner Miller's Physics Toy Set, Atomic Laboratories, 1962, NMIB, P4.................................$225.00

Junior Police Kit, 1930s, w/metal badge, whistle & wood nightstick, MIB, H12 ....$65.00

Little Miss Hasbro Brownie Mix, w/recipe book & pans, MIP, T1.................................$35.00

Little Miss Hasbro Soup Mix, w/recipe book & bowls, MIP, T1 ....$35.00

Magic Kit, Transogram, 1968, NMIB, J2 ....$50.00

Make Your Own Funnies, Jaymar, 1930s, wood construction set with Popeye, Moon Mullins, Annie, etc, EX (VG box), A, $545.00.

Master Caster, casting race car set, G (orig box), T1 ....$35.00

Microscope Set, Aristo Craft, 1950s, complete, MIB, H12 .$45.00

Mini-Dragons Thingmaker Pak, Mattel, 1965, w/heater, missing 4 bottles of goop o/w appears complete, VG+, from $60 to $65.00

Mr. Potato Head and His Tooty Frooty Friends, Hasbro, 1950s, NMIB, J6, $65.00.

Motorized Monster Maker Double Set, Topper, complete, EX (orig box), T1 ....$135.00

Motorized Monster Maker Set, Topper, 1960s, few pcs missing, EX+ (EX+ box)..$50.00

Mr & Mrs Potato Head & Pets, Hasbro, MIB $55.00

Mr Potato Head Frenchy Fry Set, very rare, few pcs missing, VG (VG box) $50.00

Mr Potato Head Funny Face Kit #2000, w/brochure, NM (EX box), from $45 to..$65.00

Mr Potato Head Ice Pops, Hassenfeld Bros, makes candied ice pops, EX+ (EX box), A..$45.00

Mr Presto Magic Transfer Set, 1983, MIB (sealed), J7 ...$200.00

Mr Tricko Magic Set, Remco, 1965, complete, NM (EX+ box), F8 ....$90.00

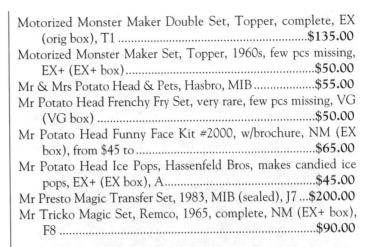

Mysto Magic Exhibition Set, Gilbert, 1920s, NM (EX box), $450.00.

Mysto Magic Exhibition Set #1.5, Gilbert, 1938, complete, NMIB, A...$100.00

Mysto Magic Set #5A, Gilbert, voucher dtd Dec 21, 1946, complete, NM (EX+ box) $350.00

Picture Maker, Hot Birds Skyway Scenes, Mattel, 1970, MIB, $75.00.

Professor Wonderful's Wonder Lab, Gilbert, 1964, MIB, from
$50 to $75.00

Shrink Machine, Wham-O, rare, MIB, T1, $85.00.

Shrunken Head Apple Sculpture Set, NMIB, J6 ....$45.00
Strange Change Machine Featuring the Lost World, Mattel,
    1967, missing orig paper mat, EX (VG+ box), T2 .....$80.00
Thingmaker Goop, Mattel, 1966, blk, M (NM card), F8 .$20.00
Thingmaker Goop, Nite-Glo, Mattel, 1965, glow-in-the-dark, M
    (NM card), F8..$25.00
Triple Thingmaker, Mattel, w/Picadoos, Fun Flowers & Zoofie
    Goofies molds & heater, EX (EX box), T1 ....$145.00
Vac-U-Form Casting Set, Mattel, orig issue, VG+ (VG box),
    T1...$65.00
Voodini Magic Set, Transogram, 1960, missing magic pencil,
    EX+ (EX+ box), F8..$25.00
Wiggly Weirdies, Hasbro, 1978, machine, molds, molding mate-
    rials & instructions, EX+ (orig box), T1 ....$50.00
Woodburning Set, American Toy, early 1950s, complete,
    NMIB, T2 ....$30.00
You Be the Magician, Earle Games/Canada, complete, NM (EX
    box), A $300.00
Young Magician's Box of Tricks, Saalfield, 1958, 31 cb punch-
    out pcs form tricks, NMIB, F8 ....$25.00
Young Nurse Medical Kit, Hasbro, 1950s, complete, MIB,
    H12..$75.00

Advertising

The assortment of advertising memorabilia geared toward
children is vast — plush and cloth dolls, banks, games, puzzles,
trucks, radios, watches and much, much more. And considering
the popularity of advertising memorabilia in general, when you
add to it the crossover interest from the realm of toys, you have a

real winning combination! Just remember to check for condition
very carefully; signs of play wear are common. Think twice about
investing much money in soiled items, especially cloth or plush
dolls. Stains are often impossible to remove.

For more information we recommend *Zany Characters of the
Ad World* by Mary Jane Lamphier; *Advertising Character Col-
lectibles* by Warren Dotz; *Advertising Dolls Identification & Value
Guide* by Joleen Ashman Robinson and Kay Sellers; *Huxford's
Collectible Advertising* by Sharon and Bob Huxford; *Pepsi-Cola
Collectibles, Vols I, II, and III,* by Bill Vehling and Michael
Hunt; and *Collectible Coca-Cola Toy Trucks* by Gael de
Courtivron.

Advisors: Jim Rash (R3), advertising dolls and plastic cereal
premiums; Larry Blodget (B2), Post Cereal cars.

**See also Bubble Bath Containers; Cereal Boxes; Char-
acter, TV and Movie Collectibles; Dakins; Disney; Fast-
Food Collectibles; Halloween Costumes; Pin-Back Buttons; Premiums; Radios; Telephones; Western; and other
specific categories.**

**Actigall, squeeze toy, Gall Bladder Doll,
Summit, 1989, vinyl, 4", M, J6, from
$35.00 to $40.00.**

Actigall, squeeze toy, Gall Bladder Doll, Summit, 1989, vinyl,
    7", M, P12 ....$65.00
Admiral Appliances, bank, The Admiral, vinyl, M, P12..$20.00
Alka-Seltzer, squeeze toy, Speedy figure, 1970s, vinyl, 8",
    VG+ $425.00
Allen's Coffee & Dainty Tea, airplane, Airking JR8, 1930s,
    balsa w/rubber-band launcher, advertising on wings, NMIB,
    A $90.00
American Corned Beef, jack-in-the-box, Germany, late 1800s,
    woman's head in lunch pail, ...Free of Trichiness, 4", EX,
    A...$345.00

American Steel & Wire Co, jigsaw puzzle, 1933, giant boots walking over farmland, Take This Step..., 9x12", EX, F9....**$65.00**

Atlantic Premium Gasoline, bank, tin gas pump, 5½", NM, A **$65.00**

Atlas Batteries, bank, shaped like 6-volt battery, red & silver on blk, 3x3x2", EX, A **$40.00**

Baby Ruth, doll, Hasbro, 1970s, beanbag body, EX **$35.00**

Baby Ruth, whistle, 2¾", NM, A **$25.00**

Barton's Candy, truck, 1950s, plastic, red & yel w/blk tires, Candy Favorite of Millions of New Yorkers, 9", EX, A.........**$100.00**

Baskin Robbins, figure, bendable spoon figure w/arms & legs, 5", M, H4 ....**$8.00**

Betty Crocker, doll, Kenner, 1974, 13", G, M15..............**$30.00**

Big Boy, bank, 1970s, vinyl, slender, sm red & wht checks, MIP, H4 ....**$35.00**

Big Boy, bank, 1994, vinyl, 10", MIP, H4 ....**$15.00**

Black Jack Chewing Gum, jigsaw puzzle, 1933, woman forcing gum into mouth of man w/armful of packages, 10x7", EX, F9..**$40.00**

Borden, doll, Elsie the Cow, stuffed body w/vinyl head & hooves, VG, M15.................................**$50.00**

Borden, figure, Elsie the Cow, bendable PVC, 3¾", M, H4.....**$18.00**

Borden, mug, 1940s, shows Elsie's face & name, ceramic, NM, P12 ....**$65.00**

Borden, place mat, Elsie w/family, M, T1 ....**$8.00**

Borden, playing cards, Elsie the Cow, NMIB, T1 ....**$20.00**

Borden, pull toy, horse-drawn milk wagon, Rich Toys, 1930s-40s, litho wood, 20", EX, A **$325.00**

Breck, doll, Bonnie Breck, Hasbro, 1972, w/accessories & booklet, 9", MIB, M15.................................**$35.00**

Buffalo Evening News, wagon, bl wooden box w/blk fr, red wheels, Yes Sir Skippy Carries a Knife Every Day..., EX, A..**$1,540.00**

Bumble Bee Tuna, bank, bee sitting on gr base, 1960s, vinyl, 7", EX, J5 ....**$45.00**

Buster Brown Shoes, Buster Brown Shoe Game, ring toss, cb, complete, MIB, A **$70.00**

Buster Brown Shoes, doll, Buster Brown, 1974, stuffed cloth, 14", NM, A **$35.00**

Buster Brown Shoes, flicker ring, C10................................**$40.00**

Buster Brown Shoes, whistle, pictures Buster & Tige, rectangular, EX+, A **$32.00**

Butter-Nut Salad Dressing, jigsaw puzzle, 1920, food & variety of dressings w/flower vase, 14x11", NM (orig envelope), A..**$22.00**

Caltex Gasoline, truck, red, cream & blk litho tin, blk rubber tires, 5½", missing 1 hubcap o/w EX, A **$55.00**

Calumet Baking Powder, bank, child atop can w/paper label, 7½", EX, A **$220.00**

Campbell's Soups, bank, Campbell Kids, AC Williams, gold-pnt CI attached figures w/gr eyes & red lips, 3½" L, EX, A **$145.00**

Campbell's Soups, cup, Campbell Girl face, F&F Mold, MIB, P12 ....**$20.00**

Campbell's Soups, doll, Campbell Boy, 1976 bicentennial, MIB, P12 ....**$75.00**

Campbell's Soups, doll, Campbell Cheerleader, 1967, vinyl, 8", EX, P6 ....**$75.00**

Campbell's Soups, doll, Campbell Girl, 1900-10, compo w/cloth clothes, w/up, 7½", VG+, M5 ....**$380.00**

Campbell's Soups, doll, Campbell Girl, 1965, vinyl & rubber, missing shoes o/w EX, 10", P6 ....**$80.00**

Campbell's Soups, doll, Campbell Kid, Horsman, 1940s, compo, NM, J6 ....**$325.00**

Campbell's Soups, dolls, Campbell Kids, 1970s, rag type, MIB, P12, pr **$95.00**

Campbell's Soups, dolls, Campbell Kids, 1988, special edition, MIB, P12, pr..**$65.00**

Campbell's Soups, game, Campbell Kids Shopping Game, Parker Bros, 1955, complete, scarce, NM (EX box), A, $300.00.

Campbell's Soups, vacuum cleaner, Pla-Vac, Mirro, 1950s, aluminum, battery-op, MIB, A, $85.00.

Cap'n Crunch, figure, General Mills, 1982, cloth, lg, EX, C17 ....$15.00

Cap'n Crunch, nodder, sm, R3 ....$75.00

Cap'n Crunch, whistle, Cap'n Crunch Bo'son, General Mills, NM, J2 ....$30.00

Caravelle Candy Bar, figure, cowboy, 1967, wood, plastic & paper w/bendable arms & legs, M, rare, P12............$195.00

Carr's Biscuits, double-decker bus biscuit tin, English, red w/red & yel advertising on sides, 10", EX, A $800.00

Ceresota Flour, doll, boy, printed cloth, name on shirt, early, 17", EX, A...$100.00

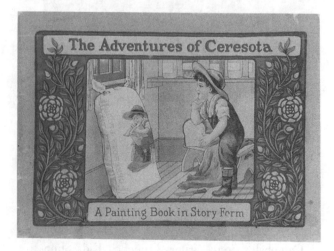

Ceresota Flour, paint book, Adventures of Ceresota, VG, $25.00.

Chevrolet, clicker, tin, 2", EX, A7 ....$15.00

Chicken of the Sea, doll, mermaid, Mattel, 1974, stuffed cloth, yarn hair, M (VG box), H4 ....$30.00

Chicken of the Sea, doll, mermaid, Mattel, 1974, stuffed cloth, yarn hair, EX, B1..$15.00

Chiffon Margarine, doll, Mother Nature, stuffed cloth w/dress, yarn hair, MIB, H4 ....$30.00

Chips Ahoy!, doll, Talbot/Nabisco, M (NM box), M5 ....$50.00

Chips Ahoy!, doll, Talbot/Nabisco, NM, J2 ....$20.00

Chips Ahoy!, figure, Keirn, bendable, NM, M5.............$12.00

Chiquita Bananas, doll, 1950s, printed material, uncut, 11x17", NM, J5 ....$45.00

Chiquita Bananas, ride-on toy, banana on wheels, M, P1 ...$35.00

Chiquita Bananas, transfers, 1950s, set of 6, M (orig mailer), V1 ....$10.00

Chocks Vitamins, doll, Charlie Chocks, 1970-71, printed cloth, 20", EX, V1 ....$25.00

Cities Service, gas station w/car, Linemar, litho tin, battery-op, NMIB, A..$475.00

Cities Service, gas truck, gr, 6", VG, A.....................$45.00

Clicquot Club Ginger Ale, bank, 1930s, half-figure of Eskimo boy holding lg bottle, 7x5½x4", M, A $420.00

Coca-Cola, bank, floor cooler, 1940s, red metal, Have a Coke on lid, Drink Coca-Cola Ice Cold on sides, 5x4", VG+, A..$1,000.00

Coca-Cola, bank, van, Toystalgia, 1980s, wood w/stamped Drink Coca-Cola logo, w/driver & cases of bottles, 7", M, A .$25.00

Coca-Cola, bank, vending machine, Marx, 1950s, red w/wht lettering, 3 drinking glasses, battery-op, EX+, A $500.00

Coca-Cola, bank/dispenser, Linemar, 1950s, EX, S19....$250.00

Coca-Cola, block puzzle, '15' Puzzle, wood, spells out Ice Cold Coca-Cola w/Drink Coca-Cola disk logo, rare, NMIB, A $310.00

Coca-Cola, bus, Sweetcentre, 1980s, red cb dbl-decker w/contour logo front & back, M, A $30.00

Coca-Cola, car, Ford Sedan, Taiyo, 1960s, red & wht tin, Refresh w/Zest lettered on sides, friction, 9", EX+, A............$195.00

Coca-Cola, cutout, Athletic Games, 1932, 10x15", EX, D10.$50.00

Coca-Cola, cutout, Toy Town, 1927, 10x15", EX, D10 ...$70.00

Coca-Cola, doll, Buddy Lee, 1950s, plastic, in uniform, no hat, VG+, A...$400.00

Coca-Cola, doll, Buddy Lee, 1950s, plastic, in uniform, w/hat, EX+, A..$650.00

Coca-Cola, doll, Santa, 1950s-60s, wht boots, holding bottle, VG, A $45.00

Coca-Cola, food stand, Playtown Hot Dogs & Hamburgers, 1950s, wood, metal & plaster, NMIB, A..................$325.00

Coca-Cola, Ford Taxi, Taiyo, litho tin, friction, 9", MIB, S19 ....$375.00

Coca-Cola, game, bingo set, complete, VG+ (orig box), A.$45.00

Coca-Cola, game, checkers, G, A $20.00

Coca-Cola, game, cribbage, complete, NMIB, A..............$50.00

Coca-Cola, game, Horse Race, complete, EX (orig box), A.....$300.00

Coca-Cola, game, Le Jeu de Sante, Canadian, 1934, commemorates 28th Anniversary, complete w/litho board, EX, A $75.00

Coca-Cola, game, Shanghai, MIB, A $20.00

Coca-Cola, game, Steps to Health, 1938, NM+ (orig envelope), M5 ....$120.00

Coca-Cola, game, Streamlined Darts, EX+ (orig box), A16.$35.00

Coca-Cola, game, Table Tennis, complete, EX+ (orig box), A..$50.00

Coca-Cola, game, Tower of Hanoi, EX+ (orig box), A..$250.00

Coca-Cola, game set, checkers, dice & backgammon, complete, VG+ (orig box), A..$40.00

Coca-Cola, game set, Milton Bradley, 1943, 2 decks of cards, cribbage board, dominos & checkers, EX (orig box), A ..$130.00

Coca-Cola, jigsaw puzzle, Crossing the Equator, EX+ (orig box), A $150.00

Coca-Cola, jigsaw puzzle, Hawaiian Beach, very rare, NMIB, A $185.00

Coca-Cola, jigsaw puzzle, Teenage Party, NMIB, A.........$90.00

Coca-Cola, jigsaw puzzle, 2000 Pieces, collage of Coke items, MIB (sealed), A $55.00

Coca-Cola, jigsaw puzzle, 2000 Pieces, collage of Coke items, NMIB, A...$20.00

Coca-Cola, puppet theater, Sid & Marty Krofft Kaleidoscope, 1968, unused, M, T1 ....$25.00

Coca-Cola, record carrying case, 1960s, Hi-Fi Club on front, vinyl w/plastic hdl, NM+, A $75.00

Coca-Cola, train set, Lionel, 1970s-80s, cars feature various Coke products, electric, NMIB, A $250.00

Coca-Cola, truck, AMBO (Italy), litho tin, plastic wheels, 1960s, EX+, S19 ....$400.00

Coca-Cola, truck, Buddy L #4969, 1970s, tractor-trailer, scarce, NM, A $75.00

Coca-Cola, truck, Buddy L #5215, 1970s, Ford, 7½", NM, A..$30.00

Coca-Cola, truck, Buddy L #5215H, 1980s, red & wht pressed steel w/big tires, MIB, A $30.00

Coca-Cola, truck, Buddy L #5216, 1962, A-frame, yel plastic, holds 8 gr & red plastic cases, EX+ (orig box), A....$425.00

Coca-Cola, truck, Buddy L #5426, 1960, Ford style, yel pressed steel w/wraparound bumper, wht-wall tires, 15", NMIB, A $550.00

Coca-Cola, truck, Buddy L #5546, 1956, International, yel pressed steel 2-tier w/red trim, w/accessories, 14", MIB, A $725.00

Coca-Cola, truck, Buddy L #5646, 1957, GMC, yel pressed steel, w/hand truck, ramp & 8 cases, 14", NMIB, A $600.00

Coca-Cola, truck, Buddy L/Aiwa #591-1350, 1980s, red pressed steel w/see-through trailer, 11", rare, MIB, A $70.00

Coca-Cola, truck, Corgi Jr, 1982 World's Fair, contour logo, NM, A...$20.00

Coca-Cola, truck, Goso #426-20, 1949, yel body w/Coca-Cola on red panel across open bed w/cases, 8", NM, A........$2,600.00

Coca-Cola, truck, Linemar, 1950s, tin, 5", NM, S19......$400.00

Coca-Cola, truck, London, 1960s, Drink Coca-Cola decal on side of open bed, 6", M, A.................................$295.00

Coca-Cola, truck, Marx, 1949, yel plastic w/red decals, side panels lift up to reveal cases of Coke, 10", EX (VG box), A .$650.00

Photo courtesy of Dunbar Gallery.

Coca-Cola, truck, Marx, 1950s, yellow and red, open divided double-decker bay with 4 cases, 12½", NM, $375.00.

Coca-Cola, truck, Marx #1090, 1956-57, yel tin w/red trim, open bed, 5 tiers of cases, red center ad panel, 17", M, D10 ....$650.00

Coca-Cola, truck, Marx #21, 1954-56, yel tin w/red stripe on hood, divided dbl-decker bay, 12½", EX+, A $200.00

Coca-Cola, truck, Marx #991, 1950s, gray pressed steel cab w/yel stake bed, Sprite boy decals, 20", rare, NMIB, A.....$900.00

Coca-Cola, truck, Marx #991, 1950s, gray pressed steel cab w/yel stake bed, Sprite Boy decals, 20", rare, NM, S19.....$650.00

Coca-Cola, truck, Marx #991, 1950s, red pressed steel cab w/ yel stake bed, Sprite boy decals, 20", EX, A $375.00

Coca-Cola, truck, Marx/Canada, 1950-54, Chevy style, red plastic w/wooden wheels, 6 yel cases w/bottles, 11", NM, A .$525.00

Coca-Cola, truck, Maxitoys/Holland, 1980s, yel & blk metal w/open-sided driver's seat, wht rubber tires, 11, NM+, A $300.00

Coca-Cola, truck, Metalcraft #171, 1932, A-frame, pressed steel, red & yel, rubber wheels, 7 bottles, 11", VG+, A....$575.00

Coca-Cola, truck, Metalcraft #171, 1932, A-frame, pressed steel, red & yel, rubber wheels, 10 bottles, 11", NM, S19.$700.00

Coca-Cola, truck, Metalcraft #215, 1933, rubber wheels, working headlights, complete w/10 bottles, NM, S19 .....$950.00

Coca-Cola, truck, Rico/Spain, 1970s, Sanson Jr, red pressed steel w/lg contour logo, 13½", VG, A $35.00

Coca-Cola, truck, Sanyo, 1960s, yel & wht tin w/red trim, enclosed cargo bay, battery-op, 13", EX (EX box), A.$300.00

Coca-Cola, truck, Siku Eurobuilt/W Germany, 1980s, Ford cargo, red diecast metal w/contour logo, 7½", MIB, A..........$40.00

Coca-Cola, truck, Siku Eurobuilt/W Germany, 1980s, Mack tractor-trailer, diecast metal, 12½", MIB, A $40.00

Coca-Cola, truck, Smith-Miller, 1944-45, A-frame, red wood & aluminum, rubber tires, wood block Coke cases, 14", EX+, A..$1,575.00

Coca-Cola, truck, Smith-Miller, 1947-53, GMC, red metal cab w/Coke bottle decals & logo on open wood bed, 14", G, A..$495.00

Coca-Cola, truck, Smith-Miller, 1979, GMC, red cast metal, 2-tier w/6 cases & bottles, only 50 made, 14", NMIB, A..$1,700.00

Coca-Cola, truck, Uni-Plast #302/Mexico, 1978-79, Repartidora, Vanet, red plastic van w/contour logo on side, NMIB, A..$35.00

Coca-Cola, truck, Winross, 1994, Collector's Club, Atlanta Convention, MIB, A...$170.00

Coca-Cola, truck set, Buddy L, 1981, Brute Coca-Cola Set, NMIB, A...$50.00

Photo courtesy of June Moon.

Coca-Cola, truck set, Buddy L #4973, 1970s, 7 pieces, MIB, J6, $85.00.

Coca-Cola, truck set, Buddy L #666, 1980s, 15 pcs, MIB, A .$35.00

Coca-Cola, van, Kennedy, 1986, Tootsietoy copy, red diecast metal w/Enjoy Coca-Cola in wht on side, M, A........$15.00

Coca-Cola, van, Lemezarugyar/Hungary, 1970s, Lendkerekes Mikrobusz (Combi-van), red plastic, friction, 7", rare, MIB, A..$200.00

Coca-Cola, van, Lemezarugyar/Hungary, 1970s, Lendkerekes Mikrobusz (Combi-van), silver plastic, friction, 7", MIB, A..$100.00

Coca-Cola, van, Roll A-Long, Durham Industries/Hong Kong, 1970s-80, NMIP, A $30.00

Coca-Cola, van, Van Goodies/Canada, 1970s, Denimachine, simulated wood w/red & wht contour logo, 12", rare, M, A $100.00

Coca-Cola, van, VW, 1950s, NM, S19 ....$275.00

Cocoa Puffs, train, 1960s, litho tin, NM, V1 ....$80.00

Comfort Inn, figure, Choice-a-saurus, PVC dinosaur, M, H4 .$8.00

Count Chocula, see General Mills

Cunningham's Drug Stores, delivery truck, CI, red, 10", G, A $100.00

Cunningham's Drug Stores, wagon, tin, red w/advertising on sides, 13", EX, A $95.00

Curad Bandages, bank, Taped Crusader figure, vinyl, 1975, 7", NM, A $55.00

Curity, doll, Dydee Bear, plush w/cloth diaper, EX, H4....$12.00

Curtiss Candy, dump truck, Marx, red plastic w/blk tires, candy rolls in cello wrap in truck bed, 9", EX+ (VG box), A $150.00

Doritos/Pepsi, doll, Dracula, inflatable, unused, M, T1 ....$25.00

Dow Bathroom Cleaner, bank, Scrubbing Bubble, ceramic, M, J2 ....$20.00

Dow Bathroom Cleaner, figure, Scrubbing Bubble, 1989, vinyl, 3½", EX, B10/M15, from $10 to $15.00

Elsie the Cow, see Borden

Energizer Batteries, doll, Energizer Bunny in sunglasses, plush, Elsie the Cow, See Bordon, mail-in premium, 24", M, P12 ....$50.00

Energizer Batteries, flashlight, Energizer Bunny, 1991, squeezable vinyl, MIP (sealed) $12.00

Eskimo Pie, doll, Eskimo Pie Man, stuffed, 16", EX, I2.....$12.00

Esso Standard, toy gas pump, tin, red w/glass bulb & hand pump, 6½", G, A $65.00

Florida Oranges, bank, Orange Bird, 1974, vinyl, MIP, J6.$35.00

Franco-American, figure, Wizard of O's, 1978, vinyl, 7½", M, from $28 ....$35.00

Franken Berry, see General Mills

Franklin Life Insurance, doll, Ben Franklin, stuffed cloth, G, H4 ....$8.00

Fruit Roll-Ups, figure, Rollupo the Wizard, bendable, 6", EX, H4 ....$12.00

Fruit Stripe Gum, figure, Yipe zebra, bendable, M, scarce, P12 ....$30.00

Funny Face Drink Mix, frisbee, set of 4, P12 ....$35.00

Funny Face Drink Mix, mug, plastic, any fruit character, P12, ea $15.00

Funny Face Drink Mix, mug, plastic, Chug A Lug Chocolate, M, scarce, P12 ....$20.00

Funny Face Drink Mix, pillow, Freckle Face Strawberry, stuffed, EX+, T1 ....$50.00

Funny Face Drink Mix, pitcher, Goofy Grape, red, R3 ..$100.00

Funny Face Drink Mix, record, Goofy Grape Sings, 1969, unused, rare, M, P12 ....$65.00

Funny Face Drink Mix, walker, Goofy Grape, no counter-balance coin o/w VG, H4 ....$35.00

Funny Face Drink Mix, walkers, P12, set of 4 w/coins....$350.00

GE Radio, figure, drum major, Cameo Toys, jointed wood with composition face, 19", NM, M5, $1,000.00.

Eveready Batteries, bank, black cat, plastic, MIB, J6, $35.00.

Fanny Farmer Candies, toy truck, Home Studio, 1950s, wht plastic w/blk lettering & tires, 10", NM (EX box), A $100.00

Farmer Jack Supermarkets, bank, Farmer Jack figure, 1986, vinyl, 7", EX, H4 ....$55.00

Flintstones Vitamins, mug, Fred or Dino, 1968, plastic, M (in mailer box), J6, ea $65.00

General Electric, doll, Marie (Aristocats), w/orig tag, M, T1 .$15.00

General Mills, bowl, Trix Rabbit, Mr Wonderful or Dudley Do-Right, R3, ea $50.00

General Mills, figure, Count Chocula, vinyl, 1975, 8", EX, P12 ....$80.00

General Mills, figure, Franken Berry, vinyl, 1975, 8", NM, P12 ....$95.00

General Mills, flicker ring, Count Chocula, C10 ....$100.00

Gerber, doll, Gerber Baby, Atlanta Toys, flirty eyes, in wicker basket w/eyelet pillow, 12", M (orig mailing box), M15...**$50.00**

Gerber, doll, Gerber Baby, 1979, stuffed body w/vinyl head, flirty eyes, 19", MIB, M15 ....**$80.00**

Gerber, doll, Gerber Baby, 1989, vinyl w/pnt eyes, bl or pk outfit, 6", MIB, M15...**$15.00**

Good Humor Ice Cream, truck, KTS, 1950s, wht w/bl & yel advertising, friction, authorized by Good Humor, 11", NMIB, A **$1,500.00**

Goodrich Silvertone Tires, truck, Metalcraft, 1930s, pressed steel w/rotating wench, red & wht w/blk tires, 13", VG, A.**$450.00**

Great Atlantic & Pacific Tea Co, delivery wagon, printed wood, enclosed, metal spoked wheels, 6", missing horse, EX, A **$1,155.00**

Green Giant, doll, Jolly Green Giant, 1966, stuffed cloth, 16", M (M plastic mailing pouch), M17 ....**$45.00**

Green Giant, doll, Little Sprout, 1970s, plush w/cloth outfit & felt leaf hair, 12", NM, H4.................................**$18.00**

Green Giant, figure, Little Sprout, 1970s, vinyl, 6½", VG, M15 ....**$12.00**

Green Giant, jump rope, Little Sprout, MIB, H4 ....**$28.00**

Heinz, figure, Heinz Ketchup Ant, bendable PVC, 4½", EX, H4 ....**$10.00**

Heinz, truck, Metalcraft, 1930s, wht pressed steel w/decals, Goodrich rubber tires, battery-op lights, 12", NMIB, A.................**$880.00**

Heinz, truck, Metalcraft, 1930s, wht pressed steel w/decals, Goodrich rubber tires, battery-op lights, 12", G (G box), A **$580.00**

Hershey's, Candee Babes doll & purse, NASTA, 1980, MOC, H4 ....**$10.00**

Hershey's, figure, Hershey's Milk Chocolate bar w/arms & legs, bendable, NM, M5...**$18.00**

Hershey's, figure, Hersheykin holding a candy bar & saw, 1980s, PVC, 3", NM, H4 ....**$4.00**

Hershey's, see also Mr Goodbar

Hi-C Fruit Drinks, pogs, 1994, complete set of 24, M & unpunched on 2 cards, orig mailer & special bonus pog, M17...**$30.00**

Hindler's Ice Cream, delivery truck, yel pressed steel, advertising showing kewpie doll eating ice cream, 22", G, A **$550.00**

Holland America Lines, doll, sailor w/vinyl head, 11", MIP, M15...**$25.00**

Hood Dairies, figure, Harry Hood, vinyl, NM, P12...........**$95.00**

Hoover Vacuum Cleaners, doll, Dust Beastie, rare, M, P12 .**$60.00**

Hush Puppies, bank, basset hound on mk base, hard vinyl, 8", missing stopper, M5 ....**$38.00**

Icee, bank, Icee Bear seated w/cup, 1974, vinyl, M, P12 ..**$35.00**

Jordache, doll, Jeans Man, Mego, 1981, 12", NRFB, M15 ...**$25.00**

Keebler, bank, Ernie the Keebler Elf, ceramic, employee premium, NM, J6 ....**$65.00**

Keebler, doll, Ernie the Keebler Elf, 1981, stuffed plush, 24", VG, M15...**$40.00**

Keebler, figure, Ernie the Keebler Elf, 1970s, vinyl, 7", M, T1 ....**$25.00**

Kellogg's, book, Funny Jungleland Moving Pictures, 1909, EX+, J2 ....**$75.00**

Kellogg's, book, Funny Jungleland Moving Pictures, 1909, G+..**$25.00**

Kellogg's, book, Jumbly Jungle, 1948, M (orig mailer), V1 .**$25.00**

Kellogg's, doll, Miss America Laurie Lea Schaefer, Mattel, 1972, walker, 11½", VG, M15 ....**$125.00**

Kellogg's, Mini 110 camera, Canadian, 1970s, M, H4 ....**$4.00**

Kellogg's, place mat, Good Manners Count, characters both sides, EX, I2 ....**$2.50**

Kellogg's Frosted Flakes, bank, Tony the Tiger, hard plastic, 8½", NM, F8 ....**$48.00**

Kellogg's Frosted Flakes, bike horn, Tony the Tiger, rare, W5 ....**$65.00**

Kellogg's Frosted Flakes, doll, Tony the Tiger, stuffed cloth, terry cloth shirt, EX+, T1 ....**$85.00**

Kellogg's Fruit Loops, figure, Toucan Sam, 1984, vinyl, 5", MIB, M5/P12 ....**$45.00**

Kellogg's Rice Krispies, figure, Crackle! from the Friendly Folks series, 1 of 5, 2", EX+, F8.....................................**$15.00**

Photo courtesy of June Moon.

Kellogg's Rice Krispies, figures, Crackle!, 1984, 5", MIB, $55.00; Snap! and Pop!, loose, M, $25.00 each.

Kellogg's Rice Krispies, figure, Pop!, 1984, vinyl, 5", MIB, M5 ....**$45.00**

Kellogg's Rice Krispies, figures, Snap!, Crackle! & Pop!, 1970s, vinyl, 8", P12 ....**$125.00**

Kellogg's Rice Krispies, friction toy, Snap! figure, Talbot Toys, 1984, M (VG card), H4.......................................**$18.00**

Kool-Aid, bank, Kool-Aid Pitcher man standing on sq base, 1970s, mechanical, 7", M, P12 ....**$50.00**

Kool-Aid, doll, Mr Kool-Aid Awesome Dude, stuffed, w/sunglasses & surfing shorts, MIP, M15.............................**$12.00**

Kool-Aid, figure, Mr Kool-Aid as weight lifter or tennis player, M, T1, ea...**$3.00**

Kraft Macaroni & Cheese, bank, Cheesasarus, mail-in premium, M, P12 ....**$35.00**

Lee, bear, 1988, wearing official Lee jeans, 15", VG, M15....**$10.00**

Levi's, doll, Knickerbocker, denim rag-type, VG+, I2 ......**$10.00**

Life Savers, pillow, stuffed candy roll, 16x10", EX+, I2 ......**$5.00**

Lion Coffee, paper dolls, Little Boy Blue, Woolsen Spice Co, ca 1900, 4 pcs, cut but unused, NM, from $60 to..........**$65.00**

Photo courtesy of June Moon.

Kraft, pull toy, cameraman on roll-about TV camera, scarce, NM, J6, from $175.00 to $200.00.

Photo courtesy of June Moon.

Libby's, doll, Mattel, 1974, pull-string talker, 15", mute otherwise EX, J6, $35.00.

Lion Coffee, paper dolls, Little Jack Horner, Woolsen Spice Co, ca 1900, 4 pcs, cut but unused, NM, from $60 to **$65.00**
Lion Coffee, paper dolls, Mary Had a Little Lamb, Woolsen Spice Co, ca 1900, 4 pcs, cut but unused, NM, from $60 to **$65.00**
Little Caesars Pizza, doll, Pizza-Pizza man, 1990, plush, EX..**$5.00**
Lucky Charms, figure, Leprechaun, General Mills, flat rubber, 2", EX+, F8..**$15.00**

Lucky Charms, ring, General Mills, C10 ....**$125.00**
Mack Trucks, doll, plush bulldog, 8", M, D4....................**$20.00**
Magic Chef, figure, vinyl, 7½", EX+, M5........................**$20.00**
Marine Bank, bank, Capt Marine, 1980s, vinyl, M, P12 ..**$55.00**
Maypo, doll, Marky Maypo, 1960s, vinyl, bl pants & shirt w/red hat & neckerchief, brn gloves & boots, 10", M, P2 ...**$55.00**
Michelin, figure, Mr Bib, w/up, MIB, P12 ....**$20.00**
Milkbone, dog, Dr Spot, stuffed, M, D8 ....**$65.00**
Mobilgas, truck, Japan, red tanker w/winged horse logos on doors, Mobilgas lettered on tanker, 9", EX+, A **$120.00**
Mobilgas, truck, Smith-Miller, red GMC tanker truck w/wht Mobilgas & winged horse logo on sides of tanker, 22", EX+, A **$870.00**
Mountain Dew, doll, Hillbilly Man, vinyl head, hands & feet w/stuffed body, poseable, w/orig tag, EX, T1 ....**$125.00**
Mr Bubble, figure, vinyl, 10", MIP, H4 ....**$40.00**
Mr Clean, figure, vinyl, EX+, P12 ....**$135.00**
Mr Goodbar, pillow, Hershey's, 1989, 4x6", NM, P3..........**$8.00**
Mr Tony's Pizza, figure, chef, vinyl, NM, P12 ....**$75.00**
Munsingwear, figure, penguin, 1970, vinyl, VG **$20.00**
Nabisco, bracelet, Straight Arrow Mystic Wrist Kit, plastic w/gold arrowhead & cowry shell, NM, J2 ....**$190.00**
Nabisco, card, Straight Arrow #21, NM, J2 ....**$15.00**
Nabisco, cards, Toy Town Carnival, complete set of 36, EX, V1 ....**$35.00**
Nabisco, doll, Mr Salty, stuffed cloth, VG+, B10/C17, from $12 to **$20.00**
Nabisco, figure, Oreo Cookie Man, bendable, EX, H4 .....**$12.00**
Nabisco, figure, Oreo Cookie Man, bendable, M, J2 ....**$15.00**
Nabisco, figures, Oreo, Fig Newton & Chips Ahoy!, MIB, P12..**$95.00**
Nabisco, playset, Barnum's animals, 3-pc, M, J2 ....**$30.00**
Nabisco, wristwatch, LeMunch Oreo Cookie, MIP, M15.**$15.00**
National Biscuit Co, doll, Uneeda Biscuit Boy, Ideal Novelties, 1914, cloth w/compo head & extremities, 15", G, A .**$130.00**
National Biscuit Co, pull toy, delivery wagon, Rich Toys, wood, articulated horse pulls enclosed wagon, 21", NMIB, A.**$880.00**
National Biscuit Co, pull toy, delivery wagon, Rich Toys, wood, articulated horse pulls enclosed wagon, 21", VG, A...**$175.00**

National Biscuit Co/Nabisco, ride-on delivery van, Roberts, metal, yellow with red stripe, 22", VG+, A, $100.00.

National Biscuit Co, pull toy, tractor-trailer, Rich Toys, litho wood, product boxes atop trailers, NMIB, A $2,310.00

Naugahyde, doll, Nauga, 1967, 4 different, M, P12 .....$35.00

Nestle Chocolate, doll, Hans, stuffed cloth, M (orig mailer), C17 ....$20.00

Nestle Quik, cup, Quik Bunny figure w/2 hdls, plastic, M, H4 ....$5.00

Nestle Quik, doll, Quik Bunny, plush, mail-in, M, P12....$20.00

Nestle Quik, figure, Quik Bunny, bendable, 6", EX, H4...$12.00

Newberry's, van, Marx, 1950s, blue and silver lithographed tin, You Always Find More in a Newberry Store, 12", NM (NM box), A, $300.00.

North American Van Lines, doll, Mary Ann, MIB, J2 .....$80.00

Northeastern Lumber Co, pocket puzzle, celluloid, You Will Get Fair Treatment..., bl on wht, rnd, EX, A....................$25.00

Northern Tissue, doll, 1986, 16", VG, M15 ....$22.00

Oscar Mayer, bank, Weinermobile, M $50.00

Oscar Mayer, Weinermobile, Hot Wheels, M, P12 ....$10.00

Oscar Mayer, Weinermobile, pedal car, NM, P12 ....$350.00

Oscar Mayer, Weinermobile, remote control, M, P12......$75.00

Oscar Mayer, whistle, 1950s, red plastic weiner shape w/yel & red pnt-on label, 2¼", NM, A....................................$10.00

Oxydol-Dreft, comic book, Archie, 1950, 7x3", EX, A3 ..$50.00

Palmolive, storybook, The Magic Parasol, 1928, H12 ......$25.00

Penn Maid Sour Cream, clicker, tin, 2½", EX, A.............$20.00

Pepsi, see also Doritos

Pepsi-Cola, dispenser, plastic, 1950s, 12x10x6", MIB, S19..$85.00

Pepsi-Cola, dolls, Pete 'N Pepsi, w/music box, NM, T1 .$125.00

Pepsi-Cola, game, Big League Baseball, 1950s-60s, EX, A.$95.00

Pepsi-Cola, hot dog wagon, 1950s, wooden cart w/tin umbrella, G, A $45.00

Pepsi-Cola, hot dog wagon, 1950s, wooden cart w/tin umbrella, MIB, S19...$150.00

Pepsi-Cola, truck, Cragstan, 1950s, tin, friction, 11", MIB, S19 ....$675.00

Pepsi-Cola, truck, Linemar, 1940s, tin, 7", EX, S19 ....$175.00

Pepsi-Cola, truck, Marx, plastic flatbed w/cases of bottles, Pepsi-Cola decals on sides of bed, 7½", NM, A $195.00

Pepsi-Cola, truck, Marx, 1945, plastic flatbed w/3 rows of bottle cases, bottle-cap logo on doors, 9", NMIB, A $310.00

Pepsi-Cola, truck, Nylint, 1950s, 16½", EX, $400.00.

Pepto Bismol, bank, 24-Hour Bug, 1970s, vinyl, 7", M, P12 .$100.00

Peters Weatherbird Shoes, clicker, tin, NM, A $20.00

Peters Weatherbird Shoes, pencil holder, cb, shaped like a lg pencil, 10½", NM, A..$45.00

Peters Weatherbird Shoes, whistle, tin, cylindrical, 2", EX, A $15.00

Philgas, doll, Buddy Lee in gray uniform, pipe in mouth, no hat o/w EX+, A $350.00

Phillips 66, doll, Buddy Lee in tan shirt & brown pants, no hat o/w EX, A $275.00

Piggly Wiggly, whistle, tin w/paper label, NM, A.............$30.00

Pillsbury, baking set, 1930s, 1 Gasoline Alley character cutter w/6 uncut cb comic characters, MIB, H12 ....$65.00

Pillsbury, doll, Poppin' Fresh, 1972, stuffed, 11", EX, I2 ...$15.00

Pillsbury, doll, Poppin' Fresh, 1982, plush, M, scarce, P12...$50.00

Pillsbury, figure, Poppin' Fresh, 1971, vinyl, 7", EX, B10 .$12.00

Pillsbury, figure, Poppin' Fresh, 1971, vinyl, 7", NM, F8 ..$15.00

Pillsbury, Poppin' Fresh Playhouse, w/4 finger puppets, lacks top floor o/w G+, T1 ....$185.00

Pillsbury, see also Funny Face Drink Mix

Planters, bank, Mr Peanut, mk Made in USA, 1960s, tan plastic, hat unlocks bank, 8½", NM, P4 ....$35.00

Planters, figure, Mr Peanut, 1940s, jtd wood, 8½", NM, M5 .$400.00

Planters, figure, Mr Peanut, 1991, bendable PVC, 6", EX, H4 ....$10.00

Planters, pop gun, paper, 1930s-40s, 9", rare, VG, A, $200.00.

Planters, w/up, Mr Peanut, plastic, 8½", EX, A $300.00

Poll-Parrot Shoes, bank, tin & cb, short can shape, 1½" dia, NM, A...$15.00

Poll-Parrot Shoes, bank, tin & cb, tall can shape, 2" dia, NM, A...$15.00

Poll-Parrot Shoes, clicker, tin, 2", NM, A........................$15.00

Poll-Parrot Shoes, figure, bsk, Poll Parrot Shoes incised on back, 3½", VG, M15 ....$55.00

Poll-Parrot Shoes, whistle, paper, All Leather..., 2½", EX, A...$15.00

Post, bowl, Mickey Mouse graphics, Beetleware/WDE, 1930s, EX, M8 ....$35.00

Post, bowl, Mickey Mouse graphics, Beetleware/WDE, 1930s, M, G16 ....$65.00

Post, Critter Card Game, Linus the Lion-Hearted, mail-in offer, complete, NM (EX box & mailer), F8 ....$45.00

Post, figure, Dr Dolittle's dog or pk snail, R3, ea.............$25.00

Post, figure, Tumbling Clown, NM (orig envelope), J2....$25.00

Post, rings, Herby, Lillums, Perry Winkle or Smokey Stover, MIP, S20, ea...$25.00

Post, rings, Smilin' Jack or Toots Toots, MIP, S20, ea $50.00

Post, vehicle, F&F Mold, Ford Crestline Fordor Sedan, Torch Red, NM, B2 ....$25.00

Post, vehicle, F&F Mold, Ford Crestline Sunliner, Torch Red, M, B2 ....$40.00

Post, vehicle, F&F Mold, Mustang GT, NM, J2 ....$20.00

Post, vehicle, F&F Mold, 1950 Ford Custom Fordor, lt bl, NM, B2 ....$50.00

Post, vehicle, F&F Mold, 1954 Ford Crestline Fordor Sedan, Cameo Coral, NM, B2..$25.00

Post, vehicle, F&F Mold, 1954 Ford Crestline Fordor Sedan, Highland Gr, NM, B2..$35.00

Post, vehicle, F&F Mold, 1954 Ford Crestline Victoria, High-land Gr, NM, B2...$30.00

Post, vehicle, F&F Mold, 1954 Ford Customline Club Coupe, Glacier Bl, NM, B2...$40.00

Post, vehicle, F&F Mold, 1954 Ford Ranch Wagon, Sierra Brn, M, B2 ....$35.00

Post, vehicle, F&F Mold, 1954 Mercury Convertible, Cameo Coral, NM, B2...$100.00

Post, vehicle, F&F Mold, 1954 Mercury Convertible, Siren Red, NM, B2 ....$100.00

Post, vehicle, F&F Mold, 1954 Mercury 4-Door Sedan, Brent-wood Brn, NM, B2..$45.00

Post, vehicle, F&F Mold, 1954 Mercury 4-Door Sedan, Cameo Coral, NM, B2...$40.00

Post, vehicle, F&F Mold, 1954 Mercury 4-Door Sedan, Golden-rod Yel, NM, B2...$30.00

Post, vehicle, F&F Mold, 1955 Ford Customline Tudor, Aqua-tone Bl, M, B2..$7.00

Post, vehicle, F&F Mold, 1955 Ford Customline Tudor, Golden-rod Yel, M, B2...$7.00

Post, vehicle, F&F Mold, 1956 Ford Gasoline Tanker, yel, rare, NM, B2 ....$20.00

Post, vehicle, F&F Mold, 1956 Ford Volume Van, red, rare, NM, B2...$20.00

Post, vehicle, F&F Mold, 1957 Ford Fairlane 500 Sunliner, Flame Red, single molding on side, rare early style, M, B2....$40.00

Post, vehicle, F&F Mold, 1959 Ford Thunderbird Convertible, Raven Blk or Flamingo, NM, B2, ea...........................$6.00

Post, vehicle, F&F Mold, 1959 Ford Thunderbird Convertible, Brandywine Red, M, B2..$15.00

Post, vehicle, F&F Mold, 1959 Ford Thunderbird Hardtop, Starlight Bl, NM, B2..$7.00

Post, vehicle, F&F Mold, 1961 Ford Thunderbird Convertible, Mint Gr or Starlight Bl, NM, B2, ea $5.00

Post, vehicle, F&F Mold, 1961 Ford Thunderbird Hardtop, Desert Gold, rare, M, B2..$15.00

Post, vehicle, F&F Mold, 1966 Ford Mustang 2+2 GT, Spring-time Yel, NM, B2..$10.00

Post, vehicle, F&F Mold, 1967 Mercury Cougar, Tiffany Bl or Fawn, rare, M, B2, ea $10.00

Post, vehicle, F&F Mold, 1967 Mercury Cougar, Traflagar Bl, M, B2...$5.00

Post, vehicle, F&F Mold, 1969 Mercury Marquis 4-Door Sedan, Lt Copper, M, B2...$10.00

Price Food Products, truck, Metalcraft, wht w/various products advertised, blk rubber tires w/yel hubs, 13", G, A....$465.00

Purex, bath toy, Touche Turtle, 1960s, 10", missing stopper o/w EX+, F8..$36.00

Puritan Dairy Ice Cream, whistle, tin, 2½", NM, A $20.00

Quaker, bowl, Quisp & Quangaroo, 1973, R3 ....$125.00

Quaker, comic book, Quisp & Quake in Plenty of Glutton, 1965, 16 pgs, 2x6", EX+, F8.......................................$40.00

Quaker, Cosmic Cloud Ray Gun, 1969, red plastic w/emb Quisp & space graphics, shoots flour, 7", EX+, F8 ....$150.00

Quaker, figure, Quisp riding unicycle, 1969, plastic, pull cord to spin, 3", EX+, F8...$45.00

Quaker, vehicle, Quake earthdigger, R3 ....$90.00

Quaker, vehicle, Quispquaft, Gemini spaceship w/Quisp parachute inside, R3 ....$150.00

Raid Bug, remote control, NM, rare, P12 ....$425.00

Raid Bug, w/up, NM, P12 ....$125.00

Ralston, doll, Chex Scarecrow, 1958, cloth & vinyl, EX, T1...$25.00

Ralston, Freakies bowl, R3..$50.00

Ralston, Freakies figure, after Carmen Miranda, R3 ....$50.00

Ralston, Freakies figures, orange or gr, R3, ea $20.00

Ralston, Moonstone magnets, 1978, R3, ea $20.00

Ralston, Space Patrol Cosmic Smoke Gun, 1950s, red plastic w/short barrel, shoots baking soda, 4½", VG, P4.....$185.00

Ralston, toy chuck wagon, vinyl, horse-drawn covered wagon w/red & wht checked top, 8", EX, A............................$15.00

Real Kill Bug Killer, clicker, tin, 2", NM, A $15.00

Red Goose Shoes, bank, red-pnt CI goose figure, 3¾", EX, A...$85.00

Red Goose Shoes, ring, glow-in-the-dark w/secret compartment, NM, C10..$195.00

Red Goose Shoes, top, tin, 1¼", NM, A..........................$20.00

Red Goose Shoes, whistle, tin, rnd, 1¼", NM, A $20.00

Red Goose Shoes, whistle, wood w/paper label, cylindrical, Blow to Beat the Band, 3½", EX, A $15.00

Reddy Kilowatt, pin, 1953, Your Favorite Pin-Up, enameled diecast metal, MOC, P4 ....$35.00

Salamander Shoes, figures, frog, salamander, lizard, mouse, elf & porcupine, jtd vinyl, complete set, 11", EX, H4.......$300.00

Salamander Shoes, figures, salamander, elf, mouse or porcupine, soft vinyl, 5", H4, ea $8.00
Scott's Fried Chicken, bank, chicken figure, vinyl, NM, P12.$65.00
Seven-Up, car, Taiyo, Ford, tin, 7-Up Your Thirst Away, bottles & logos, friction, 10", scarce, EX, A $290.00
Shakey's Pizza, doll, Pizza Chef, vinyl, red lettering on base, 9½", VG, A $35.00
Shell, gas station, Faller/Germany, plastic, red, gray & wht, 1½x3x4", EX (orig box), A $110.00
Shell, gas station, mk Made in France, masonite-type material w/plastic accessories, complete, 17", EX+, A $250.00
Shell, truck, MLB Brevattato/Italy, 1951, red & yel w/blk rubber tires, w/up, 11½", NM (EX box), A......................$2,200.00

Shell, truck, red and yellow, friction, 11", new old stock, A, $160.00.

Sherwin-Williams Paints, puzzle, McLoughlin Bros, wooden, shows home & outdoor scene, 16x12", EX, A $50.00
Shoney's, bank, bear dressed in red shirt & bl pants, plastic, head turns, 7¾", M, A..$15.00
Sinclair, bank, gas pump mk HC Gasoline, tin, 4", NM, A.$40.00
Sinclair, figure, Dino the Dinosaur, 1950s, premium giveaway w/purchase of 8 gal gas, MIP (sealed), I2......................$8.00
Sinclair, truck, Marx, tin, gr & wht Sinclair lettered on tanker, Power-X & Super Flame on doors, 2-pc, 17", EX+, A..$450.00
Smokey Bear, see US Forest Service
Snapple, nodder, Wendy the Snapple Lady, resin & vinyl, MIB, P12...$125.00
Snuggle Fabric Softener, bear, Snuggles, Lever Bros, 1986, glassine eyes, ear button & wrist tag, 16", M, H12 ....$35.00
Sprite, doll, Lucky Lymon, 1990, vinyl, talker, 7½", M, T1..$20.00
Sprite, doll, Lucky Lymon, 1990, vinyl, talker, 7½", MIB, P12...$35.00
Sprite, doll, Smilin' Sprite, vinyl, talker, NM, T1 ....$45.00
Standard Oil, checkers game, EX (orig box), A.............$100.00
Star-Kist, figure, Charlie Tuna, 1970s, vinyl, 7", MIB, P12.$125.00
Star-Kist, figure, Charlie Tuna, 1980s, inflatable, EX, H4..$20.00
Star-Kist, wristwatch, Charlie Tuna, 1977, working, EX, M17 ....$70.00
Sunbeam Bread, race car, 1970s, MIB, D8 ....$18.00
Sunoco, bank, gas pump, 4", NM, A $40.00
Sunshine Biscuits, truck, pressed steel w/stake bed, red & bl, 12", VG, A $170.00
Sweet Heart Corn, doll, 1981, vinyl w/cloth clothes, mail-in premium, 9", NM, H4...$20.00

Sun-Maid Raisins, gas-powered go-cart van, early style with brass grille and headlights, 72", M, A, $700.00.

Swiss Miss Chocolate, doll, Swiss Miss, stuffed, cloth dress & apron, yarn hair, EX, H4...$20.00
Tastee Freeze, doll, Miss Tastee Freeze, plastic w/cloth dress & banner, G, H4...$20.00
Tastee Freeze, puppet, Little-T, 1960s-70s, NM, T1.........$15.00
Tasty Food, train, tin engine & 2 tank cars, mk Tasty Foods Limited, contained coffee when sold new, 37", G, A......$200.00
Texaco, bank, plastic gas pump w/decals, wht, red, blk & silver, 8½", VG, A...$160.00
Texaco, doll, Cheerleader, red & wht outfit, complete w/raincoat & checked mini-skirt, 11½", M, A $70.00
Texaco, Fire Chief hat w/microphone & speaker, hard plastic, battery-op, NMIB, A $45.00

Texaco, jet fuel truck, red and white, 24", NMIB, A, $275.00.

Texaco, tanker, exclusive dealer offer, plastic vessel w/Texaco North Dakota decal, complete, 26", EX (EX box), A.$300.00
Tony the Tiger, see Kellogg's
Towel's Log Cabin Syrup, pull toy, Log Cabin Express, tin cabin shape, 5", VG, A..$350.00
Toys-R-Us, jack-in-the-box, Geoffrey the Giraffe, Mattel, 1978, NM, T1 ....$75.00
Travel Lodge, figure, Sleepy Bear, vinyl, M, P12 ....$45.00
Trix Cereal, figure, Trix Rabbit, General Mills, 1977, vinyl, 8½", EX, C17 ....$30.00

Trix Cereal, figure, Trix Rabbit, General Mills, 1977, vinyl, 8½", M, J6..$45.00

Trix Cereal, Magic Decoder, General Mills, M, H4............$5.00

Trix Cereal, wallet, flashes Trix Rabbit, NM, J6................$8.00

Tupperware, doll w/zippered satin bowl, 1988, stuffed, M, M15 ....$20.00

US Forest Service, bank, Smokey Bear, 1970s, hard plastic, 8", EX, P6..$50.00

US Forest Service, doll, Smokey Bear, Knickerbocker, 1972, stuffed cotton, 6", EX+ (orig box), D9 ....$20.00

US Forest Service, doll, Smokey Bear, Three Bears Inc, 1985, orig hang tag, 13", M, M15..............................$20.00

US Forest Service, doll, Smokey Bear, 1960s, stuffed, gray badge & belt buckle, EX, T1..$50.00

US Forest Service, figure, Smokey Bear, Lakeside, 1967, bendable, MIP, M17 ....$55.00

Vlasic Pickles, bank, Vlasic Stork, 1981, ceramic, NM, J2..$75.00

Wheaties, books, General Mills, Sports Library, set of 8 w/various sports rules & history, C10................................$150.00

Wizard of O's, see Franco-American

World Wide Van Lines, trucks, Japan, set of 12, EX (orig box), J2..$180.00

Wrangler, doll, Missy, 1982, in jeans w/boots & hat, 11½", NRFB, M15..$45.00

Aeronautical

Toy manufacturers seemed to take the cautious approach toward testing the waters with aeronautical toys, and it was well into the second decade of the 20th century before some of the European toy makers took the initiative. The earlier models were bulky and basically inert, but by the fifties, Japanese manufacturers were turning out battery-operated replicas with wonderful details that advanced with whirring motors and flashing lights.

See also Battery Operated; Cast Iron, Airplanes; Model Kits; Windups, Friction and Other Mechanicals.

Airmail Plane, Girard, w/up, bl tin w/red trim, 12" W, G, A.$70.00

Airmail Plane, Keystone, sheet metal, yellow and red with chrome props, 23½" wingspan, G, A, $880.00.

Airplane, early model w/single wing & ball-wheeled legs, celluloid tail blades spin, w/pilot, 6½", G, A..................$580.00

Airplane, France, 3-prop, red & yel litho tin, cut-out windows, 21" W, VG, A $1,875.00

Airplane, German, clockwork, tin w/paper rear prop, w/pilot, 3-wheeled, 5" L, VG, A $525.00

Airplane, w/up, single-prop, red & beige tin w/cut-out passenger windows, VG, A $330.00

Airplane, Wells O'London, single-prop, bl litho tin w/simulated wood paneling, red prop & wheels, 13" W, EX, A ..$385.00

Airplane, Wyandotte, pressed steel, orange & blk, 18" L, EX, A $175.00

Airship, German, clockwork, pnt tin w/double circular prop, 8" W, G, A..$1,430.00

Airship, Ladis, rubber-band drive, stained tin & wire, w/pilot, 10" L, VG (orig box), A $715.00

Airship, no mechanism, pnt tin w/paper props, motor in gondola, w/pilot, 10½" L, G, A $1,980.00

American Airlines Boeing SST, model, cast resin, decal trim, metal & resin base, 37" L, rare, EX, A $660.00

American Airlines DC-6 Flagship America, model, 4-prop, aluminum, decal trim, metal base, 27½" W, EX, A ..$2,530.00

American Airlines DC-7, 4-prop, marked N305AA on wing, silver with red and blue highlights, NM, $1,200.00.

American Airlines Electra, Holland, model, 4-prop, aluminum, decal trim, polished aluminum base, 28" W, EX, A.$715.00

American Airlines NC-2100 Flagship, 1950s, 4-prop, 27½" L, EX, A $90.00

American Airlines Passenger Biplane, scratch-built model, various materials, pnt & decal trim, 8" L, A $110.00

American Airlines Passenger Plane, Bandai, friction, 4-prop, litho tin, 11" W, NM+, A $180.00

American Airlines Passenger Plane, Linemar, battery-op, 4-prop, tin, silver w/red & bl trim, 19" W, NMIB, A..........$300.00

American Eagle Short Skyliner, scratch-built model, 2-prop, 9½" L, EX, A $75.00

American Flyer Mail Plane, 1920s, w/up, gr-pnt fuselage w/orange wings, tail & prop, decaled, EX+, A......$1,210.00

Beechcraft Airplane, TN, battery-op, tin w/plastic props, litho pilot & female passenger, MIB, L4....................$275.00

Beechcraft N1607N Skyline, TN, spin prop to start motor, litho tin & plastic, 13" W, NM (EX box), A....................$100.00

Biplane, England, 5-prop, w/up, battery-op lights, red tin w/ bl & wht trim, orange props, 21" W, G, A..................$2,200.00

Army Scout NX-110, Steelcraft, 1930s, 3-prop, gray with red wings, tail and props, Buster Brown Shoes on wing, 22" wingspan, VG+, A, $1,375.00.

Biplane, Fischer, clockwork, single-prop, litho tin, w/pilot, 8" L, VG, A..$1,210.00

Biplane, German, clockwork, pnt tin, w/pilot figure, detailed motor, 9" L, G, A.....................................$1,925.00

Biplane, German, pnt tin w/paper & cloth rear props, adjustable stabilizer, 8" L, G, A...........................$1,320.00

Biplane, Gunthermann, w/up, single prop, litho tin, pulleys on wing for string mounting, 10" W, G, A................$1,100.00

Biplane, Meccano/England, single prop, silver w/red, wht & bl trim, assembled w/screws, rubber tires, 19" W, G, A............$300.00

Biplane, rubber-band drive, cloth over wire fuselage, cloth prop, stained tin pilot, 9" L, VG, A.....................$855.00

Biplane, rubber-band drive, double rear prop, stained tin, flat tin pilot w/Am flag, 9" L, G, A....................$825.00

Biplane w/Rear Box Stabilizer, German, clockwork, double rear props, pnt tin, w/pilot, 12" L, G, A......................$2,420.00

Biplane w/Upswept Tail, German, clockwork, single paper prop, litho tin w/wire & cloth wings, w/pilot, 12" L, VG, A..$3,300.00

Biplane Z65, Zimmy, litho tin w/wooden wheels, 10½" W, prop missing otherwise VG (G box), A............$150.00

BOAC Speedbird-Salisbury Clipper Boat, Woodsman Aircraft Models Ltd, model, metal, decal trim, w/base, 21" W, EX, A..$3,190.00

Boeing 747 Jumbo Jet Plane, TN, battery-op, 17" L, M (EX box), A..$125.00

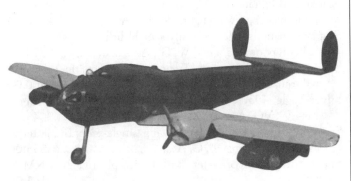

Bomber, sheet metal, single-prop, green fuselage with orange wings, cut-out windows in cockpit and bomber compartment, 26" wingspan, VG, A, $355.00.

Bomber, Tipp, w/up that allows bombs to drop, single prop, tan litho tin w/red & bl trim, 15" W, EX, A..............$1,375.00

Braniff International Airways DC-7, model, 4-prop, cast aluminum, decal trim, nameplate on metal base, 30" W, EX+, A..$880.00

Bristol Bulldog Airplane, S&E/Japan, single-prop, yellow with red, white and blue highlights, battery-operated, 14½" wingspan, NM (EX box), A, $275.00.

British Seaplane, England, single prop, red & silver litho tin, bl wings, w/decals, 11" W, EX, A..................$600.00

Canadair CL-41 Jet Trainer, Japan, model, cast resin, metal base, 9½" L, VG, A....................................$60.00

Capital Airlines Constellation, Holland, travel agency model, 4-prop, aluminum, decal trim, metal base, 28" W, EX, A..$2,640.00

Capital Airlines N7402, Linemar, friction, litho tin, levers on underside to operate props, 12" W, EX (EX box), A...$230.00

Cargo Plane, Gunthermann, w/up, single prop, silver & bl litho tin w/red prop, top wing, 10½" W, VG, A..............$330.00

Cargo Plane, Orobr, wood-grain litho tin w/red center prop & trim, NP wing props, 14" W, G, A...................$600.00

Catapult Monocoupe Plane & Hangar, Buddy L, orange plane w/overhead wing, gr 2-door hangar w/orange trim, 12" L, EX, A...$2,860.00

Cessna Sky Taxi, Japan, friction, single-prop, folding overhead wing, red, wht & yel, 10½" W, EX (VG box), A......$80.00

Comet OH-106, Modern Toys/Japan, friction, litho tin, 6½" L, G, A..$60.00

Comet-4 BOAC Airliner, Wells O'London, friction, wht w/silver wings, bl trim, 13½" W, EX (EX box), A..........$275.00

Concorde Super Sonic Transport, battery-op, 21", VG+, L4..$135.00

Constellations Airplane, Ideal #4841, 1950s, red & yel plastic w/see-through fuselage, 11", NM (VG+ box), A.....$195.00

Curtiss Jenny Trainer, S&E/Japan, friction, single-prop biplane, yel w/red, wht & bl trim, 14½" W, EX (orig box), A.......$100.00

Dirigible, Marklin, pnt tin, cream w/blk trim, celluloid rear prop, 13", EX, A $2,420.00

Douglas Caravella Experimental Jet, desk model, cast resin, hand-pnt trim, 13" W, EX+, A $300.00

Douglas Sky Rocket Jet, Bandai, friction, tin, 11" L, EX, T1.$125.00

Eastern Airlines DC-3, scratch-built model, 2-prop, primarily metal over wood fr, gas engines, 82" W, EX, A....$9,900.00

Eastern Airlines DC-7B, model, 4-prop, aluminum, decal trim, Golden Falcon on base, 28½" W, EX, A **$1,760.00**

F-80 Fighter, Japan, advances w/siren & spinning prop, tin, jutting machine guns on wings, 7", NM (VG+ box), A.........**$100.00**

Fairchild XC-120 Pack-Plane w/Jeep & Tank Cargo, Swada, 1950s, 2-prop, red plastic, 10½" L, NMIB, A **$80.00**

Fanny Passenger Plane, France, battery-op lights, red & silver tin, rear twin rudders, cut-out windows, 20" W, EX, A...**$550.00**

Fokker F-27, Verkuyl/Holland, model, 2-prop, 1-pc cast aluminum, decal trim, metal & wood base, 17½" W, EX, A **$275.00**

Folke Wolf 190, scratch-built miniature movie model, various materials, hand-pnt simulated war stress, 60" W, G+, A......**$690.00**

Grumman S-2, scratch-built model, various materials, pnt & decal trim, 20½" W, EX, A **$60.00**

High-Wing Monoplane, Wyandotte, 1930s, pressed steel, orange & blk, 12½" L, G, A...**$220.00**

Hydroplane, Alps, candle warms water in boiler allowing plane to travel, w/pilot, red, gr & wht, 5" W, EX, A......**$1,045.00**

Japan Airlines DC-8 Jet, model, cast resin w/inset celluloid windows, detailed pnt trim, 33" W, EX, A **$550.00**

Japanese Zero Fighter Plane, friction, gr tin w/Japanese symbols, pilot enclosed in plastic dome, 16" W, A **$145.00**

KLM Multi-Action Electra-Jet, TN, 4-prop, lithographed tin, battery-operated, 16" long, EX+ (EX box), A, $180.00.

Light Plane Skylark, Marusan, friction, yel plastic w/clear cockpit dome, prop spins, 13" L, EX+ (VG box), A..........**$75.00**

Lockheed Airlines 160, Marusan, w/up, litho tin, 14" W, rust on left wing & non-working, G, M5 ....**$500.00**

Lockheed F-104A Starfighter, KO, friction, tin w/plastic dome over cockpit & rubber nose cone, 11" L, EX (EX box), A...**$140.00**

Lockheed Shooting Star P-80, model, cast metal, wht metal base, 1st operational jet fighter, 9" L, EX, A............**$210.00**

Lockheed Sirius, pnt sheet metal, cream w/red wings & tail, chrome nose & prop, wheel protectors, NM, 22" W, A........**$1,540.00**

Lufthansa Boeing 707, Schuco #1024, w/up, plastic & tin, NM, A...**$200.00**

Martin 404 Coast Guard, model, 1-pc cast aluminum, pnt & decal trim, 19" W, EX+, A **$230.00**

McDonnell-Douglas DC-10, desk model, NM, T1 ....**$125.00**

Monocoupe Planes w/Hangar, Buddy L, 3 blk & orange planes, gray hangar w/4-panel folding doors, orange trim, EX, A...**$3,300.00**

Monoplane, German, clockwork, double rear props, pnt tin, 2 figures, 13" L, extremely rare, VG, A **$2,310.00**

Monoplane, Gunthermann, w/up, silver & bl tin, overhead wing, 10" W, rare, EX+, M5 ....**$675.00**

Monoplane w/Flapping Wings, Fischer, clockwork, tin w/front & rear props, rear rudder, w/pilot, 14" W, VG, A **$2,860.00**

NASA F-104 Rocket Plane, model, cast resin, pnt & decal trim, w/base, 21" L, EX, A.....................................**$120.00**

Northwest Airlines DC-6, model, 4-prop, aluminum, hand-pnt trim, metal base, 28" W, EX, A **$745.00**

Northwest Orient Constellation, model, 4-prop, solid aluminum fuselage, hollow wings, decals, metal base, 29" W, EX, A...**$140.00**

Northwest Orient 747 Jet, model, wood w/composition, decal trim, tall metal base, 1 of the 1st 747 series, 47" W, EX, A **$770.00**

Ozark DC-9 Jet, model, aluminum, decal trim, metal base, 21" W, EX, A...**$635.00**

Pan Am Clipper Flying Cloud Boeing 307, scratch-built model, various materials, pnt & decal trim, 12½" L, EX, A ...**$120.00**

Pan Am Clipper Plane, Wyandotte, pressed steel w/metal props, wood wheels, 13" W, EX, A **$285.00**

Pan Am DC-4, model, 4-prop, solid cast metal, hand-pnt trim, metal base, 19½" W, EX, A **$990.00**

Pan Am Inter-Continental Passenger Plane, Gama/Germany, 4-prop, litho tin, wht, bl & silver, 20" W, VG, A.......**$200.00**

Pan Am Vertol Helicopter, battery-op, MIB, L4 ....**$165.00**

Panther Jet, unmk, 1950s, w/up, blk & yel plastic w/aluminum wings, balloon tires, 11" L, EX, A **$175.00**

Red Baron Tri-Wing WWI Plane, German insignias, red w/2 machine guns, 10" W, VG+, A.................................**$300.00**

RSA 33 Gyro Plane, Germany, 1930s, w/up, litho tin, advances w/spinning props, 9" W, NM, A...............................**$510.00**

Seaplane, Bing, wood-look tin fuselage w/silver-tone overhead props, tail rudder & wheels, 16" W, NM, A.........**$3,190.00**

Seaplane, JEP/France, 1930s, w/up, single-prop, red, 2 pontoons, pilot in cockpit w/skylight, 19", EX, A...............**$4,950.00**

Seaplane, w/up, single prop, silver & bl litho tin, w/pilot, 2 lg balloon pontoons, 11¾" W, G-, A..........................**$275.00**

Seaplane F-NORD, Rossignol/France, w/up, 6-prop, tin, yel w/bl & red trim, detachable wing & props, 19" W, VG, A.**$6,500.00**

Silver Eagle, 1930s, w/up, 2-prop, overhead wing, blk rubber tires, 9", VG, A **$145.00**

Spirit of St Louis NX211, 1930s, w/up, single-prop, tin, lettering on overhead wing, 9", G, A **$55.00**

Super Sonic Concorde Jet, battery-op, plastic, 20", NMIB, J2 ....**$65.00**

Swallow NX211 Plane, Am National, single-prop, pressed steel, red fuselage w/gr decorated overhead wing, 32" L, VG, A **$2,200.00**

Swissair DC-7, Raise Up, Holland, model, 4-prop, aluminum, wht cross on tail, 19½" W, EX, A $440.00

Tiger Moth Biplane, scratch-built model, various materials, ENYA motor, 57" W, A $465.00

Tom Cat F-14 Jet Fighter, Son Al Toys, battery-op, tin & plastic, MIB, L4 ....$275.00

Tri-Motor Transport, Schiebles, 3-prop, sheet metal, blue fuselage with red cockpit and wings, cream props, 29" long, VG, A, $1,155.00.

TWA Airmail Plane, Marx, w/up, wht & orange litho tin, celluloid props, VG, T1 ....$225.00

United Airlines Boeing US Mail 247, dtd 1934, model, NP wht metal, decal trim, lighted interior, metal base, 22" W, A...$1,650.00

United Airlines Boeing 747 Jet Plane, stop-&-go action w/lights & sound, litho tin & plastic, 14" L, EX (EX box), A......$125.00

US Army Lockheed Constellation, model, cast resin, decal trim, metal plate, 23" W, EX+, A $300.00

US Mail Plane, Steelcraft, 3-prop, pressed steel, cream w/overhead wing, tail & hubs, chrome props, 26" W, VG, A.....$1,430.00

US Marines, Girard, single-prop, lithographed tin, windup, 17½" wingspan, rare, NM, A, $785.00.

US Navy Constellation, model, 4-prop, 1-pc cast aluminum, w/base, decal trim, 23" W, EX+, A $580.00

US Navy Douglas C-47, model, 2-prop, 1-pc heavy cast metal, pnt & decal trim, Douglas logo on base, 24½" W, EX+, A......$500.00

US Navy F-4 Jet Fighter, Memoto/Japan, model, cast resin, pnt trim, metal base, 11" L, EX, A................................$165.00

USA Defense Bomber, Wyandotte, 1930s, pressed steel, bl & red w/mc decals on wings, 13" W, VG+, A $145.00

USAF Advance F-86 Jet, model, various material w/wood & resin, pnt & decal trim, decorative base, 18" L, VG+, A.....$360.00

USAF B-29 Bomber, Yonezawa, friction, gr w/red highlights, 19" W, missing front wheel o/w EX+, M5 ....$225.00

USAF B-45 Bomber (mk FG-781), model, cast resin, pnt & decal trim, 12½" L, EX, A $110.00

USAF BK-260 Plane, Japan, friction, 4-prop, litho tin camouflage w/red trim, 2 gun stations, 16" W, A...............$330.00

USAF Boeing C-97 Strato Freighter, 1-pc cast metal, pnt & decal trim, decaled metal base, 24½" W, EX, A......$635.00

USAF C-45, att Pacific Miniatures, model, 2-prop, cast resin, decal trim, wood base, 9" L, EX, A $85.00

USAF Convair B-58 Hustler Jet, model, cast resin, decal trim, decorative metal base, 20" L, EX, A..........................$415.00

USAF Douglas DC-8 Military Air Transport Jet, model, cast aluminum, decal trim, swing-open tail, 23" W, EX, A ..$525.00

USAF Douglas D558-2 Skyrocket, model, cast resin, decal trim, resin & Lucite base, 33" L, EX+, A..........................$275.00

USAF Douglas Experimental Jet, model, cast resin, decal trim, decorative metal base, 15" W, EX+, A $330.00

USAF F-104 Lockheed Shooting Star, Japan, friction, tin, see-through fuselage, pilot under canopy, 13" L, EX, A...$95.00

USAF F-105A Fighter Jet, AAA/Japan, friction, tin, blk rubber tires, pilot w/oxygen mask, 11" L, EX, A...................$45.00

USAF F-51 Fighter Plane, SY, friction w/sparking action & spinning prop, litho tin, 7" L, NM (EX+ box), A....$135.00

USAF F-84 Jet, Republic Aviation, model, cast metal & resin, decal trim, decaled metal base, 12½" W, EX, A......$770.00

USAF Fairchild C-119, model, 1-pc cast aluminum, pnt & decal trim, wood & metal base w/plaque, 16½" W, EX+, A..$470.00

USAF Fairchild R4Q-1 Experimental, model, 2-prop, cast metal, pnt trim, metal & wood base, 17½" W, EX, A........$470.00

USAF Fighter Plane, Japan, red tin early biplane w/single wht prop, gun on fuselage, red, wht & bl tail, 11" W, A ...$135.00

USAF FS-059 Fighter Plane, TN, battery-op, piston action w/spinning props & lights, 13", EX (EX box), A $155.00

USAF FU-580 Sabre Jet Fighter, TT/Japan, friction, tin, pilot under canopy, NM+ (EX+ box), A..........................$115.00

USAF Pack Plane, lithographed tin, complete with accessories, MIB, $1,600.00.

USAF Lockheed C-130 Hercules, model, 1-pc cast metal, pnt & decal trim, decal base, 15½" W, EX+, A $190.00

USAF Lockheed C5A, model, 1-pc cast metal, decal trim & base, 18" W, EX, A.....................................$360.00

USAF MATS C-133 Air Transport, decal trim, weighted plastic base, 30" W, EX, A.....................................$770.00

USAF Northrop C-125 Air Rescue, scratch-built model, various materials, pnt & decal trim, 10½" L, EX, A...............$40.00

USAF Starfire FA-983 Lockheed Jet Fighter, Japan, friction, tin w/litho dome cockpit, silver w/red trim, 13" W, EX, A.$245.00

USAF Super Jet, Wyandotte, 1950s, friction, pressed steel w/rubber nose cone, red, 9" W, rare, EX (G box), A $135.00

USAF T-33 (mk TR-777), Memoto/Japan, model, cast resin, decal trim, resin base, 9", EX, A..............................$175.00

USAF T-34 Trainer (mk TD-224), Memoto/Japan, model, cast resin, decal trim, diecast base, 6½" L, EX, A $190.00

USAF TA-740 Trainer, model, single-prop, cast resin, pnt & decal trim, metal & wood base, 10" L, EX, A $135.00

USAF Thunder Chief F-105 Jet, Republic Aviation, model, cast metal, pnt & decal trim, metal base, 13" W, EX, A .$385.00

USAF Tornado B-45 Bomber, Bandai, friction, tin, 16" W, G, A $135.00

USAF Trainer, model, single-prop, cast resin, pnt trim, diecast base mk IWATA Tokyo, 8" L, EX, A $245.00

Varney Speed Lines Lockheed Orion, 1930, pnt paper, metal & wood, probably 1-of-a-kind sales demonstrator, 21" W, VG+, A $1,265.00

Western Airline Corvair-Liner 240, 2-prop, wood w/internal illumination, decal trim, 2-part metal base, 22" W, VG+, A $495.00

Westland G-AMHK Helicopter, battery-op, EX, L4......$200.00

WWI Fighter Biplane, Cragstan/NGS, battery-op, red tin w/German emblems, w/pilot, 14" W, EX+ (NM box), A....$435.00

Zeppelin, clockwork, litho tin w/lg cross-blade prop, w/fins that appear to be later modification, 11" L, G, A............$470.00

Zeppelin, Marx, string-held w/up, silver w/lg prop & tail fin, 11", MIB, A..$440.00

Zeppelin GRAF LZ-127, w/up, tin, 10" L, EX, A $150.00

Automobiles and Other Vehicle Replicas

Listed here are the model vehicles (most of which were made in Japan during the 1950s and '60s) that were designed to realistically represent the muscle cars, station wagons, convertibles, budget models and luxury cars that were actually being shown concurrently on showroom floors and dealers' lots all over the country. Most were made of tin, many were friction powered, some were battery operated. In our descriptions, all are tin unless noted otherwise.

When at all possible, we've listed the toys by the names assigned to them by the manufacturer, just as they appear on the original boxes. Because of this, you'll find some of the same models listed by slightly different names. All vehicles are painted or painted and lithographed tin unless noted.

Advisors: Nancy and Jim Schaut (S15).

See also Promotional Cars; specific manufacturers.

Aston Martin DB5, Hong Kong, friction, plastic w/blk rubber tires & fancy hubs, 9", NM (NM box), A................$110.00

Austin Healy Convertible, Bandai, friction, lt bl w/blk top & chrome-style trim, litho interior, 8", EX+, A...........$300.00

Austin Healy Convertible, Bandai, friction, red w/litho interior, 8", EX (EX box), from $250 to $300.00

Buick, MSK, friction, burgundy, tin w/blk rubber tires, working windshield wipers & searchlight, 7", NM (EX box), A.........$140.00

Buick, 1953, Marusan, remote control, cream w/red top, 8½", NM (EX box), M5..$265.00

Buick, 1961, Ichiko, friction, red & wht w/blk rubber tires, 18", NMIB, from $800 to..$950.00

Buick Convertible, Bandai, friction, wht w/litho interior, 6", MIB, A..$200.00

Buick Riviera Door-Matic, Haji, friction, blue, detachable top, doors and windows open, adjustable seats, 11", EX, A, $655.00.

Buick Sedan, 1959, Yonezawa, friction, tan over brn w/chrome-like fins, wht-walls, 8", EX (orig box), A $250.00

Buick Taxi No. 15, Japan, 1959, friction, 9", EX, $275.00.

Cadillac, 1950, Alps, friction, blk 4-door w/chrome grille & trim, yel & bl interior, 12½", MIB, A $1,430.00

Cadillac, 1950, Marusan, friction, wht 4-door w/chrome grille & trim, wht-walls, 12¾", MIB, A $1,870.00

Cadillac, 1952, Alps, friction, blk 2-door w/chrome trim, red interior, wht-walls, 11", NMIB..............................$900.00

Cadillac, 1954, Kiaeusa/Japan, bl-gray w/NP trim, wht-wall tires, 12½", M (worn box), A $1,210.00

Cadillac, 1959, Bandai, friction, gold 4-door w/wht & brn interior, wht-walls, 11½", NMIB, A..................$200.00

Cadillac, 1961, Y, friction, light blue with green and white lithographed interior, 14", rare color, NM (EX box), $600.00.

Cadillac Convertible, 1961, Bandai, battery-operated, gold with red interior, 17", EX (worn box), A, $525.00.

Cadillac, 1963, Bandai, friction, bl-gr 4-door, wht-walls, 11", MIB, A..$275.00

Cadillac Convertible, 1953, Alps, friction, blk 2-door w/chrome trim, red interior, wht-walls, 11", NMIB, from $900 to $950.00

Cadillac Convertible, 1960, Bandai, battery-op, gold 2-door w/red plush interior, chrome trim, wht-walls, MIB, A........$630.00

Cadillac Convertible, 1960, Bandai, friction, blk w/red interior, thin wht-walls, Caddy license plate, NM+ (EX box), A......$500.00

Cadillac Convertible, 1961, Bandai, battery-op, gold, red interior, ignition key, lights, 17", EX (orig box), A.......$525.00

Cadillac El Dorado, 1967, Ichiko, friction, red w/blk tires, rpl taillights & hubcaps, VG, M5..................$400.00

Cadillac Police Car, Ichiko, friction, roof light swivels, 6", NM (EX box mk Polizei), A..................$45.00

Cadillac Police Car, 1960, Yonezawa, battery-op, 18", G, A.$115.00

Cadillac Roadster, 1933, Bandai, friction, olive brn w/tan simulated soft top, wht-walls, 8½", EX (orig box), A........$95.00

Cadillac Sedan, Bandai, battery-op, gold w/blk top, brn interior, 10", VG (orig box), A..................$55.00

Cadillac Sedan, 1960, Bandai, friction, dk red, Caddy license plate, wht-walls, 11¼", NM (EX box), A................$300.00

Chevrolet, SKK, w/up, bl w/silver wheels, forward & reverse action, 5", NM (EX+ box), A..................$90.00

Chevrolet, 1954, Marusan, friction, beige 2-door with black roof, striped interior, 11", EX, $800.00.

Chevrolet, 1955, Linemar, friction, beige 2-door w/blk roof, yel & brn striped interior, wht-walls, 11", NMIB, A .$2,700.00

Chevrolet, 1955, Marusan, battery-operated, 2-tone green with lithographed interior, celluloid driver's head turns when door is opened, 10½", rare, NM, A, $2,800.00.

Chevrolet Astrovette, Amaze-A-Matics, Hasbro, NMIB, J6, $45.00.

Chevrolet Bel Air Station Wagon, 1961, friction, gr & wht w/plastic windshield & windows, 10", EX (EX box), A........$500.00

Chevrolet Camaro, Taiyo, battery-op, red, bump-&-go action, 9", NM (EX box), A $75.00

Chevrolet Camaro, TN, friction, bl w/red interior, 13½", EX+, M5..$90.00

Chevrolet Camaro Lightning Star Z28, battery-op, mc, 10", EX, J2..$90.00

Chevrolet Convertible w/U-Haul Trailer, Japan, friction, bl car w/litho interior, red trailer, EX (NM box), A..........$180.00

Chevrolet Corvette Sting Ray, Japan, battery-op, red w/gold & chrome trim, lights & horn, 11½", M....................$150.00

Chevrolet Impala 4-Door, 1961, Bandai, battery-op, travels in 5 patterns, wht, 11", EX+ (EX box), A $475.00

Chevrolet Nomad Station Wagon, 1958, Japan, bl w/wht top, 6", MIB..$250.00

Chevrolet Sedan, Bandai, friction, bl & wht, 6", M (EX+ box), A..$150.00

Chevrolet Station Wagon, 1960, Germany, gray over wht w/rear opening door, wht-walls, w/driver, 11", EX, A $250.00

Chevrolet Wagon, Bandai, friction, yel & red w/litho interior, 6", MIB, A $155.00

Chevrolet 2-Door, 1954, Linemar, friction, gray w/blk roof, wht & chrome trim, wht-walls, 11", EX, A $1,125.00

Chrysler, 1957, Japan, battery-op, wht & red w/chrome trim, wht-walls, 9½", EX, A..$275.00

Chrysler Imperial Convertible, 1959, Bandai, friction, gr w/litho interior, 8½", MIB..$200.00

Chrysler Imperial Convertible, 1959, Bandai, friction, maroon w/litho interior, 8", M (EX+ box), A......................$400.00

Chrysler Imperial Sedan, Bandai, friction, yel & wht w/litho interior, 8", MIB, A...$230.00

Chrysler Imperial Sedan, 1958, Bandai, friction, wht w/red roof, wht-walls, 8¼", NMIB, A $400.00

Edsel Convertible, 1958, Haji, friction, turq w/red & wht interior, 11", VG, A..$450.00

Edsel Station Wagon, TN, friction, black and red with white trim, opening rear gate, 10½", NM, A, $500.00.

Ferrari Gear Shift Car, Bandai, battery-op, silver w/red interior, blk rubber tires, 11", EX+ (G box), A....................$325.00

Fiat Convertible, Usagai, friction, blk rubber tires, rear spare, 6", NM (EX box), A $135.00

Fiat Sedan, Usagai, friction, blk rubber tires, rear spare, 6", NM (EX box), A $120.00

Firebird III, Alps, battery-op, bump-&-go w/flashing lights & sound, red & wht, 11½", NM (EX box), from $150 to $200.00

Ford Convertible, Japan, friction, beige w/yel & bl-gr interior, 12", minor scratches & wear, A $450.00

Ford Custom Ranch Wagon, box only, Bandai, #333, 11" L, EX+, A $120.00

Ford Fairlane 500 Skyliner, Cragstan, battery-op, 11", EX, M5..$110.00

Ford Fairlane 500 Skyliner, Cragstan, battery-op, 11", MIB, L4...$400.00

Ford Fire Chief Car, 1964, Taiyo, 11", M (G- box), S15..$75.00

Ford Mustang 2+2, 1960s, friction, blue, 14", MIB, J6, $150.00.

Ford Mustang Rusher Mach 1, 1969, Japan, Bruce Larson, bump-and-go action, MIB, $125.00.

Ford Red Cross Ambulance, 1956, Bandai, friction, wht w/red cross on roof, 12", EX (EX box), A $335.00

Ford T-Bird Convertible, Bandai, battery-op, red w/blk top, 11", MIB...$200.00

Hudson Jet, 1950s, Marusan, friction, blk 2-door w/wht-walls, plastic wind screen, 10", G+, A.................................$75.00

Ford Sunliner, 1962, Y, friction, red with lithographed interior, 10", NM (EX box), A, $355.00.

Ford T-Bird Convertible, West Germany, friction, blue and silver, composition driver, 13", NM (VG box), A, $150.00.

Jaguar XK-E, Bandai, battery-op, red, w/driver, 10½", EX (worn box), A..$120.00

Jaguar 3.4 Sedan, Bandai, friction, red, wht-walls, 8", MIB .$200.00

Lincoln, 1958, Bandai, friction, red w/blk top, 11½", VG, M5 .$150.00

Lincoln Continental Mark III, Bandai, friction, Model Auto Series decal on underside, red w/blk top, 11", EX, A.$185.00

Lincoln Continental Mark V Convertible, Japan, battery-op, remote control, 12", NM (G box), A.......................$500.00

Lincoln Futura, Alps, friction, red 2-door w/clear bubble roof, chrome trim, wht-walls, 11", MIB, A $4,180.00

Lincoln Zephyr Sedan, 1936, Skoglund & Olson, aluminum, blk w/wht rubber tires, 9¼", scarce, EX, A $400.00

Mercedes Benz, 1966, Japan, friction, bl w/blk rubber tires, 8", EX+ (EX box), A $85.00

Mercedes Benz 220 S/SE Sedan, Bandai, friction, gold, wht-walls, 10¼", NM (G box), A $200.00

Mercedes Benz 2203, 1950s, Cragstan, friction, 11½", rare, EX (orig box), A...$175.00

Mercedes Benz 300-SE, Ichiko, friction, red w/litho interior, blk rubber tires, 24", NM (EX+ box), A $120.00

Mercedes 190-SL Elektro-Phenomenal, Schuco #5503, battery-op, gr w/red interior & blk rubber tires, 8", NM (EX+ box), A $400.00

Mercedes Benz Racer, Taiwan, battery-operated, bump-and-go action, red, white and blue, 10", EX (G box), A, $100.00.

Mercedes 300-SL, 1950s, friction, blk w/gr interior, NP trim, 9", VG, A $190.00

Mercury Cougar Fire Chief Car, 1970, battery-op, 10", EX, J2 .$75.00

MG Midget Convertible, Bandai, friction, bright red tin w/fold-down windshield, fancy hubs mk MG, 8", NM (EX+ box), A $285.00

Nissan, Soon Cheng Toys/Taiwan, battery-op, red, wht, bl & yel, 10", EX (minor box wear), A................................$75.00

Oldsmobile Radicon Sedan, Japan, battery-op remote control, 13½", EX (G box), A $200.00

Oldsmobile Toronado, ATC, friction, bl w/litho interior, 15½", M (EX box), A...$350.00

Oldsmobile Toronado, 1966, Bandai, battery-op, red w/blk tires, 11", NM, M5..$195.00

Oldsmobile Toronado, Japan, battery-operated, yellow and black, 10", EX, $110.00.

Opel Convertible, W Germany, friction, yel w/wht-walls, 10", EX, A $100.00

Plymouth Valiant, Japan, friction, red w/litho interior, 8", scratches & soiling, A...$45.00

Porsche Carrera 10, battery-op, MIB, L4 ....$275.00

Porsche 7500 Electro-Matic, Distler, battery-op, gr, w/shift lever & on/off key, 10", non-working, VG (G box), A $220.00

Porsche 914, Daiya, mk #72, battery-op, red w/yel stripe & blk top, 8½", NM (NM box), M5 ....$150.00

Opel Kapitan Drive All Around, KS, battery-operated, white and red, complete with disks which control direction, 10½", rare, M (EX box), A, $1,400.00.

Porsche Convertible, Distler, battery-operated, 10", NM, $600.00. (For red, $700.00.)

Rambler Classic Station Wagon, 1961, Bandai, friction, bl & wht, 7½", NM (VG box), M5 ....$95.00
Rambler Station Wagon, Bandai, friction, blk over red w/wht trim, w/roof rack, wht-wall tires, 11", NM (EX box), A......$270.00

Rambler Station Wagon and Shasta Trailer, 1959, friction, blue and cream car, yellow and cream trailer, each 10", EX, $250.00.

Renault Dauphine, Bandai #786, friction, brn w/blk rubber tires & mc hubs, 8", NM (EX+ box), A..........................$365.00
Renault Floride, ATC/Japan, friction, red w/removable wht plastic top, 9½", EX+ (VG box), A $475.00
Renault Sedan, 1950s, Yonezawa, friction, bl w/gr interior, 7½", VG, A $150.00
Rolls-Royce, Bandai, battery-op, 2-tone, working lights, NMIB, A $200.00

Studebaker, 1956, battery-op, remote control, 8", G, A...$85.00
Triumph Coupe, Bandai, remote control, red & blk w/blk rubber tires & fancy hubs, 8", EX+ (EX box), A.................$110.00
Volkswagen, Globe, friction, bright gr, VW hubs, oval rear window, 7½", NM (EX+ box), A.......................................$75.00
Volkswagen Karmann Ghia, Japan, w/up, red w/wht top, blk rubber tires, 8", EX+ (EX box), A $300.00
Volkswagen Sedan, Bandai, battery-op, bl w/blk rubber tires, bump-&-go action w/full-figure driver, 10", EX (EX+ box), A $240.00

Banks

The impact of condition on the value of a bank cannot be overrated. Cast iron banks in near-mint condition with very little paint wear and all original parts are seldom found and might bring twice as much (if the bank is especially rare, up to five times as much) as one in average, very-good original condition with no restoration and no repairs. Over-painting and replacement parts (even screws) have a very negative effect on value. Mechanicals dominate the market, and some of the hard-to-find banks in outstanding, near-mint condition may exceed $20,000.00! (Here's a few examples: Girl Skipping Rope, Calamity, Mikado and Jonah and the Whale.) Modern mechanical banks are also emerging on the collectible market, including Book of Knowledge and James D. Capron, which are reproductions with full inscriptions stating that the piece is a replica of the original. Still banks are widely collected as well, with more than 3,000 varieties having been documented. Beware of unmarked modern reproductions.

For more information we recommend *The Dictionary of Still Banks* by Long and Pitman; *The Penny Bank Book* by Moore; *The Bank Book* by Norman; and *Penny Lane* by Davidson.

Advisors: Bill Bertoia, mechanicals; Dan Iannotti (I3), modern mechanicals; and Diane Patalano (P8).

See also Advertising; Battery-Operated; Character, TV and Movie Collectibles; Disney; Diecast Collector Banks; Reynolds Toys; Rock 'n Roll; Santa; Western.

Mechanical Banks

Acrobat, J&E Stevens, pnt CI, acrobat kicks clown's head & coin drops into base, EX, A...................................$6,600.00
Afghanistan Bank, att Mechanical Novelty Works or Kyser & Rex, ca 1885, CI, mk Harat, bear & lion at gate, VG, A..$1,540.00
Always Did 'Spise a Mule, Book of Knowledge, M, I3....$395.00
Always Did 'Spise a Mule, J&E Stevens, pnt CI, w/jockey, 10" brn base, rpr figure, G, A..$715.00
Always Did 'Spise a Mule, J&E Stevens, pnt CI, w/jockey, 10" base, G-, A...$200.00
Artillery Bank, J&E Stevens, copper-pnt CI, soldier shoots coin into fortress, 9" base, EX, A......................................$745.00
Artillery Bank, J&E Stevens, mc-pnt CI, soldier shoots coin from mortar into fortress, 9" base, VG, A $990.00

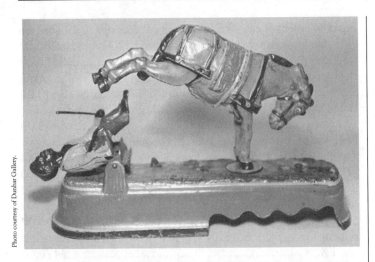

Photo courtesy of Dunbar Gallery.

Always Did 'Spise a Mule, J&E Stevens, painted cast iron, boy on bench, 10" red base, NM, $2,550.00.

Artillery Bank, Shepard Hardware, NP CI, soldier shoots coins from mortar into fortress, 8", EX, A.....................$1,155.00
Auto Bank, John Wright, 1974, orig, coin on hood flips into car, 250 made, NM, I3 ....$695.00

Photo courtesy of Dunbar Gallery.

Bad Accident, J&E Stevens, painted cast iron, boy darts in front of man on mule cart, 10" base, NM, $4,250.00.

Bad Accident, J&E Stevens, pnt CI, boy darts in front of man on mule cart, 10" base, VG, A $880.00
Bad Accident, J&E Stevens, pnt CI, boy darts in front of man on mule cart, 10" base, EX, A $1,210.00
Bad Accident, J&E Stevens, pnt CI, boy darts in front of man in mule cart, 10" base, rpt, G, A...................................$550.00
Bad Accident, James Capron, rare, NM, I3 ....$1,150.00
Bear (Slot in Chest), Kenton, ca 1870s, insert coin in bear's chest & his mouth opens & closes, VG, A..............$440.00
Bear & Tree Stump, Judd, ca 1870s, CI, place coin on tongue, tongue raises & coin slides into bank, EX, A.............$715.00
Betsy Ross, Davidson/Imswiller, 1976, orig, lady w/flag, M, I3 ....$1,075.00
Bill E Grin, J&E Stevens, pnt CI, force coin into slot & he will stick out his tongue & roll eyes upward, VG+, A ...$1,980.00

Photo courtesy of Dan Iannotti.

Betsy Ross with Trade Card (believed to be the only full-color mechanical bank trade card produced since 1891), Davidson/Imswiller, 1976, I3, $1,075.00 (bank only).

Birdie Putt, Richards/Utexiqual, M, I3 ....$425.00
Black Face Clown (Semi-Mechanical), England, litho tin clown bust, swallows coin, 5½", EX, A..............................$110.00
Blacksmith, John Deere, hammers coin into anvil, NM, I3 .$395.00

Photo courtesy of Dan Iannotti.

Bobby Clarke Slap Shot, 1977, #6 of 141 made, rare, NM, I3, $2,800.00.

Boy on Trapeze, Barton & Smith, pnt CI, boy revolves according to sz of coin deposited, VG, A $1,430.00
Boy on Trapeze, Barton & Smith, pnt CI, boy revolves according to sz of coin deposited, EX+, A.......................$2,640.00

Boy on Trapeze, Book of Knowledge, rare, NM, I3, $650.00.

Boy Scout Camp, J&E Stevens, pnt CI, Boy Scout raises flag as coin falls into bank, 10", G $1,800.00
Boy Scout Camp, J&E Stevens, pnt CI, Boy Scout raises flag as coin falls into bank, 10", rpl flag, EX, A $6,050.00
Boy Scout Camp, J&E Stevens, pnt CI, Boy Scout raises flag as coin falls into bank, 10", VG, A $3,300.00
Boy Stealing Watermelon, Kyser & Rex, 1894, pnt CI, dog attacks boy who removes hand from watermelon, rpt, G, A $550.00
Boy Stealing Watermelon, Kyser & Rex, 1894, pnt CI, dog attacks boy who removes hand from watermelon, EX.........$2,200.00

Bull Dog Bank, J&E Stevens, painted cast iron, glass eyes, blue blanket, EX, $1,100.00.

Bread Winner's Bank, J&E Stevens, ca 1886, pnt CI, 3 figures on base cause coin to fall into loaf of bread, EX+, A .$19,800.00
Bull Dog Bank, Book of Knowledge, NM+, I3...............$220.00
Bull Dog Bank, J&E Stevens, pnt CI, glass eyes, bl blanket, snaps coin from nose & swallows, G-, A..................$440.00
Bull Dog Bank, J&E Stevens, pnt CI, glass eyes, red blanket, snaps coin from nose & swallows, VG, A $660.00
Bull Dog Savings Bank, Ives Blakeslee, blk-pnt CI w/gold accents, dog takes coin from man's hand, w/up, 9", EX-, A $3,960.00
Butting Buffalo, Book of Knowledge, NM, I3 ....$385.00
Butting Buffalo, Kyser & Rex, pnt CI, buffalo butts boy up tree trunk w/raccoon atop, 7¾" base, rpl raccoon, G, A.$3,740.00
Butting Goat, Judd, ca 1870s, CI, goat butts coin into tree trunk, EX, A $470.00
Cabin Bank, Book of Knowledge, w/orig box & documents, M, I3 ....$415.00
Cabin Bank, J&E Stevens, pnt CI, Black man standing at door of slant-roof cabin, 3⅝", EX, A.............................$770.00
Cabin Bank, J&E Stevens, pnt CI, Black man standing at door of slant-roof cabin, 3½", VG...................................$475.00
Cat & Mouse, Book of Knowledge, M, I3 ....$425.00

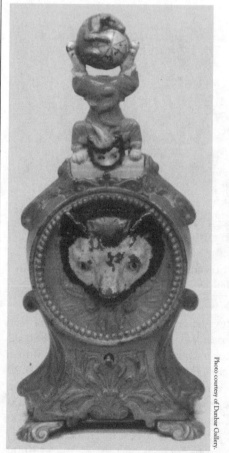

Cat and Mouse (Cat Balancing), J&E Stevens, painted cast iron, EX, from $3,000.00 to $3,500.00.

Cat & Mouse (Cat Standing), J&E Stevens, pnt CI, press lever, mouse disappears & cat appears holding mouse, VG, A..........$2,500.00
Cat Boat, Richards/Utexiqual, NM, I3 ....$895.00
Chandlers Bank, National Brass Works, coin disappears in drawer of bank, EX $225.00

Chief Big Moon, J&E Stevens, pnt CI, Indian maid in front of teepee facing frog, gold band on base, 10", EX+, A .**$4,290.00**

Chief Big Moon, J&E Stevens, pnt CI, Indian seated in front of teepee facing frog, silver band on base, 10", VG-, A.**$1,540.00**

Chief Big Moon, J&E Stevens, pnt CI, Indian seated in front of teepee facing frog, red base w/yel band, 10", NM, A.**$4,000.00**

Chief Big Moon, J&E Stevens, pnt CI, Indian seated in front of teepee facing frog, silver band on base, 10", G, A ...**$935.00**

Chimpanzee Bank, Kyser & Rex, pnt CI, scholarly monkey in front of open book at desk in domed building, rpt, A.**$310.00**

Clever Dick, Saalheimer & Strauss, dog opens his mouth & flips coin in the air & swallows, EX+, A **$2,420.00**

Clown, Chein, ca 1939, litho tin, clown bust, receives coin w/tongue, VG, A **$75.00**

Clown Bank (Arched Top), English, litho tin, tongue receives coin, EX+, A...**$155.00**

Clown on Globe, J&E Stevens, pnt CI, tan base, 9", EX, A .**$2,750.00**

Clown on Globe, J&E Stevens, pnt CI, tan base, 9", VG, A....**$1,320.00**

Clown on Globe, James Capron, NM, I3 ....**$1,200.00**

Columbian Magic, Introduction, ca 1892, CI, building w/rotunda, place coin on shelf, it disapears in bank, EX, A **$255.00**

Cragstan Jack-in-the-Box Bank, put coin in slot & clown pops up, tin, NM (EX box), M5..**$45.00**

Creedmoor, Book of Knowledge, NM+, I3 ....**$425.00**

Creedmore, J&E Stevens, pnt CI, man in gray pants shoots coin into tree trunk, 10" base, VG, A..............................**$635.00**

Creedmore, J&E Stevens, pnt CI, man in red pants shoots coin into tree trunk, 10" base, NM, A **$800.00**

Creedmore, J&E Stevens, pnt CI, man in red pants shoots coin into tree trunk, 10" base, G-, A................................**$220.00**

Cross-Legged Minstrel, Levey/England, pnt CI, insert coin, minstrel tips hat w/action from waist, EX+, A **$825.00**

Darktown Battery, J&E Stevens, pnt CI, 3 baseball players on rectangular base, 10", EX, A **$3,410.00**

Darktown Battery, J&E Stevens, pnt CI, 3 baseball players on rectangular base, 10", VG, A **$2,860.00**

Dentist, Book of Knowledge, Special Medallion Series, M, I3 ....**$350.00**

Dentist, J&E Stevens, pnt CI, dentist ready to pull Black man's tooth, ftd base, 9½", EX-, A **$11,550.00**

Destination Moon, Duro, D30, gr, gold moon ring w/inscr, w/key, rpl trap, 1960s, NM+, I3 ....**$350.00**

Dinah, English, pnt aluminum, Black bust in red dress w/wht collar, eyes roll as she swallows coin, EX+ **$400.00**

Dinah, John Harper, pnt CI, bust in yel dress, red lips, eyes roll as she swallows coin, EX, A...................................**$690.00**

Dinah, John Harper, pnt CI, bust in yel dress, red lips, eyes roll as she as she swallows coin, G, A **$330.00**

Dog on Turntable, Judd, lacquered CI w/crank hdl, dog carries penny on dish into bank building & returns, NM ...**$950.00**

Eagle & Eaglets, Book of Knowledge, eaglets chirp for food, NM, I3..**$450.00**

Eagle and Eaglets, J&E Stevens, painted cast iron, 6¾" oval base, EX, $1,540.00.

Eagle & Eaglets, J&E Stevens, pnt CI, 6¾" oval base, rpl eaglet, G, A...**$605.00**

Elephant (3 Stars), unknown, ca 1884, blk-pnt CI w/3 red stars on gold blanket, throws coin into head, VG, A **$105.00**

Elephant & Three Clowns, J&E Stevens, pnt CI, elephant on tub strikes coin w/trunk causing it to fall into tub, EX+, A.**$3,630.00**

Elephant Bank, James Capron, NM+, I3 ....**$310.00**

Elephant Bank, John Wright, w/orig box & documents, M, I3 ....**$245.00**

Elephant Swings Trunk, AC Williams, gold-pnt CI, trunk moves when coin is inserted, VG, A..........................**$95.00**

Elephant Swings Trunk, AC Williams, pnt CI, trunk moves when coin is inserted, EX+, A **$135.00**

Dog on Turntable, Judd, lacquered cast iron with crank handle, rare blue version, NM, $2,500.00.

Elephant Swings Trunk, AC Williams, pnt CI, trunk moves when coin is inserted, G, A $60.00

Elephant w/Howdah, Enterprise, pnt CI, wooden man pops out of howdah when elephant puts coin in mouth, 7", G-, A .$150.00

Football Kicker, red- & yel-pnt CI, pull back leg & push lever to kick penny into bank, G $1,200.00

Football Park, John Harper, pnt CI, player kicks coin into goal net, VG, A $2,530.00

Fowler, see Sportsman

Frog Bank (2 Frogs), J&E Stevens, pnt CI, sm frog on back flips coin into lg frog's mouth, 8¾" base, VG, A $880.00

Frog Bank (2 Frogs), J&E Stevens, pnt CI, sm frog on back flips coin into lg frog's mouth, 8¾" base, NM, A.........$4,400.00

Frog on Rock, Kilgore, 1920s, pnt CI, frog swallows coin, EX+, A $1,100.00

Frog on Round Base, J&E Stevens, pnt CI, frog swallows coin & eyes roll, VG, A $825.00

Galloping Cowboy, Y/Japan, 1950s, battery-op, cowboy on galloping wht horse, rectangular base, MIB, A.............$440.00

Girl Skipping Rope, J&E Stevens, pnt CI, yel dress, VG+, A $17,600.00

Guided Missile, Astro, D13, gray w/nose cone tip, minor fin rpr, NM+, I3 ....$85.00

Hall's Excelsior Bank, J&E Stevens, pnt CI, building w/teller in cupola, 5", EX+, A $880.00

Hall's Excelsior Bank, J&E Stevens, pnt CI building w/teller in cupola, 5", VG $600.00

Hall's Liliput Bank (w/Tray), J&E Stevens, pnt CI, cashier deposits coin into bank building, EX+, A $715.00

Hen & Chick, J&E Stevens, pnt CI, chick moves forward from under hen & pecks the coin into the bank, EX, A .$2,640.00

Hen & Chick, J&E Stevens, pnt CI, chick moves forward from under hen & pecks the coin into bank, VG, A $1,430.00

Hold the Fort (5 Holes), unknown maker, pnt CI, tan, EX, A $2,970.00

Home Bank, William Morrison, litho tin, teller behind barred window receives coin, EX+, A $550.00

Home Town Battery, Book of Knowledge, w/orig box & documents, Special Medallion Series, M, I3...................$395.00

Home Town Battery, Book of Knowledge, 1950s, CI, working, NM, M17 ....$250.00

Hoopla Bank, John Harper, pnt CI, dog jumps through clown's hoop & deposits coin into barrel, VG, A................$715.00

Humpty Dumpty, Book of Knowledge, w/orig box & documents, Special Medallion Series, M, I3 ....$375.00

Humpty Dumpty, Shepard Hardware, pnt CI, clown bust, 7½", VG+, A $1,430.00

Ice Cream Freezer, (Semi-Mechanical), John Wright,, scarce, M, I3 ....$110.00

Independence Hall Tower (Semi-Mechanical), Enterprise, pnt CI, press lever to ring bell, 9½", EX, A...................$825.00

Indian Shooting Bear, Book of Knowledge, NM, I3 ....$425.00

Indian Shooting Bear, J&E Stevens, pnt CI, brn bear, 10½" base, VG, A $1,100.00

Indian Shooting Bear, J&E Stevens, pnt CI, brn bear, 10½" base, some rpt, G, A $660.00

Initiating 1st Degree, Mechanical Novelty Works, pnt CI, butting goat, man & frog on base, EX, A $4,070.00

Initiating 2nd Degree, Mechanical Novelty Works, ca 1880, pnt CI, man on goat slings coin into frog's mouth, EX+, A $8,250.00

Jolly 'N' Bank, aluminum, ca 1920s, EX, I3 ....$425.00

Jolly 'N' Bank, Starkies, aluminum, bust of Black man in wht top hat, eyes roll as mouth flips coin, NM $450.00

Jolly 'N' Bank, Starkies, pnt CI, bust of Black man in wht top hat, eyes roll as tongue flips coin into mouth, EX, A........$330.00

Jolly 'N' Bank, Starkies/England, pnt CI, wht lips & collar, red jacket, eyes roll as mouth flips coin, G, A $110.00

Jonah & the Whale, Book of Knowledge, NM, I3..........$325.00

Photo courtesy of Dunbar Gallery.

Hall's Liliput Bank (with Tray), J&E Stevens, painted cast iron, cashier deposits coin into bank building, NM, $850.00.

Hall's Liliput Bank (w/Tray), J&E Stevens, pnt CI, cashier deposits coin into bank building, G, A $415.00

Photo courtesy of Dunbar Gallery.

Jonah and the Whale, Shepard Hardware, painted cast iron, 10¼" base, EX+, $4,500.00.

Jonah & the Whale, Shepard Hardware, pnt CI, 10¼" base, sm crack, rpr boat, A.....................$825.00

Kick Inn, Wilder Mfg/Melvisto Novelty, wood, mule kicks coin into building, G, A.....................$145.00

Leap Frog Bank, Book of Knowledge, Special Medallion, #74 of 250 made, NM+, I3.....................$395.00

Leap Frog Bank, Shepard Hardware, pnt CI, 5", G $1,400.00

Leap Frog Bank, Shepard Hardware, pnt CI, 5", VG, A .$2,200.00

Lighthouse (Semi-Mechanical), Am, ca 1891, pnt CI, 2 coin slots, bank opens when tower receives 100 nickels, VG, A.....................$1,705.00

Lion & Two Monkeys (Single Peanut), Kyser & Rex, pnt CI, monkey throws coin at lion, VG+.....................$1,500.00

Lion Hunter, J&E Stevens, pnt CI, hunter shoots coin into lion's mouth, G, A.....................$2,860.00

Little Joe, att John Harper, pnt CI bust of Black man, lifts hand to mouth, eyes roll as tongue flips coin, EX, A........$230.00

Magic Bank, J&E Stevens, painted cast iron, door opens to reveal cashier who deposits coin, EX, $1,250.00.

Magic Bank, J&E Stevens, pnt CI, door opens to reveal cashier who deposits coin, G, A.....................$525.00

Magic Bank, James Capron, NM, I3.....................$1,025.00

Magician Bank, Book of Knowledge, NM+, I3.....................$365.00

Magician Bank, J&E Stevens, pnt CI, magician at table on stepped base, 4", G, A.....................$2,090.00

Magician Bank, J&E Stevens, pnt CI, magician at table on stepped base, 4", EX, A.....................$6,050.00

Mammy & Child, Kyser & Rex, pnt CI, gr dress, 7½", scarce, rpt, A.....................$1,155.00

Mason, Blk Face, John Wright, 250 made, M, I3...........$925.00

Mason, Classic Iron (Quality Import), some rpt, NM, I3.....................$375.00

Mason, Shepard Hardware, pnt CI, 2 bricklayers on base, rpt, P, A.....................$220.00

Mason, Shepard Hardware, pnt CI, 2 bricklayers on base, rpt figure, VG, A.....................$1,650.00

Mercury Rocket, Duro, D15, silver, no pnt, buffed metal, no trap, 1960s, EX, I3.....................$55.00

Merry-Go-Round, (Semi-Mechanical), John Wright, scarce, M, I3.....................$110.00

Merry-Go-Round, Kyser & Rex, ca 1885, pnt CI, VG, A.$11,550.00

Milking Cow, Book of Knowledge, NM, I3...................$395.00

Milking Cow, J&E Stevens, pnt CI, 9¾" thin 4-ftd base, NM+, A.....................$25,300.00

Minstrel (Verse), Saalheimer & Strauss, litho tin, 'Press the lever lightly, watch my tongue appear...,' EX, A......$550.00

Monkey (Coin in Stomach), SS&SD Tillman, CI, EX, A.$580.00

Monkey & Coconut, J&E Stevens, pnt CI, monkey deposits coin into coconut, EX+, A.....................$2,200.00

Monkey & Coconut, J&E Stevens, pnt CI, monkey deposits coin into coconut, G, A.....................$770.00

Monkey & Parrot, att Saalheimer & Strauss, ca 1925, litho tin, monkey causes coin to flip into parrot's mouth, NMIB, A.....................$1,760.00

Monkey & Parrot, att Saalheimer & Strauss, ca 1925, litho tin, monkey causes coin to flip into parrot's mouth, EX....$800.00

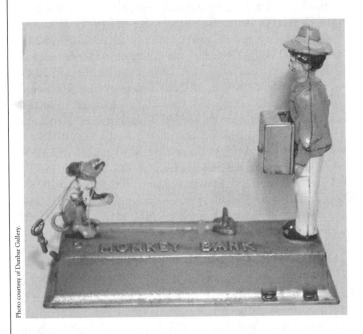

Monkey Bank, Hubley, painted cast iron, monkey leaps forward to deposit coin into organ held by man, 8¾" base, NM, $750.00.

Monkey Bank, Hubley, pnt CI, monkey leaps forward to deposit coin into organ held by man, 8¾" base, M, A......$1,375.00

Monkey Bank, Hubley, pnt CI, monkey leaps forward to deposit money into organ held by man, 8¾" base, EX, A....$440.00

Monkey Bank, James Capron, NM, I3.....................$295.00

Monkey Tips Hat, Chein, litho tin, depositing coin causes monkey to tip hat, EX, A.....................$105.00

Monkey w/Tray, German, ca 1910, litho tin, monkey standing on sq monkey house, EX, A.....................$415.00

Mosque, Judd, ca 1875, pnt CI, put coin on gorilla's tray & he deposits it into building, VG, A.....................$500.00

Mosque, Judd 1875, pnt CI, put coin on gorilla's tray & he deposits it into building, NM, A...........................$1,320.00

Mule Entering Barn, J&E Stevens, pnt CI, mule kicks legs & flips coin into barn, dog exits, 8½" base, EX, A $990.00

Mule Entering Barn, J&E Stevens, pnt CI, mule kicks legs & flips coin into barn, dog exits, 8½" base, G, A $425.00

Mule Entering Barn, James Capron, mule jumps in, dog runs out, NM, I3 ....$745.00

New Bank, att J&E Stevens, pnt CI, ca 1870s, guard exposes coin slot, deposit coin & guard returns to post, VG, A.....$250.00

Novelty Bank, J&E Stevens, pnt CI, put coin on tray, door closes & teller deposits coin into the bank, 6¼", G, A.......$385.00

Organ Bank (Boy & Girl), Book of Knowledge, NM, I3...$335.00

Organ Bank (Cat & Dog), Kyser & Rex, pnt CI, cat & dog atop crank organ turn & monkey deposits coin, 7½", EX.$1,000.00

Organ Bank w/Monkey (Medium), Kyser & Rex, pnt CI, monkey atop crank organ, 5¾", VG+, A $635.00

Organ Bank w/Monkey (Medium), Kyser & Rex, pnt CI, monkey atop crank organ, 5¾", EX+, A.....................$1,100.00

Organ Bank w/Monkey (Miniature), Kyser & Rex, pnt CI, monkey atop crank organ, VG, A $460.00

Organ Grinder, HTC/Japan, monkey atop organ w/figure turning crank on bank base, 4 actions, 8", rare, NMIB, A $660.00

Organ Grinder & Performing Bear, Kyser & Rex, ca 1890s, pnt CI, figure & house on base, G, A $250.00

Owl (Slot in Book), Kilgore, 1920s, CI, deposit coin & eyes roll, EX, A $220.00

Owl (Slot in Head), Kilgore, 1920s, CI, deposit coin & eyes roll, rpt, A $200.00

Owl (Slot in Head), Kilgore, 1920s, CI, deposit coin & eyes roll, EX $500.00

Owl (Turns Head), Book of Knowledge, M, I3...............$275.00

Owl (Turns Head), J&E Stevens, CI, brn, VG, A..........$385.00

Owl (Turns Head), J&E Stevens, CI, gray, EX, A..........$495.00

Owl (Turns Head), J&E Stevens, CI, gray, G................$300.00

Paddy & the Pig, Book of Knowledge, NM, I3 ....$385.00

Paddy & the Pig, J&E Stevens, ca 1885, pig flips coin into Paddy's mouth & he swallows, EX, A $2,090.00

Paddy & the Pig, J&E Stevens, ca 1885, pig flips coin into Paddy's mouth & he swallows, G+, A $1,485.00

Paddy & the Pig, 1970s, CI, pig flips coin into Paddy's mouth & he swallows, partial rpt, A $635.00

Pay Phone Bank, J&E Stevens, NP CI, deposit coins & phone rings, EX, A $605.00

Peg-Leg Begger, Judd, pnt copper, man seated w/hat in hand, insert coin & begger nods thanks, VG, A $1,265.00

Pelican Bank (Mammy), Trenton Lock & Hardware, japanned CI, pelican opens mouth to expose pnt figure, 8", EX+, A..$2,310.00

Penny Pineapple, Wilton, commemorating Hawaii becoming 50th state, 1st edition, NM, I3 ....$675.00

Penny Pineapple, Wilton, 2nd edition, rpr, EX, I3.........$295.00

Pig in Highchair, J&E Stevens, CI, place coin on tray & press lever, pig swallows coin, G, A $330.00

Pig in Highchair, J&E Stevens, NP CI, deposit coin on tray & press lever, pig swallows coin, EX-, A $770.00

Popeye Knockout Bank, Straits Mfg, 1930s, insert coin & Popeye knocks out Brutus on litho base, tin, 4½", EX, A.....$950.00

Presto Bank, Kyser & Rex, pnt CI, close drawer & coin disappears into domed building, G+, A..........................$275.00

Professor Pug Frog, James Capron, rare, M, I3 ....$895.00

Punch & Judy Bank, Book of Knowledge, w/orig box & documents, M, I3..$375.00

Punch & Judy Bank (Small Letters), Shepard Hardware, pnt CI, 2 figures in puppet theater, EX, A $3,740.00

Punch & Judy Bank (Small Letters), Shepard Hardware, pnt CI, 2 figures in puppet theater, G, A...........................$990.00

Rabbit, CI, sits w/penny in paws, push tail, penny drops into bank & ears wiggle, 6", rpl screw, NM, H7.............$950.00

Rabbit in Cabbage, Kilgore, ca 1925, pnt CI, ears flop when coin is deposited, VG, A $155.00

Rabbit Standing (Small), Lockwood, bronze-pnt CI, insert coin, press tail, ears move, coin falls into bank, EX, A.....$550.00

Photo courtesy of Dan Iannotti.

Race Course Runners, James Capron, NM, I3, $695.00.

Reclining Chinaman, J&E Stevens, pnt CI, yel pants, put coin in pocket, press lever, hand reveals cards, 9", rpt, A..$1,155.00

Rooster Bank, Kyser & Rex, pnt CI, drop coin in rooster's tail & his head moves, EX+, A $550.00

Santa Claus, Shepard Hardware, painted cast iron, Santa deposits coin into chimney, 4⅛" base, EX, $1,850.00.

Photo courtesy of Dunbar Gallery.

Santa Claus, John Wright, w/orig box & documents, M, I3.$325.00

Santa Claus, Shepard Hardware, pnt CI, Santa deposits coin into chimney, 4⅛" beveled base, rpt, A $605.00

Santa Claus, Shepard Hardware, pnt CI, Santa deposits coin into chimney, 4⅛" base, VG, A $1,650.00

Satelite Bank, Duro, D35, gold w/nose cone marble, inscr commemorating Spacemen, w/key, 1960s, scarce, NM, I3 ....$225.00

Scotsman, S&S/German, litho tin, push front of skirt & tongue comes out to accept coin, 7", G, A $410.00

Speaking Dog, Shepard Hardware, pnt CI, girl seated in front of dog, red dress, G, A $910.00

Speaking Dog, Shepard Hardware, pnt CI, girl seated in front of dog, red dress, NM, A $4,510.00

Sportsman (Fowler), J&E Stevens, pnt CI, hunter shoots at bird, red base, rpl bird, VG, A $15,400.00

Strato XU 232, Duro, D24, gr, w/key, NM+, I3 ....$135.00

Stump Speaker, Shepard Hardware, pnt CI, Black man w/satchel on sq base, VG+, A $1,265.00

Stump Speaker, Shepard Hardware, pnt CI, Black man w/satchel on sq base, G+, A $745.00

Tammany Bank, Book of Knowledge, Medallion Certified, Ford Collection, M, I3 ....$295.00

Tammany Bank, J&E Stevens, pnt CI, man seated in chair, hand deposits coin into pocket, EX $650.00

Tank & Cannon, Starkies, CI, place coin on platform, coin is fired into tank, EX, A $580.00

Teddy & the Bear, J&E Stevens, pnt CI, man shoots coin into tree trunk, bear pops out, 10" base, G+, A $1,100.00

Teddy & the Bear, J&E Stevens, pnt CI, man shoots coin into tree trunk, bear pops out, 10" base, EX, A $2,860.00

Teddy & the Bear, Book of Knowledge, NM, I3 ....$310.00

Toad on Stump, J&E Stevens, pnt CI, opens mouth to receive coin, M, A $1,155.00

Toad on Stump, J&E Stevens, pnt CI, opens mouth to receive coin, VG, A $440.00

Tommy Bank, John Harper, pnt CI, soldier lying on stomach fires coin into tree trunk, EX, A $4,620.00

Trick Dog, Hubley, pnt CI, dog leaps through clown's hoop & deposits coin into barrel, 6-part base, EX, A............$470.00

Trick Dog, Hubley, pnt CI, dog leaps through clown's hoop & deposits coin in barrel, solid bl base, rpr figure, A ...$150.00

Trick Dog, Hubley, pnt CI, dog leaps through clown's hoop & deposits coin into barrel, solid bl base, EX+, A $605.00

Trick Dog, Hubley, w/key, 1930, NM+, I3 ....$795.00

Trick Dog, James Capron, NM, I3 ....$625.00

Trick Pony, Book of Knowledge, w/orig box & documents, NM, I3 ....$365.00

Trick Pony, Shepard Hardware, pnt CI, deposits coin into trough, rpt, A.........................$740.00

Two Frogs, James Capron, NM, I3 ....$625.00

Uncle Remus, Book of Knowledge, Black cop chases Remus into hen house, w/orig box & documents, NM, I3 ....$395.00

Uncle Remus, Book of Knowledge, pnt CI, policeman moves toward Uncle Remus who shuts door to shed, EX, A.$150.00

Uncle Remus, Kyser & Rex, ca 1890s, policeman moves toward Uncle Remus who shuts door to shed, G, A.........$2,420.00

Uncle Sam, Book of Knowledge, NM+, I3 ....$375.00

Uncle Sam, John Wright, imported, w/orig box, M, I3 ..$235.00

Uncle Sam, Shepard Hardware, pnt CI, drops coin into carpetbag, VG, A $1,250.00

Uncle Sam, Wilton, rear trap, M, I3 ....$525.00

Photo courtesy of Dunbar Gallery.

Trick Pony, Shepard Hardware, painted cast iron, deposits coin into trough, EX, $2,500.00.

Photo courtesy of Dan Iannotti.

Uncle Sam and Arab, John Wright, commemorating 1975 Oil Embargo, 250 made, scarce, NM, I3, $1,300.00.

Uncle Tom (No Lapels), Kyser & Rex, bust of Black man, VG+, A $415.00

Uncle Tom (w/Lapels), Kyser & Rex, bust of Black man, G, A $250.00

US & Spain Bank, Book of Knowledge, w/orig box & documents..$360.00

Vending Machine, Hatwig & Vogels/Flora, litho tin, glass view front above graphics of children at play, EX, A $910.00

Vending Machine, Stollwerk Bros/Germany, tall litho tin building w/cupid in window above glass view front, EX, A $580.00

Volunteer Bank, John Harper, 1880-1890s, place coin on man's gun & he shoots it into tree trunk, rpt base, A........$285.00

Washington at Rappahannock, John Wright, orig, 1977, NM, I3 ....$750.00

Watch Bank, CL Russell Metal Novelties, silver-tone sheet metal rnd clock shape, open when filled w/25 dimes, EX, A $660.00

Watch Dog Safe, J&E Stevens, ca 1880, pnt CI, emb dog opens mouth & barks as coin in deposited, VG, A.............$360.00

Wild West Bank, Vacument/Kansas State Bank, 1960s, gun shoots coin over bandit's head who throws up hands, VG, P4 ....$85.00

William Tell, Book of Knowledge, coin rings bell in castle, NM+, I3..$340.00

William Tell, J&E Stevens, painted cast iron, NM, $1,375.00.

William Tell, J&E Stevens, pnt CI, G, A.......................$550.00

William Tell, J&E Stevens, pnt CI, VG, A....................$855.00

Wireless Bank, John Hugo, tin, CI & wood, clap hands & door deposits coin, battery-op, EX+, A $250.00

Woodpecker Bank, Bing/Germany, place coin on end of perch, turn crank, tune plays as woodpecker snatches coin, EX, A $10,730.00

World's Fair, Book of Knowledge, bronze version, M, I3...$395.00

World's Fair, J&E Stevens, pnt CI, Indian offers Columbus peace pipe, 8½" base, VG+, A...............................$1,540.00

World's Fair, J&E Stevens, pnt CI, Indian offers Columbus peace pipe, 8½" base, G $700.00

Zoo Bank, Kyser & Rex, pnt CI, red & gr lion & tiger appear when monkey's head is pushed into window, 4¼", EX, A..$1,210.00

Registering Banks

Coin Registering Bank, Kyser & Rex, ca 1889, pnt CI building w/rotating dome top, 2 slots, takes 5¢ & 10¢, EX+, A.$8,000.00

Keep' Em Sailing, Dime Register Bank, litho tin w/image of sailing ship, holds $5, octagon, scarce, VG+, A...........$200.00

Recording Bank, japanned CI w/gold lettering, stepped building w/dime register, 6½x4¼", EX, A............................$385.00

Still Banks

Amish Boy on Hay Bale, US, pnt wht metal, key lock trap, 5x3½", EX, A...$110.00

Army & Navy Bank, Kenton, CI, 2 servicemen emb on safe's double doors, 6¾", EX, A..$770.00

Baseball Player, AC Williams, 1920s, pnt CI, w/bat, 5¾", A.$385.00

Battleship Maine, Grey Iron, pnt CI, brn w/gold trim, 4½", NM, A $580.00

Battleship Oregon, J&E Stevens, pnt CI, gr w/red-trimmed stacks, 5x6", EX, A $525.00

Battleship Oregon, pewter, 5x6", rare, EX, A $635.00

Bear w/Honey Pot, Hubley, pnt CI, brn bear w/pk tongue holding bl pot, 6½", M, A...$275.00

Beauty (Horse), Arcade, blk-pnt CI, gold emb lettering, 3⅞", EX, A...$110.00

Beehive, gold CI, 3", VG, A...$120.00

Begging Bear, US, gold-pnt CI, 5⅜", EX, A $90.00

Begging Rabbit, AC Williams, pnt CI, upright pose, 5⅛", EX, A..$1,450.00

Billiken on Throne, AC Williams, gold-pnt CI w/red highlights, 6½", NM, A..$200.00

Bonzo, pot-metal figure of Bonzo w/suitcase, 5", EX, A..$100.00

Boy Scout, AC Williams, brn-pnt CI, standing figure, 6", EX, A..$100.00

Boy Scout, AC Williams, gold-pnt CI w/red trim, standing figure, 6", VG, A...$80.00

Building w/Belfry, possibly Kenton, japanned CI w/gold trim, 8x3½", EX, A...$4,620.00

Buster Brown and Tige, AC Williams, gold-painted cast iron with red trim, 5½", EX, $250.00.

Caisse Bank Building, brass w/steps & cupola, 5¼", EX, A .$110.00

Camel, AC Williams, pnt CI, gray w/gold blanket trimmed in red, 7¼", EX, A $275.00

Camel, gold-pnt CI, blk saddle, red blanket & bridle, 4½", EX, H7 ....$250.00

Camel, US, pnt CI, gray w/red blanket trimmed in gold, 4¾", EX, A $145.00

Captain Kidd, US, pnt CI, saluting figure w/shovel on tree-trunk base, 5½", EX, A...$245.00

Cat w/Ball, AC Williams, pnt CI, gray cat w/gold ball in mouth, 2½x6", EX, A $220.00

Charlie McCarthy (Movable Jaw), Vanio, wht metal w/wood jaw, sitting on seated suitcase, 5½", EX+, A............$470.00

Church Penny Bank, Chein, litho tin, slot on roof, Day By Day a Penny a Meal... on bottom trap, 4", no key o/w EX+, A .$60.00

Cinnamon Bear, German, brn-pnt wht metal, 4", EX, A.$175.00

Photo courtesy of Dunbar Gallery.

Circus Elephant, Hubley, painted cast iron, lavender pants and red polka-dot shirt, straw hat, 4", NM, $350.00.

Circus Elephant, Hubley, pnt CI, gray sitting elephant in lavender pants & red polka-dot shirt, straw hat, 4", EX+, A....$300.00

Clown, AC Williams, gold-pnt CI w/red trim, standing wearing dunce-like hat, 6", EX, A...$80.00

Clown w/Pointed Nose, German, lead, clown's head, looking up, 4", EX, A $1,485.00

Columbia Bank, Kenton, silver-pnt CI, domed building, 5¾", EX, A $440.00

Coronation, England, CI crown on tasseled base, 3", NM, A.$50.00

Cottage, George Brown, hand-pnt tin, yel 2-story house w/porch, gingerbread trim, 6½x5⅛", EX, A $690.00

Cow, AC Williams, gold-pnt CI, 4x5¼", VG, A $110.00

Decorated Egg, NP brass, etched lettering: Etta - April 5, 1893, 3½", EX, A $200.00

Dog on Tub, AC Williams, gold-pnt CI, seated pose, 4x2" dia, EX, A $175.00

Domed Mosque, Grey Iron Casting Co, gold-pnt CI, combination door in front, 5⅛", VG, A $135.00

Double Door Bank, AC Williams, CI, building w/2 doors, emb 'Bank,' 5½", EX, A $175.00

Dresser, J&E Stevens, brn-pnt CI w/cut-out 3-drawer front, wht knobs & top, 6½", M, A..$525.00

Duck on Tub, Hubley, pnt CI, wht duck w/closed blk umbrella & wearing blk top hat on rnd red base, 5⅜", EX, A $135.00

Elephant, gold-pnt CI, standing w/trunk down & curled under, 4", VG, A $65.00

Elephant on Bench on Tub, AC Williams, gold-pnt CI, 4", EX, A $110.00

Elephant on Tub, AC Williams, pnt CI, silver elephant standing upright on red tub, silver & blk trim, 5⅜", EX+, A.$275.00

Elephant on Wheels, AC Williams, CI, mounted on platform, 4", EX, A $275.00

Elk, NP CI, full antlers, standing attentively, no base, 9½", EX, A $190.00

Fidelity Trust Vaults, J Barton, 1890, CI, depicts cashiers on 3 sides, dial unlocks bank, 6½", VG, A $415.00

Fido on Pillow, Hubley, pnt CI, head & ears cocked, 7⅜" L, EX $100.00

Flat Iron Building, Kenton, CI, triangular building, 5½", EX, A $165.00

Flat Iron Building, Kenton, silver-pnt CI, 8", EX, A...$2,530.00

Four-Gable Roof Bank, gold-pnt CI, dome building w/4 gables, 2¾x4¼", EX, A $135.00

George Washington, US, pnt CI, red, wht & bl figure standing on gray base, 6", EX+, A...$110.00

Give Me a Penny, Wing, pnt CI, poor Black man in straw hat standing w/hands in pockets, 5¾", G, A..................$175.00

Globe on Arc, Grey Iron, 1900-03, red-pnt CI, globe revolves on arc, 5¼", EX, A $165.00

Good Luck Horseshoe, Arcade, CI, Buster Brown & Tige w/horse surrounded by lg horseshoe, 4x5", VG+, A..............$280.00

Goodyear Zeppelin Hangar, Ferrosteel, 1930, 2¼x7¼", EX, A $330.00

Grandpa's Hat, UB, blk- & red-pnt CI, top hat, top down, 'Grandpa's Hat,' 2¼x4", VG, A $330.00

Home Savings Bank (Dog Finial), J&E Stevens, 1891, CI, japanned & gilded, 5¾x4⅜", EX, A $245.00

Imperial Safe Deposit Bank, CI, lg blk safe w/silver emb lettering & design, w/combination lock, 9x6", EX, A.............$100.00

Independence Hall Tower, Enterprise, pnt CI, red building w/brn, gold & bl trim, 9½", EX, A........................$745.00

Indian Family, JM Harper, 1905, electroplated CI, bust of Indian chief, wife & child, 3¾", EX, A $1,100.00

Jingle Dingle See-N-Save, Rexor Toy, 1952, plastic & cb, coin rolls & rings bell, 9", NMIB, P4 ....$40.00

Kitten, Hubley, wht-pnt CI w/pk bow at side of neck, sitting upright, 4¾", EX, A $80.00

Lincoln Log, Penn, 1940s, pnt tin, hatchet & saw stuck in birch log resting on support, 8½", NM, A........................$160.00

Lion, AC Williams, gold-pnt CI, 2½x3⅝", EX, A $100.00

Lion on Tub, AC Williams, pnt CI, gold lion w/red & bl trim, 5½", EX, A $135.00

Main Street Trolley (No People), AC Williams, silver-pnt CI, red lettering, 3x6¾", rpt, A.............................$110.00

Mammy (Hands on Hips), Hubley, painted cast iron, 5¼", NM, $150.00.

Photo courtesy of Dunbar Gallery.

Mammy (Hands on Hips), Hubley, pnt CI, red dress w/wht apron, 5¼", EX+, A.............................$110.00
Mammy (w/Spoon), AC Williams, pnt CI, bl dress w/silver apron, red head scarf, 5¾", VG, A.............................$165.00
Mascot, Hubley, gold-pnt CI boy standing on red baseball, 'American National League Ball,' 6", EX, A.........$2,530.00
Metropolitan Bank, J&E Stevens, ca 1872, pnt CI, emb guard at door of safe, 6", EX, A.............................$105.00
Minuteman, Hubley, brn-pnt CI standing figure w/flesh-colored face, 6", EX, A.............................$300.00
Mulligan, AC Williams, 1950, bl, 5¾", G, A...................$80.00
Multiplying Bank, J&E Stevens, pnt CI, building w/mirrors reflecting coins making quantity seem to double, 6½", VG, A.............................$1,265.00
Mutt & Jeff, AC Williams, CI, 1 standing, 1 seated, 4x3½", EX, A.............................$145.00
Newfoundland Dog, Arcade, NP CI, standing, 3½x5¼", EX, A.............................$165.00
NY World's Fair Airplane, Dudley Crafts, blk Bakelite w/money slot on fuselage, combination lock on nose, 10" W, A........$275.00
Our Kitchener, England, japanned CI, 6¾", EX, A........$105.00
Pagoda, brass, ornate detail, 6", EX, A $580.00
Palace, Ives, japanned & pnt CI, very detailed building w/copula, 8", VG+, A.............................$1,100.00
Penny Register Pail (Still), Kyser & Rex, ca 1889, CI oaken bucket shape w/lid, 2¾", EX, A $135.00
Pig, Arcade, blk-pnt CI, 2x4", EX+, A $155.00

Policeman, Arcade, bl-pnt CI, standing, 5½", G, A.......$275.00
Prancing Horse on Platform, AC Williams, blk-pnt CI, 7¼", EX, A.............................$100.00
Puzzle Try Me Safe, Abe & Geo Abrams, patented 1868, CI, 2¾", NM, A.............................$220.00
Radio w/Combination Door, Kenton, red-pnt CI console-type radio w/combination safe door, 4½", EX, A $190.00
Radio w/Three Dials, Kenton, red-pnt CI, NP dial, 3x4⅝", EX, A.............................$230.00
Roof Bank, J&E Stevens, ca 1887, japanned CI w/gold trim, 5¼", EX, A.............................$200.00
Roosevelt New Deal, Kenton, japanned CI bust, 5", EX+, A.$495.00
Rooster, Am, blk pnt CI w/red comb & waddle, 4¾", EX, A.$120.00
Sailor, Hubley, pnt CI, saluting figure in silver uniform w/bl scarf, 5⅝", EX, A.............................$230.00
Santa w/Tree, Hubley, pnt CI, red & wht w/gold boots, holding sm gr tree, 6", EX, A.............................$965.00
Save & Smile Money Box, England, CI, blk caricature head w/red hair, bl eyes, w/ft, 4", NM, A.............................$550.00
Scotsman, pnt wht metal, standing figure w/nodding head, 8", EX+, A.............................$145.00
Seal on Rock, Arcade, blk-pnt CI, 3½x4", EX, A..........$360.00
Seated Cat w/Fine Lines, blk-pnt CI, 4x3", EX, A $220.00
Skyscraper w/Six Posts, AC Williams, CI, tall building w/6 posts on flat roof, 6½", EX, A.............................$75.00
Space Heater (Bird), England, red pnt CI, 6-sided ftd structure w/cut-out bird design, 6½", EX, A $110.00

Photo courtesy of Dunbar Gallery.

St Bernard with Large Pack, AC Williams, 7¾", EX, $225.00.

St Bernard w/Large Pack, AC Williams, 1901-1930s, 7¾", G.............................$100.00
St Bernard w/Pack (Small), AC Williams, CI, japanned w/gold trim, 3¾", EX, A.............................$30.00
Stag Deer, Arcade, gold-pnt CI, 6", VG, H7 ....$175.00
State Bank, Kenton, 1890, japanned CI, bronze trim, 3x2", EX, A.............................$55.00
State Bank, US, ca 1897, japanned CI w/gilt, 4x3", EX+, A .$85.00
State Bank, US, ca 1897, japanned CI w/gold trim, 6x4½", NM, A.............................$245.00

Tally Ho Bank, Chamberlin & Hill/England, CI, horse head surrounded by horseshoe, 4½", EX, A $145.00

Tank Bank USA 1918, AC Williams, gold-pnt CI, 3x3½", VG, A **$95.00**

Teddy Roosevelt, AC Williams, gold-pnt CI bust, 5x3½", EX, A **$330.00**

Terrier Dog, Hubley, pnt CI, wht w/blk spots, red collar, sitting upright, no base, 4½x5¾", EX, A $200.00

Trenton Trust Bank, Jacob Brubaker (Hubley)/Mary Roebling, pnt CI, lady seated in chair in front of building, M, A .. **$1,705.00**

Triangular Building, Hubley, silver-pnt CI, gold lettering, 6", EX, A **$440.00**

Two Kids (Goats), Harper, blk-pnt CI, 2 goats butting heads over tree stump, 4½", EX, A **$605.00**

Two-Faced Black Boy (Large), AC Williams, blk-pnt CI head w/gold hat & collar, 4⅛", VG, A **$80.00**

Two-Faced Black Boy (Small), AC Williams, blk-pnt CI w/gold hat & collar, 3⅛", VG, A.................................... **$65.00**

Uncle Sam, glass, pnt Uncle Sam figure attached to jar w/pnt lid, 3⅝", EX, A **$230.00**

United Banking & Trust Co, AC Williams, gold-pnt CI, flat-roofed building, 3x4x3", EX, A **$220.00**

Villa, Kyser & Rex, ca 1894, japanned CI, gold trim, red finial on roof, 5½x5", EX, A.................................... **$440.00**

Water Spaniel w/Pack (I Hear a Call), US, blk-pnt CI, silver pack, 5", EX, A **$45.00**

Westminster Abbey, England, japanned CI, 6¼x3¼", EX-, A **$190.00**

Windmill, France, brass, detailed house w/rear windmill on pebbled base, 7", EX, A.. **$200.00**

World Time Bank, Arcade, CI w/paper timetables of various cities around the world, 4⅛x2⅝", NM, A **$440.00**

Yellow Cab, Arcade, pnt CI, early blk & yel sedan w/driver, wht tires w/yel hubs, 8", EX, A................................. **$1,130.00**

Yellow Cab, Japan, yel tin w/slot atop red roof, 9", A **$470.00**

1876 Bank, Judd, 1895, japanned CI, bank building, 3⅜x3", EX, A **$135.00**

Barbie and Friends

No one could argue the fact that vintage Barbie dolls are holding their own as one of the hottest areas of toy collecting on today's market. Barbie was first introduced in 1959, and since then her face has changed three times. Her hair has been restyled over and over, she's been blond and brunette, and it's varied in length from above her shoulders to the tips of her toes. She's worn high-fashion designer clothing and pedal pushers. She's been everything from an astronaut to a veterinarian, and no matter what her changing lifestyle required, Mattel (her 'maker') has provided it for her.

Though even Barbie items from recent years are bought and sold with fervor, those made before 1970 are the most sought after. You'll need to do a lot of studying and comparisons to learn to distinguish one Barbie from another, but it will pay off in terms of making wise investments. There are several books available; we recommend them all: *The Wonder of Barbie* and *The World of Barbie Dolls* by Paris and Susan Manos; *The Collector's Encyclopedia of Barbie Dolls and Collectibles* by Sibyl DeWein and Joan Ashabraner; *The Story of Barbie* by Kitturah B. Westenhouser; *Barbie Fashion, Vol. 1, 1959-1967* by Sarah Sink Eames; *Barbie Exclusives* by Margo Rana; and *Barbie, The First 30 Years, 1959 Through 1989* by Stefanie Deutsch (all published by Collector Books).

Remember that unless the box is mentioned in the line (orig box, MIB, MIP, NRFB, etc.), values are given for loose items. As a general rule, a mint-in-the box doll is worth twice as much as one mint, no box. The same doll, played with and in only good condition, is worth half as much (or even less). Never-removed-from-box examples sell at a premium.

Advisor: Marl Davidson (D2).

Dolls

Allan, 1964, pnt red hair, orig outfit, straight legs, M, D2.**$70.00**

Allan, 1964, pnt red hair, straight legs, NRFB, D2......... **$165.00**

Barbie, #1, 1958-59, blond hair, MIB, D2 .... **$9,000.00**

Barbie, #1, 1958-59, blond hair, replica stand, MIB, D2.**$5,000.00**

Barbie, #1, 1958-59, brunette hair, MIB, D2 .... **$10,000.00**

Barbie, #2, 1959, brunette hair, MIB, D2 .... **$8,000.00**

Barbie, #3, 1960, blond hair, original swimsuit, MIB, D2, $1,500.00.

Barbie, #3, 1960, blond hair, orig swimsuit, NM+, D2 ...**$950.00**

Barbie, #3, 1960, blond hair, wearing Evening Splendor, MIB, D2 .... **$3,500.00**

Barbie, #3, 1960, brunette hair, bl eyeliner, orig swimsuit, NM, D2 .... **$1,000.00**

Barbie, #3, 1960, brunette hair, brn eyeliner, orig swimsuit, MIB, D2 ....$2,000.00

Barbie, #4, 1960, blond hair, orig swimsuit, NM, D2 .....$400.00

Barbie, #4, 1960, blond hair, replica swimsuit, NM, D2.$275.00

Barbie, #4, 1960, brunette hair, orig swimsuit, NM, D2 .$425.00

Barbie, #5, 1961, blond hair, orig swimsuit, MIB, D2....$550.00

Barbie, #5, 1961, brunette hair, orig swimsuit, EX, D2...$350.00

Barbie, #5, 1961, brunette hair, wearing Evening Splendor, MIB, D2 ....$1,950.00

Barbie, #5, 1961, red hair, orig swimsuit, EX, D2 ....$400.00

Barbie, #5, 1961, red hair, orig swimsuit, MIB, D2.........$900.00

Barbie, American, 1965, blond hair, orig swimsuit, NM+, D2 ....$1,400.00

Barbie, American Beauty Queen, 1991, NRFB (corner damaged), D12..$45.00

Barbie, American Girl, 1964, blond hair w/side part, MIB, D2 ....$3,900.00

Barbie, American Girl, 1965, brunette hair, MIB, D2...$2,800.00

Barbie, Angel Face, 1983, M (worn box), M15 ....$35.00

Barbie, Ballerina, 1983 department store special, NRFB, D2.$75.00

Barbie, Ballroom Beauty, 1991 Walmart special, NRFB, D2 .$40.00

Barbie, Beautiful Bride, foreign, 1976 department store special, NRFB, D2 ....$125.00

Barbie, Benefit Ball, 1992, NRFB, D2............................$150.00

Barbie, Blossom Beautiful, 1992 Sears special, NRFB, D2..$350.00

Barbie, Blue Rhapsody, 1986, porcelain, NRFB, D2.......$750.00

Barbie, Blue Rhapsody, 1991 department store special, NRFB, D2 ....$300.00

Barbie, Bubble-Cut, 1961, blond hair, MIB, D2 ....$450.00

Barbie, Bubble-Cut, 1961, brunette hair, original swimsuit, MIB, D2, $600.00.

Barbie, Bubble-Cut, 1961, blond hair, orig swimsuit, EX, D2 ....$175.00

Barbie, Bubble-Cut, 1961, brunette hair, replica swimsuit, NM, D2 ....$250.00

Barbie, Bubble-Cut, 1961, red hair, MIB, D2 ....$550.00

Barbie, Bubble-Cut w/side part, 1962-64, blond hair, MIB, D2 ....$900.00

Barbie, Bubble-Cut w/side part, 1962-64, brunette hair, MIB, D2 ....$1,000.00

Barbie, Bubble-Cut w/side part, 1962-64, red hair, extremely rare, M, D2 ....$650.00

Barbie, Busy Gal, 1995, NRFB, D12 ....$100.00

Barbie, California Dream, 1987 department store special, NRFB, D2..$45.00

Barbie, Chinese, 1993, NRFB, D12..................................$30.00

Barbie, Circus Star, FAO Schwarz, 1994, NRFB, D12 ...$150.00

Barbie, Color Magic, 1966, blond hair, NRFB, D2 .....$2,500.00

Barbie, Color Magic, 1966, brunette hair, MIB, D2....$4,000.00

Barbie, Crystal Rhapsody, 1992, porcelain, NRFB, D2 ..$500.00

Barbie, Czechoslovakian, 1990, NRFB, D2.....................$110.00

Barbie, Dance 'N Twirl, 1994 department store special, NRFB, D2 ....$65.00

Barbie, Dazzlin' Date, 1992 Target special, NRFB, D2 .....$35.00

Barbie, Deluxe Quick Curl, 1975 department store special, NRFB, D2 ....$50.00

Barbie, Donna Karan, 1995 Bloomingdale's limited edition, NRFB, D12 ....$175.00

Barbie, Dr, 1987 department store special, NRFB, D2......$95.00

Barbie, Dream Bride, 1991, NRFB, D12 ....$135.00

Barbie, Dreamglow, 1986, orig outfit, VG, D15................$15.00

Barbie, Dreamtime, 1988 department store special, NRFB, D2 ....$25.00

Barbie, Dutch, 1993, NRFB, D12....................................$30.00

Barbie, Egyptian Queen, 1993, NRFB, D2 ....$65.00

Barbie, Emerald Elegance, 1994, special edition, NRFB, D12..$50.00

Barbie, Empress Bride, Bob Mackie, 1992, NRFB, D2....$950.00

Barbie, Enchanted Evening, 1986, porcelain, NRFB, D2 .$500.00

Barbie, English, 1991, NRFB, D2 ....$75.00

Barbie, Evening Elegance, 1990 JC Penney special, NRFB, D2 ....$75.00

Barbie, Evening Extravaganza (Black), 1993, NRFB, D2 ...$150.00

Barbie, Evening Flame, 1991 department store special, NRFB, D2 ....$200.00

Barbie, Evergreen Princess, 1994, 2nd in series, NRFB, M15 .$130.00

Barbie, Fashion Queen, 1963, molded brunette hair, complete w/3 wigs & stand, NRFB, D2 ....$500.00

Barbie, Fashion Queen, 1963, molded brunette hair, complete w/3 wigs & stand, NM, D2 ....$150.00

Barbie, Fashion Queen, 1963, molded brunette hair, nude, NM, D2 ....$70.00

Barbie, Flight Time, 1989, NRFB, D12............................$25.00

Barbie, Goddess of the Sun, Bob Mackie, 1995, NRFB, D2 .$200.00

Barbie, Gold Sensation, 1993, porcelain, NRFB, D2......$500.00

Barbie, Golden Greetings, FAO Schwarz, 1989 department store special, NRFB, D2 ....$250.00

Barbie, Golden Winter, 1993 department store special, NRFB, D2 ....$85.00

Barbie, Great Shapes, 1983, NRFB, D12 ....$35.00

Barbie, Greek, 1985, NRFB, D2 ....$95.00

Barbie, Hair Happenin's, Sears Exclusive, 1971, orig outfit w/rpl belt, EX, D2 ....$600.00

Barbie, Hallmark Victorian Elegance, 1st in series, MIB, P12 ....$145.00

Barbie, Holiday, Canadian, 1993, NRFB, D12 ....$150.00

Barbie, Holiday, 1988, NRFB, D12 ....$750.00

Barbie, Holiday, 1989, NRFB, D2 ....$300.00

Barbie, Holiday, 1990, NFRB, D2 ....$150.00

Barbie, Holiday, 1991, NRFB, D2 ....$200.00

Barbie, Holiday, 1992, NRFB, D2 ....$125.00

Barbie, Holiday, 1993, NRFB, D2 ....$125.00

Barbie, Holiday Hostess, 1992, NRFB, D12 ....$60.00

Barbie, Holiday Memories, 1995 department store special, NRFB, D2 ....$75.00

Barbie, Ice Capades, 1989, NRFB, D12 ....$30.00

Barbie, International Holiday, 1994, NRFB, D2 ....$100.00

Barbie, International Travel, 1995 department store special, NRFB, D2 ...:...............................$75.00

Barbie, Italian, 1979, NRFB, D2 ....$200.00

Barbie, Italian, 1992, MIB, D2 ....$35.00

Barbie, Jamaican, 1991, NRFB, D2 ....$35.00

Barbie, Japanese, 1984, NRFB, D2 ....$150.00

Barbie, Kissing, 1979, orig outfit, VG, M15 ....$20.00

Barbie, Kool-Aid, 1993, 1st in series, MIB, P12 ....$195.00

Barbie, Little Debbie, 1992, limited edition, NRFB, J6, $85.00.

Photo courtesy of June Moon.

Barbie, Kraft, 1994, MIB, M15 ....$50.00

Barbie, Magic Curl, 1981 department store special, NRFB, D2 ....$40.00

Barbie, Magic Moves, 1986, orig outfit, VG, M15 ....$20.00

Barbie, Malibu, 1971, original swimsuit, MIP, $75.00.

Barbie, Malibu, 1971, orig swimsuit, VG, M15 ....$20.00

Barbie, Mardi Gras, 1987 department store special, NRFB, D2 ....$150.00

Barbie, Masquerade Ball, Bob Mackie, 1993, MIB, D2...$400.00

Barbie, Miss, 1964, pnt hair w/orange headband, complete w/3 wigs & stand, NM+, D2 ....$425.00

Barbie, Miss America, 1972, brunette hair, orig outfit, no roses o/w complete, NM, D2 ....$95.00

Barbie, Moonlight Magic, 1993 department store special, NRFB, D2.....................................$90.00

Barbie, Moonlight Rose, 1991 Hills special, NRFB, D2 ...$45.00

Barbie, Native American, 1992, 1st in series, NRFB, M15..$65.00

Barbie, Neptune Fantasy, Bob Mackie, 1992, MIB, D2.$1,000.00

Barbie, Night Sensation, FAO Schwarz, 1991 department store special, NRFB, D2 ....$225.00

Barbie, Opening Night, 1992, 2nd in Classic series, NRFB, M15.....................................$85.00

Barbie, Parisienne, 1980, 1st in International series, MIB, M15.....................................$200.00

Barbie, Party Sensation, 1990 department store special, NRFB, D2.....................................$45.00

Barbie, Peaches & Cream, 1984, NRFB, D12 ....$55.00

Barbie, Peppermint Princess, 1995, 3rd in series, NRFB, M15.$75.00

Barbie, Pepsi Spirit, 1989 department store special, NRFB, D2 ....$65.00

Barbie, Platinum, Bob Mackie, 1991, NRFB, D2............$700.00

Barbie, Polynesian, Dolls of the World series, 1994, NRFB, D12 ....$25.00

Barbie, Pretty in Purple, 1992 K-Mart special, NRFB, D12.$50.00

Barbie, Queen of Hearts, Bob Mackie, 1994, NRFB, D12.$275.00

Barbie, Royal, 1980, 2nd in International series, NRFB, M15...$200.00

Barbie, Royal Enchantment, 1995 JC Penney special, NRFB, D2...$50.00

Barbie, Royal Romance, 1992 department store special, NRFB, D2...$125.00

Barbie, Royal Splendor, 1993, porcelain, NRFB, D2......$400.00

Barbie, Russian, 1988, NRFB, D2.................................$75.00

Barbie, Savvy Shopper, 1994 Bloomingdale's department store special, NRFB, D2...$150.00

Barbie, Scottish, 1980, NRFB, D2.................................$125.00

Barbie, Scottish, 1990, NRFB, D2.................................$65.00

Barbie, Sea Holiday, 1992, NRFB, D12.........................$50.00

Barbie, Silver Screen, FAO Schwarz, 1993 department store special, NRFB, D2...$200.00

Barbie, Silver Starlight, porcelain, 1993, NRFB, D2......$500.00

Barbie, Snow Princess, foreign, 1981 department store special, NRFB, D2...$200.00

Barbie, Solo in the Spotlight, 1989, porcelain, NRFB, D2.$300.00

Barbie, Southern Belle, 1991 Sears special, NRFB, D2 ....$55.00

Barbie, Sparkling Slendor, 1993 Service Merchandise special, NRFB, D12...$45.00

Barbie, Standard, 1970, lt brn hair, orig 1-pc swimsuit, NRFB, D2...$700.00

Barbie, Starlight Waltz, 1995, NRFB, D12.................$145.00

Barbie, Swedish, 1982, NRFB, D2.................................$95.00

Barbie, Sweet Roses, 1989 department store special, NRFB, D2...$35.00

Barbie, Swirl Ponytail, 1964, blond hair, orig swimsuit, MIB, D2...$750.00

Barbie, Swirl Ponytail, 1964, blond hair, orig swimsuit, VG, D15...$245.00

Barbie, Swirl Ponytail, 1964, brunette hair, orig swimsuit, NM, D2...$475.00

Barbie, Swirl Ponytail, 1964, red hair, orig swimsuit, MIB, D2...$750.00

Barbie, Swirl Ponytail, 1964, red hair, wearing Barbie in Switzerland, M, D2...$850.00

Barbie, Talking, 1968, orig swimsuit & bows, EX, D2 ....$150.00

Barbie, Talking, 1969, brunette hair, orig swimsuit, NM+, D2...$150.00

Barbie, Talking, 1969, titian hair, NRFB, D2.................$300.00

Barbie, Truly Scrumptious, 1968, MIB, D2.................$500.00

Barbie, Twist 'N Turn, 1966, brunette hair, NMIB, D2 .$350.00

Barbie, Twist 'N Turn, 1967, blond hair, orig swimsuit, belt & hair bow, M, D2...$225.00

Barbie, Twist 'N Turn, 1967, brunette hair, orig swimsuit & hair bow, VG, M15...$95.00

Barbie, Twist 'N Turn, 1969, brunette hair, NRFB, D2 .$700.00

Barbie, Twist 'N Turn, 1969, brunette hair, nude, M, D2 .$235.00

Barbie, Vacation Sensation, 1986 department store special, NRFB, D2...$40.00

Barbie, Valentine, 1994 department store special, NRFB, D2...$50.00

Barbie, Walk Lively, 1971 department store special, NRFB, D2...$200.00

Barbie, Wedding Fantasy, 1989, NRFB, D12.................$65.00

Barbie, Winter Fantasy, FAO Schwarz, 1990 department store special, NRFB, D2...$300.00

Barbie, 35th Anniversary, 1994, blond hair, NRFB, D12.$65.00

Barbie, 35th Anniversary, 1994, brunette hair, NRFB, D12.$85.00

Barbie as Dorothy, Hollywood Legend series, 1994, NRFB, D2...$50.00

Barbie as Scarlett, Hollywood Legend series, 1994, red dress, NRFB, D2...$75.00

Barbie as Scarlett, Hollywood Legend series, 1994, gr & wht picnic dress, NRFB, D2...$55.00

Cara, Free Movin', 1975, no tennis racket, NRFB, M15 ..$55.00

Christie, Golden Dream, 1980 department store special, NRFB, D2...$40.00

Christie, Super Size, MIB, $300.00.

Christie, Superstar, 1976 department store special, NRFB, D2...$55.00

Christie, Twist 'N Turn, 1970, NRFB, D2.....................$250.00

Courtney, Cool Tops, 1990 department store special, NRFB, D2...$30.00

Courtney, Pet Pals, 1991 department store special, NRFB, D2...$35.00

Francie, Malibu, 1970, orig outfit, VG, M15 ....$45.00

Francie, 1966, blond hair, orig striped swimsuit, bendable legs, NM, D2...$90.00

Francie, 1966, brunette hair, straight legs, MIB, D2.......$450.00

Francie (no bangs), 1971, blond hair, orig orange outfit, NM, D2...$1,000.00

Ken, Busy, 1972, pnt brn hair, orig outfit & accessories, VG, M15...$65.00

Ken, Dream Date, 1982 department store special, NRFB, D2 .**$35.00**

Ken, Dream Glow, 1985 department store special, NRFB, D2..**$25.00**

Ken, Earring Magic, 1992, NRFB, M15 ....**$45.00**

Ken, Free Moving, 1975, pnt hair, orig outfit & accessories, EX+, D2 ....**$35.00**

Midge, 1965, blond hair, orig swimsuit & hair ribbon, bendable legs, NM, D2...**$300.00**

Midge, 1965, titian hair, orig swimsuit, rpl hair ribbon, bendable legs, NM, D2................................**$250.00**

Ken, Mod Hair, 1973, MIB, $45.00.

PJ, Fashion Photo, 1978, MIB, $50.00.

Ken, Sea Holiday, 1992 department store special, NRFB, D2 ....**$30.00**

Ken, Spanish Talking, 1969, pnt hair, orig outfit, no pull cord, D2 ....**$25.00**

Ken, Sport 'N Shave, 1979, NRFB, M15 ....**$35.00**

Ken, Talking, 1969, orig outfit, mute, VG, M15 ....**$50.00**

Ken, Totally Hair, 1991 department store special, NRFB, D2 ....**$55.00**

Ken, Western, 1980 department store special, NRFB, D2 ...**$35.00**

Ken, 1961, flocked blond hair, straight legs, NRFB, D2.**$350.00**

Ken, 1961, flocked brunette hair, straight legs, MIB, D2..**$250.00**

Ken, 1961, flocked hair, orig outfit, straight legs, VG (orig box), D15 ....**$145.00**

Ken, 1962, pnt blond hair, straight legs, MIB, D2 ....**$150.00**

Ken, 1962, pnt blond hair, straight legs, orig swimsuit & sandals, NM, D2...**$65.00**

Ken, 30th Anniversary, 1991, porcelain, NRFB, D2 ......**$200.00**

Ken as Rhett, Hollywood Legend series, 1994, NRFB, D2...**$65.00**

Midge, 1963, blond hair, straight legs, MIB, D2 ....**$200.00**

Midge, 1963, blond hair, straight legs, no freckles, MIB, D2 .**$500.00**

Midge, 1963, blond hair, straight legs, nude, NM, D2......**$85.00**

Midge, 1963, brunette hair, straight legs, MIB, D2 ....**$200.00**

Midge, 1963, titian hair, orig swimsuit, straight legs, NM, D2 ....**$125.00**

Midge, 1963, titian hair, straight legs, MIB, D2 ....**$225.00**

PJ, Live Action, 1971, MIB, $200.00.

PJ, Sweet Roses, 1983, NRFB, D12 ....$75.00
Ricky, 1965, MIB, D2 ....$125.00
Ricky, 1965, wearing Let's Explore, NM, D2 ....$110.00
Skipper, Dramatic Living, orig swimsuit, w/orange skooter, NRFB, D2 ....$300.00
Skipper, Dramatic Living, orig swimsuit w/rpl bows, NM, D2 ....$45.00
Skipper, Growing Up, 1975, orig outfit, VG, M15 ....$35.00
Skipper, Horse Lovin', 1982, NRFB, D12 ....$50.00
Skipper, Jewel Secrets, 1986, NRFB, D12 ....$30.00
Skipper, Western, 1980, MIB, M15 ....$35.00
Skipper, 1965, blond hair, bendable legs, NRFB, D2 .....$400.00
Skipper, 1965, blond hair, orig swimsuit, bendable legs, D2 .$75.00
Skipper, 1970, blond hair, orig swimsuit, straight legs, EX+, D2 ....$60.00
Skipper, 1970, titian hair, straight legs, MIB, D2 ....$150.00
Skipper, 30th Anniversary, 1993, porcelain, MIB, D2 .$175.00
Skooter, 1965, blond hair, straight legs, NRFB, D2........$235.00
Skooter, 1965, brunette hair, orig swimsuit, straight legs, NM, D2 ....$65.00
Skooter, 1965, red hair, replica swimsuit, straight legs, VG, D15 ....$45.00

Skooter, Funtime, 1976, MIB, $50.00.

Stacey, Talking, 1967, titian hair, orig swimsuit, NM, D2 .$165.00
Stacey, Talking, 1967, titian hair, orig swimsuit, NRFB, D2.$450.00
Stacey, Twist 'N Turn, 1967, blond hair, NRFB, D2 .....$700.00
Stacey, Twist 'N Turn, 1969, blond hair, MIB, D2 ....$325.00
Steffie, Walk Lively, 1972, brunette hair, bendable legs, orig outfit, NM, D2..$125.00
Todd, MIB, D2 ....$150.00
Tutti, 1966, blond hair, wearing Swing-a-Ling, NM, D2 .$75.00

Tutti, 1966, blond or brunette hair, NRFB, D2 ....$150.00
Whitney, Jewel Secrets, NRFB, M15 ....$100.00

Cases

Barbie, cream background, 1965, NM, $25.00.

Barbie, Francie & Skipper, 1965, Barbie wearing International Fair, rare, EX, D2 ....$25.00
Barbie & Francie, 1965, yel, oblong, VG, D2 ....$20.00
Barbie & Ken, 1962, teal gr w/lg picture of Ken & sm picture of Barbie, rectangular, G, D2 ....$15.00
Barbie & Midge Travel Pals, 1963, blk, G-, D2 ....$25.00

Skipper and Skooter, complete with dolls, NM, from $400.00 to $500.00.

Barbie in Fashion Shiner, 1965, wht, hdl broken o/w NM, D2 ....$10.00

Barbie's Playhouse Pavillion, #2914, Europe, 1978, plastic 2-room carrying case, NRFB, D2 ....$65.00

Ken in Rally Days, 1962, teal gr, G, D2 ....$15.00

Madison Avenue, FAO Schwarz, 1991, EX, D2 ....$95.00

Miss Barbie, 1963, blk patent leather w/zipper closure, no mirror o/w EX, D2 ....$95.00

Skipper, 1964, yel, dbl opening, EX, D2..........................$20.00

Skipper & Skooter, 1965, yel, oblong, rare, NM, D2........$75.00

Tutti, German, 1974, orange, NM, D2 ....$50.00

World of Barbie, 1965, dbl case w/wht flowers & 2 pictures of Barbie, EX+, D2......................................$20.00

Clothing and Accessories

After Five, Barbie, #934, complete, NM, D2 ....$65.00

All Together Elegant, Francie, #1242, complete, NM, D2.$125.00

American Airlines Captain, Ken, #779, NRFB, D2 ....$400.00

Arabian Knights, Ken, #774, NRFB, D2.........................$195.00

Arabian Nights, Barbie, #874, missing gold bracelet & pamphlet, NM, D2 ....$175.00

Barbie Baby-Sits, #953, complete, EX+, D2 ....$95.00

Barbie Fashion Favorites, #3789, 1981, silver robe, MIP, M15 .$5.00

Barbie Fashion Favorites, #3792, 1981, tricot outfit, MIP, M15 ....$4.00

Barbie in Holland, #823, no pamphlet, NM, D2 ....$95.00

Barbie in Mexico, #820, no pamphlet, NM, D2..............$85.00

Barbie Western Fashions, 1983, w/boots & hat, MIP, M15.$25.00

Beverly Hills Fashions, Barbie, #3298, 1987, NRFB, D2 ..$35.00

Bright 'N Brocade, Barbie, #1786, complete, NM, D2 .....$75.00

Campus Belle Fashion Pak, G, D2 ....$8.00

Campus Hero, Ken, #770, NRFB, D2.............................$95.00

Campus Sweetheart, Barbie, #1616, complete, NM+, D2.$600.00

Career Girl, Barbie, #954, complete, NM+, D2.............$110.00

Cheerful Chef Fashion Pak, Ken, missing hot dog, VG, D2.$50.00

Cheerleader, Barbie, #876, complete, EX, D2 ....$55.00

Chill Chaser, Skipper, #1926, complete, NM, D2 ....$45.00

Chilly Chums, Skipper, #1973, complete, M, D2 ....$40.00

Cinderella, Barbie, #872, no pamphlet, NM+, D2 ....$195.00

College Student, Ken, #1416, complete, NM+, D2........$300.00

Color Kick, Barbie, #3422, bodysuit only, NM, D2 ....$25.00

Commuter Set, Barbie, #916, complete, NM, D2...........$600.00

Concert in the Park, Francie, #1256, complete, EX+, D2 ..$65.00

Cool It Fashion Pak, Francie, complete, EX, D2...............$25.00

Cotton Casuals, Barbie, #912, dress only, G, D2 ....$15.00

Country Club Dance, Barbie, #1627, replica necklace, missing shoes, G-, D2 ....$50.00

Cruise Stripes, Barbie, #918, complete, EX, D2 ....$50.00

Dance Party, Francie, #1257, dress only, EX, D2 ....$10.00

Dancing Stripes, Barbie, #1843, complete, EX+, D2 ....$65.00

Day at the Fair, Skipper, #1911, complete, NM+, D2 ....$110.00

Dinner at Eight, Barbie, #946, complete, NM+, D2 ....$75.00

Dr Ken, #793, complete, NM, D2 ....$60.00

Dream Boat, Ken, #785, complete, NM, D2 ....$45.00

Dreamy Duo, Francie, #3450, NRFB, D2 ....$55.00

Enchanted Evening, Barbie, #983, complete, EX, D2 ....$175.00

Evening Enchantment, Barbie, #1695, complete, EX, D2.$195.00

Extravaganza, Barbie, #1844, complete, NM+, D2.........$150.00

Fancy Dancy, Barbie, #1858, complete, M, D2.............$140.00

Fancy Frills, Barbie, #3183, MOC, M15.............................$5.00

Fashion Collectibles, Ken, #1932, 1932, orange robe, MIP, M15..$3.00

Fashion Collectibles, Skipper, #1943, 1980, coat, MIP, M15.$4.00

Fashion Collectibles, Skipper, #1944, 1980, long dress, MIP, M15 ....$4.00

Color Coordinates Fashion Pak, Barbie and Midge, #1832, MOC, $65.00.

Fashion Luncheon, Barbie, #1656, complete, M, $500.00.

Fashion Luncheon, Barbie, #1656, dress only, EX, D2 .....$95.00

Fashion Shiner, Barbie, #1691, complete, NM+, D2........$95.00

Finishing Touches, Barbie, 1984, MOC, M15 ....$5.00

Floating Gardens, Barbie, #1696, complete, EX, D2 ......$225.00

Flower Girl, Skipper, #1904, complete, NM, D2 ....$50.00

Flower Showers, Skipper, #1939, NRFB, D2....................$70.00

Fraternity Dance, Barbie, #1638, complete, M, D2 ....$350.00

Friday Night Date, Barbie, #979, complete, NM, D2 ....$85.00

Frosty Fur, Francie, #3455, NRFB, D2 ....$50.00

Fun at McDonalds, Barbie, #4274, 1982, NRFB, D2 ....$30.00

Fur Out, Francie, #1262, coat only, NM, D2 ....$35.00

Furry Go Round, Francie, #1296, complete, M, D2........$350.00

Gad Abouts, Francie, #1250, complete, M, D2 ....$125.00

Garden Party, Barbie, #931, complete, NM, D2 ....$50.00

Garden Wedding, Barbie, #1658, complete, EX, D2 ......$150.00

Gay Parisienne, Barbie, #964, complete, NM, D2.......$1,000.00

Go Granny Go, Francie, #1267, missing album cover, NM+,
    D2 ....$85.00

Goin' Hunting, Ken, #1409, complete, NM, D2 ....$45.00

Going to the Ball Fashion Pak, Barbie & Midge, jacket only, EX,
    D2...$12.00

Gold Rush, Francie, #1222, complete, EX+, D2 ....$65.00

Golden Elegance, Barbie, #992, complete, NM, D2 ....$125.00

Golden Girl, Barbie, #911, complete, NM, D2 ....$65.00

Golden Glitter, Barbie, #3340, complete, M, D2.............$75.00

Groovin' Gauchos, Barbie, #1057, missing bag, NM+, D2.$75.00

Gypsy Spirit, Barbie, #1458, complete, G, D2 ....$25.00

Happy Birthday, Skipper, #1919, dress only, G, D2..........$12.00

Heavenly Holidays, Barbie, #4277, 1982, NRFB, D2 ....$75.00

Here Comes the Bride, Barbie, #1665, complete, EX, D2 .$200.00

Here Comes the Groom, Ken, #1426, missing hat, vest & gloves,
    NM, D2..$600.00

Ice Breaker, Barbie, #942, complete, NM, D2 ....$55.00

Ice Cream 'N Cake, Skipper, #1970, complete, M, D2.....$35.00

In Training, Ken, #780, complete, M, D2 ....$18.00

It's a Date, Francie, #1251, complete, NM, D2 ....$65.00

Jazz Concert, Ken, #1420, complete, NM+, D2 ....$140.00

Jump Into Lace, Barbie, #1823, complete, EX, D2 ....$45.00

Just for Fun Fashion Pak, Skipper, MOC, D2 ....$125.00

Ken in Holland, #777, complete, NM, D2.......................$115.00

Ken Western Fashions, 1983, w/boots & hat, MIP, M15 .$25.00

Knitting Pretty, Barbie, #957, bl, complete, NM, D2 ....$75.00

Lace Caper, Barbie, #1791, complete, M, D2...................$55.00

Lamb 'N Leather, Barbie, #1467, complete, M, D2 ....$150.00

Land & Sea, Skipper, #1917, NRFB, D2 ....$95.00

Learning To Ride, Skipper, #1935, complete, M, D2 .....$165.00

Leather Limelight, Francie, #1269, complete, NM+, D2..$125.00

Leather Weather, Julia, #1751, complete, M, D2 ....$85.00

Little Bow Pink, Barbie, #1483, complete, M, D2 ....$75.00

Little Red Riding Hood, Barbie, #880, complete, NM, D2 .$300.00

Lollapaloozas, Skipper, #1947, complete, NM, D2 ....$75.00

Lunch Date, Barbie, #1600, complete, NM, D2................$75.00

Lunch on the Terrace, Barbie, #1649, complete, NM, D2 .$175.00

Masquerade, Ken, #794, NRFB, D2 ....$125.00

Midi Magic, Barbie, #1869, complete, EX+, D2 ....$50.00

Midi Plaid, Francie, #3444, NRFB, D2.............................$65.00

Miss Astronaut, Barbie, #1641, uniform only, VG, D2.....$35.00

Miss Teenage Beauty, Francie, #1284, skirt only, EX+, D2 .$75.00

Mood Matchers, Barbie, #1792, complete, NM, D2 ....$75.00

Morning Work Out Fashion Pak, Ken, complete, M, D2 .$25.00

Movie Date, Barbie, #933, dress only, EX, D2 ....$25.00

Night Blooms, Francie, #1212, complete, EX, D2 ....$25.00

Night Scene, Ken, #1496, complete, NM, D2 ....$35.00

Nightly Negligee, Barbie, #965, complete, EX+, D2.........$40.00

On the Avenue, Barbie, #1644, complete, NM, D2 ....$225.00

On the Go Fashion Pak, Barbie, sheath only, M, D2........$15.00

Open Road, Barbie, #985, complete, NM, D2 ....$195.00

Let's Explore, Ricky, #1506, 1966, MIB, $75.00.

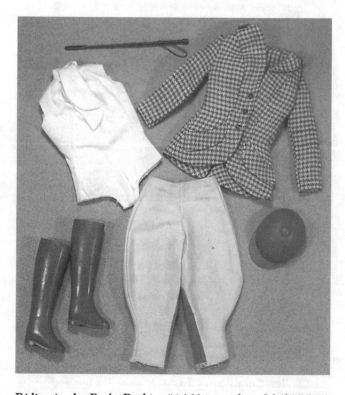

Riding in the Park, Barbie, #1668, complete, M, $275.00.

Orange Blossom, Barbie, #987, complete, NM, D2 ....$55.00

Pajama Pow, Barbie, #1806, jumpsuit only, EX, D2..........$20.00

Paris Pretty, Barbie, #1911, 1988, NRFB, D2....................$30.00

Patent 'N Pants, Skipper, #1958, NRFB, D2 ....$120.00

Picnic Set, Barbie, #967, complete, NM, D2 ....$165.00

Polka-Dots & Raindrops, Francie, #1255, complete, NM+, D2.$40.00

Poodle Parade, Barbie, #1643, missing trophy & glasses, EX+, D2 ....$300.00

Pretty as a Picture, Barbie, #1652, complete, NM, D2 ...$195.00

Pretty Frilly, Francie, #3366, missing necklace, EX, D2 ...$25.00

Rally Days, Ken, #788, complete, NM, D2 ....$35.00

Red Flare, Barbie, #939, complete, EX, D2 ....$50.00

Red Sensation, Skipper, #1901, complete, EX, D2 ....$40.00

Regal Red, Barbie, #3217, complete, rare, NM, D2........$400.00

Registered Nurse, Barbie, #991, complete, NM, D2 ....$85.00

Resort Set, Barbie, #963, missing bracelet, NM, D2 ....$50.00

Roller Skate Date, Ken, #1405, 1964 version, complete, M, D2 ....$40.00

Roman Holiday, Barbie, #968, replica compact & necklace, missing hat & hankie, EX, D2....................................$450.00

Romantic Ruffles, Barbie, #1871, missing earrings, NM, D2 ....$50.00

Satin 'N Rose, Barbie, #1611, complete, NM, D2 ....$125.00

Saturday Matinee, Barbie, #1615, complete, M, D2 ....$500.00

School Days, Skipper, #1907, complete, EX+, D2 ....$45.00

Sheath Sensation, Barbie, #986, dress only, NM, D2 ....$15.00

Shoppin' Spree, Francie, #1261, complete, EX+, D2........$65.00

Sidekick, Francie, #1273, complete, EX+, D2 ....$65.00

Silken Flame, Barbie, #977, dress only, G, D2 ....$18.00

Sissy Suit, Francie, #1228, complete, EX+, D2 ....$75.00

Skate Mates, Barbie, #1793, complete, NM, D2 ....$45.00

Skater's Waltz, Barbie, #1629, complete, M, D2 ....$175.00

Ski Queen, Barbie, #948, complete, M, D2.......................$70.00

Sleeper Set, Ken, #781, bl, complete, NM, D2 ....$40.00

Snowflake Fairy, Ballerina Barbie Fashions, 1976, MOC, M15 ....$40.00

Solo in the Spotlight, Barbie, #982, replica necklace, complete, NM, D2 ....$150.00

Sophisticated Lady, Barbie, #993, complete, NM, D2....$165.00

Sorority Meeting, Barbie, #937, replica necklace, complete, NM, D2..$60.00

Sport Shorts, Ken, #783, NRFB, D2.................................$50.00

Sportsman Fashion Pak, Ken, #1802, MOC, D2..............$75.00

Stitch 'N Style Fashion Pak, Barbie, MOC, D2 ....$25.00

Stormy Weather, Barbie, #949, missing umbrella, EX+, D2 .$20.00

Suburban Shopper, Barbie, #969, replica necklace, complete, NM, D2 ....$75.00

Sugar Sheers, Francie, #1229, missing tote, EX, D2..........$50.00

Sunflower, Barbie, #1683, missing bracelet, NM+, D2 .....$85.00

Sweater Girl, Barbie, #976, complete, NM, D2 ....$65.00

Tennis Anyone, Barbie, #941, complete, NM+, D2 ....$45.00

Tennis Tunic, Francie, #1221, complete, NM+, D2..........$35.00

Terry Togs, Ken, #784, complete, NM, D2 ....$40.00

Theater Date, Barbie, #959, complete, VG+, D2 ....$65.00

Time To Turn In, Ken, #1419, 1966-67, complete, M, $110.00.

Touchdown, Ken, #799, complete, NM, D2 ....$40.00

Triple Treat, Skipper, #1748, NRFB, D2 ....$75.00

Tropicana, Barbie, #1460, complete, NM, D2 ....$65.00

Twice as Nice, Skipper, #1735, NRFB, D2 ....$65.00

Twiggy Do's, Francie, #1725, missing purse, NM, D2 ....$50.00

Twinkle Togs, Barbie, #1854, complete, NM, D2 ....$125.00

Velvet Touch, Barbie, #2789, 1978, NRFB, D2................$35.00

Victory Dance, Ken, #1411, complete, NM, D2 ....$40.00

Wedding Day Set, Barbie, #972, gown only, G-, D2 ....$25.00

Wedding Wonder, Barbie, #1849, gown & veil only, EX, D2..$40.00

What's New at the Zoo, Skipper, #1925, complete, M, D2 .$55.00

Stripes Away, Barbie and Francie, #1775, 1967, MIB, $250.00.

Wild 'N Wintry, Barbie, #3416, jacket only, EX, D2........$12.00
Wild 'N Wooly, Francie, #1218, NRFB, D2 ....$150.00
Wild Flowers, Francie, #3456, NRFB, D2 ....$75.00
Winter Holiday, Barbie, #975, complete, EX, D2 ....$60.00
Yachtsman, Ken, #789, NRFB, D2.............................$95.00
Yellow Go, Barbie, #1816, coat only, NM, D2 ....$85.00

Furniture and Rooms

Barbie Bath 'N Beauty, #9506, Sears Exclusive, 1975, NRFB,
    D2...$10.00
Barbie Bedroom Accents, grandfather clock, #2372, 1985,
    NRFB, D2...$5.00
Barbie Dream Canopy Bed, #5641, 1987, NRFB, D2 ....$15.00
Barbie Dream Furniture, sofa & coffee table, #2475, 1978, M
    (worn box), D2 ....$10.00
Barbie Dream Furniture, vanity & stool, #2469, 1978, NRFB,
    D2...$15.00
Barbie Dream House Finishing Touches, bedroom set, #3769,
    MOC, D2...$6.00
Barbie Dream House Finishing Touches, living room set, #3769,
    MOC, D2...$6.00
Barbie Kitchen Accents, microwave, #2373, 1985, NRFB,
    D2 ....$10.00
Barbie Light-Up Vanity, #5847, Europe, 1982, NRFB, D2.$20.00
Barbie Living Room Set, 1983, wht wicker, NRFB, D2....$20.00
Barbie's Room-Fulls Country Kitchen, #7407, 1974, NRFB,
    D2...$50.00
Barbie's Room-Fulls Firelight Living Room, #7406, 1975-76,
    NRFB, D2 ....$50.00
Barbie's Room-Fulls Studio Bedroom, #7405, 1974, NRFB,
    D2...$50.00
Skipper's Dream Room, #4094, 1964, NRFB, D2...........$600.00
Skipper's Jeweled Bed, Suzy Goose, 1965, MIB, D2 ....$150.00
Skipper's Jeweled Vanity, Suzy Goose, 1965, NRFB, D2..$250.00
Skipper's Jeweled Wardrobe, Suzy Goose, #463, 1963, NM,
    D2...$50.00
Skipper's 2-in-1 Bedroom, #9282, 1975, NRFB, D2 ....$95.00
Superstar Barbie Piano Concert, 1990, NRFB, D2 ....$25.00
Tutti & Todd's Dutch Bedroom Set, 1964, M, D2 ....$800.00

Gift Sets

Army Barbie & Ken, 1993 department store special, NRFB,
    D2...$45.00
Barbie Around the Clock, 1963, complete w/brunette Barbie &
    3 outfits, NMIB, from $3,500 to $4,500.00
Barbie Color Magic Doll & Costume Set, #1043, 1965, MIB,
    D2...$4,500.00
Barbie Denim Fun, #4893, 1989, MIB, D2......................$50.00
Barbie Dream Wedding, 1993, NRFB, D2 ....$45.00
Barbie 35th Anniversary, 1993 department store special,
    brunette doll, NRFB, D2 ....$750.00
Beach Fun Barbie & Ken, 1993 department store special, NRFB,
    D2...$35.00
Birthday Fun at McDonalds, 1993, NRFB, D2.................$50.00
Cool City Blues, 1989, NRFB, D2................................$50.00
Dance Club Barbie w/Tape Player, 1989, NRFB, D2........$50.00

Ballerina Barbie on Tour, 1976, MIB, $150.00.

Barbie and Ken Campin' Out Set, 1983, MIB, $75.00.

Beautiful Blues, #3303, 1967, MIB, from $2,500.00 to $3,000.00.

Dance Sensation Barbie, 1984, NRFB, $35.00.

Dance Magic Barbie & Ken, #5409, 1990, MIB, D2 ....$45.00
Disney Barbie & Friends, 1991, NRFB, D2 ....$65.00
Disney Weekend Barbie & Ken, 1993, NRFB, D2 ....$50.00
Dolls of the World, 1995, NRFB, D2 ....$65.00
Francie Rise & Shine, #1194, 1971, NRFB $1,000.00
Midge's Ensemble, #1012, rare, NRFB, D2 ....$3,600.00
Pose 'N Play Skipper & Her Swing-a-Rounder Gym, #1179,
     1971, NRFB, D2 ....$150.00
Rollerblade Barbie Snack 'N Surf, 1992, NRFB, D2.........$45.00

Skipper Perfectly Pretty, 1968, MIB, $350.00.

Tennis Star Barbie & Ken, 1988 department store special,
     NRFB, D2 ....$50.00
Traveling Sisters Fashion Set, 1995, NRFB, D2 ....$55.00
Tutti Walking My Dolly, #3552, NRFB, D2...................$400.00
Twirly Curls, 1982 department store special, NRFB, D2..$45.00
Wedding Party Midge, 1990, NRFB, D2.........................$150.00
Western Fun Barbie w/Sunrunner, 1990, NRFB, D2 ....$75.00

Vehicles

Airplane, Barbie & Ken, Irwin, 1963, steering wheel missing o/w
     EX, rare, D2..$500.00
Austin Healy, Irwin, 1962, NM+, D2 ....$200.00
Barbie Goin' Boating, #7738, Sears Exclusive, 1973, NM, D2 .$50.00
Barbie Goin' Camping Set, #8669, 1973-75, NRFB, D2 ..$25.00
Classy Corvette, #9612, 1976, NFRB, D2 ....$35.00
Country Camper, #4994, 1970, NMIB, D2 ....$35.00
Dream Carriage w/Dapple Gray Horses, Europe, 1982, M (sepa-
     rate boxes), D2 ....$125.00
Dune Buggy, Barbie & Ken & All Their Friends, #5908, 1970,
     NRFB, D2 ....$300.00
Ferrari, #3136, 1987, red, MIB, D2.................................$50.00
Ferrari, #3564, 1988, wht, MIB, D2.................................$50.00
Mercedes, 1963, gr, NMIB, D2.......................................$150.00
Star Cycle, #2149, 1978, MIB, D2 ....$20.00
Sun 'N Fun Buggy, #1158, 1970, orange, MIB, D2 ....$75.00
Super Corvette, #1291, 1979, remote control, NRFB, D2..$75.00
Ten Speeder, #7777, 1973, MIB, D2 ....$15.00
Travelin' Trailer, #5489, 1982, NRFB, D2.......................$25.00
1957 Belair Chevy, 1989, aqua, 1st edition, MIB, D2 ....$150.00
1957 Belair Chevy, 1990, pk, 2nd edition, MIB, D2 ......$125.00

Miscellaneous

**Barbie and Francie Color Magic Fashion Designer
Set, #4040, 1966-67, MIB, $400.00.**

Photo courtesy of June Moon.

**Barbie and Ken Stand-up Dolls, Whitman, EX (VG
box), J6, $30.00.**

Autograph Book, Barbie, 1961, unused, M, D2 ....$95.00

Book, Barbie, Midge & Ken, Random House, EX, D2......$20.00

Book, Barbie & Ken, Random House, 1962, EX, D2 ....$20.00

Book, Barbie Solves a Mystery, Random House, 1962, EX, D2 ....$25.00

Book, Barbie's New York Summer, Random House, 1962, EX+, D2..$30.00

Book, Barbie's Secret, Random House, 1962, EX, D2......$20.00

Booklet, Fashion & Play Accessories by Mattel, EX, D2 ..$25.00

Booklet, World of Barbie, EX, D2 ....$30.00

Booklet, World of Barbie Fashions, #1, EX, D2 ....$10.00

Box, Allan, 1963, NM, D2 ....$75.00

Box, Bubble-Cut Barbie w/brunette hair, 1962, VG, D2 ..$85.00

Box, Ken, 1963, VG, D2..$50.00

Box, Ponytail Barbie w/blond hair, 1961, G-, D2 ....$65.00

Box, Skipper, 1963, G, D2..$35.00

Coin Purse, Skipper, 1964, bl, EX, D2 ....$30.00

Figurine, 1960 Enchanted Evening, Danbury Mint, 1994, NRFB, D2..$30.00

Figurine, 1960 Solo in the Spotlight, Danbury Mint, 1992, NRFB, D2 ....$30.00

Figurine, 1961 Ballerina, Danbury Mint, 1993, NRFB, D2..$30.00

Figurine, 1962 Red Flare, Danbury Mint, 1993, NRFB, D2..$30.00

Figurine, 1965 Fashion Editor, Danbury Mint, 1993, NRFB, D2..$30.00

Jewelry Box, 1963, red, EX, D2....................................$50.00

Lotion, Barbie, 1961, box features Barbie #1 wearing Sweater Girl outfit, MIB, D2 ....$100.00

Magazine, Barbie Bazaar, March/April, 1992, EX, D2 ......$25.00

Magazine, Barbie Bazaar, May/June, 1991, EX, D2 ....$20.00

Magazine, Barbie Bazaar, 1988, EX, D2............................$75.00

Napkins, Barbie Goes to a Party, 1964, MIP, D2 ....$50.00

Ornament, Holiday Barbie, Hallmark, 1993, 1st in series, NRFB, D2..$95.00

Ornament, Holiday Barbie, Hallmark, 1994, 2nd in series, NRFB, D2 ....$50.00

Ornament, Solo in the Spotlight, Hallmark, 1995, NRFB, D2..$35.00

Ornament, 1959 Debut Barbie, Hallmark, 1994, NRFB, D2 ..$35.00

Pattern, Sorority Tea, Sew-Free #1703, 1963, MIB, D2 ...$75.00

Pattern, Stardust, Sew-Free #1722, 1963, MIB, D2 ....$100.00

Picture Maker, Mattel, 1969, complete w/6 cards to draw scenes, NMIB, F8..$60.00

Playset, Barbie Loves McDonald's, #5559, 1982, MIB, D2 .$65.00

Playset, Barbie Pool Party, #7795, 1973, NRFB, D2 ....$25.00

Powder Puff Mitt, Barbie, 1961, MIB, D2 ....$125.00

Quick Curl Barbie Beauty Center, 1974, VG (orig box), M15 ....$25.00

Radio, Superstar Barbie, 1980, NRFB, D2 ....$10.00

Record, Barbie Sings, 1961, 45rpm, complete w/booklet, EX, I2 ....$40.00

Sheet Set, Barbie, Stevens, 1991, twin sz, MIP, M15 ....$25.00

Tea Set, Barbie's 25th Anniversary, 1984, NM, D2 ....$75.00

Tea Set, Barbie's 35th Anniversary, 1994, NRFB, M15 ...$45.00

Trading Cards, Jumbo Barbie & Ken, 1962, MIB, D2 ....$500.00

Pattern, Day 'N Night, Sew-Free #1723, 1963, MIB, $95.00.

Wallet, 1962, red vinyl, NM, J6, $55.00.

Photo courtesy of June Moon.

Wallet, Skipper in Masquerade, 1964, bl, EX, D2.............$30.00
Wristwatch, Ponytail Barbie, 1963, rpl royal bl band, working, EX, D2 ....$150.00

Battery-Operated Toys

From the standpoint of being visually entertaining, nothing can compare with the battery-operated toy. Most (probably as much as 95%) were made in Japan from the forties through the sixties, though some were distributed by American companies — Marx, Ideal and Daisy, for instance — who often sold them under their own names. So even if they're marked, sometimes it's just about impossible to identify the actual manufacturer. Though batteries had been used to power trains and provide simple illumination in earlier toys, the Japanese toys could smoke, walk, talk, drink, play instruments, blow soap bubbles and do just about anything else humanly possible to dream up and engineer. Generally, the more antics the toy performs, the more collectible it is. Rarity is important as well, but first and foremost to consider is condition. Because of their complex mechanisms, many will no longer work. Children often stopped them in mid-cycle, rubber hoses and bellows aged and cracked, and leaking batteries caused them to corrode, so very few have survived to the present intact and in good enough condition to interest a collector. Though it's sometimes possible to have them repaired, unless you can buy them cheap enough to allow for the extra expense involved, it is probably better to wait on a better example. Original boxes are a definite plus in assessing the value of a battery-op and can be counted on to add from 30% to 50% (and up), depending on the box's condition, of course, as well as the toy's age and rarity.

We have made every attempt to list these toys by the name as it appears on the original box. Some will sound very similar. Many toys were reissued with only minor changes and subsequently renamed. For more information we recommend *Collecting Toys* by Richard O'Brien (Books Americana).

Advisor: Tom Lastrapes (L4).

See also Aeronautical; Automobiles and Other Vehicle

Replicas; Boats; Marx; Robots and Space Toys.

Accordion Bear, Alps, bear w/microphone plays accordion & sways w/light-up eyes, 11", NMIB $900.00
Accordion Player Hobo, Alps, seated hobo plays accordion while plush monkey plays cymbals, MIB, L4 ....$575.00
Acrobat Motorcycle Racing Game, K/Japan, 2 cycles on rods attached to base & ramp, aerial & racing motion, 10", MIB, A..$1,650.00
Acrobot, Y, robot does acrobatics, plastic, EX, L4.........$225.00
Acrobot, Y, robot does acrobatics, plastic, MIB, L4 ....$525.00
Airmail Helicopter, KO, mystery action w/spinning rotors & sound, MIB, L4 ....$200.00
Airport Service Bus, Alps, NMIB $125.00
Albino Gorilla, MIB, L4..$525.00
All Stars Mr Baseball Jr, K, batter rotates, swings & hits ball released from batting machine, 8", EX (EX box), A.$670.00
Allis-Chalmers HD 5 Diesel Crawler, 1955, 8", EX, A ..$175.00
Anti-Aircraft Jeep, WWII jeep w/driver & rear gunner, gun revolves w/clacking noise, 9", EX (torn box), A......$150.00
Antique Gooney Car, Alps, 1960s, wht open touring car w/animated driver, 4 actions, 9", NMIB, A $330.00
Arthur-A-Go-Go, Alps, figure beats light-up drum & sways, MIB, L4..$875.00
Atom Motorcycle, Modern Toys, 1960s, rolls forward, stops & driver dismounts, litho tin, 11", EX, A $500.00
B-Z Porter, Modern Toys, 1950s, 7½", MIB, L4 ....$375.00
Baby Bertha, rare, MIB, L4 ....$1,250.00
Ball Blowing Clown, TN, ball stays suspended in air as clown wanders around, litho tin w/cloth outfit, MIB, L4..$350.00
Ball Playing Bear, Japan, bear moves head, duck & umbrella spin as balls go up tube, tin & celluloid, 9", NM, A........$385.00
Ball Playing Dog, Linemar, hits ball w/racket, tin & plush, 9", M, L4 ....$175.00

Barney Bear the Drummer Boy, Cragstan, lithographed tin and plush with cloth clothes, NMIB, $195.00.

Balloon Bunny, Y, walks, rings bell & makes sounds, remote control, MIB, rare, L4..................$275.00

Balloon Vendor, Japan, 1961, clown w/balloons & bell, tin, cloth & vinyl, 11", MIB, L4 ....$300.00

Balloon Vendor, Japan, 1961, clown w/balloons & bell, tin, cloth & vinyl, 11", EX, M5 ....$135.00

Bambi, see Walking Bambi

Barber Bear, TN, barber clips & combs child's hair as child leans forward & squeals, tin & plush, 10", NM (EX box), A.....$530.00

Batmobile, Taiwan, bump-&-go w/siren & blinking lights, litho tin w/vinyl figures, 10", NM (EX box), A.................$180.00

Bear the Cashier, Modern Toys, 7½", MIB, L4 ....$425.00

Beauty Parlor Bear, works w/curling iron & comb, bear child squeals & kicks, tin & plush, 10", NMIB, A.............$825.00

Beethoven the Piano Playing Dog, TN, plays piano & moves head, litho tin & plush, 8½", scarce, NMIB............$265.00

Big Ring Circus Truck, MT, bump-&-go action w/whistle sound, tin w/vinyl clown driver, 12", scarce, NM, A $200.00

Bingo the Clown, TN, 13", MIB, L4................................$650.00

Black Smithy Bear, TN, litho tin & plush, 9", MIB, L4.$500.00

Blacksmith Bear, AI, 1950s, 6 actions, 9½", MIB, L4 ....$400.00

Blinky the Clown, Amico, advances as he plays xylophone, light-up eyes, litho tin, remote control, 10", EX+ (VG+ box), A..$400.00

Blushing Cowboy, Y, 1960s, 4 actions, NM....................$125.00

Blushing Frankenstein, TN, sways, growls & loses his pants, tin, cloth & vinyl, 12", MIB, L4 ....$275.00

Blushing Willie, Y, 1960, man pours drink & drinks it w/lighted face & whirling eyes, tin & plastic, 10", NM, K4 ......$70.00

Blushing Willie, Y, 1960, 10", NMIB, L4 ....$100.00

Bobby the Drinking Bear, Y, MIB, L4............................$600.00

Bongo the Drumming Monkey, Alps, 1960s, 3 actions, MIB, L4...$250.00

Bowling Bank, MB Daniel, M, L4 ....$125.00

Brave Eagle, TN, beats drum, sways & makes war-whoop sound, litho tin & plastic w/cloth clothes, 12", NM+ (EX+ box), A..$125.00

Brunch Snack Bar, Japan, little chef cooks behind snack bar, litho tin & vinyl, 6", EX (EX box), A....................$410.00

Bruno Accordion Bear, Y, slides side to side while playing, light-up eyes, tin & plush, remote control, 10", MIB, A..$260.00

Bubble Blowing Boy, Y, bends forward & puts bubble maker in pan, litho tin, 7½", MIB, L4 ....$375.00

Bubble Blowing Bunny, Y, bunny blows bubbles from an eggshell, pk litho tin bunny on bl base, MIB, A......$120.00

Bubble Blowing Kangaroo, MT, mother lowers wire into pan as baby in pouch turns head, litho tin, 8½", MIB, L4..$500.00

Bubble Blowing Lion, MT, blows bubbles, head moves & eyes light up, litho tin, 7", NMIB $170.00

Bubble Blowing Monkey, Alps, 1959, plush monkey dips wand in solution & blows bubbles, eyes light, 10", NMIB, L4/M5..$150.00

Bubble Blowing Musician, Y, 1950s, man at podium blowing bubbles w/trumpet, 11", NMIB $175.00

Bump Car w/Pop-Up Clown, Criterion/Japan, clown pops out of rooftop, EX (orig box), A $135.00

Burger Chef, Y, dog shakes pan & flips burger over barbecue pit, ears raise & eyes roll, tin & plush, 10", M (G box) .$275.00

Busy Housekeeper Bear, Alps, moves forward & backwards w/vacuum, litho tin & plush, 8", NM (EX+ box), A..........$235.00

Busy Housekeeper Rabbit, Alps, moves forward & backwards w/vacuum, litho tin & plush, 8", MIB, L4 ....$425.00

Candy Vending Machine, W Toy, place coin in slot & clown turns crank & bends back & forth, 10", non-working o/w EX, A $360.00

Captain Blushwell, Y, several actions, tin, vinyl & cloth, 11", MIB, L4..$160.00

Captain Kidd Pirate Ship, Frankonia, bump-&-go, cannon shoots caps w/smoking action, tin, 13", rare, NM (EX box), A $300.00

Casino King Slot Machine, EX, L4 ....$100.00

Champion Weight Lifter, YM, monkey lifts barbells & face turns red, plush w/cloth outfit, 10", NM (EX box), M5....$140.00

Charlie the Drumming Clown, Alps, plays drums & cymbals w/several other actions, tin & plastic, 9½", NMIB, A $230.00

Charlie the Drumming Clown, Alps, 9½", MIB, L4.......$300.00

Charlie Weaver Bartender, TN, makes drinks w/several actions, 12", MIB, L4 ....$125.00

Chimp & Pup Rail Car, TN, 8", MIB, L4.......................$375.00

Chimpanzee the One-Man Drummer, Alps, 1950s, 6 actions, plush w/yel hat, 9", NMIB, A $110.00

Chippy the Chipmunk, Alps, 12", MIB, L4....................$250.00

Circus Elephant, TN, moves legs & balances ball over trunk in stream of air, plush over tin, 10", NM (EX box), A.$170.00

Circus Jet, TN, circles & fires machine gun, MIB, L4 ....$150.00

Climbing Donald Duck on His Friction Fire Engine, Linemar, Pluto driving, 18", EX (EX box) $1,500.00

Climbing Linesman, TPS, climbs up & down telephone pole, head lamp lights up, litho tin, 24", EX+ (EX+ box)..$550.00

Clown & Lion, MT, clown goes up & down spiral rod as lion roars, tin & vinyl, 13", scarce, NM (EX box), A $300.00

Bubble Blowing Popeye, Linemar, arm raises and pipe lights, lithographed tin, NMIB, A, $1,430.00.

Clown Magician, Alps, leans, tips hat & flips stack of cards, nose lights, tin, cloth & vinyl, 12", EX (VG box), A $175.00

Cock-A-Doodle Doo Rooster, Mukuni, 8", VG+, L4 ....$50.00

Cola Drinking Bear, Alps, 1950s, rare yel version, 3 actions, NMIB..$185.00

Comic Tank, Tomy, mystery action, rare, L4 ....$375.00

Concrete Mixer, Linemar, 9", NMIB, J2 ....$240.00

Coney Island Bumper Car, EX, L4 ....$250.00

Coney Island Penny Machine, Remco, complete w/turntable, bag of prizes & remote-control bucket claw, 15", EX (VG box), A..$175.00

Coney Island Rocket Ride, Alps, 1950s, spins w/ringing bell & flashing lights, litho tin, 14", rare, EX+, M5............$370.00

Coney Island Rocket Ride, Alps, 1950s, spins w/ringing bell & flashing lights, litho tin, 14", rare, MIB...............$1,000.00

Cragstan Bullfighter, TN, 1950s, litho tin, EX $95.00

Cragstan Crapshooter, Y, man w/dice cup & money stands before table, 9¼", M (worn box)..............................$125.00

Cragstan Crapshooting Monkey, NM, L4.....................$75.00

Cragstan Crapshooting Monkey, NMIB, M5...............$100.00

Cragstan Dishwasher, Alps, 1950s, tin, complete w/accessories, 9", MIB, A..$130.00

Cragstan Flying Plane, w/control tower, MIB, L4...........$400.00

Cragstan One-Armed Bandit, Y, 1960s, NMIB $275.00

Cragstan Telly Bear, S&E, dial phone for 6 actions, plush, cloth & litho tin, 9", MIB, L4 ....$575.00

Cragstan Tugboat, SAN, 13", MIB, L4 ....$225.00

Cragstan Two-Gun Sheriff, Y, 1950s, 5 actions, EX (G box) .$200.00

Cycling Daddy, Bandai, vinyl figure w/cloth clothes rides tricycle, 10", MIB, L4..$225.00

Cyclist Clown, K, travels forward & reverse w/flashing light, eyes roll, tin & cloth, remote control, 7", VG (EX box), A $235.00

Cyclist Penguin, MIB, L4 ....$575.00

Daisy the Drumming Duck, Alps, 9", MIB, L4 ....$375.00

Daisymatic No 60 Tractor 'N Trailer, MIB, L4 ....$165.00

Dandy the Happy Drumming Pup, Alps, plays drum & cymbals w/moving head & light-up eyes, tin & plush, 9", EX (VG box)..$150.00

Dennis the Menace Playing Xylophone, Rosko, 1950s, 3 actions, MIB, from $250 to..$350.00

Dentist Bear, S&E, plush bear uses lighted drill on patient who lifts cup & spits into pan, 10", MIB, L4 ....$675.00

Photo courtesy of Mike's General Store.

Dick Tracy Police Car, Linemar, tin, green, remote control, EX+ (EX box), $400.00.

Dip-ie the Whale, Japan, shoots water using plastic spout, ears flap, litho tin w/rubber ears, 13", EX+ (EX box), A..$225.00

Disney Acrobats, Linemar, 3 different versions w/Mickey, Pluto or Donald, 9", MIB, L4, ea $875.00

Disney Airliner, Italy/WDP, 1970s, Paperon de Air Lines, plastic w/decals of various characters, 15" L, EX (VG box), A.$160.00

Disneyland's Haunted House Bank, 1960s, tin & plastic, EX+, T1..$150.00

Dolly Dressmaker (Dolly Seamstress), TN, 1950s, dolly at sewing machine, 10 actions, 7", NMIB, A..............$200.00

Dozo the Steaming Clown, Rosko, sweeps floor and steam comes out hat and coat, lithographed tin with cloth clothes, NM (worn box), $500.00.

Dozo the Steaming Clown, Rosko, 13", EX (VG box), A.$255.00

Drinking Captain, S&E, 1950, MIB, L4 ....$175.00

Drinking Dog, Y, 1950s, M, L4..$125.00

Drinking Licking Cat, TN, pours & drinks from cup, plush, plastic & litho tin, MIB, L4...$325.00

Drinking Monkey, NM, L4...$100.00

Drumming Bear, Y, walks & plays drum w/light-up eyes, 12½", rare, NMIB, L4 ....$1,600.00

Drumming Clown, litho tin w/cloth clothes, 9", EX+, M5..$130.00

Dune Buggy, TPS, tin & plastic, 11", EX+, J2 ....$100.00

Electro Sonic Piano, Linemar, futuristic keyboard that plays automatically, 10x12", NMIB, A $55.00

Electro Toy Fire Engine, Linemar, MIB, L4 ....$175.00

Electro Toy Sand Loader with Conveyor, Linemar, MIB, L4.$225.00

Electrolux Vacuum Cleaner, pk & bl, 7", non-working o/w NM (NM box), M5 ....$40.00

Elektro Amphibio, Schuco #5560, red & cream, complete w/instructions, 12", NM (EX box), A $285.00

Expert Motorcyclist, Modern Toys, rider dismounts & remounts, litho tin, 11½", EX (orig box), L4 ....$1,000.00

Farmland Cup Ride, MIB, L4 ....$325.00
Father Bear, MT, rare, MIB, L4 ....$500.00
Ferris Wheel Truck, TPS, non-stop action & sound as pigs revolve w/balls inside drum, tin & plastic, 9", NM (EX box), A $120.00
Fido the Xylophone Player, Alps, dog plays xylophone & sways, litho tin & plush, 9", scarce, MIB, L4 ....$475.00
Fido the Xylophone Player, Alps, 9", EX (VG box), A ..$250.00

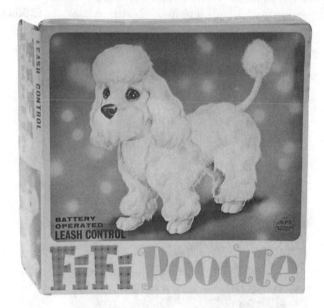

Fifi Poodle, Alps, leash control, MIB, $45.00.

Fire Chief Car, TN, bump-&-go mystery action, litho tin, 10", EX, J2 ....$140.00
Fire Dept Jeep, Daiya, mystery action, driver waves flags & lights flash, litho tin & vinyl, 9", NM (G+ box), A $160.00
Fishing Bear's Bank, Wonderful Toys, rare, MIB, L4 ..$3,200.00
Fishing Polar Bear, Alps, bear pulls fish out of pond, throws it in basket & squeals, plush & tin, 10", EX (EX box), A .$255.00

Fred Flintstone's Bedrock Band, Alps, 1962, Fred plays drum and cymbals, 8", EX (EX box), $825.00.

Flipper the Spouting Dolphin, MIB, L4 ....$125.00
Flutterbirds, Alps, 2 birds fly up & down above birdhouse as 1 chirps in door, litho tin & plush, 27", MIB, L4 ....$550.00
Forrestal Aircraft Carrier, Linemar, advances as airplane flies overhead, litho tin & plastic, 14", EX+ (EX box), A $245.00
Frankenstein Monster, see Blushing Frankenstein
Frankie the Roller Skating Monkey, Alps, remote control, 12", MIB $245.00
Fred & Barney Car, AHI, 1974, rare, NM $175.00
Funland Cup Ride, Sonsco, kids spin around in cups, MIB, from $300 to $375.00
General Patton Tank M-107, Daiya, litho tin, remote control, 7", MIB, L4 ....$275.00
Gino Neapolitan Balloon Blower, Tomiyama, 10", MIB, L4 ..$225.00

Photo courtesy of June Moon.

Good Time Charlie, MT/Japan, EX (G box), J6, $165.00.

Photo courtesy of Jeff B ubb.

Gorilla, TN, plush over tin, remote control, 9½", NM (NM box), $340.00.

Grand-Pa Panda, MT, sits in rocking chair & eats popcorn, eyes light, 9", MIB...$450.00

Grandpa Bear, Alps, sits in chair w/book, pipe lights as he rocks, litho tin & plush, 9", EX (EX box), A $275.00

Green Caterpillar, Diva, 20", EX, L4 ....$185.00

Greyhound Scenicruiser Bus, litho tin, 7", EX, M5 ....$60.00

Growling Tiger Trophy Plaque, Cragstan, tiger head mounted on plaque, pull string for actions, 10", rare, NM (EX box), A $335.00

Gypsy Fortune Teller, Ichida/Japan, 1950s, figure in blk robe & hood trimmed in red on red base, 5 actions, 12", MIB, A...$1,485.00

Happy 'N Sad Magic Face Clown, Y, moves side to side & plays accordion, face changes expression, 10", MIB $300.00

Happy Band Trio, MT, plush dog, rabbit & bear playing instruments on litho tin stage w/cb backdrop, 11", MIB, L4 ....$675.00

Happy Clown Theatre, Y, MIB, L4 ....$425.00

Happy Fiddler Clown, Alps, plays w/realistic motion & screeching sounds, litho tin w/cloth clothes, 10", EX (EX box)..$500.00

Happy Miner, Bandai, 11", MIB, L4 ....$1,350.00

Happy Naughty Chimp, Daishin, 1960, MIB, L4 ....$100.00

Happy Santa One-Man Band, Alps, 9", MIB, L4 ....$300.00

Heavy Duty Dump Truck Diesel, Japan, 1960s, red w/yel hubs, 7 actions, 10¼", EX (orig box), A...............................$90.00

High Jinks at the Circus, Alps, clown w/performing monkey, 6 actions, MIB, L4 ....$375.00

Highway Drive, TN, 16", MIB, L4 ....$125.00

Hippo Chef Cutey Cook, Y, 10", MIB, L4...................$1,275.00

Hoop Zing Girl, Linemar, girl wiggles w/hula hoop on base, celluloid figure on tin base, 12", scarce, VG (EX box), A.$535.00

Hoopy the Fishing Duck, Alps, duck pulls fish out of pond w/several actions, 10", NMIB...................................$445.00

Hooty the Happy Owl, Alps, advances w/flapping wings, hooting sound & other actions, remote control, 9", MIB, L4.$185.00

Hooty the Happy Owl, Alps, 9", NM (EX box), A.........$150.00

Hopping Pup w/Cart, Alps, advances w/light-up eyes & barking sound, plush & litho tin, 14" L, EX+ (EX box), A $85.00

Hot Rod Custom T Ford, Alps, 10½", MIB, L4.............$200.00

Hot Rod Limousine, Alps, 1960s, 4 actions, NMIB........$350.00

Huey Helicopter, MIB, L4...$100.00

Hungry Cat, Linemar, 9", MIB, L4................................$700.00

Ice Cream Baby Bear, MT, cloth bear in chair dips spoon into bowl & simulates chewing, 9", rare, EX (EX box) ...$650.00

Ice Cream Vendor, TN, rider on cycle advances in figure-8 motion w/lights & sound, litho tin, 9", EX (EX box), A $750.00

Indian Joe, Alps, plays war dance tune on drum & moves head side to side, 12", EX+ (VG box), A...........................$80.00

International Agent Car, MIB, L4 ....$200.00

Japanese Bullet Train, MT, litho tin train w/plastic track, MIB, L4..$175.00

Jet Plane Base, Yonezawa, Super Sabre jet launches from platform, litho tin, 8x11" base, EX+ (EX box), A $585.00

Jocko the Drinking Monkey, Linemar, 11", VG+, L4 ....$100.00

Jolly Bambino, Alps, 9", MIB, L4.................................$700.00

Jolly Bear w/ Robin, MT, 10", MIB, L4........................$950.00

Jolly Daddy Elephant, Marusan, 8¾", MIB, L4.............$350.00

Jolly Penguin, TN, 7", MIB, L4 ....$175.00

Jolly Pianist, TN, dog plays piano, litho tin & plush, 8", NM (EX box), A...$235.00

Jolly Santa on Snow, Alps, 1950s, skates or skis w/ringing bell, remote control, 13", MIB, L4 ....$375.00

Jolly Santa on Snow, Alps, 1950s, 13", NM (EX box), A .$285.00

Hungry Baby Bear, Y, mama bear feeds baby bear, several actions, tin and plush with cloth clothes, 9½", MIB (not shown), $275.00.

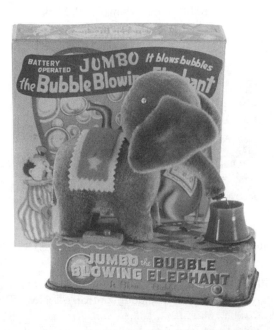

Jumbo the Bubble Blowing Elephant, Yonezawa, 1950, plush elephant on lithographed tin base, 7", MIB, $185.00.

Jumbo the Bubble Blowing Elephant, Yonezawa, 1950, 7", EX (EX box), L4 ....$85.00

Jungle Jumbo, BC, elephant advances then stops & howls while hunter shoots, remote control, 10", MIB, L4...........$775.00

Jungle Trio, Linemar, 2 monkeys & an elephant playing instruments on round platform, 8 actions, MIB, A...........$500.00

Kissing Couple, Ichida, bump-&-go car rolls as bird spins & chirps on hood, 10", EX (VG box) $220.00

Knitting Grandma, TN, 8½", M, L4..............................$250.00

Ladder Fire Engine, TN, litho tin, 13", unused, NMIB, J2.$250.00

Lady Pup Tending Her Garden, Cragstan, several actions, litho tin & cloth, 9", MIB...$475.00

Lambo, Alps, elephant picks up logs, remote control, MIB, L4...$675.00

Laughing Clown, Waco, bump-&-go action, shoulders shake & he laughs hysterically, plastic, 15", EX+ (EX box), A $350.00

Laughing Head Leprechaun, EX, L4 ....$100.00

Lightening Hot Rod, Rosko, 1950s, mystery action with flashing lights and sound, NM (VG box), J6, $225.00.

Linus Lovable Lion, Illco/Hong Kong, 1970, MIB............$40.00

Lite-O-Wheel Go Kart, Rosko Toy, MIB, $185.00.

Loop Plane, MT, advances & loops, prop spins, litho tin w/vinyl-headed pilot, remote control, 9", NM (EX box), A $155.00

Lucky Crane, Japan, crane inside window tries to catch prizes, 9", all actions not working o/w NM (NM box), A.....$1,300.00

Lucky Seven Dice Throwing Monkey, Alps, 1960, MIB, L4.$165.00

Luncheonette Bank, Alps, 12", MIB, L4.........................$450.00

M-35 Tank, MIB, L4...$175.00

Mac the Turtle, Y, rolls over barrel w/several actions, MIB, L4...$250.00

Machine Gunner Policeman, MIB, T1 ....$225.00

Loop the Loop Clown, TN, 10½", MIB, $175.00.

Magic Bulldozer, Y, bump-&-go action, w/driver, 5", MIB, L4...$175.00

Magic Man Clown, MM, advances, tips hat & smoke emits from his head, tin & cloth, remote control, 12", MIB, L4 ..$575.00

Major Tooty, Alps, drum major plays drum, 14", MIB, L4 .$275.00

Make-Up Bear, MT, 9", MIB, L4 ....$750.00

Mambo the Jolly Drumming Elephant, Alps, plays drum & cymbals, bell jingles in trunk, tin & plush, 9", EX (VG+ box) ...$200.00

Marvelous Mike Tractor, Saunders, 1965, EX, J2 ....$200.00

Mary's Little Lamb, Alps, advances w/nodding head, stops & speaks, plush & tin, 10", scarce, EX+ (EX+ box), A .$125.00

Maxwell Coffee-Loving Bear, TN, 10", NMIB, L4.........$250.00

McGregor, TN, man rises slowly from suitcase as eyes roll, smoke emits from cigar, tin & cloth, 11", NM (EX box), A $165.00

Mickey Mouse Loop the Loop, MIB, L4 ....$175.00

Miss Friday the Typist, TN, girl types and bell rings, tin and vinyl, 7", NM (NM box), M5, $275.00.

Mickey Mouse Melody Railroad, Frankonia/WDP, 1967, characters navigate as songs play, MIB, rare, L4 ....$1,600.00

Mickey the Magician, Linemar, lifts hat to reveal rabbit after many other actions, tin, 10", NM+ (EX+ box) $2,500.00

Mighty Mike the Barbell Lifter, K, lifts light-up barbells overhead, litho tin & plush, 12", EX (VG box)..............$275.00

Minnie Mouse Shopping Cart, Illco/WDP, 1960s-70s, bump-&-go action, plastic, 10", EX+ (EX box), A $65.00

Mischievous Monkey, MT, monkey scoots up & down tree w/bone in front of doghouse, litho tin, 18", NM+ (EX box), A...$300.00

Miss Friday the Typist, TN, girl types & bell rings, litho tin & vinyl, 7", EX (VG box), A $165.00

Mobile Artillery Unit, Cragstan, complete w/cannon, antiaircraft gun, radar screen & receiver, 10", NM (EX box), A .$365.00

Mobile Searchlight Unit, Thomas Toys, 1950s, bl & yel truck w/attached wagon & searchlight, 16", EX+ (EX box), A..$165.00

Mobile Space TV Unit, TN, bump-&-go w/revolving lenses on TV camera w/lighted video screen, 11", G (worn box), A $1,050.00

Mod Monster, see Blushing Frankenstein

Monkey the Shoe Maker, TN, seated monkey smokes pipe & hammers on shoe, MIB, rare, L4 ....$875.00

Mother Bear, MT, bear sits in rocking chair & knits, head nods & eyes light, plush & tin, 10", EX, L4 ....$185.00

Mother Goose, Cragstan, 1950, EX.............................$100.00

Motion-ettes, see Universal Studios Motion-ettes

Motorcycle Cop, Daiya, wht litho tin w/sidesaddles that hold batteries, NMIB, A...$375.00

Mountain Special Express, MIB, L4 ....$60.00

Movieland Drive-In Theater, Remco, plastic w/dbl-feature film strips & 4 litho tin cars, EX+ (EX box), A $195.00

Mr Baseball Jr, K/Japan, baseball player at bat hitting ball into box that acts as field, litho tin, NMIB $675.00

Mr. Magoo Car, Hubley, 1961, Mr. Magoo steers as car rocks and rattles, tin with cloth top, 9", NM (EX box), A, $425.00.

Mr Fox the Magician, Y, plush fox in blk tux at table w/patriotic hat over rabbit, 5 actions, 9", EX (orig box) $475.00

Mr Fox the Magician, Y, scarce bubble-blowing version, NMIB $525.00

Mr McPooch, SAN, 8", MIB, L4..$350.00

Mr Strong Pup, MIB, L4..$475.00

Multi-Action Dump Truck, Y, red & cream tin w/rooftop light, 11", EX, A...$145.00

Mumbo Jumbo the Hawaiian Drummer, Alps, 3 actions, 10", MIB, L4...$375.00

Musical Cadillac, Irco/Japan, plays tune as car advances, red tin w/wht roof, 9", NM, A...$170.00

Musical Jolly Chimp, CK, 10½", MIB, L4 ....$100.00

Musical Marching Bear, Alps, beats drum & blows horn, plush & tin w/cloth clothes, 11", MIB, L4 ....$700.00

Musical Showboat, Gakken, xylophone plays 'Oh Suzanna' as paddle wheeler advances, 13½", NMIB, J2..............$200.00

Nautilus Periscope, MIB, L4..$225.00

Nutty Nibs, Linemar, painted tin with red, white and black paper skirt, 12", EX (EX box), A, $850.00.

Ol' Sleepy Head Rip, Y, 9", MIB, L4..................................$450.00

Old Fashioned Hot Rod, Bandai, bump-&-go action, litho tin w/vinyl driver, 6", EX (EX box), A $110.00

Open Sleigh, MT, 2 dogs pull sled w/bump-&-go action, litho tin & vinyl, 15", NM (EX box), A..........................$750.00

Overland Express Train, TN, bump-&-go action w/whistle sound, litho tin, 16½", MIB $120.00

Overland Stagecoach, MT, galloping action & sound w/driver holding reins, litho tin & plastic, 18", MIB, L4.......$275.00

Pat O'Neill the Fun Loving Irishman, TN, hold flame to glass cigar tip for several actions, 11", rare, NMIB..........$600.00

Peppermint Twist Doll, Haji, 12", MIB, L4 ....$375.00

Performing Circus Lion, MIB, L4....................................$500.00

Periscope Firing Range, blk plastic, 11½", NM (EX box), M5..$150.00

Pet Turtle, Alps, advances w/head moving in & out of shell, pull-string action, 7", NM, L4 ....$125.00

Pete the Talking Parrot, TN, parrot perched on tree branch repeats messages, 17", EX+ $375.00

Phantom Raider, Ideal, 1964, plastic freighter changes to warship, forward & reverse action, 28", NM (VG box), A......$200.00

Piano Pooch, TN, plays piano w/sound, tin & plush, 7", NM (EX box), A $135.00

Picnic Bunny, Alps, pours carrot juice into cup & drinks it, plush over tin, NM (NM box), M5 ....$75.00

Pierrot-Monkey Cycle, MT, clown driver w/blinking nose drives crazy action cycle, monkey waves hat, 10", EX (EX box), A $360.00

Piggy Cook, Y, pig flips egg in pan, MIB, L4...................$275.00

Pilot Boat #25, Alps, litho tin, bl, yel, orange & cream, 12", EX, A $75.00

Pinky the Clown, Alps, cloth & vinyl clown blows whistle as he balances ball on nose & juggles, 10½", MIB, L4 .....$500.00

Pinky the Clown, Alps, 10½", NM, L4.............................$225.00

Pinocchio Xylophone Player, TN, plays 'London Bridge,' tin w/rubber head, 9", NM (EX box), A $245.00

Pistol Pete, Marusan, lithographed tin with cloth clothes, remote control, 11", NMIB, A, $240.00.

Playful Puppy, MT, 7½", MIB, L4....................................$300.00

Playland Octopus, Alps, gondolas undulate up & down as they spin, lights & bell sound, tin, 19", scarce, EX (VG box), A $995.00

Police Car, Ichico, litho tin w/speedometer on trunk, 13", non-working, G+, M5 ....$80.00

Police Jeep, TN, mystery action w/siren sound & working head-lights, litho tin, 13", EX (VG box), A $185.00

Police Motorcycle, Bandai, remote control, EX, L4 ....$100.00

Popcorn Vendor, S&E/Cragstan, bear pedals cart while umbrella spins & popcorn pops, 8", MIB $575.00

Popcorn Vendor, TN, duck pushes wagon w/bump-&-go action, popcorn pops inside wagon, tin, 7½", scarce, NM (EX box), A $300.00

Popeye, see also Bubble Blowing Popeye

Popeye in Rowboat, Linemar, remote control, 10", G, A .$2,750.00

Popeye in Rowboat, Linemar, remote control, 10", NMIB, A $9,000.00

Poverty Pup, Poynter, 1966, 3 actions, MIB $75.00

Professor Owl, Y, turns while chirping & raises pointer to chalk-board, litho tin, 8", NMIB, A...............................$425.00

Project Yankee Doodle, Remco, rocket & satellite take off after many actions, plastic, 16", EX+ (EX box), A $165.00

Puffy Morris, Y, 10", MIB, L4 ....$375.00

Rabbits & Carriage, S&E, mama pushes baby in buggy, MIB, L4...$425.00

Radar 'N Scope, MT, features screen w/airplanes, revolving radar antenna & lights on tower, litho tin, 10", EX+, A $195.00

Radicon Bus, T&M, remote control, MIB, L4 ....$400.00

Radio Loudspeaker, Remco, plastic truck w/revolving searchlight beam, microphone & speaker, 24", EX+ (EX+ box), A.$120.00

Radio Rex, Elmwood Button Co, 1920s, w/instructions, EX+ (partial box), J2 ....$250.00

Randy the Walking Monkey, NMIB, L4...........................$175.00

Reading Bear, Alps, 1950s, 5 actions, 9", M, L4 ....$525.00

Riverboat Queen Mary, NM, L4 ....$125.00

Roaring Gorilla, TN, advances w/roaring sounds & light-up eyes, litho tin & plush, remote control, 9", EX+ (VG+ box), A $300.00

Roaring Lion, TN, walks as his mane puffs out & he roars, plush, remote control, 12", NM (EX box), A $130.00

Rock 'N Roll Monkey, Alps, monkey plays guitar, sways & stomps foot, 12", MIB, from $300 to $325.00

Rocky (Fred Flintstone look-alike), Japan, bump-&-go action, carries club & hatchet, litho tin, 4", NM (EX+ box), A..$175.00

Royal Cub, S&E, mama bear pushes baby bear in buggy with 6 other actions, MIB, $450.00.

Sam the Shaving Man, Plaything Toy, 1960s, man in cloth suit & plush hair shaves at table w/mirror, 12", MIB, A.......$300.00

Sammy Wong the Tea Totaler, TN, man pours & drinks tea, teapot lights & smokes, tin, vinyl & cloth, 10", EX (VG+ box), A..$260.00

Santa Bank, Trim-A-Tree, H&C, 11", NMIB, L4..........$300.00

Santa Claus Phone Bank, S&E, w/pay phone, 8", EX, rare, L4 ....$500.00

Santa Copter, MT, 1960, 8½", MIB, L4 ....$150.00

Santa in His Rocking Chair, Alps, w/tree & stocking, 21", EX, rare, L4...$750.00

Santa in Sleigh, MT, advances w/lights & sound, 17", MIB, L4 ....$700.00

Photo courtesy of Mike Roscoe.

Santa on Go Kart, TM, lithographed tin with cloth hat and bag, vinyl face, 10", NM, $165.00.

Santa on Rooftop, MIB, T1 ....$150.00
Santa on Rotating Globe, HTC, 15", MIB, L4 ....$675.00
Santa on Scooter, MT, bump-&-go action w/bells & flashing lights, litho tin & vinyl, MIB $125.00
Self-Steering Electric Car, Harold Flory/England, silver w/blk tires, 10", NM (NM box), M5 ....$185.00
Serpent Charmer, Linemar, 7", NM, L4 ....$950.00
Shaking Classic Car, TN, 7", MIB, L4 ....$125.00
Shark-U-Control Racing Car, Remco, plastic, 19", NMIB, L4 ....$100.00
Shoe Shine Bear, Alps, plush bear in red cloth overalls & pipe in mouth shines shoe w/brush in each hand, 10", M, L4 .$200.00
Shoe Shine Joe w/Lighted Pipe, TN, monkey turns boot in hand as he buffs it, tin base, 9", M, L4 ....$165.00
Shooting Bear, SAN, advances & raises rifle w/sound & smoke, tin & plush, remote control, 10", scarce, M (EX+ box), A $600.00
Shooting Cowboys, dbl-barrel version, EX, L4 ....$575.00
Shooting Gallery Roaring Gorilla, MT, NMIB, L4 ....$350.00
Shutter Bug, TN, boy shuffles along & takes pictures, bulb flashes, tin, 9", NM+ (EX box), A $850.00
Shuttling Train Set, Cragstan, railroad car w/dog travels track w/several actions, litho tin, 38", MIB, A $215.00
Siren Patrol Motorcycle, Modern Toys, litho tin cycle w/spoked front wheel, rubber policeman, 12", NMIB, A $330.00
Ski Lift, Alps, goes to end of cable & changes direction, litho tin, 7", NM, M5 ....$150.00
Skipping Monkey, TN, 1960s, 2 actions, NMIB............$100.00
Sleeping Baby Bear, Linemar, alarm goes off & baby bear sits up in bed, yawns & squeals, tin & plush, 9", NM (EX box), A..$310.00

Smarty Bird, Ideal, 1964, working, EX, V1 ....$60.00
Smokey Bear Jeep, TN, forward & reverse action w/flashing light & siren sound, litho tin, rare, MIB, L4 ....$1,250.00
Smokey the Bear, Marusan, advances w/shovel & puffs on pipe, 9", NMIB $285.00
Smoking Grandpa, SAN, 1950s, eyes closed, 9", rare, MIB, L4 ....$425.00
Smoking Grandpa, SAN, 1950s, eyes open, 9", EX (EX box), A $150.00
Smoking Pa Pa Bear, SAN, 8", MIB, L4 ....$175.00
Smoky Joe Car, Marusan, driver smokes light-up pipe, litho tin, 8½", EX..$100.00
Southern Pacific Model Train, Japan, unused, MIB, J2 ..$200.00
Spanking Bear, Linemar, mama bear spanks baby, several actions, litho tin & plush, 9", NMIB, L4 ....$475.00
Sparky the Seal, MT, seal walks & balances ball in stream of air above nose, plush over tin, 8", M, L4 ....$95.00
Steam Roller w/Trailer, Japan, MIB, J6..........................$275.00

Strutting My Fair Dancer, Haji, sailor girl does jig on platform, lithographed tin and celluloid, 11", MIB, $275.00.

Super Control Anti-Craft Jeep, S&E, MIB, L4 ....$375.00
Surfing Snoopy, Mattel #3477, M, H11 ....$60.00
Suzette the Eating Monkey, Linemar, sits at table & takes a bite of meat, tin w/cloth outfit, 9", rare, NM (EX box), A ..$425.00
Swan the Queen on the Water, MIB, L4 ....$500.00
Talking Batmobile, Palitoy, 1977, press roof to play phrases, unused, M (NM box), C1................................$290.00
Teddy Bear Swing, Yonezawa, plush bear flips forward & backward on litho tin bar, 13", MIB, L4................$425.00
Teddy the Champ Boxer, Cragstan, bears hits bag, eyes roll & head moves side to side, tin & plush, 9", NM (EX box), A $355.00
Telephone Bear, MT, plush bear on litho tin chair picks up phone & chatters, 9½", MIB, L4 ....$450.00
Telephone Rabbit, MT, sits in rocking chair & picks up phone, MIB, L4 ....$275.00

Teddy the Artist, Yonezawa, Teddy simulates drawing, complete with 9 templates, NM (EX box), A, $400.00.

Tinkling Trolley, MT, 10½", MIB, L4.............................$200.00
Tom & Jerry Helicopter, MT, bump-&-go action w/spinning rotor blade, EX, L4 ....$325.00
Tom & Jerry Locomotive, MT, bump-&-go action w/ringing bell, litho tin w/vinyl figures, 9", NMIB $275.00

Tom and Jerry Vehicle, TM, lithographed tin, 10", NM, $285.00.

Topo Gigio Xylophone Player, TN, 1960s, MIB, L4...$1,450.00

Traffic Light, Linemar, lights change from gr to red on all 4 sides, 18", EX+ (EX+ box), A $145.00
Traffic Policeman, AI, policeman blows whistle & turns as light changes, 13", NM (EX box), A $310.00
Treasure Chest Bank, Illfelder, 11", MIB, L4.............$150.00
Tric-Cycling Clown, MT, 12", rare, MIB, L4 ....$875.00
Trumpet Playing Monkey, Cragstan, litho tin & plush, MIB $275.00
Turn-O-Matic Gun Jeep, TN, 10", NMIB, L4...............$175.00
Twin Racing Cars, Alps, 1950s, MIB, L4.......................$675.00
Universal Studios Motion-ettes, Wolf Man, several actions, MIB $50.00
VIP Busy Boss Bear, S&E, 8", EX, L4.............................$275.00
Volkswagen Micro Bus, MIB, L4.....................................$500.00
Volkswagen w/Visible Engine, KO, 7", MIB, L4.............$175.00
Vrroom! Cement Mixer, Mattel, working, EX+ (partial box), T1 ....$125.00
Wagon Master, MT, 18", MIB, L4 ....$375.00
Walking Bambi, MIB, L4 ....$795.00
Walking Cat, Linemar, advances w/moving head, eyes light up, meows, plush over tin, remote control, 6", EX+ (VG box), A $60.00
Western Bad Man at Red Gulch Bar, Japan, outlaw takes drink from bartender then fires gun, EX+..........................$375.00
Western Special Locomotive, Japan, late 1950s, mystery actions, 13", MIB, P4 ....$90.00
Whirly Twirly Rocket Ride, Alps, rockets spin w/flashing lights & bell sound, litho tin, 13", NM $325.00
Wild West Rodeo Bubbling Bull, Linemar, 6½", MIB, L4 .$375.00
Windy the Juggling Elephant, TN, waves feet while spinning umbrella or blows ball, plush & tin, 10½", MIB, L4.$325.00
Windy the Juggling Elephant, TN, 10½", EX, L4............$85.00
Wizard of Oz Tin Man, Remco, 21", MIB, L4 ....$375.00
Worried Mother Duck, TN, 11", MIB, L4 ....$225.00
Xylophone Bear, MIB, rare, L4..$575.00
Yo-Yo Clown, Alps, 9", NM, L4 ....$400.00

Bicycles, Motorbikes and Tricycles

The most interesting of the vintage bicycles are those made from the 1920s into the '60s, though a few even later models are collectible as well. Some from the fifties were very futuristic and styled with sweeping Art Deco lines, others had wonderful features such as built-in radios and brake lights, and some were decked out with saddlebags and holsters to appeal to fans of Hoppy, Gene and many other western heroes. Watch for reproductions.

Condition is everything when evaluating bicycles, and one worth $2,500.00 in excellent or better condition might be worth as little as $50.00 in unrestored, poor condition. But here are a few values to suggest a range.

Advisor: Richard Trautwein (T3).

Bicycles

Bowden, boy's, red futuristic design w/chrome trim, thin wht-wall tires, rear chrome carrier, wht grips, all orig, M, A .$3,850.00

BSA Paratrooper, Pat #543076, boy's, 1940, rstr, A $475.00
Columbia Century Hard Tire Safety, 1889, sprung front forks, old rstr, A $2,000.00
Columbia Chainless 2-Speed Safety, 1903, boy's, cushion fr, NP front forks, pneumatic tires, EX, A $1,300.00
Columbia Motobike, boy's, w/speedomoter & clock dashboard, front fender headlight, rear carrier, 1937, EX, A..$1,700.00
Columbia 5-Star Model R9T, 1950, wht-walls, rstr, A .$1,000.00
Eagle, boy's, pneumatic tires, no fenders, EX, A $475.00
Gamblis Hiawatha Strato Charger, boy's, headlight under handlebars, taillight under seat, rear carrier, wht-walls, G+, A $40.00

Roadmaster Luxury Liner girl's bike, metallic green with chrome fenders, 26", EX, A, $500.00.

Gene Autry girl's bike, brown and cream with horse head, gun and holster, 24", missing horseshoe taillight and handlebar streamers, minor paint wear, A, $800.00.

Grendon #7 Hard Tire Safety, Iron Wheel Co, boy's, EX, A $2,200.00
Harley-Davidson Motocyke, 1917, boy's, w/sidecar, rare, rstr, A $5,000.00
Hawthorn Comet, Montgomery Ward, boy's, front fender light, rear carrier, rear-wheel kickstand, wht-walls, 1938, EX, A $500.00
Hopalong Cassidy, girl's, front fender headlight, rear carrier & wht-walls, 26", EX, A $800.00
Huffy Radio w/Power Pack, ca 1955, boy's, front torpedo headlight, rear carrier, wht-walls, G+, A $1,400.00
JC Higgins, boy's, rear carrier, blk tires, VG, A $475.00
JC Higgins Flightlines 216, headlight in tank, chrome fenders w/rear carrier, G+, A $25.00
Mercury Deluxe, 1954, boy's, red & wht w/chrome trim, rear carrier, front fender light, wht-walls, rstr, A $650.00
Metal Specialties Speed Bike, 1930s, boy's, w/simulated motorcycle engine, leather spring seat, pneumatic tires, G, A $315.00
Monarch Super Cruiser, boy's, fender headlight, rear carrier, wht-wall tires, G+, A $650.00
Murray, boy's, chrome fenders w/front & back carriers, wht-walls, G+, A $25.00
Pacemaker Hard Tire Safety, Pat 1893, boy's, EX, A ..$1,450.00
Pennant Model 10, boy's, pneumatic tires, 1898, no seat, A.$450.00
Pierce Arrow Pneumatic Safety, boy's, spring fork & cushion fr, 1900, EX, A $950.00

Schwinn, girl's, chrome fenders, handlebar headlight, G+, A .$25.00
Schwinn, girl's, front torpedo headlight, rear carrier, wht rims, G+, A $25.00
Schwinn Black Phantom, boy's, chrome fenders w/front headlight & rear carrier, 2 bells on handlebars, wht-walls, G+, A $900.00

Schwinn Red Phantom boy's bike, red with chrome fenders, restored, A, $1,500.00.

Sears Spaceliner girl's bike, blue-green with chrome fenders, electric light and horn, 67", EX, A, $195.00.

Schwinn Cycle Truck, boy's, red w/chrome fenders, lg front wire basket, sm front tire w/lg back tire, EX, A $200.00

Schwinn Hornet, girl's, torpedo headlight on fender, rear carrier, wht-walls, G+, A $30.00

Schwinn Motobike, boy's, red & wht w/rear carrier, tool tank & horn, wht tires, EX, A $1,500.00

Shelby Flyer, boy's, front fender headlight, rear carrier, 1948, EX, A $350.00

Silver King Wing Bar, 1937, girl's, rear carrier, tool-box seat, hex handlebars, wht-walls, battery tube, rstr, A ...$1,300.00

Spaceliner, Sears, girl's, bl-gr w/chrome fenders, wht seat & grips, electric light & horn, wht-wall tires, 67", EX, A.......$195.00

Transitional Safety, flat-iron construction w/riveted joints, Victorian design w/'mustache' handlebars, orig pnt, A .$175.00

Victor Hard Tire Safety, Overman, Pat 1890, boy's, VG, A $1,200.00

Victoria Hard Tire Safety, Overman, 1890, girl's, mesh chain guard, EX, A $3,000.00

Victoria Model 35, Overman Wheel Co, girl's, wooden rear fender, EX, A $500.00

Western Strato Flyer, headlight in tank, chrome fenders w/front & rear carriers, wht-walls, G+, A $85.00

Yost's Falcon #1 Pneumatic Safety, boy's, wooden handlebars, 1893, A $800.00

Motorbikes

Monarch Super-Twin Motorbike, 1949, original black paint with red and cream highlights, EX, A, $3,200.00.

Whizzer Sportsman, 1st place winner at the Antique Auto Club of America in 1984, restored, 20", A, $5,000.00.

Elgin Motorbike/Bicycle, rear-wheel kickstand, rpl tires, G+, A $600.00

Indian Motorcycle, Citan, 1940s-50s, blk & cream w/Indian Motorcycle logo, rstr, A $4,200.00

Tricycles

Articulated Horse, wooden body w/stuffed canvas saddle on 3-wheeler w/front pedals, 36" L, EX, A $715.00

Donaldson Jockey Cycle, scooter-type handlebars, rubber tires, 24½x37", old rpt, A $8,500.00

Streamline Style, from Art Deco period, bl & cream, rstr, A .$715.00

Black Americana

Black subjects were commonly depicted in children's toys as long ago as the late 1870s. Among the most widely collected today are the fine windup toys made both here and in Germany. Early cloth and later composition and vinyl dolls are favorites of many; others enjoy ceramic figurines. Many factors enter into evaluating Black Americana, especially in regard to the hand-made dolls and toys, since quality is subjective to individual standards. Because of this you may find wide ranges in dealers' asking prices. In order to better understand this field of collecting, we recommend *Black Collectibles Sold in America* by P.J. Gibbs and *Black Dolls: 1820-1991*, and *Black Dolls, Book II*, both by Myla Perkins.

Advisor: Judy Posner (P6).

See also Battery-Operated Toys; Schoenhut; Windups, Friction and Other Mechanicals.

Acrobat Toy, articulated pnt wood native on wood fr, hand-operated, 8", VG $75.00

Banjo, Germany, 1890s, cb, litho image of Uncle Remus playing banjo while Mammy & boy dance a jig, 8x4", M, A .$120.00

Book, Kentucky Twins, Raphael Tuck, ca 1910, M Taylor illus, cb cover, full color, 8x9", EX, P6 ....$295.00

Book, Little Black Sambo, Harter Publishing, 1931, Fern Bisel Peat illus, full color, 16 pgs, EX, P6 ....$95.00

Book, Little Black Sambo, Whitman Tell-A-Tale, ca 1958, Gladys Mitchell illus, full color, 28 pgs, EX, P6.........$65.00

Book Set with Doll, All About Little Black Sambo/Mother Goose/Little Red Riding Hood, Cupples and Leon, 1906, EX+ (EX box), A, $950.00.

Book, Little Black Sambo, Whitman Tell-A-Tale #2463, 1961, rpr spine, K3.................................$40.00

Book, Little Black Sambo/The Gingerbread Man/Titty Mouse, Rand McNally, 1937, M Evans illus, full color, 64 pgs, EX, P6.................................$95.00

Book, Little Brown Koko, 1st edition, 1940, fully illus, 96 pgs, EX, P6.................................$85.00

Book, Little Washington's Holidays, Lillian E Roth, 1st edition, 1925, Paul S Jonst illus, 144 pgs, EX, P6.................$45.00

Book, Rufty Tufty Flies High, Heinemann Publishing, 1959, Ruth Ainsworth illus, EX, P6.................................$70.00

Book, Watermelon Pete (w/6 other stories), Elizabeth Gordon/Rand McNally, 1937, Clara Powers Wilson illus, EX, P6.................................$85.00

Challenge Dancer, Cromwell, 1865, jtd wood figure & platform, cloth clothes & curtain, clockwork, 10", EX (wood box), A.................................$4,890.00

Clicker Toy, Minstrel Sam, 1920s, mc litho tin, brn skin & exaggerated features, 1¾", EX, P6.................................$95.00

Clicker Toy, West Germany, 1946, clown hits golliwog w/lg mallet, 3¼x3", M.................................$150.00

Crank Toy, Dancing Ladies w/Banjo Player, DAA Buck (?), 1889, wooden cabin-shaped box, 2 dancers, 7x9", EX, A.................................$2,500.00

Crank Toy, Happy Jack Jigger, mk B&U/Germany, articulated flat litho tin figure dances when crank is turned, 7", EX+, A.................................$500.00

Crank Toy, Old Kentucky Home, Reed, 6 articulated figures referred to as Lime Kiln Club, wood, EX (orig box), A.........$4,400.00

Crank Toy, Old Plantation, Reed, turning lever activates 5 figures, litho paper on wood, 8¾", G, A.................................$470.00

Dancing Jigger, Steppin' Tom, Sturdy Mfg, pnt & stenciled articulated wood figure, yel, red, blk & wht, 13", G+.........$125.00

Dancing Sambo Magic Trick, 1940s, jtd cb figure, M (w/envelope), A.................................$45.00

Dexterity Puzzle, 1886, cake walkers celebrating US centennial, 2¼" dia, scarce, M, A.................................$240.00

Dice Toy, Alco/Britain, activate plunger to spin laughing head & dice, 2" dia, EX, A.................................$70.00

Doll, Aunt Jemima, Aunt Jemima Mills, 1917, mc litho cloth, 16½" uncut figure, complete, M, P6.................................$325.00

Doll, Belton, dk-skinned bsk socket head w/jtd wood & compo body, wht & red dress, cropped wig, pierced ears, EX, A.....$2,700.00

Doll, boy in top hat w/toothy grin, Japan, prewar, celluloid, 6", NM, A.................................$125.00

Doll, Darky, Cocheco Mfg Co, dtd Aug 15, 1893, uncut cloth w/printed directions, 15", NM+, A.................................$176.00

Doll, Germany, trade stimulator, papier-mache on wood stand, cloth suit, head nods & mouth opens, 22", VG, A.$2,530.00

Doll, girl, Effanbee, Grumpy, brn compo head w/pnt features, cotton pigtails, dressed cloth & compo body, 12", EX, A........$375.00

Doll, golliwog boy, hand-knit yarn, embroidered side-glance eyes, gr turtleneck, tweed pants, 17", EX, P6............$75.00

Doll, golliwog boy, unknown mfg, felt extremities w/applique features, fuzzy hair, blk & wht striped pants, 25", EX, P6.................................$195.00

Doll, golliwog boy, 1930s, hand-knit yarn w/felt features, red & wht striped pants, bl jacket, 17", EX, P6.................$150.00

Doll, Heubach 399-12/0, jtd vinyl w/hoop earrings & felt grass skirt, 10", EX, A.................................$175.00

Doll, molded blk leather upper body & arms, lower cloth body, blk wig, eyes & red lips, provincial costume, 17", EX, A.$1,375.00

Doll, Rasta, Cream of Wheat, early 1900s, litho cloth, EX.$295.00

Doll, Topsy, uncut cloth pattern to make 2 dolls, framed, 9x24", M, A.................................$330.00

Doll, Uncle Mose, Aunt Jemima Mills, 1917, mc litho cloth, uncut 17" figure, complete, M, P6.................................$295.00

Doll, Wade Davis, Aunt Jemima Mills, 1917, mc litho cloth, uncut 13" figure, complete, M, P6.................................$275.00

Doll Family, father, mother & boy golliwogs, stuffed cloth, button eyes, yarn hair, cloth clothed, 18" & 22", EX, A.$95.00

Doll Kit, Sambo, Bucilla Needlework, 1950s, complete, P6 .$75.00

Doll Underwear, Petit Negro, 1920s, cotton knit panties & undershirt w/woven logo label, 6" ea, EX, P6, pr.....$125.00

Dolls, golliwog boy & girl, 1930s, blk knitted yarn w/embroidered features, orange & wht clothes, 6", EX, P6, pr.$65.00

Figure, Japan, 1940s, boy w/2 lg dice on platform, celluloid w/hand-pnt features, 2", NM, A.................................$140.00

Figure, Japan, 1940s, dog chasing boy w/watermelon on platform, celluloid w/hand-pnt features, 2", NM, A.......$195.00

Game, Amos 'N Andy Card Party, AM Davis, 1930, complete, EX (VG box), A.................................$195.00

Game, De Ole Nest, rifle shoots corks at knock-down figures sitting on cabin, fiberboard & wood, complete, 14x13", EX, A.................................$425.00

Game, Four Jolly 'N' Boys, Chad Valley, 1930s, shoot at 4 boys on brick wall, gun missing o/w VG (orig box), A....$340.00

Game, Game of Dixieland, Fireside Game Co, 1897, cards, complete, EX (worn box), P6.................................$265.00

Game, Golli-Pop Target, Chad Valley, heavy cardboard with paper lithographed figure, complete, EX (EX box), A, $550.00.

Game, Little Black Sambo, Einson-Freeman, 1934, missing 2 pcs o/w complete, EX (orig box), A.................................$155.00

Game, Our Gang Tipple-Topple, All Fair Inc, box top w/wooden balls, diecut figures & fence w/targets, incomplete, G+, A..................$120.00

Game, Sambo, target game, Parker Bros, 1920s, complete, scarce, EX (G box), A.................$175.00

Game, Snake Eyes, 1957, board game w/dice & 50 illus cards, last game mfg in US, MIB, A.................$115.00

Game, Watch on de Rind, All Fair Inc, 1931, incomplete, VG (orig box), A.................$90.00

Game, Zoo Hoo, Lubbers and Bell, 1924, 3 games in 1, complete, NM (EX box), A, $165.00.

Handkerchief, 1930s, cotton print, I Love Little Pussy..., little girl gives golliwog a wagon ride, EX, P6.................$85.00

Jazz Band, British, 1890s, hand-pnt metal, 6 musicians & 6 chairs, 5" ea, EX+, A.................$485.00

Jazz Band, Mayfair Novelty, 1920s, 12 paper litho marching band figures on card, 2½" ea, MOC, A.................$40.00

Mechanical Card, bust of man in hat & earrings, move lever & eyes, hat & mouth move side to side, scarce, M, A ...$45.00

Mechanical Card, Germany, 1890s, cb, bust image of man whose eyes roll up & down & tongue that goes in & out, NM, A........$90.00

Mug, pottery, shows Santa toting bag of toys w/golliwog doll on top, EX, P6.................$75.00

Mug, Shenango China, 1930s, Golliwog's Joy Ride, unmarked, lt wear to gold at rim o/w EX, P6.................$125.00

Nodder, toddler, Germany, 1920s, dress falls to expose backside, pnt bsk, 7", EX+, H12.................$175.00

Noisemaker, Germany, 1930s, brn-skinned banjo player w/fat sax player on litho tin w/red wood hdl, 6½", EX, P6.$95.00

Noisemaker, Occupied Japan, 2" blk-skinned caricature w/lg googly eyes on 5¼" rectangle, 5¾" ratchet hdl, EX, P6....$75.00

Playette Moving Theatre, litho paper, theatre unit w/Little Black Sambo book & assorted cutouts, EX (orig box)........$225.00

Premium, Amos 'N Andy puzzle, Pepsodent Co, dtd 1932, features various characters, full color, 4 pcs missing, P6.$40.00

Premium, Golliwog Trio, Robertson's Marmalade, pnt plaster musicians, saxophone player, bass player & singer, 3", NM, A.................$115.00

Premium, Jolly Dancing Figure, Atwater Kent Radio, 1915, cb, makes 2-sided articulated figure, uncut, 7x10", M, A.................$145.00

Phonograph Jigger, Dancing Dandy, wood, EX, $225.00.

Pull Toy, pnt & stenciled wood, boy seated on wheeled platform holding reins of horse's head, 11", VG, A.................$55.00

Pull Toy, Snowflakes and Swipes, Nifty, 1920s, 8", NMIB (box not shown), $1,850.00.

Puppet, Jambo the Jiver Marionette, Talent Products, 1948, jtd wood body w/fiber hair, cloth clothes, 14", VG+ $225.00

Puppet, Lucifer, compo, peach overalls w/checked patch & shirt, neckerchief & hat, bare ft, wood base, 14", G, A $300.00

Puppet, Minstrel Mike Marionette, Hazelle's, pnt wood body w/plastic extremities, cloth clothing, 4", EX (orig box).................$150.00

Puppet, Tonga From the Congo Marionette, Talent Products, 1948, pnt wood & plastic jtd body, string skirt, 14", VG+.................$225.00

Push Toy, wooden & tin figure w/compo head in cloth pants & shirt on tin platform w/wheels, musical, 6", VG, A.$490.00

Puzzle, jigsaw, Pleasant Anticipation, 1880s, boy chasing chicken as girl watches, sold as party favor, 4x6", EX, P6.......$175.00

Roly Poly, marked Germany, 7", EX, $250.00.

Photo courtesy of Dunbar Gallery.

Scissors Toy, cloth and wood with glass eyes, EX, $250.00.

Smoke Toy, Germany, late 1800s, paper & tin disk, image of man's head w/mouth wide open, makes smoke rings, 2" dia, NM, A...$80.00

Talking Machine Toy, 1900, wood & metal, dapper referee instructs boxers on platform that attaches to phonograph, M, A $265.00

Watermelon w/Baby, hollow litho cb watermelon w/facial features opens to hold blk-skinned celluloid doll, 4", G, A $440.00

Boats

Though some commercially made boats date as far back as the late 1800s, they were produced on a much larger scale during WWI and the decade that followed and again during the years that spanned WWII. Some were scaled-down models of battleships measuring nearly three feet in length. While a few were

actually seaworthy, many were designed with small wheels to be pulled along the carpet or out of doors on dry land. Others were motor-driven windups, and later a few were even battery operated. Some of the larger manufacturers were Bing (Germany), Dent (Pennsylvania), Orkin Craft (California), Liberty Playthings (New York) and Arnold (West Germany).

Advisors: Richard Trautwein (T3); Dick Borgerding (B4)

See also Cast Iron, Boats; Battery-Operated Toys; Tootsietoys; Windups, Friction and Other Mechanicals; and other specific manufacturers.

Aeroboat, Bowman/England, wood hull w/tin bow, internal gears & orig rubber band intact, EX (orig wooden box), A...$1,375.00

Aircraft Carrier, Coral Sea, Bandai, 1950s, litho tin, 3-D jets mounted on deck, 2 radar antennas, 4 guns, 15", NMIB, A $260.00

Aircraft Carrier, Marx, battery-op, tin, lt gr & beige, 21", missing 2 missiles & 1 airplane o/w EX, M5 ....$250.00

Battleship, Bliss, paper on wood, 16 wooden guns on upper deck, 2 masts with gun towers, 36", EX, A, $4,000.00.

Battleship Dreadnaught, 1st Series, Marklin, painted tin, red, white and gray, 13 brass cannons, clockwork motor, 4 lifeboats, etc., 42", EX (professionally restored), A, $21,000.00.

Armada, Hess, litho tin battleship w/5 cruisers, w/up, VG, A $415.00
Barracuda Atomic Sub, Remco, battery-op, crew, raft, 4 missiles & 6 torpedoes, NM (EX- box), T1.........................$275.00
Battle Cruiser, Carette, 1908, pnt tin, wht over red w/gray deck & pilot's house, tower w/spotlight, w/up, 27", rst, A ..$2,310.00
Battleship, Bing, 1915, pnt tin, gray & bl, red trim, 3 observation towers on mast, 2 British flags, w/up, 19", rst, A.......$550.00
Battleship, KS/Japan, wood, wht over red, w/stacks, guns & rigging, 11½", EX (orig box), A $75.00
Battleship, Orobr, litho tin, gray & red w/twin masts, 4 gun stations, 2 lifeboats on davits, pilot house, 11", VG, A..$340.00
Battleship, Orobr, litho tin, gray w/red trim, single mast w/observation towers, 2 stacks, 14 guns, w/up, 11", EX, A .$660.00
Battleship, Radiquet, 1895, zinc hull pnt copper & blk w/woodgrain deck, steam boiler & stacks, rails, 39", EX, A .$7,370.00

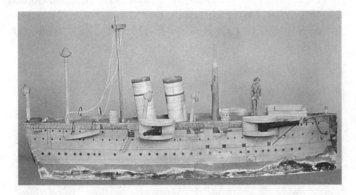

Battleship Philadelphia, Reed, 1877, paper on wood, 2 stacks, battle guns, mast poles, lifeboats and sailor, 30", VG, A, $250.00.

Battleship Texas, Orkin, litho tin w/wooden antiaircraft guns, dk olive gr, Am flag, w/up, 30", VG, A $2,750.00
Battleship USS Washington, Marx, litho tin replica, w/up activates simulated gunfire, 15", VG, A..........................$50.00
Cabin Cruiser, Japan, wood, pnt wht w/red trim & bottom, top lifts off, battery-op rudders, 11", MIB, A..................$110.00

Clipper Ship, Reed, 1877, paper on wood, 3 paper sails, 2 sailors and cargo on deck, 36", EX, A, $1,075.00.

Cabin Cruiser, Orkin/Calwis Industries Ltd CA, 1930, steel hull & cabin, wooden deck, 2-tone pnt, Am flag, 32", VG, A..$1,265.00
Clipper Ship America, Reed, paper on wood, 3 sails, sailors in dingy in simulated ocean, 31", G, A $770.00
Clipper Ship America, Reed, 1877, litho paper on wood w/cloth sails, contains barrels & crates, 42", EX, A...........$1,760.00
Cragstan Inflatable Vinyl Speedboat, battery-op outboard, MIB, L4..$185.00
Ferryboat, Gebruder, pnt & stenciled tin side-wheeler w/2 ventilator shafts, housing in center of flat deck, 16", G, A....$575.00
Ferryboat w/Circling Airplanes, C Kellerman, litho tin wheeled boat w/2 single-prop planes attached to tower, 9", EX, A $600.00
Fleetline Sea Wolf Speedboat, wood, battery-op, 15", NMIB, J2..$250.00
Gunboat, Bliss, litho paper on wood, w/4 flags & mounted guns, 4 wooden wheels, 25½", G, A $1,430.00
Motor Boat, Linemar, bl & red wood, battery-op, 11", NMIB, A..$135.00
Ocean Liner, Arnold, litho & pnt tin, red, wht & blk, 14 simulated lifeboats on davits, 2 masts & 3 stacks, 13", MIB, A $385.00
Ocean Liner, Bing, pnt tin, gold & blk w/beige deck, wht rails, 2 masts, 3 stacks, lifeboats, w/up, 15", needs rpr, A $800.00
Ocean Liner, Bing, pnt tin, red, wht & blk w/brn deck, 4 brn & red stacks, 2 masts, flags, 22", rstr, A $1,210.00
Ocean Liner, Carette, 1905, pnt tin, clockwork, 16½", masts & lifeboat missing, G pnt, A $980.00
Ocean Liner, Fleischmann, pressed steel, beige, burgundy & gray w/bl stripe, 21½", EX, A.................................$375.00
Ocean Liner, Fleishmann, pnt tin, red, wht & blk w/gr trim, 2 lifeboats, 2 masts & stacks, pilot house, 12½", M, A .$990.00
Ocean Liner, Keystone, pnt wood, 2 stacks, mast atop steering house, clockwork, VG (VG box), A $290.00
Ocean Liner Columbus, Marklin, pnt tin, wht over blk & red, 2 yel stacks, cut-out portholes, 20 lifeboats, 38", rstr, A...$8,250.00
Ocean Liner Grace, TM/Japan, red, wht & bl litho tin, battery-op whistling sounds & lights, 16", EX (orig box), A $245.00
Ocean Liner Leviathan, Bing, pnt tin, wht over blk & red, 3 blk, wht & red stacks, 3 levels, lifeboats, 36", rpt, A...$3,740.00
Ocean Liner Leviathan, 1925, wood, wht over blk & red, 3 bl, wht & red stacks, 3 levels, lifeboats, 40", rpt, A $385.00
Ocean Liner Luzern, Marklin, ca 1925, pnt tin, clockwork, 11½", missing 1 of 3 stacks & masts, G, A $1,955.00
Ocean Liner Mauretania, Fleischmann, pnt tin, wht, blk & red w/brn deck, 2 stacks, pilot house, 2 masts, 12", VG, A ...$360.00
Ocean Liner St Louis, Reed (?), 1910, paper on wood, pilot house, 2 stacks, lifeboats, simulated ocean waves, 35", EX, A...$1,980.00
Parlor Oarsman, Ives, 1869, pnt tin, maroon w/red & gold stripe, gr deck w/stripes, w/man, w/up, 11", VG, A.........$1,380.00
Phantom Rider Warship, Ideal, complete, EX (EX box), T1.$285.00
Pleasure Launch, att Fallows, pnt & stenciled tin, blk & red w/4 flags, bell, on wheels, 13", VG, A $6,820.00
Power Patrol Boat, Multiple Toymakers #2937, 1990, reissue, mc plastic, partial assembly required, 12", MIB, P4.........$10.00
Racing Boat, Carette, pnt tin, wht w/gr center band, red figure at helm, w/up, 7¾", G, A $625.00

Racing Boat Seahawk, Bowman, wood hull w/tin bow, steam-powered boiler system, 27", rpt (orig wooden box), A $330.00

Rowboat w/Oarsman, French (?), wood w/metal bow cover & crank, wood & metal figure & oars, brass hdls, 22", G-, A......$500.00

Ship w/Changable Deck, Japan, tin, changes from cruise to battleship, 12", EX......$250.00

Side-Wheeler, French, tin, blk over red w/yel trim, figures on open deck, single stack, rails at bow, w/up, 18", VG, A...$1,045.00

Side-Wheeler, Geo Brown, pnt & stenciled tin, 6¾", worn pnt, G-, A......$825.00

Side-Wheeler Betsy Green, Buffalo Toys, red, wht & gr, rear house depicts a band & dancers, 26", VG......$620.00

Side-Wheeler Columbia, Fallows, pnt & stenciled tin, base emb IXL, on wheels, 11", G, A......$3,300.00

Side-Wheeler Columbia, litho paper on wood w/tin railing & articulated walk beam, pnt stacks, 24", G-, A......$800.00

Side-Wheeler New York, Geo Brown, pnt & stenciled tin, w/flag, 6¼", pnt worn o/w VG, A......$3,300.00

Side-Wheeler Pacific, Bergmann, pnt & stenciled tin w/cast components, on wheels, 14", G, A......$3,850.00

Side-Wheeler Pilgrim, Reed, 1890s, litho paper on wood, 28", G, A......$690.00

Side-Wheeler Priscilla, Marklin, pnt tin, tan & wht w/gr bottom, 2 red & wht striped stacks, canvas top, 30", EX, A......$17,600.00

Side-Wheeler Priscilla, paper on wood, cream with green and red highlights, 2 black stacks, 37", G, A, $2,860.00.

Side-Wheeler Providence, litho paper on wood, 3 stacks, 19½", G, A......$580.00

Side-Wheeler River Queen, Reed, paper on woood, mk Gem of the Ocean, 2 decks & 2 blk stacks, 25", G, A......$440.00

Side-Wheeler Union, Bliss, paper on wood, 2 decks, 2 lg stacks, gear housing & pilot house, 23", EX, A......$1,155.00

Side-Wheeler Water Witch, Weeden, pnt tin, integral burner in keel fires steam engine, w/Am flag, 12", EX, A..$13,200.00

Speedboat, Haji, red & wht, tin w/up, 8", EX, M5......$40.00

Speedboat, Hornby/English, litho tin, bl & wht w/red trim, clockwork mechanism on stern, 16½", G-, A......$165.00

Speedboat, Japan, pnt wood, sleek design, lt bl w/red bottom, NP apparatus, 2 props, 24", EX, A......$1,705.00

Speedboat, Lionel, litho tin, cream, wht & red, orig stand, 18", VG, A......$465.00

Speedboat #43, Lionel, 1930s, pnt tin w/compo drivers, clockwork, 17½", G (VG box), A......$260.00

Photo courtesy of Dunbaar Gallery.

Speedboat, Lindstrom Outboard Motor, lithographed tin and wood, red, yellow and green, 11", EX, $450.00.

Steam Launch, Bing, pnt tin, bl & wht w/red stack & yel striping, brn seats, brass boiler, litho figure, 23", VG, A......$600.00

Steam Launch, Carette, pnt tin, gray w/brn deck & red striping, brass boiler, sm pilot house & deck rail, 19", NMIB, A......$2,090.00

Steamboat Atlantic, 1870s, pnt tin, 11¼", P, A......$175.00

Steamship Priscilla, Marklin, pnt tin, wht over red w/red trim, 2 stacks, pilot house, railing, 21", rpt, A......$2,970.00

Submarine, Marklin, pnt tin, gr w/blk trim, deck railing, w/up, 16", EX, A......$1,100.00

Submarine, Marklin, pnt tin, gr w/blk trim, deck railing, w/up, 9½", EX, A......$500.00

Submarine, Marklin, tin, gray with black stripe, large side flippers, 23", EX, A, $3,000.00.

Torpedo Boat, Bing, pnt tin, 2-tone gray w/blk trim, 2 torpedo chutes, guns, lifeboats, mast & stacks, 16", VG, A..$550.00

Tugboat, Buddy L #3000, ca 1930, pressed steel, type II, mk Buddy L Navigation Co, 28", rstr, A......$2,415.00

Tugboat, Buddy L #3000, ca 1930, pressed steel, type II, mk Buddy L Navigation Co, 28", NM, A......$12,650.00

USS Washington Battleship, Marx, w/up, travels, guns emit sparks, litho tin, 15", NM, A......$225.00

Books

Books have always captured and fired the imagination of children, and today books from every era are being collected. No longer is it just the beautifully illustrated Victorian examples or first editions of books written by well-known children's authors, but more modern books as well.

One of the first classics to achieve unprecedented success was *The Wizard of Oz* by author L. Frank Baum — such success, in fact, that far from his original intentions, it became a series. Even after Baum's death, other authors wrote Oz books until the decade of the 1960s, for a total of more than forty different titles. Other early authors were Beatrix Potter, Kate Greenaway, Palmer Cox (who invented the Brownies), and Johnny Gruelle (creator of Raggedy Ann and Andy). All were acomplished illustrators as well.

Everyone remembers a special series of books they grew up with, the Hardy Boys, Nancy Drew Mysteries, Tarzan — there were countless others. And though these are becoming very collectible today, there were many editions of each, and most are very easy to find. Generally the last few in any series will be the most difficult to locate, since fewer were printed than the earlier stories which were likely to have been reprinted many times. As is true of any type of book, first editions or the earliest printing will have more collector value.

Big Little Books came along in 1933 and until edged out by the comic-book format in the mid-1950s sold in huge volumes, first for a dime and never more than 20¢ a copy. They were printed by Whitman, Saalfield, Goldsmith, Van Wiseman, Lynn, and World Syndicate, and all stuck to Whitman's original layout — thick hand-sized sagas of adventure, the right-hand page with an exciting cartoon, well illustated and contrived so as to bring the text on the left alive. The first hero to be immortalized in this arena was Dick Tracy, but many more were to follow. Some of the more collectible today feature well-known characters like G-Men, Tarzan, Flash Gordon, Little Orphan Annie, Mickey Mouse, and Western heroes by the dozens.

Little Golden Books were first published in 1942 by Western Publishing Co. Inc. The earliest had spines of blue paper that were later replaced with gold foil. Until the 1970s the books were numbered from 1 to 600, while later books had no numerical order. The most valuable are those with dust jackets from the early forties or books with paper dolls and activities. The three primary series of books are Regular (1-600), Disney (1-140), and Activity (1-52). Books with the blue or gold paper spine (not foil) often sell at $8.00 to $15.00. Dust jackets alone are worth $20.00 and up in good condition. Paper doll books are generally valued at about $30.00 to $35.00, and stories about TV Western heroes at $12.00 to $18.00. First editions of the 25¢ and 29¢ cover-price books can be identified by a code (either on the title page or the last page); '1/A' indicates a first edition while a number '/Z' will refer to the twenty-sixth printing. Condition is important but subjective to personal standards. For more information we recommend *Collecting Little Golden Books, Vols I and II*, by Steve Santi (S8). The second edition also includes information on Wonder and Elf books.

Advisors: Ron and Donna Donnelly (D7), Big Little Books; Joel Cohen (C12), Disney Pop-Up Books; Ilene Kayne (K3), Big Golden Books, Little Golden Books, Tell-a-tale, and Wonder Books.

See also Black Americana; Coloring, Activity and Paint Books; Rock 'N Roll.

Big Little Books

Andy Panda's Vacation, #1435, EX, D8...........................$45.00
Aquaman, Whitman, 1968, EX, F8/J2.......................$15.00
Blondie, Cookie & Daisy's Pups, #1491, EX, D8 ....$25.00
Blondie, Who's Boss, #1423, VG+, D8 ....$25.00
Buccaneers, 1958, EX+, F8 ....$15.00

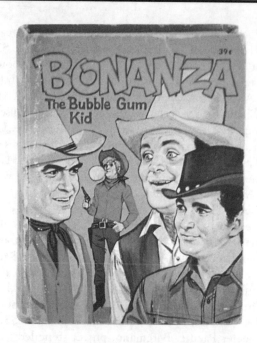

Bonanza, The Bubble Gum Kid, 1967, NM, $18.00.

Buck Jones & the Killers of Crooked Butte, G, D8...........$18.00
Buck Rogers, Planetoid Plot, #1197, 1936, EX+, M14 .....$95.00
Buck Rogers & the Depth Men of Jupiter, #1169, VG/EX, D8 ....$60.00
Buck Rogers & the Doom Comet, NM.........................$125.00
Buck Rogers & the Overturned World, #1474, VG- $50.00
Buck Rogers in the War With Planet Venus, #1437, EX ..$100.00
Buck Rogers in the 25th Century, #742, EX...................$120.00
Buck Rogers on the Moons of Saturn, #1143, EX, D8 ......$90.00
Calling W1XYZ, Jimmy Kean & the Radio Spies, #1412, VG+, D8..$35.00
Camels Are Coming, #1587, EX, D8............................$35.00
Captain Frank Hawk & the League of Twelve, #1444, VG+ .$22.00

Captain Midnight and the Moon Woman, #1452, EX, $75.00.

Chandu the Magician, #1093, EX, D8 ....$60.00

Charlie Chan of the Honolulu Police, #1478, VG+, D8 ..$35.00
Charlie McCarthy, Story of; #1456, EX, D8 ....$45.00
Chester Gump, Pole to Pole Flights, #1402, EX, D8.........$45.00
Cinderella & the Magic Wand, Walt Disney, 1950, EX...$30.00
Clyde Beatty, the Daredevil Lion & Tiger Tamer, 1938, EX,
    D8 ....$40.00
Dan Dunn on the Trail of the Counterfeiters, #1125, EX,
    D8 ....$30.00
Dan Dunn on the Trail of Wu Fang, #1454, VG+, D8.....$30.00
Danger Trail North, #1177, EX $22.00
Dick Tracy, Chains of Crime, #1185, EX...........................$60.00
Dick Tracy, Super Detective, #1488, 1939, NM..............$90.00
Dick Tracy & the Crooks in Disguise, #1479, NM $90.00
Dick Tracy & the Maroon Mask Gang Fast Action, EX, D8.$150.00

Dick Tracy and the Spider Gang, #1446, VG, $60.00.

Dick Tracy & the Tiger Lily Gang, #1460, 1949, VG,
    M14 ....$35.00
Dickie Moore in the Little Red Schoolhouse, EX, D8......$45.00
Don Winslow & the Great War Plot, EX, D8 ....$45.00
Don Winslow & the Secret Enemy Base, #1453, NM-, D8.$55.00
Donald Duck, Off the Beam, #1438, EX, D8 ....$45.00
Donald Duck & Cat Troubles, #845, 5½x5", VG+, A3 ...$25.00
Donald Duck & the Mystery of the Double X, #705-10,
    EX+ $45.00
Dumbo, Only His Ears Grew, 1941, EX $85.00
Flash Gordon & the Fiery Desert of Mongo, #1447, EX, D8.$65.00
Flash Gordon & the Forest Kingdom of Mongo, #1492, EX+,
    M14..$85.00
Flash Gordon & the Monsters of Mongo, #1166, EX, D8/M14,
    from $90 to $100.00
Flash Gordon & the Perils of Mongo, EX, D8 ....$85.00
Flash Gordon & the Red Sword Invaders, #1479, EX, D8..$75.00
Flash Gordon & the Tyrant of Mongo, #1484, EX+, from $85
    to $100.00
Flash Gordon & the Water World of Mongo, #1407, EX+,
    M14 ....$85.00
Flash Gordon & the Witch Queen of Mongo, EX, D8 .....$90.00

Frankenstein Jr, Whitman, 1968, EX $15.00
G-Man & the Radio Bank Robberies, #1434, EX, D8 ......$45.00
Gang Busters Step In, #1433, VG+, D8 ....$20.00
Gene Autry & the Gun-Smoke Reckoning, EX $65.00
Ghost Avenger, #1462, EX, D8.......................................$38.00
Go Into Your Dance (Al Jolson), #1577, EX+, M14 ....$75.00
Green Hornet Strikes!, #1453, 1940, EX+.....................$145.00
Gunsmoke, Whitman, 1958, NM, C1 ....$22.00
Hap Lee's Movie Gags, #1145, VG+ $35.00
Jack Armstrong & the Ivory Treasure, #1453, EX, D8 .....$45.00
Jackie Cooper, EX...$50.00
Jim Craig & the Kidnapped Governor, VG+ $22.00
Jim Hardy, #1180, EX, D8 ....$35.00
Joe Palooka's Greatest Adventure, #1168, NM, M14.......$70.00
Jungle Jim, #1138, 1936, NM, M14.................................$85.00
Junior Nebb on the Diamond Bar Ranch, #1422, EX, D8 ..$30.00
Kay Darcy & the Mystery Hideout, #1411, NM-, D8.......$45.00
Laughing Dragon of Oz, EX, D8 ....$250.00
Little Women, EX, D8..$65.00
Lone Ranger & the Secret Weapon, EX $50.00
Lost Patrol, #753, VG+, D8...$30.00
Major Matt Mason, Whitman, 1968, EX+, F8..................$15.00
Man From UNCLE, Whitman, 1967, EX, F8 ....$15.00
Mandrake & the Flame Pearls, #1418, VG+, D8..............$25.00
Mandrake the Magician, Mighty Solver, #1454, NM.......$65.00
Mickey Mouse & Bobo the Elephant, EX, D8 ....$85.00
Mickey Mouse & Pluto the Racer, #1128, EX, D8...........$75.00
Mickey Mouse & the Dude Ranch Bandit, #1471, EX, D8 .$65.00
Mickey Mouse & the Lazy Daisy Mystery, #1433, EX, D8.$65.00
Mickey Mouse & the Magic Lamp, 1942, EX+ $75.00
Mickey Mouse in Blaggard Castle, #726, VG+ $65.00
Mickey Mouse the Detective, #1139, VG+ $60.00
Moon Mullins & the Plushbottom Twins, VG+...............$35.00
Mutt & Jeff, #1113, NM-, D8..$95.00
Oswald the Lucky Rabbit, #1109, EX...............................$60.00
Our Gang Adventures, #1456, 1948, NM.........................$65.00
Perry Winkle & the Rinky Dink Kids, #1199, VG+, D8...$28.00
Polly & Her Pals on the Farm, #1060, VG+, D8 ....$30.00

Popeye Ghost Ship to Treasure Island, #2008, 1967, VG, $12.00.

Popeye & the Quest for the Rainbird, #1459, EX.............$75.00
Radio Patrol, #1142, EX, D8...$35.00
Radio Patrol, Outwitting the Gang Chiefs, #1496, VG-, D8.$18.00
Red Barry, Undercover Man, #1426, VG+, D8 ....$25.00
Red Ryder & Hoofs of Thunder, #1400, NM....................$70.00
Roy Rogers, King of the Cowboys, 1953, VG $30.00
Secret Agent X-9, #1144, EX $45.00
Shadow & Master of Evil, #1143, VG-, M14....................$95.00
SOS Coast Guard, EX..$30.00
Space Ghost, Whitman, 1968, EX+, F8 ....$25.00
Story of Skippy, 1934, premium, EX $55.00
Tailspin Tommy, Famous Pay-Roll Mystery, #747, EX.....$50.00
Tailspin Tommy & the Hooded Flyer, #1423, EX, D8 .....$48.00
Tailspin Tommy & the Sky Bandits, #1494, EX................$45.00
Tarzan Escapes, #1182, 1936, EX+, M14 ....$75.00
Tarzan of the Apes, #744, VG+ $65.00
Tarzan the Terrible, #1453, VG+......................................$40.00
Terry & the Pirates, #1156, NM-, D8 ....$85.00
Terry & the Pirates & the Giant's Vengeance, #1446, VG,
   M14...$37.00
Tom Beatty, Big Brain Gang, #1179, EX, D8....................$35.00
Tom Beatty Scores Again, #1420, EX, D8 ....$35.00

Tom Mix and His Circus on the Barbary Coast, 1940, EX, $45.00; Big Chief Wahoo and the Great Gusto, 1938, EX, $30.00.

Wash Tubbs in Pandemonia, #751, EX, D8 ....$35.00
Zane Grey's King of the Royal Mounted Gets His Man, #1452,
   EX, D8...$50.00
Zane Grey's King of the Royal Mounted & the Great Jewel,
   #1486, EX+, M14..$50.00

Big Golden Books

Baby Farm Animals, #10545, 23rd edition, VG-EX, K3 .....$6.00
Bambi, #10450, 9th edition, VG-EX, K3 ....$8.00
Bugs Bunny's Escape From Noddington Castle, #10827, C edi-
   tion, VG-EX, K3...$6.00
Captain Kangaroo & His Animal Friends, 1959, EX+, C1.$22.00
Dick Tracy, 1962, M, D11 ....$20.00
Gingerbread Man, #10460, 2nd edition, VG-EX, K3 ....$8.00
Great Big Car & Truck Book, #10473, 17th edition, VG-EX,
   K3...$6.00

My First Golden Dictionary, #10417, 9th edition, VG-EX,
   K3...$7.00
Peter Pan, #10453, O edition, gold on spine, K3 ....$20.00
Poky Little Puppy & Patchwork Blanket, #10387, B edition,
   VG-EX, K3...$10.00
Poky Little Puppy's First Christmas, #10395, 6th edition, VG-
   EX, K3..$10.00
Rin-Tin-Tin & the Hidden Treasure, Simon & Schuster, 1958,
   EX+, C1...$22.00
Rudolph the Red-Nosed Reindeer, #10849, 11th edition, VG-
   EX, K3..$5.00
Savage Sam, #10359, A edition, lt wear to spine, K3 ....$12.00
Sleeping Beauty, #10390, E edition, no gold on spine, K3..$6.00
Tale of Peter Rabbit, #10486, 6th edition, VG-EX, K3 ......$8.00

Little Golden Books

ABC Is for Christmas, #454-31, H edition, VG-EX, K3 .....$2.00
ABC Rhymes, #543, A edition, VG-EX, K3....................$10.00
Airplanes, #180, A edition, 28 pgs, VG-EX, K3 ....$14.00
Aladdin, #107-88, Disney, 1993, VG-EX, K3 ....$2.00
Alvin's Daydreams, #107-73, 1990, VG-EX, K3 ....$5.00
Animal Babies, #39, 1947, 1st edition, VG-, M14...........$10.00
Animal Counting Book, #584, 5th edition, VG-EX, K3 ....$4.00
Aristocats, #D122, 1st edition, VG-EX, K3 ....$12.00
Bambi, #106-60, Disney, 1992, VG-EX, K3 ....$3.00
Barbie Fairy Princess, #111-38, B edition, 24 pgs, VG-EX,
   K3...$4.00
Bear in the Boat, #397, 1st edition, 24 pgs, VG-EX, K3 .....$9.00
Bible Stories of Boys & Girls, #174, B edition, VG-EX, K3..$5.00
Blue Barry Bear Counts From 1 to 20, #203-59, 1992, VG-EX,
   K3...$3.00
Book of C, #617, A edition, VG-EX, K3 ....$4.00
Book of God's Gifts, #112, 4th edition, VG-EX, K3 ....$4.00
Bozo & the Hide 'N Seek Elephant, #598, 2nd edition, VG-EX,
   K3...$8.00
Brave Eagle, #294, B edition, VG-EX, K3.......................$7.00
Buffalo Bill Jr, #254, A edition, VG-EX, K3 ....$14.00
Bugs Bunny, #72, B edition, VG-EX, K3.........................$6.00
Bugs Bunny at the Easter Party, #183, A edition, VG-EX,
   K3...$12.00
Bugs Bunny Gets a Job, #136, 1st edition, VG-EX, K3.....$14.00
Bugs Bunny Pioneer, #111-66, C edition, VG-EX, K3........$3.00
Bullwinkle, #462, 3rd edition, VG-EX, K3 ....$12.00
Captain Kangaroo, #261, B edition, VG-EX, K3 ....$8.00
Cheyenne, #318, A edition, 24 pgs, VG-EX, K3 ....$12.00
Chip Chip, #28, C edition, VG-EX, K3 ....$8.00
Chipmunks Merry Christmas, #375, A edition, VG-EX, K3 .$10.00
Christmas Carols, #26, B edition, VG-EX, K3 ....$12.00
Christmas Carols, #26, 1946, 1st edition, EX, M14 ....$15.00
Colors Are Nice, #496, A edition, VG-EX, K3................$8.00
Counting Rhymes, #12, E edition, VG-EX, K3................$10.00
Dale Evans & the Lost Gold Mine, #213, A edition, VG-EX,
   K3...$18.00
Darkwing Duck, the Silly Canine Caper, #192-67, Disney, 1992,
   VG-EX, K3...$5.00
Davy Crockett, #D45, A edition, VG-EX, K3 ....$12.00
Dennis the Menace, #386, B edition, VG-EX, K3 ....$7.00

Dennis the Menace & a Quiet Afternoon, 1960, VG+, D9 .**$4.00**
Detective Mickey Mouse, #100-58, A edition, VG-EX, K3.**$6.00**
Donald Duck & Santa Claus, #D27, A edition, VG-EX, K3.**$15.00**
Donald Duck & the Witch, #D34, 1st edition, EX, A3 ....**$20.00**
Donald Duck in America on Parade, 3rd edition, VG-EX, K3...**$6.00**
Donald Duck's Some Ducks Have All the Luck, #102-56, Disney, 1990, VG-EX, K3......................................**$2.00**
Donald Duck's Toy Sailboat, #102-59, Disney, 1990, Chip & Dale on cover, VG-EX, K3.....................................**$4.00**
Donald Duck's Toy Train, #D18, 3rd edition, VG, A3 ......**$8.00**

Dumbo, EX, $14.00; *Snow White and the Seven Dwarfs*, EX, $12.00.

Eloise Wilkin's Mother Goose, #589, 10th edition, VG-EX, K3...**$8.00**
Elves & the Shoemaker, #307-56, B edition, VG-EX, K3 ..**$4.00**
Exploring Space, #342, A edition, 24 pgs, VG-EX, K3.....**$10.00**
First Bible Stories, #198, A edition, VG-EX, K3 ....**$22.00**
Friendly Book, #592, 3rd edition, VG-EX, K3 ....**$5.00**
Frosty the Snowman, #209-61, G edition, 24 pgs, VG-EX, K3.**$2.00**
Gingerbread Man, #437, F edition, 24 pgs, VG-EX, K3 .....**$6.00**
Hansel & Gretel, #17, D edition, VG-EX, K3 ....**$14.00**

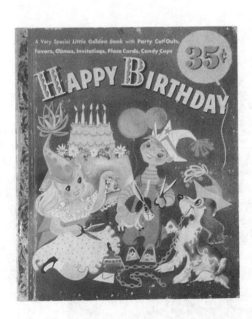

Happy Birthday, A edition, 1952, VG, $20.00.

Heidi, #207-52, G edition, 24 pgs, VG-EX, K3 ....**$2.00**
Hop Little Kangaroo, #558, A edition, 24 pgs, VG-EX, K3.**$4.00**
How To Tell Time, #285, E edition, VG-EX, K3 ....**$10.00**
Howdy Doody & Clarabell, #121, A edition, VG-EX, K3.**$18.00**

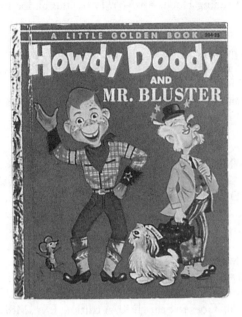

Howdy Doody and Mr. Bluster, #204, A edition, EX, $25.00.

Hymns, #34, C edition, VG-EX, K3 ....**$12.00**
I Think About God, #111, 6th edition, VG-EX, K3............**$4.00**
Jetsons, 1962, EX, J7 ....**$25.00**
Lady Lovely Locks, #107-57, C edition, VG-EX, K3 ....**$3.00**
Lassie, #415, E edition, 24 pgs, VG-EX, K3......................**$5.00**
Lion King, #107-93, Disney, 1994, VG-EX, K3 ....**$1.00**
Little Golden ABC, #101, A edition, 28 pgs, VG-EX, K3.**$12.00**
Little Golden Picture Dictionary, #369, M edition, VG-EX, K3...**$3.00**

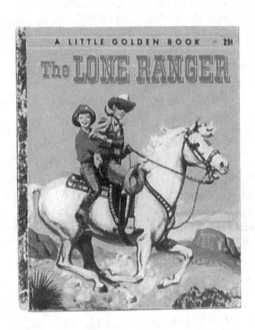

Lone Ranger, #263, A edition, EX, $22.00.

Little Lulu, #476, 2nd edition, VG-EX, K3 .... **$16.00**

Little Mermaid, #105-82, Disney, 1990, seated Ariel on cover, VG-EX, K3 .... **$7.00**

Little Pond in the Woods, #43, A edition, VG-EX, K3 .... **$23.00**

Little Red Riding Hood, #300-65, 1992, illus by Joe Evers, VG-EX, K3 .... **$4.00**

Mary Poppins, #D113, A edition, EX, K3/J7 .... **$12.00**

Merry Shipwreck, 1953, VG+, T2 .... **$5.00**

Mickey Mouse's Picnic, 1950, A edition, EX+, M8 .... **$18.00**

Mother Goose, #240, A edition, VG-EX, K3 .... **$17.00**

My Christmas Treasury, #455, A edition, 24 pgs, VG-EX, K3. **$14.00**

National Velvet, #431, A edition, VG-EX, K3 .... **$10.00**

New Pony, 1961, EX+, T2 .... **$5.00**

Noah's Ark, #109, A edition, EX+, M8 .... **$12.00**

Noises & Mr Flibberty Jib, #29, D edition, 42 pgs, VG-EX, K3 .... **$22.00**

Old MacDonald Had a Farm, #200-65, R edition, VG-EX, K3 .... **$2.00**

Old Mother Hubbard, #591, 2nd edition, 24 pgs, VG-EX, K3 .... **$5.00**

Open Up My Suitcase, #207, A edition, VG-EX, K3 .... **$16.00**

Peter Pan, #104-68, Disney, 1992, VG-EX, K3 .... **$2.00**

Pinocchio, #D8, D edition, VG-EX, K3 .... **$18.00**

Pluto the Pup Goes to Sea, #D30, A edition, EX+, M8 .... **$12.00**

Pound Puppies Pick of the Litter, #110-59, A edition, VG-EX, K3 .... **$4.00**

Raggedy Ann & the Cookie Snatcher, #107-3, 8th edition, VG-EX, K3 .... **$2.00**

Rags, #586, 2nd edition, 24 pgs, VG-EX, K3 .... **$4.00**

Rainy Day Play Book, #133, 1951, 1st ed, EX, M14 ...... **$10.00**

Rin-Tin-Tin, #304, A edition, 24 pgs, VG-EX, K3 .... **$14.00**

Robin Hood, #D126, 1st edition, VG-EX, K3 .... **$12.00**

Rudolph the Red-Nosed Reindeer, #331, A edition, VG-EX, K3 .... **$10.00**

Ruff & Reddy, #477, C edition, 24 pgs, VG-EX, K3 .... **$10.00**

Scamp, #D63, E edition, VG-EX, K3 .... **$8.00**

Seven Dwarfs Find a House, #D35, A edition, VG-EX, K3. **$17.00**

Seven Sneezes, #51, A edition, VG-EX, K3 .... **$18.00**

Shy Little Kitten's Secret Place, #372, A edition, VG-EX, K3 .... **$7.00**

Sky, #270, A edition, 24 pgs, VG-EX, K3 .... **$10.00**

Sleepy Book, #42, D edition, VG-EX, K3 .... **$9.00**

Smokey the Bear, #224, A edition, 28 pgs, VG-EX, K3 ... **$12.00**

Story of Jesus, #27, H edition, VG-EX, K3 .... **$5.00**

Surprise for Mickey Mouse, #D105, 2nd edition, VG-EX, K3.. **$4.00**

Surprise for Sally, #84, A edition, 42 pgs, VG-EX, K3 ..... **$16.00**

Swiss Family Robinson, #D95, A edition, VG-EX, K3 ..... **$12.00**

Tailspin Ghost Ship, #104-62, Disney, 1992, VG-EX, K3.. **$3.00**

Three Little Pigs, #D10, 12th edition, VG, A3 .... **$5.00**

Thumper, #D119, B edition, VG-EX, K3 .... **$15.00**

Tiny Toon Adventure of Buster Hood, #111-72, A edition, VG-EX, K3 .... **$6.00**

Tom Thumb, #353, A edition, 24 pgs, VG-EX, K3 .... **$9.00**

Top Cat, #453, A edition, VG-EX, K3 .... **$18.00**

Toy Soldiers, #D99, C edition, VG-EX, K3 .... **$10.00**

Tweety's Global Patrol, #110-82, A edition, VG-EX, K3 ... **$5.00**

Uncle Wiggily, #148, A edition, VG-EX, K3 .... **$14.00**

Up in the Attic, #53, A edition, VG-EX, K3 .... **$17.00**

Velveteen Rabbit, #307-68, 1993, VG-EX, K3 .... **$3.00**

We Help Daddy, 1962, VG+, T2 .... **$5.00**

We Help Mommy, #208-2, 12th edition, VG-EX, K3 .... **$5.00**

We Like Kindergarten, #205-53, E edition, VG-EX, K3 .... **$3.00**

Welcome to Little Golden Book Land, #370, A edition, VG-EX, K3 .... **$3.00**

Whales, #308-41, F edition, 24 pgs, VG-EX, K3 .... **$2.00**

When Bunny Grows Up, #311-71, 1992, VG-EX, K3 ...... **$2.00**

Winnie the Pooh & the Missing Bullhorn, #101-61, Disney, 1991, VG-EX, K3 .... **$4.00**

Wizard of Oz, #310-2, 6th edition, VG-EX, K3 .... **$3.00**

Woodsy Owl, #107, 1st edition, VG-EX, K3 .... **$8.00**

Woody Woodpecker at the Circus, #111-43, H edition, 24 pgs, VG-EX, K3 .... **$2.00**

Wyatt Earp, #315, A edition, 24 pgs, VG-EX, K3 .... **$15.00**

Year on the Farm, #37, D edition, 42 pgs, VG-EX, K3 ..... **$14.00**

Yogi Bear, #395, G edition, 24 pgs, VG-EX, K3 .... **$7.00**

Zorro, #D68, B edition, VG-EX, K3 .... **$14.00**

101 Dalmatians, #105-81, Disney, 1985, VG-EX, K3 .... **$2.00**

Pop-Up Books

Abenteur der Mickey Maus, Bollmann/Walt Disney, Zurich, 1936, 1st German edition, octavo, 2 pop-ups, 29 pgs, EX+, B12 .... **$750.00**

Buck Rogers in a Dangerous Mission, Blue Ribbon Press/Dille, 1934, blk & wht illus, 60 pgs, EX, A **$210.00**

Buck Rogers Strange Adventures in the Spider-Ship, Blue Ribbon/Caulkins, 1935, 3 full-color pop-ups, VG **$450.00**

Dick Tracy, Capture of Boris Arson, Pleasure Books, c 1935, 3 pop-ups of Tracy in action scenes, EX **$375.00**

Flash Gordon Tournament of Death, Pleasure Books, 1935, 3 pop-ups, EX **$450.00**

Goldilocks & the Three Bears, Blue Ribbon, 1934, 3 pop-ups, 14 pgs, EX+, B12 .... **$275.00**

Happy Families & Their Tales, Ernest Nister/EP Dutton, 1898, oblong quarto, 5 stories, illus & pop-ups, EX+, B12.. **$1,350.00**

Hopalong Cassidy and Lucky at the Double X Ranch, Garden City, 1950, 2 pop-ups, EX, $65.00.

Hopalong Cassidy Lends a Helping Hand, Bonnie Books/Golden, 2 pop-ups, VG, J5 ....$25.00

Jack the Giant Killer, Blue Ribbon, 1933, Pop-Up Classics Series, 1st edition, octavo, 20 pgs, EX+, B12..........$265.00

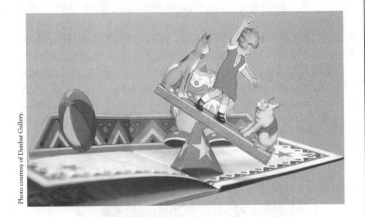

Little Orphan Annie, 1930s, NM, $275.00.

Little Red Riding Hood, Blue Ribbon, 1934, octavo, blk & wht illus w/3 pop-up scenes, 10 pgs, EX+, B12 ....$275.00

Little Showman's Series No 2, Summer, McLoughlin Bros, 1884, 3-tier foldout w/tab movable, lt rubbed o/w EX+, B12 ...$375.00

Lothar Meggendorfer's Internationaler Circus, Schreiber, 1887, 8-panel panorama w/6 pop-ups, rpl replica pcs o/w EX, B12..$3,750.00

Lucky Little People, Rumplestiltskin, Scholastic Book Services, 1973, artist Gorey, tab movable, 1 pop-up, EX+, B12 ..$85.00

Mickey Mouse, Blue Ribbon, 1933, 3 pop-ups, EX, B12..$375.00

Monsters: A Pop-Up Book, Ottenheiner Pub, 1987, 6 pop-ups, 6½x9½", EX+, D9 ....$5.00

New Adventures of Tarzan, Pleasure Books, 1935, 3 pop-ups, EX+ $600.00

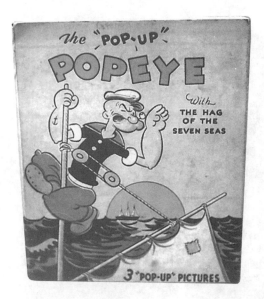

Popeye With the Hag of the Seven Seas, 1935, EX, $450.00.

Popeye & the Pirates, Duenewald, 1945, 4 pop-ups, hardbound, rare, EX, A...$225.00

Terry & the Pirates in Shipwrecked, 1935, by Milton Caniff, 20 pgs, 3 pop-ups, 8x9", NM, rare $450.00

Tim Tyler in the Jungle, Pleasure/KFS, 1935, 3 pop-ups of jungle animals, EX+, A...$160.00

Winnie the Pooh & Eeyore's Tail, Methuen/London, no date, artist EH Shepard, 4 pop-ups, spiral-bound boards, EX, B12 ....$300.00

Wizard of Oz, Hallmark, 1976, 22 pgs, 7½x10½", NM, very scarce, S6 ....$53.00

Tell-a-Tale

Bambi, Whitman #2548, 1972, VG-EX, K3 ....$4.00

Beany (& Cecil) & His Magic Set, 1953, EX+, C1 ....$22.00

Bedknobs & Broomsticks, Whitman #2541, 1971, VG-EX, K3 ....$5.00

Buffy & the New Girl, Whitman #2526, 1969, VG-EX, K3 .$7.00

Chicken Little, Golden #2464-46, A edition, VG-EX, K3 .$3.00

Cinderella, Whitman #2552, 1954, VG-EX, K3 ....$7.00

Daktari's Judy & the Kitten, Whitman #2506, 1969, VG-EX, K3 ....$7.00

Dale Evans & Buttermilk, VG, J5 ....$15.00

Dennis the Menace Takes the Cake, Golden #2451-46, B edition, VG-EX, K3 ....$3.00

Donald Duck & the New Birdhouse, #2520, 1956, VG-EX, K3 ....$8.00

Duck Tales-Silver Dollars for Uncle Scrooge, Golden #2454-49, A edition, VG-EX, K3 ....$3.00

Fat Albert & the Cosby Kids, Whitman #2598, 1975, VG-EX, K3 ....$7.00

Fat Albert & the Cosby Kids, 1975, EX, J7 ....$8.00

Fuzzy Duckling, Whitman #912, 1952, VG-EX, K3 ....$7.00

Gene Autry Goes to the Circus, EX, J5.......................$10.00

Goofy & the Tiger Hunt, Whitman #2612, 1954, EX $8.00

Hooray for Lassie, 1964, EX.....................................$8.00

Howdy Doody & the Monkey Tale, Whitman #2594, 1953, torn spine, K3 ....$15.00

Johnny Appleseed, Whitman #808, 1949, VG-EX, K3 ....$18.00

Land of the Lost, 1975, EX.......................................$8.00

Lassie Finds a Friend, Whitman #2571, 1960, VG-EX, K3.$7.00

Mary Poppins, Whitman #2606, 1964, illus by Jan Neely, VG-EX, K3 ....$7.00

No Sit-Ups for Porky Pig, Golden #2453-46, 1991, VG-EX, K3 ....$1.50

Peter's Pencil, 1953, VG+...$3.00

Roy Rogers at the Lane Ranch, 1950, photo cover, EX+, D8.$28.00

Roy Rogers Sure 'Nough Cowpoke, VG, J5 ....$15.00

Surprise for Howdy Doody, Whitman #2573, 1950, VG-EX, K3 ....$20.00

Tom & Jerry & the Toy Circus, 1953, EX, A3 ....$10.00

Tom & Jerry's Big Move, Golden #2451-38, A edition, VG-EX, K3 ....$3.00

Tweety & Sylvester at the Farm, Whitman #2642, 1978, VG-EX, K3 ....$3.00

Woody Woodpecker's Peck of Troubles, Whitman #2562, 1951, VG-EX, K3 ....$6.00

Yogi Bear & the Super Scooper, 1961, EX+, T2 ....$5.00
Yogi Bear Takes a Vacation, Whitman #2406, 1965, VG-EX, K3 ....$10.00

Whitman

Littlest Outlaw, activity book, 1955, w/stickers, EX, J7 ....$20.00
A Horse for Henry, Cozy Corner #2098, 1952, VG-EX, K3...$6.00
Beverly Hillbillies & Saga of Wildcat Creek, 1963, 5½x7½", EX, D9...$10.00
Big Valley (from TV series), hardcover, NM, D8 ....$10.00
Blondie & Dagwood's Secret Service, by Chic Young, 1942, blk & wht illus, hardcover, complete, EX $9.00
Bonanza, Killer Lion, TV Authorized Edition, EX+, F8 .....$5.00
Bozo, King of the Ring, 1960, EX, F8 ....$6.00
Bozo & the Hide 'N Seek Elephant, 1968, EX, F8 ....$4.00
Brave Little Tailor, Whitman #1058, 1939, EX+, M8......$55.00
Captain Kangaroo's Too-Small House, 1958, EX, F8..........$4.00
Cheyenne & Lost Gold of Lion Park, 1958, TV Authorized Edition, NM, C1 ....$22.00
Combat, The Counterattack; 1964, TV Authorized Edition, NM, C1 ....$22.00
Crusader Rabbit, Bubble Trouble, 1960, Tip-Top Tale, EX .$18.00
Dale Evans & Buttermilk, 1956, TV Authorized Edition, EX+, F8 ....$12.00
Dale Evans & Danger in Crooked Canyon, VG, J5 ....$15.00
Dick Tracy Meets the Night Crawler, by Chester Gould, 1945, blk & wht illus, 247 pgs, hardcover, complete, G, A6.$5.00
Dick Tracy Meets the Night Crawler, 1945, hardcover, EX, D11 ....$15.00
Disney's Pinocchio, 1961, Tip-Top Tale, EX $8.00
Donald Duck & the New Birdhouse, 1956, hardcover, 5x6", VG+, T2 ....$5.00
Dragnet, 1957, TV Authorized Edition, EX, J7 ....$20.00
Flintstones & Dino, 1961, Top-Top Tale #2460, VG-EX, K3.$7.00
Gene Autry & the Big Valley Grab, 1952, NM w/NM dust jacket, C1 ....$36.00
Gene Autry & the Ghost Riders, 1955, EX+, D8/F8 ....$12.00
Gene Autry & the Redwood Priates, 1946, w/dust jacket, EX+ $25.00
Gingerbread Man, 1960, Top-Top Tale #2472, VG-EX, K3 .$8.00
Gnome-Mobile, 1967, TV Authorized Edition, EX, J7.....$12.00
Gumby & Pokey to the Rescue, 1969, EX+, F8 ....$5.00
Gunsmoke, hardcover, NM, D8 ....$18.00
Have Gun Will Travel, hardcover, NM, D8.....................$15.00
Hawaii Five-O's Top Secret, 1969, TV Authorized Edition, NM, C1..$15.00
Huckleberry Hound Giant Story Book, 1961, 20 illus stories, EX, F8 ....$25.00
Huckleberry Hound Helps a Pal, 1960, Tip-Top Tale, EX, J7 .$15.00
I Love Lucy & the Madcap Mystery, 1963, TV Authorized Edition, hardcover, EX+, T2.................................$10.00
Ironside, 1969, TV Authorized Edition, Raymond Burr on cover, EX+, F8 ....$6.00
Janet Lennon, Adventure at Two Rivers, 1961, TV Authorized Edition, EX, J7 ....$12.00
Jetsons & the Birthday Surprise, 1963, EX+, F8 ....$18.00
King Leonardo's Royal Contest, 1962, EX+, F8................$18.00

Lassie, Wild Mountain Trail, 1966, TV Authorized Edition, EX, J7 ....$15.00
Lassie & the Treasure Hunter, 1960, VG, M16 ....$12.00
Leave It to Beaver, 1962, TV Authorized Edition, VG-, J7.$10.00
Lone Ranger & War Horse, Cozy-Corner, VG, J5............$15.00
Loopy De Loop & the Odd Jobber, 1964, EX, F8 ....$8.00
Man From UNCLE #1, The Gentle Saboteur, 1966, TV Authorized Edition, EX, F8 ....$5.00
Man From UNCLE #2, Gunrunner's Gold, 1967, EX+, F8 ..$9.00
Marcus: The Tale of a Monkey, 1950, Cozy Corner #2036, VG-EX, K3..$20.00
Maverick, hardcover, EX+, D8......................................$15.00
Mickey Mouse Alphabet Book, 1936, illus, hardbound, NM, A $175.00

Photo courtesy of June Moon.

Mickey Mouse and Tanglefoot, 1934, EX, J6, $55.00.

Mickey Mouse in Pigmy Land, 1936, softcover, 7x10", EX+, A3 ....$200.00

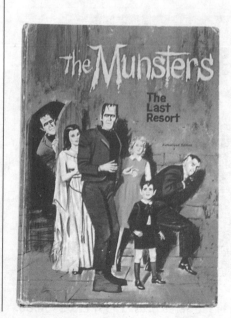

Munsters, The Last Resort, Authorized Edition, VG, $15.00.

Mickey Mouse's Summer Vacation, 1948, Story Hour Series, 6½x5", G+, A3 ....$16.00

Mission Impossible & the Priceless Particle, 1969, NM, F8.$7.00

Monkees & Who's Got the Button, 1968, TV Authorized Edition, EX+, F8/T2, from $12 to....................................$15.00

Munsters & the Great Camera Caper, TV Authorized Edition, F8/T2, from $12 to...$15.00

Mush Mouse & Punkin Puss, Country Cousins, 1964, EX+, F8.$7.00

National Velvet, 1962, Tip-Top Tale, EX, from $8 to $12.00

Patrick the Fuzziest Bunny, 1946, Fuzzy Wuzzy #5071, w/dust jacket, VG-EX, K3...$35.00

Patty Duke & Mystery Mansion, TV Authorized Edition, EX, J7 ....$20.00

Peter Potamus & the Pirates, 1968, Tiny-Tot Tale #2942, VG-EX, K3...$7.00

Peter Potamus Meets the Black Knight, 1965, EX+, F8......$7.00

Pixie & Dixie & the Make-Believe Mouse Child's Book, 1961, Top-Top Tales, EX+, T2 ....$20.00

Quick-Draw McGraw Badmen Beware, 1960, Top-Top Tales, EX+, T2 ....$20.00

Rifleman, 1959, Authorized Edition, EX, $25.00.

Rin-Tin-Tin's Rinty, hardcover, EX+, D8 ....$15.00

Roy Rogers & Dale Evans, Big Toppers, Cozy-Corner, VG, J5 ....$15.00

Roy Rogers & the Gopher Creek Gunman, hardcover, w/dust jacket, EX..$25.00

Ruff 'n Reddy Go to a Party, 1958, EX, F8 ....$5.00

Sea Hunt, 1960, TV Authorized Edition, VG+, J7...........$12.00

Spin & Marty, hardcover, EX+, D8................................$10.00

Super Chief in the Big City, 1965, missing spine, G, F8.....$4.00

Swiss Family Robinson, 1969, TV Authorized Edition, EX, J7 ....$12.00

Sword in the Stone, Top-Top Tales, hardcover, VG+, T2.$6.00

The Rebel, 1961, TV Authorized Edition, EX+, C1.........$24.00

Voyage to the Bottom of the Sea, 1965, TV Authorized Edition, NM+, C1 ....$25.00

Zorro, 1958, TV Authorized Edition, hardcover, 5½x8", EX+, D9...$10.00

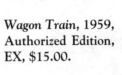
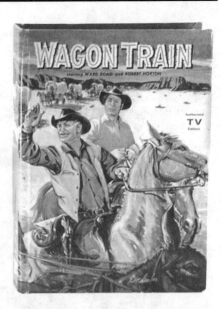

Wagon Train, 1959, Authorized Edition, EX, $15.00.

Wonder Books

Alvin's Lost Shoe, #824, 1963, VG-EX, K3 ....$6.00

Baby Elephant, #541, 1950, VG-EX, K3 ....$6.00

Barbie the Babysitter, 1964, hardcover, EX, T2 ....$7.00

Billy & His Steam Roller, #537, 1951, VG-EX, K3 ....$5.00

Blowaway Hat, #554, 1946, VG-EX, K3.............................$8.00

Can You Guess, #7018, 1953, VG-EX, K3 ....$5.00

Cinderella, #640, 1954, illus Ruth Ives, VG-EX, K3...........$9.00

Copycat Colt, #545, 1951, illus Charlotte Steiner, VG-EX, K3 ....$10.00

Cowardly Lion From Wizard of Oz, 1956, EX, J7.............$20.00

Dick Whittington & His Cat, 1958, illus Dellwyn Cunningham, VG-EX, K3..$8.00

Favorite Nursery Tales, #1504, 1953, sculptured cover, VG-EX, K3 ....$9.00

Fred Flintstone's Surprising Corn, #918, 1976, VG-EX, K3..$6.00

Giraffe Who Went to School, #551, 1951, VG-EX, K3 .....$7.00

Heckle & Jeckle, 1957, EX, J7...$15.00

Helpful Friends, 1955, hardcover, 7x8", EX, T2.................$7.00

Herman & Katnip, 1961, Herman pretends to be from outer space, EX+, F8...$7.00

How Peter Cottontail Got His Name, #668, 1957, by Thornton Burgess, VG-EX, K3..$7.00

Huckleberry Hound, Handy Hound, 1975, Stand-Up Story Book, EX+, F8...$5.00

Little Dog Who Forgot How To Bark, #504, 1946, VG-EX, K3 ....$6.00

Little Peter Cottontail, #641, 1956, by Thorton W Burgess, VG-EX, K3..$7.00

Little Schoolhouse, #310, 1958, VG-EX, K3 ....$5.00

Man From UNCLE, 1965, softcover, 8x11", EX, D9 ....$8.00

Mister Magoo, 1958, EX+, F8...$9.00

Mod Squad Assignment: The Hideout, 1970, NM, F8 ....$9.00

Peter Goes to School, #600, 1953, EX, K3/T2 ....$5.00

Playtime for Nancy, #560, 1951, EX+, M14 ....$12.00

Raggedy Andy's Surprise, #604, 1953, tape rpr on spine, K3 ....$3.00

Roly-Poly Puppy, #549, 1950, VG-EX, K3 ....$7.00

Romper Room Do-Bee Book of Manners, 1960, hardcover, 7x8", VG+, T2.....................$5.00

Sleeping Beauty, #635, 1956, VG-EX, K3 ....$5.00

Sonny the Bunny, #591, 1952, VG-EX, K3.....................$6.00

Soupy Sales & the Talking Turtle, #860, 1965, VG-EX, K3 .$10.00

Story of Babar, #590, VG-EX, K3.................................$14.00

A Surprise For Felix, 1959, NM, J6, $14.00.

Tom Corbett's Trip to the Moon, 1950s, NM, J2 ....$35.00

Tom Terrific's Greatest Adventure, 1959, NM, F8 ....$25.00

Too-Little Fire Engine, 1950, hardcover, 7x8", NM, T2 ....$7.00

Traveling Twins, 1953, hardcover, 7x8", NM, T2.............$8.00

Trick on Deputy Dawg, 1964, writing on 1 pg & loose cover o/w EX, F8...$4.00

Miscellaneous

Adventures of Mickey Mouse, David McKay Publishing/WDP, c 1931, 1st US Mickey Mouse book, 8½x6½", EX, A $125.00

Aladdin & the Wonderful Lamp, McLoughlin Bros #838, 1940, illus by Corinne Malvern, VG+, K3...........................$18.00

Alice Through the Looking Glass, Maxton, 1947, mc illus, w/illus dust jacket, EX+, F8 ....$8.00

Astronut & the Flying Bus, Wonder, 1965, EX, F8 ....$4.00

Ave Maria, 1940, 1st edition, Disney's Fantasia art, hardcover, EX+, from $100 to...$125.00

Babar Learns To Cook, Random House, 1978, VG-EX, K3..$7.00

Baby Chipmunk, Miss Frances' Ding-Dong School Books #208, A edition, VG+, K3...$7.00

Batman With Robin the Boy Wonder & Superman British Annual, 1973, hardcover, stories & comics, NM, C1 .$22.00

Bobby Bear's Busy Day, Saalfield #4212, 1952, VG-EX, K3 .$14.00

Book-Collected Works of Buck Rogers, Chelsea, 1969, illus from many Sunday comic pgs, 370 pgs, NM (EX dust jacket), A $85.00

Bringing Up Father, Bonanza/King Features, 1973, blk & wht comic strips, 179 pgs, 9x11", NM, A6 ....$15.00

Bringing Up Father, Cupples & Leon, 1926, Big Book #1, hardcover, 142 pgs, 10x10", NM (EX+ dust jacket), A3 ..$550.00

Bringing Up Father, 1921, by George McManus, EX, G16 .$65.00

Brownie the Bear Who Liked People, McLoughlin Bros #824, 1939, VG+, K3 ....$18.00

Buffalo Bill, Dean London, 1900, illus, EX, A $220.00

Carousel, Figment Press, no date, by D Weiss, edition of 100, musical, w/fold-out 10-animal carousel, 2x2¾", EX+, B12.$375.00

Celebrated Cases of Dick Tracy, Chelsea House, 1970, illus w/Chester Gould strips, hardcover, 291 pgs, NM, from $15 to $25.00

Cinderella, Treasure Books #879, 1954, illus by Ruth Ives, VG-EX, K3 ....$8.00

Cowboy Book, 1940s, diecut cover of cowboy on bucking bronco, turn diecut to move, 3-D sky back cover, VG+, M16...$50.00

Davy Crockett & Danger From the Mountain, Triple Nickle Books, 1955, 64 pgs, 5x7", EX, M16.........................$16.00

Dick & Jane, Guess Who Reader, 1962, EX, J6 ....$45.00

Dick Tracy, His Greatest Cases #1, Pruneface; Fawcett, 1975, NM, D11 ....$15.00

Dick Tracy, His Greatest Cases #2, Shaky; Fawcett, 1975, NM, D11...$15.00

Dick Tracy, Tempo, 1970, William Johnston, paperback, EX+, D11...$15.00

Dick Tracy Meets Angeltop, Tempo, 1979, NM, D11 .....$10.00

Disneyana, by Cecil Munsey, 1974, 385 pgs, NM (w/dust jacket), A..$140.00

Don Winslow Breaks the Spy Net, Grosset & Dunlap, 1940s, 211 pgs, 5x7", w/VG complete dust jacket, NM, A6 ...$7.50

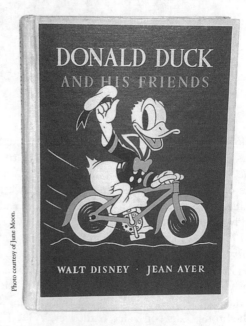

Donald Duck and His Friends, Jean Ayer, 1939, NM, J6, $45.00.

Donald Duck & the Hidden Gold, Simon & Schuster, 1940s, Young Reader's Library, 7½x5", VG, A3.................$15.00

Dumbo of the Circus Health Book, 1948, EX, M8............$20.00

Felix on Television, Treasure Books #904, 1956, VG-EX, K3 .$12.00

Felix the Cat, Treasure Books, 1953, EX, F8......................$8.00

Flintstones Featuring Pebbles, Hanna-Barbera, 1963, 1st printing, paperback w/comic strip illus, complete, VG, A6.$6.50

Grimms' Fairy Tales, Studibilt Books, 1948, VG-EX, K3 .$12.00

Hansel & Gretel, Samuel Lowe, 1944, soft cover, VG-EX, K3..$10.00

Hardy Boys & the Secret of the Caves, Grosset & Dunlap, 1929, 1st series, brn covers, EX, M14 ....$25.00

Horton Hatches the Egg, Random House, 1940, by Dr Seuss, EX+, F8..$16.00

I Go Pogo, Walt Kelly, 1952, NM, J6......................$24.00

Incompleat Pogo, Walt Kelly, 1954, NM, J6......................$15.00

Jack & the Beanstalk, McLoughlin Bros #808, 1938, VG+, K3..$10.00

Jolly Bunny Book, Jolly Book #209, 1953, VG-EX, K3.......$9.00

Larry & the Dinosaur, Storytime Book #B113, 1978, VG-EX, K3 ....$3.00

Leave It to Beaver, Here's Beaver!, 1961, 2nd novel based on TV show, paperback, EX+, F8......................$12.00

Let's Play Nurse & Doctor, Treasure Book #863, 1953, VG-EX, K3..$10.00

Little Orphan Annie in the Circus, Cupples & Leon, 1927, hardcover, 7x9", VG, A3......................$65.00

Lonely Doll Learns a Lesson, 1961, EX, G16 ....$35.00

Mad Scientist's Club Book, Scholastic Books, 1965, 188 pgs, 5x7", EX, T2......................$6.00

Mandrake the Magician, by Lee Falk, Tempo Books/King Features, 1979, paperback w/comic strip illus, complete, EX, A6......................$7.50

Mickey Mouse Wee Little Book Set, EX (in box), D8 ...$250.00

Mighty Mouse Storybook, McGraw-Hill, 1964, cb pgs, 8x10", EX, F8......................$18.00

Nancy Drew Mystery Stories, Bungalow Mystery, by Carolyn Keene, 1960, EX, $6.00.

Our Daddy Is a Lumberman, Kitty Kat Publishing, VG-EX, K3 ....$10.00

Peter Pan, Grosset & Dunlap, 1942, hardcover, 7x9", EX+, T2......................$15.00

Pogo, Simon & Schuster/Walt Kelly, 1951, 182 pgs, 5x8", EX, P6......................$38.00

Pogo Stepmother Goose, Simon & Schuster, 1954, EX+, T2.$22.00

Positively Pogo, Simon & Schuster, 1957, 1st edition, 198 pgs, EX+, M14......................$25.00

Puffy Plays Baseball, Little Owl Book #104, 1954, VG-EX, K3......................$10.00

Raggedy Ann, Johnny Gruelle's Golden Book, PF Volland, 1925, blk & wht illus, 96 pgs, 10x12", EX, J6 ....$85.00

Raggedy Ann & Andy & the Camel w/the Wrinkled Knees, Bobbs Merrill, 1960, EX+, F8......................$12.00

Robin Family, Miss Frances' Ding-Dong School Books #215, A edition, VG+, K3......................$7.00

Robin Hood, Rand McNally, 1955, Richard Green art from British TV series, EX+, F8......................$12.00

Rock-A-Bye Stories, McLoughlin Bros #833, 1940, illus by Geraldine Clyne, VG+, K3 ....$12.00

Runaway Robot Book, Scholastic Books, 1965, by Lester Del Ray, VG+, T2......................$8.00

Rusty the Pup Who Wanted Wings, McLoughlin Bros #821, VG+, K3......................$14.00

Sammy the Seal, I Can Read Book, 1959, hardcover, 6x9", EX+, D9......................$4.00

School Days in Disneyville Health Book, 1939, EX, M8..$25.00

Scooby Doo & the Haunted Doghouse, Rand McNally, 1975, hardcover, VG, D9......................$4.00

Shirley Temple on the Movie Lot, Saalfield, 1936, 17 pgs of sepia photos of Shirley at work, softcover, 6x8", EX, P6......................$60.00

Shirley Temple's Favorite Tales of Long Ago, 1958, hardcover, 8x11", EX+, F8......................$20.00

Skippy, Grosset & Dunlap, 1929, by Percy Grosby, blk & wht illus, 335 pgs, complete, EX, A6 ....$7.50

Snow White & the Seven Dwarfs, Rand McNally, 1937, artist B Livings, 4x6", EX, M14......................$20.00

Spoodles, Jolly Book #201, 1952, VG-EX, K3......................$7.00

Steele of the Royal Mounted, 1911, by James Oliver Curwood, hardcover, missing dust jacket o/w VG+, M16..........$45.00

Steve Canyon & Operation Convoy, Grosset & Dunlap, 1959, 179 pgs, w/dust jacket, NM, A6 ....$12.50

Story of Happy Hooligan, McLoughlin Bros, 1932, 20 pgs, 10x13", EX, A3......................$150.00

Supergirl, GP Putnam, 1984, mc movie photos, EX+, D9 ..$3.00

Tarzan & the Jewel of Kah, Superscope Story Teller Books #ST37, 1977, VG-EX, K3......................$8.00

Tennessee Tuxedo & the Sailboat Race, Saalfield #1022, 1964, soft cover, VG-EX, K3 ....$12.00

Three Little Pigs Who's Afraid of the Big Bad Wolf, David McKay/Disney, 1933, 8½x6¼", EX, P6 ....$125.00

Tom Terriffic w/Mighty Manfred the Wonder Dog, CBS, 1958, hardcover, missing 1 pg at back o/w EX+, D9............$12.00

Tom Thumb, Platt & Munk #3000H, 1934, soft cover, VG+, K3 ....$6.00

Travels of Dr Dolittle, Beginner Books, 1967, hardcover, 7x9", EX+, D9 ....$3.00

TV Pals, Little Owl Book #101, VG-EX, K3......................$5.00

Valentine Writer Book, England, 1810, features poems for gents w/fold-out hand-colored picture, EX, A...................$300.00

Victory March, Random House, 1942, movable parts w/tabs, EX+, M8 ....$145.00

Walt Disney Parade, Shepard & Newman Printing of Australia, 1940, VG, M8...$30.00

Walt Disney's Seven Dwarfs Find a House, See-Saw Books #S-2, A edition, VG-EX, K3 ....$15.00

Walt Disney's Story of the Reluctant Dragon, Garden City, 1941, EX illus, hardcover, 9¼x10¾", EX, scarce, P6.$95.00

Walt Disney's Surprise Package, Giant Golden, 1944, 5th printing, w/dust jacket, NM, M8......................................$85.00

Walt Disney's Version of Pinocchio, Grosset & Dunlap, 1939, mc illus, hardcover, 9x7", EX, P6 ....$55.00

Who Was That Masked Man, Lone Ranger, NM, D8......$15.00

Wonderful Treasure Hunt, Treasure Book #853, 1952, VG-EX, K3 ....$5.00

Yogi Bear & the Colorado River, Modern Promotions #39018, 1972, VG+, K3...$3.00

Your Friend the Policeman, Miss Frances' Ding-Dong School Books #200, VG+, K3 ....$8.00

003.5: The Adventures of James Bond Jr, Random House, 1968, Authorized Teen Edition, EX+, F8 ....$20.00

Breyer

Breyer collecting seems to be growing in popularity, and though the horses dominate the market, the company also made dogs, cats, farm animals, wildlife figures, dolls, and tack and accessories such as barns for their models. They've been in continuous production since the fifties, all strikingly beautiful and lifelike in both modeling and color. Earlier models were glossy, but since 1968 a matt finish has been used, though glossy and semi-glossy colors are now being re-introduced, especially in special runs. (A special run of Family Arabians was done in the glossy finish in 1988.) Condition and rarity are the most important worth-assessing factors.

Advisor: Carol Karbowiak Gilbert (G6), author of *Model Horses: A Guide to Collecting*, to be released September 1996, as well as several articles on model collecting, values and care for *The Model Horse Gazette*. Note: values are based on examples in excellent to near-mint condition.

Classic Scale Models

Andalusian Foal, matt dk chestnut, 1979-93, G6 ....$15.00

Andalusian Mare, matt alabaster, 1984, Sears, G6 ....$25.00

Andalusian Stallion, matt dapple gray, 1984, Sears, G6...$25.00

Arabian Foal, matt lt bay, complete w/cookie tin, 1988 (signing parties), G6 ....$65.00

Arabian Mare, matt chestnut, 1973-91, G6 ....$15.00

Arabian Stallion, matt sorrel, 1973-91, G6........................$15.00

Black Beauty, matt blk, 1980-93, G6 ....$15.00

Black Stallion, matt blk, 1983-93, G6................................$15.00

Bucking Bronco, matt gray, 1961-67, G6..........................$200.00

Duchess, matt bay, 1980-93, G6...$15.00

Ginger, matt chestnut, 1980-93, G6 ....$15.00

Hobo (on base), matt buckskin, w/book & carrying case, G6.$55.00

Jet Run, matt bay, 1980-93, G6...$15.00

Johar, matt alabaster, 1983-93, G6....................................$15.00

Keen, matt chestnut, 1980-93, G6......................................$15.00

Kelso, matt or semi-gloss bay, 1975-90, G6, ea $30.00

Lipizzan Stallion, matt alabaster, 1975-80, G6 ....$50.00

Man O' War, matt red chestnut, 1975-90, G6...................$30.00

Merrylegs, matt dapple gray, 1980-93, G6.........................$10.00

Mesteno, Charging; matt dk buckskin, 1995-present, G6..$15.00

Mesteno, Fighting; matt dk buckskin, 1994-present, G6..$15.00

Mesteno, matt dk buckskin, 1992-present, G6 ....$15.00

Mesteno the Foal, matt lt dun, 1993-present, G6 ....$7.00

Mesteno's Mother, matt buckskin, 1993-present, G6.......$15.00

Mighty Tango, matt dapple gray, 1980-91, G6 ....$20.00

Mustang Foal, matt chestnut, 1976-90, G6......................$10.00

Mustang Mare, matt chestnut pinto, 1976-90, G6...........$20.00

Mustang Stallion, matt chestnut, 1976-90, G6.................$20.00

Polo Pony (on base), matt bay, 1976-82, G6.....................$75.00

Quarter Horse Foal, matt lt bay, 1974-93, G6...................$15.00

Quarter Horse Mare, matt bay, 1974-93, G6 ....$25.00

Quarter Horse Stallion, matt palomino, 1974-93, G6 ......$25.00

Rearing Stallion, matt palomino, 1965-85, G6..................$30.00

Rojo, matt red dun, 1995-present, G6................................$15.00

Ruffian, matt dk bay, 1977-90, G6 ....$30.00

Sagr, matt sorrel, 1983-93, G6...$20.00

Silky Sullivan, matt brn, 1975-90, G6 ....$30.00

Sombra, matt grulla, 1994-present, G6 ....$15.00

Swaps, matt chestnut, 1975-90, G6....................................$30.00

Terrang, matt dk brn, 1975-90, G6 ....$30.00

Traditional Scale

Action Stock Horse Foal, matt chestnut, 1984-86, G6 ....$22.00

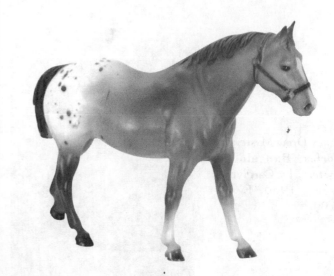

Appaloosa Gelding, #97, 1971-80, $35.00.

Appaloosa Performance Horse, matt chestnut roan appaloosa, G6 ....$44.00

Belgian, matt chestnut, 1965-80, G6 ....$45.00

Black Stallion, semi-gloss blk, G6.....................................$35.00

Buckshot, matt grulla, 1971-73, G6 ....$45.00
Cantering Welsh Pony, matt chestnut w/no ribbon, 1979-81, G6..$30.00
Clydesdale Mare, matt chestnut, 1969-89, G6................$25.00
Clydesdale Stallion, glossy bay w/gold ribbons, muscular, 1958-63, G6..$140.00
Family Arabian Mare, matt alabaster, 1967-73, G6..........$30.00

John Henry, matt dk bay, 1988-90, G6............................$35.00
Justin Morgan, matt red bay, 1977-89, G6......................$40.00
Kipper, matt chocolate brn, 1986, G6............................$80.00
Lady Roxana, matt alabaster, 1986-88, G6......................$40.00
Midnight Sun, matt blk, red & wht ribbon, 1972-87, G6...$40.00

Moose, #79, 1966-95, $25.00.

Five-Gaiter, #52, 1963-86, sorrel, $35.00.

Morgan, matt blk w/diamond star, 1965-87, G6...............$40.00
Mustang, glossy alabaster w/red eyes, semi-rearing, 1961-66, G6 ....$150.00

Foal, #909, woodgrain, $75.00.

Old Timer, #200, 1966-76, alabaster, missing hat, $40.00.

Friesian, matt blk, 1992-95, G6..$25.00
Fury Prancer, glossy blk pinto, 1954-63, G6....................$90.00
Gem Twist, matt alabaster, 1993-95, G6 ....$25.00
Hackney Pony, matt bay, 1995-present, G6......................$20.00
Halla, matt bay, 1977-85, G6 ....$50.00
Ideal American Quarter Horse, matt chestnut, Special Run, 1995, G6 ....$25.00

Pacer, matt or semi-gloss, dk bay, 1967-87, G6................$40.00
Performing Misty, ceramic, glossy palomino w/stool, 1993, G6 ....$40.00
Pluto, matt lt gray, 1991-95, G6......................................$20.00
Proud Arabian Stallion, matt or semi-gloss mahogany bay, 1971-80, G6 ....$50.00
Quarter Horse Gelding, glossy bay, 1959-66, G6............$125.00
Quarter Horse Yearling, matt liver chestnut, 1970-80, G6.$40.00

Racehorse, matt woodgrain, 1958-66, G6.......................$200.00
Roy the Belgian, matt sorrel, 1989-90, G6......................$40.00
Running Foal, glossy Copenhagen (rare), 1963-65, G6 ..$1,000.00
Running Mare, glossy Florentine (rare), 1963-64, G6...$1,100.00

**Running Mare, 1963-73, glossy dapple gray, $75.00;
Running Foal, 1963-73, glossy dapple gray, $45.00.**

Running Stallion, glossy charcoal, 1968-71, G6............$225.00
San Domingo, matt chestnut pinto, 1978-87, G6.............$40.00
Scratching Foal, matt blk blanket appaloosa, 197-86, G6 ..$30.00
Secretariat, matt chestnut, 1987-95, G6 ....$20.00
Sham, matt red bay, 1984-88, G6.....................................$45.00
Sherman Morgan, matt chestnut, 1987-90, G6 ....$50.00
Shire, matt honey sorrel, 1972-76 & 1978-80, G6 ....$60.00

St Bernard, #328, 1972-80, $35.00.

Stock Horse Mare, matt blk appaloosa, 1983-88, G6 ....$40.00
Stock Horse Stallion, matt bay blanket appaloosa, 1981-86,
 G6 ....$35.00

Stud Spider, matt blk blanket appaloosa, G6...................$40.00
Western Pony, glossy blk, 1956-63, G6............................$70.00

Bubble Bath Containers

Since back in the 1960s when the Colgate-Palmolive Company produced the first Soaky, hundreds of different characters and variations have been marketed, bought on demand of the kids who saw these characters day to day on TV by parents willing to try anything that might make bathtime more appealing. Purex made their Bubble Club characters, and Avon and others followed suit. Most Soaky bottles came with detachable heads made of brittle plastic which cracked easily. Purex bottles were made of a softer plastic but tended to loose their paint.

Rising interest in US bubble bath containers has created a collector market for those made in foreign countries, i.e, UK, Canada, Italy, Germany and Japan. Licensing in other countries creates completely different designs and many characters that are never issued here. Foreign containers are generally larger and are modeled in great detail, reminiscent of the bottles that were made in the US in the sixties. Prices may seem high, considering that some of these are of fairly recent manufacture, but this is due to their limited availablity and the costs associated with obtaining them in the United States. We believe these prices are realistic, though many have been reported much higher. Rule of thumb: pay what you feel comfortable with — after all, it's meant to be fun. And remember, value is affected to a great extent by condition. Unless noted otherwise, our values are for examples in near-mint condition. Bottles in very good condition are worth only about 60% to 65% of these prices. For slip-over styles, add 100% if the bottle is present.

Advisors: Matt and Lisa Adams (A7); Jon Thurmond (T1).

Brutus and Popeye, Colgate, 1960s, NM, A7, $40.00 each.

Photo courtesy of Matt and Lisa Adams.

Alvin (Chipmunks), Colgate-Palmolive, 1960s, wht w/red cap head, NM, A7/J2 ....$25.00

Baloo Bear (Jungle Book), Colgate-Palmolive, 1960s, slipover only, NM, A7..................................$25.00

Bambi, EX $30.00

Bamm-Bamm, Purex, 1960s, blk & wht, NM, A7/T2.......$30.00

Barney Rubble, Purex, 1960s, brn & yel, NM, A7............$30.00

Batman, Avon, MIB $25.00

Batman, Soaky, VG $50.00

Beatles, Paul McCartney, Colgate-Palmolive, red, EX, B3.$110.00

Beatles, Ringo Starr, bl, EX, B3/R2, from $100 to $125.00

Big Bad Wolf, Tubby Time, 1960s, gray & red w/cap head, NM, A7 ....$35.00

Bozo the Clown, VG................................$25.00

Broom Hilda, VG..$35.00

Bugs Bunny, Colgate-Palmolive, slipover only, NM, A7..$25.00

Bugs Bunny, Colgate-Palmolive, 1960s, gray, wht & orange, cap ears, NM, A7 ....$30.00

Bugs Bunny, Colgate-Palmolive, 1960s, lt bl & wht, NM, A7 ....$35.00

Bugs Bunny, leaning against egg, VG................$15.00

Cecil Sea Serpent, Purex, 1960s, gr, NMIB (w/1 of 9 disguises), A7 ....$75.00

Cement Truck, Colgate-Palmolive, 1960s, bl & gray w/movable wheels, NM, A7..................................$40.00

Cinderella, Colgate-Palmolive, 1960s, movable arms, NM, A7..$35.00

Creature From the Black Lagoon, NM..................$95.00

Deputy Dawg, Colgate-Palmolive, gray, yel & bl, cap hat, sm, NM, A7..$30.00

Deputy Dawg, Colgate-Palmolive, 1960s, brn & yel outfit, lg, NM, A7/C17..................................$30.00

Dick Tracy, Soaky, 1965, 10", EX+, D11 ....$45.00

Donald Duck, Colgate-Palmolive, 1960s, wht, bl & yel w/cap head, NM, A7..................................$25.00

Donald Duck, Colgate-Palmolive, 1960s, wht & bl, NM, A7 .$30.00

Dopey, Colgate-Palmolive, 1960s, bank, purple & yel, NM, A7 ....$30.00

Dopey, Colgate-Palmolive, 1960s, purple, yel & red, NM, A7 ....$30.00

Dum Dum, VG..$25.00

El Cabong, Knickerbocker, 1960s, blk, yel & wht, rare, NM, A7 ....$75.00

Elmer Fudd, VG..$25.00

Explosives Truck, Colgate-Palmolive, 1960, red & gray w/movable wheels, NM, A7 ....$40.00

Felix the Cat, red, VG..................................$35.00

Fire Truck, Colgate-Palmolive, 1960s, red w/hose & movable wheels, NM, A7..................................$40.00

Fire Truck, Colgate-Palmolive, 1960s, red w/ladder & movable wheels, NM, A7..................................$40.00

Fred Flintstone, Colgate-Palmolive, EX, C17 ....$20.00

Fred Flintstone, Purex, 1960s, blk & red, NM, A7 ....$30.00

Goofy, Colgate-Palmolive, 1960s, red, wht & blk w/cap head, NM, A7..$25.00

Gravel Truck, Colgate-Palmolive, 1960s, orange & gray w/movable wheels, NM, A7 ....$40.00

Gumby, Perma Toy, No More Tears, 1987, 9½", M (sealed) .$20.00

Huckleberry Hound, Knickerbocker, 1960s, powder/bank, red & blk, 15", NM, A7..................................$50.00

Jiminy Cricket, Colgate-Palmolive, 1960s, gr, blk & red, NM, A7 ....$30.00

King Louie (Jungle Book), Colgate-Palmolive, 1960s, slipover only, NM, A7..................................$25.00

Lippy the Lion, Purex, 1960s, EX $55.00

Magilla Gorilla, Purex, 1960s, movable or non-movable arm, NM, A7, ea $60.00

Mickey Mouse, band leader, Colgate-Palmolive, 1960s, red, NM, A7 ....$30.00

Mickey Mouse, w/red shirt, VG..................$20.00

Frankenstein, Soaky, EX, $90.00.

Mighty Mouse, Colgate-Palmolive, 1960s, yellow, red and black with cap head, NM, $30.00.

Mousketeer Girl, Colgate-Palmolive, 1960s, red outfit w/orange or yel hair, NM, A7, ea..................................$25.00

Mr Jinx w/Pixie & Dixie, Colgate-Palmolive, EX, B10/T2, from $30 to $35.00

Mr Jinx w/Pixie & Dixie, Purex, 1960s, orange w/gray mice, NM, A7...$30.00

Mummy, Colgate-Palmolive, 1960s, wht & gr, NM, A7..$100.00

Mush Mouse, EX $50.00

Muskie, Soaky, 1960s, NM, C1/J2, from $25 to...............$35.00

Oil Truck, Colgate-Palmolive, 1960s, gr & gray w/movable wheels, NM, A7 ....$40.00

Panda Bear, Tubby Time, 1960s, wht & blk w/cap head, NM, A7 ....$30.00

Pebbles Flintstone, Purex, 1960s, brn w/gr or purple shirt, cap head, NM, A7, ea $35.00

Peter Potomus, Purex, NM, $25.00.

Pinocchio, Colgate-Palmolive, 1960s, red w/removable head, EX, C17...$20.00

Punkin' Puss, NM, $40.00.

Pinocchio, Soaky, 1960s, NM $20.00

Pluto, Colgate-Palmolive, 1960s, orange w/cap head, NM, A7 ....$25.00

Pokey, 1987, M (sealed) $20.00

Popeye, Soaky, 1960s, EX $30.00

Porky Pig, Colgate-Palmolive, w/removable head, EX, C17/T2 ....$20.00

Quick Draw McGraw, Purex, 1960s, orange & bl or orange only, NM, A7, ea $40.00

Ricochet Rabbit, Purex, 1960s, movable or non-movable arm, NM, A7, ea $50.00

Rocky Squirrel, Soaky, 1960s, w/removable head, EX, C17 .$35.00

Sailor, Avon, VG...$10.00

Santa Claus, EX $15.00

Secret Squirrel, Purex, 1960s, yel & purple, NM, A7.......$60.00

Simon (Chipmunks), Colgate-Palmolive, 1960s, bl shirt, NM, A7 ....$30.00

Smokey the Bear, Colgate-Palmolive, bl pants, yel cap hat, NM, A7 ....$30.00

Snaggle Puss, Purex, 1960s, pk w/gr hat, NM, A7 ....$50.00

Snoopy, Avon, retains orig label, 5½", EX, D9................$15.00

Snow White, Colgate-Palmolive, 1960s, bank, bl & yel, NM, A7 ....$30.00

Speedy Gonzales, Colgate-Palmolive, 1960s, bl & red, NM, A7 ....$30.00

Spouty the Whale, retains orig tag, M..............................$25.00

Squiddly Diddly, Purex, 1960s, purple & pk, NM, A7......$60.00

Superman, Avon, 1978, 8", NM, minimum value $35.00

Tennessee Tuxedo, 1960s, NM, T2....................................$30.00

Three Little Pigs, Tubby Time, 1960s, bl, red or yel overalls, NM, A7, ea $35.00

Thumper (Bambi), Colgate-Palmolive, 1960s, lt bl & wht, NM, A7 ....$30.00

Tidy Toy Race Car, red or bl w/movable wheels, NM, A7, ea.$50.00

Top Cat, 1960s, NM, $45.00.

Top Cat, 1960s, standing on garbage can, NM $45.00

Touche Turtle, Purex, 1960s, turquoise or red w/purple feather, lying down, NM, A7, ea $50.00

Tweety Bird, Colgate-Palmolive, 1960s, slipover only, NM, A7 ....$25.00

Wally Gator, Purex, 1960s, powder, lying on stomach, gr, NM, A7 ....$50.00

Wendy the Witch, Colgate-Palmolive, 1960s, red and yellow, NM, $30.00.

Winsome Witch, Purex, 1960s, bl & blk, NM, A7...........$30.00

Wolfman, EX, from $75.00 to $95.00.

Woodsy Owl, Lander Co, early 1970s, brn, gr & yel, NM, A7 ....$30.00

Woody Woodpecker, Colgate-Palmolive, 1960s, bl, yel & wht w/red flume cap, NM, A7 ....$25.00

Yakky Doodle Duck, 1976, retains orig tag, M.................$25.00

Yogi Bear, Knickerbocker, 1960s, powder/bank, brn, 14", NM, A7 ....$30.00

Yogi Bear, Purex, 1960s, powder/bank, blk or gr hat, NM, A7, ea $30.00

Foreign

Action Man (Battle Force), Rosedew Ltd/UK, 1994, camouflage outfit, kneeling w/machine gun, 8½", NM, A7 ....$35.00

Action Man (Night Creeper), Rosedew Ltd/UK, 1994, Topper, w/suction cups & silver gun, 9", NM, A7....................$15.00

Alf, PE/Germany, unknown date, brn & tan, opens at neck, 7", NM, A7..$40.00

Alice in Wonderland, Aidee International Ltd/UK, 1993, standing in grass w/rabbit, 10", NM, A7 ....$35.00

Aliens, Grosvenor/UK, 1993, Topper, Plasma Foam Bath, 9", NM, A7..$25.00

Ariel (Little Mermaid), Damascar/Italy, 1995, sitting on purple rock, 8", NM, A7 ....$35.00

Asterix, Euromark/Switzerland, 1992, wing-headed man w/yel moustache & gr belt, 9½", NM, A7, from $50 to......$75.00

Barbie, Grosvenor/UK, 1995, pk & wht wedding dress w/heart tag, 9", NM, A7 ....$30.00

Barney Rubble (Flintstones), Damascar/Italy, 1995, wearing Water Buffalo hat w/bowling ball, 9", NM, A7 ....$35.00

Batman, Grosvenor/UK, 1992, c DC Comics, gray suit & blk cape, 11", NM, A7 ....$35.00

Batman Forever, Prelude/UK, 1995, blk w/beige face, movable arms, comes apart at waist, 11", NM, A7 ....$35.00

Beano (Dennis the Menace), Rosedew Ltd/UK, 1990, red & blk-striped outfit, blk curly hair, 10", NM, A7.................$35.00

Bear (Forever Friends), Grosvenor/UK, 1995, in tub of bubbles, 5", NM, A7 ....$30.00

Beast (Beauty & the Beast), Centura/Canada, 1993?, Topper, hand under chin, 9", NM, A7 ....$15.00

Beast (Beauty & the Beast), Prelude/UK, 1994, movable arms, comes apart at waist, lg, NM, A7 ....$35.00

Belle (Beauty & the Beast), Centura/Canada, 1994, yel gown & gloves, 10", NM, A7 ....$25.00

Benjamin Bunny (Beatrix Potter), Grosvernor/UK & Canada, 1991, Topper, gr & red hat, holding bag & onion, 7", NM, A7 ....$30.00

Big Bird (Sesame Street), Grosvenor/UK, 1995, Topper, sitting in bubbles w/teddy bear, 8", NM, A7 ....$15.00

Bubbly Bear, Belvedere/Canada, 1995, bank, bl, 8½", NM, A7...$15.00

Bugs Bunny, Centura/Canada, 1994, purple robe, holds carrot, 11", NM, A7 ....$30.00

Captain Scarlet (Thunderbirds), Euromark/UK, 1993, red & blk outfit, kneeling w/blk gun, 9½", NM, A7 ....$35.00

Casper the Friendly Ghost, Damascar/Italy, 1995, sitting on pumpkin, glow-in-the-dark, 7½", NM, A7 ....$35.00

Cinderella, Damascar/Italy, 1994, gray & wht gown, 9½", NM, A7 ....$35.00

Clown, Impulse Notions/Canada & US, 1990s, bl or pk, 9", NM, A7, ea..$15.00

Cookie Monster (Sesame Street), Jim Henson PI/UK, 1995, w/bl & wht cloth towel, 8½", NM, A7 ....$30.00

Daffy Duck, Prelude/UK, 1994, wearing shark suit, 10½", NM, A7 ....$35.00

Desperate Dan, DC Thompson/UK, 1991, lumberjack w/dog, 10½", NM, A7...$40.00

Dewey (Donald Duck's nephew), Rosedew Ltd/UK, 1990s, bl outfit & hat, 8½", NM, A7 ....$35.00

Dino (Flintstones), Damascar/Italy, 1995, standing on food dish w/giant bone, 9½", NM, A7.......................$35.00

Dino (Flintstones), Rosedew Ltd/UK, 1993, w/collar, 9", NM, A7 ....$35.00

Dirt Movers, Prelude/UK, yel construction vehicle w/movable wheels, 7", NM, A7 ....$30.00

Donald Duck, Centura/Canada, 1994, standing on red base, 9½", NM, A7 ....$30.00

Donald Duck (Mickey & Pals), Centura/Canada, 1995, driving yel boat, 9", NM, A7 ....$25.00

Dr X (Action Man), Rosedew Ltd/UK, 1994, Topper, bald man w/X on back of head, 8", NM, A7 ....$15.00

Fairy, Delagar/UK & Canada, 1994, bl dress w/3 yel stars, holds wand, wings at back, 10", NM, A7 ....$30.00

Florence (Magic Roundabout), Grosvenor/UK, 1993, girl w/flower, orange & bl outfit, bow in hair, 8½", NM, A7 ....$35.00

Fred Flintstone (Flintstones), Damascar/Italy, 1994, stands w/golf club, 8½", NM, A7 ....$35.00

Genie (Aladdin), Prelude/UK, 1994, sitting w/arms crossed, 10", NM, A7...$35.00

Hello Kitty, Bandai/Japan, 1992, wht cat w/red ribbon, 5", NM, A7 ....$30.00

Jasmin (Aladdin), Prelude/UK, 1994, gr outfit, holds bird on hand, 9", NM, A7 ....$35.00

Jerry (Tom & Jerry), Euromark/UK, 1989, standing on Swiss cheese, holding his full stomach, 7½", NM, A7 ....$35.00

John Smith (Pocahontas), Centura/Canada, 1995, sitting on gray rock, opens at waist, 8½", NM, A7 ....$25.00

Little Mermaid, Prelude/UK, 1994, sitting in clear bubbles, opens at center, 8", NM, A7.............................$30.00

Magic Princess, Boots Co/UK, 1990s, blond woman w/wings, basket & purple-flowered dress, 9½", NM, A7 ....$30.00

Mario (Mario Brothers), Grosvenor/UK, 1992, red & bl outfit w/red hat, 8", NM, A7 ....$35.00

Martin the Pig (Creature Comforts), Rosedew Ltd/UK, 1995, pk pig w/yel shower cap & beige towel, 6½", NM, A7 ...$35.00

Mickey Mouse, Disney/Canada, 1994, blk tuxedo, red pants & yel tie, 8½", NM, A7 ....$30.00

Mickey Mouse, Prelude/UK, 1994, Topper, pie-eyed w/legs crossed, 7½", NM, A7 ....$15.00

Mickey Mouse (Fantasia), Centura/Canada, 1994, red robe, bl star & moon hat, 9½", NM, A7 ....$30.00

Minnie Mouse, Disney/Canada, 1994, pie-eyed, traditional 1930s outfit, 8½", NM, A7..............................$35.00

Mowgli & Kaa (Jungle Book), Prelude/UK, 1994, snake wrapped around boy, 7", NM, A7 ....$35.00

Mr Blobby, Rosedew Ltd/UK, 1994, Topper, pk blob w/yel polka-dot dogs & tie, 7½", NM, A7 ....$15.00

Mumfie (Magic Adventures of Mumfie), Euromark/UK, 1995, gray & pk elephant waving bl scarf w/trunk, 9½", NM, A7 ....$35.00

Musical Bears, Delagar/Canada & US, 1989, band leader, accordion or drummer, NM, 7", A7, ea $15.00

Nala (Lion King), Centura/Canada, 1994, sitting on pk base, 8", NM, A7...$30.00

Noddy Elf, Grosvenor/UK, 1994, Topper, gray beard, waving pose w/cat, 8½", NM, A7 ....$15.00

Olive Oyl (Popeye), Damascar/Italy, 1995, sitting w/clasped hands, 8½", NM, A7 ....$35.00

Oscar the Grouch (Sesame Street), Grosvenor/UK, 1995, Topper, in trash can w/I Hate Baths sign, 8½", NM, A7 .$15.00

Pablo the Parrot (Creature Comforts), Rosedew Ltd/UK, 1993, Topper, gr, yel, red, purple & bl, 8½", NM, A7.........$15.00

Paddington Bear, Cottsmore Ltd/UK, 1995, Topper, bl or red raincoat w/suitcase & sandwich, 9", NM, A7, ea.......$35.00

Papa Smurf, IMPS Brussels/Germany, 1991, bl w/red pants & hat, wht beard, 9½", NM, A7 ....$40.00

Percy (Thomas the Tank), Grosvenor/UK, 1994, Topper, sitting on blk tracks w/gray bricks, 6½", NM, A7 ....$15.00

Peter Rabbit (Beatrix Potter), Grosvenor/US & Canada, 1991, bl coat, 8½", NM, A7 ....$30.00

Piglet (Winnie Pooh), Prelude/UK, 1990s, Topper, waving w/scarf flapping in wind, 10", NM, A7......................$20.00

Pingu, Grosvenor/UK, 1994, penguin standing on igloo, 6½", NM, A7 ....$30.00

Pippa (Budgie), Euromark/UK, 1994, Topper, girl in airplane, 8", NM, A7 ....$15.00

Pocahontas, Centura/Canada, 1995, sitting on rock in grass, 8½", NM, A7..$25.00

Pocahontas, Grosvenor/UK, 1995, Topper, in canoe w/racoon, 10", NM, A7 ....$15.00

Pogo (101 Dalmatians), Grosvenor/UK, 1994, father dog w/pup on head & between legs, 9½", NM, A7 ....$35.00

Popeye, Rosedew Ltd/Uk, 1987, holds spinach can, blk base, 10", NM, A7...$40.00

Postman Pat, Rosedew Ltd/UK, 1991, mailman w/lg brn bag, 9", NM, A7...$35.00

Pumba (Lion King), Centura/Canada, 1994, Topper, warthog eating worm, 9", NM, A7 ....$15.00

Pumba (Lion King), Prelude/UK, 1994, warthog, 7", NM, A7 ....$35.00

RoboCop, Euromark/UK, 1995, movable arms, standing on gray bricks, 12", NM, A7.................................$35.00

Rupert Bear, unknown maker/UK, 1995, Topper, in yel airplane, 8", NM, A7 ....$20.00

Scrappy Doo (Scooby Doo), Damascar/Italy, 1995, dog coming out of well w/water creature, 7", NM, A7 ....$35.00

Simba (Lion King), Prelude/UK, 1994, cub w/raised paw, sitting on gray rock, 8", NM, A7 ....$35.00

Sindy (UK version of Barbie), Rosedew Ltd/UK, 1995, blond girl w/pk & gold dress, 10½", NM, A7 ....$35.00

Skates, unknown maker/Canada, 1990s, turtle on skates w/bl hat, mk #1 on back, 8", NM, A7................$20.00

Sleeping Beauty, Damascar/Italy, 1994, standing w/roses, 10½", NM, A7..$35.00

Smurf, IMPS Brussels/German, 1991, bl w/wht pants & hat, 9½", NM, A7...$40.00

Sneezy & Sleepy, Grosvenor/UK, 1994, Topper, Fairy Tale Fragrance Foam Bath, 7½", NM, A7..............$15.00

Snoopy, Grosvenor/UK, 1990s, on stomach w/cap nose, 8½", NM (clear box w/card), A7 ....$35.00

Snow White, Rosedew Ltd/UK, 1994, standing w/crossed arms & long dress, 10", NM, A7 ....$35.00

Sonic Hedgehog, Matey/UK, 1990s, standing on red & bl game button, 9", NM, A7 ....$35.00

Space Precinct Tan Monster, Euromark/UK, 1995, Topper, 8", NM, A7 ....$15.00

Spider-Man, Euromark/UK, 1995, walking over trash can & tire, 9", NM, A7 ....$35.00

Spot, Grosvenor/UK, 1993, dog w/ball on nose, 8", NM, A7 ....$35.00

SPV (Thunderbirds), Euromark/UK, 1993, gray, bl, wht & blk vehicle from cartoon, 8", NM, A7 ....$35.00

Super Soaker Gun, Larami/Cosrich/Canada, 1992, 7", NM, A7 ....$30.00

Sylvester, Prelude/UK, 1995, cloth hand puppet slips over bottle, 9", NM, A7 ....$35.00

Sylvester & Tweety, Prelude/UK, 1995, cat w/mean look holds bird, 10", NM, A7 ....$35.00

Tasmanian Devil, Centura/Canada, 1994, gray whirlwind on rock, opens at waist, 7", NM, A7 ....$30.00

Thomas the Tank, Bandai/Japan, 1991, red & bl engine, 3½", NM, A7 ....$30.00

Thunderbird 2, ITC Ent/UK, 1992, gr, 8", NM (orig box), A7 ....$35.00

Tilly (Tots TV), Euromark/UK, 1994, Topper, red hair, bl overalls, 8", NM, A7 ....$15.00

Tom (Tots TV), Euromark/UK, 1994, Topper, bl hair, gr overalls, 8", NM, A7 ....$15.00

Truck (4x4 Matchbox), Grosvenor/UK, 1995, Topper, Fast Lane, on lg rock, 6½", NM, A7 ....$15.00

Two-Face (Batman), Prelude/UK, 1995, head w/purple bottle, 9", NM, A7 ....$15.00

Vampire (Horror Bubbles!), Jackel International/UK, 1994, cartoon-like child vampire, 7½", NM, A7 ....$25.00

Wakko (Animaniacs), Prelude/UK, 1995, Topper, baseball cap, 10½", NM, A7 ....$15.00

Warrior Dude, Belvedere/Canada, 1995, bank, Teenage Mutant Ninja Turtle knockoff, 9", NM, A7 ....$15.00

Wilma Flintstone (Flintstones), Damascar/Italy, 1995, washing clothes in pelican's bill, 9", NM, A7 ......$35.00

Wilma Flintstone (Flintstones), Rosedew Ltd/UK, 1993, Topper, cartoon outfit, 8½", NM, A7 ....$20.00

Winnie the Pooh, Boots Co/UK, 1990s, yel bear on blk base, cap at bottom, 7", NM, A7 ....$35.00

Wombles (Uncle Bulgaria), Euromark/UK, 1994, full figure, 8", NM, A7 ....$35.00

Woodstock (Peanuts), unknown maker/UK, unknown date, yel w/blk heart-shaped glasses, red scarf, flying plane, 5", NM, A7 ....$35.00

Yakko (Animaniacs), Prelude/UK, 1995, Topper, blk & wht w/red nose, 10½", NM, A7 ....$15.00

Zebedee (Magic Roundabout), Grosvenor/UK, 1992, spiral body, yel jacket w/red head & moustache, 10", NM, A7 ....$35.00

Buddy L

First produced in 1921, Buddy L toys have escalated in value over the past few years until now early models in good original condition (or restored, for that matter) often bring prices well into the four figures when they hit the auction block. The business was started by Fred Lundahl, founder of Moline Pressed Steel Co., who at first designed toys for his young son, Buddy. They were advertised as being 'Guaranteed Indestructible,' and indeed they were so sturdy and well built that they just about were. Until wartime caused a shortage, they were made of heavy-gauge pressed steel. Many were based on actual truck models; some were ride-ons, capable of supporting a grownup's weight. Fire trucks with hydraulically activated water towers and hoisting towers that actually worked kept little boys entertained for hours. After the war, the quality of Buddy Ls began to decline, and wood was used to some extent. Condition is everything. Remember that unless the work is done by a professional restorer, overpainting and amateur repairs do nothing to enhance the value of a toy in poor condition. Professional restorations may be expensive, but they may be viable alternatives when compared to the extremely high prices we're seeing today. In the listings that follow, toys are all pressed steel unless noted.

See also Advertising; Boats.

Cars and Busses

Bus, gr w/gold stripe, 28x7½x7¾", G, A $2,050.00

Country Squire Wagon, 1964, VG+ $175.00

Coupe, blk, silver tires w/red spoked wheels, 10½", G, A.$415.00

Flivver Coupe, blk hardtop, w/full running boards & working steering, aluminum tires w/red spoked wheels, 11", EX, A...$1,155.00

Flivver Coupe #210B, 1920s, blk w/balloon tires & red spoked wheels, 11", G+, A $690.00

Greyhound Bus #755, MIB..$550.00

Greyhound Bus #844, bl & wht w/Greyhound decals, 17", minor rust, G, A $230.00

Greyhound Bus #955, NMIB..$475.00

Yogi, Cindy and Boo Boo, Damascar/Italy, 1994-95, NM, A7, $35.00 each.

Greyhound Bus, #855, blue and white with decals, windup with battery-operated taillights, 17", NM, A, $600.00.

Passenger Bus, lt sage gr w/red & yel stripe, silver tires w/gr disk hubs, side spares, 22 chairs & 2 benches, 29", G, A **$2,070.00**

PPR Passenger Bus, maroon w/gray roof, gray tires w/lime gr disk wheels, 22 chair seats, side spares, 28", rstr, A $2,080.00

Scarab #711, red futuristic vehicle w/chrome lights & grille, blk rubber tires, w/up, 10", G, A $300.00

Station Wagon, pnt wood, maroon & yel w/simulated wood-grain side panels, opening front & rear doors, 19", VG, A...$285.00

Construction

Aerial Tower Tramway, 2 towers connected by cords supporting blk grab bucket, hand-crank controls, 33½", EX, A.........$2,970.00

Cement Mixer, gr w/blk crank, gear board & wheels, w/decals, 10¾", EX, A $275.00

Cement Mixer, light gray with black steel wheels, includes water tank with brass faucet, folding crank and gear raises hopper, 18", restored, A, $575.00.

Cement Mixer, olive gr w/blk water tank, brass faucet, operating hopper, wheels in crawling treads, 16x18", VG, A .$1,980.00

Cement Mixer #5464, 1965, EX.....................................$200.00

Derrick, red boom on blk spoked base, 21½", G, A........$230.00

Digger, red & blk w/seat on twin skids, hand levers control bucket, 27", G-, A $40.00

Hoisting Tower, gr w/blk hoist bucket, hand crank, 39", EX, A..$1,100.00

Hoisting Tower, w/3 chutes, 37½x15x12", missing 3 long chutes, rpl nuts & screws o/w G-, A.......................$700.00

Mack Quarry Dump Truck, yel, EX.................................$65.00

Marion Steam Shovel, 14½", G, A...............................$95.00

Road Roller, green and red, chain-driven roller, spoked wheels, 20", G, A, $2,640.00.

Road Roller, steam type w/2 working pistons & gear-type stearing mechanism, 19x9¾x7¼", G, A $2,250.00

Steam Shovel, blk w/red corrugated roof & base, upright boiler, crank-op shovel & boom, 13", G, A $245.00

Steam Shovel, w/treads, 18½", G, A $1,050.00

Traveling Overhead Crane, red & blk, 43", EX, A $2,090.00

Firefighting

Aerial Hook & Ladder Truck, pnt wood, yel cab w/red fenders, red base w/natural wood ladders, 30", EX, A $880.00

Aerial Ladder Truck, red w/NP ladders & brass hand wheel & bell, hand wheel erects extension ladders, 39", VG, A $955.00

Aerial Ladder Truck, red w/open cab, NP ladders that extends 4½' on rotating base, disk wheels, 39", G-, A..........$770.00

Fire Hose & Water Pumper Truck, 1940s, 12x3¾x4½", missing 1 ladder holder o/w VG (G box), A..........................$75.00

Fire Wrecking Truck, red, brass railing, open driver's seat, w/crane, 26", VG, A...$880.00

Fire Wrecking Truck, red w/open cab & brass railing, side ladders & hose reel, w/crane, rubber disk wheels, 26", NM, A $2,090.00

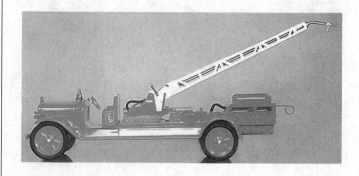

Water Tower Truck, red, silver latticework water tower, tank inside body, electric lights, 45", restored, A, $1,050.00.

Insurance Patrol Truck, red w/open cab, brass rail & rear platform, aluminum tires w/red hubs, 26", G, A.........$1,650.00

Water Pumper, red w/open cab, brass gong & rear handrails, w/boiler & pump flywheels, aluminum disk wheels, 23", VG, A.................$990.00

Outdoor Trains

Ballast (Side Dump Car), blk w/4 discharge doors on ea end, EX, A.................$1,100.00

Boxcar #35407, red w/blk trucks, sliding center doors, ladders on 1 end, 22½", NM, A.................$1,540.00

Caboose, red w/blk trucks, hinged opening doors at ea end, 20¼", G, A.................$550.00

Caboose, red w/blk trucks, opening door at ea end, 20¼", EX+, A.................$1,650.00

Coal Car (Gondola) #70836, blk w/ladders on both ends, 22½", VG, A.................$935.00

Coal Car (Gondola) #96834, blk w/ladders on 1 end, 22½", rare, EX, A, from $1,100 to.................$1,200.00

Flatcar #35047, blk w/5 stake pockets on each side, 18", VG, A.................$2,530.00

Flatcar #68502, blk w/6 stake pockets, couplers on both ends, 22½", G, A.................$465.00

Locomotive & Tender, blk w/brass handrails & bell, opening fire box, 72-oz water tank w/drain plug, 26"/19", EX, A.................$2,420.00

Pile Driver, blk w/corrugated roof, geared hand wheel rotates cab on flatcar base, 22½", rstr, A, from $900 to.........$1,300.00

Railway Dredge, blk open cab on flatcar base w/red corrugated roof, clamshell dredge bucket, 22½", EX, A.........$4,070.00

Railway Improved Steam Shovel, blk w/red corrugated roof, rotating cab on flat bed, 22½", VG, A.................$4,400.00

Roundhouse & Turntable, 3 trapezoid-shaped stalls attached to turntable by tracks, mk Outdoor Railroad, 33" W, EX, A.................$1,980.00

Single-Truck Construction Car, dk gr, tilting dump bed mounted on supports, mk Outdoor Railroad, 12¾", rare, VG, A.................$2,750.00

Stock Car #12457, red, sliding center doors, ladders on 1 end, 22½", VG, A.................$635.00

Stock Car #12457, red w/blk trucks, sliding center doors w/ladders on 1 end, 22½", EX, A.................$1,100.00

Tank Car, red with black frame, restraining straps fastened with brass bolts, 19½", EX, A, $1,870.00.

Trucks and Vans

Allied Van Lines Moving Van, orange and black with black disk wheels, roof lifts open, 29", EX, A, $715.00.

Baggage Truck, blk w/red chassis, yel stake bed, aluminum tires w/red hubs, doorless enclosed cab, 26½", G, A....$1,980.00

Baggage Truck #203B, 1927-29, blk cab w/red chassis & wheels, yel stake bed, w/3 gray cans, 26", EX, A.............$3,738.00

Circus Truck, pnt wood, red & yel cab attached to red, gr & yel cage w/animals, mk Big Top on Wheels, 25", MIB, A......$1,210.00

City Dray Truck, blk enclosed cab w/doors, red chassis, yel stake bed, blk tires (rear dual) w/red hubs, 24", G, A....$1,980.00

Coal Truck, blk w/red chassis, aluminum tires w/red hubs, doorless enclosed cab, detachable chute, 25", rstr, A ..$3,190.00

Coal Truck, 24", G, A.................$1,375.00

Coke-Cola Delivery Truck, yel w/red logo, wht-wall tires, VG.................$200.00

Delivery Truck, blk w/enclosed cab, roof over bed supported by posts, drop-down tailgate, red spoke wheels, 14", VG, A.................$2,860.00

Dump Truck, blk enclosed cab w/doors, red chassis & bed, blk tires w/red hubs, brass hydraulic cylinder, 25", VG, A....$1,045.00

Dump Truck, blk open cab w/red chassic, aluminum tires w/red hubs, crank action, 25", G, A.................$580.00

Dump Truck, blk open cab w/red chassis, aluminum wheels w/red hubs, crank/chain-drive dump action, 25", EX, from $850 to.................$950.00

Dump Truck, gr & wht enclosed cab, wht dump bed w/decaled sides, brass hydraulic cylinder, NP hubs, 22", MIB, A.$660.00

Dump Truck, orange w/red bed & hubs, 11½", G, A..$1,100.00

Dump Truck, 1960s, 13", VG, N2.................$30.00

Dump Truck (Jr Line), blk open cab w/red chassis & dump bed, blk rubber tires w/red hubs, lever action, 24", EX, A $2,420.00

Dump Truck #10, 1935, blk cab, red dump bed, hydraulic dump mechanism, 25", G, A.................$545.00

Photo courtesy of Dunbar Gallery.

Express Truck, black with red chassis, aluminum tires with red spoked wheels, open cab, 24", EX, $1,760.00.

Dump Truck w/Snow Plow, late model, orange, door reads Hydraulically Operated, 16", EX, A $70.00

Express Semi, red tractor w/gr van trailer, blk tires w/red hubs, removable roof w/drop-down rear door, EX, A $600.00

Express Truck, blk w/red chassis, aluminum tires w/red hubs, open cab w/extended roof, rear doors open, 25", EX, A ..$1,980.00

Express Truck, blk w/red chassis, aluminum tires w/red spoked wheels, open cab, drop-down tailgate, 24", EX, A...$1,760.00

Express Truck, dk gr van w/roof extending over blk doorless cab, red chassis, aluminum wheels, red hubs, 23", VG, A $1,100.00

Express Van, blk w/red chassis, removable blk mesh van top, aluminum tires w/red disk hubs, 25", G, A $1,430.00

Express Van, blk w/red chassis, removable gr mesh van top, blk rubber tires w/red hubs, VG, A $4,070.00

Farm Supply Dump Truck #634, 1949, rpt, EX..............$180.00

Flat Tire Wrecker #5427, 1963, w/tools & spare tire, G.$100.00

Flivver Dump Truck, blk w/open cab, aluminum tires w/red spoked wheels, lever-action dump bed, 11", EX, A $2,530.00

Flivver Pickup, blk w/aluminum tires, red spoke wheels, drop-down tailgate, 12", VG, A.......................................$550.00

Flivver Truck, blk w/simulated folding soft top, aluminum tires w/red spoked wheels, 12", EX, A..........................$1,430.00

Flivver 1-Ton Express Truck, blk w/aluminum tires, red spoked wheels, flared rail w/stake pockets, 14", EX, A.....$3,520.00

Ford Dump Truck, blk w/open cab, sm tapering dump compartment w/latch release, aluminum tires w/red spokes, 13", G, A...$1,760.00

Ford 1-Ton Delivery Truck, blk enclosed cab, extended roof over bed w/post sides, aluminum tires, red spokes, 14", EX, A...$6,050.00

GMC Bell Telephone Truck, w/retractable lift and trailer, EX.$200.00

Lumber Truck, blk w/red chassis & 2 solid stake sides, aluminum tires, red hubs, crank action, lumber, 25½", rstr, A .$1,760.00

Lumber Truck, pnt wood tractor & trailer w/wood peg stakes holding lumber, blk & yel cab, yel bed, rear crank, 25", M, A $330.00

Milk Delivery Truck, blk enclosed cab w/doors, red chassis w/bl-gray stake bed, blk dual rear tires, red hubs, 24", G, A......$1,980.00

Milk Delivery Truck #2002, 1930s, blk cab w/gr stake bed, w/6 milk cans, 24", VG+, A $2,185.00

Mister Buddy Ice Cream Truck, wht w/bl base, EX+, S15.$100.00

Oil Tanker, blk enclosed cab w/doors, red chassis, gr tank w/blk fill caps & brass faucet, rear dual wheels, 25", EX, A....$4,400.00

Ol' Buddys' Pie Wagon, MIB..$100.00

Repair-It Wrecker, 15", VG..$165.00

Robotoy Truck, red enclosed cab w/litho robot driver, blk chassis & fenders, gr dump bed, w/transformer, 21½", M, A ...$1,430.00

Sand & Gravel Truck, blk w/red chassis, aluminum wheels w/red hubs, operational steering wheel, 4 doors, 26", G-, A...$1,320.00

Sand & Gravel Truck, blk w/red chassis, aluminum wheels w/red hubs, doorless enclosed cab, 26", VG, A $1,650.00

Shell Fuel Oil Delivery Truck, 1930s, yel & red, 22", NM (EX box), A $2,400.00

Shell Gas Truck, orange & red, open cab & fender wells, G.$300.00

Stake Truck, blk w/red chassis & solid stake bed, aluminum wheels w/red hubs, open cab, w/bales of wire, 25", EX, A...$1,925.00

Stake Truck, blk w/red chassis & stake bed, aluminum tires w/red disk wheels, open cab, 25", EX, A...............$1,760.00

Stake Truck, gr C-style cab w/blk fenders & running boards, red chassis, natural wood stake bed, red hubs, 25", rstr, A.$600.00

Supermarket Delivery Truck, wht, open bed w/miniature grocery bags, 13", NM, A $230.00

Ice Truck, black with yellow bed, ice blocks and tongs, new canvas cover, 26", restored, EX, A, $600.00.

Ice Truck #207, 1926, blk cab w/yel bed & red hubs, 12½x26", rpt o/w EX..$1,650.00

International Dump Truck Deluxe Rider, bl & beige cab w/bl pull hdl, bl bed w/removable seat, red hubs, 25½", EX, A..$2,090.00

International Harvester Truck, solid red, aluminum tires w/red spoked wheels, doorless enclosed cab, 24½", rstr, A .$1,650.00

Tank Line Truck, black with red chassis, aluminum wheels with red hubs, 23", NM, $1,600.00.

Tank Line Truck, blk body w/red chassis, dk gr tank, aluminum wheels w/red hubs, brass faucet in rear, 23", EX, A.$1,430.00

Tank Line Truck, blk w/gr tank, pk fr & front bumper, wht tires w/pk disk hubs, 24", rst, EX, A $770.00

Tank Line Truck, blk w/red chassis, gr tank, aluminum tires, red hubs, operational steering wheel, doorless, 23", VG, A $1,265.00

Tank Line Truck, wht balloon tires, 24", EX, A............$880.00

Texaco Tanker, old, C10...$125.00
US Mail Truck, blk enclosed cab w/doors, red chassis & van body,
    NP front bumper, blk tires w/red hubs, 22", rstr, A..$1,540.00
US Mail Truck, brn w/wht van roof, Buy Defense Bonds decal,
    blk tires w/chrome hubs, 21", M, A.........................$825.00
US Mail Truck #5345, 1964, VG+ $200.00
Wrecker, blk open cab w/red chassis & body, brass railing, hand
    lever controls winch & crane, 28", EX, A $3,080.00

Wrecker, black open cab with red chassis and crane body, black rubber tires with red simulated spoked wheels, 26½", EX, A, $2,300.00.

Wrecker, pnt wood, brn & gr sleek design, crank hdl operates
    detachable crane, wooden wheels, 17¾", EX, A $210.00
Wrecker, wht & gr, Buddy L Towing Service yel decal, 25", EX,
    A $385.00
Wrecker Deluxe Rider, blk tires w/red emb spokes, 25½", no
    seat, rpt, A $495.00
Wrigley Spearmint Railway Express Agency, red cab w/gr van,
    blk tires w/red hubs, 23", EX, A............................$1,320.00
Wrigley Spearmint Tractor & Trailer, 1940s, gr & yel w/logo,
    23x9x6", VG, A $1,000.00

Building Blocks and Construction Toys

Toy building sets were popular with children well before television worked its mesmerizing influence on young minds; in fact, some were made as early as the end of the eighteenth century. Important manfacturers include Milton Bradley, Joel Ellis, Charles M. Crandall, William S. Tower, W.S. Read, Ives Manufacturing Corporation, S.L. Hill, Frank Hornby (Meccano), A.C. Gilbert Brothers, The Toy Tinkers, Gebruder Bing, R. Bliss, S.F. Fischer, Carl Brandt Jr., and F. Ad. Richter (see Richter Anchor Stone Building Sets). Whether made of wood, paper, metal, glass, or 'stone,' these toys are highly prized today for their profusion of historical, educational, artistic, and creative features. For further information on Tinker Toys, read *Collector's Guide to Tinker Toys* by Craig Strange (Collector Books).

Richter's Anchor (Union) Stone Building Blocks were the most popular building toy at the beginning of the twentieth century. As early as 1880, they were patented in both Germany and the USA. Though the company produced more than six hundred different sets, only their New Series is commonly found today (these are listed below). Their blocks remained popular until WWI, and Anchor sets were one of the first toys to achieve international 'brand name' acceptance. They were produced both as basic sets and supplement sets (identified by letters A, B, C, or D) which increased a basic set to a higher level. There were dozens of stone block competitors, though none were very successful. During WWI the trade name Anchor was lost to A.C. Gilbert (Connecticut) who produced Anchor blocks for a short time. Richter responded by using the new trade name 'Union' or 'Stone Building Blocks,' sets considered today to be Anchor blocks despite the lack of the Richter's Anchor trademark. The A.C. Gilbert Company also produced the famous Erector sets which were made from about 1913 through the late 1950s.

Note: Values for Richter's blocks are for sets in very good condition.

Advisors: Arlan Coffman (C4); George Hardy (H3), Richter's Building Blocks.

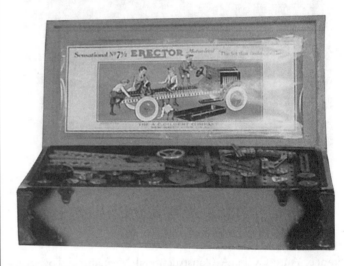

Erector, #7½, AC Gilbert, builds a truck, comes with catalog which demonstrates building a rocket launcher, EX (red wood box), from $250.00 to $350.00.

Erector, #10, Merry-Go-Round and Parachute Jump, ca 1946, EX (EX metal box), from $170.00 to $200.00.

Artwood Toy Mfg, #6050, 1930s, builds boats w/blocks, EX (EX box), P3...$25.00

Astrolite, 1960s, builds futuristic city w/lights, near complete, EX (EX box), T1.....................................$65.00

Block City, #B-300, 152-pc, no roofing o/w VG, T1........$25.00

Block City, #B-500, w/brochure, no roof o/w EX (EX canister), J6..$40.00

Capsela, #400, motorized, NMIB, J6...........................$38.00

DA Pachter, Build-A-Set, 1943, cb & wood, 170-pc, unused, NM (water-stained box w/sm tear), S16..................$50.00

Dux Airplane Construction Set, Germany, metal, EX (EX box), A...$100.00

Elgo, #96, Skyline, EX+, T1.......................................$75.00

Erector, #06½, w/manual, EX (orig box) $45.00

Fisher-Price, Construx #6331, Mobile Missiles Military series, NMIB, from $40.00 to $60.00.

France, Auto-Cycle, A Constructional Mechanical Toy, complete w/instructions, EX (orig box), A.....................$360.00

Gilbert, #10063, complete w/rocket, pcs & booklet, NM (NM metal box), S15...$120.00

Halsam, American Plastic Bricks, #705, w/brochure, NM (canister), J6..$35.00

Halsam, American Plastic Bricks, #715, M (canister) $40.00

Halsam, American Plastic Bricks, #735, VG+, T1 ....$55.00

Ideal, Supercity Town & Country, VG (orig box), T1.....$45.00

Kenner, #07, Bridge & Turnpike Girder & Panel Building Set, EX+ (EX box), J2..$50.00

Kenner, #08, Constructioneer Girder & Panel Set, VG, T1...$65.00

Kenner, #11, Hydro-Dynamic Building Set, MIB, from $125 to...$200.00

Kenner, #14, Build-A-Home, NM (VG box) $55.00

Kenner, #16, Build-A-Home, Subdivision, NMIB, J6....$125.00

Kenner, #17, Sky Rail Girder & Panel Set, NMIB, minimum value...$125.00

Kenner, #72050, Skyscraper Girder & Panel Set, complete w/elevator, EX (rpr box), S15................................$40.00

Make-It, similar to Tinkertoy, VG (canister box), T1......$25.00

Marklin, Construction Set, #1012, complete, VG (orig box), A...$95.00

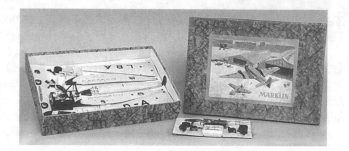

Marklin, D-A LBA Transport Plane Kit #1151, painted metal parts with tools and clockwork mechanisms, EX (EX box), A, $2,000.00.

Marx, Masterbuilder Kit of the White House, w/35 presidents, w/information booklet, unbuilt, M (EX box), T1....$185.00

Meccano, Aeroplane Constructor, G (orig box), A $300.00

Meccano, Motor Car Constructor, England, complete w/tools & metal parts for building sports cars, EX (orig box)...$500.00

Metalcraft, Spirit of St Louis, builds over 25 airplanes, complete, VG (VG box), A.....................................$385.00

Metalcraft, Train Kit, builds stock car, caboose & trucks, w/instructions, VG, S15......................................$200.00

Riviton, #200, MIB, J6...$45.00

Spalding Tinkertoy, #166, 1950s, w/electric motor, EX+ (canister), N2..$125.00

Spalding Tinkertoy, #630, Curtain Wall Builder, with metal girders, NM (NM canister), $75.00.

Tinkertoy, #116, 1950s, VG (orig cb & metal canister), N2 .$20.00

Town & Country, USA, similar to Block City, MIB (sealed tall canister), J6..$36.00

Transogram, Construct-All #100, plastic, appears complete, NMIB, T1...$45.00

Wannatoy, Construction Kit, 1950s, M (VG box), T1 ....$75.00

Super City Skyscraper Building Set, Ideal, 1960s, NM (VG box), T1, $135.00.

Richter Anchor Stone Building Sets

DS, Set #E3, w/metal parts & roof stones, H3 ....$60.00
DS, Set #03A, w/metal parts & roof stones, H3.................$50.00
DS, Set #05, w/metal parts & roof stones, H3 ....$100.00
DS, Set #05A, w/metal parts & roof stones, H3 ....$150.00
DS, Set #07, w/metal parts & roof stones, H3 ....$250.00
DS, Set #07A, w/metal parts & roof stones, H3 ....$200.00
DS, Set #09A, w/metal parts & roof stones, H3 ....$250.00
DS, Set #11, w/metal parts & roof stones, H3 ....$675.00
DS, Set #11A, w/metal parts & roof stones, H3 ....$300.00
DS, Set #13A, w/metal parts & roof stones, H3 ....$325.00
DS, Set #15, w/metal parts & roof stones, H3 ....$1,500.00
DS, Set #15A, w/metal parts & roof stones, H3 ....$475.00
DS, Set #17A, w/metal parts & roof stones, H3 ....$475.00
DS, Set #19A, w/metal parts & roof stones, H3 ....$900.00
DS, Set #21A, w/metal parts & roof stones, H3 ....$975.00
DS, Set #23A, w/metal parts & roof stones, H3 ....$750.00
DS, Set #25A, w/metal parts & roof stones, H3 ....$1,500.00
DS, Set #27, w/metal parts & roof stones, H3 ....$6,000.00
Fortress Set #402, H3...$100.00
Fortress Set #402A, H3...$130.00
Fortress Set #404, H3...$250.00
Fortress Set #404A, H3 ....$275.00
Fortress Set #406, H3...$500.00
Fortress Set #406A, H3...$400.00
Fortress Set #408, H3 ....$1,000.00
Fortress Set #408A, H3 ....$800.00
Fortress Set #410, H3 ....$1,800.00
Fortress Set #410A, H3 ....$1,000.00
Fortress Set #412A, H3 ....$1,500.00
Fortress Set #414, H3 ....$5,000.00
GK-NF, Set #06, H3...$120.00

GK-NF, Set #06A, H3...$100.00
GK-NF, Set #08, H3...$220.00
GK-NF, Set #08A, H5...$100.00
GK-NF, Set #10, H3...$300.00
GK-NF, Set #10A, H3...$120.00
GK-NF, Set #12, H3...$500.00
GK-NF, Set #12A, H3...$195.00
GK-NF, Set #14A, H3...$200.00
GK-NF, Set #16, H3...$800.00
GK-NF, Set #16A, H3...$240.00
GK-NF, Set #18A, H3...$375.00
GK-NF, Set #20, H3...$1,500.00
GK-NF, Set #20A, H3...$450.00
GK-NF, Set #22A, H3...$450.00
GK-NF, Set #24A, H3...$500.00
GK-NF, Set #26A, H3 ....$1,125.00
GK-NF, Set #28, H3...$3,875.00
GK-NF, Set #28A, H3 ....$1,000.00
GK-NF, Set #30A, H3 ....$1,125.00
GK-NF, Set #32B, H3 ....$1,600.00
GK-NF, Set #34, H3...$6,000.00
GK-NK, Great-Castle, H3 ....$9,950.00
KK-NF, Set #05, H3...$45.00
KK-NF, Set #05A, H3...$55.00
KK-NF, Set #07, H3...$100.00
KK-NF, Set #07A, H3...$90.00
KK-NF, Set #09A, H3...$100.00
KK-NF, Set #11, H3...$275.00
KK-NF, Set #11A, H3...$275.00
KK-NF, Set #13A, H3...$300.00
KK-NF, Set #15A, H3...$450.00
KK-NF, Set #17A, H3...$750.00
KK-NF, Set #19A, H3...$1,500.00
KK-NF, Set #21, H3...$3,500.00
Modern House & Country House Set #206, H3.............$600.00
Modern House & Country House Set #208, H3.............$600.00
Modern House & Country House Set #210, H3.............$700.00
Modern House & Country House Set #301, H3.............$500.00
Modern House & Country House Set #301A, H3..........$500.00
Modern House & Country House Set #303, H3.............$800.00
Modern House & Country House Set #303A, H3 ......$2,000.00
Modern House & Country House Set #305, H3 ....$2,500.00
Neue Reihe, Set #102, H3...$75.00
Neue Reihe, Set #104, H3...$100.00
Neue Reihe, Set #106, H3...$150.00
Neue Reihe, Set #108, H3...$250.00
Neue Reihe, Set #110, H3...$500.00
Neue Reihe, Set #112, H3...$600.00
Neue Reihe, Set #114, H3...$1,000.00
Neue Reihe, Set #116, H3...$1,500.00

California Raisins

The California Raisins made their first TV commercials in the fall of 1986. The first four PVC figures were introduced in 1987, the same year Hardee's issued similar but smaller figures, and three 5½" Bendees became available on the retail market.

In 1988 twenty-one more Raisins were made for retail as well as promotional efforts in grocery stores. Four were graduates identical to the original four characters except standing on yellow pedestals and wearing blue graduation caps with yellow tassels. Hardee's increased their line by six.

In 1989 they starred in two movies: *Meet the Raisins* and *The California Raisins — Sold Out*, and eight additional characters were joined in figurine production by five of their fruit and vegetable friends from the movies. Hardee's latest release was in 1991, when they added still four more. All Raisins issued for retail sales and promotions in 1987 and 1988 (including Hardee's) are dated with the year of production (usually on the bottom of one foot). Of those released for retail sales in 1989, only the Beach Scene characters are dated, and these are actually dated 1988. Hardee's 1991 series are also undated. For more information, see *The Flea Market Trader, Revised Tenth Edition*, by Sharon and Bob Huxford.

Advisors: Ken Clee (C3) and Larry DeAngelo (D3).
Other Sources: W6, P10

Applause, Captain Toonz, w/bl boom box, yel glasses & sneakers, Hardee's Second Promotion, 1988, sm, M $3.00

Applause, FF Strings, w/bl guitar & orange sneakers, Hardee's Second promotion, 1988, sm, M.....................$3.00

Applause, Michael Raisin (Jackson), w/silver microphone & studded belt, Special Edition, 1989, M $20.00

Applause, Rollin' Rollo, w/roller skates, yel sneakers & hat mk H, Hardee's Second Promotion, 1988, sm, M $3.00

Applause, SB Stuntz, w/yel skateboard & bl sneakers, Hardee's Second Promotion, 1988, sm, M $3.00

Applause, Trumpy Trunote, w/trumpet & bl sneakers, Hardee's Second Promotion, 1988, sm, M $3.00

Applause, Waves Weaver 1, w/yel surfboard connected to foot, Hardee's Second Promotion, 1988, sm, M $4.00

Applause, Waves Weaver 2, w/yel surfboard not connected to foot, Hardee's Second Promotion, 1988, sm, M $4.00

CALRAB, Blue Surfboard, board connected to foot, Unknown Promotion, 1988, M.....................$35.00

CALRAB, Blue Surfboard, board in right hand, not connected to foot, Unknown Promotion, 1987, M $50.00

CALRAB, Guitar, red guitar, First Commercial Issue, 1988, M, $8.00.

CALRAB, Hands, left hand points up, right hand points down, Post Raisin Bran Issue, 1987, M $4.00

CALRAB, Hands, pointing up w/thumbs touching head, First Key Chains, 1987, M $7.00

CALRAB, Hands, pointing up w/thumbs touching head, Hardee's First Promotion, 1987, sm, M $3.00

CALRAB, Microphone, right hand in fist w/microphone in left, Post Raisin Issue, 1987, M $6.00

CALRAB, Microphone, right hand points up w/microphone in left, Hardee's First Promotion, 1987, sm, M.................$3.00

CALRAB, Microphone, right hand points up w/microphone in left, First Key Chains, 1987, M....................................$7.00

CALRAB, Santa, red cap & gr sneakers, Christmas Issue, 1988, M...$9.00

CALRAB, Saxophone, gold sax, no hat, First Key Chains, 1987, M..$7.00

CALRAB, Saxophone, gold sax, no hat, Hardee's First Promotion, 1987, sm, M..$3.00

CALRAB, Saxophone, inside of sax pnt red, Post Raisin Bran Issue, 1987, M..$4.00

CALRAB, Singer, microphone in left hand not connected to face, First Commercial Issue, 1988, M.......................$8.00

CALRAB, Sunglasses, holding candy cane, gr glasses, red sneakers, Christmas Issue, 1988, M $9.00

CALRAB, Sunglasses, index fingers touching face, orange glasses, Hardee's 1st Promotion, 1987, M.....................$3.00

CALRAB, Sunglasses, index fingers touching face, orange glasses, First Key Chains, 1987, M...............................$7.00

CALRAB, Sunglasses, right hand points up, left hand points down, orange glasses, Post Raisin Bran Issue, 1987, M ..$4.00

CALRAB, Sunglasses 1, eyes visible, aqua glasses & sneakers, First Commercial Issue, 1988, M...............................$16.00

CALRAB, Sunglasses 2, eyes not visible, aqua glasses & sneakers, 1988, First Commercial Issue, 1988, M..................$8.00

CALRAB, Winky, in hitchhiking pose & winking, First Commercial Issue, 1988, M $8.00

CALRAB-Applause, AC, 'Gimme-5' pose, tall pompadour & red sneakers, Meet the Raisins Second Edition, 1989, M .$85.00

CALRAB-Applause, Alotta Stile, w/purple boom box, pk boots, Hardee's Fourth Promotion, 1991, sm, MIP.............$12.00

CALRAB-Applause, Anita Break, shopping w/Hardee's bags, Hardee's Fourth Promotion, 1991, sm, MIP.............$12.00

CALRAB-Applause, Bass Player, w/gray slippers, Second Commercial Issue, 1988, M $8.00

CALRAB-Applause, Benny, w/bowling ball, orange sunglasses, Hardee's Fourth Promotion, 1991, sm, MIP.............$12.00

CALRAB-Applause, Boy in Beach Chair, orange glasses, brn base, Beach Theme Edition, 1988, M $10.00

CALRAB-Applause, Boy w/Surfboard, purple board, brn base, Beach Theme Edition, 1988, M $10.00

CALRAB-Applause, Drummer, blk hat w/yel feather, Second Commercial Issue, 1988, M $8.00

CALRAB-Applause, Girl w/Boom Box, purple glasses, gr shoes, brn base, Beach Theme Edition, 1988, M..................$10.00

CALRAB-Applause, Girl w/Tambourine, gr shoes & bracelet, Raisin Club Issue, 1988, M......................................$12.00

CALRAB-Applause, Girl w/Tambourine (Ms Delicious), yel shoes, Second Commercial Issue, 1988, M $12.00

CALRAB-Applause, Hands, Graduate w/both hands pointing up & thumbs touching head, Graduate Key Chains, 1988, M...$35.00

CALRAB-Applause, Hip Band Guitarist (Hendrix), w/headband & yel guitar, Third Commercial Issue, 1877, M $22.00

CALRAB-Applause, Hip Band Guitarist (Hendrix), w/headband & yel guitar, Second Key Chains, 1988, sm, M $35.00

CALRAB-Applause, Hula Girl, yel shoes & bracelet, gr skirt, Beach Theme Edition, 1988, M $10.00

CALRAB-Applause, Microphone, right hand points up, microphone in left, Graduate Key Chains, 1988, M............$35.00

CALRAB-Applause, Microphone (Female), yel shoes & bracelet, Third Commercial Issue, 1988, M $9.00

CALRAB-Applause, Microphone (Female), yel shoes & bracelet, Second Key Chains, 1988, sm, M................$25.00

CALRAB-Applause, Microphone (Male), left hand extended w/open palm, Third Commercial Issue, 1988, M $9.00

CALRAB-Applause, Microphone (Male), left hand extended w/open palm, Second Key Chains, 1988, sm, M........$25.00

CALRAB-Applause, Mom, yel hair & pk apron, Meet the Raisin Second Promotion, 1989, M $95.00

CALRAB-Applause, Piano, bl piano, red hair, gr sneakers, Meet the Raisins First Edition, 1989, M...............................$20.00

CALRAB-Applause, Saxophone, black beret, blue eyelids, Second Key Chains, 1988, small, M, $35.00.

Photo courtesy of Larry DeAngelo.

CALRAB-Applause, Saxophone, blk beret, bl eyelids, Third Commercial Issue, 1988, M..$15.00

CALRAB-Applause, Saxophone, Graduate w/gold sax, no hat, Graduate Key Chain, 1988, M $35.00

CALRAB-Applause, Singer (Female), reddish purple shoes & bracelet, Second Commercial Issue, 1988, M $12.00

CALRAB-Applause, Sunglasses, Graduate w/index fingers touching face, orange glasses, Graduate Key Chains, 1988, M...$35.00

CALRAB-Applause, Valentine, Be Mine, girl holding heart, Special Lover's Issue, 1988, M....................................$8.00

CALRAB-Applause, Valentine, I'm Yours, boy holding heart, Special Lovers Issue, 1988, M......................................$8.00

Claymation-Applause, Banana White, yel dress, Meet the Raisins 1st Edition, 1989, M...$12.00

Claymation-Applause, Lick Broccoli, gr & blk w/red & orange guitar, Meet the Raisins 1st Edition, M.....................$12.00

Claymation-Applause, Cecil Thyme, Meet the Raisins Second Edition, 1989, M, $85.00.

Photo courtesy of Larry DeAngelo.

Claymation-Applause, Rudy Bagaman, vegetable w/cigar, purple shirt & flipflops, Meet the Raisins First Edition, 1989, M $12.00

Claymation-CALRAB, Hands, Graduate on yel base, Post Raisin Bran Issue, 1988, M $40.00

Claymation-CALRAB, Saxophone, Graduate on yel base, Post Raisin Bran Issue, 1988, M $40.00

Claymation-CALRAB, Singer, Graduate on yel base, Post Raisin Bran Issue, 1988, M $40.00

Claymation-CALRAB, Sunglasses, Graduate on yel base, Post Raisin Bran Issue, 1988, M $40.00

Miscellaneous

Air Freshener, several styles, M, C3, ea..............................$5.00

Photo courtesy of Larry DeAngelo.

AM/FM Radio, Nasta, poseable arms and legs, MIB, from $150.00 to $175.00.

Bendy, flat body, bl sneakers, orange sunglasses or microphone, C3, ea $7.00

Bendy, plush, 5", M, D4, set of 4 ....$20.00

Book Tote, M (w/tag), P12 ....$30.00

Bookmark, diecut U or punched hole at top, different styles, M, C3, ea $5.00

Can, product label with 1 California Raisin on side, M, C3 ..$12.00

Colorforms, M, C3 ....$25.00

Colorforms, MIB (sealed), P12 ....$30.00

Computer Game, IBM, M, C3 ....$22.00

Doorknob Hangers, 6 different styles, M, C3, ea $6.00

Eraser, rubber, set of 2, MOC, C3 ....$15.00

Lapel Pin, PVC figure, MOC, C3, set of 3 ....$19.00

Paper Plates, MIP, C3 ....$15.00

Party Invitations, M, C3 ....$15.00

Pens, orange, wht or blk ballpoints w/sm PVC figure at top, set of 3, M, C3 ....$24.00

Puzzle, 75-pc, MIB (sealed), P12 ....$20.00

Record, Rudolph the Red-Nosed Reindeer, 45 rpm, M (w/picture sleeve), C3 ....$12.00

Record, Signed Sealed Delivered I'm Yours, 45 rpm M (w/picture sleeve) C3 ....$12.00

Record, When a Man Loves a Woman, 45 rpm, M (w/picture sleeve), C3 ....$12.00

Sandwich Music Box, Hands, mk 1987 CALRAB, both hands out to side w/fingers pointing, M.................................$25.00

Sandwich Music Box, Microphone, mk 1987-CALRAB, both hands out as if to hug, M $25.00

Sandwich Music Box, Sunglasses, mk 1987-CALRAB, both hands out as if to hug, M $25.00

Scarf, Raisin Chorus Line printed on fabric, M, C3 ....$20.00

Trading Cards, World Tour Series #1, complete set, M, C3 .$15.00

Video, Hip To Be Fit, M, C3 ....$15.00

Winross Truck, New America Highway Series, 1989, red Ford long-nose tandem axle with dual stacks, features Champion Raisins, M, $125.00.

Wrapping Paper, M, C3...$15.00

Wristwatch, w/second hand, EX+, T1..............................$35.00

Candy Containers

As early as 1876, candy manufacturers used figural glass containers to package their candy. They found the idea so successful that they continued to use them until the 1960s. The major producers of these glass containers were Westmoreland, West Bros., Victory Glass, J.H. Millstein, J.C. Crosetti, L.E. Smith, and Jack and T.H. Stough. Some of the most collectible and sought after today are the character-related figurals such as Amos 'N Andy, Barney Google, Santa Claus, and Jackie Coogan, but there are other rare examples that have been known to command prices of $1,000.00 and more. Some of these are Black Cat for Luck, Black Cat Sitting, Quick Firer Cannon (with original carriage), and Mr. Rabbit with Hat (that books for $1,800.00 even in worn paint). There are many reproductions; know your dealer. For a listing of these reproductions, refer to *Schroeder's Antiques Price Guide*.

'L' numbers in the listings that follow refer to *An Album of Candy Containers, Vols 1 and 2*, by Jennie Long; 'E&A' numbers correlate with *The Compleat American Glass Candy Containers Handbook* by Eikelberner and Agadjanian, revised by Adele Bowden. Watch for a comprehensive information and value guide written by our advisor Doug Dezso and Leon and Rose Poirier.

Advisor: Doug Dezso (D6).

For other types of candy containers, see Halloween; Pez Dispensers; Santa Claus.

Amos 'N Andy Fresh Air Taxi, clear glass car w/pnt figures & wheels, EX, A $440.00

Angeline Coach, L #398 (E&A #166)............................$450.00

Basket, clear glass w/grape design, L #223 (E&A #81) $35.00

Battleship on Waves, L #335 (E&A #96)........................$175.00

Black Cat for Luck, L #4 (E&A #136-1), $1,800.00.

Felix on the Pedestal, L #87 (E&A #211-1), 1923, worn paint, $4,000.00.

Bulldog, 4⅛", G, A $45.00
Chicken, fancy closure, L #9 ....$500.00
Chicken in Sagging Basket, L #8 (E&A #148) $65.00
Decorettes, L #655 ....$125.00
Dog w/Glass Hat, L #22 (E&A #181), lg $25.00
Fish, L #34 ....$400.00

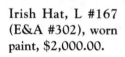

Flossie Fisher's Bed, L #127 (E&A #234), EX, $2,000.00.

Irish Hat, L #167 (E&A #302), worn paint, $2,000.00.

House, orig pnt, closure, L #75 (E&A #324) $165.00
Lantern, domed closure, L #576 ....$25.00
Lantern, oval panels, L #570 ....$25.00
Laundry Truck, L #606 (E&A #785) $750.00
Locomotive 888, no wheels, L #395 (E&A #485) $45.00
Lynne Clock Bank, L #119 (E&A #159) $500.00
Mantel Clock #1, L #115 (E&A #164) $150.00
Mule Pulling Barrel, L #38 (E&A #539) $85.00
Poodle Dog, glass head, L #471....................................$20.00
Pumpkin Head Witch, L #165 (E&A #594)..................$565.00
Rabbit, seated upright, E&A #618, 6¼", G, A $25.00
Rabbit Running on Log, gold pnt, L #42 (E&A #603)...$200.00
Refrigerator, Victory Glass Co, L #266 (E&A #650) ..$3,800.00
Scottie Dog, L #17 (E&A #184) $12.00
Suitcase, clear, L #217 (E&A #207)................................$35.00
Telephone, Stough's #3, L #308 (E&A #751) $40.00
Volkswagon, L #373 (E&A #58)..$35.00

Skookum by Stump, L #106 (E&A #681), ca 1916, $250.00.

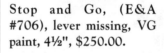

Stop and Go, (E&A #706), lever missing, VG paint, 4½", $250.00.

Cast Iron

Realistically modeled and carefully detailed cast-iron toys enjoyed their heyday from about the turn of the century (some companies began production a little earlier) until about the 1940s when they were gradually edged out by lighter-weight toys that were less costly to produce and to ship. (Some of the cast irons were more than 20" in length and very heavy.) Many were vehicles faithfully patterned after actual models seen on city streets at the time. Horse-drawn carriages were phased out when motorized vehicles came into use.

Some of the larger manufacturers were Arcade (Illinois), who by the 1920s was recognized as a leader in the industry; Dent (Pennsylvania); Hubley (Pennsylvania); and Kenton (Ohio). In the 1940s Kenton came out with a few horse-drawn toys which are collectible in their own right but naturally much less valuable than the older ones. In addition to those already noted, there were many minor makers; you will see them mentioned in the listings.

For more detailed information on these companies, we recommend *Collecting Toys* by Richard O'Brien (Books Americana).

Advisor: John McKenna (M2).

See also Banks; Pull and Push Toys.

Airplanes

Air Express, Dent, trimotor, gr w/NP props, 2 disk wheels, 12" W, rpt, EX, A $3,850.00

Air Ford Monoplane, 1930s, gr, 3¼", VG, A..................$135.00

America, Hubley, gray w/2 pilots in open cockpit, NP rotating props, blk tires w/yel hubs, 13", G-, A $1,760.00

America, Hubley, trimotor w/rubber tires, nickel props, 2 pilots, motor clicker, 17" W, G, A..................................$4,100.00

Friendship Seaplane, Hubley, trimotor, yel w/Friendship & Fokker in bl lettering, NP props, rubber tires, 13", G, A $5,170.00

Lindy, Hubley, cream with red lettering, nickel-plated propeller and wheels, 9½" long, EX, $2,200.00.

Lindy (Spirit of St Louis), Hubley, gray w/NP prop, new wheels, 11", A...$935.00

Monoplane, AC Williams, red & silver, 3", no prop, wht rubber tires rpl, A..$25.00

Travel Air Mystery Plane, Kilgore, 1930s, blue with nickel-plated propeller and wheels, 7" wingspan, EX, $950.00.

Question Mark Airplane, Dent, trimotor, yel w/Question Mark on wings & '?' on fuselage, NP props, 12", EX, A.$3,960.00

Trimotor Airplane, Dent/USA, ca 1929, salesman's sample w/tag, silver w/red trim, Ford on tailfin, 11½", rpt, A $3,410.00

Boats

Battleship, gray w/blk bottom, 2 gun turrets & center stack, 4 wheels, 9½", EX, A...$175.00

City of New York Paddleboat, Wilkins, wht w/blk stacks, red trim, 15", G, A $1,020.00

Penn-Yan Speedboat, Hubley, 1930, pnt CI, med bl w/outboard motor, on wheels, w/4 passengers & captain, 14", VG, A $8,800.00

Puritan Paddleboat, Wilkins, wht w/blk stack, red trim, 10½", VG, A $1,045.00

Racing Scull, US Hardware, 4 oarsmen, 4 spoked wheels, G-, A..$800.00

Racing Scull, US Hardware, 8 oarsmen, yel & blk scull w/4 red spoked wheels, 14", rpt, A...$2,035.00

Racing Scull, Wilkins, 1890, 4 oarsmen & coxswain in red scull w/4 yel star-spoked wheels, 10", EX, A.................$1,375.00

Sidewheel Riverboat, Hubley, ca 1910, cream, 6", heavy paint wear, $350.00.

Character

Andy Gump Car, red with green trim, white tires with green and red hubs, figure in black jacket and red tie, 7", EX (this toy sold for $5,720.00 at the Bertoia auction in 1995, a world-record price realized due to its condition).

Amos 'N Andy Fresh Air Taxi, 3 figures in open auto, blk tires w/spoked wheels, 6", NM, A $1,900.00

Andy Gump Car, Arcade, red car, wht tires w/gr hubs, mk 348 on grille, 7", G, A $1,760.00

Andy Gump Car, Arcade, red car w/NP figure & tires, mk 348 on grille, Licensed by Sidney Smith emb inside, 7", EX, A..............$2,600.00

Happy Hooligan Car, red car w/silver spoked wheels, yel & bl figure w/articulated head, 6", rpt, A......................$1,100.00

Happy Hooligan in Mule Cart, Kenton, 1900s, head nods as 2-wheeled cart is pulled, 10¼", rpt body, A.................$300.00

Happy Hooligan Police Patrol Wagon, Kenton, 3 figures in yel wagon w/red spoke wheels, 2 blk horses, 18", EX, A......................$2,530.00

Jonah & the Whale, mc figure riding atop blk whale on axle w/2 spoked wheels, mouth opens, 5", rpt, A...................$500.00

Mama Katzenjammer Spanking Child in Horse-Drawn Cart, Kenton, Captain driving, 2 lg spoked wheels, 12", EX, A $3,850.00

Popeye Spinach Delivery Cycle, red 3-wheeler w/blk rubber tires, 5¼", G, A $825.00

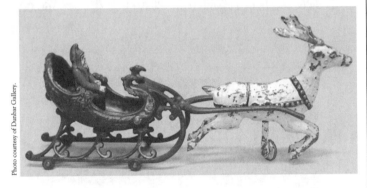

Santa and Sleigh, Hubley, blue version, white reindeer, 15", EX, $1,550.00.

Circus and Accessories

Overland Circus Band Wagon, Kenton, 1920s, 15", 3 new & 2 old musicians, 2 rpt horses, seat missing, A $100.00

Overland Circus Band Wagon, Kenton, 6 musicians & driver on red wagon, yel spokes, 2 riders on wht horses, 16", M, A...$1,210.00

Overland Circus Bear Cage, Kenton, red w/yel spoke wheels, w/driver & 2 wht horses, 14", VG, A.......................$245.00

Overland Circus Wagon, Kenton, 1930s, pulled by 2 white horses, 14", NM, $950.00.

Overland Circus Lion Cage, Kenton, 1920s, red w/wht wheels, gold-trimmed hubs, 10", rpt, A $525.00

Overland Circus Polar Bear Wagon, Kenton #231, 1940s, w/driver & riders on 2 wht horses, 14", MIB, A $575.00

Royal Circus Band Wagon, Hubley, red wagon w/gold trim pulled by 4 blk horses, w/8 band members & driver, 29", rpt, A...$2,530.00

Royal Circus Bear Cage, Hubley, gr wagon w/gold trim pulled by 2 blk horses, w/2 bears & driver, 15", G-, A $770.00

Royal Circus Calliope, Hubley, bl wagon w/gold trim pulled by 4 blk horses, w/driver, 24", EX, A $2,420.00

Royal Circus Clown Van, Hubley, bl wagon w/gold trim & oval mirror pulled by 2 blk horses, w/driver & clown, 16", EX, A ...$2,090.00

Royal Circus Farmer's Van, Hubley, gr w/gold emb rhinos, gold trim, wagon driver & 2 blk horses, 16", VG, A $2,530.00

Royal Circus Farmer's Van, Hubley, gr wagon w/emb rhinos, bobbing farmer's head, 2 blk horses, 16", EX, A...$2,970.00

Royal Circus Giraffe Cage, Hubley, wht wagon w/red trim pulled by 4 blk horses, w/2 giraffes & driver, 24", EX, A.$2,310.00

Royal Circus Lion Cage, Hubley, red wagon w/gold trim pulled by 2 blk horses, w/lion & driver, 15½", EX, A $1,430.00

Royal Circus Polar Bear Cage, Hubley, bl wagon w/gold trim pulled by 2 blk horses, w/2 bears & driver, 15", G, A $690.00

Royal Circus Rhino Cage, Hubley, wht wagon w/gold trim pulled by 2 blk horses, w/2 rhinos & driver, 16", rpt, A $630.00

Royal Circus Tiger Cage, Hubley, red wagon w/gold trim pulled by 4 blk horses, w/2 tigers & driver, 23", rpt, A.......$600.00

Royal Circus Wagon, Hubley, red w/gold trim, emb rhino in oval, pulled by 4 blk horses, w/driver, 23", rpt, A.$1,760.00

Construction

Buckeye Ditcher, Kenton, red & gray, chain-driven shovel & treads, 11¾", EX, A..$1,375.00

Cement Mixer, Kenton, orange & bl, 6¾", G, A...........$275.00

Cement Mixer, Kenton, red and green with white rubber tires, 8½", EX, $2,500.00.

Contractor's Auto Coal Wagon, Kenton, red open cab w/gr dump bed, NP tires w/yel spokes, w/driver, 8¼", VG, A $525.00

Contractor's Auto Coal Wagon, Kenton, red w/NP tires & yel spokes, 3 dumping compartments, fender lights, 8½", NM, A.................................$1,430.00

Contractor's Dump Truck, Kenton, red w/silver buckets hinged into truck bed, disk wheels, w/driver, 8½", G-, A ...$250.00

Jaeger Cement Mixer, Kenton, yel & bl w/red spoked wheels & trim, w/driver, crank action, 7", rpt, A.....................$45.00

Road Roller, Hubley, gr 'Huber' spoked wheels & front roller, 7½", missing driver, EX, A.................................$525.00

Road Roller, Hubley, orange w/scrolled spoke wheels, 7½", rpl figure, NM, A $525.00

Road Roller, Hubley, w/NP water tank & clicker, daisy-design spoked wheels, 14½", EX, A $1,000.00

Steam Shovel, Hubley, 5", EX, A...........................$75.00

Steam Shovel Truck, Hubley, gr & red w/NP shovel, wht rubber tires w/red hubs, 8", rpl tires, EX, A $500.00

Steam Shovel Truck, Hubley, gr & red w/NP shovel, wht rubber tires w/red hubs, 9¾", G, A $440.00

Steam Shovel Truck, Hubley, green and red with nickel-plated shovel, white rubber tires with red hubs, 10", EX, $950.00.

Firefighting

Only motor vehicles are listed here; see also Horse-Drawn.

Fire Pumper, Kenton, ca 1927, red with white rubber tires, integral driver, 10", EX, $1,100.00.

Fire Pumper, Hubley, take-apart model, red w/wht rubber tires, 5", EX, A.................................$190.00

Hose Truck, Kenton, yellow with open cab, nickel-plated wheels with red hubs, integral driver, 7", EX, $850.00.

Hose Truck, Kenton, yel w/open cab, red spoked wheels, railed body & rear bumper, emb Hose, 8¼", G, A.............$360.00

Ladder Truck, AC Williams, red with nickel-plated spoked wheels, integral figures, 7½", EX, $225.00.

Ladder Truck, AC Williams, red, wht rubber tires, w/driver, 8", G-, A.................................$45.00

Ladder Truck, Arcade, 1933, red, wht rubber tires, w/3 firemen, 2-pc, 16¼", 2 rpl ladders, G, A $275.00

Ladder Truck, Dent, red, w/driver, 18½", rpl ladder, G, A..$220.00

Ladder Truck, Hubley, early open frame-type truck w/3 wooden ladders, w/driver & rear fireman, 17", VG, A.......$1,100.00

Ladder Truck, Hubley, red, w/driver, 10¾", 1 rpl ladder, G, A $155.00

Photo courtesy of Dunbar Gallery.

Ladder Truck, Arcade, red and yellow with white rubber tires, 3 integral figures, 15½", EX, $950.00.

Ladder Truck, Hubley, red, 6½", rpl ladders & wht rubber tires, G, A $65.00

Ladder Truck, Hubley, 1930s, red, wht rubber tires, w/2 firemen, 8½", G-, A $95.00

Ladder Truck, Hubley, 2 NP drivers & 2 ladders, 3½x9", rpl wht rubber tires, EX, H7 ....$425.00

Mack Fire Apparatus Truck, red, gold striping, NP ladder rack & hose reel, dual rear wheels, ringing bell, 18", rpt, A ..$440.00

Mack Ladder Truck, Arcade, red, 2 figures, 20", rpl metal spoked wheels, G, A $255.00

Mack Ladder Truck, Arcade, red w/NP rack, hose, ladders & driver, wht rubber tires w/red wheels, 17¾", EX+, A............$1,320.00

Pumper, AC Williams, red, spoked wheels, w/driver, 6¼", G, A ..$140.00

Pumper, AC Williams, 1920s, red, wht rubber tires, w/driver, 6¼", rpl tires, G-, A......................................$90.00

Pumper, Arcade, red, blk rubber tires, w/6 firemen, 13", missing hose o/w VG, A $660.00

Pumper, Arcade, red open cab w/silver trim, NP hose reel, rubber tires, 6 bl firemen, 13", VG, A $935.00

Pumper, Hubley, red, blk rubber tires w/spoked wheels, 11⅛", rpl driver, G, A $275.00

Pumper, Hubley, red long-nose w/open cab, emb gauges on boiler, rubber spoked wheels, 10½", overpt, A $195.00

Horse-Drawn (and Other Animals)

Adams Express Wagon, Ives, gr open wagon w/gold lettering on sides, red spoked wheels, w/driver & horse, 18½", VG, A $1,045.00

Ambulance Wagon, Kenton, brn enclosed wagon mk 2nd Regiment..., red spoked wheels, copper-flashed horse, 15", EX, A $3,300.00

Back-to-Back Trap, Kenton, lady passenger w/back to driver in blk wagon w/yel spoke wheels, wht & blk horse, 13", EX+, A..$2,750.00

Bakery Wagon, Kenton, wht open-door van w/red spoked wheels pulled by 2 blk & silver horses, no driver, 12¾", rpt, A..$265.00

Barouche, Pratt & Letchworth, blk w/gold upholstery, red spoked wheels, w/driver, 1 brn & 1 wht horse, 17", rpt, A $990.00

Barouche, Wilkins, blk w/yel spoke wheels & side lanterns, driver in blk, yel spoke wheels, wht horse, 15", EX, A......$1,265.00

Beer Wagon (32), Kenton, gr w/flanged sides, 4 red spoked wheels, 2 blk horses, w/driver, 15", G, A $500.00

Boys Express Wagon, Wilkins, red w/high upholstered seat, 4 yel spoked wheels, 2 blk horses, w/driver, 16½", VG, A ..$1,210.00

Brake (2-Seat), Hubley, red w/yel spoked wheels, 1 couple & 2 drivers, 1 blk & 1 wht horse, 17", G, A $3,410.00

Brake (3-Seat), Hubley, blk w/gold trim, 2 couples & 2 drivers, 2 brn horses, 18", some rpt, A $4,950.00

Brake (3-Seat), Hubley, red w/yel spoked wheels, 2 couples & 3 drivers, 4 wht horses, 18", some rpt, A $9,570.00

Brake (4-Seat), Hubley, blk wagon w/yel spoked wheels, 3 couples & 2 drivers, 2 blk & 2 wht horses, VG, A.....$4,950.00

Brewery Wagon, Ives, dk gr w/flanged sides & 4 red spoked wheels, 1 wht & 1 blk horse, Blk driver, 18½", VG, A $2,860.00

Brownie Wagon, single horse pulls 2-wheeled cart w/driver, spoked wheels, 5", VG, A...$150.00

Buckboard, Hubley, red open-sided wagon w/center seat, yel spoked wheels, w/mc driver & blk horse, 13½", G-, A.............$360.00

Cairo Express Cart, Kenton, wht box type w/2 spoked wheels pulled by gray elephant, w/driver, 10", G, A............$550.00

Carl Jenson Co Dray Wagon, Pratt & Letchworth, yel stake sides w/4 red spoked wheels, blk horse, w/driver, 13", G, A........$1,045.00

Chaise, Kenton, w/single horse, lady driver, 12", G-, A ..$315.00

City Express Wagon, Kenton, red w/4 yel spoked wheels pulled by trotting wht horse, Blk driver, 17", G, A $525.00

City Truck, Harris, red dray wagon w/low stake sides, 4 yel spoked wheels, 1 wht & 1 brn horse, w/driver, 15", VG, A..$1,925.00

City Truck, Harris, yel & red dray wagon w/low stake sides, 4 red spoked wheels, 2 blk mules, w/driver, 15", VG, A .$1,700.00

Coal Dump Cart, Ives, Pat 1896, red box w/tin Ives logo, 4 blk spoked wheels, 2 blk donkeys, Blk driver, 18", VG, A...$1,210.00

Coal Wagon, Hubley, blk w/flared solid sides & 2 yel spoked wheels pulled by blk mule, w/Blk driver, 11", G, A..$440.00

Coal Wagon, Hubley, red box type w/rear trap door & Coal on sides, 4 yel spoked wheels, 2 horses, Blk driver, 15", VG, A ...$500.00

Coal Wagon, single horse pulls wagon mk Coal, spoked wheels, w/driver, 9", G, A $80.00

Contractor's Dump Wagon, Arcade, red box type w/spoked wheels pulled by 2 blk horses, w/driver, 13½", G, A .$320.00

Contractor's Dump Wagon, Kenton, red w/3 dump sections, 4 red spoked wheels, 2 blk horses, no driver, 15½", G-, A...$385.00

Covered Wagon, Kenton #170, 1940s, 1 wht & 1 blk horse, w/driver, MIB, A $400.00

Doctor's Cart, Pratt & Letchworth, blk w/red spoke wheels, tan horse w/yel mane, 11", VG, A $1,155.00

Dray Wagon, Ives, stake-bed wagon holding 4 barrels, red spoked wheels, blk articulated horse, w/driver, 15", EX, A...$1,320.00

Dray Wagon, Kenton, gr open wagon w/red spoke wheels, 1 blk & 1 wht horse, Blk driver, 15", EX, A $160.00

Express Wagon, Kenton, gr w/simulated stake sides, open back, 4 yel spoked wheels, silver horse, w/driver, 12", VG, A..$170.00

Farm Cart, Kenton, blk w/contoured sides & 4 yel spoked wheels pulled by 2 yoked blk steers, w/Blk driver, 13", rpt, A..$300.00

Farm Wagon, Ives, blk w/box sides & 2 red spoked wheels pulled by 2 blk long-horned steers, w/Blk driver, 12", EX, A $715.00

Farm Wagon, Ives, Pat 1883, blk w/open box bed w/red trim & 2 red spoked wheels, 2 blk steers, no driver, 12", VG, A........$275.00

Farm Wagon, Kenton, red box type w/4 yel spoked wheels pulled by 2 yoked steers, w/Blk driver, 16", rpl seat, rpt, A ..$285.00

Farm Wagon, Kenton, red box type w/4 yel spoked wheels pulled by 2 blk horses w/silver tails, w/Blk driver, 18", G, A $210.00

Fire Aerial Wagon, Wilkins, 1895, blk long flat bed w/hose reel behind driver, red spoked wheels, 3 horses, 43", VG, A $3,850.00

Fire Chief's Wagon, red wagon w/red spoked wheels, wht galloping horse, w/driver, 14½", EX, A $1,430.00

Fire Hook & Ladder Wagon, Dent, open wagon w/scrollwork, side-mount ladders, front & rear seats, 2 figures, 30", EX, A...$1,760.00

Fire Hook & Ladder Wagon, Ives, blk open-fr wagon w/red ladders & spoked wheels, 2 firemen, wht & blk horses, 28", VG, A $580.00

Fire Hook & Ladder Wagon, Ives, blk scrolled fr, red spoked wheels, front & rear drivers, w/2 horses, 34", VG, A $2,750.00

Fire Hook & Ladder Wagon, Wilkins, blk open-fr wagon w/red ladders & spoked wheels, 2 horses & firemen, 19½", EX, A $690.00

Fire Hook & Ladder Wagon #126, Hubley, 1906, wht open wagon, red ladders & trim, 2 firemen, 3 blk/wht horses, 34", VG, A $330.00

Fire Hose Reel Wagon, Ives, blk w/gold trim, spoked wheels, w/driver & rear rider, galloping horse, oversized, VG, A............$4,950.00

Fire Hose Reel Wagon, Ives, brn seat on blk fr, gold trim, spoked wheels, w/driver & wht horse, 15½", rpt hitch, A...$550.00

Fire Hose Tower Wagon, red open-fr wagon w/wht 4-sided tower, yel spoked wheels, 2 bl horses, 13", rpt, A $65.00

Fire Patrol Wagon, Harris, red wagon w/rails & rear step, yel spoked wheels, 4 firemen, 1 blk & 1 wht horse, 19", EX, A..$1,705.00

Fire Patrol Wagon, Hubley, driver & 6 seated firemen in red wagon w/yel spoked wheels, 1 wht & 2 blk horses, 14", VG, A..$1,320.00

Fire Patrol Wagon, Ives, bl open wagon w/rails & rear step, red spoked wheels, 7 firemen, 3 blk/wht horses, 21", rpt, A...............$470.00

Fire Patrol Wagon, Ives, blk w/gold letters, red spoked wheels, 6 firemen & driver, 1 wht & 1 blk horse, 21", EX, A ..$1,980.00

Fire Patrol Wagon, Ives, blk w/railing & rear step, red spoked wheels, 7 firemen, 2 horses, fr mk Phoenix, 21", rpt, A..............$550.00

Fire Patrol Wagon, Kenton, red open wagon w/bench seats & rails, yel spoked wheels, 2 men & 2 wht horses, 12", G, A..$170.00

Fire Patrol Wagon, Kenton, yel open wagon w/red spoked wheels, w/3 riders & driver, 1 blk horse, 12", G, A $360.00

Fire Patrol Wagon, Wilkins, red wagon w/blk spoked wheels, driver & 6 firemen, 2 blk horses, gold trim, 20½", VG, A ..$1,265.00

Fire Patrol Wagon, Wilkins, wht wagon w/yel spoked wheels, driver & 6 firemen, 1 wht & 2 blk horses, 20", EX, A............$965.00

Fire Pumper, Arcade, 3 horses pull pumper, spoked wheels, 4", EX, A $85.00

Fire Pumper, Hubley, NP boiler & seat w/red spoked wheels, red driver, 3 blk & wht horses, 22", G, A $1,045.00

Fire Pumper, Ives, blk w/gold trim, ornamental eagle, red spoked wheels, rear rider & driver, 2 horses, oversized, VG, A..$5,170.00

Fire Pumper, red, yel & gold pumper w/driver, 2 blk horses, 13½", EX, H7 ....$350.00

Fire Pumper, Wilkins, blk wagon w/silver-tone boiler, red spoked wheels, driver & 3 blk & wht horses, 25", rare, rpt, A..$2,420.00

Fire Water Tower Wagon, Kenton, ca 1915, bl open-fr wagon w/wht tower, yel spoked wheels, 2 horses, w/driver, 32", G, A $440.00

Goat Cart, Harris, red open-seat cart, yel spoked wheels, wht goat, driver, 9½", VG, A....................................$1,485.00

Hansom Cab, Ives, blk w/yel trim, red spoked wheels, rear-mounted driver's seat, brn articulated horse, 18", VG, A $3,520.00

Hansom Cab, Kenton #162, 1940s, w/driver & lady passenger, 14", MIB, A $575.00

Hansom Cab, Pratt & Letchworth, blk w/yel spoked wheels, single blk horse w/brn saddle, gold trim, 12", EX+, A $1,430.00

Hay Wagon, Kyser & Rex, yel w/flared stake sides & 2 red spoked wheels, pulled by blk & wht steer, w/driver, 12", EX, A...$1,100.00

Hay Wagon, Kyser & Rex, red cart w/flared stake sides, yel spoked wheels, pulled by 2 steers, w/driver, 13", EX, A $1,595.00

Huckster Wagon, Wilkins, red tin wagon w/yel spoked wheels, w/driver & 2 blk horses w/gold trim, EX, A $1,870.00

Ice Wagon, Hubley, 1920, red w/yel top & spoked wheels, Ice emb on sides, w/driver, 2 blk horses, 15", rpt, A......$575.00

Ice Wagon, Kenton, ca 1929, red & yel wagon pulled by 1 horse, 6½x16", VG, H7..$1,850.00

Ice Wagon, Shimer, brn w/Ice emb in gold, 4 red spoked wheels, no driver, 2 silver horses, 13", rpt, A........................$330.00

Log Wagon, Hubley, dk gr log on red fr w/4 red spoked wheels, w/Blk driver, pulled by 2 steers, 15", rpt, A $465.00

Log Wagon, Kenton, brn log on yel fr w/4 yel spoked wheels, Blk driver, pulled by 2 blk horses, 15", rpt, A.................$385.00

Milk Wagon (Eagle Milk & Cream), Hubley, red open-door van w/4 yel spoked wheels, w/driver, blk horse, 12½", rpt, A......$250.00

Panama Wagon, Wilkins, red sheet-metal dumpster wagon w/yel spoked wheels, w/driver & 2 blk horses, 19", G, A $330.00

Plantation Cart, Ives, red w/flared stake sides & 2 yel spoked wheels pulled by blk mule, 10½", rpl Blk figure, A .$145.00

Plantation Cart, Kenton, red w/flared stake sides & 2 yel spoked wheels pulled by wht ox, w/Blk driver, 11", G, A....$600.00

Plantation Cart, Wilkins, red w/flared stake sides & 2 yel spoked wheels pulled by blk mule, Blk driver, 10½", G-, A ..$230.00

Police Patrol Wagon, Hubley, bl open wagon w/railing & rear step, red spoked wheels, 3 figures, 3 blk horses, 18", G, A...$715.00

Pony Cart, Wilkins, ca 1895, red cart w/2 yel spoke wheels, single blk pony, w/Blk driver, 10", EX, A $990.00

Sand & Gravel Wagon, gr w/4 red spoked wheels, 1 wht & 1 blk horse, w/driver, 15", G, A.......................................$175.00

Sleigh, Dent, gr sleigh w/yel runners & trim, w/rider & wht horse, 15½", rpt, A $910.00

Sleigh, Hubley, gr w/gold trim, lady rider, 1 gold & 1 blk horse w/gold trim, 13½", rpt, A $660.00

Sleigh, Hubley, gr w/gold trim, w/rider, 1 brn & 1 blk horse, 13½", VG, A..$1,265.00

Stake Wagon, Kenton, gr w/red spoked wheels, w/driver, 1 gold- & 1 silver-trimmed blk horse, 15", M, A $165.00

Stake Wagon, Wilkins, yel fr w/2 yel spoked wheels, red seat w/driver, 2 mules, 16½", G, A................................$525.00

Sulky, Pratt & Letchworth, blk horse w/front pivotal wheel, w/driver, 8½", G, A..$910.00

Surrey, Pratt & Letchworth, 1900, blk w/yel spoked wheels, no top, w/driver & horse, 15", rpt, A $635.00

Photo courtesy of Dunbar Gallery.

Hansom Cab, Kenton, 1930s, yellow and blue with black horse, with driver and lady passenger, 14", NM, $500.00.

Photo courtesy of Dunbar Gallery.

Surrey, Pratt and Letchworth, original paint, 15", EX, $2,450.00.

Transfer Wagon, Dent, gr open wagon w/red spoked wheels, w/driver & 4 blk & wht horses on wheels, 24½", VG, A.............$910.00

Transfer Wagon, Dent, red wagon w/yel emb lettering, yel spoked wheels, 1 wht & 1 blk horse, w/driver, 21", EX, A....$1,045.00

Trolley, Wilkins, 1895, gold w/cut-out windows, on 4 sm wheels, 2 wheeled horses, 17", rpt, A.......................$880.00

Trolley, Wilkins, 1895, red w/cut-out windows, on 4 sm wheels, wheeled horse mk World's Fair Street RR, 13", G, A...$800.00

Trolley #712, Wilkins, 1896, red & blk w/cut-out windows on 4 sm wheels, 1 blk & 1 wht horse on wheels, 17", VG, A.$1,045.00

Motor Vehicles

Note: Description lines for generic vehicles may simply begin with 'Bus,' 'Coupe,' or 'Motorcycle,' for example. But more busses will be listed as 'Coach Bus,' 'Coast-To-Coast,' 'Greyhound,' 'Interurban,' 'Mack,' or 'Public Service' (and there are other instances); coupes may be listed under 'Ford,' 'Packard,' or some other specific car company; and lines describing motorcycles might also start 'Armored,' 'Excelsior-Henderson,' 'Delivery,' 'Policeman,' 'Harley-Davidson,' and so on. Look under 'Yellow Cab' or 'Checker Cab' and other cab companies for additional 'Taxi Cab' descriptions. We often gave any lettering or logo on the vehicle priority when we entered descriptions, so with this in mind, you should have a good idea where to look for your particular toy. Body styles (Double-Decker Bus, Cape-Top Roadster, etc.) were also given priority.

American Oil Co Gasoline Truck, Dent, red C-style cab & bed fr w/bl tank, yel spoked wheels, 15¼", rpt, A.......$1,155.00

American Oil Co Gasoline Truck, Dent, red w/C-style cab, gold trim, NP wheels w/red hubs, factory stock, 11", rpt, A..$632.00

Auto Dray, Kenton, yel w/open cab & stake sides, red spoked wheels, w/driver & rear standing passenger, 9", G-, A.............$1,650.00

Auto Express, Hubley, blk w/gold lettering, open cab w/post-supported extended roof, red spoked wheels, 9½", VG, A.................................$990.00

Auto Express, Hubley, red w/open cab & rear, gold trim, yel spoked wheels, 9½", EX, A $1,870.00

Auto Express, Kenton, orange w/blk trim, red spoked wheels, w/driver, 9¼", EX, A...$3,520.00

Baby Dump Truck, Arcade, red, metal disk wheels, w/driver, 10", missing boom, rst, A $175.00

Baby Dump Truck, Arcade, red w/blk rubber tires & red disk hubs, 11", EX $950.00

Photo courtesy of Dunbar Gallery.

Bell Telephone Truck and Trailer, Hubley, ca 1930, C-style cab, olive green with white rubber tires, embossed lettering, 19", NM, $1,650.00.

Bell Telephone Truck, Hubley, gr w/wht rubber tires, emb gold lettering, complete w/NP ladder & 3 tools, 9", EX+, A $530.00

Bell Telephone Truck, Hubley, open top deck, wht rubber tires, 9", 2 rpl tires, G, A $110.00

Bell Telephone Truck, Hubley, red w/emb wht lettering, wht rubber tires w/red hubs, fully equipped, 12", EX, A .$990.00

Bell Telephone Truck, Hubley, red w/wht rubber tires, pole carrier, 2 ladders & 3 NP tools, 9¾", EX, A $980.00

Bell Telephone Truck, 6¼", EX, A $90.00

Bus, AC Williams, yel, spoked wheels, 7¾", G-, A........$100.00

Bus, Arcade, Fregol Safety, 12", rst, A $220.00

Bus, Hubley, silver & red, 7½", rpl wht rubber tires, VG, A $120.00

Camouflage Tank, Arcade, orig treads, 8", M, A............$875.00

Car Carrier, AC Williams, metal spoked wheels, 2 Austin cars, 12½", 2 rpl wheels, G-, A..$220.00

Photo courtesy of Dunbar Gallery.

Car Carrier, AC Williams, red and green with nickel-plated spoked wheels, carries 3 Austin cars, 12½", EX, $850.00.

Car Carrier, Hubley, 1938, red w/2 bl & 2 gr cars, rubber tires, 10", G, A..$490.00

Car Carrier, rubber tires, w/4 cars, 14", rpl tires on tractor, G-, A $365.00

Chevrolet Landau Coupe, Arcade, 1927, blk over bl w/blk fenders & running board, rear spare, 8¼", EX, A........$1,210.00

Chevrolet Roadster, Arcade, blk, 6½", rst, A.................$420.00

Chrysler Airflow, Hubley, ca 1935, tan w/NP grille & bumper, rubber tires, 4½", G, A $115.00

Chrysler Airflow, Hubley, gr sedan w/electric lights, rear spare, 8", EX, A $2,750.00

Chrysler Airflow, Hubley, yellow with nickel-plated grille, white rubber tires and spare, 6", VG, $450.00.

Chrysler Airflow, Hubley, tan w/wht rubber tires & spare, battery-op lights, NP grille & bumpers, 8", VG, A ...$1,250.00

Chrysler Airflow, Hubley, 1930s, pk w/NP grille, rear bumper & spare tires, 4½", VG, A $145.00

City Ambulance, Arcade, 1932, bl w/gold trim, wht rubber tires, 6", NM, A...$715.00

City Service Truck, Kenton, 1923, bl C-style cab, silver tires w/red hubs, 10¼", VG, A $2,750.00

Coach Bus, Kenton, 1930s, Nite Coach, orange with nickel-plated wheels, 7½", EX, $600.00.

Coupe, AC Williams, bl, NP spoked wheels, 5", G, A, from $65 to $80.00

Coupe, AC Williams, blk w/silver metal wheels, 5⅛", G, A...$165.00

Coupe, AC Williams, yel, metal spoked wheels, 4¾", G-, A $105.00

Coupe, Arcade, bl, rubber tires, 4½", scarce, G-, A..........$45.00

Coupe, Arcade, bl, 4⅞", rpl metal spoked wheels, G-, A .$65.00

Coupe, Hubley, 1930, gr w/wht rubber tires, 6", EX, A ..$160.00

Coupe, take-apart model, gr & blk, 4¼", rpt, rpl wht rubber tires, A, from $45 to...$65.00

Coupe w/Rumble Seat, AC Williams, bl, spoked wheels, 6", G .$120.00

Coupe w/Rumble Seat, Kilgore, red w/NP wheels, 8", driver & steering wheel missing, A.......................................$200.00

Crash Car Motorcycle, Hubley, orange, NP wheels, 4½", EX, A..$230.00

Crash Car Motorcycle, Hubley, red w/NP wheels, driver & open wagon, 4¾", G, A..$145.00

Delivery Van, JL Hudson, blk & gr, rubber tires w/disk hubs, 7¾", VG, A $100.00

Deluxe Sedan, Arcade, 1940, w/red & silver striping, driver & passenger, orig decal & clicker, 8¼", EX, A.........$1,840.00

Double-Decker Bus, Arcade, gr w/blk rubber tires, NP headlights & bumper, 2 passengers, 8", EX, A..........................$600.00

Double-Decker Bus, Kenton, ca 1928, red and green with white rubber tires and red hubcaps, 2 passengers, 6½", EX, minimum value, $1,100.00.

Double-Decker Bus, Kenton, gr w/red trim, wht tires w/yel hubs, rear staircase, 6", VG-, A..$470.00

Dump Truck, Arcade, bl, lift-up bed, 12", EX, A............$800.00

Dump Truck, Arcade, w/driver, wht rubber tires, 10½", rstr, A..$135.00

Dump Truck, Arcade, 1920s-30s, red & gr, 5½", VG, A..$120.00

Dump Truck, Arcade, 1923, yel-orange, wht rubber tires w/yel-orange hubs, w/NP driver, 10½", rpt, A...................$450.00

Dump Truck, Champion, red & bl, wht rubber wheels, 8", rpl wheels, G-, A..$220.00

Dump Truck, Dent, red w/C-style cab, blk dump bed, yel spoked wheels, tailgate opens, 15¼", VG, A...................$1,430.00

Dump Truck, Hubley, red & gr, wht rubber tires, 6½", rpl wheels, G, A...$40.00

Dump Truck, Hubley, red w/NP dump bed, wht rubber tires, 7½", EX, A..$455.00

Dump Truck, Hubley, red w/silver bed, wht rubber tires, 4½", G, A...$60.00

Ford Model A Coupe, Arcade, 1928, red, wht rubber tires, 5", VG, A...$260.00

Ford Model A Truck w/Stake Wagon, Arcade, 1931, gr enclosed truck w/red wagon, NP spoked wheels, 11", EX, A..$990.00

Ford Model T Express Truck, AC Williams, blk cab w/simulated wood bed, spoked wheels, 7¼", rpt, A $145.00

Ford Model T Express Truck, AC Williams, red simulated wood body w/blk roof, spoke wheels, 7", VG, A...............$275.00

Ford Model T Sedan, Arcade, blk, gold & wht, wht rubber tires w/spoked wheels, 6½", VG, A.................................$230.00

Ford Model T Sedan, Arcade, blk, wht tires w/blk spoked wheels, NP driver, 6½", rpt, A................................$100.00

Ford Model T Sedan, Arcade, blk 1923 model w/center door, spoked wheels, 6½", G, A $145.00

Ford Model T Touring Car, Arcade, blk, metal spoked wheels, 6¼", rpl driver & wheels, G, A $155.00

Ford Sedan, Dent, blk w/red running boards & fenders, metal spoked wheels, 4", VG, A....................................$55.00

Ford Wrecker, 1928, Arcade, red w/enclosed cab, NP spoked wheels, w/driver, 8¼", rpt, hoist missing, A...............$95.00

Ford 1-Ton Truck, Arcade, bl w/enclosed cab, wht rubber tires w/NP spoked wheels, low sides, w/driver, 8½", rpt, A..$250.00

Ford 1-Ton Truck, Motorcade, red w/enclosed cab, wht rubber tires w/NP spoked wheeks, low sides on bed, 8½", EX, A....$100.00

Gas & Motor Oil Truck, Champion, 1930s, red tanker, 8", rpl rubber tires, G-, A $200.00

Gas & Motor Oil Truck, Champion, 1930s, red w/metal spoked wheels, C-style cab, 8", EX, A $600.00

Gasoline Truck, AC Williams, red, spoked wheels, 5", G, A...$60.00

Gasoline Truck, AC Williams, red w/C-style cab, NP spoked wheels, sides mk Gasoline, 7", G-, A $175.00

Greyhound Bus, Arcade, marked Century of Progress, Chicago-1933, green and cream with rubber tires, 12½", EX, $450.00.

Greyhound Bus, Arcade, 1933 Century of Progress, rubber tires, 10½", VG+, A..$230.00

Greyhound Bus, Arcade, 1933 Century of Progress, rubber tires, 10½", 2 rpl tires, G, A..$135.00

Greyhound Bus, Arcade, 1933 Century of Progress, rubber tires, 7", 2 missing & 4 rpl tires, G-, A.................................$90.00

Greyhound Bus, Arcade, 1933 Century of Progress, 7½", EX, A...$175.00

Greyhound Bus, Arcade, 1937, GMC, red & gold stripe, rubber tires, 7½", EX, A $460.00

Harley-Davidson Motorcycle, Hubley, bl, rubber tires, spoked wheels, w/driver, 5½", G, A, from $300 to..............$350.00

Harley-Davidson Motorcycle, Hubley, gr, rubber tires, spoked wheels, driver w/swivel head, 7", VG+, A...............$600.00

Harley-Davidson Motorcycle, orange w/silver handlebars, blk rubber tires, w/separate driver, 8¾", VG, A.............$715.00

Harley-Davidson Motorcycle, Hubley, orange with white rubber tires, integral driver, 6", NM, $750.00.

Harley-Davidson Motorcycle w/Sidecar, Hubley, olive gr, driver & passenger, separate handlebars, rubber tires, 9", VG, A...$1,430.00

Harley-Davidson Motorcycle w/Sidecar, red w/bl sidecar, gold lettering, wht rubber tires, 5¼", VG, A $145.00

Hathaway's Bakery Truck, Arcade, 2-tone w/advertising on sides, wht rubber tires, 9½", G, A.........................$1,600.00

Hershey's Ford V-8 Tanker, wht w/brn running boards & fenders, brn advertising, wht-walls & spare, 9¾", NM, A $40.00

Huckster Truck, Motorcade Toy, gr, wht rubber tires w/spoke wheels, open-sided vegetable bay w/scales, driver, 9", M, A..$175.00

Ice Truck, Arcade, bl, wht rubber tires, 6¾", G, A $220.00

Ice Truck, Arcade, red w/enclosed cab, railed side bed, NP grille, wht rubber tires w/NP hubs, 6¾", NMIB, A............$690.00

Ice Truck, Dent, red open cab, rails, w/Ice emb on sides, NP wheels, 6", G, A...$155.00

Indian Motorcycle, Hubley, red w/blk rubber tires, w/driver, 9", rare, EX, A $500.00

Indian Motorcycle w/Sidecar, Hubley, 1930, red w/blk rubber tires & spoked wheels, 8½", rpr handlebars, A........$375.00

Indian Traffic Car, Hubley, red and green with white rubber tires, nickel-plated spoked wheels, integral driver, 9", EX, $1,475.00.

Indian 3-Wheel Crash Cycle, red, rubber tires, w/driver, 4½", EX, A $212.00

Indian 4-Cylinder Motorcycle, Hubley, 1930, red w/NP motor & handlebars, 9", G, A $800.00

International Dump Truck, Arcade, ca 1928, red with nickel-plated tires and driver, red hubcaps, 10½", EX, $950.00.

International Baby Dump Truck, 1923, Arcade, red, wht rubber tires w/red hubs, labeled door, 10½", VG, A $935.00

International Pickup Truck, Arcade, yel, 9¼", G-, A $220.00

International Pickup Truck, 1941, Arcade, bright yel, blk rubber tires w/chrome hubs, Arcade sticker, 9¼", EX, A....$855.00

International Stake Truck, Arcade, 1941, red w/blk rubber tires, 11", G-, A $360.00

J&B Express Stake Truck, yel w/open cab, red spoked wheels, w/6 milk cans & driver, 16½", rpl tin floor, G, A ...$825.00

Jr Supply Co Express Truck, Dent, red w/C-style cab, yel spoked wheels, cut-out grids on van body, 15½", rpt, A ..$2,750.00

Jr Supply Co Express Truck (Double Dent), Dent, New York to Philadelphia, red w/yel spoked wheels, gr driver, 16", EX, A $2,800.00

Lakeshore Lines Bus, Fageol, red w/blk top, metal tires, 12⅛", VG, A $600.00

Limousine, Dent, bl, blk & gold 2-door w/red spoked wheels, 7½", EX, A $690.00

Limousine & Trailer, Julian Thomas, maroon car w/wht rubber tires & side spare, silver camping trailer, 24", EX, A $660.00

Lincoln Sedan, AC Williams, gr 4-door, metal spoked wheels, rear spare, 9", G, A $255.00

Lincoln Touring Car, AC Williams, 2-door, open side windows, spoked wheels w/rear spare, 7", VG, A $330.00

Lincoln Town Car, Hubley, take-apart model, gr w/wht rubber tires, NP grille, headlights, bumpers & running boards, 7", NM, A $1,600.00

Lincoln Zephr, Hubley, 1937, gr w/wht rubber tires, 5", NM, A $310.00

Mack Coal Dump Truck, Arcade, red w/Coal stenciled in wht, blk rubber tires, tilting dump bed, 10", G, A $800.00

Mack Dump Truck, Arcade, 1925, C-style cab, bl w/rubber tires, 12", missing front tires & axle o/w G, A $545.00

Mack Dump Truck, Champion, red C-style cab w/bl dump bed, NP tires, 7¾", G, A $175.00

Mack Gas & Motor Oil Tanker, Champion, orange w/C-style cab, wht rubber tires w/orange hubs, rpt, A $190.00

Mack Gasoline Truck, Arcade, gr w/gold trim, NP tires w/gr spoked wheels, tin tank, 12½", G, A $1,320.00

Mack Gasoline Truck, Arcade, 1925, red, wht tires (rear dual tires) w/red spoked wheels, 13", VG, A $1,870.00

Mack Ice Truck, Arcade, bl w/NP wheels, Ice stenciled on sides of railed bed, w/driver, ice cube & tongs, 10½", EX, A $3,740.00

Mack Ice Truck, Arcade, bl w/silver trim, NP spoked wheels, w/driver, ice cube & tongs, 7", EX, A $450.00

Mack Ice Truck, Arcade, 1930, bl NP tires w/bl spokes, Ice in wht, opening tailgate, 2 cubes & tongs, 10½", EX, A $3,520.00

Mack Lubrite Gasoline Truck, Arcade, bl & red cab w/red tank, gold trim, rear dual tires, red spoked wheels, 12", G, A......$1,100.00

Mack Lubrite Gasoline Truck, Arcade, red w/3 gold filler caps, red spoked wheels, 13", rpt, A...............................$715.00

Mack Milk Stake Truck, Arcade, 1929, gr w/gold trim, wht rubber tires (rear duals) w/gr hubs, 11½", G, A.........$1,870.00

Mack T-Bar Dump Truck, Arcade, gray w/gold trim, wht tires w/gray spoked wheels, Mack Bulldog Int Mfg decal, 12", EX+, A $2,860.00

Mack T-Bar Dump Truck, Arcade, 1928, gr w/gold trim, enclosed cab, wht rubber tires w/rear duals, gr hubs, 12", EX, A $525.00

Mack T-Bar Dump Truck, Arcade, 1928, red w/gold trim, NP wheels w/red hubs, rear dual tires, 12", VG, A $250.00

Mack Wrecker and Service Truck, Arcade, red and green with nickel-plated spoked wheels, 13", EX, $2,750.00.

Milk Cream Truck, Hubley, 1930, wht, rubber tires, 3¾", VG, A..$315.00

Motor Express, Hubley, red, gr & silver, wht rubber tires, 2-pc, 7½", rpl tires, G, A $155.00

Motorcycle, Champion, bl w/wht rubber tires, integral driver, 7", EX, A $180.00

Motorcycle, Champion, 1930s, bl, metal wheels, w/driver, 4½", G, A $110.00

Motorcycle, Hill Climber; Hubley, swivel-head driver in racing position, orig rubber tires, 6½", G, A........................$400.00

Motorcycle, Hubley, red, rubber tires, electric lights, 6", VG, A..$300.00

Motorcycle, Hubley, red w/rubber tires, 2 riders, 4", EX+, A $250.00

Motorcycle, Hubley, 1930s, yel, no rider, 3¾", G, A $120.00

Motorcycle, Speed Racing; Hubley, red, w/driver in racing position, spoked CI wheels, 4¼", G, A $550.00

Motorcycle Crash Car, Hubley, red w/rubber tires, integral driver, 5", EX, A $160.00

Mack Ice Truck, Arcade, blue with nickel-plated spoked wheels, with driver, ice cube and tongs, 8½", EX, $1,850.00.

Motorcycle w/Sidecar, Hubley, bl, w/driver & passenger, 4", G, A $85.00

Motorcycle w/Sidecar, Hubley, red w/blk rubber tires & spoked wheels, separate bl driver & passenger, 9", VG, A ..$580.00

New York World's Fair Streetcar, Arcade, 1939, NP trim, 10¼", EX, A $800.00

Nu Car Transport, Hubley, 1932, red & silver, rubber tires, 16", EX, A $575.00

Oil & Gas Truck, Kenton, gr w/gold trim & filler caps, yel spoked wheels, emb Oil/Gas, w/driver, 10", VG, A $1,705.00

Patrol Wagon, Dent, gr, metal hub wheels, w/driver, 6¼", VG, A $250.00

PDQ Delivery Motorcycle, Vindex, red w/NP handlebars, motor exhaust, rubber tires w/NP spoked wheels, 9", EX, A...$500.00

Phaeton, Dent, red open car w/gold striping & 4 gold lanterns, yel spoke wheels, 2 figures, 8½", rpt, A $195.00

Pickup Truck, AC Williams, blk, spoked wheels, 7", G, A..$415.00

Pickup Truck, Champion, red, wht rubber tires, 7½", VG, A..$360.00

Pickup Truck, Hubley, orange w/tan roof, blk fenders, NP grille, rubber tires, 6¼", EX, A $430.00

Pierce Arrow Sedan, 1934, red, 7", rpl rubber tires, G, A.$250.00

Plymouth Coupe, Arcade, bl, w/rumble seat, rubber tires, G-, A $145.00

Plymouth Stake Truck, Arcade, bl, rubber tires, 4½", G, A.$230.00

Police Motorcycle, Champion, bl, rubber tires, w/driver, 7", VG+, A...$250.00

Police Motorcycle, Champion, bl figure & motorcycle w/wht rubber tires, red wheels, 7⅛", G, A.............................$265.00

Police Motorcycle, Champion, bl w/NP spoked tires, integral driver, 7", NM (G box), A....................................$1,250.00

Police Motorcycle, dk bl cycle w/battery-op headlight, wht rubber tires w/red hubs, w/driver, 6¼", VG, A $415.00

Police Motorcycle, Hubley, red, w/driver, 4⅛", G, A......$70.00

Police Motorcycle, Winters, bl, rubber tires, w/driver, 6", G, A $155.00

Police Motorcycle with Sidecar, Hubley, red with black rubber tires and nickel-plated spoked wheels, 8½", EX, $1,300.00.

Police Motorcycle w/Sidecar, Hubley, yel, metal spoked tires, w/driver & passenger, 4", VG, A.............................$200.00

Police Patrol, Kenton, 1933, red & bl, wht rubber tires, w/driver & 3 officers, 9½", G, A $825.00

Racer, Arcade, 1920s, red w/gold spoked wheels, no driver, 6½", VG, A $230.00

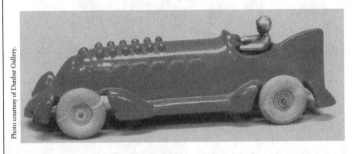

Racer, Boat-Tail; Hubley, orange with white rubber tires, nickel-plated driver, 8½", M, $750.00.

Racer, Boat-Tail; Hubley, orange w/wht rubber tires, w/driver, 7", EX, A...$250.00

Racer, Champion, 1930s, red & bl, 6", rpl wht rubber tires, G, A...$85.00

Racer, Hubley, gr, 7¼", rpl wht tires, G.........................$180.00

Racer, Hubley, movable pistons, w/driver, 8½", new rubber tires & hubs, G, A $400.00

Racer #5, Hubley, gr rubber tires w/spoked wheels, w/driver, 9¾", EX, A...$1,100.00

Racer #5, Hubley, yel w/blk fr, blk rubber tires, disk hubs, w/driver, 9¾", G, A...$1,300.00

Reo Coupe, Arcade, gray, w/rumble seat, wht rubber tires w/side spare, w/driver, 9¼", VG, A $5,750.00

Roadster, Hubley, open, bl, wht rubber tires, 4½", 3 rpl tires, A $50.00

Sedan, AC Williams, red, metal wheels, 5", G, A.........$120.00

Sedan, Arcade, bl, rubber tires, 4", G, A......................$80.00

Sedan, Arcade, gr, metal spoked wheels, 5", VG, A.......$190.00

Sedan, Arcade, 1940, red, rubber tires, 5½", VG+, A....$210.00

Sedan, Champion, red, 6½", rpl wht rubber tires, G, A ...$85.00

Sedan, Dent, 1920, beige w/blk roof, silver trim, chromed tires, rear spare, 7½", rpt, A $190.00

Sedan, Hubley, gr w/rubber tires, NP grille, 4", EX+, A.$165.00

Sedan, Hubley, take-apart model, red w/wht rubber tires, NP grille & bumper, 4½", EX+, A $230.00

Sedan, Hubley, yel w/red running boards & fenders, 4¾", 2 rubber tires rpl, VG, A...$145.00

Seeing New York Bus #899, Kenton, open 5-seat bus w/5 comical characters, red spoked wheels, 10½", rare, rstr, A $2,750.00

Sports Car, Hubley, red roadster w/blk rubber tires, 9", NMIB (box missing end flap), A $100.00

Stake Truck, AC Williams, gr, NP spoked wheels, 4¾", G, A $90.00

Stake Truck, Champion, red C-style cab w/NP spoked wheels, 7½", VG, A...$375.00

Stake Truck, Dent, red C-style cab, yel spoked wheels, chains link stakes together, w/4 milk cans, 15½", VG, A $3,740.00

Stake Truck, Hubley, bl & yel w/6 wht rubber tires, 5", EX, A $350.00

Stake Truck, Hubley, red, 3½", G-, A.............................$50.00

Photo courtesy of Dunbar Gallery.

Stake Truck, Hubley, ca 1935, red with nickel-plated bumper and sideboards, white rubber tires, 8½", M, $550.00.

Stake Truck, Hubley, red & silver, wht rubber tires, 4¾", G, A..$90.00

Stake Truck, Hubley, red w/wht rubber tires, NP stake bed, grille & bumper, 7", EX, A $185.00

Stake Truck, Hubley, 5½", rpt, rpl wht rubber tires, G-, A ..$95.00

Photo courtesy of Dunbar Gallery.

Stake Truck, Kenton, 1930s, red with white rubber tires, 7", VG+, $325.00.

Stake Truck, Kenton, 2-pc, 8", rpl wht rubber tires, G-, A ..$190.00

Stake Truck, 5 Ton; Hubley, gr w/open cab, red trim, yel spoked wheels, w/driver, 17", rpt, A $525.00

Studebaker, Hubley, take-apart model, red w/wht rubber tires, NP grille, lights, bumpers & running boards, 7", EX, A...$890.00

Taxi, Dent, blk over orange w/silver tires & orange hubs, w/driver, 7½", EX+, A $1,265.00

Taxi, Freidag, blk & orange, orange hubs, w/driver, 7½", G-, A $195.00

Taxi, Freidag, 1920s, orange & blk w/spare tire, riveted driver, 7½", G-, A $415.00

Touring Car, Hubley, gr open car w/yel spoked wheels, father driving mother & child, 10", VG, A $1,430.00

Touring Car, Kenton, yel w/red trim, blk single seat, center steering wheel, 2 lanterns, spoke wheels, 6½", rpt, A $165.00

Traffic Car Motorcycle, Hubley, red w/bl stake body, rubber tires w/spoked wheels, w/driver, 9", A.............................$900.00

Transport Service, Arcade, red & yel, rubber tires, 7", G-, A..$220.00

White Dump Truck, Arcade, red w/blk hood & fenders, wht rubber tires, w/driver, 11½", NM, A $15,000.00

White Ice Truck, Arcade, 1941, red w/NP grille, rubber tires, VG+, A...$375.00

World's Fair People Mover, Arcade, 1939, tractor w/NP driver, 3 canopied cars, EX tractor/G cars, A $345.00

Wrecker, Arcade, red w/metal spoked wheels, 5½", pnt loss & soiling, A $110.00

Wrecker, Arcade, Weaver, metal spoked wheels, 8½", missing boom, rpl driver, G-, A..$110.00

Wrecker, Arcade, Weaver, red & gr, 10", G, A..............$255.00

Wrecker, Champion, red, wht rubber tires, 7½", VG, A..$520.00

Wrecker, Hubley, red & beige, wht rubber tires, 3⅞", 2 rpl tires, G, A $100.00

Wrecker, Hubley, take-apart model, red w/wht rubber tires, NP hook, 5", EX, A..$165.00

Wrecker, Hubley, 1930s, gr open cab w/NP hook, wht rubber tires, 5", G+, A $85.00

Photo courtesy of Dunbar Gallery.

Yellow Cab, Arcade, single stripe version, nickel-plated tires with yellow hubcaps, 5", EX, $1,100.00.

Yellow Cab, Arcade, 1936, yel Parmalee w/blk roof, NP grille & license plate, wht rubber tires, 8", VG+, A $4,025.00

Yellow Cab, Arcade, 1941, yel w/bl trim, blk rubber tires, 8¼", G, A...$200.00

Yellow Coach Double-Decker Bus, Arcade, shaded brn & blk, seats on top, 11½", rpl rubber tires, EX, A $2,750.00

Yellow Coach Double-Decker Bus, Arcade, 2-tone brn w/blk trim, blk rubber tires, disk hubs, 13½", EX, A......$2,300.00

Trains

Big 6 Locomotive w/Tender & 2 UPRR cars, red & blk loco, red tender & 2 wagon-type cars, 21", EX, A...............$1,430.00

Keystone Express, blk loco w/tender & 2 passenger coaches, 42", VG, A $525.00

Locomotive w/Tender & Passenger Coach, Hubley, bl, 9¾", VG, A $60.00

PRR No 6 Locomotive w/3 America Coaches, Hubley, 1921, 8¼" loco, 6½" coaches, VG, A $545.00

Pullman Railplane, Arcade, 1935, 8¾", G-, A $50.00

Miscellaneous

Bobsled, 2-Man; Germany, w/2 compo figures, 5", EX, A .$50.00

Box, for 1939 New York World's Fair Bus, Greyhound Lines, #3780, retains Expo Souvenir Inc sticker, 11", rare, EX+, A....$375.00

Cradle, Ives, allover cut-out filigree design, dk red, 7", EX, A..$550.00

Football Kicker, figure w/articulated leg on metal base, when activated he kicks ball, 7", G, A $130.00

Monkey Riding Tricycle, brn articulated monkey on red trike w/wht rubber tires, red spokes, 7", EX, A..............$3,630.00

Sign, Don't Park Here, red & wht lollipop on pedestal base, 4½", A..$45.00

Sign, Men Working, gr vertical rectangle on post, 3¾", G, A...$30.00

Sign, Railroad, red lollipop on post, 3¾", G, A $30.00

Sign, Stop, red octagon, 3½", G, A...............................$30.00

Sign, Turn, yel diamond on post, 3¾", G-, A....................$30.00

Toonerville Trolley, Dent, 1920s, green and orange with rider, EX, $1,775.00.

Photo courtesy of Jeff Bubb.

Catalogs

In any area of collecting, old catalogs are a wonderful source for information. Toy collectors value buyers' catalogs, those from toy fairs, and Christmas 'wish books.' Montgomery Ward issued their first Christmas catalog in 1932, and Sears followed a year later. When they can be found, these 'first editions' in excellent condition are valued at a minimum of $200.00 each. Even later issues may sell for upwards of $75.00, since it's those from the fifties and sixties that contain the toys that are now so collectible.

Advisor: Bill Mekalian (M4)

American Character, 1965, 31 pgs, H12 ....$45.00

American Flyer Trains, 1933, 8 pgs, VG+ $20.00

American Flyer Trains, 1952, mc, EX, J5 ....$25.00

American Mechanical Toy Co, 1915, model building, 80 pgs, G...$32.00

BCM Die Cast Toys, ca 1965-67?, blk & wht, 16 pgs, P4.$18.00

Capitol Records, 1965, Santa Claus on cover holding Beatles' Help! LP, shows all 8 LPs, NM, R2.........................$30.00

Carnell Manufacturing Co, Authentic Western Holsters Dealer Catalog, 1956, blk & wht, 16 pgs, P4......................$35.00

Charles C Merzback, 1968, trains & accessories, 56 pgs, VG+ ...$32.00

Corgi, 1966, NM, F5..$20.00

Corgi, 1967, NM, F5..$20.00

Corgi, 1972, NM, F5..$8.50

Corgi, 1978, NM, F5..$6.50

Corgi, 1979, NM, F5..$6.50

Effanbee Dolls, 1983, 1984 or 1985, M, M15, ea $5.00

Firestone, 1950s, toys, dolls, playthings & recreational items, 67 pgs, H12 ....$38.00

Fisher-Price, pamphlet, 1941-42, fold-out type w/24 illus, NM, A $90.00

Gilbert Hall of Science, 1948, features Superman cover & toys, 8½x5½", EX, A3......................................$175.00

Horikawa Toys, SH/Japan, 1968, features robots & space toys, EX+, A...$110.00

Horikawa Toys, SH/Japan, 1971, features photo of Fire Robot, also other robots & space toys, EX+, A....................$225.00

Horikawa Toys, SH/Japan, 1975, features robots & remote control cars, EX, A $110.00

Horsman, 1880-81, rare, VG, A, $500.00.

Horsman, 1963, features Poor Pitiful Pearl, Gloria Jean, Baby Buttercup & more, H12.......................................$35.00

Hot Wheels International Collectors Catalogue, 1969 or 1970, NM, M17, ea...$25.00

Hubley Dealer Catalog, 1950, 8 pgs, P4 ....$25.00

Hubley Dealer Catalog, 1953, 8 pgs, P4 ....$25.00

Hubley Dealer Catalog, 1955, 12 pgs, P4 ....$35.00

Hubley Dealer Catalog No 17, 6 pgs, P4 ....$20.00

Hubley Gun Catalog, 1958, 4 color, 16 pgs, P4 ....$35.00

Huffy, 1961, bicycles, 9 pgs, 8½x11", VG $35.00

Ideal Dolls, 1967, 12 mc pgs, features Betsy Wetsy, Giggles, Thumbelina & Super Heroines, H12........................$45.00

J&E Stevens Toys & Banks, early edition, 52 pgs, EX, A $65.00

JC Penney, Christmas 1987, EX, I2 ....$5.00

Lionel, 1939, mc, EX, J5 ....$65.00

Lionel, 1939, 52 mc pgs, NM, M17................................$100.00

Lionel, 1941, 1948 or 1949, EX, J5, ea..........................$45.00

Lionel, 1955, 1956 or 1957, EX, J5, ea $45.00

Lionel, 1958, trains & accessories, 54 pgs, G $37.00

Lionel, 1962, trains & accessories, 40 pgs, 8x11", VG......$22.00

LH Smith Woodenware, 1923, 72 pages, EX, A, $100.00; LH Smith Toys, 1939, 148 pages, EX, A, $185.00.

Marx Toys, 1964, magazine format, 2-color, 80 pgs, features figures, playsets, trains & prototype Stony Smith, EX+, F5 .....$250.00

Marx Toys, 1969, magazine format, 2-color, 72 pgs, features playsets, slot cars, trains, figures & space toys, EX, F5 ....$220.00

Mattel, 1962, 8 pgs, 2x6", EX+, F8.................$12.00

Mattel Thing-Maker, 1967 & 1969, 2½x5" & 3x4", EX+, F8, pr ...$20.00

Milton Bradley Game & Toy Catalog, 1964, 56 pgs, NM, M17 ....$115.00

Montgomery Wards, Christmas 1943, 144 pgs, 8x11", G+ $50.00

Montgomery Wards, Christmas 1976 or Christmas 1978, NM, J2, ea $25.00

New Toys, DSK/Japan, 26 pgs, EX, A $140.00

Oscar Strasburger & Co, New York, 1880, wholesale prices on toys & banks w/Am tin & clockwork, Crandall & Reed, VG, A $440.00

Parker Brothers, 1929, games, 12 pgs, 6x9", G $40.00

Playskool, 1931, learning toys, 38 pgs, 3¼x7¼", G $45.00

Prang Crayons, 1930s, diecut, H12 ....$14.00

Roucher Playthings, 1939, model ship building, 68 pgs, VG+ $15.00

Sears, Christmas Wish 1989, EX, I2 ....$10.00

Sears Roebuck, Christmas 1949, 268 pgs, 8½x11", G $72.00

Sears Roebuck, 1938, H12 ....$65.00

Selchow & Righter, 1887, Weeden, Ives, Reed, etc, 70 pgs, VG, A $210.00

Spiegel, Fall & Winter, 1941, 10x14", 663 pgs, H12 ....$48.00

Stevens & Brown, 1872, Am tin & iron toys & banks, 104 pgs, G, A $660.00

Weimann & Muench Catalog of Holiday Goods, 1899, wholesale prices on CI, Am tin, squeak toys, etc, VG, A $195.00

William A Harwood, 1877, wholesale toy prices, no pictures, 36 pgs, EX, A $220.00

William K Walthers, 1948, HO & O gauge trains, 100+ pgs, 6x9", VG $35.00

Cereal Boxes and Premiums

This is an area of collecting that attracts crossover interest from fans of advertising as well as character-related toys. What makes a cereal box interesting? Look for Batman, Huckleberry Hound, or a well-known sports figure like Larry Bird or Roger Marris on the front or back. Boxes don't have to be old to be collectible, but the basic law of supply and demand dictates that the older ones are going to be expensive! After all, who saved cereal boxes from 1910? By chance if Grandma did, the 1910 Corn Flakes box with a printed-on baseball game could get her $750.00. Unless you're not concerned with bugs, it will probably be best to empty the box and very carefully pull apart the glued flaps. Then you can store it flat. Be sure to save any prize that might have been packed inside. For more information we recommend *Cereal Box Bonanza, The 1950s, ID and Values*, by Scott Bruce (Collector Books). Unless noted, our values are for boxes in mint condition, whether full or folded.

Advisor: Jon Thurmond (T1).

General Mills Cheerios, 1980, Lone Ranger on rearing Silver, M, from $45 to $50.00

General Mills Cheerios, 1987, free M&M's inside, NM, T1 ..$3.00

General Mills Cherrios, Mr Peabody, front panel only, G, J2 ..$25.00

General Mills Count Chocula, 1986, Bela Lugosi w/Star of David pendant on front, limited issue, NM, from $25 to $30.00

General Mills Franken Berry, 1985, free Wacky Racers offer, NM, T1 ....$5.00

General Mills Jets, rocket ships & space station kit offer, VG ...$56.00

General Mills Kix, 1951, rodeo cattle chute cutout on box, uncut, M, J2 ....$50.00

General Mills Lucky Charms, 1989, w/new red balloon marshmallows, NM, T1 ....$2.00

General Mills Trix, Corvair Sweepstakes offer, EX $20.00

General Mills Urkelo's, 1992, Urkel for President, limited issue, M, P3 ....$6.00

General Mills Wheaties, 1987, Minnesota Twins, M, M15 ..$18.00

General Mills Wheaties, 1990, Michael Jordon, M, P3/T2, from $10 to $12.00

General Mills Wheaties, 1992, Lou Gehrig, NM, T1 ....$10.00

Kellogg's Apple Jacks, 1986, Starbot offer, NM, T1 ....$6.00

Kellogg's Cocoa Krispies, 1958, Jose the Monkey, front panel only, 9½", from $75 to $100.00

Kellogg's Cocoa Krispies, 1973, Ogg the Caveman on front, Great Civilizations comics on back, NM, scarce, T2 ....$120.00

Kellogg's Cocoa Krispies, 1981, free Sneaky Squeaker, NM, T1..$5.00

Kellogg's Corn Flakes, Bonnie Blair, Gold Medalist, NM, P3 ..$8.00

Kellogg's Corn Flakes, Clara Barton, 1973 Biography Scenes, EX, from $15 to $20.00

Kellogg's Corn Flakes, Corny & Friend in Another Tall-Up Tale, back panel only, EX, J2 ....$20.00

Kellogg's Corn Flakes, Huckleberry Hound & Yogi Bear, EX ..$45.00

Kellogg's Corn Flakes, Norman Rockwell girl on front, Cheer & Bubble Blower offer on back, EX $30.00

Kellogg's Corn Flakes, Superman w/Satellite Gun ad, front panel only, from $40 to $50.00

Kellogg's Corn Flakes, Yogi Bear Cartoon Printing Set, back panel only, EX, J2 ....$20.00

Kellogg's Corn Flakes, Yogi Bear cup offer, EX, from $20 to...$25.00

Kellogg's Corn Flakes, 1955, Dragnet whistle offer on front panel ...$100.00

Kellogg's Corn Flakes, 1957, Woody Woodpecker contest, front panel only, from $50 to.................$75.00

Kellogg's Corn Flakes, 1970s, Fernando Valenzuela on front, Spalding baseball offer on back, NM, from $20 to.....**$25.00**

Kellogg's Fruit Loops, 1963, 1st year of Oot-Fray Opps-Lay ad, missing back & top panel o/w EX, from $40 to.........**$50.00**

Kellogg's Honey Smacks, 1967, Bertie the Bee on front, Pepsi sweepstakes on back, NM......................................**$75.00**

Kellogg's Pep Whole Wheat Flakes, 1940s, story of Superman and the Terrible Underseas Monster on back, scarce, NM, A, $895.00.

Kellogg's Raisin Bran, Woody Woodpecker & Turbo Beam Car offers, VG...**$75.00**

Kellogg's Raisin Bran, 1960, skin diver w/harpoon offer on back, cut side coupon, no top flaps o/w EX, from $40 to.....**$50.00**

Kellogg's Raisin Bran, 1984, free bumper stickers offer, NM, T1 ....**$5.00**

Kellogg's Rice Krispies, Dennis the Menace fan club offer, EX ...**$65.00**

Kellogg's Rice Krispies, Pitch & Hit Baseball Game, front & back panels only, EX, J2 ....**$25.00**

Kellogg's Rice Krispies, Woody Woodpecker's Secret Message Contest, 1960, missing end flaps o/w EX, J2 ....**$40.00**

Kellogg's Rice Krispies, 1950s, NY/Canadian issue, Annie Oakley doll offer & recipe, 7x10", NM, scarce, T2 ....**$100.00**

Kellogg's Rice Krispies, 1981, free initial ring, NM, T1 ......**$6.00**

Kellogg's Rice Krispies, 1988, Win, Lose or Draw, NM, T1..**$4.00**

Kellogg's Sugar Corn Pops, 1953, Jingles on front panel .**$125.00**

Kellogg's Sugar Pops, Sugar Pop Pete w/gun on front, US Frogmen offer on back, EX **$45.00**

Nabisco Rice Honeys, Buffalo Bee & Rin-Tin-Tin mask, M..**$55.00**

Nabisco Rice Honeys, 1956, Sky King statuette, front & back panels only **$100.00**

Nabisco Shredded Wheat, Rin-Tin-Tin cover, 1955, cavalry rifle-pen offer on back w/Rusty & Rinty, VG, M16 ....**$88.00**

Nabisco Spoon Size Shredded Wheat, cereal w/3 Spoonmen on front, US President plaque offer on back, M..............**$45.00**

Nabisco Wheat Honeys, Buffalo Bee & Mr Banana Face, M ..**$45.00**

Post Alpha-Bits, Twirl-A-Cane, front & back panels, w/Twirl-A-Cane, EX+, J2...**$45.00**

Post Cocoa Krispies, 1985, free Hot Wheels car offer, NM, T1 ..**$10.00**

Post Raisin Bran, 1953, Roy Rogers w/western ring offer, front & back panels only, from $200 to **$250.00**

Post Raisin Bran, 1961, mc free baseball card offer on front, missing back & top flaps o/w EX, T2....................**$20.00**

Post's Raisin Bran, 1950s, Roy Rogers and Trigger advertising Pop Out Card, sample cards on back, scarce, NM, $250.00.

Post Sugar Corn-Fetti, 1957, Captain Jolly on front panel...**$100.00**

Post Sugar Crisp, bears on front, Oil Can Harry mask (from Mighty Mouse cartoons) on back, EX **$75.00**

Post Sugar Crisp, Sugar Bear w/Bugs Bunny offer on front, Sylvester mask on back, EX................................**$75.00**

Post Sugar Crisp, 1957, Mighty Mouse offer, front & back panels, 10½" **$100.00**

Post Sugar Crisp, 1960, contest to win electric train on back, 7x9", no top flaps o/w EX, T2 ....**$50.00**

Post Sugar Crisp, 1960, Yogi Berra & free baseball card offer on front, no back panel or top flaps o/w EX, T2 ....**$22.00**

Post Sugar Rice Krinkles, 1955, clown & top offer on front panel..**$45.00**

Post Toasties, Mickey Mouse Band Concert, 1935, back panel only, EX, from $25 to.....................................**$35.00**

Post Toasties, Pinocchio, 1939, EX, from $200 to.........**$300.00**

Post Toasties, 1935, Mickey Mouse Band Concert, back panel only, EX, from $25 to.....................................**$35.00**

Post Toasties, 1937, Snow White & the Seven Dwarfs, back panel only, EX, from $25 to.....................................**$35.00**

Post 40% Bran Flakes, Li'l Abner & Name Honest Abe's Sweetheart contest, VG **$65.00**

Quaker Life, Shari Lewis finger puppets offer, EX.............**$55.00**

Quaker Pettijohns Rolled Wheat, EX, J2 ....**$20.00**

Quaker Puffed Rice, Sgt Preston, early 1950s, pictures to color, M, J2...**$95.00**

Quaker Puffed Wheat, Sgt Preston Yukon Trail #5, back panel only, EX, J2 ....**$80.00**

Quaker's Quisp, 1990, space trivia game on back, 7x10", NM, T2..**$25.00**

Ralston Hot Wheels Cereal, 1990, Super Changers offer, NM, T1...**$10.00**

Ralston Jetsons Cereal, 1990, free lunar launcher, NM, T1..**$5.00**

Ralston Prince of Thieves, 1991, free target game, NM, T1...**$4.00**

Ralston Purina Wheat Chex, 1950s, Cadet Happy on front, side panel w/offer for Space Patrol Microscope, EX, scarce, A...**$250.00**

Ralston Shredded Wheat, 1940s-1950s, EX, J2................**$40.00**

Ralston Teenage Mutant Ninja Turtles Cereal, 1989, free comic book offer, NM, T1 ....**$6.00**

Character and Promotional Drinking Glasses

Once given away by fast-food chains and gas stations, a few years ago, you could find these at garage sales everywhere for a dime or even less. Then, when it became obvious to collectors that these glass giveaways were being replaced by plastic, as is always the case when we realize no more (of anything) will be forthcoming, we all decided we wanted them. Since many were character-related and part of a series, we felt the need to begin to organize these garage-sale castaways, building sets and completing series. Out of the thousands available, the better ones are those with super heroes, sports stars, old movie stars, Star Trek, and Disney and Walter Lantz cartoon characters. Pass up those whose colors are worn and faded. Unless another condition or material is indicated in the description, values are for glass tumblers in mint condition. Cups are plastic unless noted otherwise.

There are some terms used in our listings that may be confusing if you're not familiar with this collecting field. 'Brockway' style tumblers are thick and heavy, and they taper at the bottom. 'Federal' is thinner, and top and diameters are equal.

Advisors: Mark E. Chase (C2) and Michael J. Kelly, authors of *Collectible Drinking Glasses* (Collector Books, 1995). See also Clubs, Newsletters and Other Publications.

Other Sources: B3, C1, C10, C11, D9, D11, F8, J2, H11, I2, J7, M8, M16, P3, P6, P10, R2, S20, T1, T2

Al Capp, Li'l Abner, Sneaky Pete's Hot Dogs, 1975, indent base, from $40 to..$80.00
Al Capp, Li'l Abner, 1975, Brockway, any of 6 different except Joe Btsfplk, ea, from $30 to.................................$50.00
Al Capp, Li'l Abner & Daisy Mae, Kickapoo Joy Juice, 1977, from $10 to...$15.00
Al Capp, Unwashable Jones/Schmoos, 1949, Federal, 4¾", A..$22.00
Andy Panda, Walter Lantz/Pepsi, 1970s, Brockway, from $100 to.$125.00
Andy Panda & Miranda, Dbl Character Series, Walter Lantz/Pepsi, late 1970s-80s, 6⅛", from $20 to $30.00
Aquaman, Super Moon Series, Pepsi, 1976, c NPP or DC Comics, ea, from $8 to...$12.00
Archies, Betty & Veronica Give a Party, Welch's, 1971, 4¼", from $3 to...$5.00
Atlanta Falcons, McDonald's/Dr Pepper, 1981, 4 different, ea, from $4 to..$6.00
Batgirl, Pepsi, Super Moon Series, 1976, 6½", NM, D9 ...$12.00
Batman, DC Comics Super Heroes, Pepsi, 1978, Brockway, 6¼", from $8 to..$12.00
Batman, Ultramar Petroleum/Canadian, 1989-1990, 6 different, ea, from $3 to $6.00
Battlestar Galactica, Universal Studios, 1979, 4 different, ea, from $7 to...$10.00
BC Ice Age, Arby's, 1981, 6 different, ea, from $3 to $5.00
Beaky Buzzard & Cool Cat, Interaction Series, Warner Bros/Pepsi, 1976, Brockway, from $8 to....................$10.00
Beatles, Dairy Queen/Canadian, group photo & signatures in wht burst, from $75 to...$100.00
Beatles, mc photo w/insulated coating at middle, VG+, R2..$125.00

Beatles/Mopheads, Yea! Yea! Yea!, Canadian, 6½", A.....$30.00
Big Baby Huey, Action Series, Harvey/Pepsi, late 1970s, 5", from $8 to...$12.00
Big Boy, 50th Anniversary, 1986, from $5 to.....................$7.00
Blue Fairy (Pinocchio), bl image w/verse on bk, 1940, 4⅜"...$20.00
Bobby Benson, H-O Ranger, Howdy Pard, cowboy on bucking bronco, 4¾", A...$30.00
Boris Badenov, PAT Ward/Holly Farms/Pepsi, 1975, Brockway, Holly Farms logo, limited distribution, from $60 to...$80.00
Broom Hilda, Sunday Funnies, 1976, rare, from $100 to..$150.00

Bugs Bunny, 50th Anniversary, Ultramar/Canadian, from $5.00 to $7.00 each.

Bugs Bunny, Static Pose Series, Warner Bros/Pepsi, 1973, wht letters, Federal, from $6 to..$10.00
Bugs Bunny & Marvin Martian, Interaction Series, Warner Bros/Pepsi, 1976, Brockway, from $45 to $65.00
Bullwinkle, Bicentennial Series, Arby's, 1976, crossing the Delaware, 5", from $10 to..$12.00
Bullwinkle, Static Pose Series, PAT Ward/Pepsi, late 1970s, 5", from $25 to...$30.00
Burger Chef & Jeff, Burger Chef, no date, Now We're Glassified, from $15 to..$25.00
Burger Chef & Jeff, Burger Chef, 1975, from $8 to..........$10.00
Burger Chef & Jeff, Friendly Monster Series, Burger Chef, 1977, 6 different, ea, from $25 to $35.00
Buzz Buzzard & Space Mouse, Dbl Character Series, Walter Lantz/Pepsi, late 1970s-80s, 6⅛", from $25 to $35.00
Captain America & The Falcon, Super Heroes, 7-Eleven/Marvel Comics, 1977, from $15 to $25.00
Care Bears, Pizza Hut, 1983, any of 6 except Good Luck Bear or Friend Bear, ea $1.00
Care Bears, Pizza Hut, 1983, Friend Bear or Good Luck Bear, ea, from $7 to..$10.00
Casper the Friendly Ghost, Static Pose Series, Harvey/Pepsi, 1970s, 5", from $12 to...$15.00
Charlie Chaplin, Actors Series, Arby's, 1979, smoke-colored glass w/silver trim, from $3 to $5.00
Chilly Willy, Walter Lantz/Pepsi, 1970s, Brockway, from $35 to...$55.00
Clara Peller, Where's the Beef?, Wendy's, 1984, 6", from $5 to...$8.00
Cool Cat, Static Pose Series, Warner Bros/Pepsi, 1973, logo on side, blk letters, Federal, from $8 to...........................$12.00
Creature From the Black Lagoon, Universal Studios Monsters, early 1980s, short, from $65 to $85.00

Currier & Ives, Collector Series, Arby's, 1978, 4 different, 4½", ea, from $3 to **$5.00**

Daffy Duck, Static Pose Series, Warner Bros/Pepsi, 1973, Brockway, from $5 to...............................**$7.00**

Daffy Duck & Pepe Le Pew, Interaction Series, Warner Bros/Pepsi, 1976, Brockway, from $5 to **$7.00**

Davy Crockett, Holiday Freeze, 7", from $10 to...............**$15.00**

Davy Crockett, Welch's, emb character on bottom, from $7 to **$10.00**

Dick Tracy, Domino's Pizza, mid-1970s, Brockway, from $100 to **$125.00**

Donald Duck, bl figure w/vertical name, 1930s, 4⅜", NM, M8 ....**$45.00**

Dracula, Universal Studios Monsters, early 1980s, short, from $65 to **$85.00**

Dudley Do-Right, Action Series, PAT Ward/Pepsi, late 1970s, Brockway, from $8 to.................................**$10.00**

Elmer Fudd, Static Pose Series, Warner Bros/Pepsi, 1973, wht letters, Federal, from $5 to **$8.00**

Empire Strikes Back, Burger King/Coca-Cola, 1980, 4 different, ea, from $3 to **$7.00**

Esso Tiger, Put a Tiger in Your Tank emb in 8 different languages, pitcher w/8 glasses, 1950s, V1 ....**$115.00**

ET, AAFES (Army & Air Force Exchange Service), 1982, 4 different, ea, from $5 to **$10.00**

ET, Collector's Series, Pizza Hut/Pepsi, 1982, 4 different, ea, from $2 to..**$3.00**

Flash, DC Comics Super Heroes, Pepsi, 1978, Brockway, 6¼", from $8 to...**$12.00**

Flintstones, Hanna-Barbera/Flintstones Children's Chewable VItamins, 3¾", from $10 to.............................**$15.00**

Flintstones Kids, Pizza Hut, 1986, 4 different, ea, from $2 to...**$3.00**

Foghorn Leghorn & Marc Antony, Interaction Series, Warner Bros/Pepsi, 1976, Brockway.....................................**$40.00**

Great Muppet Caper, McDonald's, 1981, 4 different, ea, from $1 to **$2.00**

Green Lantern, Super Moon Series, Pepsi, 1976, c DC, from $40 to **$60.00**

Happy Days, The Fonz, Pizza Hut/Dr Pepper, 1977, indent base, from $10 to..**$15.00**

Henery Hawk, Static Pose Series, Warner Bros/Pepsi, 1973, logo under name, Federal, 15-oz, ea, minimum value......**$150.00**

Henery Hawk, Static Pose Series, Warner Bros/Pepsi, 1973, side logo, blk letters, Federal, from $25 to.....................**$40.00**

Henery Hawk, Static Pose Series, Warner Bros/Pepsi, 1973, side logo, wht letters, Brockway, 16-oz, ea, from $25 to....**$40.00**

Heritage Bicentennial Collector Series, Coca-Cola, 1976, set of 4, A **$28.00**

Holly Hobbie, Happy Talk Series, Coca-Cola, undated, indent base, 6 different, ea, from $2 to.....................**$5.00**

Hopalong Cassidy, Western Series, mk Wm Boyd, Indian scenes & symbols around image of Hopalong, 5", scarce, NM, A ..**$65.00**

Hopalong Cassidy, 2-color action scene on milk glass, flared top, rolled base, from $20 to **$25.00**

Horace Horsecollar, Musical Notes, Disney, 1937, red & bl, 4¼", A...**$85.00**

Howard the Duck, Super Heroes, 7-Eleven/Marvel Comics, 1977, from $15 to...**$18.00**

Huckleberry Hound & Yogi Bear, Hanna-Barbera/Pepsi, 1977, from $15 to...**$25.00**

Incredible Hulk, Super Heroes, 7-Eleven/Marvel Comics, 1977, from $20 to...**$25.00**

Indiana Jones & the Temple of Doom, 7-Up, 1984, distributed by 4 restaurants, 4 different, ea, from $6 to **$12.00**

James Bond 007, 1985, 4 different, from Roger Moore movies, ea, from $10 to **$15.00**

Josie & the Pussycats, Hanna-Barbera/Pepsi, 1977, from $15 to ..**$25.00**

Jungle Book, Bagheera, WDP/Pepsi, late 1970s, from $60 to **$90.00**

Gasoline Alley, Sunday Funnies, 1976, from $8.00 to $15.00.

Photo courtesy of Collector Glass News..

Jungle Book, Canadian, 3 from a set of 6, from $35.00 to $50.00 each.

Go-Go Gophers, Leonardo TTV/Pepsi, 6", from $15 to...**$20.00**

Goofy in Adventureland, McDonald's, 1989, Missouri test market, from $8 to **$12.00**

Jungle Book, Colonel Hathi, WDP/Pepsi, late 1970s, from $50 to **$60.00**

King Kong, Coca-Cola, 1976, 4 different, ea, from $5 to....**$8.00**

Little Orphan Annie, Sunday Funnies, 1976, from $8 to .**$15.00**

McDonaldland, Action Series, McDonald's, 1977, 6 different, ea, from $3 to $5.00

McDonaldland, Adventure Series, McDonald's, 1980, 6 different, ea, from $10 to.................................$15.00

Mickey Mouse, Bosco, 1930s, blk graphics on clear ground, 3" $45.00

Mickey Mouse, Christmas Carol, Mickey as Cratchit, Goofy as Marley & Scrooge McDuck, 1983, M, M8, set of 3 ...$30.00

Mickey Mouse, Happy Birthday, WDP/Pepsi, 1978, from $6 to $8.00

Mickey Mouse, vertical name, 1930s, 4¼", NM, M8........$45.00

Mickey Mouse & Minnie & Pluto, All-Star Parade, 1939, 4¼", NM, M8 ....$45.00

Mickey Mouse Through the Years, Sunoco, 1988, 6 different, ea, from $5 to..$7.00

Mighty Mouse, Terrytoons/Pepsi, Brockway, very rare, from $500 to...$600.00

Minnie Mouse, Disney/Hook's Drugs, 1984, from $12 to .$15.00

Monstro the Whale, bl image w/verse on back, 1940, 4¾"..$20.00

Mummy, Universal Studios, 1960s, tall, from $35.00 to $45.00.

Photo courtesy of June Moon.

Natasha, Static Pose Series, PAT Ward/Pepsi, late 1970s, 5", from $10 to..$15.00

NFL Helmets/Logos, Mobil, 1988, Washington Redskins, NY Giants or Tampa Bay Buccaneers, ea, from $3 to.........$5.00

Nursery Rhymes, Big Top Peanut Butter, 1950s, ea, from $3 to $5.00

Oklahoma Indians, Knox Industries, 1950s, frosted, 8 different, ea, from $6 to...$10.00

Pac-Man, Arby's, 1980, 4½", from $2 to $4.00

Peanuts, Camp Snoopy Series, McDonald's, 1983, 5 different, ea, from $1 to...$2.00

Peanuts, Kraft Jelly, 1988, 4 different, ea.........................$2.00

Petunia Pig, Static Pose Series, Warner Bros/Pepsi, 1973, logo under name, Federal, 15-oz, minimum value $50.00

Petunia Pig, Static Pose Series, Warner Bros/Pepsi, 1973, side logo, Brockway or Federal, 16-oz, from $6 to...........$8.00

Pierre the Bear, LK's, 1977, 4 different, ea, from $3 to $5.00

Pinocchio, red image w/verse on back, 1940, 4¾" $20.00

Pittsburgh Penguins, Elby's Big Boy, 1989, 4 different, ea, from $6 to $8.00

Pittsburgh Steelers Superbowl 13, McDonald's, 1978, 4 different, ea, from $5 to..$8.00

Pluto at Disneyland, Coca-Cola, A $10.00

Popeye, Kollect-A-Set Series, Coca-Cola, 1975, indent base, 6 different, ea $5.00

Popeye, Popeye's Famous Fried Chicken, 1979, 4 different, ea, from $10 to..$20.00

Porky Pig, Static Pose Series, Warner Bros/Pepsi, 1973, logo under name, Federal, 15-oz, from $15 to...................$20.00

Rescuers, Bianca or Penny, WDP/Pepsi, 1977, ea, from $10 to......$12.00

Rescuers, Madame Medusa, WDP/Pepsi, 1977, from $25 to...........$30.00

Return of the Jedi, Burger King/Coca-Cola, 1983, 4 different, ea, from $2 to..$5.00

Richie Rich, Harvey/ Pepsi, 1973, Brockway, from $8.00 to $10.00.

Richie Rich, Static Pose Series, Harvey/Pepsi, late 1970s, 6", from $15 to...$20.00

Riddler, Super Moon Series, Pepsi, 1976, c DC Comics, from $40 to $60.00

Riddler, Super Moon Series, Pepsi, 1976, c NPP (National Periodical Publications), from $20 to $40.00

Road Runner, Static Pose Series, Warner Bros/Pepsi, 1973, Brockway, from $8 to...$10.00

Robin, Super Moon Series, Pepsi, 1976, from $10 to........$15.00

Rockwell, Norman; Saturday Evening Post Covers, Arby's, indent base, 6 different, ea...$2.00

Rockwell, Norman; Summer Scenes, Arby's, 1987, indent base, 4 different, ea, from $3 to $5.00

Roy Rogers & Trigger, mk Many Happy Trails, shows Roy on rearing Trigger, 5", scarce, NM, A $72.00

Shazam!, DC Comics Super Heroes, Pepsi, 1978, rnd bottom, 5⅝", from $15 to..$25.00

Sleeping Beauty, Disney/Canadian, 1959, Briar Rose & forest friends, blk & wht, 5", A $30.00

Sleeping Beauty, Disney/Canadian, 1959, fairies making dress, pk & blk, 5"...$30.00

Slow Poke Rodriguez, Warner Bros/Pepsi, 1973, from $30.00 to $50.00.

Snidely Whiplash, Static Pose Series, PAT Ward/Pepsi, late 1970s, 6", from $15 to..$20.00

Snoopy, Sports Series, Dolly Madison, 4 different, ea.........$5.00

Snow White & the Seven Dwarfs, Disney/Bosco, 1938, A $37.00

Space Mouse, Walter Lantz/Pepsi, 1970s, Brockway, from $150 to..$200.00

Speedy Gonzales, Static Pose Series, Warner Bros/Pepsi, 1973, · blk letters, Federal, from $6 to...................................$10.00

Spider-Man, Super Heroes, 7-Eleven/Marvel Comics, 1977, from $25 to $30.00

Spike (Tom & Jerry), MGM/Pepsi, 1975, wht or blk letters, Brockway, from $10 to...$12.00

Star Trek, Dr Pepper, 1976, 4 different, ea, from $15 to...$20.00

Star Trek III: The Search for Spock, Taco Bell/Coca-Cola, 1984, 4 different, ea, from $3 to $5.00

Star Trek: The Motion Picture, Dr Pepper, 1980, 3 different, ea, from $20 to...$30.00

Star Wars, Burger King/Coca-Cola, 1977, 4 different, ea, from $5 to $7.00

Sunday Funnies, Gasoline Alley, 1976, 5½", from $8 to..$10.00

Supergirl, Super Moon Series, Pepsi, 1976, c NPP or DC Comics, ea, from $10 to..$15.00

Superman, DC Comics Super Heroes, Pepsi, 1978, Brockway, 6¼", from $8 to...$12.00

Superman the Movie, DC Comics, 1978, 6 different, ea, from $5 to $10.00

Sylvester & Tweety, Interaction Series, Warner Bros/Pepsi, 1976, Brockway, from $5 to...$7.00

Tasmanian Devil, Static Pose Series, Warner Bros/Pepsi, 1973, side logo, Brockway or Federal, 16-oz, from $15 to....$20.00

Tasmanian Devil, Static Pose Series, Warner Bros/Pepsi, 1973, logo under name, Federal, 15-oz, minimum value ...$100.00

Thought Factory, Sports Collector Series, Pepsi, 1979, bowling, soccer, tennis or fishing, ea, from $15 to...................$25.00

Tom & Jerry, Action Series, MGM/Pepsi, 1975, 2 different, 5", ea, from $6 to...$10.00

Ultimate Warrior, World of Wrestling, Schwartz's Peanut Butter, 1989, from $2 to $3.00

Underdog, Action Series, Leonardo TTV/Pepsi, 5", from $15.00 to $20.00.

Urchins, American Greetings/Coca-Cola, 1976-78, 6 different, ea, from $3 to..$5.00

Wile E Coyote, Static Pose Series, Warner Bros/Pepsi, 1973, side logo, Brockway or Federal, 16-oz, ea, from $3 to..........$5.00

Wile E Coyote, Static Pose Series, Warner Bros/Pepsi, 1973, logo under name, Brockway or Federal, 15-oz, ea, from $15 to $20.00

Winnie the Pooh, Disney World Souvenir Series, WDP/Sears, 1970s, scarce, from $15 to $25.00

Winnie the Pooh for President, WDP/Sears, 1970s, from $7 to.....$10.00

Wizard of Id, Arby's, 1983, 6 different, ea, from $7 to......$10.00

Wizard of Oz, Swift & Co, Scarecrow, wavy bottom, wht, 5", from $12 to..$18.00

Wizard of Oz, Swift & Co, Tinman, plain bottom, gr, from $12 to $18.00

Wizard of Oz, Swift & Co, Toto, plain bottom, bl, 5", from $12 to $18.00

Wizard of Oz, Swift & Co, Witch of the North, fluted bottom, frosted color, 5", A..$18.00

Wolfman, Universal Studios Monsters, early 1980s, short, from $65 to $85.00

Wonder Woman, DC Comics Super Heroes, Pepsi, 1978, rnd bottom, 5⅝", from $10 to...$15.00

Woody Woodpecker, Walter Lantz/Pepsi, 1970s, Brockway, from $10 to $20.00

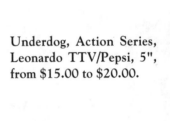

Character and Promotional Mugs (left column continues from glasses)

Wyatt Earp, OK Corral, blk, gold & gr, 4⅞", A................$25.00
1982 Knoxville World's Fair, McDonald's, flared top, 5½", from $3 to $5.00

Character and Promotional Mugs

Bamm-Bamm, 1972, plastic, 8-oz, EX+, N2 ....$12.00
Batman, McDonald's, 1995, Batman, Riddler, Two Face or Robbin, P10, ea..$5.00
Batman, 1966, M, D8...$15.00
Beatles, Nems/London, ceramic w/mc fired-on decal, 4¼", EX, B3 ....$280.00
Big Al, Disney World Theme Park, from $5 to $7.00
Campbell Kid, plastic, 8-oz, EX, N2 ....$15.00
Chicago Bears, Fisher Nuts, team helmet on clear, fluted base, tall, from $2 to $4.00
Davy Crockett, Indian Fighter; Hazel Atlas, milk glass, from $5 to $7.00
Dino (Flintstones), 1972, plastic, 8-oz, EX..................$5.00
Donald Duck, Dan Brechner, 1961, mk WDP, EX+, M8 .$20.00

Donald Duck, Walt Disney Productions, Pepsi, milk glass, from a set of four, from $8.00 to $10.00 each.

Dukes of Hazzard, 1981, plastic, 10-oz, EX, N2 ....$8.00
ET, Avon, 1983, NM...$10.00
Felix the Cat, 1960s, pk, sipping style, NM, T1................$15.00
Flintstones, British, 1989, MIB, J7 ....$30.00
Fred Flintstone, 1969, plastic, 8-oz, EX $5.00
Funny Face Chocolate, Pillsbury, M, P12 ....$20.00
Funny Face Lemon, Orange, Tutti-Frutti, Punch or Watermelon, Pillsbury, M, P12, ea........................$15.00
Garfield, McDonald's, c 1978, distributed 1987, 4 different, P10, ea...$2.00
Green Hornet, milk glass, NM, T2...........................$65.00
Happy Days/The Fonz, 1976, plastic, EX, J7 ....$12.00
Hershey's Time for Chocolate, 1992, mail-in offer, w/unpunched lid, NM, P3...$4.00
Hopalong Cassidy, red, blk, gr or bl graphics on milk glass, ea, from $20 to...$30.00
Howdy Doody, Shake-Up, NM, J6.............................$24.00
Incredible Hulk, Deka, 1977, plastic, 10-oz, EX, from $10 to $12.00
Jiminy Cricket, Walt Disney, bl plastic w/flasher eyes, 4", EX+, D9..$10.00
Josie & the Pussycats, 1971, bl plastic w/mc decal, EX, J5 ..$15.00

Keebler Elf, 1972, plastic, 8-oz, EX+, N2 ....$12.00
Kliban Cat, M, S15..$15.00
Ludwig Von Drake, Dan Brechner, 1961, mk WDP, EX+, M8 .$16.00
McDonald's, Good Morning, milk glass, P10 ....$2.00
Mickey Mouse, America on Parade, Coca-Cola, 1976, from $5 to $7.00
Mickey Mouse, Enesco, 1960s, Behind Every Great Man..., NM, M8..$45.00
Mickey Mouse, Single Character Series, Pepsi/Anchor Hocking, milk glass, from $8 to $10.00
Mickey Mouse, Through the Years Collector Series, WDP/Pepsi, 1980, 4 different, ea, from $8 to $10.00
Mickey Mouse Club, 1950s, plastic, EX, J7 ....$15.00
Mighty Mouse, 1977, plastic, 10-oz, EX $15.00
Mowgli, Enesco, 1965, EX+, M8 ....$17.00
Olive Oyl, 1971, plastic, 10-oz, EX+ $15.00
Olive Oyl, 1980, hand-pnt ceramic, M, J2 ....$20.00
Orphan Annie, Ovaltine/Beetleware, 1930s, Shake-Up, beige hard plastic w/orange lid, EX, P6........................$55.00
Pebbles, 1972, plastic, 8-oz, EX, N2 ....$14.00
Ponderosa Ranch/Bonanza, metal, EX, J7 ....$10.00
Porky Pine (Pogo), wht plastic, NM, I2 ....$6.00
Quick Rabbit, Nestle's, 1992-93, bl plastic w/emb bunny, MIP, P3 ....$5.00
Rocket Ship, Hong Kong, remove nose cone to insert straw, clear plastic w/space graphics, 7½", EX, D9 ....$5.00
Rocketeer, Applause/Disney, Korea, 1991, mc ceramic, lg, MIB....$10.00
Rockwell, Norman; Good Old Days, Japan/HMI, 1982, decal on china w/gold trim, 4 different, ea..................$4.00
Roy Rogers, Quaker Oats, 1950s, 4½", EX, C10/M16, from $40 to $45.00
Smurf, 1980, plastic, 10-oz, EX, N2 ....$8.00
Snoopy, Vote for the American Beagle, milk glass, from $5 to $8.00
Speedy Alka Seltzer, folding plastic, w/Speedy on lid, S15.$5.00
Spider-Man, Deka, 1977, plastic, 10-oz, EX, N2 ....$12.00
Tony Tiger, 1960s, plastic, 8-oz, EX+, N2 ....$15.00
Winnie the Pooh, Disney World Souvenir Series, 1970s, available for limited time, from $20 to..................$30.00
Zorro, 1950s, bl plastic boot w/decal on side, Z-form hdl, 4½", EX+, M8..$25.00

Character Bobbin' Heads

Frequently referred to as nodders, these papier-mache dolls reflect accuracte likenesses of the characters they portray and have become popular collectibles. Made in Japan throughout the 1960s, they were sold as souvenirs at Disney, Universal Studios, and Six Flags amusement parks. They were available at roadside stops as well. Papier-mache was was used until the mid-'70s when ceramic composition came into use. They were very susceptible to cracking and breaking, and it's difficult to find mint specimens — little wonder, since these nodders were commonly displayed on car dashboards!

Our values are for nodders in near-mint condition. To calculate values for examples in very good condition, reduce our prices by 25% to 40%. Advisors: Matt and Lisa Adams (A7).

Bugs Bunny, Foghorn Leghorn, Porky Pig, Wile E. Coyote, Speedy Gonzales, Elmer Fudd, Tweety, Yosemite Sam, NM, A7, from $100.00 to $150.00 each.

Beetle Bailey, NM, A7 ....$125.00
Charlie Brown (Peanuts), Japan, 1970s, ceramic w/gr baseball
 cap & mitt, NM, A7..$75.00
Charlie Brown (Peanuts), Lego, blk sq base, NM, A7......$75.00
Charlie Brown (Peanuts), 1970s, no base, sm, NM, A7 ...$40.00
Colonel Sanders, Kentucky Fried Chicken, 2 different, NM, A7,
 ea..$100.00
Danny Kaye, kissing, NM, A7..$100.00
Danny Kaye & Girl, kissing, NM, A7, pr $150.00
Dobie Gillis, NM, A7, from $250 to $300.00
Donald Duck, Walt Disney World, sq wht base, NM, A7..$75.00
Donald Duck, 1970s, rnd gr base, NM, A7 ....$75.00
Donny Osmond, wht jumpsuit w/microphone, NM, A7, from
 $100 to..$125.00
Dr Ben Casey, from 1960s TV show, NM, A7, from $100 to.$125.00
Dr Kildare, from 1960s TV show, NM, A7, from $100 to..$125.00
Dumbo, rnd red base, NM, A7 ....$100.00
Eisenhower, bl coat, NM, A7, from $100 to $125.00
Goofy, Disneyland, arms at side, wht base, NM, A7.........$75.00

Goofy, Walt Disney World, arms folded, sq wht base, NM, A7.....$75.00
Linus (Peanuts), Japan, 1970s, ceramic, baseball catcher w/gr
 cap, NM, A7...$75.00
Little Audrey, NM, A7, from $100 to $125.00
Lt Fuzz (Beetle Bailey), NM, A7 ....$125.00
Lucy (Peanuts), Japan, 1970s, ceramic w/gr baseball cap & bat,
 NM, A7...$75.00
Lucy (Peanuts), Lego, sq blk base, lg, NM, A7 ....$75.00
Lucy (Peanuts), 1970s, no base, sm, NM, A7 ....$40.00
Mammy (Dogpatch USA), NM, A7 ....$75.00
Maynard Krebs (Dobie Gillis), holds bongos, NM, A7, from
 $250 to..$300.00
Mickey Mouse, Disneyland, red, wht & bl outfit, sq wht base,
 NM, A7...$100.00
Mickey Mouse, Walt Disney World, bl shirt & red pants, NM,
 A7...$75.00
Mickey Mouse, yel shirt & red pants, rnd gr base, NM, A7 .$75.00
Mr Peanut, moves at waist, w/cane, NM, A7..................$175.00
New York World's Fair, boy & girl in fair outfits, kissing, NM,
 A7...$125.00
New York World's Fair, 1964, globe, NM, A7 ....$75.00
Oodles the Duck (Bozo the Clown), NM, A7 ....$150.00
Pappy (Dogpatch USA), NM, A7...$75.00
Peppermint Patti (Peanuts), Japan, 1970s, ceramic w/gr baseball
 cap & bat, NM, A7...$75.00
Phantom of the Opera, sq brn base, NM, A7.................$500.00
Phantom of the Opera, Universal Studios of California, gr face,
 NM, A7...$150.00
Pig Pen (Peanuts), Lego, sq blk base, lg, NM, A7............$75.00
Pluto, 1970s, rnd gr base, NM, A7 ....$75.00
Raggedy Andy, bank, mk A Penny Earned, NM, A7 ....$75.00
Raggedy Ann, bank, mk A Penny Saved, NM, A7...........$75.00
Roy Rogers, NM, A7, from $150 to $200.00
Schroeder (Peanuts), Lego, sq blk base, lg, NM, A7.........$75.00
Sgt Snorkel (Beetle Bailey), NM, A7 ....$125.00
Smokey the Bear, holds lowered shovel, rnd base, NM, A7, from
 $125 to..$150.00
Smokey the Bear, holds shovel in raised hand, sq base, NM, A7,
 from $125 to $150.00
Snoopy (Peanuts), Japan, 1970s, ceramic w/gr baseball cap &
 mitt, NM, A7..$75.00
Snoopy (Peanuts), Lego, sq blk base, lg, NM, A7.............$75.00
Snoopy (Peanuts), 1970s, as Flying Ace, no base, sm, NM, A7...$40.00
Snoopy (Peanuts), 1970s, as Joe Cool, no base, sm, NM,
 A7...$40.00
Snoopy (Peanuts), 1970s, Christmas outfit, no base, sm, NM,
 A7 ....$40.00
Snoopy (Peanuts), 1970s, no base, sm, NM, A7 ....$40.00
Space Boy, blk spacesuit & helmet, NM, A7 ....$75.00
Three Little Pigs, bl overalls & yel cap, rnd red base, NM, A7,
 ea..$100.00
Topo Gigio, standing w/out fruit, standing w/apple, orange or
 pineapple, NM, A7, ea $75.00
Winnie the Pooh, 1970s, rnd gr base, NM, A7, from $100 to .$125.00
Wolfman, sq gr base, NM, A7...$500.00
Woodstock (Peanuts), Japan, 1970s, ceramic w/bat, NM, A7.$75.00
Woodstock (Peanuts), 1970s, no base, sm, NM, A7.........$40.00
Zero (Beetle Bailey), NM, A7 ....$125.00

Linus, Lego, black base, NM, $75.00.

Character Clocks and Watches

Clocks and watches whose dials depict favorite sports and TV stars have been manufactured with the kids in mind since the 1930s, when Ingersoll made both a clock and a wristwatch featuring Mickey Mouse. The #1 Mickey wristwatch came in the now-famous orange box illustrated with a variety of Disney characters. The watch itself featured a second hand with three revolving Mickey figures. It was available with either a metal or leather band. Babe Ruth stared on an Exacta Time watch in 1949, and the original box contained not only the watch but a baseball with a facsimilie signature.

Collectors prize the boxes about as highly as they do the watches. Many were well illustrated and colorful, but most were promptly thrown away, so they're hard to find today. Be sure you buy only watches in very good condition. Rust, fading, scratches or other signs of wear sharply devaluate a clock or a watch. Hundreds have been produced, and if you're going to collect them, you'll need to study *Comic Character Clocks and Watches* by Howard S. Brenner (Books Americana) for more information.

Note: Our values are typical of high retail. A watch in exceptional condition, especially an earlier model, may bring even more. Dealers (who will generally pay about half of book when they buy for resale) many times offer discounts on the more pricey items, and package deals involving more than one watch may sometimes be made for as much as a 15% discount.

Advisor: Bill Campbell (C10).

See also Advertising; California Raisins.

Clocks

Aristocats Alarm Clock, Bayard/France, 1960, cat's head nods & ticks off seconds, 5", NM (M box), A $300.00
Bambi Animated Alarm Clock, Bayard/France/WDP, 1964, Bambi, Thumper & Flower, animated butterfly, bl case, VG, P4 ....$225.00
Batman & Robin, 1980s, action pose on dial face, w/up alarm, 4½", M, A6 ....$15.00

Bugs Bunny Talking Alarm Clock, Janex, 1974, Eh, Wake Up Doc, MIB, $75.00.

Batman Talking Alarm Clock, Janex, 1974, mc plastic w/Batman & Robin in Batmobile before Gotham City, 7x7x3", EX, M17 ....$90.00
Beatles' Yellow Submarine, Sheffield, mc psychedelic sides, w/alarm, needs pin o/w VG+, B3 ....$720.00
Betty Boop Alarm Clock, China, Betty, Koko & Bimbo on red & yel rnd dial, rnd case, 6", EX (orig box), A $55.00
Bugs Bunny Alarm Clock, Ingraham, 1940, Bugs eating carrot, sq dial, cream-colored sq case, 5", EX (orig case) $325.00
Bugs Bunny Talking Alarm Clock, 1974, Eh Wake Up Doc, EX, J7 ....$30.00
C-3PO & R2-D2 Talking Alarm Clock, Bradley, 1980, MIB..$100.00
Charlie McCarthy Alarm Clock, Gilbert, 1940, head on red dot, rnd dial, cream-colored cathedral case, 6", VG+, A..$550.00
Cinderella, France, 1940, Cinderella in coach w/moving donkey's head, rnd dial, wht case, 6", EX, A..................$120.00
Disney Alarm Clock, Phinney Walker, 1960s, Mickey & Donald w/instruments on face, plastic, 4½" dia, MIB, A $200.00
Disney Time Traveling Alarm Clock, Phinney Walker, 1960s, Mickey on face, metal w/red tin flip-top case, 3" dia, MIB............$150.00
Donald Duck, Glen Clock of Scotland, image of Donald in flower garden w/bird in hand, head moves, 5½" sq, EX $250.00
Donald Duck, 1960s, pendulum weight w/moving eyes, NM (EX+ box) $100.00
Donald Duck Alarm Clock, Bayard/France, Donald holding pointers for hands, rnd dial, bl case, 5", EX (orig box), A....$200.00
Dr Seuss Alarm Clock, ca 1978, Cat in the Hat w/swinging arms as clock hands on rnd dial, 2-bell, 6", EX, A..............$70.00
Early Bird, Canadian, animated, C10..............................$325.00
Green Sprout, talking alarm, M, V1................................$36.00
Hopalong Cassidy Alarm Clock, EX, C10 ....$500.00
Howdy Doody Alarm Clock, It's Howdy Doody Time, numbers & Howdy's head at 12-3-6-9, rnd dial, 2-bell, 6", EX, A ..$65.00
Mickey Mouse & Goofy Alarm Clock, Bradley/WDP, red numbers surround Mickey & Goofy on rnd dial, red case, 5", EX, A....$100.00
Mickey Mouse #1 Electric Alarm Clock, 1933, Mickey on dial, character strip on case, NM, C10............................$850.00
Mickey Mouse Alarm Clock, Bayard/France, 1960s, Mickey in running position on rnd face, red base, 5", M (EX box), A .$200.00
Mickey Mouse Alarm Clock, Bradley, 1960, Mickey flanked by name on oval dial, red case, 2 yel bells, 3½", EX, A ..$45.00
Mickey Mouse Alarm Clock, Bradley/WDP, 1970s, MIB (sealed), M8..$90.00

Mickey Mouse Alarm Clock, Ingersoll, 1933-34, lg Mickey w/sm Mickeys on dial, sq gr case, 5", EX (box), from $850 to **$1,000.00**

Mickey Mouse Alarm Clock, Ingersoll, 1940, Mickey on rnd dial, cream-colored tombstone-shaped case, 5", EX (orig box), A..**$300.00**

Mickey Mouse Alarm Clock, Ingersoll, 1940s, Mickey on rnd dial, yel tombstone-shaped case, 5", EX, A **$85.00**

Mickey Mouse Alarm Clock, Ingersoll/US Time, 1950s, Mickey on rnd dial, 5", EX (orig box)...................................**$300.00**

Mickey Mouse Alarm Clock, 1940s, Mickey Mouse playing the piano on rnd dial, ribbed case, flat base, 3½", EX, A.**$75.00**

Mickey Mouse Clock, Germany, 1960, lg face of Mickey on rnd dial w/blk tin ears atop, red case, 5", EX, A **$35.00**

Minnie Mouse Alarm Clock, Bradley/Germany, Minnie w/lg red hands, rnd dial, yel rnd case, 2 red bells, 7", EX, A ...**$90.00**

Mr Magoo Alarm Clock, China, Mr Magoo w/fishing pole in 1 hand, trying to grab fish in the other, 5", EX, A......**$100.00**

Pinocchio Alarm Clock, Baynard/France, 1940, bust of Pinocchio surrounded by 12 friends, rnd dial, bl case, 5", EX **$175.00**

Pluto Alarm Clock, Baynard/France, 1964, blue case, 5", EX, $250.00.

Photo courtesy of Dunbar Gallery.

Popeye Alarm Clock, New Haven, 1940, Popeye w/moving arms on rnd dial w/seconds dial, Popeye & Wimpy on case, 4", EX, A **$770.00**

Popeye Alarm Clock, Smith Alarm Co/British, 1940, Popeye & Sweet Pea, red, yel & bl numbers, rnd, 5", EX (orig box), A **$360.00**

Roy Rogers & Trigger Alarm Clock, Ingraham, 1950s, desert scene, gr square case, 5", EX (orig box), A...............**$440.00**

Roy Rogers & Trigger Alarm Clock, Ingraham, 1950s, desert scene, galloping motion ticks off seconds, 4x4", EX, A **$175.00**

Scrooge McDuck Alarm Clock, Bayard/France, 1950, gold coins surround a strolling Scrooge, rnd dial, wht case, 5", EX, A **$155.00**

Smokey the Bear Alarm Clock, Germany, 1960s, Prevent Forest Fires!, Smokey w/shovel on rnd dial, 2-bell, 7", EX, A .**$100.00**

Smurf Alarm Clock, Bradley, Have a Smurfy Day!, a Smurf & bl numbers on yel rnd dial, 2 yel bells, 6½", EX, A **$20.00**

Snoopy Alarm Clock, Blessing/Germany, 1972, dancing on blk face w/chrome, 5", EX, H11....................................**$55.00**

Snoopy Alarm Clock, United Features Syndicate, 1958, Snoopy playing tennis, rnd dial, 4", EX-, A **$35.00**

Snoopy Alarm Clock, United Features Syndicate, 1958, Snoopy playing baseball, rnd dial, 5", EX, A...........................**$55.00**

Snoopy Doghouse Alarm Clock, Salton, LED, 6", M, H11..**$40.00**

Three Little Pigs, Ingersoll, 1934, Three Little Pigs surround lg image of the Big Bad Wolf, red rnd dial, 4", EX, A .**$385.00**

Tom Mix Alarm Clock, Germany, 1950s, name & bust image w/red numbers on rnd dial, gold case, 3½", EX, A.....**$75.00**

Toppie Alarm Clock, 1940, pk & wht checked elephant w/bl blanket, Toppie on rnd dial, rnd base, 4¾", EX, A .**$220.00**

Woody Woodpecker Alarm Clock, W Lantz, 1st issue, Woody in chef's hat in front of Woody's Cafe tree, EX (EX box), $300.00.

Watches

Aladdin's Genie, battery-op, MIB, B10............................**$10.00**

Alien, w/wraparound tail band, 1980s, MOC, T1/D8.......**$20.00**

Archie, Cheval/Archie Comic Pub, Hong Kong, 1989, plastic case, Betty & Veronica orbit Archie, plastic band, MIB, P4.**$30.00**

Babe Ruth, Exacta Time, 1950s, Official Sports Watch of Champions, expansion band, NM (w/ball & orig box)...**$1,100.00**

Babe Ruth, Exacta Time, 1950s, Official Sports Watch of Champions, expansion band, NM **$500.00**

Bambi, M (birthday box), C10.......................................**$500.00**

Bambi Birthday Series, Ingersoll/WDP, 1949, Bambi on face, gr band, complete w/pen, NM (EX box), A.................**$625.00**

Bart Simpson, Nelsonics, LCD, 5-function, mc plastic, MOC, K1..**$12.00**

Batman, Fossil/DC Comics, 1989, lg gold-tone bezel, chrome bk, running Batman, quartz, brn leather band, M, P4 .....**$60.00**

Batman Action Watch, Gilbert, 1965, MIB, M17 ....**$390.00**

Batman Binky Flasher, 1960s-70s, face switches from Batman to Robin, NM+, C1 ....**$15.00**

Beauty & the Beast, Disney, 1994, quartz, limited edition, logo on dial, gold-tone bezel, blk leather strap, M, P4.....**$150.00**

Boris & Natasha, A&M Hollywood/PAT Ward, 1984, chrome case, sweep second hand, quartz, VG, P4.................**$100.00**

Bozo the Clown, 1971, MOC, J7.......................................**$20.00**

Bugs Bunny, MZ Berger/Warner Bros, Swiss movement, gold-tone bezel, sweep second hand, VG, P4.....................**$90.00**

Bugs Bunny, Timex/Warner Bros, 1955, carrots as hands, C10..**$325.00**

Buzz Corey Space Patrol, US Time, 1950, shows military & standard time, w/working compass, MIB, C10 ....**$750.00**

Campbell's Soup Kid (boy), 1982, 50th Anniversary, working, EX, P6 ....**$48.00**

Capt Marvel, Fawcett, 1948, Capt Marvel holding airplane on face, NM (EX box) **$650.00**

Capt Marvel, w/orig band, unused, M, C10 ....**$350.00**

Child's Play's Chucky, MOC, T1 ....$35.00

Cinderella, US Time, 1951, pink band, complete with Cinderella figure, MIB, from $250.00 to $400.00.

Dale Evans, Ingraham-Bradley, 1957, Dale posing on brn, rnd bezel w/rectangular chrome case, rpl leather band, VG, P4....$85.00

Dale Evans Queen of the West, Bradley, 1950s, features Dale & Buttermilk on face, leather band, NM (EX pop-up box), A..$395.00

Dan Quayle, his tie as hands that run backward, M (orig 'Quayle' egg-carton box), C10 ....$150.00

Dick Tracy, New Haven, 1947, working, orig band, VG+, D11 ....$125.00

Dick Tracy, Omni, electronic digital & musical, w/papers, NM (orig space coupe pkg), D11 ....$125.00

Dick Tracy, Omni, 1981, digital, NM (orig mc cb police car box w/movable plastic wheels)...$100.00

Dick Tracy Moving Gun Wristwatch, Chicago Tribune/USF/ New Haven, 1951, Swiss, lg chrome case, NM, P4 .$275.00

Disney, Official 1995 Disneyana Convention, Fantasma, 1995, Japan movement, lg gold-tone case, blk leather band, MIB, P4 ....$135.00

Disney Credit Card Exclusive, 1993, limited to 5,000, Sorcerer Mickey w/star circle on face, leather strap, MIB, M8..$100.00

Disney New Fantasyland Cast Members, 1993, limited to 1,000, Pinocchio, Jiminy & Figaro w/Cleo second hand, M (M pouch), M8..$125.00

Disney's Haunted Mansion Cast Member, 1994, limited edition of 999, M(orig tin box), M8 ....$300.00

Disneyana Convention Walt Disney World, 1994, Sorcerer Mickey w/broom, limited to 3,000, M (wood box), M8........$75.00

Disneyland Matterhorn 35th Anniversary, 1994, limited to 1,000, M (M blk velvet pouch), M8 ....$150.00

Disneyland Tower of Terror, 1995, w/certificate & countertop display, sold to public at opening, M, M8 ....$90.00

Disneyland 35 Years Anniversary, Lorus, 1990, quartz, blk plastic case, sweep second hand, blk leather band, M, P4..$30.00

Donald Duck, box only (for pocket watch), Ingersoll, 1939, Donald & Mickey listen to watch tick, bl background, 2x2", EX $200.00

Donald Duck, 1934, pocket watch, Mickey decal on back, orig box, C10 ....$1,100.00

Donald Duck Birthday Watch, Bradley/WDP, Donald on face, bl band, w/warranty, unused, NM (NM box), A $180.00

Dukes of Hazzard, Unisonic, 1981, LCD quartz, w/stainless steel band, NRFB, H4 ....$40.00

Ernest, unknown maker/Cardin & Cherry Advertising Agency, 1987, Japan movement, blk acrylic case & band, VG, P4................$35.00

Flash Gordon, Bradley/King Features, 1979, Swiss movement, chrome case, sweep second hand, M (M plain Bradley box), P4 ....$200.00

Gene Autry Moving Gun Wristwatch, New Haven, 1951, Swiss movement, lg chrome case, western-style leather band, VG, P4 ....$225.00

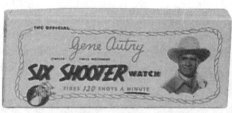
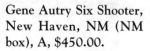

Gene Autry Six Shooter, New Haven, NM (NM box), A, $450.00.

Goofy, Lorus/Walt Disney, 1991, Japan movement, gold-tone bezel, numbers reversed, runs backwards, M, P4 ....$30.00

Hopalong Cassidy, box only, US Time, 1950, blk & wht photo image of Hoppy, red background, w/insert, 7x4", EX+, A...........$150.00

Hopalong Cassidy, US Time/William Boyd, sm rnd chrome case, Good Luck From Hoppy on back, lt wear to orig band, VG, P4 ....$80.00

Hopalong Cassidy, 100th Anniversary, w/neckerchief & steer-head slide, MIB, C10..$100.00

Howdy Doody, display only, Ingraham/Kagran, 1954, diecut cb Howdy w/hand outstretched to hold watch, 7", EX, A....$250.00

James Bond 007, Gilbert-Eon/Glidrose Prod, 1965, Swiss movement, lg cycolac case, world time dial, velcro band, VG, P4 ....$165.00

Jetsons, w/George & Astro, MIP, T1................................$25.00

Jetsons the Movie, 1990, digital quartz, purple, MOC, I2...$8.00

Joe Carioca, US Time, 1950s, Birthday series, Joe Carioca parrot on face, yel band, rare, NM (EX+ box), A...............$420.00

Jughead, Cheval/Archie Comic Pub, Hong Kong, 1989, plastic case, burger & soda orbit Jughead, plastic band, MIB, P4..........$30.00

Lion King, Fantasma/Company D, Japan, 1994, quartz, artist's proof (1 of 5), Mufasa on dial, Simba on crystal, M, P4 ....$300.00

Little Orphan Annie, New Haven, 1935, Annie on face, maroon band, NM (EX box) $350.00

Little Orphan Annie, New Haven/Harold Gray/News Syndicate, 1948, chrome case, rpl brn leather band, NMIB, P4 ..$325.00

Little Orphan Annie & Sandy, 1970s, comic-strip illus on dial, gold-tone band, M, A6 ....$28.00

Little Rascals, LCD, MOC, T1....................................$30.00

Madonna, MOC, T1..$35.00

Major Moon Moonstones, Ralston, 1983, med chrome case w/sweep second hand, vinyl denim band, NM, P4 ..$100.00

Mary Marvel, Fawcett, 1948, Mary on face, pk band, NM (EX box), A...$290.00

Mickey Mouse, box only, Ingersoll, bl w/image of Mickey atop red banner, VG, M5 ....$150.00

Mickey Mouse, box only, Ingersoll, 1938, w/red image of Mickey w/cane & top hat, 7x4", EX, A $400.00

Mickey Mouse, Classic Moments/Bulova/Walt Disney, 1991, lg silver case, Mickey painting self-portrait, MIB, P4 ....$90.00

Mickey Mouse, for lapel, w/button, orig box, C10 ......$1,650.00

Mickey Mouse, Fossil/Disney, 1993, limited edition, Mickey as rodeo star, w/rodeo kerchief, M (wood box & cover), P4...$110.00

Mickey Mouse, Ingersoll, early 1930s, Mickey second hand, metal band w/stamped Mickeys, EX (VG box w/Mickeys), A..$490.00

Mickey Mouse, Ingersoll, early 1930s, Mickey second hand, metal band w/stamped Mickeys, EX (EX blk plastic box), A......$635.00

Mickey Mouse, Ingersoll, 1933, full-figure Mickey on face, diecut metal Mickeys on band, orig box, C10 ....$700.00

Mickey Mouse, Ingersoll, 1947, measles face, MIB, C10 ...$350.00

Mickey Mouse, Ingersoll/Canadian import, 1933, w/orig insert & papers, NM (illus box), C10.....................................$850.00

Mickey Mouse, light-up display, US Time, 13" diameter, M, $1,700.00.

Mickey Mouse, WDP, 1954, Mickey on face, red band, box mk Mouseketeers, complete w/cb Mickey figure, EX+ (EX+ box), A $375.00

Mickey Mouse, 1939, w/laser repro insert, orig box, C10 .$400.00

Minnie Monroe, Disney/Pedre, 1989, prototype, quartz, dress blowing up, sweep second hand, red leather band, MIB, P4 ....$450.00

Minnie Mouse, Brio, Walt Disney World Showcase of Dolls 1990, limited edition, gold-tone case, leather band, MIB, P4 ....$150.00

Minnie Mouse, Timex, 1958, Minnie on face, yel band, complete w/celluloid plaque, MIB, A $355.00

New Kids on the Block, metal w/leather band, working, EX, I2 ....$12.00

Nightmare Before Christmas/Burger King, 1993, Christmastown, Halloweentown, Pumpkins & Cats w/Pumpkins, M, M8, set of 4 ....$50.00

Pink Panther, w/warranty, MIB, C10.............................$250.00

Popeye, box only (for pocket watch), KFS, Montgomery Ward USA No 45-9686, red, w/insert, 3x3", scarce, EX+, A $395.00

Popeye, 1948, NMIB, C10 ....$1,000.00

Real Ghostbusters, flasher style, M, T1 ....$10.00

Rocketeer, Disney/Hong Kong/China, 1991, Swiss movement, limited edition to Disney employees, MIP, P4.........$350.00

Rocketeer, Hope/Walt Disney Co, 1991, 5-function LCD, gold-tone case, bl vinyl band, MOC, P4/J2 ....$35.00

Rocketter, sweep second hand, tan leather band, Disney chanel premium, MIP, T1 ....$25.00

Roger Rabbit, Lorus/Disney-Amblin, 1990, Japan movement, Ta-Dah silhouette, gold-tone case, blk leather band, MIB, P4 ....$35.00

Roy Rogers, Ingraham, 1951, Roy & Trigger on face, expansion band, scarce, NM+ (EX+ box), A.............................$225.00

Roy Rogers, Ingraham, 1951, Roy on Trigger on face, leather band, w/box insert & instruction slip, NM (NM box), A $355.00

Six Million Dollar Man, Berger/Universal, 1976, Swiss movement, gold-tone bezel, bl leather band, VG, P4.........$75.00

Smitty, New Haven, 1935, Smitty on face, red band, scarce, EX (EX box), A $575.00

Snoopy, Armitron, 1989, LCD, yel case w/bl strap, MOC, H11 ....$15.00

Snoopy, Armitron, 1989, quartz, gold face w/leather band, M, H11 ....$80.00

Snoopy Hero-Time Watch, Determined, Snoopy on red dial with red band, with blue It's Hero Time patch, MIB, $100.00.

Snoopy, Timex #86211, playing tennis, tennis ball as second hand, M, H11 ....$100.00

Snoopy Tennis Player, Timex/UFS, 1970s, Swiss movement, silver bezel, stainless back, leather band, VG, P4..........$75.00

Snow White, Fantasma/Company D, 1994, Japan movement, artist's proof (1 of 5), Wicked Queen on bezel, M, P4 .**$300.00**
Snow White, 1955, w/statue, rare plastic case, C10 ....**$125.00**
Snow White & Dopey, Timex/WDP, 1958, sm rnd chrome case, Snow White at 10:00; Dopey at 4:00, rpl leather band, VG, P4 ....**$65.00**
Snow White & the Seven Dwarfs, 1993, battery-op, MIP, B10.....**$12.00**
Superman, Death of; NMIB, C10..................................**$500.00**
Superman, New Haven, lg sz, EX+, C10........................**$475.00**

Photo courtesy of Dunbar Gallery.

Three Little Pigs, Ingersoll, 1935, wolf's eyes move and tick off seconds, NM (EX box), $2,500.00.

Tom & Jerry, Armitron/Warner Bros, 1991, Looney Tunes 3-D Series, over-sz blk acrylic case & band, quartz, MIB, P4 .**$30.00**
UNCLE Secret Agent, Bradley/MGM, 1966, sm gold-tone aluminum case, Girl Agent on pk dial, red vinyl band, VG, P4 ....**$110.00**
UNCLE Secret Agent, Bradley/MGM, 1966, Swiss movement, Man Agent & glow-in-dark dots on dial, leather band, VG, P4 ....**$95.00**
007 Secret Service Wristwatch, Imperial, 1984, dial lights, MOC, M17...**$56.00**

Character, TV and Movie Collectibles

To the baby boomers who grew up glued to the TV set and addicted to Saturday matinees, the faces they saw on the screen were as familiar to them as family. Just about any character you could name has been promoted through retail merchandising to some extent; depending on the popularity they attain, exposure may continue for weeks, months, even years. It's no wonder, then, that the secondary market abounds with these items or that there is such wide-spread collector interest. For more information, we recommend *Collector's Guide to TV Memorabilia, 1960s & 1970s* by Greg Davis and Bill Morgan; *Howdy Doody* by Jack Koch; *Character Toys and Collectibles, Vols I and II* by David Longest; and *Cartoon Friends of the Baby Boom Era* by Bill Bruegman.

Note: Though most characters are listed by their own names, some will be found under the title of the group, movie, comic strip, or dominate character they're commonly identified with. The Joker, for instance, will be found in the Batman listings.

Advisors: Lisa Adams (A7), Dr. Dolittle; Jerry and Ellen Harnish (H4); Larry Doucet (D11), Dick Tracy; Trina and Randy Kubeck (K1), The Simpsons; Norm Vigue (V1); TV Collector (T6); Casey's Collectible Corner (C1); Bill Stillman (S6), Wizard of Oz.

See also Action Figures; Battery-Operated; Books; Chein; Character Clocks and Watches; Coloring, Activity and Paint Books; Comic Books; Dakins; Disney; Dolls, Celebrity; Fast-Food Collectibles; Fisher-Price; Games; Guns; Halloween Costumes; Lunch Boxes; Marx; Model Kits; Paper Dolls; Pin-Back Buttons; Plastic Figures; Playsets; Puppets; Puzzles; Records; Toothbrush Holders; View-Master; Western; Windups, Friction and Other Mechanicals.

A-Team, air freshener, Mr T, 1983, MIP, J7 ....**$8.00**
A-Team, Colorforms Adventure Set, 1983, NMIB, J7 .....**$20.00**
A-Team, dinnerware set, 1983, plastic, MIB (sealed), J7 .**$25.00**
A-Team, party hat, set of 4 different, EX, J7 ....**$8.00**
A-Team, tray, 1983, litho metal, 17x12", EX, J7 ....**$15.00**
A-Team, vehicle, 1983, diecast, 1/64 scale, M (NM card), H4..**$5.00**

Addams Family, bank, Thing, Pointer Products, 1964, hand pops out to grab coin, battery-operated, EX (EX box), $45.00.

Alf, doll, stuffed, 17", EX, I2..**$5.00**
Aliens, pinball machine sticker/poster, Konami, 1990, 28x18", EX, H4..**$30.00**
All in the Family, doll, Joey Stivic, Ideal, 1976, NMIB, C17.**$45.00**
Alphonse & Gaston, handkerchief, ca 1902, 6-panel comic strip on silk, signed F Opper, 12x12", EX+, A3 ....**$125.00**
Alvin & the Chipmunks, Curtain Call Theater, Ideal, 1983, MIB, B10...**$25.00**
Alvin & the Chipmunks, doll, Alvin, 1987, stuffed, 7", EX, J7 .**$6.00**
Alvin & the Chipmunks, On Tour Van, Ideal, 1983, MIB, B10..**$28.00**
Alvin & the Chipmunks, outfit, Ideal, 1983, plush, for 10" doll, EX, B10...**$8.00**
Alvin & the Chipmunks, soap dispenser, Helm Products, 1984, MIB, B10..**$10.00**
Amos 'N Andy, tablet, C10...**$40.00**
Annie (Movie), ball, High Bounce, 1981, MOC, J7 ....**$10.00**
Annie (Movie), belt, 1981, leather, EX, J7 ....**$8.00**
Annie (Movie), doll, Applause, 1982, porcelain, MIB.....**$30.00**
Annie (Movie), doll, Knickerbocker, 1982, w/party dress & shoes, MIB, from $25 to..**$35.00**

Annie (Movie), napkins, 1980s, Happy Birthday, MIP (sealed), J7 ....$6.00

Annie (Movie), tray, 1982, litho metal, 17x12", EX, J7...$15.00

Annie, see also Little Orphan Annie

Arachnophobia, Big Bob Spider, Remco, 1990, MOC, H4 ..$8.00

Archies, carrying case, Marx, EX, H4/J7, from $30 to $35.00

Archies, figure, Ronson, 1920s, tin, pull string to make eyes spark, needs new flint, 9x6", H12............................$225.00

Archies, Gang at Pop's Color & Play Time Activity Set, Whitman, 1970, M (NM box), H4............................$30.00

Archies, Iron-On Transfer Book, Golden, 1977, 6 different full pgs, unused, NM, C1 ....$27.00

Aristocats, Colorforms, 1960s, NM (EX box), F8.............$38.00

Bamm-Bamm, see Flintstones

Banana Splits, Kut-Up Kit, Larami, 1973, MIP (sealed), F8 ....$8.00

Banana Splits, tambourine, MIP, T1 ....$35.00

Barney Google, sheet music, ...Goo Goo Goo-Gilly Eyes, 1923, mc graphics, VG+, A3...................................$35.00

Barney Rubble, see Flintstones

Bart Simpson & other Simpson characters, see Simpsons

Batgirl, slipper socks, 1979, knit w/red soles, unused, M, C1 .$36.00

Batman, air freshener, 1970s, mc diecut, unused, MIP, T1.$6.00

Batman, bank, Penguin bust, Mego, w/orig sticker, NM, P12..$60.00

Batman, Batchute, CDC, 1966, official figure w/27" chute, M (NM card), D9..$38.00

Batman, Batmobile, Aurora, HO scale, M (orig clear plastic case), H4...$150.00

Batman, Batmobile, Ertl, 1989, 1/64 scale, M (silhouette card), H4..$8.00

Batman, bread bag, 1960s, M, D8..................................$18.00

Batman, charm bracelet, DC Comics, 1966, 5 mc character charms on gold-tone chain, EX, A3 ....$50.00

Batman, coin purse, 1991, orange soft plastic w/logo & carry clip, M, T2 ....$7.00

Batman, coins, 1966, complete set of 20, MIP, T1 ....$65.00

Batman, Colorforms, 1966, NMIB, F8 ....$40.00

Batman, doll, Joker, hard head w/stuffed body, 13", EX, J7..$40.00

Batman, doll, Penguin, Applause, vinyl, 10", M, D4 ....$10.00

Batman, figure, China, vinyl w/cloth cape, all blk version, EX details, 12", M (orig bag w/header card), H4 ....$25.00

Batman, figure, 1973, bendable, NM, H4 ....$25.00

Batman, film, 1960s, The Adventures of Batman, 8mm, 200-ft, EX+ (orig box), A3...$20.00

Batman, Helicopter, Empire Toys, 1977, EX (EX box), H4 ..$30.00

Batman, lamp, 1966, mc figure w/cloth cape, 11", NM, C17..$125.00

Batman, lamp, Vanity Fair Industries, plastic, 7½" wide with expandable arm for light, EX, $135.00.

Batman, magazine, Look, 1966, EX+, D8.........................$45.00

Batman, magic slate, Golden, 1989, MIP (sealed), P3........$3.00

Batman, Make-A-Show refill kit, 1973, MIB, D8.............$55.00

Batman, makeup kit, Joker, 1989, MIB, J7 ....$8.00

Batman, milk bottle stopper, C10 ....$40.00

Batman, Paint-By-Number Set, Hasbro, 1973, partially painted canvas, NMIB, F8 ....$34.00

Batman, party hat, Amscan/Canada, 1972, cb, 7", unused, M, T2.$10.00

Batman, patch, Batman or Robin, 1966, C10, ea $35.00

Batman, pencil, w/Penguin topper, NM, P3 ....$2.00

Batman, pillow, Batman Returns, 18" sq, NM, P3 ....$10.00

Batman, print, Dayco/Pilgrim, sturdy cb w/cartoon scene over Gotham City, 16x20", lt edge wear o/w EX, J5 ....$40.00

Batman, sleeping bag, 1975, 2 sm tears o/w EX+, F8 ....$48.00

Batman, snow-cone cup, 1960s, cb, unused, 5½", M, M5...$4.00

Batman, spoon & fork, Imperial Knife/NPPI, 1966, stainless steel w/raised image, mk Batman, unused, NM (EX+ card), A $65.00

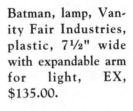

Batman, stand-up store display figure from 1st movie, cb, 60", EX, H4 ....$45.00

Batman, String Art Kit, Smith, 1976, MIB (sealed), F8 ...$65.00

Batman, sunglasses, licensed 1966, w/paper label, scarce, M $90.00

Batman, Thing-Maker, Mattel, 1965, makes bats & insignia, working, EX+, F8 ....$55.00

Batman & Superman, bicycle spoke cover, DC Comics, 1966, plastic disk w/decal ea side, 3" dia, NM, C1 ....$30.00

Battlestar Galactica, Colorforms Adventure Set, 1978, deluxe version, NM (EX+ box) $30.00

Battlestar Galactica, Poster Art Set, Craft Master, 1978, 2 posters, 6 pens & instructions, MIP (sealed), H4 ....$30.00

Battlestar Galactica, wall plaque, Richard Hatch, EX, J7 .$20.00

Beany & Cecil, doll, Beany, Mattel, 15", missing propeller o/w VG+, I2 ....$30.00

Beany & Cecil, music box, Mattel, M, S15 ....$150.00

Beany & Cecil, music box, Mattel, not working o/w EX, J7 ....$40.00

Ben Casey, charm bracelet, Sears, 1962, steel w/plastic pearls, NMOC, F8 ....$25.00

Photo courtesy of June Moon.

Ben Casey, doctor kit, Transogram, 1960s, includes 8 accessories, EX, $30.00.

Betty Boop, doll, Cameo Doll/Fleischer Studios, jtd wood body w/compo head, molded blk dress, 13½", EX $800.00

Betty Boop, fan, prewar Japan, image of Betty w/moving eyes, paper & wood, 5", M, A $175.00

Betty Boop, figures, prewar Japan, bsk, set of 4 w/Betty playing instruments, 3½", NM, A $475.00

Betty Boop, tablet, Fleischer Studios, shows Betty as teacher w/Bimbo & Koko as students, scarce, EX, A $250.00

Betty Boop, tea set, Fleischer Studios, 1930s, lustreware, blond Betty, complete, EX, from $500 to $600.00

Betty Boop & Mickey Mouse, fan, 1930s, shows Mickey sawing chair that Betty sits on, wood hdl, 7", scarce, EX+, A $1,100.00

Betty Rubble, see Flintstones

Beverly Hillbillies Car, Ideal, bl & red plastic w/seated characters, 23", EX (orig box), A $470.00

Bewitched, tablet, 1964, 8x10", unused, M, from $15 to ..$22.00

Big Bird, see Sesame Street

Bimbo (Betty Boop's Dog), pitcher, Spain, 1930s, ceramic, Bimbo balances on base mk Recuerdo..., 8", rare, EX, A $685.00

Bionic Woman, Paint-By-Number Set, MIB, T1 ....$45.00

Bionic Woman, Tatoos & Stickers, Kenner, 1976, 8 stickers & 1 sheet of 28 tatoos, MOC, D9 ....$8.00

Blondie, figure, Alexander, King Features, dtd 1944, pnt compo, 3½", NM A6 ....$25.00

Blondie, sandwich bag, 1952, Dagwood making sandwiches, 7x5", unused, M, T2 ....$25.00

Blue Knight, toy watch, 1976, MOC, B3 ....$12.00

Bonanza, hat, Little Joe, C10 ....$55.00

Bonnie Braids, see Dick Tracy

Bonzo, bank, Elastolin/Germany, compo, VG, S15 ....$325.00

Bonzo, figure, Occupied Japan, rectangular opening at back probably for pincushion, 4", M, P6 ....$85.00

Bonzo, figure, 1930s, chalkware w/mc highlights, 7", EX, P6 ....$60.00

Bonzo, valentine, Germany, 1920s, mc litho, M, P6 ....$35.00

Boo Boo, see Yogi Bear

Photo courtesy of Dunbar Gallery.

Bozo the Clown, bank, 1960s, composition, 19", VG, $85.00.

Bozo the Clown, bank, 1972, vinyl, EX, J2 ....$25.00

Bozo the Clown, Colorforms, 1962, NM (EX+ box), F8 ..$28.00

Bozo the Clown, doll, Capitol Records, 1960s, stuffed, EX, J7 ....$25.00

Bozo the Clown, doll, Knickerbocker, 1960s, stuffed body, rubber head w/orange yarn hair, 20", EX+, F8 ....$40.00

Bozo the Clown, doll, Mattel, talker, MIB $150.00

Bozo the Clown, doll, Mattel, talker, working, NM, J2 ....$90.00

Bozo the Clown, doll, Mattel, talker (non-working), G ...$10.00

Bozo the Clown, figure, Super Flex, MOC, J7 ....$20.00

Bozo the Clown, party favors, MIP, J7 ....$12.00

Bozo the Clown, toy watch, Japan, 1960s, plastic, tin & paper, MIP, P4 ....$6.00

Brady Bunch, Fishing Fun Set, 1973, MOC, J7 ....$40.00

Buck Rogers, Astral Heroes Printing Set, Stamperkraft/JFD, 1930s, complete, scarce, NM (NM box), A $825.00

Buck Rogers, cassette, Mark 56 Records, 1970s, MIP (sealed), A6 ....$8.50

Buck Rogers, Communications Set, HG, 1979, working walkie-talkies & other pcs, no code wheel, MIP $50.00

Buck Rogers, Magic Erasable Dot Pictures, Transogram, 1950s, complete, NM (EX box), A..$80.00

Buck Rogers, pencil box, Dille, 1935, emb w/12 characters & spaceships naming ea on side panel, 10", EX, A $85.00

Buck Rogers, Super Sonic Glasses (binoculars), EX+ (VG box), T1..$145.00

Buck Rogers, 25th Century Electronic Walkie-Talkies, Remco, NMIB, T1 ....$250.00

Buffy & Mrs Beasley, doll, Mattel, talker, MIB..............$250.00

Buffy & Mrs Beasley, doll, Mattel, talker (non-working), G...........$50.00

Bugs Bunny, bank, Homecraft, 1972, mc vinyl, 13", EX, C17........$25.00

Bugs Bunny, bookends, 1970, EX, J7, pr..........................$20.00

Bugs Bunny, Cartoon Pals Paint-By-Number, Craft, 1979, MIB (sealed), C1...$22.00

Bugs Bunny, cookie mold, 1978, EX, J7...........................$5.00

Bugs Bunny, cup dispenser, 1989, MIP..........................$8.00

Bugs Bunny, desk lamp, figure atop rnd base, T1 ....$45.00

Bugs Bunny, doll, Mattel, 1972, talker, 12", working, EX, C17 ......$50.00

Bugs Bunny, doll, Mattel, 1976, Chatter Chum, 10", EX, B10.......$25.00

Bugs Bunny, doll, Mighty Star, stuffed, 18", NM, C17 .....$15.00

Bugs Bunny, doll, 1964, rubber head w/stuffed body, talker, not working o/w EX, J7 ....$35.00

Bugs Bunny, figure, Mattel, 1978, plastic, talker, 8", S15.$10.00

Bugs Bunny, invitations, Warner Bros, 1981, MOC, J7......$6.00

Bugs Bunny, jack-in-the-box, Mattel, 1970s, VG, C17....$15.00

Bugs Bunny, magic slate, Golden, 1987, MIP (sealed), P3 P3...$4.00

Bugs Bunny, pencil case, 1975, vinyl, EX, C17..................$15.00

Bugs Bunny, planter, Shaw, 1940s, 5x4", EX, P6............$125.00

Bugs Bunny, shakers, Warner Bros, 1950s, ceramic, EX, P6, pr $225.00

Bugs Bunny, slippers, EX, J7, pr..$10.00

Bugs Bunny, tray, 1982, litho metal, 17x12", EX, J7.........$10.00

Bugs Bunny & Elmer Fudd, tote bag, 1978, vinyl, VG, C17 ....$15.00

Bugs Bunny & Sniffles, figure, glazed ceramic, Sniffles sitting at Bugs Bunny's ft, 9", EX+, A $140.00

Bullwinkle, doll, Mighty Star, 1980s, stuffed plush w/tag, 18", EX, C17...$18.00

Bullwinkle, figure, General Mills, 1969, rubber, 2", EX+, F8...$15.00

Bullwinkle, figure, Wham-O, 1972, bendable, EX, J7.......$20.00

Bullwinkle, Peabody & Sherman, flicker card, Wheat Hearts, 1960, 1" sq, M, F8...$9.00

Bullwinkle, Spelling & Counting Board, Larami, 1969, M (EX card), C1 ....$28.00

Bullwinkle, see also Rocky & Bullwinkle

Buster Brown & Tige, doll, 1924, mc print cloth, uncut, 18x42", EX, A3...$275.00

Buzz Sawyer, Christmas card, 1950s, unused, NM+, C1 ...$14.00

Cabbage Patch Kids, tray, 1983, 17x12", EX, J7 ....$12.00

Capt Caveman, figure, 1970s, plastic, 3", EX+, F8 ....$25.00

Capt Marvel, bank, registers dimes, C10........................$300.00

Capt Marvel, figure, 1970s, pnt ceramic, 2", M, A6...........$4.00

Capt Marvel, Magic Flute, Lee-Tex Rubber/Fawcett, 1946, EX (orig card), A...$170.00

Capt Marvel, party horn, 1946, heavy cb w/plastic mouthpiece, yel w/illus & logo, 4½", EX, A3...........................$150.00

Capt. Kangaroo, doll, Mattel, 1967, pull-string talker, mute, otherwise EX, J6, $55.00.

Photo courtesy of June Moon.

Capt Marvel, pennant, 1940s, bl felt w/name & graphics, 15", EX, A3 ....$250.00

Capt Marvel, Power Siren display, Fawcett Pub, 1940, Capt Marvel & Whiz Comics above 12 attached whistles, scarce, NM, A $2,400.00

Capt Marvel, tie clip, Fawcett, 1946, gold-tone metal w/bust image, EX (orig card), K4 ....$70.00

Capt Video, Supersonic Spaceships, Lido, complete w/8 plastic spaceships in various colors, NM (EX display box), A..$235.00

Casper the Friendly Ghost, bank, 1970s, plastic w/decals, 1 age crack o/w EX, C17 ....$20.00

Casper the Friendly Ghost, candy bucket, plastic, EX+, T1.$30.00

Casper the Friendly Ghost, doll, Mattel, talker, MIB.....$225.00

Casper the Friendly Ghost, doll, Mattel, talker (non-working), G..$25.00

Casper the Friendly Ghost, doll, Talk Ups, Mattel, MIB .$75.00

Casper the Friendly Ghost, doll, Talk Ups, Mattel, non-working, G $15.00

Casper the Friendly Ghost, doll, 1960s, stuffed plush w/Casper sweater, VG, C17...$20.00

Casper the Friendly Ghost, figure, 1970s, bendable, EX, C17 ....$12.00

Casper the Friendly Ghost, Harvey Comics advertising sign, HFS, 1957, images of Casper in Santa hat & turban, EX+, A $75.00

Casper the Friendly Ghost, lamp shade, mc character cast, orig cellophane wrappers, H12 ....$45.00

Cecil the Seasick Serpent, doll, Mattel, talker, MIB......$300.00

Cecil the Seasick Serpent, doll, Mattel, talker (non-working), G $45.00

Charlie Brown, see Peanuts

Charlie Chaplin, pencil box, 1930s, tin, EX, J2...............$60.00

Charlie McCarthy, doll, Effanbee, cloth body w/compo head & extremities, orig blk suit & hat, 19", EX, A $550.00

Charlie's Angels, Colorforms, 1978, missing 1 gun, NM (EX box), F8..$28.00

Charlie's Angels, cosmetic kit, 1970s, w/mirror & bag, MIB, H12 ....$65.00

Charlie's Angels, jewelry set, Fleet, 1977, M (NM card), C1 .$50.00

Charlie's Angels, necklace, Farrah, 1977, MOC, J7 ....$30.00

Charlie's Angels, purse, vinyl box style, blk names on beige, 8" L, NM, B3 ....$20.00

Charlie's Angels, underwater action gear, MIB, J7 ....$45.00

Charlie's Angels, 3-D viewer, Fleet, 1977, 4 strips w/viewer, M (NM card), C1 ....$45.00

Child's Play, doll, Chucky, 1991, 18", M, from $20 to $25.00

Chilly Willy, bank, Royalty, 1972, vinyl w/felt hat, unlicensed, 12", NM, F8 ....$45.00

Chilly Willy, movie, Yukon Have It, 1960s, 8mm blk & wht 50-ft cartoon, NMIB, F8 ....$10.00

Chimp on the Farm, movie, Castle Films No 623, 16mm, EX; Andy Panda, movie, Castle Films No 485, 16mm, EX, J6, $24.00 each.

CHiPs, Emergency Medical Kit, 1980, complete w/mc photo case, MIB, C1 ....$36.00

Clarabell, see Howdy Doody

Creature From the Black Lagoon, 3-D viewing glasses, unused, M, T1 ....$15.00

Daddy Warbucks, rubber stamp, 1932, 2¼", complete, EX, A6.$4.00

Daffy Duck, place mat, Warner Bros/Pepsi, EX, J7 ....$7.00

Dennis the Menace, Stuff 'n Lace Doll, Standard Toycraft, MIP, J6, $35.00.

Dennis the Menace, curtains, M, V1, pr $70.00

Dennis the Menace, doll, 14", EX, J2.............................$100.00

Dennis the Menace, figure, Hall Syndicate, 1959, vinyl, 8", EX, P6 ....$85.00

Dennis the Menace, helmet, Ideal, 1950s, unused, MIB, J2 .$75.00

Dennis the Menace, Mischief Kit, Hassenfeld Bros, 1955, MIB, M17..$80.00

Dennis the Menace, night light, w/Ruff, T1 ....$55.00

Deputy Dawg, Colorforms, M (VG box), C17 ....$30.00

Dick Tracy, belt buckle, 1960s, mc plastic profile mounted on gold- or silver-toned metal, EX+, D11, ea..................$20.00

Dick Tracy, braces (suspenders), early 1950s, w/badge, magnifying glass & whistle, NMIB, D11 ....$90.00

Dick Tracy, business card, preprinted for Rick Fletcher, artist from 1961-1983, dtd 1979, M, D11 ....$10.00

Dick Tracy, calendar, Copy Express of Woodstock, 1988, blk & wht cover, NM, D11 ....$25.00

Dick Tracy, calendar, Copy Express of Woodstock, 1988, mc cover, NM, D11 ....$45.00

Dick Tracy, calendar poster, 1990, This Year They're Out To Get Him, w/logo, scarce, D11 ....$75.00

Dick Tracy, camera, Seymour Sales, 1950s, 127mm, Dick Tracy & profile on lens, EX (orig box missing 1 flap), D11 .$75.00

Dick Tracy, candy wrapper, Schutter Candy Co, early 1950s, NM, D11 ....$25.00

Dick Tracy, charms, Sam Catchem, Gravel Gertie or Sparkle Plenty, from gumball machine, D11, ea $20.00

Dick Tracy, Christmas tree light bulb, 1940s, mc glass, 3¼", EX+, D11 ....$65.00

Dick Tracy, coin, 1980s, nearly pure silver w/emb Tracy, limited edition, uncirculated, MIP (sealed), D11 ....$40.00

Dick Tracy, Colorforms Adventure Kit, 1962, NMIB, J7 .$65.00

Dick Tracy, Crime Stoppers Set, Laramie, 1967, complete, EX+ (orig bubble pkg), D11..................................$35.00

Dick Tracy, display card, Criss Cross Card Machine, 1930s, w/5 penny cards & 6 for 5¢ sign, NM, scarce, D11.........$100.00

Dick Tracy, doll, Bonnie Braids, EX, T1 ....$100.00

Dick Tracy, Electric Casting Outfit, Allied Mfg/FAS, incomplete, VG (VG+ box), A..$200.00

Dick Tracy, figure, Bonny Braids, Charmore, 1951, plastic, 1¼", EX+ (EX card), D11 ....$50.00

Dick Tracy, figure, Jr, Rubb'r Niks, 1968, poseable w/magnetic space car, 6", NM (orig bubble card), D11 ....$35.00

Dick Tracy, figure, Tracy, Rubb'r Niks, 1968, poseable w/gun, wrist radio & holster, 6", NM (orig bubble card), D11 ....$45.00

Dick Tracy, figures, Dick Tracy, Jr & Chief Brandon, 1930s, cast lead, 3½", D11 ....$75.00

Dick Tracy, flashlight, 1950s, etched Tracy on side, bl body w/red top, 3x1x½", EX+ (orig box), D11 ....$50.00

Dick Tracy, Handcuffs for Jr, John Henry #800, early 1940s, metal, EX (red card), D11 ....$50.00

Dick Tracy, holster, Mattel, 1961, rubber, NM, D11.......$20.00

Dick Tracy, iron-on transfer, NY Daily News, Aug 1975, comic section w/mc profile inside, NM, D11 ....$25.00

Dick Tracy, lithograph, Chester Memorial Library, 1990, limited edition of 500, 8½x11", D11 ....$20.00

Dick Tracy, magazine, NEMO, Chester Gould & Dick Tracy Special Issue, February 1986, NM, D11 ....$15.00

Dick Tracy, magazine ad, Saturday Evening Post, March 1966, Ford Autolite w/Piston Puss, full pg, D11 ....$10.00

Dick Tracy, magnifying glass, Laramie, 1979, MOC, C1..$20.00

Dick Tracy, newspaper ad, Quaker Radio Show, 1938, Get Dick Tracy's Secret Detecto Kit, 10x14", EX, D11 ....$20.00

Dick Tracy, newspaper ad, Quaker Radio Show, 1938-39, shows available premiums, 10x14", NM, D11 ....$25.00

Dick Tracy, note pad, 1970s, Tracy profile & Rick Fletcher signature on cover, 3½x7x¼", M, D11 ....$15.00

Dick Tracy, postcard, Reuben Award Winner Series, 1987, Dick Tracy in 3-D, NM, D11 ....$20.00

Dick Tracy, postcard, Reuben Award Winner Series, 1987, Tracy in lab w/Wormy, TV Wiggles & Mrs Frost, NM, D11...$20.00

Dick Tracy, postcard, Reuben Award Winner Series, 1987, Tracy in lab w/Measles, Sleet & Larceny Lou, NM, D11 ....$20.00

Dick Tracy, postcard, 1943, pilot w/Tracy in praying pose in airplane, NM, rare, D11.................................$100.00

Dick Tracy, poster, San Diego Comic Co, 1970s, mylar, 19x25", NM, D11...$100.00

Dick Tracy, press kit, Dick Tracy Movie, 9 glossy photos, 56-pg booklet & mc folder, NM, scarce, D11 ....$75.00

Dick Tracy, Sparkle Paints, Kenner, 1963, 6 pictures & pnt bottles, MIB (sealed), D11.................................$80.00

Dick Tracy, stickers, 1970s, 17 different of Tracy & villains, 3½x¾", D11 ....$20.00

Dick Tracy, store display, Dick Tracy Movie, 1990, for video tapes, mc illus 3-part, 3-D standee, 14x10x6", D11 ...$30.00

Dick Tracy, tie tack, Dick Tracy Jr Detective Agency, 1930s, EX, scarce, D11 ....$90.00

Dick Tracy, TV Watch, Ja-Ru-Toys, plastic wristwatch viewer w/2 boxes of paper filmstrips, NMIP, D11.................$20.00

Dick Tracy, wallet, 1973, blk vinyl w/Tracy profile, 3½x2½", w/6 Crime Stopper Textbook cards, NM, D11 ....$20.00

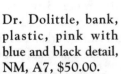

Dr. Dolittle, bank, plastic, pink with blue and black detail, NM, A7, $50.00.

Dick Tracy, wallpaper section, 1950s, shows 3 rows of drawings of 6 characters, 19x19", EX+, D11, from $50 to $75.00

Dick Tracy, wrist radio, Da Myco, ca 1947, unused w/clips & papers, scarce, MIB, D11......................................$1,000.00

Dino, see Flintstones

Dr Dolittle, bank, Sea Snail, AJ Renzi Plastic Corp, 1971, pk, NM, A7...$50.00

Dr Dolittle, Cartoon Kit, Colorforms #456, NMIB, A7 ...$40.00

Dr Dolittle, doll, Dr Dolittle, Mattel #5349, talker, 24", NMIB, A7...$150.00

Dr Dolittle, doll, Dr Dolittle w/Polynesia, Mattel #3575, poseable, 6", NMIB, A7......................................$60.00

Dr Dolittle, Fun Sponge Bath Toy, Amsco #1591, NMIB, A7...$30.00

Dr Dolittle, hat, Jacobson Hat Co, beany type in animal print, NMIP, A7...$20.00

Dr Dolittle, jack-in-the-box, working, NM, T1 ....$85.00

Dr Dolittle, lawn shower-spray toy, Sea Snail, AJ Renzi Plastic Corp, 1975, pk, NMIB, A7..................................$50.00

Dr Dolittle, medical kit, Hasbro #1345, NMIB, A7..........$75.00

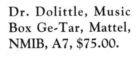

Dr. Dolittle, Music Box Ge-Tar, Mattel, NMIB, A7, $75.00.

Dr Dolittle, music box, Giraffe, Mattel #4747, jack-in-the-box style, NMIB, A7...$50.00

Dr Dolittle, party centerpiece, Hallmark, NMIP, A7 ....$20.00

Dr Dolittle, party plates, Hallmark, w/animals & their names, MIP, A7 ....$15.00

Dr Dolittle, periscope, Bar-Zim #609, NMIP, A7 ....$30.00

Dr Dolittle, projector, Ugly Mugly, Remco #1937, w/slides from movie, NMIB, A7...$50.00

Dr Dolittle, pull-string toy, Pushmi-Pullyu, Mattel, 1967, plush 2-headed llama, mute o/w MIB (sealed), J6.............$140.00

Dr Dolittle, Spelling & Counting Board, Bar-Zim #1059, NMIP, A7 ....$35.00

Dr Dolittle, stick horse, Toggle the Horse, AJ Renzi Plastic Corp, 1972, NMIP, A7...$40.00

Dr Dolittle, Stitch-a-Story, Hasbro #1520, NMIP, A7.....$25.00

Dr Dolittle, tablet, NMIP, A7 ....$15.00

Dr Suess, book bag, Cat in the Hat, 1970s-80s, cloth, 9x11", unused, NM, F8 ....$12.00

Dr Suess, doll, Cat in the Hat, Mattel, talker, rag & plush, MIB..$300.00

Dr Suess, doll, Cat in the Hat, Mattel, talker (non-working), rag & plush, G $100.00

Dr Suess, doll, Horton the Elephant, sitting on elf & nest, w/orig tag, M, T1 ....$50.00

Dr Suess, doll, Lorax, Coleco, MIB, H4 ....$40.00

Dr Suess, jack-in-the-box, Cat in the Hat, 1970, plays For He's a Jolly Good Fellow, working, EX+, F8.................$120.00

Dr Suess, rocking chair, Cat in the Hat, for infant, slightly worn pnt o/w EX, I2 ....$50.00

Dracula, figure, Universal Studios, bendable, MOC, B10....$8.00

Dragnet, badge, Sergeant Los Angeles Police 714, EX, I2 .$20.00

Dragnet, Talking Police Car, Ideal, 1955, plastic, crank in trunk provides talking action, 14", EX+ (EX box), A $260.00

Dukes of Hazzard, cereal bowl, EX, J7 ....$12.00

Dukes of Hazzard, Etch-A-Sketch Fun Screens, 1981, MIP, J7 ......$15.00

Dukes of Hazzard, guitar, 1981, EX, J7 ....$45.00

Dukes of Hazzard, tray, 1981, litho metal, 17x12", EX, J7 ..$20.00

Elmer Fudd, pencil holder, 1940s, diecast figure, NM, T1...........$125.00

Ernest Goes to Camp, doll, Ernest P Worrel, Kenner, 1989, talker, 17", NRFB, M15 ....$25.00

Ernie, see Sesame Street

ET, book bag, faux leather w/buckles & adjustable shoulder strap, EX+, T1..$50.00

ET, Colorforms, 1982, MIB $20.00

ET, doll, Showtime, 1982, plush, 8", NM, P3 ....$6.00

ET, figure, poseable arms, neck extends, 4", MOC, D4 ....$10.00

ET, key chain, figural, M, D4..$3.00

ET, ring, 1982, EX, J7 ....$5.00

ET, stickers, Stick-On Fuzzies, 1982, MOC, J7 ....$6.00

ET, tray, 1982, litho metal, 17x12", EX, J7 ....$15.00

Fall Guy, truck, Fleetwood, 1981, motorized, break-apart model, MOC..$12.00

Family Affair, doll, Mrs Beasley, Mattel, 1976, stuffed body, 10", talker (non-working), G $50.00

Family Affair, hat box, Buffy, 1969, EX, J7 ....$50.00

Family Matters, doll, Steve Urkel, Hasbro, 1991, 18", EX, B10...$10.00

Family Matters, doll, Steve Urkel, Hasbro, 1991, 18", NRFB, M15..$32.00

Fantastic Four, notebook, 1975, EX, J2 ....$20.00

Felix the Cat, box, unmk, various images of Felix & mouse on pk fabric cover, 8" L, EX, A....................................$110.00

Felix the Cat, dexterity game, mk Germany, 1920s, litho of Felix trying to trap mouse, 2" dia, NM, A.......................$200.00

Felix the Cat, dish, unmk, 1930s, china w/2 illus of Felix, 5" dia, EX, A $25.00

Felix the Cat, doll, stuffed felt w/bendable arms & tail, 15", NM+, A $150.00

Felix the Cat, doll, unmk European, stuffed felt w/glass eyes, tail can be used for balancing, 13", NM, A $120.00

Felix the Cat, doll, 1920s-30s, stuffed mohair w/hump back, movable arms & legs, 14", NM, A..........................$50.00

Felix the Cat, figure, 1920s-30s, wood w/leather ears, jtd, 8", VG+, J5 ....$395.00

Felix the Cat, pencil box, C10 ....$165.00

Felix the Cat, valentine, Germany, mechanical, EX, P6 ..$50.00

Felix the Cat (unauthorized), pump, Japan, pressed steel w/wooden plunger hdl, 7", EX+, A $195.00

Flash Gordon, Christmas light shade set, Flash Gordon Cheers, General Electric/Texolite, 1934, set of 8, NM (VG box), A..$225.00

Flash Gordon, Colorforms, 1980, MIB, M17 ....$30.00

Flash Gordon, compass, 1950s, silver plastic w/yel wristband, MOC, P4 ....$55.00

Flash Gordon, space outfit, Esquire, 1952, jacket and cumberbund with Flash silkscreen, NM (EX box), A, $250.00.

Flash Gordon, space outfit, Esquire Novelty, 1952, cloth vest & vinyl shoulder pads, EX (EX box), A $150.00

Flash Gordon, tray, 1979, mc litho w/Flash battling lizard creatures, 17½x13", EX, D9 ....$8.00

Flintstones, bank, Barney, Homecraft, 1973, w/bowling ball, NM, C17...$30.00

Flintstones, bank, Barney & Bamm-Bamm, 1971, Money Lover, vinyl, 12", NM, C1 ....$45.00

Flintstones, bank, Fred, Homecraft, 1973, NM, C17.......$35.00

Flintstones, bank, Pebbles, Homecraft, 1973, sitting in chair, NM, C17...$30.00

Flintstones, bank, Pebbles, vinyl, sleeping pose, EX+, T1...$25.00

Flintstones, bowl, 1978, plastic, EX, J7 ....$15.00

Flintstones, cake decorations, 1960s-70s, plastic, set of 4, 2", NMIP (sealed), F8 ....$25.00

Flintstones, clothes hanger, Bamm-Bamm, 1975, EX, J7..$20.00

Flintstones, dinnerware set, 1986, Melamine, 3-pc, MIB (sealed), J7 ....$25.00

Flintstones, doll, Barney, Knickerbocker/Hanna-Barbera, vinyl w/curly fur outfit, 17", EX, A $40.00

Flintstones, doll, Dino, Knickerbocker, 1960s, plush w/vinyl head, NM, T1 ....$85.00

Flintstones, doll, Pebbles, Mighty Star Ltd, 1982, vinyl head, arms & legs, stuffed cloth body, 12", MIB, H4..........$55.00

Flintstones, dolls, Pebbles & Bamm-Bamm, Ideal, 1960s, 12", missing club & bone, VG+, C17 ....$75.00

Flintstones, earring tree, Fred, EX+, T1 ....$35.00

Flintstones, Felt Picture Kit, 1976, MIB (sealed), V1 ....$20.00

Flintstones, figure, Bamm-Bamm, Hanna-Barbera, rubber, 1", EX, J7 ....$5.00

Flintstones, figure, Barney, Mattel, 1993, Barney w/lawn mower, MOC, B10..$5.00

Flintstones, figure, Barney, 1960, vinyl w/jtd head, VG, T1 ....$55.00

Flintstones, figure, Dino, Post, rubber, NM, H4..................$3.00

Flintstones, Flintmobile, Mattel, 1993, MIB, B10 ....$10.00

Flintstones, Funny Pumper Play-Doh, 1970s, missing Play-Doh, EX+ (EX box), F8...$78.00

Flintstones, Moulding & Colour Kit, Sculptorcraft, 1960s, complete, scarce, EX (EX display card), A $125.00

Flintstones, night light, Barney Rubble Electricord, 1979, MOC, H4..$6.00

Flintstones, ornament, Hallmark, Fred & Barney in car, MIB...$30.00

Flintstones, Pebbles Fortune Teller, MIP, T1.....................$5.00

Flintstones, pull toy, Pebbles and Wilma, Transogram, 1963, 11", scarce, NM (EX+ box), A, $660.00.

Flintstones, squeeze toy, Barney, 1962, vinyl w/gr hair, 6", EX, B10...$12.00

Flintstones, Super Putty, 1980, MOC, J7...........................$15.00

Flintstones, tablecloth, 1974, MIB (sealed), J7.................$12.00

Flintstones, wall plaque, Bedrock City, 1976, EX, J7........$20.00

Flintstones, Wonder Slate, 1973, MIP (sealed), T1..........$15.00

Flying Nun, Flying Nun Kit, Rayline, 1970, figure w/lg propeller launches 100 ft in air, MIB, M17.......................$200.00

Forbidden Planet, press book, Movie Press Kit, 1956, features Robby on cover, opens to 17x34", scarce, EX+, A ..$200.00

Forbidden Planet, press book, Movie Press Kit, 1956, features Robby to color on front, opens to 17x34", scarce, EX+, A $225.00

Foxy Grandpa, papier-mache w/tin eyeglasses, press stomach & tongue sticks out, 12", EX+, H12 ....$425.00

Foxy Grandpa, postcard, leather, dtd 1906, unused, M, P6.$35.00

Frank Webb, cartooning kit, 1946, unused, EX (EX box), J2 .$40.00

Fred Flintstone, see Flintstones

Freddy Krueger, see Nightmare on Elm Street

Friday the 13th, spitball, Jason, 1989, MOC, J7 ....$10.00

Full House, doll, Michelle, Meritus, 1991, talker, 15", NRFB, M15...$40.00

Geoffrey, music box, Toys R Us, 1975, EX, J7 ....$25.00

Ghidrah, movie, 8mm, NM, J6...$24.00

Ghostbusters, figure, Sta-Puft, 1984, vinyl, movable arms & legs, 7", EX+, D9..$10.00

Ghostbusters, iron-on transfers, 1984, MOC, J7..............$10.00

Ghostbusters, patch, 1986, cloth, MOC, P3 ....$3.50

Ghostbusters, sticker, I Ain't Afraid of No Ghost w/ghost logo, Ralston, 1986, EX+, P3..$4.00

Gilligan's Island, tablet, 1965, 8x10", unused, EX+, T2 ...$18.00

Godzilla, bop bag, 1985, inflatable, 48", MIB, B10...........$18.00

Goldilocks, doll, Storybook Small Talk, Mattel, MIB $85.00

Goldilocks, doll, Storybook Small Talk, Mattel, non-working, G...$10.00

Good Times, doll, JJ Dyn-O-Mite!, Shindana Toys, 1975, talker, 23", non-working o/w M (EX box), M17.....................$120.00

Green Hornet, bag, Vernor's promotion, EX+, D8.........$125.00

Green Hornet, balloons w/strings, 20th Century Fox, 1960s, M (orig card), H12...$175.00

Green Hornet, charm bracelet, w/5 charms, NMOC, B3 .$90.00

Green Hornet, pin, Agent, EX, D8 ....$25.00

Green Hornet, rub-ons, Hasbro, rare, M (NM box), T2 .$425.00

Green Hornet, spoon, 1966, NM, D8.................................$25.00

Gremlins, doll, Gizmo, Spain, plush, 14", MIB, D4........$195.00

Gremlins, figure, 1984, hard rubber, 4", EX, J7 ....$7.00

Gremlins, night light, EX, J7..$10.00

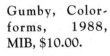

Gumby, Color-forms, 1988, MIB, $10.00.

Gumby, cowboy outfit, MOC, D8 ....$18.00

Gumby, figure, Pokey, Lakeside, 1965, bendable, MOC, M17...$55.00

Gumby, figure, Pokey, Prema Toys, 1984, bendable, 12", EX, B10...$10.00

Happy Face, pencil sharpener, EX, J2................................$25.00

Hardcastle & McCormick, handcuffs, JaRu, 1983, MOC, C1 ....$18.00

Harry & the Hendersons, doll, Harry, Galoob, 1990, talker, 24", NRFB, M15..$50.00

Harry & the Hendersons, figure, Harry, bendable, 8", MOC, B10...$8.00

Heathcliff, doll, Knickerbocker, 1981, stuffed, 12", VG, M15 ......$8.00

Hector Heathcote, Colorforms, 1964, missing 3 pcs & booklet, EX (EX box), F8...$28.00

Hogan's Heroes, Signal Sender & Compass, 1977, MOC, J7/L4...$25.00

Hogan's Heroes, tablet, 1965, 8x10", unused, NM, from $20 to...$25.00

Homey the Clown, see In Living Color

Hong Kong Phooey, tablecloth, 1975, MIP, J7.................$15.00

Howdy Doody, Air-O-Doodle, Plasticraft/Kagran, yel & red, 8", NM (NM card), A...$315.00

Howdy Doody, Air-O-Doodle Circus Train, Plasticraft/Kagran, vehicle pulls 3 caged cars, 17", scarce, NM (EX+ box), A $950.00

Howdy Doody, bank, Lefton, 1950s, Howdy sitting on barrel, hand pnt, 6", NM, A $335.00

Howdy Doody, bank, mk Bob Smith USA, 1950s, ceramic, Howdy atop pig, 7", no trap closure o/w NM, A......$235.00

Howdy Doody, bread label album, Continental Bakers/Wonder Bread, Balloon Series, 2 labels attached, EX+, K4....$50.00

Howdy Doody, bubble pipe, Clarabell, plastic, 5", NM, J2 ..$35.00

Howdy Doody, Color TV Set, Am Plastic Toy/Kagran, w/7 boxes of film, scarce, NM (EX+ box), A $1,150.00

Howdy Doody, crayon set, Milton Bradley, 1950, complete w/crayons & paper, scarce, unused, NM (EX+ box), A.................$200.00

Howdy Doody, dexterity puzzle, Japan, 1950s, shows Howdy holding marionettes of Mr Bluster & Dilly, 3" dia, EX, A...$155.00

Howdy Doody, Doodle Slate, Stickless Corp./Kagran, 9x10", EX+, A, $155.00.

Howdy Doody, figure set, Put on Your Own Tee-Vee Show, Kagran, 1950s, set of 5, 4", M (EX+ window box), A, $260.00.

Howdy Doody, game, Howdy Doody's Comic Circus Animals, Poll Parrot-Shoes/Kagran, spin & match up heads, 9", EX+, A...$150.00

Howdy Doody, Howdy Doody's One Man Band, Trophy Products/Kagran, complete w/4 plastic instruments, rare, EX (VG box), A...$950.00

Howdy Doody, key chain, puzzle style, M, from $30 to $40.00

Howdy Doody, laundry bag w/complete set of material & instructions to make Clarabell, Kagran, 1950s, NM (NM box), A..$115.00

Howdy Doody, pen, Leadworks/NBC/KFS, 1988, articulated plastic figure, 6", M, P4...................................$5.00

Howdy Doody, pencil holder, Leadworks/NBC/KFS, 1988, ceramic Howdy in cowboy hat, 6", MIB, P4.............$45.00

Howdy Doody, pencil topper, Leadworks/NBC, 1988, vinyl, 1½", M, P4..$5.00

Howdy Doody, pin-back light, EJ Kahn/Kagran, 1950s, plastic figure w/pull-string for light, 3", EX, A $65.00

Howdy Doody, Sand Forms, Ideal/Kagran, 1952, complete w/4 plastic molds of various characters & shovel, NM (EX+ card), A..$125.00

Howdy Doody, shower curtain, 1950s, mc circus scenes on plastic, EX, P6...$75.00

Howdy Doody, stringing beads, Stahlwood Prod/Kagran, mc wooden beads in soft plastic container, rare, NM, A..$620.00

Howdy Doody, swim ring, vinyl, VG, V1.................$20.00

Howdy Doody, toy wristwatch, Ever Tick Corp/Kagran, 1950s, movement causes Howdy's head to move, EX+ (EX+ card), A...$250.00

Howdy Doody, Uke, ukulele, Emenee/Kagran, plastic, pictures Howdy & Clarabell singing & playing, 16", NM (EX box), A...$175.00

Howdy Doody, wallpaper border, 1950s, scenes featuring carnival parade of Howdy & friends, 9-ft, EX, A.............$270.00

Huckleberry Hound, Animated Cartoon Cel Paint Kit, Spumco Inc/Hanna-Barbera, 1995, MIB (sealed), P4.............$20.00

Huckleberry Hound, bowling pin, hollow plastic figure, 7", VG, D9...$2.00

Huckleberry Hound, Cartoon Kit, Colorforms, 1960, complete w/booklet, EX+ (EX+ box), F8.................$48.00

Huckleberry Hound, charm bracelet, Hanna-Barbera, 1959, metal, MOC, from $50 to...................................$60.00

Huckleberry Hound, doll, Boo Boo, Knickerbocker, 1960s, vinyl head w/plush body, 10", EX, C17.................$30.00

Huckleberry Hound, doll, 1959, rubber head w/stuffed body, EX, J7...$40.00

Huckleberry Hound, game, Flip Face, Kellogg's, 1960, EX+, T2...$12.00

Huckleberry Hound, pencil box, Hanna-Barbera, 1960s, cb, VG+, T1...$45.00

Huckleberry Hound, rug, 1950s, mc, VG, C17 ....$35.00

Huckleberry Hound, Wonder Slate, Hamlyn, 1973, unused, MIP (sealed), C1...$20.00

Huckleberry Hound & Yogi Bear, bank, Royal Russell School, England, 1960s, Help Us Help the Children, rare, 9", EX, A...$490.00

Huckleberry Hound & Yogi Bear, glasses case, 5", EX, J7...$8.00

I Love Lucy, hat, w/orig tag, NM, J6 ....$48.00

In Living Color, doll, Homey the Clown, Acme, 1992, 24", MIP, M15..$18.00

Incredible Hulk, contact paper, 1978, comic book format, 8x18" roll, M (orig shrink wrap), A3..............................**$65.00**

Incredible Hulk, figure, Marvel Comics, 1979, hand-pnt ceramic, 3", M, A6...**$4.00**

Incredible Hulk, figure, 1979, rubber, 5", EX, J7.................**$8.00**

Incredible Hulk, paint set, 1981, MIB (sealed), V1..........**$17.00**

Incredible Hulk, playing cards, Marvel Comics, 1979, plastic coated, MIB, A6...**$5.00**

Incredible Hulk, Rub 'N Play Set, Colorforms, 1979, MIB, from $15 to..**$18.00**

Incredible Hulk, switchplate, 1976, glow-in-the-dark w/3-D illus, MIP (sealed), C1......................................**$22.00**

Inspector Gadget, Shrinky Dinks, Colorforms, 1983, MIB, C1...**$27.00**

James Bond, beach towel, 1964, portrait & facsimile autograph, M, J6...**$85.00**

James Bond, Bond-X Automatic Shooting Camera, w/bullets, missing pistol handle grip o/w EX, H4........................**$20.00**

James Bond, figures, Sonora, 1960s, header card mk Fantastic Bond, set of 10, EX+ (EX card), A...........................**$120.00**

James Bond, ID tags, Imperial, 1980s, MOC, C1..............**$22.00**

James Bond, press book, Thunderball, NM, D8................**$75.00**

James Bond, sign, Gilbert, 1960s, features blk & white photo of Sean Connery, advertises 3 sets of toys, 6x19", VG+, A................**$150.00**

James Bond, talcum powder, 1960s, NM, D8....................**$35.00**

James Bond, tie tack, Agent 007, no mk, NM, J6.............**$40.00**

James Bond 007, deodorant stick, Colgate, blk & silver cylinder w/blk, bl & silver graphics, full/contents shrunken, B3......**$39.00**

Jerry Mahoney & Paul Winchell, pamphlet, How To Be a Ventriloquist, H12..**$8.00**

Jetsons, cap, EX, J7..**$8.00**

Jetsons, socks, Elroy, 1980, EX, J7, pr............................**$10.00**

Jingle Dingle, Ring-O-Bell Set, Gilmar, 1954, ring toss w/figure, missing bar to stand o/w EX+, F8.............................**$48.00**

Joe Palooka, display box, 1940s, held transfer pictures & possibly candy or prizes, mc diecut, EX, M17.....................**$750.00**

Joe Palooka, figure, Germany, bsk, 7", H12....................**$65.00**

Joe Palooka, Sok-o-Bag, 1940s?, 2 inflatable punching bags, MOC, M17..**$60.00**

King Kong, bank, Ricogen Inc, 1977, vinyl figure atop Empire State Bldg, train in 1 hand, house in other, 13", EX, H4...**$40.00**

King Leonardo & Tennessee Tuxedo, Easy Show Film, Kenner, 1966, 8mm, MOC (sealed), F8...................................**$15.00**

Knight Rider, diecast car, Ertl, 1982, 1/25 scale, NRFB, H4..........**$20.00**

Knight Rider, diecast car, Ertl, 1982, 1/64 scale, MOC, H4 .**$6.00**

Krazy Kat, figure, Chein, jtd wood figure w/indented toothy grin, bulbous body, flat hands w/3 fingers, 7", EX, A.......**$425.00**

Land of the Giants, Movie Viewer, Chemtoy, 1969, MOC, M17...**$110.00**

Land of the Giants, Movie Viewer, Kenner, 1969, NMOC (sealed), F8..**$36.00**

Land of the Lost, figure, Christa, Krofft, 1991, bendable, MOC, B10...**$8.00**

Lariat Sam, Colorforms, 1962, some pcs missing o/w EX+ (VG+ box), F8..**$45.00**

Lassie, doll, Knickerbocker, 1965, stuffed plush w/felt-like face, 24", EX+, F8...**$48.00**

Laugh-In, Butt-On Kit, 1968, 3 metal buttons w/changeable sayings & stickers, MOC (sealed), F8..............................**$25.00**

Laughing Sam, sheet music, 1906, VG+, A3....................**$65.00**

Laurel & Hardy, bank, Hardy, Play Pal, 1974, 7", VG, M15 .**$22.00**

Laurel & Hardy, chair, Rico Spain, 1930, Laurel & Hardy playing ukelele on backrest, tin, on wheels, 11", rare, VG, A...**$675.00**

Laurel and Hardy, figure, Stan, 1972, plastic, 14", NM, J6, $28.00.

Knight Rider, KITT Dashboard, Illco, battery-operated, NMIB, J6, $65.00.

Laurel & Hardy, figure, Stan, Dell, 1962, rubber, squeeze & hat pops up, 7", EX+, F8...**$26.00**

Li'l Abner, barrette, Occupied Japan, hard plastic, mk #31, EX, P6...**$28.00**

Li'l Abner, poster, Git Mad, Buy War Stamps Here-Now!, ca 1943, mc, 14x18", sm crease o/w EX, A3................**$275.00**

Li'l Abner, tray, Dogpatch USA, 1968, EX, T1.............**$45.00**

Lil' Abner, tattoo sheet, Orange-Crush, 1950, mc comic strip characters, orig envelope, M17..................................$40.00

Linus, see Peanuts

Linus the Lionhearted, doll, Mattel, MIB......................$100.00

Linus the Lionhearted, doll, Mattel, talker (non-working), G $10.00

Little Bo Peep, doll, Storybook Small Talk, Mattel, MIB..$85.00

Little Bo Peep, doll, Storybook Small Talk, Mattel, non-working, G $10.00

Little Bo Peep, record player, England, pie-slice shaped metal, old, I2 ....$40.00

Little House on the Prairie, Paint-By-Number Set, 1979, MIB, J7 ....$45.00

Little King, figure, Jaymar, wood, pull top & he scoots around, 4", NM (EX box), M5 ....$110.00

Little Lulu, bank, Play Pal Plastics, 7½", no trap o/w NM, J6 ....$45.00

Little Lulu, jewelry box, Larami, 1973, NMIP (sealed), F8 ..$12.00

Little Nemo, song sheet, 1980, artist Windsor McCay, 1" tear o/w NM, A3..$250.00

Little Orphan Annie, charm, 1930s, celluloid, NM, V1 ..$20.00

Little Orphan Annie, clothespins, Transogram, 1930s, NMIP, $125.00.

Little Orphan Annie, figure, Sandy, 1930s, mk Sandy, jtd wood, 3½", scarce, M, A...$120.00

Little Orphan Annie, figures, Annie, Sandy, Harold Teen & Lillums, bsk, NM (NM box), C10 ....$190.00

Little Orphan Annie, stove, Marx, 1930s, Annie at top & on ea of 3 doors, 8x9½x5", working, NM, C1 ....$130.00

Little Orphan Annie & Sandy, dolls, jtd wood, 5½", EX+, H12, pr $225.00

Little Red Riding Hood, bank, European, 1920s-30s, cottage w/removable roof, tin, 7" L, G, A $100.00

Lord of the Rings, bank, Samwise or Frodo, MIB, J6, ea...$35.00

Love Boat, Barber Kit, MOC, T1 ....$15.00

Lucy, see Peanuts

M*A*S*H, wallet, MOC, J2 ....$20.00

MAD, notebook, Scout Rules for Ghouls, NM, J2 ....$150.00

Magnum PI, tray, 1982, litho metal, 17x12", EX, J7........$15.00

Mammy & Pappy Yokum, bank, Capp Enterprises Inc Dogpatch USA, 1975, mc compo figure, 7¼", M, P6 ....$95.00

Man From UNCLE, Secret Cap Shooting Lighter, EX, H4.$45.00

Margie, travel case, 1962, blk vinyl w/Margie dancing & drinking soda, EX+, F8...$18.00

Masters of the Universe, bank, HG Toys Ltd., MIB, $6.00.

Masters of the Universe, toothpaste topper, MOC, J7......$15.00

Masters of the Universe, tray, 1982, litho metal, 17x12", EX, J7..$12.00

Miss Piggy, see Muppets

Moon Mullins, figures, N Shure/FAS, 1930s, bsk, complete w/Moon Mullins, Kayo, Uncle Willie & Emmy, EX+ (VG+ box), A...$195.00

Mork & Mindy, doll, Mork, rag-type talker, non-working o/w EX, C17..$12.00

Mork & Mindy, Magic Show, Colorforms, MIB, V1 ....$30.00

Mortimer Snerd, doll, Ideal, jtd legs & arms, clothed in shirt & tie w/sports jacket & pants, 12", G, A $105.00

Mortimer Snerd, doll, mk Ideal Doll/Made in USA, dressed in clown outfit, hand-pnt compo w/movable head, 13", EX, A $130.00

Mother Goose, doll, Mattel, talker, rag & plush, MIB ...$125.00

Mother Goose, doll, Mattel, talker (non-working), rag & plush, G..$5.00

Mother Goose, jack-in-the-box, Mattel, 1971, working, EX+, F8 ....$25.00

Mother Goose, nodder, she w/papier-mache head & cloth armature body on cloth-covered papier-mache goose, 26", EX, A...$3,960.00

Mrs Beasley, doll, Mattel, talker, rag & plush, MIB.......$175.00

Mrs Beasley, doll, Mattel, talker (non-working), rag & plush, G $5.00

Mummy, head, glow-in-the-dark, 2", M, J2....................$15.00

Munsters, baby figure, Ideal, 1964, Lilly or Eddie, nude, EX, H4, ea...$25.00

Photo courtesy of June Moon.

Munsters, doll, Herman, vinyl w/stuffed body, talker, non-working o/w EX, T1 ....$225.00

Munsters, doll, Lurch, Remco, vinyl, M (EX+ box), T1.$400.00

Munsters, gift bag, M, J2 ....$20.00

Muppets, oven mitt, Miss Piggy, 1981, EX, J7 ....$8.00

Muppets, shoes, child sz 5, EX, J7 ....$10.00

Muppets, vehicle, Miss Piggy car, Tomy, 1983, EX, J7 ....$6.00

Mush Mouse, doll, Ideal, 1960s, vinyl head w/stuffed felt body, poseable, 9", EX+, F8 ....$70.00

Mutley (Dastardly), figure, 1970s, plastic w/movable head, 3", EX+, F8 ....$25.00

Mutt & Jeff, figures, A Boucherer/Swiss, metal ball-jtd bodies w/compo heads & limbs, cloth clothes, 6" & 8", NM, A $440.00

New Zoo Revue, doll, Freddie the Frog, bean bag, EX, C17 ..$25.00

Nightmare on Elm Street, doll, Freddy Krueger, Matchbox, 1989, talker, 18", NRFB, M15 ....$40.00

Nightmare on Elm Street, figure, Stick-Up, 4", MOC, T1 .$6.00

Nightmare on Elm Street, glove, Freddy Krueger, M (EX+ card), P3 ....$18.00

Olive Oyl, doll, Columbia Toy Prod/KFS, 1940s, stuffed cloth w/fabric clothes, hand-pnt features, 18", scarce, EX+, A $275.00

Olive Oyl, ponytail holder, King Features, 1958, MOC, M17 ....$30.00

Olive Oyl, see also Popeye & Olive Oyl

Our Gang, rowboat, Mego, 1975, plastic, NM (original box), $40.00.

Our Gang, school box, 1930, gold & blk on emb red w/group illus, 8½x4½", EX+, A3 ....$225.00

Partridge Family, shopping bag, 1972, M, V1 ....$12.00

Peanuts, bank, Lucy, Quadifuglio, Florence Italy, ceramic, 7", EX, H11 ....$50.00

Peanuts, bank, Snoopy, Leonard #9669, silverplate, MIB, H11..$30.00

Peanuts, bank, Snoopy on soccer ball, ceramic, 1960s, NM, V1 ....$17.00

Peanuts, bank, Snoopy's doghouse, Korea, papier-mache, slot on side, 6", EX, H11 ....$10.00

Peanuts, banner, Snoopy, America You're Beautiful on wht, 13x28", M, H11 ....$20.00

Peanuts, bell, Snoopy, Schmid, Christmas 1973, atop doghouse, EX, H11 ....$60.00

Peanuts, bicycle horn, Snoopy, 1958, NM, V1 ....$18.50

Peanuts, bicycle license plate, Hallmark, Powered by Woodstock on red, MOC, H11 ....$10.00

Peanuts, bookends, Snoopy, Hong Kong, red plastic hearts, EX, H11, pr $18.00

Peanuts, cake pan, Charlie Brown, Wilton, aluminum w/plastic face, M, H11 ....$25.00

Peanuts, centerpiece, Snoopy, Hallmark, Halloween, w/Woodstock & broom, 16", MIP, H11 ....$6.00

Peanuts, charm bracelet, Applause, gold-tone metal w/5 cloisonne charms, M, H11 ....$20.00

Peanuts, crib toy, Snoopy Baby Funtime, Hasbro #8272, VG, H11 ....$7.00

Peanuts, cymbals, Chein, 1969, silver w/red wood knob, 4½" dia, EX, H11, pr $45.00

Peanuts, doll, Charlie Brown, Hungerford, 8", VG, H11..$110.00

Peanuts, doll, Linus, Hungerford, w/red shirt & hand held out, 7", VG, rare, H11 ....$100.00

Peanuts, doll, Linus, 1950s, vinyl, 9", EX+, J2 ....$40.00

Peanuts, doll, Snoopy, Applause, China Beach Beagle, w/bl visor, M, H11 ....$20.00

Peanuts, doll, Snoopy, Determined, 1969, blk & wht plush w/red necktie, 10", MIP, T2 ....$40.00

Peanuts, doll, Snoopy, Ideal #1410, rag type w/plastic nose, bl jeans & red shirt, 14", VG, H11 ....$10.00

Peanuts, doll, Snoopy, United Features, 1968, cloth w/cloth clothes, 7", EX, H4 ....$14.00

Peanuts, dolls, Pocket Dolls, Boucher, 1960s, jtd w/cloth clothes, 7", VG to EX, H4, any, from $22 to $25.00

Peanuts, doormat, Snoopy & Woodstock, wht & yel on gray, 14x26", M, H11 ....$15.00

Peanuts, earring tree, Snoopy, 1979, enameled metal doghouse, 5", MIB, H11..$10.00

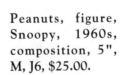

Peanuts, figure, Snoopy, 1960s, composition, 5", M, J6, $25.00.

Photo courtesy of June Moon.

Peanuts, figure, Snoopy, Silverdeer #00131, valentine w/red heart, cut glass, 30mm, M, H11 ....$70.00

Peanuts, fishing rod, Snoopy, Zebco, VG, H11................$10.00

Peanuts, harp, Snoopy, 1969, from movie A Boy Named Charlie Brown, MIB, H11 ....$20.00

Peanuts, jack-in-the-box, Mattel, Where Did My Little Dog Go?, M, H11 ....$60.00

Peanuts, jack-in-the-box, Snoopy, NMIB, J2.................$75.00

Peanuts, magic slate, Super Slate, Saalfield, 1967, MOC (sealed), F8..$15.00

Peanuts, megaphone, Snoopy, Chein, 1970, Head Beagle, VG, rare, H11 ....$25.00

Peanuts, music box, Snoopy, Schmid, 1985, plays Home Sweet Home, 5", M, H11 ....$50.00

Peanuts, pajama bag, Snoopy figure, w/button, EX, J6..$28.00

Peanuts, pin, Lucy, Knott's Camp Snoopy, 1992, gold-tone, 2¾", M, H11 ....$30.00

Peanuts, scissors, Snoopy Snippers, Mattel #7410, battery-op, blades in mouth, VG, H11 ....$20.00

Peanuts, Skiddidler figure (only), Charlie Brown, Lucy or Snoopy w/aviator cap, EX, H4, ea $30.00

Peanuts, Snoopy's Scooter Shooter, Child Guidance #51720, MIB, H11 ....$40.00

Peanuts, soap dish, Snoopy, Avon, rubber, w/soap, 7½", MIB, H11 ....$15.00

Peanuts, wastebasket, Snoopy & Lucy, Chein, That WWI Act of Yours..., 13", EX, H11...$50.00

Pebbles Flintstone, see Flintstones

Pee-Wee's Playhouse, doll, Pee-Wee Herman, Matchbox, 1987, talker, unused, NM (EX+ 10x20" box), D9 ....$27.00

Pee-Wee's Playhouse, Pee-Wee's Ball Darts, Herman Toys/Hong Kong, 1987, balls, foam board, etc, MIB (sealed), P4..$35.00

Penelope Pitstop, jewelry set, Larami, 1971, matching necklace, ring, headband & belt, MOC (sealed), F8 ....$12.00

Penguin, see Batman

Peter Potamus, bank, 12", EX $65.00

Peter Potamus, movie, Stars on Mars, 1966, 8mm blk & wht 50-ft film, NMIB $10.00

Peter Rabbit, Magician Magic Set, Strathmore, complete, NM (NM box), A $155.00

Pink Panther, jewelry set, 1989, MOC, J7 ....$12.00

Pink Panther, valentines, 1980, w/riddles, MIB (sealed), J7...$8.00

Planet of the Apes, Astronaut Virdon Mix 'N Mold Casting Set, Catalog Shoppe, 1974, M (EX+ box), D9.................$35.00

Planet of the Apes, bank, plastic, M, T1 ....$45.00

Planet of the Apes, Dress-Up Playset, MIB, rare, P12 ......$65.00

Planet of the Apes, movie, Beneath the Planet of the Apes, 8mm, NM, J6...$10.00

Planet of the Apes, plaque, Milton Bradley, 1975, 3-D, orig box, J7 ....$75.00

Pokey, see Gumby

Popeye, bank, dime register, King Features, c 1929, litho tin, 2½" sq, VG, A..$55.00

Popeye, bank, holds gumballs, T1.................................$45.00

Popeye, bowl, cereal; 1979, plastic, EX, J7 ....$8.00

Popeye, charm, 1930s, celluloid, NM, V1 ....$22.00

Popeye, Cheer Light, light bulb, Aerolux, 1930s, metal Popeye w/torch glows in center of bulb, EX+ (G+ scarce box), A..............$185.00

Popeye, Colorforms, 1959, The Weatherman, missing booklet o/w complete, NMIB, F8 ....$30.00

Popeye, dinnerware, Taylor Smith & Taylor, 1935, mc plate, bowl & mug, unused, M, P6, 3-pc set.....................$300.00

Popeye, doll, mk Popeye KFS on chest, movable head, hands & legs, hand pnt, 14", NM, A $890.00

Popeye, fan, prewar Japan, image of Popeye w/moving eyes, paper & wood, 5", M, A $200.00

Popeye, figure, Jaymar, pnt & jtd wood body w/compo head, blk shirt & bl pants, red trim, brn shoes, pipe, 8", VG, A..$65.00

Popeye, figure, Lakeside, 1967, bendable, NRFP, C17 .....$20.00

Popeye, figure, prewar Japan, Popeye holding his pipe, celluloid, 5", EX, A $130.00

Popeye, figure, 1930s, jtd & pnt wood, EX, 5", EX, A $65.00

Popeye, flashlight, Larami, 1983, pocket sz, MOC, C1.....$16.00

Popeye, Foto Fun Printing Kit, Fun Bilt, 1958, MIB, M17 ..$55.00

Popeye, jack-in-the-box, Mattel, missing pipe, otherwise EX, $80.00.

Popeye, knapsack, 1979, mc canvas w/tags, M, C17.........$12.00

Popeye, mechanical pencil, Eagle/KFS, 1930s, metal w/illus & testimonial statement, 10", EX, K4 ....$35.00

Popeye, muffler, box only, KFS, 1936, pictures snow scene w/Popeye talking to kids, Blow Me Down Kids!..., 9x11", NM, A $160.00

Popeye, pencil box, King Features Syndicate, 1934, EX, $55.00.

Popeye, Numbered Pencil Coloring Set, Hasbro, 1950, NMIB, T2..$90.00

Popeye, paint set, Popeye Paints, Am Crayon, 1933, unused, MIB, A..$130.00

Popeye, pen, Lyric, set of 4, EX, J7 ....$15.00

Popeye, pin, 1930s, diecut metal Popeye at helm, NM, V1 .$20.00

Popeye, pocketknife, image of Popeye on faux pearl hdl, 3", EX+, M5 ....$48.00

Popeye, Power Strength Toy, 1950s, MIP, V1 ....$60.00

Popeye, pull toy, unmk, paper litho on wood, Popeye & various characters on the SS Popeye, 16", EX......................$250.00

Popeye, pull toy, 1940-50s, Popeye plays xylophone w/Sweet Pea on his back, Bluto on front, wood & tin, 12", NM..$400.00

Popeye, rattle, Japan, celluloid, wood & rubber, lg bells attached to arms, 6", NM, A $150.00

Popeye, record player, Dynamite Music Machine, EX, J7.$25.00

Popeye, trinket box, 1980, hand-pnt ceramic Popeye on spinach crate, M, J2..$30.00

Popeye, wall sculpture, figural light-up, 24", NM, J6........$55.00

Popeye, wallet, vinyl w/flasher sq, NM, J2 ....$55.00

Popeye & Olive Oyl, bank, sitting on spinach can, ceramic, VG, I2 ....$8.00

Popeye & Olive Oyl, Slinky Handcar, Linemar, 1950s, 6½", VG, A $770.00

Popeye & Olive Oyl, valentine, early, EX, J2 ....$25.00

Popeye & Other King Features Syndicate Characters, Cartoon Charm Set, Prevue/KFS, 1964, complete, EX+ (EX box)..$175.00

Porky Pig, bank, 1972, 16", EX, B10 ....$26.00

Porky Pig, cookie mold, 1978, EX, J7 ....$5.00

Porky Pig, doll, Mattel, talker, MIB $175.00

Porky Pig, doll, Mattel, talker (non-working), G..............$10.00

Porky Pig, figure, Warner Bros, rubber, 1", EX, J7..............$5.00

Prince Valiant, shield, 1950s, mc illus & logo on metal, 12", 1 hasp on back undone o/w VG+, A3..........................$40.00

Punky Brewster, doll, Punky, Galoob, 1984, 18", NRFB, M15 ....$40.00

Punky Brewster, jewelry, pendant w/pearls, MOC, J7.........$8.00

Quick Draw McGraw, Magic Rub-Off Picture Set, Whitman, 1960, used, missing crayons & tissue, EX box, J5.......$25.00

Quick Draw McGraw, Flintstones and Huckleberry Hound, wastebaskets, lithographed tin, EX, $60.00 each.

Raggedy Andy, doll, Playschool, 1987, 12", MIB, M15 ....$12.00

Raggedy Ann, doll, Georgene Novelties, 1930s-40, w/orig tag, 14", missing clothes o/w NM, G16............................$60.00

Raggedy Ann, doll, Hasbro, 1983, 17", MIB, M15 ....$25.00

Raggedy Ann, doll, Knickerbocker, 1970s, 14", NM, J6, $30.00.

Raggedy Ann, doll, newer (?), stuffed cloth, yarn hair, red triangle nose, blk button eyes, floral dress, 16", EX, A $20.00

Raggedy Ann, figure, 1988, bsk, 4", M, M15....................$15.00

Raggedy Ann & Andy, camper, Buddy L, MIB $300.00

Raggedy Ann & Andy, coat rack, wall-type, 18x20", EX, I2..$18.00

Raggedy Ann & Andy, dolls, early 1940s, hand-made stuffed cloth, w/provenance, 8", NM, G16, pr.......................$85.00

Rat Finks, decal, 1990, mc, 8", M, B10...............................$7.00

Rat Finks, gumball machine paper insert, EX, B10 ....$8.00

Rat Finks, ring, sm, M, from $7 to $10.00

Rat Patrol, hat, 1966, red w/logo, EX, J7.........................$85.00

Reg'lar Fellers, paint set, American Toy Works, 1932, used & possibly incomplete in EX 12x16" mc illus box, J5..$255.00

Reginald Racoon, soap dish, Avon, EX, B10 ....$12.00

Richie Rich, plastic zip bag, 1981, EX, J7...........................$8.00

Richochet Rabbit, change purse, early 1960s, pk vinyl, NMOC, C17..$50.00

Ricochet Rabbit, plate, Melmac, 1960s, 8", EX, F8 ....$25.00

Robin, see Batman

Robin Hood, shoes, C10...$225.00

Rocky, diecast figure, Ertl, 1981, 2", MOC, from $12 to ..$18.00

Rocky & Bullwinkle, figure, Snydley Whiplash, Wham-O, 1971, bendable, MOC, H4 ....$28.00

Rocky & Bullwinkle, magic slate, Whitman, 1972, w/pencil, EX+, F8 ....$30.00

Rocky & Bullwinkle, marbles, 1988, MIP $3.00

Rocky & Bullwinkle, sewing cards, 1961, EX, J7 ....$25.00

Rocky Squirrel, figure, pnt ceramic, 2½", NM, F8...........$45.00

Rocky the Flying Squirrel & Commander Peachfuzz, sewing cards, 1961, EX, J7...$25.00

Rodan, figure, Toho Co, 1979, lg, EX/NM, J6 ....$85.00

Romper Room, jack-in-the-box, 1970, working, EX, J7 ...$20.00

Romper Room, tambourine, Mr Doo Bee, early 1960s, EX, C17..$25.00

Rookies, Crime Buster Set, 1975, MOC $18.00

Rookies, movie viewer w/film, 1975, MOC $18.00

Sandy, see Little Orphan Annie

Saturday Night Live, doll, Conehead, Broadway Video, 1991, w/tag & stand, 10", EX, B10 ....$12.00

Scooby Doo, bank, vinyl w/felt vest, NM, T1 ....$25.00

Scooby Doo, doll, Mattel, talker, MIB $175.00

Scooby Doo, doll, Mattel, talker (non-working), G $35.00

Scooby Doo, stamper, Hanna-Barbera, 1983, MOC, B10...$5.00

Secret Sam Shooter, pipe, MIB, T1................................$20.00

Sesame Street, boot rack, Big Bird, 1982, MIB, J7...........$12.00

Sesame Street, doll, Big Bird, Ideal, talks w/tape player, 25", VG, M15 ....$50.00

Sesame Street, doll, Big Bird, Playskool, 1970s, pull-string talker, 22", VG, M15 ....$25.00

Sesame Street, doll, Ernie, stuffed, 18", EX, J7 ....$10.00

Sesame Street, tray, 1971, litho metal, 17x12", EX, J7 ...$12.00

Sherman & Peabody, sewing cards, EX, J7 ....$25.00

Shmoo, figures, Al Capp's Soapy Shmoo, Kirk Guild, 1948, box lid shows Abner, Daisy & Shmoo, set of 5, EX+ (EX box), A $155.00

Simpsons, airwalker, Anagram International, Mylar, MIP, K1 ....$12.00

Simpsons, bank, Bart, Street Kids, standing plastic figure, MIB, K1..$12.00

Simpsons, Crayon-By-Numbers, Rose Art, w/6 pictures & numbered crayons, MIB, K1...................................$6.00

Simpsons, doll, Bart, Dandee, stuffed body w/vinyl head, arms & legs, 16", MIB, K1 ....$15.00

Simpsons, doll, Bubble Blowin' Lisa, Mattel, 18", w/4-oz bubble solution, MIB, K1 ....$35.00

Simpsons, figures, Jesco, bendable, 5 different, MOC, K1, ea..$5.00

Simpsons, frisbee, Betras Plastics, wht w/Radical Dude, MIP, K1...$4.00

Simpsons, Fun Dough Model Maker, Rose Art, w/2 molds, 3 cans dough & accessories, MIB, K1.......................$20.00

Simpsons, paper plates, Chesapeake, 9", 8 per pkg, MIP, K1 .$4.50

Simpsons, socks, Pel-Bar, wht cotton-nylon blend w/dk bl band at top ribbing, emb Bart at side, MIP, K1, pr $6.00

Six Million Dollar Man, Bionic Video Center, w/2 movie cartridges, EX (EX box), H4..$50.00

Six Million Dollar Man, Give-A-Show Projector, 1977, MIB, B10..$25.00

Smitty, Christmas bulb, 1930s, pnt glass figure, lt pnt wear, o/w EX, P6...$35.00

Smokey & the Bandit, diecast figure, Bandit, Ertl, 1982, M (EX+ card), H4...$12.00

Smurfs, doll, Smurfette, 1981, stuffed, 8", EX, B10..........$10.00

Smurfs, figures, PVC, several different, NM, B10, ea, from $2 to...$4.00

Smurfs, music box, 1982, walking figure, lt pnt wear, B10..$10.00

Smurfs, record player, 1982, EX, I2 ....$20.00

Smurfs, zipper pull, Brainy or Smurfette, hard plastic w/clip, 2½", P10, ea $5.00

Snidley Whiplash, see Rocky & Bullwinkle

Sniffles, figure, Shaw/Warner Bros, 1940s, w/paper label, 6", EX, P6 ....$95.00

Snoopy, see Peanuts

Snuffy Smith, poster, Time's a Wastin'! Buy War Stamps Here-Now!, 1943, mc on yel, 14x18", EX, A3 ....$450.00

Soupy Sales, doll, Knickerbocker, 1966, stuffed, w/vinyl head, EX-, H4 ....$80.00

Space: 1999, bank, Commander Koenig/Martin Landau, 1975, vinyl figure w/slot at back, 11", EX+ $30.00

Space: 1999, Sonic Powered Megaphone, Vanity Fair, 1970s, battery-op, VG (orig box), J5.................................$25.00

Speedy Gonzales, doll, Mighty Star, 1971, cloth, EX+, J2..$20.00

Spider-Man, book bag, canvas, EX, I2............................$12.00

Spider-Man, comb & brush set, 1970s, MIB, H12 ....$45.00

Spider-Man, latch hook pillow kit, 1970s, MIB, D8.........$55.00

Sluggo and Nancy, dolls, Georgene Novelties, 1949, MIB, $1,450.00 for the pair.

Photo courtesy of Dunbar Gallery.

Spider-Man, Mix 'N Mold Set, 1970s, MIB, D8 ....$45.00

Spider-Man, Official Gumball Pocket Pack Dispenser, 3-D figure, Superior Toy, 1984, MIP (sealed), A6 ....$7.00

Spider-Man, pencil sharpener, Nasta, 1980, 4", MOC (sealed), A6..$5.00

Spider-Man, roller skates, 1979, red, blk & bl plastic, EX, I2 ...$15.00

Spider-Man, scissors, Nasta, 1980, figural hdl w/metal blades, 3½", MOC (sealed), A6 ....$4.00

Spider-Man, sign, 1977, promotes beginning of comic strip in newspaper, card stock, 11x17", EX, A3...................$350.00

Spider-Man, stapler, Nasta, 1980, M (EX card), C1 ....$18.00

Spider-Man, vehicle set, Buddy L, 1984, MIB, J2 ....$35.00

Spider-Man, wallet, 1978, MOC, D8 ....$25.00

Spike Jones, drum, Junior City Slickers, 19" dia, EX, J6, $85.00.

Sta-Puft, see Ghostbusters

Steve Canyon, T-shirt, membership card & wings, C10 ..$150.00

Steve Urkle, see Family Matters

Super Heroes, beach tote bag, 1978, EX, J7 ....$15.00

Super Heroes, Contact Paper, DC Comics, 1973, w/Batman, Robin, Superman & Wonder Woman, covers 50 sq ft, MIP, A6 ....$25.00

Super Heroes, flashlight, Mighty Thor, Marvel Comics, 1978, 3½", MIP (sealed), A6..$3.00

Super Heroes, postcard book, DC Comics, 1981, perforated, shows miscellaneous characters, EX+, D9 ....$10.00

Super Heroes, stamp set, Fleetwood, 1978, set of 8 different w/stamp pad, MIP (sealed), A6 ....$8.00

Super Heroes, stick-ons, Our Way Studios, 1973-1974, M (M 13x9" pkg), D9, ea, from $15 to $17.00

Super 7, balloons, Web Woman, Bubb-A-Loons, 1979, plastic, set of 7, MIP, J7 ....$15.00

Superman, bank, Mego, 1974, plastic, EX, C17 ....$30.00

Superman, belt buckle, 1970s, heavy bronze, 4", M, A6.....$7.50

Superman, belt buckle, 1970s, mc, NM $25.00

Superman, bread bag, 1966, NM, D8 ....$15.00

Superman, Colorforms/NPPI, 1964, unused, NM (EX+ box), K4 ....$40.00

Superman, coupon card, ca 1939, from candy, collect for premiums, 2½x3", EX, A3 ....$75.00

Superman, doll, Mego, 1978, stuffed, 18", EX, C17 ....$28.00

Superman, doll, soft stuffed poseable figure, 18", M (VG box), H4 ....$70.00

Superman, doll box, Ideal Novelty & Toy, cb w/blk & wht paper label on end, 13", rare, EX+, A.............................$2,600.00

Superman, film viewer, Acme, 1940, w/3 boxed films, EX (EX orig mc diecut 7½x5" box), A3 ....$650.00

Superman, hood ornament, emb LW Lee Mfg/Nat'l Comic Pub, 1940s, silvered figure of Superman in classic pose, 11", NM, A...$2,400.00

Superman, horseshoe set, Super Slim Inc, 1954, EX (VG- box), T2 ....$40.00

Superman, iron-on, 1950s, lg red & blk image w/logo, 9x14", EX, J5 ....$35.00

Superman, kite, 1971, MIP, D8...$22.00

Superman, Kryptonite Rock, DC Comics, 1978, glows in the dark, MIB, from $20.00 to $30.00.

Superman, ornament, Hallmark, MIB, D9/T1 ....$35.00

Superman, Paint-By-Number Set, 1977, MIB, D8............$28.00

Superman, party hat, 1977, EX, J7......................................$6.00

Superman, pencil case, Mattel, 1966, EX, D8 ....$28.00

Superman, pencil sharpeners, 1980, set of 5, D8..............$30.00

Superman, scissors, 1973, MOC, D8 ....$16.00

Superman, spoon, Imperial/NPP Inc, ca 1960, stainless steel, 6", M, P4..$10.00

Superman, sticker, 1939-40, promoting radio station KECA, mc figure w/logo, 4", unused, NM, rare, A3...................$500.00

Superman, Sunday pages, from 1940s tabloid, EX, D8......$25.00

Superman, swim fins, National Comics Pub Co, gr w/metal hooks on sides for straps, 10", missing straps o/w EX, I2, pr..$15.00

Superman, tote bag, 1982, EX, J7 ....$12.00

Superman, valentine, diecut Superman holding heart, To Me It Would Be Fine To Be Your Super Valentine, 4", NM, A .$60.00

Superman, valentine, 1940, Superman w/children peeking through brick wall, folding, EX+, A3 ....$75.00

Superman, wallet, 1976, brn leather, M, I2...................$10.00

Superman, wastebasket, 1978, litho tin w/Christopher Reeve photo, EX, I2..............................$35.00

Superman, wood-burning set, American Toy & Furniture Co, 1979, appears complete, VG (G box), I2 ....$12.00

SWAT, bullhorn, 1975, EX, J7 ....$12.00

Sweeney & Son, figure, Sweeney, Chicago Tribune, late 1940s, pnt plaster w/name on rnd base, EX, A3 ....$40.00

Swee' Pea, tile, mc emb image, hangs on wall, 4⅛x3", M, P6 ..$35.00

Sylvester, blow-up figure, 1970, 8", EX, J7 ....$8.00

Sylvester, doll, velour, 5", VG, B10...............................$8.00

Sylvester, rattle, 1975, EX, J7 ....$6.00

Tarzan, Cartoon Kit, Colorforms, 1965, EX (EX box), J2...$25.00

Tarzan, magic slate, 1968, EX, J2 ....$20.00

Tarzan, tennis bag, 1975, EX, J7 ....$30.00

Tarzan, Thingmaker, mold only, EX+, T1 ....$50.00

Tasmanian Devil, doll, 1980, stuffed, 13", EX, J7 ....$12.00

Teddy Ruxpin, 1986, talks w/tape player, 14", MIB, M15 ..$70.00

Teenage Mutant Ninja Turtles, valentines, Grand Award, 1991, set of 42, MIB (sealed), P3................................$5.00

Three Stooges, beanie, mk NMP (Norman Maurer Prod), 1959, red & wht w/blk & wht photo image, 8" dia, scarce, EX, A $300.00

Three Stooges, Colorforms, 1959, missing 2 pcs o/w complete w/booklet, NMIB, F8...................................$95.00

Three Stooges, film, Thud & Blunder, Excell 8mm Home Movies, 1940s, EX (EX box), P6 ....$45.00

Three Stooges, flicker ring, NM, H4, any character $20.00

Three Stooges, folder, Bright-Ideals, 1984, 9½x12", NM, D9 ....$12.00

Three Stooges, Jolly Theatre, Excell, 1947, w/toy movie projector, no film, EX (EX box), A $195.00

Three Stooges, membership kit, Maurer TV, 1959, letter, 2 photos w/2 sticker & card sheets, uncut, M (orig mailer), A3 ....$450.00

Three Stooges, photos, 1977, set of 4, 11x14", NM, J2.....$48.00

Tillie the Toiler, portrait, King Features/Punch Comic Weekly, early, scarce, V1 ....$80.00

Tom & Jerry, doll, Mattel, talker, rag & plush, MIB $175.00

Tom & Jerry, doll, Mattel, talker (non-working), rag & plush, G..$25.00

Tom & Jerry, squeak toy, Jerry, Lanco, 1960s, as cowboy, NM, C17...$20.00

Tom Corbett Space Cadet, binoculars, Sport Glass, 1950s, bl metal w/decals, M, A $135.00

Tom Corbett Space Cadet, book bag, 1950s, EX, J2.......$150.00

Tom Corbett Space Cadet, Cosmic Vision Helmet, Practi-Cole, 1950, see-thru plastic, EX (EX box), A....................$450.00

Topo Gigio, bank, ceramic figure sitting between pineapples, w/orig hang tag, MIB, V1.....................................$80.00

Tweety Bird, doll, Mighty Star, 1971, stuffed, EX, C17....$15.00

Tweety Bird & Sylvester, bowl, plastic, EX, J7.................$4.00

Tweety Bird & Sylvester, figure, Warner Bros, 1980, EX, B10..$10.00

Uncle Walt, charm, 1930s, celluloid, NM, V1 ....$18.00

Uncle Wiggly, doll, Georgene Averill, tan cloth body w/pk ears, red shirt w/yel vest, print pants, 20", EX, A.............$470.00

Uncle Wiggly, Hollow Stump Bungalow, papier-mache tree-stump house on cb platform w/10 cut-out cb figures, VG+, A $125.00

Underdog, harmonica, 1975, emb Simon Bar Sinister or Under-dog at ea end, 8", NM+ $15.00

Underdog, pillow, wht inflatable vinyl, EX, B10 ....$23.00

V, Walkie Talkies, Power Tronic by Nasta, MIB, $75.00.

Wacky Racers, Penelope Pitstop Jump & Go Friction-Powered Buggy, Laramie, 1973, plastic, M (NM+ box), C1.....$40.00

Welcome Back Kotter, calculating wheel, 1976 M (M photo-illus card), V1 ....$12.50

Welcome Back Kotter, desk calendar, Horshack, 1977, EX, J7..$35.00

Welcome Back Kotter, greeting card, set of 6, MIB (sealed), V1..$25.00

Wheel of Fortune, wristwatch, Sharp/Merv Griffin Ent, 1990, gold-tone case w/animated disk, blk leather band, M, P4 ....$45.00

Where's Waldo? doll, Waldo or Wenda, Mattel, 1991, 18", M (NM box), B3, ea...$18.00

Wimpy, doll, Columbia Toy Prod/KFS, 1940s, stuffed cloth w/fabric clothes, hand-pnt features, 18", scarce, EX+, A....$565.00

Tom and Jerry, skooter, plastic, friction, 4½", NM (NM box), M5, $140.00.

Photo courtesy of Mike's General Store.

Wimpy, figure, Syroco, 1944, pressed wood, about 4", EX...$150.00

Wimpy, pin, Wheatena, 1930s, cloisonne, EX (orig card), V1 ......$115.00

Winnie Winkle, figure, Bill Wright, Chicago Tribune, late 1940s, plaster w/name on rnd base, EX, A3 ....$25.00

Wizard of Oz, bank, Dorothy, Arnart Imports, 1960s, hand pnt, w/paper tag, 7", NM+ (orig 4x7" box), S6 ....$826.00

Wizard of Oz, bank, Scarecrow, Arnart Imports, 1960s, hand pnt, w/orig paper tag, 7", NMIB, S6 ....$100.00

Wizard of Oz, bank, Tin Woodman, Arnart Imports, 1960s, hand pnt, 7", MIB, S6 ....$135.00

Wizard of Oz, doll, Dorothy, Presents, 14", MIB, D4 ....$35.00

Wizard of Oz, doll, Glenda, Presents, 15", MIB, D4 ....$45.00

Wizard of Oz, doll, Lowes Inc, 1988, 6 different, MIB, ea, B10/P4, from $20 to..$30.00

Wizard of Oz, doll, Scarecrow, MD toilet tissue premium, 1960s, 16", NM, H4 ....$25.00

Wizard of Oz, doll, Wicked Witch, Presents, 14", MIB, D4 .$40.00

Wizard of Oz, figure, Dorothy, Justoys, bendable, MOC, B10 .$6.00

Wizard of Oz, foaming bath beads, Ansehi, 1976, complete set of 12 in plastic tray, EX+ (4¾x14½" window box), S6 .$73.00

Wizard of Oz, handbill, British rerelease, distributed by theaters, dtd 1945 on orig 1939 stock, 8x20", EX, S6 ....$125.00

Wizard of Oz, magazine, Hollywood, Behind Scenes on Set 4-pg article, 7 movie stills, August 1939, 8½x11", NM, rare, S6..$135.00

Wizard of Oz, music box lid, 1960s, pnt ceramic, 4x4", NM, S6 ....$50.00

Wizard of Oz, pressbook, 1955, for 3rd release, 12 pgs, w/sample herald (10½x16¼"), 12x17", NM, S6........................$80.00

Wizard of Oz, puppet, Proctor & Gamble, ca 1965-69, premium, molded plastic head w/vinyl hand cover, 7x10", EX+, S6 ....$52.00

Wizard of Oz, sheet music, Rainbow Orchestration, 1 of 5,000 copies, incomplete, in 6¾x10½" folder, VG, scarce, S6..$50.00

Wizard of Oz, valentine, Am Colortype Co, 1940-41, Dorothy w/Toto & Scarecrow on yel brick road, 3x5", EX, S6 .$120.00

Wizard of Oz, valentine, Am Colortype Co, 1940-41, Scarecrow & Crabby Appletree, 3x5", NM, S6......................$110.00

Wizard of Oz, valentine, Am Colortype Co, 1940-41, Scarecrow & Tin Woodman, 3x5", EX, S6 ....$114.00

Wizard of Oz, wastebasket, Cheinco, 1975, characters & Oz map graphics, 10x13", G, S6 ....$265.00

Wolfman, eraser top, 1960s, rubber w/hole at bottom for pencil, 1", NM, F8 ....$12.00

Wolfman, pencil sharpener, UP Co, 1960s, gr plastic bust w/sharpener base, 3", NM, F8.............................$25.00

Wolfman, statue lamp, Universal Studios, 1973, plaster, 19", EX, H4 ....$200.00

Wonder Woman, music box, 1978, ceramic, working, NM, C17 ....$50.00

Woody Woodpecker, banjo, MIB, T1 ....$25.00

Woody Woodpecker, bank, Applause, ceramic, MIB, J2 ..$25.00

Woody Woodpecker, doll, Mattel, talker, MIB $200.00

Woody Woodpecker, doll, Mattel, talker (non-working), G..$25.00

Woody Woodpecker, flanel board set, VG, T1 ....$45.00

Woody Woodpecker, Magnetic Puzzle Set, 1973, MOC, J6...$14.00

Woody Woodpecker, note pad, EX, J7 ....$6.00

Woody Woodpecker, sheet music, 1974, mk As Recorded by Kay Kyser, EX+, F8 ....$12.00

Yogi Bear, blow-up chair, 1980, MIP (sealed), J7 ....$20.00

Yogi Bear, camera, 1960s, MIB, from $50.00 to $60.00.

Yogi Bear, camera, 1976, NMOC, J2 ....$20.00

Yogi Bear, chalk board, w/Boo Boo, EX, J7 ....$20.00

Yogi Bear, chime toy, 1965, Yogi on scooter, pull-string action, complete w/DW Thompson ad, 12", scarce, EX, A .$535.00

Yogi Bear, doll, Boo Boo, Mighty Star, 1979, stuffed cloth, 12", NM, C17 ....$25.00

Yogi Bear, figure, stuffed felt, 5", EX, J7 ....$7.00

Yogi Bear, spoon, Old Company Plate, late 1960s-70s, figure w/name on hdl, 6", EX, D9...........................$15.00

Yogi Bear & Boo Boo, curtains, 1967, brn chenille w/fuzzy red letters, 67x38", EX, J5, pr $85.00

Yosemite Sam, doll, 1971, stuffed, 17", EX, J7 ....$15.00

Ziggy, figure, postman, card in special delivery bag, 19", NM ..$25.00

Ziggy, trinket box, ceramic, J6..$14.00

Zippy the Chimp, film, Hot Shot Hero, Castle, 1950s, 8mm or 16mm, unused, EX (orig box), P6, ea......................$28.00

Zogg (from Electro Man), Ideal, 1977, half man/half monster, plastic, missing gun o/w EX, J2 ....$35.00

Chein

Though the company was founded shortly after the turn of the century, this New Jersey-based manufacturer is probably best known for the toys it made during the thirties and forties. Windup merry-go-rounds and Ferris wheels as well as many other carnival-type rides were made of beautifully lithographed tin even into the fifties, some in several variations. The company also made banks, a few of which were mechanical and some that were character-related. Mechanical, sea-worthy cabin cruisers, space guns, sand toys, and some Disney toys as well were made by this giant company; they continued in production until 1979.

Advisor: Scott Smiles (S10).

See also Banks; Disney.

Windups, Frictions and Other Mechanicals

Aquaplane, advances w/spinning prop, litho passengers in windows, 8", NM (EX+ box), A....................................$525.00

Barnacle Bill, 1930s, advances in waddling motion, 6", EX, A .$300.00

Bear, 1938, advances w/twisting action, 5", EX, A $100.00

Bonzo on Scooter, gray dog on gr & red scooter, 7", G-, A .$275.00

Broadway Trolley, 1935, 8", NM....................................$350.00

Cabin Cruiser, 1950s, 15", key needs work o/w MIB, H12.$100.00

Clown Floor Puncher, clown punches bag, litho tin w/celluloid punching bag, 8", VG+ $575.00

Clown w/Spinners, early mk, balances rod on nose & moves in circular vibrating motions, 8", EX+ $175.00

Disneyland Roller Coaster, 2 cars travel down track & stop, 19", NM (EX box), from $750 to......................................$850.00

Drummer Boy, 1930s, drum major beats drum, 9", EX+ (EX+ box)...$225.00

Duck, 1930s, 3½", non-working o/w EX, A $30.00

Ferris Wheel, 1930s, 6 gondolas spin w/bell sound, 17", NM (VG box), from $600 to $650.00

Greyhound Bus, plate mk Coast To Coast, 2-tone gr w/red tires, 9", EX...$325.00

Hand-Standing Clown, balances on hands and moves back and forth, purple pants with white polka-dots, 5", EX, from $125.00 to $150.00.

Photo courtesy of Scot Smiles.

Happy Days Cash Register, press keys for several actions, 4", EX, A $100.00

Happy Hooligan, 1932, vibrates & moves side to side, 6", EX (VG+ box), A $1,550.00

Helicopter, unused, 12", NMIB, J2....................................$225.00

Hercules Jazz Band, early, complete, 13", rare, EX (G- box), A....$825.00

Junior Truck, mk 220 on doors, gr & red w/yel tires, half-figure driver, 8", EX $275.00

Junior Truck, mk 420 on doors, gr w/red tires, half-figure driver, 8", EX...$350.00

Merry-Go-Round, kids spin around on horses w/bell noise, 10", NM (EX+ box), A $800.00

Musical Aero Swing, 4 cars fly out as canopy spins w/musical notes, orig flag, 10", NM (G box), A $825.00

Peggy Jane Sailboat, mk Hercules, complete, 23", scarce, VG, A...$250.00

Penguin, advances in waddling motion, 4", EX................$75.00

Pig, advances w/twisting action, 5", EX, A $100.00

Playland Merry-Go-Round, 5 carousel horses w/riders & 5 swans around perimeter, 11" dia, EX+ (EX box), A..........$800.00

Playland Whip, 4 cars w/riders circle corners w/bobbing heads & bell sound, 20", NM (EX box), from $675 to...........$750.00

Popeye, litho tin figure w/molded arms looking sideways, 6", non-working, G, A..$175.00

Popeye Floor Puncher, litho tin figure on platform hits celluloid bag on rod, 7½", EX (flaps missing on box) $1,500.00

Popeye Floor Puncher, litho tin figure on platform hits celluloid bag on rod, 7½", EX, from $950 to $1,050.00

Popeye Overhead Puncher, 1930s, lithographed tin, 10", M, from $2,500.00 to $3,000.00.

Photo courtesy of Dunbar Gallery.

Rabbit, advances w/twisting action, 5", EX, A................$100.00

Rabbit w/Cart, rabbit pulls cart w/litho ducks riding in Express vehicle & rabbit flying an airplane, 8", NM, A $175.00

Rabbit w/Cart, rabbit pulls cart w/litho rabbits carrying a pumpkin & other animal scenes, 8", NM, from $125 to...$150.00

Racer #5, 1930, red & yel w/driver & attached spare tire, 9½", scarce, EX...$400.00

Raggedy Ann Musical Top, features Raggedy Ann, jack-in-the-box, rocking horse & teddy bear, 10" dia, VG+, A....$55.00

Ride-A-Rocket Carousel, figures in 4 rockets attached to top of rotating disk, 18", G, A $100.00

Roller Coaster, 1930s, w/2 cars & bell, 19", EX, from $275 to...$325.00

Roller Coaster, 1930s, w/2 cars & bell, 19", EX (orig box), from $325 to $375.00

Roller Coaster, 1950s, w/2 cars, 19", NM, from $225 to.$275.00

Roller Coaster, 1950s, w/2 cars, 19", NMIB, from $250 to.$300.00

Ski-Ride #320, kids travel ride & go to the top, 19½", NM (EX box), A $1,100.00

Miscellaneous

Bank, clown receives & deposits coin, mc metal, 7", NM .$100.00

Cathedral Organ, turn crank & music plays, litho tin, 9½", NMIB...$175.00

Hercules Motor Express Truck, blk C-style cab, blk chassis, yel stake bed
w/name panel, wht wheels, red hubs, 22", EX.....................$1,000.00
Popeye Sparkler, 1959, sparks fly behind clear red window inserts,
plunger action, needs flint o/w EX (VG box), A......$260.00
Rabbit Roly Poly, 6", EX...$75.00

Chinese Tin Toys

China has produced toys for export since the 1920s, but most of their tin toys were made from the 1970s to the present. Collectors are buying them with an eye to the future, since right now, at least, they are relatively inexpensive.

Government-operated factories are located in various parts of China. They use various numbering systems to identify types of toys, for instance, ME (metal-electric — battery operated), MS (metal-spring — windup), MF (metal friction), and others. Most toys and boxes are marked, but some aren't; and since many of the toys are reproductions of earlier Japanese models, it is often difficult to tell the difference if no numbers can be found.

Prices vary greatly depending on age, condition, availability and dealer knowledge of origin. Toys currently in production may be discontinued at any time and may often be as hard to find as the earlier toys. Records are so scarce that it is difficult to pinpoint the start of production, but at least some manufacture began in the 1970s and '80s. If you have additional information (toy name and number; description as to size, color variations, actions, type, etc.; and current market), please contact our advisor. In the listings below, values are for new-in-the-box items.

Advisor: Steve Fisch (F7)

#ME021, police car, current, 16½x5x5", F7, from $55 to .$125.00
#ME060, tank, remote control, 1970s, 7x4x4", F7, from $35
to...$75.00
#ME072, open-door police car, 9½x4x4", F7, from $35 to...$100.00
#ME084, jet plane, current, 13x14x4½", F7, from $35 to...$75.00
#ME086, Shanghai bus, MIB, F7, from $85 to.................$150.00
#ME087, jetliner, 1980s, 19x18x3", F7, from $55 to......$125.00
#ME089, Universe car, 1950s, MIB, F7, from $85 to......$150.00
#ME093, open-door trolley, current, 10x5x4", F7, from $25
to $35.00
#ME095, fire chief car, current, 12½x5x5", F7, from $35 to .$75.00
#ME097, Police car, 13x5x5", F7, from $35 to..................$75.00
#ME099, UFO spaceship, current, 8x8x5", F7, from $35 to.$75.00
#ME100, robot, current, 12x4x6", F7, from $35 to.........$125.00
#ME102, spaceship, blows air, current, 13x5x4", F7, from $35
to...$75.00
#ME104, locomotive, 15½x4x7", F7, from $35 to.............$75.00
#ME105, locomotive, 9½x5½x5½", F7, from $35 to $75.00
#ME610, hen laying eggs, current, 7x4x6", F7, from $25 to..$50.00
#ME611, News Car or World Cap Car, 5x16½x5", MIB, F7, ea,
from $55 to $125.00
#ME614, automatic rifle, current, 23x2x8", F7, from $25 to....$35.00
#ME677, Shanghai convertible, 1970s, 12x5x3", F7, from $60
to $100.00
#ME679, dump truck, discontinued, 13x4x3", F7, from $25
to $50.00

Photo courtesy of Steve Fisch.

#ME603, hen and chicken, MIB, F7, from $25.00 to $50.00.

#ME699, fire chief car, 10x5x2", F7, from $25 to $50.00
#ME756, anti-aircraft armoured tank, MIB, F7, from $50 to ..$100.00
#ME767, Universe boat, current, 10x5x6", F7, from $35 to ...$75.00
#ME767, Universe boat, 1970s, 10x5x6", F7, from $75 to..$150.00
#ME770, Mr Duck, current, 9x7x5", F7, from $25 to $50.00
#ME774, tank, remote control, 1970s, 9x4x3", F7, from $45
to..$75.00
#ME777, Universe Televiboat, current, 15x4x7", F7, from $35
to..$75.00
#ME777, Universe Televiboat, 1970s, 15x4x7", F7, from $75
to..$150.00
#ME801, Lunar explorer, 1970s, 12x6x4", F7, from $75 to ..$125.00
#ME809, anti-aircraft armoured car, 1970s, 12x6x6", F7, from
$75 to..$100.00
#ME821, Cicada, 1970s, 10x4x4", F7, from $50 to.........$125.00
#ME824, Patrol car, 1970s, 11x4x3½", F7, from $35 to ...$75.00
#ME842, camel, discontinued, 10x4x7", F7, from $35 to .$50.00
#ME884, Police car, VW bug style, current, 11½x5x5", F7, from
$35 to $75.00
#ME895, fire engine, 1970s, 10x4x4", F7, from $50 to $85.00
#MF032, Eastwind sedan, current, 6x2x2", F7, from $8 to .$15.00
#MF033, pickup truck, current, 6x2x2", F7, from $8 to....$15.00
#MF044, sedan, Nissan style, 1980s, 9x3½x3", F7, from $10
to..$25.00
#MF046, sparking carbine, current, 18x5x1", F7, from $20 to....$35.00
#MF052, sedan, 8x3x2", F7, from $15 to..........................$25.00
#MF083, sedan, current, 6x2x2", F7, from $8 to...............$15.00
#MF104, passenger plane, current, 9x10x3", F7, from $15 to ..$25.00
#MF107, airplane, 6x6x2", F7, from $20 to......................$35.00
#MF111, ambulance, current, 8x3x3", F7, from $15 to $20.00
#MF127, Highway patrol car, 9½x4x3", F7, from $20 to..$50.00
#MF132, ambulance, 1980s, 10x4x4", F7, from $15 to.....$35.00
#MF134, tourist bus, current, 6x2x3", F7, from $15 to $25.00
#MF135, red flag convertible, MIB, F7, from $35 to.........$75.00
#MF136, double-decker train, current, 8x2x3", F7, from $15
to..$20.00
#MF146, VW, 5x2x2", F7, from $10 to............................$20.00
#MF151, Shanghai pickup, 1970s, 12x4x4", F7, from $50
to $100.00

#MF154, tractor, 1970s, 5x3x4", F7, from $25 to $50.00

#MF155, airplane, 14x11½x4", F7, from $30 to $35.00

#MF162, motorcycle, 6x2x4", F7, from $15 to..................$35.00

#MF163 fire truck, current, 6x2x3", F7, from $8 to $15.00

#MF164, construction truck, 1970s, 7x3x5", F7, from $35 to.$75.00

#MF164, VW, current, 4x2x3", F7, from $10 to..................$15.00

#MF170, train, current, 10x2x4", F7, from $15 to............$25.00

#MF171, convertible, current, 5x2x2", F7, from $8 to $15.00

#MF184, coach bus, 12½x4x4", F7, from $15 to $30.00

Photo courtesy of Steve Fisch.

#MF185, double-decker bus, current, 11x5x3", F7, from $15.00 to $25.00.

#MF193, soft-cover truck, 1970s, 11x3x4", F7, from $50 to.$75.00

#MF201, oil tanker, current, 14x4x4", F7, from $15 to $25.00

#MF202, jetliner, discontinued, 9x4x3", F7, from $15 to .$25.00

#MF203, sedan, 10½x4x2½", F7, from $20 to $50.00

#MF206, panda truck, current, 6x3x2", F7, from $10 to...$20.00

#MF216, airplane, discontinued, 9x9x3", F7, from $15 to ..$35.00

#MF234, sedan, 6x2x2", F7, from $15 to...........................$25.00

#MF239, tiger truck, current, 10x3x4", F7, from $15 to ...$30.00

#MF240, passenger jet, 13x11x4", F7, from $30 to $35.00

#MF249, flying boat, 1970s, 6x6x2", F7, from $35 to $75.00

#MF254, Mercedes sedan, current, 8x4x3", F7, from $15 to .$25.00

#MF274, tank, 1970s, 3x2x2", F7, from $8 to $15.00

#MF298, traveling car, 8½x4x3½", F7, from $15 to.........$25.00

#MF304, race car, discontinued, 10x4x3", F7, from $15 to..$35.00

#MF309, sedan, 9x2x3½", F7, from $20 to $35.00

#MF310, Corvette, current, 3x2x3", F7, from $10 to........$15.00

#MF316, 1953 Corvette, F7, from $20 to..........................$50.00

#MF317, Corvette convertible, current, 10x4x3", F7, from $20 to $50.00

#MF320, Mercedes sedan, current, 7x3x2", F7, from $10 to..$10.00

#MF321, Buick convertible, current, 11x4x3", F7, from $20 to...$50.00

#MF322, Buick sedan, current, 11x4x3", F7, from $20 to...$50.00

#MF326, Mercedes gull-wing sedan, 9x3x2", F7, from $15 to $25.00

#MF329, 1956 Corvette convertible, 10x4x4", F7, from $20 to...$50.00

#MF330, Cadillac sedan, current, 11x4x3", F7, from $20 to $50.00

#MF334, helicopter, 10x2x4", F7, from $15 to $35.00

#MF339, 1956 Corvette sedan, 10x4x4", F7, from $20 to ...$50.00

#MF340, Cadillac convertible, current, 11x4x3", F7, from $20 to $50.00

#MF341, convertible, 12x4x3", F7, from $20 to $50.00

Photo courtesy of Steve Fisch.

#MF333, Thunderbird convertible, current, 11x4x3", F7, from $20.00 to $50.00.

#MF342, sedan, 12x4x3", F7, from $20 to.......................$50.00

#MF712, locomotive, current, 7x2x3", F7, from $10 to....$15.00

#MF713, taxi, current, 5x2x2", F7, from $8 to..................$15.00

#MF714, fire chief car, current, 5x2x2", F7, from $8 to....$15.00

#MF716, ambulance, 1970s, 8x3x3", F7, from $15 to.......$30.00

#MF717, dump truck, discontinued, 10x3x5", F7, from $15 to...$35.00

#MF718, ladder truck, current, 10x3x4", F7, from $15 to...$35.00

#MF721, light tank, current, 6x3x3", F7, from $15 to $20.00

#MF722, jeep, current, 6x3x3", F7, from $15 to $20.00

#MF731, station wagon, current, 5x2x2", F7, from $8 to....$15.00

#MF732, ambulance, current, 5x2x2", F7, from $8 to $15.00

#MF735, rocket racer, current, 7x3x3", F7, from $15 to...$35.00

#MF742, flying boat, current, 13x4x4", F7, from $15 to...$35.00

#MF743, Karmann Ghia sedan, current, 10x3x4", F7, from $15 to...$45.00

#MF753, sports car, current, 8x3x2", F7, from $15 to.......$25.00

#MF782, circus truck, current, 9x3x4", F7, from $15 to ...$25.00

#MF787, Lucky open car, current, 8x3x2", F7, from $15 to..$25.00

#MF798, patrol car, current, 8x3x3", F7, from $15 to.......$25.00

#MF800, race car #5, current, 6x2x2", F7, from $10 to $20.00

#MF804, locomotive, current, 16x3x5", F7, from $15 to..$25.00

#MF844, double-decker bus, current, 8x4x3", F7, from $15 to...$20.00

#MF861, space gun, 1970s, 10x2x6", F7, from $45 to.......$75.00

#MF893, animal van, current, 6x2x3", F7, from $15 to....$20.00

#MF900, police car, current, 6x3x2", F7, from $8 to $15.00

#MF910, airport limo bus, current, 15x4x5", F7, from $20 to ...$35.00

#MF923, torpedo boat, current, 8x3x3", F7, from $15 to .$25.00

#MF951, fighter jet, 1970s, 5x4x2", F7, from $15 to.........$20.00

#MF956, sparking tank, current, 8x4x3", F7, from $15 to ..$20.00

#MF957, ambulance helicopter, 7½x2x4", F7, from $15 to ...$35.00

#MF958, poultry truck, current, 6x2x2", F7, from $15 to .$20.00

#MF959, jeep, discontinued, 9x4x4", F7, from $15 to $20.00

#MF962, station wagon, 1970s, 9x3x3", F7, from $25 to..$45.00

#MF974, circus truck, current, 6x2x4", F7, from $15 to....$20.00

#MF985, fowl transporter, current, 8x2x3", F7, from $15 to $20.00

#MF989, noisy locomotive, 1970s, 12x3x4", F7, from $25 to ..$50.00

#MF993, mini car, current, 5x2x2", F7, from $8 to...........$15.00

#MF998, sedan, current, 5x2x2", F7, $8 to $15.00

#MS002, jumping frog, current, 2x2x2", F7, from $8 to ...$15.00

#MS006, pecking chick, 1970s, 2x1x1", F7, from $8 to....$15.00

#MS011, roll-over plane, current, 3x4x2", F7, from $10 to...$18.00

#MS014, single-bar exerciser, 1970s, 7x6x6", F7, from $25 to...$50.00

#MS057, horse & rider, 1970s, 6x2x5", F7, from $18 to..$35.00

#MS058, old-fashioned car, current, 3x3x4", F7, from $12 to $20.00

#MS082, jumping frog, current, 2x2x2", F7, from $8 to ...**$15.00**

#MS083, jumping rabbit, current, 3x3x2", F7, from $8 to ...**$15.00**

#MS085, xylophone girl, current, 7x3x9", F7, from $18 to **$35.00**

#MS107, jumping Bambi, current, 5x1½x6", F7, from $12 to $20.00

#MS134, sparking jet, current, 5x5x3", F7, from $15 to ...**$30.00**

#MS166, crawling baby, vinyl head, current, 5x4x5", F7, from $12 to $20.00

Photo courtesy of Steve Fisch.

#MS203, train, current, 11x2x2", F7, from $8.00 to $15.00.

#MS405, ice cream vendor, current, 4x3x4", F7, from $8 to $20.00

#MS405, jumping zebra, current, 5x2x4", F7, from $8 to .**$20.00**

#MS565, drumming panda/wheel, current, 5x3x5", F7, from $8 to $20.00

#MS568, sparrow, current, 5x2x2", F7, from $8 to **$15.00**

#MS569, oriole, current, 5x2x2", F7, from $8 to **$15.00**

Photo courtesy of Steve Fisch.

#MS575, bear with camera, current, 6x3x4", F7, from $15.00 to $35.00.

#MS702, motorcycle, current, 7x4x5", F7, from $15 to ..**$35.00**

#MS704, bird music cart, 1970s, 3x2x5", F7, from $15 to ..**$25.00**

#MS709, motorcycle w/sidecar, current, 7x4x5", F7, from $15 to $35.00

#MS710, tricycle, current, 5x3x5", F7, from $15 to..........**$20.00**

#MS713, washing machine, current, 3x3x5", F7, from $15 to ..**$20.00**

#MS765, drummer, current, 5x3x6", F7, from $15 to.......**$25.00**

#MS827, sedan, steering, 1970s, 9x3x3", F7, from $50 to...**$75.00**

#MS858, girl on goose, current, 5x3x3", F7, from $15 to.....**$25.00**

#PMS102, rolling cart, current, 3x2x1", F7, from $15 to..**$20.00**

#PMS105, jumping dog, current, 3x2x6", F7, from $15 to..**$25.00**

#PMS106, jumping parrot, current, 3x2x6", F7, from $15 to $25.00

#PMS108, duck family, current, 10x2x3", F7, from $15 to..............**$25.00**

#PMS113, Fu dog, current, 4x2x3", F7, from $15 to........**$25.00**

#PMS119, woodpecker, current, 3x2x6", F7, from $15 to ..**$25.00**

#PMS210, clown riding bike, current, 4x2x5", F7, from $15 to..$25.00

#PMS212, elephant on bike, current, 6x3x8", F7, from $15 to..$35.00

#PMS213, duck on bike, current, 6x3x8", F7, from $15 to ..**$35.00**

#PMS214, lady bug family, current, 13x3x1", F7, from $15 to..**$25.00**

#PMS215, crocodile, current, 9x3x1", F7, from $12 to.....**$20.00**

#PMS217, jumping rabbit, current, 3x2x6", F7, from $15 to..**$25.00**

#PMS218, penguin, current, 3x2x6", F7, from $15 to **$30.00**

#PS013, boy on tricycle, current, 2x4x4", F7, from $12 to...**$25.00**

Circus Toys

If you ever had the opportunity to go to one of the giant circuses as a child, no doubt you still have very vivid recollections of the huge elephants, the daring trapeze artists, the clowns and their trick dogs, and the booming voice of the ringmaster, even if that experience was a half century ago. Most of our circus toys are listed in other categories.

See also Battery-Operated Toys; Cast Iron, Circus; Chein, Windups; Marx, Windups; Windups, Friction and Other Mechanicals.

Acrobats Gravity Toy, Germany, 2 tin acrobats descend rod which can be reversed for continuous play, 11", EX, A..........$470.00

Britain's Mammoth Circus, complete, NM (EX box), A, $800.00.

Circus Performers, Webber, 1912, jtd wood base w/center slots to fit cb clown w/drum & other figures, 14", EX......$150.00

Clever Clowns, Greycraft, Grey Iron Casting Co, 1930s, diecast figures, EX (EX box), D10...$750.00

Clicker, circus elephant, mk Made in Japan, litho tin elephant balancing on a log, 2½", NM.....................................$125.00

Elephant in Hoop, Fallows, gray circus elephant w/red blanket in blk-pnt hoop, tin, 11½" dia, rstr, A $440.00

Ringling Bros Toy Circus, Mattel, MIB, W5 ....$85.00

Zirkus, East Germany, wood figures, set of 48, EX (orig box), T1 ....$45.00

Coloring, Activity and Paint Books

Coloring and activity books from the early years of the twentieth century are scarce indeed, and when found can be expensive if they are tied into another collectibles field such as Black Americana or advertising; but the ones most in demand are those that represent familiar movie and TV stars of the 1950s and '60s. Condition plays a very important part in assessing worth, and though hard to find, unused examples are the ones that bring top dollar — in fact, as much as 50% to 75% more than one partially used.

Advisor: Diane Albert (T6).

See also Advertising.

ABC Book To Color, Saalfield #2105, 1935, few pgs colored, VG, M14 ....$20.00

Agent Zero M, coloring book, Whitman, 1966, M, F8 .....$28.00

Alice in Wonderland, coloring book, Whitman, 1951, several pgs colored o/w EX+, F8 ....$18.00

Andy Panda, coloring book, Whitman, 1944, few pgs colored o/w EX+, F8 ....$25.00

Andy Panda, paint book, Whitman, 1946, EX, A3 ....$40.00

Annette, coloring book, Whitman, 1961, several pgs colored o/w VG+, F8 ....$10.00

Archie & Jughead, coloring book, Whitman, 1972, 10 pgs colored o/w EX+, F8 ....$15.00

Barney Rubble, activity book, Watkins-Strathmore, 1961, neatly applied stickers, EX, T2 ....$20.00

Bat Masterson, coloring book, Saalfield, 1959, EX+, F8...$25.00

Batman, coloring book, Vroom Screee, 1966, 6 pgs colored o/w EX, A3 ....$25.00

Battlestar Galactica, activity book, Grosset & Dunlap, 1979, NM, C1 ....$14.00

Beatles, coloring book, Saalfield, unused, EX, B3 ....$80.00

Ben Casey, coloring book, Saalfield, 1963, EX+, F8.........$15.00

Ben Casey, coloring book, Saalfield, 1963, unused, M $25.00

Big John, Little John, coloring book, 1972, unused, M, J7..$15.00

Black Hole, activity book, 1979, unused, NM, F8 ....$15.00

Bobby Benson's B-Bar-Riders, coloring book, Whitman, 1950, unused, EX, J5 ....$15.00

Bonanza, coloring book, Saalfield, 1965, unused, M, J7 ...$50.00

Boots & Saddles, coloring book, 1958, unused, M, V1 .....$48.00

Brady Bunch, coloring book, Whitman, 1974, 11 pgs colored o/w EX+, F8 ....$36.00

Buck Rogers, coloring & activity book, Whitman, 1979, NM, C1...$14.00

Calvin & the Colonel, coloring book, 1962, unused, M, V1 ....$35.00

Candid Camera, coloring book, Lowe, 1963, several pgs colored o/w EX+, F8 ....$25.00

Captain Gallant, coloring book, Lowe, 1956, features Buster Crabbe & Cuffy on cover, NM..................................$50.00

Captain Marvel Fun Book, activity book, 1944, unused, NM, rare, A3 ....$250.00

Charlie Chaplin, coloring book, Saalfield, 1941, 3 pgs colored o/w EX, A3 ....$125.00

Charlie McCarthy Coloring Set, Whitman, 1938, complete w/coloring book & crayons, unused, MIB, A...........$150.00

Charmin' Chatty, coloring book, unused, L6....................$35.00

Chatty Baby, coloring book, unused, L6 ....$35.00

Chilly Willy, coloring book, Whitman, 1957, unused, EX+, A3 ....$30.00

Chipmunks, coloring book, 1963, unused, M, from $25 to ...$30.00

Chitty-Chitty Bang-Bang, coloring book, Watkins-Strathmore, EX, F8..$12.00

Batman, coloring book, Whitman, 1967, NM, $25.00.

Elizabeth Taylor, coloring book, few pages colored otherwise EX, $22.00.

Colt .45, coloring book, 1959, unused, M, V1 ....$45.00

Coronation, coloring book, Saalfield, 1953, EX+, D9 ......$38.00

Curious George, coloring book, Artcraft, 1973, EX+, F8 .$15.00

Daisy Duck Cut-Out Coloring Book, Pocket Books, 1953, EX+, M8...$35.00

Dick Tracy, coloring book, Saalfield #399, 1946, EX, D11 ..$35.00

Dick Tracy Junior Detective Kit, punch-out book, 1962, 5 pgs, 13½x7½", M, D11..$20.00

Disney's Fantasyland, coloring book, Whitman, 1955, Tinkerbell on cover, several pgs colored o/w NM, F8..................$18.00

Disney's Its a Small World, coloring book, Whitman, 1966, NM, F8..$12.00

Double Deckers, coloring book, 1971, M, V1 ....$16.00

Dr Kildare, coloring & activity book, Lowe, 1963, NM, C1 .$36.00

Dudley Do-Right, coloring & activity book, Whitman, 1972, EX, H4...$12.00

Family Affair, coloring book, Whitman, 1974, 14 pgs colored o/w EX, F8...$15.00

Famous San Diego Chicken, coloring book, 1978, photo cover, EX, J7 ....$8.00

Felix the Cat Elf Book To Color, Rand McNally, 1955, NM, C1 ....$45.00

Flash Gordon, coloring book, Saalfield, 1958, several pgs colored o/w EX+, F8 ....$30.00

Flash Gordon, coloring book, Saalfield, 1958, unused, M, V1 ..$50.00

Flash Gordon, coloring book, 1979, unused, M, J7...........$15.00

Flash Gordon, coloring book, A McWilliams, 1952, M, $75.00.

Flintstones, activity book, Hear-See-Do, 1973, unused, M, J7 ....$30.00

Flintstones, punch-out book, A Great Big Punchout, Whitman, 1961, unused, NM $35.00

Flipper, coloring book, Whitman, 1965, EX, F8 ....$15.00

Freckles, coloring book, Saalfield, 1952, unused, VG+, A3....$35.00

Gene Autry, paint book, 1940, EX, J2................................$45.00

Gene Autry Adventures To Color, 1941, 14 pgs colored o/w EX, I2 ....$50.00

George of the Jungle, coloring book, Whitman, 1969, EX, F8 .$24.00

Get Smart, coloring book, Artcraft, 1965, 10 pgs colored o/w EX+, F8..$48.00

Gilligan's Island, coloring book, Whitman, 1964, EX+, scarce, T2...$60.00

Green Hornet, coloring book, Whitman, 1960s, NM, from $40 to $50.00

Gremlin's Sticker Fun, 1984, unused, J7 ....$8.00

Gulliver's Travels, coloring book, Saalfield, 1939, 11 pgs colored o/w EX, F8..$24.00

Gumby & Pokey Dot Book, activity book, Whitman, 1970, EX+, F8..$16.00

Hopalong Cassidy, coloring book, Funtime, 1954, 1 pg neatly colored o/w NM, C1 ....$45.00

Hopalong Cassidy, coloring book, Whitman, Authorized Edition, 1951, NM, from $55.00 to $75.00.

I Learn My Colors, coloring book, 1950s, EX, H12.............$8.00

Incredible Hulk, activity book, Whitman #2169, 1979, complete & unused, M $10.00

Jack & the Beanstalk, coloring book, Clover Pub, 1964, NM, T2..$12.00

Jackie Gleason, coloring book, 1956, unused, EX+, A3 ...$50.00

Jetsons, coloring book, Rand McNally, 1986, NM, H4.......$6.00

Jetsons, coloring book, 1971, unused, M, from $15 to $20.00

Johnny Quest Meets Judy Jetson, coloring book, 1977, EX, J2...$30.00

Judy Garland, paint book, 1930s, unused, VG+, from $40 to $50.00

Just Kids Comics, coloring book, King Features, 1928, unused, VG, A3 ....$75.00

Kit Carson, coloring book, Lowe, 1957, 26 pgs colored o/w EX+, F8..$25.00

Korg, coloring book, Artcraft, 1975, EX, H4 ....$15.00

Lady & the Tramp, coloring book, Whitman, 1954, 20 pgs colored o/w EX, F8..$18.00

Land of the Giants, coloring book, Whitman, 1969, 13 pgs colored o/w EX, F8...$28.00

Lassie, Magic Paint Book, 1957, unused, NM, J7..............$40.00

Laugh-In, punch-out & paste book, 1968, unused, EX, J2 ...$15.00

Laverne & Shirley, coloring book, Playmore, 1983, NM, F8 ..$4.00

Lawman, coloring book, 1959, unused, M, V1 ....$65.00

Little Lulu, coloring book, Whitman, 1944, 2 pgs colored o/w NM, C1 ....$82.00

Little Lulu Sticker Fun, Whitman, 1973, unused, NM.....$10.00

Little Orphan Annie, coloring book, McLoughlin, 1933, several pgs colored o/w EX+, A3 ....$125.00

Little Orphan Annie Paint & Crayon Book, 1937, artist Harold Gray, several pgs colored o/w VG, A3 ....$60.00

Lone Ranger, coloring book, Whitman, 1950s, NM........$25.00

MacKenzie's Raiders, coloring book, 1960, unused, M, V1 ..$48.00

Margie TV Show Cynthia Pepper Cut-Out Book, Watkins-Strathmore, 1963, photo cover, NM, C1 ....$32.00

Marlin Perkins, A Trip to the Zoo, coloring book, Lowe, 1954, EX+, F8 ....$12.00

Mary Poppins Merry-Go-Round, coloring book, 1964, M, V1 ....$15.00

Masquerade Horror Masks, punch-out book, 1969, unused, EX, J2 ....$30.00

Mighty Mouse, coloring book, Treasure, 1957, 5 pgs colored o/w EX, F8 ....$15.00

Monroes, coloring book, Artcraft, 1966, EX+, F8 ....$45.00

Mork From Ork, activity book, 1978, unused, EX, J7 ....$12.00

Mrs Beasley Color & Read, activity book, 1972, unused, M, J2 ....$35.00

My Favorite Martian, coloring book, Whitman, 1964, unused, M, J7 ....$50.00

My Favorite Martian, coloring book, Whitman, 1964, 11 pgs colored o/w EX, F8 ....$26.00

My Three Sons, coloring book, Whitman, 1967, photo cover, NM, C1 ....$36.00

Nanny & the Professor, coloring book, Artcraft, 1971, 6 pgs colored o/w EX+, F8 ....$25.00

National Velvet, coloring book, Whitman, 1961, EX+, T2/F8 ....$15.00

Northwest Passage, coloring book, 1959, unused, M, J7 ...$40.00

Our Gang, coloring book, Saalfield, 1933, few pgs colored, cover torn o/w EX, P6 ....$55.00

Partridge Family, coloring & activity book, Artcraft, 1973, unused, M $25.00

Peanuts, coloring book, Saalfield, 1965, G+, A3 ....$8.00

Planet of the Apes, coloring book, 1974, 1st version, unused, M $15.00

Popeye, coloring book, Lowe, 1962, 10 pgs colored o/w EX+, F8 ....$20.00

Popeye, paint book, McLoughlin Bros, 1932, artist Segar, EX+, A3 ....$140.00

Raggedy Ann Color 'N Read, Whitman, 1972, NM, J6 ...$12.00

Ramar of the Jungle, coloring book, Saalfield, 1956, 20 pgs colored o/w EX+, F8 ....$25.00

Red Ryder, coloring book, Whitman, 1952, unused, EX+, A3 ....$150.00

Reg'lar Fellers Story Paint Book, Gene Byrnes, 1932, 12x9", unused, EX, P6 ....$295.00

Restless Gun, coloring book, 1958, unused, M, V1 ....$50.00

Roy Rogers & Dale Evans, punch-out book, Whitman/Roy Rogers Enterprises, 1954, scarce, unused, NM, A $245.00

Scooby-Doo's All-Star Laff-a-Lympics, coloring book, Rand McNally, 1978, NM, C1 ....$28.00

Sid & Marty Krofft's Kaleidoscope Puppets, punch-out activity book, Kaleidoscope/Coca-Cola, 1968, unused, NM, J5 .$75.00

Sigmond & the Sea Monsters, coloring book, Rand McNally, 1974, NM, C1 ....$25.00

Skeezix, coloring book, McLoughlin Bros, 1929, 10x10", EX+, A3 ....$60.00

Smokey the Bear, coloring book, Whitman, 1958, few pgs colored o/w EX, J5 ....$15.00

Soupy Sales Fun & Activity Book, Treasure Books, 1965, NM, C1...$18.00

Space Mouse, coloring book, Saalfield, 1962, Walter Lantz characters, 5 pgs colored o/w EX+, F8 ....$15.00

Space: 1999, activity book, Saalfield, 1975, NM $15.00

Spider-Man's Oyster Mystery, coloring book, Whitman, 1976, NM, C1...$20.00

Steve Canyon, coloring book, Saalfield, 1952, EX+, C1 ..$50.00

Strange World of Mr Mum, coloring book, 1962, unused, M, V1 ....$35.00

Sugarfoot, coloring book, 1959, unused, M, V1 ....$65.00

Superman, coloring book, Saalfield, 1940, several pgs colored o/w G+, A3...$120.00

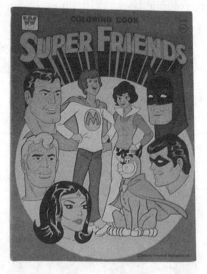

Super Friends, coloring book, Whitman, 1975, NM, $12.00.

Superman, cut-out book, Saalfield/Superman Inc, 1940, unused, scarce, NM, A $865.00

Suzy Homemaker, coloring book, Whitman/Topper, 1971, unused, EX $25.00

Tarzan, coloring book, Whitman, 1952, G+, A3 ....$20.00

Terry & the Pirates, coloring book, Saalfield, 1946, unused, VG, A3 ....$40.00

That Girl, coloring book, Saalfield, 1967, NM, C1 ....$50.00

Three Stooges, coloring & activity book, Playmore, 1983, 2 pgs colored, H4 ....$12.00

Thunderbirds, coloring book, Whitman, 1968, 2 pgs colored o/w VG, J5 ....$25.00

Tom & Jerry, coloring book, Whitman, 1952, 20 pgs colored o/w EX, F8 ....$12.00

Tom Corbett Space Cadet, punch-out book, Saalfield, 1952, unused, NM, A $95.00

Tonto, coloring book, Whitman, 1957, 14 pgs colored o/w EX, F8 ....$16.00

Top Cat, coloring book, Whitman, 1971, unused, M, V1 ..$18.00

Underdog, coloring book, Whitman, 1972, 9 pgs colored o/w EX, F8...$12.00

Underdog, coloring book, 1974, unused, M $25.00

Universal Studios: Virginian/McHale's Navy/Wagon Train, unused, M, J7 ....$50.00

US Marshall & Heroes of the West, coloring book, James & Jonathan, 1955, unused, NM, T2 ....$25.00

Wizard of Oz, activity book, Whitman, 1976, M, H4 ....$12.00

Wonderbug, coloring book, unused, M, J2 ....$15.00

Zedo Into Space, coloring book, 1950s, EX, J2 ....$20.00

Zorro, coloring book, Whitman, 1960s, EX $20.00

101 Dalmatians, coloring book, Whitman, 1960, several pgs colored o/w EX $5.00

Comic Books

For more than a half a century, kids of America raced to the bookstand as soon as the new comics came in for the month and for 10¢ an issue kept up on the adventures of their favorite super heroes, cowboys, space explorers, and cartoon characters. By far most were eventually discarded — after they were traded one friend to another, stacked on closet shelves, and finally confiscated by Mom. Discount the survivors that were torn or otherwise damaged over the years and those about the mundane, and of those remaining, some could be quite valuable. In fact, first editions of high-grade comics books or those showcasing the first appearance of a major character often bring $500.00 and more. Rarity, age, and quality of the artwork are prime factors in determining value, and condition is critical. If you want to seriously collect comic books, you'll need to refer to a good comic book price guide such as Overstreet's. The examples we've listed here are worth from $5.00 and up; many are worth much less.

Other Sources: A3, P3, K1 (Simpson's Comics)

Adventures of Rex the Wonder Dog, #11, VG, M14 ....$30.00

Adventures of the Jaguar, Archie #7, 1962, EX+, F8 ....$9.00

Alice's Adventures in Wonderland & Through the Looking Glass, King Classics Comic, 1978, NM, A6 ....$2.50

Amazing Spider-Man, Marvel Comics #1, 1963, EX, $5,400.00.

All-Star Comics, #27, 1945, EX+, M14 ....$450.00

Alley Oop, #12, 1948, EX, F8 ....$34.00

Alvin & the Chipmunks, Dell #15, 1966, VG+, F8 ....$4.00

Andy Panda, Dell New Funnies #118, EX, M14 ....$15.00

Annie Oakley, #10, NM, C1 ....$27.00

Annie Oakley & Tagg, Dell #5, EX-, T2 ....$12.00

Archie's Mad House, Comic Book Annual #2, 1964-65, EX+, F8 ....$15.00

Archie's Mad House, Comic Book Annual #9, VG, M14 ..$10.00

Archies, #166, 1965, EX+, Beatles on cover, F8 ....$5.00

Avengers, Gold Key #1, 1968, VG+, T2 ....$45.00

Avengers, Marvel #15, VG, M14 ....$20.00

Banana Splits, Gold Key, April 1971, G, H4 ....$12.00

Batman, #1, 1970s, H12 ....$35.00

Battlestar Galactica, Marvel #1, 1979, EX+, F8 ....$3.00

Ben Casey, Dell #2, 1962, EX, T2 ....$12.00

Beneath the Planet of the Apes, Gold Key Movie Comics, 1962, NM, M14 ....$28.00

Beverly Hillbillies, Dell #17, EX, F8 ....$8.00

Blackhawk, #39, Kinstler Art, 1951, EX+, C1 ....$200.00

Bonanza, #4, EX, C1 ....$35.00

Bonanza, #7, EX, J7 ....$25.00

Bonanza, Dell Four Color #01-210, G+, T2 ....$20.00

Bonanza, Gold Key #10, 1964, EX, T2 ....$12.00

Bonanza, Gold Key #37, 1970, EX, F8 ....$5.00

Brave Eagle, Dell Four Color #770, EX, T2 ....$10.00

Buck Jones, #589, VG+, D8 ....$25.00

Buffalo Bill Jr Comics, #356, G+, D8 ....$12.00

Bugs Bunny, #200, 1948, EX+, C1 ....$45.00

Bugs Bunny Finds the Frozen Kingdom, Dell Four Color #164, VG, M14 ....$30.00

Bugs Bunny Halloween Parade, Dell Giant #1, 1953, EX+, M14 ....$115.00

Bullwinkle, Gold Key #2, 1963, EX, T2 ....$25.00

Bullwinkle & Rocky, Whitman #5, 1972, EX, F8 ....$14.00

Captain Marvel, #35, 1942, Comix Cards on back neatly cut off o/w EX, C1 ....$45.00

Captain Marvel Adventures, Fawcett #24, EX+, M14 ...$160.00

Captain Midnight, Fawcett #37, EX+, M14 ....$65.00

Dark Shadows, Gold Key #15, 1972, EX, $10.00.

Captain Venture, Gold Key #1, 1968, EX, F8.................$15.00
Casper the Friendly Ghost, Harvey #18, VG, M14..........$18.00
Cave Kids, Gold Key #2, EX+, T2...........................$8.00
Charlie Chan, Dell #1, 1965, EX+, F8....................$24.00
Charlie McCarthy's Rocket Ship, Dell #6, 1950, VG, F8...$8.00
Cheyenne, Dell #22, 1961, EX, F8.........................$8.00
Cheyenne, Dell #6, EX+, D8..............................$30.00
Circus Boy, Dell Four Color #759, VG, T2................$18.00
Cisco Kid, #17, VG+, D8.................................$18.00
Colt .45, Dell #5, 1960, EX+, T2........................$20.00
Comic Cavalcade, #16, 1946, Green Lantern, Flash, Wonder
    Woman & others, EX+, M14...........................$295.00
Conqueror, Dell, 1956, John Wayne cover, EX, T2.........$40.00
Daniel Boone, Gold Key #10, 1967, EX, F8................$5.00
Dark Shadows, Gold Key #1, 1961, 1st issue, no poster o/w EX,
    H4...$30.00
Dark Shadows, Gold Key #2, 1969, EX, F8................$14.00
Dick Tracy, Dell Four Color #133, EX, D11..............$75.00
Dick Tracy, Dell Monthly #5, EX+, D11..................$80.00
Dick Tracy, Dell Monthly #6, EX, D11...................$70.00
Dick Tracy, Dell Super Comics #112, 1947, EX, M14.....$20.00
Dick Tracy, Feature Showcase - The Great Classic Newspaper
    Comic Strips #213, Alan Light, 1974, NM, D11.......$25.00
Dick Tracy, Harvey Monthly #111, NM, D11...............$40.00
Dick Tracy, Harvey Monthly #139, EX+, D11..............$35.00
Dick Tracy, Harvey Monthly #51, EX+, D11...............$30.00
Dick Tracy, Harvey Monthly #78, EX, D11................$30.00
Dick Tracy, Little Orphan Annie & Other Super Comics, #87,
    1945, NM, C1.......................................$45.00
Dinky Duck, St Johns #2, 1952, VG, F8...................$6.00
Dirty Dozen, Dell Movie Classic, 1967, EX, F8..........$15.00
Doc Savage, #12, 1943, EX+, C1.........................$92.00
Don Winslow, #61, 1948, EX+, C1........................$26.00
Donald & Mickey in Disneyland, Dell Giant #1, VG, M14...$50.00

Donald Duck Christmas on Bear Mountain, Dell Four Color #178, 1947, VG, A, $185.00; Donald Duck in The Golden Christmas Tree, Dell Four Color #203, 1948, VG, A, $130.00.

Donald Duck in Frozen Gold, Dell Four Color #62, EX+, M14..$750.00
Donald Duck in Ghost of the Grotto, Dell Four Color #159,
    1947, EX, M14......................................$325.00

Dr Who & the Daleks, Dell, 1966, VG+, T2...............$25.00
F-Troop, Dell #2, 1966, EX, F8..........................$8.00
Fantastic Four, Marvel #8, G+, M14....................$120.00
Flash Gordon, Dell Four Color #10, 1943, 2nd series, 6 photos at
    home & studio, EX+, M14...........................$225.00
Flintstones, Gold Key #33, 1966, VG+, T2................$8.00
Flipper, Top Comics #1, EX, J7.........................$20.00
Francis the Talking Mule, Dell Four Color #465, EX+,
    M15..$15.00
Fury, Dell Four Color #1296, 1962, EX, F8..............$20.00

Gene Autry Comics, #1, Fawcett, 1941, rare, EX, A, $2,000.00.

Gene Autry, Dell #24 through #44, EX+, D8, ea, from $30
    to...$35.00
Gene Autry, Dell #54, EX+, D8..........................$25.00
Gene Autry, Dell #59 through #74, EX+, D8, ea, from $18
    to...$22.00
Gene Autry, Dell #78 to #104, EX, D8, ea...............$18.00
Gentle Ben, Dell #4, 1968, EX, F8.......................$5.00
George of the Jungle, Dell #2, 1969, EX+, T2...........$30.00
George of the Jungle, Gold Key #2, 1969, EX, F8........$22.00
Get Smart, Dell #1, 1965, EX+, T2......................$10.00
Gidget, Dell #2, 1966, EX+, T2.........................$20.00
Girl From UNCLE, Gold Key #2, 1967, VG+, T2.............$5.00
Governor & JJ, #1, EX, J7..............................$20.00
Green Hornet, #2, EX, J7...............................$75.00
Green Hornet, #44, 1949, VG, C1........................$32.00
Gunsmoke, Dell Four Color #679, NM, C1.................$80.00
Hardy Boys, Dell Four Color #760, 1956, 1st issue, EX+, F8..$45.00
Heckle & Jeckle, Dell #3, 1967, VG, F8..................$5.00
Hennesey, Dell Four Color #1200, 1961, VG+, T2.........$10.00
Henry, Dell #12, 1950, EX, F8..........................$10.00
High Chaparral, Gold Key #1, 1968, VG+, T2..............$8.00
Honey West, Gold Key #1, 1966, NM, M14.................$65.00
Howdy Doody, Dell #18, 1952, VG, F8....................$15.00
HR Pufnstuf, Gold Key #1, 1970, VG+, T2................$20.00
HR Pufnstuf, Gold Key #8, EX, F8.......................$15.00
Huckleberry Hound, Dell #16, 1962, EX, F8..............$12.00
Huey, Dewey & Louie Back to School, Dell Giant #1, EX+,
    M14..$45.00
I Spy, #5, EX, J7......................................$25.00

Hi-Yo Silver The Lone Ranger to the Rescue, Dell, 1939, EX, $255.00; Heigh-Yo Silver The Lone Ranger, Whitman, 1938, EX, $255.00.

Incredible Hulk #2, 1976, NM, A6 ....$5.00
Invaders, Gold Key #3, 1968, EX+, F8 ....$10.00
It's About Time, Gold Key #1, EX+, F8 ....$18.00
Jace Pearson's Tales of the Texas Rangers, Dell #17, EX, F8 ....$10.00
Jerry Lewis, DC Comics #108, 1968, EX, F8 ....$5.00
Jetsons, Charlton #6, 1971, EX, F8 ....$6.00
Jetsons, Gold Key #6, 1963, EX, T2 ....$15.00
Jiggs & Maggie, Standard #12, 1949, EX, F8 ....$15.00
Jo Jo, #23, C10 ....$60.00
John Wayne the Cowboy Trouble-Shooter, C10..........$65.00
Johnny Mack Brown, Dell Four Color #645, EX, D8........$30.00
Journey Into Mystery, Marvel #116, VG+, M14 ....$12.00
Jungle Jim, Standard Comics #12, 1949, VG, M14............$8.00
Katy Keene, Archie #45, 1959, Christmas issue, G+, F8 ..$15.00
Kid Colt, Marvel #5, G, D8 ....$18.00
King of the Royal Mounted, Dell #8, G+, D8..................$15.00
Krazy Kat, Dell Four Color #454, EX, M14 ....$16.00
Lady & the Tramp, Dell Giant #1, 1955, VG+, M14.......$40.00
Lancelot Link Secret Chimp, #4, EX, J7 ....$12.00
Lancer, Gold Key #1, 1968, EX+, T2 ....$10.00
Land of the Giants, #2, NM, C1................................$36.00
Laramie, Dell Four Color #1125, 1960, 1st issue, photo cover, EX, F8..$25.00
Lassie, Dell #10, 1950, EX, M14 ....$12.00
Lassie, Gold Key #59, 1962, EX+, F8........................$5.00
Lawman, Dell #7, 1961, EX+, F8..............................$15.00
Lidsville, Gold Key #1, 1972, EX, C1 ....$18.00
Linus the Lionhearted, Gold Key #1, 1965, EX, T2..........$25.00
Little Audrey, Harvey #2, 1957, 2nd issue, EX, F8 ......$12.00
Little Monsters, Gold Key #13, 1964, EX, F8................$3.00
Little Orphan Annie, Sparkie #2, C10..........................$65.00
Lone Ranger, #126, EX, D8 ....$35.00
Lone Ranger, #61 through #74, EX+, D8, ea $30.00
Lone Ranger, #75 through #83, D8, ea........................$25.00
Lone Ranger, Dell #24, 1950, EX, F8........................$45.00
Lost World, Dell, 1960, Jill St John cover, EX+, T2.........$50.00
Magilla Gorilla Vs Yogi Bear for President, Gold Key #3, 1964, EX, T2..$12.00
Man From UNCLE, Gold Key #13, 1966, EX, T2 ....$8.00

Man in Space, Dell Four Color #716, binder holes o/w VG+, T2 ....$8.00
Margie, Dell #2, 1962, VG, F8..................................$4.00
Marvel Super Heroes Tales Annual, #1, 1964, EX, C1.....$64.00
Mary Poppins, Gold Key, 1964, EX+, T2 ....$18.00
Maverick, Dell #7, EX+, D8....................................$40.00
Maverick, Dell #9, EX, D8......................................$25.00
Maverick, Dell Four Color #930, VG+, D8 ....$25.00
Melvin Monster, Dell #4, 1966, EX, F8......................$15.00
Men Into Space, Dell Four Color #1083, EX+, F8.............$45.00
Mickey Mouse & the House of Many Mysteries, Dell Four Color #116, 1946, EX+, M14..................................$125.00
Mickey Mouse & the Seven-Colored Terror, Dell Four Color #27, 1943, G+, very scarce, M14..................$195.00
Mickey Mouse Summer Fun, Dell Giant #1, 1958, EX+, M14 ....$48.00
Mighty Mouse, Pines, May 1957, EX+, F8 ....$20.00
Mission Impossible, Dell #3, VG+, T2 ....$10.00
Moby Dick, Dell #717, 1956, G+, T2 ....$10.00
Mod Squad, Dell #4, 1970, G, F8..............................$2.00
Moses & the Ten Commandments, Dell Giant #1, 1957, EX+, M14..$40.00
Mr Ed, Gold Key #2, 1963, G, F8..............................$5.00
Munsters, Gold Key #1, EX, J7................................$100.00
Munsters, Gold Key #4, VG, M14..............................$14.00
Mutt & Jeff, DC Comics #34, 1948, clipped corner o/w EX, F8 ....$12.00
My Favorite Martian, Gold Key #8, EX, C1................$18.00
My Little Margie's Boy Friends, Charlton #2, 1955, G, F8 .$4.00
New People, #2, EX, J7..$10.00
Outer Limits, Dell #1, EX, M14................................$30.00
Phantom, Gold Key #8, EX, M14..............................$10.00
Playful Little Audrey, Harvey #1, EX+, M14 ....$75.00

Pogo Possum, Dell #8 and #9, 1952, NM, $75.00 each.

Popeye, Dell #48, 1959, EX+, F8 ....$18.00
Popeye the Sailor, Gold Key #79, Feb 1966, VG, A6........$3.50
Prize Comics Western, #76, 1949, Randolph Scott cover, 52 pgs, EX, M14..$22.00
Queen of the West, Dale Evans, Dell #5, NM, M14.........$40.00
Range Rider, Dell #8, 1955, VG, T2 ....$10.00
Rawhide Kid, Marvel Comics #73, Dec 1969, VG, A6.......$2.50
Red Ryder, Dell #69, 1949, EX, F8............................$25.00

Restless Gun, Dell Four Color #1089, VG, D8 ....$12.00
Restless Gun, Dell Four Color #934, 1st issue, G+, D8.....$25.00
Restless Gun, Dell Four Color #986, VG+, D8................$18.00
Rex Allen, Dell #13, EX+, D8 ....$28.00
Rifleman, Dell #5, EX, J7 ....$30.00
Rifleman, Dell #5, VG+, D8..$18.00
Rin-Tin-Tin, Dell #10, 1955, VG, F8 ....$8.00
Rin-Tin-Tin & Rusty, Dell #18, April 1957, EX+, J5 ......$15.00
Rocky Lane Western, Fawcett/Charlton #42, VG+, M14 ..$20.00
Roy Rogers, Dell #16, G+, D9 ....$20.00
Roy Rogers, Dell #27, VG+, D8...................................$25.00
Roy Rogers, Dell #68 through #80, EX+, D8, ea..............$30.00
Roy Rogers, March of Comics #131, 1955, VG, M16.......$20.00
Ruff 'N Ready, Dell #7, 1960, VG, F8..........................$6.00
Run Buddy Run!, Gold Key #1, 1967, photo cover, G, F8 .$3.00
Secret Agent, Gold Key #1, 1966, EX, F8......................$36.00
Sgt Preston, Dell #20 through #27, G+, D8, ea $15.00
Shadow Pulp, Jan 1, 1938, C10...................................$125.00
Shotgun Slade, #111, G, D8..$12.00
Son of Flubber, Gold Key, 1963, EX, F8........................$6.00
Spin & Marty, Dell Four Color #767, EX+, T2 ....$20.00
Spin & Marty w/Annette, Dell Four Color #826, 1957, VG+,
     F8...$40.00
Sports Thrills, Accepted #12, 1951, G, F8 ....$8.00
Star Trek, Gold Key #4, EX, J7 ....$65.00
Sugarfoot, #1098, G+, D8...$18.00
Super Cops, Red Circle #1, July 1974, NM, A6.................$3.50

Superman's Girl-friend Lois Lane, DC Comics #1, 1958, EX, $195.00.

Superman's Pal, Jimmy Olsen, DC Comics #64, 1962, EX,
     F8 ....$5.00
Tales From the Crypt, #26, EX+, M14...........................$145.00
Tales of Suspense, Marvel #10, EX, M14 ....$70.00
Tales of the Texas Rangers, #19, EX+, D8 ....$25.00
Tales of Wells Fargo, Dell Four Color #876, 1st issue, photo
     cover, EX..$45.00
Target: The Corruptors, Dell #2, 1962, VG, F8 ....$5.00
Tarzan, Dell #10, 1949, VG, F8........................$40.00

Tarzan, Dell #2, 1948, NM, C1 ....$350.00
Tarzan, Dell #28, 1952, photo cover, EX+, T2 ....$65.00
Tarzan, Gold Key #162, 1966, 1st issue w/Ron Ely cover, EX+,
     F8...$13.00
Tarzan's Jungle Annual, Dell #7, 1958, VG+, T2............$10.00
Ted Horton, Super Green Beret, Wilson #1, April 1967, VG,
     A6...$3.50
Terry & the Pirates, Dell Four Color #101, VG+, M14....$75.00
Tex Ritter Western, Fawcett/Charlton #33, EX, M14......$28.00
Tex Taylor, #4, VG+, D8...$25.00
Tex Taylor, #9, EX+, D8...$55.00
Texas Rangers in Action, #63, VG+, D8 ....$5.00
Texas Rangers in Action, #8, VG+, D8 ....$12.00

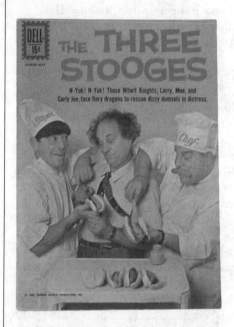

Three Stooges, Dell, 1962, EX, $30.00.

Three Stooges, Dell #12, 1963, G, T2 ....$20.00
Three Stooges, Dell Comic Album #3, 1958, VG+, M14 ..$15.00
Three Stooges, Gold Key #29, NM, C1 ....$32.00
Three Stooges, Gold Key #47, photo cover, EX, F8..........$12.00
Three Stooges, St John, 1953, 3-D, no glasses, G-, T2 .....$30.00
Time Machine, Classics Illus #133, June 1964, EX, A6......$3.50
Tippy's Friends & Go-Go Animal, Tower #7, 1967, EX, F8 ..$12.00
Tom & Jerry, Dell #136, 1955, VG+, F8..........................$4.00
Tom & Jerry, Gold Key #222, Feb 1965, VG, A6..............$2.50
Tom Corbett Space Cadet, #9, C10.................................$25.00
Top Cat, #25, EX, J7..$10.00
Twilight Zone, #13, EX, J7...$15.00
Uncle Scrooge in Only a Poor Old Man, Dell Four Color #386,
     EX+, M14 ....$290.00
Underwater City, Dell Four Color #1328, 1961, photo cover,
     EX+, F8..$15.00
Untouchables, Dell #876-210, 1962, VG, T2 ....$20.00
Voyage to the Bottom of the Sea, Gold Key #8, 1967, EX,
     T2 ....$10.00
Wagon Train, Gold Key #3, 1964, photo cover, EX, F8 ...$15.00
Walt Disney's Merry Christmas, Dell Giant #39, NM,
     M14...$170.00
Western Marshall, #613, G+, D8 ....$12.00

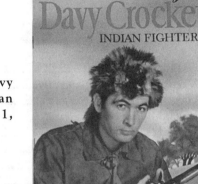

Walt Disney's Davy Crockett Indian Fighter, Dell #631, EX, $38.00.

Western Roundup, #1, VG+, D8.................................$55.00
Wyatt Earp, #4, EX, J7..$25.00
Wyatt Earp, #8, VG+, D8...$18.00
Zane Grey's Stories of the West, Dell Four Color #632, 1955, EX+, D8..$24.00
Zorro, Dell Four Color #617, 1955, G+, T2.............$15.00

Corgi

Corgi vehicles are among the favorites of the diecast collectors; they've been made in Great Britain since 1956, and they're still in production today. They were well detailed and ruggedly built to last. Some of the most expensive Corgi's on today's collector market are the character-related vehicles, for instance, James Bond (there are several variations), Batman, and U.N.C.L.E.

Values are for mint-in-the-box examples.
Advisor: Irwin Stern (S3)
Other Sources: G2, L1, N3, W1

#050, Massey-Ferguson 50B Tractor................................$40.00
#050, Massey-Ferguson 65 Tractor................................$110.00
#051, Massey-Ferguson Tipper Trailer............................$20.00
#053, Massey-Ferguson Tractor Shovel...........................$100.00
#054, Fordson Half-Track Tractor..................................$160.00
#054, Massey-Ferguson Tractor Shovel...........................$50.00
#055, David Brown Tractor..$50.00
#055, Fordson Major Tractor..$100.00
#056, Plough..$25.00
#057, Massey-Ferguson Tractor & Fork............................$110.00
#058, Beast Carrier...$30.00
#060, Fordson Power Major Tractor................................$100.00
#061, Four-Furrow Plough..$15.00
#062, Ford Tipper Trailer...$20.00
#064, Conveyor on Jeep..$75.00
#066, Massey-Ferguson Tractor......................................$85.00
#067, Ford Super Major Tractor.....................................$90.00
#069, Massey-Ferguson Tractor Shovel..........................$100.00

#071, Fordson Disc Harrow..$20.00
#072, Ford 5000 Tractor & Trencher..............................$125.00
#073, Massey-Ferguson Tractor & Saw.............................$125.00
#074, Ford 5000 Tractor & Scoop..................................$100.00
#100, Dropside Trailer..$20.00
#101, Platform Trailer..$20.00
#102, Pony Trailer..$25.00
#104, Dolphin Cabin Cruiser...$30.00
#107, Batboat & Trailer..$125.00
#109, Penny Burn Trailer..$50.00
#112, Rice Horse Box..$45.00
#150, Surtees TS9...$35.00
#150, Vanwall...$70.00
#150s, Vanwall..$75.00
#151, Lotus XI..$80.00
#151, McLaren Yardley M19A..$30.00
#152, BRM Racer...$80.00
#152, Ferrari 312 B2..$35.00
#153, Bluebird Record Car..$125.00
#153, Team Surtees..$35.00
#154, Ferrari Formula I...$50.00
#154, Lotus John Player...$40.00
#154, Lotus Texaco Special..$40.00
#155, Shadow F1 Racer...$40.00

#156, Cooper-Maserati, $50.00; #155, Lotus Climax Racer, $50.00.

#156, Shadow F1, Graham Hill.......................................$40.00
#158, Lotus Climax..$50.00
#158, Tyrrell-Ford Elf..$40.00
#159, Cooper Maserati...$50.00
#159, Indianapolis Racer..$40.00
#160, Hesketh Racer...$40.00
#161, Elf-Tyrrell Project 34..$50.00
#161, Santa Pod Commuter..$40.00
#162, Quartermaster Dragster..$40.00
#163, Santa Pod Dragster..$50.00
#164, Wild Honey Dragster...$50.00
#165, Adams Bros Dragster...$40.00
#166, Ford Mustang..$45.00
#167, USA Racing Buggy..$35.00
#169, Starfighter Jet Dragster......................................$40.00
#170, John Wolfe's Dragster...$40.00
#190, Lotus John Player Special.....................................$60.00
#191, McLaren Texaco-Marlboro.......................................$65.00
#200, BMC Mini 1000...$50.00
#200, Ford Consul, dual colors.....................................$200.00
#200, Ford Consul, solid colors....................................$175.00

#200m, Ford Consul, w/motor	$200.00
#201, Austin Cambridge	$175.00
#201, Saint's Volvo	$120.00
#201m, Austin Cambridge, w/motor	$200.00
#202, Morris Cowley	$175.00
#202, Renault R16	$40.00
#202m, Morris Cowley, w/motor	$200.00
#203, Detomaso Mangust	$40.00
#203, Vauxhall Velox, dual colors	$200.00
#203, Vauxhall Velox, solid colors	$175.00
#203m, Vauxhall Velox, w/motor, dual colors	$300.00
#203m, Vauxhall Velox, w/motor, red or yel	$200.00
#204, Morris Mini-Minor, bl	$150.00
#204, Morris Mini-Minor, metallic bl	$100.00
#204, Rover 90, other colors	$175.00
#204, Rover 90, wht & red, 2-tone	$300.00
#204m, Rover 90, w/motor	$175.00
#205, Riley Pathfinder, bl	$175.00
#205, Riley Pathfinder, red	$130.00
#205m, Riley Pathfinder, w/motor, bl	$175.00
#205m, Riley Pathfinder, w/motor, red	$225.00
#206, Hillman Husky, metallic bl & silver, 2-tone	$175.00
#206, Hillman Husky Estate, solid colors	$130.00
#206m, Hillman Husky Estate, w/motor	$200.00
#207, Standard Vanguard	$125.00
#207m, Standard Vanguard, w/motor	$175.00
#208, Jaguar 2.4 Saloon	$160.00
#208m, Jaguar 2.4 Saloon, w/motor	$200.00
#208s, Jaguar 2.4 Saloon, w/suspension	$100.00
#209, Riley Police Car	$120.00
#210, Citroen DS19	$90.00
#210s, Citroen DS19, w/suspension	$100.00
#211, Studebaker Golden Hawk	$100.00
#211m, Studebaker Golden Hawk, w/motor	$175.00
#211s, Studebaker Golden Hawk, w/suspension	$125.00
#213, Jaguar Fire Chief	$150.00
#213s, Jaguar Fire Chief, w/suspension	$200.00
#214, Ford Thunderbird	$95.00
#214m, Ford Thunderbird, w/motor	$300.00
#214s, Ford Thunderbird, w/suspension	$100.00
#215, Ford Thunderbird Sport	$100.00
#215s, Ford Thunderbird Sport, w/suspension	$100.00
#216, Austin A-40, red & blk	$175.00
#216, Austin A-40, 2-tone bl	$100.00
#216m, Austin A-40, w/motor	$300.00
#217, Fiat 1800	$80.00
#218, Aston Martin DB4	$100.00
#219, Plymouth Suburban	$80.00
#220, Chevrolet Impala	$80.00
#221, Chevrolet Impala Cab	$90.00
#222, Renault Floride	$80.00
#223, Chevrolet Police	$70.00
#224, Bentley Continental	$100.00
#225, Austin 7, red	$100.00
#225, Austin 7, yel	$300.00
#226, Morris Mini-Minor	$100.00
#227, Mini-Cooper Rally	$300.00
#228, Volvo P-1800	$80.00

#229, Chevrolet Corvair	$70.00
#230, Mercedes Benz 220	$75.00
#231, Triumph Herald	$100.00
#232, Fiat 2100	$75.00
#233, Heinkel Trojan	$100.00
#234, Ford Consul Classic	$75.00
#235, Oldsmobile Super 88	$75.00
#236, Motor School, right-hand drive	$90.00
#237, Oldsmobile Sheriff's Car	$100.00
#238, Jaguar Mk10, gr or silver	$200.00
#238, Jaguar Mk10, metallic gr, red or bl	$100.00
#239, VW Karman Ghia	$90.00
#240, Fiat 500 Jolly	$125.00
#241, Chrysler Ghia	$90.00
#242, Fiat 600 Jolly	$175.00
#245, Buick Riviera	$75.00
#246, Chrysler Imperial, metallic turq	$250.00
#246, Chrysler Imperial, red	$100.00
#247, Mercedes Benz 600 Pullman	$65.00
#248, Chevrolet Impala	$70.00
#249, Morris Mini-Cooper, wicker	$130.00
#251, Hillman Imp	$100.00
#252, Rover 2000, metallic bl	$80.00
#252, Rover 2000, metallic maroon	$150.00
#253, Mercedes Benz 220 SE	$90.00
#255, Motor School, left-hand drive	$225.00
#256, VW 1200 East Africa Safari	$200.00

#258, Saint's Volvo P1800 ....$175.00
#259, Citroen Le Dandy, bl $200.00
#259, Citroen Le Dandy, maroon.......................$120.00
#259, Penguin Mobile.................................$50.00
#260, Renault R16 ....$40.00

#260, Superman Police car, Metropolis Buick, $60.00.

#261, James Bond's Aston Martin DBS $200.00
#261, Spiderbuggy.......................................$100.00
#262, Captain Marvel's Porsche $65.00
#262, Lincoln Continental Limo, bl $200.00
#262, Lincoln Continental Limo, gold $100.00
#263, Captain America's Jetmobile.......................$50.00
#263, Rambler Marlin....................................$50.00
#264, Incredible Hulk...................................$75.00
#264, Oldsmobile Toronado $65.00
#265, Supermobile.......................................$65.00
#266, Chitty-Chitty Bang-Bang, original $350.00
#266, Chitty-Chitty Bang-Bang, replica $125.00
#266, Superbike $50.00
#267, Batmobile, red 'Bat' hubs.........................$400.00
#267, Batmobile, w/red whizzwheels $500.00
#267, Batmobile, w/whizzwheels $150.00

#268, Green Hornet, $400.00.

#268, Batman's Bat Bike $70.00
#269, James Bond's Lotus $100.00
#270, James Bond's Aston Martin, w/tire slashers, 1/43 scale ...$250.00
#270, James Bond's Aston Martin, w/whizzwheels, 1/43 scale $100.00
#271, Ghia Mangusta De Tomaso $50.00
#271, James Bond's Aston Martin $90.00
#272, James Bond's Citroen 2CV $60.00
#273, Honda Driving School............................$40.00
#273, Rolls Royce Silver Shadow.......................$100.00
#274, Bentley Mulliner $80.00
#275, Mini Metro, colors other than gold $20.00
#275, Mini Metro, gold................................$75.00
#275, Rover 2000 TC, gr $75.00
#275, Rover 2000 TC, wht $160.00
#275, Royal Wedding Mini Metro $25.00
#276, Oldsmobile Toronado $70.00
#276, Triumph Acclaim $15.00
#277, Monkeemobile....................................$300.00
#277, Triumph Driving School $25.00
#279, Rolls Royce Corniche $30.00
#280, Rolls Royce Silver Shadow $50.00
#281, Metro Datapost $20.00
#281, Rover 2000 TC $150.00
#282, Mini Cooper Rally Car $90.00
#283, DAF City Car....................................$40.00
#284, Citroen SM $40.00
#284, Mercedes Benz 240D $25.00
#285, Mercedes Benz 240D $20.00
#286, Jaguar XJ12C $40.00
#287, Citroen Dyane...................................$25.00
#288, Minissima $20.00
#289, VW Polo $25.00
#290, Kojak's Buick, no hat...........................$100.00
#290, Kojak's Buick, w/hat $75.00
#291, AMC Pacer $20.00
#291, Mercedes Benz 240 Rally $35.00
#292, Starsky & Hutch's Ford Torino $60.00
#293, Renault 5TS.....................................$20.00
#294, Renault Alpine $20.00
#298, Magnum PI's Ferrari $50.00
#299, Ford Sierra 2.3 Ghia............................$20.00
#300, Austin Healey Sports Car, bl....................$300.00
#300, Austin Healey Sports Car, red or cream..........$150.00
#300, Chevrolet Corvette $70.00
#300, Ferrari Daytona $25.00
#301, Iso Grifo 7 Litre...............................$50.00
#301, Lotus Elite $25.00
#301, Triumph TR2 Sports Car $150.00
#302, Hillman Hunter Rally, kangaroo..................$130.00
#302, MGA Sports Car $130.00
#302, VW Polo $20.00
#303, Mercedes Benz 300SL.............................$100.00
#303, Porsche 924 ....$20.00
#303, Roger Clark's Ford Capri $75.00
#303s, Mercedes Benz 300SL, w/suspension $100.00
#304, Chevrolet SS350 Camaro..........................$65.00
#304, Mercedes Benz 300SL, yel & red..................$100.00

#304, Mercedes Benz 300SL, yel	$150.00
#304s, Mercedes Benz 300SL, w/suspension	$100.00
#305, Mini Marcos GT 850	$50.00
#305, Triumph TR3	$135.00
#306, Fiat X1/9	$20.00
#306, Morris Marina	$55.00
#307, Jaguar E Type	$125.00
#307, Renault	$20.00
#308, BMW M1 Racer, gold plated	$100.00
#308, BMW M1 Racer, yel	$25.00
#308, Monte Carlo Mini	$100.00
#309, Aston Martin DB4	$125.00
#309, Aston Martin DB4, w/spoked hubs	$200.00
#309, VW Turbo	$20.00
#310, Chevrolet Stingray, bronze	$175.00
#310, Chevrolet Stingray, red or silver	$65.00
#310, Porsche 924	$20.00
#311, Ford Capri, orange	$125.00
#311, Ford Capri, red	$80.00
#311, Ford Capri, w/gold hubs	$150.00
#312, Ford Capri S	$35.00
#312, Jaguar E Type	$100.00
#312, Marcos Mantis	$40.00
#313, Ford Cortina, bronze or bl	$100.00
#313, Ford Cortina, yel	$300.00
#314, Ferrari Berlinetta Le Mans	$65.00
#314, Supercat Jaguar	$30.00
#315, Lotus Elite	$25.00
#315, Simca Sports Car, metallic bl	$200.00
#315, Simca Sports Car, silver	$65.00
#316, Ford GT70	$50.00
#316, NSU Sport Prinz	$90.00
#317, Mini Cooper Monte Carlo	$200.00
#318, Jaguar XJS	$25.00
#318, Lotus Elan, copper	$300.00
#318, Lotus Elan, metallic bl	$90.00
#318, Lotus Elan, wht	$160.00
#319, Jaguar XJS	$35.00
#319, Lamborghini P400 GT Miura	$35.00
#319, Lotus Elan, gr or yel	$140.00
#319, Lotus Elan, red or bl	$100.00
#320, Saint's Jaguar XJS	$70.00
#321, Monte Carlo Mini Cooper, 1965	$300.00
#321, Monte Carlo Mini Cooper, 1966, w/autographs	$600.00
#321, Porsche 924, metallic gr	$70.00
#321, Porsche 924, red	$25.00
#322, Rover Monte Carlo	$200.00
#323, Citroen DS19 Monte Carlo	$200.00
#323, Ferrari Daytona 365 GTB4	$25.00
#324, Marcos Volvo 1800 GT	$70.00
#325, Chevrolet Caprice	$50.00
#325, Ford Mustang Competition	$80.00
#326, Chevrolet Police Car	$30.00
#327, Chevrolet Caprice Cab	$30.00
#327, MGB GT	$130.00
#328, Hillman Imp Monte Carlo	$125.00
#329, Ford Mustang Rally	$50.00
#329, Opel Senator, bl or bronze	$30.00

#329, Opel Senator, silver	$50.00
#330, Porsche Carrera 6, wht & bl	$120.00
#330, Porsche Carrera 6, wht & red	$50.00
#331, Ford Capri Rally	$90.00
#332, Lancia Fulvia Sport, red or bl	$50.00
#332, Lancia Fulvia Sport, yel & blk	$125.00
#332, Opel, Doctor's Car	$50.00
#333, Mini Cooper Sun/Rac	$400.00
#334, Ford Escort	$20.00
#334, Mini Magnifique	$100.00
#335, Jaguar 4.2 Litre E Type	$125.00
#336, James Bond's Toyota 2000 GT	$350.00
#337, Chevrolet Stingray	$65.00
#338, Chevrolet SS350 Camaro	$65.00
#338, Rover 3500	$30.00
#339, Rover 3500 Police Car	$30.00
#339, 1967 Mini Cooper Monte Carlo, w/roof rack	$300.00
#340, Rover Triplex	$25.00
#340, 1967 Sunbeam Imp Monte Carlo	$135.00
#341, Chevrolet Caprice Racer	$25.00
#341, Mini Marcos GT850	$60.00
#342, Lamborghini P400 GT Miura	$50.00
#342, Professionals Ford Capri	$80.00
#342, Professionals Ford Capri, w/chrome bumpers	$100.00
#343, Pontiac Firebird	$50.00
#344, Ferrari 206 Dino Sport	$50.00
#345, Honda Prelude	$25.00
#345, MGC GT, orange	$300.00
#345, MGC GT, yel	$125.00
#346, Citroen 2 CV	$20.00
#347, Chevrolet Astro 1	$50.00
#348, Pop Art Mustang Stack Car	$150.00
#348, Vegas Ford Thunderbird	$75.00
#349, Pop Art Morris Mini	$1,500.00
#350, Thunderbird Guided Missile	$125.00
#351, RAF Land Rover	$80.00
#352, RAF Vanguard Staff Car	$100.00
#353, Road Scanner	$50.00
#354, Commer Military Ambulance	$100.00
#355, Commer Military Police	$135.00
#356, VW Personnel Carrier	$135.00
#357, Land Rover Weapons Carrier	$200.00
#358, Oldsmobile Staff Car	$100.00
#359, Commer Army Field Kitchen	$165.00
#370, Ford Cobra Mustang	$20.00
#371, Porsche Carrera	$40.00
#373, Peugeot 505	$20.00
#373, VW 1200 Police Car, Polizie	$130.00
#373, VW 1200 Police Car, Polizei	$50.00
#374, Jaguar 4.2 Litre E Type	$70.00
#374, Jaguar 5.3 Litre	$70.00
#375, Toyota 2000 GT	$60.00
#376, Chevrolet Stingray Stock Car	$50.00
#377, Marcos 3 Litre, wht & gray	$100.00
#377, Marcos 3 Litre, yel or bl	$60.00
#378, Ferrari 308 GT	$25.00
#378, MGC GT	$140.00
#380, Alfa Romeo P33	$40.00

#380, Beach Buggy	$40.00
#381, Renault Turbo	$20.00
#382, Lotus Elite	$20.00
#382, Porsche Targa 911S	$50.00
#383, VW 1200, red or orange	$80.00
#383, VW 1200, Swiss PTT	$130.00
#383, VW 1200, yel ADAC	$200.00
#384, Adam Bros Probe 15	$40.00
#384, Renault 11 GTL, cream	$20.00
#384, Renault 11 GTL, maroon	$40.00
#384, VW 1200 Rally	$70.00
#385, Porsche 917	$40.00
#386, Bertone Runabout	$40.00
#387, Chevrolet Corvette Stingray	$100.00
#388, Mercedes Benz C111	$40.00
#389, Reliant Bond Bug 700, gr	$100.00
#389, Reliant Bond Bug 700 ES, orange	$60.00
#391, James Bond's 007 Mustang	$250.00
#392, Bertone Shake Buggy	$40.00
#393, Mercedes Benz 350 SL, wht or bl	$50.00
#393, Mercedes Benz 350SL, metallic gr	$100.00
#394, Datsun 240Z, East African Safari	$45.00
#396, Datsun 240Z, US Rally	$45.00
#397, Can Am Porsche Audi	$35.00
#400, VW Driving School, bl	$65.00
#400, VW Driving School, red	$140.00
#401, VW 1200	$60.00
#402, Ford Cortina GXL, wht w/red stripe	$80.00
#402, Ford Cortina GXL Police, wht	$50.00
#402, Ford Cortina GXL Polizei	$150.00
#403, Bedford Daily Express	$200.00
#403, Thwaites Dumper	$45.00
#403m, Bedford KLG Plugs, w/motor	$230.00
#404, Bedford Dormobile, cream, maroon & turq	$110.00
#404, Bedford Dormobile, yel & 2-tone bl	$200.00
#404, Bedford Dormobile, yel w/bl roof	$125.00
#404m, Bedford Dormobile, w/motor	$160.00
#405, Bedford Utilicon Fire Dept, red	$200.00
#405, Bedford Utilicon Fire Tender, gr	$160.00
#405, Chevrolet Superior Ambulance	$40.00
#405, Ford Milk Float	$25.00
#405m, Bedford Utilicon Fire Tender, w/motor	$200.00
#406, Land Rover	$80.00
#406, Mercedes Ambulance	$35.00
#406, Mercedes Benz Unimog	$50.00
#407, Karrier Mobile Grocers	$150.00
#408, Bedford AA Road Service	$150.00
#409, Allis Chalmers Fork Lift	$30.00
#409, Forward Control Jeep	$50.00
#409, Mercedes Dumper	$40.00
#411, Karrier Lucozade Van	$160.00
#411, Mercedes 240D, orange	$80.00
#411, Mercedes 240D Taxi, cream or blk	$60.00
#411, Mercedes 240D Taxi, orange w/blk roof	$30.00
#412, Bedford Ambulance, split windscreen	$130.00
#412, Bedford Ambulance, 1-pc windscreen	$250.00
#412, Mercedes Police Car, Police	$50.00
#412, Mercedes Police Car, Polizei	$40.00

#413, Karrier Bantam Butcher Shop	$150.00
#413, Karrier Bantam Butcher Shop, w/suspension	$200.00
#413, Mazda Maintenance Truck	$50.00
#414, Bedford Military Ambulance	$120.00
#414, Coastguard Jaguar	$35.00
#415, Mazda Camper	$50.00
#416, Buick Police Car	$40.00
#416, Radio Rescue Rover, bl	$125.00
#416, Radio Rescue Rover, yel	$400.00
#416s, Radio Rescue Rover, bl	$100.00
#416s, Radio Rescue Rover, yel	$400.00
#417, Land Rover Breakdown	$80.00
#418, Austin Taxi	$40.00
#419, Ford Zephyr, Politie	$300.00
#419, Ford Zephyr, Rijks Politie	$350.00

#419, Ford Zephyr Police Car, white, $100.00.

#419, Jeep	$30.00
#420, Airborne Caravan	$100.00
#421, Bedford Evening Standard	$200.00
#422, Bedford Van, Corgi Toys, bl w/yel roof	$500.00
#422, Bedford Van, Corgi Toys, yel w/bl roof	$200.00
#422, Riot Police Wagon	$30.00
#423, Rough Rider Van	$30.00
#424, Ford Zephyr Estate	$85.00
#424, Security Van	$20.00
#425, London Taxi	$25.00
#426, Chipperfield's Circus Booking Office	$300.00
#426, Pinder's Circus Booking Office	$50.00
#428, Mister Softee's Ice Cream Van	$175.00
#428, Renault Police Car	$25.00
#429, Jaguar Police Car	$40.00
#430, Bermuda Taxi, metallic bl & red	$400.00
#430, Bermuda Taxi, wht	$120.00
#430, Porsche 924 Polizei	$30.00
#431, Vanatic Van	$30.00
#431, VW Pickup, metallic gold	$300.00
#431, VW Pickup, yel	$100.00
#432, Vanatic Van	$30.00
#433, VW Delivery Van	$100.00
#434, VW Kombi	$100.00
#435, Karrier Dairy Van	$125.00
#435, Superman Van	$50.00

#436, Citroen Safari	$100.00	#470, Greenline Bus	$20.00
#436, Spider Van	$50.00	#471, Karrier Snack Bar, Joe's Diner	$125.00
#437, Cadillac Ambulance	$100.00	#471, Karrier Snack Bar, Patates Frites	$300.00
#437, Coca-Cola Van	$40.00	#471, Silver Jubilee Bus	$40.00
#438, Land Rover, gr	$60.00	#471, Woolworth Silver Jubilee Bus	$40.00
#438, Land Rover, Lepra	$400.00	#472, Public Address Land Rover	$130.00
#439, Chevrolet Fire Chief	$100.00	#474, Ford Musical Walls Ice Cream Van	$250.00
#440, Ford Cortina Estate, w/golfer & caddy	$170.00	#475, Citroen Ski Safari	$150.00
#440, Mazda Pickup	$25.00	#477, Land Rover Breakdown	$60.00
#441, Jeep	$25.00	#478, Forward Control Jeep, Tower Wagon	$50.00
#441, VW Toblerone Van	$135.00	#479, Mobile Camaro Van	$150.00
#443, Plymouth US Mail	$100.00	#480, Chevrolet Impala Cab	$80.00
#445, Plymouth Suburban	$90.00	#480, Chevrolet Police Car	$80.00
#447, Renegade Jeep	$20.00	#482, Chevrolet Fire Chief Car	$100.00
#447, Walls Ice Cream Van	$250.00	#482, Range Rover Ambulance	$40.00
#448, Police Mini Van, w/dog & handler	$200.00	#483, Dodge Tipper	$50.00
#448, Renegade Jeep	$20.00	#483, Police Range Rover, Belgian	$75.00
#450, Austin Mini Van	$100.00	#484, AMC Pacer Rescue	$25.00
#450, Austin Mini Van, w/pnt grill	$160.00	#484, AMC Pacer Secours	$40.00
#450, Peugeot Taxi	$25.00	#484, Livestock Transporter	$60.00
#452, Commer Lorry	$130.00	#484, Mini Countryman Surfer	$175.00
#453, Commer Walls Van	$200.00	#485, Mini Countryman Surfer, w/unpnt grille	$225.00
#454, Commer Platform Lorry	$130.00	#486, Chevrolet Kennel Service	$100.00
#455, Karrier Bantam 2-ton	$120.00	#487, Chipperfield's Circus Parade	$200.00
#456, ERF Dropside Lorry	$100.00	#489, VW Police Car	$30.00
#457, ERF Platform Lorry	$100.00	#490, Caravan	$25.00
#457, Talbot Matra Rancho, gr or red	$25.00	#490, VW Breakdown Truck	$80.00
#457, Talbot Matra Rancho, wht or orange	$45.00	#491, Ford Escort Estate	$100.00
#458, ERF Tipper Dumper	$75.00	#492, VW Police Car, Polizei	$300.00
#459, ERF Moorhouse Van	$375.00	#492, VW Police Car, Polizei	$80.00
#459, Raygo Road Roller	$40.00	#492, VW Police Car, wht w/gr mudguards	$300.00
#460, ERF Cement Tipper	$90.00	#493, Mazda Pickup	$25.00
#461, Police Vigilant Range Rover, Police	$35.00	#494, Bedford Tipper, red & silver	$175.00
#461, Police Vigilant Range Rover, Politie	$80.00	#494, Bedford Tipper, red & yel	$70.00
#462, Commer Van, Co-op	$125.00	#495, Opel Open Truck	$15.00
#462, Commer Van, Hammonds	$170.00	#497, Man From UNCLE, bl	$250.00
#463, Commer Ambulance	$100.00	#497, Man From UNCLE, wht	$600.00
#464, Commer Police Van, City Police	$300.00	#499, Citroen, 1968 Olympics	$175.00
#464, Commer Police Van, County Police, bl	$100.00	#500, US Army Rover	$400.00
#464, Commer Police Van, Police, bl	$100.00	#503, Circus Giraffe Transporter	$125.00
#464, Commer Police Van, Police, gr	$750.00	#506, Sunbeam Imp Police	$100.00
#464, Commer Police Van, Rijks Politie, bl	$300.00	#508, Holiday Minibus	$100.00
#465, Commer Pickup Truck	$65.00	#509, Porsche Police Car, Polizei	$80.00
#466, Commer Milk Float, Co-op	$170.00	#509, Porsche Police Car, Rijks Politie	$125.00
#466, Commer Milk Float, wht	$70.00	#510, Citroen Tour De France	$125.00
#467, London Routemaster Bus	$70.00	#511, Chipperfield's Circus Poodle Pickup	$600.00
#468, London Transport Routemaster, Design Centre, red	$250.00	#513, Alpine Rescue Car	$350.00
#468, London Transport Routemaster, Gamages, red	$200.00	#647, Buck Roger's Starfighter	$75.00
#468, London Transport Routemaster Bus, Church's Shoes, red	$200.00	#648, Space Shuttle	$50.00
#468, London Transport Routemaster Bus, Corgi Toys, brn, gr or cream	$1,000.00	#649, James Bond's Space Shuttle	$80.00
#468, London Transport Routemaster Bus, Corgi Toys, red	$100.00	#650, BOAC Concorde, all others	$25.00
#468, London Transport Routemaster Bus, Madame Tussand's, red	$200.00	#650, BOAC Concorde, gold logo on tail	$100.00
#468, London Transport Routemaster Bus, Outspan, red	$60.00	#651, Air France Concorde, all others	$50.00
#470, Disneyland Bus	$40.00	#651, Air France Concorde, gold tail design	$140.00
#470, Forward Control Jeep	$60.00	#652, Japan Air Line Concorde	$400.00
		#653, Air Canada Concorde	$300.00
		#681, Stunt Bike	$250.00
		#700, Motorway Ambulance	$20.00

#701, Intercity Minibus $15.00
#703, Breakdown Truck $20.00
#703, Hi Speed Fire Engine $20.00
#801, Ford Thunderbird $25.00
#801, Noddy's Car $450.00
#801, Noddy's Car, w/blk-face golly.............$1,000.00
#802, Mercedes Benz 300SL $20.00
#802, Popeye's Paddle Wagon $500.00
#803, Beatle's Yellow Submarine $500.00
#803, Jaguar XK120 ....$20.00
#804, Jaguar XK120 Rally $20.00
#804, Jaguar XK120 Rally, w/spats $50.00
#804, Noddy's Car, Noddy only $275.00
#804, Noddy's Car, w/Mr Tubby $350.00
#805, Hardy Boys' Rolls Royce.....................$300.00
#805, Mercedes Benz 300SC $20.00
#806, Lunar Bug...$150.00
#806, Mercedes Benz 300SC $20.00
#807, Dougal's Car.......................................$300.00
#808, Basil Brush's Car $200.00
#809, Dick Dastardly's Racer $150.00
#810, Ford Thunderbird $20.00
#811, James Bond's Moon Buggy..................$500.00
#831, Mercedes Benz 300SL $20.00
#851, Magic Roundabout Train $350.00
#852, Magic Roundabout Carousel $800.00
#853, Magic Roundabout Playground.............$1,500.00
#859, Mr McHenry's Trike $250.00
#900, German Tank......................................$50.00
#901, British Centurion $50.00
#902, American Tank....................................$50.00
#903, British Chieftain Tank $50.00
#904, King Tiger Tank $50.00
#905, SU100 Tank Destroyer $50.00
#906, Saladin Armoured Car $50.00
#907, German Rocket Launcher $60.00
#908, French Recovery Tank.........................$75.00
#909, Quad Gun Tractor, Trailer & Field Gun $60.00
#920, Bell Helicopter $30.00
#921, Hughes Helicopter $30.00
#922, Sikorsky Helicopter.............................$30.00
#923, Sikorsky Helicopter Military $30.00
#924, Rescue Helicopter................................$30.00
#925, Batcopter $60.00
#926, Stromberg Helicopter $60.00
#927, Chopper Squad Helicopter $60.00
#928, Spidercopter $90.00
#929, Daily Planet Helicopter........................$50.00
#930, DAAX Helicopter.................................$60.00
#931, Jet Police Helicopter............................$50.00

Corgitronics

#1001, Corgitronics Firestreak......................$80.00
#1002, Corgitronics Landtrain $50.00
#1003, Ford Torino.......................................$30.00
#1004, Corgitronics Beep Beep Bus...............$40.00
#1005, Police Land Rover..............................$30.00

#1006, Roadshow, Radio $50.00
#1007, Land Rover & Compressor $50.00
#1008, Chevrolet Fire Chief $40.00
#1009, Maestro MG1600 ....$50.00
#1011, Firestreak...$40.00

Major Packs

#1100, Carrimore Low Loader, red cab $140.00
#1100, Carrimore Low Loader, yel cab...........$225.00
#1100, Mack Truck $80.00
#1101, Carrimore Car Transporter, bl cab $250.00
#1101, Carrimore Car Transporter, red cab $100.00
#1101, Hydraulic Crane $50.00
#1102, Crane Fruehauf Dumper $50.00
#1102, Euclid Tractor, gr $150.00
#1102, Euclid Tractor, yel $200.00
#1103, Airport Crash Truck $75.00
#1103, Euclid Crawler Tractor $125.00
#1104, Machinery Carrier $150.00
#1104, Racehorse Transporter $100.00
#1105, Berliet Racehorse Transporter $60.00
#1106, Decca Mobile Radar Van $160.00
#1106, Mack Container Truck $75.00
#1107, Berliet Container Truck $60.00
#1107, Euclid Tractor & Dozer, gr $150.00
#1107, Euclid Tractor & Dozer, orange $300.00
#1107, Euclid Tractor & Dozer, red $375.00
#1108, Bristol Bloodhound & Launching Ramp...........$125.00
#1108, Michelin Container Truck $50.00
#1109, Bristol Bloodhound & Loading Trolley.............$130.00
#1109, Michelin Truck $50.00
#1110, JCB Crawler Loader $60.00
#1110, Mobilegas Tanker $300.00
#1110, Shell Tanker......................................$3,000.00
#1111, Massey-Ferguson Harvester $150.00
#1112, Corporal Missile on Launching Ramp.............$160.00
#1112, David Brown Combine $120.00
#1113, Corporal Erector & Missile..................$375.00
#1113, Hyster $50.00
#1113, Hyster Sealink...................................$125.00

#1121, Chipperfield's Circus Crane, $250.00.

#1115, Bloodhound Missile $110.00
#1116, Bloodhound Missile Platform $100.00
#1116, Refuse Lorry $30.00
#1117, Bloodhound Missile Trolley....................$65.00
#1117, Faun Street Sweeper $30.00
#1118, Airport Emergency Tender $70.00
#1118, International Truck, Dutch Army.............$300.00
#1118, International Truck, gr $150.00
#1118, International Truck, US Army $275.00
#1119, HDL Hovercraft.....................................$100.00
#1120, Midland Coach $250.00
#1121, Corgimatic Ford Tipper $50.00
#1123, Chipperfield's Circus Animal Cage..........$120.00
#1124, Corporal Missile Launching Ramp $80.00
#1126, Ecurie Ecosse Transporter.....................$200.00
#1126, Simon Snorkel Fire Engine.....................$50.00
#1127, Simon Snorkel Fire Engine.....................$100.00
#1128, Priestman Cub Shovel $50.00
#1129, Mercedes Truck.....................................$25.00
#1129, Milk Tanker $250.00
#1130, Chipperfield's Circus Horse Transporter............$275.00
#1130, Mercedes Tanker, Corgi $25.00
#1131, Carrimore Machinery Carrier..................$135.00
#1131, Mercedes Refrigerated Van $20.00
#1132, Carrimore Low Loader $250.00
#1132, Scania Truck $20.00
#1133, Troop Transporter $250.00

#1134, Army Fuel Tanker, $400.00.

#1135, Heavy Equipment Transporter $400.00
#1137, Ford Tilt Cab w/Trailer $100.00
#1138, Carrimore Car Transporter, Corgi.....................$135.00
#1139, Chipperfield's Circus Menagerie Truck $500.00
#1140, Bedford Mobilgas Tanker $300.00
#1140, Ford Transit Wrecker............................$25.00
#1141, Milk Tanker..$250.00
#1142, Holmes Wrecker $150.00
#1143, American LaFrance Rescue Truck $125.00
#1144, Berliet Wrecker.....................................$80.00
#1144, Chipperfield's Circus Crane Truck..........$600.00
#1145, Mercedes Unimog Dumper $50.00
#1146, Tri-Deck Transporter $170.00
#1147, Ferrymaster Truck.................................$100.00
#1148, Carrimore Car Transporter....................$160.00
#1150, Mercedes Unimog Snowplough $60.00
#1151, Scammell Co-op Set...............................$350.00

#1151, Scammell Co-op Truck $250.00
#1152, Mack Truck, Esso Tanker $75.00
#1152, Mack Truck, Exxon Tanker $140.00
#1153, Priestman Boom Crane $80.00
#1154, Priestman Crane $85.00
#1154, Tower Crane $75.00
#1155, Skyscraper Tower Crane $60.00
#1156, Volvo Concrete Mixer............................$60.00
#1157, Ford Esso Tanker...................................$50.00
#1158, Ford Exxon Tanker $75.00
#1159, Ford Car Transporter $60.00
#1160, Ford Gulf Tanker $55.00
#1161, Ford Aral Tanker $85.00
#1163, Circus Cannon Truck $70.00
#1164, Dolphinarium.......................................$125.00
#1169, Ford Guiness Tanker..............................$60.00
#1170, Ford Car Transporter $60.00

Exploration Models

#2022, Scanotron..$60.00
#2023, Rocketron...$60.00
#2024, Lasertron...$60.00
#2025, Magnetron..$60.00

Gift Sets

#01, Car Transporter Set................................$900.00
#01, Ford Sierra & Caravan..............................$40.00
#01, Ford 500 Tractor & Beast Trailer...............$160.00
#02, Land Rover & Horsebox............................$150.00
#02, Unimog Dumper $150.00
#03, Batmobile & Batboat, w/Bat hubs $400.00
#03, Batmobile & Batboat, w/whizzwheels $200.00
#03, RAF Land Rover & Missile $250.00
#04, Country Farm Set.....................................$75.00
#04, RAF Land Rover & Missile $500.00
#05, Agricultural Set $400.00
#05, Country Farm Set, w/no hay......................$100.00
#05, Racing Car Set..$300.00
#06, Rocket Age Set.......................................$1,000.00
#06, VW Transporter & Cooper Maserati $175.00
#07, Daktari Set...$150.00
#07, Tractor & Trailer Set $130.00
#08, Combine Harvester Set $400.00
#08, Lions of Longleat $200.00
#09, Corporal Missile & Launcher $600.00
#09, Tractor w/Shovel & Trailer $200.00
#10, Centurion Tank & Transporter $120.00
#10, Rambler Marlin, w/kayaks $200.00
#11, ERF Truck & Trailer $200.00
#11, London Set, no Policeman $125.00
#11, London Set, w/Policeman...........................$60.00
#12, Circus Crane & Cage $300.00
#12, Glider Set...$80.00
#12, Grand Prix Set..$450.00
#13, Fordson Tractor & Plough..........................$150.00
#13, Peugeot Tour De France.............................$90.00

#13, Renault Tour De France $150.00
#14, Giant Daktari Set $500.00
#14, Tower Wagon $100.00
#15, Giant Daktari Set $500.00
#15, Land Rover & Horsebox..$100.00
#15, Silverstone Set..$1,600.00
#16, Ecurie Ecosse Set $500.00
#17, Land Rover & Ferrari $200.00
#17, Military Set...$90.00
#18, Emergency Set $80.00
#18, Fordson Tractor & Plough.....................................$135.00
#19, Chipperfield's Circus Rover & Elephant Trailer $350.00
#19, Emergency Set $80.00
#19, Flying Club Set $85.00
#20, Car Transporter Set...$1,000.00
#20, Emergency Set $80.00
#20, Golden Guinea Set..$300.00
#21, Chipperfield's Circus Crane & Trailer $1,600.00
#21, ERF Milk Truck & Trailer $400.00
#21, Superman Set...$250.00
#22, Farm Set $1,100.00
#22, James Bond Set $300.00
#23, Chipperfield's Circus Set, w/Booking Office $1,000.00
#23, Chipperfield's Circus Set, w/giraffe truck...............$750.00

#23, Spider-Man Set, $200.00.

#24, Construction Set $150.00
#24, Mercedes & Caravan $50.00
#25, Shell or BP Garage Set..$2,000.00
#25, VW Transporter & Cooper Maserati $160.00
#26, Beach Buggy Set..$50.00
#26, Matra Rancho & Racer...$75.00
#27, Priestman Shovel Set...$180.00
#28, Mazda & Dinghy $50.00
#28, Transporter Set $800.00
#29, Ferrari Racing Set $80.00
#29, Tractor & Trailer $140.00
#30, Grand Prix Set $250.00
#30, Pinder's Circus Rover & Trailer $100.00
#31, Buick Riviera & Boat $225.00
#31, Safari Set $75.00
#32, Tractor & Trailer $170.00
#35, Chopper Squad $60.00
#35, London Set $175.00
#36, Tarzan Set..$250.00

#36, Tornado Set...$250.00
#37, Fiat & Boat...$60.00
#37, Lotus Racing Team $500.00
#38, Jaguar & Powerboat $60.00
#38, Mini Camping Set $75.00
#38, Monte Carlo Set $800.00
#40, Avenger Set, w/Bentley, gr...................................$800.00
#40, Avenger Set, w/Bentley, red..................................$650.00

#40, Batman Set, $250.00.

#41, Ford Transporter Set..$800.00
#41, Silver Jubilee State Landau....................................$40.00
#42, Agricultural Set..$80.00
#43, Silo & Conveyor $70.00
#44, Police Rover Set...$70.00
#45, All Winners Set..$800.00
#46, All Winners Set..$600.00
#46, Super Karts $30.00
#47, Ford Tractor & Conveyor.......................................$180.00
#47, Pony Club Set $50.00
#48, Ford Transporter Set..$600.00
#48, Jean Richard's Circus Set $200.00
#48, Scammell Transporter Set $900.00
#49, Flying Club Set $50.00

Huskies

Huskies were marketed exclusively through the Woolworth stores from 1965 to 1969. In 1970, Corgi Juniors were introduced. Both lines were sold in blister packs. Models produced up to 1975 (as dated on the package) are valued from $15.00 to $30.00 (MIP), except for the character-related examples listed below.

#1001A, James Bond Aston Martin, Husky on base.......$200.00
#1001B, James Bond Aston Martin, Junior on base, MIP..$175.00
#1002A, Batmobile, Husky on base, MIP $200.00
#1002B, Batmobile, Junior on base, MIP $175.00
#1003A, Bar Boat, Husky on base, MIP $125.00
#1003B, Bat Boat, Junior on base, MIP $85.00
#1004A, Monkeemobile, Husky on base, MIP $200.00
#1004B, Monkeemobile, Junior on base, MIP $175.00
#1005A, UNCLE Car, Husky on base, MIP $175.00
#1005B, UNCLE Car, Junior on base, MIP..................$1,500.00
#100-6A, Chitty-Chitty Bang-Bang, Husky on base, MIP .$200.00
#1006B, Chitty-Chitty Bang-Bang, Junior on base, MIP...$175.00
#1007, Ironsides Police Van, MIP $125.00
#1008, Popeye Paddle Wagon, MIP $250.00
#1010 James Bond VW, MIP $200.00

#1011, James Bond Bobsleigh, MIP................................$300.00
#1012, Spectre Bobsleigh, MIP $300.00
#1013, Tom's Go-Kart, MIP.....................................$75.00
#1014, Jerry's Banger, MIP $75.00
#1017, Ford Holmes Wrecker, MIP................................$175.00

Dakins

Dakin has been an importer of stuffed toys as far back as 1955, but it wasn't until 1959 that the name of this San Francisco-based company actually appeared on the toy labels. They produced three distinct lines: Dream Pets (1960 - early 1970s), Dream Dolls (1965 - mid-1970s), and licensed characters and advertising figures, starting in 1968. Of them all, the latter series was the most popular and the one that holds most interest for collectors. Originally there were seven Warner Brothers characters. Each was made with a hard plastic body and a soft vinyl head, and all were under 10" tall. All in all, more than fifty cartoon characters were produced, some with several variations. Advertising figures were made as well. Some were extensions of the three already existing lines; others were completely original.

Goofy Grams was a series featuring many of their character figures mounted on a base lettered with a 'goofy' message. They also utilized some of their large stock characters as banks in a series called Cash Catchers. A second bank series consisted of Warner Brothers characters molded in a squatting position and therefore smaller. Other figures made by Dakin include squeeze toys, PVCs, and water squirters.

Advisor: Jim Rash (R3).

Alice in Wonderland, set of 3 w/Alice, Mad Hatter & the
    White Rabbit, artist Faith Wick, 18", EX+ $300.00
Baby Puss, Hanna-Barbera, 1971, EX+, R3....................$100.00
Bambi, Disney, 1960s, MIP, R3.......................................$35.00
Bamm-Bamm, Hanna-Barbera, w/club, 1970, EX, R3 ......$35.00

Banana Splits, Fleegle, 1970, 7", NM, $75.00.

Barney Rubble, Hanna-Barbera, 1970, EX, R3/B10, from $35
    to $40.00
Benji, 1978, name emb on brass tag, 10", VG, M15 ....$15.00
Bozo the Clown, Larry Harmon, 1974, EX, R3 ....$35.00
Bugs Bunny, Warner Bros, 1971, MIP, R3 ....$30.00
Bugs Bunny, Warner Bros, 1976, MIB (cartoon theater box),
    R3 ....$40.00
Bugs Bunny, Warner Bros, 1978, MIP (fun farm bag), R3 .$20.00
Bull Dog, Dream Pet, EX $15.00
Bullwinkle, Jay Ward, 1976, MIB (cartoon theater box), R3...$60.00
Cool Cat, Warner Bros, w/beret, 1970, EX+, R3 ....$40.00
Daffy Duck, Warner Bros, 1968, EX, R3 ....$30.00
Daffy Duck, Warner Bros, 1976, MIB (cartoon theater box),
    R3 ....$40.00
Deputy Dawg, Terrytoons, 1977, EX, R3 ....$40.00
Dewey Duck, Disney, red shirt, straight or bent legs, EX,
    R3 ....$30.00
Dino Dinosaur, Hanna-Barbera, 1970, EX, R3 ....$40.00
Donald Duck, Disney, 1960s, straight or bent leg, EX, R3 ..$20.00
Donald Duck, orig tag, NMIP, M5 ....$30.00
Dudley Do-Right, Jay Ward, 1976, MIB (cartoon theater box),
    R3...$75.00
Dumbo, Disney, EX+, J2...$20.00
Dumbo, Disney, 1960s, cloth collar, MIB, R3..................$25.00
Elmer Fudd, Warner Bros, 1968, in hunting outfit w/rifle, EX,
    R3...$125.00
Elmer Fudd, Warner Bros, 1968, in tuxedo, EX, R3.........$30.00

Elmer Fudd, Warner Bros, 1968, in hunting outfit, EX, $125.00.

Elmer Fudd, Warner Bros, 1978, MIP (fun farm bag), R3...$35.00
Foghorn Leghorn, Warner Bros, 1970, EX+, R3 ....$75.00
Fred Flintstone, Hanna-Barbera, 1970, EX, R3/B10, from $35
    to $40.00
Goofy, Disney, 1960s, EX, R3.......................................$20.00
Goofy Gram, Bloodhound, You Think You Feel Bad!, EX,
    R3 ....$20.00
Goofy Gram, Dog, You're Top Dog!, EX, R3 ....$20.00
Goofy Gram, Fox, Wanna See My Etchings?, EX, R3 ......$20.00

Goofy Gram, Kangaroo, World's Greatest Mom!, EX, R3 ..$20.00

Goofy Gram, Lion, Sorry You're Feeling Beastly!, EX, R3..$20.00

Hawaiian Hound, Dream Pets, w/orig tag & surfboard, EX..$25.00

Hokey Wolf, Hanna-Barbera, 1971, EX+, R3 ....$250.00

Hoppy Hopperoo, Hanna-Barbera, 1971, EX+, R3 ....$100.00

Huckleberry Hound, Hanna-Barbera, 1970, EX+, R3 ......$75.00

Huey Duck, Disney, gr shirt, straight or bent legs, EX, R3..$30.00

Jack-in-the-Box, bank, 1971, EX, R3 ....$25.00

Kangaroo, Dream Pet, w/camera, wearing beret, EX, H4..$25.00

Lion in a Cage, bank, 1971, EX, R3 ....$25.00

Louie Duck, Disney, bl shirt, straight or bent legs, EX, R3...$30.00

Merlin the Magic Mouse, Warner Bros, 1970, EX+, $25.00.

Mickey Mouse, Disney, 1960s, cloth clothes, EX, R3 ....$20.00

Midnight Mouse, Dream Pet, w/orig tag, missing 1 slipper o/w EX, H4 ....$22.00

Mighty Mouse, Terrytoons, 1978, EX, R3......................$100.00

Minnie Mouse, Disney, 1960s, cloth clothes, EX, R3 ....$20.00

Monkey on a Barrel, bank, 1971, EX, R3 ....$25.00

Olive Oyl, King Features, 1974, cloth clothes, MIP, R3...$50.00

Olive Oyl, King Features, 1976, MIB (cartoon theater box), R3 ....$40.00

Oliver Hardy, Larry Harmon, 1974, EX+, R3 ....$30.00

Opus, 1982, cloth, 12", EX, B10 ....$15.00

Pebbles Flintstone, Hanna-Barbera, 1970, EX, R3............$35.00

Pepe Le Peu, Warner Bros, 1971, EX+, R3 ....$75.00

Pink Panther, Mirisch-Freleng, 1971, EX+, R3 ....$50.00

Pink Panther, Mirisch-Freleng, 1976, MIB (cartoon theater box), R3 ....$50.00

Pinocchio, Disney, 1960s, cloth clothes, EX, R3 ....$20.00

Popeye, King Features, 1974, cloth clothes, MIP, R3 ....$50.00

Popeye, King Features, 1976, MIB (cartoon theater box), R3 ..$50.00

Porky Pig, Warner Bros, 1968, EX+, R3..........................$30.00

Porky Pig, Warner Bros, 1975, stuffed, NM, C17 ....$15.00

Porky Pig, Warner Bros, 1976, MIB (cartoon theater box), R3 ....$40.00

Ren & Stimpy, water squirters, Nickelodeon, 1993, EX, R3, ea $10.00

Road Runner, Warner Bros, 1968, EX+, R3 ....$30.00

Road Runner, Warner Bros, 1976, MIB (cartoon theater box), R3 ....$50.00

Rocky Squirrel, Jay Ward, 1976, MIB (cartoon theater box), R3 ....$60.00

Scooby Doo, Hanna-Barbera, 1980, EX, R3.....................$75.00

Scrappy Doo, Hanna-Barbera, 1982, EX+, R3 ....$75.00

Seal on a Box, bank, 1971, EX, R3 ....$25.00

Second Banana, Warner Bros, 1970, EX, R3 ....$35.00

Smokey Bear, 1974, MIP, R3...$20.00

Smokey Bear, 1976, MIB (cartoon theater box), R3 ....$30.00

Snagglepuss, Hanna-Barbera, 1971, EX, R3.....................$100.00

Speedy Gonzalez, Warner Bros, MIB (cartoon theater box), R3 ....$50.00

Stan Laurel, Larry Harmon, 1974, EX+, R3 ....$30.00

Swee' Pea, beanbag doll, King Features, 1974, VG, R3 ....$35.00

Sylvester, Warner Bros, 1968, EX+, R3 ....$20.00

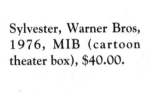

Sylvester, Warner Bros, 1976, MIB (cartoon theater box), $40.00.

Sylvester, Warner Bros, 1978, MIP (fun farm bag), R3 ....$20.00

Tasmanian Devil, Warner Bros, 1978, R3, EX (fun farm bag) $400.00

Tiger in a Cage, bank, 1971, EX, R3 ....$25.00

Top Banana, NM, C17 ....$25.00

Tweety Bird, Warner Bros, 1966, EX+, R3 ....$20.00

Tweety Bird, Warner Bros, 1968, EX, C17 ....$15.00

Tweety Bird, Warner Bros, 1976, MIB (cartoon theater box), R3 ....$40.00

Tweety Bird, Warner Bros, 1978, MIP (fun farm bag), R3 .$20.00

Uncle Bugs Bunny, Warner Bros, 1975, EX+, R3 ....$50.00

Underdog, Jay Ward, 1976, MIB (cartoon theater box), R3...$150.00

Wile E Coyote, bank, 1971, on top of crate w/bomb, missing tail o/w EX, C17 ....$28.00

Wile E Coyote, Warner Bros, 1968, MIB, R3 ....$30.00

Wile E Coyote, Warner Bros, 1976, MIB (cartoon theater box), R3 ....$40.00

Yogi Bear, Hanna-Barbera, 1970, EX, R3........................$60.00

Yosemite Sam, Warner Bros, 1968, MIB, R3 ....$30.00

Yosemite Sam, Warner Bros, 1968, missing hat o/w VG+, I2 .$10.00

Yosemite Sam, Warner Bros, 1976, MIP (fun farm bag), R3 ...$40.00

Advertising

Bay View Eagle, bank, 1976, EX+, R3..........................$30.00
Big Foot Sasquatch Savings, bank, 10", EX, H4................$65.00
Bob's Big Boy, 1974, missing hamburger o/w VG, H4 ......$80.00
Bob's Big Boy, 1974, w/hamburger, EX+, R3 ....$190.00
Christian Brothers Brandy St Bernard, 1982, 12", VG, M15 ...$30.00
Crocker National Bank's Spaniel, 1979, w/metal dog chain &
     orig tag, 12", EX, M15 ....$20.00
Diaparene Baby, Sterling Drug Company, 1980, EX, R3 ..$40.00
Freddie Fast, 1976, M, P12 ....$95.00
Glamour Kitty, 1977, wht or blk w/gold crown, EX, R3, ea...$150.00
Kernal Renk, American Seeds, 1970, rare, EX+, R3 ......$350.00
Li'l Miss Just Rite, 1965, EX+, R3 ....$75.00
Miss Liberty Belle, 1975, w/hat, MIP, R3.................$75.00
Quasar Robot, bank, 1975, NM, R3.........................$150.00
Sambo's Boy, 1974, EX+, R3 ....$75.00
Sambo's Tiger, 1974, EX+, R3 ....$125.00
Woodsy Owl, 1974, MIP, R3.............................$60.00

Diecast

Diecast replicas of cars, trucks, planes, trains, etc., represent a huge corner of today's collector market, and their manufacturers see to it that there is no shortage. Back in the 1920s, Tootsietoy had the market virtually by themselves, but one by one other companies had a go at it, some with more success than others. Among them were the American companies of Barclay, Hubley and Manoil, all of whom are much better known for other types of toys. After the war, Metal Masters, Smith-Miller and Doepke Ohlsson-Rice (among others) tried the market with varying degrees of success. Some companies were phased out over the years, while many more entered the market with fervor. Today it's those fondly remembered models from the fifties and sixties that many collectors yearn to own. Solido produced well-modeled, detailed little cars; some had dome lights that actually came on when the doors were opened. Politoy's were cleanly molded with good detailing and finishes. Mebetoys, an Italian company that has been bought out by Mattel, produced several; and some of the finest come from Brooklyn, whose Shelby (signed) GT-350H Mustang can easily cost you from $900.00 to $1,000.00 when you can find one.

In 1968 the Topper Toy Company introduced its line of low-friction, high-speed Johnny Lightning cars to be in direct competition with Mattel's Hot Wheels. To gain attention, Topper sponsored Al Unser's winning race car, the 'Johnny Lightning,' in the 1970 Indianapolis 500. Despite the popularity of their cars, the Topper Toy Company went out of business in 1971. Today the Johnny Lightnings are highly sought after and a new company, Playing Mantis, is reproducing many of the original designs as well as several models that never made it into regular production.

If you're interested in Majorette Toys, we recommend *Collecting Majorette Toys* by Dana Johnson, as well as his *Collector's Guide to Diecast Toys and Scale Models*; ordering information is given with Dana's listing under Diecast, in the section called Categories of Special Interest in the back of the book.

Other sources: P3, N3

See also Corgi; Dinky; Diecast Collector Banks; Farm Toys; Tootsietoy; Hot Wheels; Matchbox; Tekno.

Aurora Cigarbox, Chaparral, turq, #7, M, B10 ....$14.00
Aurora Cigarbox, Dino Ferrari, red w/wht stripes, M, B10 .$14.00
Aurora Cigarbox, Ferrari Berlinetta, red w/wht stripes, M,
     B10...$14.00
Aurora Cigarbox, Ferrari GTO, wht w/red stripe, VG, B10 ..$8.00
Aurora Cigarbox, Ford GTO, wht w/blk stripes, M, B10..$14.00
Aurora Cigarbox, Ford J Car, red w/blk stripe, M, B10.....$12.00
Aurora Cigarbox, Ford Lola GT, red w/wht stripe, VG+, B10...$8.00
Aurora Cigarbox, Porsche 904, gr w/wht stripe, M, B10...$12.00
Benbros, Electric Milk Trolley, dk bl, orig man, 1950s, NM (box
     missing 2 flaps), W1.............................$20.00
Best Box, 1919 Ford Model T, gr & red, blk plastic tires, 1960s,
     EX..$10.00
Budgie, #11 Royal Mail Truck, red, metal wheels, 1950s, EX+,
     W1..$18.00
Budgie, #18 Dump Truck, red chassis, gray dump, blk plastic
     tires, 1960s, EX, W1..............................$6.00
Budgie, #216 Renault Truck, red & yel w/canvas cover mk Fresh
     Fruit Daily, NM (EX box), M5.....................$70.00
Budgie, #22 Cattle Truck, tan, blk plastic tires, 1960s, NM,
     W1..$8.00

Budgie, Austin A95, orange, blk plastic tires, 1960s, EX, W1..$6.00

Cragstan, Model Car Miniatures, HO scale, boxed set of 12, NM (VG box), A $110.00

Crescent, #1285 BRM, gr, NMIB, L1 ....$75.00

Crescent, #1288 Jaguar, dk gr, NM, L1 ....$95.00

Diapet, Sunny Coupe 1200 GL, red, blk rubber tires, 1960s, MIB, W1 ....$20.00

Ertl, A-Team Van, blk, blk plastic tires, 1980s, EX+, W1..$4.00

Ertl, Chevy Fleetside Pickup, brn w/Cooter's Garage labels, blk plastic tires, 1980s, NM+, W1 ....$14.00

Ertl, Dick Tracy Coupe, blk or red, blk rubber tires, 1980s, M, W1 ....$10.00

Ertl, Dukes of Hazzard Boss Hogg's Cadillac, 1/64 scale, 1981, MOC, M15 ....$12.00

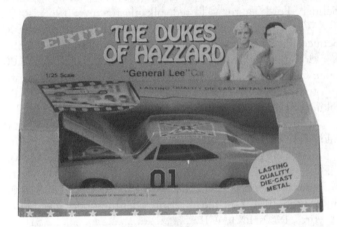

Ertl, Dukes of Hazzard General Lee Car, orange with black plastic tires, 1/25 scale, 1981, MIB, $65.00.

Ertl, Dukes of Hazzard Pontiac Bonneville Hazzard County Sheriff Car, wht, blk plastic tires, 1980s, NM+, W1 ....$20.00

Ertl, Richard Petty Superstock Race Car, 1/25 scale, MIB, M5 ....$110.00

Ertl, Turbo Firebird, blk, blk plastic tires, 1980s, EX, W1..$4.00

Ertl, 1980 Mountain Dew NASCAR Stocker, wht, blk plastic tires, MBP (card creased, blister partially loose), W1 ..$80.00

Goodee, Ford Gas Tanker Truck, red, blk rubber tires, 1950s, VG, W1...$8.00

Goodee, Ford Gas Tanker Truck, yel, blk rubber tires, 1950s, NM, W1...$12.50

Goodee, Ford Sedan, yel, blk rubber tires, 1950s, EX, W1..$10.00

Goodee, Jeep, olive, blk rubber tires, 1950s, NM, W1......$12.50

Goodee, Moving Van, dk bl, blk rubber tires, 1950s, VG+, W1 ....$10.50

Goodee, Station Wagon, lt gr, blk rubber tires, 1950s, VG+, W1 ....$8.00

Goodee, Studebaker Sedan, gr, blk rubber tires, 1950s, NM, W1 ....$12.50

Goodee, Truck, red, blk rubber tires, 1950s, EX+, W1 .....$10.50

Impy, Chrysler Imperial, bl w/bl interior, blk plastic tires, 1960s, EX+, W1...$44.00

Impy, Ford Corsair, purple, blk rubber tires, 1970s, EX+, W1.$30.00

Impy, Ford Zodiac Station Wagon, yel, blk rubber tires, 1970s, NM+, W1 ....$25.00

Impy, Mercedes Benz 220SE, lt bl w/wht interior, opening doors, hood & trunk, blk plastic tires, 1970s, EX+, W1 ....$14.00

Impy, Rolls Royce Silver Cloud Convertible, silver, blk plastic tires, missing windshield o/w NM, W1.....................$14.00

Impy, 1960s Alfa Romeo Giulia 1600 Spider Convertible, bl w/tan interior, blk plastic tires, 1970s, M (NM+ box), W1 ....$30.00

Impy, 1960s Corvette Stingray Gran Turismo, aqua w/orange interior, opening doors, blk plastic tires, 1970s, MIB, W1 ....$50.00

Jet Wheel, Buick Riviera, gr w/cream interior, blk plastic wheels, 1960s, NM, W1 ....$20.00

Johnny Lightning, Baja, gold, orig canopy, G+, W1........$17.00

Johnny Lightning, Big Rig, metallic aqua, complete, EX, W1..$44.00

Johnny Lightning, Condor, metallic bl, grayish bottom, VG, W1..$40.00

Johnny Lightning, Custom Dragster, metallic olive, no-canopy version, M (NM card), W1 ....$50.00

Johnny Lightning, Custom Ferrari, metallic lime w/red interior, EX, W1..$22.00

Johnny Lightning, Custom Mako Shark, metallic orange w/wht interior, M (abrasions on EX card), W1 ....$150.00

Johnny Lightning, Custom Spoiler, metallic purple, orig wing, missing canopy, EX, W1 ....$12.00

Johnny Lightning, Custom Thunderbird, metallic magenta w/wht interior, pnt touched up, scarce, EX+, W1 ...$100.00

Johnny Lightning, Custom Toronado, metallic red w/wht interior, open doors, rare mirror finish, NM+, W1 ....$295.00

Johnny Lightning, Custom Turbine, metallic olive, unpnt interior, M (sm abrasion on EX+ card), W1......................$60.00

Johnny Lightning, Custom XKE, metallic red w/wht interior, VG+, W1 ....$18.00

Johnny Lightning, Double Trouble, metallic olive, missing pipes, G+, W1...$20.00

Johnny Lightning, Flame Out, metallic red, complete, VG+, W1 ....$24.00

Johnny Lightning, Hairy Hauler, metallic purple, orange exhaust covers & stickers, missing top & hook o/w VG+, W1.$22.00

Photo courtesy of June Moon.

Johnny Lightning, Indy 500 racing set, NRFB, J6, $425.00.

Johnny Lightning, Leapin' Limo, metallic magenta, orig pipes, missing engine & engine cover, VG+, W1 ....$16.00

Johnny Lightning, Mad Maverick, metallic red, orig engine & pipes, missing steering wheel, EX+, W1 ....$18.00

Johnny Lightning, Monster, metallic bl w/wht interior, VG+, W1 ....$22.00

Johnny Lightning, Movin' Van, metallic gr, orig engine, pipes & stickers, missing steering wheel, EX-, W1 ....$17.50

Johnny Lightning, Nucleon, metallic purple, complete, EX+, W1 ....$35.00

Johnny Lightning, Sand Stormer, metallic aqua, orig engine, EX, W1 ....$20.00

Johnny Lightning, Sling Shot, metallic magenta, dragster front wheels, complete, EX, W1 ....$35.00

Johnny Lightning, Stilletto, EX, W1 ....$22.00

Johnny Lightning, Triple Threat, dk metallic orange, complete, EX+, W1 ....$26.00

Johnny Lightning, Vulture, metallic gr, orig engine, missing blower & wings, VG, W1 ....$20.00

Johnny Lightning, Wasp, metallic rose, missing 1 engine blower, EX+, W1 ....$24.50

Johnny Lightning, Whistler, metallic lime, orig windshield, added sticker, VG, W1 ....$16.00

Johnny Lightning, Wild Winner, metallic purple, orig engine, side pieces, stickers, slicks, missing both wings, NM, W1 .....$30.00

JRD, #152 Citroen DS 19 Convertible, orange w/cream interior, M, L1 ....$250.00

JRD, #153 Mercedes 220S, metallic charcoal, M, L1 .....$145.00

Lledo, Fire Truck, MIB, T1 ....$8.50

Lledo, Red Crown Bulk Delivery Truck, MIB, T1 ....$8.50

Lledo, Red Crown Gasoline Truck, MIB, T1 ....$5.00

Lledo, Refinery Fire Truck, MIB, T1 ....$5.00

Lledo, RPM Motor Oil Truck, MIB, T1 ....$5.00

Lledo, Standard Oil Barrel Delivery Truck, MIB, T1 ....$8.50

Majorette, BMW 3.0 CSI, lime, blk plastic tires, 1970s, M, W1 ....$30.00

Majorette, Fiat 127, lt gr, blk plastic tires, 1970s, NM+, W1 .$20.00

Majorette, F1 Racing Car, on orange trailer, lt bl, blk plastic tires, 1960s, NM+, W1 ....$22.00

Majorette, Vacation Trailer, cream, blk plastic tires, 1960s, 3 sm cracks in front window o/w NM, W1 ....$6.00

Marx, Jaguar XKE, red, litho tin interior, blk plastic tires, no-window version, 1 orig label, 1970s, MIB, W1 ....$40.00

Mercury, #29 Rolls Royce Silver Cloud, dk gray, M, L1.$195.00

Mercury, #30 Bentley S Sedan, gray, M, L1 ....$195.00

Mercury, #31-2 Maserati (old type), red, NM, L1 ....$150.00

Mercury, #91 Viberti Shell, yel & red, rare, M, L1........$300.00

Mercury Miniatures, Chevy Compressor Truck, red, blk rubber tires, orig jackhammer, 1960s, NM, W1 ....$50.00

Midgetoy, Army Ambulance, olive, blk rubber tires, 1950s, G+, W1 ....$10.00

Midgetoy, Army Amphibious Vehicle & Cannon Trailer, olive, blk rubber tires, 1950s, VG, W1 ....$10.00

Midgetoy, Army Truck, olive, blk rubber tires, 1950s, EX+, W1 ....$10.00

Midgetoy, Convertible, bl, blk rubber tires, 1950s, EX+, W1.$16.00

Midgetoy, Corvette, yel, blk plastic tires, 1950s, VG, W1.$10.00

Midgetoy, Jeep, olive, crimped axles, 1950s, NM, W1.......$4.00

Midgetoy, Pickup, Jeep cab-over, bl, blk rubber tires, 1950s, NM, W1 ....$16.00

Playart, Man From UNCLE Car, lime, both orig spotlights, blk plastic tires, 1970s, NM, W1 ....$60.00

Playart, VW Bus, lime, 1960s style w/sunroof & eyebrow windows, blk plastic tires, 1970s, M, W1 ....$50.00

Playart, 1965 Mustang, orange w/lt bl interior, blk roof, blk plastic tires, 1970s, EX+, W1 ....$24.00

Politoys, #518 Rolls Royce, silver, opening doors, hood & trunk, blk rubber tires, 1960s, M (EX+ box), W1 ....$40.00

Politoys, #532 Alfa Romeo GS Zagato, cream, blk fenders & rubber tires, orig top & instructions, 1960s, M (EX+ box), W1 ....$40.00

Politoys, #538 VW 1600 Fastback, metallic aqua, opening door, hood & trunk, blk rubber tires, 1960s, M (EX+ box), W1..........$40.00

Schuco, Ford Taurus GT, red, blk plastic tires, 1960s, MIB, W1 ....$40.00

Schuco, Piccolo Mercedes Bus, bl, litho tin interior, blk rubber tires, removable top, 1950s, VG+, W1 ....$18.00

Siku, Citroen DS 21, gr, yel interior, opening doors, blk plastic tires, 1960s, EX+, W1 ....$18.00

Siku, Ford F500 Pickup, dk gr, wht interior, red chassis, blk plastic tires, 1960s, EX+, W1 ....$24.00

Siku, Ford OSI TS (Sports Car), red w/cream interior, opening doors, blk plastic tires, 1960s, EX+, W1 ....$18.00

Siku, Ford 15M, lt gr, yel interior, opening doors, blk plastic tires, 1960s, EX+, W1 ....$18.00

Siku, Ford 20M, tan, red interior, opening doors, blk plastic tires, 1960s, EX+, W1 ....$18.00

Siku, Opel Rekord Coupe, wht, opening doors, blk plastic tires, 1960s, 1 seatback cracked loose o/w NM+, W1........$14.00

Siku, Pontiac GTO Convertible, lt bl w/orange interior, opening doors, blk plastic tires, 1960s, EX, W1 ....$30.00

Siku, Porsche Carrera 906, wht, orig decals, blk plastic tires, 1960s, NM+, W1 ....$24.00

Siku, Porsche 901, bl, blk plastic tires, 1960s, NM+, W1.$24.00

Siku, VW 1300 Bug, yel, opening doors, blk plastic tires, 1960s, NM+, W1 ....$40.00

Tekno, #927 Jaguar XKE, red, blk top, opening doors, hood & trunk, blk rubber tires, 1960s, NMIB, W1 ....$100.00

Tomica, Datsun 1200, bl, 1974, M (NMBP), W1 ....$20.00

Tomica, Datsun 240Z, silver, 1974, NM, W1 ....$8.00

Tomica, Datsun 240ZG, maroon, 1975, NM+, W1 ....$10.00

Tomica, Datsun 510, red, 1974, M (NMBP), W1............$20.00

Tomica, Dodge Colt, lt metallic olive, 1974, M (NMBP), W1..$20.00

Tomica, Furukawa Wheel Loader, orange, 1974, M (NMBP), W1 ....$20.00

Tomica, Hino Cement Mixer Truck, red, 1974, M (NMBP), W1 ....$20.00

Tomica, Hino Dump Truck, gr, 1974, M (NMBP), W1 ...$14.00

Tomica, Hitachi Dump Truck, orange, 1974, M (EX BP) W1.$20.00

Tomica, Honda Civic, brn, 1974, M (NMBP), W1.........$20.00

Tomica, Honda Pepsi Truck, wht, 1974, M (NMBP), W1 ..$30.00

Tomica, Komatsu Fork Lift, yel, 1974, M (NMBP), W1 ..$14.00

Tomica, Mazda Light Bus, pk, 1974, M (NMBP), W1 .....$20.00

Tomica, New Toyota Mk II, wht, 1974, M (NMBP), W1 ..$20.00

Tomica, Toyota Celica, lime, 1974, NM+, W1 ....$10.00

Tomica, Toyota 2000GT, gray, 1974, NM+, W1 ....$14.00

Tri-ang Minic Ships, M892, 1960, features SS United States, complete with booklet, NMIB, $300.00.

Diecast Collector Banks

Thousands of banks have been produced since Ertl made its first model in 1981, the 1913 Model T Parcel Post Mail Service #9647. The Ertl company was founded by Fred Ertl, Sr., in Dubuque, Iowa, back in the mid-1940s. Until they made their first diecast banks, most of what they made were farm tractors. Today they specialize in vehicles made to specification and carrying logos of companies as large as Texaco and as small as your hometown bank. The size of each 'run' is dictated by the client and can vary from a few hundred up to several thousand. Some clients will later add a serial number to the vehicle; Ertl does not. Other numbers that appear on the base of each bank are a 4-number dating code (the first three indicate the day of the year up to 365 and the fourth number is the last digit of the year, '5' for 1995, for instance.) The stock number is shown only on the box, never on the bank, so it is extremely important that you keep them in their original boxes.

Other producers of these banks are Scale Models, incorporated in 1991, First Gear Inc., and Spec-Cast, whose founders at one time all worked for the Ertl company.

In the listings that follow, unless another condition is given, all values are for banks mint and in their original boxes. (#d) indicates a bank that was numbered by the client, not Ertl.

Advisors: Art and Judy Turner (H8).

Other Sources: S5

Key:

JLE — Joseph L. Ertl

Ertl

A&W RootBeer, 1923 Chevy Van, #B544, H8 .... $35.00
A&W RootBeer #2, 1905 Ford Delivery Van, #9827, H8.. $45.00
Aberfoyle Antique Market, 1938 Chevy Van, #4868, H8.. $35.00
AC Spark Plugs, 1950 Chevy Panel Truck, #2901, H8 .... $35.00
Ace Hardware, 1913 Ford Model T, #9409, H8 .... $30.00
Ace Hardware, 1955 Chevy Cameo Pickup, #B384, H8 .. $22.00
Adamstown MD Carrol Manor, 1926 Seagrave Fire Engine, #7693, D13 .... $28.00
Agway #1, 1913 Ford Model T, #9444 .... $275.00
Alan Kulwicki Chrome, 1940 Panel, JLE, #6021, H8 .... $75.00

Alex Cooper, 1913 Ford Model T, #9201, D13 .... $55.00
Allen Organs, 1931 Hawkeye, #9892, H8 .... $45.00
Alliance Racing, R Presley, 1913 Ford Model T, #2174, H8 ... $95.00
Allied Van Lines, 1917 Ford Model T, #2119, D13 .... $60.00
Allis Chalmers, Vega Plane, #35023, H8 .... $24.00
Alzheimers Assn #1, 1913 Ford Model T, limited edition, #9680, H8 .... $65.00
American Quarter Horse Assn, 1948 Diamond T Tractor Trailer, #2780, H8 .... $28.00
American Red Cross #11, Grumman Step Van, #3821, H8... $25.00
American Vets, 1913 Ford Model T, #107, D13 .... $25.00
Amoco, 1938 Dodge Airflow, JLE, #7000, H8 .... $35.00
Amoco Certicare, 1913 Ford Model T, #9151, H8 .... $50.00
Amoco Certicare, 1932 Ford Panel Truck, #7668, H8 ..... $45.00
Amoco Food Shop, 1918 Ford Barrel, #9288, D13 .... $30.00
Amoco Quality Parts, 1905 Ford Delivery Van, #1333, D13 .. $85.00
Amoco Stanolind Polarine #3, 1926 Mack Truck, #9383, H8 .... $140.00
Amsouths, 1913 Ford Model T, #9454, H8 .... $45.00
Angelo's Liquors, 1955 Chevy Cameo Pickup, #B969, H8 ... $25.00
Anheuser-Busch #1, 1918 Ford Runabout (silver spokes), #9766, H8 .... $125.00
Anheuser-Busch #5, 1931 Hawkeye, #9056, H8 .... $25.00
Anheuser-Busch #8, 1932 Ford Panel Truck, #9552, H8 . $22.00
Antique Power, 1923 Chevy Van, #9282, H8 .... $30.00
Ar-Jay Sales, 1938 Chevy Van, #B072, H8 .... $20.00
Arkansas Sesquicentennial, 1913 Ford Model T, #9367, H8 .... $28.00
Arm & Hammer, 1913 Model T, #9486, D13 .... $100.00
Arm & Hammer, 1931 Hawkeye, #7523, H8 .... $30.00
Armour All, 1905 Ford Delivery Van, #9738, D13 .... $40.00
Arrow Dist Co Solon OH #3, 1918 Ford Runabout, #9328, H8 .... $24.00
Ashville Office Supply, 1931 Hawkeye, #9118, D13/H8, from $20 to $25.00
Atlanta Falcons, 1913 Ford Model T, #1248, H8 .... $35.00
Atlas Van Line, 1926 Mack Truck, #9514, H8 .... $40.00
Auto Palace, 1955 Chevy Cameo Pickup, #2773, H8 ...... $40.00
Auto Palace, 1960 Ford Pickup, #4582, H8 .... $30.00
Baker Oil Tools, 1926 Mack Truck, #9210, rare, H8 ..... $695.00
Baltimore Fire Department, 1926 Seagrave Fire Engine, #9262, D13.................... $45.00
Baltimore Gas & Electric #5, 1931 Hawkeye, #9848, H8.$34.00
Barnsdale (sampler), 1930 Diamond T Tanker, #9629, H8.. $32.00
Barq's Root Beer, 1918 Ford, #9054, H8 .... $25.00
Barq's Root Beer, 1932 Ford Panel, #9072, H8 .... $45.00
Baseball, Cincinnati Reds, 1905 Ford Delivery Van, #B231, H8 .... $18.00
Baseball, Oakland A's, 1905 Ford Delivery Van, #3242, H8.$18.00
Baseball II, Baltimore Orioles, 1917 Ford Model T, #B353, H8.................... $22.00
Baseball II, Cleveland Indians, 1917 Ford Model T, #B373, H8.................... $22.00
Baseball II, Milwaukee Brewers, 1917 Ford Model T, #B377, H8.................... $18.00
Beckman High School, 1913 Ford Model T, #1656, D13/H8 .$22.00
Bell, Horse & Wagon, #2141, D13.................... $75.00
Bell Telephone of Canada, 1913 Ford Model T, #1327, D13 .$60.00

Bell Telephone of Canada, 1905 Ford Delivery Van, #7609, H8 ....$25.00

Bell Telephone System, 1905 Ford Delivery Van, #7610, D13/H8, from $20 to $25.00

Bell Yellow Pages, 1926 Mack Truck, #2142, H8 ....$45.00

Bi-County Ambulance, 1923 Chevy Van, #9093, H8 ......$28.00

Big A Auto Parts #4, 1918 Ford Truck, #1324, H8........$28.00

Big Apple D Marcis, 1913 Ford Model T, #2975, D13 ...$225.00

Big Brothers/Big Sister Elastimold, 1932 Ford Panel Truck, #9853, H8 ....$110.00

BJR Radiator Service, 1913 Ford Model T, #9500, H8.....$55.00

Blue Ball National Bank, 1913 Ford Model T, #9029, H8.$45.00

Bobby Allison, 1940 Ford, JLE, #6014, H8 ....$65.00

Boulder Beer, 1918 Ford Barrel Truck, #9623, H8...........$28.00

Branson MO, Music City, 1920 International, JLE, #3044, H8..$30.00

Breyer's Ice Cream, 1905 Ford Delivery Van, #9028, H8.$65.00

Briggs & Stratton, 1937 Ford Tractor Trailer, #9509, H8 ..$45.00

British American Oil #1, 1931 Hawkeye Tanker, #9512, H8..$45.00

Bud Light, Gamma, #F241, D13..................................$25.00

Buffalo Oil Co, 1931 Hawkeye Tanker, #9578, H8.........$22.00

Bumper to Bumper, 1923 Chevy Van, 1992, MIB, $30.00.

Bussman Fuses, 1918 Ford Runabout, #9333, H8 ....$45.00

CA Lessig Oil, 1931 Hawkeye, #B063, H8 ....$65.00

Campbell's Beans, 1918 Ford Runabout, #9184, D13 ....$70.00

Campbell's Tomato Juice, 1931 Hawkeye, #7537, H8......$35.00

Canada Dry, 1913 Ford Model T, #2133, D13/H8 ....$125.00

Canada Ontario, 1913 Ford Model T, #9217, D13 ....$30.00

Carl Budding, 1913 Ford Model T, #2106, H8 ....$55.00

Carlisle Production Spring Car Show, 1950 Chevy Panel Truck, #2977, H8 ....$24.00

Carlos Leffer, Propane Truck, #B691, D13 ....$25.00

Carnation, 1913 Ford Model T, #9178, H8 ....$34.00

Castrol Oil #2, 1926 Mack Tanker, #9464, H8................$50.00

Castrol Oil GTX, 1926 Kenworth, #9701, H8..................$28.00

Cedarburg Fire Department, 1926 Seagrave Fire Engine, #9271, D13..$35.00

Central Tractor Farm & Family, 1938 Chevy Van, #3836, H8.$20.00

Chambersburg PA Fire Engine, 1926 Seagrave Fire Engine, #9762, D13 ....$225.00

Champlin Sampler, 1930 Diamond T Tractor Trailer, #9133, H8..$110.00

Check the Oil IPCA #1, 1937 Ford Tanker, #7548, D13..$150.00

Chevrolet Bow Tie, 1923 Chevy Van, #9316, H8...........$28.00

Chevrolet Fire Department #1, 1926 Seagrave Fire Engine, #9823, D13..$25.00

Chevrolet Heartbeat, 1950 Chevy Panel Truck, bl, #9761, H8 ....$28.00

Chevrolet Super Service, 1923 Chevy Van, #9667, H8 ..$24.00

Chevron #1, 1930 Diamond T Tractor Trailer, #2768, H8..$95.00

Chicago Cubs, 1926 Mack Truck, #7545, H8/D13 ....$40.00

Chiquita Bananas, 1913 Ford Model T, #9662, D13 ....$65.00

Christmas #4, Horse & Wagon, #9780, H8 ....$25.00

Circus in America-200 Years, 1925 Kenworth, #3747, H8..$30.00

Citgo #4, 1930 Diamond T Tractor Trailer, #9692, D13..$90.00

Citgo Lubricants #2, 1918 Ford, #9456, H8.....................$75.00

Clark's Super Gas, Liberty Classics, limited edition, M, $30.00.

Clearkote Protector, 1940 Ford, JLE, #6061, H8 ....$32.00

Clemson University, 1918 Ford Runabout, #9523, H8.....$38.00

Clyde Beatty Circus, 1937 Ford Tractor Trailer, #9391, D13.$36.00

Co-op the Farm Store, 1913 Ford Model T, #9245, H8....$30.00

Coast to Coast Hardware, 1925 Kenworth Truck, #B037, H8..$25.00

Coca-Cola, Air Express Plane, #B318, H8......................$40.00

Coca-Cola, 1931 International Tanker, JLE, #4075, D13 .$55.00

Cohen & Sons, 1926 Mack Truck, #9339, H8 ....$38.00

Conoco Oil #1, 1926 Mack Tanker, #9750, H8 ....$225.00

Conoco Oil #3, 1937 Ford Tractor Trailer, #9500, H8.....$35.00

Continental Insurance, 1918 Ford, #2766, H8 ....$24.00

Coors Malted Milk, 1931 Hawkeye, #B233, H8 ....$18.00

Corona, 1918 Ford Barrel Truck, #9254, D13..................$30.00

Country Fresh, 1923 Chevy Van, #2944, D13 ....$25.00

Country Fresh, 1925 Kenworth, #B069, H8.....................$22.00

County Store, 1925 Kenworth, #3283, H8 ....$24.00

Crown Petroleum #4, 1925 Kenworth Stake Truck, #B966, H8 ....$28.00

Cub Foods, 1931 Hawkeye, #9042, D13/H8 ....$30.00

Cumberland Valley #2, 1932 Ford Panel, #9657, H8 ....$35.00

Dairy Queen, 1938 Chevy Panel Van, #3256, D13 ....$35.00

Dairy Queen #13, 1913 Ford Model T, #B306, H8...........$28.00

Dairy Queen #2, 1937 Ford Tractor Trailer, #9284, D13 .$95.00

Dairy Queen #7, 1950 Chevy Panel Truck, #9178, D13/H8, from $160 to $170.00

Darrell Waltrip Western Auto, 1950 Chevy, #7553, H8..$24.00

Delco Radio, 1950 Chevy Panel Truck, #9082, D13/H8..$100.00

Diamond Walnut Growers, 1931 Hawkeye, #9881, H8....$20.00

Diamond Walnuts, 1925 Kenworth, #B788, H8 ....**$34.00**

Dixie Brewing, 1918 Ford Barrel Truck, #9073, H8 ....**$65.00**

Dobyns-Bennett High School Tennessee, 1950 Chevy Panel Truck, #7516, D13/H8 ....**$100.00**

Downtown MC Seatle WA, 1931 Hawkeye, #B103, H8..**$42.00**

Dr Pepper, 1926 Mack Truck, #9235, H8 ....**$65.00**

Drag Specialties #1, 1931 Hawkeye, #9084, H8 ....**$195.00**

Drake Hotel, 1913 Ford Model T, #2113, H8..................**$125.00**

Drake Oil Well, 1931 International Tanker, JLE, #4059, D13 ....**$50.00**

Dubuque Golf & Country Club, 1912 Ford Open Front Panel, #2904, H8 ....**$65.00**

Dutch Girl Ice Cream, 1931 Hawkeye, #9049, D13/H8 ...**$30.00**

Dyersville Fire Chief, 1940 Ford, JLE, #0005, H8 ....**$95.00**

Dyersville Historical Society, 1918 Ford Runabout, limited edition, #9883, D13 ....**$35.00**

EAA Oshkosh 1992 Air Show, Hubley Plane, #5004, H8..**$30.00**

Eastman #2, 1932 Ford Panel, #3806, D13 ....**$65.00**

Eastview Pharmacy, 1950 Chevy Panel Truck, #1317, D13/H8, from $125 to **$130.00**

Eastwood #1 (1989), 1950 Chevy Panel Truck, #9325, D13/H8 ....**$600.00**

Eastwood #4, 1937 Ford Tractor Trailer, #7664, D13/H8..**$225.00**

Eastwood #7, 1947 International Tractor Trailer, #9122, H8..**$80.00**

Eastwood #9, 1955 Chevy Cameo Pickup, #9747, D13 ...**$26.00**

Edelbrock #1, 1932 Ford Panel Truck, #9027, D13/H8..**$325.00**

Elmira Maple Festival #2, 1905 Ford Delivery Van, #9759, D13/H8 ....**$32.00**

Elmira Maple Festival #6, 1918 Ford Runabout, #B403, H8.**$28.00**

Entenmann's #1, 1913 Ford Model T, #9455, H8.............**$65.00**

Ephrata Fair #3, 1932 Ford Panel Truck, #9730, H8 ....**$28.00**

Ertl Air Express, Air Express Plane, #B270, H8 ....**$34.00**

Ertl Christmas #4 (1992), Horse & Wagon, #9780, D13..**$15.00**

Ertl Collectors Club (Replica), 1931 Hawkeye, #2088, H8 ..**$25.00**

Ertl Collectors Club (Replica), 1938 Chevy Panel Van, #B048, D13...**$30.00**

Ertl Collectors Club (Replica), 1950 Chevy Panel Truck, #9064, H8 ....**$80.00**

Ertl Safety, 1913 Ford Model T, #7554, D13 ....**$100.00**

Ethyl Gasoline, 1931 International, JLE, #4006, H8 ....**$28.00**

Fanny Farmer Candies, 1913 Ford Model T, #2104, H8...**$30.00**

Farm Progress Show, 1930 International, JLE, #5008, H8 ..**$20.00**

Farm Toy Capitol #1, 1913 Ford Model T, #9233, D13 ...**$90.00**

FDR Associates, 1905 Ford Delivery Van, #9378, D13 ....**$45.00**

Fergus Truck Show, 1948 Diamond T Tractor Trailer, #B559, H8 ....**$40.00**

Fina Employees Only, 1917 Ford Model T Van, #9456, D13.**$145.00**

Fina Oil, 1905 Ford Delivery Van, #9043, H8 ....**$30.00**

Firehouse Films, 1950 Chevy Panel Truck, #9369, H8...**$125.00**

Food City, 1905 Ford Delivery Van, #9857, H8 ....**$25.00**

Food Lion, 1013 Ford Model T, #9279, D13....................**$30.00**

Football II-Denver Broncos, 1955 Chevy Cameo Pickup, #3568, H8 ....**$18.00**

Football III-Carolina Panthers, 1951 GMC, #B844, H8 ..**$20.00**

Football III-Jacksonville Jaguars, 1951 GMC, #B845, H8...**$20.00**

Football-Atlantic Falcons, 1931 Hawkeye, #B164, H8.....**$22.00**

Football-Dallas Cowboys, 1931 Hawkeye, #3566, H8 ......**$50.00**

Football-LA Rams, 1931 Hawkeye, #B162, H8 ....**$22.00**

Ford #2, 1913 Ford Model T, limited edition, #1322, D13 .**$100.00**

Ford Motorsports, 1918 Ford Runabout, #2151, D13........**$35.00**

Ford Motorsports, 1932 Ford Panel Truck, #9693, H8 .....**$45.00**

Ford-New Holland, 1917 Ford Model T, #0374, D13.......**$20.00**

Ford-New Holland, 1960 Ford 4x4, #0721, H8................**$24.00**

Ford Runabout, 1918, MIB, $35.00.

Franco-American, 1926 Mack Truck, #9302, D13 ....**$60.00**

Frito Lay, 1950 Chevy Panel Truck, #9633, H8 ....**$35.00**

Gates Hardware & Supply, 1955 Chevy Cameo Pickup, #9982, D13...**$30.00**

GDS Fair, 1917 Ford Model T, #2996, H8......................**$24.00**

Georgia Tech, 1932 Ford Roadster, NB, #9251, D13 .....**$120.00**

Gilbertville Community Day, 1932 Ford Panel Truck, #9368, H8 ....**$50.00**

Glendale Medical, 1913 Ford Model T, #9266, D13 ....**$60.00**

Goody's, 1931 International, JLE, #5037, D13 ....**$45.00**

Graceton Store, 1913 Ford Model T, #7566, H8 ....**$24.00**

Graduation 1993, 1905 Ford Delivery Van, #9453, D13..**$15.00**

Granny Goose Chips, 1913 Ford Model T, #9979, H8.....**$50.00**

Grapette Soda, 1932 Ford Panel Truck, #9885, D13 ....**$60.00**

Grapette Soda, 1940 Ford, JLE, #6001, D13 ....**$75.00**

Grauer's Paint & Decorating #1, 1932 Ford Panel Truck, #2139, H8 ....**$28.00**

Gulf Oil, 1926 Mack Tanker, #7652, H8 ....**$45.00**

Gulf Oil, 1926 Mack Truck, #9158, H8 ....**$50.00**

Gulf Oil, 1932 Ford Panel Truck, #9879, H8...................**$30.00**

Hamm's Beer, 1913 Ford Model T, #2145, H8 ....**$75.00**

Hamm's Beer, 1926 Mack Truck, #7619, D13 ....**$75.00**

Hamm's Beer, 1938 Chevy Panel Truck, #B985, D13 ......**$18.00**

Hancock Oil Co, 1930 Diamond T Tractor Trailer, #2795, H8...**$32.00**

Harbor Freight Tools, 1931 Hawkeye, #B730, D13 ....**$25.00**

Harley-Davidson, 1933 Motorcycle w/Sidecar, #99199, H8 .**$85.00**

Harley-Davidson #1, 1918 Ford Runabout, #9784, D13.**$700.00**

Harleys 'R' US Schott Cycle, 1932 Ford Panel, #2763, D13/H8, from $150 to **$160.00**

Heartland Popcorn, 1905 Ford Delivery Van, #9250, H8/D13, from $24 to...**$30.00**

Henderson Motorcycles, 1920 International, JLE, H8......$35.00

Henny Penny, 1918 Ford Runabout, #9945, D13/H8, from $20 to..$25.00

Hershey Antique Auto Club, 1950 Chevy Panel Truck, #9198, H8...$75.00

Hershey's, 1931 International Tanker, #F104, D13..........$20.00

Hershey's Chocolate Syrup, Horse & Wagon, #9511, D13..$25.00

Hershey's Kisses, 1950 Chevy Panel Truck, chrome, #2126, D13...$125.00

Hershey's 100th Anniversary, Trolley, #B310, H8...........$20.00

Hershey's 100th Anniversary, 1929 Lockheed, #B311, H8..$38.00

Hey! Rube Jim Beam, 1918 Ford Runabout, #2182, D13..$25.00

Hills Bank & Trust, 1938 Chevy Panel Truck, #B271, D13..$50.00

Hills Dept Store, 1913 Ford Model T, #9768, H8.............$24.00

Hires Root Beer, 1918 Ford Barrel Truck, #9435, D13....$40.00

Holly Farms #3, 1926 Mack Truck, #9849, D13...............$35.00

Hollycliff Farms, 1926 Mack Truck, #9477, H8................$45.00

Home Hardware, 1913 Ford Model T, #1356, D13.........$180.00

Home Savings & Loan, 1926 Mack, #9292, D13...............$40.00

Homestead Collectibles, 1905 Ford Delivery Van, #9651, H8..$20.00

Hormel Meats, 1917 Ford Model T, #9451, D13..............$65.00

Howards, 1913 Ford Model T, #1366, D13......................$30.00

Humble Oil #1 (regular run), 1931 Hawkeye, #9073, D13..$48.00

Humma Pharmacy, 1932 Ford Panel Truck, #7674, H8...$20.00

HWI Christmas #1, 1905 Ford Delivery Van, #2761, D13..$30.00

I-70 Speedway, 1950 Chevy Panel Truck, #1319, D13.....$35.00

Ideal Truck Line, 1937 Ford Tractor Trailer, #2963, D13..$35.00

IGA, 1931 Hawkeye, #7696, H8.......................................$25.00

IGA, 1950 Chevy Panel Truck, #9015, H8........................$25.00

IGA #2, 1926 Mack Truck, #2138, D13............................$45.00

IGA #8, 1931 Hawkeye, #7696, D13................................$25.00

Imperial Oil #3, 1925 Kenworth Stake Truck, #B414, H8..$30.00

Imperial Palace #2, 1926 Mack Truck, #9943, D13..........$40.00

Indian Motorcycle, Vega Plane, #35009, H8....................$69.00

Indian Motorcycle, 1932 Ford Panel Truck, #1345, no spare, D13...$160.00

Intercourse PA, 1923 Chevy Van, #3917, D13.................$25.00

Iowa Hawkeyes #1, 1913 Ford Model T, #1311, D13.....$300.00

Iowa 113th Firemans Assn, 1926 Seagrave Fire Engine, #9201, D13...$175.00

Irishtown Fire Department, 1926 Seagrave Fire Engine, #2923, D13...$30.00

It's a Girl, Horse & Wagon, #B247, D13..........................$15.00

Jack Daniels, 1931 Kenworth, #9342, D13.......................$60.00

Jackson Brewery, 1905 Ford Delivery Van, #9050, D13...$40.00

JC Penney, 1905 Ford Delivery Van, #1326, D13.............$50.00

JC Penney, 1925 Kenworth, #9636, H8............................$25.00

JC Penney, 1937 Ahrens-Fox Fire Engine, #9635, D13/H8..$26.00

JF Good Co, 1913 Ford Model T, #9524, H8....................$40.00

JI Case, 1931 International, #0734, H8.............................$20.00

JI Case, 1955 Chevy Cameo Pickup, #4626, D13.............$20.00

JI Kraft, 1913 Ford Model T, #2147, D13........................$80.00

Jim Beam, 1932 Ford Panel Truck, #7661, D13...............$60.00

Jim Beam District 5-1986 #1, 1913 Ford Model T, #9412, D13...$175.00

Jim Beam District 5-1991 #6, 1931 Hawkeye, #9319, H8..$35.00

Jim Beam International #3, GMC Tractor Trailer, #T421, NB, H8...$35.00

Jim Beam Rockford, 1905 Ford Delivery Van, #9832, D13.$30.00

Jimmy's Goodyear, 1932 Ford Panel Truck, #9381, D13..$35.00

John Deere #6, 1926 Mack Stake Truck, #5689, D13......$20.00

John Deere Window Box, 1926 Mack Truck, #5534, D13/H8, from $115 to...$125.00

Johnson Gasoline, 1920 International, JLE, #4047, H8...$25.00

Johnson Gasoline (sampler), 1920 International, JLE, #4046, H8...$40.00

Jolt Cola, 1913 Ford Model T, #9232, D13.....................$40.00

Kansas Basehor, 1905 Ford Delivery Van, #9007, H8.......$50.00

Kansas State Fair, 1913 Ford Model T, #9272, red & wht, H8...$50.00

Kerr-McGee, 1926 Kenworth, #9773, D13/H8.................$65.00

Kerr-McGee, DC-3 Plane, #B538, H8...............................$95.00

Key Aid Distributors, 1913 Ford Model T, #9175, H8......$65.00

Key Federal Savings Bank, 1932 Ford Panel Truck, #9703, D13/H8...$35.00

Keystone Wood Specialists, 1950 Chevy Panel Truck, #9110, D13/H8...$35.00

Kingsport Press, 1923 Chevy Van, #2933, H8.................$50.00

Kingsport TN, #1, 1918 Ford Runabout, limited edition, #9174, D13...$100.00

Kiwanis Club, 1905 Ford Delivery Van, #9884, D13........$25.00

Kodak, 1905 Ford Delivery Van (gold spokes), #9985, H8..$245.00

Kraft Dairy Group, 1917 Ford Model T, #9675, D13........$35.00

Kralinator Filters, 1955 Chevy Cameo Pickup, #1347, D13.$50.00

Kroger #1, 1913 Ford Model T, #9511, H8......................$45.00

Kyle Petty (sampler), 1950 Chevy Panel Truck, #2881, H8.$75.00

Lake of the Ozarks, 1923 Chevy Van, #B380, H8............$30.00

Lake Speed, 1931 International, JLE, #5056, H8...............$45.00

Lawson Products #1, 1950 Chevy Panel Truck, #9117, H8.$55.00

Lennox-Heatcraft, 1923 Chevy Van, #9379, D13.............$20.00

Lion Coffee #1, 1913 Ford Model T, #9306, H8...............$50.00

Lipton Tea #2, 1932 Ford Panel Truck, #9087, H8..........$35.00

Lone Star Beer, 1926 Mack Truck, #9168, H8.................$55.00

Long Island Fire Department, 1937 Ahrens-Fox Fire Engine, #2905, D13...$40.00

Loon Mountain, 1940 Ford, JLE, #6044, H8....................$50.00

M&M Oil, 1931 Kenworth, #9595, D13............................$50.00

Madison Electric, 1913 Ford Model T, #9589, H8............$75.00

Marathon Oil, 1929 International Tanker, #4044, H8.......$30.00

Massey-Ferguson, 1926 Mack Truck, #1348, H8.............$22.00

Maurice's, 1932 Ford Panel Truck, #9476, D13...............$35.00

McAnany Oil, 1931 Kenworth, #9594, D13......................$50.00

Mead Paper, 1923 Chevy Van, #B196, D13.....................$60.00

Merit Oil, 1926 Mack Tanker, #9980, H8........................$75.00

Michelin Tires #1, 1931 International, JLE, #5046, H8...$30.00

Miller Beer, 1950 Chevy Panel Truck, #9269, H8............$30.00

Miller Beer, 1950 Chevy Tractor Trailer, #9270, H8........$25.00

Miller Beer #1, 1905 Ford Delivery Van, #2116, H8........$40.00

Minnesota State Police 65th Anniversary, 1932 Ford Panel Truck, #4943, H8...$50.00

Minnesota Vikings, 1913 Ford Model T, #1246, D13.......$50.00

Mobil Oil, 1937 Ford Tanker, #9971, D13.......................$75.00

Mobil Oil, 1939 Dodge Airflow, #4863, H8......................$32.00

Mobil Oil (#d), 1913 Ford Model T, #9743, D13/H8, from $80 to..$85.00

Mobil Oil #3, 1926 Mack Truck, #9760, D13..................$65.00

Mobilgas-Magnolia Petroleum, 1935 Sterling, JLE, #4021-22, H8 ....$95.00

Monagan PA 30th Anniversary, 1937 Ahrens-Fox Fire Engine, #7556, D13 ....$35.00

Monroe Shocks, 1931 Hawkeye, #9350, H8 ....$22.00

Montgomery Ward #1, 1913 Ford Model T, #9542, H8 ...$150.00

Montgomery Ward #5, 1932 Ford Panel Truck, #2110, H8 ..$40.00

Moorsmans Mfg Co, 1905 Ford Delivery Van, #9585, H8..$95.00

Morton Salt, 1905 Ford Delivery Van, #9787, H8...........$42.00

Mustang Club #2, 1913 Ford Model T, #B388, D13/H8, from $30 to $35.00

Nash Finch, 1913 Ford Model T, #9347, D13 ....$155.00

National Motorcycle Museum, 1931 Hawkeye, #3545, H8 .$35.00

National Van Lines, 1937 Ford Tractor Trailer, #B284, D13/H8 ....$30.00

Nestle Butterfinger #3, 1932 Chevy Panel Truck, #1318, H8 ....$35.00

New Holland, 1913 Ford Model T, #9397, H8 ....$75.00

New York City Fire Department #1, 1926 Seagrave Fire Engine, #9640, D13..$50.00

NFL Cowboys, 1931 Hawkeye, #3566, D13 ....$45.00

Nintendo (#d), 1913 Ford Model T, #2113, D13 ....$60.00

North Pole Fire Department, 1926 Seagrave Fire Engine, #2906, D13...$60.00

Northwest Hardware Co, 1955 Chevy Cameo Pickup, #3859, H8 ....$22.00

Oakwood Mobile Homes, 1917 Ford Model T, #9822, H8..$20.00

Oil Can Henry, 1931 Kenworth, #9897, D13 ....$100.00

Old El Paso, 1905 Ford Delivery Van, #7636, H8............$45.00

Old Forester, 1917 Ford Model T, #1350, H8 ....$28.00

Old Milwaukee Beer, 1950 Chevy Panel Truck, #9175, H8 .$28.00

Olivet University, 1905 Ford Delivery Van, #2115, H8 ...$20.00

Otasco #3, 1926 Mack Truck, #2134, H8 ....$55.00

Pan American Air, 1931 International, #4081, H8 ....$32.00

Penn State Nittany Lions #1, 1917 Ford Model T, #9263, D13 ....$150.00

Pennzoil, 1955 Chevy Cameo Pickup, #7648, D13 ....$30.00

Pennzoil (#d), 1913 Ford Model T, #9019, H8 ....$30.00

Pepsi-Cola, Trolley Car, #B655, H8.............................$40.00

Pepsi-Cola, 1931 International, #5027, H8 ....$45.00

Pez Candy, 1931 International, JLE, #5083, H8 ....$95.00

Phillips 66 Super Clean, 1920 International Tanker, JLE, #4020, H8 ....$35.00

Prairie Farms Milk, 1920 International, JLE, #3009, D13...$20.00

Quakertown National Bank #3, 1905 Ford Delivery Van, #9979, H8 ....$65.00

Rawlings: The Mark of a Pro, 1935 Mack Truck, #8017, H8 ..$30.00

Renninger-FL, 1905 Ford Delivery Van, #9713, H8.........$30.00

Ringling Bros Circus, 1913 Ford Model T, #9027, H8 ...$145.00

Route 66 Anniversary (sampler), 1950 Chevy Panel Truck, #7625, H8 ....$75.00

Ryder Truck Rental, 1931 International, #5054, H8........$30.00

Schneider's Meats, 1950 Chevy Panel Truck, #9445, H8.$150.00

Shell Oil Co, 1935 Mack Tanker, JLE, #3011, H8 ....$40.00

Shoprite, 1926 Mack Truck, #9666, H8...........................$22.00

Signal Oil Co, 1931 Hawkeye, #1321, H8 ....$25.00

Simpson Racing Equipment, #1, 1940 Ford, JLE, #6012, H8..$70.00

Star Enterprises, 1935 Mack Tanker, JLE, #3009, D13 ..$150.00

Sun Holiday Travel, 1918 Ford, #9618, H8 ....$25.00

Tabasco Sauce, 1905 Ford Delivery Van, #9878, H8........$40.00

Texaco, 1925 Kenworth stake truck, 1992, MIB, $30.00.

Texaco #4, 1905 Ford Delivery Van, #9321, H8 ....$165.00

Texaco-Bruce's in Tulsa (sampler), 1931 International, #4102, H8 ....$65.00

Tip-U-Town, 1950 Chevy Panel Van, #9034, H8............$95.00

Tonka, 1913 Ford Model T, #9739, H8 ....$35.00

Toy Farmer Country Store, 1913 Ford Model T, #9483, H8.$20.00

Tractor Supply Co #5, 1950 Chevy Panel Truck, #9207, H8.$65.00

True Value Hardware #3, 1950 Chevy Panel Truck, #1296, H8 ....$75.00

United Van Lines, 1917 Ford Model T, #9715, 1988, M, $30.00.

United Van Lines, 1918 Ford, #9096, H8 ....$28.00

US Army Air Corps, Vega Plane, #12700, H8 ....$35.00

US Mail, 1923 Chevy Van, #1352, H8 ....$25.00

Utz Potato Chips, 1923 Chevy Van, #9398, H8 ....$25.00

Valvoline, 1950 Chevy Panel Truck, #9340, H8 ....$25.00

Vintage Chevrolet Club, 1923 Chevy Van, #9245, H8....$18.00

White Castle #1, 1931 International, JLE, #5045, H8......$32.00

Wix Filters, 1932 Ford Panel Truck, #9810, H8 ....$150.00

WR Meadows, 1923 Chevy Van, #9437, H8 ....$30.00

First Gear

AAA Towing, 1957 International Wrecker, #19-1321, T4 ..$35.00

Adley Shipping, 1960 B-Mack, #19-1299, T4 ....$90.00

Akers, 1960 B-Mack, #19-1468, T4 ....$60.00

Alaska Railroad, 1953 Ford, #19-1522, T4 ....$35.00
All State, 1960 B-Mack, #19-1469, T4 ....$58.00
American Flyer, 1951 Ford Crates, #19-0118, T4 ....$50.00
Ar-Jay Sale #1, 1951 Ford DGV, #19-1008, T4 ....$100.00
Atlantic, 1951 Ford Tanker, #10-1290, H8/T4, from $35 to.$40.00
Atlas Van Line, 1957 International Moving Truck, #19-1310,
    T4 ....$90.00
Auto Parts, 1951 Ford DGV #10-0102, T4 ....$30.00
Bare Trucking, 1957 International Wrecker, #19-1457, H8 ..$38.00
Bitburger Beer, 1953 Ford DGV, #19-1569, T4 ....$32.00
Bloomington Gold, 1952 GMC Tanker, #19-1257, H8 ...$40.00
Boston Engine 54, 1957 International, #19-1371, T4 ......$50.00
Boston Fire Dept, 1953 Ford Pickup, #19-1551, H8 ....$30.00
Boston Globe, 1951 Ford DGV, #29-1064, T4 ....$70.00
Boston Tow Co, 1957 International Wrecker, #19-1460,
    T4 ....$40.00
Cambell's Family of Brands, 1957 International, #19-1313,
    H8 ....$40.00
Campbell's, Horse & Sled, #39-0109, T4 ....$30.00
Campbell's Soup, 1957 International DGV, #19-1313, T4 ..$36.00
Cape Cod Chips, 1960 B Mack, #19-1279, H8/T4 ....$60.00
Carlisle Anniversary, 1952 GMC Wrecker, #19-1256, T4.$38.00
Central Tractor Farm & Family, 1957 International Grain
    Truck, #19-1263, H8 ....$34.00
Charles Town Races, 1957 International Moving Van, #19-
    1323, T4 ....$48.00
Chicago Fire Dept, 1957 International Tanker, #19-1723,
    T4 ....$32.00
Civil Defense, 1949 Chevy Panel, #19-1355, T4 ....$30.00
Columbian Moving, 1957 International Wrecker, #19-1527,
    T4 ....$45.00
Country Store, 1951 Ford Stake Truck, #10-1232, T4 .....$28.00
Covan Moving, 1957 International Moving, #19-1287, T4.$45.00
Custom Chrome, 1951 Ford Stake Truck, #18-1161, T4/H8 .$55.00
Dahlkes, 1957 International Moving, #18-1487, T4 ....$45.00
Dart Towing, 1957 International Wrecker, #19-1322, T4.$34.00
Dave's Towing #2, 1957, International Wrecker, #18-1185,
    T4...$50.00
Double Cola, 1951, Ford Pop Truck, #19-1190, T4..........$32.00

Eagle Snacks #4, 1960 B-Mack, #19-1394, T4.................$50.00
Eastern Express, 1953 Ford DGV, #19-1481, H8/T4 ....$32.00
Eastwood Co, 1952 GMC Wrecker, #19-0109, H8 ....$80.00
Eastwood Museum, 1951 Ford DGV, #19-1010, T4 ....$70.00
Eastwood 15th Anniversary, 1952 GMC Van, #19-0115,
    H8 ....$50.00
Erin Brewing, 1960 B-Mack, #19-1176, T4 ....$100.00
Eslinger Beer, 1952 GMC Full Stake Truck, #19-1244, H8 ..$40.00
Esso, 1960 B-Mack, #19-1670, T4.................................$55.00
Falstaff, 1949 Chevy Panel, #19-1546, T4......................$32.00
Farmall International Harvester, 1957 International DGV, #19-
    1577, T4...$35.00
Fire Deptartment New York, 1960 B-Mack, #18-1451, T4.$55.00
First Gear (Eastwood), 1951 Ford Half Rack, #19-0120, T4 .$40.00
Ford Economy Set, 1951 Ford Hauler, #19-1343, T4 ....$50.00
Ford Jubilee, 1953 Ford DGV, #19-1513, T4 ....$35.00
Ford Tractor, 1953 Ford Pickup, #10-1547, T4...............$25.00
Genuine Chevrolet, 1949 Chevy Panel, #10-1328, T4 ....$30.00
GMC Sales & Service, 1952 GMC Wrecker, #10-1548,
    H8/T4 ....$35.00
Gulf Oil, 1957 International Fire Truck, #19-1334, H8 ..$40.00
Gulf Oil, 1957 International Tanker, #29-1335, T4.........$35.00
Gulf Oil #1, 1957 International Wrecker, #19-1336, H8.$75.00
Hamm's Beer, 1953 Ford DGV, #29-1480, H8/T4............$35.00
Hennis, 1960 B-Mack, #18-1489, T4 ....$55.00
Hershey's, Horse & Wagon, #39-0105, T4 ....$30.00
Hershey's Anniversary, 1960 B-Mack, #19-1288, T4 ....$80.00
Hershey's Chocolate, 1959 International, #19-1283, H8 .$36.00
Hershey's Cocoa, 1952 GMC/Sacks, #19-1273, H8 ....$38.00
Hershey's Syrup, 1951 Ford Stake Truck, #19-1499, T4...$38.00
Hostess Cupcakes, 1949 Chevy Panel, #19-1494, H8/T4.$32.00
Hostess Cupcakes, 1960 B-Mack, #19-1530, T4 ....$55.00
International Golden Anniversary, 1957 Internationl DGV,
    #10-1411, T4 ....$35.00
International Harvester, 1957 International Fire Truck, #19-
    1289, T4...$35.00
Interstate, 1960 B-Mack, #19-1606, T4 ....$55.00
J Levy & Sons, 1949 Chevy Panel, #18-1409, T4 ....$32.00
J Levy & Sons, 1960 B-Mack, #18-1519, T4...................$55.00
Jax Beer, 1953 Ford DGV, #29-1461, T4 ....$35.00
JC Whitney #4, 1951 Ford Flatbed, #19-1386, H8/T4 .....$60.00
JC Whitney #5, 1949 Chevy, #19-1387, T4 ....$34.00
Kendall, 1949 Chevy Panel, #18-1385, T4 ....$32.00
LA Fire Department, 1957 International Fire Truck, #19-1539,
    T4..$32.00
Leffler Oil, 1951 Ford Oil, #28-1213, T4 ....$25.00
Lionel Trains #1, 1951 Ford Box Truck, #19-0104, H8..$125.00
Lone Star Beer, 1952 GMC DGV, #10-1258, T4 ....$38.00
M Schultz Co, 1957 International Van, #19-1332, T4.....$35.00
M&M, 1960 B-Mack, #18-1365, T4 ....$70.00
Mack Trucks, Mack B061 Tractor Trailer, #19-0117, H8 .$135.00
Madison Hardware, 1953 Ford, #19-1396, T4 ....$48.00
Marathon, 1953 Ford Tanker, #29-1588, T4 ....$35.00
Marx Toys, 1957 International Fire Truck, #19-0113, T4 ..$38.00
Maryland Heights, 1949 Chevy, #19-1463, T4 ....$30.00
Maryland Heights Fire Dept, 1957 IHC Fire Truck, #19-1178,
    H8 ....$32.00
Mayfield Ice Cream, 1952 GMC Insulated Van, #10-1492, T4.$32.00

Eagle Snacks, 1951 Ford F-6, 1992, MIB, $32.00.

Mayflower Moving, 1957 International Moving Van, #18-1471, T4 ....$50.00

Mayflower Moving, 1960 B-Mack, #18-1532, T4 ....**$55.00**

McConnelsburg Fire Dept, 1926 Seagrave Fire Engine, #35037, H8 ....$32.00

Mechanicsburg PA 100th Anniversary, 1918 Ford, #B683, H8 ....$30.00

Mercer, 1960 B-Mack, #18-1397, T4 ....$60.00

Mercury Marine, Mack B-61 Tractor Trailer, #19-1266, H8..$75.00

Mercy Ambulance, 1949 Chevy Panel, #19-1402, T4......$30.00

Michelin Tires, 1960 B-Mack, #19-1502, T4....................$50.00

Miss Budweiser, 1952 GMC DGV, #10-1271, T4 ....$25.00

Miss Pepsi, 1951 Ford Truck, #19-1567, T4......................$34.00

Mobil Gas, 1953 Ford Tanker, #29-1501, T4...................$35.00

Mobil Oil, 1949 Chevy, #19-1500, H8 ....$38.00

Mobil Oil, 1957 International Tanker, #19-1405, T4 ......$35.00

Mobil Oil, 1957 International Wrecker, #18-1381, H8....$35.00

Morton Salt, 1952 GMC Sack Truck, #19-1130, H8/T4 .**$32.00**

Moxie, 1952 GMC Pop Truck, #19-0119, T4...................$35.00

Moyer & Sons, 1957 International Moving Van, #19-1515, T4 ....$45.00

Mushroom, 1960 B-Mack, #19-1507, T4 ....$65.00

Nehi Soda Bottle, 1951 Ford Pop Truck, #18-1074, T4 ...$34.00

Nitro Cola, 1951 Ford Pop Truck, #19-0114, T4.............$35.00

North Pacific, 1953 Ford Pickup, #19-1559, T4 ....$30.00

NY Central Systems, 1953 Ford DGV, #19-1436, T4.......$38.00

NY City Police, 1949 Chevy Panel, #19-1377, T4 ....$30.00

NY Fire Department, 1957 International Wrecker, #19-1401, T4..$34.00

O'Doul's Non-Alcohol Brew, 1952 GMC Van, #19-1352, H8 ....$35.00

Pepsi-Cola Santa, 1951 Ford Bottle Truck, #19-1092, H8 ..**$95.00**

Phillips 66, 1951 Ford Tanker, #19-1034, H8...................$50.00

Phillips 66 Pipe Line, 1951 Ford Flatbed, #19-1427, H8 ..**$60.00**

Police Department, 1957 International Wrecker, #19-1264, H8..$35.00

Radio Flyer, Mack B-61 Tractor Trailer, #10-1346, H8.**$125.00**

Railway Express Agency, 1960 B-Mack, #19-1654, T4 ....$28.00

Rock Island Motor Transit, 1957 International R-190, MIB, $35.00.

Ralph Moody, 1956 Stock Car, #19-1512, T4 ....$55.00

Red Ball Moving, 1957 International Moving Van, #19-1466, T4..$55.00

Remington-Goose, 1952 GMC Van, #10-1134, H8.........$30.00

Roadway Express, Mack B-61 Tractor Trailer, #10-1211, H8..**$75.00**

Roadway Safety, 1949 Chevy Panel, #10-1479, T4 ....$30.00

Rock Solid Chevy, 1949 Chevy Panel, #10-1329, T4 ......$30.00

Rockies Brewery, 1951 Ford Barrel Truck, #19-1235, T4 .$35.00

Rolling Thunder Cycles, 1951 Ford Van, #28-1141, H8 ..**$45.00**

Santa Barbara, 1957 International Fire Truck, #19-1408, T4 ....$35.00

Seekonk Speedway, 1951 Ford Stock Car, #19-1516, T4 .**$45.00**

Shell Aviation Fuel, 1957 International R-190 with Fuel Tanker, MIB, $38.00.

Shell Oil Co, 1952 GMC Tanker, #28-0105, H8 ....$50.00

Shell Oil Co #10, 1957 International Stake Truck, #19-1565, H8/T4..$35.00

Shell Oil Co #6, 1957 International Tanker, #29-1270, H8/T4 ....$32.00

Shell Oil Co #8, 1951 Ford Flatbed, #19-1433, H8/T4 ....$50.00

Slinky's 50th Anniversary, 1952 GMC Stake Truck, #19-1315, H8 ....$50.00

Smith & Wesson, Mack B-61 Tractor Trailer, #18-1219, H8 ....$75.00

Southern Pacific Line, 1960 B-Mack, #19-1526, T4 ....$55.00

Squirt, 1951 Ford Pop Truck, #18-1180, T4 ....$30.00

St Johnsbury, 1960 B-Mack, #19-1341, T4 ....$60.00

Star Pianos, 1957 International Moving Van, #19-1340, T4..$35.00

Statewide Towing, 1957 International Wrecker, #18-1553, T4 ....$48.00

Storey Wrecker, 1952 GMC Wrecker, #18-1068, H8 ......$35.00

Stroh's Beer, 1952 GMC Insulated Van, #10-1353, T4....$35.00

Sunshine Biscuits, 1960 B-Mack, #10-1472, T4 ....$52.00

Tippett Richardson, 1957 International Moving Van, #19-1566, T4..$55.00

TNT Overland Express, 1957 International DGV, #19-1474, T4 ....$32.00

Tollway, 1957 Fire Truck, #19-1438, T4............................$30.00

True Value, 1952 GMC DGV, #10-1196, T4.....................$30.00

US Air Force, 1957 International Wrecker, #19-1431, T4..**$35.00**

US Army, 1957 International Fire Truck, #29-1380, T4 .**$35.00**

US Army Ambulance, 1949 Chevy Panel, #19-1388, T4 .$32.00
US Mail, 1952 GMC Sack Truck, #19-1103, H8 ....$32.00
US Mail, 1953 Ford DGV, #19-1441, T4.........................$30.00
US Mail, 1960 B-Mack, #19-1302, T4............................$68.00
Vic Irwin Shell, 1956 Ford Stock Car, #19-1425, T4 ....$50.00
Von De Ahe #2, 1957 International Moving Van, #19-1448,
      T4 ....$40.00
Wayne Oil Co, 1951 Ford Oil, #19-1015, T4 ....$25.00
West Coast Freight, 1952 GMC Box Truck, #19-1007, H8..$32.00
Wonder Bread, 1949 Chevy Panel, #19-1493, T4 ....$30.00
Wooster, 1960 B-Mack, #19-1208, T4...........................$180.00
Yellow Freight, 1960 B-Mack, #10-1293, T4...................$55.00
Zephyr Gasoline, 1957 International DGV, #19-1166, T4.$20.00
Zephyr Petroleums, 1957 International Wrecker, #19-1135,
      H8 ....$32.00

Racing Champions

AC Delco, Kenworth Tractor Trailer, #250, D13.............$35.00
Alliance Racing/Seltzer #59, 1934 Biplane, #386, D13 ....$40.00
Army Desert Storm/Kulwicki #7, T-Bird, #478, D13........$55.00
Atlanta Speedway/Hooters 500, 1934 Biplane, #253, D13.$75.00
Brickyard 400, Chevy Lumina, #457, D13 ....$40.00
Chad Chaffin #16, Chevy Lumina, #2832, D13 ....$30.00
Chevy Thunder, 1931 Travel Air, #0656, D13.................$40.00
Coca-Cola 600/Charlotte #1, Model A Pickup, #200, D13 .$175.00
Coca-Cola 600/Charlotte #6, Model A Tanker, #226, D13 ...$45.00
Curt Turner, Vega Airplane, #320, D13 ....$75.00
Darlington Speedway, Model A Panel, #201, D13 ....$70.00
Daytona International Speedway, Model A Pickup, #255,
      D13 ....$30.00
Dupont Racing/J Gordon #24, Kenworth Tractor Trailer, #367,
      D13..$40.00
Family Channel/T Kendall #7, T-Bird, #414, D13 ....$45.00
First Union 400 (4/18/93), Model A Panel, #218, D13 ....$25.00
Ford Motorsports, 1934 Biplane, #460, D13 ....$60.00
French's Mustard/Black Flag #43, Pontiac, #462, D13......$35.00
Goodwrench/D Earnhardt, 1955 Panel, #467, D13 ....$50.00
Goodyear #1, Chevy Lumina, #318, D13 ....$70.00
Harry Gant #33, Model A Pickup, #228, D13 ....$40.00
Hooters 500 Atlantic Speedway, Model A Panel, #208, D13.$90.00
Jim Brown, T-Bird, #2253, D13....................................$20.00
Kodak Film Racing/Ernie Irvan #4, Chevy Lumina, #344,
      D13 ....$40.00
LA Raiders, T-Bird, #552, D13.....................................$25.00
Mac Tools/Harry Gant #7, Chevy Lumina, #376, D13.....$50.00
Martinsville, Kenworth Tractor Trailer, #244, D13 ....$35.00
Meineke Muffler/Spencer #12, T-Bird, D13 ....$65.00
Mello Yello/Charlotte, Kenworth Tractor Trailer, #248,
      D13..$35.00
Motorcraft, Kenworth Tractor Trailer, #306, D13............$55.00
Nascar #93, Pontiac, #436, D13 ....$40.00
Nascar Racing, Model A Panel, #314, D13.....................$30.00
North Wilkesboro, Kenworth Tractor Trailer, #246, D13..$35.00
Petty Enterprises/Wilson #44, 1937 Chevy Pickup, #362,
      D13 ....$35.00
Pontiac/R Wallace #2, Pontiac, #428, D13....................$160.00
Racing Champs #51, Chevy Lumina, #317, D13 ....$40.00

Santa Mobile #25, T-Bird, #286, D13 ....$50.00
STP/Richard Petty #43, Pontiac, #346, D13...................$100.00
Tide/R Rudd #5, Chevy Lumina, #336, D13...................$40.00
Valvoline/Reece #6, T-Bird, #2210, D13.........................$25.00
Western Auto, 1955 Chevy Sedan DEL, #236, D13...........$45.00
Western Auto/D Waltrip, 1955 Chevy Convertible, #475,
      D13 ....$25.00
Winn Dixie/M Martin #60 Busch, T-Bird, #328, D13......$75.00
World of Outlaws/S Kinser, Helmet, #808, D13 ....$40.00

Spec-Cast

AGCO White Collector's Edition, Model A Roadster, #1534,
      D13..$25.00
Allied Van Lines, 1934 Biplane, #37506, D13................$45.00
Amoco, Model A Tanker, #2015, D13 ....$30.00
Amoco #1, Vintage Plane, #0805, H8 ....$110.00
Amoco Blue Lead Free Regular, Model A Tank, #2001B,
      D13 ....$35.00
Amoco w/Santa, Model A Roadster, #1530, D13 ....$40.00
Buick Motor Sport, Model A Pickup, #1020, D13............$25.00
California Highway Patrol #1, 1929 Ford, #2585, H8.......$30.00
Cambell's Soup, 1937 Chevy, #10004, H8.......................$22.00
Campbell's Soup, 1957 Chevy Pickup, #50013, D13..........$30.00
Canadian Tire, Model A Panel, #2501C, D13...................$35.00
Case Best of All Worlds, Kenworth Tractor Trailer, #ZJD712,
      D13 ....$30.00
Chevrolet KY, 1937 Chevy Pickup, #12506, H8 ....$20.00
Chevy Factory Service, 1937 Chevy Pickup, #15011, D13.$25.00
Chicago Auto Show, 1937 Chevy Roadster, #10017, D13.$25.00
Citgo, Studebaker Tanker, #27502, D13..........................$30.00
Clark Oil Refining #1, Model A Roadster, #1544, D13....$25.00
Classic Rods w/Mags, Model A Roadster, #1563, D13 .....$25.00
Coca-Cola 600, Kenworth Tractor Trailer, #30001, H8 ..$50.00
Collectors World, 1913 Ford Model T, #9137, H8...........$34.00
Cooper Tire, Kenworth Tractor Trailer, #30028, D13 .....$25.00
Daytona Bike Week #2, Model A Panel, #2589, D13 ....$100.00
Drive Magazine, 1957 Chevy Pickup, #50042, D13.........$30.00
Eastwood #10 w/Santa, 1929 Roadster, #1928, D13 ....$35.00
Eastwood Auto Club #1-11600, Model A Wrecker, #1043,
      D13...$25.00
Eastwood Co #1, Vintage Plane, #1715, H8 ....$195.00
Evers Toy Store #1, Model A Roadster, #1507, D13 ....$25.00
Fina, Model A Tanker, #2004, D13 ....$30.00
Golden Rule Lumber Center, 1937 Chevy, #12515, H8 ..$20.00
Goodyear, 1937 Chevy Pickup, #15001, D13..................$40.00
Hamm's Beer, Model A Pickup, #1014, D13...................$30.00
Harley-Davidson, Kenworth Tractor Trailer, #99197, H8..$75.00
Harley-Davidson, 1933 Motorcycle w/Sidecar, #99199,
      D13..$150.00
Harry Gant #33, 1929 Ford, #0228, H8 ....$44.00
Heinz 57, Model A Pickup, #1018, D13.........................$25.00
Heinz 57, 1916 Studebaker, #22502, H8........................$22.00
Indian Motorcycle, #1, Airplane, #40017, D13...............$55.00
Indian Motorcycle, 1955 Chevy Convertible, #55014, H8..$25.00
James Dean, 1913 Ford Model T, #9344, H8 ....$25.00
JC Whitney, 1952 GMC, #110-1215, H8 ....$35.00
Jeff Gordon/Dupont #24, Vintage Plane, #0426, H8........$45.00

Jewel Tea, 1931 Ford, #2584, H8 ....$65.00
Lennox, 1916 Studebaker, #22510, H8........................$40.00
Lion's Club Farm Show #2, Model A Panel, #2530, D13 .$30.00
Massey Ferguson, Kenworth Tractor Trailer, #30007, D13..$25.00
Mic Ford Motorcraft, Airplane, #40028, D13 ....$30.00
Minneapolis Moline, Model A Roadster, #1513, D13 ......$20.00
Nabisco #1, Model A Panel, #2508, D13 ....$25.00
Nascar, 1929 Ford, #0314, H8 ....$22.00
Neil Bonnett/Citgo #21, 1929 Ford, #0300, H8................$65.00
New York Fire Dept Chief #1, Model A Roadster, #1556, D13..$40.00
NTPA Fort Recovery, Model A Pickup, #1021, D13 ....$45.00
Oliver Farm Equipment, Kenworth Tractor Trailer, #30005, D13 ....$30.00
Olympia Beer, Kenworth Tractor Trailer, #30020, D13 ...$25.00
Olympia Beer, 1929 Ford, #2528, H8 ....$20.00
Pabst Beer, 1937 Chevy, #1019, H8.................................$25.00
Pabst Blue Ribbon, Model A Roadster, #1512, D13 ....$35.00
Pennzoil, Model A Crate, #1061, D13 ....$30.00
Pennzoil, 1929 Ford, #1062, H8 ....$30.00
Pepsi-Cola, F-16, #46001, D13 ....$50.00
Pepsi-Cola, 1916 Studebaker Pickup, #22519, H8.............$30.00
Police #3, Model A Roadster, #1522, D13 ....$30.00
Police Department, 1937 Chevy Panel, #15008, D13 ......$20.00
Police Department, 1937 Chevy Panel, #50002, D13 ......$20.00
Red Crown Gas, Model A Wrecker, #02036, D13 ....$25.00
Red Crown Gas, Plane, Orion, #42504, D13 ....$45.00
Red Crown Gas, 1940 Ford Tanker, #65502, H8..............$25.00
Richman's Ice Cream, 1916 Studebaker, #25018, H8 ......$35.00
Santa-Seasons Greetings, 1929 Ford, #1569, H8 ....$20.00
Sentry Hardware, 1955 Chevy, #50030, H8 ....$20.00
Sheriff w/Lights, 1937 Chevy, #15017, D13 ....$30.00
Snap-On Tools, 1929 Ford, #2598, H8 ....$85.00
Spec-Cast, Model A Fire Truck, #2013, H8......................$65.00
Spur Gasoline, 1948 Diamond T Tractor Trailer, #3903, H8..$25.00
Standard Oil #1 Humble, Biplane, #37509, D13 ....$45.00
State Patrol, 1937 Chevy, #15007, H8..............................$30.00
Sunmaid Raisins, 1937 Chevy, #12505, D13/H8..............$25.00
Sunsweet, 1916 Studebaker Roadster, #20001, D13 ....$25.00
Sunsweet, 1955 Chevy Convertible, #55001, H8 ....$22.00
Sweet & Low, 1929 Ford Roadster, #1554, H8 ....$30.00
Tanya Tucker, 1937 Chevy, #10021, D13 ....$20.00
Texaco Havoline Oil, Model A Panel, #2529, D13..........$50.00
Texaco Sales, Model A Roadster, #1537, D13 ....$50.00
Thunderbirds, F-16, #46002, D13 ....$50.00
Thunderhills, 1916 Studebaker, #25016, H8 ....$35.00
True Test, Model A Panel, #2547, D13 ....$20.00
True Value Master Mechanic, Model A Pickup, #1203, D13..$20.00
Trustworthy Hardware, Studebaker Panel, #22500, D13..$20.00
Trustworthy Hardware, 1929 Ford, #1013, H8 ....$25.00
US Army Staff Car, 1937 Chevy, #10015, H8..................$25.00
US Mail, Biplane, #37522, D13 ....$35.00
Valvoline, Vega Plane, #35032, D13 ....$35.00
Village of Chevy #1, 1937 Chevy Pickup, #12506, D13...$20.00
Winchester, 1929 Ford, #02601, H8 ....$25.00
Wix Filters, 1955 Chevy, #50001, H8.............................$30.00
Wix Parts Plus, 1957 Chevy Pickup, #50006, D13 ....$35.00
Wrigley's Doublemint Gum, Kenworth Tractor Trailer, #30021, D13...$30.00

Dinky

Dinky diecasts were made by Meccano (Britain) as early as 1933, but high on the list of many of today's collectors are those from the decades of the fifties and sixties. They made commercial vehicles, firefighting equipment, farm toys, and heavy equipment as well as classic cars that were the epitome of high style, such as the #157 Jaguar XK120, produced from the mid-fifties through the early sixties. Some Dinkys were made in France; since 1979 no toys have been produced in Great Britain. Values are for examples mint and in the original packaging unless noted otherwise.

Advisor: Irwin Stern (S3).

#100, Lady Penelope's Fab 1, luminous pk $400.00
#100, Lady Penelope's Fab 1, pk.....................................$250.00
#101, Sunbeam Alpine...$200.00
#101, Thunderbird II & IV, gr $300.00
#101, Thunderbird II & IV, metallic dk gr $400.00
#102, Joe's Car $170.00
#102, MG Midget $300.00
#103, Austin Healey 100 ....$350.00
#103, Spectrum Patrol Car $160.00
#104, Aston Martin DB3S...$250.00

#104, Spectrum Pursuit Vehicle, $200.00.

#105, Maximum Security Vehicle....................................$170.00
#105, Triumph TR2..$250.00
#106, Austin Atlantic, bl or blk $200.00
#106, Austin Atlantic, pk..$350.00
#106, Prisoner Mini Moke...$300.00
#106, Thunderbird II & IV...$150.00
#107, Stripey, The Magi Mini $400.00
#107, Sunbeam Alpine..$150.00
#108, MG Midget $200.00
#108, Sam's Car, gold, red or bl.....................................$160.00
#108, Sam's Car, silver $120.00

#109, Austin Healey 100 ....$160.00
#109, Gabriel Model T Ford $150.00
#110, Aston Martin DB3S...........................$150.00
#110, Aston Martin DB5 ....$125.00
#111, Cinderella's Coach.............................$50.00
#111, Triumph TR2 ....$160.00
#112, Austin Healey Sprite $125.00
#112, Purdey's Triumph TR7.....................$75.00
#113, MGB $100.00
#114, Triumph Spitfire, gray, gold or red $125.00
#114, Triumph Spitfire, purple $170.00
#115, Plymouth Fury.................................$125.00
#115, UB Taxi...$85.00
#116, Volvo 1800S $100.00
#117, Four Berth Caravan $60.00
#118, Tow-Away Glider Set........................$250.00
#120, Happy Cab..$75.00
#120, Jaguar E-Type $110.00
#121, Goodwood Racing Gift Set $2,000.00
#122, Touring Gift Set.............................$2,000.00
#122, Volvo 265 Estate Car $50.00
#123, Mayfair Gift Set.............................$3,000.00
#123, Princess 2200 HL $50.00
#124, Holiday Gift Set $1,000.00
#124, Rolls Royce Phantom V $90.00
#125, Fun A'Hoy Set $300.00
#126, Motor Show Set.............................$2,000.00
#127, Rolls Royce Silver Cloud III..............$140.00
#128, Mercedes Benz 600 ....$8.00
#129, MG Midget $500.00
#129, VW 1200 Sedan...................................$80.00
#130, Ford Consul Corsair $100.00
#131, Cadillac El Dorado............................$200.00
#131, Jaguar E-Type 2+2 ....$160.00
#132, Ford 40-RV..$60.00
#132, Packard Convertible $200.00
#133, Cunningham C-5R.............................$150.00
#133, Ford Cortina $110.00
#134, Triumph Vitesse $100.00
#135, Triumph 2000....................................$100.00
#136, Vauxhall Viva $80.00
#137, Plymouth Fury...................................$150.00
#138, Hillman Imp......................................$100.00
#139, Ford Cortina $130.00
#139a, Ford Fordor Sedan, cream & red, or pk & bl.......$300.00
#139a, Ford Fordor Sedan, solid colors..................$160.00
#139a, US Army Staff Car $350.00
#139b, Hudson Commodore Sedan, dual colors.............$350.00
#139b, Hudson Commodore Sedan, solid colors............$225.00
#140, Morris 1100 ....$60.00
#141, Vauxhall Victor $80.00
#142, Jaguar Mark 10..................................$100.00
#143, Ford Capri..$125.00
#144, VW 1500...$100.00
#145, Singer Vogue......................................$100.00
#146, Daimler V8 ....$125.00
#147, Cadillac 62...$125.00
#148, Ford Fairlane, gr...............................$125.00

#148, Ford Fairlane, metallic gr.................$225.00
#149, Citroen Dyane.....................................$50.00
#149, Sports Cars Gift Set.......................$1,800.00
#150, Rolls Royce Silver Wraith $100.00
#150, Royal Tank Corps Personnel $250.00
#151, Royal Tank Corps Med Tank Set........$600.00
#151, Triumph 1800 Saloon $150.00
#151, Vauxhall Victor 101 ....$100.00
#151a, Med Tank $250.00
#151b, Six-Wheeled Covered Wagon............$180.00
#151c, Cooker Trailer.................................$100.00
#151d, Water Tank Trailer $100.00
#152, Rolls Royce Phantom V.......................$65.00
#152, Royal Tank Corps Light Tank Set $600.00
#152a, Light Tank $160.00
#152b, Reconnaissance Car.........................$175.00
#152c, Austin 7 Car.....................................$250.00
#153, Aston Martin $100.00
#153, Standard Vanguard-Spats $160.00
#153a, Jeep...$160.00
#154, Ford Taunus 17m $65.00
#155, Ford Anglia $140.00
#156, Mechanized Army Set $5,000.00
#156, Rover 75, dual colors........................$300.00
#156, Rover 75, solid colors........................$150.00
#156, Saab 96..$100.00
#157, BMW 2000 Tilux.................................$100.00
#157, Jaguar XK120, wht or dual colors $400.00
#158, Riley $160.00
#158, Rolls Royce Silver Shadow.................$100.00
#159, Ford Cortina MK II.............................$100.00
#159, Morris Oxford, dual colors $300.00
#159, Morris Oxford, solid colors $170.00
#160, Austin A30...$150.00
#160, Mercedes Benz 250 SE.........................$80.00
#160, Royal Artillery Personnel $300.00
#161, Austin Somerset, dual colors.............$300.00
#161, Austin Somerset, solid colors $150.00
#161, Ford Mustang $70.00
#161, Mobile Antiaircraft Unit $1,000.00
#161a, Lorry w/Searchlight.........................$500.00
#161b, Antiaircraft Gun on Trailer $150.00
#162, Ford Zephyr......................................$150.00
#162, Triumph 1300......................................$75.00
#162a, Light Dragon Tractor......................$150.00
#162b, Trailer...$40.00
#162c, 18-Pounder Gun................................$50.00
#163, Bristol 450 Coupe $100.00
#163, VW 1600 TL, metallic bl $150.00
#163, VW 1600 TL, red $75.00
#164, Ford Zodiac MKIV, bronze $200.00
#164, Ford Zodiac MKIV, silver $100.00
#164, Vauxhall Cresta.................................$150.00
#165, Ford Capri..$100.00
#165, Humber Hawk $180.00
#166, Renault R16 ....$60.00
#166, Sunbeam Rapier.................................$150.00
#167, AC Aceca, all cream $300.00

#167, AC Aceca, dual colors	$160.00
#168, Ford Escort	$100.00
#168, Singer Gazelle	$160.00
#169, Ford Corsair	$100.00
#169, Studebaker Golden Hawk	$170.00
#170, Ford Fordor, dual colors	$300.00
#170, Ford Fordor, solid colors	$100.00
#170, Lincoln Continental	$120.00
#170m, Ford Fordor US Army Staff Car	$350.00
#171, Austin 1800	$100.00
#171, Hudson Commodore, dual colors	$350.00
#172, Fiat 2300 Station Wagon	$80.00
#172, Studebaker Land Cruiser, dual colors	$300.00
#172, Studebaker Land Cruiser, solid colors	$180.00
#173, Nash Rambler	$110.00
#173, Pontiac Parisienne	$75.00
#174, Hudson Hornet	$160.00
#174, Mercury Cougar	$80.00
#175, Cadillac El Dorado	$100.00
#175, Hillman Minx	$150.00
#176, Austin A105, cream or gray	$160.00
#176, Austin A105, cream w/bl roof, or gray w/red roof	$250.00
#176, NSU R80, metallic bl	$180.00
#176, NSU R80, metallic red	$80.00
#177, Opel Kapitan	$100.00
#178, Mini Clubman	$60.00

#178, Plymouth Plaza, blue with white roof, $400.00.

#178, Plymouth Plaza, pk, gr or 2-tone bl	$170.00
#179, Opel Commodore	$70.00
#179, Studebaker President	$170.00
#180, Packard Clipper	$170.00
#180, Rover 3500 Sedan	$30.00
#181, VW	$100.00
#182, Porsche 356A Coupe, cream, red or bl	$130.00
#182, Porsche 356A Coupe, dual colors	$325.00
#183, Fiat 600	$100.00
#183, Morris Mini Minor	$125.00
#184, Volvo 122S, red	$130.00
#184, Volvo 122S, wht	$375.00
#185, Alpha Romeo 1900	$125.00
#186, Mercedes Benz 220	$65.00
#187, De Tomaso Mangusta 5000	$65.00
#187, VW Karmann-Ghia Coupe	$120.00

#188, Ford Berth Caravan	$60.00
#188, Jensen FF	$75.00
#189, Lamborghini Marzal	$65.00
#189, Triumph Herald	$130.00
#190, Caravan	$60.00
#191, Dodge Royal Sedan, cream w/bl flash	$300.00
#191, Dodge Royal Sedan, cream w/brn flash, or gr w/blk flash	$170.00
#192, Desoto Fireflite	$200.00
#192, Range Rover	$50.00
#193, Rambler Station Wagon	$130.00
#194, Bentley S Coupe	$140.00
#195, Jaguar 3.4 Litre MKII	$150.00
#195, Range Rover Fire Chief	$60.00
#196, Holden Special Sedan	$100.00
#197, Morris Mini Traveller, dk gr & brn	$400.00
#197, Morris Mini Traveller, lime gr	$300.00
#197, Morris Mini Traveller, wht & brn	$130.00
#198, Austin Countryman, orange	$325.00
#198, Rolls Royce Phantom V	$125.00
#199, Austin Countryman, bl	$125.00
#200, Matra 630	$50.00
#201, Plymouth Stock Car	$85.00
#201, Racing Car Set	$750.00
#202, Customized Land Rover	$40.00
#202, Fiat Abarth 2000	$40.00
#203, Customized Range Rover	$40.00
#204, Ferrari	$40.00
#205, Lotus Cortina	$125.00
#205, Talbot Lago, in bubble pkg	$325.00
#206, Customized Corvette Stingray	$50.00
#206, Maserati, in bubble pkg	$360.00
#207, Alfa Romeo, in bubble pkg	$300.00
#207, Triumph TR7	$40.00
#208, Cooper-Bristol, in bubble pkg	$300.00
#208, VW Porsche 914	$50.00
#209, Ferrari, in bubble pkg	$300.00
#210, Alfa Romeo 33	$50.00
#210, Vanwall, in bubble pkg	$200.00
#211, Triumph TR7	$80.00
#212, Ford Cortina Rally	$135.00
#213, Ford Capri	$75.00
#214, Hillman Imp Rally	$100.00
#215, Ford GT Racing Car	$70.00
#216, Ferrari Dino	$50.00
#217, Alfa Romeo Scarabeo	$40.00
#218, Lotus Europa	$65.00
#219, Jaguar XJS Coupe	$65.00
#220, Ferrari P5	$50.00
#221, Corvette Stingray	$40.00
#222, Hesketh Racing Car, dk bl	$50.00
#222, Hesketh Racing Car, Olympus Camera	$100.00
#223, McLaren M8A Can-Am	$40.00
#224, Mercedes Benz C111	$40.00
#225, Lotus Formula I Racer	$40.00
#226, Ferrari 312/B2	$40.00
#227, Beach Bunny	$40.00
#228, Super Sprinter	$40.00

#236, Connaught Racer......................................$125.00
#237, Mercedes Benz Racer.............................$140.00
#238, Jaguar Type-D Racer...............................$160.00
#239, Vanwall Racer..$100.00
#240, Cooper Racer $70.00
#240, Dinky Way Gift Set..................................$100.00
#241, Lotus Racer $80.00
#241, Silver Jubilee Taxi....................................$50.00
#242, Ferrari Racer..$90.00
#243, BRM Racer...$90.00
#243, Volvo Police Racer $40.00
#244, Plymouth Police Racer.............................$40.00
#245, Superfast Gift Set....................................$200.00
#246, International GT Gift Set $200.00
#249, Racing Car Gift Set.............................$1,500.00
#249, Racing Car Gift Set, in bubble pkg..................$1,800.00
#250, Mini Coopers Police Car $75.00
#251, USA Police Car, Pontiac...........................$80.00
#252, RCMP Car, Pontiac.................................$100.00
#254, Austin Taxi, yel......................................$120.00
#254, Police Range Rover $50.00
#255, Ford Zodiac Police Car $100.00
#255, Mersey Tunnel Police Van......................$100.00
#255, Police Mini Clubman................................$50.00
#256, Humber Hawk Police Car........................$150.00
#257, Nash Rambler Canadian Fire Chief Car $100.00
#258, USA Police Car, Cadillac, Desoto, Dodge or Ford...$150.00
#259, Bedford Fire Engine $130.00
#260, Royal Mail Van..$160.00
#260, VW Deutsch Bundepost $185.00
#261, Ford Taunus Polizei $300.00
#261, Telephone Service Van.............................$170.00
#262, VW Swiss Post PTT Car, casting #129 ....$300.00
#262, VW Swiss Post PTT Car, casting #181 ....$500.00
#263, Airport Fire Rescue Tender $70.00
#263, Superior Criterion Ambulance.................$100.00
#264, RCMP Patrol Car, Cadillac.....................$175.00
#264, RCMP Patrol Car, Fairlane $150.00
#265, Plymouth Taxi..$170.00
#266, ERF Fire Tender...$75.00
#266, ERF Fire Tender, Falck............................$100.00

#269, Ford Transit Police Accident Unit, Falck Zonen, $60.00.

#266, Plymouth Taxi, Metro Cab $200.00
#267, Paramedic Truck..$50.00
#267, Superior Cadillac Ambulance $100.00
#268, Range Rover Ambulance...........................$40.00
#268, Renault Dauphine Mini Cab $150.00
#269, Jaguar Motorway Police Car $160.00
#270, AA Motorcycle Patrol.............................$100.00
#270, Ford Panda Police Car $70.00
#271, Ford Transit Fire, Appliance $100.00
#271, Ford Transit Fire, Falck..........................$150.00
#271, TS Motorcycle Patrol $300.00
#272, ANNB Motorcycle Patrol........................$350.00
#272, Police Accident Unit................................$60.00
#273, RAC Patrol Mini Van..............................$200.00
#274, AA Patrol Mini Van.................................$250.00
#274, Ford Transit Ambulance $50.00
#274, Mini Van, Joseph Mason Paints.............$750.00
#275, Brink's Armoured Car, no bullion $75.00
#275, Brink's Armoured Car, w/gold bullion $200.00
#275, Brink's Armoured Car, w/Mexican bullion........$1,000.00
#276, Airport Fire Tender $100.00
#276, Ford Transit Ambulance $60.00
#277, Police Land Rover $40.00
#277, Superior Criterion Ambulance.................$100.00
#278, Plymouth Yellow Cab $40.00
#278, Vauxhall Victor Ambulance $100.00
#279, Aveling Barford Diesel Roller....................$80.00
#280, Midland Mobile Bank.............................$140.00
#281, Fiat 2300 Pathe News Camera Car $200.00
#281, Military Hovercraft...................................$50.00
#282, Austin 1800 Taxi....................................$100.00
#282, Land Rover Fire, Appliance......................$50.00
#282, Land Rover Fire, Falck.............................$80.00
#283, BOAC Coach...$150.00
#283, Single-Decker Bus....................................$80.00
#284, London Austin Taxi $60.00
#285, Merryweather Fire Engine $80.00
#285, Merryweather Fire Engine, Falck............$150.00
#286, Ford Transit Fire, Appliance $100.00
#286, Ford Transit Fire, Appliance, Falck........$160.00
#288, Superior Cadillac Ambulance $80.00
#288, Superior Cadillac Ambulance, Falck....................$150.00
#289, Routemaster Bus, Esso, purple $750.00
#289, Routemaster Bus, Esso, red $100.00
#289, Routemaster Bus, Festival of London Stores.........$200.00
#289, Routemaster Bus, Madame Tussaud's...................$150.00
#289, Routemaster Bus, Silver Jubilee.................$40.00
#289, Routemaster Bus, Tern Shirts or Schweppes........$150.00
#290, Double-Decker Bus..................................$175.00
#290, SRN-6 Hovercraft.....................................$40.00
#291, Atlantean City Bus $70.00
#292, Atlantean Bus, Regent or Ribble $150.00
#293, Swiss Postal Bus $50.00
#294, Police Vehicle Gift Set............................$200.00
#295, Atlantean Bus, Yellow Pages....................$70.00
#296, Duple Luxury Coach.................................$40.00
#296, Police Accident Unit...............................$100.00
#297, Police Vehicles Gift Set $200.00

#297, Silver Jubilee Bus, National or Woolworth $40.00
#298, Emergency Services Gift Set $1,300.00
#299, Crash Squad Gift Set $70.00
#299, Motorway Services Gift Set $1,600.00
#299, Post Office Services Gift Set $650.00
#300, London Scene Gift Set $100.00
#302, Emergency Squad Gift Set.....................................$100.00
#303, Commando Gift Set $120.00
#304, Fire Rescue Gift Set $120.00
#305, David Brown Tractor $100.00
#308, Leyland 384 Tractor..$75.00
#309, Star Trek Gift Set $150.00
#319, Week's Tipping Farm Trailer $40.00
#320, Halesowen Harvest Trailer $50.00
#321, Massey-Harris Manure Spreader $60.00
#322, Disc Harrow $50.00
#323, Triple Gang Mower $50.00
#324, Hay Rake $50.00
#325, David Brown Tractor & Harrow $150.00
#340, Land Rover $100.00
#341, Land Rover Trailer...$40.00
#342, Austin Mini Moke $70.00
#342, Moto-Cart $75.00
#344, Estate Car $80.00
#344, Land Rover Pickup..$40.00
#350, Tony's Mini Moke $150.00
#351, UFO Interceptor..$90.00
#352, Ed Straker's Car, red $100.00
#352, Ed Straker's Car, yel or gold-plated.......................$140.00
#353, Shado 2 Mobile $100.00
#354, Pink Panther $60.00
#355, Lunar Roving Vehicle..$60.00
#357, Klingon Battle Cruiser $80.00
#358, USS Enterprise $75.00
#359, Eagle Transporter $75.00
#360, Eagle Freighter $75.00
#361, Galactic War Chariot $75.00
#362, Trident Star Fighter $75.00
#363, Cosmic Zygon Patroller, for Marks & Spencer........$80.00
#364, NASA Space Shuttle, w/booster $100.00
#366, NASA Space Shuttle, w/no booster.........................$50.00
#367, Space Battle Cruiser...$80.00
#368, Zygon Marauder $80.00
#370, Dragster Set...$70.00
#371, USS Enterprise, sm version $50.00
#372, Klingon Battle Cruiser, sm version...........................$50.00
#380, Convoy Skip Truck..$20.00
#381, Convoy Farm Truck...$20.00
#382, Convoy Dumper...$20.00
#382, Wheelbarrow..$25.00
#383, Convoy NCL Truck..$30.00
#384, Convoy Fire Rescue Truck $25.00
#384, Grass Cutter...$25.00
#385, Convoy Royal Mail Truck..$30.00
#385, Sack Truck $25.00
#386, Lawn Mower $125.00
#390, Customized Transit Van $50.00
#398, Farm Equipment Gift Set $2,000.00

#399, Farm Tractor & Trailer Set $200.00
#400, BEV Electric Truck...$70.00
#401, Coventry-Climax Fork Lift, orange $70.00
#401, Coventry-Climax Fork Lift, red...............................$500.00

#402, Bedford Coca-Cola Truck, $250.00.

#404, Conveyancer Fork Lift..$50.00
#405, Universal Jeep $50.00
#406, Commer Articulated Truck......................................$200.00
#407, Ford Transit, Kenwood or Hertz.............................$120.00
#408, Big Bedford Lorry, bl & yel, or bl & orange..........$350.00
#408, Big Bedford Lorry, maroon & fawn $200.00
#408, Big Bedford Lorry, pk & cream $2,000.00
#409, Bedford Articulated Lorry $175.00
#410, Bedford Van, Danish Post or Simpsons.................$125.00
#410, Bedford Van, MJ Hire, Marley or Collectors Gazette..$50.00
#410, Bedford Van, Royal Mail $30.00
#411, Bedford Truck...$160.00
#412, Austin Wagon..$500.00
#412, Bedford Van AA...$40.00
#413, Austin Covered Wagon, lt & dk bl, or red & tan.$650.00
#413, Austin Covered Wagon, maroon & cream, or med bl & lt
    bl $200.00
#413, Austin Covered Wagon, red & gray, or bl & cream..$450.00
#414, Dodge Tipper, all colors other than royal bl $125.00
#414, Dodge Tipper, royal bl..$200.00
#415, Mechanical Horse & Wagon....................................$200.00
#416, Ford Transit Van..$50.00
#416, Ford Transit Van, 1,000,000 Transits $200.00
#417, Ford Transit Van..$50.00
#417, Leyland Comet Lorry...$150.00
#418, Leyland Comet Lorry...$175.00
#419, Leyland Comet Cement Lorry..................................$200.00
#420, Leyland Forward Control Lorry................................$100.00
#421, Hindle-Smart Electric Lorry.....................................$100.00
#422, Thames Flat Truck, bright gr...................................$200.00
#422, Thames Flat Truck, dk gr or red $100.00
#424, Commer Articulated Truck......................................$250.00
#425, Bedford TK Coal Lorry $200.00
#428, Trailer, lg..$50.00
#429, Trailer...$50.00
#430, Commer Breakdown Lorry, all colors other than tan &
    gr...$1,000.00

#430, Commer Breakdown Lorry, tan & gr...................$200.00
#430, Johnson Dumper $40.00
#431, Guy 4-Ton Lorry..$600.00
#432, Foden Tipper...$50.00
#432, Guy Warrior Flat Truck..................................$500.00
#433, Guy Flat Truck w/Tailboard...........................$350.00
#434, Bedford Crash Truck $150.00
#435, Bedford TK Tipper, gray or yel cab $125.00
#435, Bedford TK Tipper, wht, silver & bl $250.00
#436, Atlas COPCO Compressor Lorry......................$100.00
#437, Muir Hill Loader $40.00
#438, Ford D 800 Tipper, opening doors....................$50.00
#439, Ford D 800 Snow Plough & Tipper...................$75.00
#440, Petrol Tanker, Mobilgas $200.00
#441, Petrol Tanker, Castrol $200.00
#442, Land Rover Breakdown Crane $50.00
#442, Land Rover Breakdown Crane, Falck $70.00
#442, Petrol Tanker, Esso...$200.00
#443, Petrol Tanker, National Benzole......................$200.00
#448, Chevrolet El Camino w/Trailers $400.00
#449, Chevrolet El Camino Pickup $120.00
#449, Johnston Road Sweeper $70.00
#450, Bedford TK Box Van, Castrol $200.00
#450, Trojan Van, Esso...$200.00
#451, Johnston Road Sweeper, opening doors $70.00
#451, Trojan Van, Dunlop..$200.00
#452, Trojan Van, Chivers $200.00
#453, Trojan Van, Oxo...$300.00
#454, Trojan Van, Cydrax..$200.00
#455, Trojan Van, Brooke Bond Tea $200.00
#465, Morris Van, Capstan.......................................$325.00
#470, Austin Van, Shell-BP......................................$200.00
#471, Austin Van, Nestle's $225.00
#472, Austin Van, Raleigh Cycles $225.00
#475, Ford Model T $100.00
#476, Morris Oxford $100.00
#477, Parsley's Car $100.00
#480, Bedford Van, Kodak $180.00
#481, Bedford Van, Ovaltine $180.00
#482, Bedford Van, Dinky Toys $200.00
#485, Ford Model T w/Santa Claus...........................$200.00
#486, Morris Oxford, Dinky Beats............................$200.00
#490, Electric Dairy Van, Express Dairy $100.00
#491, Electric Dairy Van, NCB or Job Dairies.............$150.00
#492, Electric Mini Van $350.00
#492, Loudspeaker Van $125.00
#501, Foden Diesel 8 Wheel, 1st cab $1,000.00
#501, Foden Diesel 8 Wheel, 2nd cab $600.00
#502, Foden Flat Truck, 1st or 2nd cab $1,000.00
#503, Foden Flat Truck, 1st cab............................$1,200.00
#503, Foden Flat Truck, 2nd cab, bl & orange $400.00
#503, Foden Flat Truck, 2nd cab, bl & yel $1,200.00
#503, Foden Flat Truck, 2nd cab, 2-tone gr.............$3,000.00
#504, Foden Tanker, red..$800.00
#504, Foden Tanker, 1st cab, 2-tone bl.....................$500.00
#504, Foden Tanker, 2nd cab, red.............................$600.00
#504, Foden Tanker, 2nd cab, 2-tone bl..................$3,500.00
#505, Foden Flat Truck w/Chains, 1st cab................$3,000.00

#505, Foden Flat Truck w/Chains, 2nd cab $450.00
#511, Guy 4-Ton Lorry, red, gr or brn.........................$900.00
#511, Guy 4-Ton Lorry, 2-tone bl...............................$350.00
#512, Guy Flat Truck, all colors other than bl or red $750.00
#512, Guy Flat Truck, bl or red...................................$400.00
#513, Guy Flat Truck w/Tailboard $400.00
#514, Guy Van, Lyons...$2,000.00
#514, Guy Van, Slumberland $600.00
#514, Guy Van, Spratt's $600.00

#514, Guy Van, Weetabix, $3,500.00.

#521, Bedford Articulated Lory.....................................$200.00
#522, Big Bedford Lorry, bl & yel................................$350.00
#522, Big Bedford Lorry, maroon & fawn $175.00
#531, Leyland Comet Lorry, all colors other than bl or brn .$300.00
#531, Leyland Comet Lorry, bl & brn............................$500.00
#532, Bedford Comet Lorry w/Tailboard $300.00
#533, Leyland Cement Wagon......................................$200.00
#551, Trailer..$60.00
#555, Fire Engine, w/extension ladder $100.00
#561, Blaw-Knox Bulldozer $100.00
#561, Blaw-Knox Bulldozer, plastic..............................$500.00
#562, Muir-Hill Dumper...$40.00
#563, Blaw-Knox Heavy Tractor $100.00
#564, Elevator Loader..$100.00
#571, Coles Mobile Crane $120.00
#581, Horse Box, British Railway $150.00
#581, Horse Box, Express Horse Van $800.00
#582, Pullmore Car Transporter..................................$160.00
#591, AEC Tanker, Shell..$225.00
#601, Austin Para Moke $100.00
#602, Armoured Command Car $50.00
#603, Army Personnel, box of 12 ....$100.00
#604, Land Rover Bomb Disposal Unit..........................$70.00
#604, Royal Tank Corps...$250.00
#609, 105mm Howitzer & Gun Crew $50.00
#612, Commando Jeep...$50.00
#615, US Jeep & 105mm Howitzer................................$60.00
#616, AEC Articulated Transporter & Tank...................$90.00
#617, VW KDF w/Antitank Gun..................................$100.00
#618, AEC Articulated Transporter & Helicopter.........$100.00
#619, Bren Gun Carrier & Antitank Gun $50.00

#620, Berliet Missile Launcher	$170.00
#621, 3-Ton Army Wagon	$100.00
#622, Bren Gun Carrier	$40.00
#622, 10-Ton Army Truck	$140.00
#623, Army Covered Wagon	$80.00
#624, Daimler Military Ambulance	$300.00
#625, Austin Covered Wagon	$500.00
#625, 6-Pounder Antitank Gun	$40.00
#626, Military Ambulance	$100.00
#640, Bedford Military Truck	$400.00
#641, Army 1-Ton Cargo Truck	$75.00
#642, RAF Pressure Refueler	$150.00
#643, Army Water Carrier	$120.00
#650, Light Tank	$160.00
#651, Centurion Tank	$90.00
#654, Mobile Gun	$40.00
#656, 88mm Gun	$40.00
#660, Tank Transporter	$150.00
#661, Recovery Tractor	$150.00
#662, Static 88mm Gun & Crew	$40.00
#665, Honest John Missile Erector	$175.00
#666, Missile Erector Vehicle w/Corporal Missile & Launching Platform	$400.00
#667, Armored Patrol Car	$40.00
#667, Missile Servicing Platform Vehicle	$250.00
#668, Foden Army Truck	$50.00
#669, US Army Jeep	$450.00
#670, Armoured Car	$45.00
#671, MKI Corvette (boat)	$25.00
#671, Reconnaissance Car	$175.00
#672, OSA Missile Boat	$25.00
#672, US Army Jeep	$160.00
#673, Scout Car	$45.00
#674, Austin Champ, olive drab	$60.00
#674, Austin Champ, wht, UN version	$500.00
#674, Coast Guard Missile Launch	$25.00
#675, Motor Patrol Boat	$20.00
#675, US Army Staff Car	$35.00
#676, Armoured Personnel Carrier	$60.00
#676, Daimler Armoured Car, w/speedwheels	$40.00
#677, Armoured Command Vehicles	$100.00
#677, Task Force Set	$70.00
#678, Air Sea Rescue	$30.00
#680, Ferret Armoured Car	$30.00
#681, DUKW	$30.00
#682, Stalwart Load Carrier	$30.00
#683, Chieftain Tank	$50.00
#686, 25-Pounder Field Gun	$25.00
#687, Convoy Army Truck	$25.00
#687, Trailer	$20.00
#688, Field Artillery Tractor	$50.00
#689, Med Artillery Tractor	$100.00
#690, Mobile Antiaircraft Gun	$100.00
#690, Scorpion Tank	$30.00
#691, Field Gun Unit	$350.00
#691, Striker Antitank Vehicle	$60.00
#692, Leopard Tank	$60.00
#692, 5.5 Med Gun	$60.00
#693, 7.2 Howitzer	$60.00
#694, Hanomag Tank Destroyer	$60.00
#694, Howitzer & Tractor	$300.00
#696, Leopard Antiaircraft Tank	$60.00
#697, 25-Pounder Field Gun Set	$150.00
#698, Tank Transporter & Tank	$250.00
#699, Leopard Recovery Tank	$70.00
#699, Military Gift Set	$500.00
#700, Seaplane	$200.00
#700, Spitfire MKII RAF Jubilee	$200.00
#701, Shetland Flying Boat	$650.00
#702, DH Comet Jet Airliner	$200.00
#704, Avro York Airliner	$200.00
#705, Viking Airliner	$100.00
#706, Vickers Viscount Airliner, Air France	$200.00
#708, Vickers Viscount Airliner, BEA	$200.00
#710, Beechcraft S35 Bonanza	$100.00
#712, US Army T-42A	$100.00
#715, Beechcraft C-55 Baron	$60.00
#715, Bristol 173 Helicopter	$70.00
#716, Westland Sikorsky Helicopter	$60.00
#717, Boeing 737	$100.00
#718, Hawker Hurricane	$100.00
#719, Spitfire MKII	$100.00
#721, Junkers Stuka	$100.00
#722, Hawker Harrier	$100.00
#723, Hawker Executive Jet	$60.00
#724, Sea King Helicopter	$75.00
#725, Phantom II	$135.00
#726, Messerschmitt, desert camouflage	$135.00
#726, Messerschmitt, gray & gr	$200.00
#727, US Air Force F-4 Phantom II	$350.00
#728, RAF Dominie	$80.00
#729, Multi-Role Combat Aircraft	$80.00
#730, US Navy Phantom	$130.00
#731, SEPECAT Jaguar	$80.00
#731, Twin-Engine Fighter	$50.00
#732, Bell Police Helicopter, M*A*S*H	$100.00
#732, Bell Police Helicopter, wht & bl	$60.00
#733, German Phantom II	$200.00
#733, Lockheed Shooting Star Jet Fighter	$50.00
#734, P47 Thunderbolt	$200.00
#734, Submarine Swift	$60.00
#735, Glouster Javelin	$60.00
#736, Bundesmarine Sea King	$100.00
#736, Hawker Hunter	$60.00
#737, P1B Lightning Fighter	$100.00
#738, DH110 Sea Vixen Fighter	$60.00
#739, Zero-Sen	$120.00
#741, Spitfire MKII	$100.00
#749, RAF Avro Vulcan Bomber	$3,500.00
#750, Telephone Call Box	$50.00
#751, Lawn Mower	$100.00
#751, Police Box	$50.00
#752, Goods Yard Crane	$70.00
#753, Police Controlled Crossing	$120.00
#755-6, Standard Lamp, single or dbl arm	$30.00
#760, Pillar Box	$30.00

#766, British Road Signs, Country Set A	$100.00
#767, British Road Signs, Country Set B	$100.00
#768, British Road Signs, Town Set A	$100.00
#769, British Road Signs, Town Set B	$100.00
#770, Road Signs, set of 12	$200.00
#771, International Road Signs, set of 12	$160.00
#772, British Road Signs, set of 24	$300.00
#773, Traffic Signal	$25.00
#777, Belisha Beacon	$20.00
#778, Road Repair Warning Boards	$25.00
#781, Petrol Pumping Station, Esso	$100.00
#782, Petrol Pumping Station, Shell	$100.00
#784, Dinky Goods Train Set	$60.00
#785, Service Station	$270.00
#786, Tyre Rack	$60.00
#787, Lightning Kit	$35.00
#796, Healey Sports Boat	$40.00
#798, Express Passenger Train	$170.00
#801, Mini USS Enterprise	$60.00
#802, Mini Klingon Cruiser	$60.00
#815, Panhard Armoured Tank	$150.00
#816, Berliet Missile Launcher	$275.00
#817, AMX 13-Ton Tank	$125.00
#822, M3 Half-Track	$125.00
#884, Brockway Bridge Truck	$300.00
#893, UNIC Boilot Car Transporter	$175.00
#893, UNIC Pipe-Line Transporter	$175.00
#900, Building Site Gift Set	$1,500.00
#901, Foden Diesel 8 Wheel, see #501	
#902, Foden Flat Truck, see #502	
#903, Foden Flat Truck w/Tailboard, see #503	
#905, Foden Flat Truck w/Chains, see #505	
#908, Mighty Antar w/Transformer	$750.00
#911, Guy 4-Ton Lorry, see #511	
#912, Guy Flat Truck, see #512	
#913, Guy Flat Truck w/Tailboard, see #513	
#914, AEC Articulated Lorry	$200.00
#915, AEC & Flat Trailer	$80.00
#917, Mercedes Benz Truck & Trailer	$120.00
#917, Mercedes Benz Truck & Trailer, Munsterland	$300.00

#918, Guy Van, Ever Ready, $350.00.

#919, Guy Van, Golden Shred	$1,000.00
#920, Guy Warrior Van, Heinz	$3,000.00
#921, Bedford Articulated Lorry	$200.00
#922, Big Bedford Lorry	$200.00
#923, Big Bedford Van, Heinz Baked Beans can	$600.00
#923, Big Bedford Van, Heinz Ketchup bottle	$2,000.00
#924, Aveling-Barford Dumper	$75.00
#925, Leyland Dump Truck	$250.00
#930, Bedford Pallet-Jekta Van, Dinky Toys	$300.00
#931, Bedford Comet Lorry, bl & brn	$500.00
#931, Leyland Comet Lorry, all colors other than bl or brn	$300.00
#932, Leyland Comet Wagon w/Tailboard	$300.00
#933, Leyland Cement Wagon	$200.00
#934, Leyland Octopus Wagon, all colors other than bl or yel	$400.00
#934, Leyland Octopus Wagon, bl & yel	$2,000.00
#935, Leyland Octopus Flat Truck w/Chains, bl cab	$3,000.00
#935, Leyland Octopus Flat Truck w/Chains, gr & gray	$2,000.00
#936, Leyland 8-Wheel Test Chassis	$150.00
#940, Mercedes Benz Truck	$60.00
#941, Foden Tanker, Mobilgas	$750.00
#942, Foden Tanker, Regent	$600.00
#943, Leyland Octopus Tanker, Esso	$500.00
#944, Shell-BP Fuel Tanker	$300.00
#944, Shell-BP Fuel Tanker, red wheels	$500.00
#945, AEC Fuel Tanker, Esso	$150.00
#945, AEC Fuel Tanker, Lucas	$175.00
#948, Tractor-Trailer, McLean	$300.00
#949, Wayne School Bus	$350.00
#950, Foden S20 Fuel Tanker, Burmah	$100.00
#950, Foden S20 Fuel Tanker, Shell	$100.00
#951, Trailer	$50.00
#952, Vega Major Luxury Coach	$150.00
#953, Continental Touring Coach	$400.00
#954, Fire Station	$400.00
#954, Vega Major Luxury Coach, no lights	$130.00
#955, Fire Engine	$100.00
#956, Turntable Fire Escape, Bedford	$150.00
#956, Turntable Fire Escape, Berliet	$250.00
#957, Fire Services Gift Set	$600.00
#958, Snow Plough	$300.00
#959, Foden Dumper, w/bulldozer blade	$125.00
#960, Lorry-Mounted Concrete Mixer	$125.00
#961, Blaw-Knox Bulldozer, see #561	
#961, Vega Major Luxury Coach	$250.00
#962, Muir-Hill Dumper	$40.00
#963, Blaw-Knox Heavy Tractor	$100.00
#963, Road Grader	$50.00
#964, Elevator Loader	$100.00
#965, Euclid Rear Dump Truck	$80.00
#965, Terex Dump Truck	$275.00
#966, Marrel Multi-Bucket Unit	$160.00
#967, BBC TV Mobile Control Room	$200.00
#967, Muir-Hill Loader & Trencher	$50.00
#968, BBC TV Roving Eye Vehicle	$225.00
#969, BBC TV Extending Mast Vehicle	$225.00
#970, Jones Cantilever Crane	$100.00
#971, Coles Mobile Crane	$120.00

#972, Coles 20-Ton Lorry, mounted crane, yellow and orange, $100.00.

#972, Coles 20-Ton Lorry, mounted crane, yel & blk $200.00
#973, Eaton Yale Tractor Shovel $50.00
#973, Goods Yard Crane...$70.00
#974, AEC Hoyner Transporter.....................................$100.00
#975, Ruston Bucyrus Excavator...................................$375.00
#976, Michigan Tractor Dozer......................................$50.00
#977, Commercial Servicing Platform Vehicle $250.00
#977, Shovel Dozer..$50.00
#978, Refuse Wagon $80.00
#979, Racehorse Transport $450.00
#980, Coles Hydra Truck...$60.00
#980, Horse Box Express $800.00
#981, Horse Box, British Railways $200.00
#982, Pullman Car Transporter.....................................$160.00
#983, Car Carrier & Trailer $350.00
#984, Atlas Digger $60.00
#984, Car Carrier...$225.00
#985, Trailer for Car Carrier..$80.00
#986, Mighty Antar Loader & Propeller.........................$400.00
#987, ABC TV Control Room..$375.00
#988, ABC TV Transmitter Van $375.00
#989, Car Carrier, Autotransporters $2,000.00
#990, Transporter Set...$2,500.00
#991, AEC Tanker, Shell Chemicals..............................$225.00
#992, Avro Vulcan Delta Wing Bomber $3,000.00
#994, Loading Ramp for #992.......................................$30.00
#997, Caravelle Air France $400.00
#998, Bristol Britannia Canadian Pacific.......................$350.00
#999, DH Comet Jet...$200.00

Disney

Through the magic of the silver screen, Walt Disney's characters have come to life, and it is virtually impossible to imagine a child growing up without the influence of his genius. As each classic film was introduced, toy manufacturers scurried to fill department store shelves with the dolls, games, battery-ops and windups that carried the likeness of every member of its cast. Though today it is the toys of the 1930s and '40s that

are bringing exorbitant prices, later toys are certainly collectible as well, as you'll see in our listings. Even characters as recently introduced as Roger Rabbit already have their own cult following.

For more information we recommend *Character Toys and Collectibles, First and Second Series,* and *Antique & Collectible Toys, 1870-1950* by David Longest; *Stern's Guide to Disney Collectibles* by Michael Stern (there are three in the series); *The Collector's Encyclopedia of Disneyana* by Michael Stern and David Longest; *Disneyana* by Cecil Munsey (Hawthorne Books, 1974); *Disneyana* by Robert Heide and John Gilman; *Walt Disney's Mickey Mouse Memorabilia* by Hillier and Shine (Abrams Inc., 1986); *Tomart's Disneyana Update Magazine*; and *Elmer's Price Guide to Toys* by Elmer Duellman (L-W Books).

Advisors: Joel J. Cohen (C12); Don Hamm (H10), Rocketeer; Allen Day (D1), Roger Rabbit.

See also Battery-Operated; Books; Bubble Bath Containers; Character and Promotional Drinking Glasses; Character Clocks and Watches; Chein; Coloring, Activity and Paint Books; Dakins; Fisher-Price; Games; Lunch Boxes; Marx; Paper Dolls; Pez Dispensers; Pin-Back Buttons; Plastic Figures; Puppets; Puzzles; Records; Toothbrush Holders; ViewMaster; Western; Windups, Friction and Other Mechanicals.

Alice in Wonderland, figure, Tweedle Dum, Shaw, 1940s, w/paper label, EX, P6..$275.00
Alice in Wonderland, figure, Walrus or Mad Hatter, Shaw, 1940s, EX, P6, ea...$475.00
Alice in Wonderland, movie promo packet, 1974, NM, J2...$50.00
Alice in Wonderland, planter, Leeds/WDP, ceramic, dbl style, 7", NM, P6...$135.00
Alice in Wonderland, sheet music, I'm Late, 1951, NM, M8..$22.00
Alice in Wonderland, tea set, early, unused, MIB, J2.......$70.00
Babes in Toyland, Colorforms, WDP, 1961, unused, NM (NM box)..$20.00
Babes in Toyland, Printer Set, Colorforms, 1960, EX (orig box), T2..$20.00
Bambi, figure, American Pottery, 1940s, Bambi looking forward w/head tilted to left, 7½", EX................................$175.00
Bambi, figure, Goebel, 1950s, standing on base beside tree stump, bee-in-V mk, 4", M.......................................$250.00
Bambi, figure, Shaw, 1940s, 7¾", M, P6 ....$135.00
Bambi, handkerchief & storybook set, 1942, 6-pg book w/4 handkerchiefs, NM+, M8.......................................$125.00
Bambi, milk pitcher, Shaw, 1940s, M, P6 ....$175.00
Bambi, perfume lamp, Goebel, figure w/applied glass eyes, stylized bee mk, paper foil label, 6½", M, P6.................$475.00
Bambi, plate, Beswick, 1955, Disneyland souvenir w/mc graphics, 7", M, P6...$85.00
Bambi, printing set, Multi Print of Milano, Italy, 1970s, 7 stamps & ink pad, EX+, M8..$45.00
Bambi, sheet music, Twitterpated, 1942, EX+ $50.00
Big Bad Wolf, figure, bsk, 1930s, 3½", EX $95.00
Black Hole, wastebasket, 1979, litho metal, 11x6½", G, D9.$12.00
Cinderella, cream pitcher, Gus, Weetman Cinderella Ware, England, 1950s, figural china, 3", NM, rare, M8........$75.00
Cinderella, doll, Effanbee, 1985, MIB, J2.....................$50.00
Cinderella, doll, Storybook Small Talk, Mattel, MIB.......$85.00

Cinderella, doll, Storybook Small-Talk, Mattel, non-working, G...$10.00

Cinderella, pattern, for apron, early, unused, M, J2..........$25.00

Cinderella, sheet music, A Dream Is a Wish Your Heart Makes, 1949, EX+, M8...$16.00

Disney, chime toy, possibly German, 1930, features Mickey, Minnie & Felix holding hands, litho tin, 2x2" dia, G, A...$300.00

Disney, colored pencil set, 1950s, MIB, J7.......................$40.00

Disney, feeding set, Dan Brechner paper label, 3-pc set w/mc graphics on bowl, plate & tumbler, unused, M, P6....$95.00

Disney, Happy Birthday Tin Rotating Candle Set, EX, J2..$75.00

Disney, Scramble 4 Faces, Halsam Products, paper lithograph on wood, complete, VG (worn box), $50.00.

Disney, Sleepy Symphonies Slumberwear, Beautex/England, 1938, 2 pr of pajamas featuring Mickey, Donald & Goofy, NMIB, A...$300.00

Disney, song sheet, You Belong to My Heart, 1943, Donald Duck, Panchito & Jose cover, VG+, A3....................$10.00

Disney, tea set, Patriot China, Mickey & friends on teapot, creamer & sugar w/4 place settings, EX (orig box)..$850.00

Disney, tray, Ohio Art, 1935, tin, several characters on gr background, wavy rim, 5x7", NM, A................................$455.00

Disney, tray, Walt Disney, 1961, litho metal w/characters watching Professor Von Drake on TV, 17x12", VG+, D9..$10.00

Disney, tray, 1961, Disney's Wonderful World of Color, litho metal, 17x12", NM...$30.00

Disney, TV tray, 1960s, Mickey & friends on bl background, faces surround yel rim, 9½x14", NM+, M5................$14.00

Disney, Walt Disney Paint Set, Toykraft, 1940, complete, NM (NM box), A...$450.00

Disneyland, hard hat, BF McDonald, 1950s, bl & red, Adventureland, Fantasyland & Frontierland, child sz, EX+, rare, M8...$95.00

Disneyland, lamp, drum-form tin w/mc litho graphics, working, EX, P6...$225.00

Disneyland, Metal Tooling Kit, NM, T1.........................$35.00

Photo courtesy of Dunbar Gallery.

Disneyland Tea Set, 1950s, MIB, D10, $250.00.

Disneyland, tray, mc litho tin w/very primitive map, EX..$75.00

Disneyland, xylophone, mc litho tin w/Main Street & Carousel scenes, EX (NM box), P6.....................................$135.00

Donald Duck, bowl, Post Grape-Nuts Flakes, 1930s, red plastic w/alphabet rim, Beetleware, EX+, M8......................$45.00

Donald Duck, bowls, France/WD, 1940s, hand-pnt & glazed pottery, set of 4, 7" dia (largest), M, M8.......................$250.00

Donald Duck, brush, Henry L Hughes Co, 1930s, image on metal over wood, EX+, M8.....................................$115.00

Donald Duck, bubble pipe, 1950s, w/soap powder & spoon, 8", MIB...$45.00

Donald Duck, cake pan mold, Wilton, 1970s, head only w/orig advertising papers, EX+, M8..................................$35.00

Donald Duck, charm, 1930s, mc enamel figure w/long bill, EX, P6...$95.00

Donald Duck, dexterity game, Germany, 1937, get balls in Donald's eyes, 2¼" dia, EX, A......................................$150.00

Donald Duck, doll, Lars of Italy, wears artist smock w/Le Vagan on sign, felt & wire, 13", EX+, P6..........................$250.00

Donald Duck, figure, bsk, 1930s, w/bugle, 3", NM, M8..$100.00

Donald Duck, figure, celluloid, prewar Japan, w/wooden horse, 6", scarce, NM, A.......................................$2,100.00

Donald Duck, figure, celluloid, Walt Disney, 1930s, long billed, strung body, 4", NM, G16.................................$175.00

Donald Duck, figure, ceramic, Brayton Laguna, EX, P6.$525.00

Donald Duck, figure, compo, WDE, 1930s, 6", rare, VG+, M5...$650.00

Donald Duck, figure, rubber, WD, long-billed w/side-glancing eyes, 5", G, A...$80.00

Donald Duck, lamp base, Leeds, 1940s, ceramic figure standing on base, w/fixture, EX+, M8...............................$125.00

Donald Duck, Man-Egg-Kins book, Paas Dye Co, 1938, complete w/20 cutouts to put on Easter eggs, rare, NM, A........$250.00

Donald Duck, Mini Molding Set, w/orig box, T1.............$65.00

Donald Duck, night light, 1938, 2-D Donald on round base w/cylindrical light, litho tin & paper, 3¾", VG, A.$260.00

Donald Duck, roly poly, Japan, ca 1940, movable arms & legs, chimes when moved, 4", NM, A...............................$260.00

Donald Duck, squeeze toy, 1986, Donald as baby, 7", EX, J7.$8.00

Donald Duck, suspenders, Flying Cadet All Elastic Kiddie Braces, 1950s, w/metal clips, NMOC, M8.................$75.00

Donald Duck, swim goggles, Auburn Rubber, late 1950s-early 1960s, M (EX card), D9 ....$35.00

Donald Duck, toilet soap, box only, Cussons, shows Donald scratching his chin in thinking pose, VG+, K4 ....$35.00

Donald Duck, tractor, Sunruco/Canada, Donald driving tractor, rubber, 5", EX+, M5 ....$115.00

Donald Duck, transfers, McCall's, 1940, 2 patterns to sew, EX+ (orig envelope), M8 ....$60.00

Donald Duck, transfers booklet, England, 1940s, illus cover w/diecut Donald-shaped top, scarce, unused, M, M8.$75.00

Donald Duck, tray, lap type, Casey Jr, 1961, VG+, J6 ......$24.00

Donald Duck, xylophone, WDP, letters of the notes incised on ea musical bar, litho tin, w/orig stick, 4x10", EX, A ..$65.00

Donald Duck & Mickey Mouse, Giant Crayons, Transogram, 1949, different characters on labels, set of 10, NM (M box), A $50.00

Donald Duck & Nephews, wall plaques, WDP, set of 4, 15" Donald/10" Nephews, VG/EX, A $20.00

Donald Duck's Nephew, charm, Huey, Delta, 1940s, sterling silver w/name, ½", rare, NMOC, M8 ....$50.00

Donald Duck's Nephew, figure, vinyl, Japan/WD, movable head, 9", EX $24.00

Duck Tales, stickers, Panini, 1987, complete set of 140 w/book, NM, M8 ....$28.00

Dumbo, bank, Leeds, 1940s, pastels, EX, 6½", P6 ....$95.00

Dumbo, bank, 1950s, metal figure, M, V1 ....$26.00

Elmer & Tillie the Tiger, figure, Goebel, Elmer wrapping his trunk around Tillie as they kiss, 4", scarce, NM $425.00

Fantasia, figure, Satyr #2, Vernon Kiln, 1940, mk on bottom, 3 tiny chips on base o/w M, M8 ....$160.00

Fantasia, figure, Sprite, American Pottery, 1940s, EX, P6 ..$225.00

Ferdinand the Bull, animation cel, 1930s, Courvoisier background, $1,500.00.

Ferdinand the Bull, model sheet, Picador's Horse Model, 1937, orig studio animator sheet, EX, P6 ....$275.00

Ferdinand the Bull, pin, 1930s, mc enamel figure w/rhinestone fence, EX, P6 ....$125.00

Ferdinand the Bull, sheet music, 1938, EX+, M8 ....$20.00

Figaro, see Pinocchio

Gepetto, see Pinocchio

Goofy, figure, bsk, 1930s, 1⅞", EX+, M8 ....$90.00

Goofy, figurine, Goebel, multicolored, NM, $60.00.

Goofy, plaque, Kemper-Thomas, 1940s, Goofy in the hot sun, no thermometer, 4¼x4¼", NM, M8 ....$35.00

Happiest Millionaire, sheet music, 1967, pk illus cover, NM, M8 ....$5.00

Horace Horsecollar, plate, vintage, mc enamel, EX, P6 .$175.00

Jiminy Cricket, see Pinocchio

Jungle Book, doll, Baba Looey, Knickerbocker, 1960s, vinyl head w/plush body, rpl neckerchief, 14", VG, C17 ....$30.00

Lady & the Tramp, dolls, Schuco, Noah's Ark, 3" L, MIB, pr 375.00

Lady & the Tramp, dolls, Schuco, 9" & 13", NM, pr 425.00

Lady & the Tramp, figure, Lady, Hagen-Renaker, 1950s, 3", EX $48.00

Lady & the Tramp, napkin ring, sterling silver w/raised images, oval, NM, rare, M8 ....$125.00

Ludwig Von Drake, umbrella, NM, T1 ....$75.00

Mad Hatter, see Alice in Wonderland

Mary Poppins, bracelet, 1960s, mc charms on gold-tone metal, EX, P6 ....$48.00

Mary Poppins, figure, 1964, ceramic, orig tag, 8", NM, M5 .$65.00

Mary Poppins, nodder, Disneyland, 1960s, pnt wood head & hands on springs, 5", very scarce, M, P6 ....$95.00

Mary Poppins, rug, Mary & Friends, Sears, 45x56", EX+, P6 .$375.00

Mary Poppins, tea set, Chein/WDP, 1964, kettle & tray w/4 table settings, EX, P6 ....$125.00

Mary Poppins, transfers, Rub-Ons, Hasbro, 1964, set of 3, complete, NM (EX+ box), F8 ....$22.00

Mickey Mouse, action toy, celluloid Mickey on wooden hobby horse attached to steel spring rod on wooden base, 5", NM, A $1,000.00

Mickey Mouse, bank, France, ceramic figure of Mickey kneeling w/hands clasped together by smiling face, 6", NM, A ..$225.00

Mickey Mouse, bank, 1971, head form, 12", EX, B10.......$25.00

Mickey Mouse, Big Little Set, Whitman, 1935, Mickey Mouse To Draw & Color, contains 154 of 160 cards, NM (EX box), A...$250.00

Mickey Mouse, birthday card, Hallmark, 1930s, Mickey as sailor, EX+...$50.00

Mickey Mouse, blotter, Post-O Wheat Cereal, 1930s, Mickey w/spoon saying Get My Swell Silverplated Spoon, 3½x6", M8...$50.00

Mickey Mouse, box, Henry L Hughes Co, 1930s, held brush, hinged cover w/walking Mickey, EX+, scarce, M8 ..$115.00

Mickey Mouse, brush & comb set, wood & litho tin brush & plastic (Superior) comb, EX (EX box), A................$115.00

Mickey Mouse, cake mold, Wilton, 1970s, Mickey as band leader, 14", EX+, M8 ....$35.00

Mickey Mouse, calendar, 1930, France, pictures Mickey talking to 2 girls w/umbrellas, celluloid, 5x6", EX, A..........$175.00

Mickey Mouse, camera, Kodak/WDE, early box-type w/image of Mickey & name around view finder, leather hdl, 5x4", EX $250.00

Mickey Mouse, cane, Borgfeldt, 1930s, wood w/compo Mickey at top, 29", EX, A $300.00

Mickey Mouse, colored pencils, Dixon, 1930s, Mickey, Minnie & Horace on box, set of 6, EX+ (EX+ box), M8 .....$165.00

Mickey Mouse, cup, Safetyware, 1930s, pie-eyed Mickey on yel plastic, 3", EX, M8 ....$40.00

Mickey Mouse, dish set, litho metal, w/tray, 7 pcs, EX, G16.$125.00

Mickey Mouse, doll, cloth & vinyl Mouseketeer, 11", M, B3..$18.00

Mickey Mouse, doll, Dean, stuffed cloth, w/toothy grin, 5 fingers & shoe-button eyes, 6", rare, EX $450.00

Mickey Mouse, doll, Gund, 1940s, molded stockinette face w/plush head, body & limbs, felt ears & clothes, 14", VG, A $290.00

Mickey Mouse, doll, Knickerbocker/WDE, 1930s, stuffed cotton w/compo shoes & rubber tail, w/orig ad card, 12", NM.$750.00

Mickey Mouse, doll, Mattel, 1976, Chatter-Chum talker, working, EX, I2 ....$26.00

Mickey Mouse, doll, Playskool, 1988, baseball player w/suction cups, 12", MIB, M15 ....$15.00

Mickey Mouse, doll, Steiff, 1930s, felt w/leatherette eyes, pnt features, gr shorts, yel gloves, no tag, 5", EX, A.......$800.00

Mickey Mouse, doll, Steiff, 1930s, velveteen w/leatherette eyes, pnt features, red shorts, yel gloves, no tag, 7", EX, A $1,150.00

Mickey Mouse, doll, Talk Ups, Mattel, MIB $125.00

Mickey Mouse, doll, Talk Ups, Mattel, non-working, G..$10.00

Mickey Mouse, doll, Tweak 'N Squeak, Gund, 1940s, 12", EX, J6 ....$120.00

Mickey Mouse, doll, Tweak 'N Squeak, Gund, 1940s, 14", NM, J6 ....$95.00

Mickey Mouse, doll, Worlds of Wonder, talker w/movement, working, EX $50.00

Mickey Mouse, doll, 1930s, stuffed cotton sateen & felt, oil-pnt face w/pie eyes & pointed nose, neck ribbon, 12", EX, A..$460.00

Mickey Mouse, Dominoes, Halsam, ea w/raised image of Mickey & WDE, EX+ (EX+ box), A...................................$125.00

Mickey Mouse, fan, prewar Japan, image of Mickey w/moving eyes, paper & wood, 5", M, A...................................$150.00

Mickey Mouse, figures, bisque, set of 4 with Mickey holding different instruments, MIB, $950.00.

Mickey Mouse, figure, bsk, as conductor, Germany, 3", M, A .$185.00

Mickey Mouse, figure, bsk, pie-eyed, gr shorts & brn shoes, Japan, 1¾", P6 ....$75.00

Mickey Mouse, figure, bsk, playing drum, 3", NM, A $70.00

Mickey Mouse, figure, bsk, standing before cactus, Germany, 2¼", M, A..$200.00

Mickey Mouse, figure, bsk, standing w/hands on hips, 2¾", EX, M8...$75.00

Mickey Mouse, figure, bsk, standing w/left hand on hip & right hand extended, 6¾", VG, A $150.00

Mickey Mouse, figure, celluloid, on wooden hobbyhorse, Japan, 6", NM, A...$1,800.00

Mickey Mouse, figure, ceramic, Goebel, 1950s, sitting w/book on log, bee-in-V mk, 3½", NM $425.00

Mickey Mouse, figure, ceramic, Leeds, 1940s, 6½", NM ..$65.00

Mickey Mouse, figure, ceramic, Rosenthal, standing w/toothy smile & drawing gun from holster, 3¼", M, A $300.00

Mickey Mouse, figure, papier-mache w/pipe-cleaner-type arms & legs, 1930s, 3", missing parasols, EX, pr, A $100.00

Mickey Mouse, figure, plastic & rubber, Durham, Naval outfit w/cap & bag, VG, I2..$18.00

Mickey Mouse, figure, rubber, Seiberling, 1930s, 3½", NM, A $100.00

Mickey Mouse, figure, rubber, 1930s, pie-eyed Mickey looking upward & smiling, 9", EX, A $325.00

Mickey Mouse, figure, vinyl, Dell, hiking pose w/sack & pole at shoulder, jtd head, 9", VG, D9 ....$15.00

Mickey Mouse, gas mask, Happynak, series #50, dated November 19, 1936, extremely rare, VG (VG container), A, $3,000.00.

Mickey Mouse, figure, wood, 1930s, fiber tail, disk hands, 4¾", G, A $290.00

Mickey Mouse, figure, wood, 1930s, pop-up head w/leatherette ears, rope arms, bead hands, name on chest decal, 7", G, A $315.00

Mickey Mouse, figure, wood, 1930s, red, blk, yel & white, ball hands & ears, 6", NM, H7 ....$350.00

Mickey Mouse, figures, bsk, Mickey playing drum, saxophone or horn, mc w/gold & gr trim, set of 3, 3", M, P6 ....$295.00

Mickey Mouse, film, Mickey's Quick Exit, Hollywood Film Ent, 16mm, EX+ (EX+ box), M8 ....$22.00

Mickey Mouse, handkerchiefs, WDE, 1930s, shows Mickey in different poses, set of 3, EX (EX box) $200.00

Mickey Mouse, Jax, 1976, w/carrying box, MOC, J6 ......$24.00

Mickey Mouse, joke book, Wheaties/WD, H12 ....$18.00

Mickey Mouse, kaleidoscope, VG, T1 ....$50.00

Mickey Mouse, lamp, Dan Brechner, 1961, 8" ceramic base w/orig mc shade, sm dent o/w EX $125.00

Mickey Mouse, lamp, WDE, 1938, Mickey w/sheath & canteen saluting on base, generic shade, EX $125.00

Mickey Mouse, Lantern Outfit w/Full Color Slides, Ensign Ltd/England, complete, rare, EX (orig box), A $1,000.00

Mickey Mouse, Magic Lantern, Ensign Ltd/WD, 1930s, metal w/separate tin plate w/image of Mickey, 12" L, VG+ (VG box), A $140.00

Mickey Mouse, medallion/key chain, America on Parade, 1976, pewter, NMIB (plastic box), M8 ....$75.00

Mickey Mouse, Mousegetar, Mattel, 1950s, red plastic w/Mickey's face at center, w/booklet, NM (EX+ box), C1 ....$95.00

Mickey Mouse, Movie Jecktor, c WDE, includes 6 orig packaged films, 10½", VG (orig box), A $300.00

Mickey Mouse, Movie Projector #E-18, Keystone, 1930s, w/4 16mm films, 8½", VG (G- box), A $230.00

Mickey Mouse, necklace, WDP, emb image of Mickey on rnd pendant, 1¼" dia, EX, A $10.00

Mickey Mouse, nodder, Disneyland, 1960s, pnt wood head & hands on springs, 3¾", EX, P6 ....$65.00

Mickey Mouse, pencil box, Dixon/WDE, 1935, red w/image of Mickey sleeping on wharf & Donald in boat, 6½x9½", EX, A $100.00

Mickey Mouse, perfume bottle, full-length figure w/hands in pockets, head pulls off to reveal screw cap, 6", NM, A $950.00

Mickey Mouse, pin, Syrocco, 1930s, Mickey as drummer, EX, P6 ....$95.00

Mickey Mouse, pin, 1990s, enameled Mickey w/attached initial, NM, M8 ....$5.00

Mickey Mouse, pin, 2nd Disneyana Convention, 1993, cloisonne, Mickey as band leader, NM, M8 ....$10.00

Mickey Mouse, popcorn popper, Mickey figure moves back & forth as wire mesh popper is shaken, 18", VG+, A ..$210.00

Mickey Mouse, Print Shop, Fulton Specialty #195, wood letters & numbers, EX+ (EX box), M8 ....$95.00

Mickey Mouse, purse, 1930s, cloth w/silkscreened pictures of Mickey playing guitar, tipping hat, etc, 16x13", VG, A $475.00

Mickey Mouse, sheet music, 1942, Der Fuehrer's Face, stamp mk o/w NM, M8 ....$50.00

Mickey Mouse, Shoo-Fly, WDP, 1950s, rocker, image of Mickey in bent-over running postion on sides, 32", VG, A.$200.00

Mickey Mouse, Shooting Gallery, 1970s, MOC, J6 ....$12.00

Mickey Mouse, soda bottle label, Mickey Mouse Lime Rickey, 1940s, mc paper w/Have One With Me, 3¼x4", EX+, rare, M8 ....$135.00

Mickey Mouse, spoon, Post Toasties, 1930s, silverplate, EX+, M8 ....$25.00

Mickey Mouse, stamp pad, WDE, 1930s, mc litho tin, EX, P6 ....$70.00

Mickey Mouse, stroller, RSA/Spain, tin w/circular image of Mickey on seat back, 10", EX, A $700.00

Mickey Mouse, tablet, Whitman/WD, 1940s, w/Mickey, Bongo, the Flying Gauchito & others on cover, EX+, scarce, M8 ....$40.00

Mickey Mouse, tea set, Happynak #651, litho tin, complete w/10x6" cb tray, NMIB, A $125.00

Mickey Mouse, tea set, Japan, 1930s, mc porcelain w/Mickey at different activities, service for 6, M (tape rpr box), P6.....$675.00

Mickey Mouse, tie rack, early 1930s, wood, 9½", rare, EX+, M8 ....$250.00

Mickey Mouse, Tinkersand Pictures, Toy Tinkers/WDE, 1938, 10 various characters to fill w/sand, complete, VG (VG box), A $75.00

Mickey Mouse, tray, litho metal, 11" dia, EX, J7 ....$12.00

Mickey Mouse, wall plaque, as Sherlock Holmes, WDP, 14", EX, A $25.00

Mickey Mouse, Yarn Sewing Set, Marks Bros/WDE, 1930s, sewing cards, yarn & needle, incomplete, EX (VG+ box), A $325.00

Mickey Mouse & Betty Boop, fan, 1930s, shows Mickey sawing chair that Betty is on, wood hdl, 7" dia, scarce, EX+, A $1,100.00

Mickey Mouse & Donald Duck, fire engine, WDP, 1930s, rubber, red, yel & blk, 6½", EX $75.00

Mickey Mouse & Donald Duck, magazine, Cine-Filo, 1937, mc illus cover, EX, J5 ....$45.00

Mickey Mouse & Donald Duck, map, Race to Treasure Island, Standard Oil, 1939, complete w/stickers, 20x27", rare, EX, A $165.00

Mickey Mouse & Donald Duck, night light, Haunted House, Enesco, 1988, MIB, J2 ....$50.00

Mickey Mouse & Donald Duck, rug, Alexander Smith & Sons, 1935, embroidered snowball fight scene, 42x26½", EX, M8...$225.00

Mickey Mouse & Donald Duck & Pluto, tin, England, 1950s, w/other characters on lid, 8-sided, 4x5½", EX+, M8 .$125.00

Mickey Mouse & Minnie, composition book, Powers Paper, 1930s, Mickey & Minnie ride banister rail, VG, scarce, M8....$45.00

Mickey Mouse, pistol, Mickey Mouse Bubble Buster, Kilgore, 1930s, 7", NM, D10, $275.00.

Mickey Mouse & Minnie, cream pitcher, 1930s, pk lustreware w/crude images, crack starting o/w EX+, M8 ....$85.00

Mickey Mouse & Minnie, figures, bsk, bl & red nightshirts, 4", rpt o/w EX+, M8, pr..$275.00

Mickey Mouse & Minnie, figures, wood, 1930s, pnt & jtd w/pie eyes, ball hands, stick legs, 4", VG+, A $200.00

Mickey Mouse & Minnie, hairbrush, Hughes, 1930s, wood hdl mk c WD, EX, P6...$70.00

Mickey Mouse & Minnie, sled, mk WDE, 1930s, wood w/litho image of Minnie beside Mickey on sled, 28", VG, A ..$275.00

Mickey Mouse & Minnie, tapestry, 1930s, mc Mickey serenading Minnie on velvet ground, 16½x17", M, P6 ....$150.00

Mickey Mouse & Minnie, tea set, Chein/WDP, 1940s, litho tin, 12 pcs, EX, P6...$225.00

Mickey Mouse & Minnie & Donald Duck, ruler, Dixon, 1930s, wood, EX, M8 ....$35.00

Mickey Mouse & Minnie, tea set, Nifty/Germany, lustreware, 18 pcs, incomplete, VG+ (orig box), A $165.00

Mickey Mouse & Minnie & Donald Duck & Goofy, Springees, Multiple/WDP, plastic, w/instruments, 4", NM (NM box), A...100.00

Mickey Mouse & Minnie & Donald Duck & Horace, top, Fritz Bueschel, 1930s, litho tin, 9" dia, working, EX, M8 ....$325.00

Mickey Mouse & Minnie & Horace & Pluto, cup & saucer, Faiencerie D'Onnaing, 1930s, china, EX+, rare, M8.$175.00

Mickey Mouse & Minnie & Pluto, figures, wood, Fun-E-Flex, Mickey & Minnie on sled pulled by Pluto, 11", VG+, A...$1,800.00

Mickey Mouse & Minnie & Pluto, tin, French, 1930s, mc litho, 6¼" dia, very rare, NM, M8 ....$325.00

Mickey Mouse & Pluto, figure, Mickey riding Pluto, 2¼", NM, M8...$100.00

Mickey Mouse & Pluto, pin, 1930s, mc enamel, EX, P6..$125.00

Mickey Mouse Club, bank, Mattel, 1957, tin & plastic, EX, I2 ....$70.00

Mickey Mouse Club, Dance-A-Tune, Jaymar, MIB, $125.00.

Mickey Mouse Club, doll stroller, Adco Liberty/WDP, 1950s, litho tin w/mc graphics, 20", EX+, P6......................$295.00

Mickey Mouse Club, Mouseketeer handbag kit, Connecticut Leather/WDP, complete, EX+ (EX box), A...............$50.00

Mickey Mouse Club, nameplate, 1950s, plastic w/Mickey Mouse Club Member & personalized 1st name, 2¼x4", EX+, M8, ea $4.00

Mickey Mouse Club, Plastic Palette Coloring Set, 1950s, plastic figure as palette w/pnt, brushes & pictures, MIP, M8 .$25.00

Mickey Mouse Club, tray, litho tin, 17x12", NM, J7........$40.00

Mickey Mouse Club House, bank, compo, MIB, T1........$25.00

Minnie Mouse, action toy, celluloid Minnie on wooden hobby-horse attached to steel spring rod on wooden base, 5", NM, A $900.00

Minnie Mouse, doll, Dean's Rag, 1930s, orig clothes & label, 8½", EX, P6..$550.00

Minnie Mouse, doll, Lars of Italy, 1940s, blk & wht felt body w/mc outfit, shoes & gloves, 12", EX, P6 ....$325.00

Minnie Mouse, doll, Mattel, 1991, hug to play Twinkle Little Star, lights flash, 16", NRFB, M15 ....$40.00

Mickey Mouse Club, CB Radio, Durham Industries, 1977, MIB, J6, $25.00.

Minnie Mouse, pillowcase, embroidered, framed, 23x20", D10, $150.00.

Minnie Mouse, doll, Sun Rubber, 1950s, 10", VG, M15 ..$65.00

Minnie Mouse, figure, bsk, playing mandolin, 3½", NM, A .$80.00

Minnie Mouse, figure, celluloid, prewar Japan, on wooden hob-byhorse, attached bell, 5", NM, A $1,800.00

Minnie Mouse, figure, wood, Fun-E-Flex, 1930s, 4", EX, A ..$115.00

Minnie Mouse, ring, silver face, EX, B10 ....$48.00

Nightmare Before Christmas, doll, Oogie Boogie, cloth, NM, J6..$30.00

Nightmare Before Christmas, doll, Santa, Applause, 12", M, D8 ....$30.00

Nightmare Before Christmas, dolls, Sally and Jack Skelling-ton, MIB, J6, $350.00 (for Sally); $225.00 (for Jack).

Nightmare Before Christmas, figure, Jack Skellington, Applause, 10", MIP, H4 ....$25.00

Nightmare Before Christmas, figures, PVC, set of 5, M, D8 ..$18.00

Nightmare Before Christmas, pencil topper, figural, J6, ea .$6.00

Nightmare Before Christmas, postcard book, M, H4 ....$14.00

Peter Pan, bell, Tinkerbell, figure stands on globe & jewelled star dangles from her hand, 3½", EX, P6 ....$55.00

Peter Pan, booklet, Admiral Appliances, 1953, promotional item, NM, M17 ....$35.00

Peter Pan, change purse, Tinkerbell, vinyl, EX+, T1 ....$25.00

Peter Pan, Christmas-tree topper, Tinkerbell, Disney, MIB, T1 ....$100.00

Peter Pan, figure, Tinkerbell, Goebel, stylized bee mk, 5½", M, P6 ....$495.00

Peter Pan, music box, Tinkerbell, 1950s, plays It's a Small World, 6½", EX, P6 ....$125.00

Peter Pan, pin, Tinkerbell, 1950s, gr & yel on gold-tone metal, 2", EX, P6 ....$65.00

Peter Pan, pirate ship, Hallmark, 1950s, paper, w/lg Never-Never Land Map, unassembled, NM (orig envelope), A3 ....$225.00

Peter Pan, plate, Tinkerbell, Disneyland, 1960s, flying over cas-tle, 4", NM, M8...$20.00

Peter Pan, record player, G, W5 ....$40.00

Pinocchio, doll, Pinocchio, early 1960s, vinyl head w/bean-bag body, C17...$20.00

Pinocchio, figure, Figaro, Brayton Laguana, 1940s, 3", M, P6.$125.00

Pinocchio, figure, Figaro, Knickerbocker, 1950s, compo w/hand-pnt features, movable head & limbs, 8", VG+, A....$325.00

Pinocchio, figure, Gepetto, Multi-Products, 1940s, wood compo, 5¾", EX $125.00

Pinocchio, figure, Jiminy Cricket, Ideal Novelty/WD, 1940s, jtd wood w/hand-pnt features, 8", scarce, VG+, A $175.00

Pinocchio, figure, Jiminy Cricket, Multi-Products, 1952 United Community Fund Campaign Award, 5½", EX $225.00

Pinocchio, figure, Pinocchio, bsk, 1940s, EX+, M8 ....$50.00

Pinocchio, figure, Pinocchio, ceramic, 1940s, 2½", EX, A3..$25.00

Pinocchio, figure, Pinocchio, compo, Crown Disney USA, jtd arms, 9½", EX, A..$360.00

Pinocchio, figure, Pinocchio, wood compo, Multi-Products, 1940s, 2⅛", M..$75.00

Pinocchio, music box, France, 1950s, red & yel litho tin, turn crank for music, 2½" dia, M, A $110.00

Pinocchio, rug, w/Jiminy Cricket & other characters, 40x19½", EX, I2 ....$40.00

Pinocchio, shovel, Pinocchio & Jiminy Cricket, shovel, Italy, litho tin w/wood hdl, 16", NM, scarce, M8.............$125.00

Pinocchio, squeak toy, Cleo the Goldfish, Sun Rubber, EX, J2 ....$45.00

Pinocchio, stationery sheet, 1940, mc Pinocchio at top, lined, unused, 5¼x4", NM, M8..$20.00

Pinocchio, wall mural, West Germany, 1950s, 150x53", MIB, L4 ....$175.00

Pluto, bank, compo figure, MIB, T1 ....$65.00

Pluto, doll, early 1960s, vinyl head w/beanbag body, EX ..$25.00

Pluto, doll, Schuco, plush, 6", NM, A...........................$150.00

Pluto, doll, 1980, stuffed, 16", EX, J7................................$8.00

Pluto, figure, ceramic, Brayton Laguna, 1930s, sitting or crouch-ing & sniffing, NM, M8, ea $165.00

Pluto, figure, lead, Allied Toys, 1933, mc pnt, 2½", M (original envelope), P6 ....$65.00

Pluto, figure, rubber, Seiberling/WDE, 1935, 7½", rare, EX, A $125.00

Pluto, figure, wood, Fun-E-Flex, 1930s, felt ears, 7", EX, A ..$315.00

Pluto, jump rope, 1970s, MOC, J6 ....$12.00

Pluto, trivet, early, 6", MIB, J2 ....$50.00

Rocketeer, airplane, The Gee Bee, Spectra Star, 1991, yel plas-tic, rubber-band powered replica, 16" W, MIB, P4 ....$35.00

Rocketeer, backpack, leather-like, promo for AMC Theatres, H10 ....$75.00

Rocketeer, beach towel, 2 designs, promo for AMC Theatres, H10, ea..$25.00

Rocketeer, candy container, Topps, plastic helmet, 2½", M, P4 ....$3.00

Rocketeer, Fan Club Membership Button, H10.................$2.00

Rocketeer, Fan Club Membership Card, H10...................$10.00

Rocketeer, figure, bendable PVC, Justoys/Disney, 1991, 6", MOC, P4 ....$5.00

Rocketeer, figure, vinyl, Applause, standing, 9", H10 ......$20.00

Rocketeer, Poster Pen Set, Rose Art #1921, 1991, w/2 11x16" posters & 6 markers, MOC, from $20 to $30.00

Rocketeer, umbrella, Pyramid Handbag Co, H10............$45.00

Rocketeer, wallet, Pyramid Handbag Co, H10 ....$40.00

Roger Rabbit, see Who Framed Roger Rabbit

Roo the Kangaroo, see Winnie the Pooh

Scrooge McDuck, bank, D Brechner, 1950s, EX, M8 ....$65.00

Scrooge McDuck, bank, gum-ball machine, Superior/WD, 1989, 9½", MIB, P4 ....$20.00

Silly Symphony, fan, 1930s, cb on wood stick, advertiser's premium w/scenes on both sides, EX+, scarce, M8.......$110.00

Sleeping Beauty, booklet, Walt Disney's Sleeping Beauty Castle, 1957, EX+, M8...$50.00

Sleeping Beauty, Dress Designer, Colorforms, 1959, EX+ (EX+ box), T2 ....$30.00

Sleeping Beauty, dress-up outfit, Walt Disney, 1950s, MIP, P6 ....$85.00

Sleeping Beauty, Guest Towels To Embroider, Walt Disney, 1950s, MIB, P6 ....$95.00

Sleeping Beauty, Magic Bubble Wand, Gardner, 1959, NMIP (sealed), M8..$25.00

Sleeping Beauty, sewing set, Transogram, complete w/accessories & clothes, EX+ (EX+ box), M8 ....$75.00

Sleeping Beauty, sheet music, 1954, I Wonder, EX+, scarce, M8...$25.00

Sleeping Beauty, squeeze toy, Dell, 1959, kneeling w/forest animals, rubber, EX+, M8 ....$45.00

Snow White, doll, Storybook Small Talk, Mattel, MIB ...$85.00

Snow White, doll, Storybook Small Talk, Mattel, non-working, G $10.00

Snow White & the Seven Dwarfs, booklet, Bendix Appliances, 1953, promotional item, NM, M17......................$35.00

Snow White & the Seven Dwarfs, booklet, Knitting Instructions for Dwarf's Cap, England, 1930s, diecut cover, 9½", M8 ....$165.00

Snow White & the Seven Dwarfs, bracelet, 1938, mc enamel charms on gold-tone metal, EX...............................$250.00

Snow White and the Seven Dwarfs, candy containers, papier mache with mica, $350.00 for the set.

Snow White & the Seven Dwarfs, cereal bowl, WDE, 1930s, red graphics on milk glass, 5" dia, NM, M8......................$75.00

Snow White & the Seven Dwarfs, doll, Ideal, 1937, stuffed cloth, Dopey w/compo head, 12", missing Sleepy o/w 6 dolls, G...$500.00

Snow White & the Seven Dwarfs, dolls, Bashful or Doc, Chad Valley, 1939, stuffed cloth, orig tag, 7", EX+, A, ea .$125.00

Snow White & the Seven Dwarfs, figure, Dopey, Enesco, 1960s, w/name label, 4½", NM, M8 ....$45.00

Snow White & the Seven Dwarfs, figure, Sleepy, bsk, 1930s, EX+, M8..$50.00

Snow White & the Seven Dwarfs, figure, Sleepy, Evan K Shaw, EX $225.00

Snow White & the Seven Dwarfs, figure, Snow White, bsk, 1940s, 4", EX, M8..$50.00

Snow White & the Seven Dwarfs, figure, Snow White, Evan K Shaw, M, P6..$650.00

Snow White & the Seven Dwarfs, figure, Snow White, G Leonardi, holds sides of shirt, hand-pnt ceramic, 12", VG, A..$45.00

Snow White & the Seven Dwarfs, figures, Borgfeldt, 1938, set of 8, 3¼" Snow White, 2½" Dwarfs, EX (VG box).....$825.00

Snow White and the Seven Dwarfs, figures, Seiberling, hard rubber, some faded paint, set of 7, $540.00; Snow White, figure, Seiberling, 1939, hollow rubber, G, $900.00.

Snow White & the Seven Dwarfs, figures, Heissner/W Germany/WDP, pnt ceramic, set of 8, 8" Snow White/6" Dwarfs, EX, A $250.00

Snow White & the Seven Dwarfs, handkerchief, WDE, 1938, mc printed cotton, EX, P6..$48.00

Snow White & the Seven Dwarfs, ironing board, Wolverine, litho metal, 24", EX $35.00

Snow White & the Seven Dwarfs, lantern slide, Silly Symphonies, VG (orig box), A3 ....$50.00

Snow White & the Seven Dwarfs, napkin ring, Bakelite, 1930s, EX+ $45.00

Snow White & the Seven Dwarfs, Par-T-Mask, Dopey or Doc, Einson Freeman/WDE, 1937, paper, M, M8, ea.........$25.00

Snow White & the Seven Dwarfs, planter, Snow White, Leeds, EX+, M8...$45.00

Snow White & the Seven Dwarfs, sheet music, Australia, 1938, complete w/gr cover, VG, M8 ....$12.00

Snow White & the Seven Dwarfs, squeeze toy, Dopey, 1960s, pnt rubber, 4", EX, F8 ....$45.00

Snow White & the Seven Dwarfs, stove, MIB.................$75.00

Snow White & the Seven Dwarfs, tablet, White & Wyckoff, 1930s, illus cover, 8x5", EX, M8...............................$75.00

Snow White & the Seven Dwarfs, tea set, Marx/WDP, china, 23-pc, EX (VG box), A $370.00

Snow White & the Seven Dwarfs, viewer, ca 1940, w/lg film strip, EX+ (EX+ box), A3 ....$120.00

Three Caballeros, sheet music, Australia, 1943, You Belong to My Heart, EX+, M8..................................$10.00

Three Little Pigs, bank, WDE, 1930s, metal, images & We Save Our Coins... on leather cover, 4", scarce, EX+ (EX box), A $175.00

Three Little Pigs, figures, bsk, 1930s, set of 3, EX, P6 ....$145.00

Three Little Pigs, figures, painted bisque, with instruments, 2½", MIB, D10, $450.00.

Three Little Pigs, greeting card, Hallmark, mid-1930s, trifold diecut, EX+, A3 ....$35.00

Three Little Pigs, lantern slides, Silly Symphonies, mid-1930s, set of 24, VG (G box), A3..................................$75.00

Three Little Pigs, tea set plate, Fifer Pig or Fiddler Pig, Japan, lustreware w/tan border, 4⅜", EX, P6, ea $32.00

Tinkerbell, see Peter Pan

Tweedle Dum, see Alice in Wonderland

Uncle Scrooge, rug, 1950s, mc figure watching TV, w/fringe, 34x21", EX, P6..................................$145.00

Walrus, see Alice in Wonderland

Who Framed Roger Rabbit, doll, Roger Rabbit, stuffed, 18", M $55.00

Who Framed Roger Rabbit, figure, Benny the Cab, plush, MIB $50.00

Who Framed Roger Rabbit, figure, Eddie Valiant, LJN, bendable, 6", MOC..................................$5.00

Who Framed Roger Rabbit, figure, Jessica, LJN, bendable, 6", MOC..................................$30.00

Who Framed Roger Rabbit, figure, Judge Doom, LJN, bendable, 6", MOC..................................$5.00

Who Framed Roger Rabbit, figure, Roger Rabbit, Applause, PVC, M $5.00

Who Framed Roger Rabbit, figure, Smart Guy, LJN, bendable, 6", MOC..................................$5.00

Who Framed Roger Rabbit, party bags for party favors, plastic, MIP $20.00

Who Framed Roger Rabbit, party pack, Unique/Disney-Amblin, 1987, complete, MIP, P4 ....$5.00

Winnie the Pooh, ceiling light cover, EX, J2 ....$40.00

Winnie the Pooh, doll, 1960s, stuffed velvet, 6", NM, G16 .$65.00

Winnie the Pooh, jack-in-the-box, working, EX, T1 ....$85.00

Winnie the Pooh, night light, ceramic, w/characters sleeping under lg mushroom, EX, H4 ....$40.00

Winnie the Pooh, rug, Sears, 1964, w/Winnie the Pooh & Eeyore, mc cotton, 34x62", EX, P6 ....$95.00

Winnie the Pooh, bookends, Enesco, 1960s, painted ceramic, M, $425.00.

Winnie the Pooh, squeeze toy, Roo the Kangaroo, NM, T1 ..$28.00

Winnie the Pooh, switch plate, WDP, EX+, I2 ....$6.00

Winnie the Pooh, tea set, Sears, 1964, MIB, P6.............$145.00

Winnie the Pooh, toy box, vinyl, 16x30x15", EX, I2 ....$35.00

101 Dalmatians, poster, 1972, 27x41", NM, J5 ....$15.00

101 Dalmatians, squeeze toy, EX+, T1 ....$25.00

Dollhouse Furniture

Back in the forties and fifties, little girls often spent hour after hour with their dollhouses, keeping house for their imaginary families, cooking on tiny stoves (that sometimes came with scaled-to-fit pots and pans), serving meals in lovely dining rooms, making beds, and rearranging furniture, most of which was plastic, much of which was made by Renwal, Ideal, Marx, Irwin, and Plasco. Jaydon made plastic furniture as well, but sadly never marked it. Tootsietoy produced metal items, many in boxed sets.

Of all of these manufacturers, Renwal and Ideal are considered the most collectible. Renwal's furniture was usually detailed; some pieces had moving parts. Many were made in more than one color, often brightened with decals. Besides the furniture, they made accessory items as well as 'dollhouse' dolls of the whole family. Ideal's Petite Princess line was packaged in sets with wonderful detail, accessorized down to the perfume bottles on the top of the vanity. Ideal furniture and parts are numbered, always with an 'I' prefix. Most Renwal pieces are also numbered.

Advisor: Judith Mosholder (M7).

Acme, Ferris wheel, red w/bl base, 4 yel chairs w/gr seats, M7.$45.00

Acme, rocker, shoofly; red w/wht horsehead, M7 ....$8.00

Acme, rocker, yel w/red trim, M7..................................$4.00

Acme, stroller, pk, M7..................................$6.00

Acme, wagon, gr w/red wheels & hdl, M7 ....$20.00

Allied, highboy, red, M7..................................$3.00

Allied, refrigerator, wht, M7..................................$3.00

Allied, sink, wht, M7 ....$3.00

Allied, table, wht, M7..................................$3.00

Allied, vanity w/bench, red, M7..................................$5.00

Best, cradle, pk, M7...$6.00

Bestmade, corner cupboard, bl, M7 ....$4.00

Blue Box, vanity, tan w/heart-shaped mirror, M7 ....$3.00

Century Products, seesaw, gr w/2 hard plastic babies, bl base, moves & spins, M7 ....$18.00

Commonwealth, watering can, red, M7 ....$6.00

Durham Industries, hobby horse, metal, wht & gr, ½" scale, M7..$8.00

Durham Industries, hutch, metal, bl & wht, doors & drawers open, ½" scale, M7.....................................$8.00

Durham Industries, kitchen cupboard, metal, brn & wht, doors & drawers open, ½" scale, M7 ....$8.00

England, vacuum cleaner, metal, 1920s, 4", EX+, H12.....$35.00

F&F, refrigerator, turq, ½" scale, M7...........................$2.00

F&F, stove, wht, ½" scale, M7..................................$2.00

F&F, trash compactor, lt brn, ½" scale, M7 ....$2.00

Fisher-Price, dresser, wht, 3 drawers w/mirror, M7..............$3.00

Galoob, phonograph w/2 speakers, M7.......................$8.00

Gerber, doll, girl, sitting, yel, M7................................$8.00

Grand Rapids, bed, wood w/stained finish, 1½" scale, M7..$12.00

Grand Rapids, dresser w/mirror, wood w/stained finish, 1½" scale, M7 ....$15.00

Ideal, bed, turq spread, 1969, M7...............................$6.00

Ideal, buffet, dk brn, M7 ....$10.00

Ideal, chair, dining; brn w/yel seat, M7 ....$5.00

Ideal, chair, kitchen; ivory w/red seat, M7 ....$4.00

Ideal, china cupboard, dk marbleized maroon, M7 ....$10.00

Ideal, hamper, ivory, M7...$4.00

Ideal, highboy, ivory w/bl trim, cb back, M7.................$17.00

Ideal, night stand, brn, M7 ....$6.00

Ideal, piano bench, brn, M7.......................................$3.00

Ideal, refrigerator, ivory w/blk trim, M7 ....$15.00

Ideal, sink, ivory w/blk trim, M7 ....$15.00

Ideal, sink, yel & bl, M7 ....$35.00

Ideal, stove, ivory w/blk trim, M7 ....$15.00

Ideal, table, coffee; brn, M7......................................$8.00

Ideal, table, dining; dk maroon swirl, M7....................$15.00

Ideal, table, kitchen; ivory, M7..................................$6.00

Ideal, vacuum, gr upright w/red base, yel hdl, no bag, M7 .$20.00

Ideal, vanity, dk maroon, worn mirror, M7 ....$15.00

Ideal, vanity bench, brn w/red seat, M7 ....$4.00

Ideal Petite Princess, boudoir chaise lounge, #4408-1, bl, M7 .$18.00

Ideal Petite Princess, dining room table, #4421-4, M7 .....$15.00

Ideal Petite Princess, dressing table chair, #4417-2, pk or bl, M7, ea $5.00

Ideal Petite Princess, Grandfather clock, #4423-0, M7 ....$18.00

Ideal Petite Princess, guest dining chair, #4414-9, M7 .....$10.00

Ideal Petite Princess, host dining chair, #4413-1, M7.........$8.00

Ideal Petite Princess, lyre table set, #4426-3, complete, M7..$25.00

Ideal Petite Princess, pedestal table set, #4427-1, M7.......$22.00

Ideal Petite Princess, rolling tea cart, #4424-8, complete, M7 ..$25.00

Ideal Petite Princess, Royal buffet, #4419-8, no accessories, M7 ....$12.00

Ideal Petite Princess, Royal grand piano, #4425-5, no accessories, M7 ....$25.00

Ideal Petite Princess, salon drum chair, #4411-5, gold, M7....$15.00

Ideal Petite Princess, salon wing chair, #4410-7, ivory w/gold brocade, M7 ....$15.00

Ideal Petite Princess, treasure trove cabinet, #4418-0, M7..$12.00

Ideal Young Decorator, armoire, reddish brn swirl, M7 ....$25.00

Ideal Young Decorator, bed, wht w/rose spread, M7 ....$35.00

Ideal Young Decorator, buffet, dk marbleized reddish brn, M7 ....$15.00

Ideal Young Decorator, diaper pail, yel & bl, M7 ....$25.00

Ideal Young Decorator, sofa, straight section, rose, M7 ....$10.00

Ideal Young Decorator, sweeper, bl, red & yel, M7...........$20.00

Ideal Young Decorator, vanity, reddish brn swirl, M7 ......$20.00

Ideal Young Decorator, vanity bench, wht w/rose seat, M7 ..$8.00

Imagination, console TV, gr, M7.................................$2.00

Imagination, patio set w/picnic table, umbrella, pole, bench & BBQ pit, M7 ....$15.00

Imagination, refrigerator, yel, M7..............................$2.00

Imagination, toilet, yel, M7 ....$2.00

Irwin, mop & pail, orig NM card, M7 ....$18.00

Jaydon, buffet, reddish brn, M7..................................$4.00

Jaydon, corner cupboard, reddish brn, M7....................$4.00

Jaydon, sofa, red w/brn trim, M7 ....$10.00

Jeryco, stroller, pk, orig box, M7.................................$8.00

JP Co, hutch, brn, M7...$4.00

Lundby, kitchen set, sink w/upper cabinets & stove w/upper cabinets, orig box, M7 ....$25.00

Marx, bathroom set w/tub, toilet, sink & chair, soft plastic, lt bl, NM, F5...$16.50

Marx, bathroom set w/tub, toilet, sink & hamper, hard plastic, ivory, ¾" scale, M7 ....$20.00

Marx, bed, bright yel, hard plastic, ¾" scale, M7 ....$5.00

Marx, bedroom set w/bed, vanity & bench, chair, highboy, nightstand & lamp, hard plastic, yel, ¾" scale, M7 ...$30.00

Marx, buffet, dk maroon swirl, hard plastic, ¾" scale, M7 ..$5.00

Marx, buffet, med maroon swirl, hard plastic, ½" scale, M7..$2.00

Marx, chair, armless; pale bl, hard plastic, ½" scale, M7.....$2.00

Marx, chair, captain's; red, soft plastic, ½" scale, M7 ....$3.00

Marx, chair, living room; red w/decal, tufted back style, hard plastic, ¾" scale, M7 ....$5.00

Marx, china cupboard, dk brn, hard plastic, ½" scale, M7..$2.00

Marx, crib, pk, soft plastic, ¾" scale, M7....................$3.00

Marx, dining room set w/table, buffet, china cupboard & 1 chair, hard plastic, maroon swirl, ¾" scale, M7...................$15.00

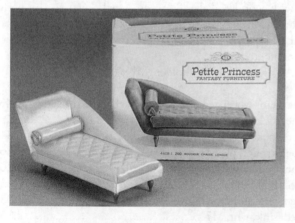

Ideal Petite Princess, boudoir chaise lounge, #4408-1, pink, MIB, $25.00.

Marx, dining room set w/table, hutch, 2 host & 2 side chairs, soft plastic, brn, ¾" scale, M7......................$18.00

Marx, dresser, pk, low style, hard plastic, ½" scale, M7 ......$2.00

Marx, end table, red, hard plastic, ¾" scale, M7 ....$5.00

Marx, hamper, ivory, hard plastic, ½" scale, M7................$2.00

Marx, hamper, lt yel, soft plastic, ½" scale, M7.................$3.00

Marx, hamper, peach, hard plastic, ¾" scale, M7...............$5.00

Marx, highboy, yel, hard plastic, ½" scale, M7..................$2.00

Marx, highboy, yel, hard plastic, ¾" scale, M7..................$5.00

Marx, kitchen set w/sink, stove, refrigerator, counter & 4 chairs, hard plastic, ivory, ¾" scale, M7 ....$32.00

Marx, laundry basket, dk chartreuse, soft plastic, ¾" scale, M7...$3.00

Marx, night stand, ivory, hard plastic, ¾" scale, M7...........$5.00

Marx, night stand, yel, hard plastic, ½" scale, M7 ....$2.00

Marx, patio & utility room, 11-pc set, lt gr soft plastic, MIP, F5 ....$30.00

Marx, playpen, bl, hard plastic, ¾" scale, M7.....................$5.00

Marx, playpen, pk w/emb Donald Duck, hard plastic, ½" scale, M7...$8.00

Marx, potty chair, pk, soft plastic, ¾" scale, M7 ....$3.00

Marx, refrigerator, wht, hard plastic, ½" scale, M7 ....$2.00

Marx, sink, bl, hard plastic, ¾" scale, M7...........................$5.00

Marx, sink, wht, hard plastic, ½" scale, M7 ....$2.00

Marx, sofa, bl, hard plastic, ¾" scale, M7............................$5.00

Marx, sofa, gr, hard plastic, ½" scale, M7 ....$2.00

Marx, sofa, red, soft plastic, ¾" scale, M7...........................$3.00

Marx, sofa, 2-pc sectional; lt bl, soft plastic, ½" scale, M7..$3.00

Marx, sofa, 3-pc sectional; pale bl, hard plastic, ½" scale, M7 ..$5.00

Marx, stool, pk, hard plastic, ftd, ¾" scale, M7 ....$4.00

Marx, toilet, dk ivory, hard plastic, ½" scale, M7 ....$2.00

Marx, toilet, lt yel, soft plastic, ½" scale, M7 ....$2.00

Marx, toilet, pk, hard plastic, ¾" scale, M7.........................$5.00

Marx, tub, corner; lt yel, soft plastic, ½" scale, M7 ....$3.00

Marx, tub, corner; pk w/fish decal, hard plastic, ¾" scale, M7...$5.00

Marx, tub, ivory, hard plastic, ½" scale, M7.......................$2.00

Marx, TV/phonograph combination, bl, hard plastic, ¾" scale, M7...$5.00

Marx, vanity, lt yel, hard plastic, ¾" scale, M7 ....$5.00

Marx, vanity, yel, hard plastic, ½" scale, M7 ....$2.00

Marx, washer, wht, front-load style, hard plastic, ¾" scale, M7...$5.00

Marx Little Hostess, chair, ivory w/bright pk trim, M7.......$8.00

Marx Little Hostess, chest of drawers, block front, MIB, M7..$12.00

Marx Little Hostess, vanity w/3-way mirror, ivory, M7 ....$12.00

Mattel Littles, armoire, M7..$8.00

Mattel Littles, chair, kitchen; M7...$3.00

Mattel Littles, cradle, M7 ....$3.00

Mattel Littles, dresser, M7 ....$8.00

Mattel Littles, kitchen sink/ice box, M7 ....$10.00

Mattel Littles, sofa, M7..$8.00

Plasco, bathroom set w/sink, tub, toilet, hamper, vanity, bench & paper floor plan, no insert, w/orig box, M7............$75.00

Plasco, buffet, brn or tan, M7, ea $4.00

Plasco, buffet w/top, dk maroon, M7 ....$8.00

Plasco, chair, dining; brn, M7..$3.00

Plasco, chair, living room; yel, no-base style, M7................$3.00

Plasco, crib, dk peach, M7 ....$25.00

Plasco, dining set w/table, buffet, 4 chairs & 2 side tables, brn, no insert, w/orig box, M7 ....$65.00

Plasco, fireplace w/andirons, brn & ivory, M7 ....$12.00

Plasco, hamper, pk, lid opens, M7 ....$4.00

Plasco, highboy, tan w/yel trim, M7 ....$8.00

Plasco, kitchen counter, wht w/bl base, rectangular style, M7 ..$5.00

Plasco, night stand, marbleized, med brn, M7 ....$3.00

Plasco, night stand, mauve, M7 ....$4.00

Plasco, refrigerator, wht, no-base style, M7 ....$3.00

Plasco, sink, bathroom; pk, M7..$4.00

Plasco, sink, kitchen; pk, no-base style, M7 ....$3.00

Plasco, sofa, lt bl w/dk trim, M7..$8.00

Plasco, stove, wht w/bl base, M7 ....$5.00

Plasco, table, coffee; brn, M7...$3.00

Plasco, table, dining; brn, M7..$8.00

Plasco, table, kitchen; lt bl, M7..$5.00

Plasco, table, patio; bl w/ivory legs, no umbrella, M7 ....$4.00

Plasco, vanity, bright pk, no mirror, M7................................$5.00

Plasco, vanity, pk, rnd mirror style w/bench, M7 ....$8.00

Plasco, vanity bench, wht, M7..$3.00

Pyro, refrigerator, ivory, M7...$3.00

Renwal, bathroom scale, #10, red or ivory, M7, ea $8.00

Renwal, bed, #81, brn w/ivory spread, M7...........................$8.00

Photo courtesy of Judith Mosholder.

Renwal, bedroom set, dresser, $20.00; beds, $8.00 each; night stand, $4.00; lamp, $8.00; vanity, $18.00; bench, $3.00.

Renwal, buffet, #D55, brn, drawer opens, M7 ....$8.00

Renwal, chair, barrel; #77, ivory & brn, M7 ....$8.00

Renwal, chair, club; #76, pk w/metallic red trim, M7.......$10.00

Renwal, chair, folding; #109, metallic gold w/dk bl seat, M7..$15.00

Renwal, chair, teacher's; #35, bl, M7 ....$15.00

Renwal, china closet, #K52, ivory, door opens, M7..........$10.00

Renwal, clock, kitchen; #11, ivory or red, M7, ea.............$20.00

Renwal, clock, mantel; #14, red or ivory, M7, ea..............$10.00

Renwal, desk, teacher's; #34, brn, M7 ....$20.00

Renwal, doll, baby, #8, pk, no pnt, M7..................................$8.00

Renwal, doll, brother, #42, tan suit, metal rivets, M7.......$28.00

Renwal, doll, father, #44, tan, plastic rivets, M7 ....$25.00

Renwal, doll, mother, #43, flesh, plastic rivets, no pnt, M7.$25.00

Renwal, doll, mother, #43, rose dress, M (NM box), M7 .$55.00

Renwal, doll, nurse, #43, no-cap style, M7.........................$50.00

Renwal, hamper, #T98, pk, lid opens, M7............................$4.00

Renwal, highboy, #85, brn, drawers open, M7 ....$8.00

Renwal, ironing board, #32, w/iron, pk & bl, M7 ....$22.00

Renwal, kiddie car, #27, yel w/red & bl trim, M7 ....$55.00

Renwal, lamp, table; #71, yel or brn w/ivory shade, M7 ...$8.00

Photo courtesy of Judith Mosholder.

Renwal, Jolly Twins living room set, complete, MIB, M7, from $100.00 to $125.00.

Renwal, night stand, #B84, pk, M7 ....$4.00
Renwal, piano/vanity bench, #75, brn or lt brn swirl, M7, ea.$3.00
Renwal, playpen, #118, pk & bl, M7................................$15.00
Renwal, radio, floor; #79, brn, M7.................................$8.00
Renwal, radio, table; #16, brn, M7...............................$12.00
Renwal, refrigerator, #66, lt turq, door does not shut completely, M7...$10.00
Renwal, server, #D54, brn, drawer opens, M7.....................$8.00

Photo courtesy of Judith Mosholder.

Renwal, sewing machine, #89, $30.00; garbage can with dustpan, #64, $25.00; sister, #41, $25.00.

Renwal, sink, #T96, dk turq w/blk trim, M7 ....$8.00
Renwal, sink, #68, ivory w/blk door, no moving parts, M7.$10.00
Renwal, smoking stand, #13, red & ivory, M7 ....$12.00
Renwal, sofa, #78, metallic gold w/metallic red base, M7.$15.00
Renwal, stool, #12, red w/ivory seat, M7...........................$12.00
Renwal, stove, #K69, ivory w/blk door, no moving parts, M7.$8.00
Renwal, table, cocktail; #72, lt reddish brn, M7 ....$8.00
Renwal, table, dining; #D51, brn, M7 ....$15.00
Renwal, table, end; #L73, brn w/stencil design, rnd, M7 ....$8.00
Renwal, table, folding; #108, turq, M7.............................$15.00
Renwal, table, kitchen; #67, yel, brn or gr, M7, ea $8.00
Renwal, toilet, #T97, pk, no-hdl style, M7 ....$10.00
Renwal, tricycle, #7, red w/bl seat, yel wheels & handlebars, M7...$20.00
Renwal, tub, #T95, pk w/bl trim, M7 ....$7.00

Renwal, vacuum cleaner, yel w/red hdl, worn decal, M7..$15.00
Renwal, vanity, #82, brn w/mirror & finials, M7 ....$18.00
Renwal, washing machine, #31, bl or pk w/decal, M7, ea.$30.00
Strombecker, bathroom set, unfinished w/sandpaper & instructions, 1936, 6-pc, unused, orig box, M7 ....$90.00
Strombecker, bed, pk, ¾" scale, M7 ....$12.00
Strombecker, bedroom set, pk pnt wood, complete 10-pc set, ¾" scale, NRFB, H12 ....$150.00
Strombecker, bedroom set, 2 pnt wood single beds, vanity, bench, night stand, chair, lamps & clock, ¾" scale, MIB, H12 ....$125.00
Strombecker, dresser, pk, tall style, ¾" scale, M7 ....$15.00
Strombecker, kitchen set, unfinished w/sandpaper & instructions, 5-pc set, unused, orig box, M7 ....$75.00
Strombecker, living room set, finished hardwood & velour, 1950s, 5-pc set, MIB, H12 ....$135.00
Strombecker, living room set, unfinished w/sandpaper & instructions, 1936, 5-pc set, orig box, M7 ....$75.00
Strombecker, night stand, pk, ¾" scale, M7 ....$5.00
Strombecker, rocking chair, 1950s, for 8" doll, MIB, H12.$65.00
Strombecker, school room, pnt wood, 1930s-40s, MIB, H12 ....$225.00
Strombecker, sink, bathroom; lt gr, ¾" scale, M7 ....$8.00
Strombecker, tub, lt gr, ¾" scale, M7 ....$8.00
Strombecker, vanity bench, pk, ¾" scale, M7 ....$5.00
Superior, chest of drawers, lt bl, low style, ¾" scale, M7.....$5.00
Superior, hutch, pk, ¾" scale, M7 ....$5.00
Superior, tub, bl, ¾" scale, M7...$5.00
Thomas, doll, baby w/diaper, 2", M7 ....$4.00
Thomas, doll, girl w/raised hand, M7 ....$4.00
Thomas, stroller, bl, M7...$6.00
Tomy Smaller Homes, bathtub, M7 ....$8.00
Tomy Smaller Homes, bentwood rocker, M7.......................$6.00
Tomy Smaller Homes, dresser, w/3 hangers, M7...............$14.00
Tomy Smaller Homes, high wall cabinet, for living room, M7...$8.00
Tomy Smaller Homes, refrigerator, 3 drawers, M7............$12.00
Tomy Smaller Homes, speakers, M7, ea $3.00
Tootsietoy, bathroom set w/tub, sink, toilet, stool & medicine cabinet, ivory, M7 ....$110.00
Tootsietoy, bed, lt pk, open headboard & footboard, M7.$18.00
Tootsietoy, buffet, lt brn, M7 ....$18.00
Tootsietoy, cupboard, ivory, M7.......................................$20.00
Tootsietoy, sofa, gold simulated cane w/red cushions, M7.$25.00
Tootsietoy, table, dining; ivory, M7 ....$15.00
Tootsietoy, telephone, blk metal, 1930s, H12 ....$35.00
Tootsietoy, towel bar, lavender, M7..................................$12.00
Tootsietoy, vanity, pk w/3 mirrors, M7 ....$25.00
Tootsietoy, Victrola, gold, M7..$35.00
Unknown, picnic set, early, 2 blown glasses w/bottle, cheese, bread, plates & checked blanket, MIB, H12............$125.00

Dollhouses

Dollhouses were first made commercially in America in the late 1700s. A century later, Bliss and Schoenhut were making wonderful dollhouses that even yet occasionally turn up on the market, and many were being imported from Germany. During the forties and fifties, American toy makers made a variety of cottages; today they're all collectible.

Advisor: Bob and Marcie Tubbs (T5).
Other Sources: M15

American, side-by-side detailed kitchen unit w/taller living room unit, 2-part litho paper on wood, 16", VG+, A.....**$1,870.00**

Bliss, 1½-story, red slanted roof with attic dormers, extensive front porch with steps, paper lithograph on wood, 20x18", G, A, $1,760.00.

Bliss, 2½-story, 3 dormers & 2 chimneys, balcony & 3-sided porch, paper litho, pnt & stained wood, 1905, VG, A..$3,080.00
Bliss, 2-story, bay window & attic gable, front opens to upper & lower room, paper litho on wood, VG, A $375.00
Bliss, 2-story, bl roof, arched glassine windows w/lace curtains, paper litho on wood, ¾ scale, 14", EX, A $635.00
Bliss, 2-story, yel clapboard, full-length porch & upper balcony w/pediment, 4 rooms, paper litho on wood, 23x20", EX, A $990.00
Christian Hacker, 2-story, cream w/balcony over full-length porch, opens to 4 rooms, stepped base, 1900s, 23x23", EX, A $3,520.00
English, 3-story, beige w/wht trim, 2 bay windows, front opens 3 ways to 6 rooms & hallway w/stairs, 1865, 60x23", G, A $11,000.00
German, 2-story, brick (red) w/red gabled roof, 2 chimneys, wht lattice on 2nd-story porch, 1900, 19x13", EX, A.....$880.00
German, 2-story, brick w/bl roof, half-porch, 2nd story & attic balconies, 4 rooms, 1890, 23x23", EX, A.................$990.00
German, 2-story, brick w/gables, railed porch over front door, basement windows, 1905, 25", EX, A...................$1,650.00

German, 2-story city building, tower entrance, red & gold w/bl roof, glass windows, wood, 17", EX, A.................$2,970.00
German, 2-story stable, center dormer & 2 other front windows, open lower level w/columns, 21x32", EX, A............$550.00
German, 2-story townhouse, red & gold roof w/tower-type dormer, attached fence, wood, 30", EX, A...........$7,700.00
German, 3-story, cream-pnt wood w/red gabled roof & dormers, 2 balconies, lattice trim, 8 rooms, ca 1920, 23x38", VG, A...$825.00
Jayline, 2-story, gr siding over wht w/red bricks, purple roof, 1 chimney, 5 rooms, litho tin, 18½x15", VG, T5.........$50.00
Keystone, similar to No 1229F, w/light & fireplace, 3 front awning hangers, 1 cloth awning, rpt, M7...................$80.00
Marx, Colonial Doll House w/Disney Character Nursery, battery-op lights, EX+, F5......................................$70.00
Marx, split-level, wht roof, gray siding & yel brick, w/fireplace & breakfast bar, set of steps, EX, M7 ....$80.00
Marx, split-level, wht roof, gray siding & yel brick, w/pool & 42-pc furniture set, EX (orig box), M7 ....$120.00
Marx, 2-story, gray roof, red siding & gray stone, patio above utility room, EX, M7......................................$80.00
Marx, 2-story, red roof, patio above garage, ABC nursery, ½" scale, EX, M7 ....$50.00

Photo courtesy of Bob and Marcie Tubbs.

Marx, 1952, lithographed tin, 2-story with 7 rooms, white clapboard over multicolored stone, red roof, 14x38", VG, T5, $95.00.

Marx, 2-story, red roof, patio above utility room, ABC nursery, ½" scale, EX (orig box), M7 ....$75.00
McLoughlin, 2-story, collapsible litho cb w/fold-down garden front, 2 lg rooms, 2 chimneys, 19x17", VG, A.........$580.00
McLoughlin, 2-story, Dolly's Playhouse, open front, interior graphics, 1900, 18x12", EX (orig box), A $440.00
Meritoy, Cape Cod, clapboard & gray stone w/red roof, 3 dormers, 1 chimney, 5 windows, litho tin, 1949, 21x15", M, T5 ....$200.00
Rich, bungalow, wht w/red roof, 4 windows, 2 chimneys, Arts & Crafts-style litho cb, 1930s, 32x21", VG, T5...........$200.00
Rich, 2-story, red roof, bl shutters, 2 porch benches, 2 chimneys, 4 rooms, litho fiberboard, 1940s, 24x16x9", VG, T5....$135.00
Schoenhut, 2-story, brick & stone w/red roof, porch w/turned columns, glass windows, removable roof & side, 23x23", G, A...$1,045.00
Schoenhut, 2-story, brick w/red roof, porch w/litho columns, 2 rooms, 16½x12½", G, A $660.00

T Cohn, 2-story, 6 rooms, 2 patios w/furniture, garage w/car, 4 windows, litho tin, 1951, 28½x13x10", VG, T5 .....$195.00

Tootsietoy, 2-story, cream w/red roof, bl shutters, fold-out attic windows, 2 chimneys, furniture, cb, 1927, 17", EX, A $635.00

Unknown Maker, cupboard-style w/trompe l'oeil brick facade opening to 4 lg rooms, early 1800s, 23x34", G, A ...$575.00

Unknown Maker, 2-story, pitched roof, chimney, yel w/gr, pk & gold trim, opens to 4 furnished rooms, 1890, 45x24", EX, A $29,700.00

Unknown Maker, 2-story, sand-pnt finish, dk gr chamfered trim, hinged front opens to 4 rooms, 1890, 27x12", EX, A..$3,410.00

Unknown Maker, 2-story farmhouse, bl wood clapboard w/gray roof, porch, side is open to 6 furnished rooms, 23x41", VG, A..$2,640.00

Unknown Maker, 2-story Georgian, blk hinged roof, gray w/wht trim, front opens to 4 rooms, 2 chimneys, 23x23", G, A..$715.00

Unknown Maker, 2-story Victorian, gables & gr gingerbread trim, turrets & porches, open back, late 1800s, 23x23", EX, A...$33,000.00

Unknown Maker, 3-story, wht slat-board w/gr gabled roof, sm balcony & 2 porches, 2 lg papered rooms, 34x21x30", EX, A...$330.00

Unknown Maker, 3-story Victorian, wht & gr w/red trim, railed slate-look roof lifts off, papered interior, EX, A....$4,180.00

Unknown Maker (shown in FAO Schwarz), 2½-story, gambrel roof, cream w/gr chamfered wood trim, 1897, 23x52", EX, A $27,500.00

Unknown Maker (shown in FAO Schwarz), 2-story Victorian, hinged front, papered walls, furnished, 1890, 39", EX, A $6,600.00

Wolverine, Colonial Mansion, no garage, ½" scale, EX, M7..$45.00

Wolverine, Country Cottage No 800, 1986, ½" scale, EX, M7..$45.00

Shops and Single Rooms

Butcher's Shop, Germany, lithographed wood with cut-out door and window, complete with figure and meats, 10x15", EX, A, $3,500.00.

Stable, 4 roofless stalls w/metal bar, 3 basket hay feeders, 2 horses pnt on marquee, pnt wood, Germany, 29x44", EX, A.......$3,300.00

Victorian Room, litho columns flank 3-sided room w/bl, red & gold walls & floors, w/table, ca 1900, 7x12x7½", EX, A $250.00

Dolls and Accessories

Obviously the field of dolls cannot be covered in a price guide such as this, but we wanted to touch on some of the later plastic dolls from the fifties and sixties, since so much of the collector interest today is centered on those decades. For in-depth information on dolls of all types, we recommend the many lovely doll books written by authority Pat Smith; all are available from Collector Books. For Ideal dolls, refer to *Collector's Guide to Ideal Dolls* by Judith Izen.

See also Action Figures; Barbie and Friends; Character, TV and Movie Collectibles; GI Joe; and other specific categories.

Baby Dolls

Aimee, Hasbro, 1972, plastic & vinyl, rooted hair, 18", EX .$55.00

Baby Big Eyes, Ideal, 1954-59, soft vinyl, rooted curly hair, orig blanket & nightie, 20", EX..$50.00

Baby Brother Tenderlove, Mattel, 1969, anatomically correct, 16", MIB, M15 ....$35.00

Baby Giggles, Ideal, 1967-69, vinyl, rooted blond hair, pull hands together & she giggles, 18", EX $120.00

Baby Grows Up, Mattel, 1978, grows from 16" to 18", MIB, M15 ....$35.00

Baby Laugh Alot, Remco, 1970, plastic & vinyl, all orig, 16", EX...$30.00

Baby Luv, Eegee, 1973, rare dk hair, all orig, 15", VG, M15 .$25.00

Baby Skates, Mattel, 1982, 15", MIB, M15 ....$35.00

Baby Talk, Galoob, 1986, 18", NRFB, M15 ....$60.00

Baby Wet & Care, Kenner, complete w/accessories, 13", MIB, H12 ....$85.00

Baby's First Baby, Horsman, 1960s, drinks & wets, sleep eyes, 12", MIB, H12..$95.00

Betsy Wetsy, Ideal, 1959, plastic & vinyl, molded hair, redressed, EX...$55.00

Bobbie, Fisher-Price #243, brunette, NRFB, M15 ....$25.00

Bye-Bye Diapers, Mattel, 1981, uses potty chair & claps hands, NRFB, M15...$25.00

Bylo Baby, Horsman, 1972, issued for Montgomery Ward 100th Anniversary, 14", MIB, M15 ....$60.00

Chatterbox, Madame Alexander, 1961, 23", MIB, M15...$215.00

Chew Suzy Chew, Ideal, 1980, 15", NRFB, M15 ....$25.00

Corky, Playmate, 1985, talks w/tape player, 27", MIB, M15 .$165.00

Crissy, Ideal, 1969, orange dress, 19", MIB, M15 ....$40.00

Crissy, Magic Hair; Ideal, 1977, w/5 hairpieces, MIB, M15 ..$100.00

Crissy, Teeny Baby; Ideal, 1992, blond hair, 10", NRFB, M15.$30.00

Crissy, Twirly Bead; Ideal, 1971, 19", MIB, M15.............$45.00

Dancerella, Mattel, 1978, 17", NRFB, M15 ....$35.00

Dream Dancer, Tomy, 1984, twirls, kicks & pirouettes on battery-op stand, 12", NRFB, M15 ....$30.00

Elizabeth, Fisher-Price #210, 1973, Blk version, NRFB, M15..$50.00

First Love, Marx, 1979, bl eyes, poseable, baby powder scent, 16", MIB, M15 ....$35.00

Gabbigale, Kenner, 1972, plastic & vinyl, blond hair, all orig, 18", EX $45.00

Gabbigale, Kenner, 1972, w/tape recorder to repeat what you say, 19", MIB, M15 ....$55.00

Ginny Baby, Vogue, 1960s, vinyl & plastic, rooted blond hair, M $45.00

Jumpsey, Remco, 1970, jumps rope, 15", MIB, M15 ....$75.00

Kathy Tears, Madame Alexander, 1959-62, vinyl, 15", EX..$70.00

Kerry, Ideal, 1971, 19", NRFB, M15.................................$65.00

Kissy, Ideal, 1962, 23", NRFB, M15 ....$155.00

Li'l Drowsy Beans, Mattel, 1980, blond hair, 11", NRFB, M15 ....$20.00

Living Baby Love 'N Touch, Mattel, 1981, fingers move & grasp, Blk version, 14", NRFB, M15......................$30.00

Look-Around Velvet, Ideal, 1972, pull-string movement, 16", 16", MIB, M15 ....$55.00

Magic Baby Tenderlove, Mattel, 1978, complete w/all accessories, 14", MIB, M15 ....$30.00

My First Precious Moments Baby, Rose Art, 1992, 8", NRFB, M15 ....$15.00

New Arrival, Horsman, w/crying voice, MIB, J6 ....$45.00

Newborn Thumbelina, Ideal, 1968-72, vinyl & cloth, rooted blond hair, 9", EX $30.00

Posie, Ideal, 1967, foam-filled with vinyl head and arms, sleep eyes, original dress, EX, $40.00.

Photo courtesy of Pat Smith.

Rub-A-Dub Dolly, Ideal, 1979-80, Blk version, 16", NRFB, M15...$50.00

Sunbonnet Baby, Knickerbocker, 1975, 7", MIP, M15.....$15.00

Teeny Tiny Tears, Playmate, 1991, rare red hair, 10", NRFB, M15...$25.00

Tender Love & Kisses, Mattel, 1976, 14", MIB, M15.......$25.00

Tickletoes, Ideal, 1931-39, stuffed cloth w/rubber arms & legs, organdy dress, 15", EX $100.00

Tiny Baby Tenderlove, Mattel, 1971, molded hair, all orig, M...$20.00

Tippee Toes, Mattel, 1967, w/trike & horse, 16", MIB, M15...$100.00

Tumbling Tomboy, Remco, 1969, plastic & vinyl, all orig, 16", EX...$25.00

Twinkle Eyes, Ideal, 1957-60, soft vinyl, rooted saran ponytail, orig pinafore & bonnet, 19", EX..............................$55.00

Wee Li'l Miss Blk Ballerina, Mattel, 1990, 7", NRFB, M15......$15.00

Wendy Walker, Playgroup, 28", MIB, M15.....................$25.00

Betsy McCall

The tiny 8" Betsy McCall doll was manufactured by the American Character Doll Co. from 1957 through 1963. She was made from high-quality hard plastic with a bisque-like finish and hand-painted features. Betsy came in four hair colors — tosca, red, blond and brunette. She had blue sleep eyes, molded lashes, a winsome smile, and a fully jointed body with bendable knees. On her back there is an identification circle which reads McCall Corp. The basic doll wore a sheer chemise, white taffeta panties, nylon socks, and Maryjane-style shoes and could be purchased for $2.25.

There were two different materials used for tiny Betsy's hair. The first was a soft mohair sewn into fine mesh. Later the rubber scullcap was rooted with saran which was more suitable for washing and combing.

Betsy McCall had an extensive wardrobe with nearly one hundred outfits, each of which could be purchased separately. They were made from wonderful fabrics such as velvet, taffeta, felt, and even real mink. Each ensemble came with the appropriate footwear and was priced under $3.00. Since none of Betsy's clothing was tagged, it is often difficult to identify other than by its square snap closures (although these were used by other companies as well).

Betsy McCall is a highly collectible doll today but is still fairly easy to find at doll shows. The prices remain reasonable for this beautiful clothes horse and her many accessories.

Advisor: Marci Van Ausdall (V2).

See also Clubs and Newsletters.

Case, Standard Plastics Products Inc, 1962, w/bed, bedding & canopy, EX, V2 ....$50.00

From the collection of Marci Van Ausdall. Photo courtesy of Leslie Robinson.

Doll, starter kit #9300, blond hair with side-part, complete, EX (worn card), $175.00.

Doll, Uneeda, all orig, 11½", V2 ....$45.00
Doll, w/2 hair clips, G color, nude, EX, V2, minimum value $100.00
Doll, 1st year bridal outfit, complete, EX, V2 ....$150.00
Doll, 1958, printed nylon teddy, socks & wht shoes, all orig, 8", MIB, minimum value $195.00
Outfit, Cotillion #1, complete w/slip & panties, for 8" doll, EX, V2 ....$75.00
Outfit, School Days, dress & hat, 1958, for 14" Am Character doll, EX, V2 ....$50.00
Outfit, Sweet Dreams, for 8" doll, VG, V2 ....$35.00
Outfit, Zoo Time, w/blk tights, for 8" doll, VG, V2 ....$45.00
Pattern, McCalls #2239, for 8" doll, unused, M, V2 ....$10.00
Record, Sing Along w/Betsy, McCall's, 33⅓ rpm, EX, V2..$25.00
Starter Set #9300, MOC, V2 ....$175.00

Celebrity and Personality Dolls

Celebrity and character dolls have been widely collected for many years, but they've lately shown a significant increase in demand. Except for the rarer examples, most of these dolls are still fairly easy to find at doll shows, toy auctions, and flea markets, and the majority are priced under $100.00. These are the dolls that bring back memories of childhood TV shows, popular songs, favorite movies and familiar characters. Mego, Mattel, Remco and Hasbro are among the largest manufacturers.

Condition is a very important worth-assessing factor, and if the doll is still in the original box, so much the better! Should the box be unopened (NRFB), the value is further enhanced. Using mint as a standard, add 50% for the same doll mint in the box and 75% if it has never been taken out. On the other hand, dolls in only good or poorer condition drop at a rapid pace.

Henri Yunes (Y1).

Andy Gibb, Ideal, 1979, w/disco dancing stand, 7½", M (EX+ box), B3 ....$50.00

Angie Dickinson (Police Woman), Horsman, 1976, 9", MIB, $40.00.

Photo courtesy of June Moon.

Beatles, Remco, 1964, ea member w/instrument, vinyl & plastic w/lg heads, MIB, ea from $150 to $200.00
Brooke Shields, LJN, 1982, 1st issue, sweater outfit, 11½", MIB $50.00
Brooke Shields, LJN, 1983, 2nd issue, suntan & swimsuit, 11½", rare, NRFB $95.00

Brooke Shields, Prom Party, LJN, 1983, 3rd issue, 11½", rare, MIB, $100.00.

Photo courtesy of Henri Yunes.

Cher, Mego, 1976, 1st issue, pk dress, 12¼", NRFB, M15 ..$45.00
Cher, Mego, 1976, 2nd issue, w/growing hair, 12¼", M (EX+ box), B3 ....$65.00
Cher, Mego, 1981, 3rd issue, red swimsuit, 12¼", M (M box) $45.00
Diahann Carroll (Julia), Mattel, 1969, 1st issue, reddish brn hair, 2-pc nurse outfit, 11½", NRFB $200.00
Diahann Carroll (Julia), Mattel, 1969, 1st issue, reddish brn hair, gold & silver jumpsuit, talker, 11½", NRFB....$250.00
Diahann Carroll (Julia), Mattel, 1970, 2nd issue, dk Afro hair, 1-pc outfit, 11½", NRFB $175.00
Diahann Carroll (Julia), Mattel, 1971, 2nd issue, dk Afro hair, talker, 11½", NRFB..$175.00
Dolly Parton, Eegee, 1980, 1st issue, red jumpsuit, 11½", MIB $55.00
Dolly Parton, Eegee, 1987, new face mold, cowgirl outfit or blk jumpsuit, 11½", MIB, ea...$45.00
Dolly Parton, World Doll, 1987, red gown, 18", NRFB, M15 ....$90.00
Donny & Marie Osmond, Mattel, 1976, gift set, MIB....$100.00
Donny Osmond, Mattel, 1976, 11½", MIB....................$50.00
Dorothy Hamill outfit, Warm Up, 1977, MOC, M15 ......$12.00
Elizabeth Taylor, The Bluebird, Horsman, 1976, w/3 outfits, 12", NRFB $150.00
Elvis Presley, Eugene, 1984, issued in 6 different outfits, 12", MIB, ea, from $60 to..$65.00
Elvis Presley, Hasbro, 1993, Teen Idol, Jail House Rock or '68 Special, ea from numbered edition, 12", MIB, B3, ea ..$40.00

Elvis Presley, World Doll, 1984, Burning Love, vinyl, 21", VG+, I2 ....$110.00

Farrah Fawcett (Jill from Charlie's Angels), Hasbro, 1977, jumpsuit w/scarf, 8½", MOC, D9 ....$35.00

Farrah Fawcett (Jill from Charlie's Angels), Mego, 1976, wht jumpsuit, 12", MIB, M15 ....$50.00

Farrah Fawcett (Jill from Charlie's Angels), Mego, 1981, lavender swimsuit, 12", rare, M (photo box) $65.00

Flip Wilson/Geraldine, Shindana, 1976, stuffed cloth, 16", MIB, M15 ....$65.00

Flo-Jo, LJN, 1989, in pk & bl athletic outfit w/bag, 11½", MIB, M17 ....$60.00

Flo-Jo, outfit, LJN, 1989, 6 different, for 11½" doll, NRFB, ea..$20.00

Groucho Marx, Effanbee, 1983, 17", MIB, M15 ....$90.00

Jaclyn Smith (Charlie's Angels), Hasbro, 1977, 8½", MOC, $35.00.

James Dean, DSI, 1994, Rebel Rouser or City Streets outfit, NRFB, M15, ea $75.00

John Travolta (On Stage...Superstar), Chemtoy, 1977, 12", MIB $55.00

John Wayne, Effanbee, 1981, 1st issue, Legend Series, Spirit of the West Cowboy outfit, 17", MIB $125.00

John Wayne, Effanbee, 1982, 2nd issue, Legend Series, Guardian of the West Calvary outfit, 18", MIB $120.00

Judy Garland (Wizard of Oz), Effanbee, 1984, Great Legends series, w/basket & vinyl Toto, 14½", MIB, M15 ....$95.00

Julie Andrews (Mary Poppins), Horsman, 1964, w/Michael & Jane dolls, 3-pc set, 10", NRFB, C17 ....$150.00

Kate Jackson (Sabrina from Charlie's Angels), Hasbro, 1977, jumpsuit & scarf, 8½", MOC $35.00

Kate Jackson (Sabrina from Charlie's Angels), Mattel, 1978, 11½", M (M box) $50.00

Linda Carter (Wonder Woman), Mego, 1976, 1st issue, includes military uniform, 12", MIB (w/photo)......................$85.00

Linda Carter (Wonder Woman), Mego, 1977, 2nd issue, no extra outfit, MIB (no photo) $60.00

Macaully Caulkin (Kevin from Home Alone), vinyl, screams, MIB, T1 ....$20.00

Madonna, Applause, 1990, Breathless Mahoney, blk evening gown w/gold trim & heels, 10", M17....................$40.00

Mae West, Effanbee, 1982, Legend Series, 18", vinyl, M (EX+ box), B3 ....$70.00

Marie Osmond, Mattel, 1976, 11", MIB..........................$50.00

Marie Osmond, Mattel, 1976, 30", MIB, M15 ....$115.00

Marilyn Monroe, DSI, 1993, issued in 6 different outfits, 11½", NRFB, ea $60.00

Marilyn Monroe, Tri-Star, 1982, issued in 4 different outfits, 16", MIB, ea $110.00

Marilyn Monroe, Tri-Star, 1982, issued in 8 different outfits, 11½", NRFB, ea, from $50 to $100.00

Michael Jackson, LJN, 1984, issued in 4 different outfits, NRFB, ea, from $40 to $50.00

Michael Jackson, outfit, LJN, 1984, American Music Awards, MOC...$25.00

Michael Jackson, outfit, LJN, 1984, Thriller or Billy Jean, for 11½" doll, MOC, ea $25.00

Mr. T, Galoob, 1983, 1st issue, 12", MIB, $50.00.

Mr T, Galoob, 1983, 2nd issue, vinyl, vest & jeans outfit w/accessories, talker, 12", MIB $65.00

New Kids on the Block, 1990, 1st issue, Hangin' Loose, 5 different, vinyl, 12", MIB, ea.......................................$15.00

New Kids on the Block, 1990, 2nd issue, In Concert, 5 different, vinyl, 12", w/casette tape, MIB, ea $20.00

OJ Simpson, Shindana, 1975, football uniform w/ball, 9½", MIB...$95.00

Patty Duke (Patty/Cathy Lane from The Patty Duke Show), Horsman, 1965, vinyl, w/phone, 12½", rare, NRFB ..$400.00

Prince Charles, Goldberger, 1982, vinyl, palace guard or military wedding outfit, 12", NRFB, ea................................$80.00

Prince Charles, Peggy Nesbit/England, 1984, royal admiralty wedding attire, 8", MIB, M17 ....$100.00

Princess Diana, Danbury Mint, 1985, pk gown, shoes, earrings & rose, w/stand, 15", M, H4 ....$110.00

Princess Diana, Goldberger, 1982, vinyl, silver or wedding gown, 11½", NRFB, ea..$80.00

Princess Diana, London Antiques, pnt porcelain w/dk bl lace gown & hat, 16", MIB, M15......................................$60.00

Princess Diana, Peggy Nesbit/England, 1984, wedding outfit, 8", M, M17...$100.00

Real Models Collection (Beverly Johnson), Matchbox #54613, 1989, 11½", NRFB, M15...$35.00

Real Models Collection (Cheryl Tiegs), Matchbox #54612, 1989, NRFB...$35.00

Real Models Collection (Christie Brinkley), Matchbox #54611, 1989, 11½", NRFB..$35.00

Rex Harrison (Dr Dolittle), Mattel, 1967, 1st issue, vinyl w/Polynesia (parrot), 6", MIB...$60.00

Rex Harrison (Dr Dolittle), Mattel, 1967, 2nd issue, w/Pushmi-Pullyu & Polynesia, MIB...$90.00

Rex Harrison (Dr Dolittle), Mattel, 1969, 3rd issue, stuffed body w/vinyl limbs, talker, 24", MIB $130.00

Robert Vaughn (Napoleon Solo from Man From UNCLE), Gilbert, 1965, vinyl, w/accessories, 12½", MIB.......$215.00

Roger Moore (James Bond from Moonraker), Mego, 1979, vinyl, 12", MIB, D8...$95.00

Sally Field (Flying Nun), Hasbro, 1967, vinyl, 5", MIB....$80.00

Sarah Stimson (Little Miss Marker), Ideal, 1980, vinyl, 12", MIB, M17...$40.00

Shaun Cassidy (Joe Hardy from The Hardy Boys), Kenner, 1978, vinyl, 12", NRFB...$50.00

Shirley Temple, Ideal, 1957, flocked bl & pk dress w/tag, 12", VG, M15...$150.00

Shirley Temple, Ideal, 1982, vinyl, issued in 6 different outfits, 8", MIB, ea...$60.00

Shirley Temple, Ideal, 1984, Glad Rags to Riches outfit, 16", M (damaged box), M15 ....$125.00

Shirley Temple, outfit #9770, 1950s, red & wht velvet party dress w/hat & accessories, for 12" doll, complete, MIB, H12.$150.00

Sonny, Mego, 1976, vinyl, wht shirt & jeans, 12", MIB...$65.00

Sonny, outfit, Mego, 1976, 6 different issued, for 12" doll, MIB, ea...$20.00

Suzanne Sommers (Crissy from Three's Company), Mego, 1975, 12½", MIB...$50.00

Suzie Moppet, Tammy Faye Baker, 1985, NRFB, H4.....$45.00

Twiggy, outfit, Trimfit Net Tights, 1967, MOC, J7..........$25.00

Vanilla Ice, THQ (Toy Headquarters), 1991, issued in 3 different outfits, 12", NRFB, ea...$25.00

Vanna White, Pacific Media/Home Shopping Network, 1990, issued in 20 different outfits, NRFB, ea.....................$50.00

Vanna White, Pacific Media/Home Shopping Network, 1992, Special Limited Edition, blk gown, 11½", NRFB......$65.00

Wayne Gretsky, Mattel, 1982, vinyl, The Great Gretsky/Le Magnifique, 11½", M (French & English text on box).....$100.00

Chatty Cathy

In their book, *Chatty Cathy Dolls, An Identification & Value Guide,* authorities Kathy and Don Lewis (L6) tell us that Chatty Cathy (made by Mattel) has been the second most popular doll ever made. She was introduced in the 1960s and came as either a blond or a brunette. For five years, she sold very well. Much of her success can be attributed to the fact that Chatty Cathy talked. By pulling the string on her back, she could respond with eleven different phrases. During her five years of fame, Mattel added to the line with Chatty Baby, Tiny Chatty Baby and Tiny Chatty Brother (the twins), Charmin' Chatty, and finally Singing' Chatty. Charmin' Chatty had 16 interchangeable records. Her voice box was activated in the same manner as the above-mentioned dolls, by means of a pull string located at the base of her neck. The line was brought back in 1969, smaller and with a restyled face, but it was not well received.

Advisor: Kathy and Don Lewis (L6).

See Also Coloring, Activity and Paint Books; Paper Dolls; Puzzles.

Armoire, Chatty Cathy, L6 ....$170.00

Bedspread, Chatty Cathy, twin-sz, L6 ....$200.00

Carrying Case, Chatty Baby, pk or bl, L6......................$20.00

Carrying Case, Tiny Chatty Baby, bl or pk, L6................$20.00

Cover & Pillow Set, Tiny Chatty Baby, L6 ....$55.00

Crib, Tiny Chatty Baby, MIB, L6 ....$200.00

Doll, Black Chatty Baby, M, L6....................................$325.00

Doll, Black Chatty Baby, w/pigtails, M, L6....................$700.00

Doll, Black Chatty Cathy, 1962, pageboy-style hair, M, L6 ....$600.00

Doll, Black Tiny Chatty Baby, M, L6 ....$300.00

Doll, Charmin' Chatty, aburn or blond hair, bl eyes, 1 record, M, L6..$95.00

Doll, Chatty Baby, brunette hair, red pinafore over wht romper, orig tag, MIB, L6...$200.00

Doll, Chatty Baby, open speaker, blond hair, bl eyes, M, L6 ..$75.00

Doll, Chatty Baby, open speaker, brunette hair, bl eyes, M, L6..$90.00

Doll, Chatty Baby, open speaker, brunette hair, brn eyes, M, L6..$125.00

Doll, Chatty Cathy, brunette hair, brn eyes, M, L6........$150.00

Twiggy, Mattel, 1967, rare, MIB, $350.00.

Photo courtesy of Henri Yunes.

Doll, Chatty Cathy, later issue, open speaker grille, blond hair, bl eyes, M, L6 ....$130.00

Doll, Chatty Cathy, later issue, open speaker grille, brunette hair, bl eyes, M, L6 ....$150.00

Doll, Chatty Cathy, later issue, open speaker grille, brunette hair, brn eyes, M, L6 ....$175.00

Doll, Chatty Cathy, mid-year or transitional, brunette hair, brn eyes, M, L6 ....$135.00

Doll, Chatty Cathy, mid-year or transitional, brunette hair, bl eyes, M, L6 ....$125.00

Doll, Chatty Cathy, mid-year or transitional, open speaker, blond hair, bl eyes, M, L6 ....$120.00

Doll, Chatty Cathy, patent pending, brunette hair, bl eyes, M, L6 ....$150.00

Doll, Chatty Cathy, patent pending, cloth over speaker or ring around speaker, blond hair, bl eyes, M, L6..............$150.00

Doll, Chatty Cathy, porcelain, 1980, MIB, L6, $700.00.

Photo courtesy of Kathy Lewis.

Doll, Chatty Cathy, reissue, blond hair, bl eyes, M, L6 ....$55.00

Doll, Chatty Cathy, soft face, w/pigtails, blond, brunette or auburn hair, M, L6....................................$200.00

Doll, Chatty Cathy, unmk prototype, brunette hair, bl eyes, M, L6 ....$145.00

Doll, Chatty Cathy, unmk prototype, brunette hair, brn eyes, M, L6 ....$200.00

Doll, Chatty Cathy, unmk prototype, cloth over speaker, blond hair, bl eyes, M, L6 ....$150.00

Doll, early Chatty Baby, blond hair, bl eyes, ring around speaker, M, L6....................................$90.00

Doll, early Chatty Baby, brunette hair, bl eyes, M, L6......$85.00

Doll, early Chatty Baby, brunette hair, brn eyes, M, L6.$125.00

Doll, Singin' Chatty, blond hair, M, L6 ....$100.00

Doll, Singin' Chatty, brunette hair, M, L6 ....$125.00

Doll, Tiny Chatty Baby, blond hair, bl eyes, M, L6 ....$75.00

Doll, Tiny Chatty Baby, brunette hair, bl eyes, M, L6......$90.00

Doll, Tiny Chatty Baby, brunette hair, brn eyes, M, L6.$125.00

Doll, Timey Tell, blond hair, bl eyes, M, L6 ....$55.00

Jewelry Set, Chatty Cathy, MIP, L6.............................$150.00

Nursery Set, Chatty Baby, NRFB, L6............................$150.00

Outfit, Charmin' Chatty, Cinderella, MIP, L6 ....$75.00

Outfit, Charmin' Chatty, Let's Go Shopping, MIP, L6 ....$75.00

Outfit, Charmin' Chatty, Let's Play Birthday Party, MIP, L6....................................$75.00

Outfit, Charmin' Chatty, Let's Play Nurse, MIP, L6 ....$75.00

Outfit, Charmin' Chatty, Let's Play Pajama Party, MIP, L6..$75.00

Outfit, Charmin' Chatty, Let's Play Tea Party, MIP, L6 ..$90.00

Outfit, Charmin' Chatty, Let's Play Together, MIP, L6 ...$75.00

Outfit, Chatty Baby, Coverall Set, pk or bl, MIP, L6 ....$50.00

Outfit, Chatty Baby, Dots-n-Dash, MIP, L6 ....$125.00

Outfit, Chatty Baby, Leotard Set, MIP, L6 ....$75.00

Outfit, Chatty Baby, Outdoors, MIP, L6........................$75.00

Outfit, Chatty Baby, Party Pink, MIP, L6......................$100.00

Outfit, Chatty Baby, Playtime, MIP, L6..........................$40.00

Outfit, Chatty Baby, Sleeper Set, MIP, L6.......................$50.00

Outfit, Chatty Cathy, Nursery School, MIP, L6 ....$85.00

Outfit, Chatty Cathy, Party Coat, MIP, L6......................$90.00

Outfit, Chatty Cathy, Party Dress, bl gingham, MIP, L6 ..$150.00

Outfit, Chatty Cathy, Pink Peppermint Stick, MIP, L6.$150.00

Outfit, Chatty Cathy, Sleepytime, MIP, L6 ....$80.00

Outfit, Chatty Cathy, Sunday Visit, MIP, L6.................$150.00

Outfit, Chatty Cathy, Sunny Day, MIP, L6....................$150.00

Outfit, Tiny Chatty Baby, Bye-Bye, MIP, L6...................$60.00

Outfit, Tiny Chatty Baby, Fun Time, MIP, L6 ....$100.00

Outfit, Tiny Chatty Baby, Night-Night, MIP, L6............$60.00

Outfit, Tiny Chatty Baby, Party Dress, bl gingham, MIP, L6....................................$150.00

Outfit, Tiny Chatty Baby, Pink Frill, MIP, L6 ....$80.00

Pattern, Chatty Baby, uncut, L6....................................$15.00

Pattern, Chatty Cathy, uncut, L6...................................$15.00

Pencil-Point Bed, Chatty Cathy, L6 ....$200.00

Play Hats, Charmin' Chatty, L6 ....$55.00

Play Table, Chatty Baby, L6..$150.00

Record, VG, M15..$12.00

Stroll-a-Buggy, Chatty Baby, 9-way, complete, L6 ....$225.00

Stroller, Chatty Cathy, 5-way, complete, L6 ....$175.00

Stroller, Chatty Walk'n Talk, L6 ....$175.00

Tea Cart, Chatty Cathy, 2 trays, L6..............................$100.00

Teeter-Totter, Tiny Chatty Baby Twins, L6.................$250.00

Dawn

Dawn and her friends were made by Deluxe Topper, ca 1970s. They're becoming highly collectible, especially when mint in the box. Dawn was a 6" fashion doll, part of a series sold as the Dawn Model Agency. They were issued in boxes already dressed in clothes of the highest style, or you could buy additional outfits, many complete with matching shoes and accessories.

Advisor: Dawn Parrish (P2).

Case, orig issue, NM, C17...$20.00

Dawn's Apartment, w/furniture, MIB................................$50.00

Doll, Dancing Dawn, gr dress w/long red fringe, NRFB, P2 ..$35.00

Doll, Daphne, Dawn Model Agency, gr & silver dress, NRFB, P2....................................$75.00

Doll, Connie Majorette, NRFB, $75.00.

Photo courtesy of Pat Smith.

Doll, Dawn, 2nd issue, NRFB, P2 ....$20.00
Doll, Dawn & Her Music Box, MIB.................................$55.00
Doll, Dawn Head to Toe, pk & silver dress, NRFB, P2 ....$90.00
Doll, Dawn Majorette, NRFB, P2....................................$90.00
Doll, Denise, Dawn Model Agency, gold dress w/fur, MIB (no
    cellophane), P2 ....$40.00
Doll, Gary, NRFB, C17 ....$40.00
Doll, Glori, 2nd version, w/bangs, NRFB, P2...................$30.00
Doll, Kip Majorette, NRFB, P2 ....$35.00
Doll, Longlocks, NRFB...$30.00
Doll, Maureen, Dawn Model Agency, red & gold dress, MIB (no
    cellophane), P2 ....$50.00
Doll, Melanie, Dawn Model Agency, pk & silver dress, NRFB,
    P2 ....$85.00
Outfit, Bluebelle, dress only, EX, P2 ....$5.00
Outfit, Bride, MIP..$25.00
Outfit, Cupid's Beau, dress, boots & hat, M, P2..................$5.00
Outfit, Gala Go-Go, #0621, NRFB, P2 ....$30.00
Outfit, Glamour Jams, #8124, NRFB, P2 ....$25.00
Outfit, Green Slink, dress only, EX, P2 ....$5.00
Outfit, Midnight Lace, nightie & robe, G, P2.....................$3.00
Outfit, Pajama Drama, top & pants, M, P2 ....$10.00
Outfit, Peek-A-Boo Poncho, top & pants, M, P2 ....$8.00
Outfit, Silver Sparkler, #8120, NRFB, P2 ....$25.00
Outfit, Up, Up & Away!, #8394, missing shirt, P2...........$15.00

Flatsys

Flatsy dolls were a product of the Ideal Novelty and Toy Company. They were produced from 1968 until 1970 in 2", 5" and 8" sizes. There was only one boy in the 5" line; all were dressed in seventies' fashions, and not only clothing but accessory items such as bicycles were made as well.
    Advisor: Dawn Parrish (P2).

Bonnie Flatsy, sailing, NRFB (tear in cellophane), P2 .....$55.00

Candy Mountain Flatsy, lavender ice cream truck w/pk wheels,
    P2 ....$15.00
Cookie Flatsy, w/bl & red stove, P2.................................$12.00
Dale Fashion Flatsy, hot pk maxi, NRFB, P2 ....$60.00
Fall Mini Flatsy Collection, NRFB, P2.............................$65.00
Filly Flatsy, cowgirl outfit slightly faded, P2 ....$10.00
Flatsy Casey, NRFP, C17...$65.00
Flatsy Townhouse, house only, P2...................................$35.00
Flower Time Mini Flatsys, missing plastic fr, EX, C17......$40.00
Gwen Fashion Flatsy, 1973, gr hair, peach poncho & boots, 9",
    NRFB, P2 ....$65.00
Nancy Flatsy, nurse w/baby carriage, P2..........................$15.00
Rally Flatsy, w/car in picture fr, 5", VG, M15 ....$35.00
Sandy Flatsy, beach outfit, faded, NRFB, P2.....................$50.00

Spinderella Flatsy, 1970, M, $30.00.

Holly Hobbie

About 1970 a young homemaker and mother, Holly Hobbie, approached the American Greeting Company with some charming country-styled drawings of children. Since that time over four hundred items have been made with almost all being marked HH, H. Hobbie, or Holly Hobbie. See also Clubs and Newsletters.
    Helen McCale (M13)

Activity Table, Holly Hobbie decal, 1976, VG $20.00
Bench/Toy Chest, Holly Hobbie & Heather decal, 1976,
    VG $30.00
Bookcase/Toy Chest, Holly Hobbie & Heather decal, 1976,
    VG $35.00
Cash Register, Holly Hobbie, VG $12.00
Craft Kit, Holly Hobbie Bake-A-Craft, 1976, VG $5.00
Craft Kit, Holly Hobbie Country House, 1976, VG $8.00
Craft Kit, Holly Hobbie or Heather Cast 'N Paint, 1976, VG,
    ea...$10.00
Cricket Rocker, Holly Hobbie decal, 1976, VG $25.00
Doll, Country Fun Holly Hobbie, 1989, 16", NRFB........$20.00

Doll, Amy, 6", MIB, $6.00.

Doll, Grandma Holly, Knickerbocker, cloth, 14", MIB $15.00
Doll, Grandma Holly, Knickerbocker, cloth, 24", MIB $25.00
Doll, Holiday Holly Hobbie, 1988, berry scented, 18", NRFB ..$35.00
Doll, Holly Hobbie, Heather, Amy or Carrie, Knickerbocker, cloth, 6", MIB, ea $6.00
Doll, Holly Hobbie, Heather, Amy or Carrie, Knickerbocker, cloth, 9", MIB, ea $10.00
Doll, Holly Hobbie, Heather, Amy or Carrie, Knickerbocker, cloth, 16", MIB, ea $20.00
Doll, Holly Hobbie, Heather, Amy or Carrie, Knickerbocker, cloth, 27", MIB, ea $30.00
Doll, Holly Hobbie, Heather, Amy or Carrie, Knickerbocker, cloth, 33", MIB, ea $40.00
Doll, Holly Hobbie, 1987, apple scented, 12", NRFB, M15 ..$15.00
Doll, Holly Hobbie Bicentennial, Knickerbocker, cloth, 12", MIB $25.00
Doll, Holly Hobbie Day 'N Night, Knickerbocker, cloth, 14", MIB $15.00
Doll, Holly Hobbie Dream Along, Holly, Carrie or Amy, Knickerbocker, cloth, 9", MIB, ea $10.00
Doll, Holly Hobbie Dream Along, Holly, Carrie or Amy, Knickerbocker, cloth, 12", MIB, ea $15.00
Doll, Holly Hobbie Talker, Knickerbocker, cloth, 4 sayings, 16", MIB $25.00
Doll, Little Girl Holly, Knickerbocker, 1980, cloth, 15", MIB ...$25.00
Doll, Robby, Knickerbocker, cloth, 1981, 16", MIB $25.00
Doll, Robby, Knickerbocker, cloth, 1981, 9", MIB $15.00
Gazebo Garden House, 1976, hinged cb sides open to 25" play area, VG $25.00
Highchair, wood w/any of 3 different decals, VG, ea $25.00
Jewelry Box, 1976, Holly Hobbie w/umbrella, musical, 9x4", VG $10.00
Phonograph w/Gramophone Horn, Holly Hobbie decal, battery-op & electric, 1976, VG $30.00
Piano, Vanity Fair, Holly Hobbie, VG $12.00
Playset, Amy, for 6" Amy, Carrie or Holly Hobbie, MIP, ea ..$8.00
Playset, Holly Hobbie, w/house, rocker, hobbyhorse & doghouse, MIP $15.00

Radio, Holly Hobbie sitting in rocking chair, plastic base, VG $20.00
Radio, jewelry/trinket box, bl w/flowers & girl w/parasol, VG $20.00
Radio, old-style radio w/Holly standing to 1 side, VG $20.00
Radio, Sing-A-Long, battery-op, w/microphone, 4¾x6¾x2", VG $20.00
Table & Chairs, Holly Hobbie decal, 1976, 3-pc set, VG $50.00
Tea Set, metal, 1976, 44-pc set, VG $15.00
Teddy Bear, Knickerbocker, pastel, 14", MIB $15.00
Tote Bag, Heather, old-time print, VG $6.00
Tote Bag, Holly Hobbie, patchwork print, VG $6.00
Typewriter, Holly Hobbie, 1977, VG $12.00
Wastebasket, 1974, litho tin, EX, N2 ....$25.00

Jem

The glamorous life of Jem mesmerized little girls who watched her Saturday morning cartoons, and she was a natural as a fashion doll. Hasbro saw the potential in 1985 when they introduced the Jem line of 12" dolls representing her, the rock stars from Jem's musical group, the Holograms, and other members of the cast, including the only boy, Rio, Jem's road manager and Jerrica's boyfriend. Each doll was poseable, jointed at the waist, head and wrists, so that they could be positioned at will with their musical instruments and other accessory items. Their clothing, their makeup, and their hairdos were wonderfully exotic, and their faces were beautifully modeled. The Jem line was discontinued in 1987 after being on the market for only two years. Our values are given for mint-in-box dolls. All loose dolls are valued at about $8.00 each.

Aja, bl hair, w/accessories, complete, MIB $40.00
Ashley, curly blond hair, w/stand, 11", MIB $20.00
Banee, waist-length straight blk hair, w/stand, MIB $20.00
Clash, straight purple hair, complete, MIB $40.00

Jem/Jerrica, Glitter and Gold, MIB, $50.00.

Photo courtesy of Lee Garmon.

Danse, pk & blond hair, invents dance routines, MIB......$40.00

Jem, Roll 'N Curl, 12", NRFB, M15 ....$25.00

Jem Roadster, AM/FM radio in trunk, working, scarce, EX.$150.00

Jem Soundstage, Starlight House #17, from $40 to...........$50.00

Jetta, blk hair w/silver streaks, complete, MIB..................$40.00

Kimber, red hair, w/stand, cassette, instrument & poster, 12½",
    MIB $40.00

Krissie, dk skin w/dk brn curly hair, w/stand, 11", MIB $20.00

Pizzaz, Misfits (bad girls), chartreuse hair, complete, MIB ..$40.00

Raya, pk hair, complete, MIB..$40.00

Rio, Glitter & Gold, complete, 12½", MIB $50.00

Roxy, blond hair, complete, MIB $40.00

Shana, member of the Holograms band, purple hair, complete,
    EX, from $30 to..$40.00

Stormer, curly bl hair, complete, MIB...............................$40.00

Tape Player, piano form w/keyboard, pk, blk & wht plastic
    w/accessories, working, M15......................................$50.00

Video, band member who makes audio tapes, MIB $40.00

Liddle Kiddles

From 1966 to 1971, Mattel produced Liddle Kiddle dolls and accessories, typical of the 'little kid next door.' They were made in sizes ranging from a tiny ¾" up to 4". They were all poseable and had rooted hair that could be restyled. Eventually there were Animiddles and Zoolery Jewelry Kiddles, which were of course animals, and two other series that represented storybook and nursery-rhyme characters. There was a set of extraterrestrials, and lastly in 1979, Sweet Treets dolls were added to the assortment. Loose dolls, if complete and with all their original accessories, are worth about 25% less than the same mint in the box. Dressed, loose dolls with no accessories are worth 75% less. For more information, refer to *Little Kiddles, Identification and Value Guide* by Paris Langford (Collector Books).

    Advisor: Dawn Parrish (P2).

    Other Sources: S14

Alice in Wonderliddle Playset, w/vinyl fold-out playcase, Alice
    & rabbit w/watch, used, VG+, H4 ....$150.00

Anabelle Autodiddle, #3770, car only, P2 ....$12.00

Anabelle Autodiddle, #3770, complete, P2 ....$35.00

Apple Blossom Kologne, #3707, complete w/stand, P2 ....$25.00

Babe Biddle, #3505, complete, P2 ....$55.00

Photo courtesy of Cindy Sabulis.

Babe Biddle and Her Car, #3503, EX, $65.00.

Photo courtesy of Cindy Sabulis.

Alice in Wonderliddle, #3533, missing storybook otherwise complete and EX, $75.00.

Baby Din-Din, #3820, doll only, P2 ....$25.00
Baby Liddle, #3587, complete w/pk carriage, P2.............$130.00
Baby Rockaway, #3819, complete, M, P2 ....$110.00
Beat-A-Diddle, #3510, doll & blk pants, P2 ....$60.00
Blue Beauty, #3585, MIP, P2 ....$35.00
Bluebelle Kologne, #3709, complete w/stand, P2 ....$50.00
Bluey Blooper Kozmic Kiddle, MIP (no hang tag), P2 ...$180.00
Bunson Burnie, #3501, complete, P2 ....$55.00
Calamity Jiddle, missing boots, EX, P2.............................$55.00

Photo courtesy of Cindy Sabulis.

Cases, all EX, from $20.00 to $40.00 each.

Case, #3567, rectangular w/zipper, gr, EX, P2 ....$35.00
Case, #3567, sq train style, hot pk, M, P2 ....$40.00
Case, Kiddle Zoo, NM, V1 ....$22.00
Case, Little Kiddle Klub, EX, M15 ....$22.00
Case, pk vinyl, rectangular, holds 16 dolls, EX $20.00
Case, rnd w/zipper, bl, gr or purple, EX, P2, ea................$35.00
Charlie Brown Skediddler, #3632, complete, P2 ....$20.00
Cinderiddle, #3528, w/gown & broom, VG, P2 ....$75.00
Clown'n, #LK4, red & yel outfit, MIP, P2 ....$35.00
Cook'n, #LK8, MIP, P2 ....$35.00
Dainty Deer, #3637, complete w/tail & pin, P2 ....$35.00
Donald Duck Skediddler, #3628, MIP, P2 ....$75.00
Florence Niddle, #3507, complete, EX, P2 ....$60.00
Flower-Bracelet Jewelry Kiddle, #3447, 1967, EX............$15.00
Flower-Charm Bracelet Jewelry Kiddle, #3747, charm only, P2..$7.00
Flower-Charm Bracelet Jewelry Kiddle, #3747, MIP, P2 ..$25.00
Flower-Pin Kiddle, #3741, complete, P2 ....$20.00
Flower-Ring Kiddle, #3744, complete, P2 ....$20.00
Flower-Ring Kiddle, #3744, MIP, P2.................................$45.00
Freezy Sliddle, #3516, missing boots, G, P2 ....$30.00
Frosty Mint Kone, #3653, complete w/both stands, P2.....$60.00
Gardenia Kologne, #3710, complete w/stand, P2 ....$40.00
Goodnight Kiddle, #3848, w/furniture (missing 1 chair) & pk
    bedspread, P2 ....$50.00
Goofy Skediddler, #3627, MIP (split cellophane), P2 ......$70.00
Gretta Grape, #3728, complete, P2 ....$45.00
Harriet Helididdle, #3768, missing goggles, P2 ....$35.00
Heart Ring, #3744, P2 ....$20.00
Heart-Charm Bracelet Jewelry Kiddle, #3747, MIP, P2....$25.00
Henrietta Horseless Carriage, #3641, dressed doll only, P2...$20.00
Howard Biff Boodle, #3502, complete w/wht shirt & yel wagon,
    P2 ....$65.00

Photo courtesy of Cindy Sabulis.

Jewelry Kiddles, loose, from $10.00 to $20.00 each.

Kiddle Komedy Theatre, #3592, MIP, P2 ....$25.00
King & Queen of Hearts Storybook Sweethearts, #3784, MIP,
    P2 ....$165.00
Kleo Kola, #3729, complete, P2 ....$45.00
Lady Lace Tea Party Kiddle, 1969, MIP, H4..................$100.00
Laffy Lemon Kola Kiddle, #3732, complete, C17/P2 ....$45.00
Laffy Lemon Kola Kiddle, #3732, English/French version, MIP,
    P2 ....$75.00
Laverne Locket, #3718, MIP, P2 ....$25.00
Lenore Limousine, #3643, missing feather & shawl, worn shoe
    pnt, P2 ....$60.00
Liddle Biddle Peep, #3544, w/storybook, P2 ....$65.00
Liddle Diddle, #3503, polka-dot pajamas, complete, P2 ...$60.00
Liddle Kiddle Kolony, #3571, MIP $50.00
Liddle Kiddle Kolony, #3571, missing umbrella, M, P2 ....$25.00
Liddle Middle Muffet, #3545, w/cape & both hair ribbons,
    P2 ....$30.00
Liddle Red Riding Hiddle, #3546, faded hood, missing book,
    P2 ....$75.00
Lily of the Valley Kologne, #3706, MIP, P2.......................$50.00
Lola Liddle, #3504, dressed doll w/hat, P2 ....$25.00
Lolli-Grape, #3656, MIP, P2 ....$100.00
Lolli-Mint, #3658, complete w/both stands, P2 ....$45.00
Lolli-Mint, #3658, MIP, P2 ....$75.00
Lorelei Locket, #3717, 1976, MIP, P2 ....$25.00
Loretta Locket, #3722, 1976, MIP, P2 ....$25.00
Lottie Locket, #3719, 1976, MIP, P2 ....$25.00
Lou Locket, #3537, doll & locket, P2................................$20.00
Lucky Lion, #3635, complete w/tail & pin, P2 ....$40.00
Lucky Lion, #3635, missing tail & pin, P2 ....$25.00
Lucy Skediddler, #3631, complete, P2 ....$20.00
Luscious Lime, #3733, non-glitter version, complete, P2 .$45.00
Luvvy Duvvy Kiddle, #3596, w/pin, M, P2 ....$35.00
Mickey Mouse Skediddler, #3629, MIP, P2 ....$75.00
Millie Middle, #3509, complete w/pail & shovel, P2........$85.00
Mini-Kiddles Pop-Up Gingerbread House w/Gretel, #3777,
    loose, P2 ....$30.00
Miss Mouse, #3638, complete w/tail & pin, P2.................$40.00
Nurse'n, #LK7, Totsy outfit, MIP (name sticker missing),
    P2 ....$30.00
Olivia Orange, #3730, complete, P2 ....$35.00

Orange Blossom Kologne, #3711, MIP, P2 ....$60.00

Orange Ice Kone, #3554, MIP, P2....................................$90.00

Orange Meringue, #3585, MIP (name sticker missing), P2...$25.00

Paper Dolls, Liddle Kiddles, #1951, 9 dolls, uncut, M, P2..$50.00

Paper Dolls, Lucky Locket Kiddles, #1992, 7 dolls, uncut, flocked cover, M, P2..$75.00

Paper Dolls, Storybook Kiddles, #1981, uncut, flocked cover, M, P2..$100.00

Peter Paniddle, #3547, w/crocodile, missing feather for hat, P2...$50.00

Pink Funny Bunny, #3532, complete, P2 ....$25.00

Pink Funny Bunny, #3532, MIP, P2 ....$85.00

Posies 'N Pink, #3585, MIP, P2 ....$25.00

Pretty Parlor, #3847, w/3 tables, P2 ....$50.00

Pretty Priddle, #3549, complete w/bl T-strap shoes, M, P2..$75.00

Rah Rah Skediddle, #3788, doll & dress, P2.....................$25.00

Robin Hood & Maid Marion Storybook Sweethearts, #3785, MIP, P2..$150.00

Robin Hood & Maid Marion Storybook Sweethearts, #3785, missing feather o/w M, P2.......................................$75.00

Rolly Twiddle, #3519, missing hair ribbon, P2 ....$165.00

Romeo & Juliet Storybook Sweethearts, #3782, MIP, P2 ...$150.00

Rosebud Kologne, #3702, glitter version, complete w/stand, P2 ....$45.00

Rosemary Roadster, #3642, dressed doll w/hair ribbon, P2 .$22.00

Santa Kiddle, #3596, no gold hoop, P2 ....$20.00

Shelia Skediddle, #3765, MIB, $60.00.

Shirley Skeddiddle, #3766, complete, P2 ....$25.00

Sleeping Biddle, #3527, complete w/castle & variant storybook, P2 ....$200.00

Slipsy Sliddle, #3754, complete, P2................................$60.00

Snap Happy Patio Furniture, #5171, MIP, P2...................$35.00

Soapy Siddle, #3518, robe w/belt, slippers & hair ribbon, P2 ....$25.00

Suki Skediddle, #3767, MIP, P2.....................................$60.00

Surfy Skiddle, #3517, complete w/towel & glasses, P2 .....$65.00

Sweet Pea Kologne, #3705, complete w/stand, P2 ....$25.00

Sweet Pea Kologne, #3705, MIP, P2 ....$50.00

Teeter-Time Baby, #3817, complete, M, P2 ....$75.00

Teeter-Time Baby, #3817, MIP (creased), P2.................$150.00

Tiny Tiger, #3635, complete w/tail & pin, P2 ....$40.00

Totsy, outfit, Out'n #LK6, red jacket, blk hat & gr purse, MIP, P2 ....$35.00

Totsy, outfit, Shop'n #LK2, red jacket, bl skirt & blk hat, MIP, P2 ....$35.00

Totsy, outfit, Sleep'n #LK5, MIP, P2 ....$35.00

Tutti-Frutti Kone, #3655, MIP, P2 ....$75.00

Vanilly Lilly, #2819, MIP, P2 ....$25.00

Violet Kologne, #3703, complete w/stand, P2 ....$25.00

Windy Fliddle, #3514, yel plane, MIP, P2 ....$200.00

Yellow Funny Bunny, #3532, MIP, P2 ....$100.00

Littlechap Family

In 1964 Remco Industries created a family of four fashion dolls that represented an upper-middle class American family. The Littlechaps family consisted of the father, Dr. John Littlechap, his wife, Lisa, and their two children, Judy and Libby. Their clothing and fashion accessories were made in Japan and are of the finest quality. Because these dolls are not as pretty as other fashion dolls of the era and their size and placement of arms and legs made them awkward to dress, children had little interest in them at the time. This lack of interest during the 1960s has created shortages of them for collectors of today. Mint and complete outfits or outfits never-removed-from box are especially desirable to Littlechap collectors. Values listed for loose clothing are for ensembles complete with all their small accessories. If only the main pieces of the outfit are available, then the value could go down significantly.

Advisor: Cindy Sabulis (S14).

Remco's Littlechap Family, Libby (front), Judy (left), John (back), and Lisa (right), EX, $15.00 to $20.00 each.

Case, EX, S14...$20.00

Doll, Doctor John, EX, S14 ....$20.00
Doll, Doctor John, NRFB, S14 ....$60.00
Doll, Judy, EX, S14 ....$20.00
Doll, Judy, NRFB, S14 ....$65.00
Doll, Libby, EX, S14 ....$15.00
Doll, Libby, NRFB, S14 ....$45.00
Doll, Lisa, EX, S14 ....$20.00
Doll, Lisa, NRFB, S14 ....$60.00
Family Room, Bedroom, or Dr John's Office, EX, S14, ea .$125.00
Outfit, Dr John, complete w/accessories, EX, S14, from $15
     to $30.00
Outfit, Dr John, NRFB, S14, from $30 to $50.00
Outfit, Judy, complete w/accessories, EX, S14, from $15 to ..$30.00
Outfit, Judy, NRFB, S14, from $25 to' $50.00
Outfit, Libby, complete w/accessories, EX, S14, from $15 to ..$30.00
Outfit, Libby, NRFB, S14, from $30 to $50.00
Outfit, Lisa, complete w/accessories, EX, S14, from $25 to ...$40.00
Outfit, Lisa, NRFB, S14, from $40 to $75.00

Mattel Talking Dolls

When a range is given, the low side is the suggested value for nonworking, played-with dolls, while the high side is for dolls still mint in box.
     Advisor: Kathy Lewis (L6).
     See also Disney; Character, TV and Movie Memorabilia.

Baby First Step, MIB, L6 ....$150.00
Baby Secret, 1965, vinyl w/foam body, red hair, pull-string
     talker, 18", EX $45.00
Baby See 'N Say, MIB, L6 ....$125.00
Baby Small Talk, MIB, L6 ....$75.00
Matty-Mattel the Talking Boy, L6, MIB $200.00
Sister Belle, MIB, L6 ....$200.00
Sister Small Talk, 1967, plastic & vinyl, rooted blond hair, 10",
     EX $30.00
Teachy Keen, MIB, L6 ....$125.00
Timey Tell, MIB, L6 ....$100.00

Strawberry Shortcake

Strawberry Shortcake came on the market with a bang around 1980. The line included everything to attract small girls — swimsuits, bed linens, blankets, anklets, underclothing, coats, shoes, sleeping bags, dolls and accessories, games, and many other delightful items. Strawberry Shortcake and her friends were short lived, lasting only until the mid-1980s.
     Advisor: Geneva Addy (A5).

Clock, Learn To Tell Time $20.00
Doll, Almond Tea, 5½", MIB $25.00
Doll, Apple Dumpling, cloth, 12", G $25.00
Doll, Cafe Ole, 5½", MIB $25.00
Doll, Merry Berry Worm, MIB $20.00
Doll, Mint Tulip, 5½", MIB $25.00
Doll, Strawberry Shortcake, strawberry scented, 12", NRFB ..$25.00
Doll, Strawberry Shortcake, 15", NM $35.00
Doll Furniture, many items available, ea, from $8 to $10.00

Doll, Raspberry Tart, MIB, $22.00.

Dollhouse $65.00
Record, Sweet Songs, NM, J6 ....$8.00
School Desk, w/attached seat $45.00
School Desk, w/seperate chair $45.00
Stroller, Berry Buggy, Coleco, 1981, M, J6 ....$85.00
Tray, 1981, litho metal, EX $15.00

Tammy

In 1962 the Ideal Novelty and Toy Company introduced their teenage Tammy doll. Slightly pudgy and not quite as sophisticated-looking as some of the teen fashion dolls on the market at the time, Tammy's innocent charm captivated consumers. Her extensive wardrobe and numerous accessories added to her popularity with children. Tammy had a car, a house, and her own catamaran. In addition, a large number of companies obtained licenses to issue products using the 'Tammy' name. Everything from paper dolls to nurse's kits were made with Tammy's image on them. Her success was not confined to the United States; she was also successful in Canada and several other European countries.
     Values quoted are for mint-in-box dolls. Loose dolls are generally about half mint-in-box value, as they are relatively common. Values for other items are for examples in mint condition but without their original packaging.
     Advisor: Cindy Sabulis (S14).

Case, Pepper & Dodi, 1960s, vinyl, EX+, C17 ....$50.00
Catamaran, M, S14 ....$150.00
Colorforms, 1964, missing a few pcs o/w EX, C17 ....$35.00
Doll, Black Tammy, MIB, S14 ....$225.00
Doll, Bud, MIB, S14 ....$325.00
Doll, Dodi, 1964, MIB, S14 ....$65.00
Doll, Dodi, 1964, orig dress w/tag, 9", VG $25.00
Doll, Dodi, 1977, suntan version, 9", MIB, M15 ....$40.00
Doll, Glamour Misty, MIB, S14 ....$90.00

Doll, Grown-Up Tammy, MIB, S14 ....$55.00
Doll, Grown-Up Tammy, 1965, redressed, 12", VG, M15 ..$28.00
Doll, Patty (Montgomery Ward's Exclusive), MIB, S14 .$125.00
Doll, Pepper, 1963, 9", MIB, S14 ....$40.00
Doll, Pepper, 1965, slimmer body, MIB, S14 ....$50.00
Doll, Pos'n Dodi, MIB, S14 ....$75.00
Doll, Pos'n Pepper, 1964, orig clothes, 9", VG $20.00
Doll, Pos'n Pete, MIB, S14 ....$80.00
Doll, Pos'n Salty, MIB, S14 ....$80.00
Doll, Pos'n Tammy & Her Phone Booth, MIB, S14 ....$65.00
Doll, Tammy, MIB, from $45 to $50.00

Doll, Tammy dressed in Snow Bunny outfit #9211, 12", EX, $50.00.

Photo courtesy of Pat Smith.

Doll, Tammy's Dad, MIB, S14 ....$50.00
Doll, Tammy's Mom, MIB, S14 ....$50.00
Doll, Ted, 1964, redressed, 12½", VG $25.00
Doll, Ted (Tammy's brother), 1964, MIB, S14 ....$50.00
Tammy's Car, M, S14, minimum value $75.00
Tammy's Ideal House, M, S14, minimum value $100.00
Tea Set, M, S14 ....$150.00

Tonka

The Aurora line of fashion dolls made by Tonka in 1987 are unique in that their Barbie-like bodies are metallic. There were four in the line, Aurora herself, Crysta, Lustra and Mirra. Their costumes are futuristic, and their eyes are inset, faceted jewels. Their long tresses are shockingly bright – Aurora's is gold, Crysta's is pink, Mirra's blue, and Lustra's lavender. Mattel made a very similar line of dolls; the most notable difference is that they lacked the jewel eyes. Mattel's are dated 1975. Dolls from either series are valued at about $25.00 each, mint in box.

Tressy

American Character's Tressy doll was produced in this country from 1963 to 1967. The unique thing about this 11½"

fashion doll was that her hair 'grew' by pushing a button on her stomach. Tressy also had a 9" little sister named Cricket. These two dolls had numerous fashions and accessories produced for them. Never-removed-from box Tressy and Cricket items are rare, so unless indicated, values listed are for loose, mint items. A never-removed-from box item's worth is at least double its loose value.

Advisor: Cindy Sabulis (S14).

Apartment, M, S14 ....$150.00
Beauty Salon, M, S14 ....$125.00
Case, features Cricket, M, S14 ....$25.00
Case, features Tressy, M, S14 ....$20.00
Doll, Cricket, M, S14 ....$25.00
Doll, Pre-Teen Tressy, M, S14 ....$50.00
Doll, Tressy, M, S14 ....$20.00

Doll, Tressy in Miss America Character outfit, NM, $50.00.

Doll, Tressy w/Magic Makeup Face, M, S14 ....$20.00
Doll Clothes Pattern, M, S14 ....$6.00
Gift Paks w/Doll & Clothing, NRFB, S14, ea, minimum
    value $100.00
Hair Accessory Paks, NRFB, S14, ea $20.00
Hair Dryer, M, S14 ....$40.00
Hair or Cosmetic Accessory Kits, M, S14, ea, minimum value .$50.00
Millinery, M, S14 ....$150.00
Outfits, MOC, S14, ea $20.00
Outfits, NRFB, S14, ea, mimimum value $40.00

Upsy Downsys by Mattel

The Upsy Downsy dolls were made by Mattel during the late 1960s. They were small, 2½" to 3½", made of vinyl and plastic, and some of the group were 'Upsies' that walked on their feet, while others were 'Downsies' that walked or rode fantasy animals while upsidedown.

Advisor: Dawn Parrish (P2).

Baby So-High, #3828, playland board only, P2.................$16.00
Downy Dilly, #3832, NRFB (worn), P2.......................$135.00
Downy Dilly, #3832, playland board only, P2..................$15.00
Flossy Glossy, #3827, doll & playland, P2......................$25.00
Flossy Glossy, #3827, playland board only, P2................$15.00
Miss Information, #3831, NRFB, P2............................$150.00
Mother What Now, #3829, NRFB, P2..........................$150.00
Pocus Hocus, #3820, playland board only, P2.................$16.00
Pudgy Fudgy, #3826, NRFB, P2................................$150.00
Tickle Pickle, #3825, doll, car, bridge, stop sign, connector &
    playland, P2 ....$45.00

Farm Toys

It's entirely probable that more toy tractors have been sold
than real ones. They've been made to represent all makes and
models, of plastic, cast iron, diecast metal, and even wood.
They've been made in at least 1/16th scale, 1/32nd, 1/43rd, and
1/64th. If you buy a 1/16th-scale replica, that small piece of
equipment would have to be sixteen times larger to equal the size
of the real item. Limited editions (meaning that a specific number will be made and no more) and commemorative editions
(made for special events) are usually very popular with collectors.
Many models on the market today are being made by the Ertl
company; Arcade made cast-iron models in the '30s and '40s.

Advisor: John Rammacher (S5).

Agco Allison 6690 Tractor w/Duals, Ertl, 1/64th scale, #1215,
    MIB, S5 ....$3.00
Allis Chalmers Disc Harrow, Am Precision, early 1950s, orange,
    9", G..$65.00
Allis Chalmers Model C Tractor, Am Precision, orange, 7½",
    EX, A $140.00
Allis Chalmers Model U Tractor w/Earth Hauler, Arcade, 1/20
    scale, CI, 1930, 8", MIB $675.00
Allis Chalmers Model WC Tractor, Hubley, red w/bl driver,
    1939, 7", EX...$320.00

**Allis Chalmers Tractor and Manure Spreader, Arcade,
1930s, cast iron, red and green with white rubber tires,
integral driver, 8", EX, D10, from $200.00 to $350.00.**

Allis Chalmers Tractor w/Dump Trailer, CI, red tractor w/gr
    hook trailer, 12", 2 rpl rubber tires, VG, A $85.00

Allis Chalmers 220 Landhandler 4-WD, Ertl, 1995 Toy Farmer,
    1/16th scale, #2623, MIB, S5 ....$80.00
Antique Pump, Ertl, 1/16 scale, red, #4553, MIB, S5 ....$16.00
Avery Tractor Model 18-36, Hubley, 1920, blk, 4¼", VG...$170.00
Case Combine, Vindex, CI, red & silver, revolving cutter reel,
    imitation motor exhaust, 1930, 12", rare, EX, A..$4,625.00
Case IH Forage Harvester, Ertl, 1/64th scale, #201, MIB, S5 .$2.50
Case IH Grain Drill, Ertl, 1/16th scale, #269, MIB, S5 ....$13.50
Case IH Gravity Wagon, Ertl, red, 1/64th scale, #1864, MIB,
    S5 ....$2.50
Case IH Hay Rake, Ertl, 1/64th scale, #210, MIB, S5........$3.00
Case IH Historical Set, Ertl, 1/64th scale, #238, MIB, S5 ..$5.50
Case IH Maxxum 5120 w/Duals, Ertl, 1/64th scale, #241, MIB,
    S5 ....$38.00
Case IH Milk Truck, Ertl, 1/64th scale, #648, MIB, S5 ......$6.00
Case IH Mixer Mill, Ertl, 1/64th scale, #480, MIB, S5 ....$2.50
Case IH Self-Propelled Windrower, Ertl, 1/64th scale, #4405,
    MIB, S5 ....$8.00
Case IH 1660 Combine, Ertl, 1/64th scale, #655, MIB, S5.$10.50
Case IH 1844 Cotton Picker, Ertl, 1/64th scale, #211, MIB,
    S5 ....$6.00
Case IH 2188 Combine, Ertl, 1995 Farm Show Edition, 1/64th
    scale, #4607, MIB, S5 ....$15.00
Case IH 2594 Tractor, Ertl, 1/64th scale, #227, MIB, S5 ...$3.00
Case IH 5130 Row Crop, Ertl, 1/64th scale, #229, MIB, S5 .$3.00
Case IH 66 Series #3 Special Edition, Ertl, 1/64th scale, #4636,
    MIB, S5 ....$28.00
Case IH 7130 Magnum Tractor, Ertl, 1/64th scale, #458, MIB,
    S5 ....$3.00
Case IH 7140 Mechanical Front Drive Tractor, Ertl, 1/64th
    scale, #616, MIB, S5 ....$3.00
Case IH 7150 Front Wheel Assist, Ertl, 1/64th scale, 1992 Farm
    Show Edition, #285, MIB, S5 ....$10.00
Case IH 7250 Magnum Mechanical Front Drive, Ertl, 1/64th
    scale, #4757, MIB, S5 ....$8.00
Case IH 9260 4-WD Tractor, Ertl, 1/64th scale, #231, MIB,
    S5 ....$4.50
Case L Tractor, Ertl, 1/43rd scale, #2554, MIB, S5 ....$5.00
Case L Tractor, Ertl, 150 Year Collector's Edition, 1/16th scale,
    #252, MIB, S5..$35.00
Case 3-Bottom Plow, Vindex, CI, red w/lime gr spoke wheels,
    1930, 10", very rare, EX, A $1,375.00
Case 500 Tractor, Ertl, 1/43rd scale, #2510, MIB, S5 ....$5.00
Case 800, Ertl, Collector's Edition, 1/16th scale, #693, MIB,
    S5 ....$40.00
Case-O-Matic 800, Ertl, National Show Tractor 1990, 1/43rd
    scale, #2616, MIB, S5 ....$26.00
Caterpillar Diesel Tractor, Arcade, 1936, w/driver, pnt CI, yel
    w/metal tracks, exposed engine & radiator, 7", EX..$1,200.00
Co-op E3 Tractor, Advanced Products, orange, 7", EX, A .$250.00
Cockshutt 30 Tractor, Lincoln Products, narrow front, 7", EX,
    A $290.00
Corn Binder, Arcade, 1-row, gr & yel, 3", VG, A $130.00
Corn Binder, Slik, 2-row, aluminum, 5", G, A $15.00
Deutz Allis Mixer Mill, Ertl, 1/64th scale, #2208, MIB, S5...$2.00
Deutz Allis Planter, Ertl, 1/64th scale, #1212, MIB, S5 ......$3.50
Deutz Allis R-50 Combine, Ertl, 1/64th scale, #1284, MIB,
    S5 ....$13.00

Deutz Allis 6260 All Wheel Drive Tractor, Ertl, 1/64th scale, #2232, MIB, S5 ....$3.00

Deutz Allis 7085 Tractor, Ertl, 1/64th scale, #1260, MIB, S5..$3.00

Deutz Allis 7085 Tractor w/Duals, Ertl, 1/64th scale, #2234, MIB, S5 ....$4.00

Deutz Allis 9150 Orlando Show Tractor, Ertl, 1/16th scale, #1280, MIB, S5 ....$190.00

Disk Harrow, Tru-Scale, red with yellow decals, MIB, A, $80.00; Fordson Major Tractor, Chad Valley, blue and red with black tires, 3-point hookup, NMIB, A, $445.00.

Ertl 50th Anniversary 6-pc Tractor Set, 1/64th scale, #4496, MIB, S5 ....$28.00

Farm Set, Hubley, 1950s, w/tractor, 2-wheeled wagon & plow, 6", EX (orig box), A $80.00

Farmall Cub, Ertl, 1/16th scale, 1956-58, #235, MIB, S5 .$20.00

Farmall F-20 Precision Classic, Ertl, 1/16th scale, #294, MIB, S5 ....$95.00

Farmall H w/Man, Ertl, 50th Anniversary Collection, 1/16th scale, #4453, MIB, S5 ....$38.00

Farmall Model M, Arcade, 7½", rpl tires, G, A $245.00

Farmall Model M Tractor, Arcade, gr w/wooden rear wheels, 5½", VG, A $200.00

Farmall Regular Tractor, Arcade, red, 6", VG $800.00

Farmall 140 Tractor, Ertl, 1995 Farm Show Edition, 1/16th scale, #4741, MIB, S5 ....$35.00

Farmall 350 Tractor w/Wide Front End, Ertl, 1/43rd scale, #2244, MIB, S5 ....$5.00

Ferguson TO 20 Tractor, Advanced Products, 3-point hookup, MIB, $560.00.

Ford F Tractor, Ertl, Collector's Edition, 1/16th scale, #872, MIB, S5 ....$45.00

Ford F-250 Pick-Up w/Livestock Trailer, Ertl, 1/64th scale, #311, MIB, S5 ....$5.00

Ford Harvestor Tractor w/Heritage Cards, Ertl, 1/64th scale, #809, MIB, S5 ....$10.00

Ford Holland Forage Harvestor, Ertl, 1/64th scale, #372, MIB, S5 ....$2.50

Ford Model 9N Tractor, Arcade, 1939, CI, gray w/blk rubber tires, integral driver, 6½", EX, A $465.00

Ford Model 9N Tractor & Scoop Trailer, Arcade, CI, red w/blk rubber tires, silver hitch w/dump release, 15", EX, A.......$1,100.00

Ford Model 961 Tractor w/Plow, Hubley, red & gray, 15", G, A $250.00

Ford New Holland TR97 Combine, Ertl, 1/64th scale, #815, MIB, S5 ....$10.00

Ford Precision Classic 8N, Ertl, 1/16th scale, #352, MIB, S5 ....$95.00

Ford Tractor, Ertl, 1950s, metal, red & beige w/red decals, plastic rims & rubber tires, 7½", EX, A $110.00

Ford 4000 Tractor, Hubley, bl & gray, wide front, 3-point hitch, 10½", MIB, A $295.00

Ford 5640 w/Loader, Ertl, 1/64th scale, #334, MIB, S5.......$4.00

Ford 6640 Row Crop, Ertl, 1/64th scale, #332, MIB, S5 .....$3.00

Ford 7740 Row Crop, Ertl, Collector's Edition, 1/16th scale, #873, MIB, S5 ....$50.00

Ford 7840, Ertl, 1/64th scale, #336, MIB, S5 ....$3.00

Ford 8340 w/Duals, Ertl, 1/64th scale, #388, MIB, S5.........$4.00

Ford 8730 w/Loader, Ertl, 1/64th scale, #303, MIB, S5.......$4.50

Ford 8830 Tractor w/Front Wheel Drive Assist, Ertl, 1/64th scale, #854, MIB, S5 ....$3.00

Ford 901, Ertl, Dealer Demo Tractor Collector's Edition, 1/16th scale, #363, MIB, S5 ....$38.00

Fordson Model F Tractor, Ertl, 1/16th scale, #301, MIB, S5 ..$18.00

Fordson Tractor, Arcade, CI, gr w/red spoke wheels, NP integral driver, 5¾", VG, A $130.00

Fordson Tractor, Bing, tin w/up, silver w/red spoked tires, 8", driver missing 1 arm o/w VG+, M5 ....$210.00

Fordson Tractor w/Hay Rake, Arcade, CI, gr & red w/NP wheels on hay rake, 8½", EX, A $475.00

Fordson Tractor w/Loader, Hubley, gr, 2 versions, 9", very rare, VG, A $1,500.00

Genesis 8770 Tractor, Ertl, 1/64th scale, #391, MIB, S5 ....$3.00

Hay Rake, Tru-Scale, 8", M, A $5.00

Hesston Forage Harvester, Ertl, 1/64th scale, #2262, MIB, S5.$2.50

Hesston Forage Wagon, Ertl, 1/64th scale, #2266, MIB, S5..$2.50

Hesston SL-30 Skid Steer Loader, Ertl, 1/64th scale, #2267, MIB, S5 ....$4.00

IH Anhydrous Ammonia Tank, Ertl, 1/64th scale, #1550, MIB, S5 ....$2.50

IH Cub Tractor, Ertl, 1976-79, 1/16th scale, #448, MIB, S5 ..$18.00

IH I-59 Tractor, Ertl, 1993 Farm Show Edition, 1/16th scale, #4611, MIB, S5 ....$36.50

IH 1568 V-8 Tractor w/Duals, Ertl, Collector's Edition, 1/16th scale, #4630, MIB, S5 ....$40.00

IH 1586 Tractor, Ertl, 1/16th scale, #463, MIB, S5 ....$18.50

IH 1586 w/Loader, Ertl, 1/16th scale, #416, MIB, S5 ....$22.00

John Deere Bale Processor, Ertl, 1/64th scale, #5571, MIB, S5.$2.50

John Deere Bale Throw Wagon, Ertl, 1/64th scale, #5755, MIB, S5 ....$3.00

John Deere Barge Wagon, Ertl, 1/64th scale, #5529, MIB, S5.$2.50

John Deere Cotton Picker, Ertl, 1/80th scale, #1000, MIB, S5 ..$6.00

John Deere D, Ertl, Minneapolis Branch Collection, 1/16th scale, #5817, MIB, S5..........................$100.00

John Deere Dealership Set, Ertl, 1993, MIB, T1..............$25.00

John Deere E Engine, Ertl, 1/16th scale, #4969, battery-op, MIB, S5 ....$22.00

John Deere Farm Wagon, Vindex, CI, gr & red w/2 blk horses, running gear has working parts, 7½", scarce, EX, A.......$1,300.00

John Deere Fertilizer Spreader, Ertl, 1/64th scale, #5565, MIB, S5 ....$3.50

John Deere Flare Box Wagon, Ertl, 1/43rd scale, #5637, MIB, S5..$5.00

John Deere Forage Harvester, Ertl, 1/64th scale, #566, MIB, S5 ....$3.00

John Deere Gas Engine, Vindex, CI, gr w/yel logo, features working pulley & flywheels, EX, A.......................$1,175.00

John Deere GP Wide, Ertl, 1/16th scale, #5787, MIB, S5 .$26.00

John Deere Grain Drill, Ertl, 1/64th scale, #5528, MIB, S5..$3.00

John Deere Gravity Wagon, Ertl, 1/64th scale, #5552, MIB, S5 ....$3.00

John Deere LP Tractor, Ertl, 1/43rd scale, #5599, MIB, S5 .$5.00

John Deere Model A General Purpose Tractor, Ertl, Collector's Edition, MIB, $75.00.

John Deere Model A Tractor, Arcade, NP driver, 7", EX, A..$675.00

John Deere Model A Tractor, Ertl, 1/16th scale, #539, MIB, S5 ..$18.00

John Deere Model A Tractor, Ertl, 1/43rd scale, #5598, MIB, S5 ....$5.00

John Deere Mower Conditioner, Ertl, 1/64th scale, #5657, MIB, S5 ....$3.00

John Deere Mulch Tiller, Ertl, 1/64th scale, #578, MIB, S5 .$3.00

John Deere Overtime Tractor, Ertl, 1/16th scale, #5811, MIB, S5 ....$24.00

John Deere Skid Loader, Ertl, 1/64th scale, #5536, MIB, S5..$4.50

John Deere Skid Steer Loader, Ertl, 1/16th scale, #569, MIB, S5 ....$18.00

John Deere Sprayer, Ertl, 1/64th scale, #5558, MIB, S5 .....$3.00

John Deere Thresher, Vindex, CI, gr & silver w/yel wheels, removable straw stacker & grain pipe, 15", rare, NM, A.....$3,100.00

John Deere Tractor w/Front Wheel Drive, Ertl, 1/64th scale, #5612, MIB, S5 ....$3.50

John Deere Van Brunt Drill, Vindex, CI, red & yel w/NP dril l disks, 9¾", rare, NM, A $2,900.00

John Deere Waterloo Engine, Ertl, 1/16th scale, #5645, MIB, S5..$20.00

John Deere 12 A Combine, Ertl, Collector's Edition, 1/16th scale, #5601DA, MIB, S5..$44.00

John Deere 12 A Combine, Ertl, shelf model, 1/16th scale, #5601DO, MIB, S5..$24.00

John Deere 12-Row Planter, Ertl, 1/64th scale, #576, MIB, S5..$4.50

John Deere 1930 GP Tractor, Ertl, 1/16th scale, #5801, MIB, S5..$25.00

John Deere 1949 Model AR Tractor, Ertl, 1/16th scale, #5680, MIB, S5 ....$22.00

John Deere 2640, Ertl, Field of Dreams Collection, 1/16th scale, #516, MIB, S5..$40.00

John Deere 3010, Ertl, Collector's Edition, 1/16th scale, #5635, MIB, S5 ....$38.00

John Deere 338 Rectangular Baler, Ertl, 1/64th scale, #5646, MIB, S5 ....$3.00

John Deere 4010 Diesel Tractor, Ertl, National Toy Show 1994, 1/43rd scale, #5725, MIB, S5..$25.00

John Deere 4020 Precision #3, Ertl, 1/16th scale, #5638, MIB, S5 ....$95.00

John Deere 630 LP Tractor, Ertl, 1/16th scale, #5590, MIB, S5...$18.00

John Deere 6400 Mechanical Front Wheel Drive, Ertl, Collector's Edition, 1/16th scale, #5667, MIB, S5..............$36.00

John Deere 6400 w/Duals, Ertl, 1/64th scale, #5734, MIB, S5 ....$3.00

John Deere 6910 Self-Propelled Harvester, Ertl, 1/64th scale, #5658, MIB, S5..$10.00

John Deere 70 Tractor, Ertl, 1/16th scale, #5611, MIB, S5 ....$20.00

John Deere 7800, Ertl, Demonstrator Tractor, 1/16th scale, #5719, MIB, S5..$85.00

John Deere 7800 w/Duals, Ertl, 1/64th scale, #5649, MIB, S5 ....$4.00

John Deere 7800 w/Loader, Ertl, 1/64th scale, #5652, MIB, S5 ....$5.00

John Deere 820 Diesel Tractor, Ertl, 1/16th scale, #5705, MIB, S5 ....$20.00

John Deere 8560 4-WD Tractor, Ertl, 1/64th scale, #5603, MIB, S5 ....$5.00

John Deere 8870 4-WD Tractor, Ertl, 1/64th scale, #5791, MIB, S5 ....$5.00

Knudson 4400 4-WD Tractor w/Duals, Ertl, 1/64th scale, #4400, MIB, S5 ....$20.00

Massey-Ferguson Challenger, Ertl, 1/16th scale, #1103, MIB, S5 ....$20.00

Massey-Ferguson 3070 Front Wheel Drive, Ertl, 1/64th scale, #1107, MIB, S5..$3.50

Massey-Ferguson 3120 Tractor, Ertl, 1/64th scale, #1177, MIB, S5 ....$3.00

Massey-Ferguson 3120 w/Loader, Ertl, 1/64th scale, #1109, MIB, S5 ....$4.50

Massey-Ferguson 44 Special Tractor, Ertl, 1/16th scale, #1115, MIB, S5 ....$18.00

Massey-Ferguson 699 w/Loader, Ertl, 1/64th scale, #1125, MIB, S5 ....$5.00

Massey-Harris Challenger Tractor, Ertl, 1/43rd scale, #2511, MIB, S5 ....$5.00

Massey-Harris Combine, Lincoln Products, self-propelled, 11½", VG, A $295.00

Massey-Harris 44 Tractor, Lincoln Toys/Canada, red & yel w/blk tires, 11½", EX, M5 ....$140.00

Massey-Harris 55, Ertl, 1/43rd scale, #1131, MIB, S5 ....$5.50

Massey-Harris 55, Ertl, 1992 National Toy Show, 1/16th scale, #1292, MIB, S5 ....$80.00

Massey-Harris 745 D Tractor, red, rubber tires w/beige rims, 8½", EX, A $360.00

McCormick-Deering Dump Rake, Arcade, 5", G, A $75.00

McCormick-Deering Farm Wagon, Arcade, CI, dk gr box-type w/center seat, 4 red spoked wheels, 2 blk horses, 12", VG, A $690.00

McCormick-Deering Farmall AV, Ertl, 1992 Lafayette Farm Toy Show Edition, 1 of 3,000, stock #250TA, MIB, $60.00.

McCormick-Deering M Engine, Ertl/JC Penney's, MIB, T1 ..$25.00

McCormick-Deering Spreader, Arcade, CI, red body w/NP gears & spoked wheels pulled by oxen, 15", VG, A..........$385.00

McCormick-Deering Thresher, Arcade, CI, bl w/NP wheels, 9", EX $465.00

McCormick-Deering 10-20 Tractor, Arcade, CI w/spoke wheels, 6½", G-, A..$180.00

Minneapolis-Moline G750, Ertl, National Toy Show, 1/16th scale, #4375, MIB, S5 ....$80.00

Monarch Tractor, Hubley, 1933, CI, olive-colored crawler, 4½", VG $180.00

New Holland Box Spreader, Ertl, 1/64th scale, #308, MIB, S5 ..$3.00

New Holland Mower Conditioner, Ertl, 1/64th scale, #322, MIB, S5 ....$3.00

New Holland Skid Loader, Ertl, 1/64th scale, #381, MIB, S5..$4.00

Oh Boy Tractor Crawler, Kilgore, CI, orange & red w/NP wheels, 6", EX, A..$900.00

Oliver Hay Baler PTO, Slik, 10", rare, G, A..................$110.00

Oliver Orchard Tractor, Hubley, lt gr, 5", G, A $100.00

Oliver 1655 w/Wide Front, Ertl, 1/16th scale, #4472, MIB, S5 ....$20.00

Oliver 70 Tractor, Arcade, red, 7", VG $200.00

Publix 1913 Model T Dari-Fresh '92, Ertl, 1/43rd scale, #2105, MIB, S5 ....$8.00

Sickle Mower, Tru-Scale, 9", M, A $20.00

Tractor, Hubley, compo w/NP CI driver's head, red w/blk tires, 5½", EX (EX box), A $125.00

Tractor, Lincoln Toys/Canada, orange w/blk tires, 6½", VG+, M5 ....$115.00

Tractor w/Attachments, Slik/Lansing, w/disc harrow, cultivator & dragger, new old stock, MIB, A $250.00

Tractor w/Dump Wagon, Arcade, red tractor, gr 2-wheeled wagon w/arched hook-up bars, wht rubber tires, 8", EX, A $200.00

Wagon, Arcade, red w/CI wheels, 6½", VG, from $65 to...$85.00

Whitehead & Kales Wagon, Arcade, 8½", very rare, VG ..$60.00

Fast-Food Collectibles

Fast-food collectibles are attracting a lot of attention right now — the hobby is fun and inexpensive (so far), and the little toys, games, buttons and dolls originally meant for the kids are now being snatched up by adults who are much more likely to appreciate them. They were first included in kiddie meals in the late 1970s. They're often issued in series of up to eight or ten characters; the ones you'll want to watch for are Disney characters, popular kids' icons like Barbie dolls, Cabbage Patch Kids, My Little Pony, Star Trek, etc. But it's not just the toys that are collectible. So are the boxes, store signs and displays, and promotional items (like the Christmas ornaments you can buy for 99¢). Supply dictates price. For instance, a test market box might be worth $20.00, a box from a regional promotion might be $10.00, while one from a national promotion could be virtually worthless.

Toys don't have to be old to be collectible, but if you can find them still in their original package, so much the better. Though there are exceptions, a loose toy is worth one-half to two-thirds the value of one mint in package. For more information we recommend *McDonald's® Happy Meal® Toys — In the USA* and *McDonald's® Happy Meal® Toys — Around the World* by Joyce and Terry Losonsky, and *Tomart's Price Guide to Kid's Meal Collectibles* by Ken Clee. Both are listed under Fast-Food Collectibles in the Categories of Special Interest section of this book.

Advisors: Bill and Pat Poe (P10); Scott Smiles (S10), Foreign. Other Sources: C3, C11, I2, K1 (Simpsons), M8, P3

Arby's

Babar's Posters, 1991, ea $3.00

Babar's World Tour Finger Puppets, 1990, ea $2.00

Babar's World Tour License Plates, 1990, ea...................$2.00

Babar's World Tour Pull-Back Racers, 1992, ea $3.00

Babar's World Tour Squirters, 1992, ea........................$2.00

Babar's World Tour Stampers, 1991, MIP, ea $4.00

Babar's World Tour Storybooks, 1991, MIP, ea $3.00

Babar's World Tour Vehicles, 1990, MIP, ea $3.00

Little Miss, 1981, 9 different, ea $4.00

Looney Tunes Car Tunes, 1989, 6 different, ea................$3.00

Looney Tunes Characters, 1987, oval base, 6 different, ea .**$3.00**
Looney Tunes Fun Figures, 1989, Sylvester, Tasmanian Devil or
 Daffy Duck, ea..**$4.00**
Looney Tunes Ring, Porky Pig, MIP **$10.00**
Mr Men, 1981, 10 different, ea, from $4 to **$5.00**
Yogi Bear Fun Squirters, 1994, MIP, ea...........................**$4.00**

Burger King

Action Figures, 1991, MIP, ea **$3.00**
Aladdin, 1992, MIP, ea...**$3.00**
Aladdin Hidden Treasures, 1994, 5 different, MIP, ea **$2.00**
Archies, 1991, 4 different, MIP, ea...................................**$4.00**
Barnyard Commandos, 1993, 4 different, all recalled, MIP,
 ea...**$3.00**
Beach Party, 1994, 5 different, MIP, ea...........................**$3.00**
Beatlejuice, 1990, 6 different, ea **$2.00**
Beauty & the Beast, 1991, Belle, Chip, Cogsworth or The Beast,
 MIP, ea...**$4.00**
Bone Age, 1989, 4 different, ea **$5.00**
Bonkers, 1993, Toots, Fall About Rabbit, Bonkers, Jitters, or
 Detective Lucky Piquel, ea **$3.00**
Capitol Critters, 1992, 4 different, MIP, ea......................**$2.00**
Captain Planet, 1991, 4 different, MIP, ea.......................**$2.00**
Chipmunk Adventure, 1987, sparkle rubber ball, MIP.......**$6.00**
Cool Stuff, 1995, 5 different, MIP, ea, from $2 to.............**$3.00**

Dino Crawlers, Tyrann-O-Crawler, 1994, MIP, $2.00.

Dino Crawlers, 1994, 5 different, MIP, ea..........................**$2.00**
Gargoyles, 1995, MIP, ea, from $2 to **$3.00**
Glow-in-the-Dark Troll Patrol, 1993, 4 different, ea..........**$2.00**
Go-Go Gadget Gizmos, 1991, 4 different, MIP, ea.............**$3.00**
Good Goblin, 1989, Zelda Zoombroom, Frankie Steen or
 Gourdy Goblin, ea **$3.00**
Goof Troop Bowlers, 1992, Goofy, Max, Pete or PJ, MIP, ea.**$3.00**
Goofy & Max Adventures, 1995, water raft, fishing boat, water
 skiers, bucking bronco or red runaway car, MIP, ea **$3.00**
It's Magic, 1992, 4 different, MIP, ea................................**$2.00**
Kid Transporters, 1990, 6 different, ea **$1.00**
Life Savers Freaky Fellas, 1992, w/o Lifesavers, ea **$2.00**
Lion King, 1994, 7 different, MIP, ea................................**$4.00**
Lion King Finger Puppets, 1995, 6 different, MIP, ea **$3.00**
Little Mermaid, 1993, 4 different, MIP, ea........................**$3.00**

Goof Troop Bowlers, Max, 1992, MIP, $3.00.

McGruff Cares for You, 1991, 4 different songbook & tape sets,
 MIP, ea..**$6.00**
Mini Record Breakers, 1989, 6 different, ea **$2.00**
Mini Sports Games, 1993, 4 different, MIP, ea **$3.00**
Nerfuls, 1989, Officer Bob, Bitsy Ball or Scratch, ea..........**$4.00**
Pinocchio Summer Inflatables, 1992, 5 different, MIP, ea..**$4.00**
Pocahontas, 1995, 8 different, MIP, ea..............................**$3.00**
Pranksters, 1994, 5 different, MIP, ea................................**$3.00**
Purrtenders, 1988, Free Wheeling Cheese Rider or Flip Top Car,
 ea **$2.00**
Purrtenders Sock-Ems, Christmas 1987, 4 different stuffed plush
 animals, ea..**$5.00**
Save the Animals, 1993, 4 different w/animal cards, MIP,
 ea...**$4.00**
Silverhawks, 1987, pencil topper......................................**$5.00**
Simpsons, 1990, Lisa, Homer, Maggie, Marge or Bart, ea ...**$2.00**
Spacebase Racers, 1989, Super Shuttle, Moonman Rover, Star-
 ship Viking or Cosmic Copter, ea **$3.00**
Sports All-Stars, 1994, Kid Vid, Boomer, Jaws, Snaps or IQ,
 MIP, ea...**$4.00**
Surprise Celebration Parade, 1992, 4 different, MIP, ea **$4.00**
Teenage Mutant Ninja Turtles Bike Gear, 1993, MIP, ea..**$3.00**
Thundercats, 1986, Snarf...**$5.00**
Top Kids Wild Spinning Tops, 1994, 4 different, MIP, ea..**$2.00**
Trak-Pak Golden Jr Classic Books, 1988, My Little Book of
 Trains, The Circus Train or Roundabout Train, G, ea..**$4.00**
World Travel Adventure Kid, 1991, Kid Vid, Lingo, Jaw or
 Snap, MIP, ea...**$5.00**
Z-Bots w/Pogs, 1994, 5 different, MIP, ea.........................**$2.00**

Carl's Jr.

Addams Family, MIP, ea **$8.00**
Amazing Mazes, MIP, ea **$5.00**
Bone-A-Fide Friends, MIP, ea **$4.00**
Crazy Doodlers, 1994, MIP, ea..**$4.00**
Eek! Stravaganza, MIP, ea...**$6.00**
Flyin' Away, MIP, ea..**$4.00**
Hair Dudes, 1995, 4 different w/pkgs of rye grass seed to grow
 hair, MIP, ea..**$5.00**
Reptile Inflatables, MIP, ea...**$6.00**
Rollerblade, 4 different, MIP, ea..**$5.00**

Dairy Queen

Alvin & Chipmunks Music Makers, 4 different, MIP, ea ...**$5.00**
Baby's Day Out Books, 4 different, M, ea..........................**$12.00**
Bobby's World, 4 different, MIP, ea.................................**$5.00**
Circus Train, set of 4, MIP **$22.00**
Radio Flyer, 1991, red Radio Flyer miniature wagon, M......**$5.00**
Rock-A-Doodle, 1991, 6 different, MIP, ea **$7.00**
Space Shuttle, 6 different, MIP, ea.................................**$3.00**
Tom & Jerry, 1993, 6 different, MIP, ea............................**$6.00**

Denny's

Adventure Seekers Activity Packet, 1993, MIP, ea...........**$2.00**
Dino-Makers, 1991, 6 different, MIP, ea **$3.00**
Flintstone Dino-Racers, 1991, 6 different, MIP, ea.............**$4.00**
Flintstone Fun Squirters, 1991, 5 different, MIP, ea **$4.00**
Flintstone Glacier Gliders, 1990, Barney, Pebbles, Bamm-Bamm
    or Hoppy, ea..**$3.00**
Flintstone Rock 'N Rollers, 1991, Fred w/guitar or Barney w/sax,
    ea..**$4.00**
Flintstone Vehicles, 1990, Fred, Dino, Pebbles or Bamm-Bamm,
    ea..**$4.00**
Jetson's Space Cards, 6 different, 1992, MIP, ea **$4.00**
Jetsons Go Back to School, 1992, 4 different, MIP, ea **$3.00**
Jetsons Space Travel Fun Books, 1992, 6 different, M, ea ..**$3.00**
Jetsons Space-Age Puzzle Ornaments, 1992, MIP, ea **$3.00**

Dominos Pizza

Avoid the Noid, 1988, Noid w/jackhammer, Noid w/boxing
    gloves or Noid as magician, ea.....................................**$4.00**
Keep the Noid Out, 1987, Clown Noid pulling ears or Noid
    holding bomb, ea...**$4.00**
Noid, figure, bendable, 1988, 7", NM...............................**$10.00**
Noid Glider w/Power Prop, 1989, MIP.............................**$20.00**

Frisch's Big Boy

Monster in My Pocket, MIP, ea......................................**$3.00**
Racers, 1992, ea..**$5.00**
Safari Fun, MIP, ea...**$4.00**
Sports Figures, 1990, ea...**$5.00**
Time Capsule, MIP, ea..**$5.00**

Hardee's

Apollo 13 Rocket, 1995, 3 different, MIP, ea.....................**$4.00**
Breakman's World, 1995, 4 different, MIP, ea, from $2 to .**$3.00**
Camp California, 1994, 4 different, MIP, ea **$3.00**
Days of Thunder Racers, 1990, 4 different, MIP, ea............**$5.00**
Dinobend Buddies, 1994, 4 different, MIP, ea...................**$3.00**
Dinosaur in My Pocket, 1993, 4 different, MIP, ea.............**$3.00**
Doodletop Jr's, 1996, 4 different, MIP, ea **$3.00**
Eek! The Cat, 1995, 6 different, MIP, ea...........................**$3.00**
Eureka Castle Stampers, 1994, 4 different, MIP, ea **$3.00**
Fender Bender 500 Racers, 1990, 5 different, MIP, ea, from $2
    to...**$3.00**

Flintstones First 30 Years, 1991, 5 different, MIP, ea..........**$5.00**
Gremlin Adventures Read-Along Book & Record, 1984, 5 dif-
    ferent, M, ea..**$6.00**
Kazoo Crew Sailors, 1991, 4 different, MIP, ea **$3.00**
Marvel Super Heroes in Vehicles, 1990, 4 different, MIP, ea..**$3.00**
Mickey's Christmas Carol, 1984, 5 different, M, ea **$6.00**
Micro Super Soakers, 1994, 4 different, MIP, ea...............**$3.00**
Muppet Christmas Carol Finger Puppets, 1993, 4 different, MIP,
    ea, from $3 to **$4.00**
Nicktoons Cruisers, 1994, 8 different, MIP, ea **$3.00**
Pound Puppies, 1986, stuffed plush, 4 different, ea **$5.00**
Smurfs Funmeal Pack, 1990, 6 different, ea......................**$3.00**
Swan Princess, 1994, 5 different, MIP, ea **$4.00**
Tattoads, 1995, 4 different, MIP, ea **$3.00**
Tune-A-Fish, 1994, 4 different fish-shaped whistles, MIP, ea...**$3.00**
Waldo & Friends Holiday Ornaments, 1991, 3 different, MIP, ea...**$4.00**
Waldo & Friends Straw Buddies, 1990, 4 different, ea........**$3.00**
Walt Disney Animated Film Classic, 1985, 4 different plush
    toys, ea..**$6.00**
X-Men, 1995, 6 different, MIP, ea....................................**$3.00**

Jack-in-the-Box

Bendable Buddies, 1991, 5 different, MIP, ea....................**$8.00**
Bendable Buddies, 1994, 5 different, MIP, ea....................**$6.00**
Garden Fun, 3 different seed pkgs, MIP, ea **$5.00**
Jack Pack Make-A-Scene, 3 different, MIP, ea..................**$4.00**
Star Trek Generations, 6 different, MIP, ea, from $4 to **$5.00**

Long John Silver's

Berenstain Bears Books, 4 different, ea..............................**$3.00**
Fish Car, 1989, plastic fish-shaped car, ea **$3.00**
Free Willy 2, 5 different, ea...**$4.00**
I Love Dinosaurs, 4 different, ea **$4.00**
Map Activities, 1991, Solar System, USA or The World, MIP,
    ea **$4.00**
Once Upon a Forest, 1993, 5 different, MIP, ea..................**$4.00**
Sea Watchers, 1991, miniature kaleidoscope, MIP **$5.00**
Treasure Trolls, 1992, pencil toppers, MIP, ea...................**$3.00**
Water Blasters, 1990, Billy Bones, Long John Silver, Captain
    Flint or Ophelia Octopus, ea **$4.00**

McDonald's

Adventures of Ronald McDonald, 1981, hard rubber figure, 7
    different, M, ea..**$10.00**
Airport, 1986, 5 different, MIP, ea **$5.00**
Amazing Wildlife, 1995, 8 different, MIP, ea.....................**$3.00**
American Tale Storybook, 1986, ea **$2.00**
Astrosniks, 1983, Regional, any of 8 except Robo or Snikapota-
    mus, ea, minimum value **$8.00**
Astrosniks, 1983, Regional, Robo or Snikapotamus, ea....**$12.00**
Astrosniks, 1984, Regional, 6 different, ea.....................**$14.00**
Barbie/Hot Wheels, 1991, any Barbie except under age 3, Cos-
    tume Ball or Wedding Day Midge, MIP, ea.................**$4.00**
Barbie/Hot Wheels, 1991, any Hot Wheels except under age 3,
    MIP, ea...**$4.00**

Barbie/Hot Wheels, 1993, any Barbie/Hot Wheels except under age 3, MIP, ea....................$3.00

Barbie/Hot Wheels, 1994, any Barbie except Camp Teresa or under age 3, MIP, ea, from $4 to $5.00

Barbie/Hot Wheels, 1995, any Barbie w/rooted hair except under age 3, MIP, ea....................$3.00

Barbie/Mini Streex, 1992, Barbie under age 3, Sparkle Eyes, MIP....................$4.00

Barbie/Mini Streex, 1992, Mini Streex, under age 3, Orange Arrow, MIP....................$4.00

Barnyard (Old McDonald's Farm), 1986, 6 different, ea.....$8.00

Batman, 1992, 4 different, MIP, ea....................$3.00

Bedtime, 1989, foam wash mitt, MIP $5.00

Berenstain Bears Books, 1990, 8 different story or activity books, ea....................$2.00

Boats & Floats, 1987, Fry Kids Raft or McNuggets Lifeboat w/sticker sheet, ea, from $8 to $15.00

Cabbage Patch Kids, Lindsay Elizabeth and Mimi Kristina, 1992, MIP, $3.00 each.

Cabbage Patch Kids/Tonka Trucks, 1992, any Cabbage Patch Kid except under age 3, MIP, ea....................$3.00

Circus Parade, 1991, Regional, Ronald, Birdie, Fry Guy or Grimace, MIP, ea $5.00

Crazy Creatures w/Popoids, 1985, 4 different, ea $5.00

Dink the Little Dinosaur, 1990, Regional, 6 different, ea...$5.00

Dinosaur Days, 1981, 6 different, available in several colors, ea..$2.00

Ducktails I, 1987, MIP, ea, from $5 to....................$6.00

Flintstone Kids, 1988, 4 different, MIP, ea, from $6 to.......$8.00

Flintstones, 1994, under age 3, Rocking Dino, MIP $5.00

Friendly Skies, 1992, Ronald or Grimace in UAL plane, MIP, ea $10.00

Fun w/Food, 1989, 4 different, MIP, ea $8.00

Gravedale High, 1991, Regional, Frankentyke, Sid, Vinnie Stoker or Cleofatra, MIP, ea....................$5.00

Halloween McNuggets, 7 different, MIP, ea, from $3 to.....$4.00

Halloween Pails, 1990, ea....................$2.00

Happy Birthday 15 Years, 1994, Barbie #2, recalled, MIP ..$6.00

Happy Birthday 15 Years, 1994, under age 3, Ronald McDonald, MIP....................$4.00

Hook, 1991, 4 different, MIP, ea $3.00

Jungle Book, 1990, Baloo, King Louie, Kaa or Shere Khan, MIP, ea $4.00

Jungle Book, 1990, under age 3, Junior or Mowgli, MIP, ea..$9.00

Lego Building Set, 1986, race car, 16-pc set, MIP....................$6.00

Lego Motion, 1989, 10 different, MIP, ea, from $5 to.........$6.00

Little Golden Book, 1982, 5 different, EX, ea $3.00

Little Mermaid, 1989, 4 different, MIP, ea....................$5.00

McDonaldland Band, 1986, Fry Kid Trumpet, Pan Pipes or Grimace Saxophone, ea $3.00

Mickey & Friends Epcot '94 Adventure, 1994, any of 9 except under age 3, MIP, ea....................$3.00

Mickey's Birthdayland, 1988, any of 6 except under age 3, ea..$2.00

Moveables, 1988, 6 different, ea, from $8 to $9.00

Muppet Workshop, 1995, 4 different, MIP, ea....................$1.50

Nature's Helper, 1991, 5 different & under age 3, MIP, ea, from $2 to $3.00

New Archies, 1988, 6 different, ea $8.00

Piggsburg Piggs, 1991, Regional, 4 different, MIP, ea $5.00

Potato Heads, 1992, 8 different, ea....................$4.00

Power Rangers, 1995, 5 different, MIP, from $3 to $4.00

Runaway Robots, 1987, 6 different, ea $3.00

Santa Claus the Movie Storybook, 1986, ea $3.00

Stomper Mini 4X4, 1986, MIP, ea....................$15.00

Super Mario Brothers, 1990, 5 different except under age 3, MIP, ea....................$3.00

Totally Toys, 1993, Magic Nursery, Attack Pack, Polly Pocket, Sally Secrets, Tatoo Machine, or Mighty Max, MIP, ea .$3.00

Wild Friends, 1992, Regional, any except under age 3, MIP, ea..$4.00

Zoo Face, 1988, Toucan, Monkey, Tiger or Alligator, MIP, ea $4.00

101 Dalmatians, 1991, 4 different, MIP, ea $4.00

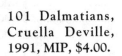

101 Dalmatians, Cruella Deville, 1991, MIP, $4.00.

Pizza Hut

Air Garfield, Inflatable Spaceball, Parachute or Flying Disk, MIP, ea $6.00

Beauty & the Beast Hand Puppets, 1992, rubber Beast, Belle, Chip or Cogsworth, MIP, ea....................$5.00

Brain Thaws, 4 different, MIP, ea......................................$4.00
Eureeka's Castle Hand Puppets, 1992, rubber Batley, Eureeka or
    Magellan, MIP, ea...$5.00
Fievel Goes West, 1991, Fievel or Cat R Waul, ea $5.00
Marvel Comics, 4 different, MIP, ea..................................$4.00
Mascot Misfits, 4 different, MIP, ea...................................$4.00
Pagemaster, 4 different, MIP, ea.......................................$4.00
Squirt Toons, 5 different, MIP, ea $5.00

Roy Rogers

Animals II, 4 different, MIP, ea...$3.00
Beakman's World, 4 different, MIP, ea...............................$5.00
Doddletop Jr, 4 different, MIP, ea.....................................$4.00
Eek! The Cat, 6 different, MIP, ea, from $4 to...................$5.00
Gator Tales, 1989, 4 different, MIP, ea, from $8 to $9.00
Ickky Stickky Bugs, 4 different, MIP, ea.............................$4.00
Space Meals, 4 different, MIP, ea $4.00
Swan Princess, 4 different, MIP, ea, from $5 to..................$6.00
Tootin' Jammers, 4 different, MIP, ea $5.00

Sonic

All-Star Mini-Baseballs, 5 different, MIP, ea $4.00
Animal Straws, 4 different, MIP, ea, from $4 to $5.00
Brown Bag Bowlers, 1994, 4 different, MIP, ea $5.00
Brown Bag Juniors, 1989, 4 different, ea............................$5.00
Flippin' Food, 1995, 3 different, MIP, ea $3.00
Go Wild Balls, 1995, MIP, 4 different, MIP, ea $3.00
Holiday Kids, 1994, 4 different, MIP, ea, from $4 to...........$5.00
Squishers, 4 different, MIP, ea $5.00
Wacky Sackers, 1994, 6 different, MIP, ea.........................$4.00

Subway

Battle Balls, 1995-96, 4 different, MIP, ea.........................$3.00
Bump in the Night, 4 different, MIP, ea.............................$5.00
Cone Heads, 1993, 4 different, MIP, ea..............................$4.00
Explore Space, 1994, 4 different, MIP, ea $4.00
Hackeysack Balls, 1991, 5 different, MIP, ea.......................$4.00
Hurricanes, 1994, 4 different, MIP, ea...............................$4.00
Inspector Gadget, 1994, 4 different, MIP, ea.......................$4.00
Monkey Trouble, 1994, 5 different, MIP, ea $3.00

Taco Bell

Happy Talk Sprites, Spark, Twink or Romeo, plush, ea $6.00
Hugga Bunch, Fluffer, Gigglet, or Tuggins, plush, ea..........$8.00
Milk Caps, MIP, ea $3.00
Pebble & the Penguin, 3 different, MIP, ea.........................$5.00
Sticker Sheets, Undersea Scene, MIP $3.00

Target Markets

Adventure Team Window Walkers, 1994-95, 4 different, MIP,
    ea $4.00
Muppet Twisters, 3 different, MIP, ea $4.00
Roll-O-Fun Coloring Kit, 3 different, MIP, ea....................$4.00

Targeteers, 1992, 4 different figures or vehicles, MIP, ea....$5.00
Targeteers, 1994, 6 different figures or 6 different vehicles, MIP,
    ea $4.00

Wendy's

Alf Tales, 1990, 6 different, MIP, ea $4.00
All Dogs Go to Heaven, 1989, 6 different, MIP, ea.............$4.00
Ballsasaurus, 1992, 4 different, MIP, ea.............................$4.00
Definitely Dinosaurs I, 1988, 4 different, MIP, ea, from $5 to...$6.00
Definitely Dinosaurs II, 1989, 6 different, MIP, ea, from $5 to...$6.00
Furskins Bears, 1986, plush, 4 different, ea, from $5 to.......$6.00
Gear-Up, 5 different, MIP, ea...$3.00
Jetsons Space Vehicles, 1989, 6 different, MIP, ea..............$5.00
Jetsons: The Movie, 1990, 5 different, MIP, ea $3.00
Kids 4 Parks, 5 different, MIP, ea, from $3 to....................$4.00
Potato Head II, 1988, 5 different, ea.................................$4.00
Rocket Writers, 1992, 5 different 4" vehicles, ea $2.00
Too Kool for School, 1992, 5 different, MIP, ea $3.00

Wacky Windups,
1991, MIP, from
$3.00 to $4.00.

Wacky Windups, 1991, 5 different, MIP, ea, from $3 to.....$4.00
World of Teddy Ruxpin, 1987, Teddy, Grubby, Professor or
    Wolly What's It, ea...$4.00
World Wild Life, 1988, 4 different books, ea $3.00

White Castle

Bow Biters, 1989, Blue Meany, MIP................................$5.00
Camp White Castle, 1990, MIP, ea..................................$4.00
Castle Meal Friends, 1991, Wendell, Princess or Woofles, MIP,
    ea $9.00
Castleburger Dudes, 1991, 4 different, MIP, ea $4.00
Glow-in-the-Dark Monsters, 3 different, MIP, ea $4.00
Holiday Huggables, 1990, 4 different, MIP, ea...................$6.00
Super Balls, 1994, 4 different, MIP, ea, from $4 to $5.00

Boxes and Bags

Burger King, Bone Age, 1989, ea......................................$7.00
Burger King, Critter Carton/Punch-Out Paper Masks, 1985,
    ea $18.00
Burger King, Trak-Pak, 1988, ea......................................$8.00

Burger King, Tricky Treaters, 1989, ea..............................$5.00
Denny's, Jetsons Fun Book & Menu, 1992, ea $1.00
Hardee's, Days of Thunder, 1990.......................................$3.00
Hardee's, Eureka's Castle, 1994 ....$2.00
Hardee's, Fender Bender 500 Racers, 1990......................$3.00
Hardee's, Muppet Christmas Carol, 1993 ....$2.00
McDonald's, Amazing Wildlife, 1995, ea..........................$1.00
McDonald's, Back to the Future, 1992, ea.........................$2.00
McDonald's, Barbie/Mini Streex, 1992, ea........................$1.00
McDonald's, Bobby's World, 1994, ea...............................$1.00
McDonald's, Camp McDonaldland, 1990, ea.....................$3.00
McDonald's, Ducktails, 4 different, M, set of 4 ....$8.00
McDonald's, Fry Benders Clubhouse, 1990........................$5.00
McDonald's, Good Friends, 1987, ea.................................$4.00
McDonald's, Halloween McNugget Buddies, 1993, ea $1.00
McDonald's, Looney Tunes Quack-Up Cars, 1993, ea $1.00
McDonald's, Making Movies, 1994, ea...............................$1.00
McDonald's, McDonaldland Dough, 1990, set of 2, M.......$6.00
McDonald's, McNugget Buddies, 1988, ea.........................$4.00
McDonald's, Mickey & Friends/Epcot, 1994, ea.................$1.00
McDonald's, Muppet Workshop, 1995, ea..........................$1.00
McDonald's, Oliver & Co, 1988, ea $5.00
McDonald's, Peanuts, 1990, ea $2.00
McDonald's, Rain or Shine, 1989, ea.................................$3.00
McDonald's, Real Ghostbusters, 1987, ea $5.00
McDonald's, Santa Claus the Movie, 1985, M, ea.............$2.50
McDonald's, Snow White & Seven Dwarfs, 1993, ea.........$2.00
McDonald's, Tiny Toon Adventures, 1992, ea $1.00
McDonald's, Zoo Place, 1988, ea......................................$5.00
McDonald's, 101 Dalmatians, 1991, ea $3.00
Shoney's, Shoney Bear & Friends Comic Book, 1991, ea...$1.00
Wal-Mart, Lisa Frank, 1993, ea $2.00
Wendy's, Carmen Sandiego, Code Cracker, 1994, ea.........$2.00
Wendy's, Fast Food Racers, 1990, ea................................$4.00
Wendy's, Jetsons: The Movie, 1990, ea.............................$4.00
Wendy's, Wendy & the Good Stuff Gang, 1989, ea $3.00
Wendy's, Wizard of Wonders, 1991, ea.............................$2.00
Wendy's, Yogi Bear & Friends, 1990, ea...........................$4.00

Foreign

Burger King (European), Cinderella, set of 3, MIP $50.00
Burger King (European), Flintstones, set of 4, MIP, S10 ..$30.00
Burger King (European), Glow-in-the-Dark Trolls, set of 4, MIP,
    C3...$22.00
Burger King (European), Goof Troop, set of 4, MIP.........$20.00
Burger King (European), Peter Pan, set of 5, MIP, C3/P10..$35.00
Burger King (European), Power Rangers, set of 5, MIP $30.00
Burger King (European), Sports All-Star Action Figures, set of 5,
    MIP, C3 ....$22.00
Burger King (European), Tasmania Crazies, set of 4, MIP,
    S10 ....$30.00
Burger King (European), Tiny Toons, set of 4, MIP, C11/S10..$25.00
Burger King (New Zealand), Snow White, set of 4, MIP, C3..$48.00
McDonald's (Australia), Aladdin Straw Grippers, 1994, set of 4,
    MIP, P10 ....$35.00
McDonald's (Australia), Disney Finger Puppets, 1994, set of 4,
    MIP $40.00

McDonald's (Australia), Flintstone Gadgets, 1994, set of 4, MIP,
    P10...$35.00
McDonald's (Australia), Flintstone Stationery Series, 1994, set
    of 4, MIP, P10..$35.00
McDonald's (Australia), Sports Ball, set of 4, MIP, C3 ....$28.00
McDonald's (Australia), Summer Fun Toys, 1995, set of 4, MIP,
    P10...$30.00
McDonald's (Australia), World Cup, 1994, set of 4, MIP, P10..$35.00
McDonald's (Canadian), Barbie/Attack Pack, set of 8, MIP,
    C3...$32.00
McDonald's (Canadian), Farm Animals, set of 8, MIP, C3 ..$20.00

Photo courtesy of Terry and Joyce Losonsky.

McDonald's (Canadian), figures, 1985, set of 4, from $4.00 to $6.00 each.

McDonald's (Canadian), Garfield, set of 4, MIP, C3 ....$24.00
McDonald's (Canadian), Jungle Animals, set of 6, MIP, C3..$24.00
McDonald's (Canadian), Kid's Floss, set of 2, MIP, C3 ....$10.00
McDonald's (Canadian), Looney Tunes, set of 4, MIP, C3....$23.00
McDonald's (Canadian), Muppet Babies, set of 4, MIP, C3 ..$29.00
McDonald's (Canadian), Peanuts, set of 4, MIP, C3 ....$30.00
McDonald's (Canadian), Yo Yogi, set of 4, MIP, C3 ....$24.00
McDonald's (European), Airport, 1995, set of 4, MIP,
    C3/P10...$27.00
McDonald's (European), Aladdin, 1994, set of 4, MIP,
    C11/S10..$25.00
McDonald's (European), Aristocats, 1994, set of 4, MIP,
    S10...$20.00
McDonald's (European), Asterix, 1994, set of 4, MIP $30.00
McDonald's (European), Astromac, set of 4, MIP, C3 .....$30.00
McDonald's (European), Barbie/Hot Wheels, set of 8, MIP,
    C3...$60.00
McDonald's (European), Beauty & the Beast, set of 4, MIP,
    C3/S10 ....$35.00
McDonald's (European), Big Top Circus, 1991, set of 4,
    P10...$18.00
McDonald's (European), Bontempi Music, set of 4, MIP, C3..$25.00
McDonald's (European), Connect-A-Car, 1991, set of 4,
    MIP...$25.00
McDonald's (European), Draakjes (Dragonettes), set of 4, MIP,
    from $20 to...$25.00
McDonald's (European), Dragonettes, set of 4, MIP, C3/S10..$25.00
McDonald's (European), Euro Disney, 1992, set of 4, EX.$25.00
McDonald's (European), Euro Disney, 1992, set of 4, MIP ...$35.00
McDonald's (European), Fly & Drive, 1995, set of 4, MIP,
    P10...$28.00
McDonald's (European), Intergalactic Adventure, 1995, set of 4,
    MIP $25.00

McDonald's (European), Jungle Book, 1993, set of 4, MIP.$25.00

McDonald's (European), Legos, 1994, set of 5 includes under age 3, MIP, P10..$28.00

McDonald's (European), Lion King Puzzles, set of 4, MIP..$25.00

McDonald's (European), McMusic, 1994, set of 4, MIP, P10..$28.00

McDonald's (European), McRockin' Foods, set of 4, MIP..$20.00

McDonald's (European), McRodeo, set of 4, MIP, C11/S10..$25.00

McDonald's (European), Play-Doh, set of 4, MIP, C3......$28.00

McDonald's (European), Rev Ups, set of 4, EX $20.00

McDonald's (European), Sonic the Hedgehog, set of 4, MIP ..$25.00

McDonald's (European), Space Launchers, 1992, set of 4, MIP..$25.00

McDonald's (European), Tail Spins, set of 4, MIP, C11...$25.00

McDonald's (European), Tale Spins, set of 4, MIP...........$30.00

McDonald's (European), Weather Station, 1993, set of 4, MIP, P10..$28.00

McDonald's (European), Winter Sports, 1994, set of 4, MIP, C3/P10, from $32 to..$35.00

McDonald's (European), World of Dinosaurs, 1993, set of 4, MIP, P10..$25.00

McDonald's (France), Growing Figures, set of 3, MIP, C3 .$18.00

McDonald's (Germany), Bontempi Music, set of 4, MIP, C3...$25.00

McDonald's (Germany), Bubble Games, set of 3, MIP, C3 .$25.00

McDonald's (Germany), Dinosaurier Memory, set of 4, MIP, C3..$30.00

McDonald's (Germany), Garfield, set of 4, MIP, C3........$32.00

McDonald's (Germany), Lion King Erasers, set of 4, MIP, C3..$16.00

McDonald's (Germany), Verruckte Knete, set of 4, MIP, C3..$22.00

McDonald's (Germany), Water Pistols, 1993, 4 different, P10, ea..$10.00

McDonald's (Germany), World Cup, set of 4, MIP, C11 .$25.00

McDonald's (Germany), Young Astronauts, set of 4, MIP, C3..$25.00

McDonald's (Holland), Oranjepakket, 1994, set of 3, MIP, P10..$12.00

McDonald's (Mexico), McRodeo, 1995, set of 4, MIP, P10..$30.00

McDonald's (New Zealand), Disney Fun Riders, 1994, set of 4, MIP, C3/P10, from $30 to..$35.00

McDonald's (New Zealand), Vehicle Windups, set of 4, MIP, C3..$48.00

Miscellaneous

This section lists items other than those that are free with kids' meals — for instance, store displays and memorabilia such as Christmas ornaments and plush dolls that can be purchased at the counter.

Arby's, employee badge, 1993, Yogi & Friends Adventure Meal, P10..$8.00

Arby's, ring, Porky Pig, MIP, P10................................$10.00

Burger King, bear, 1986, Crayola Christmas series, plush, P10, ea..$5.00

Burger King, cassette tape, 1989, Christmas Sing-A-Long series, MIB, P10, ea..$3.00

Burger King, doll, Burger King, 1980, 18", EX $15.00

Burger King, doll, Magical Burger King, w/ring & disappearing hamburger, 20", MIB, J6..$65.00

Burger King, doll, 1972, stuffed cloth, EX, C17................$10.00

Denny's, placemats, 1989, set of 4, EX..........................$12.00

Denny's, plate, 1989, plastic w/Flintstones graphics, EX, ea .$5.00

Domino's, pin-back button, Avoid the Noid, Call Domino's Pizza, 2¼", P10..$2.00

Dominos, bookmark, 1989, Noid, P10..........................$10.00

Hardee's, backpack, orange, MIP, P10..........................$3.00

Hardee's, car, #2 Hardee's Racer, bl, P10 ....$5.00

Hardee's, doll, Gilbert Giddy-Up, stuffed cloth, 15", EX, H4..$12.00

Jerry's Restaurants, flicker ring, 1960s, H4......................$12.00

Little Caesar's, figure, Meatsa-Meatsa Man, stuffed, M, C3/P10.$4.00

Long John Silvers, book, 1991, Adventure on Volcano Island, pnt w/water, M, P10..$3.00

McDonald's, action figure, Big Mac, Remco, MOC (unpunched), H4..$50.00

McDonald's, address/phone book, 1992, pocket-sz.............$3.00

McDonald's, bank, 1993, Ronald Happy Times, 7½", EX ..$15.00

McDonald's, bop bag, 1978, Grimace, 8", MIP..............$4.00

McDonald's, calendar, 1994, Ronald & Friends fund raiser for North Carolina, M, L2..$3.00

McDonald's, cap, 1992, Season's Greetings $3.00

McDonald's, cards, 1993, NBA Fantasy, set of 50 ....$25.00

McDonald's, Christmas stocking, 1981, Ronald & graphics on vinyl, P10..$5.00

McDonald's, coin board, 1988, Fiesta w/actual coins from other countries, MIP, L2..$4.00

McDonald's, comb, 1980-1988, various characters & colors, ea..$1.50

McDonald's, cookie cutter, 1978, Ronald or Grimace, plastic, ea..$3.00

McDonald's, display, Barbie/Hot Wheels, 1991, w/plastic dome & premiums, C11..$150.00

McDonald's, display, Funny Fry Friends, 1990, w/plastic dome & premiums, from $100 to..$125.00

McDonald's, display, Garfield, 1989, w/plastic dome & premiums, C11..$125.00

McDonald's, display, Hook, 1991, w/plastic dome & premiums, C11..$90.00

McDonald's, display, Jungle Book, 1990, w/plastic dome & premiums, C11..$125.00

McDonald's, display, Mickey & Friends/Epcot Center '94 Adventure, w/premiums, C11................................$60.00

McDonald's, display, Peanuts, 1990, w/plastic dome & premiums, C11..$100.00

McDonald's, display, Space Rescue, 1995, w/4 premiums, from $10 to..$20.00

McDonald's, display, Tiny Toon Adventures I, 1991, flip cars, w/plastic dome & premiums, from $90 to................$100.00

McDonald's, doll, Hamburglar, 1972, vinyl & cloth, 16", NM..$12.00

McDonald's, doll, Ronald, inflatable, 14", EX, from $8 to...$10.00

McDonald's, doll, Ronald, 1978, plastic head w/whistle, cloth body, 24", EX, B10..$35.00

McDonald's, doll, Ronald McDonald or Professor, Remco, 1976, 8", VG, M15, ea..$25.00

McDonald's, eraser, 1991, Ronald, Grimace or Hamburglar, ea..$2.00

McDonald's, football, Regional, Georgia Bulldogs or Georgia Tech Yellow Jackets, ea $5.00

McDonald's, Fun Set, from K-Mart, Wal-mart, etc., EX, $3.00.

McDonald's, ornament, Cinderella's Jacque Mouse, 1987, MIB, from $3.00 to $4.00.

McDonald's, game, 1993, Ronald Ring Toss, MIB $10.00

McDonald's, game cards, $40,000,000 Dick Tracy Crime Stopper Game, 12 different, unscratched, M, set of 12 .....$12.00

McDonald's, hand puppets, 1993, Ronald, Grimace & Hamburglar, set of 3, MIB..$25.00

McDonald's, Ken Griffey Jr Golden Moments, set of 3, MOC, P10 ....$8.00

McDonald's, kite, 1983-84, McDonald's & 7-Up logos on wht, rare, P10 ....$50.00

McDonald's, music box, 1990, McDonald's restaurant plays Silent Night & Jingle Bells, 2¼x2¼", MIB, P10 ....$25.00

McDonald's, ornament, Bernard or Miss Bianca, MIB, B10, ea ..$6.00

McDonald's, ornament, Enesco, 1990, Over One Million Holiday Wishes, MIB, P10...$25.00

McDonald's, ornament, Enesco, 1990-1991, 'Twas the Night Before Christmas, MIB, P10 ....$20.00

McDonald's, ornament, Enesco, 1992-1993, Mc Ho Ho Ho, MIB, P10...$20.00

McDonald's, ornament, 1982, Norman Rockwell, brass, MIP, from $7 to...$10.00

McDonald's, ornament, 1987, Cinderella's Jacque Mouse or Gus, MIB, from $3 to $4.00

McDonald's, ornament, 1988, Dodger, plush, MIB, from $3 to...$4.00

McDonald's, ornament, 1989, Little Mermaid's Flounder, MIB, from $3 to...$4.00

McDonald's, pen, 1990, Holiday Greetings, M, P10...........$2.00

McDonald's, pin-back button, Garfield, 3", C11.................$3.00

McDonald's, pin-back button, I Support Ronald McDonald House, 3", P10...$2.00

McDonald's, pin-back button, Low Fat Yogurt, 3½", P10 ..$2.00

McDonald's, pin-back button, Make It Mac Tonight, 2" sq, C11 ....$3.00

McDonald's, pin-back button, Make It Mac Tonight, 3", C11 ....$3.00

McDonald's, pin-back button, McButton, 2", P10..............$2.00

McDonald's, pin-back button, McDonald's McRib Pack, 3", P10..$2.00

McDonald's, pin-back button, McLean Deluxe, 91% Fat Free, 3", P10...$2.00

McDonald's, pin-back button, Michael Jordan, 2 Sweet 2 Repeat, P10 ....$5.00

McDonald's, pin-back button, NBA Hoops, 2¼", C11 ......$2.00

McDonald's, pin-back button, Visit With Ronald, 3", P10...$2.00

McDonald's, pin-back button, Wayne Giffey Jr, 1991, sold in Washington state as fund-raiser, MOC, L2, set of 3 ..$10.00

McDonald's, pin-back button, World's Largest Drive-Thru, 1990, special fund-raiser in Sacramento, 3", M, L2......$3.00

McDonald's, Pinata, Fry Girl or Fry Guy, 13", ea, from $8 to $10.00

McDonald's, plate, 1989, Ronald Rhyme, Melamine, 9", M ..$5.00

McDonald's, plate, 1993, any carnival scene, Melamine, 9½", ea, M...$5.00

McDonald's, playset, Playskool, 1970s, MIB, from $50 to ..$60.00

McDonald's, pog, Ronald McDonald House, Hawaii..........$2.00

McDonald's, popsicle mold, 1989, Ronald figure w/hdl......$3.00

McDonald's, poster, 1991, Florida Marlins, Welcome to Major League Baseball $5.00

McDonald's, puppet, Uncle O'Grimacey, inflatable, from Happy Meal Test IV, uncut, L2.................................$7.00

McDonald's, ring, Ronald's face or Spaceship Friendship, ea, from $3 to..$5.00

McDonald's, ring, silver w/emblem at top, restaurant on side, EX, B10...$50.00

McDonald's, ruler, 1981, Ronald, plastic, 6" $2.00

McDonald's, shoe lace ornament, 1986, Fry Girl $2.00

McDonald's, sipper, 1991, Minute Maid, plastic.................$2.00

McDonald's, sunglasses, Ronald, Birdie or Hamburglar, MIP, ea $4.00

McDonald's, telephone, 1994, replica of #27 race car, tone or pulse dialing, MIB...$45.00

McDonald's, translite, Play Dick Tracy Crime Stopper Game, plastic w/Tracy & wristwatch, 21½x21½", from $8 to........$10.00

McDonald's, translite, Raggedy Ann & Andy, sm, C3 .....$15.00

McDonald's, translite, Super Looney Tunes, sm, from $5 to....**$10.00**

McDonald's, translite, Tiny Toons Adventure, sm, from $5 to **$10.00**

McDonald's, travel kit, Ronald McDonald, NMIB, J2 .....**$35.00**

McDonald's, whistle, 1985, McDonald Tootler, gr **$2.00**

McDonald's (Foreign), clip pin, Grimace, Santa Claus or Snowman, M, P10, ea **$3.00**

McDonald's (Foreign), rub-off decal, various characters, MIP, P10 ....**$2.00**

McDonald's (Foreign), snow dome, Ronald skating or w/snowman, P10, ea..**$8.00**

Pizza Hut, pin-back button, Pizza Hut's Book It, M, P10 ....**$3.00**

Pizza Hut, pizza cutter, plastic, P10.............................**$3.00**

White Castle, magnet, Castleburger, M, P10 ....**$4.00**

Fisher-Price

Fisher-Price toys are becoming one of the hottest new trends in the collector's marketplace today. In 1930 Herman Fisher, backed by Irving Price, Elbert Hubbard and Helen Schelle, formed one of the most successful toy companies ever to exist in East Aurora, NY. The company has seen many changes since then, the most notable being the changes in ownership. From 1930 to 1968, it was owned by the individuals mentioned previously and a few stockholders. In 1969 the company was acquired by Quaker Oats, then in June of 1991 it became independently owned. But in November of 1993, one of the biggest undertakings in the toy industry took place: Fisher-Price became a subdivision of Mattel.

There are a few things to keep in mind when collecting Fisher-Price toys. You should count on a little edge wear as well as some paint fading or wear. The prices in the listings are for toys in that kind of condition. Pull toys found in mint condition are truly rare and command a higher value, especially if you find one with its original box. This also applies to playsets, but to command the higher prices, they must also be complete, with all pieces present. Another very important rule to remember is there are no set colors for pieces that came with a playset. Fisher-Price often substituted a piece of a different color when they ran short. Please note that dates on the toys indicate their copyright date and not the date they were manufactured.

The company put much time and thought into designing their toys. They took care to operate by their 5-point creed: to make toys with (1) intrinsic play value, (2) ingenuity, (3) strong construction, (4) good value for the money, and (5) action. Some of the most sought-after pull toys are those bearing the Walt Disney logo.

The ToyFest limited editions are a series of toys produced in conjunction with ToyFest, an annual weekend of festivities for young and old alike held in East Aurora, NY. It is sponsored by the 'Toy Town USA Museum' and is held every year in August. Fisher-Price produces a limited-edition toy for this event. (For more information on ToyFest and the museum, write to Toy Town Museum, P.O. Box 238, East Aurora, NY 14052.) For more information on Fisher-Price toys we recommend *Fisher-Price, A Historical Rarity Value Guide* by John J. Murray and Bruce R. Fox, and *Modern Toys, American Toys, 1930-1980* by Linda Baker.

Additional information may be obtained through the Fisher-Price Collectors' Club who publish a quarterly newsletter; their address may be found in the Directory under Clubs, Newsletters and Other Publications.

Advisor: Brad Cassidy (C13). (Brad asks that he be allowed to thank his wife and three daughters, his brother Beau, Jeanne Kennedy and Deanna Korth, all of whom he feels have been very instrumental in his life and hold a special place in his heart.)

Note: Prices are for examples that show only a little edge and paint wear and minimal fading (EX).

Other Sources: J2, J6, N2, O1, S20, T1

#0005 Bunny Cart, 1948, C13 ....**$75.00**

#0007 Doggy Racer, 1942, C13 ....**$200.00**

#0007 Looky Fire Truck, 1950, C13.............................**$100.00**

#0008 Bouncy Racer, 1960, C13 ....**$40.00**

#0010 Bunny Cart, 1940, C13.......................................**$75.00**

#0012 Bunny Truck, 1941, C13.....................................**$75.00**

#0015 Bunny Cart, 1946, C13.......................................**$75.00**

#0020 Animal Cutouts, 1942, duck, elephant, pony or Scotty dog, C13, ea **$50.00**

#0028 Bunny Egg Cart, 1950, C13 ....**$75.00**

#0050 Baby Chick Tandem Cart, 1953, no number on toy, C13 ....**$100.00**

#0052 Rabbit Cart, 1950, C13.......................................**$75.00**

#0075 Baby Duck Tandem Cart, 1953, no number on toy, C13 ....**$75.00**

#0100 Dr Doodle, 1931, C13.......................................**$700.00**

#0100 Musical Sweeper, 1950, plays Whistle While You Work, C13 ....**$250.00**

#0101 Granny Doodle, 1931, C13 ....**$700.00**

#0102 Drumming Bear, 1931, C13 ....**$700.00**

#0102 Drumming Bear, 1932, fatter & taller version, C13...**$700.00**

#0103 Barky Puppy, 1931, C13 ....**$700.00**

#0104 Looky Monk, 1931, C13 ....**$700.00**

#0105 Bunny Scoot, 1931, C13 ....**$700.00**

#0109 Looky Monk, 1932, C13 ....**$700.00**

#0110 Chubby Chief, 1932, C13 ....**$700.00**

#0111 Play Family Merry-Go-Round, 1972-76, plays Skater's Waltz, w/4 figures, C13 ....**$40.00**

#0112 Picture Disk Camera, 1968-71, w/5 picture disks, C13 ...**$40.00**

#0114 Music Box TV, 1967, plays London Bridge & Row Row Row Your Boat as pictures pass screen, C13...............**$20.00**

#0114 Sesame Street Music Box TV, 1984-87, plays People In Your Neighborhood, C13 ....**$10.00**

#0118 Tumble Tower Game, 1972-75, w/10 marbles, C13 ....**$15.00**

#0120, Cackling Hen, 1958, wht, C13 ....**$40.00**

#0121 Happy Hopper, 1969-76, C13............................**$25.00**

#0122 Bouncing Buggy, 1974-79, 6 wheels, C13 ....**$10.00**

#0123 Cackling Hen, 1967, red litho, C13 ....**$40.00**

#0125 Music Box Iron, 1967-69, C13 ....**$50.00**

#0125 Uncle Timmy Turtle, 1956, red shell, C13..........**$100.00**

#0130 Wobbles, 1964-65, dog wobbles when pulled, C13..**$50.00**

#0131 Milk Wagon, 1965-72, truck w/bottle carrier, C13...**$55.00**

#0131 Toy Wagon, 1951, driver's head pops up & down when pulled by 2 musical horses, C13 ....**$250.00**

#0132 Dr Doodle, 1958, C13......................................$100.00

#0132 Molly Moo Cow, 1972-78, C13.....................$35.00

#0135 Play Family Animal Circus, 1974-76, complete, C13 ..$50.00

#0136 Play Family Lacing Shoe, 1966-69, complete, C13.$50.00

#0137 Pony Chime, 1962, pk plastic wheels, C13 ....$50.00

#0138 Jack-in-the-Box Puppet, 1970-73, C13 ....$30.00

#0139 Tuggy Tooter, 1967-73, C13 ....$40.00

#0139 Tuggy Turtle, 1959, C13 ....$100.00

#0140 Coaster Boy, 1941, C13 ....$700.00

#0142 Three Men in a Tub, 1970-73, C13 ....$20.00

#0145 Humpty Dumpty Truck, 1963, rnd heads w/wood nose, C13...$40.00

#0146 Play Family Pull-A-Long Lacing Shoe, 1970-75, w/6 figures & 50" rnd lace, C13 ....$45.00

#0148 TV-Radio, 1959-67, Jack 'N Jill, wood & plastic, C13..$40.00

#0149 Dog Cart Donald, 1936, C13................................$700.00

#0150 Pop-Up-Pal Chime Phone, 1968-78, C13.............$40.00

#0150 Teddy Totter, 1940, C13 ....$400.00

#0150 Timmy Turtle, 1953, gr shell, C13 ....$100.00

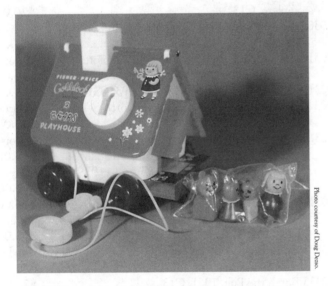

#0151 Goldilocks and the Three Bears Playhouse, 1967-71, complete with figures and plastic key, $60.00.

#0152 Road Roller, 1934, C13 ....$700.00

#0154 Frisky Frog, 1971-83, squeeze plastic bulb & frog jumps, C13 ....$20.00

#0154 TV-Radio, 1964-67, Pop Goes the Weasel, wood & plastic, C13 ....$25.00

#0155, TV-Radio, 1968-70, Jack 'N Jill, wood & plastic w/see-through window on back, C13 ....$40.00

#0155 Skippy Sam, 1934, C13 ....$850.00

#0156 Circus Wagon, 1942, band leader in wagon, C13..$400.00

#0156 Jiffy Dump Truck, 1971-73, squeeze bulb & dump moves, C13...$30.00

#0156 TV-Radio, 1966-67, Baa-Baa Black Sheep, wood & plastic $50.00

#0158 Katie Kangaroo, 1976-77, squeeze bulb & she hops, C13 ....$30.00

#0158 TV-Radio, 1967, Little Boy Blue, wood & plastic, C13...$50.00

#0159 TV-Radio, 1961-65 & Easter 1966, Ten Little Indians, wood & plastic, C13 ....$20.00

#0160 Donald & Donna Duck, 1937, C13 ....$700.00

#0161 Creative Block Wagon, 1961-66, 18 building blocks & 6 wooden dowels fit into pull-along wagon, C13 ....$75.00

#0161 Looky Chug-Chug, 1949, C13 ....$250.00

#0161 TV-Radio, 1968-70, Old Woman Who Lived in a Shoe, wood & plastic w/see-through window on back, C13..$30.00

#0162 Roly Poly Sailboats, 1968-69, C13 ....$15.00

#0164 Chubby Cub, 1969-72, C13................................$20.00

#0164 Mother Goose, 1964-66, C13 ....$40.00

#0166 Bucky Burro, 1955, C13 ....$250.00

#0166 Piggy Bank, 1981-82, pk plastic, C13 ....$20.00

#0166 TV-Radio, 1963-66, Farmer in the Dell, C13 ....$20.00

#0168 Magnetic Chug-Chug, 1964-69, C13 ....$50.00

#0168 Snorky Fire Engine, 1960, gr litho, 4 wooden firemen & dog, C13...$125.00

#0169 Snorky Fire Engine, 1961, red litho, 4 wht wooden firemen, C13 ....$100.00

#0170 Change-A-Tune Carousel, 1981-83, music box w/crank hdl, 3 molded records & 3 child figures, C13..............$40.00

#0171 Toy Wagon, 1942, ponies move up & down, bell rings, C13 ....$300.00

#0172 Roly Raccoon, 1980-82, waddles side to side, tail bobs & weaves, C13 ....$15.00

#0175 Gold Star Stagecoach, 1954, w/2 litho wood mail pouches, C13 ....$250.00

#0175 Kicking Donkey, 1937, C13 ....$450.00

#0175 TV-Radio, 1971-73, Winnie the Pooh, Sears distribution only, C13 ....$25.00

#0177 Donald Duck Xylophone, 1946, 2nd version w/'Donald Duck' on hat, C13 ....$300.00

#0177 Oscar the Grouch, 1977-84, C13 ....$30.00

#0178 What's in My Pocket, 1972-73, 10-pg cloth book w/8 pockets & 8 plastic replicas of boys' pocket items, C13 ....$20.00

#0181 Snoopy Sniffer, 1971, MIB, $50.00.

#0183 Play Family Fun Jet, 1970-80, 1st version, red plastic wings w/bl engines, 4 wooden figures, no hole for gas, C13 ....$15.00

#0185 Donald Duck Xylophone, 1938, mk WDE, C13..$800.00

#0189 Pull-A-Tune Blue Bird Music Box, 1968-79, hangs on crib, plays Children's Prayer, C13 ....$350.00

#0190 Gabby Duck, 1939, C13 ....$350.00

#0190 Pull-A-Tune Pony Music Box, 1969-72, hangs on crib, plays Shubert's Cradle Song, C13 ....$100.00

#0191 Golden Gulch Express, 1961, C13 ....$100.00

#0192 Playland Express, 1962, C13............................$100.00

#0194 Push Pullet, 1971-72, 16" push stick, C13..............$25.00

#0195 Double-Screen TV Music Box, 1965-69, Mary Had a Little Lamb, wood & plastic, C13 ....$20.00

#0195 Teddy Bear Parade, 1938, C13 ....$600.00

#0196 Double-Screen TV Music Box, 1964-69, Hey Diddle Diddle, wood & plastic, C13 ....$30.00

#0200 Mary Doll, 1974-78, vinyl face & hands w/cloth body, removable apron & skirt, C13 ....$40.00

#0200 Winky Blinky Fire Truck, 1954, C13 ....$100.00

#0201 Jenny Doll, 1974-78, vinyl face & hands w/cloth body, removable skirt, C13........................$40.00

#0201 Woodsy-Wee Circus, 1931, complete, C13 ....$650.00

#0202 Natalie Doll, 1974-78, vinyl face & hands w/cloth body, removable skirt & bonnet, C13........................$40.00

#0203 Audrey Doll, 1974-78, vinyl face & hands w/cloth body, removable jeans, C13 ....$40.00

#0204 Baby Ann Doll, 1974-78, vinyl face & hands w/cloth body, removable nightgown & diaper, C13 ....$40.00

#0205 Black Elizabeth Doll, 1974-78, vinyl face & hands w/cloth body, removable skirt, C13........................$40.00

#0205 Woodsy-Wee Zoo, 1931, complete w/camel, giraffe, lion, bear & elephant, C13 ....$650.00

#0206 Joey Doll, 1975, vinyl face & hands w/cloth body, w/jacket, lace & tie sneakers, C13........................$40.00

#0207 Woodsy-Wee Pets, 1931, complete w/goat, donkey, cow, pig & cart, C13 ....$650.00

#0208 Honey Bee, 1978, yel & wht, C13........................$10.00

#0209 Woodsy-Wee Dog Show, 1932, complete w/5 dogs, C13 ....$650.00

#0215 Fisher-Price Choo-Choo, 1955, engine w/4 cars, C13 ..$85.00

#0234 Nifty Station Wagon, 1960, removable roof, 4 wooden family figures & dog, C13 ....$250.00

#0250 Big Performing Circus, 1932, complete w/figures, animals & accessories, C13........................$950.00

#0250 Dollhouse, 1978-79, 3-story w/5 rooms, spiral staircase, 2 figures, wallpaper & instructions, C13 ....$40.00

#0251 Dinette, 1978, pedestal table w/4 chairs, C13, ea.....$2.00

#0252 Kitchen Appliances, 1978, oven range w/exhaust, refrigerator & sink, C13, ea........................$2.00

#0253 Bathroom, 1978, sink, toilet unit & shower stall, C13, ea........................$2.00

#0254 Chair & Fireplace, 1978, C13, ea $2.00

#0255 Bedroom Set, 1978, brass bed w/cover, dresser w/mirror & 3 drawers, C13, ea........................$2.00

#0256 Living Room Set, 1978, sofa w/cushion & coffee table, C13, ea........................$2.00

#0257 Baby's Room, 1978, baby, crib, dresser & rocking horse, C13, ea........................$2.00

#0258 Music Room, 1978, grand piano w/stool & stereo center, C13, ea........................$2.00

#0259 Patio Set, 1978, redwood-type chair, chaise lounge, grill & collie dog, C13, ea........................$2.00

#0260 Bed Set, 1979, bunkbed w/mattress & female figure, C13, ea........................$2.00

#0261 Desk Set, 1980, roll-top desk w/swivel chair & spinning globe, C13, ea........................$2.00

#0262, Grandfather Clock & Rocker, 1980, C13, ea..........$2.00

#0263 Deluxe Decorator Set w/Lights, 1981, hutch w/2 compartments for AA batteries, 2 lamps, C13, ea....................$2.00

#0264 Dining Room Set, butterfly drop-leaf table w/wht bowl & 4 chairs, C13, ea........................$2.00

#0265 Dollhouse Family, dad, mom & 2 daughters, C13, ea........................$2.00

#0268 Wing Chair & Rug Set, chair w/footstool, lg potted plant & Oriental-style rug, C13, ea $2.00

#0280 Dollhouse w/Lights, 1981, same as #250 but lighted, has battery compartment & 7 outlets, C13 ....$30.00

#0302 Chick Basket Cart, 1957, C13........................$40.00

#0303 Adventure People Emergency Rescue Truck, 1975-78, complete, C13........................$15.00

#0303 Bunny Push Cart, 1957, C13 ....$75.00

#0304 Adventure People Safari Set, 1975-78, complete, C13 ..$25.00

#0304 Running Bunny Cart, 1957, C13........................$75.00

#0306 Adventure People Sport Plane, 1975-80, orange & wht plane w/gold pilot, C13........................$8.00

#0307 Adventure People & Their Wilderness Patrol, 1975-79, complete, C13........................$20.00

#0309 Adventure People & Their TV Action Team, 1977-78, complete, C13........................$25.00

#0310 Adventure People & Their Sea Explorer, 1975-80, complete, C13........................$15.00

#0310 Mickey Mouse Puddle Jumper, 1953, C13 ....$125.00

#0312 Adventure People & Their North Woods Trailblazer, 1977-82, complete, C13 ....$15.00

#0318 Adventure People Daredevil Sports Van, 1978-82, complete, C13........................$15.00

#0322 Adventure People Dune Buster, 1979-82, complete, C13 ....$12.00

#0323 Aero-Marine Search Team, 1978-83, complete, C13..$15.00

#0325 Adventure People Alpha Probe, 1980-84, complete, C13 ....$15.00

#0325 Buzzy Bee, 1950, 1st version, dk yel & blk litho, wooden wheels & antenna tips, C13 ....$40.00

#0333 Butch the Pup, 1951, C13 ....$75.00

#0334 Adventure People Sea Shark, 1981-84, complete, C13 ..$8.00

#0345 Penelope the Performing Penguin, 1935, w/up, C13 ..$700.00

#0350 Adventure People Rescue Team, 1976-79, complete, C13 ....$12.00

#0350 Go 'N Back Mule, 1931, w/up, C13 ....$800.00

#0351 Adventure People Mountain Climbers, 1976-79, complete, C13........................$12.00

#0352 Adventure People Construction Workers, 1976-79, complete, C13........................$12.00

#0353 Adventure People Scuba Divers, 1976-81, complete, C13 ....$12.00

#0354 Adventure People Daredevil Skydiver, 1977-81, complete, C13........................$12.00

#0355 Adventure People White Water Kayak, 1977-80, complete, C13........................$12.00

#0355 Go 'N Back Bruno, 1931, w/up, C13................$800.00

#0356 Adventure People Cycle Racing Team, 1977-81, complete, C13........................$6.00

#0357 Adventure People Fire Star 1, blk & silver rocket sled, life-support cable & pilot figure, C13 ....$8.00

#0358 Adventure People Deep Sea Diver, 1980-84, complete, C13 ....$8.00

#0358 Donald Duck Back-Up, 1936, w/up, C13 ....$800.00

#0360 Go 'N Back Jumbo, 1931, w/up, C13 ....$800.00

#0365 Puppy Back-Up, 1932, w/up, C13 ....$800.00

#0367 Adventure People Turbo Hawk, 1982-83, complete, C13 ....$8.00

#0368 Adventure People Alpha Interceptor, 1982-83, wht 2-stage space vehicle, astronaut & tether, C13 ....$8.00

#0375 Bruno Back-Up, 1932, w/up, C13 ....$800.00

#0377, Adventure People Astro Knight, 1979-80, foam plastic space glider & figure, C13.................................$6.00

#0400 Donald Duck Drum Major, 1946, C13 ....$275.00

#0400 Donald Duck Drum Major Cart, 1946, C13 ....$275.00

#0404 Bunny Egg Cart, 1949, C13 ....$50.00

#0405 Lofty Lizzy, 1931, Giraffe Pop-Up Kritter, C13 ...$225.00

#0407 Chick Cart, 1950, C13 ....$50.00

#0407 Dizzy Dino, 1931, Dinosaur Pop-Up Kritter, C13.$225.00

#0410 Stoopy Stork, 1931, Pop-Up Kritter, C13 ....$225.00

#0415 Lop-Ear Looie, 1934, Mouse Pop-Up Kritter, C13.$225.00

#0415 Super Jet, 1952, C13...$225.00

#0420 Sunny Fish, 1955, C13 ....$225.00

#0422 Jumbo Jitterbug, 1940, Elephant Pop-Up Kritter, C13 ..$225.00

#0425 Donald Duck Pop-Up, 1938, C13 ....$400.00

#0432 Mickey Mouse Choo-Choo, 1938, C13 ....$600.00

#0432-532 Donald Duck Drum Major Cart, 1948, C13 ...$300.00

#0433 Dizzy Donkey, 1939, Pop-Up Kritter, C13 ....$100.00

#0434 Ferdinand the Bull, 1939, C13 ....$600.00

#0440 Goofy Gertie, 1935, Stork Pop-Up Kritter, C13..$225.00

#0440 Pluto Pop-Up, 1936, mk WDE, oilcloth ears, C13..$225.00

#0440 Pluto Pop-Up, 1936, mk WDP, C13 ....$100.00

#0444 Queen Buzzy Bee, 1959, red litho, C13 ....$40.00

#0445 Nosey Pup, 1956, C13.......................................$75.00

#0448 Mini Copter, 1971-83, bl litho, C13 ....$25.00

#0450 Donald Duck Choo-Choo, 1941, 8½", C13.........$400.00

#0450 Donald Duck Choo-Choo, 1942, bl hat, C13 ......$200.00

#0450 Music Box-Radio, 1981-83, Teddy Bear Picnic, plastic, C13...$15.00

#0454 Donald Duck Drummer, 1949, C13 ....$300.00

#0460 Dapper Donald Duck, 1936, C13 ....$600.00

#0460 Movie Viewer, 1973-90, crank hdl, C13 ....$5.00

#0461 Movie Viewer Cartridge, 1973-90, color, C13, ea....$6.00

#0469 Donald Cart, 1940, C13 ....$400.00

#0474 Bunny Racer, 1942, C13....................................$225.00

#0476 Cookie Pig, 1967, C13 ....$50.00

#0476 Mickey Mouse Drummer, 1941, C13 ....$300.00

#0477 Dr Doodle, 1940, C13 ....$225.00

#0478 Pudgy Pig, 1962, C13..$50.00

#0480 Leo the Drummer, 1952, C13.............................$225.00

#0485 Mickey Mouse Choo-Choo, 1949, new litho version of #432, C13 ....$100.00

#0488 Popeye Spinach Eater, 1939, C13 ....$600.00

#0494 Pinocchio, 1939, C13 ....$600.00

#0499 Kitty Bell, 1950, C13...$100.00

#0500 Donald Duck Cart, 1937, no number on toy, 3 colors, C13 ....$700.00

#0500 Donald Duck Cart, 1951, no baton, gr litho background, C13 ....$350.00

#0479 Donald Duck and Nephews, Walt Disney Productions, 1941, $475.00.

#0500 Donald Duck Cart, 1953, w/baton, new litho w/yel background, C13 ....$350.00

#0500 Pick-Up & Peek Puzzles, 1972-86, C13, ea $10.00

#0510 Strutter Donald Duck, 1941, C13 ....$300.00

#0530 Mickey Mouse Band, 1935, C13 ....$800.00

#0533 Thumper Bunny, 1942, C13................................$500.00

#0544 Donald Duck Cart, 1942, C13............................$300.00

#0557 Toy Lunch Kit, 1957, red, wht & gr plastic barn shape, no litho, C13...$40.00

#0604 Bunny Bell Cart, 1954, C13 ....$100.00

#0605 Donald Duck Cart, 1954, C13............................$300.00

#0605 Horse & Wagon, 1933, C13 ....$600.00

#0605 Woodsey Mayor Goodgrub Mole Book, 1981, 32 pgs, C13 ....$20.00

#0606 Woodsey Bramble Beaver, 1981, 32 pgs, C13 ....$20.00

#0607 Woodsey Very Blue Bird Book, 1981, 32 pgs, C13..$20.00

#0615 Tow Truck, 1960, C13..$75.00

#0616 Chuggy Pop-Up, 1955, C13, $100.00.

#0616 Patch Pony, 1963, C13 ....$50.00

#0617 Prancing Pony, 1965-70, C13.............................$40.00

#0625 Playful Puppy, 1961, w/shoe, C13......................$50.00

#0626 Playful Puppy, 1963, w/shoe, C13......................$50.00

#0629 Fisher-Price Tractor, 1962, C13 ....$50.00

#0630 Fire Truck, 1959, C13..$50.00

#0634 Drummer Boy, 1967-69, drummer beats hollow drum w/spring-mounted mallets, plastic base, C13 ....$50.00

#0641 Toot-Toot Engine, 1962, bl litho, C13 ....$75.00

#0641 Toot-Toot Engine, 1964-87, red litho, C13 ....$3.00

#0642 Dinky Engine, 1959, blk litho, C13.....................$75.00

#0642 Smokie Engine, 1960, blk litho, C13....................$75.00

#0649 Stake Truck, 1960, C13.................................$50.00

#0653 Allie Gator, 1960, C13................................$100.00

#0654 Tawny Tiger, 1962, C13................................$100.00

#0656 Bossy Bell, 1960, w/bonnet, C13 ....$60.00

#0656 Bossy Bell, 1961, no bonnet, new litho design, C13.$50.00

#0658 Lady Bug, 1961-62, C13 ....$55.00

#0659 Puzzle Puppy, 1976, 8-pc take-apart & put-together dog, C13..$15.00

#0662 Merry Mousewife, 1962, C13.............................$50.00

#0677 Picnic Basket, 1975-79, plastic w/accessories & cotton tablecloth, C13 ....$30.00

#0678 Kriss Krickey, 1955, C13.............................$100.00

#0685 Car & Boat, 1968-69, wood & plastic, 5 pcs, C13 .$40.00

#0686 Car & Camper, 1968-70, wood & plastic, 5 pcs, C13..$50.00

#0686 Perky Pot, 1958, C13..................................$50.00

#0695 Pinky Pig, 1956, missing wooden eyes, C13.........$100.00

#0695 Pinky Pig, 1958, litho eyes, C13.....................$100.00

#0698 Talky Parrot, 1963, C13..............................$100.00

#0700 Cowboy Chime, 1951, C13 ....$250.00

#0700 Popeye, 1935, hitting bell, C13......................$700.00

#0700 Woofy Wowser, 1940, C13..............................$400.00

#0703 Bunny Engine, 1954, C13..............................$100.00

#0703 Popeye the Sailor, 1936, C13.........................$700.00

#0705 Mini Snowmobile, 1971-73, w/sled, 2 figures & dog, C13 .$50.00

#0705 Popeye Cowboy, 1937, on horse, C13...................$700.00

#0711 Cry Baby Bear, 1967-69, C13...........................$40.00

#0711 Huckleberry Hound, 1961, Sears only, C13.........$300.00

#0711 Raggedy Ann & Andy, 1941, C13........................$700.00

#0712 Fred Flintstone Xylophone, 1962, Sears only, C13 ..$250.00

#0712 Teddy Tooter, 1957, C13..............................$250.00

#0714 Mickey Mouse Xylophone, 1963, Sears only, C13 .$250.00

#0715 Ducky Flip Flap, 1964-65, 21" push stick, C13 ......$40.00

#0715 Peter Bunny Engine, 1941, C13........................$225.00

#0717 Ducky Flip Flap, 1937-40, Easter only, C13.........$400.00

#0718 Tow Truck & Car, 1969-70, wood & plastic, C13.$30.00

#0719 Cuddly Cub, 1973-77, head turns & chimes when rocked, C13..$20.00

#0719 Fisher-Price Choo-Choo, 1963, engine, 3 cars, 3 figures & dog, C13..$40.00

#0720 Fisher-Price Fire Engine, 1969, w/driver & 2 firemen, C13..$20.00

#0720 Pinocchio, 1939, C13.................................$500.00

#0721 Peter Bunny Engine, 1949, C13........................$200.00

#0724 Jolly Jalopy, 1965-78, circus clown's roadster, C13 ..$15.00

#0725 Play Family Bath/Utility Room Set, 1972, 4 wooden figures & accessories, C13...................................$20.00

#0726 Play Family Patio Set, 1970, 3 figures w/dog & accessories, C13..$20.00

#0728 Buddy Bullfrog, 1959, yel body w/red litho coat, C13 ..$75.00

#0728 Buddy Bullfrog, 1961, gr coat w/red & wht pants, C13...$75.00

#0728 Play Family House Decorator Set, 1970, 4 figures w/accessories, C13..$20.00

#0729 Fisher-Price Cash Register, 1960, w/3 wooden coins, C13..$50.00

#0732 Happy Hauler, 1968-70, wooden garden tractor w/plastic cart, C13..$40.00

#0733 Mickey Mouse Safety Patrol, 1956, C13.............$250.00

#0734 Teddy Zilo, 1964-66, C13..............................$45.00

#0735 Juggling Jumbo, 1958, C13............................$225.00

#0736 Humpty Dumpty, 1972-79, plastic, C13.................$8.00

#0737 Galloping Horse & Wagon, 1948, C13................$250.00

#0737, Ziggy Zilo, 1958, $75.00.

#0738 Dumbo Circus Racer, 1941, rubber arms, C13.....$700.00

#0738 Shaggy Zilo, 1960, C13................................$75.00

#0739 Poodle Zilo, 1962, C13................................$75.00

#0741 Teddy Zilo, 1967, C13.................................$40.00

#0741 Trotting Donald Duck, 1937, C13......................$800.00

#0745 Elsie's Dairy Truck, 1948, w/2 bottles, C13 ....$400.00

#0746 Pocket Radio, 1977-78, It's a Small World, wood & plastic, C13...$25.00

#0750 Hot Dog Wagon, 1938, C13.............................$400.00

#0750 Space Blazer, 1953, C13..............................$400.00

#0752 Teddy Zilo, 1946, 1st version, clown outfit w/red cheeks, C13..$350.00

#0752 Teddy Zilo, 1948, 2nd version, no outfit, C13.....$325.00

#0756 Pocket Radio, 1973, 12 Days of Christmas, wood & plastic, C13...$25.00

#0757 Humpty Dumpty, 1957, C13.............................$225.00

#0758 Pocket Radio, 1970-72, Mulberry Bush, wood & plastic, C13..$20.00

#0759 Pocket Radio, 1969-73, Do-Re-Me, wood & plastic, C13..$20.00

#0760 Peek-A-Boo Block, 1970-79, C13.......................$20.00

#0761 Play Family Nursery Set, 1973, family of 4 w/baby & accessories, C13..$8.00

#0762 Pocket Radio, 1972-77, Raindrops, wood & plastic, C13..$15.00

#0763 Music Box, 1962, Farmer in the Dell, yel litho, C13 ..$50.00

#0763 Pocket Radio, 1978, Whistle a Happy Tune, wood & plastic, C13...$20.00

#0764 Music Box, 1960-61 & Easter 1962, Farmer in the Dell, red litho, C13...$50.00

#0764 Pocket Radio, 1975-76, My Name Is Michael, C13 .$15.00

#0765 Pocket Radio, 1976, Humpty Dumpty, wood & plastic, C13..$25.00

#0765 Talking Donald Duck, 1955, C13 ....$125.00

#0766 Pocket Radio, 1968-70, Where Has My Little Dog Gone?, wood & plastic, C13...$20.00

#0766 Pocket Radio, 1977-78, I'd Like To Teach the World To Sing, C13..$20.00

#0767 Pocket Radio, 1977, Twinkle Twinkle Little Star, C13..$20.00

#0768 Pocket Radio, 1971-76, Happy Birthday, wood & plastic, C13..$15.00

#0772, Pocket Radio, 1974-76, Jack & Jill, C13 ....$15.00

#0774 Pocket Radio, 1967-71, Twinkle Twinkle Little Star, wood & plastic, C13...$20.00

#0775 Pocket Radio, 1967-68, Sing a Song of Six Pence, C13...$25.00

#0775 Pocket Radio, 1973-75, Pop Goes the Weasel, wood & plastic, C13..$15.00

#0777 Squeaky the Clown, 1958, C13........................$250.00

#0778 Ice Cream Wagon, 1940, C13 ....$350.00

#0778 Pocket Radio, 1967-68, Frere Jacques, wood & plastic, C13..$20.00

#0779 Pocket Radio, 1976, Yankee Doodle, wood & plastic, C13..$20.00

#0784 Mother Goose Music Cart, 1955, C13 ....$100.00

#0785 Blackie Drummer, 1939, C13 ....$450.00

#0786 Perky Penguin, 1973-75, C13 ....$30.00

#0790 Tote-A-Tune Radio, 1979, Let's Go Fly a Kite, plastic, C13..$15.00

#0792 Music Box, 1980-81, Teddy Bear's Picnic, plastic, C13 ....$15.00

#0793 Jolly Jumper, 1963, C13...................................$50.00

#0793 Tote-A-Tune Radio, 1981, When You Wish Upon a Star, plastic, C13..$10.00

#0794 Tote-A-Tune Radio, 1982-91, Over the Rainbow, plastic, C13...$5.00

#0795 Mickey Mouse Drummer, 1937, pie-eyed, C13....$700.00

#0795 Musical Duck, 1952, C13................................$100.00

#0795 Tote-A-Tune Radio, 1984-91, Toyland, C13 ....$10.00

#0798 Chatter Monk, 1957, C13 ....$100.00

#0798 Mickey Mouse Xylophone, 1939, 1st version, w/hat, C13 ....$400.00

#0798 Mickey Mouse Xylophone, 1942, 2nd version, no hat, C13 ....$400.00

#0800 Hot Diggety, 1934, w/up, C13 ....$700.00

#0810 Hot Mammy, 1934, w/up, C13 ....$700.00

#0909 Play Family Rooms, 1972, Sears only, 4 figures w/dog & accessories, C13 ....$75.00

#0910 Change-A-Tune Piano, 1969-72, Pop Goes the Weasel, This Old Man & The Muffin Man, C13...................$40.00

#0915 Play Family Farm, 1968-91, 1st version, 4 wooden figures w/plastic animals & accessories, masonite base, C13.$30.00

#0916 Fisher-Price Zoo, 1984-87, 6 figures w/accessories, C13 ....$35.00

#0919 Music Box Movie Camera, 1968-70, plays This Old Man, w/5 picture disks, C13...$40.00

#0923 Play Family School, 1971-78, 1st version, roof & side hinge open, 5 figures & accessories, C13 ....$20.00

#0926 Concrete Mixer, 1959, C13................................$250.00

#0928 Play Family Fire Station, 1980-82, w/3 figures, dog & accessories, C13 ....$75.00

#0929 Play Family Nursery School, 1978-79, 6 figures & accessories, removable roof, 13¾x10x5½", C13 ....$70.00

#0930 Play Family Action Garage, 1970-85, 1st version, w/elevator, ramp, 4 cars & 4 figures, masonite & plastic, C13 ..$20.00

#0931 Amusement Park, 1963, park map, 6 wooden figures, musical merry-go-round & accessories, C13 ....$300.00

#0931 Play Family Hospital, 1976-78, w/figures & accessories, C13 ....$115.00

#0932 Ferry Boat, 1979-80, 3 figures, 2 cars & 2 life preservers, C13 ....$25.00

#0934 Play Family Western Town, 1982-84, 4 figures & accessories, C13 ....$75.00

#0937 Play Family Sesame Street Clubhouse, 1977-79, w/4 Sesame Street characters & accessories, C13...........$75.00

#0938 Play Family Sesame Street, 1975-78, w/8 Sesame Street characters & accessories, C13.............................$75.00

#0940 Sesame Street Characters, 1977, C13, ea $3.00

#0942 Play Family Lift & Load Depot, 1977-79, w/3 figures & accessories, C13 ....$50.00

#0945 Offshore Cargo Base, 1979-80, 3 platforms, 4 figures & accessories, C13 ....$50.00

#0952 Delivery Truck, 1969-71, 1st version, cb moving truck for yel-roof house, 'Fisher-Price Movers' on side, C13 ....$50.00

#0952 Play Family House, 1969-79, 1st version, 2-story w/yel roof, figures & accessories (packed in cb truck), C13 ....$75.00

#0952 Play Family House, 1969-79, 1st version, 2-story w/yel roof, figures & accessories (no cb delivery truck), C13.........$25.00

#0952 Play Family House, 1980-87, 2nd version, new style litho & brn roof, no staircase, C13 ....$15.00

#0952 Play Family House, 1987-88, 2-story w/yel roof, gr plastic base, complete, C13...$15.00

#0960 Woodsey's Log House, 1979, w/figures, accessories & 32-pg book, C13...$40.00

#0961 Woodsey's Store, 1980, hollow tree w/figures, accessories & 32-pg book, C13...$40.00

#0962 Woodsey's Airport, 1980, airplane, hangar, 1 figure & 32-pg book, C13...$40.00

#0969 Musical Ferris Wheel, 1966-72, 1st version w/4 wooden straight-body figures, rods in seats, C13 ....$50.00

#0969 Musical Ferris Wheel, 1973-80, 2nd version, 4 figures w/shaped bodies, no rods in seats, C13.......................$25.00

#0979 Dump Trucker Playset, 1965-70, w/3 figures & accessories, C13 ....$75.00

#0982 Hot Rod Roadster, 1983-84, riding toy w/4-pc take-apart engine, C13...$65.00

#0983 Safety School Bus, 1959, w/6 figures, Fisher-Price Club logo, C13 ....$250.00

#0985 Play Family Houseboat, 1972-76, w/2 deck lounges, figures & accessories, C13..$40.00

#0987 Creative Coaster, 1964-81, riding toy w/18 blocks & 6 wooden dowels, C13 ....$75.00

#0990 Play Family A-Frame, 1974-76, w/4 figures, dog & accessories, C13 ....$75.00

#0991 Play Family Circus Train, 1973-78, 1st version, w/figures, animals & gondola car, C13 ....$25.00

#0991 Play Family Circus Train, 1979-86, 2nd version, w/figures & animals, no gondola car, C13 ....$15.00

#0992 Play Family Car & Camper, 1980-84, camper unfolds to tent, 4 figures & accessories, C13 ....$30.00

#0993 Play Family Castle, 1974-77, 1st version, w/6 figures & accessories, C13 ....$100.00

#0994 Play Family Camper, 1973-76, w/4 figures & accessories, C13 ....$75.00

#0996 Play Family Airport, 1972-76, 1st version, bl airport w/clear look-out tower, 6 figures & accessories, C13 .$70.00

#0997 Play Family Village, 1973-77, 2-pc village w/bridge, 8 figures, dog & accessories, C13 ....$75.00

#2500 Little People Main Street, 1986-90, w/figures & accessories, C13 ....$40.00

#2525 Little People Playground, 1986-90, w/2 figures & accessories, C13 ....$15.00

#2526 Little People Pool, 1986-88, w/2 figures & accessories, C13 ....$15.00

#2551 Little People Neighborhood, 1988-90, 2-pc playset connects w/tree house, 4 figures & accessories, C13 ....$55.00

#2552 McDonald Restaurant, 1990, 1st version, bl car, trash can, fry coaster, arches & 5 figures, C13 ....$100.00

#2552 McDonald Restaurant, 1991-92, 2nd version, same pcs as 1st version but lg-sz figures, C13 ....$50.00

#5000 Dr Doodle, 1993-94, 1st Fisher-Price limited edition, 1 of 5,000, C13 ....$125.00

#6145 Jingle Elephant, 1993, ToyFest limited edition, 1 of 5,000, C13 ....$75.00

#6550 Buzzy Bee, 1987, ToyFest limited edition, 1 of 5,000, C13 .$130.00

#6558 Snoopy Sniffer, 1988, ToyFest limited edition, 1 of 3,000, C13 ....$625.00

#6575 Toot-Toot, 1989, ToyFest limited edition, 1 of 5,000, C13 ....$135.00

#6588 Snoopy Sniffer, 1990, Fisher-Price Commemorative limited edition, 1 of 3,500, Ponderosa pine, C13 ....$225.00

#6590 Prancing Horses, 1990, ToyFest limited edition, 1 of 5,000, C13 ....$60.00

#6592 Teddy Bear Parade, 1991, ToyFest limited edition, 1 of 5,000, C13 ....$50.00

#6593 Squeaky the Clown, 1995, ToyFest limited edition, 1 of 5,000, C13 ....$100.00

#6599 Molly Bell Cow, 1992, ToyFest limited edition, 1 of 5,000, C13 ....$150.00

#8121 My Friend Karen Doll, 1990, was never produced, only 200 made, C13 ....$125.00

Furniture

Any item of furniture imaginable has been reduced to child size, and today these small-scale dressers, washstands, chairs, and tables are especially popular with doll collectors who use them to display a favorite doll. If you'd like to learn more, we recommend *Children's Glass Dishes, China, and Furniture, Vol I and II*, by Doris Anderson Lechler.

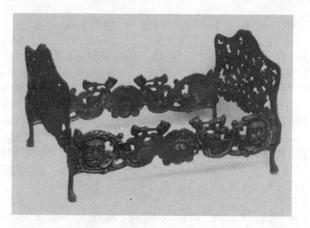

Bed, black-painted cast iron, ornate design with 2 children playing horns and 3 scowling faces on sides, 31", EX, A, $600.00.

Bed, Victorian, poplar w/cherry stain, ornate headboard & footboard, 17x29", EX, A $175.00

Bed, walnut, scalloped & pointed headboard & footboard w/cutout in headboard, tall legs, late 1800s, 19", EX, A $275.00

Bedroom Set, hand-pnt wood, bed, mirrored dresser, spindled chairs w/rnd seats, lamp table & chest, 6" to 14" EX, A $550.00

Chair, Morris, early 1900s, all orig, 10", minor upholstery, G16 ....$400.00

Chair, Victorian, wood w/rnd cane seat & rnd open back, 22½", EX, A $120.00

Chairs, contemporary bl upholstered wingback style, 30", EX, A, pr $550.00

Crib, maple, Jenny Lind style w/removable rockers, ca 1860, 27", EX, A $200.00

Cupboard, southern pine, 2 upper hinged glass doors, 2 lower drawers & 1 hinged glass door, ca 1900, 39", EX, A .$300.00

Desk, cherry, folding table top w/inkwell & letter compartments, 9x11", EX, A $40.00

Desk, poplar, spinet type w/compartments, ca 1930, 26x28", EX, A $65.00

Dresser, walnut-stained poplar, 3-drawer Victorian style w/mirror & candle stands, ornate trim, 45x26", EX, A $470.00

Dressing Mirror, floor-standing Empire style w/wood fr, 29", EX, A $165.00

Highchair, Amsco, bl & yel pnt metal w/EX rpt, 25", VG, M15 ....$35.00

Highchair, bentwood w/wicker, 28", EX, A $120.00

Phonograph, Garford, blk upright wood & tin cabinet w/side crank, storage area mk Baby Cabinet, w/7 records, 17", EX, A $525.00

Piano Stool, wood w/turned legs & adjustable seat, possible salesman's sample, 9x7", EX+, H12.........................$225.00

Rocking Chair, ca 1900, oak, floral padded seat, spindle back, 25", EX, A $165.00

Rocking Chair, Gardner, wood, armless folding type, 1870s, 24", EX, A $155.00

Rocking Chair, mahogany, upholstered Empire style, ca 1850, 24", EX, A $220.00

Rocking Chair, stenciled wood w/shaped seat & spindle back, ca 1835, 35", EX, A $300.00

Table, drop-leaf, walnut, removable spindle legs, 10", VG+, A $145.00

Table, gate-leg, oak, 29" L, EX, A $100.00

Table, gate-leg drop-leaf, contemporary, cherry, 34" (extended), EX, A..$485.00

Table, walnut Victorian style w/contoured marble top, ca 1870, 13", EX, A..$200.00

Table & Chairs, tilt-top, wood, 33½" dia table & 4 26" ladder-back chairs w/wicker seats, EX, A $360.00

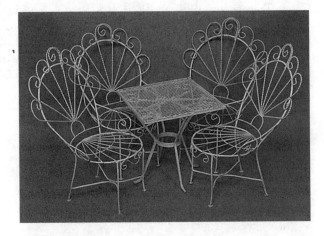

Table and Chairs, white metal with lattice table top, ice-cream parlor-type chairs with scrolled backs and trim, EX, A, $70.00.

What-Not Stand, walnut, Victorian corner-type w/4 shelves, ca 1870, 42", EX, A...$300.00

Wicker Set, 2 settees, 4 chairs & rnd table, natural, 5" to 8", EX, A $60.00

Games

Early games (those from 1850 to 1910) are very often appreciated more for their wonderful lithographed boxes than their 'playability,' and you'll find collectors displaying them as they would any fine artwork. Many boxes and boards were designed by commercial artists of the day.

After a two-year decline, baby-boomer game prices have leveled off. Some science fiction and rare TV games are still in high demand. Games produced in the Art Deco era between the World Wars have gained in popularity — especially those with great design. Victorian games have become harder to find; their prices have also grown steadily. Condition and rarity are the factors that most influence game prices.

When you buy a game, check to see that all pieces are there. Look on the instructions or in the box lid for a listing of contents. For further information we recommend *Baby Boomer Board Games* by Rick Polizzi (Collector Books) and *Board Games of the '50s, '60s and '70s*, distributed by L-W Book Sales.

Advisor: Paul Fink (F3).

A-Team Grenade Toss, Playco, 1983, MIB, J7 ....$25.00

A-Team Moving Knock-Down Target, Arco, MIB, J7 .....$25.00

Acme Bible Book Game, card game, Goodenough & Woglow, 1930s, VG, S16..$45.00

Acquire, 3M, 1968, EX (M box), M6........................$30.00

Across the Continent, board game, Parker Bros, 1952, complete, EX (EX box), J6/F8, from $30 to $45.00

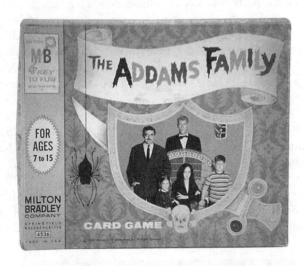

Addams Family, card game, Milton Bradley, 1965, MIB, $45.00.

Addams Family, board game, Milton Bradley, 1973, unused, MIB, C1 ....$72.00

ADT Delivery Boy, board game, Milton Bradley, early, complete, EX (EX box), A $145.00

Adventureland Game, Parker Bros, 1956, VG (EX box), M6 .$45.00

Aggravation, CO-5, 1960s, VG (EX box), M6 ....$30.00

Alfred Hitchcock Presents Why, Milton Bradley, 1958, complete, NM (EX box)...$30.00

Alien, board game, Kenner, 1979, M (EX box), M17.......$65.00

All in the Family, Milton Bradley, 1972, complete, VG (EX box), M6 ....$30.00

Alley Oop, 1937, appears complete, EX (orig canister), A3 .$75.00

Alphabet Soup, Parker Bros, 1992, complete, EX (M box), M6..$25.00

Amazing Dunninger Mind Reading, Hasbro, 1967, EX (orig box), J6...$16.00

Annette's Secret Passage Game, Parker Bros, 1958, based on Disney TV show, EX (orig box) $50.00

Annie, Parker Bros, 1981, complete, EX (EX box), M6/S16.$25.00

Annie Oakley, board game, Milton Bradley, 1955, NMIB, C1 ....$100.00

Annie Oakley, board game, Milton Bradley, 1955, VG (VG box), S16...$70.00

Ants in the Pants, Schaper, 1970, complete, VG (VG box), M6 ....$30.00

Apples Way, Milton Bradley, 1974, VG (VG box), S16 ..$20.00

Aquanauts, Transogram, 1961, missing 2 pcs, NMIB, F8 .$60.00

Archie Bunker's Card Game, Milton Bradley, 1972, NM, J6..$12.00

Around the World, Milton Bradley, 1962, complete, VG (VG box), M6 ....$30.00

Around the World in 80 Days, Transogram, 1957, complete, NMIB, F8 ....$25.00

Arrest & Trial, Transogram, 1963, complete, MIB (sealed), F8 .$70.00

Art Linkletter House Party, Whitman, unused, MIB, V1.**$25.00**

Art of Parqueter (title in English, French & German), 1830s, 60 pcs w/6 instruction pgs, EX (orig wood box), B12 ..**$1,250.00**

Assembly Line, Selchow & Righter, 1953, NMIB, S15....**$45.00**

At The Fort, target game, Milton Bradley, 1906, mk A War Game With Pistols & Ammunition, soldier targets, EX (EX box), A...**$580.00**

Auto Race, video game, 1970s, NM, J6.............................**$30.00**

Bagatelle, Morrill & Silsby, mid-1800s, litho paper on wood, 2 hand-colored harbor scenes, 23¾", G, A................**$200.00**

Bagatelle Pinball Game, Marx, early 1960s, Dick Tracy character graphics, NM, D11 ....**$75.00**

Bali, card game, Selchow & Righter, 1954, complete, G+ (VG box), M6...**$25.00**

Bantu, Parker Bros, 1955, complete, EX (EX box), M6....**$75.00**

Baretta, Milton Bradley, 1976, EX (EX box), T2/S16, from $15 to **$20.00**

Barney Google An' Snuffy Smith Time's A-Wastin'!, Milton Bradley, 1963, NM (EX box), C1...............................**$45.00**

Barney Miller, Parker Bros, 1977, M (NM box), M17......**$25.00**

Photo courtesy of Dunbar Gallery.

Barnyard Tiddledy Winks, Parker Bros, 1930, complete, MIB, from $50.00 to $95.00.

Baseball, Baker, 1920s, w/mechanical players, includes instructions, 26½" sq, G (G box), A...................................**$800.00**

Baseball, electronic hand-held game, Mattel, MIB, J6 .....**$24.00**

Baseball, video game, 1970s, NM, J6.............................**$30.00**

Baseball Game, Parker Bros, 1950, complete, EX (EX box), A..**$125.00**

Bash! Knockout Game, Milton Bradley, 1965, EX+ (EX+ box), F8 ....**$25.00**

Bat Masterson, Lowell, 1956, missing instructions, EX+ (orig box), S16...**$95.00**

Batman Game, University Games, 1989, 50th-Anniversary edition, EX (orig box), S16 ....**$40.00**

Bats in the Belfry, Mattel, 1964, missing 1 pc, NMIB, F8 ....**$90.00**

Battle of the Planets, Milton Bradley, 1979, VG (VG box), S16 ....**$65.00**

Battle Stations, Burleson, 1952, NM (EX+ box), T2........**$50.00**

Battleship, Milton Bradley, 1971, complete, MIB (sealed), M6..**$25.00**

Battlestar Galactica Bagatelle, 1978, MIB, V1.................**$25.00**

Battlestar Galactica/L'Astro Guerre des Galactica, Parker Bros, 1978, Canadian edition, missing 1 pc, EX (EX box), S16 ....**$60.00**

Beany & Cecil Match It, Mattel, 1961, missing 4 pcs, EX (EX box), F8 ....**$25.00**

Beatles Flip Your Wig, Milton Bradley, 1964, complete, VG+ (VG box), B3...**$110.00**

Ben Casey, Transogram, 1961, NMIB, from $25 to **$35.00**

Betsy Ross Flag Game, Transogram, 1960s, EX+ (EX+ box), F8 ....**$25.00**

Beverly Hillbillies, Standard Toycraft, 1963, complete, NMIB, F8 ....**$55.00**

Bewitched, board game, Game Gems, 1965, MIB, $55.00.

Big Foot the Giant Snowman Monster, Milton Bradley, 1977, MIB, H4...**$10.00**

Billionaire, Parker Bros, 1972, VG (orig box).................**$30.00**

Bingo-Matic, Transogram, 1954, M (box missing 1 flap), H12..**$35.00**

Bionic Crisis, Parker Bros, 1975, EX (EX box), S16 ....**$20.00**

Photo courtesy of June Moon.

Bionic Woman, board game, Parker Bros, 1976, complete, MIB, $30.00.

Bionic Woman, Parker Bros, 1976, VG (orig box) **$15.00**

Bit, card game, Parker Bros, 1919, lt edge wear o/w VG, S16..**$22.00**

Black Experience, Theme Prod, 1971, complete, VG (M box), M6..**$50.00**

Blast-Away, Hasbro, 1950s, complete, G (EX box), M6..**$100.00**

Blockade, Corey, 1941, Deluxe Edition, missing 1 pc, VG (VG box), S16...**$90.00**

Blondie, Parker Bros, 1969, missing 3 cards, EX+ (EX box), F8 ....$25.00

Blue Line Hockey, 3M, 1969, complete, EX (EX box), M6 ..$60.00

Bobbsey Twins, board game, Milton Bradley, 1957, MIB, $65.00.

Bonanza Michigan Rummy, Parker Bros, 1964, complete, NM (EX box), F8 ....$35.00

Boob Tube Race, Milton Bradley, 1962, M (NM box), T2..$30.00

Booby Trap, Parker Bros, 1965, NM (EX+ box) $20.00

Bozo, card game, Ed-U Cards, 1972, complete, EX+ (EX+ box), F8 ....$12.00

Brass Monkey, Master Spy, 1973, unused, MIB, V1 ....$28.00

Break the Bank, 1955, unused, MIB, V1 ....$20.00

Bret Ball, Keltner, 1981, complete, EX (EX box), M6......$60.00

Bridge Keno, Milton Bradley, 1930, complete, VG (EX box), M6..$25.00

Bringing Up Father, Embee, 1920, EX+ (VG envelope), A3.$650.00

Buccaneers, Transogram, 1957, NMIB, F8.....................$60.00

Buck Rogers Game of the 25th Century AD, board game, Dille, 1935, no playing pcs, NM (EX box), A $355.00

Bug-A-Boo, Whitman, 1968, litho tin lady bug moves to advance play, complete, EX+ (EX+ box), F8............$25.00

Bugaloos, Milton Bradley, 1971, EX (VG box), S16 ....$25.00

Bugs Bunny & Looney Tunes Race, Milton Bradley, 1968, complete, NMIB, F8 ....$48.00

Buy or Sell Stock Market, board game, KMS, 1967, NMIB, J6 ....$25.00

Calling All Cars, board game, Parker Bros, 1938, VG (VG box), S16 ....$30.00

Camelot Battle, Parker Bros, 1961, VG+ (VG+ box), T2.$20.00

Camp Granada, Milton Bradley, 1965, EX (EX box) $45.00

Camp Runamuck Game, Ideal, 1965, complete, VG (EX box), M6..$45.00

Candyland, Milton Bradley, 1955, complete, G (VG box), M6..$35.00

Capt America, board game, Milton Bradley, 1966, EX (EX box), J2..$30.00

Capt America, board game, Milton Bradley, 1977, NMIB, A6..$15.00

Capt Gallant of the Foreign Legion, Transogram, copied instructions & missing 1 pc, EX+ (EX+ box), F8..................$45.00

Capt Video, board game, Milton Bradley, 1950, complete, M (EX box), A $100.00

Car 54 Where Are You?, board game, Allison, 1961, NM (EX box), F8..$195.00

Careers, Parker Bros, 1957, complete, EX (EX box), M6..$35.00

Careers, Parker Bros, 1957, complete, VG (worn box), S16 ..$25.00

Cargos, Selchow & Righter, 1934, 1st version, NM (EX gr box), F8 ....$60.00

Carnival Shooting Gallery, target game, Ohio Art, missing dart gun, NM (EX box), A $165.00

Carrier Pigeon Geographical Game, Jannin/Paris, 1860s, hand-colored litho in 3 languages, magnetic, EX (orig box), B12 ....$1,000.00

Carrier Strike, Milton Bradley, 1977, VG (VG box), S16..$25.00

Casey Jones Railroad Game Box, Saalfield, 1959, unused, M (NM box), F8..$55.00

Casper & His TV Pals, card game, Ed-U Cards, 1960s, missing 2 cards & instructions, EX+ (EX box), F8..................$8.00

Casper the Friendly Ghost, Milton Bradley, 1959, complete, EX+ (EX+ box)..$20.00

Casper's Goodies, card game, Warren, 1960s-70s, NMIB, F8 ....$12.00

Catchword, Whitman, 1954, complete, G (EX box), M6..$30.00

Cattlemen, Selchow & Righter, 1977, VG (VG box), S16.$40.00

Champion Game of Baseball, Proctor Amusement Co, MIB, $550.00.

Championship Fight Game, Frankie Goodman, 1940s, VG (M box), M6 ....$60.00

Charlie McCarthy Put & Take Bingo, Whitman, 1938, complete, MIB, A..$85.00

Charlie McCarthy Snatch the Hat, 1938, mc wood hats w/cards, MIB, H12..$125.00

Charlie's Angels, board game, Milton Bradley, 1977, NM, J6..$20.00

Checkers, 1940s, wood, 24-pc set, MIB, H12.....................$5.00

Cherry Ames Nursing Game, Parker Bros, 1959, missing few pcs, EX (EX box), F8..$35.00

Chevyland Sweepstakes, Milton Bradley, 1968, complete, EX (EX box), M6..$90.00

Cheyenne, Milton Bradley, 1958, EX (EX box), J2 ....$60.00

Children's Hour, Parker Bros, 1946, VG (VG box), M6..$50.00

Ching Gong, Samuel Gabriel, 1937, VG (VG box), S16.$85.00

Chiromagica, McLoughlin Bros, 1870s, 3 rnd magnetized question cards & 3 overlays w/metal pointer, EX+ (orig box), B12..$850.00

Chit Chat, board game, Milton Bradley, 1963, MIB $15.00

Chrysler Corporation Test Driver, Milton Bradley, 1956, missing 3 pcs, timer not working o/w EX+ (EX box), F8........$25.00

Chuggedy Chug, Milton Bradley, 1955, VG (orig box), S16..$125.00

Chutes & Ladders, Milton Bradley, 1956, EX (EX box), M6....$40.00

Cinderella, board game, 1934, missing 1 token, EX (EX box), T1 ....$65.00

Circus Game, Parker Bros, 1910s, complete, EX (VG+ box), A $185.00

Civil War, Avalon Hill, 1961, VG (VG box), M6 ....$75.00

Classic Major League Baseball, Game Time Ltd, 1987, missing several cards, EX (orig box), S16................................$70.00

Cloak & Dagger, Ideal, 1984, EX (EX box), M6...............$50.00

Close Encounters of the Third Kind, Parker Bros, 1978, copied instructions, EX+ (EX box), F8 ....$16.00

Cold Feet, squirt game, Ideal, 1967, EX (EX box), J2 ....$25.00

Collector's Series Chess Set, Classic Games, 1963, EX (EX box), M6..$50.00

Columbo, board game, Milton Bradley, 1973, NM, J6 .....$14.00

Combat, Ideal, 1963, VG (EX box), M6 ....$40.00

Comic Card Game, Milton Bradley, 1972, NM (EX+ box), F8 ....$36.00

Commercial Traveler, board game, McLoughlin Bros, 1890s, complete, EX (EX box), A $275.00

Concentration, Milton Bradley, 1959, orig edition, missing 1 minor pc, VG (orig box), S16 ....$45.00

Concentration, Milton Bradley, 1961, 4th edition, NM (EX+ box), F8..$15.00

Coney Island, Sel-Right, 1956, complete, scarce, NM (EX+ box), A...$190.00

Confucius Say, card game, Milton Bradley, ca 1937, VG+, S16 ....$50.00

Countdown, The Adventure in Space Game, ES Lowe, 1967, EX (EX box), H4 ....$30.00

Countdown Arithmetic, Whitman, 1962, NM (EX box), D9.$12.00

Cover 'Em Up, Parker Bros, 1891, VG (orig box), S16 ..$220.00

Crandall's Jack Straws, wooded straws w/tab ends depicting letters of the alphabet, 6¼", EX (EX wood canister), A $385.00

Creature Features, Athol Research, 1975, based on monster movies, plays like Monopoly, EX (orig box), S16....$145.00

Criss Cross Spelling Slips, McLoughlin Bros, 1900, complete, NM (EX box), A $165.00

D-Day, Avalon Hill, 1965, VG (EX box), M6..................$25.00

Dan Dare Spaceship Construction, board game, Chad Valley, missing 2 dice, EX+ (VG+ box), A..........................$210.00

Dan Dare Treasure Hunt, Pepys Party Game, Pepys/Eagle, 1950s, complete, NM (EX+ box), A $60.00

Daniel Boone, card game, Ed-U Cards, EX (EX plastic box), J5 ....$15.00

Dark Shadows, Barnabas Collins, Milton Bradley, 1969, missing fangs, NMIB, from $30 to..............................$45.00

Dark Shadows Mysterious Maze, Whitman, 1968, complete, EX (EX box), F8 ....$30.00

Dark Tower Fantasy, Milton Bradley, 1981, EX+ (EX+ box), F8 ....$60.00

Dauntless, Avalon Hill, 1977, EX+ (EX+ box), T2 ....$20.00

Davy Crockett Frontier Target Game, Am Toys, complete, NM (VG box), A $75.00

De Whirst Music, card game, 1936, MIB, H12 ....$25.00

Dennis the Menace Tiddlywinks, EX, V1 ....$20.00

Derby Day, Parker Bros, 1930, complete w/hurdles, G- (VG box), M6 ....$40.00

Descent on Crete, SPI, 1978, G (M box), M6 ....$60.00

Detectives Exciting Game of Deduction, Transogram, 1961, NMIB, F8...$60.00

Dice Ball, Milton Bradley, 1934, VG (orig box w/2 split corners), S16 ....$75.00

Dick Tracy Crime Stopper, Ideal, 1963, EX (EX box), J7..$50.00

Dick Tracy Double Target, Marx, 1941, complete, M (EX box), A, $175.00.

Dick Tracy Master Detective Game, Selchow & Righter, 1961, NMIB, D11 ....$50.00

Dick Tracy Sunday Funnies Game, Ideal, 1972, complete, EX (orig box), D11 ....$50.00

Dick Tracy Target Board, FAS, 1950s, litho cb, 17" dia, EX, K4 ....$50.00

Dick Van Dyke Show, Standard Toykraft, 1962, complete, NMIB, rare, F8..$195.00

Dig, Parker Bros, 1940s, EX (EX box), M6....................$35.00

Digital Derby Auto Raceway, electronic hand-held game, MIB, J6 ....$24.00

Dino the Dinosaur, Transogram, 1961, VG (VG box), S16 .$60.00

Disney Derby, racing game, Metal-Wood Repetitions Co/Sydney Australia, 1940s, complete, EX (orig box), A..........$140.00

Disney's Wonderful World of Color, board game, Parker Bros, 1962, complete, NM (EX+ box), F8 ....$45.00

Disneyland Riverboat, Parker Bros, 1950s, complete, NMIB, M8 ....$40.00

Dispatcher, Avalon Hill, 1961, EX (EX box), M6..........$125.00

Don't Spill the Beans, Schaper, 1967, VG (VG box), M6 .$30.00

Donald Duck's Party Game, Parker Bros, 1938, EX (VG+ box), A3 ....$150.00

Down You Go, Selchow & Righter, 1954, VG (VG box) ..$25.00

Dr Who Game of Time & Space, Games Workshop, 1980, MIB (sealed), F8/J6, from $35 to $45.00

Dragnet Badge 714 Puzzle Game, Transogram, 1955, EX+ (EX box), F8..$26.00

Driver Training Game, Decor Note, 1959, VG (EX box), M6 ....$30.00

Duck Shoot, target game, Superior, 1950s, complete, EX (orig box), A $45.00

Duck Shooting, Parker Bros, ca 1901, missing cork gun, VG (orig box), S16 ....$75.00

Dukes of Hazzard, Ideal, 1981, NRFB, H4..................$25.00

Dunce, Schaper, 1955, EX (EX box), M6 ....$45.00

Dune, board game, Parker Brothers, 1984, MIB (sealed), C1 .$36.00

Dungeon Dice, Parker Bros, 1977, EX (EX box), M6 ....$25.00

Easy Money, Milton Bradley, 1936, G (G- box), M6 ....$25.00

Economic Chess-Board..., PM Roget/Appleton, 1840s, folding board w/cb pcs that fit in slots at side, EX (orig case), B12 ....$600.00

Ed Wynn the Fire Chief, board game, Selchow & Righter, complete, EX+ (EX box), A $75.00

Electric Bunny Run, Prentice, 1951, NM (EX+ box), T2..$50.00

Electric Target Game, Marx, 1940, complete, EX (EX box), A $175.00

Eliot Ness & the Untouchables, Transogram, missing instructions, EX (EX box), D9..$25.00

Ellsworth Elephant, Selchow & Righter, 1960, unused, M (NM box), T2 ....$295.00

Elm Hills Golf, 1946, MIB, V1 ....$36.00

Emergency!, Milton Bradley, 1974, complete, EX+ (EX box), F8 ....$25.00

Endangered Species, Teaching Concepts, 1976, missing 1 pc, EX (EX box), S16 ....$40.00

Errand Boy, board game, McLoughlin Bros, 1891, box shows street fight w/errand boy retreating, complete, EX (EX box), A $175.00

Escape From Colditz, British Parker, 1960s, based on BBC TV series & book, w/booklet about Colditz, VG (orig box), S16 ....$170.00

ET, board bame, Parker Bros, MIB (sealed), J6................$12.00

Everest, J&L Randall Ltd, England, 1961, missing 4 pcs, VG (orig box), S16 ....$60.00

Eye Guess, board game, Milton Bradley, 1966, NM J6 .....$32.00

Fall Guy, Milton Bradley, 1982, VG+ (orig box), S16 .....$20.00

Fall of Tobruk, Conflict Games, 1975, EX (EX box), M6...$45.00

Fang Bang, Milton Bradley, 1967, EX (EX box), M6........$75.00

Fantastic Voyage, board game, Milton Bradley, 1968, NMIB, F8 ....$25.00

Farmer Electric Maps, a Game of Tokens, Farmer, 1938, EX (EX box), P3..$55.00

Fascination, Remco, 1968, VG (EX box), M6 ....$45.00

Fat Albert & the Cosby Kids, Milton Bradley, 1973, complete, EX+ (EX+ box), F8..$36.00

Ferdinand the Bull, card game, Whitman, 1938, NMIB, M8..$75.00

Fess Parker Trail Blazer, Milton Bradley, EX (damaged box), J5 ....$25.00

Fibber McGee, 1940, VG+ (orig box), J6 ....$20.00

Finance, Parker Bros, 1962, VG (EX box), M6................$30.00

Fishin' Around Mickey Mouse, board game, Chad Valley, complete, EX (orig box), A $350.00

Flag Game, card game, McLoughlin Bros, 1887, missing few cards & instructions, G (orig wood box), S16 ....$60.00

Flight to Paris, board game, Milton Bradley, 1927, complete, EX (EX box), A $175.00

Flinch, Parker Bros, 1934, VG (VG box), M6 ....$25.00

Flintstones & Yogi Bear, card game, Ed-U Cards, 1961, EX+ (EX box), F8 ....$18.00

Flintstones Big Game Hunt, Whitman, 1962, complete, NMIB, C1/F8, from $50 to $100.00

Flintstones Break Ball Game of Skill, Whitman, 1962, MIB (sealed), F8 ....$135.00

Flintstones Penny Arcade Target Game, complete, VG (VG box), B10 ....$26.00

Flintstones Stone Age Game, 1961, NM (EX+ box), C1 .$65.00

Flip a Basket, Hasbro, 1969, EX+ (EX+ box), F8.............$48.00

Flora's Bower, England, 1850s, 100 hand-colored pictures & text cards, w/spinner & instructions, EX+ (orig box), B12 .$585.00

Flying Nun, Milton Bradley, 1968, missing 2 cards, EX+ (EX box), F8..$28.00

Flying the Beam, Parker Bros, 1941, complete, NMIB ...$100.00

Foil, 3M, 1969, EX (EX box), M6 ....$35.00

Follow the Flag to Glory, Geo F Cram Co, 1942, G (VG box), M6..$60.00

Fonz, Milton Bradley, 1967, MIB $30.00

Foo Chu Fortune Telling Sticks, Lakeside, 1965, missing 1 stick, EX+ (EX+ box), F8..$25.00

Football Target, Eagle Toys, Canadian, tin, few minor dings o/w EX, M5 ....$40.00

Foto-Electric Football, Cadaco, 1958, VG (EX box), M6..$50.00

Fox Hunt, ES Lowe, 1940s, NMIB, V1 ....$35.00

Frosty the Snowman, Parker Bros, 1979, missing 1 pc & spinner arrow, VG (orig box), S16................................$30.00

Feeley Meeley, Milton Bradley, 1967, EX+ (EX box), $48.00.

Fugitive Game, Ideal, 1960s, complete, EX (EX box), F3, $125.00.

Fun on the Farm, Milton Bradley, 1940s, EX (EX box), T2..$42.00

Fun With Phonics Dog House Game, 1960s, MIB, H12 ..$25.00

Game of Bird Watchers, 1958, unused, M, V1................$30.00

Game of Famous Paintings, card game, 1897, NM, V1.....$22.00

Game of Flags, card game, 1896, NM, V1 ....$22.00

Game of Jaws, Ideal, 1976, complete, EX (EX box), M6 ..$45.00

Game of Moon Tag, Parker Bros, 1957, missing 3 pcs, G+ (orig box), rare, S16 ....$100.00

Game of Nations, card game, McLoughlin Bros, 1898, EX, S16 ....$85.00

Game of Old Maid, board game, McLoughlin Bros, 1904, complete, EX (G box), A...$225.00

Game of Pegity, Parker Bros, 1939, complete, EX (EX box) ..$35.00

Game of Pegity, Parker Bros, 1953, complete, EX+ (EX+ box), T2..$15.00

Game of Politics, Parker Bros, 1952, VG (orig box), S16.$55.00

Game of Pony Express, Polygon, 1947, M $50.00

Game of Santa Fe, Stroll & Edwards, 1924, NMIB, V1....$75.00

Game of State Capitals, Milton Bradley, 1960, complete, VG (EX box), M6...$35.00

Game of the States, Milton Bradley, 1940s, 2nd edition, VG (orig box), S16...$70.00

Game of Time & Space, 1980, MIB (sealed), J6...............$55.00

Gene Autry Bandit Trail Game, Kenton Hardware, complete, EX (EX box), from $150 to $200.00

Geographical Game of Europe, D Carvalho/England, 1810, canvas-backed foldout, EX (EX paper sleeve), A $825.00

Gestiefelte Kater: Ein Gesellschafts Spiel..., Mode Verlag/Berlin, ca 1850, w/instructions, EX+ (orig case w/ties), B12..$950.00

Gettysburg, Avalon Hill, 1961, G (VG box), M6 ....$25.00

Global War, SPI, 1975, EX (EX box), M6 ....$45.00

Go, ES Lowe, 1951, VG (EX box) $30.00

Go to Texas, Bright Ideas, 1979, VG (EX box), M6.........$35.00

Godfather, Family Games Inc, 1971, VG (orig box), S16 ..$32.00

Godzilla Game, Mattel, 1978, figure jumps up & eats spaceships, missing 1 ship & instructions, VG (orig box), S16..$125.00

Going to Jerusalem, Parker Bros, 1955, EX (EX box), M6..$50.00

Gomer Pyle, Transogram, 1966, copied instructions, complete, EX+ (EX+ box), F8..................................$48.00

Good Neighbor Game, Whitman, 1942, VG (EX box), M6..$40.00

Goodbye Mr Chips, Parker Bros, 1969, MIB (sealed), F8.$25.00

Grand Auto Race, board game, Atkins, 1915, complete, rare dbl set, EX+ (EX box) $150.00

Grandmama's Useful Knowledge, McLoughlin Bros, 1900, EX (EX box) $50.00

Green Hornet, card game, blk & wht TV photos, MIB, T2 ....$45.00

Groucho Marx TV Quiz, Pressman, 1954, EX (VG+ box) ..$100.00

Halma, board game, EI Horsman, ca 1888, VG (VG box) .$50.00

Hands Down, Ideal, 1964, VG (VG box), M6....................$25.00

Happy Little Train Game, Milton Bradley, 1957, VG (EX box) $20.00

Harlem Globetrotters, Milton Bradley, 1971, NM (EX+ box), F8 ....$35.00

Harlequin, board game, McLoughlin Bros, 1890, complete, EX (EX box), A..$635.00

Have Gun Will Travel, Parker Bros, 1959, NM (VG+ box)..$75.00

Hialeah, Milton Bradley, ca 1940, EX (VG+ box) $35.00

Hickety Pickety, Parker Bros, 1954, VG (EX box), M6....$40.00

Hide 'N Thief, board game, Whitman, 1965, NM, J6 ......$12.00

High Bid, 3M, 1965, VG (EX box), M6............................$25.00

Hike the Camping Game, Milton Bradley, 1950s, NMIB, V1...$25.00

Hippety-Hop, Corey Games, 1940, VG (VG box) $50.00

Hippodrome, Milton Bradley, 1900, complete, NM (EX box), A..$210.00

Hollywood Squares, board game, Ideal, 1974, NM, J6......$12.00

Hollywood Squares, board game, Western Publishing, 1967, NMIB, J6, $35.00.

Hometeam Baseball, NM (EX box), V1 ....$35.00

Hopalong Cassidy, board game, Milton Bradley, 1950, EX (EX box), J2..$90.00

Hopalong Cassidy Canasta, 1950, 2 complete decks of playing cards, missing rules & score sheet, EX+ (EX box), F8.$90.00

Hopalong Cassidy Chinese Checkers, Milton Bradley, 1950, 1 marble not orig o/w complete & NM (EX box), A..$165.00

Hopalong Snap, card game, Chad Valley, 1953, complete, EX (VG box), A...$215.00

Horse Race Game, France, 1900s, 4 CI jockeys on horses move around groove on sq wooden base, lever action, 10" sq, VG, A ...$345.00

Hot Spot, Parker Bros, 1961, G (M box), M6...................$35.00

How Silas Popped the Question, Parker Bros, 1915, VG (orig box), S16...$40.00

Howdy Doody Quiz Show, Multiple/Kagran, 1951, litho tin, 12" dia, NM, A..$245.00

Howdy Doody's Bowling, Parker Bros, 1949, NM (EX+ box), F8 ....$110.00

Howdy Doody's TV Game, board game, Milton Bradley/Kagran, 1950s, complete, M (EX box), A $150.00

Howdy Doody's 3-Ring Circus, Harett-Gilmar/Kagran, electric game w/spinner, complete, NM (VG+ box), A.........$80.00

Huckleberry Hound Bumps, Transogram, 1961, complete, NM (EX box), F8 ....$48.00

Huckleberry Hound Juggle Roll, Transogram, 1960, EX+ (EX+ box), T2 ....$32.00

Huggin' the Rail, Selchow & Righter, 1948, complete, NMIB, A..$50.00

I Dream of Jeannie, Milton Bradley, 1965, EX (VG box), M6/S16, from $50 to...$75.00

I Spy, board game, Ideal, 1965, missing 1 disk, EX+ (EX+ box), F8 ....$75.00

Image, 3M, 1972, EX (EX box), M6................................$30.00

Improved Game of Tiddlywinks, McLoughlin Bros, 1890, complete, EX (EX box), A $50.00

India, board game, McLoughlin Bros, 1895, complete, EX (EX box mk An Oriental Game), A $155.00

India Bombay, board game, Cutler & Saleby, 1910, complete, EX (EX box), A $110.00

Indian Traveller, board game, L'Orient/David Ogilvy, 1846, complete, EX, A $715.00

Ironside, Ideal, 1967, complete, NM (EX+ box), F8........$70.00

Jackie Gleason's 'And Awa-a-a-a-y We Go!' TV Fun, Transogram, 1956, complete, NM (EX+ box), F8 ....$145.00

James Bond Secret Agent 007, board game, Milton Bradley, 1964, NMIB, C1 ....$55.00

James Bond Thunderball, Milton Bradley, 1965, complete, NMIB, F8 ....$70.00

James Bond 007, card game, Milton Bradley, 1966, complete, EX+, F8 ....$45.00

James Bond 007: Assault!, Victory, 1986, MIB (sealed), J2..$15.00

James Bond 007: Goldfinger, Milton Bradley, 1966, EX (shrink-wrapped box), M6..$65.00

Jeep Patrol, Lido Toy, 1940s, unused, MIB, V1 ....$30.00

Jeopardy, Milton Bradley, 1962, 2nd edition, VG (M box), M6...$25.00

Jeopardy, Milton Bradley, 1964, 3rd edition, missing 1 card, EX+ (EX box), F8 ....$12.00

Jeu en Demands & Responses Enfantines, Eigenthum/Germany, ca 1850, 36 cards in 3 languages, EX+ (orig box), B12 ..$1,650.00

Jolly Clown, Milton Bradley, 1932, MIB, H12 ....$45.00

Jumping DJ Surprise Action Game, MIB, L4................$125.00

Junior Auto Race Game, board game, All-Fair, 1929, complete, NM (EX+ box), A $400.00

Justice Courtroom Game, Lowell, 1955, complete, NM (EX+ box), F8..$88.00

Kentucky Derby, Whitman, 1960, EX (EX box), V1........$20.00

Key to the Kingdom, Golden, 1992, EX (M box), M6......$30.00

Kick Back, Schaper, 1965, EX (EX box), M6..................$40.00

King Kong, Ideal, 1976, complete (VG box), H4 ....$8.00

King of the Hill, Schaper, 1960s, complete (G box), H4 .$25.00

King Oil, Milton Bradley, 1974, VG (EX box), M6 ....$45.00

Photo courtesy of Bob Gottuso.

KISS On Tour, board game, complete, EX (EX box), B3, $50.00.

Knight in Armor, target game, MT, litho tin, battery-op, MIB, L4 ....$450.00

Knight Rider, video game, Aklaim, 1989, hand-held arcade type w/sounds & multiple skill levels, MIP (sealed), C1 ...$32.00

Knight Rider High Speed Adventure, Parker Bros, 1983, missing 1 minor pc, EX+ (EX box), F8..............................$12.00

Kojak, Milton Bradley, 1975, unused, M (worn box), S16 ....$30.00

Kooky Carnival Game, Milton Bradley, 1969, EX+ (EX+ box), F8 ....$48.00

Kopeefun, Embree Mfg, 1946, EX (EX box), M6.............$45.00

Korg: 70,000 BC, Milton Bradley, 1974, complete, EX+ (EX+ box), F8/H4, from $20 to...$25.00

Kreskin's ESP Advanced Edition, board game, Milton Bradley, 1967, NM, J6...$25.00

Kukla & Ollie, board game, Parker Bros, 1962, EX (orig box), J6 ....$32.00

Land of the Lost, Milton Bradley, 1975, M (EX box), C17, from $25 to $35.00

Last Straw, Schaper, 1966, VG (EX box), M6 ....$30.00

Laugh-In's Squeeze Your Bippy Game, Hasbro, 1968, NMIB, F8 ....$55.00

Laurel & Hardy Delightfully Funny Game of Monkey Business, Transogram, 1962, missing box insert, EX+, F8.........$45.00

Laverne & Shirley, 1977, EX (EX box), I2 ....$20.00

Leave It to Beaver Ambush Game, Hasbro, 1959, EX (VG box)...$65.00

Leave It to Beaver Money Maker Game, Hasbro, 1959, NM (EX+ box), F8...$60.00

Leave It to Beaver Rocket to the Moon Space Game, Hasbro, 1959, complete, NM (EX+ box), F8 ....$65.00

Let's Go (Walt Disney's Big Track Meet...), Ontex Games, 1940s, complete, EX (orig box), A $40.00

Let's Take a Trip, Milton Bradley, 1962, VG (EX box) ...$20.00

Lie Detector TV Studio Mystery, Mattel, 1964, EX+ (EX+ window box), F8..$50.00

Lincoln Highway & Checkers, board game, Parker Bros, 1925, complete, EX (EX box), A $165.00

Lindy the New Flying Game, card game, EX (EX box) $45.00

Lippy the Lion Flips, Transogram, 1962, copied instructions, EX+ (EX+ box), F8...$75.00

Little House on the Prairie, Parker Bros, 1978, M (NM box), M17..$30.00

Little House on the Prairie, Parker Bros, 1978, missing 3 cards, VG (VG box), S16 ....$20.00

Little Red Hen, Corey Games, 1941, VG (EX box), M6..$50.00

Logomarchy or War of Words, McLoughlin Bros/FA Wright, 1874, 66 cards w/instructions, EX (wood box) $100.00

London Cabbie Game, Intellect, 1971, NM (EX+ box), F8 ....$25.00

Lone Ranger, board game, Parker Bros, 1938, NMIB, from $50 to $100.00

Lone Ranger Double Target, Marx, 1939, complete, NM (G box), A...$175.00

Lost in Space, Milton Bradley, 1966, EX (EX box), T2....$90.00

Loterij Van Don Quichot en Sanche Panche, card game, Netherlands, 1820s?, 93 cards w/instructions, EX+ (orig box), B12..$1,250.00

Love Boat, board game, 1980, EX (orig box), J6...............$12.00

Ludwig Von Drake Ball Toss, EX+ (EX+ box), T1..........$55.00

M*A*S*H, Milton Bradley, 1981, complete, EX+ (EX+ box), M6/M17, from $25 to $30.00

MacDonald's Farm Game, Selchow & Righter, 1948, VG (EX box)...$45.00

MAD Magazine, card game, Parker Bros, 1980, MIB (minor wear), H4 ....$30.00

MAD's Spy Vs Spy, board game, Milton Bradley, 1986, missing 1 pc, EX+ (EX box), F8 ....$30.00

Magic Circus-Roll, Am Toys Inc, 1950s, complete, MIB, A .$35.00

Magilla Gorilla, board game, Ideal, 1964, NMIB, F8........$55.00

Mail, Express or Accomodation, board game, McLoughlin Bros, 1895, complete, EX (EX box), A $580.00

Make-A-Million, card game, Parker Bros, 1945, complete, VG (VG box) $20.00

Man From UNCLE, card game, Milton Bradley, 1965, NM (EX+ box), F8 ....$14.00

Managing Your Money, CNA Mutual Ins, 1970, complete, EX (EX box), M6 ....$30.00

Mandrake the Magician, board game, Transogram, 1966, NM (EX+ box), F8 ....$48.00

Mansion of Happiness, board game, Ives, 1864, board has latch, 9x14½", EX, A $300.00

Mansion of Happiness, board game, McLoughlin Bros, 1895, complete, EX (EX box), A $1,155.00

Marathon, Sports Games Co, 1978, VG (orig box), S16..$20.00

Marble Game, Arcade, wood & CI w/3 dog targets, spring-loaded trigger activates shooter, 29", VG, A..............$85.00

Margie, Milton Bradley, 1961, EX (EX box), A3/S1, from $30 to $40.00

Marlin Perkins Zoo Parade, Cadaco-Ellis, 1955, EX+ (EX+ box), F8 ....$50.00

Mary Hartman, Mary Hartman, Life in Fernwood, Reiss, 1977, character pawns, complete, NMIB, F8 ....$45.00

Masquerade Party, Bettye-B, 1955, EX (EX box)..............$75.00

Masterpiece, Parker Bros, 1970, complete, EX (EX box), M6..$45.00

Match Game, Milton Bradley, 1963, complete, G (VG box), M6..$30.00

Mattel's Flea Circus, Mattel, 1965, EX+ (EX box), F8 .....$80.00

Meet the Presidents, Selchow & Righter, 1965, complete, EX (VG box) $20.00

Melvin the Moon Man, Remco, 1959, missing instructions, EX+ (EX+ box) $50.00

Men in Space, Milton Bradley, 1960, missing 1-pc, EX+ (orig photo box), S16..$100.00

Men of Destiny, Milton Bradley, 1942, complete, G (EX box) $30.00

Mickey Mouse Ball Trapp, Migra Jeux/France, figures of Mickey, Minnie, Pluto, Horace & Clarabelle, EX (EX box), A .$225.00

Mickey Mouse Bean Bag Game, Marks Bros/WDE, 1930s, throw bean bags through barrels on board, VG+ (EX box), A $295.00

Mickey Mouse Coming Home, Marx, 1930s, complete w/dice, shaker & instructions, EX+ (EX+ box)....................$200.00

Mickey Mouse Old Maid, 1937, complete, NM (EX box) .$100.00

Mickey Mouse Pin the Tail on Mickey Party, Hallmark, 1930s, complete, EX+ (EX+ envelope), M8..........................$95.00

Mickey Mouse Ping Pong Table, WDE, 1938, masonite foldout w/2 full-color decals, complete, 84" L, EX, A $135.00

Mickey Mouse Quoits, target game, Mickey pictured in center of numbered bull's-eye target, 11" sq, EX, A................$100.00

Mickey Mouse Scatter Ball Game, Marks Bros, 1930s, complete, EX+ (EX rstr box), rare, M8..................................$375.00

Photo courtesy of Dunbar Gallery.

Mickey Mouse Circus Game, Marks Bros, Boston, 1936, EX (orig box), from $800.00 to $1,500.00.

Mickey Mouse Spin-N-Win, Northwestern Products, 1957, all litho tin pcs, EX+, M8..$95.00

Mighty Mouse Playhouse Rescue Game, Harett Gilman, 1956, appears complete except instructions, EX (EX box), S16..$100.00

Milton the Monster, board game, Milton Bradley, 1966, NM (NM box)..$45.00

Mingo, Hasbro, 1956, complete, VG (EX box), M6........$40.00

Miss America Pageant, Parker Bros, 1974, EX+ (EX box), F8 ....$15.00

Mister Magoo, 3-D Game, Oh Magoo, You've Done It Again!, Warren, 1978, complete, NM (EX+ box), F8...........$25.00

Monopoly, Parker Bros, 1936, complete, VG (EX box), M6..$35.00

Monster Mash, Parker Bros, 1987, complete, EX (EX box), M6..$30.00

Monster Squad, Milton Bradley, 1977, complete, NM (EX box), F8/P3, from $20 to $25.00

Moon Blast Off, Schaper No 543, 1970s, MIB (sealed), P4..$25.00

Mork & Mindy, board game, Parker Bros, 1979, complete, NMIB $30.00

Mother Goose Target Game, Reed, paper litho on wood, pop-up targets, complete, 18", EX, A $600.00

Mr Doodles Dog, Selchow & Righter, 1940s, Junior edition, missing few pcs & instructions, VG (orig box), S16..$30.00

Mr President, 3M, 1967, complete, NMIB, T2 ....$35.00

Mr Ree, Selchow & Righter, 1946, missing 1 pc, VG (VG box), S16..$35.00

Murder She Wrote, Warren, 1985, EX (EX box), S16 .....$35.00

Mutuels, Mutuels Inc/Los Angeles, 1938, missing 3 pcs & instructions, VG (VG box), S16..............................$195.00

My Favorite Martian, Transogram, 1963, M (EX box), M17..$135.00

Mystery Date, board game, Milton Bradley, 1965, NM, J6....$68.00

Mystic Skull Game of Voodoo, Ideal, 1964, complete, EX (EX box), F8/M6, from $50 to $60.00

Name That Tune, Milton Bradley, 1957, complete, G (VG box), M6..$30.00

Nancy & Sluggo, board game, Milton Bradley, 1944, missing playing pcs & dice, NM (EX box), A......................$140.00

Nascar Daytona 500 Race Game, Milton Bradley, 1990, MIB (sealed), M6..$35.00

New Game of Knight & Dragon, card game, England?, 1840s, w/counters & instructions, EX+ (orig varnished wood box), B12...$650.00

New Game of Pictorial Authors, McLoughlin Bros, 1888, complete, NM (EX box), A $175.00

No Time for Sergeants, Ideal, 1964, complete, EX+ (EX+ box), F8...$50.00

Noma Party Quiz, Noma Electronics, 1947, complete, VG (EX box), M6 ....$40.00

Nutty Mad Pinball, Marx, 7x13", EX, J2...........................$48.00

Official Baseball Game, Milton Bradley, 1969, M (EX box), M17..$150.00

Oh-Wah-Ree, 3M, 1966, complete, VG (EX box), M6 ...$45.00

Operation, Milton Bradley, 1965, complete, EX (EX box), M6...$35.00

Orbit, board game, Parker Bros, NMIB $50.00

Ouija, Parker Bros, 1970s, complete, VG (EX box), M6 ..$30.00

Our Gang Tipple-Topple Game, All Fair, 1930, complete, NM (EX box) $600.00

Pan American World Jet Flight, Hasbro, 1961, EX+ (EX+ box) $35.00

Panorama of London, J Harris/London, 1809, 50 hand-colored scenes on board, complete (orig cb case), B12.........$850.00

Parachute Jump, board game, Milton Bradley, 1936, complete, EX (EX box), A $95.00

Parcheesi, Selchow & Righter, 1942, complete, VG (VG box), M6...$35.00

Park & Shop, Milton Bradley, 1960, missing 1 pawn & 2 cars, EX+ (EX box), F8 ....$25.00

Parlor Keeps Marble Game, EJ Ingwerson, wood w/applied litho tin label picturing boys playing marbles, 14", VG, A..$255.00

Partridge Family, board game, Milton Bradley, 1971, NM (EX+ box), F8...$25.00

Password, 2nd Edition, Milton Bradley, 1962, complete, EX (EX box) $10.00

Pathfinder, board game, Milton Bradley, 1977, NM, J6 ...$12.00

Patty Duke, board game, Milton Bradley, 1963, complete, NMIB, from $40.00 to $45.00.

Peanuts, board game, Selchow & Righter, 1959, NM, J6 .$30.00

Peg Baseball, Parker Bros, 1930s, VG (EX box), M6 ....$70.00

Perquackey, Lakeside, 1965, complete, EX (EX box) $10.00

Perry Mason's Case of the Missing Suspect, Transogram, 1959, complete, NMIB $50.00

Peter Coddle & His Trip to New York, Parker Bros, 1886, EX (EX box) $50.00

Peter Pan, board game, Parker Bros, 1969, complete, NM (EX+ box), F8...$30.00

Peter Pan, board game, Transogram, 1953, complete, NMIB, J6...$45.00

Phalanx, Whitman, 1964, VG (VG box), S16 ....$25.00

Pink Panther, board game, Cadaco, 1981, NM, J6............$8.00

Pirate & the Traveler, Milton Bradley, 1940s, complete, VG (EX box), M6..$50.00

Pit, Parker Bros, 1919, complete, EX (EX box)................$12.00

Planet of the Apes, board game, Milton Bradley, 1974, complete, EX+ (EX box) $35.00

Plant 'Em, Selchow & Righter, 1930s-40s, missing 3 pcs, EX+ (EX box), F8 ....$25.00

Play Football, Whitman, 1934, complete, G (G box), M6..$50.00

Play Sheriff, Milton Bradley, 1958, missing 1 card, EX+ (EX+ box)..$20.00

Point of Law, 3M, 1972, complete, EX (EX box), M6 ......$35.00

Popeye Pipe Toss Game, Rosebud Art/KFS, 1935, diecut cb Popeye w/pipe & rings, unused, NM (EX box), A $65.00

Popeye's Game, Parker Bros, 1948, missing few tiddlywinks, NM (EX box), A $200.00

Popeye's Good Time Game, Built-Rite, 1950s, NM (EX+ box), F8...$30.00

Popeye's Sliding Boards & Ladders, Built-Rite, 1958, missing 1 marker, NM (EX+ box), F8............................$30.00

Poppin' Popeye, 1930s, paper lithograph on wood, 12x18", EX, $100.00 to $200.00.

Premium Game of Logomachy, Milton Bradley, 1930s, VG, S16 ....$20.00

Pro Playoff, NBC/Hasbro, 1969, complete, EX (EX box), M6...$55.00

Probe, Parker Bros, 1964, complete, EX (EX box)............$15.00

Puck Luck Hockey, Schaper, 1950s, NMIB, T2................$35.00

Puss in the Corner, Samuel Gabriel, 1940s, complete, EX (VG+ box), S16..$90.00

Put & Take, Schaper, 1950s, VG (EX box), M6...............$30.00

Quick Draw McGraw Moving Target, Knickerbocker, 1960, complete, scarce, EX+ (EX box), A $200.00

Quick Draw McGraw Private Eye, board game, Milton Bradley, 1960, NM (EX+ box), C1 ....$62.00

Quick Wit, Game Gang, 1987, complete, EX (M box), M6 ..$40.00

Rack-O, Milton Bradley, 1961, H12/T2, from $12 to.......$20.00

Radio Amateur Hour Game, Milton Bradley, 1930s, VG (orig box), S16..$90.00

Raffles, Corey Games Co, 1939, complete, VG (VG box), M6...$40.00

Raggedy Ann Magic Pebble Game, 1941, EX (EX box), V1...$50.00

Raiders of the Lost Ark, board game, Kenner, 1981, complete, NMIB, F8...$25.00

Ranger Commandos, Parker Bros, 1944, complete, VG (VG box)...$55.00

Red Herring, Cadaco-Ellis, 1945, complete, G (VG box), M6...$35.00

Restless Gun, board game, Milton Bradley, 1959, complete, EX+ (EX+ box)...$40.00

Rex Mar's Space Target Game, Marx, complete, NM (EX box), A...$325.00

Rich Uncle, Parker Bros, 1955, VG (VG box) $35.00

Rifleman, board game, Milton Bradley, 1959, complete, EX+ (EX box), F8...$70.00

Rin-Tin-Tin, Transogram, 1955, NMIB, M17...............$60.00

Rip Van Winkle, board game, Parker Bros, 1900, complete, scarce, NM (EX box), A...$235.00

Rival Policeman, McLoughlin Bros, 1896, complete, rare, EX (EX box), F3, $4,500.00.

Rivers, Roads & Rails, Ravensburger, 1985, complete, EX (EX box), M6...$40.00

Road Runner, board game, Milton Bradley, 1968, NM (NM box), C1...$65.00

Robin Hood, Parker Bros, 1973, Walt Disney cartoon version, VG (orig box), S16.......................................$38.00

Robin Hood 3-D Magic Window Game, Bettye-B, 1956, complete, NM (EX+ box w/Richard Greene & cast photo), F8...$150.00

Robin the Boy Wonder, card game, Russell's Mfg Co, 1977, EX+ (EX box), D9...$15.00

Rock 'Em Sock 'Em Robots, Marx, 1973, complete, NM+ (EX box), A...$180.00

Rocket Darts, target game, Am Toy Works, 1950s, complete, scarce, VG+ (VG+ box), A.....................................$95.00

Rocket Patrol Magnetic Target Game, G (G box), A $25.00

Rocky, board game, Super Star, 1985, MIB (sealed), J6 ...$18.00

Role Master, ICE, 1984, complete, EX (EX box), M6 .....$30.00

Rook, Parker Bros, 1936, complete, EX (EX box)...........$15.00

Rootie Kazootie Word Game, card game, Ed-U Cards, 1953, complete, NMIB...$20.00

Roulette Baseball, Bar-Zim Toy, 1930, complete, G- (G box), M6...$45.00

Roulette Wheel Game, England, CI base depicting seated child supporting brass wheel, marble lands in slot, 12", EX, A...$580.00

Route 66 Travel Game, Transogram, 1962, complete, NM (EX box), A...$370.00

Roy Rogers Horseshoe Set, Ohio Art, complete, EX (VG box), A...$100.00

Russian Front, Avalon Hill, 1970s, EX+ (EX+ box), T2 ..$20.00

Safari, Selchow & Righter, 1950, complete, VG (EX box), M6...$45.00

Santa Claus Ring Game, Spear, early 1900s, toss rings onto Santa's nose, complete, EX (VG+ box), A.............$280.00

Say When!, Parker Bros, 1961, complete, VG (EX box), M6...$40.00

Scarlet O'Hara Marble Game, Marietta, 1939, complete, MIB, A...$80.00

Scooby-Doo & Scrappy-Doo, Milton Bradley, 1983, VG+ (orig box), S16...$20.00

Screwball: The Mad Mad Mad Game, Transogram, 1960, missing instructions, VG (VG box), S16....................$45.00

Scribbage, ES Lowe, 1963, complete, EX (EX box), M6 ..$30.00

See the USA, Cadaco, 1968, complete, G (VG box), M6 .$30.00

Shakespeare, Avalon Hill, 1966, complete, EX (M box), M6...$35.00

Shari Lewis' Shariland Game, Transogram, 1959, complete, NM (EX+ box), F8...$70.00

Sheriff of Dodge City, Parker Bros, 1966, missing 1 card, EX+, F8...$25.00

Sherlock Holmes, card game, Parker Bros, 1904, VG (orig box), S16...$45.00

Shindig, Remco, 1965, VG+ (VG+ box), S16 ....$65.00

Sid & Marty Krofft Bugaloos Music Game, 1971, NMIB, V1...$40.00

Siege of Havana, board game, Parker Bros, 1898, complete, EX (EX box), A, $690.00.

Silly Sidney the Absent-Minded Elephant, Transogram, 1963, complete, NM (EX+ box), F8 ....$48.00

Sinbad, Cadaco, 1978, complete, EX (EX box), M6.........$70.00

Situation 4, Parker Bros, 1968, complete, EX (EX box), M6...$35.00

Six Million Dollar Man, Parker Bros, 1975, EX+ (EX box), T2...$10.00

Skirmish, American Heritage Series, Milton Bradley, 1975, VG (orig box), S16......................................$38.00

Skittle Score-Ball, Aurora, 1971, EX (EX box), P3 ....$40.00

Skunk, Schaper, 1953, complete, EX (EX box) $25.00

Smurf Game, Milton Bradley, 1981, VG (orig box), S16..$32.00

Snagglepuss Fun at the Picnic, Transogram, 1961, NMIB, F8..$70.00

Snake's Alive, Ideal, 1967, complete, EX (EX box), M6..$45.00

Snoopy & the Red Baron Skill & Action, board game, Milton Bradley, 1970, complete, NMIB, F8..........................$40.00

Snoopy's Doghouse, Milton Bradley, 1971, MIB, J7.........$25.00

Snow White & the Seven Dwarfs, board game, Milton Bradley, 1937, EX (orig box), A...$230.00

Snow White & the Seven Dwarfs, Cadaco, 1977, missing instructions, EX (orig box), S16............................$20.00

Sod Buster, D Santee, 1980, complete, EX (EX box), M6..$30.00

Solarquest, Western Publishing, 1986, VG+ (orig box), S16...$35.00

Soldiers, SPI, 1972, complete, EX (EX box), M6.............$50.00

Sorry, Parker Bros, 1958, complete, VG (EX box)............$15.00

Soupy Sales Sez Go-Go-Go, Milton Bradley, 1960s, missing few cards, EX (VG box), H4..$35.00

Space Bug Game, Drueke, 1959, missing 1 pc, EX+ (EX+ box), F8 ....$25.00

Space Mouse, card game, Fairchild, 1964, missing 2 cards, EX+ (EX+ box), F8...$18.00

Space 1999, Milton Bradley, 1976, VG (orig box), S16...$38.00

Spartan, SPI, 1975, complete, EX (M box), M6 ....$75.00

Spingo & Whirlette, Transogram, 1940, complete, VG (EX box), M6..$40.00

Spot Shot, Wolverine Supply, 1930s, EX (EX box), M6 ..$110.00

Spot-A-Plane, Toy Creations, 1942, 2nd series, missing 5 plastic pcs, VG (worn box), S16.....................................$225.00

Spudsie Hot Potato Game, Ohio Art, 1960s, MIB, M6....$50.00

Square Mile, Milton Bradley, 1962, complete, EX (EX box), M6..$70.00

Stage, card game, 1904, 66 actor/actress photo cards, scarce, V1...$55.00

Steady Eddie Balancing Game, Milton Bradley, 1962, NMIB, T2...$25.00

Steppe, TSR, 1988, VG (M box), M6..............................$30.00

Steve Canyon Air Force Game, 1959, complete, NMIB, F8 .$50.00

Stock Market, Whitman, 1968, EX+ (EX+ box), S16/T2, from $35 to $40.00

Stocks & Bonds, 3M, 1964, complete, VG (EX box), M6.$35.00

Stratego, Milton Bradley, 1962, complete, VG (EX box), M6..$30.00

Strategy Poker, Milton Bradley, 1968, complete, VG (EX box), M6..$25.00

Streamlined Train Game, Rexall, EX (EX box), A...........$65.00

Stump the Stars, 1962, MIB, V1 ....$20.00

Sub Search, Milton Bradley, 1977, complete, VG (EX box), M6..$45.00

Submarine, Avalon Hill, 1977, EX+ (EX+ box), T2........$20.00

Submarine Chase, board game, Milton Bradley, 1939, complete, NM (EX box), A...$130.00

Sudden Déath!, Gabriel, 1978, complete, EX (EX box), M6..$45.00

Super Galaxy Invader, electronic hand-held game, Bandai, 1970s, MIB, J6...$35.00

Super Heroes, card game, Milton Bradley, 1978, complete, MIB, A6...$15.00

Superman Comic Connection, 1979, EX (EX box), D8...$35.00

Superman Flying Bingo, 1966, EX (EX box), D8.............$65.00

Superman III, board game, Parker Brothers, 1982, NMIB, C1/S16, from $20 to...$30.00

Superman Quoit Game, 1950s, w/orig papers, MIB, H12.$28.00

Superman Senior Rubber Horseshoe Set, Super Swim, 1950s, complete, VG (EX box), A..$65.00

Superman Speed Game, board game, Milton Bradley, complete, EX (EX box), A...$170.00

Superstar Baseball, Avalon Hill, 1978, MIB (sealed), J6..$24.00

Susceptibles, board game, McLoughlin Bros, 1891, complete, EX (EX box), A..$500.00

Swayze, Milton Bradley, 1950s, VG (VG box), S16.........$35.00

Tactics II, Avalon Hill, 1961, EX+ (EX+ box), T2 ....$25.00

Take 12, Phillips Pub, 1959, complete, EX (EX box), M6.$25.00

Tantalizer, Northern Signal, 1958, complete, EX (EX box), M6..$55.00

Tarzan to the Rescue, board game, Milton Bradley, 1977, NMIB, C1/M17, from $25 to...$30.00

Ten-To-Tal, Selchow & Righter, EX (EX box), P3..........$45.00

Thinking Man's Golf, 3M, 1967, complete, EX (EX box), M6..$45.00

Three Musketeers, Milton Bradley, 1958, complete, EX (VG box), S16...$22.00

Three Stooges Fun House, rare, NM (VG box), T1 ....$325.00

Thunderbirds, Parker Bros, 1967, NMIB, F8 ....$125.00

Tic-Tac-Dough, Transogram, 1957, complete, G (VG box), M6..$30.00

Tight Squeeze, the Snuggle-Struggle Game, Mattel, 1967, M (NM box), T2...$20.00

Tip-I-Tip Marble Game, Reed, Pat 1892, litho paper on wood, G, A $145.00

Touring, card game, Parker Bros, complete, EX (worn box), $25.00.

Tip-It Wackies Balancing Game, Ideal, 1965, EX+ (EX+ box), F8 ....$25.00

To the Wolf's Lair, People's War, 1983, complete, EX (M box), M6 ....$45.00

Tom Savini's Gotcha!, card game, Imagine, 1988, MIB (sealed), D9 ....$18.00

Tootsie Roll Train, Hasbro, 1969, orig candy missing o/w complete, EX (orig box), H4 ....$40.00

Top Scholar, Cadaco, 1957, complete, EX (EX box), M6 ..$40.00

Tortoise & the Hare, Russell, 1922, VG (worn box), S16 ..$125.00

Toy Town Post Office, Milton Bradley, 1910, complete, G (VG box), M6 ....$155.00

Toy Town Target, Milton Bradley, 1911, complete, EX (EX box), A $200.00

Travel With Woody Woodpecker, Walter Lantz/ Cadaco, 1956, complete, NM (EX box), A, $145.00.

Treasure Hunt, Cadaco-Ellis, 1942, complete, VG (VG box), M6 ....$50.00

Treasure Island, Harett-Gilmar, 1954, missing instructions, NM (EX box), F8 ....$25.00

Tripoly Junior, Cadaco-Ellis, 1962, complete, EX (EX box), M6 ....$45.00

Trivial Pursuit, Selchow & Righter, 1981, complete, EX (EX box), M6 ....$35.00

Troke, Selchow & Righter, 1967, complete, VG (VG box), M6 ....$30.00

Truth or Consequences, Gabriel, 1955, 1st issue, unused, NMIB, F8 ....$36.00

Tumbling Tom the Soldier, board game, Milton Bradley, 1930s, complete, NM (EX box), A $170.00

Twist, 3M, 1962, complete, VG (VG box), M6 ....$35.00

UFO Master Blaster Station, electronic hand-held game, MIB, J6 ....$24.00

Ultimate Golf, Ultimate Golf Co, 1985, complete, VG (EX box), M6 ....$45.00

Ultra 7: The Great 30 Monsters, Bandai/Japan, complete, M (NM box), F8 ....$75.00

Uncle Jim's Question Bee, Toy Creations, 1940s, VG (VG box) $25.00

Uncle Sam's Mall, board game, Milton Bradley, 1910, incomplete, EX (EX box), A $100.00

Undersea World of Jaques Cousteau, Parker Bros, 1968, NMIB, C1 ....$55.00

Untouchables, board game, Transogram, 1961, NM (EX box), C1 ....$110.00

Verdict II, Avalon Hill, 1961, complete, VG (EX box), M6 ....$60.00

Vest Pocket Checkers, Emb Co, 1929, EX (VG+ box), P3 ....$25.00

Viking, 3M, 1975, complete, EX (M box), M6 ....$75.00

Vox Pop, Milton Bradley, 1938, based on Vox Poppers radio show, VG (orig box), S16 ....$35.00

Voyage Interplanetaire, board game, France, 1950s, complete, NM (EX box), A $195.00

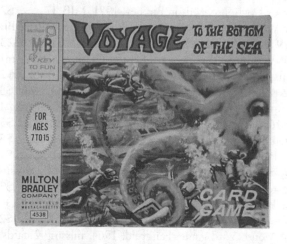

Voyage to the Bottom of the Sea, Milton Bradley, 1964, NMIB, $70.00.

Wallis's New Game of Genius, Wallis/London, 1832, hand-colored paper on linen, w/instruction book, EX (orig case), B12 ....$1,500.00

Walt Disney's Big Track Meet, Ontex/Canada, 1940s, complete, EX+ (EX box), M8 ....$85.00

Walt Disney's Ski-Jump Target Game, Am Toy Works, 1938, complete, NM (EX box), A $725.00

Walt Disney's Steps & Chutes, 1960, unpunched, EX (EX box), V1 ....$35.00

Walt Disney's Treasure Island, Gardner, EX (EX box), V1 ...$30.00

Waltons, Milton Bradley, 1974, NMIB, M17 ....$28.00

Waterloo: A Battle Game, Parker Bros, 1895, G (orig box), A $385.00

Waterworks, Parker Bros, 1972, complete, EX (EX box), M6 ....$30.00

Web of Gold, TSR, 1989, complete, MIB, M6 ....$30.00

Welfare, Jedco, 1978, complete, VG (VG box), M6 ....$55.00

Wendy's Hearts, card game, Warren, 1960s-70s, NM (EX+ box), F8 ....$12.00

What Shall I Be?, Selchow & Righter, 1968, VG (orig box), S16 ....$32.00

Whatzit, Milton Bradley, 1987, complete, VG (EX box), M6 ....$30.00

Wheeler Dealer, Ranco Games, 1977, complete, VG (EX box), M6 ....$45.00

Which Witch, Milton Bradley, 1970, NM (EX box), P3 .$20.00

Whirl Out Game, Milton Bradley, 1971, complete, EX (EX box), M6 ....$40.00

White Shadow, Cadaco, 1970s, EX (orig box), S16 ....$115.00

Who Am I?, card game, Ed-U-Cards, 1954, features Pinky Lee, VG (orig box), S16 ....$125.00

Wildcatter, Kessler, 1981, complete, MIB, M6 ....$80.00

Wildlife, ES Lowe, 1971, VG (orig box), S16 ....$50.00

Winner Spinner, Whitman, 1956, complete, EX (EX box), M6 ....$35.00

Winnie the Pooh, board game, Parker Bros, 1933, complete, EX (EX box), A $125.00

World Flag Game About the United Nation, Parker Bros, 1961, complete, VG (EX box), M6 ....$50.00

World War III, SPI, 1975, complete, EX (M box), M6 ....$50.00

WOW Pillow Fight Game, Milton Bradley, 1969, complete, VG (VG box), M6 ....$45.00

Yogi Bear, card game, Ed-U Cards, rummy, NMIB, F8 .....$12.00

Yogi Bear Go Fly a Kite, Transogram, 1960s, missing instructions, EX, J5 ....$45.00

You Don't Say, Milton Bradley, 1963, MIB, S16 ....$25.00

Zorro, board game, Parker Bros, 1966, M (NM box), D9...$65.00

4-Cycle, Milton Bradley, 1967, EX (EX box), M6 ....$30.00

6 Family Fun Games, Transogram, 1958, VG (EX box), M6 ....$25.00

12 O'Clock High, Ideal, 1965, EX+ (EX+ box), D9 ....$45.00

77 Sunset Strip, Lowell, 1960, complete, NM (EX+ box), F8 ....$40.00

Gasoline-Powered Toys

Two of the largest companies to manufacture gas-powered models are Cox and Wen Mac. Since the late fifties they have been making faithfully detailed models of airplanes as well as some automobiles and boats. Condition of used models will vary greatly because of the nature of the miniature gas engine and damage resulting from the fuel that has been used. Because of this, 'new in box' gas toys command a premium.

Advisor: Danny Bynum (B7).

Cameron Rodzy, green with Oilzum logo, Cameron .19 engine, EX, $325.00.

Cox, A-25 Dive Bomber, 1965-67, olive drab, EX, B7 .....$65.00

Cox, Acro Piper Cub, 1971-72, orange & wht, EX, B7 ....$35.00

Cox, AD-6 Skyraider, 1967-69, tan, wht & bl, EX, B7 ....$45.00

Cox, Aerobat 150, E-Z Flyer Series, 1988-93, wht, M, B7 ..$25.00

Cox, Airwolf, 1987-89, blk helicopter, EX, B7 ....$25.00

Cox, Army P-51B Mustang, 1963-70, olive drab, w/molded landing gear, EX, B7 ....$35.00

Cox, Attack Cobra, 1993-95, blk helicopter, M, B7.........$25.00

Cox, Avion Shinn, 1962, all yel w/red wing numbers, EX, B7 ....$65.00

Cox, Baron, Wings Series, 1980-81, blk, M, B7..............$25.00

Cox, Black Widow Pinto Funny Car, S15 ....$75.00

Cox, Blue Angel, Wings Series, 1981-86, bl, M, B7 ....$25.00

Cox, Buick Riviera, 1964, Thimbledrome motor, NMIB, S15 ....$150.00

Cox, Bushmaster, 1973-74, red & wht, w/pontoons & skis, EX, B7 ....$40.00

Cox, Cessna 150, Sure Flyer Series, 1976-78, wht w/red mks, EX, B7 ....$20.00

Cox, Combat Mustang, 1974-77, olive drab, P-51 w/side-mounted engine, EX, B7..$25.00

Cox, Commanche, 1960-64, tan, cream, maroon & chrome, .15 engine, EX, B7 ....$75.00

Cox, Corsair, 1969-70, red, Thompson Trophy Racer, EX, B7 ....$45.00

Cox, Corsair II, 1970-72, chrome w/red & wht checkerboard on wing, M, B7 ....$65.00

Cox, Crusader, 1976-79, wht & bl w/NASA mks, EX, B7 .$25.00

Cox, Curtiss Pusher, 1960-62, blk & orange, Wright Bros biplane, 1960-62, EX, B7 ....$70.00

Cox, Desert Defender, 1991-93, tan, M, B7 ....$25.00

Cox, F-1 Sport Trainer, 1973-81, pk w/bl canopy, EX, B7..$30.00

Cox, F-15 Eagle, Wings Series, 1977-79, wht, EX, B7 ......$15.00

Cox, FA-18 Hornet, 1991-95, lt gray, EX, B7 ....$20.00

Cox, Falcon, Wings Series, 1977-79, wht, EX, B7 ....$15.00

Cox, Firebird, E-Z Flyer Series, 1993-95, red w/muffler, M, B7 ....$25.00

Cox, Flying Circus, 1958-61, wht w/red checkerboard on wing, metal tank, EX, B7..$45.00

Cox, Flying Trainer, red & bl or bl & yel, Profile fuselage, EX, B7 ....$45.00

Cox, Fokker Triplane, 1973-74, red, German WWI fighter, EX, B7 ....$35.00

Cox, Fokker-D, 1972-74, red & bl, EX, B7 ....$30.00

Cox, Hustler, Wings Series, 1977-79, red, EX, B7 ....$15.00

Cox, Invader, Buck Rogers Series (flying saucer), 1980 only, blk, EX, B7 ....$35.00

Cox, JU87D Stuka, 1962-65, gr w/molded landing gear, EX, B7 ....$50.00

Cox, L-4 Grasshopper, 1963-70, olive drab, Army Piper Cub, EX, B7 ....$45.00

Cox, Lil Stinker, 1958-64, red & wht biplane, .020 engine, EX, B7 ....$45.00

Cox, Mantis, Wings Series, 1977-79, yel, EX, B7 ....$15.00

Cox, Marine Corsair, 1978, bl, side-mounted engine, EX, B7 ....$30.00

Cox, Mini Stunt Biplane, 1969-70, lime gr, .020 engine, EX, B7 ....$45.00

Cox, P-39 Airacobra, Sure Flyer Series, 1976-79, bl, EX, B7 .$20.00

Cox, P-40 Flying Tiger, 1959-60, tan, mk Flying Tiger on fuselage, inverted engine, EX, B7 ....$55.00

Cox, P-40 Kitty Hawk, 1964-65, gr w/yel tail & lettering, EX, B7 ....$60.00

Cox, P-40 Warhawk, 1961-68, tan w/inverted engine & pnt pilot, EX, B7 ....$45.00

Cox, P-51 Bendix Racer, 1963-64, red & yel, molded landing gear, EX, B7 ....$65.00

Cox, P-51 Miss America, 1972-75, red, wht & bl, 2nd version w/bolt-on landing gear, EX, B7 ....$35.00

Cox, P-51 Mustang, Red Baron Air Race, 1981 only, EX, B7 ....$35.00

Cox, P-51 Mustang, 1979-80, olive drab, upright engine, EX, B7 ....$30.00

Cox, P-51D Mustang, olive drab, w/bubble canopy & bolt-on landing gear, M, B7 ....$50.00

Cox, Piper Commanche, Sure Flyer Series, 1976-77, wht w/gr mks, EX, B7 ....$20.00

Cox, Pitts Special, 1968, wht, .020 powered biplane, EX, B7 ....$45.00

Cox, Pitts Special, 1996 only, 50th Anniversary Biplane, metallic gold, 3,000 produced, M, B7 ....$100.00

Cox, QZ PT-19, 1966-69, red & wht, Quiet Zone Muffler, EX, B7 ....$45.00

Cox, RAF Spitfire, 1966-69, dk gr w/camo, EX, B7 ....$40.00

Cox, Red Devil, Wings Series, 1980, red, EX, B7 ....$15.00

Cox, Red Knight Biplane, 1970-72, dk red, .020 engine, EX, B7 ....$45.00

Cox, Rivets Racer, 1971-73, red & yel w/pilot figure, NM, B7 ....$50.00

Cox, Ryan PT-20, 1969-70, olive drab & yel, .020 engine, EX, B7 ....$45.00

Cox, Ryan ST-3, wht & bl, .020 engine, 2 pilots, M, B7..$65.00

Cox, SB2C Navy Helldiver, 1963-66, lt & dk bl, EX, B7.$55.00

Cox, Sky-Copter, 1976-79, yel & orange, plastic fuel tank & .020 engine, EX, B7 ....$30.00

Cox, Sky-Jumper, 1989-95, olive drab helicopter w/pilot & parachute, M, B7 ....$35.00

Cox, Sky-Ranger, Coast Guard Helicopter, 1980-89, wht, M, B7 ....$35.00

Cox, Skymaster, Sure Flyer Series, 1976-79, orange, twin tail, blk stickers, EX, B7 ....$20.00

Cox, Skymaster, 1953-59, red, yel, bl or wht, aluminum wing, diecast engine w/metal tank, EX, B7 ....$85.00

Cox, Sopwith Camel, 1972-74, yel & bl, EX, B7 ....$30.00

Cox, Spook, 1964, wht flying wing kit w/engine, EX, B7 .$55.00

Cox, Star Cruiser, Wings Series, 1978-79, wht, flying saucer, EX, B7 ....$25.00

Cox, Starfighter, Buck Rogers Series, 1980 only, wht, EX, B7 ....$35.00

Cox, Stealth Bomber, 1987-89, blk, EX, B7.....................$25.00

Cox, Stuka, 1974-80, blk w/landing gear bolted on wing, side-mounted engine, EX, B7 ....$40.00

Cox, Super Cab 105, Civil Air Patrol version, yel & bl w/inverted engine, M, B7 ....$90.00

Cox, Super Cab 150, 1961-62, red & cream, upright engine, metal tank, EX, B7 ....$45.00

Cox, Super Sabre F-100, 1958-63, wht or gray, .020 engine, EX, B7 ....$55.00

Cox, Super Sport II, 1982-90, yel, M, B7 ....$30.00

Cox, Super Stunter, 1974-79, EX, B7.............................$30.00

Cox, T-28 Trainer, 1966-67, yel, EX, B7 ....$45.00

Cox, Thunderbolt, E-Z Flyer Series, 1993-95, blk w/muffler, M, B7 ....$25.00

Cox, Top Gun, 1988-1990, gray, M, B7 ....$30.00

Dooling Mercury, prewar racer, 18" long, NM, $2,500.00.

Wen-Mac, Aeromite, 1950-53, blk, Baby Spitfire engine, EX, B7 ....$55.00

Wen-Mac, AT-6, 1963-64, olive drab, EX, B7 ....$45.00

Wen-Mac, B-33 Debonair, 1962-64, gr, yel & chrome, EX, B7 ....$45.00

Wen-Mac, Basic Trainer, 1962-64, red, bl, yel, blk & chrome, EX, B7 ....$45.00

Wen-Mac, Beechcraft M-35, 1958-64, bl, gr, yel & wht, EX, B7 ....$40.00

Wen-Mac, Bomber, 1962-64, yel & orange, EX, B7 ....$45.00

Wen-Mac, Cessna 175 Trainer, 1962-64, red & wht, EX, B7 ....$40.00

Wen-Mac, Cutlass, 1958-60, bl, blk & yel, EX, B7...........$45.00

Wen-Mac, Earth Satellite, 1960-64, red, flying saucer, EX, B7 ....$45.00

Wen-Mac, Falcon, 1963-64, red, wht & bl, EX, B7 ....$40.00

Wen-Mac, Fan/Jet XL600, 1958-60, red, Delta wing, rear engine, EX, B7 ....$45.00

Wen-Mac, Flying Platform, 1956-58, olive drab, w/USN emblems, EX, B7 ....$65.00

Wen-Mac, Giant P-40 Flying Tiger, 1959-60, wht, EX, B7 ..$40.00

Wen-Mac, Giant P-51 Mustang, Vacuum Formed, 1959-60, wht, EX, B7 ....$40.00

Wen-Mac, Hawk, 1963-64, yel & wht, EX, B7 ....$40.00

Wen-Mac, Navy Corsair, 1958-64, bl, EX, B7 ....$40.00

Wen-Mac, Navy SNJ-3, 1963-64, lt bl, EX, B7 ....$45.00

Wen-Mac, Night Fighter, 1952-55, bl, Wen-Mac engine, EX, B7 ....$50.00

Wen-Mac, P-26 Pursuit, 1958-62, bl & yel, EX, B7..........$65.00

Wen-Mac, P-38 Lightning, 1959-64, red, gray, tan & chrome, 2 engine, EX, B7 ....$85.00

Wen-Mac, RAF Day Fighter, 1963-64, wht, EX, B7.........$45.00

Wen-Mac, RCAF Banshee Raider, 1963-64, blk, EX, B7.$45.00

Wen-Mac, SBD-5 Navy Dive Bomber, 1962-64, EX, B7..$45.00

Wen-Mac, Thunderbird, Flying Wings, lt bl & wht, EX, B7 ....$40.00

Wen-Mac, Turbojet, 1958-64, red & cream, red & chrome, EX, B7 ....$40.00

Wen-Mac, US Army Hovercraft, 1960-64, olive drab, EX, B7 ....$40.00

GI Joe

GI Joe, the most famous action figure of them all, has been made in hundreds of variations since Hasbro introduced him in 1964. The first of these jointed figures was 12" tall; they can be identified today by the mark each carried on his back: GI Joe T.M. (trademark), Copyright 1964. They came with four different hair colors: blond, auburn, black, and brown, each with a scar on his right cheek. They were sold in four basic packages: Action Soldier, Action Sailor, Action Marine, and Action Pilot. A Black figure was also included in the line. There were also representatives of many nations as well — France, Germany, Japan, Russia, etc. These figures did not have scars and are more valuable. Talking GI Joes were issued in 1967 when the only female (the nurse) was introduced. Besides the figures, uniforms, vehicles, guns, and accessories of many varieties were produced. The Adventure Team series, made from 1970 to 1976, included Black Adventurer, Air Adventurer, Talking Astronaut, Sea Adventurer, Talking Team Commander, Land Adventurer, and several variations. Joe's hard plastic hands were replaced with kung fu grips, so that he could better grasp his weapons. Assorted playsets allowed young imaginations to run wild, and besides the doll-size items, there were wristwatches, foot lockers, toys, and walkie-talkies made for the kids themselves. Due to increased production costs, the large GI Joe was discontinued in 1976.

In 1982, Hasbro brought out the 'little' 3¾" GI Joe figures, each with its own descriptive name. Of the first series, some characters were produced with either a swivel or straight arm. Vehicles, weapons, and playsets were available, and some characters could only be had by redeeming flag points from the backs of packages. This small version proved to be the most successful action figure line ever made. Loose items are common; collectors value those still mint in the original packages at two to four times higher.

In 1993 Hasbro reintroduced the 12" line while retaining the 3¾" size. The highlights of the comeback are the 30th anniversary collection of 6 figures which are already selling in the collector's market at well above retail ($29.00): Soldier, $80.00; Sailor, $80.00; Marine, $50.00; Pilot, $80.00; Black Soldier, $180.00; and Green Beret, $285.00.

Production of the 3¾" figures came to an end in December 1994, but we may see GI Joe again in 1996. For more information we recommend *Collectible Male Action Figures* by Paris and Susan Manos (Collector Books); *Encyclopedia to GI Joe* and *The 30th Anniversary Salute to GI Joe* both by Vincent Santelmo; *Official Collector's Guide to Collecting and Completing, Official Guide To Completing 3¾" Series* and *Hall of Fame: Vol II*, and *Official Guide To GI Joe: '64-'78*, all by James DeSimone. There is also a section on GI Joe in *Dolls in Uniform*, a publication by Joseph Bourgeois (Collector Books). Note: all items are American issue unless indicated otherwise. (Action Man was made in England by Hasbro circa 1960 to the 1970s.)

Advisor: Cotswold Collectibles (C6).
Other Sources: D4, D8, M15, O1, P3, S17, T1, T2

See also Games; Lunch Boxes; Windups, Friction and Other Mechanicals.

Key: A/M – Action Man

12" GI Joe Figures and Figure Sets

Action Marine, #7700, missing few accessories, M, $150.00.

Action Pack: Escape From Danger, complete Rescue Raft & Escape Car, ea w/booklet, 1971, NM (VG box), C6 .$95.00
Action Pilot, complete w/flight suit, boots, cap, dog tags, club & manual, #7800, EX (EX box) $450.00
Action Sailor, complete w/shirt & trousers, boots, cap, dog tags, club & manual, #7600, EX (EX box) $225.00
Action Soldier, complete w/fatigues, boots, cap, dog tags, club & manual, #7500, EX+ (EX box), C6 ....$290.00
Air Force Dress Doll, complete w/accessories, EX (EX+ box), H4 ....$330.00
Astronaut, complete w/accessories, silver space suit, NM, H4 ....$175.00
Australian Jungle Fighter, complete w/accesories, #8205, M (VG, resealed, narrow box), C6 ....$800.00
Australian Jungle Fighter, complete w/accessories, EX, C6 ....$270.00
Black Adventurer, shirt w/decal, trousers, boots, shoulder holster & pistol, EX (G box), C6 ....$270.00
British Commando, helmet, jackets, trousers & boots, #8204, M (EX narrow box), C6.................................$1,100.00
British Commando w/Chevrons, complete w/accessories, VG, C6 ....$295.00
British Infantry Major, jacket, trouser, cap, scarf, binoculars, belt, boots, laynard, .45/holster, A/M, MIP, C6.........$65.00
Combat Soldier, Army sweater, trousers, boots, beret, rifle, belt, A/M, M (VG box), C6 ....$95.00
Crash Crew, complete w/accessories, EX, C6 ....$180.00
Deep Freeze, complete w/accessories, VG, C6 ....$210.00
Deep Sea Diver, complete w/accesories, #7620, M (G box, reshrink-wrapped), C6..$885.00

Deep Sea Diver, complete w/accessories, VG, H4 ....$160.00

Duke, Hall of Fame, Desert Storm fatigues, MIB, $70.00.

Fighter Pilot, complete, EX, H4 ....$420.00

French Resistance Fighter, complete w/accesories, #8103, M (M reproduced box), C6.......................................$525.00

French Resistance Fighter, complete w/accessories, NM, C6..$275.00

German Soldier, complete w/accessories, #8100, M (G box, reshrink-wrapped), C6 ....$1,750.00

German Stormtrooper, complete w/accessories (rpl sling), VG, C6 ....$295.00

Green Beret, complete w/accessories, VG, H4 ....$220.00

Japanese Imperial Soldier, complete w/accessories, M, C6..$625.00

Japanese Soldier, complete w/accessories, #8201, M (EX narrow box), C6...$975.00

Joseph Colton Arctic Explorer, complete w/accessories, #783, M..$190.00

Landing Signal Officer, complete w/accessories, VG, C6..$230.00

Man of Action, shirt, trousers, brn boots, gr cap, dog tags, hard hands, EX (G box), C6.......................................$180.00

Marine Demolition, complete w/accessories, EX, C6 .....$150.00

Marine Jungle Fighter, complete w/accessories, no patch over pockets, pants faded, VG, H4 ....$240.00

Military Police, brn outfit, complete w/accessories, VG, H4..$160.00

Military Police, complete w/accessories, rpl strap in helmet, VG, C6 ....$225.00

Navy Attack, complete w/accessories, EX, C6...............$225.00

Race Car Driver, rpl strap on goggles, VG, C6 ....$150.00

Russian Infantryman, complete w/accessories, #8102, M (EX reshrink-wrapped lg window box w/stain), C6 .....$2,700.00

Sabotage Set, Action Marine w/complete accessories, EX, H4..$250.00

Scramble Pilot, missing oxygen mask & gr tinted visor o/w complete, EX, H4 ....$190.00

Sea Adventurer, dog tags, shoulder holster & pistol, hard hands, EX (VG box), H4 ....$130.00

Sea Adventurer, shirt w/insignia, dungarees, boots, shoulder holster & pistol, hard hands, EX (EX box), C6.............$190.00

Shore Patrol, complete w/accessories, VG, C6 ....$265.00

Ski Patrol, complete, VG, H4 ....$180.00

Space Ranger Captain, complete w/accessories, A/M, M (G box), C6 ....$90.00

Space Ranger Patroller, complete w/accessories, A/M, M (VG box), C6 ....$50.00

Special Forces, complete w/accessories, #7532, M (NM+ box), C6 ....$975.00

Special Talking GI Joe Adventure Pack, French Resistance Fighter outfit, complete, #9083, 1967, M (G box), C6........$1,350.00

Talking Action Pilot, foreign head, all orig paperwork, missing stickers, NM (NM box), H4...............................$790.00

Talking Action Soldier (EX voice), complete w/accessories, #7590, NM (VG box), C6..$350.00

Talking Astronaut, blonde hair, no beard, hard hands, wht coveralls, space boots, VG+, H4 ....$110.00

West Point Cadet, complete w/accessories, EX, H4 ....$210.00

West Point Cadet, complete w/accessories, M (EX window box), C6 ....$1,000.00

Accessories for 12" GI Joe

Action Soldier Flame Thrower, gr, w/helmet sticker, 1960s, A/M, M (EX card), C6 ....$60.00

Adventure Team Dog Tags, plastic, w/chain, EX, H4 ......$16.00

Air Cadet, #7822, complete, M (EX box), C6 ....$1,450.00

Air Cadet Hat, EX, H4...$25.00

Air Cadet Jacket, VG+, H4..$40.00

Air Force Dress Jacket, no helmet sticker, MOC, C6.....$200.00

Air Force Dress Uniform, #7803, complete, M (EX box), C6..$1,450.00

Airbourne Military Police Pants, tan, VG+, H4..............$25.00

Ammo Pouch (for belt), gr, EX, H4 ....$4.00

Annapolis Cadet, #7264, complete, MIB (sealed), C6..$1,250.00

Annapolis Cadet Hat, EX, H4..$25.00

Annapolis Cadet Jacket, G, H4..$25.00

Army Communications Radio, gr, EX, H4........................$15.00

Army Field Jacket, VG $24.00

Army Helmet, gr, w/strap, EX, H4..................................$20.00

Army Poncho, gr, EX, H4..$10.00

Army Tent, gr, complete, EX, H4 ....$35.00
Backpack, gr, EX, H4 ....$12.00
Backyard Patrol Sandstorm Survival Equipment, complete
     w/accessories, M (in bag), H4..............................$45.00
Bear Trap, EX, H4..$5.00
Belt, blk, cloth, EX, H4..$6.00
Belt, gr, EX, H4..$10.00
Belt, gray, cloth, EX, H4 ....$3.00
Belt, tan, plastic, EX, H4 ....$4.00
Belt, w/pouches, gr, EX, H4...$12.00
Belt, wht, cloth, EX, H4...$4.00
Billy Club, EX, H4...$2.00
Binoculars, red, EX, H4..$2.00
Bivouac Machine Gun Set, #7514, MOC, C6..................$60.00
Bivouac Sleeping Bag, #7515, MOC, C6..........................$55.00
British Commando Equipment, #8304, M (card has cello tear),
     C6 ....$245.00
British Greatcoat, w/knit cap, A/M, MOC, C6 ....$30.00
Canteen, w/cover, EX, H4...$12.00
Carbine, w/.45 & 6 grenades, A/M, MIP, C6....................$12.00
Chain Saw, EX, H4..$5.00
Cobra Rifle Range Set, complete, 1985, EX, H4..............$6.00
Combat Camouflage Netting Set, #7511, MOC, C6........$25.00
Combat Sand Bags Set, no sticker, #7508, MOC, C6 ......$25.00
Command Post Poncho, gr, #7519, MOC, C6..................$55.00
Communications Field Set, #7703, MOC, C6..................$85.00
Coveralls, camo, EX, H4...$4.00
Crash Crew Ax, EX, H4..$3.00
Crash Crew Jacket, VG, H4 ....$15.00
Crash Crew Pants, VG...$20.00
Crash Crew Set, #7820, M (VG box), C6 ....$260.00
Deep Sea Diver's Foot Weights, EX, pr $10.00
Deep Sea Divers Outfit, complete, VG, H4 ....$90.00
Demolition Set, complete, M (EX box), C6 ....$85.00
Detonator Gun, w/detonator, A/M, MIP, C6....................$5.00
Diver's Gloves, EX $6.00
Diver's Helmet, EX $15.00
Diver's Hoses, EX, pr, H4...$5.00
Diver's Sledge Hammer, EX, H4 ....$12.00
Diver's Weighted Belt, EX..$24.00
Dress Uniform, #7803, complete, scarce, NM (EX+ box),
     A $800.00
El Alamein Weapons Arsenal, Lewis machine gun, Sten sub
     machine gun, Mausser, Ger & Brit grenades, A/M, M (VG+
     card), C6 ....$70.00
Entrenching Tool w/Cover, EX $25.00
Fatigue Hat, bl, EX, H4...$15.00
Fatigue Hat, gr, EX $5.00
Field Pack, wht, EX, H4...$16.00
Fire Fighter Accessories, backpack extinguisher, lg axe, A/M, M
     (VG+ card), C6 ....$17.00
Flare Gun, EX, H4...$3.00
Flotation Collar, Sear's Exclusive Space Capsule, EX, H4 ..$80.00
Footlocker, gr, w/tray & inner lid illustration, EX $40.00
French Greatcoat, French Foreign Legion, A/M, MOC,
     C6 ....$30.00
French 7.65 Lt Machine Gun, w/Beretta & combat knife, A/M,
     MIP, C6 ....$15.00

French 7.65 Lt Machine Gun, w/brn shoulder holster &
     revolver, A/M, MOC, C6....................................$22.00
German Stormtrooper Equipment, complete w/accessories,
     #8300, M (card has cello tear), C6 ....$265.00
Goggles, for Desert Patrol Jeep, yel tinted, EX, H4..........$25.00
Gold Treasure Chest, EX, H4..$8.00
Gravity Boots, dk gray boots w/canteen & tan pouch that
     attaches to belt, A/M, MOC, C6...........................$8.00
Grease Gun, EX, H4...$14.00
Green Beret Bazooka, w/2 shells, EX, H4.......................$32.00
Green Beret Hat, w/emblem, EX, H4.............................$45.00
Green Beret M-16 Rifle, w/strap, EX.............................$20.00
Green Beret Pants, BH, H4..$20.00
Green Beret/French Radio, EX, H4...............................$14.00
Grenade Launcher, w/lugar, silencer & removable stock, MOC,
     C6 ....$30.00
Grenade Launcher Rifle, w/strap, EX, H4 ....$45.00
Grenades (4), EX, H4 ....$2.00
Heavy Weapon's Vest, EX, H4......................................$80.00
Highway Hazard Accessories, jack, axe, bolt cutters, fire extin-
     guisher, A/M, M (VG card), C6............................$21.00
Highway Hazards Uniform, bl coveralls, visibility vest, A/M,
     MOC, C6 ....$20.00
HK-MP5, w/.45 & holster, A/M, MIP, C6........................$10.00
Ice Pick/Climbing Tool, EX, H4.....................................$5.00
Idol, from the Search for Stolen Idol set, EX, H4 ....$10.00
Indian Brave, shirt & trousers, moccasins, belt, headband, wig,
     tomahawk, knife, musket, A/M, M (EX box), C6......$60.00
Indian Chief, shirt, trousers, moccasins, wampum bag, peace
     pipe, headdress, campfire, tomahawk, A/M, M (VG box),
     C6 ....$60.00
Jacket, from the Mouth of Doom, EX, H4.......................$12.00
Jacket, from the White Tiger Hunt, gr, EX, H4 ....$7.00
Jet Pack Accessories Pack, fits around waist, EX, H4.........$8.00
Jettison To Safety, blk shirt, yel pants, red mobile terrain
     scanner, red & gray rocket pack, Canadian, M (VG box),
     C6 ....$110.00

Jungle Survival, GI Joe Adventure Team, 1972-75, MIB, $95.00.

Karate, shirt & trousers, 3 belts, mat, break-apart brick & stand, manual, M (EX box), C6 ....$90.00

Knife & Scabbard, EX, H4..$15.00

Land Mine Disk, metal, EX, C6/H4...$3.00

Landing Signal Officer Set, no sticker, #7626, MOC, C6...$115.00

Laser Rescue Set, complete, EX, H4...$6.00

Life Ring, MOC, C6 ....$45.00

M-1 Carbine, w/strap, EX, H4 ....$12.00

M-60 Machine Gun, no bipod, EX, H4...................................$30.00

Machine Gun, 30 caliber, tripod & ammo box, EX, H4...$30.00

Map Case, w/map, yel, EX, H4 ....$5.00

Marine Camo Communication Radio, EX, H4.................$14.00

Marine Dress Cap, EX...$7.00

Marine Dress Jacket & Pants, VG $55.00

Marine Field Phone, camo, vinyl, EX, H4........................$12.00

Marine Flame Thrower, gr, EX, H4 ....$25.00

Marine Flame Thrower, M (card has cello tear), C6 ....$80.00

Marine Helmet, camouflage, w/strap, EX, H4..................$20.00

Marine Parachute Pack, no helmet sticker, MOC, C6 .....$75.00

Marine Parachute Set, parachute, carbine, knife/scabbard, grenades, first aid kit, canteen, manual, #7705, M (NM box), C6...$225.00

Marine Poncho, camouflage, EX, H4 ....$20.00

Marine Tent Camouflage Set, #7708, MOC, C6..............$55.00

Mask, from Radiation Detection Set, EX, H4 ....$4.00

Medic Armband, EX, H4..$15.00

Medic Box, red, sm, EX, H4..$6.00

Medic Crutch, EX, H4...$3.00

Medic Helmet, w/strap, EX, H4...$40.00

Medic Shoulder Bag, EX, H4...$15.00

Mess Kit, EX, H4...$8.00

Military Police, #7521, complete, M (NM box), C6...$1,025.00

Military Police Duffle Bag, #7523, MOC, C6 ....$40.00

Military Police Jacket, brn, MOC, C6 ....$115.00

Military Police Jacket, brn, VG $25.00

Military Police Trousers, brn, MOC, C6..........................$70.00

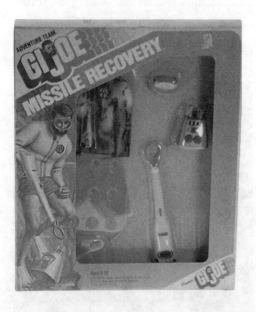

Missile Recovery, GI Joe Adventure Team, #7348, MIB, $40.00.

Mine Detection Set, mine detector & case, headset, battery pack, land mines, A/M, M (G box w/cello torn), C6.........$145.00

Mortar, complete w/3 shells, A/M, M (G+ card), C6.......$65.00

Mortar Launch Base, VG+, H4 ....$4.00

Mountain & Artic Set, complete w/accessories, A/M, M (VG box), C6 ....$55.00

Mountain Troops, #7530, complete, M (EX+ box), C6 .$175.00

NATO Night Maneuvers Arsenal, complete w/accessories, A/M, MOC, C6 ....$70.00

Navy Attack Semaphore Flags, EX, H4 ....$35.00

Navy Basics, no sticker, #7628, MOC, C6........................$100.00

Navy Frogman Scuba Tanks, #7606, MOC, C6................$45.00

Navy Frogman Set, #7602, complete, MIB (sealed), C6...$765.00

Octopus, EX, H4...$10.00

Parachute, wht, cloth, w/strings, EX, H4...........................$25.00

Parachute Regiments, complete w/accessories, A/M, M (VG+ pkg), C6 ....$75.00

Paths of Danger, Super Joe Adventure Team, MOC, $55.00.

Pick, from Mummy's Tomb, EX, H4......................................$4.00

Pilot Survival Set, #7801, complete, MIB, C6...............$950.00

Pistol, reg or French, EX, H4 ....$9.00

Plasma Bottle, EX, H4..$4.00

Polar Explorer, complete w/accessories, A/M, MIP, C6....$55.00

Poncho, camouflage, EX $15.00

Pursuit Craft Pilot, gr flight suit, gr helmet w/visor, shoulder holster & Beretta, blk boots, A/M, M (VG+ pkg), C6 ...$70.00

Radar Unit, yel, EX, H4 ....$8.00

Radioactive Satellite, EX, H4 ....$5.00

Raft, orange, EX, H4 ....$5.00

Raft, yel, w/oars, EX, H4 ....$12.00

Rescue Raft Backpack, EX (VG box), H4.............................$25.00

Rifle w/Scope, blk, EX, H4 ....$8.00

Royal Air Force, A/M, complete, M (EX box), C6...........$70.00

Royal Air Force, complete w/accessories, A/M, M (EX box), C6..$70.00

Russian Infantry Equipment, #8302, MOC, C6.............$290.00

Russian Lt Machine Gun, w/bipod & ammo disc, A/M, MOC, C6...$45.00

Russian Soldier Equipment, #8302B, M (sm cello tear), C6...$250.00

Sabotage Set, #7516, complete, EX (VG photo box), C6...$725.00

Sabotage Set, complete w/accessories, A/M, M (VG pkg), C6 ....$50.00
Sailor Hat, EX $10.00
Sand Bags, EX, ea $4.00
SAS Secret Mission, complete w/accessories, A/M, M (EX box), C6 ....$85.00
Scramble Pilot Air Vest & Accessories, MOC, C6 ....$90.00
Scramble Pilot Coveralls, gray, G $40.00
Scramble Pilot Life Vest, orange, vinyl, EX, H4 ....$10.00
Scramble Pilot Parachute Pack, MOC, C6 ....$70.00
Scramble Pilot Set, #7807, complete, M (NM box), C6 ..$645.00
Scuba Bottom, #7604, MOC, C6 ....$60.00
Scuba Flippers, blk or orange, EX, H4, pr $2.00
Scuba Mask, blk, EX $5.00
Scuba Mask, orange, EX $15.00
Scuba Mask, red, EX, H4 ....$2.00
Scuba Tank, w/straps & hoses, wht, EX $8.00
Sea Rescue Set, #7601, complete, MIB, C6 ....$650.00
Search for the Abominable Snowman, complete, MIB (sealed, C6 ....$295.00
Searchlight, battery-operated, A/M, MIB, C6 ....$19.00
Searchlight, for Jeep, EX, H4 ....$15.00
Secret Mountain Outpost, complete, M (G box), C6 ....$125.00
Secret of the Mummy's Tomb, complete, EX, H4 ....$70.00
Secret of the Mummy's Tomb Set, complete except missing instructions, comics & inserts, EX+ (EX+ box), H4 ..$180.00
Shark, EX, H4 ....$8.00
Shell for Jeep Cannon, EX, H4 ....$50.00
Shirt, Man of Action, gr, EX, H4 ....$3.00
Shirt, Mike Powers, EX, H4 ....$5.00
Shore Patrol Dress Pants, no sticker, #7641, MOC, C6 ...$65.00
Shore Patrol Pants, VG, H4 ....$15.00
Shore Patrol Sea Bag, #7615, MOC, C6 ....$40.00
Shore Patrol Set, #7612, complete, M (EX box), C6 ..$1,000.00
Shorts, camo, VG+, H4 ....$4.00
Shorts, gr or tan, EX, H4, ea $2.00
Shorts, Mike Powers, brn, EX, H4 ....$5.00
Shoulder Holster, blk, EX $25.00
Shoulder Holster, brn, EX $18.00
Shovel, from Mummy's Tombs set, EX, H4 ....$4.00
Signal Light, EX, H4 ....$3.00
Ski Patrol Boots, EX, H4, pr $15.00
Ski Patrol Gloves, EX, H4, pr $12.00
Ski Patrol Jacket, EX, H4 ....$18.00
Ski Patrol Skis, EX, H4, pr $22.00
Sleeping Bag, EX, H4 ....$9.00
Snow Shoes, red, EX $25.00
Space Coveralls, wht, VG, H4 ....$20.00
Space Rifle, A/M, MIP, C6 ....$10.00
Special Operations Kit, complete w/accessories, A/M, M (VG card), C6 ....$40.00
Squid, EX, H4 ....$10.00
Stethoscope, EX, H4 ....$8.00
Trench Coat, brn, EX, H4 ....$10.00
Underwater Demolition Set, EX, H4 ....$9.00
US Air Force Dress Uniform, #7803, complete, M (EX box), C6 ....$1,450.00
Walkie-Talkie, EX, H4 ....$5.00

West Point Cadet Hat, no plume, EX, H4 ....$12.00
West Point Cadet Scabbard, EX, H4 ....$25.00
West Point Cadet Uniform, complete, EX, H4 ....$150.00
Wet Suit Bottoms, orange, rubber, VG, H4 ....$14.00
White Tiger, in cage, EX $16.00
Wire Roll, blk, EX, H4 ....$5.00
Workshop Accessories, A/M, M (VG+ card), C6 ....$20.00
Wrist Camera, EX, H4 ....$9.00

1964-1969 Paperwork

Air Manual for Action Pilot, narrow, EX, C6 ....$10.00
Air Manual for Action Pilot, wide, EX, C6 ....$7.00
Army Manual for Action Soldier, narrow, VG, C6 ....$7.00
Army Manual, wide, EX+, C6 ....$5.00
Counter Intelligence Manual, EX, H4 ....$20.00
Instructions, Cave, C6 ....$3.00
Instructions, Danger of the Depths, C6 ....$4.00
Instructions, Signal Flasher, in color, C6 ....$4.00
Intelligence Manual, A/M (same as GI Joe's), 1960s, EX, C6 ...$25.00
Marine Manual, wide, EX+, C6 ....$8.00
Marine Manual for Action Marine, narrow, VG, C6 ....$10.00
Navy Manual for Action Sailor, narrow, EX+, C6 ....$10.00
Navy Manual for Action Sailor, wide, EX+, C6 ....$8.00
Official Gear & Equipment Manual, color pictures, EX, H4 ..$15.00
Pamphlet, Join the GI Joe Club, C6 ....$5.00

Vehicles for 12" GI Joe

Action Backpack Escape Car, w/instructions, EX, H4 ......$15.00
Action Pack Turbo Copter, complete, MIB (very sm tear), H4 ....$50.00
Action Pilot Official Space Capsule, complete w/doll, record & instructions, M (EX box), H4 ....$230.00
Adventure Team Desert Patrol Adventure Jeep, tan, missing poles for tent, w/instructions, EX+ (EX box), H4 ....$250.00
Adventure Team Helicopter, yel, complete, EX (EX box) .$115.00
Adventure Team Sandstorm Survival Adventure Jeep, gr, missing tent poles, EX (EX box), H4 ....$190.00
Amphibious Duck, complete, EX (EX+ box), H4 ....$750.00
Ampicat, 6-wheeled vehicle, MIB, H4 ....$75.00
Armoured Jeep, Browning MG, camo net, shovel, wire cutters, jerry cans, A/M, EX (G box), C6 ....$90.00
Avenger Pursuit Craft, no instructions o/w complete, EX+ (EX+ box), H4 ....$200.00
Big Trapper Vehicle, complete, EX, H4 ....$75.00
Capture Copter, NRFB, H4 ....$200.00
Desert Patrol Attack Jeep, complete, NM (EX+ box), H4 ..$800.00
Desert Patrol Attack Jeep, complete w/accessories, EX ..$500.00
Devil of the Deep Turbo Swamp Craft, complete w/accessories, M (VG box), H4 ....$125.00
Fate of the Trouble Shooter Vehicle, no accessories, EX, H4 ....$30.00
Fire Engine, holds 1 figure, extending ladder, operating pump & hose, A/M, MIP, C6 ....$75.00
German Staff Car, blk plastic, holds 4 figures, no spare tire, #5652, EX (P illus box), C6 ....$695.00
Iron Knight Tank, A/M, M (NM box), C6 ....$175.00

Iron Knight Tank, complete, #9031, EX (EX box), C6 ..$245.00
Jeep Trailer, A/M, missing canopy o/w MIB, C6 ....$55.00
Jet Helicopter, complete, EX (EX+ box), H4 ....$450.00
Panther Jet Plane, complete w/instructions, EX+ (VG box), H4 ....$900.00
Sea Wolf Sub, missing mirror device & comic, no inserts, VG+ (EX+ box), H4 ....$80.00
Space Speeder, spacecraft converts to 4 vehicles, A/M, M (EX box), C6 ....$65.00
Survival, yel life raft w/anchor, complete w/accessories, A/M, MIB, C6 ....$45.00
Team Vehicle, yel ATV, winch, hook, rope, VG+ (VG- box), C6 ....$85.00
Underground Rescue Accessories, A/M, MOC, C6 ....$25.00
Windboat, bl w/yel mast & sail, Canadian issue, M (NM box), C6 ....$60.00

3¾" GI Joe Figures

Ace, complete w/accessories, 1983, MIP, C6 ....$25.00
Airborne, complete w/accesories, 1983, MIP, C6 ....$47.00
Airtight, complete w/card & accessories, 1985, EX $10.00
Alley Viper, complete w/accessories, 1989, EX, C6 ....$6.00
Alpine, complete w/accessories, 1985, EX $12.00
Alpine, complete w/accessories, 1986, MIP, C6 ....$30.00
Annihilator, complete w/accessories, 1989, MIP, C6 ....$14.00
Astro Viper, complete w/ID card & accessories, 1988, EX, H4 ....$6.00
Astro Viper, 1988, MIP, C6 ....$12.00
Astro Viper, 1993, M (pkg faults), C6 ....$9.00
Barbecue, complete w/accessories, 1985, EX $10.00
Barbecue, 1983-85, MIP, H4/C6 ....$26.00
Baroness, complete w/accessories, 1984, C6 ....$25.00
Bazooka, 1983-85, MIP $35.00
Beachhead, 1983-85, MIP $32.00

Beachhead, 1986, not original backpack otherwise complete, $10.00.

Big Boa, complete w/accessories, 1986, EX $10.00
Big Boa, 1987, MIP, C6 ....$25.00
Blizzard, complete w/accessories, 1988, C6.......................$8.00

Blow Torch, complete w/ID card & accessories, 1984, EX ..$13.00
Breaker, 1983, M (pkg faults), C6 ....$42.00
Buzzer, 1985, MIP, C6 ....$35.00
Capt Grid Iron, 1990, MIP, C6 ....$11.00
Charbroil, red eyes, 1988, M (pkg faults), C6 ....$14.00
Chuckles, complete w/accessories, 1986, EX.....................$7.00
Chuckles, 1987, M (pkg faults), C6...................................$18.00
Clutch, complete w/accessories, 1988, C6 ....$18.00
Cobra Commander, Chinese pkg, 1983, MIP, C6 ....$25.00
Cobra Commander, mail-in, complete w/ID card & accessories, 1983, EX, H4 ....$15.00
Cobra Commander, 1983, MIP, C6 ....$125.00
Cobra Officer, 1983, MIP, H4 ....$62.00
Cobra Soldier, 1983, MIP, C6 ....$62.00
Cobra Stinger Driver, w/ID card, 1982, M (factory bag) ..$12.00
Countdown, 1989, MIP, C6 ....$18.00
Countdown, 1993, M (pkg faults), C6 ....$14.00
Cover Girl, complete w/accessories, 1983, C6 ....$25.00
Crazylegs, 1987, M (pkg faults), C6.................................$18.00
Crimson Guard, complete w/accessories, 1985, EX..........$10.00
Crimson Guard, 1985, MIP, H4 ....$42.00
Croc Master, 1987, M (pkg faults), C6..............................$22.00

Crystal Ball Cobra Hypnotist, 1986, MOC, $15.00.

Cutter, complete w/accessories, 1984, C6 ....$15.00
D-Day, 1995, MIP, C6 ....$7.00
Darklon, complete w/ID card & accessories, 1989, EX $10.00
Dee Jay, complete w/ID card & accessories, 1988, EX, H4 .$6.00
Dee Jay, 1989, MIP, C6 ....$13.00
Deep Six, 1989, MIP, C6 ....$14.00
Deep Six w/Finback, 1992, MIP, C6 ....$15.00
Destro, complete w/accessories, 1983, C6 ....$15.00
Dial Tone, Chinese pkg, 1988, MIP, C6 ....$16.00
Dial Tone, complete w/ID card & accessories, 1986, EX, H4..$8.00
Doc, complete w/accessories, 1983, C6 ....$16.00
Dojo, 1992, MIP, C6 ....$9.00
Downtown, 1989, MIP, C6 ....$14.00
Dr Mindbender, complete w/accessories, 1986, C6............$9.00
Dr Mindbender, 1983-85, MIP $28.00

Duke, 1984, MIP, C6...$105.00

Dusty, missing bipod, 1984, EX $10.00

Dusty, 1985, MIP, C6..$40.00

Dynomite, 1995, MIP, C6..$7.00

Eels, complete w/accessories, 1985, EX $15.00

Eels, 1985, MIP, C6..$52.00

Eels, 1992, MIP, C6..$10.00

Fast Draw, complete w/accessories, 1987, C6............$8.00

Firefly, complete w/accessories, 1984, EX $18.00

Firefly, 1984, M (pkg faults), C6 ....$90.00

Flash, complete w/accessories, 1982, C6 ....$17.00

Flint, 1985, MIP, C6...$55.00

Footloose, complete w/accessories, 1985, EX $10.00

Footloose, 1985, M (pkg faults), C6 ....$30.00

Frag Viper, 1989, MIP, C6...$14.00

Fridge, complete w/accessories, mail-in, 1986, C6 ....$19.00

Fridge, w/ID card, 1986, M (factory bag), H4 ....$30.00

Frostbite, complete w/accessories, 1985, EX.............$12.00

Gen Flagg, 1992, MIP, C6 ....$6.00

Gnawgahyde, 1989, MIP, C6...$20.00

Grunt, complete w/accessories, 1982, EX, H4...........$20.00

Gung Ho, complete w/accessories, 1983, C6.............$16.00

Hardball, 1988, MIP, C6 ....$18.00

Hardtop, complete w/accessories, 1987, C6 ....$18.00

Hawk, complete w/accessories, 1987, C6 ....$13.00

Heavy Duty, 1991, MIP, C6...$8.00

Ice Viper, w/1993 Convention sticker, MIP, C6 ....$19.00

Iceberg, mail-in, 1987, M (pkg faults), C6 ....$9.00

Iceberg, 1983-85, MIP...$32.00

Iceberg, 1986, MIP, C6...$32.00

Interrogator, complete w/accessories, 1991, C6 ....$6.00

Iron Grenadiers, 1988, MIP, C6....................................$18.00

Jinx, complete w/ID card & accessories, 1987, EX.............$9.00

Jinx, mail-in, 1986, MIP, C6..$12.00

Jinx, w/ID card, 1987, M (factory bag)...........................$12.00

Keel Haul, complete w/accessories, mail-in, 1989, M (pkg

    faults), C6 ....$10.00

Lady Jaye, 1985, MIP, C6 ....$75.00

Lamprey, complete w/accessories, 1985, C6....................$10.00

Leatherneck, 1983-85, MIP..$32.00

Leatherneck, 1986, M (pkg faults), C6 ....$22.00

Lifeline, Chinese pkg, 1986, MIP, C6 ....$18.00

Lifeline, complete w/ID card & accessories, 1986, EX, H4 .$8.00

Lift Ticket, incomplete, 1986, C6 ....$10.00

Lightfoot, 1988, M (pkg faults), C6.............................$14.00

Lowlight, complete w/accessories, 1986, EX $10.00

Lowlight, 1983-85, MIP...$32.00

Lowlight, 1991, MIP, C6...$10.00

Mainframe, 1986, MIP, C6...$32.00

Major Attitude, 1991, M (pkg faults), C6 ....$9.00

Major Bludd, complete w/ID card & accessories, 1983, EX .$14.00

Manta Windsurfer, mail-in, 1993 Convention sticker, 1984,

    MIP, C6 ....$18.00

Maverick, 1988, MIP, C6..$27.00

Mega Marine Blast-Off, 1993, MIP, C6 ....$11.00

Mega Marine Clutch, 1993, M (pkg faults), C6.................$9.00

Mega Marine Cyber-Viper, 1993, MIP, C6...................$11.00

Mega Marine Mega-Viper, 1993, MIP, C6.......................$11.00

Mega Marine Mirage, 1993, MIP, C6...........................$11.00

Mega Monster Bio-Viper, 1993, MIP, C6 ....$15.00

Mega Monster Monstro-Viper, 1993, MIP, C6................$15.00

Metal-Head, 1990, MIP, C6..$15.00

Monkey Wrench, complete w/accessories, 1986, C6 ....$7.00

Monkey Wrench, 1983-85, MIP, H4 ....$20.00

Motor Viper, complete w/ID card & accessories, 1986, EX..$10.00

Motor Viper, 1986, MIP, C6...$22.00

Muskrat, complete w/ID card & accessories, 1986, EX $9.00

Mutt & Junkyard, 1984, M (pkg faults), C6................$35.00

Night Creeper, complete w/accessories, 1990, C6.............$6.00

Night Force Outback, complete w/accessories, 1988, C6 .$14.00

Night Viper, complete w/accessories, 1989, C6 ....$7.00

Ninja Force Banzai, 1993, M (pkg fault), C6 ....$4.00

Ninja Force Bushido, 1993, MIP, C6............................$5.00

Ninja Force Lt Falcon, complete w/accessories, 1988, C6 ..$6.00

Ninja Force Night Creeper, 1993, MIP, C6 ....$5.00

Ninja Force Snake Eyes, 1993, MIP, C6......................$6.00

Ninja Force Zartan, 1993, MIP, C6...............................$6.00

Nitro Viper, 1993, M (pkg faults), C6.........................$5.00

Outback, 1987, M (pkg faults), C6...............................$18.00

Ozone, 1993, M (pkg faults), C6 ....$5.00

Payload, complete w/accessories, 1987, C6 ....$23.00

Psyche-Out, 1987, missing some accessories, NM, $5.00.

Psyche-Out, 1987, MIP, C6...$22.00

Quick Kick, 1985, MIP, C6...$35.00

Range-Viper, 1990, MIP, C6...$11.00

Rapid-Fire, w/video tape, 1990, M (pkg faults), C6..........$14.00

Raptor, complete w/ID card & accessories, 1987, EX $8.00

Raptor, 1987, MIP, C6...$20.00

Recoil, 1989, MIP, C6..$15.00

Recondo, complete w/ID card & accessories, 1984, EX $13.00

Recondo, 1989, MIP, C6...$40.00

Repeater, complete w/accessories, 1988, C6................$7.00

Rip Cord, w/ID card, missing parachute pack, 1984, EX, H4 .$10.00

Rip Cord, 1984, MIP, C6...$45.00

Ripper, 1985, MIP, C6...$36.00

Road Pig, complete w/ID card & accessories, 1988, EX $8.00
Road Pig, 1988, MIP, C6 ....$20.00
Roadblock, complete w/accessories, 1984, C6 ....$16.00
Roadblock, machine gun & tripod only, 1986, EX, H4 ......$7.00
Roadblock, 1986, MIP, C6 ....$36.00
Rock 'N Roll, complete w/accessories, 1983, C6 ....$17.00
Rock 'N Roll, complete w/ID card & accessories, 1989, EX..$7.00
Rock Viper, Chinese pkg, MIP, C6 ....$8.00
Rolling Thunder, English pkg, 1988, M (pkg faults), C6..$29.00
Rumbler, incomplete, 1987, C6 ....$9.00
Salvo, complete w/accessories, 1990, C6 ....$8.00
Scarlett, complete w/accessories, 1982, C6 ....$25.00
Sci-Fi, missing hose, 1986, EX, H4 ....$5.00
Sci-Fi, 1991, MIP, C6 ....$9.00
Scoop, 1989, MIP, C6 ....$15.00
Scrap Iron, India pkg, 1984, M (pkg faults), C6 ....$16.00
Scrap Iron, w/accessories, 1984, EX................................$13.00
Sergeant Savage, 1995, MIP, C6 ....$6.00
Sgt Slaughter, Drill Instructor, w/ID card, 1985, M (factory
     bag) $28.00
Sgt Slaughter, mail-in, complete w/ID card & accessories, 1985,
     EX $18.00
Sgt Slaughter, 1988, MIP, C6 ....$9.00
Shipwreck, complete w/ID card & accessories, 1985, EX .$14.00
Shipwreck, w/parrot, 1985, MIP, C6 ....$60.00
Shockwave, 1988, MIP, C6 ....$22.00
Short Fuse, complete w/accessories, 1982, EX, H4 ....$20.00
Short Fuse, complete w/accessories, 1983, C6..................$18.00
Skid Mark, complete w/ID card & accessories, 1988, EX .$10.00
Sky Patrol Airwave, w/Parachute Pack, tan, 1990, M (pkg
     faults), C6 ....$16.00
Sky Patrol Drop Zone, w/Parachute Pack, brn, 1990, MIP,
     C6..$18.00
Slaughter's Marauders Footloose, 1989, MIP, C6 ....$18.00
Slaughter's Renegades Mercer/Taurus/Red Dog, 1987, MIP,
     C6..$30.00
Slip Stream, complete w/accessories, 1986, C6.................$10.00
Snake Armor, gray, India pkg, M (pkg faults), C6 ....$30.00
Snake Eyes, complete w/ID card & accessories, 1982, EX,
     H4 ....$45.00
Snake Eyes, complete w/ID card & accessories, 1989, EX, H4...$7.00
Snake Eyes, 1985, M (pkg faults), C6................................$95.00
Snake Eyes, 1989, MIP, C6...$30.00
Snow Job, complete w/accessories, 1984, EX, H4 ....$15.00
Snow Serpent, complete w/accessories, 1985, EX............$14.00
Snow Serpent, 1985, M (pkg faults), C6 ....$42.00
Sonic Fighter Dial-Tone, 1990, MIP, C6 ....$18.00
Stalker, complete w/accessories, 1983, C6 ....$18.00
Stalker, complete w/ID card & accessories, 1989, EX $10.00
Stalker, Japan pkg, 1983, M (pkg faults), C6 ....$18.00
Steeler, 1983, MIP, C6 ....$35.00
Storm Shadow, complete w/ID card & accessories, 1988,
     EX...$12.00
Strato Viper, mail-in, 1988, M (pkg faults), C6 ....$9.00
Street Fighter Blanka, 1993, M (pkg faults), C6 ....$5.00
Street Fighter Chun-Li, 1993, M (pkg faults), C6..............$7.00
Street Fighter Guile, 1993, M (pkg faults), C6 ....$5.00
Street Fighter Ken, 1993, M (pkg faults), C6.....................$6.00

Street Fighter M Bison, 1993, M (pkg faults), C6 ....$6.00
Street Fighter Ryu, 1993, M (pkg faults), C6 ....$6.00
Stretcher, 1990, MIP, C6..$15.00
Sub-Zero, 1990, MIP, C6 ....$10.00
Super Trooper, complete w/accessories, mail-in, 1988, C6 .$20.00
T'Jbang, 1992, MIP, C6 ....$10.00
Talking Battle Commander Cobra Commander, 1991, MIP,
     C6..$12.00
Talking Battle Commander Stalker, 1991, MIP, C6 ....$12.00
TARGAT, 1989, MIP, C6 ....$18.00
Techno-Viper, complete w/accessories, 1987, C6..............$8.00
Techno-Viper, 1986, MIP $23.00
Tele-Viper, 1985, MIP, C6 ....$42.00
Tele-Viper, 1989, MIP, C6 ....$13.00
Thrasher, complete w/accessories, 1986, C6 ....$8.00
Thunder, mail-in, 1987, M (pkg faults), C6 ....$9.00
Tiger Force Duke, complete w/accessories, 1988, C6........$12.00
Tiger Force Lifeline, complete w/accessories, C6 ....$10.00
Tiger Force Roadblock, complete w/accessories, 1988, C6 .$8.00
Tiger Force Skystriker, incomplete, 1988, C6 ....$8.00
Tiger Force Tiger Shark, 1988, MIP, C6 ....$18.00
Tiger Force Tripwire, complete w/accessories, 1988, C6 ..$10.00
Tomax, complete w/ID card & accessories, 1985, EX.......$10.00
Topside, 1990, MIP, C6..$10.00

Torch, missing back-pack and cutting torch, 1984, $6.00.

Torch, 1985, M (pkg faults), C6 ....$32.00
Torpedo, 1983, MIP, C6...$47.00
Toxo Viper, 1988, M (pkg faults), C6 ....$14.00
Tripwire, complete w/accessories, 1983, EX.....................$12.00
Tripwire, 1983, M (pkg faults), C6....................................$38.00
Tunnel Rat, 1987, MIP, C6...$25.00
Vapor, 1990, MIP, C6...$15.00
Voltar, w/Condar, 1988, MIP, C6 ....$17.00
Wet Suit, complete w/ID card & accessories, 1986, EX....$13.00
Wet Suit, 1986, MIP, C6...$45.00
Wild Bill, complete w/ID card & accessories, 1983, EX,
     H4 ....$12.00

Wild Bill, 1992, MIP, C6..............................$5.00
Wild Weasel, complete w/accessories, 1984, C6.............$15.00
Wolverine, w/Cover Girl, tow hook, complete w/accessories, C6..............................$42.00
Zandar, complete w/accessories, 1986, C6....................$6.00
Zandar, 1983-85, MIP, H4..............................$18.00
Zap, olive drab gr, India pkg, M (pkg faults), C6 ....$15.00
Zarana, no earrings, 1985, EX, H4..............................$10.00
Zartan, complete w/accessories, 1984, C6 ....$35.00
Zartan, w/Swamp Skier, 1984, M (pkg faults), C6 ....$85.00

Vehicles and Accessories for 3¾" GI Joe

Air Defense Battle Station, 1985, EX (orig pkg), C6........$12.00
Ammo Dump Unit, 1985, EX (orig pkg), C6....................$10.00
Armadillo Mini Tank, 1984, EX..............................$8.00
Artic Blast, w/instructions, 1988, EX, H4 ....$12.00
Attack Vehicle Vamp, w/Clutch, 1982, EX, H4..............$40.00
Battle Gear Accessory Pack #1, 1983, MIP......................$16.00
Battlefield Robot Devastator, missing 1 rocket, 1986, EX, H4..............................$5.00
Bomb Disposal, 1984, EX, H4..............................$12.00
Bomb Disposal Unit, 1985, MIP..............................$8.00
Bomb Disposal Vehicle, no accessories, 1986, EX, H4........$3.00
Cobra Claw, 1984, EX $10.00
Cobra Ferret, 1984, EX, H4..............................$12.00
Cobra HISS, w/driver & ID card, 1983, EX, H4..............$35.00
Cobra HISS Tank, mail-in, 1983, M (pkg faults), H4 ......$12.00
Cobra Night Attack 4-WD w/Driver, Canadian pkg, MIP, H4 ....$55.00
Cobra Pom Pom Gun, 1983, EX, H4..............................$12.00
Cobra Rifle Range Set, complete, EX, H4........................$6.00
Cobra Thunder Machine, w/Thrasher, ID card, 1985, EX, H4 ....$20.00
Cobra Wolf, w/Ice Viper, 1985, EX..............................$17.00
Condor Z25, w/instructions, decals worn, 1989, EX, H4 ..$25.00
Dictator, w/instructions, 1989, EX, H4 ....$9.00
Dragonfly Helicopter, w/Wild Bill, 1983, complete, EX, H4 ....$40.00
Dreadnok Thunder Machine, w/Thrasher, 1985, NRFB (EX box), H4..............................$40.00
Evaser, w/Darklon, complete w/instructions, 1989, EX, H4 ....$25.00
Falcon Glider, w/Grunt, complete w/ID card, EX (glider G), H4 ....$60.00
Fang II, complete w/instructions, 1989, EX, H4.................$9.00
Flame Thrower, EX, H4 ....$5.00
Forward Observer Unit, 1985, complete w/accessories, EX, C6..............................$8.00
Heavy Artillery Laser, w/Grand Slam, 1982, NRFB.......$110.00
Hovercraft, mail-in, 1984, M (pkg faults), C6 ....$40.00
Jet Pack JUMP & Platform, Canadian pkg, 1982, MIP, C6..$50.00
LCV Recon Sled, complete, 1983, EX, H4 ....$5.00
Locust, complete w/instructions, 1989, EX, H4 ....$9.00
Machine Gun, EX, H4..............................$5.00
Manta Windsurfer, mail-in, MIB..............................$18.00
Missile Defense Unit, 1984, MIP..............................$20.00
Missile Launcher, EX, H4 ....$5.00

Mobile Missile System, complete w/Hawk, EX $45.00
Mobile Support Vehicle, no accessories, VG, H4.............$40.00
Motorized Battle Wagon, 1991, MIP, C6......................$35.00
Mountain Climber Motorized Action Pack, 1986, EX, H4.$4.00
Mountain Howitzer, 1984, complete w/accessories, EX $8.00
P-40 Warhawk, w/Pilot Savage, 1995, MIP, C6 ....$33.00
Pac/Rat Machine Gun Mini Vehicle, M (mailer bag), H4 .$10.00
Pac/Rat Missile Launcher Mini Access Vehicle, M (mailer bag), H4 ....$10.00
Parasite, cobra personnel carrier, 1991, EX, H4 ....$8.00
Pathfinder, 1990, MIP, C6..............................$11.00
Persuader, w/Backstop, complete w/instructions, 1987, EX, H4 ....$18.00
Pogo, complete w/instructions, EX, H4..............................$8.00
Polar Battle Bear, mail-in, 1983, M (pkg faults), C6 ....$10.00
Python Conquest, complete w/instructions, 1988, EX, H4 .$15.00
Python Stun, complete w/instructions, 1988, EX, H4 ......$10.00
Q Force Battle Gear, Action Force, MIP, C6....................$4.00
Rope Crosser Action Pack, 1987, MOC..............................$5.00
SAS Parachutist Attack, Action Force, MIP $25.00
Sea Ray, w/Sea Slug, complete w/instructions, EX, H4 ....$15.00
Serpentors Air Chariot, 1985, EX, H4 ....$5.00
SHARK, w/Deep Six, complete w/ID card, EX, H4..........$25.00
Sky Patrol Airwave, w/parachute pack, 1990, MIP, C6....$18.00
Sky Patrol Drop Zone, w/parachute pack, brn, 1990, MIP, C6..............................$18.00
Skyhawk, complete w/accessories, EX (G box) $18.00
Snow Cat, w/Frostbite, 1984, EX, H4..............................$25.00
Space Force Battle Gear, Action Force, MIP, C6 ....$3.00
Swamp Skier Vehicle, w/Zartan, complete w/ID card, EX, H4 ....$45.00
Tiger Fish, complete w/instructions, 1988, EX, H4.............$9.00
Tiger Shark, complete w/instructions, 1988, EX, H4........$12.00
Transportable Tactical Battle Platform, 1985, complete w/accessories, 1985, EX, C6..............................$22.00
Weapons Transport, 1984, EX, H4..............................$12.00
Whirlwind, twin battle gun, 1983, EX $15.00

Miscellaneous

GI Joe Activity Box, Whitman, 1965, complete, MIB, $125.00.

Combat Watch, Gilbert, 1965, shows standard & military time, w/compass & sighting lens, MIB, A $265.00

Comic, Danger Ray Detection, French or English, C6, ea..$6.00

Dog Tag, w/chain, GI Joe Club, child sz, EX, H4 ....$40.00

Puzzle, Action Sailor Navy Attack, Whitman, 1965, complete (G- box), H4 ....$15.00

Record & Book Set, Secret Spy Mission to Spy Island, C6, set $25.00

Super Joe Adventure Team Laser/Communicator, Hasbro, 1978, plastic, battery-op, w/sound alarm, 10", MIB (sealed), P4 ....$55.00

Guns

Until WWI, most cap guns were made of cast iron. Some from the 1930s were nickel-plated, had fancy plastic grips and were designed with realistic details like revolving cylinders. After the war, a trend developed toward using cast metal, a less expensive material. These diecast guns were made for two decades, during which time the TV western was born. Kids were offered a dazzling array of weapons, endorsed by stars like the Lone Ranger, Gene, Roy and Hoppy. Sales of space guns, made popular by Flash Gordon and Tom Corbett, kept pace with the robots coming in from Japan. Some of these early tin lithographed guns were fantastic futuristic styles that spat out rays of sparks when you pulled the trigger. But gradually the space race lost its fervor, westerns were phased out, and guns began to be looked upon with disfavor by the public in general and parents in particular. Since guns were meant to see lots of action, most will show wear. Learn to be realistic when you assess condition; it's critical when evaluating the value of a gun.

Advisor: Bill Hamburg (H1).

Other Sources: C10, I2, H7, K4, M16.

Actoy Restless Gun .38, EX, H1 ....$150.00

Aids Inc/Target, Atomic Airblaster Space Gun, EX, J2 ...$60.00

American Silent Ray Gun, blk, 11", EX, J2 ....$75.00

Atom Buster Air Blaster, 1950s, w/atomic target, NMIB..$100.00

Barton Space-Jet Water Ray Gun, Hong Kong, 1968, gr translucent plastic, 3½", MIP, P4...$15.00

BCM Space-Outlaw Atomic Pistol, England, 1960s, silver with red plastic windows, 10", MIB, $300.00.

Photo courtesy of Plymouth Rock Toy Co.

BCM Space-Outlaw Cap Firing Ray Gun, England, 1960s, silver w/reciprocating barrel, red plastic windows, 10", MIB ..$300.00

Belco Gun, Made in USA, solid metal, 3½", NM, I2 ....$18.00

Daisy, Stagecoach Strong Box/Gun, 1960s, opens w/2 keys & gun fires, plastic & steel, working, sm chip o/w EX+, F8 ....$70.00

Daisy Bull's Eye, bl fr, wood grips, no bullets, EX, H1 ......$95.00

Daisy Model 12 Soft-Air Gun, Japan, 1993, fires .25 cal soft-air pellets, w/10 cartridges & bag of pellets, MIB.........$125.00

Daisy Model 870 Soft-Air Shotgun, Japan, 1993, replica of Remington 870 Wingmaster, w/5 shells & bag of pellets, M, P4 ....$145.00

Daisy Rocket Dart Pistol, 1950s, litho tin, 7½", missing darts, lt scratches o/w VG...$100.00

Daisy Spittin' Image Six-Gun, bronze finish w/plastic walnut wood-grained grips, ejector lever missing o/w EX, H1 .$45.00

Duncan Astro-Light Spinning Space Ship #3910, 1970s, plastic, battery-op lights & jet sounds, MOC, P4..................$35.00

Edison Susanna, Italian, 1960s, long barrel similar to Colt .38, MIB, H1 ....$35.00

Elvin Atomic Sparking Ray Gun, Japan, 1960s, litho tin, mk T, 4", NMIP, P4..$55.00

Elvin Space Universe Sparking Ray Gun, Japan, 1960s, bl, wht & yel litho tin, mk T, 4", NMIP, P4 ....$45.00

Empire Plastics Corp Astronaut Space Gun, spinning gears & sound, friction, 11", needs new flint o/w EX (EX box), A $95.00

Empire Plastics Corp Guided Missiles & Launcher No 189, 1950s, blk plastic, fires 5" missile cap bombs, MIB, P4............$90.00

Esquire Action Miniatures No 10 Authentic Derringer, 1960s, bronze diecast, fires caps, 2", MOC, P4.....................$15.00

Haji Atomic Sparking Ray Gun, 1969, red, gray & yel litho tin w/plastic muzzle, sparking action, 9", M, P4...............$55.00

Halco Texan Holster Set w/Cap Pistols, diecast w/plastic grips, NM (NM card), A $75.00

Hamilton Invaders Pistol, w/2 grenades, EX $75.00

Hero Toy Co Friction Ray Gun, Japan, red, yel & bl litho tin, sparking, 7", M, P4...$55.00

Hiller Atom Ray Gun Water Pistol, 1948, red pnt diecast, 6", gasket hardened, trigger tip missing, lt pnt loss, VG..**$75.00**

Hubley Army .45 Repeater Cap Gun, metal w/plastic grips, NP CI trigger, unused, 6½", M (G box).......................**$125.00**

Photo courtesy of Dunbar Gallery.

Hubley Atomic Disintegrator Cap Pistol No 270, 1954, diecast with zinc finish, red plastic grips, 8", MIB, $350.00.

Hubley Automatic Cap Pistol No 290, diecast w/brn-checkered plastic grips, pop-up magazine, 6½", VG **$75.00**

Hubley Chief Single-Shot Cap Gun, 7½", MOC **$20.00**

Hubley Colt .38 Cap Pistol w/Chest Holster & Suspenders, 1959, diecast pistol, unused, NM (VG card), A **$85.00**

Hubley Colt .45 Cap Pistol, 1959, diecast, lever-removable revolving cylinder for 6 2-pc bullets, 13½", VG......**$125.00**

Hubley Cowboy Dummy Cap Pistol No 275, 1950s, swing-out revolving cylinder, release on barrel, wht plastic grips, NM **$175.00**

Hubley Cowboy Gold Cap Pistol No 275, 1950s, diecast, swing-out revolving cylinder, blk plastic grips, 12", VG....**$125.00**

Hubley Cowboy Repeating Cap Pistol, metal cap gun w/plastic inset hdls, 11½", EX (G box), A...............................**$175.00**

Hubley Dagger Derringer, metal w/slide-out plastic dagger, barrel rotates, 7", NMOC, A **$140.00**

Hubley Dick Cap Pistol, 1950, NP diecast, automatic style, side loading, unfired, 4¼", MIB..**$45.00**

Hubley Electra-Matic 50 Pistol, plastic machine gun, shoots caps, battery-op, 8", M (EX box), A.........................**$130.00**

Hubley Flintlock Jr Pistol, unused, NMIB.......................**$45.00**

Hubley Flintlock Pistol No 280, 1954, 2-shot, single action, dbl barrel, brn swirl plastic stock, unfired, 9", MIB........**$100.00**

Hubley Panther Pistol, metal derringer attached to spring-loaded leather wrist strap, shoots caps, 4", NM (G box).....**$125.00**

Hubley Pirate Cap Pistol, 1950, diecast fr w/cast dbl hammers & trigger, flintlock style, unfired, NMIB.....................**$225.00**

Hubley Remington .36 Cap Pistol, 1959, diecast w/blk plastic grips, revolving cylinder w/6 2-pc bullets, 8", VG **$75.00**

Hubley Rifleman Flip Special, 1959, diecast & plastic, pop-down cap magazine, lever action, unfired, 32½", NM.......**$175.00**

Hubley Rodeo, diecast, M, H1....................................**$45.00**

Hubley Sharp Shooter Rifle, 1965, NP w/gr plastic stock, bolt action, roll caps, not repeater, 37", NMIB...............**$150.00**

Hubley Texan .38 Cap Pistol, late 1958, diecast w/wht plastic grips, revolving cylinder w/6 brass bullets, 10", VG..**$125.00**

Hubley 2-in-1 Cap Pistol w/Short Barrel, EX, J2 ....**$50.00**

HY See-Thru Sparking Ray Gun, 1970s, rose translucent plastic, 3 wheels at top rotate, orange muzzle, 8½", VG, P4 ..**$25.00**

Imperial Toy Space Water Gun No 5, 1974, lime-gr translucent plastic, 7", M, P4...**$15.00**

Hubley Texan Jr. Repeating Cap Pistol, 1950s, nickel-plated cast iron with embossed steer on plastic inset grips, 9", MIB, A, $200.00.

Invincible New 50 Shot Cap Gun, CI, 5", VG, A............**$75.00**

J Rosenthal Toys Tunderbird 100-Shot Variable Direction Water Pistol, 1966, bright orange w/swivel nozzle, 8", MIP, P4 ....**$65.00**

Jyesa Pistola Sideral, Spain, 1960s, mc litho tin w/reciprocating action, 9¾", lt rust on chrome trim o/w NMIB **$75.00**

Kilgore American Cap Pistol, MIB **$400.00**

Kilgore Avenger Cap Pistol, diecast pistol in plastic shell, complete w/ammo, 3", NMOC, K4.....................................**$22.00**

Kilgore Border Patrol Cap Pistol, 1935, NP CI, side-loading automatic, 4½", lt rust o/w VG, P4 ....**$45.00**

Kilgore Captain 50-Shot, 4¼", M (torn box) **$75.00**

Kilgore Dude Derringer Cap Pistol, Italy, 1974, silver diecast single shot, blk plastic grips, 4", MOC, P4.....................**$25.00**

Kilgore Eagle, plastic grips, set of 2 w/dbl holster, EX+, J2..**$165.00**

Kilgore Mountie Cap Pistol, 1950, blk metal fr w/silver trim & blk grips, lever-release pop-up cap magazine, 6", MIB, P4 ....**$45.00**

Kilgore Ra-Ta-Tat Machine Gun, 1930s, NP CI, shoots caps, 5½", unused, M (G box), A **$265.00**

Kilgore Rawhide Cap Whip, ca 1960, 15" plastic tube w/firing cap insert, crack 24" rawhide whip to fire, w/caps, MIP, P4 ....**$45.00**

Kilgore Wagon Train Gun & Holster Set, 2 Pinto roll-cap guns, 6 plastic bullets, w/silver buckle on belt, VG+ **$150.00**

Kilgore Western Squirt Water Pistol, red plastic, 8", unused, NMIB, J2...**$65.00**

KO Mars Rifle, litho tin w/red plastic barrels, sparking action & sound, VG (orig box), A **$65.00**

KO Space Jet Friction Ray Gun, Japan, 1957, litho tin & plastic, sparks, reciprocating rocket in gr barrel, 9", VG........**$50.00**

KO Space Pilot X-Ray Gun, plastic w/simulated satellite openings, flashing lights & sound, friction, 8", NM (EX+ box), A **$110.00**

KO Space Super Jet Gun, 1957, litho tin & plastic, reciprocating barrel, friction sparking action, 9½", MIB, P4...**$125.00**

KO Super Jet Ray Gun, Japan, late 1960s, translucent plastic w/many gears, sparking friction action, 9", MIB, P4 ..**$55.00**

Kusan Western Heritage Texan, diecast, MOC, H1........**$25.00**

Langston Super Nu-Matic Jr Paper Popper, ca 1949, metallic-gray diecast ray-gun style, shoots paper roll, 6", VG, P4 ....$55.00

Langston Super Nu-Matic Paper Buster Gun, diecast w/plastic nose extension, 5", NM (EX box), A $35.00

Leslie-Henry Smoky Joe Texas Longhorn Cap Pistol, 1950s, coppered metal, lever release, break-to-front, 9", VG $65.00

Leslie-Henry Texas Cap Pistol, diecast, extra-long barrel, wht grips, unfired, M $65.00

Lido Cosmo Pistol in Space No 891, Hong Kong, 1970s, plastic w/battery-op lights & laser sound, 10", MIB, P4 ....$45.00

Lone Star Cork .45 Cork Gun, England, 1960s, bl pnt diecast w/wht horse-head grips, fires 1 cork, 6½", M, P4 ....$22.00

Lone Star English Outlaw Buntline Special, 1950s, Wyatt Earp gun replica, emb Indian on plastic hdls, NM (EX+ box), A $190.00

Lone Star Space Ranger Cap Pistol, 1960s, bl pnt diecast w/red & wht trim, pop-up cap magazine, lt wear, VG $200.00

M&L Space Rocket Gun, 1950s, plastic w/raised planet design on hdl, 9", no firing spheres o/w EX+ (EX box), A....$95.00

Marx Blue & Gray Shell Shooting Civil War Cavalry Pistol, 1960, plastic w/diecast works & plastic bullets, 10", MOC...$75.00

Marx Bullet Shooting 9mm Luger, ca 1960, plastic w/diecast works, shoots red plastic bullets, 7¼", NMIP, P4 ......$55.00

Marx Desert Patrol Luger Pistol & Silencer, 1960s, plastic w/diecast works, dk gray body, brn grips, 10", MOC, P4 ....$30.00

Marx Famous Firearms, set of 9 miniature historic guns w/4 holsters, NM (VG+ box) $100.00

Marx Security Pistol, 1970s, MOC, T1 ....$20.00

Marx Snub-Nose .38 Shell Firing Pistol, ca 1960, plastic w/diecast works, fires plastic bullet, 6½", VG, P4 ......$35.00

Marx Tommy Gun, 24", EX..$50.00

Marx Western Double Holster & Gun Set No 2382, 1961, loads plastic bullets or caps, 10", w/dbl vinyl holsters, NMIB .$100.00

Matley Pirate Pistol, w/soap, EX+ (orig box), T1 ....$65.00

Mattel Agent Zero-M Rifle, EX, J2 ....$35.00

Mattel Agent Zero-M Snap-Shot Camera Gun, fires caps, M (NM box), M5 ....$80.00

Mattel Agent Zero-W Smoking Fanner 50, #5503, 1965, fires roll caps, dura-hyde holster mk Zero-W, 9", NM (NM box), A $150.00

Mattel Burp Gun, ca 1955, pressed steel & plastic, fires perforated roll caps, 23" w/stock extended, NMIB..........$100.00

Mattel Cowboy in Africa Black Fanner 50 Gun & Holster Set, antelope head on grips, lt rust on rivets & buckle, EX, H1 ....$100.00

Mattel Official Winchester Saddle Rifle, ca 1960, plastic w/diecast works, fires Greenie roll caps, 33", VG, P4.................$110.00

Mattel Shootin' Shell Buckle Gun Western Belt Set, #932, diecast Remington Derringer, cartridges & bullet noses, NMIB, A..$75.00

Mattel Shootin' Shell Snub-Nose .38 Cap Pistol, 1960s, diecast w/revolving cylinder, brn plastic grips, 7", VG $45.00

Mattel Tommy-Burst Machine Gun, early 1960s, plastic w/diecast works, brn stock, blk body, fires roll caps, 25", VG $75.00

Mercury Industries Repeating Marble-Shooting Gun, pressed steel, machine gun form, 17½", EX, H1....................$35.00

Mini-Mag X-200 Multi-Matic Spy Rifle, NMOC, J2 ....$30.00

Newell Airfire Sub-Machine Gun, 1950s, aluminum & plastic w/brn plastic stock & grip, fires ping-pong balls, 25", VG $35.00

Nichols Buccaneer Shell-Firing Flintlock Pistol No 210, 1958, diecast, shoots red plastic bullets, 3½", MOC...........$25.00

Nichols Dyna-Mite Derringer Cap Gun, EX (EX box), J2..$60.00

Nichols Mustang 500 Cap Gun, metal w/gold-toned trigger, simulated cowhide grips, 12", M (EX+ box), A.............$265.00

Nichols Stallion .38 Cap Pistol, 1950s, diecast w/revolving cylinder, blk plastic grips, 8", MIB $150.00

NK Razer Ray Gun, Hong Kong, 1980s?, gold plastic w/gr spark window, red translucent barrel, 14", MIP, P4 ....$45.00

Park Plastics Squirt Ray Atomic Repeater Water Gun, 1950-60s, brass nozzle w/solid rubber plug, 5½", M, P4..............$20.00

Park Plastics Squirt Ray Water Guns, 1950s, set of 9, 5", NM (NM box), A $100.00

Parris Straitshooter Lever Action Cork Pistol No 6, 1950s, pressed steel & plastic, red plastic grips, 11", NMIB..$75.00

Playcraft Co Atom-Matic Water Rocket Gun, ca 1949, pressed aluminum, brass & plastic, rubber stopper, 7", VG....$75.00

Product Engineering Co Frontier Smoker Cap Gun, complete w/pkg of smoking powder, 9", EX+ (EX box), A $165.00

Remco B-52 Electronic Ball Turret Gun, battery-op, complete w/ammunition belt, EX+ (EX box), A....................$165.00

Remco Electronic Space Gun, 1950s, gray plastic w/red trim, battery-op light w/4-color wheel, MIB....................$175.00

Remco Jupiter 4-Color Signal Gun No 600, 1950s, blk plastic w/red trim, internal color wheel, 9", MIB $65.00

Renwal .38 Military & Police Automatic Revolver No 265, 1960s, gray plastic, spring-loading w/12 bullets, NMIB, P4 ....$65.00

Schmidt Buck 'N Bronc-Marshal Cap Pistol, 1950s, diecast, copper grips w/flower logo, has been fired, 10", VG $95.00

Schmidt Buck 'N Bronc-Marshal Cap Pistol, 1950s, diecast w/copper stag grips, lever release, unfired, 10", VG $9.50

Smart Style Real Texan Gun & Holster Set, 1950s, 2 simulated leather holsters & diecast Echo pistols, EX (EX box), A $45.00

Stevens Jet Jr Space Cap Gun, 1949, diecast w/sliding door in grip, 6⅜", VG $195.00

Stevens Ranger, ca 1946, cast aluminum w/blk grips, single shot, 7½", w/holster mk Cowboy, NMIB, H1 ....$75.00

Stevens Sheriff Cap Gun, NP CI w/plastic inset grips featuring cowboy & horse head, 8½", M (G box)..................$150.00

Stevens 49-ER Cap Pistol, 1940, gold-tone CI, repeating action, roll caps, sliding magazine door in grip, 9", NMIB, P4.........$350.00

Tigrett Atom Flash Zoomeray Space Gun, 1950s, red plastic, wrist motion fires rolled paper wad w/message, 7", NMIB, P4 ....$45.00

Tim-Mee Laser Ray Gun, plastic, 10", MIB, J2................$55.00

TN Circle 8 Space Gun, ball attached to barrel reciprocates & lights, tin, battery-op, 7", scarce, NM, A $125.00

TN Flashy-Ray Gun, Japan, 1950s, mc space graphic litho tin, pull trigger & battery-op light flashes, 18½", MIB.....$150.00

TN Space Control Ray Gun, 1950s, litho tin, friction-sparking action, disintegrated flint, 3¾", MIB $50.00

TN Space Rocket Pistol, tin w/up, shoots w/machine gun noise & sparks, 9½", NM (EX+ box), A $215.00

Topper/Deluxe-Reading Cane Shooter No 8003, 1966, blk plastic w/gold lion head top, 31", MOC, P4 .... $55.00

Topper/Deluxe-Reading Multi-Pistol 09, NMIB $75.00

Topper/Deluxe-Reading Secret Sam Bomb Binoculars, 1966, plastic, use nose trigger to fire cap bomb, 5", MIB, P4 .... $45.00

Topper/Deluxe-Reading Secret Sam Pipe Shooter, 1966, blk & brn plastic, squeeze w/teeth to fire, 6", MIB, P4 .... $30.00

Twentieth Century Products Super Site Magic Bullet Gun, 1950s, plastic, telescopic sight, whistle in grip, 9", VG, P4 .... $20.00

Unknown Maker, A Tom Hick Ray Gun, 1950s, cb, wrist action snaps paper insert, 8", lt wear, VG, P4 .... $75.00

Unknown Maker, Clicker Ray Gun, 1950s, plastic, rocket & planet graphics on grips, 5", M, P4 .... $25.00

Unknown Maker, Jet Gun Sparking Ray Gun, Japan, 1957, litho tin w/red windows & space graphics, sparks, 6", MIP, P4 ...... $35.00

Unknown Maker, Jet Star Sparking Galaxy Gun, Hong Kong, 1970s, wht plastic, removable sight, sparks, 10¾", MIB, P4 .... $45.00

Unknown Maker, Potato Gun, Hong Kong, 1970s?, blk & red ray gun-styled plastic, fires potato plugs, 6½", M, P4. $20.00

Unknown Maker, Radar Clicker Ray Gun, 1950s, rose plastic, gr spaceman moves when gun clicks, 6¼", M, P4 .... $30.00

Unknown Maker, Rapid Fire Squirt Gun, 1900, NP CI w/rubber bulb hdl, 5", NM (EX box), A $85.00

Unknown Maker, Repeating Ray Gun Cap Pistol, Hong Kong, 1970s, plastic w/pop-up metal magazine & trigger, 8", MOC, P4 .... $55.00

Unknown Maker, Rota-Matic Special Water Ray Gun No 741, 1970s, bright orange plastic w/castle logo, 8", M, P4 . $25.00

Unknown Maker, See Through Astro Ray Gun, Japan, early '60s, plastic, visible gears, antenna at top, sparks, 9", MIB, P4 .... $35.00

Unknown Maker, Signal Flash Ray Gun, 1960s, wht plastic w/orange trim, battery-op, 6", discolored, o/w VG, P4 ... $25.00

Unknown Maker, Space Cap Gun, Hong Kong, 1970s, solid bl plastic, pop-up cap magazine, 8½", MIP, P4 .... $45.00

Unknown Maker, Space Control Clicker Ray Gun, ca 1956, red plastic & tin w/space graphics, 5½", M, P4 .... $30.00

Unknown Maker, Space Outlaw Water Pistol #111, 1970s, bl plastic, 6", MIP, P4 .... $65.00

Unknown Maker, Space Outlaw Water Pistol #999, 1970s, plastic version of BCM Space Outlaw cap gun, 10", M, P4 .. $135.00

Unknown Maker, Space Pilot Jet Ray Gun, 1970s?, copper plastic w/gr & red windows, friction sparks, 11½", M, P4 .... $45.00

Unknown Maker, Space Scout Potato Gun, 1960s?, blk & wht plastic, fires potato plugs, 6½", M, P4 .... $30.00

Unknown Maker, Space Sparking Ray Gun, 1970s, brn, yel, silver & red litho tin, 5", flint not working o/w VG, P4 .... $25.00

Unknown Maker, Space Water Gun, 1950s, copper-brn plastic w/brass nozzle, 6", VG, P4 .... $65.00

Unknown Maker, Space Water Pistol, 1950s, pk plastic, 4", EX, J2 .... $25.00

Unknown Maker, Whistle Clicker Ray Gun, 1950s, hard plastic w/space designs, whistle at back, 5", M, P4 .... $25.00

US Plastic Flying Saucer Space Gun, 1950s, EX+ (EX+ box), J2 .... $110.00

US Plastic Space Patrol Dart Gun, blk plastic w/raised logo design on hdl, complete, 10", EX+, A $95.00

US Plastic Space Patrol Dart Gun, red plastic w/raised logo design on hdl, complete, 10", EX+, A $95.00

Wes-Ko Thompson Automatic Sub-Machine Gun Jr, 1950s, plastic, Tommy-gun style fires hard plastic balls, 26", MIB $50.00

WF Friction Ray Gun, Hong Kong, 1970s, bl translucent plastic, sparks, 7", M, P4 .... $25.00

Wham-O Air Blaster, 1960s, blk plastic w/rubber diaphragm, shoots blast of air, working, 10" w/orig gorilla target, EX $75.00

Wyandotte Dart Pistol, 1950s, MIB, J2 .... $70.00

Wyandotte Pop Ray Gun, ca 1937, red-pnt pressed steel, internal cork, 7", lt scratches o/w VG, P4 .... $185.00

Character

Bat Masterson Gun & Holster, 1958, MIP, J7 .... $150.00

Batman Bat Ray Gun, Remco, 1977, VG (VG+ box), T1.. $65.00

Batman Bat Ray Projector Pistol, 1977, battery-op, EX (EX box), T1 .... $65.00

Batman Escape Gun, Australia, 1966, MOC, J7 .... $75.00

Beetle Bailey Ping Pong, Janu, 1981, tinted clear plastic w/3 ping-pong balls, M (bag w/NM header), C1 .... $20.00

Billy the Kid Repeating Pistol, Stevens, metal, Billy the Kid & buffalo emb on grips, 7½", M (G box), A $125.00

Buck Rogers Atomic Pistol U-235, Daisy, 1947, gold-pnt pressed steel, red spark windows, flint working, 10", VG $175.00

Buck Rogers Pop Gun, Daisy, metal, Buck inscr on hdl, 9½", EX, A $225.00

Buck Rogers Sonic Ray Flashlight Gun, Norton-Honer, 1952, blk plastic body w/red & yel trim, battery-op, 7", VG $50.00

Buck Rogers Sonic Ray Flashlight Gun, Norton-Honer, 1952, red plastic w/gr & yel trim, battery-op, 7¼", MIB ... $145.00

Buck Rogers Sonic Ray Gun, Commonwealth, 1950, plastic signal gun, battery-op, 8", NM+ (EX+ box), A $215.00

Buck Rogers Space Gun, Daisy, 1930s, steel w/chrome finish, 9½", NM $250.00

Buck Rogers Venus Duo-Destroyer MK 24L, Tootsietoy, 1937, diecast w/yel & red finish, 4¾", VG $160.00

Buck Rogers XZ-31 Rocket Pistol Pop Gun, Daisy, 1934, pressed steel w/bl finish, 9½", VG $225.00

Buck Rogers XZ-38 Disintegrator Pistol, Daisy, 1935, pressed steel w/copper finish, 9½", VG $250.00

Buck Rogers XZ-44 Liquid Helium Water Pistol, Daisy, pressed steel w/copper finish, 7½", VG $200.00

Buck Rogers XZ-44 Liquid Helium Water Pistol, Daisy, red & yel litho, pressed steel, 7½", VG $175.00

Buffalo Bill Cap Pistol, CI w/6" barrel, 9", NM $150.00

Captain Space Solar Scout Atomic Ray Gun, Marx, 1950s, red plastic, flashes red, gr or clear light, 27", NMIB $200.00

Cheyenne Singin' Saddle Gun, Daisy/Warner Bros, 1959, plastic & metal rifle, 32", NM (EX box), A $140.00

Daniel Boone Cork/Flint Gun, unknown maker, 1950s, litho tin, breaks to cock, w/cork, 10", non-working spark o/w VG, P4 .... $145.00

Davy Crockett Clicker Pistol, Wyandotte, 1950s, mc litho tin revolver, 8", VG $25.00

Dick Tracy Automatic Water Gun, Larami, 1972, w/3 refillable cartridges, NMBP, D11..............................$35.00

Dick Tracy Bullet Gun, Ja-Ru-Toys, lugar w/6 bullets & mc Tracy passport, NMBP, D11..............................$20.00

Dick Tracy Crimestopper Machine Gun, Larami, 1973, plastic w/plastic bullets, 14", EX+ (orig mc pkg), D11..........$40.00

Dick Tracy Special Agent, Larami, 1972, w/badge & handcuffs, NMOC, D11..............................$35.00

Photo courtesy of Dunbar Gallery.

Dick Tracy Sub-Machine Water Gun, 1950s, plastic, MIB, $225.00.

Dragnet Snub Nose Cap Pistol, Knickerbocker, 1960s, blk plastic w/gold Dragnet, #714 badge on grip, unfired, 7", M, P4.$55.00

Equalizer 25-Shot Pistol, 1985, MOC $20.00

Flash Gordon Air Ray Gun, Budson, 1950s, pressed steel, hdl at top cocks mechanism, missing rubber diaphragm, 10", G $75.00

Flash Gordon Radio Repeater Click Pistol, Marx, 1935, red & silver litho, 10", MIB..............................$450.00

Flash Gordon Signal Pistol, Marx, early 1950s, pressed steel w/fly-wheel mechanism, sounds, shoots sparks, 7", VG $350.00

Flash Gordon Stun Gun, Hong Kong/King Features, 1979, plastic, battery-op reciprocating light, mk Tommy Z, 18", MIB..$50.00

G-Man Machine Gun, Exelo, operates w/sound, battery-op, 10", EX (EX box), A $175.00

G-Man Sparking Sub-Machine Gun, Marx, 1950s, litho tin, detachable drum magazine, red & yel plastic stock, 25", VG ..$100.00

Gangbusters Crusade Against Crime Machine Gun, Marx, 1930s, metal & wood, cartridge rotates w/sound, 23", VG, A..............................$120.00

Gene Autry Cap Pistol, Kenton, 1950, NP CI, friction break-to-front, 6½", rpl wht grips o/w NM..............................$125.00

Gene Autry Cap Pistol, Leslie-Henry, 1950s, diecast w/wht plastic horse-head grips, rpl hammer, 9", unfired, NM, P4....$110.00

Gene Autry Cap Pistol, Leslie-Henry, 1950s, NP diecast, lever release, wht plastic horse grips, 9", MIB..................$275.00

Gene Autry Golden Pistol, Leslie-Henry, gold finish, 7½", EX+ (EX+ box), A..............................$255.00

Gene Autry Repeating Cap Pistol, Kenton, plastic grips w/facsimile signatures, 6", EX+ (EX box), A....................$265.00

George Washington Pistol, Marx of Great Britain, ca 1960, diecast & plastic flintlock, 4½", MOC, P4 ....$25.00

Green Avenger Hidden Hand Gun, Barton, 1960s-70s, MOC (sealed), F8..............................$25.00

Gunsmoke Holster Set, Halco, Matt Dillon & Gunsmoke on holster, complete w/2 9" Smoky Joe cap guns, EX (G box), A..............................$300.00

Hopalong Cassidy Clicker Gun, unknown maker, 1950s, blk-pnt pressed steel w/wht-pnt grips, 8½", VG $125.00

Hopalong Cassidy Gun & Holster, Wyandotte, M..........$500.00

ISA (International Secret Agent) O7-11 Spy Gun Set, Marx, missing grenade o/w EX (EX box), J2......................$110.00

James Bond 007 Cap Gun, Spain, 1978, diecast, Hideaway or Sting, w/ID, NMIB, D8, ea......................$45.00

James Bond 007 Gun & Shoulder Holster Set, Lone Star, 1985, MIB, M17......................$15.00

James Bond 007 Moonraker Space Gun, Lone Star, 17", M (NM box), M5 ....$70.00

James Bond 007 Secret Service Flasher Gun, Imperial, 1984, MOC, M17......................$75.00

Johnny West Ranch Rifle, Marx, 26", unused, MOC, J2..$75.00

Kit Carson Cap Gun, Kilgore, NM, J2 ....$60.00

Lone Ranger Action Water Gun, 1974, mc plastic, MOC, P6......................$45.00

Lone Ranger Gun 'N Holster, Larami #6112-0, 1980s, NM, S18......................$15.00

Matt Dillon/Gunsmoke Cap Guns, Leslie-Henry, copper-clad grips, EX+, J2, pr......................$300.00

Photo courtesy of Plymouth Rock Toy Co.

Matt Dillon Cap Pistol, Leslie-Henry, 1950, nickel-plated diecast with steer on copper grips, 10", M, $225.00.

Matt Dillon/Gunsmoke Double Holster Set, Leslie-Henry, diecast, wht grips w/oval insert, leather holsters, VG $275.00

Matt Dillion, see also Gunsmoke

Maverick Double Gun & Holster Set, C10 ....$225.00

Paladin Have Gun Will Travel Holster Set, Halco, complete w/2 Buffalo Bill cap guns, NM+ (G box), A............$350.00

Pawnee Bill Cap Gun, silver-toned CI w/emb design & lettering, 8", unused, M......................$250.00

Popeye Cap Pistol, Halco/KFS, 1961, dbl holster w/2 diecast pistols, diecut card shows Popeye on horse, NMOC, A.$115.00

Punch & Judy, Ives, blk CI, Punch figure bumps Judy w/nose causing cap to explode, 5", EX $700.00

Red Ranger Clicker Pistol, Wyandotte, mc litho tin revolver, 8", VG, P4 ....$45.00

Red Ranger Engraved-Gold Repeating Cap Pistol, gold-plated diecast w/blk plastic grips, 8", NM (EX box) $200.00

Red Ranger Six-Shooter Repeater Pistol, Wyandotte, steel, plastic grips emb w/bust images, 10", scarce, M (G box), A..$215.00

Return of the Saint Gun, Handcuffs & Badge, Crescent of Great Britain, ca 1978, diecast, MIB, M17 ....$150.00

Return of the Saint 100-Shot Metal Pistol, Crescent of Great Britain, ca 1978, MOC, M17 ....$145.00

Rex Mars Planet Patrol Sparking Space Gun, Marx, early 1950s, mc litho tin w/red plastic stock & grips, 22", NMIB..$250.00

Rookies Clicker Gun Set, 1975, MOC, J7 ....$30.00

Roy Rogers Cap Gun, Kilgore, 10", EX, J2 ....$200.00

Roy Rogers Carbine Rifle, Marx, Roy Rogers on hdl, shoots caps, 26", MIB, A $275.00

Roy Rogers Mini Cap Pistol, 6", EX, J2 ....$65.00

Roy Rogers Riders Signal Gun, Langston, diecast, Morse code on grips, 5", EX+ (EX box), A.........................$190.00

Roy Rogers Shootin' Iron, Classy, metal cap gun w/plastic grips, 10", MOC, A $350.00

Roy Rogers Tuckaway Gun, C10.........................$35.00

Spider-Man Supersonic Pistol, Larami/Marvel Comics, 1974, red & wht plastic, 4", MOC (sealed), A6.........................$8.00

Starsky & Hutch Repeater Cap Gun, 1977, MOC, J7......$40.00

Starsky & Hutch 9mm-Clicker Gun Set, 1977, MOC, J7 .$40.00

Superman Cinematic Pistol, Daisy, raised figure on barrel, EX+ $300.00

Superman Krypto-Ray Gun No 94, Daisy, 1939, battery inside filmstrip assembly, adjustable lens, 7", unusual, VG ..$200.00

SWAT Clicker Gun Set, 1975, MOC, J7 ....$30.00

SWAT Pump-Action Rifle, 1976, MIP, J7 ....$40.00

Texas Ranger Gun and Holster, Leslie-Henry, 1946, gold-plated metal gun with plastic grip, embossed leather holster, MIB, A, $200.00.

Texas Ranger Gun & Holster, Leslie Henry, 1946, gold-plated metal cap gun w/plastic grip, emb leather holster, MIB, A $200.00

Tom Corbett Space Cadet Clicker Gun, Marx, 1950s, litho tin, pull trigger to click, 10", VG $150.00

Tom Corbett Space Cadet Sparking Ray Gun, Marx, early 1950s, mc litho tin w/red & yel plastic stock & grips, 22", NM...$200.00

Wanted Dead or Alive Official Mares Laig, 5¼", EX, I2..$45.00

Wild Bill Hickok .44 Cap Gun, metal, clear amber-colored grips w/emb horse head, complete w/leather holster, 11", NM $200.00

Wild Bill Hickok .44 Cap Pistol, Leslie-Henry, 1950s, diecast w/wht horse-head plastic grips, side loading, 11", VG .$135.00

Wild West Cap Rifle, Marx, w/sight, 30", NM, J2..........$100.00

Wyatt Earp Buntline Special, Hubley, diecast w/plastic grip, shoots caps, 11", NM (VG photo card), A $215.00

Zorro Flintlock Pistol, Marx, 1950s, plastic, fires caps, 11", NMOC, A..$70.00

BB Guns

Values are suggested for BB guns that are in excellent condition. Advisor: Jim Buskirk.

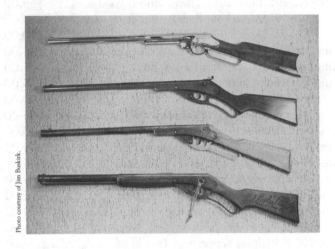

Photo courtesy of Jim Buskirk.

Daisy '1000 Shot,' (often referred to by collectors as the 'Bennett'), lever action, wood stock, $150.00; King Model 5536, lever action, wood stock, $40.00; Daisy No 102, Model 36, lever action, wood stock, $25.00; Daisy No 111, Model 40, Red Ryder, iron lever, $70.00.

Daisy (Early), break action, wire stock, B6 ....$350.00

Daisy (Early), top lever, wire stock, B6 ....$450.00

Daisy '500 Shot Daisy,' lever action, wood stock, B6 .....$125.00

Daisy Model A, break action, wood stock, B6 ....$125.00

Daisy Model B, lever action, wood stock, B6 ....$65.00

Daisy Model C, break action, wood stock, B6................$100.00

Daisy Model H, lever action, wood stock, B6 ....$75.00

Daisy Model 21, 1968, dbl barrel, plastic stock, B6 ....$250.00

Daisy Model 094, Red Ryder, plastic stock, 1955, B6.......$35.00

Daisy Model 1938B, Christmas Story/Red Ryder, B6 ....$65.00

Daisy No 11, lever action, wood stock, B6 ....$50.00

Daisy No 12, break action, wood stock, B6 ....$50.00

Daisy No 25, pump action, pistol-grip wood stock, B6 .....$35.00

Daisy No 25, pump action, straight wood stock, B6..........$50.00

Daisy No 30, lever action, wood stock, B6 ....$40.00

Daisy No 40, 'Military,' lever action, wood stock, B6.....$100.00

Daisy No 40, 'Military', w/bayonet, lever action, wood stock, B6..$250.00

Daisy No 50, copper-plated, lever action, blk wood stock, B6..$80.00

Daisy No 100, Model 38, break action, wood stock, B6....$25.00

Daisy No 101, Model 33, lever action, wood stock, B6 ....$25.00

Daisy No 101, Model 36, lever action, wood stock, B6 ....$25.00

Daisy No 103, Model 33, Buzz Barton, B6 ....$175.00

Daisy No 103, Model 33, lever action, wood stock, B6 ..$100.00

Daisy No 104, dbl barrel, wood stock, B6 ....$450.00

Daisy No 105, 'Junior Pump Gun,' wood stock, B6...........$90.00
Daisy No 106, break action, wood stock, B6 ....$25.00
Daisy No 107, 'Buck Jones Special,' pump action, wood stock, B6...$80.00
Daisy No 107, pump action, plastic stock, B6 ....$20.00
Daisy No 108, Model 39, 'Carbine,' lever action, wood stock, B6...$65.00
Daisy No 111, Model 40, Red Ryder, aluminum lever, B6.$50.00
Daisy No 111, Model 40, Red Ryder, plastic stock, B6 .....$30.00
Daisy No 140, 'Defender,' lever action, wood stock, B6.$120.00
Daisy No 195, Buzz Barton, lever action, wood stock, B6.$65.00
Daisy No 195, Model 36, Buzz Barton, lever action, wood stock, B6..$70.00
King Model 5533, lever action, wood stock, B6................$35.00
King No 1, break action, all wood, B6.............................$45.00
King No 2, break action, wood stock, B6 ....$45.00
King No 4, lever action, wood stock, B6...........................$80.00
King No 5, 'Pump Gun,' wood stock, B6...........................$65.00
King No 5, lever action, wood stock, B6...........................$80.00
King No 10, break action, wood stock, B6 ....$30.00
King No 17, break action, wood stock, B6 ....$65.00
King No 21, lever action, wood stock, B6 ....$55.00
King No 22, lever action, wood stock, B6 ....$55.00
King No 24, lever action, wood stock, B6 ....$65.00
King No 55, lever action, wood stock, B6 ....$35.00
King No 2136, lever action, wood stock, B6 ....$20.00
King No 2236, lever action, wood stock, B6 ....$20.00
Markham/King 'Chicago,' break action, all wood, B6 ....$150.00
New King, repeater, break action, wood stock, B6............$80.00
New King, single shot, break action, wood stock, B6 ....$75.00

Related Items and Accessories

Box, Cowboy Repeating Cap Pistol, Hubley, 5x11", EX, J2..$45.00
Box, Daisy Bull's Eye Six Gun No 90 26 3300, ca 1960, NM..$15.00
Box, Roy Rogers & Trigger Official Holster Outfit, Classy, 3 images on lid, 12x13", EX..$150.00
Box, Texan Holster, Halco, early, EX $20.00
Bullets, Mattel Shootin' Shell Bullets, 1958, 3 brass cartridges w/35 gray plastic bullets, MOC, P4 ....$25.00
Bullets, Nichols Stallion Bullets, 1950s, 2-pc w/brass casing, set of 6, M (on wht plastic strip), P4 ....$20.00
Caps, Hubley Texan .38 Round Caps, 1950s, 100 per box, MIB, P4 ....$4.00
Caps, Kilgore Disc Caps, 20 per box, MIB, P4 ....$3.00
Caps, Kilgore Round Caps on Roll No 514, ca 1960, 3 rolls per box, MIB, P4 ....$3.00
Caps, Kilgore Stick-On Round Cap Rolls No 533, ca 1960, 3 rolls (120 shots) per box, MIB, P4.........................$3.00
Caps, Marx Thundercaps-Supersound Perforated Roll Caps, late 1950s, 5 rolls per box, MIB, P4.............................$5.00
Caps, Mattel Bullet Pak No 637, 1958, For All Mattel Western & Shootin' Shell Guns, 8 play bullets, MOC, P4......$25.00
Caps, Mattel Greenie Perforated Roll Caps No 635, 5 rolls per box, MIB, P4 ....$5.00
Caps, Mattel Greenie Stick-M-Caps No 633, 1958, 2 sheets of 60 (120 caps) per box, MIB, P4 ....$5.00

Caps, Mattel Greenie Stick-M-Caps No 634, 1958, 8 sheets of 60 (480 caps) per box, MIB, P4...............................$10.00
Caps, Nichols Fury 500-Shot Roll Caps, for all 500 Series guns, 1 roll per box, MIB, P4 ....$5.00
Caps, Nichols Stallion Round Caps, 1950s, fit all Nichols cap cartridges, 100 per box, MIB, P4 ....$5.00
Caps, Nichols Tophand 250-Shot Roll Caps, 250-shot continuous perforated roll, 1 roll per box, MIB, P4 ....$5.00
Holster, Kilgore Fast Draw, vinyl, no belt, NM (G box), T1..$35.00
Holster, Lone Ranger, dbl w/belt, blk rubber, 1978, VG+, M16..$22.00
Holster, Maverick, Carnell, wht & blk leather w/jewels & studs, unused, NM (worn box) $175.00
Holster, Maverick, dbl w/dbl belt, no bullets, EX-, J6 ....$145.00
Holster, Red Ranger, Wyandotte, leather w/studs, single, EX, J6..$55.00
Holster, Roy Rogers, dbl, EX, J2...................................$225.00
Holster, Roy Rogers Tiny Tots Holster Set, Hubley, EX, J2..$85.00
Holster, Wild Bill Hickok, dbl, leather, EX, J2..............$100.00
Molotov Cocktail Tank Buster Cap Bomb No 1940, Mace, 1964, plastic & diecast, 6", MIB (sealed), P4.............$20.00

Halloween

Halloween is a uniquely American holiday melded from the traditions of superstitions brought to the new world from Germany and Scotland. St. Matrimony was reportedly the patron saint of this holiday as it was at this time of the year when the harvest was safely in that betrothals and weddings took place. Most activity for the holiday focused on getting young eligible people married. Trick or Treat was a way of getting rid of bothersome younger siblings. Robert Burns, the poet of Scotland was a major influence on the folklore of the holiday. In this country today, Halloween is a holiday with little or no association with earlier religious rites of any group. It's an evening of fun, frolic and fantasy filled with lots of sugar and calories!

Note: Our values are prices realized at a high-profile, specialty auction and should be considered high retail, though certainly valid.

Advisor: Pamela E. Apkarian-Russell, The Halloween Queen (H9).
See also Halloween Costumes.

Banner, paper w/orange, blk & yel scenes, German, 1930s, 60", NM, A..$180.00
Bridge Score Card, blk cat pictured, 1930s, unused, M (orig envelope), A...$25.00
Bridge Score Pad, blk & orange w/4 jack-o'-lantern tallies, 1930s, unused, M, A $50.00
Candy Box, Clark's Black Jack Caramel, blk, wht & orange, ca 1950, 10x9", EX, A $40.00
Candy Box, Curtiss' Caramel Roll Trick or Treats, jack-o'-lanterns, witches & goblins, 5x10x2", EX, A...........$130.00
Candy Box, Oh Henry, wht, orange & blk w/trick or treaters, 9x7x2", EX, A..$95.00
Candy Container, blk cat, compo w/glass eyes & pk nose, removable head, German, 1920s, 4", NM, A..........$325.00

Candy Container, blk cat atop pumpkin, compo, German, 1920s, 6½", NM, A $700.00

Candy Container, blk cat on jack-o'-lantern, papier-mache, 3", EX, A $275.00

Candy Container, boot w/jack-o'-lantern happy face, orange w/blk at top rim, mk Germany on sole, 1920s, 5", NM, A $210.00

Candy Container, clown w/yel outfit, compo w/hat on spring, German, 1920s, 7", NM, A $170.00

Candy Container, devil's head in top hat, papier-mache & cb, orange w/blk hat, 5", EX, A $440.00

Candy Container, German, rnd paper-covered cb w/wood spinners, animated facial features, 2½" dia, NM, A $470.00

Candy Container, Harlequin boy, U-Neak, bsk figure in orange & blk crepe-paper costume on rnd orange cb box, 7", EX+, A $415.00

Candy Container, owl, mc pulp w/glass eyes & blk base, Am, 1920s, 11", EX, A $235.00

Candy Container, witch sits atop pumpkin, pulp, Am, 1940s, 6", NM, A $195.00

Candy Container, witch's head in blk shoe, pnt papier-mache, gr hat w/red band, 4", EX, A $660.00

Centerpiece, blk cat w/gold trim, crepe-paper & cb w/accordion body, late 1930s-40s, 10", unused, M, A $70.00

Cooky Cutters, metal, MIB, from $50.00 to $65.00.

Diecut, jack-o'-lantern goblin face, blk w/orange & wht trim, German, 1920s, 11x9", rare, EX, A $160.00

Figure, blk cat carrying parrot cages, celluloid, 6", sm dent in head o/w NM, A $465.00

Figure, blk cat w/red bow tie scratches ear, celluloid w/brass bell, 1930s, 4", NM, A $110.00

Figure, cowboy w/rope & pistol, orange & blk plastic, 3½", M, A $100.00

Figure, Halloween clown w/bl collar, red buttons & hat, on gr cart w/yel wheels, plastic, 1950s, 5", M, A $45.00

Figure, orange jack-o'-lantern on gr cart w/yel wheels, plastic, 1950s, 6x5", NM, A $100.00

Flour Bag, jack-o'-lantern w/children dancing in pumpkin patch, 12x18", M, A $255.00

Haunted House, tin, folk-art style, witch weathervane, tall turrets, 12x20x17", EX, A..$1,200.00

Horn, cb & crepe-paper w/jack-o'-lanterns, witches & blk cats, Marks Bros, Boston Mass, 1921, 10", EX, A $90.00

Horn, orange jack-o'-lantern w/blk trim & hat, German, 1920s, 8", NM, A $425.00

Horn, tin, Wizard of Oz characters, US Metal Co, 1940s, 13", NM, A $190.00

Invitation, jack-o'-lantern w/fortune teller, orange w/blk & yel trim, 1930s, EX, A $20.00

Jack-o'-Lantern, blk cat w/red bow, cb w/paper insert, German, 1920s, 4", EX, A $350.00

Jack-o'-Lantern, cb w/Durante-style molded nose & paper insert features, German, 1920s, 5", EX, A..........................$200.00

Jack-o'-Lantern, cb w/insert, Seneca Falls Folding Box Co, Pat 1902, 9x10x3", NM, A..$475.00

Jack-o'-Lantern, plastic dbl-sided 'Trick' w/frowning face & 'Treat' w/happy face, 8", NM, A..................................$70.00

Jack-o'-Lantern, pulp w/paper insert, orange w/gr eyebrows, American, 1940s, 8", EX, A $255.00

Jack-o'-Lantern, tin w/paper face, Am, 1900s, 7", lt wear to pnt o/w EX, A $760.00

Lamp Shade, Casper the Ghost & friends on merry-go-round, 1960s, 8x8", M, A $50.00

Lantern, accordion style, German, cardboard and paper, 10", EX, $175.00.

Lantern, jack-o'-lantern funny face, accordion style, orange w/purple eyes & gr nose, 1930s, 6", unused, M, A ...$120.00

Lantern, owl, orange tin w/molded wings, candle holder & bail hdl, 1920s, 6x10" (hdl extended), EX+, A $235.00

Lantern, skull on blk pole, wht plastic w/plug-in base, 12", EX, A $50.00

Lantern, watermelon w/paper insert features, cb w/papier-mache wash, German, 1920s, 3", NM, A $900.00

Lantern, watermelon w/paper insert features, cb w/2-tone gr papier-mache wash, German, 1920s, 5½x3½", EX, A $1,300.00

Noisemaker, compo ratchet style w/witch, detailed face, German, 1910-20s, 4x6", EX, A $350.00

Noisemaker, mc tin windup w/witches, bats & cats, 1940s, oval, 4", EX, A $150.00

Planter, jack-o'-lantern scarecrow w/gr coat & hat, blk pants & shoes, pnt ceramic, Japan, 1950s, 6", NM, A............$50.00

Planter, witch in blk on orange pumpkin carriage, pnt ceramic, Japan, 1950s, 6", NM, A................................$60.00

Postcard, Halloween Greetings, shows smiling pumpkin & apples w/candle, 1920s, lt creases o/w EX, A $25.00

Rattle, cb & paper w/dbl-sided compo faces of jack-o'-lantern & devil, wood hdl, German, ca 1915, 10", M, A $385.00

Scissors Toy, vegetable person w/compo squash head & crepe-paper bow, wood base, mk Germany, 1920s, 12", NM, A $700.00

Stickpin, blk cat face, compo, Japan, 1930s, rare, 1", EX, A...$45.00

Tambourine, blk & orange litho tin, Chein, 7" dia, EX, A ..$120.00

Tambourine, orange jack-o'-lantern w/red lips, German, 1920s, 7" dia, EX, A...$275.00

Tambourines, EX, from $35.00 to $50.00 each.

Photo courtesy of Dunbar Gallery.

Halloween Costumes

During the fifties and sixties Ben Cooper and Collegeville made Halloween costumes representing the popular TV and movie characters of the day. If you can find one in excellent to mint condition and still in its original box, some of the better ones can go for over $100.00. MAD's Alfred E. Neuman (Collegeville, 1959-60) usually carries an asking price of $150.00 to $175.00, and The Green Hornet (Ben Cooper, 1966), $200.00. Earlier handmade costumes are especially valuable if they are 'Dennison-Made.'

Advisor: Pamela E. Apkarian-Russell, The Halloween Queen (H9).

Alfred E Neuman, 1960s, mask only, NM, P12 ....$50.00
Alien, mask only, M, unused $10.00
Andromeda Lady Space Fighter, EX (EX box), J2 ....$35.00
Aquaman, Ben Cooper, 1967, NMIB.............................$75.00
Ark II, 1977, NMIB, J7...$40.00
Astronaut, 1962, NMIB..$55.00
Bart Simpson, Ben Cooper/Canadian, 1989, MIB, K1 .....$15.00
Batgirl, Ben Cooper, 1973, EX (EX orig box) $45.00
Batman, Ben Cooper, 1970, EX (EX box)......................$95.00
Batman, DC Comics, 1989, full rubber mask w/bat insignia, 21x7", EX+, D9...$45.00
Beatles, Paul McCartney, mask & suit, EX (VG+ box)..$300.00
Beatles, Ringo Starr, mask only, G $40.00
Bossie the Cow, 1950s, cheesecloth mask w/skull cap, blk & wht suit, EX+ (EX+ box) $50.00
Bullwinkle, Ben Cooper, 1970, mask only, EX (orig box), J5 ..$25.00
Captain America, Ben Cooper, 1967, MIB.....................$75.00
Cecil (Beany & Cecil), Ben Cooper, 1950, EX+ (EX box), F8 ....$70.00
Cinderella, Ben Cooper, EX+ (EX box), J2 ....$30.00
Close Encounters of the Third Kind, Extra Terrestrial, Imagineering, 1978, mask only, NRFB (sealed).................$10.00
Daffy Duck, Collegeville, 1960s, EX (EX box).................$40.00
Daniel Boone, Ben Cooper, mask w/cloth suit, EX..........$65.00
Dick Tracy, mask only, plastic w/hinged movable jaw, 1960s, NM, D11 ....$25.00
Doctor Doom, Ben Cooper, gr & yel 1-pc suit, MIP (sealed), T2 ....$95.00
Dr Dolittle, Ben Cooper, NMIB, A7..............................$50.00
Father Murphy, 1981, NMIB, J7...................................$30.00
Fin Man (monster), gr rubber, glow-in-the-dark, EX, I2 ..$60.00
Flash Gordon, Esquire Novelty, unused, MOC, J2 ....$200.00
Fred Flintstone, 1973, NMIB.......................................$50.00
GI Joe, 1982, mask only, EX $10.00
GI Joe, 1989, NMIB...$35.00
Green Hornet, mask & felt hat, 1966, EX.......................$75.00
Green Hornet & Kato, mask set, MOC, T2 ....$295.00
Green Lantern, Ben Cooper, 1967, EX (EX box) $80.00

Addams Family, Morticia, Ben Cooper, 1965, MIB, $95.00.

Photo courtesy of John and Sheri Pavone.

KISS, Gene Simmons, Collegeville, 1978, MIB, $95.00.

Photo courtesy of June Moon.

Hanging Witch, Ben Cooper, 1960s, EX, J2 ....$30.00
HR Pufnstuf, Witchie Poo, 1970, NMIB, J7 ....$75.00
I Dream of Jeannie, costume only, EX, J7 ....$35.00
Jaws (Moonraker), 1970s, NM, T1.................................$25.00
Johnny Tremain, Ben Cooper, EX+ (EX box), J2..............$25.00
King Kong, Ben Cooper, 1976, MIB (cellophane window
     cracked), H4 ....$20.00
Laura Ingalls, NM, V1 ....$25.00
Little Orphan Annie, 1930s, mk Leapin' Lizards! Its' Little
     Orphan Annie, complete w/bag & party favors, EX+ (EX
     box), A $175.00
Lucy (Peanuts), MIB, T1 ....$20.00

Man from UNCLE, Halco, complete, EX+ (EX+ box), $45.00.

Maverick, 1959, mask, skull cap & jumpsuit, EX, F8........$45.00
Max Headroom, 1986, mask only, unused, M, from $15 to .$25.00
Moe (Three Stooges), NM, T1...$95.00
Moon Man, Collegeville, 1960s, glow-in-the-dark mask, w/alien-
     illus jumpsuit, EX (EX box), F8 ....$30.00
Mork From Ork, MIB, T1 ....$20.00
Mummy, Ben Cooper, 1963, mask & suit, M, T2 ....$60.00
Mummy, Don Post, 1977, full-head rubber mask, 11½", NM,
     D9 ....$45.00
Phantom, Ben Cooper, 1963, EX (G+ box) $95.00
Pushmi-Pullyu, Ben Cooper, NMIB, A7 ....$50.00
R2-D2, Ben Cooper, NMIB...$12.00
Scooby Doo, 1970s, MIB, from $30 to $40.00
Shazzam!, mask w/light, VG+, J7 ....$15.00
Spark Plug, Collegeville, 1950s, NM (VG box), F8.........$78.00
Spider-Man, Ben Cooper, 1950s, 5-pc playsuit w/plastic mask,
     NMIB, M17 ....$135.00
Spider-Man, Ben Cooper, 1972, MIB, J7 ....$35.00
Super President, 1968, NMIB, J7 ....$75.00
Superman, Ben Cooper, 1970s, EX (EX box), D8............$35.00
Tarzan, 1975, NM...$20.00
Tarzan, 1975, NMIB..$45.00
Top Cat, Ben Cooper, EX, J2 ....$20.00
Willow, 1988, NMIB, J7...$15.00
Wolfman, Groovy Goohlies, orig tag, M...........................$30.00
Wonder Woman, 1975, playsuit, complete, NMIB, C17..$45.00
Woody Woodpecker, Collegeville, 1950s, cheesecloth mask, red
     skull cap & suit, EX (EX box) $45.00

Underdog, Ben Cooper, 1969, MIB, $40.00.

Yoda, vinyl, EX $25.00
Zorro, Ben Cooper, MIB, C10...$150.00

Hartland Plastics, Inc.

Originally known as the Electro Forming Co., Hartland Plastics, Inc. was founded in 1941 by Ed and Iola Walters. They first produced heels for military shoes, birdhouses and ornamental wall decor. It wasn't until the late 1940s that Hartland produced their first horse and rider. Figures were hand painted with an eye for detail. The Western and Historic Horsemen, Miniature Western Series, Authentic Scale Model Horses, Famous Gunfighter Series, and the Hartland Sports Series of Famous Baseball Stars were a symbol of the fine workmanship of the '40s, '50s and '60s. The plastic used was a virgin acetate. Paint was formulated by Bee Chemical Co., Chicago, Illinois, and Wolverine Finishes Corp., Grand Rapids, Michigan. Hartland figures are best known for their uncanny resemblance to the TV Western stars who portrayed characters like the Lone Ranger, Matt Dillon and Roy Rogers. For more information we recommend *Hartland Horses and Riders* by Gail Fitch. See Also Clubs, Newsletters and Other Publications.

Advisor: Judy and Kerry Irvin (K5).

Alkine Ike, NM, K5..$150.00
Annie Oakley, NM, K5 ....$275.00
Bat Masterson, NMIB, K5 ....$500.00
Bill Longley, NM, K5 ....$600.00
Brave Eagle, NM, K5 ....$200.00
Brave Eagle, NMIB, K5 ....$300.00
Bret Maverick, miniature series, NM, K5.........................$75.00
Bret Maverick, NM, K5 ....$150.00
Bret Maverick, NMIB, K5 ....$750.00
Bret Maverick, w/Coffeedunn horse, NM, K5 ....$650.00
Bret Maverick, w/gray horse, rare, NM, K5....................$700.00
Buffalo Bill, NM, K5..$300.00
Bullet, NM, K5...$45.00
Bullet, w/tag, NM, K5...$75.00
Cactus Pete, NM, K5..$150.00
Champ Cowgirl, NM, K5 ....$150.00
Cheyenne, miniature series, NM, K5 ....$75.00

Cheyenne, w/tag, NM, K5 ....$190.00
Chief Thunderbird, rare shield, NM, K5 ....$150.00
Chris Colt, NM, K5 ....$150.00
Clay Holister, NM, K5 ....$225.00
Cochise, NM, K5 ....$150.00
Commanche Kid, NM, K5 ....$150.00
Dale Evans, gr, NM, K5 ....$125.00
Dale Evans, purple, NM, K5 ....$300.00
Dale Evans, rare bl version, NM, K5 ....$400.00
Dan Troop, NM, K5 ....$400.00
Davy Crockett, NM, K5 ....$550.00
General Custer, NMIB, K5 ....$200.00
General Custer, repro flag, NM, K5 ....$150.00
General George Washington, NMIB, K5 ....$175.00
General Robert E Lee, NMIB, K5 ....$175.00
Gil Favor, prancing, NM, K5 ....$800.00
Gil Favor, semi-rearing, NM, K5 ....$600.00
Hoby Gillman, NM, K5 ....$225.00
Jim Bowie, w/tag, NM, K5 ....$250.00
Jim Hardy, NM, K5 ....$150.00
Jim Hardy, NMIB, K5 ....$275.00
Jockey, NM, K5 ....$150.00
Jockey, repro crop, NM, K5 ....$100.00
Johnny McKay, NM, K5 ....$800.00
Josh Randle, NM, K5 ....$650.00
Lone Ranger, champ, blk breast collar, NM, K5 .....$125.00
Lone Ranger, miniature series, NM, K5 ....$75.00
Lone Ranger, NM, K5 ....$150.00
Lone Ranger, rearing, NMIB, K5 ....$300.00
Matt Dillon, w/tag, NMIB, K5 ....$275.00
Paladin, NM, K5 ....$400.00
Paladin, NMIB, K5 ....$350.00
Rebel, miniature series, repro hat, NM, K5 ....$100.00
Rebel, NMIB, K5 ....$1,200.00
Rifleman, miniature series, repro rifle, EX, K5 ......$75.00
Rifleman, NMIB, K5 ....$350.00

Roy Rogers, semi-rearing, NMIB, K5 ....$350.00
Roy Rogers, walking, NMIB, K5 ....$250.00
Seth Adams, NM, K5 ....$275.00
Sgt Lance O'Rourke, NMIB, K5 ....$250.00
Sgt Preston, repro flag, NM, K5 ....$750.00
Tom Jeffords, NM, K5 ....$175.00
Tonto, miniature series, NM, K5 ....$75.00
Tonto, NM, K5 ....$150.00
Tonto, rare semi-rearing, NM, K5 ....$650.00
Vint Bonner, w/tag, NMIB, K5 ....$650.00
Warpaint Thunderbird, w/shield, NMIB, K5 ....$350.00
Wyatt Earp, NM, K5 ....$200.00
Wyatt Earp, w/tag, NMIB, K5 ....$275.00

Hoop Toys

Nineteenth-century toys with figures of animals or people balanced within a hoop designed to be rolled down the hallway or along the ground were among some of the earliest manufactured toys in America. They're extremely rare today and when found in even poor condition can command hefty prices.

Balance Hoop w/Girl, att George Brown, pnt tin, girl atop balance mechanism above hoop, 10", some rstr, G, A $1,870.00
Boy on Base & Horse In Hoop (Mechanical Patent Model), William Sellers, Pat Sept 12, 1871, 8", G, A........$4,950.00
Horse, George Brown, pnt tin, 5¾", G-, A $600.00

Horse, Merriam, painted tin, 4", G, A, $550.00.

Horse, Hull & Stafford, ca 1875, pnt tin, w/flag, 6" dia, G-, A .$575.00
Horse & Rider, Bergmann, pnt tin, wht horse w/red blanket, lady rider, 8", G, A $580.00
Horse w/Circus Rider, att Hull & Stafford, pnt tin, acrobat in wide stance on back of wht horse, G, A $1,540.00
Horse w/Circus Rider, pnt tin, sm figure balancing on 1 leg on rear of wht trotting horse, 12", G, A....................$2,750.00
Monkey Pushing Hoop, pnt tin monkey on 2-wheeled platform pushing hoop, 4", G+, A......................................$1,210.00

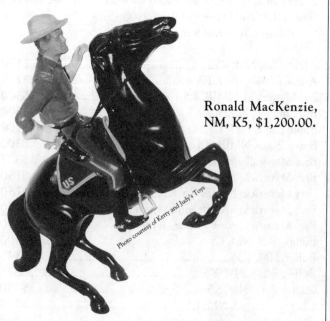

Ronald MacKenzie, NM, K5, $1,200.00.

Photo courtesy of Kerry and Judy's Toys

Horses

Horse riding being the order of the day, many children of the 19th century had their own horses to ride indoors; some were wooden while others were stuffed, and many had glass eyes and real horsehair tails. There were several ways to construct these horses so as to achieve a galloping action. The most common types had rocker bases or were mounted with a spring on each leg.

Gliding Horse, glass eyes, hair mane & tail, leather tack, 1900s, 32½", pnt & leather wear, A......................................$575.00

Horse, blk cloth-covered & stuffed, hair mane & tail, 4-wheeled wood platform, 20", VG, A $230.00

Horse & Cart, early, 2-wheeled sulky w/front wheel on dapple gray horse, rachet action propels cart, 35", EX, A ...$415.00

Platform Horse, German (?), blk cloth-covered w/leather saddle, platform w/metal spoked wheels, 21", VG, A $500.00

Platform Horse, stuffed brn burlap w/hair mane & tail, glass eyes, saddle, wood platform w/CI wheels, 25", EX, A $525.00

Riding Horse, orange-pnt wood, keyhole-shaped seat w/carved horse head, 3-wheeled, 17", VG, A............................$50.00

Riding Horse, 2-pc wood hinged at neck, wht w/blk mane & tail, red saddle seat, front wheels close together, 23", VG, A $100.00

Rocking Horse, cream horse w/dappled effect, glass eyes & blk hooves, leatherette saddle, 4-legged platform, 34", VG+, A $400.00

Rocking Horse, hand-pnt wht carved wood w/applied stick legs on red rockers, blk leather bit & saddle, 47", EX, A..$580.00

Rocking horse, W. Reed, wood with dapple gray paint, horsehair tail and mane, oilcloth saddle, leather tackle, red rockers, 47" long, VG+, A, $2,970.00.

Rocking Horse, wood, dapple gray, glass eyes, hair mane, orig saddle, wooden fr w/metal rockers, 28x32", EX, A..$440.00

Shoofly Rocking Horse Seat, Am, pnt wood, 2 horses on rockers flank upholstered seat, 36", G, A $155.00

Hot Wheels

When they were introduced in 1968, Hot Wheels were an instant success. Sure, their racy style and flashy custom paint jobs were instant attention-getters, but what the kids loved most was the fact that they were fast! The fastest on the market! It's estimated that more than two billion Hot Wheels have been sold to date — every model with a little variation, keeping up with new trends in the big car industry. The line has included futuristic vehicles, muscle cars, trucks, hot rods, racers, and some military vehicles. Lots of these can still be found for very little, but if you want to buy the older models (collectors call them 'Red Lines' because of their red sidewall tires), it's going to cost you a little more, though many can still be found for under $25.00. By 1971, earlier on some models, black-wall tires had become the standard.

A line of cars with Goodyear tires called Real Riders were made from 1983 until about 1987. (In 1983 the tires had gray hubs with white lettering; in 1984 the hubs were white.) California Customs were made in 1989 and 1990. These had the Real Rider tires, but they were not lettered 'Good Year' (and some had different wheels entirely).

Chopcycles are similar to Sizzlers in that they have rechargable batteries. The first series was issued in 1973 in these models: Mighty Zork, Blown Torch, Speed Steed, and Bruiser Cruiser. Generally speaking, these are valued at $35.00 (loose) to $75.00 (MIB). A second series issued in 1974 was made up of: Ghost Rider, Rage Coach, Riptide, Sourkraut, and Triking Viking. This series is considerably harder to find and much more expensive today; expect to pay as much as $250.00 to $350.00 for a mint-in-box example.

Though recent re-releases have dampened the collector market somewhat, cars mint and in the original packages are holding their values and are still moving well. Near mint examples (no package) are worth about 40% to 50% of MIP prices, excellent condition only about 25% to 35%.

Advisor: Steve Stephenson.

'31 Doozie, red line tires, orange, orig top, no tampo, 1977, NM+, W1 ....$30.00

'32 Ford Delivery, blk walls, yel, 1986, MBP.....................$10.00

'34 Ford 3-Window Coupe, blk walls, red, 1980, EX+, S15 ..$10.00

'34 Ford 3-Window Coupe, Real Rider tires w/gray Goodyear, blk, 1984, MBP $35.00

'34 Ford 3-Window Coupe, Real Rider tires w/wht Goodyear, blk, 1984, MBP $150.00

'55 Chevy, blk walls, blk w/wht & orange '3' tampo, M (NM card), W1 ....$15.00

'56 Hi-Tail Hauler, blk walls, lt bl, 1979, MBP.................$15.00

'57 Chevy Convertible, blk walls, brn, 1990, MIP, S15......$5.00

'57 T-Bird, blk walls, blk w/red, magenta & bl tampo, M (EX+ card), W1 ....$12.00

'57 T-Bird, gray hubs w/wht Goodyear, metal-flake red, M..$25.00

'63 Split Window Corvette, blk walls, gray, 1980, NM+, S15 ..$15.00

'63 Vette, California Custom, Real Rider tires w/yel hubs, hot pk, MIP, S15 ....$10.00

'65 Mustang, blk walls, red, 1984, MBP..................$6.00

'80 Firebird, blk walls, wht, Chuck E Cheese promo, M, W1 ..$10.00

Alive '55, red line tires, chrome, 1970, G+, S15 ....$15.00

American Hauler, red line tires, bl, 1976, EX+................$12.00

AMX/2, red line tires, metallic red, 1971, NM, W1........$24.50

Army Funny Car, blk walls, wht, 1978, MBP....................$32.00

Backwoods Bomb, red line tires, gr, 1975, G......................$4.00

Backwoods Bomb, red line tires, lt bl, gray windshield, orig top, G+, W1 ....$11.50

Baja Breaker, blk walls, metal-flake orange, yel, bl & wht tampo, gray Goodyear tires, MBP (top of card cut off), W1 ..$10.00

Banshee, California Customs, turbo wheels, gold, 1990, MIP, S15 ....$10.00

Beach Bomb, red line tires, metallic gr, dk interior, 1969, M (NM+ card) $120.00

Black Lightning, blk walls, blk w/wht, yel & red '3' tampo, gray Goodyear tires, M (EX card), W1 ....$15.00

Brabham Repco F1, red line tires, metallic gr, blk interior, orig decals, 1969, NM, W1 ....$14.00

Bronco 4-Wheeler, blk walls, red, wht Goodyear tires, yel, bl & wht '21' tampo, wht camper, M (VG+ card), W1 .....$26.00

Bugeye, red line tires, metallic magenta, blk interior, very lt toning, NM+, W1 ....$34.00

Buzzoff, red line tires, dk bl, blk interior, yel pinstripe, EX+, W1 ....$20.00

Byefocal, red line tires, metallic magenta, dk interior, orig decals, EX+..$55.00

Bywayman, blk walls, maroon, 1989, MBP......................$8.00

Cadillac Seville, blk walls, gray, 1982, MBP $8.00

Camaro Z-28, Gold Wheels, red w/bl, blk & yel tampo, M (NM card), W1 ....$6.00

Carabo, red line tires, metallic magenta, blk interior, 1970, EX+..$15.00

CAT Earth Mover, blk walls, yel, 1987, MBP $14.00

CAT Forklift, blk walls, yel, 1980, MBP.........................$25.00

Chaparral 2G, red line tires, ice bl, 1969, NM..................$22.00

Chevy Monza 2+2, red line tires, Super Chrome, yel & blk tampo, 1975, EX+, W1 ....$12.50

Chief Special, red line tires, red, 1975, EX+ $18.00

Classic '31 Woodie, red line tires, metallic lt bl, cream interior, smooth blk roof, 1969, NM, W1 ....$26.00

Classic '32 Vicky, red line tires, metallic magenta, cream interior, smooth blk roof, 1969, NM+ $25.00

Classic '35 Caddy, wht walls, metal-flake silver, pk fenders, beige interior, MBP, W1 ....$15.00

Classic '36 Coupe, red line tires, metallic red, blk interior, smooth blk roof, 1969, EX+, W1..................$24.00

Classic '36 Ford Coupe, red line tires, gr, 1969, NM $18.00

Classic '57 Bird, red line tires, metallic bl, cream interior, 1969, EX+, W1 ....$20.00

Classic '57 T-Bird, red line tires, gr, 1969, NM+ $25.00

Classic Cobra, blk walls, bl, wht tampo, gray hubs w/wht Goodyear, M, W1 ....$24.00

Classic Cobra, Real Rider, red, 1986, MBP.......................$18.00

Classic Cord, red line tires, rose, 1971, NM..................$120.00

Classic Nomad, red line tires, metallic gr, lt interior, M (EX+ card), W1 ....$134.00

Classic Nomad, red line tires, turq, 1969, VG, S15 ....$15.00

Classic Nomad, red line tires, yel, w/flowers, 1971, NM+...$35.00

Cockney Cab, red line tires, metallic magenta, blk interior, orig sticker, 1971, M, W1 ....$64.00

Cool One, red line tires, plum, 1976, NM+ $38.00

Corvette Stingray, blk walls, wht w/red, bl & blk '35' tampo, M (NM card), W1 ....$14.00

Corvette Stingray, red line tires, red w/bl, yel & wht ribbon tampo, 1976, EX+ $20.00

Custom AMX, red line tires, metallic orange, cream interior, 1969, NM, W1 ....$34.00

Custom Barracuda, red line tires, gold, cream interior, 1968, EX+, W1 ....$60.00

Custom Camaro, red line tires, metallic lime, cream interior, smooth blk roof, 1968, EX+, W1....................$60.00

Custom Charger, red line tires, metallic magenta, cream interior, 1969, NM+, W1 ....$110.00

Custom Continental Mk III, red line tires, metallic pk, cream interior, 1969, NM, W1.............................$50.00

Custom Corvette, red line tires, metallic red, cream interior, 1968, NM+, W1 ....$80.00

Custom Cougar, red line tires, metallic gr, med interior, lt toning, 1968, EX+, W1 ....$50.00

Custom Cougar, red line tires, olive, blk roof, 1968, NM+ ..$85.00

Custom Eldorado, red line tires, bl, wht interior, 1968, NM...$25.00

Custom Eldorado, red line tires, metallic aqua, blk roof, dk interior, England, M (NMBP), W1 ....$150.00

Custom Eldorado, red line tires, metallic purple, cream interior, smooth blk roof, 1968, NM, W1 ....$38.00

Custom Firebird, red line tires, bl, bl interior, EX............$14.00

Custom Firebird, red line tires, metallic bl, cream interior, 1968, NM, W1..$40.00

Custom Firebird, red line tires, metallic red, lt interior, England, 1968, M (NMBP), W1 ....$270.00

Custom Fleetside, red line tires, metallic purple, dk interior, smooth blk roof, 1968, EX, W1 ....$20.00

Custom Mustang, red line tires, bl, wht interior, 1968, EX+..$42.00

Custom Mustang, red line tires, metallic red, scarce red interior, blk steering wheel, 1968, rare, VG, W1..................$170.00

Custom Police Cruiser, red line tires, blk & wht, clear light, 1969, M (creased card)................................$140.00

Chopcycles Blown Torch, 1973, MIB, $75.00.

Custom Police Cruiser, red line tires, wht, red light, 1969, EX+ $12.00

Custom T-Bird, red line tires, metallic brn, med interior, smooth blk roof, 1968, EX+, W1.............................$29.00

Custom VW, red line tires, metallic bl, cream interior, rare version w/no sunroof, 1968, EX, from $150 to.............$250.00

Custom VW, red line tires, metallic magenta, cream interior, 1968, NM+, W1 ....$32.00

Datsun 200SX, Gold Wheels, gold, 1982, MIP, S15...........$8.00

Demon, red line tires, bl, 1970, NM.....................................$15.00

Demon, red line tires, metallic lt gr, dk interior, blk roof, 1970, EX+, W1 ....$9.50

Deora, red line tires, metallic aqua, lt interior, 1968, M (EX+ card), W1...$224.00

Deora, red line tires, purple, 1969, NM+ $50.00

Dixie Challenger, blk walls, orange, 1981, NM, S15........$10.00

Double Header, red line tires, dk bl, blk interior, 1973, G+, W1 ....$40.00

Double Vision, red line tires, flourescent lime, cream interior, 1973, M, W1...$130.00

Dream Van XGW, Real Rider, gr, 1985, MBP.................$20.00

Dump Truck, red line tires, metallic bl, blk interior, 1970, NM, W1 ....$34.00

Dumpin' A, blk walls, orange, 1980, MBP $12.00

Dune Daddy, red line tires, yel, cream interior, 1973, VG+, W1 ....$50.00

Emergency Squad, red line tires, red, 1975, EX+ $10.00

Evil Weevil, red line tires, metallic gr, cream interior, orig stickers, 1971, NM $55.00

Ferrari F40, Ultra Hot Wheels, red, 1988, MIP, S15 ....$5.00

Ferrari Testarossa, Ultra Hot Wheels, red w/blk & yel tampo, tan & red interior, MIB, W1 ....$5.00

Fiero 2M4, Gold Wheels, red, 1988, MIP, S15 ....$5.00

Fire Chaser, blk walls, red w/yel, blk & wht '5' tampo, blk interior, M (NM card), W1 ....$10.00

Fire Eater, red line tires, red, 1977, NM $8.00

Fire Eater #51, blk walls, red, 1988, MBP..........................$8.00

Fire Engine, red line tires, metallic red, blk interior, complete, NM, W1...$30.00

Firebird Funny Car, blk walls, yel w/orange, magenta & bl '2' tampo, M (NM card), W1 ....$10.00

Flame Stopper, blk walls, red w/yel & wht tampo, silver construction tires, M (NM card), W1 ....$7.00

Ford J-Car, red line tires, metallic lt bl, blk interior, orig stickers, some darkening, 1968, EX+, W1...............$14.00

Ford Mk IV, red line tires, lt gr, 1969, NM+.....................$22.00

Ford Mk IV, red line tires, metallic orange, blk interior, orig stickers, 1969, NM, W1...$10.00

Formula 5000, red line tires, wht w/bl & red '76' tampo, 1976, EX+, W1 ....$10.00

Fuel Tanker, red line tires, wht enamel, 1971, NM+........$70.00

Funny Money, red line tires, gray, complete, 1972, NM, W1 ..$44.00

Good Ol' Pick-Em-Up, Real Rider, plum, M $50.00

Grasshopper, red line tires, metallic magenta, blk interior, orig top, 1971, EX+, W1..$30.00

Grasshopper (2 engines), red line tires, purple, 1975, EX, S15 ..$10.00

Gremlin Grinder, Super Chrome, red, gr & blk tampo, 1976, Canada, M (NM+ card), W1 ....$34.00

Grand Prix Series Indy Eagle, red line tires, in common colors, MBP, from $30.00 to $40.00; in Gold Chrome, MBP, from $150.00 to $200.00.

Greyhound Bus, marked Hong Kong, M, $15.00 (MBP, $25.00). For the Mexican model, M, from $30.00 to $40.00 (MBP, from $50.00 to $100.00).

GT Racer, blk walls, purple, 1989, MBP $5.00

Gun Bucket, red line tires, olive, wht tampo, 1976, EX, W1 ....$14.00

Gun Slinger, red line tires, olive, 1976, EX+ $15.00

Hairy Hauler, red line tires, metallic magenta, cream interior, 1971, NM, W1...$24.00

Hare Splitter, blk walls, wht w/red, blk & plum '3' tampo, M, W1 ....$10.00

Heavy Chevy, red line tires, metallic red, cream interior, orig stickers, 1970, NM, W1.......................................$40.00

Heavyweights, Ambulance, red line tires, red, 1970, NM ..$22.00

Heavyweights, Moving Van, red line tires, gr, 1970, NM...$22.00

Heavyweights, Scooper, red line tires, gr, 1971, NM+......$75.00

Heavyweights, Tow Truck, red line tires, gr, 1970, NM+.$25.00

Heavyweights, Waste Wagon, red line tires, olive, 1971, NM ..$55.00

Hiway Hauler, blk walls, gr, Mountain Dew logo, NM+, W1..$24.00

Hiway Robber, red line tires, dk bl, blk interior, 1973, EX+, W1..$90.00

Hot Heap, red line tires, metallic lt magenta, cream interior, 1968, M (NM+ card)...$50.00

Ice T, red line tires, lt gr, blk interior, orange & olive tampo, 1974, NM, W1...$44.00

Incredible Hulk Scene Machine, blk walls, wht, M (NM card), W1 ....$60.00

Jack Rabbit Special, red line tires, wht, wht interior, 1970, NM, W1 ....$13.00

Jeep Scrambler, blk walls, metal-flake bl, 1987, MBP.......$10.00

Jet Threat, red line tires, metallic yel, complete, 1971, NM, W1 ....$36.00

Jet Threat II, red line tires, plum, yel tampo, orig top, 1976, EX, W1 ....$12.00

Khali Kooler, red line tires, olive, wht tampo, plastic base, 1976, NM, W1 ....$18.00

King Kuda, red line tires, bl, blk roof, 1970, NM.............$50.00

Landlord, blk walls, orange, 1982, MIP, S15....................$10.00

Large Charge, red line tires, gr w/blk, yel & orange tampo, 1975, NM, W1 ....$26.00

Large Charge, Super Chrome, blk, yel & orange tampo, NM+, W1 ....$10.00

Letter Getter, blk walls, red, wht & bl, 1979, NM, S15......$8.00

Lickety Six, blk walls, bl, 1978, NM, S15 ....$10.00

Light My Firebird, red line tires, metallic olive, dk tan interior, complete, 1970, EX, W1..$30.00

Lola GT70, red line tires, red, 1969, NM........................$12.00

Lotus Turbine, red line tires, metallic aqua, blk interior, orig decals, 1969, NM, W1 ....$14.00

Lotus Turbine, red line tires, orange, 1969, NM+ $20.00

Lowdown, red line tires, gold chrome, 1976, NM+ $36.00

Lowdown, red line tires, lt bl, blk interior, plum, yel & wht tampo, 1976, VG+, W1..$18.00

Malibu Grand Prix, Real Rider, blk, M $14.00

Mantis, red line tires, metallic gr, lt interior, M (NM card), W1 ....$40.00

Mantis, red line tires, red, dk interior, 1970, NM+..........$25.00

Maserati Mistral, red line tires, metallic gr, 1969, EX+, W1..$38.00

Maxi Taxi, red line tires, yel, 1976, NM $28.00

McLaren M6A, red line tires, metallic magenta, blk interior, orig stickers, 1969, NM, W1..$10.00

Mercedes C-111, red line tires, metallic magenta, blk interior, toning, 1972, EX+, W1 ....$50.00

Mighty Maverick, red line tires, aqua, 1970, M $50.00

Mighty Maverick, red line tires, metallic bl, blk interior, complete, 1970, NM+, W1 ....$44.00

Mighty Maverick, red line tires, turq, 1969, G+, S15.......$15.00

Minitrek, blk walls, wht, 1983, MIP, S15........................$10.00

Mirada Stocker, blk walls, red, 1981, NM, S15................$10.00

Mod Quad, red line tires, metallic yel, blk interior, some toning, 1970, NM+, W1 ....$27.00

Mongoose, red line tires, red, complete, 1970, EX, W1 ....$24.00

Mongoose II, red line tires, metallic bl, complete, 1971, EX, W1 ....$52.00

Mongoose Rear Engine Dragster, red line tires, bl, blk front wheels, 1972, missing engine cover & stickers, VG, W1 ....$20.00

Monster Vette, blk walls, yel, 1987, MBP $10.00

Monte Carlo Stocker, red line tires, yel w/red, wht & bl '38' tampo, 1975, EX, W1 ....$18.00

Moving Van, red line tires, metallic bl, wht interior, wht trailer, complete, 1970, EX+, W1 ....$18.00

Mustang Boss Hoss, red line tires, metallic brn, lt interior, M (NM card)..$175.00

Mutt Mobile, red line tires, metallic aqua, blk interior, complete, 1971, EX+, W1 ....$36.00

Mutt Mobile, red line tires, purple, 1970, G+, S15...........$20.00

Neet Streeter, blk walls, bl w/orange, bl & wht tampo, NM+, W1 ....$12.50

Neet Streeter, blk walls, maroon, 1975, NM, S15 ....$10.00

Nitty Gritty Kitty, red line tires, metallic gr, cream interior, complete, 1970, EX+, W1..$32.00

Noodlehead, red line tires, metallic red, cream interior, 1971, NM, W1 ....$50.00

Open Fire, red line tires, metallic aqua, blk interior, toning, 1972, NM..$85.00

Oshkosh Snowplow, blk walls, orange, metal cab, orange construction tires, M (EX+ card), W1..$5.00

P-928, Gold Wheels, red w/yel & orange tampo, M (NM card), W1 ....$12.00

Packin' Pacer, blk walls, yel, 1978, MBP..................$10.00

Paramedic, blk walls, yel w/red & wht tampo, metal base, NM, W1 ....$14.50

Peeping Bomb, red line tires, metallic lt gr, blk interior, 1970, NM, W1 ....$10.00

Peterbuilt Cement Mixer, blk walls, red, straight exhaust, M (NM card), W1 ....$7.00

Phantomachine, blk walls, chrome, 1987, MBP..................$7.00

Pit Crew Car, red line tires, wht, orig stickers, 1971, EX+, W1..$44.00

Poison Pinto, red line tires, lt gr w/yel, blk & wht tampo, 1976, NM, W1 ....$22.00

Police Cruiser, red line tires, wht enamel, 1976, EX $8.00

Porsche 917, red line tires, magenta, 1970, EX+.............$14.00

Porsche 917, red line tires, metallic lt gr, cream interior, orig stickers, 1970, EX+, W1 ....$12.50

Power Pad, red line tires, metallic magenta, blk interior, orig top, 1970, NM, W1 ....$40.00

Prowler, red line tires, orange, 1974, NM+ $42.00

Python, red line tires, metallic purple, med interior, smooth blk roof, 1968, EX+, W1..$15.00

Quick Trick, blk walls, metallic magenta, 1984, MBP......$10.00

Racer Rig, red line tires, wht, orig stickers, 1971, VG, W1 ..$28.00

Ramblin' Wrecker, red line tires, wht, gray-tinted windows, 1975, NM..$25.00

Rear Engine Mongoose, red line tires, bl, 1972, NM+, from $120 to..$140.00

Road King Truck, red line tires, yel, complete, rare, 1974, NM+, W1 ....$700.00

Road Torch, blk walls, red, 1987, MBP..........................$25.00

Rock Buster, red line tires, yel, 1975, EX, S15 ....$10.00

Rodger Dodger, red line tires, gold chrome, 1977, NM+ ..$42.00

Rodger Dodger, red line tires, plum, orange & yel flame tampo, metal base, 1974, NM+, W1 ....$40.00

Royal Flash, blk walls, orange, 1982, MIP, S15..................$10.00

S'Cool Bus, red line tires, yel, orig blower, prop, seats & stickers, 1971, EX from $50 to..$70.00

Sand Crab, red line tires, metallic bl, blk interior, 1970, NM, W1 ....$12.50

Sand Crab, red line tires, metallic pk, 1969, G+, S15.........$8.00

Sand Drifter, red line tires, yel, blk interior, orange & magenta flame tampo, 1975, NM, W1..$32.00

Science Friction, blk walls, wht, 1978, MBP..................$14.00

Scooper, red line tires, metallic gr, blk interior, complete, 1971, EX, W1..$50.00

Sheriff Patrol, blk walls, blk & wht, 1982, MIP, S15........$10.00

Short Order, red line tires, metallic lt gr, 1971, MBP.....$135.00

Show Off, red line tires, red, 1973, NM+......................$105.00

Side Kick, red line tires, metallic magenta, blk rear louvers, toning, 1972, EX+, W1 ....$60.00

Silhouette, red line tires, metallic gr, 1968, EX+, W1 ....$5.00

Sir Rodney Roadster, red line tires, yel, red flame tampo, orig top, added blk trim, 1974, EX+, W1 ....$20.00

Sir Rodney Roadster, red line tires, yel, 1974, NM+ $40.00

Six Shooter, red line tires, aqua, 1971, NM+....................$45.00

Six Shooter, red line tires, metallic yel, cream interior, 1971, NM+, W1 ....$80.00

Snake, red line tires, yel, orig cage & prop, repro stickers, 1970, NM+, W1 ....$50.00

Snake Rail Dragster, red line tires, wht, orig blk front wheel & wheelie wheels, missing rear sticker, 1971, EX+, W1 ..$36.00

Snorkel, red line tires, metallic gr, blk interior, 1971, EX+, W1........................$50.00

Special Delivery, red line tires, lt bl, 1971, NM+ $30.00

Special Delivery, red line tires, metallic bl, wht interior, orig stickers, toning, 1971, NM, W1 ....$32.00

Speed Seeker, blk walls, wht, 1987, MBP $10.00

Spider-Man Scene Machine, blk walls, wht, M (NM card), W1........................$60.00

Splittin' Image, red line tires, gold, cream interior, 1969, NM+, W1 ....$20.00

Splittin' Image, red line tires, red, 1969, NM....................$12.00

Spoiler Sport, red line tires, lt gr, 1977, NM+ $28.00

Staff Car, red line tires, olive, blk interior, wht tampo, rare, 1976, NM........................$550.00

Steam Roller, red line tires, wht, 1974, NM+ $38.00

Steam Roller, red line tires, wht w/red & bl '3' tampo, 3 stars, 1974, NM, W1........................$25.00

Steam Roller, Super Chrome, yel & bl '3' tampo, NM+, W1..$28.00

Sting Red, blk walls, olive, 1988, MBP $7.00

Street Rodder, blk walls, blk w/red & yel flame tampo, EX+, W1........................$15.00

Street Rodder, red line tires, blk, red & yel flame tampo, 1976, VG+, W1 ....$12.00

Street Snorter, red line tires, yel, 1973, NM, W1 ....$160.00

Strip Teaser, red line tires, aqua, 1971, NM+ $45.00

Strip Teaser, red line tires, metallic bl, blk interior, 1971, NM ...$50.00

Sugar Caddy, red line tires, metallic bl, blk interior, orig stickers, 1971, NM, W1........................$40.00

Super Scraper, blk walls, blk, 1983, MBP........................$12.00

Super Van, red line tires, wht, orig baggie, rare Toy Fair Super Van, 1975, MIB........................$550.00

Sweet Sixteen, red line tires, flourescent gr, 1973, EX+ ...$38.00

Swingin' Wing, red line tires, metallic lt gr, cream interior, orig wing, 1970, NM+, W1........................$25.00

T-Totaler, blk walls, brn, 1979, EX, S15 ....$15.00

T-4-2, red line tires, metallic aqua, dk gray interior, orig top, 1971, NM, W1........................$38.00

T-4-2, red line tires, yel, 1971, M........................$42.00

Tank Gunner, blk walls, olive, M, W1........................$5.00

Team Trailer, red line tires, metallic red, blk interior, orig stickers, missing door, 1971, VG, W1........................$20.00

Thunder Burner, blk walls, wht, 1987, MBP..................$20.00

Thunderbird Stocker, Gold Wheels, wht, '21' tampo, M (NM+ card), W1........................$50.00

TNT Bird, red line tires, metallic aqua, dk gray interior, smooth blk roof, complete, lt toning, 1970, NM, W1 ....$34.00

TNT Bird, red line tires, red, 1970, NM+......................$30.00

Top Eliminator, red line tires, dk bl, orig seats, orange, gr & yel tampo, 1974, EX+, W1 ....$40.00

Torero, red line tires, metallic magenta, cream interior, 1969, NM, W1........................$12.00

Torino Stocker, blk walls, blk, '3' tampo, NM, W1 ....$18.00

Torino Stocker, blk walls, blk, 1982, MBP $28.00

Torino Stocker, red line tires, red, blk interior, '23' tampo, 1975, NM, W1........................$40.00

Tough Customer, red line tires, olive, complete, 1975, NM+, W1 ....$20.00

Tow Truck, red line tires, metallic aqua, wht interior, complete, 1970, EX+, W1........................$17.50

Tri Baby, red line tires, metallic yel, cream interior, 1970, NM, W1 ....$12.00

Tricar X, blk walls, red, 1983, MIP, S15........................$8.00

Truckin' A, blk walls, yel, 1977, NM, S15......................$10.00

Turbo Streak, blk walls, flame red, '1' tampo, bl wing label, NM, W1 ....$28.00

Turbo Streak, Real Rider, yel, M........................$10.00

Turbofire, red line tires, gr, wht interior, 1969, NM $10.00

Turismo #10, blk walls, red, 1981, NM, S15 ....$10.00

Twinmill, red line tires, gold, cream interior, 1969, EX+, W1 ....$4.00

Vega Bomb, red line tires, orange w/red, yel & bl tampo, missing interior, VG, W1........................$18.00

Vette Van, blk walls, red, 1982, MBP $14.00

VW Beach Bomb, red line tires, orange, 1969, NM+ $68.00

VW Gulf, blk walls, wht w/pk, gr & bl tampo, NM+, W1..$40.00

Waste Wagon, red line tires, metallic bl, complete, 1971, NM+, W1 ....$68.00

What 4, red line tires, metallic aqua, med interior, overall toning, complete, EX+, W1........................$50.00

Whip Creamer, red line tires, metallic pk, blk interior, complete, darkening, 1970, EX+, W1........................$22.50

Whip Creamet, red line tires, pk, 1970, NM+ $28.00

Winnipeg, red line tires, yel, '33' tampo, 1974, missing wing o/w EX+, W1 ....$36.00

Xploder, red line tires, lt gr, blk interior, 1973, G+, W1 ..$22.50

Z Whip, red line tires, gray, 1977, M........................$28.00

Rumblers

Bold Eagle, yel, missing driver & front tire, 1972, EX $44.00

Choppin' Chariot, yel, 1972, NM, W1........................$40.00

Devil's Deuce, yel, orig driver, 1972, EX+........................$50.00

High Trailer, red, missing driver & training wheels, EX, W1 ....$18.00

Mean Machine, orange, 1971, NM, W1 ....$30.00

Revolution, yel, 1972, NM, W1........................$50.00

Rip Code, bl, 1973, NM+, W1........................$150.00

Rip Snorter, red, 1971, NM, W1........................$30.00

Road Hog, orange or dk bl, 1971, NM, W1 ....$20.00

Roamin' Candle, bronze, 1971, NM+, W1 ....$40.00

Straight Away, yel, missing driver, broken handlebars, 1972, EX, W1 ....$12.00

Torque Chop, red, 1971, EX+, W1 ....$20.00

3 Squealer, metallic gr, 1971, NM, W1.........................$30.00

Sizzlers

Angeleno M-70, metallic dk gr, chipped orig wing, darkening, EX+ (NM box), W1 ....$15.00

Angelino, olive, NM....................................$35.00

Anteater, metallic pk, loose chassis, EX+, W1............$20.00

Co-Motion, gold, NM....................................$38.00

Ferrari Can-Am, red, NMIB....................................$75.00

Flat Out, gold, EX+....................................$25.00

Ford Mk IV, gr, NMIB....................................$50.00

Hot Head, metallic gr, NM (NM box), W1 ....$22.50

Hot Wings, gold, MIB....................................$80.00

Indy Eagle, bl, MIB....................................$40.00

Live Wire, metallic gold, NM+ (NM box), W1 ....$24.00

March Formula I, orange, M....................................$65.00

Mustang Boss 302, gold, orig wing, EX, W1 ....$30.00

Revvin' Heaven, metallic orange, NM (EX+ box), W1 ...$22.50

Revvin' Heaven, lt gr, MIB....................................$80.00

Spoil Sport, metallic rose, orig wing, EX, W1 ....$14.00

Spoil Sport, red, M....................................$40.00

Straight Scoop, metallic bl, NM (NM box), W1 ....$24.00

Up Roar, red, NM....................................$40.00

Van, chrome, EX....................................$20.00

Accessories

Action City, 1968, NM+, W1....................................$130.00

Bridge Set, 3-pack, MIB....................................$20.00

Button, metal, Chaparral 2G, EX+, W1 ....$2.00

Button, metal, Classic '36 Coupe, VG+, W1 ....$1.00

Button, metal, Classic Nomad, NM, T2 ....$5.00

Button, metal, Custom Barracuda, NM, T2 ....$5.00

Button, metal, Custom Corvette, NM....................................$4.00

Button, metal, Custom Dodge Charger, NM....................................$4.00

Button, metal, Custom Firebird, EX+, W1 ....$2.00

Button, metal, Custom Mustang, EX+, W1 ....$3.50

Button, metal, Custom T-Bird, NM $2.00

Button, metal, Deora, EX+....................................$2.00

Button, metal, Evil Weevil, EX $2.00

Button, metal, Heavy Chevy, NM, W1....................................$5.00

Button, metal, Indy Eagle, NM+....................................$2.00

Button, metal, Jack Rabbit Special, NM+, W1 ....$2.00

Button, metal, King Kuda, NM....................................$2.00

Button, metal, Light-My-Firebird, NM $2.00

Button, metal, Mongoose Funny Car, EX+ $6.00

Button, metal, Police Cruiser, NM....................................$2.00

Button, metal, Python, NM, T2....................................$2.00

Button, metal, Silhouette, NM, W1....................................$2.50

Button, metal, Swingin' Wing, NM $2.00

Button, plastic, Grasshopper, M....................................$2.00

Button, plastic, Short Order, M, W1....................................$8.50

California 500 Track Layout, MIB $80.00

Case, Collector's, 1969, 24-car, adjustable, VG+, W1.....$20.00

Case, Collector's, 1970, 48-car, EX+, W1 ....$30.00

Case, Collector's, 1975, 24-car, NM, J6 ....$24.00

Case, Super Rally, 1969, 24-car, VG+, W1 ....$10.50

Catalog, 1970 International Collector's Catalog, NM, $20.00.

Dare Devil Loop, MIB....................................$30.00

Drive It Clean Car Wash, 1988, MIB $15.00

Dual Lane Lap Counter, MIB....................................$36.00

Dual Lane Rod Runner, MIB....................................$55.00

Dual-Lane Speed Brake & Esses Pak, Sizzlers, MIB, M5...$30.00

Dual-Lane Speedometer, MIB (sealed), M5....................................$30.00

Full Curve, MIB....................................$24.00

Half Curve, MIB....................................$24.00

Juice Machine, MIB....................................$20.00

Lap Blastin' Bridge Blaster, MIB....................................$35.00

Mini-Market Stop & Go Set, #5464, w/White Passion, MBP, W1 ....$20.00

Plaque, Car Carrier Showcase, 1969, bl, new but dirty, M (EX card), W1 ....$28.00

Shift Kicker's Leap of Flame Stunt, MIB....................................$40.00

Sky Show Airplane, yel, orig nose pc, NM, W1 ....$30.00

Speedometer (single lane), MIB....................................$36.00

Super-Charger, NM+ (EX+ box), M5....................................$40.00

Tresle 5-pack, MIB....................................$24.00

Housewares

Back in the dark ages before women's lib and career-minded mothers, little girls emulated mommy's lifestyle, not realizing that by the time they grew up, total evolution would have taken place before their very eyes. They'd sew and bake, sweep, do laundry and iron (gasp!), and imagine what fun it would be when *they* were big like mommy. Those little gadgets they played with are precious collectibles today, and any child-size houseware item is treasured, especially those from the forties and fifties. Values are suggested for items in excellent condition unless noted otherwise. If you're interested in learning about toy sewing machines, we recommend *Toy and Miniature Sewing Machines* by Glenda Thomas (Collector Books).

Advisor: Lorraine Punchard (P13) author of *Playtime Kitchen Items and Table Accessories*.

See also **Furniture**.

Cleaning and Laundry

Boiler, 1910s, tin w/lid, 6", NM, G16 ....$135.00
Dust Pans, George Brown, bl tin w/gold stenciling, set of 2, VG, A $130.00
Iron, Wolverine, 1950s, electric, MIB, H12.....................$35.00
Ironing Set, Wolverine, 1940s, iron, doll cutouts & clothes, wood pins & line, unused & uncut, MIB, H12 ....$35.00
Kitchenette Set, Johnny & Mary, 1950s, dish drainer, dishes, tablecloth & sample boxes of soap, MIB, H12...........$55.00
Laundry Set, wood, table mk Peerless w/2 washtubs, clothes wringer, washboard & 9 clothespins, 15½" table, G, A................$770.00
Laundry Set, 1930s, tin basin w/hand wringer, washboard, basket, clothesline & clothespins, MIB, H12 ....$100.00

Maytag Washing Machine, Ertl, 1993, marked 100 Year Anniversary, M, $50.00.

Photo courtesy of Nate Stoller.

Sweeper, Little Queen, Bissell, tin w/wood hdl, functional, 25½", EX, A...$50.00
Washboard, tin & wood, H12 ....$20.00
Washing Machine, Geo Combs, Pat 1869, mahogany w/hinged dome lid, 4 stick legs, agitates against washboards, 8", EX, A...$800.00

Cooking

Baking set, Mother's Little Helper, early, complete w/rolling pin, egg beater, bowls, cutters & baking sheets, MIB, H12 ....$145.00
Baking Set, Standard Toycraft Inc, MIB, V2 ....$50.00
Betty's Pastry Set, Transogram, 1940, wood rolling pin, pestles, cutting boards & egg beaters, EX+ (EX box) $50.00

Canister Set, Wolverine, tin, MIB, G16 ....$130.00
Coffee Grinder, Daisy, 1900s, w/orig paper label, 2½" sq, NM, G16 ....$95.00
Cookie Mold Set, 1920s, stainless steel Heart, Club, Spade & Diamond, M (Art Deco-styled box), H12................$25.00
Cooking Set, Mirro, 1940s, 16 pcs, MIB, H12 ....$150.00
Kandy Kitchen Marshmallow & Gumdrop Maker, Transogram, 1966, complete w/molds & trays, NMIB, T2 ....$20.00
Refrigerator, Wolverine, Frost Free, litho tin, 15", VG, from $15 to $20.00
Spice Set, china, 6 lg & 6 sm containers w/wall-mounted salt box, iridescent wht w/gold trim, miniature, EX, A..$275.00
Stove, Bing, ftd bl steel 4-burner w/polished trim, alcohol fired, w/4 pcs bl & wht enamelware, 16", VG.................$600.00
Stove, Buck's Jr Range, St Louis MO, new body & pnt, recast parts, 26"..$850.00
Stove, Cresent, plated CI & steel 4-burner w/ornate front, stovepipe & shelf, 4-ftd w/4 pcs CI cookware, 12", EX.................$230.00
Stove, Dainty, Reading Stove Works, PA, 7x13x8", VG .$150.00
Stove, Eagle, plated CI & steel 6-burner w/ornate front, stovepipe w/shelf, 11", G...$110.00
Stove, Eagle, sm, EX...$200.00
Stove, Eclipse, EX..$175.00
Stove, ftd ornate CI w/stovepipe shelf, 16", G-.................$85.00
Stove, Grand Jewel, plated CI w/utensils & top covers, allover ornate emb design, 4-ftd w/side grates, 18", G, A....$150.00
Stove, Ideal, CI flat-top w/stovepipe, 6 burners, Baby lettered across oven door, 8x16", NM, A $525.00
Stove, Karr, pnt sheet metal w/bl & wht finish, NP trim & iron accessories, removable grill, 21", NM $3,000.00
Stove, Karr, Qualified, Belleville, IL, bl porcelain w/nickel, 1925, EX (repro in 1960s, same value for repro as orig) ..$2,500.00
Stove, Kenton/Royal, CI & steel 4-burner w/ornate front & working grates, 10", rpt, no stovepipe, G $45.00
Stove, Kenton/Royal, polished CI & steel ftd 4-burner w/ornate pipe shield, 10", no stovepipe, VG.........................$100.00

Stove, Lionel, cream and green porcelain and cast iron, electric cord, 32x26", EX, A, $550.00.

Stove, Little Fanny, EX $300.00

Stove, Little Giant, unmk/unidentified, 7½x8½x11", EX...$675.00

Stove, Little Willie, EX $75.00

Stove, Queen, 15" L, no shelves, EX............................$1,000.00

Stove, Queen, 9" L, no shelves, EX...............................$500.00

Stove, Rival, top warmers & oven, several accessories, 14", NM $1,350.00

Stove, Rival, 12" L, no shelves, EX $900.00

Stove, Royal, sm, EX $200.00

Stove, saleman's sample, mk Bono Magnetic No 6C, Southern Robertson Co, CI, fully functional, 20", EX+, A.....$440.00

Stove, saleman's sample, mk The Range Eternal, Engman Mathews, South Bend Ind, sheet metal & CI, flat bottom, 30", VG, A...$1,760.00

Stove, Susie Homemaker, VG+, T1 ....$65.00

Stove/Heater, Dolly #6, Keely Stove Co, CI, Victorian style w/4 mica windows, 28", EX, A $385.00

Utensil Set, rolling pin, slotted spoon, spatula, masher, wire soap holder, etc, wht-pnt wood hdls, 9 pcs, VG, A $45.00

Waffle Iron, pnt & plated CI w/wooden hdls, 7¾", EX, from $100 to $125.00

Nursery

Carriage, all wood construction w/flared spoked sides & 4 wheels, flat sun-block roof, G, A.............................$500.00

Carriage, att Joel Ellis, red-pnt wood horizontal seat w/striping & decor, orig upholstery, 4 spoked wheels, 47", EX, A.$320.00

Carriage, gold-pnt wood body w/red leather upholstered seat, blk collapsible top, wooden spoke wheels, 25", orig pnt, A..$415.00

Carriage, Joel Ellis type, aqua-pnt wood w/fringed canopy, leather cushioned seat, wooden spoke wheels, 28x38", EX, A..$385.00

Carriage, Joel Ellis type, blk wood w/blk & orange fringed top, wooden spoke wheels, 22", orig pnt, A $275.00

Carriage, Joel Ellis type, blk wood w/folding leather hood, 2 wooden spoke wheels, 22" w/38" front hdl, orig pnt, A.............$320.00

Carriage, Kelly Bros, wicker w/side compartments & cloth parasol, metal spoke wheels, upholstered interior, rstr, EX, A $715.00

Carriage, orange-pnt wood w/railed sides, collapsible fringed top, wooden spoke wheels, 22", orig pnt, A $275.00

Carriage, orig blk pnt w/striping & decor, folding buggy-type top w/rear window, turned hdl, 4 spoked wheels, 47", EX, A.$600.00

Carriage, red wooden body w/blk leather collapsible top, stenciled trim, 3 wooden spoked wheels, 24x33", rpt (?), A $165.00

Carriage, Wakefield (?), wicker seat shaped like early shoe, 4 spoked wheels, 40", EX, A $1,100.00

Carriage, wht wicker, 2 lg rear & 2 sm front blk spoked wheels, for 27-30" dolls, 26½", EX, A...................................$100.00

Carriage, wicker, horizontal upholstered seat w/delicate scrolled & beaded sides, 4 spoked wheels, turned hdl, 35", G, A $180.00

Carriage, 1890s, 2 fringed canopies over horizontal twin seat on spring-mounted & metal-covered wheels, 44", EX, A.$1,250.00

Carriage, 2-wheeled pull type, wooden chair w/upper half of back cane-woven, metal spoked wheels, pull hdl, 40", VG, A...$250.00

Cradle, France, blk scrolled wrought iron w/wht lace covering & head drape, 27x19", EX, A $210.00

Grooming Set, 1920s, hand-pnt celluloid brush, comb & rattle w/bl ribbon flowers, M (M floral box), H12.............$125.00

Swing, 1920s-30, bl & cream metal, 10x6", G16 ....$45.00

Table Service

Decanter Set, solid brass, 6 goblets, decanter w/lid, fruit bowl, bucket & serving tray, MIB, H12 ....$38.00

Dinner Set, allover bl floral design, 2 entree bowls, 2 gravy boats, 2 tureens, serving bowl, 10 plates, etc, EX, A...........$390.00

Dinner Set, England, wht china w/intricate allover brn pattern, 2 tureens, gravy boat, plates & platter, 21 pcs, EX, A..$275.00

Dishes, Ohio Art, 1930s, litho metal w/wedding scene, 31 pcs, MIB, H12..$250.00

Lemonade Set, Mirro, 1930s, 6 glasses w/pitcher, hammered tray, 6 spoons & straws, MIB, H12..........................$125.00

Platter, Blue Willow, oval, 6", H12 ....$45.00

Silverware Set, Banner Metallone Tableware, 4 place settings w/butter knife & cake server, MIB, H12 ....$55.00

Tea Service, bl graniteware, early 1900s, teapot (spout missing), creamer, sugar bowl & 5 cups w/saucers, minor chips, G16 ....$150.00

Tea Set, Doole & Roache, stamped Quadruple Plate, teapot, creamer & sugar bowl, w/2 2-hdl vessels, EX, A $35.00

Tea Set, English (?), 1870s, wht china w/rose design, gold trim, service for 4 w/jam cup & underplate, 1 rpr, H12....$175.00

Tea Set, European, rose, aqua & gr clover pattern, gold trim on emb & scalloped edge, service for 4, H12 ....$325.00

Tea Set, florals on caramel lustreware, 1920s, service for 6 w/soup tureen, meat platter & shakers, complete w/lids, H12 ....$265.00

Tea Set, French, orange-banded wht china w/gold trim, service for 5 w/cups & plates, 15 pcs, EX, A $120.00

Tea Set, Ideal, cranberry, gold & wht fleur-de-lis pattern, tin & hard plastic, 4 place settings w/extra pcs, MIB, H12 .$165.00

Tea Set, KT&K, wht w/mice on fruit, colonial couple & coaches, teapot, creamer & sugar, 6 cups, plates & saucers, EX $145.00

Tea Set, mk Bavaria, wht w/children at play or on skis, teapot, creamer & sugar, 6 cups, saucers & plates, EX, A....$415.00

Tea Set, Noritake, yel & blk Art-Deco motif w/gold trim, service for 4, MIB, H12..$350.00

Tea Set, Staffordshire, red sponged design, teapot, cream & sugar, 6 cups, plates, saucers & waste bowl, EX, A ..$580.00

Tea Set, wht china w/Dutch floral design, service for 5 w/plates, cups & saucers, spoons, EX, A................................$165.00

Tea Set, wht china w/floral design & girl holding apples, teapot, creamer & sugar bowl, 6 cups, plates & saucers, EX, A.$145.00

Tea Set, wht china w/gold floral design, fluted teapot, creamer & sugar bowl, 4 straight-sided cups, 6 plates, EX, A $135.00

Teapot, Blue Willow, 3x3", H12 ....$45.00

Sewing

Sewing Basket, sq wicker basket w/lid on 4 tall legs w/bottom shelf, 17x9", EX, A $55.00

Sewing Cabinet, Martha Washington, ca 1930, dk wood w/3 drawers, 2 flip-top side compartments, 18", EX, A ..$245.00

Sewing Kit, lid illus w/Victorian girls & Christmas pram, w/mirror, needles, thread, thimble & button, MIB, H12 ..$135.00

Sewing Machine, Betsy Ross, 1930s, all metal, working, H12 ....$52.00

Sewing Machine, English, 1948, bl pressed steel w/gray trim, working, 7x8", EX, A $30.00

Sewing Machine, Foley & Williams, early, CI, working, EX (orig wood box), A $550.00

Sewing Machine, Singer Sewhandy No. 20, 1940s, pressed steel and cast iron, M (worn box), from $75.00 to $100.00.

Miscellaneous

Dresser Set, china, brn & purple floral design, water pitcher & bowl, soap dish, lotion, powder & pin containers, EX, A........$250.00

Dresser Set, 1930s, celluloid mirror, brush, comb & hair receiver, doll sz, MIB, H12 ....$200.00

Lawn Mower, Arcade, push-type w/wooden hdl, CI cutter, 22", VG, A $55.00

Sink, France, bl-pnt & stenciled tin, bowl on pedestal base, back board w/canted corners, fully functional, 29", EX, A.$100.00

Spinning Wheel, early, oak, fully functional, 28", EX, A .$255.00

Telephone, red metal w/bell, Speed Phone, NM, J6.........$65.00

Telephone, Zimphone, Vintage Products, 1950s, hard blk plastic, ringer & rotary dial, uses D batteries, NMIB, T2.$15.00

Tool Set, Ideal, 1960s, diecast metal, 5-pc set, MIB, H12 .$15.00

Trunk (Footlocker), tin- & paper-covered wood, blk w/metal corner & edge trim, removable tray, 10", EX, A........$35.00

Typewriter, Smith Corona, 1950s, MIB, H12 ....$38.00

Wall Clock, Gilbert, ca 1870, rosewood veneer octagonal shape w/paper label on reverse, 6½" dia, EX, A.................$110.00

Wheelbarrow, Am, natural wood w/image of horse on sides, front spoked wheel, 25", EX, A $220.00

Jack-in-the Boxes

Very early jack-in-the-box toys were often made of papier-mache and cloth, fragile material to withstand the everyday wear and tear they were put through, so these vintage German exam-

ples are scarce today and very expensive. But even those from the '50s and '60s are collectible, especially when they represent well-known TV or storybook characters.

See also Character, TV and Movie Collectibles; Disney.

Blippy (Spaceman), Mattel, 1968, EX+, J2 ....$90.00

Chimney Sweep, wood & wire figure w/blk paper clothes & papier-mache head, brick paper-covered wood box, 6", VG+, A...$300.00

Clippo the Clown, Effanbee, 6", G-, A $45.00

Leprechaun, German, papier-mache & cloth figure, paper-covered box, 3½" sq, G, A..$115.00

Man in Gray Top Hat, German, papier-mache head w/gray hair, lg nose, paper & wood box, no squeaker, 4½" sq, EX, A..$360.00

Man in Red Top Hat, German, papier-mache head w/gray furry hair, paper-covered wood box, enclosed squeaker, 5" sq, EX, A $440.00

Policeman, German, papier-mache head with blue hat and brown mustache, paper-covered box, with squeaker, 4" square, VG+, A, $245.00.

Poodle Wearing Glasses, German, wht papier-mache head w/wht fur trim, paper label on wood box, w/squeaker, 4" sq, EX, A $290.00

Keystone

Though this Massachusetts company produced a variety of toys during their years of operation (ca 1920-late '50s), their pressed-steel vehicles are the most collectible, and that's what we've listed here. As a rule they were very large, with some of the riders 30" in length.

Aerial Ladder Truck, red open cab, long body w/ladder supports, red side ladders w/chromed extension ladder, 31", VG, A $1,045.00

Air Mail Plane, gray fuselage w/red wings, prop, tail & hubs, red grip hdl, side compartment opens, 26", G, A $3,300.00

American Railway Express Truck, blk w/red chassis, aluminum hubs, doorless cab, enclosed screen bed, 26", EX, A .$1,155.00

Army Truck, gr open cab & base, canvas top stenciled US Army, 27", G $350.00

Chemical Pump Engine, red, open cab, hand-operated siren, 28",
    G, A...$1,595.00
Coast-to-Coast Bus, lt bl w/cream hinged roof w/blk wooden steer-
    ing hdl, blk rubber tires w/bl hubs, 31", VG, A........$2,090.00
Dump Truck, blk w/red chassis hubs, doorless cab, lever controls,
    26", VG, A...$660.00

**Dump Truck, Packard, black with red chassis, black rubber
tires with red hubs, front hand lever, 26", EX, A, $745.00.**

Dump Truck, rider, gr cab & chassis w/red grip hdl, red bed
    w/wooden seat, red tires & hubs, 25", G, A.............$230.00
Fire Department Combination Truck #49 w/2 Ladders & Bell,
    T-type steering wheel & seat, 28", G, A..................$325.00
Greyhound Bus, bl w/blk rubber tires, destination plate mk Lim-
    ited, front plate mk 228, w/up, 17", scarce, VG, A..$650.00
Koaster Truck, blk open cab w/red flat bed used for riding, blk
    rubber tires w/red hubs, 26", VG, A......................$635.00
Locomotive, rider, red & blk, mk Keystone RR 6400,
    wooden handlebar, 2 front rubber tires w/red hubs, 24",
    NM, A...$415.00
Locomotive #1400, rider, 1941, red & blk, VG.............$250.00
Police Patrol Truck, w/all decals & EX pnt, 28x11x8", EX,
    A...$1,400.00
Pullman Car, hinged roof for steering, 25", rstr, EX, A ..$145.00
Railroad Engine, rider, red & blk, EX, A.....................$275.00
Steam Roller #60, blk w/corrugated red roof & trim, w/stack &
    brass bell, simulated spoked wheels, 19½", EX, A ...$660.00
Steam Shovel, rider, red & blk w/metal wheels, 21",
    VG...$150.00
US Army Troop Carrier, open cab w/gr canvas top over bed,
    26", rstr, A $200.00

**Water Tower Truck, ca 1928, red, black rubber tires with
black hubs, 33", EX, from $1,100.00 to $1,500.00.**

Water Tower Truck, rider, red w/open cab, hand-operated siren,
    30", G, A $715.00

Photo courtesy of Dunbar Gallery.

Lehmann

Lehmann toys were made in Germany as early as 1881.
Early on they were sometimes animated by means of of an
inertia-generated flywheel; later, clockwork mechanisms were
used. Some of their best-known turn-of-the-century toys were
actually very racist and unflattering to certain ethnic groups. But
the wonderful antics they perform and the imagination that
went into their conception have made them and all the other
Lehmann toys favorites with collectors today. Though the company faltered with the onset of WWI, they were quick to recover
and during the war years produced some of their best toys, several of which were copied by their competitors. Business
declined after WWI. Lehmann died in 1934, but the company
continued for awhile under the direction of Lehmann's partner
and cousin, Johannes Richter.

Advisor: Scott Smiles (S10).

Windups, Frictions and Other Mechanicals

Adam the Porter, man pushing trunk on handcart, 8", EX ..$600.00
AHA Delivery Van, driver in early van w/open cab, red w/yel
    chassis, 5", EX..$650.00
Ajax, acrobat, litho tin figure w/cloth costume, 9", EX+, from
    $1,000 to..$1,250.00
Alabama Coon Jigger, Blk man dances on platform, 10", EX,
    A..$655.00
Alabama Coon Jigger, Blk man dances on platform, 10", VG,
    from $450 to $500.00
ALSO Automobile, w/driver, 4", EX, from $350 to........$400.00
ALSO Automobile, yel & red open auto w/driver at center
    steering wheel, 4", M, from $550 to $600.00
Anxious Bride, hand-pnt & litho tin, 8½", EX+.........$2,200.00
Auto #420, horseless-carriage style, spoked wheels w/balloon
    tires, EX $500.00
Autobus, dbl-decker w/rear stairs leading to open seats, red, wht
    & yel litho tin, spoked wheels, 7", NMIB, A $2,310.00
Autobus, red w/yel striping, 8", EX, M5.....................$1,475.00

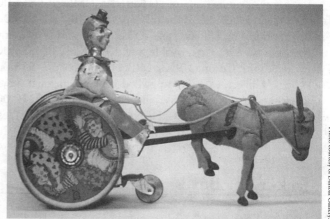

Photo courtesy of Dunbar Gallery.

**Balky Mule, clown bounces up and down as he drives
mule cart, 7½", EX, from $400.00 to $500.00.**

Autohutte, gr sedan w/spoked wheels rolls out of wht garage w/red roof & litho detail, tin, 6", EX.........................$750.00

Baker & Sweep, baker on front of 3-wheeled cart w/sweep on back, hand-pnt & litho tin, 5½", NM, A.............$4,620.00

Baldur Limousine, blk over yel litho tin w/driver, tin wht-walls w/yel hubs, 10", EX, A $1,650.00

Balky Mule, clown bounces up & down as he drives mule cart, 7½", VG, from $300 to.................................$350.00

Buster Brown, seated in open car w/center steering wheel, yel & red, hand-pnt & litho tin, 4", VG, A......................$825.00

Cat & Mouse, lg blk & wht cat appears to chase sm mouse, tin, NM, A...$1,375.00

Climbing Monkey, monkey climbs up string when finger loops are pulled, hand-pnt & litho tin, 8", NM, from $225 to..$250.00

Couple Walking Down Broadway, EPL #260, man & woman walking dog on a leash, 6½", EX, from $3,500 to.$3,750.00

Couple Walking Down Broadway, EPL #260, man & woman walking dog on a leash, 6½", G, from $2,500 to ..$2,750.00

Crocodile, activated walking & jaw movement, real-life colors, tin, 9½", NM, A...$415.00

Dancing Sailor, cloth-dressed tin figure, 7½", EX+ (EX box, M5...$900.00

Dancing Sailor, cloth-dressed tin figure in Navy hat, 7½", rpl clothes, G, from $500 to....................................$600.00

Dancing Sailor, litho tin figure in cloth suit, cap reads SMS Bradenburg, 7", MIB $1,250.00

Dare Devil, figure on cart pulled by zebra, 7", VG.........$475.00

Drive Porter Pushing Lady in 2-Wheeled Chair, lady in bl dress holding fan, porter in striped pants & bl coat, 7", G, A $300.00

DUO Rooster & Rabbit, rabbit atop 2-wheeled egg pulled by rooster, litho tin, 6½", M, from $800 to $900.00

Echo Motorcycle, EPL #725, green with brown rider, 8½", VG, $1,650.00.

EHE & Co, litho tin truck w/open bed & cab, wht w/red chasis, yel bed interior, wht tires w/spoke wheels, 7", VG, A $385.00

EPL-1 Dirigible, 2 observation decks, rear tail blade, 7½", EX, from $225 to $250.00

EPL-11 Zeppelin, gold tin w/celluloid props, 7¼", NM (EX box) $750.00

Express, porter pulling trunk on 2-wheeled cart, 6" G, from $350 to...$400.00

Flying Bird, bird is suspended from 2 strings, hand-pnt tin w/pasteboard wings, 10" W, NM, from $375 to.......$400.00

Galop Racer #1, yel w/bl stripe, w/driver, 5½", EX+, from $500 to...$550.00

Galop Racer #1, yel w/bl stripe, w/driver, 5½", VG, from $400 to $450.00

Gustav the Miller, pull string & figure climbs pole to mill, litho tin, 18", EX, from $200 to $250.00

Halloh Rider on Cycle, flywheel mechanism, 8", M, from $3,500.00 to $4,000.00.

Heavy Swell, lg man in long checked cloth coat, wht hat, red scarf & holding cane & key, pnt tin body, 8½", NM, A ..$4,620.00

Heini, boy on scooter w/back-&-forth motion, 5x6", EX .$600.00

Ikarus Airplane, litho tin fuselage & tail wings, wire-framed paper wings, w/pilot in open cockpit, 10½", EX, A $2,860.00

ITO Sedan, EPL #679, red w/blk roof, bl driver, spoked wheels, 7", VG+, A..$1,265.00

Kadi, 2 Chinese men carrying tea chest, hand-pnt tin, 7", NM, A $1,375.00

Lana Sedan, yel & blk litho tin, 7", EX, A $2,500.00

Lila Hansom Cab, w/driver & 2 lady passengers, litho tin, 5½", EX, from $1,500 to $1,750.00

Lolo Automobile, wht & gr open auto w/driver at center steering wheel, litho tin, 3¾", EX+, A.........................$1,430.00

Lu Lu Delivery Van, gr hood & chassis w/yel simulated wood paneling, rack atop, wht tires w/spoke wheels, 7", EX.$3,600.00

Mandarin, Chinese man in sedan chair carried by 2 other Chinese men, hand-pnt tin, 7", EX+, A $3,520.00

Masayama (Rickshaw), 1927, w/driver & passenger, litho tin, 6¾", NM, from $1,550 to...................................$1,750.00

Mikado Family, man pulling female passenger in rickshaw, hand-pnt & litho tin, 7", EX+, A.............................$1,375.00

Mixtum, crazy car w/3 spiral wheels driven by wobbly Peter, hand-pnt & litho tin, 4", M..................................$3,200.00

Motorcoach, w/driver, pnt & litho tin, 5", NM.............$700.00

Motorcoach, w/driver, pnt & litho tin, 5", VG...............$500.00

NA-OB, donkey cart w/driver advances as offset wheels cause wagon to move erratically, 6", EX............................$485.00

Naughty Boy, 1903, wht & bl open auto w/driver & boy facing each other at center wheel, 5", G, from $650 to......$750.00

Naughty Boy, 1903, wht & bl open auto w/driver & boy facing each other at center wheel, 5", NM, from $1,200 to.........$1,300.00

New Century Cycle, man holds umbrella over driver on 3-wheeled vehicle, 5", EX, from $700.00 to $800.00.

New Century Cycle, man holding umbrella over driver, litho tin, 5", NM, from $900 to $1,000.00

Nu-Nu, Chinese man pulling tea chest, hand-pnt tin, 5", NM, A $1,265.00

OHO, open auto w/driver at center steering wheel, litho tin, 3¾", EX, A $500.00

Paak-Paak (Quack-Quack) Duck Cart, mother duck pulling 3 ducklings in 2-wheeled cart, 7", G $350.00

Paak-Paak (Quack-Quack) Duck Cart, mother duck pulling 3 ducklings in cart, 7", NM, A $465.00

Paddy the Pig, man moves sideways on pig that moves in circles, hand-pnt tin w/cloth clothes, 5½", NM, from $2,000 to $2,250.00

Paddy the Pig, man moves sideways on pig that moves in circles, hand-pnt tin w/cloth clothes, 5½", VG, from $1,250 to.........$1,500.00

PANNE Touring Car, driver in gray & red open car, wht tires w/red spokes, 6½", EX, A......................................$1,000.00

Performing Sea Lion, advances moving front & rear flippers, tin, 7½", NM (G box)..$350.00

Playing Mice, 2 mice on spiral rod that revolves when turned upside down, hand-pnt & litho tin, VG $100.00

Rad Cycle, driver on 3-wheeled delivery cycle w/spoked wheels, 5", EX...$1,300.00

Rigi 900 Cable Car, 1950, w/passengers, EX, from $250 to ..$300.00

Royal Mail Truck, EPL-585, ca 1972, red & beige litho tin, 6½", EX, A $2,300.00

Sedan, gr w/wht trim, 5½", EX, A..................................$450.00

Skirolf, man in gray brimless hat & bl suit on skis, hand-pnt & litho tin, 7", NM $2,000.00

Snik-Snak, man in checked jacket & yel hat walking 2 balking dogs, litho tin, 8x16", EX+, A $7,700.00

Stubborn Donkey, clown drives mule cart w/tumbling clowns lithoed on wheels, 7½", NM (G box), from $600 to.$650.00

Take-Apart Airplane, WWII plane w/camouflage pnt & Nazi insignia, 7¼" W, NM, A $250.00

Take-Apart Heinkel-Blitz Airplane, w/instructions, 5½" W, NMIB, A..$450.00

Tap-Tap Man with Wheelbarrow, 6½", EX, from $350.00 to $450.00.

Tap-Tap Man w/Wheelbarrow, wht hat & pants, bl coat & blk boots, 6½", NM (EX box), from $600 to $650.00

Terra Towing Co, EPL-720, red w/blk roof, bl driver, spoked wheels, 10", G, A...$635.00

Tut-Tut, man in open car blowing horn, hand-pnt & litho tin, 6½", EX, from $1,000 to $1,100.00

Tut-Tut, man in open car blowing horn, 6½", VG, from $800 to.$900.00

Two-Car Garage, wht w/red roof, gr trim, 6½", EX, A ...$350.00

Tyras Walking Dog, tin poodle, 6", EX+, A $525.00

UHU Amphibious Car, w/driver, hand-pnt tin, 9", M, from $1,750 to..$1,850.00

Vineta, monorail car w/gyroscope stabilizer, red, wht & bl litho tin, 9½", NM, A..$1,210.00

Walking Doll, cloth-dressed w/celluloid head, revolving base, moves in realistic manner, 9", EX, A.....................$1,150.00

Waltzing Doll, cloth-dressed w/celluloid head, 8½", M, A ..$1,870.00

Wild West Bucking Bronco, rider & horse on platform, 6", NMIB, from $1,200 to..$1,300.00

Zig-Zag, 2 men seated facing each other between 2 lg wheels, hand-pnt & litho tin, 4¼", NM, from $2,000 to..$2,200.00

Zulu Ostrich Mail, driver on ostrich-driven 2-wheeled cart, yel litho w/red trim, 6", NM (EX+ box), from $1,500 to.........$1,600.00

Zulu Ostrich Mail, driver on ostrich-driven 2-wheeled cart, yel litho tin w/red trim, 7", NM, from $1,400 to........$1,500.00

Lunch Boxes

When the lunch box craze began in the mid-1980s, it was only the metal boxes that so quickly soared to sometimes astronomical prices. But today, even the plastic and vinyl ones are collectible. Though most lunch box dealers agree that with few exceptions, prices have become much more reasonable than they were at first, they're still holding their own and values seem to be stabilizing. So pick a genre and have fun. There are literally hundreds to choose from, and just as is true in other areas of character-related collectibles, the more desirable lunch boxes are those with easily recognized, well-known subjects — western heroes, TV, Disney and other cartoon characters, and famous entertainers. Thermoses are collectible as well. In our listings, values are just for the box unless a thermos is mentioned in the description. If you'd like to learn more about them, we recommend *A Pictorial Price Guide to Metal Lunch Boxes and Thermoses* and a companion book *A Pictorial Price Guide to Vinyl and Plastic Lunch Boxes* by Larry Aikins. For more pricing information, Philip R. Norman (Norman's Olde Store) has prepared a listing of hundreds of boxes, thermoses and their variations. He is listed in the Categories of Special Interest under Lunch Boxes.

Advisor: Terri Ivers (I2).

Other Sources: C10, J6, J7, M15, T1

Metal

A-Team, 1983, VG+, N2 ....$14.00
A-Team, 1985, w/thermos, unused, M, C1 ....$45.00
Adam-12, Aladdin, 1972, EX+ $50.00
Addams Family, VG $55.00
Addams Family, 1974, NM, C1 ....$115.00
Airline, 1968, VG+ $40.00
Animal Friends, 1975, blk letters, VG+ $28.00
Animal Friends, 1975, yel letters, VG+, N2 ....$25.00
Annie, 1981, VG+, N2 ....$10.00
Annie, 1981, w/thermos, M $38.00
Archies, 1969, EX+, J2 ....$75.00
Archies, 1969, some wear, w/thermos, VG+, I2..............$68.00
Astronaut, dome top, w/thermos, EX+, M5 ....$160.00
Atom Ant, Secret Squirrel, 1966, G+, I2 ....$58.00
Back in '76, 1975, VG+ $28.00
Basket Weave, 1968, VG+, N2 ....$20.00
Battle Kit, EX $80.00
Battlestar Galactica, 1978, w/thermos, EX, I2 ....$40.00
Beaver's Box, 1950s, gray & red, w/Universal ribbed thermos, VG+, N2 ....$25.00
Bedknobs & Broomsticks, 1972, EX- $42.00
Bee Gees, Maurice, Barry or Robin, unused, NM+ $65.00
Betsy Clark, 1975, bl, VG, N2 ....$14.00
Betsy Clark, 1976, yel, w/thermos & coupons, M (old store stock), I2 ....$40.00
Black Hole, 1979, EX+, I2 ....$35.00
Black Hole, 1979, w/plastic thermos, NM, C1 ....$55.00
Blondie, 1969, wht pnt splotches, G, N2 ....$25.00
Bobby Sherman, 1972, w/thermos (EX), G+, I2 ....$52.00
Bonanza, 1965, EX $95.00
Bond XX, VG, M5 ....$80.00
Buccaneer, 1957, dome top, VG+, N2 ....$150.00
Buck Rogers, 1979, VG, N2 ....$18.00
Bugaloos, 1971, EX+, from $85 to $95.00
Bugaloos, 1971, w/thermos, VG+, T1 ....$65.00

Cabbage Patch Kids, 1983, w/thermos, EX, N2 ....$15.00
Campus Queen, 1967, VG+, N2, from $22 to $30.00
Canadian Train, NM $35.00
Care Bear Cousins, 1985, EX, N2..............................$15.00
Care Bears, 1983, VG+, I2 ....$10.00
Cartoon Zoo Lunch Chest, 1963, VG........................$120.00
Chan Clan, 1973, w/thermos (NM), EX, I2 ....$80.00

Charlie's Angels, blue rim, NM, J6, $65.00.

Charlie's Angels, w/thermos, EX, V1 ....$35.00
Christmas Carousel, 1990s, 2-hdl, EX, N2 ....$9.00
Color Me Happy, EX, J2 ....$65.00
Corsage, 1964, G+, I2 ....$20.00
Cowboy Lassoing a Steer, 1950s, decoupage, VG+, N2 .$250.00
Curiosity Shop, 1972, VG+, N2 ....$45.00
Cyclist, 1979, VG+, N2 ....$28.00
Daniel Boone, red rim, w/thermos, EX, M5 ....$150.00

Daniel Boone, 1965, yellow rim, EX, $150.00.

Dark Crystal, 1982, w/thermos, M, N2........................$20.00
Davy Crockett, 1955, gr rim, VG+, N2.........................$89.00

Debutante, 1958, VG+ $50.00
Dick Tracy, 1967, EX, D11...$125.00
Disney Express, 1979, slight wear, plastic thermos, EX+, I2 ..$20.00
Disney Express, 1979, VG+, N2 ....$12.00
Disney Fire Fighter, 1969, dome top, VG+ $80.00
Disney School Bus, Aladdin, orange, dome top, EX+, I2 .$60.00
Disney School Bus, Aladdin, orange w/litho characters, dome top, w/plastic thermos, NM $80.00
Disneyland Castle, 1957, rims pnt beige (not bad), VG, N2 ..$75.00
Disneyland Monorail, 1960, VG+, N2 ....$185.00
Donald Duck, Fyna Foods/Australia, Donald & his nephews, EX, A $200.00
Dr Dolittle, 1967, VG+ $60.00
Drag Strip, 1975, w/plastic thermos, EX, I2 ....$45.00
Dragon's Lair, 1983, VG+/EX, I2/N2, from $18 to $25.00
Drummer Boy, 1975, M, N2 ....$90.00
Dukes of Hazzard, 1980, w/thermos, VG, I2......................$20.00
Dukes of Hazzard, 1983, VG+, N2 ....$33.00
Dynomutt, 1976, EX, I2...$38.00
Dynomutt, 1976, VG, N2 ....$20.00
Early West Indian Territory, 1982, VG+, N2 ....$39.00

Early West Pony Express, Ohio Art, 1982, orange and red rim, NM, $65.00.

Empire Strikes Back, bl rim, VG, M5.............................$22.00
ET, 1982, w/thermos, EX+, N2 ....$27.00
Evel Knievel, red rim, EX $45.00
Evel Knievel, 1974, w/thermos, G+, N2 ....$20.00
Exciting World of Metrics, 1976, few scratches, EX, I2 ....$22.00
Fall Guy, 1981, EX, I2...$20.00
Fall Guy, 1981, w/thermos, VG+ $25.00
Family Affair, 1969, w/thermos, red cup, EX, I2 ....$90.00
Fantastic World of Hanna Barbera, 1977, VG+, N2 ....$32.00
Fireball XL-5, 1964, VG+, N2.......................................$85.00
Flag, 1973, NM, C1 ....$55.00
Flag, 1973, VG+, N2 ....$38.00
Flintstones, Canadian, yel rim, w/thermos, EX+, M5 .....$125.00
Flintstones & Dino, orange rim, EX+, M5 ....$80.00
Fox & the Hound, 1981, w/thermos, EX, I2.....................$26.00
Fraggle Rock, 1984, w/thermos, EX, I2............................$18.00

Fraggle Rock, 1984, w/thermos, NM $30.00
Fruit Basket, 1975, EX $25.00
Fruit Basket, 1975, VG, N2 ....$15.00
Gene Autry Melody Ranch, Universal, 1954, no hdl, lt rust w/thermos (w/cork but no cup o/w EX), VG, I2 ......$200.00
Gene Autry Melody Ranch, Universal, 1954, w/unused thermos, NM+ $500.00
Ghostland, Ohio Art, 1977, w/spinner game on back, VG, I2..$25.00
GI Joe, 1967, VG+, N2...$75.00

GI Joe, Thermos, 1982, green rim, VG, $18.00.

Goober & the Ghost Chasers, 1974, EX $35.00
Great Wild West, 1959, VG+, N2.................................$395.00
Gremlins, 1984, VG back, EX front, I2 ....$9.00
Gremlins, 1984, w/thermos, VG+, N2 ....$15.00
Grizzly Adams, Aladdin, 1977, dome top, w/plastic thermos (EX), NM..$110.00
Gunsmoke, 1972, VG $50.00
Gunsmoke, 1973, stagecoach scene on back, NM, I2 ....$90.00
Hair Bear Bunch, 1971, VG+, N2.................................$25.00
Hansel & Gretel, 1982, EX...$45.00
Happy Children, 1974, bl, VG+, N2 ....$125.00
Hardy Boys, 1977, G+, N2 ....$12.00
Harlem Globetrotters, 1971, some flaking, w/thermos (EX+), VG+, I2 ....$40.00
Heathcliff, 1982, w/thermos (EX+), EX, I2....................$21.00
Hogan's Heroes, 1966, dome top, EX+, J2 ....$235.00
Holly Hobbie, 1973, orange rim, VG+, N2....................$15.00
Home Town Airport, 1960, dome top, EX, J2 ....$800.00
Hopalong Cassidy, 1950, bl w/mc decal, VG, J5 ....$65.00
Hopalong Cassidy, 1950, red, w/thermos, EX+, M5 ....$200.00
Hopalong Cassidy, 1954, full-face litho version, EX.......$225.00
Hot Wheels, 1969, lt rim wear & scratches, EX+, I2........$60.00
How the West Was Won, 1978, VG+, N2 ....$25.00
Howdy Doody, 1954, lt rust, EX, I2...............................$290.00
HR Pufnstuf, Aladdin, 1970, G, D9 ....$25.00
Huckleberry Hound & His Friends, 1961, yel background, VG+ $70.00
Indiana Jones, 1984, brn, VG+.......................................$20.00
Indiana Jones, 1984, G, N2...$8.00

Jonathan Livingston Seagull, 1973, w/thermos, VG+, N2 .$50.00
Julia, Thermos, 1969, EX+ $90.00
Jungle Book, 1968, EX, T1 ....$60.00
Junior Miss, 1956, girl w/big hat, VG, N2......................$15.00
Kid Power (Wee Pals), 1974, VG+, I2 ....$24.00
King Kong, 1976, NM...$50.00
Knight Rider, 1982, VG+, N2 ....$15.00
Kong Phooey, 1974, VG, N2...$33.00
Korg, 1975, VG+, N2...$27.00
Krofft Supershow, Aladdin, 1976, EX+, F8.....................$60.00
Krofft Supershow, Aladdin, 1976, w/thermos (G), VG+, I2 ..$45.00
Kung Fu, 1974, VG, N2...$25.00
Lamb w/Red Bow, 1980s, 2-hdl, EX, N2 ....$12.00
Land of the Giants, Aladdin, 1969, NM, C1 ....$155.00
Land of the Lost, 1975, sm dents, VG+, I2 ....$45.00
Lassie, Magic of; Thermos, 1978, NM, C1 ....$75.00
Laugh-In, 1968, helmet scene, w/thermos, EX, N2 ....$125.00
Little House on the Prairie, 1978, VG+ $50.00
Lone Ranger, 1954, red trim, EX+, M5...........................$260.00
Lone Ranger, Legend of, 1980, VG+, N2 ....$22.00
Looney Tunes TV Set, 1959, G+, M5...............................$60.00
Lost in Space, 1967, dome top, lt rubbing, EX+, I2 ....$350.00
Magic Kingdom, 1980, VG+, N2 ....$12.00
Marvel Comics Super Heroes, 1976, VG, N2 ....$15.00
Mary Poppins, 1964, VG+, N2..$60.00

Masters of the Universe, Aladdin, 1983, with thermos, NM, $10.00.

Mickey Mouse, unmk, 1929, Mickey & Minnie dancing & other Mickey figures playing instruments, pk background, rare, EX, A $1,700.00
Mickey Mouse Club, 1976, wht rim, EX $55.00
Mickey Mouse Club, 1977, red rim, VG, N2 ....$14.00
Miss America, 1972, G, N2 ....$14.00
Mod Tulips, 1962, dome top, EX, J2 ....$275.00
Monroes, 1967, EX, I2...$130.00
Mork & Mindy, King Seeley, 1979, w/plastic thermos, NM, C1...$65.00
Mork & Mindy, King Seeley, 1979, w/thermos, EX+, I2 ..$45.00
Mr Merlin, 1981, w/thermos, M $50.00
Mr Merlin, 1981, w/thermos, VG+ $30.00

Munsters, King Seeley Thermos, 1965, black rim, VG, J6, $195.00.

Muppet Babies, 1985, EX+, I2..$13.00
Muppet Show, 1978, EX, I2..$17.00
Muppets (Fozzie Bear), 1979, VG+, N2 ....$15.00
NC State University, old, pnt dome top, VG+, N2..........$35.00
NFL, 1975, stripes on band, VG, N2.................................$13.00
NFL, 1978, VG, I2 ....$12.00
Osmonds, 1973, EX, I2 ....$46.00
Pac-Man, 1980, w/thermos, M..$28.00
Pac-Man, 1980, w/thermos, no cup, EX, I2 ....$15.00
Paladin, 1960, EX+, M5 ....$170.00
Partridge Family, 1971, VG+...$35.00
Peanuts Baseball, 1980, w/thermos, NM...........................$25.00
Pebbles & Bamm-Bamm, 1971, red rim, w/thermos, EX, M5 ....$70.00
Pete's Dragon, 1977, VG+, N2...$28.00
Pigs in Space, 1977, VG-, N2 ....$14.00
Pink Panther & Sons, 1984, w/thermos, EX, N2 ....$25.00
Pit Stop, 1968, VG+ $90.00
Plaid, 1960s, no clasp, EX, N2...$20.00
Police Patrol, 1978, EX $135.00
Popeye, Aladdin, 1980, w/plastic thermos, NM................$40.00
Popeye, 1964, EX, N2 ....$150.00
Popeye, 1980, VG+, N2..$24.00
Racing Wheels, 1977, VG+, N2..$25.00
Raggedy Ann, 1973, w/thermos, VG+, N2 ....$20.00
Rambo, 1985, w/thermos, EX+, I2 ....$20.00
Rat Patrol, Canadian, yel rim, w/thermos, VG+, M5 ....$75.00
Red Barn, Thermos, 1958, dome top, open doors, NM+, C1 ....$82.00
Rescuers, 1977, VG+, I2 ....$25.00
Return of the Jedi, 1983, VG $20.00
Return of the Jedi, 1983, w/thermos, EX, I2/M5 ....$40.00
Rifleman, 1960, VG+ $190.00
Road Runner, 1970, lavender, EX $45.00
Road Runner, 1970, lavender, VG, M5 ....$30.00
Road Runner, 1970, lavender, w/thermos, yel cup, EX, I2..$60.00
Robin Hood, 1956, VG, N2 ....$75.00
Robin Hood, 1974, VG+, N2..$28.00

Ronald McDonald Sheriff of Cactus Canyon, Aladdin, 1982, with thermos, EX, $22.00.

Roscoe Recycling, NM $95.00
Rough Rider, 1972, VG+, N2...$37.00
Roy Rogers, 1955, rearing Trigger, w/thermos, EX, N2 ..$175.00
Roy Rogers & Dale Evans, 1954, Canadian, bl rim, w/thermos, VG+, M5 ....$90.00
Roy Rogers & Dale Evans Double R Bar Ranch, w/thermos (no cup), EX, J2..$150.00
Saddlebags, 1977, NM, N2...$140.00
Satellite, American Thermos, 1958-62, w/thermos, missing red cap, VG..$80.00
School Days, 1960, VG+ $45.00
Scooby Doo, 1973, EX..$45.00
Scotch Plaid, 1959, VG+, N2...$15.00
Secret Agent, 1968, EX+ $60.00
Secret of the Nimh, 1982, EX, N2 ....$15.00
Secret Wars, 1984, VG+, N2 ....$19.00
Sesame Street, 1979, G, I2..$9.00
Singer Sewing Machine, 1980s, 2-hdl, M $20.00
Six Million Dollar Man, 1978, VG+, N2.........................$17.00
Snow White, 1977, w/game, VG+, N2 ....$25.00
Solid Red, 1980s, 2-hdl, VG, N2......................................$6.00

Star Wars, 1977, with thermos, EX, J6, $65.00.

Space Shuttle Orbiter Enterprise, 1977, VG....................$25.00
Speed Buggy, 1973, VG, I2/N2.......................................$17.00
Sport Goofy, 1984, VG+, N2 ....$15.00
Sports Afield, 1957, VG-, N2..$58.00
Sports Skwirts, 1972, baseball, EX, N2............................$25.00
Stars & Stripes, 1970, dome top, EX, N2 ....$60.00
Steve Canyon, 1959, lt scratches, EX, I2 ....$180.00
Strawberry Shortcake, 1980, w/thermos, EX, I2/V1.........$15.00
Submarine, 1960, rope hdl, G+, I2..................................$30.00
Super Powers, 1983, EX+, I2 ....$25.00
Superman, 1978, w/thermos, VG, N2 ....$30.00
Tapestry, 1963, VG+ $25.00
Tarzan, Aladdin, 1966, NM, C1.....................................$125.00
Teenager, 1957, dome top, NM, I2 ....$75.00
Thundercats, 1985, EX $20.00
Thundercats, 1985, w/thermos, M....................................$30.00
Tom Corbett Space Cadet, 1952, bl, minor chips on decal o/w VG $85.00
Tom Corbett Space Cadet, 1952, red w/decal, incorrect thermos cap o/w EX, A $180.00
Tom Corbett Space Cadet, 1952, red w/decal, VG $100.00
Train, CP Rail, Canadian, 1970, M, N2 ....$35.00
Transformers, 1986, w/thermos, VG, N2 ....$17.00
Traveler, 1962, red trim, VG+ $25.00
UFO, Thermos, 1973, EX+, C1......................................$76.00
Universal Highway Markers, 1968, 1st design, VG+, N2 .$60.00
Universal's Movie Monsters, Aladdin, 1979, EX+, D9.....$50.00
US Mail, 1969, dome top, EX, N2, from $48 to...............$60.00
US Space Corps, 1961, w/thermos (no cup), NM $350.00
Valentine, 1980s, 2-hdl, EX, N2 ....$16.00
VW Bus, 1960s, dome top, lt scratches, w/thermos (M), EX, I2 ....$500.00
VW Bus, 1960s, rare, NM, T1.......................................$465.00
Wagon Train, 1964, VG, I2...$72.00
Walt Disney World, 1972, EX, I2.....................................$18.50
Waltons, 1975, EX, C1 ....$45.00
Waltons, 1984, w/thermos, VG+......................................$40.00
Weave Pattern, 1972, EX+ $20.00
Wild Frontier, 1977, VG+, N2 ....$30.00
Wonderful World, 1980, VG+, N2 ....$18.00
Woody Woodpecker, 1972, EX $90.00
Yankee Doodles, 1975, VG-, N2 ....$10.00
Ye Old Inn, 1950s, oval, 2-hdl, lg, VG+, N2 ....$25.00
Yogi Bear, 1974, purple rim, EX+, M5 ....$75.00
18 Wheeler, 1975, EX, N2...$44.00

Plastic

Alf, Thermos, 1987, red, w/thermos, EX-, I2 ....$10.00
Batman, 1982, bl, Joker w/1 wht glove, w/thermos, EX, I2 .$8.00
Batman, 1982, dk bl, no glove, w/thermos, VG+, N2.......$14.00
Batman Returns, 1992, blk, odd-shaped, w/thermos, complete, NM, C2 ....$9.00
Beauty & the Beast, 1991, purple, w/thermos, EX, I2 ....$7.00
Bozostuffs, 1988, red, w/thermos, EX, I2 ....$20.00
Bozostuffs, 1988, red, w/thermos, M, N2 ....$30.00
Cabbage Patch, 1983, yel, w/thermos, EX+, I2 ....$8.00
Ecology, 1980, dome top, w/thermos, EX, N2..................$35.00

Photo courtesy of June Moon.

Duck Tales, Aladdin, 1986, decal on blue, NM, $8.00.

Elephant, Hippo & Lion, 1986, EX, N2 ....$20.00
Flav-O-Rich, 1990, Atlantic Braves, EX, N2 ....$20.00
Garfield, 1978, Odie kissing Garfield, w/thermos, EX+, I2 .$8.00
Gumby, 1986, VG+, N2 ....$25.00
Jabber Jaw, 1977, aqua, puffy decal, EX, I2 ....$22.00
Jem, 1986, purple, w/thermos, EX, I2 ....$5.00
Jetsons: The Movie, 1990, w/thermos, M, N2 ....$25.00
Kellogg's Corn Flakes, 1985, w/thermos, EX+, N2 ....$50.00
Little Orphan Annie, 1988, w/thermos, NM $30.00
Lunch 'N Tunes, 1986, bear on beach, works, EX, N2 .....$40.00
Mickey & Donald, 1986, on seesaw, w/thermos, EX, I2......$5.00
Mickey Mouse on Skateboard, 1980, red, w/thermos, EX, I2 .$4.50
Minnie Mouse (head), 1992, thick, EX $20.00
Mr T, 1984, orange, w/thermos, EX, I2 ....$12.00
Muppets, 1981, dome lid, w/thermos, EX, I2 ....$9.00
New Kids on the Block, 1990, orange, w/thermos, EX, I2 ..$8.00
Pee-Wee's Playhouse, 1987, pk, w/thermos, complete, EX+, I2..$18.00
Punky Brewster, 1984, w/thermos, EX, I2 ....$15.00
Pup Named Scooby Doo, 1988, w/thermos, M, N2 ....$23.00
Real Ghostbusters, 1986, purple, EX, I2 ....$4.00
Return of the Jedi, 1983, red, R2-D2 & Wicket pictured, EX, I2..$20.00
Ring Raiders, 1988, Aladdin, bl, w/thermos (G), EX, I2 ....$3.00
Rocketeer, Aladdin/Disney, 1991, bl, w/mc thermos, M, P4.$20.00
Shirt Tales, 1980, bl, EX, I2..$4.00
Sky Box, blk, 7 ads on box, EX, N2 ....$20.00
Snoopy, 1978, dome lid, bl, EX, I2 ....$8.00
Star Com US Space Force, 1987, w/thermos, M, N2........$20.00
Teenage Mutant Ninja Turtles, 1990, bl, w/decaled thermos, EX, I2...$5.00
Tom & Jerry: The Movie, 1992, VG+, N2 ....$20.00
Wizard of Oz, 1989, w/thermos, VG, N2...........................$25.00
Yogi's Treasure Hunt, 1987, w/thermos, NM, N2.............$28.00
101 Dalmatians, 1990, red, w/thermos, EX, I2 ....$8.00

Vinyl

Alvin & the Chipmunks, 1963, gr, EX+, I2....................$250.00

Annie, 1981, w/thermos, NM...$40.00
Ballerina on Lily Pad, 1960s, pk, VG+, N2 ....$125.00
Banana Splits, w/metal thermos, NM, M5 ....$360.00
Barbarino, 1977, bl, brunch bag, w/thermos, EX+, I2.....$175.00
Beatles, brunch bag, bl w/zippered top & oval form, mc photo on front, EX-, B3...$410.00
Boston Red Sox, 1960, EX...$60.00
Bullwinkle, 1962, yel, sm split on bottom o/w VG, I2....$400.00
Captain Kangaroo, 1964, EX, N2.....................................$300.00
Carousel, 1962, bl, w/thermos (G), EX, I2.......................$270.00
Deputy Dog, Thermos, 1962, EX, J2.................................$350.00
Donny & Marie, 1977, long hair, NM, J2...........................$90.00
Donny & Marie, 1978, short hair, EX, N2 ....$75.00
First Union Bank, 1980s, soft, zippered, EX, N2 ....$20.00
Leo Lion, 1978, drawstring, NM, N2 ....$75.00
Liddle Kiddles, 1968, bl, w/metal thermos (NM+), EX+, I2..$200.00
Lion in the Cart, 1985, puffy, VG+ $40.00
Lion in the Van, 1978, M..$120.00
Love, 1974, wht, brunch bag, 1 girl, w/thermos, EX+, I2 .$165.00
Peanuts, 1969, red, Snoopy looking into mailbox, NM, N2..$89.00
Peanuts, 1969, red, Snoopy looking into mailbox, VG+, N2...$50.00
Psychedelic, 1968, brunch bag, tall, EX, I2 ....$35.00
Roy Rogers Saddlebag, 1960, brn, EX+, I2 ....$225.00
Saturday Evening Post, 2-hdl, EX, N2................................$35.00
Skipper, lt bl, minor tears o/w EX, M5 ....$65.00
Snoopy, 1977, yel, brunch bag, EX, N2 ....$65.00
Speedy Turtle, 1978, drawstring, EX, N2 ....$39.00
Tic Tac Toe, 1970s, red, VG+, N2 ....$35.00
Twiggy, brunch bag, EX+ $230.00
Twiggy, 1967, rectangular, EX+ $150.00
Wizard & the Van, 1978, VG, N2 ....$45.00

Thermoses

Addams Family, 1974, plastic, no cup, EX, I2..................$15.00
Aladdin (Disney's), plastic, full litho, complete, EX, I2 .....$3.00
Auto Race, 1967, metal, NM $30.00
Beverly Hillbillies, 1963, metal, EX, J2 ....$45.00
Biker Mice From Mars, 1994, plastic, full litho, EX, I2.......$3.00
Bionic Woman, 1978, G..$12.00
Boating, 1959, metal, EX, J2..$70.00
Bonanza, 1963, metal, no cup, EX....................................$40.00
Buccaneer, metal, brn cap, EX+, M5.................................$65.00
Chuck Wagon, 1958, metal, no cup, sm dent, EX, I2 ....$42.00
Corsage, 1958, no cup, EX, J2..$20.00
Dick Tracy: The Movie, plastic, EX, I2 ....$2.00
Dino-Riders, 1988, plastic, complete, EX, I2......................$4.00
Disco, 1979, plastic, cracked orange cup, EX, I2 ....$12.00
Disneyland, 1959, metal, w/riverboat scene, NM, I2/J2....$60.00
Donny & Mary, 1976, plastic, long-hair version, w/yel cup, no stopper, NM, I2...$12.00
Flintstones, 1964, metal, yel, picnic table scene, EX $45.00
Flintstones, 1964, metal, yel, picnic table scene, G, I2.....$28.00
Flying Nun, 1968, metal, no cup or stopper, VG+, I2 ......$33.00
Go-Go, 1966, NM, J2..$40.00
Green Hornet, 1967, metal, red cup, EX+, I2.................$80.00
Hee Haw, 1970, NM..$45.00
Holly Hobbie, 1979, plastic, complete, EX-, I2 ....$6.00

Hong Kong Phooey, 1975, plastic, no cup, lt litho wear, EX-, I2...$10.00

Hopalong Cassidy, 1954, full litho, w/cup but no stopper, EX+, I2...$90.00

Hopalong Cassidy, 1954, no cup or stopper, VG, J2.........$45.00

Hot Wheels, 1969, EX, J2...$25.00

Hot Wheels, 1969, NM, C1...$40.00

Howdy Doody, 1977, plastic, dk red cup, EX, I2...............$12.00

HR Pufnstuf, 1970, plastic, complete, NM, I2..................$35.00

Huckleberry Hound, Aladdin, 1961, NM+.......................$58.00

It's a Small World, metal, wht cup, EX+, I2.....................$38.00

James Bond 007, 1966, metal, NM, I2..............................$60.00

Junior Nurse, 1963, metal, EX+, I2.................................$45.00

Kewtie Pie, all metal, red cap, no cup, EX, I2.................$45.00

King Kong, 1977, plastic, NM+, I2...................................$13.50

Land of the Giants, 1968, plastic w/glass liner, EX+.........$28.00

Life & Times of Grizzly Adams, 1977, plastic, complete, EX, I2...$15.00

Looney Tunes, 1959, no cup, EX.......................................$40.00

Mary Poppins, 1964, metal, sm dents, EX-, I2..................$32.00

Nintendo Super Mario Bros, 1988, plastic, EX+, I2............$2.00

Partridge Family, King Seeley, 1971, metal, NM..............$35.00

Peanuts, 1966, metal, playing baseball, gr cup, EX, I2......$11.00

Pinocchio, 1971, NM, I2...$30.00

Princess, 1962, metal, red cap, wht cup, EX, I2...............$15.00

Road Runner, Thermos, 1970-73, metal, NM...................$35.00

Robin Hood, 1956, gr cap, EX, M5..................................$40.00

Rocketeer, 1990, plastic, M, I2..$8.00

Scooby Doo, 1973, plastic, NM.......................................$15.00

Sigmund & the Sea Monsters, 1974, plastic, no cup, EX+, I2...$30.00

Six Million Dollar Man, 1974, plastic, NM, I2....................$9.00

Space: 1999, 1976, plastic, EX...$15.00

Star Wars, 1978, plastic, EX..$15.00

Superman, Canadian, red cap, rare, EX+, M5...................$45.00

Superman, plastic, NM..$10.00

Tammy, 1964, metal, NM...$45.00

Tarzan, Canadian, red cap, EX+, M5...............................$35.00

Tarzan, 1966, EX, J2...$40.00

Yellow Submarine, NM, J6, $140.00.

Photo courtesy of June Moon.

Tom Corbett Space Cadet, 1952, metal, no cup, lt rubbings, VG, I2...$45.00

Universal Movie Monsters, 1979, plastic, no cup, NM, I2 .$20.00

Wild Bill Hickok, 1955, Canadian, red cap, EX $40.00

Wild Bill Hickok, 1955, no top or cup, EX $35.00

18 Wheeler, 1978, plastic, sipper stopper, worn litho, G, I2 ..$2.00

19th Hole, golf motif, built-in straw, soft vinyl, golf ball-shaped top, EX, I2...$9.00

Marbles

Antique marbles are divided into several classifications: 1) Transparent Swirl (Solid Core, Latticinio Core, Divided Core, Ribbon Core, Lobed Core, and Coreless); 2) Lutz or Lutz-type (with bands having copper flecks which alternate with colored or clear bands); 3) Peppermint Swirl (made of red, white, and blue opaque glass); 4) Indian Swirl (black with multicolored surface swirls); Banded Swirl (wide swirling bands on opaque or transparent glass); 6) Onionskin (having an overall mottled appearance due to its spotted, swirling lines or lobes); 7) End of Day (single pontil, allover spots, either 2-colored or multicolored); 8) Clambroth (evenly spaced, swirled lines on opaque glass); 9) Mica (transparent color with mica flakes added); 10) Sulphide (nearly always clear, colored examples are rare, containing figures). Besides glass marbles, some were made of clay, pottery, china, steel, and even semiprecious stones.

Most machine-made marbles are still very reasonable, but some of the better examples may sell for $50.00 and up, depending the colors that were used and how they are defined. Guineas (Christensen agates with small multicolored specks instead of swirls) sometime go for as much as $200.00. Mt. Peltier comic character marbles often bring prices of $100.00 and more with Betty Boop, Moon Mullins and Kayo being the rarest and most valuable.

From the nature of their use, mint-condition marbles are extremely rare and may be worth as much as three to five times more than one that is near-mint, while chipped and cracked marbles may be worth half or less. The same is true of one that has been polished, regardless of how successful the polishing was. If you'd like to learn more, Everett Grist has written three books on the subject that you will find helpful: *Antique and Collectible Marbles*, *Machine Made and Contemporary Marbles*, and *Everett Grist's Big Book of Marbles*.

Artist-made, crown filigree & peppermints, contemporary, by Bill Burchfield, 1", M..$35.00

Artist-made, swirl or end-of-day, contemporary, by Mark Matthews, 1½", M...$60.00

Banded Opaque, gr & wht, 2", M...............................$1,200.00

Banded Opaque, red & wht, 1¾", M..........................$1,200.00

Banded Opaque, red & wht, ¾", M..................................$95.00

Banded Opaque, semiopaque w/translucent pk bands, ¾", NM...$40.00

Banded Transparent Swirl, bl, ¾", M...............................$75.00

Banded Transparent Swirl, lt gr, 1¾", M.........................$600.00

Bennington, bl, 1¾", M..$40.00

Bennington, brn, 1¾", M $30.00

Bennington, fancy, 1¾", M $80.00
China, decorated, glazed, w/apple, 1¾", M $800.00
China, decorated, glazed, w/rose, 1¾", M $800.00
China, decorated, glazed, wht w/geometrics, 1¾", M $125.00
China, decorated, unglazed, w/geometrics & flowers, ¾", M..$200.00
Clambroth, opaque, bl & wht, 1¾", M $2,600.00
Clambroth, opaque, bl & wht, ¾", M $250.00
Clambroth, opaque blk base w/wht stripes, ¾", M...........$60.00
Comic, Andy Gump, M..$90.00
Comic, Betty Boop, M......................................$150.00
Comic, Cotes Bakery, M....................................$700.00
Comic, Kayo, rare, M......................................$150.00
Comic, Little Orphan Annie, M.............................$100.00
Comic, Moon Mullins, M....................................$175.00
Comic, Popeye, M...$70.00
Comic, set of 12, M.....................................$1,500.00
Comic, Skeezix, M...$100.00
Comic, Tom Mix, M.......................................$1,800.00

Comic Strip Characters, Peltier Glass, complete set of 20, MIB, $2,000.00.

Divided Core Swirl, bl-tinted glass w/mc inner & outer bands, 1⅞", NM..$150.00
Divided Core Swirl, bl-tinted glass w/red, wht & bl inner bands, wht outer bands, 1¼", NM.............................$80.00
End-of-Day, bl & wht, 1¾", M...........................$1,100.00
End-of-Day, onionskin lutz, pk & wht core, ½", NM.......$90.00
End-of-Day, onionskin w/mica, opaque core w/transparent bl & red splotches, 1½", EX.............................$110.00
End-of-Day, onionskin w/mica, yel w/2 red & gr panels, 1½", NM..$75.00
Goldstone, ¾", M...$35.00
Indian, slag-type, opaque blk base w/dk red bands, ¾", NM .$40.00
Indian Swirl, lutz-type, gold flakes, ¾", M...............$600.00
Indian Swirl, 1¾", M....................................$1,500.00
Latticinio Core, bright orange core, mc outer bands, ⅝", NM+, A...$90.00
Latticinio Core, broken-cane core swirl, mc outer bands, ground bottom pole, 1⅛", NM, A.............................$345.00
Latticinio Core, orange core, clear w/tiny stretched bubbles, transparent outer bands, ¾", NM+, A....................$85.00
Latticinio Core, wht & yel core, red- & bl-banded outer layer, 2", EX+, A...$155.00

Latticinio Core, wht core, transparent purple & gr outer bands, 1⅜", EX+, A..$50.00
Latticinio Core, wht core swirl, orange & blk outer bands, 1", EX+, A...$40.00
Latticinio Core, 4 mc bands on wht outer layer, wide core, 2", VG, A..$65.00
Machine-made, carnelian oxblood, Akro Agate, ½" to ¾", M...$100.00
Machine-made, lemonade & oxblood, Akro Agate, ½" to ¾", M..$75.00
Machine-made, lt aqua slag w/rotating wht spirals, MF Christensen & Sons, ⅝", M.....................................$50.00
Machine-made, oxblood swirl, Akro Agate, ½" to ¾", M.$20.00
Machine-made, purple slag, melted pontil, ⅞", NM........$40.00
Machine-made, red & wht, Am Christensen Agate, ⅝", M .$65.00
Machine-made, transparent brn w/opaque swirls, MF Christensen & Sons, ¾", M..$35.00
Onionskin, wht w/bl, red & gr specks, 1⅜", M.............$150.00
Onionskin, 16-lobe, unusual, 1¾", M....................$1,800.00
Onionskin, 4-lobe, 1¼", M................................$450.00
Opaque Swirl, gr, ¾", M...................................$75.00
Opaque Swirl, lutz-type, bl, yel & gr, ¾", M.............$325.00
Peppermint Swirl, opaque, red, wht & bl, 1¾", M $3,000.00
Peppermint Swirl, opaque, red, wht & bl, ¾", M $125.00

Peppermint Swirl, pink and blue bands, ¾", NM, A, $50.00.

Pottery, 1¾", M..$45.00
Ribbon Core, 2 wide mc bands form core, 1¾", NM (polished), A...$75.00
Solid Core, opaque orange interior w/wht strands, mc bands form outer layer, 1¼", NM (polished), A $70.00
Solid Core, opaque wht w/transparent mc strands, mc outer layer, ⅞", NM, A...$35.00
Solid Core, opaque wht w/yel strands in middle, mc outer bands, 1¾", VG+, A...$85.00
Sulfide, alligator, 1¾", M...............................$160.00
Sulfide, angel face w/wings, 1¾", M....................$1,000.00
Sulfide, bear, upright, begging, gr tint to glass, 2¼", NM+, A..$210.00
Sulfide, bird, below average detail, 1⅞", EX+, A.........$100.00
Sulfide, bird, 2", EX.....................................$150.00
Sulfide, boar, 1⅞", EX...................................$160.00
Sulfide, bust of George Washington, 2⅜", NM.............$650.00
Sulfide, bust of Jenny Lind, 1½", G+, A..................$260.00
Sulfide, bust statue, off-center, 1½", M, A..............$625.00
Sulfide, cat, 1¼", M.....................................$100.00
Sulfide, child sitting, 1¾", M...........................$600.00

Sulfide, child w/hammer, 1¾", M $600.00
Sulfide, child w/sailboat, 1¾", M $650.00
Sulfide, circus bear, 2", NM+, A $140.00

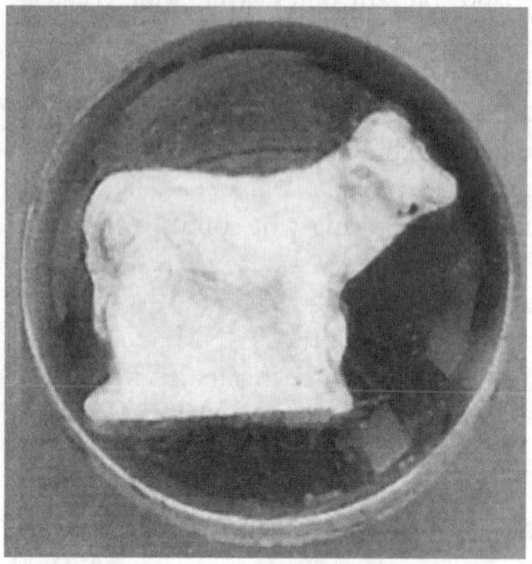

Sulfide, cow, 1⅞", NM, A, $200.00.

Sulfide, crucifix, 1¾", M $600.00
Sulfide, dbl eagle, rare, 1¾", M $675.00
Sulfide, dog, 1¾", M $125.00
Sulfide, dog w/bird in mouth, 1¾", M....................................$900.00
Sulfide, donkey, 2", NM, A $130.00
Sulfide, dove, 1⅝", M $160.00
Sulfide, duck, seated, 1¾", M, A $90.00
Sulfide, duck seated on mound of grass, 1¼", NM............$50.00
Sulfide, eagle w/half-spread wings, 1¾", NM, A............$130.00
Sulfide, elephant, standing, sea gr glass, 1¾", NM, A $400.00
Sulfide, fish, 1½", NM+, A $170.00
Sulfide, fox, 1½", EX $130.00
Sulfide, goat, standing, 2¼", VG+, A $160.00
Sulfide, goat, 1¾", M....................................$125.00
Sulfide, hen, 1⅛", M $100.00
Sulfide, horse, lg, prancing, off-center, 1½", NM, A......$185.00
Sulfide, horse, rearing, below average detail, 1⅞", M (polished), A $75.00
Sulfide, lamb, lt amber, 1¾", M $1,600.00
Sulfide, lamb, 1¾", NM....................................$125.00
Sulfide, lion, seated male, lt rose-colored glass, 1⅞", EX+, A...$550.00
Sulfide, lion, standing, off-center, 1½", M....................................$130.00
Sulfide, lion, standing, 1¾", NM+, A....................................$285.00
Sulfide, lion w/see-through hole under stomach, 1¼", M, A $170.00
Sulfide, Little Boy Blue, 1¾", M $700.00
Sulfide, monkey seated on drum, above average detail, 1⅜", NM, A $200.00
Sulfide, mythical figure, kneeling on 1 leg w/hands under chin, tall rabbit-like ears, 1¼", EX+, A $130.00
Sulfide, Nipper dog, lt sea foam gr-colored glass, 1¾", NM-, A $350.00
Sulfide, otter, 1½", M....................................$135.00
Sulfide, owl, standing, 2", NM, A $130.00
Sulfide, owl w/wings spread, 1¾", M....................................$375.00
Sulfide, papoose, 1¾", M....................................$700.00
Sulfide, pig, 2", M $180.00
Sulfide, pony, 1¾", M....................................$200.00
Sulfide, rabbit, crouching, ears intact, 1½", M, A $110.00
Sulfide, rabbit, sprinting over grass, 1⅞", NM $150.00
Sulfide, raccoon, 2", M $200.00
Sulfide, rooster, 1¾", M....................................$150.00
Sulfide, Santa Claus, 1¾", M $1,200.00
Sulfide, sheep, 1¾", M....................................$150.00
Sulfide, squirrel, standing, 1¾", M $170.00
Sulfide, squirrel w/nut, 2", EX $200.00

Marx

Louis Marx founded his company in New York in the 1920s. He was a genius not only at designing toys but also marketing them. His business grew until it became one the largest toy companies ever to exist, eventually expanding to include several factories in the United States as well as other countries. Marx sold his company in the early 1970s; he died in 1982. Though toys of every description were produced, collectors today admire his mechanical toys above all others.

Advisor: Scott Smiles (S10), windups; Tom Lastrapes (L4), battery-ops.

See also Advertising; Banks; Character, TV and Movie Collectibles; Dollhouse Furniture; Games; Guns; Plastic Figures; Playsets; and other categories. For toys made by Linemar (Marx's subsidiary in Japan) see Battery-Operated Toys; Windups, Friction and Other Mechanicals.

Battery-Operated

Agent .012 Car, 1960s, MIB, M17 ....$125.00
Aircraft Carrier, 20", EX, L4 ....$375.00
Alley the Roaring Stalking Alligator, MIB, L4...............$475.00
Amphibious Military Vehicle w/Soldiers, forward & reverse action, plastic, complete, 9", EX+ (EX+ box), A $145.00
Atomic Submarine, advances w/lights, press buttons to release rockets, tin, remote control, 14", rare, NM (EX box), A $260.00

Big Parade, soldiers march together with drum in front, 15" long, MIB, $300.00.

Bengal Tiger, NM, L4.......................................$100.00

Brewster the Rooster, plush rooster travels around, lifts head, opens beak & crows, 10", MIB $225.00

Buttons the Puppy w/a Brain, non-working o/w VG, I2 .$110.00

Clang-Clang Locomotive, early 1960s, advances w/lights & sound, 13", MIB $85.00

Colonel Hap Hazard, walks while arms move & antenna spins, mostly tin, 12", NMIB.......................$1,500.00

Electric Convertible, forward & reverse action, red & wht, litho tin, 20", EX+ (VG box), A...........................$335.00

Electric Robot, side-to-side motion w/light-up eyes & buzzing sound, red & blk plastic, 15", NMIB.......................$425.00

Electric Robot & Son, advances & lifts baby robot up & down, light-up eyes & buzzer, plastic, 16", EX (orig box) ..$450.00

Flashy Flickers, plastic picture gun shows 16 comic characters on flat surface, complete w/5 films, 16", MIB, A $110.00

Fred Flintstone on Dino, plush, tin and plastic, 19", MIB, $795.00.

Futuristic Airport, plane circles airport, remote control, 16x16" base, EX (orig box), A................................$385.00

G-Man Car, 1930s, red & cream pressed steel w/rubber tires, working lights, 14", VG+, T1...................................$465.00

Great Garbo Robot, w/orig medallion, working, EX+, T1 .$500.00

Hootin' Hollerin' Haunted House, litho tin, NM, T1 ..$1,150.00

Marx-A-Copter, 1958, plastic copter circles pylon, bombs sub & rescues men, missing tower & battery cover, NMIB, P4......$50.00

Marx-A-Serve Table Tennis, MIB, rare, L4 ....$200.00

Mickey Mouse on Big-Wheel, advances w/sound, NMIB..$275.00

Mickey the Musician, 1950s, plastic Mickey leans over & plays tin xylophone on sq tin base, 12", VG, A................$260.00

Mighty Kong, advances in chains, beats chest & moves mouth, plush, tin & vinyl, remote control, 11", NM (EX+ box), A $615.00

Moon Scout Helicopter, MIB, L4 ....$150.00

Mr Mercury, walks, bends over & grasps objects, tin & plastic, remote control, 13", EX, A.........................$345.00

Nutty Mad Car, vinyl head flips around in litho car w/crazy actions & engine noise, 9", working, lt rust o/w EX+, T1 ....$285.00

Nutty Mad Indian, Indian rocks while beating drum, tongue moves as war hoops are made, tin & vinyl, 12", MIB, M17 ...$175.00

Whistling Spooky Kooky Tree, bump-&-go w/swinging arms, mouth emits whistling sound, tin & vinyl, 13", NM (EX box), A $2,000.00

Pressed Steel

Army Transport Truck, mk USA 41573147, orig canvas top, 13½", NM...$250.00

Auto Transport, Cross Country Transportation Service decals, truck carries cars on top, 23", EX+ (EX box), A......$265.00

Auto Transport, 1950s, truck w/ramps carries 2 plastic Yellow Cabs, 13", NM (EX+ box), A...................................$250.00

Caterpiller Tractor w/Snow Blade & Wagon, 1930s, w/driver, 20", VG, A...$200.00

Delivery Truck, 1950s, Inter-City Delivery Service on side, red & white, w/2-wheeler & ad boxes, 16", EX (EX box), A $475.00

Deluxe Delivery Truck Rider, 1940s, 25", NM, A..........$400.00

Earth Hauler w/Scoop, ca 1964, heavy gauge steel, F5 .....$90.00

Fire Hose Truck, American-La France, 21", EX $300.00

Fire Truck Rider, 1950s, crank-action siren sound, litho tin side plates mk VFD, 30", NM, A...................................$425.00

Garbage Truck, wht w/blk & red letters on van, rear door slides open, litho tin wheels, 13", VG+ $220.00

Giant Reversing Tractor Truck, w/plastic driver & accessories, 14", EX+ (VG+ box), A...................................$350.00

Gold Star Hauler w/Van & Trailer, 1950s, red & wht w/plastic tires, rear doors open, 21", NM (EX box) $330.00

Highway Emergency Truck with Blinker Lights, marked Day-Night Service, black and white with black Lumar tires, 18", NM (EX box), A, $400.00.

Ice Truck, red & yel w/Polar Ice Co decal, tin balloon tires, complete w/ice cubes & tongs, 12", MIB $545.00

Ice Truck, red cab w/wht dump, ICE on sides, lg headlights & molded fender skirts, VG...................................$100.00

Lumar Coal Truck, red & bl, blk tires w/red hubs, 11¼", G ...$40.00

Lumar Contractors Load & Dump Truck, 1950s, red, yel & wht, 15", NM (VG+ box), A $260.00

Lumar Utility Service Truck & Accessories, complete, NM (EX box), A...$435.00

Lumar Wrecker Service Truck, Dial Lumar 1-234 on door, bright litho w/blk-pnt Lumar tires, 16", NM, A $285.00

Marx-A-Haul Dump Truck, NM (EX+ box), T1 ....$125.00

Stake Bed Truck w/Advertising Cartons & Banks, #1008, blk w/red plastic stake bed, Lumar tires, 19", NM (NM box), A $300.00

Steam Roller, ca 1940, chrome-plated, 11", EX...............$65.00

Studebaker Steam Shovel Truck, VG+ $165.00

Toy Town Express Van Lines Deluxe Service, red, wht & bl, open cab, molded fender skirts, VG......................$175.00

US Army Jeep w/Searchlight Trailer, blk Lumar tires, 22", NM (NM box) $275.00

US Navy Jeep w/Searchlight Trailer, 1950s, trailer w/plastic engine & battery-op searchlight, 21", MIB.............$585.00

Utility Service Truck, 1950s, mk Public Utility Service, complete w/tarpaulin & accessories, 17", EX+ (VG+ box), A.................$425.00

Willys Jeep w/Lights & Trailer, red & bl w/blk rubber tires, battery-op lights, 21", NM (EX box), A.......................$350.00

Wrecker Truck Rider, 1950s, mk 24 Hour Radio Dispatched Towing Service, red, wht & bl, 31", EX+ (EX box), A.................$560.00

Windups, Frictions and Other Mechanicals

Amos 'N Andy Fresh Air Taxi, 1930s, Amos 'N Andy w/dog in open car, crazy action, litho tin, 8", EX $800.00

Amos 'N Andy Fresh Air Taxi, 1930s, Amos 'N Andy w/dog in open car, crazy action, litho tin, 8", NM+ (G box).$1,700.00

Amos Walker, litho tin figure wearing 'Taxi' hat, eyes move, 11", EX (orig box) $800.00

Archie Jalopy, Mexico, litho tin w/comical sayings in Spanish, 7", EX+, A.......................$300.00

Archie Jalopy, 1975, mc plastic, MIB $125.00

Army Staff Car, early 1950s, EX, J6, $85.00.

Army Truck, 1920s, litho tin w/cloth cover mk USA Army Truck, C-style cab w/simulated spoked wheels, 10½", EX, A $300.00

Automatic Car Wash Garage, mk Mid Town, car goes in & out of car wash, litho tin & plastic, EX+ (VG+ box) $350.00

Balky Mule, 1950s, donkey pulls farmer in 2-wheeled cart w/crazy action, litho tin, 8", EX+ $150.00

Ballerina, 1930s, pull rod out & she spins, litho tin, 6", EX+ (G box)..................$200.00

Bedrock Express, 1962, train w/litho Flintstones characters advances, 12", EX+, A..................$250.00

BO Plenty, advances while holding baby Sparkles, tips his hat, litho tin, 8", EX $200.00

BO Plenty, advances while holding baby Sparkles, tips his hat, litho tin, 8", MIB..................$350.00

Buck Rogers Rocket Police Patrol, 1927, advances w/sparks & sound, litho tin, 11½", NM+ (VG rare box)........$2,000.00

Buck Rogers Rocket Police Patrol, 1927, advances w/sparks & sound, litho tin, 11½", VG $1,000.00

Buck Rogers 25th Century Rocket Ship, 1930s, advances w/sound & sparks, tin w/celluloid shield, 13", EX (EX box) $1,400.00

Buck Rogers 25th Century Rocket Ship, 1930s, advances w/sound & sparks, tin w/celluloid shield, 13", G $800.00

Busy Miners, coal cart w/2 miners travels track from station house to coal mine, litho tin, 16", NM (EX box) $350.00

Camouflage Fighting Tank, advances on tread w/moving gun & firing sounds, 9", EX $150.00

Careful Johnnie, Johnnie drives car w/non-fall action, plastic & tin, 6½", EX.................$100.00

Champion Skater, 1930s, pull out rod & skater spins, litho tin, 6", rare, NM (VG box), A.................$400.00

Charleston Trio, 1921, G $500.00

Charleston Trio, 1921, jigger dances, boy plays violin & dog w/cane jumps atop cabin w/litho audience, 10", EX ..$900.00

Charlie McCarthy and Mortimer Snerd Coupe, 1930s, travels with actuated bumpers, heads turn, lithographed tin, 15", EX, $1,800.00.

Charlie McCarthy in His Benzine Buggy, 1938, advances in erratic motion as Charlie's head spins, 7", EX (orig box) $1,000.00

Charlie McCarthy in His Benzine Buggy, 1938, 7", EX..$700.00

Charlie McCarthy Walker, moves side to side as jaws open & close, 8", EX.................$350.00

Charlie McCarthy Walker, moves side to side as jaws open & close, 8", NM+ (VG box).................$650.00

Chicken Snatcher, see Hey-Hey Chicken Snatcher

Climbing Fireman, plastic & tin, NM (G box) $250.00

Coo-Coo Car, 1931, advances in circular motion w/full-figure driver moving up & down, 8", EX, from $650 to $750.00

Cowboy Rider, ca 1939, rearing horse vibrates as cowboy spins lariat overhead & aims gun, 8¼", MIB, from $350 to.....$400.00

Dagwood Aeroplane, 1935, travels w/crazy action as Dagwood's head bobs, litho tin, 9", NMIB, from $1,500 to....$1,600.00

Dagwood the Driver, Dagwood in crazy car, litho tin, 8", NMIB, from $1,300 to $1,400.00

Dapper Dan Coon Jigger, 1925, w/up & insert coin in slot & jigger dances on stage, litho tin, 10", VG, from $500 to.......$550.00

Daredevil Motor Drome & Car, place car in drome & shove for action, litho tin w/plastic drome, NM (EX+ box), A ..$400.00

Dick Tracy Siren Squad Car, metallic gr w/various characters lithoed in windows, battery-op light, 11", NMIB $450.00

Dick Tracy Sparkling Riot Car, mk Squad Car No 1, various characters in windows, litho tin, friction, 6", EX (EX box), A.................$245.00

Dippy Dumper, 1930s, travels in circles as driver gets thrown out & dumpster lifts, tin & celluloid, 9", EX (G box), A....$1,800.00

Disney Parade Roadster, tin w/plastic Minnie, Goofy, Donald & Nephew, 11", NM+ (EX+ box), A $1,200.00

Disney Turnover Tank, WDP/Mexico, 1950s, Goofy creates turnover action, Daisy litho on turret, 4", rare, EX, A $750.00

Disneyland Jeep, litho tin w/fold-down windshield, friction, 9", EX (EX box), A $250.00

Donald Duck Duet, 1946, Goofy dances atop base as Donald plays drum, lithographed tin, 11", EX, $750.00.

Donald Duck Duet, 1946, lg Goofy & sm Donald standing on drums, litho tin, 10", MIB.....................................$1,300.00

Donald Duck Duet, 1946, 10", M $1,000.00

Donald Duck Twirly Tail, 1950s, vibrates around as tail spins, plastic, 6", NM (EX+ box) $300.00

Donald Duck Twirly Tail, 1950s, 6", EX+ $150.00

Donkey Cart, 1950, 2 donkeys pull wagon w/litho barrels, tin, 10", NM (G box)...$200.00

Dopey Walker, 1938, advances in vibrating motion as his eyes move up & down, litho tin, 8", EX, A $350.00

Dopey Walker, 1938, 8", VG $250.00

Doughboy Tank, 1930s, advances w/erratic motion, guns move & soldier pops up, litho tin, 9", EX+ (EX+ box), from $500 to..$550.00

Dumbo Carousel, 3 Dumbos travel in circle, 1 w/mallet hits musical keys, litho characters on top & base, 7" dia, EX, A $650.00

Farm Set w/Tractor & Mower, NMIB.............................$200.00

Ferdinand the Bull, 1938, vibrates around w/spinning tail, tin, 6", EX (NM box), from $250 to $300.00

Fighting Tank, travels on blk rubber treads w/gun noise, 10", needs new flint o/w EX (G box)...............................$250.00

Fire Chief Car, 1949, advances w/siren sound & battery-op roof light, litho tin, 11", EX, A...$200.00

Fire House, 1930s, Fire House & General Alarm garages on base, pull alarm box levers & cars exit, tin, EX (EX box) ..$325.00

Flash Gordon Rocket Fighter, 1939, litho tin, 12", G $300.00

Flintstone Flivver, 1962, Fred as driver, litho tin w/vinyl figure, 4", EX (orig box)..$650.00

Flintstone Friction Car, Barney in tin replica of his car w/log body, canopy & granite wheels, friction, 7", EX, A.$300.00

Flintstone Pals, Barney riding Dino, litho tin & vinyl, 8½", VG $325.00

Flintstone Pals, Fred riding Dino, litho tin & vinyl, 8½", EX $450.00

Flintstones, see also Bedrock Express, Fred Flintstone Tricycle, Hopping Dino, Hopping Fred Flintstone

Flippo the Jumping Dog, 1930s, performs somersaults, blk & wht litho tin, 4", NM (EX box), from $300 to $325.00

Flutterfly, 1930s, wings flap, litho tin w/celluloid wings, 5", VG+ (VG scarce box)...$75.00

Fred Flintstone Tricycle, litho tin, 4", NM (worn box)..$500.00

Funny Face Walker, smiling Black man w/lg head, 11", G $400.00

Funny Flivver, 1926, eccentric car w/comical driver advances in erratic motion, 7", EX+ (EX+ box) $900.00

Golden Pecking Goose, advances & pecks ground, comes w/4 eggs to insert near tail, litho tin, 9½", EX (NM box)........$250.00

Goofy the Gardener, Goofy pushes cart, litho tin, EX, from $475 to..$500.00

Harold Lloyd Funny Face Walker, 1929, face changes expressions as he advances, 11", rpl arms, VG $650.00

Hee-Haw the Balky Mule, mk England, litho tin, NM (EX box), H7 ....$350.00

Hey Hey Chicken Snatcher, 1927, lithographed tin, 8½", VG, from $1,100.00 to $1,200.00.

Honeymoon Express, 1930, locomotive & cars circle base w/3 tunnels & station house, litho tin, EX, from $175 to $200.00

Honeymoon Express, 1930, locomotive & cars circle base w/3 tunnels & station house, litho tin, EX (G box), from $225 to $250.00

Honeymoon Express, 1950, train circles track w/tunnels & station, plane circles above, tin, 9½" dia, EX, from $150 to $175.00

Hop-A-Long Cassidy, rider w/lariat on rocking base, arms move depicting bucking horse, 10", VG, A $400.00

Hopping Astro, litho tin, 4½", EX $350.00
Hopping Dino, litho tin, 4", G, M5 .... $80.00

Hopping Elroy, 1963, lithographed tin, 4", MIB, $1,000.00.

Hopping Fred Flintstone, litho tin, 3½", EX+ $325.00
Hopping Rosie the Robot, litho tin, 4", scarce, NM, from $400 to $450.00
Hot Rod, 1950s, mk Super 777, advances w/battery-op lights in engine, litho tin, friction, 11", rare, EX, A $275.00
Hovercraft, mk SRN6, advances w/siren sound, plastic, friction, 6", EX+ (EX box) $50.00
Huckleberry Hound Car, 1962, litho tin w/vinyl figure, friction, 4", NM (EX box), A $295.00
Jetsons, see also Hopping Elroy and Hopping Rosie the Robot
Jetsons Express Choo Choo, litho tin w/characters riding in cars & engine, VG+ $250.00
Joe Penner & His Duck Goo Goo, 1934, advances w/shuffling motion as his hat tips, litho tin, 8½", MIB $850.00
Joe Penner & His Duck Goo Goo, 1934, 8½", EX $600.00
Joy Rider, ca 1930, tractor-type vehicle travels in erratic motion as driver's head spins, tin, 7", NM+ (EX box) $900.00
Jumpin' Jack Car, litho tin, friction, 8", G, A $50.00
Jumpin' Jeep, litho tin, EX+ $200.00
Jumpin' Jeep, litho tin, non-working, G $75.00
King Racer, 1920s, yel w/bl trim, gr wheels, w/driver, 8½", M $750.00
Knockout Champs, 2 boy boxers on revolving disk in boxing ring, celluloid & litho tin, 7x7", NMIB, A $350.00
Limping Lizzie, advances in swaying motion w/rattling sound, tin w/litho graffiti, 7", VG (EX box) $450.00
Little Orphan Annie Skipping Rope, 1930s, litho tin, 6", EX .$600.00
Little Orphan Annie Skipping Rope, 1930s, litho tin, 6", NMIB $1,200.00
Little Orphan Annie's Dog Sandy, dog w/suitcase in mouth, litho tin, 5½", EX (orig box missing side flaps), A ..$500.00
Lizzie of the Valley Jalopy, blk litho tin w/allover wht lettering, 7", VG, A $275.00

Magic Garage and Car, garage door flies open upon impact of car, lithographed tin, 10" garage, NMIB, $300.00.

Magic Garage & Car, Dick Tracy version, 1950, litho tin, friction, 10", rare, M (EX box), A $400.00
Magic Garage & Car, garage door flies open upon impact of car, litho tin, 10" garage, VG+ $150.00
Mammy's Boy, ca 1925, Black man w/cane sways as eyes shift, litho tin, 11", EX, A $600.00
Merry Makers, 1929, 3 mice band members w/band leader atop piano, no marquee, 9¼", EX, from $1,000 to $1,100.00
Merry Makers, 1929, 3 mice band members w/band leader atop piano, w/marquee, 9¼", EX (orig box), from $1,500 to $1,600.00
Mickey Mouse, see also Whirling Tail Mickey Mouse
Mickey Mouse & Donald Duck Handcar, 1950s, Mickey & Donald navigate track, litho tin & plastic, 22" base, EX (VG box), A $600.00
Mickey Mouse Dipsy Car, 1949, head bobs while crazy car advances, litho tin w/plastic figure, 6", MIB, from $700 to $800.00

Mickey Mouse Express, 1950s, Mickey flies above track with Disneyville station in center, lithographed tin, 9" dia, NMIB, from $900.00 to $1,000.00.

Mickey the Musician, 1950s, Mickey leans over & plays the xylophone on sq tin base, 12", EX (worn box) $350.00

Milton Berle Car, 1950, Milton's head spins while driving crazy car, litho tin, plastic hat, 5½", EX (EX box) $450.00

Milton Berle Car, 1950s, Milton's head spins while driving crazy car, litho tin, plastic hat, 5½", MIB $550.00

Miniature Train Set, 1950, train travels around base w/city scene, litho tin, 15" train, NM (G box), A..............$200.00

Moon Mullins & Kayo Handcar, 1930s, flat litho tin figures work handlebars, 6", NM (EX box), from $1,100 to.......$1,200.00

Moon Mullins & Kayo Handcar, 1930s, 6", VG.............$500.00

Mortimer Snerd Tricky Auto, 1939, advances w/erratic motion, Mortimer's head swivels in complete circle, 7", VG+, A...$500.00

Mortimer Snerd Walker, 1939, advances in vibrating motion while tipping his hat, litho tin, 8", EX, A................$400.00

Motorcycle Delivery, 1930s, litho tin w/full-figure driver, 9½", NM+ (EX box), A..$925.00

Mountain Climber, futuristic bus travels track & up mountain, litho tin, 33" base, MIB, A.................................$300.00

Mystery Spaceship, fires rockets w/gyro power using propulsion lever, plastic, complete w/accessories, EX+ (EX box), A...$150.00

Mystic Motorcycle, 1930s, non-fall action, w/driver, litho tin, 4", NM+ (VG box), A $250.00

New Flivver, full-figure driver, tin w/spoked wheels, 7", EX (EX box), A...$640.00

Old Jalopy, blk, red & yel litho tin, 7", EX, S10 ....$200.00

Old Mother Goose, 1930, Mother Goose & her cat ride goose, litho tin, 9", NM (VG rare box), A.....................$1,925.00

PD Motorcycle w/Sidecar, 1930s, stop-&-go action, tin w/full-figure driver, 3½", NM...$250.00

PD Siren Motorcycle, #2688, litho tin, 6x8", EX $350.00

Peter Rabbit Eccentric Car, litho tin & plastic, 8", NM (EX box)...$450.00

Pinched, 1927, truck goes in circle under 2 bridges, tunnel & station, includes cops & restaurant, 10" sq base, EX $750.00

Pinocchio, see Walking Pinocchio

Pluto, see also Rollover Pluto

Pluto the Drum Major, 1940s, wearing hat & holding baton, litho tin, 6", M, A...$275.00

Police Motorcycle, 1930, travels in circle w/siren sound, litho tin, 8½", NM+ (EX box), from $500 to...................$550.00

Police Motorcycle, 1940, officer in gray shirt w/red & yel pants on yel motorcycle w/red trim, 8", EX $350.00

Police Motorcycle w/Sidecar, 1930s, litho tin w/celluloid shield, electric light & siren, w/driver, 8", VG, from $300 to .$350.00

Police Tip-Over Motorcycle, 1933, travels in circle, tips over & gets up, 8", EX, A..$400.00

Popeye, see also Walking Popeye

Popeye & Olive Oyl Jiggers, 1934, Olive Oyl plays accordion & sways while Popeye dances on roof, 10", EX.........$1,200.00

Popeye & Olive Oyl Jiggers, 1934, Olive Oyl plays accordion & sways while Popeye dances on roof, 10", NMIB ...$1,700.00

Popeye Express, 1935, train travels under bridges as Popeye circles in plane overhead, tin, 9½" dia, NM (G box)........$1,250.00

Popeye Express w/Parrot, parrot pops out of crate & wheelbarrow pushed by Popeye, 8½", EX....................................$850.00

Popeye Express w/Parrot, 8½", G $475.00

Popeye Handcar, Olive Oyl standing & Popeye sitting on spinach crate, tin w/rubber figures, 7", EX base (VG+ box), A...$525.00

Popeye the Champ, Popeye and Bluto on revolving platform in ring, lithographed tin ring and celluloid figures, 7x7", EX, $2,000.00.

Popeye the Pilot (Popeye Eccentric Airplane), 1930s, Popeye flies bl & red single-prop plane w/2 lg wheels, 7", NMIB $1,800.00

Porky Pig, 1939, vibrates as he twirls umbrella, litho tin, 8½", EX, A...$300.00

Porky Pig, 1939, vibrates as he twirls umbrella, litho tin, 8½", NMIB, A...$525.00

Porky Pig Cowpuncher, 1949, vibrates around as lasso spins, litho tin, 9", scarce, NM..$725.00

Porky Pig w/Top Hat, 1939, waves top hat as umbrella spins, litho tin, 9", rare, EX+, A..$725.00

Racer #7, red litho tin w/driver, balloon tires, 6", VG+ .$125.00

Range Rider, 1938, Lone Ranger on Silver swings his lasso, rocker base, litho tin, 11", VG+, from $350 to........$400.00

Red Cap Porter, 1930, litho tin Black man w/toothy grin & fast-moving legs carrying 2 bags, 8", VG, from $650 to..$750.00

Red the Iceman, 1930s, litho tin, complete w/ice tongs & wooden block of ice, 8½", scarce, NM (VG box), A $3,400.00

Reversible Climbing 6-Wheel DeLuxe Tractor, 1931, forward & reverse action, w/driver, 12", VG+ (VG box) $200.00

Reversible Coupe, 1936, bump-&-go action, red tin w/aluminum plating, 16", EX (G+ box), from $550 to $600.00

Ring-A-Ling Circus, ringmaster & 4 circus figures on rnd platform, litho tin w/pk base, 7", EX..........................$1,500.00

Road Roller, 1930, driver stands in red & blk vehicle w/lg simulated spoked wheels, roller on front, 8½", EX, A.....$175.00

Rollover Plane, pilot in litho tin plane, 6" wingspan, G, from $150 to...$175.00

Rollover Plane, pilot in litho tin plane, 6" wingspan, M, from $250 to...$275.00

Rollover Pluto, 1939, Pluto advances & rolls over, tail spins, litho tin, 9", EX $300.00

Rookie Pilot, 1940, advances in erratic motion, red and yellow lithographed tin, EX, from $500.00 to $550.00.

Photo courtesy of Scott Smiles.

Royal Bus Lines, features roof rack, spare tire, jutting headlights & luggage box, red & yel litho tin, 10", VG+, A **$400.00**

Royal Bus Lines, gr & pk w/bl tires, 10", rare color variation, 10", NM, A..**$725.00**

Royal Bus Lines, red & yel w/blk tires, 10", MIB, A.......**$750.00**

Sam the City Gardener, 1940, jtd plastic figure pushes litho tin wheelbarrow, 7½", MIB, from $225 to **$250.00**

Sandy, see Little Orphan Annie

Sheriff Sam Whoopee Car, advances w/crazy action, tin & plastic, 6", NM, A...**$125.00**

Smokey Joe the Climbing Fireman, 1930s, fireman climbs ladder attached to base, lithographed tin, 11½", EX (EX box), from $350.00 to $375.00.

Smokey Joe the Climbing Fireman, 1930s, articulated fireman climbs ladder, 11½", EX (EX box), from $350 to **$375.00**

Solar Rocket, futuristic rocket w/disk in center, plastic, friction, 12", scarce, NM (EX box), A **$225.00**

Somstepa, 1925, Black man performs jig on stage, litho tin, 8", EX **$650.00**

Space-Mobile, futuristic space bus travels track & up lunar mountain, litho tin, 33" base, MIB, A **$350.00**

Sparkling Climbing Fighting Tank, advances w/sparks & gun sound, litho tin, 9", NM (EX box) **$400.00**

Sparkling Rocket Fighter Ship, advances w/sparks & sound, litho tin w/pilot, 12", NM+ (VG box), A **$1,125.00**

Sparkling Soldier Motorcycle, 1930s, travels in circles w/sparking action, litho tin, 8½", NM+ (EX+ box), A.......**$750.00**

Sparkling Tank, 1935, advances w/sparks, camouflaged top tank w/dbl guns, litho tin, 8", EX+ (G box).....................**$300.00**

Sparkling Tank, 1940, advances w/sparks, litho tin, 4", EX (EX box)..**$200.00**

Speed Boy Delivery Cycle, 1935, driver on cycle pulling wagon, litho tin, 10", EX, A **$400.00**

Speed Racer #2, litho tin w/oversized balloon tires, 6", EX (EX+ box), from $175 to......................................**$200.00**

Spic & Span, 1924, 2 Black minstrels on stage mk The Hams What Am, litho tin, 10½", NM **$2,500.00**

Spic & Span, 1924, 2 Black minstrels on stage mk The Hams What Am, litho tin, 10½", VG **$1,300.00**

Streamlined Speedway, 1930s, 2 cars circle track, EX (EX box) .**$250.00**

Super Sonic Jet, 1960s, plastic, friction, EX, J2................**$50.00**

Superman Rollover Plane, 1940, Superman revolves in back & turns plane over, litho tin, 5", NM+ (EX+ box) ..**$1,200.00**

Tidy Tim, figure pushes barrel w/broom & shovel, litho tin, 9", EX, from $750 to **$800.00**

Tidy Tim, figure pushes barrel w/broom & shovel, litho tin, 9", NM, from $850 to...**$900.00**

Tom Corbett Space Cadet Rocket Ship, 1930s, advances w/sparks & sound, litho tin, 12", EX **$600.00**

Toyland Milk Wagon, brn horse pulls gray wagon w/red roof, disk wheels, 10½", MIB..**$450.00**

Toytown Dairy Wagon, dapple-gray horse pulls red & yel wagon, EX, H7 ....**$300.00**

Tricky Fire Chief, 1930s, car navigates litho tin base w/non-fall action, EX (VG+ box)..**$400.00**

Tricky Motorcycle, 1930s, travels w/non-fall action, litho tin, 4", EX (EX box), from $250 to **$275.00**

Tricky Taxi, 1940, travels to end of table & turns around, litho tin, 5", scarce, NM+ (EX+ box), from $300 to........**$325.00**

Trumpton Climbing Fireman, European-style fireman climbs ladder, plastic, 9", NM (EX box), A.....................**$225.00**

Tumbling Monkey, 1942, circus monkey flips between 2 chairs, litho tin, 6", NM (EX box), A.....................................**$300.00**

Turnover Tank, 1935, advances & turns over, litho tin, 8", NM (G box), A...**$350.00**

Uncle Wiggily Car, 1935, travels w/crazy action as Uncle Wiggily's head turns, Easter motif on car, 7", NM, A **$825.00**

US Army Command Car, litho tin, friction w/battery-op lights & siren, 19", EX+ (VG+ box), A.............................**$350.00**

US Army Fighter Plane, (non-sparking version), dbl guns on ea wing, tin w/balloon tires, 7", EX+, A **$175.00**

US Army Fighter Plane, (sparking version), dbl guns on ea wing, tin w/balloon tires, 7", EX+ **$225.00**

US Army Truck, tin w/canvas top, 5", EX, A $175.00

Wacky Taxi, litho tin w/nervous passengers in windows, friction, 7", VG+ $100.00

Walking Astronaut, VG+, T1 ....$45.00

Walking Cow, 1950s, hard plastic, lift tail to milk, H12 ..$30.00

Walking Pinocchio, WDE/1939, eyes move as he walks, litho tin, 8½", EX (partial box) $450.00

Walking Popeye, King Features, 1935, carries 2 cages w/lithoed parrots, 8¼", EX, from $450 to................................$500.00

Walt Disney's Television Car, litho tin, friction, 7½", EX, A..$450.00

Western Tricycle, tin, unused, MIB, J2 ....$100.00

Whirling Tail Mickey Mouse, plastic figure, tail spins when activated, 7", NMIB, A $300.00

Whoopee Car, 1930s, jalopy w/2 flapper girls sitting on trunk, crazy action, litho tin, 7", VG+ (G box) $1,000.00

Whoopee Cowboy, 1932, cowboy moves up & down as crazy car travels, happy cow faces on wheels, 8", NM, H7 .....$425.00

World Famous Racers, set of 6 plastic open-wheel racers w/drivers, friction, 6", NM (EX box), A $185.00

Miscellaneous

Fix-All Tractor, take apart & reassemble w/tools, 9½", VG (orig box), A..$45.00

Glendale Station, litho tin, bi-level base, 10x20½", VG $285.00

Grand Central Station, litho tin, gold finish, 2-wheel trailer, front canopy & opening doors, 11x17", VG $145.00

Happi-Time Service Station, 1950s, appears unused, NM+ (EX+ box), A..$350.00

Hauler & Low-Side Stake Trailer, Tri-City Freight decals on sides, litho tin w/blk-pnt tires, 19", NM (EX+ box), A $215.00

Hometown Movie Theatre #170, 1925, turn knobs to view paper roll movie on litho tin theatre, 5", MIB, A..............$420.00

Little Orphan Annie Stove, 1930s, electric, Annie & Sandy graphics, 3 oven doors, 8x9½x5", working, NM......$225.00

Pet Shop Delivery Truck, sides flip up to show 6 cubicles holding 6 dogs, plastic, 11", EX (EX box) $200.00

Press Lever Top Set, complete w/2 litho tin globes, EX+ (VG box)..$175.00

Typewriter, De-Luxe Dial, tin, VG, J6 ....$85.00

Roadside Rest Service Station, lithographed tin, complete with Lubster car and water can, 14" long, VG, A, $400.00.

Universal Freight Station, litho tin, complete, EX (EX box), A..$175.00

Walt Disney's Television Playhouse #4349, Marx, litho tin stage w/various Disney characters, EX (VG box), A $400.00

Matchbox

The Matchbox series of English and American-made autos, trucks, taxis, Pepsi-Cola trucks, steamrollers, Greyhound buses, etc., was very extensive. By the late 1970s, the company was cranking out more than 5 million cars every week, and while those days may be over, Matchbox still produces about 75 million vehicles on a yearly basis.

Introduced in 1953, the Matchbox Miniatures series has always been the mainstay of the company. There were 75 models in all but with enough variations to make collecting them a real challenge. Larger, more detailed models were introduced in 1957; this series, called Major Pack, was replaced a few years later by a similar line called King Size. To compete with Hot Wheels, Matchbox converted most models over to a line called SuperFast that sported thinner, low-friction axles and wheels. (These are much more readily available than the original 'regular wheels,' the last of which were made in 1969.) At about the same time, the King Size series became known as Speed Kings; in 1977 the line was reintroduced under the name Super Kings.

In the early '70s, Lesney started to put dates on the baseplates of their toy cars. The name 'Lesney' was coined from the first names of the company's founders. The last Matchboxes that carried the Lesney mark were made in 1982. Today many models can be bought for less than $10.00, though a few are priced much higher.

In 1988, to celebrate the company's 40th anniversary, Matchbox issued a limited set of five models that except for minor variations were exact replicas of the originals. These five were repackaged in 1991 and sold under the name Matchbox Originals. In 1993 a second series expanded the line of reproductions.

Another line that's become very popular is their Models of Yesteryear. These are slightly larger replicas of antique and vintage vehicles. Values of $20.00 to $60.00 for mint-in-box examples are average, though a few sell for even more.

Sky Busters are small-scale aircraft measuring an average of 3½" in length. They were introduced in 1973. Models currently being produced sell for about $4.00 each.

To learn more, we recommend *Matchbox Toys, 1948 to 1993* by Dana Johnson, and a series of books by Charlie Mack: *Lesney's Matchbox Toys* (there are two: *Regular Wheel Years* and *Super Fast Years*) and *Universal Years*.

To determine values of examples in conditions other than given in our listings, based on MIB or MOC prices, deduct a minimum of 10% if the original container is missing, 30% if the condition is excellent, and as much as 70% for a toy graded only very good. In the following listings, we have added zeroes ahead of the numbers to avoid the idiosyncrasies of computer sorting.

Advisors: Mark Giles (G2) 1-75 Series; Dan Wells (W1) King Size, Speed Kings and Super Kings; Matchbox Originals; Models of Yesteryear; Skybusters.

Other Sources: C18, N3

Key:
LW — Laser Wheels (introduced in 1987)
reg — regular wheels (Matchbox Miniatures)
SF — SuperFast

1-75 Series

01-A, Diesel Road Roller, reg, dk gr, 1953, M (NM box)..$50.00
01-B, Road Roller, reg, lt gr, tan driver, 1955, M (NM- box) ..$75.00
01-C, Road Roller, reg, dk gr, 1958, EX+, W1.................$50.00
01-D, Aveling Barford Road Roller, reg, 1962, NM, W1...$14.00
01-F, Mercedes Truck, SF, olive, tan canopy, bl windows, 5-spoke wheels, 1970, NM, W1 ....$3.00

01-G, Mod Rod, yellow with red interior, 1971, MIB, $10.00.

02-A, Dumper, reg, orig driver, metal wheels, 1953, NM-, W1 ....$34.00
02-C, Muir Hill Dumper, reg, Laing decal, blk wheels, M (NM box), W1..$29.00
02-D, Mercedes Trailer, reg, orange canopy, blk wheels, 1968, M (NM box)..$11.00
02-F, Jeep Hot Rod, SF, pk, lt gr base, cream interior, 4-spoke wheels, 1970, M, W1 ....$13.00
02-G, Hovercraft, SF, gr, tan hull, silver scoop, Rescue label, 1976, M $9.00
03-A, Cement Mixer, reg, metal wheels, 1953, NM-, W1.$22.00
03-B, Bedford Tipper, reg, gray w/red dumper, M $15.00
03-B, Bedford Tipper, reg, red dumper, 1961, M (NM+ box)..$25.00
03-C, Mercedes Ambulance, reg, decals, orig patient, blk walls, 1968, M (NM box) $15.00
03-E, Monteverdi Hai, SF, orange, 1973, MIB, from $5 to..$8.00
03-F, Porsche Turbo, SF, brn, cream interior, blk base, 1978, M (EX box), from $6 to...$12.00
04-B, Massey Harris Tractor, reg, no fenders, orig driver, missing smoke stack, metal wheels, 1957, EX, W1 ....$22.00
04-C, Triumph Motorcycle & Sidecar, reg, blk walls, 1960, NM+, W1 ....$44.00
04-D, Dodge Stake Truck, reg, gr stakes, blk wheels, 1967, M (NM- box), W1...$13.00
04-E, Stake Truck, SF, yel, 4-spoke wheels, 1970, M (EX+ box) $13.00
04-F, Gruesome Twosome, SF, unpt base, purple windshield, cream interior, 1971, M, W1 ....$8.00
04-G, Pontiac Firebird, SF, lt bl, dot-dash wheels, 1975, NM+...$5.00
04-H, '57 Chevy, SF, lt purple, 1979, MBP (cracked blister & wrinkled card), from $4 to $5.00

05-A, London Bus, reg, metal wheels, 1954, NM, W1 .....$60.00
05-B, London Bus, reg, Buy Matchbox Series decals, gold wheels, 1957, EX..$34.00
06-A, Quarry Truck, reg, metal wheels, 1954, M (EX- box), from $35 to $40.00
06-C, Euclid Quarry Truck, reg, solid tires, blk wheels, M (EX+ box), from $35 to $40.00
06-D, Ford Pickup Truck, reg, wht grille, orig top, blk wheels, M (EX box) $12.00
06-F, Mercedes 350SL, orange, 1976, M (VG box) $9.00
07-A, Milk Float, reg, wht letters/driver/bottles, metal wheels, 1954, NM..$77.00
07-B, Ford Anglia, reg, gold wheels, 1961, NM $28.00
07-C, Ford Refuse Truck, reg, gray dumper, M $14.00
07-C, Ford Refuse Truck, reg, straight side plates, blk walls, 1966, M (EX+ box), W1 ....$16.00
07-E, Hairy Hauler, SF, bronze, blk base, amber windshield, 5 yel side labels, 5 on hood label, NMIB, W1 ....$13.00
08-A, Caterpillar Tractor, reg, yel, orig treads, 1955, M (NM-box) $60.00

08-E, Ford Mustang, regular wheels, white with black wheels, 1966, EX, $16.00.

08-E, Ford Mustang, reg, wht, blk walls, 1966, NM-, W1.$19.00
08-F, Ford Mustang, SF, orange, ivory interior, MIB $35.00
08-G, Wildcat Dragster, SF, pk & orange w/blk base, yel & orange Wildcat labels, 1971, NM, W1 ....$10.00
09-A, Dennis Fire Escape, reg, no # cast, metal wheels, 1955, EX-...$30.00
09-C, Merryweather Marquis Fire Engine, reg, gold ladder, blk walls, 1959, NM..$24.00
09-D, Boat & Trailer, reg, blk walls, 1966, NM+ $15.00
10-C, Sugar Container Truck, reg, no crown decal, blk walls, 1961, NM+ $38.00
10-D, Pipe Truck, reg, silver grille, 7 pipes still on tree, blk wheels, 1966, M (NM+ box) $18.00
11-A, Road Tanker, reg, red, Esso decal on rear, metal wheels, 1955, M (NM box) $50.00
11-C, Jumbo Crane, reg, red or yel weight box, blk wheels, 1965, M (NM box) $17.00
11-D, Scaffolding Truck, reg, complete, blk walls, 1969, M (EX+ box), W1 ....$20.00
11-F, Flying Bug, SF, gray windows, heart decal on hood, 5-spoke wheels, 1972, NM+, W1 ....$15.00
12-A, Land Rover, reg, missing driver, metal wheels, 1955, NM...$40.00
12-C, Safari Land Rover, reg, bl, tan luggage, blk walls, 1965, M (NM- box), W1 ....$15.00

12-D, Land Rover Sedan, SF, gold, tan luggage, 1970, NM+, W1 ....$19.00

12-E, Setra Coach, SF, burgundy, wht roof, gr windshield, 1970, M (NM+) $9.00

12-H, Pontiac Firebird, SF, red, tan interior, clear windshield, 1982, MBP (wrinkled card), W1 ....$6.00

13-B, Bedford Wreck Truck, reg, no # cast, metal wheels, 1958, M (EX+ box) $65.00

13-C, Thames Wreck Truck, reg, outlined letters, silver metal hook, blk walls, 1961, M (NM- box) $55.00

Photo courtesy of Dana Johnson.

13-D, Dodge BP Wreck Truck, regular wheels, green and yellow, black wheels, 1965, MIB, $24.00.

13-F, Baja Dune Buggy, SF, gr, flower label, 1971, M (VG box).$10.00

13-G, Hi Ho Silver VW Bug, SF, pearl silver, 1981, EX, W1 ....$3.00

14-A, Daimler Ambulance, reg, w/cross, metal wheels, 1956, M (EX box) $50.00

14-C, Bedford Ambulance, reg, blk wheels, 1962, M, W1.$29.00

14-D, Iso Grifo, reg, blk walls, 1968, M (EX+ box) $14.00

14-D, Iso Grifo, reg, dk bl, M...$12.00

14-F, Mini Ha Ha, SF, red, pk driver, brn helmet, 4 color labels, Maltese cross on front wheels, 1975, M........................$9.00

15-A, Prime Mover, reg, orange, metal wheels, 1956, M (EX+ box)..$36.00

15-C, Tippax Refuse Truck, reg, peep hole, slanted edge decal, blk walls, 1963, M (EX- box), W1 ....$23.00

15-D, VW 1500 Saloon, reg, labels, blk walls, 1968, NM+..$15.00

15-E, VW 1500, SF, red, missing labels, front bumper decals, 1969, EX...$13.00

16-C, Scammell Mountaineer Snow Plow, reg, orange w/wht decal, blk wheels, 1964, NM $37.00

16-D, Case Bulldozer, reg, orig top & treads, 1969, NM...$26.00

17-A, Bedford Removals Van, reg, gr, solid letters, metal wheels, 1956, NM, W1 ....$34.00

17-C, Austin Taxi, reg, complete, 1960, NM+ $44.00

17-D, Hoveringham Tipper, reg, blk or red base, blk wheels, 1963, NMIB...$25.00

17-E, Horse Box, reg, horses on tree, blk walls, 1969, M (NM box)..$13.00

17-E, Horse Box, SF, red, no horses, 1970, M (NM+ box) .$19.00

17-F, Londoner Bus, SF, red, blk base, 5-spoke wheels, Berger Paints, 1972, M..$10.00

18-B, Caterpillar Bulldozer, reg, orig treads, 1958, M $40.00

18-E, Field Car, reg, unpnt base, red hubs, orig top, blk wheels, 1969, M (NM box), W1 ....$17.00

18-G, Hondarora Motorcycle, SF, gr, 1975, MBP, W1.......$6.00

19-A, MG Sports Car, reg, cream, complete, metal wheels, 1956, M (NM+ box)..$50.00

19-D, Lotus Racing Car, reg, gr, decals, blk wheels, 1966, NM+.$18.00

19-F, Road Dragster, SF, red/orange, '8' labels, 1970, NM..$13.00

20-B, ERF 686 Truck, reg, gold wheels, 1959, VG+ $14.00

20-C, Chevrolet Impala Taxi, reg, orange w/red interior, label, unpnt base, blk walls, 1965, M (NM box), W1 ....$24.00

20-D, Lamborghini Marzal, SF, red, no labels, 1969, M (NM box), W1 ....$12.00

21-B, Long Distance Coach, reg, missing decals, metal wheels, 1958, NM+ $35.00

21-C, Commer Milk Float, reg, gr windows, cow decals, blk walls, 1961, M (NM+ box), W1....................$37.00

21-D, Foden Concrete Truck, reg, blk walls, 1968, NM+..$15.00

22-C, Pontiac Grand Prix Sports Coupe, reg, blk walls, 1964, NM, W1..$16.00

22-E, Freeman Intercity Commuter, magenta, unpnt base, ivory interior, w/labels, 1970, NM+, W1.......................$8.00

23-B, Berkeley Cavalier Trailer, reg, pale bl, no # cast, metal wheels, 1958, M (NM box) $33.00

23-D, House Trailer Caravan, reg, pk, blk walls, 1965, NM..$13.00

24-A, Weatherhill Hydraulic Excavator, reg, yel, metal wheels, 1956, EX- $24.00

24-C, Rolls Royce Silver Shadow, reg, blk walls, 1967, NM+, W1..$9.00

24-F, Shunter, SF, gr, red undercarriage & base, tan panel, 'Rail Freight' label, 1978, MIB, W1 ....$9.00

25-A, Dunlop Van, reg, decals 98%, gold wheels, 1956, NM+ $35.00

25-B, VW 1200 Bug, reg, gr windows, blk walls, 1960, NM..$39.00

25-C, BP Petrol Tanker, reg, gr, blk wheels, 1964, complete, M (EX+ box), W1 ....$25.00

25-D, Ford Cortina, reg, no-roof version, blk wheels, 1968, M (NM- box) $14.00

25-E, Ford Cortina, SF, bl, tacky pnt, 1970, NM+ $12.00

26-A, Concrete Truck, reg, silver grille, gold wheels, 1956, M (NM- box)..$45.00

26-B, Foden Concrete Truck, reg, orange barrel, blk walls, 1961, M $34.00

26-C, GMC Tipper Truck, reg, red cab, silver tipper, M, J1 .$12.00

27-A, Bedford Lowloader, reg, gr & tan, metal wheels, 1956, NM, W1..$54.00

27-C, Cadillac Sixty Special, reg, lilac w/pk roof, blk base, blk wheels, 1960, EX+ $32.00

27-D, Mercedes 230SL, reg, blk walls, 1966, NM+..........$16.00

28-A, Bedford Compressor Truck, reg, yel, metal wheels, 1956, M (NM box) $38.00

28-B, Thames Compressor Truck, reg, blk walls, 1959, EX..$26.00

28-D, Mack Dump Truck, reg, red hubs, blk walls, 1968, M (NM box), W1 ....$22.00

28-E, Mack Dump Truck, SF, gr, unpnt base, spiro wheels, 1970, M (EX+ box) $18.00

28-F, Stout Armoured Vehicle, SF, olive, blk base, blk hubs, 1974, M $8.00

28-G, Lincoln Continental Mk V, SF, red, unpnt base, tan interior, wht roof, 1979, NM, W1................................$7.00

29-A, Bedford Milk Delivery Van, reg, metal wheels, 1956, NM- $32.00

29-B, Austin A55 Cambridge Sedan, reg, blk walls, 1961, M $26.00

29-C, Fire Pumper, reg, plain sides, blk walls, 1966, M $17.00

30-C, 8-Wheel Crane Truck, reg, yel hook, blk walls, 1965, M (EX+ box), W1 ....$15.00

30-E, Beach Buggy, SF, pk, unpnt base, yel-splattered interior, 1970, NM+ $13.00

31-A, Ford Station Wagon, reg, yel, no windows, metal wheels, 1957, NM $32.00

31-C, Lincoln Continental, reg, aqua, blk walls, 1964, M (NM box) $17.00

31-D, Lincoln Continental, SF, gr & gold, 1970, NM+ ...$16.00

32-A, Jaguar XK140, reg, cream, metal wheels, 1957, NM- ..$37.00

32-B, E-Type Jaguar, reg, clear windows, wire wheels, blk walls, 1962, NM (EX box) $33.00

32-E, Maserati Bora, SF, burgundy, dk gr base, '8' label, no tow hook, 1972, MBP, W1 ....$11.00

33-A, Ford Zodiac Mk II Sedan, reg, dk gr, no windows, metal wheels, 1957, NM+ $40.00

33-C, Lamborghini Miura, reg, yel, red interior, blk walls, M (NM-) $13.00

33-D, Lamborghini Miura, gold, unpnt base, ivory interior, 1969, M, W1 ....$15.00

33-E, Datsun 126X, SF, yel, orange base, no tampo, 1973, M (EX box), W1 ....$11.00

34-C, VW Camper, reg, silver, raised roof, blk walls, 1967, M $25.00

34-E, Formula 1 Racing Car, SF, pk, yel label, 4-spoke wheels, 1971, NM+, W1 ....$9.00

34-F, Vantastic, SF, orange, labels, 1975, M (EX box), W1..$4.00

34-G, Chevy Pro Stocker, SF, wht, 1981, M (NM box), W1..$6.00

35-B, Snowtrac Tractor, reg, plain sides, orig treads, 1964, M (EX box w/loose flap) $30.00

35-C, Merryweather Fire Engine, SF, red, gray base, 2 clips, 5-spoke wheels, 1970, MIP, W1 ....$13.00

35-D, Fandango, SF, red, unpnt base, clear windows, ivory interior, bl prop, 1975, NM+ $8.00

35-E, Zoo Truck, SF, red, blk base, gray cage, tan lions, 5-arch wheels, complete, 1982, NM $11.00

36-A, Austin A50, reg, metal wheels, 1957, NM $33.00

36-B, Lambretta Scooter & Sidecar, reg, blk walls, 1961, NM $36.00

36-D, Opal Diploma, SF, dk gold, blk base, silver trim, 1970 ....$16.00

36-E, Hot Rod Draguar, SF, red, unpnt base, ivory interior, clear windshield, trunk label, 1970, NM+ $13.00

37-A, Coca-Cola Lorry, reg, no base, sm letters, even load, metal wheels, 1956, M (NM box) $57.00

37-C, Dodge Cattle Truck, reg, orig cattle on tree, blk walls, 1966, M (NM+ box)..$18.00

37-E, Cattle Truck, SF, orange, orig cattle on tree, 1970, M $14.00

37-F, Soopa Coopa, SF, pk, unpnt base, flower label, Maltese Cross wheels, 1972, EX+, W1 ....$8.00

38-A, Karrier Refuse Collector, reg, gray, metal wheels, 1957, M, W1 ....$34.00

37-J, Jeep 4x4, red, white and blue, black wheels, 1984, MIB, $4.00.

38-B, Vauxhall Victor Estate Car, reg, red interior, blk walls, 1963, NM+ $34.00

38-C, Honda Motorcycle & Trailer, reg, yel trailer, labels, blk walls, 1967, NM+ $16.00

38-D, Honda Motorcycle & Trailer, SF, pk bike, yel trailer, 5-spoke wheels, 1970, NM+ $14.00

38-E, Stingeroo Motorcycle, SF, purple, 1972, NM+, W1..$10.00

38-F, Jeep, bl, wht base, US Mail tampo, wht roof, silver hubs, 1976, M $7.00

39-A, Ford Zodiac Convertible, reg, turq interior, metal wheels, complete, 1957, M (EX box) $41.00

39-B, Pontiac Convertible, reg, yel, ivory steering wheel, blk base, blk wheels, 1962, NM+.................................$32.00

39-C, Ford Tractor, reg, bl & yel, blk walls, 1967, NM+..$13.00

39-D, Clipper, magenta, gr base, yel interior, amber windshield, silver pipes, 1973, NM+, W1 ....$10.00

40-A, Bedford Tipper Truck, reg, blk walls, 1957, NM $37.00

40-B, Leyland Royal Tiger Coach, reg, blk wheels, 1961, M ..$26.00

40-D, Vauxhall Guildsman, pk, gr base, gr windows, flames label, 5-spoke wheels, 1971, M, W1 ....$13.00

41-A, D-Type Jaguar, reg, complete, 1 pnt chip on front fender, metal wheels, 1965, M (NM box) $400.00

41-D, Ford GT, wht w/blk base, '6' label, 5-spoke wheels, 1970, M, W1 ....$12.00

41-E, Siva Spyder, SF, red, no tampo, cream interior, blk strap, 5-spoke wheels, 1972, M, W1...............................$10.00

41-F, Ambulance, SF, wht, unpnt base, gray interior, red 'Pacific Ambulance' tampo, 1978, M $5.00

42-A, Bedford Evening News, reg, blk walls, 1957, M (NM box) $50.00

42-B, Studebaker Lark Wagonaire, reg, orig hunter & dog, blk walls, 1965, NM-, W1/J1 ....$23.00

42-C, Iron Fairy Crane, reg, blk walls, 1969, NM............$17.00

43-A, Hillman Minx, reg, bl & gray w/gray roof, metal wheels, 1958, M (NM- box)...$45.00

43-D, Pony Trailer, SF, yel, lt or dk gr base, orig horses, 1970, M $14.00

43-E, VW Bug Dragon Wheels, SF, gr, NM+, W1............$9.00

44-A, Rolls Royce Silver Shadow, reg, gold wheels, 1958, NM+ $32.00

44-B, Rolls Royce Phantom V, reg, blk wheels, 1964, M .$33.00

44-C, GMC Refrigerator Truck, reg, blk wheels, 1967, M..**$17.00**

44-D, GMC Refrigerator Truck, SF, yel, red container, blk axle covers, 1970, NM+ **$17.00**

44-E, Boss Mustang, SF, dk gr, 'Cobra' limited edition, 1972, MOC (blister crack o/w EX), W1.................................**$9.00**

45-A, Vauxhall Victor, reg, yel, no windows, gold wheels, 1958, NM- **$27.00**

45-C, Ford Group 6, gr, unpnt base, clear windows, silver motor, rnd '7' label, 1970, MIB, W1.................................**$15.00**

45-D, BMW 3.0 CSL, SF, orange, label, gr window, 1976, M (NM- box) **$8.00**

45-E, Kenworth Cab-Over Semi Truck, SF, wht, 1982, M, W1 ..**$2.00**

46-A, Morris Minor, reg, dk gr, metal wheels, 1958, NM+ ...**$53.00**

46-B, Pickford's Removal Van, reg, gr, 3-line decal, blk wheels, 1960, M, W1...**$38.00**

46-C, Mercedes Benz 300 SE, reg, gr, blk walls, 1968, M (EX box), W1 ....**$24.00**

46-D, Mercedes 300 SE, SF, gold, unpnt base, solid doors, no labels, 5-spoke wheels, 1970, M (NM- box) **$18.00**

46-E, Stretcha Fetcha, SF, lime, wht base, amber window, blk/wht 'Viper Van' tampo, Maltese Cross wheels, M (NM pkg), W1 ....**$11.00**

47-A, 1-Ton Trojan Van, reg, gold wheels, 1958, EX+, W1 ..**$36.00**

47-B, Commer Ice Cream Canteen, reg, cream, oval roof, plain side decal, blk wheels, 1963, NM+.............................**$39.00**

47-D, Dipper Truck, SF, silver & yel, 1970, M **$16.00**

47-E, Beach Hopper, SF, dk bl, windscreen, pk base, orange interior, tan driver, 1974, M **$11.00**

48-B, Sport Boat & Trailer, reg, wht deck, red hull, dk bl trailer, gold motor, blk walls, 1961, NM+.............................**$27.00**

48-C, Dodge Dump Truck, reg, full-length base, blk wheels, 1966, MIB **$9.00**

49-A, M3 Personnel Carrier, reg, metal rollers, new treads, gold wheels, 1958, NM+ **$29.00**

49-B, Unimog, reg, bl & red, blk walls, 1967, MIB, W1...**$19.00**

49-C, Unimog, SF, bl & gr, plain grille, red base, spiro wheels, 1970, M...**$16.00**

49-D, Chop Suey, SF, magenta, red handlebars, 1973, M, W1 ....**$13.00**

50-A, Commer Pickup Truck, reg, tan, metal wheels, 1958, NM+ (VG box) **$40.00**

50-B, John Deere Tractor, reg, gold wheels, 1964, MIB, W1 ....**$32.00**

50-C, Kennel Truck, reg, wht grille, dogs on tree, blk wheels, tacky base pnt, 1969, MIB..**$13.00**

50-D, Kennel Truck, SF, gr, blk base, silver grille, orig top, 7 dogs, 1970, M..**$12.00**

51-B, John Deere Trailer, reg, complete, barrels on tree, blk walls, 1964, M (NM box), W1 ....**$20.00**

51-E, Citroen SM, SF, bronze, cream interior, unpnt base, no labels, 5-spoke wheels, 1972, NM-, W1 ....**$7.00**

52-A, Maserati 4CLT Racer, reg, yel, decal, complete, blk walls, 1958, NM- **$39.00**

52-B, BRM Racing Car, reg, scarce red, decals, blk walls, 1965, NM+ **$21.00**

52-C, Dodge Charger, SF, red, gr base, 5 labels, 1970, M ..**$12.00**

53-A, Aston Martin, reg, metallic lt gr, metal wheels, 1958, NM+ **$38.00**

53-B, Mercedes Benz 220 SE, reg, red, blk wheels, 1963, NM...**$25.00**

53-C, Ford Zodiac Mk IV, reg, silver & bl, blk wheels, 1968, MIB...**$17.00**

53-D, Ford Zodiac, SF, lt gr, 1970, M (NM- box).............**$12.00**

53-E, Tanzara, SF, orange, unpnt base, silver interior, amber windows, no tampo, 1972, M **$10.00**

53-F, Jeep CJ6, red, beige top, yel interior, 1977, M (EX box), W1 ....**$4.00**

54-C, Cadillac Ambulance, SF, wht, blk base, silver grille, 1970, NM+ **$17.00**

54-D, Ford Capri, SF, purple, ivory interior, 5-spoke wheels, 1971, M..**$9.00**

55-A, DUKW, reg, metal wheels, 1958, EX (VG+ box) ..**$42.00**

55-D, Mercury Police Car, reg, bl dome, blk walls, 1968, NM, W1 ....**$23.00**

55-E, Mercury Police Car, SF, wht, bl dome light, 1970, NMIB...**$12.00**

55-F, Mercury Police Station Wagon, SF, wht, unpnt base, hood & side shield labels, red light, MBP (dirty card)........**$13.00**

55-G, Hellraiser, SF, wht, unpnt base, cream interior, clear windows, stars & stripes label, 1975, NM, W1.................**$6.00**

56-A, London Trolley Bus, reg, red poles, decals 95%, gold wheels, 1958, NM+, W1 ....**$52.00**

56-B, Fiat 1500 Sedan, reg, aqua, brn luggage, blk walls, 1965, MIB, W1 ....**$18.00**

56-G, Peterbuilt Tanker, SF, bl, wht tank, clear windows, 'Milk' tank & door tampo, 1982, NM+ **$3.50**

57-A, Wolseley 1500, reg, pale gr, silver grille, gold wheels, 1958, NM...**$38.00**

57-B, Chevrolet Impala, reg, blk base, gold wheels, 1961, EX-, W1 ....**$24.00**

57-C, Land Rover Fire Truck, reg, decals, orig ladder, blk walls, 1966, M (EX+ box), W1 ....**$23.00**

58-A, BEA Coach, reg, decals, gold wheel, 1962, EX+ **$32.00**

58-C, DAF Girder Truck, reg, complete, girders on tree, blk wheels, 1968, M (NM box), W1 ....**$19.00**

58-E, Whoosh 'n Push, SF, yel, red interior, 2 labels, Maltese Cross wheels, 1972, M (EX- box), W1.....................**$11.00**

59-B, Ford Fairlane Fire Chief Car, reg, blk walls, 1963, EX...**$20.00**

Photo courtesy of Dana Johnson.

61-B, Alvis Stalwart BP Exploration Truck, regular wheels, green hubs, black wheels, 1966, MIB, $25.00.

59-E, Mercury Fire Chief Car, SF, red, unpnt base, clear window/dome light, ivory interior, dot-dash wheels, label, NM+ $14.00

60-B, Site Hut Truck, reg, blk walls, 1966, M (NM- box) ..$18.00

60-D, Lotus Super Seven, SF, orange, flame labels, 1971, EX+, W1..$6.00

60-E, Holden Pickup, SF, red, yel interior/bikes, amber windows, '500' labels, 1977, M, W1 ....$10.00

61-A, Ferret Scout Car, reg, M (EX- box).........................$37.00

61-C, Blue Shark, SF, dk bl, clear window, unpnt base, '86' label, 1971, EX+..$8.50

62-A, General Service Lorry, reg, blk walls, 1959, NM, W1 ..$33.00

62-D, Mercury Cougar, SF, gr, 1970, roof has box rub, NM+ (EX+ box) $11.00

63-A, Ford Service Ambulance, reg, blk walls, 1959, EX ..$30.00

63-B, Foamite Airport Crash Tender, reg, gold nozzle, complete, blk wheels, M (EX+ box) $32.00

63-C, Dodge Crane Truck, reg, red hook, blk walls, 1968, MIB $15.00

63-D, Dodge Crane Truck, SF, yel, blk axle covers, 1970, M (NM box) $17.00

63-H, Snorkel Fire Engine, SF, red, pnt base insert, 1982, M, W1..$5.00

64-A, Scammell Breakdown Truck, reg, gray plastic hook, blk walls, 1959, NM+ $34.00

64-B, MG 1100 Sedan, reg, blk wheels, 1966, M (EX+ box), W1..$16.00

64-C, MG 1100, SF, rare gr body, 1970, NM+ (NM box) ..$175.00

65-A, Jaguar 3.8 Litre Saloon, reg, red, blk walls, 1962, NM+..$26.00

65-C, Claas Combine Harvester, reg, blk wheels, 1967, NM+ ..$12.00

66-B, Harley-Davidson Motorcycle & Sidecar, reg, blk walls, 1962, MIB $65.00

66-C, Greyhound Bus, reg, amber windows, labels, blk wheels, 1967, M (NM box) $21.00

67-A, Saladin Armoured Car, reg, blk walls, 1959, M, W1 .$26.00

67-C, VW 1600TL Fastback, SF, purple, 1970, NM+ $17.50

67-D, Hot Rocker, SF, orange & red, unpnt base, 5-spoke wheels, 1973, M (EX+ card).......................................$13.00

68-A, Austin Mk II Radio Truck, reg, blk wheels, 1959, NM+..$40.00

68-B, Mercedes Coach, reg, orange, blk walls, 1965, MIB, W1..$20.00

68-C, Porsche 910, SF, red, amber windows, '68' hood label only, 1970, EX+ $7.00

69-A, Commer 30 CWT Nestle's Van, reg, decals 100%, gold wheels, 1959, MIB $45.00

69-B, Hatra Tractor Shovel, reg, yel, MIB $32.00

69-C, Rolls Royce Silver Shadow Coupe, SF, gold, ivory interior, blk tonneau, blk base, 1969, M.....................$16.00

70-A, Ford Thames Estate Car, reg, gr windows, blk walls, 1959, NM+ $34.00

70-D, Dodge Dragster, SF, pk, lavender base, lt gr snake label, spoked wheels, 1971, M...............................$13.00

71-B, Jeep Gladiator Pickup, reg, wht interior, blk walls, 1964, NM...$25.00

72-A, Fordson Tractor, reg, orange hubs, blk walls, 1959, EX $29.00

72-D, Hovercraft, SF, wht, blk base, bl windows, labels, 1972, M..$10.00

73-B, Ferrari F1 Racer, reg, gray driver, blk wheels, 1962, NM .$29.00

73-C, Mercury Station Wagon, reg, blk wheels, 1968, NM+.$13.00

73-F, Weasel, SF, olive, gr base & insert, blk hubs, 1974, NM $7.00

74-A, Mobile Refreshment Canteen, reg, silver, bl base & interior, gold wheels, 1959, EX+, W1 ....$35.00

74-B, Daimler Bus, reg, red, labels, blk wheels, 1966, M (EX box) $21.00

75-A, Ford Thunderbird, reg, cream & pk w/blk base, gold wheels, 1960, EX+ $36.00

75-B, Ferrari Berlinetta, reg, gr, wire wheels, blk wheels, 1965, NM+, W1 ....$9.00

75-D, Alfa Carabo, SF, pk, yel base, tampo, 5-spoke wheels, 1971, NM+..$4.50

75-F, Seasprite Helicopter, SF, wht, red base, bl window, 'Rescue' labels, 1977, MIP...$35.00

King Size, Speed Kings and Super Kings

K-01B, Hoveringham Tipper Truck, MIB, W1 ....$49.00

K-01C, O&K Excavator, SF, red & wht labels, VG-, W1 ..$3.00

K-02B, Kenworth Dump Truck, yel, NM, W1 ....$18.00

K-02C, Scammell Heavy Wreck Truck, wht, gr windows, EX, W1 ....$19.00

K-03B, Hatra Tractor Shovel, orig insert, M (NM window box), W1 ....$42.00

K-04A, International Tractor, red plastic wheels, NM+, W1 ....$39.00

K-04B, GMC Tractor & Freuhof Hopper Train, orig insert/price sticker, M (NM- window box), W1 ....$52.00

K-04C, Leyland Tipper, 'LE Transport' labels, G+, W1 .....$5.00

K-04D, Big Tipper, metallic red body, yel dump, 3 stripe labbels, orig insert, M (EX+ window box), W1 ....$19.00

K-05B, Racing Car Transporter, 2 cracks in roof plastic, EX+, W1 ....$14.00

K-05C, Muir Hill Tractor/Trailer, yel body, red chassis, bl driver, amber windows, labels, 1972, NM (EX window box), W1 ....$19.00

K-06B, Mercedes Ambulance, decals, orig stretcher & blanket, windshield crack, EX, W1............................$7.00

K-06C, GMC Cement Mixer, bl body, red chassis, yel barrel, blk box atop cab, orig insert, 1971, M (EX window box), W1 ....$19.00

K-07A, Curtis Wright Rear Dumper, missing 1 bed pin & 1 broken, G, W1 ....$8.00

K-07B, Refuse Truck, 1967, NM, W1 ....$22.00

K-07C, Racing Car Transporter, yel, red tailgate, amber windshield & top, no car, EX-, W1 ....$5.00

K-08C, CAT Traxcavator, yel body, orange bucket, blk rollers & treads, orig insert, NM+ (EX- window box), W1 ..$14.00

K-09B, Claas Combine Harvester, gr body, red blade, gr/wht labels, wht driver, orig insert, 1967, M (EX window box), W1 ....$42.00

K-09C, Fire Tender, blk extension, NM, W1 ....$9.00

K-10A, Aveling Barford Tractor Shovel, aqua, red wheels, w/air cleaner, no side decals, VG, W1 ....$15.00

K-10B, Pipi Truck, orig insert, 1967, NM+ (EX window box), W1 ....$44.00

K-10C, Car Transporter, clear windows, 'Auto Transport' labels, NM, W1 ....$12.50

K-101A, Sherman Tank, gold body, 'USA 48350' labels, orig gray treads, M, W1 ....$15.00

K-106A, Tank Transporter, lt gr cab, w/K-102A tank, NM+, W1 ....$29.00

K-108A, M3A1 Half Track, metallic gr body, charcoal gray base, orig top & treads, NM, W1 ....$12.00

K-11A, Fordson Tractor/Farm Trailer, bl steering wheel, orange plastic wheels, 1 rear wheel broke, 1 tire gone, EX, W1..$9.50

K-11C, Breakdown Truck, yel, blk base, wht booms, red hooks, 'AA' labels, NM+, W1 ....$13.00

K-115A, Army Petrol Tanker, complete, NM+, W1........$19.00

K-12A, Heavy Breakdown Truck, red hubs, no roof lights, no hook, EX+, W1 ....$12.00

K-12C, Hercules Mobile Crane, yel, red hook, 'Laing' labels, EX+, W1 ....$9.00

Photo courtesy of Dana Johnson.

K-13A, Readymix Concrete Truck, red with decals, red hubs, 1963, MIB, $30.00.

K-14A, Taylor Jumbo Crane, red weight box, orig insert, 1964, M (NM window box), W1 ....$42.00

K-14C, Heavy Breakdown Truck, amber windows, NM, W1 .$12.00

K-15A, Merryweather Fire Engine, label, orig insert, M (EX+ window box), W1 ....$50.00

K-15C, The Londoner, labels, 1982, M (NM- window box), W1 ....$17.00

K-16A, Dodge Tractor w/Twin Tippers, rear trailer missing dump & 2 tires, G+, W1....................................$9.00

K-17A, Lowloader w/Bulldozer, 'Taylor Woodrow' decals, no bulldozer, EX-, W1 ....$19.00

K-17B, Articulated Container Truck, metallic red cab, red trailer chassis, wht containers w/bl roofs, labels, NM, W1 ....$14.00

K-18A, Articulated Horse Box, gr interior, no horses, VG+, W1 ....$6.00

K-19A, Scammell Tipper Truck, 1967, EX-, W1..............$12.00

K-20C, Peterbuilt Wrecker, dk gr, unpnt roof mount & base, red lights, M (NM window box), W1....................$24.00

K-21A, Mercury Cougar, red interior, w/insert, 1968, M (EX+ window box), W1 ....$33.00

K-22A, Dodge Charger, orig insert, 1969, NM+ (EX+ window box), W1 ....$54.00

K-23A, Mercury Police Commuter, NM, W1 ....$12.00

K-31A, Bertone Runabout, gr windows, orig insert, M (NM window box), W1 ....$17.00

K-31B, Peterbuilt Refrigerator Truck, 'Burger King' label, orig insert, MIB, W1 ....$89.00

K-34A, Thunderclap, yel background '34' labels, orig insert, NMIB, W1 ....$14.00

K-35A, Lightning, red, '35 Team Matchbox' hood label, 'Firestone' wing label, '35' side label, orig insert, MIB, W1 ....$18.00

K-39B, Snorkel Fire Engine, 4 orig men, NM (EX- window box), W1 ....$19.00

K-40A, Trail Blazer, red body, yel base & interior, amber windows, blk antenna, bl lights, EX+, W1....................$9.00

K-41A, Fuzz Buggy, wht body, blk base, clear windows, yel interior, amber lights, wht steering wheel, EX+, W1 ....$9.00

K-42A, Nissan 270ZX, 2 cracks in gr windows, EX, W1.....$7.00

K-48A, Mercedes 350 SLC, bronze, silver & gray base, yel interior, amber windows, M (EX box), W1 ....$19.00

K-49A, Ambulance, wht body, red roof & interior, blk base, clear windows, bl light, orig stretcher & blanket, NM, W1 ....$12.00

K-51A, Barracuda, bl body, yel interior & spoiler, clear windshield, wht driver, '5' labels, NM+, W1 ....$10.00

K-53A, Hot Fire Engine, blk driver w/gold helmet, no rider, right front fender bent o/w NM+, W1 ....$10.00

K-62A, Doctor's Emergency Car, silver & gray base, NM, W1..$10.00

K-63A, Mercedes Ambulance, dk bl windows, orig stretcher, blanket & insert, NMIB, W1 ....$15.00

K-64A, Range Rover Fire Engine, wht ladder, 'Fire Control' labels, NM+, W1 ....$12.00

K-65A, Plymouth Trail Duster, red, wht base, amber windows, 'Emergency Rescue' labels, orig stretcher & blanket, NM, W1 ....$10.00

K-66A, Jaguar XJ12 Police Patrol, brn interior, bl lights, Maltese Cross wheels, stripe tampo, amber windows, NM+, W1 ....$15.00

Photo courtesy of Dana Johnson.

K-67A, Dodge Monaco Fire Chief Car, yellow with red and blue detail, 1978, MIB, $10.00.

K-78A, Gran Fury Police Car, bl & wht body, bl lights, 'Polizie' decals, orig key, no insert, M (NM window box), W1 ....$14.00

K-2001A, Raider Command, orig treads, rockets missing 1 tip o/w NM+, W1..$20.00

K-2002A, Flight Hunter, NM, W1.................................$20.00

K-2003A, Crusader Tank, orig treads, NM, W1 ....$17.00

Models of Yesteryear

Y-01A, 1925 Allchin Traction Engine, diagonal unpnt treads, gold boiler door, 1956, NM+, W1 ....$58.00

Y-01B, 1911 Ford Model T, blk roof, seats & grille, 12-spoke 13-mm brass wheels, 1 brake lever, MIB, W1 ....$31.00

Y-01C, 1936 Jaguar SS, cream, blk seats & tires, 1977, NM+, W1..$9.00

Y-02A, 1911 B-Type London Bus, red, unpnt wheels, bl driver, 8 over 4 windows, 1956, EX+, W1 ....$52.00

Y-02B, 1911 Ford Model T, red, blk roof, blk seats & grille, red steering wheel, 12-spoke wheels, 1964, NM+, W1 .....$15.00

Y-02B, 1911 Renault 2-Seater, gr, 3-prong spare, gr metal steering wheel, 1963, M (VG+ box), W1 ....$21.00

Y-02C, 1914 Prince Henry Vauxhall, red, blk chassis/radiator, silver hood, red 12-spoke wheels, wht-walls, 1970, NM+, W1...$19.00

Y-03A, 1907 London E Class Tramcar, wht roof, new decals (99%), 1956, M, W1 ....$83.00

Y-03B, 1910 Benz Limo, cream, gr roof, seats & grille, metal steering wheel, high lights, 1966, EX+, W1..............$19.00

Y-04A, 1928 Sentinel Steam Wagon, bl, blk chimney, gold rim & box, crimped axles, decals 100%, 1956, NM+ (EX+ box), W1 ....$109.00

Y-04A, 1928 Sentinel Steam Wagon, bl, rare blk plastic wheels, 1956, NM-, W1...$270.00

Y-04B, 1905 Shand Mason Horse-Drawn Fire Engine, red, blk horses, gold 'London' decals & boiler, 1960, NM, W1 .$110.00

Y-04C, 1909 Opel Coupe, wht, tan roof, red seats & radiator, 1967, M, W1...$13.00

Y-04D, 1930 Duesenberg, red, blk roof & seats, 24-spoke wheels, 1976, NM, W1...$16.00

Y-05A, 1929 LeMans Bentley, gold radiator, gr grille & tonneau, silver steering wheel, 1958, NM, W1 ....$67.00

Y-05B, 1929 4.5 Litre Bentley, gr, silver radiator, '5' decal, C base, M (EX- box), W1..$39.00

Y-05C, 1907 Peugeot, yel, blk roof, red seats & grille, amber windows, 1969, M, W1..$13.00

Y-05D, 1927 Talbot Van, yel, 1 'Merita' label & spare missing, VG+, W1...$4.00

Y-06A, 1916 AEC Y-Type Lorry, dk gray, decals 98%, 1957, NM+, W1...$106.00

Y-06B, 1926 Type 35 Bugatti, red, wht dash & floor, '6' decal, 1961, M, W1..$46.00

Y-06C, 1913 Cadillac, gold, dk red roof, seats & radiator, brass wheels, '1913' on base, 1967, M, W1 ....$14.00

Y-06C, 1913 Cadillac, gold, maroon roof, grille & seats, '1913' on base, 1967, NM+, W1.....................................$49.00

Y-07A, 1918 4-Ton Leyland Van, red-brn, cream roof, full decal, 1957, NM-, W1...$66.00

Y-07B, 1913 Mercer Raceabout, lilac, short spotlight, fine tread, 1961, NM+, W1...$44.00

Y-07C, 1912 Rolls Royce, gold, red base, red roof, blk seats & grille, 12-spoke silver wheels, 1968, NM+, W1 ....$17.00

Y-08A, 1926 Morris Bullnose Cowley, tan, gold trim, unplated wheels, NM, W1..$64.00

Y-08B, 1914 Sunbeam Motorcycle & Sidecar, dk gr seat, 1962, M, W1..$34.00

Y-09A, 1924 Fowler Big Lion Showman Engine, marked Lesney's Modern Amusement, maroon base, MIB, $100.00.

Y-09A, 1924 Fowler Big Lion Showman Engine, gold boiler door & roof supports, maroon base, VG+, W1...................$26.00

Y-09B, 1912 Simplex, gr, red seats, dk red grille, seat pins, brass wheels, no roof, EX+, W1...$7.00

Y-10A, 1908 GP Mercedes, cream, gr seats, plated wheels, gold trim, 2 exhaust webs, riveted axles, NM+, W1 ....$64.00

Y-10B, 1928 Mercedes Benz 36/220, wht, beige dash, single spare, NM-, W1 ....$13.00

Y-11A, 1920 Aveling & Porter Steam Roller, blk roof supports & flywheel, gold trim, MIB, W1 ....$125.00

Y-11B, 1912 Packard Landaulet, dk red seats, blk seats, brass wheels, radiator & steering wheel, 3-prong spare, NM+, W1 ....$17.00

Y-11C, 1938 Lagonda Drophead Coupe, copper, gold chassis, blk seats & radiator, silver 24-spoke wheels, NM+, W1 ....$8.00

Y-12B, 1909 Thomas Flyabout, bl, tan top, red seats, seat pins, B base, M, W1..$15.00

Photo courtesy of Dana Johnson.

Y-13B, 1911 Daimler, yellow with red seats, 4-spoke steering wheel, open spare recess, MIB, $50.00.

Y-13B, 1911 Daimler, yel, red seats, 4-spoke steering wheel, open spare recess, D base, no radiator o/w M, W1 .....$15.00

Y-13C, 1918 Crossley RAF Tender, bl, tan roof & canopy, wht seats/olive radiator, silver 24-spoke wheels, M (EX box), W1 ....$62.00

Y-14B, 1911 Maxwell Roadster, turq, blk roof, dk red seats, copper tank & fire extinguisher, no radiator, NM, W1 .....$5.00

Y-15A, 1907 Rolls Royce Silver Ghost, metallic lt gr, blk seats, brass C wheels, 1960, M (VG box), W1 ....$27.00

Y-16A, 1904 Spyker, mustard yel, yel radiator & seats, fine tread, M (EX- box), W1 ....$31.00

Y-16B, 1928 Mercedes Benz SS Coupe, bl w/gray side panels, 1972, MIB $20.00

Y-16B, 1928 Mercedes Benz SS Coupe, red body, 1972, M ..**$15.00**

Y-20A, 1937, Mercedes Benz 540K, silver, 1981, M.........**$15.00**

Y-22A, 1930 Ford Model A Van, Maggi, 1982, M **$12.00**

Y-22A, 1930 Ford Model A Van, Oxo, 1982, M **$10.00**

Y-22A, 1930 Ford Model A Van, Palm Toffee, 1982, M..**$15.00**

Y-22A, 1930 Ford Model A Van, beige with red and cream detail, 1982, MIB, $18.00.

Y-23A, 1922 AEC S-Type Omnibus, 1982, M **$15.00**

Y-23B, 1930 Mack Tanker, 1989, M (NM box) **$14.00**

Y-24A, 1927 Bugatti T44, 1983, M..................................**$12.00**

Y-25A, 1910 Renault Type AG, 1983, M.......................**$15.00**

Y-26A, 1918 Crossley Beer Lorry, 1983, M.....................**$10.00**

Y-40A, 1931 Mercedes Benz Type 770, gray w/bl roof, 1991, M..**$10.00**

Skybusters

SB-01, Learjet, wht, US Air Force, MBP **$4.00**

SB-02B, Airbus A300, Lufthansa, wht & gray, NM, W1 ...**$7.00**

SB-04, Mirage F1, thick axles, bull's-eye labels, NM, W1 ..**$5.00**

SB-06, MIG 21, silver metal-flake, EX-, W1......................**$3.00**

SB-10, Boeing 747, Pan Am, wht, pearly silver underside, Macau, M, W1...**$12.00**

SB-12, Skyhawk 1-4F, dk bl, wht base & wings, thick axles, 'Marines' labels, EX, W1..**$5.00**

SB-13, DC-10, wht & gray, United, NM+, W1...............**$10.00**

SB-15, Boeing 747, blue and white, MIB, $4.00.

SB-16, F4U-4 Corsair, bl, Navy, MIB **$10.00**

SB-20, Helicopter, Army gr, MBP....................................**$10.00**

SB-21, Lightning, olive gr, MBP **$10.00**

SB-22, Tornado, lt gray, wht base, F132 ornate design, Thailand, NM ,W1...**$4.00**

SB-23, Supersonic Transport, Air France, fuselage tampo, tall label, Macau, EX+, W1...**$7.00**

SB-28, Airbus A300, Lufthansa, M (EX+ box), W1........**$10.00**

SB-31, Boeing 747-400, gray & bl, MBP.............................**$3.00**

SB-32, Fairchild A-10, gray & gr camo, MBP....................**$4.00**

SB-34, Lockheed C-130 Hercules, wht & silver, USCG, MIB..**$4.00**

SB-36, F-117 Stealth Fighter, blk, MBP.............................**$4.00**

SB-38, BAE 146, wht, MIB..**$4.00**

Model Kits

While values for military kits seem to have leveled off and others may have actually gone down, this is certainly not the case with the Aurora monster and character kits which are continuing to increase in value.

Though model kits were popular with kids of the fifties who enjoyed the challenge of assembling a classic car or two or a Musketeer figure now and then, when the monster series hit in the early 1960s, sales shot through the ceiling. Made popular by all the monster movies of that decade, ghouls like Vampirella, Frankenstein and the Wolfman were eagerly built up by kids everywhere. They could (if their parents didn't object too strongly) even construct an actual working guillotine. Aurora had other successful series of figure kits, too, based on characters from comic strips and TV shows as well as a line of sports stars.

But the vast majority of model kits were vehicles. They varied in complexity, some requiring much more dexterity on the part of the model builder than others, and they came in several scales, from 1/8 (which might be as large as 20" to 24") down to 1/43 (generally about 3" to 4"), but the most popular scale was 1/25 (usually between 6" to 8"). Some of the largest producers of vehicle kits were AMT, MPC, and IMC. Though production obviously waned during the late 1970s and early '80s, with the intensity of today's collector market, companies like Ertl (who now is producing 1/25 scale vehicles using some of the old AMT dies) are proving that model kits still sell very well.

As a rule of thumb, assembled kits (built-ups) are priced at about 25% to 50% of the price range for a boxed kit, but this is not always true on the higher-priced kits. One mint in the box with the factory seal intact will often sell for up to 15% more than if the seal were broken, though depending on the kit, a sealed perfect box may add as much $100.00. Condition of the box is crucial. For more information, we recommend *Aurora History and Price Guide* by Bill Bruegman, *Collectible Figure Kits of the 50s, 60s & 70s* by Gordy Dutt and *Classic Plastic Model Kits* by Rick Polizzi.

Advisors: Mike and Kurt Fredericks (F4); John and Sheri Pavone (P3).

Other Sources: B10, J7, T1, P4

See also Plasticville.

Adams, Aerial Missile Transporter, 1958, M (EX+ box), D9..**$45.00**

Adams, Hawk Missile Batter #154, 1958, 1/40, MIB, G5 .$75.00

Adams, Honest John w/Launcher #150, 1958, 1/40, MIB, G5 ....$140.00

Adams, Thor Rocket #162, 1958, 1/87, MIB, G5...........$150.00

Addar, Planet of the Apes, Cornelius, 1973, MIB (sealed), from $35 to $45.00

Addar, Planet of the Apes, Dr Zaius, 1973, MIB, from $30 to $40.00

Addar, Planet of the Apes, Dr Zaius, 1973, MIB (sealed), from $55 to $65.00

Addar, Planet of the Apes, Scenes in a Bottle, Treehouse, 1975, MIB (sealed), H4 ....$35.00

Addar, Rendezvous in Space, Scenes in a Bottle, 1975, M (EX+ box), D9 ....$25.00

Addar, Spirit in a Bottle (phantom-like monster in cemetery), Super Scenes, 1975, MIB, D9/H4, from $30 to..........$35.00

Addar, WWI Dogfight, Super Scenes, 1975, M (EX+ box), D9...$32.00

AEF Designs, Aliens, Burke #AC-4, 1980s, 1/35, MIB, G5 ..$20.00

AEF Designs, Aliens, Queen Egg Chamber, MIB, E3.....$200.00

AEF Designs, Aliens, Warrior Alien C (kneeling) #AX-3, 1980s, 1/35, MIB, G5..$40.00

Airfix, Anne Boleyn, Famous Women in History, 1974, partially assembled, 1 sm pc pnt, w/instructions (EX+ box), D9 ....$15.00

Airfix, Henry VIII, 1960s, M (EX+ box), D9...................$30.00

Airfix, High Chaparral Set #38, 1/75, MIB, G5.................$8.00

Airfix, Lunar Module #3013, 1979, 1/72, MIB, D9/G5 ....$20.00

Airfix, Mayflower, 1972, M (EX+ box), D9......................$10.00

Airfix, Moonraker James Bond, 1979, M (VG+ box), H4..$35.00

Airfix, Star Wars, Snowspeeder #10172, 1983, 1/35, MIB, G5 ....$15.00

Alabe, Neanderthal Man #2963, 1976, 1/8, MIB, G5 ......$45.00

AMT, Apollo Spacecraft #955, 1970, 1/200, MIB (sealed), G5 ....$12.00

AMT, Big Hit?, Hang-Out #615, late 1960s, MIB, D9/G5, from $30 to...$35.00

AMT, Flintstone's Family Sedan, MIB (sealed), J2 ....$90.00

AMT, Flintstone's Rock Cruncher, 1974, MIB (sealed), D9...$43.00

AMT, Flintstone's Sports Car, 1970s, MIB (sealed), J2....$90.00

AMT, Get Smart Sunbeam Car #925, 1967, 1/25, MIB.$150.00

AMT, Intrepid Civil War Balloon, 1960-70s, M (EX 8½x10" box), D9 ....$17.00

AMT, KISS Custom Chevy Van, 1977, MIB (sealed), D9.$45.00

AMT, Munsters' Coach, 1964, orig issue, NMIB, J2 ......$240.00

AMT, Pacer Wagon Kit #T484, NMIB, J2 ....$25.00

AMT, Star Trek, Klingon Battle Cruiser, 1968, MIB (sealed), D9...$58.00

AMT, Star Trek, Klingon Battle Crusier (Klingon Warrior Empire), 1974, MIB, H4 ....$40.00

AMT, Star Trek, Motion Picture Enterprise #970, 1979, 1/500, w/lights, MIB (sealed), G5/J6, from $60 to $65.00

AMT, Star Trek, Space Ship Set, 1976, includes USS Enterprise, Klingon Battle Cruiser & Romulan Bird of Prey, MIB, D9..$15.00

AMT, Star Trek, Spock w/Snakes, 1970s, assembled & pnt, needs rpr, D9...$45.00

AMT, Star Trek, Spock w/Snakes, 1970s, 1/12, MIB, G5 ..$95.00

AMT, Star Trek, USS Enterprise #951, MIB (sealed), E3..$55.00

AMT, Star Trek, USS Enterprise Command Bridge, 1975, MIB (sealed), C1/D9, from $60 to.................................$75.00

AMT, Star Trek, USS Enterprise Exploration Set, 1974, MIB (sealed), D9...$40.00

AMT, Star Trek (The Motion Picture), Vulcan Shuttle, 1979, MIB (sealed), D9...$35.00

AMT, 1937 Chevy Coupe Street Rod #A137-250, 1/25, MIB, M19..$30.00

AMT, 1949 Ford Coupe #T290, 1/25, wht, MIB, M19 ....$25.00

AMT, 1949 Ford Sedan 2-Door #T149-149, 1/25, gray, MIB, M19..$55.00

AMT, 1953 Chevy Corvette Convertible #T310, 1/25, wht, MIB, M19...$15.00

AMT, 1953 Corvette T-310, M (VG box), S15 ....$25.00

AMT, 1962 Corvette, NMIB, J2 ....$20.00

AMT, 1963 Buick Electra Convertible #06-513-149, 1/25, wht, MIB, M19 ....$150.00

AMT, 1977 Ford Pinto 2-Door #T485, 1/25, wht, MIB, M19..$20.00

AMT/Ertl, Airwolf Helicopter #6680, 1984, 1/48 scale, MIB, D9/G5, from $20 to $25.00

AMT/Ertl, Batman, Batmobile #6877, 1989, 1/25, MIB, E3/G5, from $15 to..$20.00

AMT/Ertl, Deep Space 9, Runabout, MIB, E3.........$15.00

AMT/Ertl, Dick Tracy Coupe #6107, 1990, 1/25, MIB, G5 ....$10.00

AMT/Ertl, Ghostbusters II ECTO 1-A #6017, 1989, 1/25, MIB, D9............$12.00

AMT/Ertl, Joker Goon Car/Gotham City Police Car, 1989, MIB (sealed), from $10 to............$12.00

AMT/Ertl, Munsters, Koach & Dragula Cars #8059, 1991, 1/25, MIB, from $55 to............$60.00

AMT/Ertl, Robo 1 Police Car, MIB (sealed), D9............$10.00

AMT/Ertl, Star Trek, USS Enterprise, 1983, MIB (sealed), D9............$15.00

AMT/Ertl, Star Trek, 3-Ship Enterprise Set #6618, 1988, 1/2200, MIB, from $8 to............$10.00

AMT/Ertl, Star Trek (IV), USS Enterprise #6693, 1986, 1/500, MIB, from $15 to............$20.00

AMT/Ertl, Star Trek: The Next Generation, Klingon Battle Cruiser #6812, 1991, MIB, from $12 to............$18.00

AMT/Ertl, Star Trek: The Next Generation, USS Enterprise #6619, MIB, from $10 to............$15.00

AMT/Ertl, 1964 American La France Pumper #6669, 1/25, MIB, M19............$35.00

Aoshima, Delorian #1800, 1990, 1/24, MIB, G5............$25.00

Argonauts, Robocop 2, Robocop, 1990, 1/8, MIB, G5............$90.00

Arii, Macross, Destroid Defender #302, 1/100, MIB, G5/E3, from $12 to............$20.00

Atlantic, Geronimo & the Apaches #4002, 1/75, MIB, G5..$16.00

Aurora, AH-IG Assault Copter, NMIB, J2............$30.00

Aurora, Alfred E Neuman, 1965, M (NM box), from $300 to............$350.00

Aurora, Alfred E Neuman, 1965, partially assembled, missing about 5 pcs, VG box, D9............$165.00

Aurora, Allosaurus, Prehistoric Scenes, 1971, missing 1 ft pc & 2 hands, partially assembled o/w complete, EX+ box, D9.$70.00

Aurora, Amazing Spider-Man, 1966, M (NM box), from $300 to............$350.00

Aurora, Black Knight of Nurnberg #1580, 1956, 2nd issue, M (EX+ box), $65.00.

Photo courtesy of June Moon.

Aurora, American Astronaut #AMS409, 1967, 1/12, MIB (sealed), from $140 to............$185.00

Aurora, Aston Martin DB4, 1965, M (EX+ box), D9............$25.00

Aurora, Batman, Comic Scenes, MIB, E3............$65.00

Aurora, Batman, 1964, M (NM box), E3, from $200 to.$250.00

Aurora, Blue Knight of Milan #B472, 1963, M (EX+ box), D9............$16.00

Aurora, Blue Knight of Milan #1520, 1956, M (EX 1st issue box), D9............$50.00

Aurora, British Spitfire WWII Airplane, NMIB, J2............$48.00

Aurora, Captain Action #480, 1966, 1/12, MIB, G5............$330.00

Aurora, Captain America, Comic Scenes, MIB (sealed), T2............$195.00

Aurora, Cave, Prehistoric Scenes, M (poor box), T2............$30.00

Aurora, Cave, Prehistoric Scenes, 1972, M (NM sealed 2nd issue box), D9............$45.00

Aurora, Chevy Custom Pick-Up Model Kit, 1963, MIB (sealed), D9............$25.00

Aurora, Chinese Girl, 1957, NMIB, D9............$70.00

Aurora, Chinese Junk, 1962, M (EX+ box), D9............$35.00

Aurora, Chinese Mandarin, 1957, M (EX+ box), D9............$70.00

Aurora, Chitty-Chitty Bang-Bang, 1968, missing 6 sm detail pcs o/w complete, EX+ (EX+ box), F8............$55.00

Aurora, Corsair American Privateer, 1959, M (G box), D9..$20.00

Aurora, Creature From the Black Lagoon, Monsters of the Movies, MIB (sealed), T2............$250.00

Aurora, Cro-Magnon Man, Prehistoric Scenes, 1971, M (M sealed Canadian box), D9............$35.00

Aurora, Customized Corvette, 1963, MIB (sealed), D9....$26.00

Aurora, Customizing Monster Kit #1, 1963, M (EX+ 5x13" box), T2............$140.00

Aurora, Dick Tracy, 1968, MIB, D11/T2, from $175 to.$225.00

Aurora, Dick Tracy Space Coupe, 1968, M (sealed box), C1............$310.00

Aurora, Dr Jekyll, Glow-in-the-Dark, 1969, MIB, from $150 to............$175.00

Aurora, Dr Jekyll, Monsters of the Movies, MIB (sealed), T2, from $95 to............$125.00

Aurora, Dr Jekyll as Mr Hyde, Glow-in-the-Dark, 1972, MIB (sealed), from $125 to............$175.00

Aurora, Dracula, Glow-in-the-Dark, 1972, assembled, NM, J2............$35.00

Aurora, Dracula #424, Monsters of the Movies, 1962, MIB (sealed), T2............$295.00

Aurora, Dracula #424, 1962, EX (EX box), J2............$220.00

Aurora, Dracula #454, Frightening Lightening, Glow-in-the-Dark, MIB, from $275 to............$325.00

Aurora, Famous Fighters, Regulus II Guided Missile, 1958, 1/48, MIB, P4............$225.00

Aurora, Fantastic Voyage, Voyager, orig issue, MIB (sealed), T2............$895.00

Aurora, Ferrari Tiger Shark Customizing Kit, 1960, MIB (sealed), D9............$35.00

Aurora, Fokker D-7 WWII Airplane, MIB, J2............$38.00

Aurora, Forgotten Prisoner, Glow-in-the-Dark, 1969, MIB, T2............$300.00

Aurora, Frankenstein, Glow-in-the-Dark, 1972, MIB, T2, from $120 to............$150.00

Aurora, Frankenstein, Monster Scenes, MIB, from $125 to..**$150.00**

Aurora, Frankenstein, orig issue, M (M 1½" thick box), from $325 to...**$400.00**

Aurora, Frankenstein, orig issue, M (M 2" thick box), from $250 to...**$325.00**

Aurora, Giant Bird, Prehistoric Scenes, 1972, MIB, J2/T1, from $50 to..**$60.00**

Aurora, Giant Bird, Prehistoric Scenes, 1972, missing 1 eggshell half & baby bird o/w complete, EX (VG box), D9 ....**$40.00**

Aurora, Giant Wooly Mammoth, 1972, M (EX+ box), D9 .**$100.00**

Aurora, Gladiator #V406, 1964, 1/8, MIB (sealed), G5 .**$245.00**

Aurora, Godzilla, Glow-in-the-Dark, 1964, assembled, EX, J6...**$55.00**

Aurora, Godzilla, Glow-in-the-Dark, 1972, MIB, T2.....**$285.00**

Aurora, Gold Knight, Historical, M (EX+ box w/torn seal), T2..**$195.00**

Aurora, Great Moments in Sport, Dempsey Vs Firpo, 1965, M (NM box), D9...**$125.00**

Aurora, Green Beret, 1966, M (EX+ box), D9 ....**$85.00**

Aurora, Gruesome Goodies #634, Monster Scenes, MIB, T2..**$125.00**

Aurora, Gruesome Goodies #634, Monster Scenes, 1971, 2 pcs pnt, orig instructions missing, EX Canadian issue box, D9..**$45.00**

Aurora, Hanging Cage, Monster Scenes, 1974, w/1 photocopied instruction sheet o/w complete, M (EX+ box), D9....**$45.00**

Aurora, Hulk, Comic Scenes, MIB, T2 ....**$75.00**

Aurora, Hunchback of Notre Dame, Glow-in-the-Dark, 1972, MIB, from $100 to...**$150.00**

Aurora, Hunchback of Notre Dame, 1963, assembled, EX+, J2...**$55.00**

Aurora, Hunchback of Notre Dame, 1963, M (EX+ box w/Anthony Quinn art), from $300 to **$350.00**

Aurora, Indian Chief, 1957, M (EX+ box), D9 ....**$100.00**

Aurora, Invaders Flying Saucer, 1975, missing base & instructions (EX+ 2nd issue box), D9 ....**$40.00**

Aurora, Invaders UFO, assembled, missing 6 landing gear pcs, 15% pnt, w/7 figures, D9 ....**$35.00**

Aurora, James Bond 007-Goldfinger, James Bond #414, 1966, 1/8, MIB, G5..**$519.00**

Aurora, John F Kennedy, Great American Presidents, 1965, MIB (sealed), C1, from $180 to **$210.00**

Aurora, John F Kennedy #851, Great American Presidents, 1965, 1/8, EX (EX box), D9.....................................**$90.00**

Aurora, King Kong #K465, 1972, 1/25, MIB, G5, from $250 to...**$300.00**

Aurora, Land of the Giants Snake Scene #816, assembled & partially pnt, complete, D9, from $170 to.....................**$200.00**

Aurora, Land of the Giants Spindrift Space Ship, 1968, assembled, 40% pnt, missing stand leg, needs rpr, w/3 figures, D9 ....**$180.00**

Aurora, Lone Ranger, Comic Scenes, 1974, MIB (sealed), C1/T2, from $35 to...**$45.00**

Aurora, Lost in Space, Robot, orig issue, assembled, complete, T2, from $275 to..**$330.00**

Aurora, Madame Tussad's Chamber of Horrors Guillotine, few pcs only (EX box), J2...**$275.00**

Aurora, Man From UNCLE, Napoleon Solo #411, 1966, VG (VG box), H4 ....**$130.00**

Aurora, Moscow-Russian Aircraft Missile Ship, 1972, MIB (sealed), J2 ....**$45.00**

Aurora, Mummy, Glow-in-the-Dark, 1972, partially assembled, complete (EX box), $50.00.

Aurora, Mummy #427, 1963, 1/8, NMIB, J2, minimum value...**$265.00**

Aurora, Munster's Living Room, MIB **$1,290.00**

Aurora, Neanderthal Man, Prehistoric Scenes, EX+ (EX+ 1st issue box), J2...**$55.00**

Aurora, Pan-Am Boeing 747 Jumbo Jet, 1971, NMIB, J2..**$40.00**

Aurora, Pendulum, Monster Scenes, M (NM box), T2..**$125.00**

Aurora, Phantom of the Opera, Glow-in-the-Dark, 1969, assembled, w/instructions, EX+ (orig box), from $100 to.**$135.00**

Aurora, Phantom of the Opera, Glow-in-the-Dark, 1972, MIB (sealed), T2, from $120 to.......................................**$150.00**

Aurora, Phantom of the Opera, 1963, 1/12-scale, Lon Chaney as Phantom, M (EX+ box), T2......................................**$280.00**

Aurora, Rat Patrol, 1967, M (EX+ box), D9....................**$98.00**

Aurora, Robin the Boy Wonder, original issue, MIB, $150.00.

Aurora, Robin, Comic Scenes, MIB (sealed), T2 ....$125.00

Aurora, Russian Stalin Tank #323, 1972, M (G box), S15..$35.00

Aurora, Russian-TV-104 Jet Airliner, NMIB, J2 ....$50.00

Aurora, Silver Knight of Ausberg #471, 1963, MIB (sealed), D9...$45.00

Aurora, Silver Knight of Ausberg #471, 1963, 1/8, partially assembled, orig box, G5...$22.00

Aurora, Spartacus, 1965, 1/8, MIB, scarce, T2 ....$360.00

Aurora, Stanley Steamer Car, 1961, NMIB, J2.................$30.00

Aurora, Superboy, Comic Scenes, 1974, MIB, D9/E3, from $60 to...$70.00

Aurora, Superboy, Comic Scenes, 1974, MIB (sealed), T2..$100.00

Aurora, Superman, Comic Scenes, 1974, MIB, D9/E3, from $40 to...$55.00

Aurora, Superman, Comic Scenes, 1974, MIB (sealed), D9, from $40 to..$60.00

Aurora, Tarzan #181, 1967, assembled, 85% pnt, needs rpr, D9...$23.00

Aurora, Thoroughbred Horse Race, 1972, M (EX+ box), D9 .$15.00

Aurora, Tonto #183, Comic Scenes, 1974, MIB (sealed), D9/T2, from $30 to...$35.00

Aurora, Tucumari Hydrofoil, Young Model Builders Club, 1974, MIB, D9 ....$55.00

Aurora, Viking Ship #H30, 1957, 1/80, MIB, G5.............$70.00

Aurora, Viking Ship #320, 1962, 1/80, MIB, G5..............$60.00

Aurora, White-Tail Deer, 1962, M (EX+ box), D9 ....$35.00

Aurora, Witch #470, Glow-in-the-Dark, 1969, MIB, T2 ..$175.00

Aurora, Witch #470, Glow-in-the-Dark, 1972, MIB (torn seal), from $175 to $200.00

Aurora, Wolf-man, assembled, M, $225.00.

Photo courtesy of June Moon.

Aurora, Wolfman, Monsters of the Movies, 1975, MIB (sealed), from $250 to $300.00

Aurora, Wolfman, 1962, EX+ (NM 1st issue box), from $250 to..$300.00

Aurora, Wonder Woman #FS479, 1965, 1/12, MIB, G5..$550.00

Aurora, WWI British SE-5 Scout, 1956, M (VG+ 10x4" box), D9...$25.00

Aurora, Zorro, 1965, orig issue, M (EX+ box), from $200 to.$250.00

Aurora, Zorro, 1965, orig issue, MIB (sealed), from $275 to...$325.00

Bachmann, Americana, Bowlers #6001, 1962, 1/15, MIB, G5...$75.00

Bachmann, Animals of the World, Lion #7101, 1959, 1/12, MIB, G5..$40.00

Bachmann, Birds of the World, Baltimore Oriole #9000, 1959, 1/1, MIB, G5...$25.00

Bachmann, Birds of the World, Bohemian Waxwing #9011, 1959, 1/1, MIB, G5...$32.00

Bachmann, Dogs of the World, Basset Hound, 1960s, M (EX+ box), D9 ....$26.00

Bachmann, Dogs of the World, Standard Poodle #8007, 1959, 1/6, MIB, G5...$25.00

Bachmann, Dogs of the World, Wire-Haired Terrier, 1960s, M (EX+ box), D9 ....$25.00

Bachmann, Douglas DC-8 Airliner, 1960s, MIB, T2........$15.00

Bachmann, German Messerschmitt Me-109, 1960s, MIB, T2..$15.00

Bachmann, German WWII Focke-Wulf 90, 1960s, MIB, T2...$15.00

Bachmann, Storytown USA, Humpty Dumpty, 1950s, M (VG box), T2 ....$70.00

Bachmann, Storytown USA, Three Men in a Tub, 1950s, 2 pcs glued o/w unassembled, EX (EX 6x9" box), T2..........$80.00

Bachmann, US WWII B-29 Super Fortress, 1960s, MIB, T2 ..$15.00

Bachmann, USS WWII B-24 Liberator, 1960s, MIB, T2 .$15.00

Bandai, Baltanseizin #0503524, 1984, 1/350, MIB, E3/G5, from $15 to $18.00

Bandai, Godzilla #0003526, 1990, 1/350, MIB, G5 ....$55.00

Bandai, Gundam Mobile Suit F91 #0032347, 1991, 1/100, MIB, G5 ....$20.00

Bandai, Lotus 47GT #8027-600, 1/20, yel, MIB, M19......$25.00

Bandai, Star-Blazers, Space Cruiser #0031253, 1/500, MIB, G5 ...$75.00

Bandai, Ultraman #0003523, 1990, 1/350, MIB, G5 ....$16.00

Billiken, Creature From the Black Lagoon, MIB, H4 .....$120.00

Billiken, Frankenstein, MIB, H4 ....$110.00

Billiken, Godzilla, minor partial assembly (EX+ box), D9..$45.00

Billiken, 7th Voyage of Sinbad, Cyclops, 1984, MIB, G5 ..$200.00

Comet, Spad Biplane #3105, balsa wood, 12", MIB, G5.....$6.00

Dark Horse, Frankenstein, vinyl, MIB, E3 ....$90.00

Dark Horse, King Kong #K1092, 1992, MIB, G5..............$70.00

Dark Horse, Predator, MIB, E3..$225.00

Delux Vacumform, Fantastic Voyage, Proteus, 1980s, MIB, G5 ....$25.00

Eldon, Invader Show Car, 1st issue, EX (EX box), J2 ....$15.00

Eldon, Match Kit, ME-109E Messerschmitt, 1967, 1/100, MIP (sealed), S15 ....$10.00

Eldon, Match Kit, P-51D Mustang, 1967, 1/100, MIP (sealed), S15 ....$10.00

Entex, 1912 Model T Ford Tin Lizzy #B469, 1/16, blk, MIB, M19..$50.00

ESCI, Flag Raising on Iwo Jima #8062, 1/72, MIB, G5 ....$12.00

Fun Dimensions, Colossal Mantis, MIB, E3 ....$95.00

Fun Dimensions, Six Million Dollar Man, Bionic Bustout, 1974, missing instructions o/w complete, EX+ box, D9.......$25.00

Fun Dimensions, Space 1999, Alien, 1975, w/10x5" base, M (EX+ box), D9 ....$25.00

Fun Dimensions, Space 1999, Alpha Moonbase, 1976, M (EX+ box), D9...$75.00

Geometric, Fiend Without a Face, MIB, E3 ....$100.00

Geometric, Star Trek: The Next Generation, Jean-Luc Picard, 1990s, 1/6, MIB, E3 ....$45.00

Geometric, Star Trek: The Next Generation, Lt Commander Data, 1993, 1/6, MIB, E3/G5.....................................$50.00

Glencoe, Lunar Lander #05003, 1993, 1/96, MIB, G5 .....$25.00

Graphitti, Lobo Statue, MIB, E3.....................................$125.00

Graphitti, Superman Statue, MIB, E3................................$110.00

Graven Images, Judge Dredd, MIB, E3.............................$40.00

Guilow, Spirit of St Louis, balsa wood, ¾" scale, unbuilt, MIB, T1...$50.00

Halcyon, Alien, Alien Face Hugger #V02, 1991, 1/1, vinyl, MIB, G5...$112.00

Halcyon, Alien, Alien Warrior, vinyl, MIB, E3...............$75.00

Halcyon, Alien, Alien Warrior w/Egg #04, plastic, 1991, 1/9, MIB, G5...$30.00

Halcyon, Alien, Nostromo #HT03, 1992, 1/960, vinyl & plastic, MIB, from $155 to...$165.00

Hamilton Gifts, Frankenstein, Universal Monsters, 1991, assembled & pnt, 15", orig box, G5.....................................$25.00

Hasegawa, Space Shuttle w/Boosters #001, 1985, 1/200, MIB, G5 ....$20.00

Hawk, Chaparral II Race Car #03, 1/32, wht, MIB, M19 .$15.00

Hawk, Explorer 18 Earth Satellite, NMIB......................$35.00

Hawk, Frantic Cats, Frantics, 1965, M (EX+ box), D9 ....$70.00

Hawk, Lotus Race Car #02, 1/32, gr, MIB, M19 ....$10.00

Hawk, Silly Surfers, Hodad Makin' the Scene, 1954, MIB (sealed), T2..$125.00

Hawk, Silly Surfers, Hot Dogger & Surf Bunny Riding Tandem, 1965, MIB (sealed), from $75 to.............................$100.00

Hawk, Silly Surfers, Hot Dogger Hangin' Ten #541, 1964, MIB, G5 ....$100.00

Hawk, Silly Surfers, Woodie on Surfari, 1960s, M (EX+ box), T2...$110.00

Hawk, Vanguard Satellite #515, 1958, 1/5, MIB, G5 ....$75.00

Hawk, Weird-Ohs, Davy the Way-Out Cyclist, 1963, M (EX box), D9...$85.00

Hawk, Weird-Ohs, Digger the Way-Out Dragster #530, 1963, MIB, D9/G5, from $85 to...$90.00

Hawk, Weird-Ohs, Drag Hag #536, 1960s, MIB, E3/G5 ..$100.00

Hawk, Weird-Ohs, Drag Hag #536, 1960s, MIB (sealed), T2...$150.00

Hawk, Weird-Ohs, Huey's Hut Rod #538, 1963, MIB, from $35.00 to $40.00.

Hawk, Weird-Ohs, Endsville Eddie #537, 1963, MIB, from $75 to...$100.00

Hawk, Weird-Ohs, Francis the Foul #535, 1960s, M (EX+ box), T2...$60.00

Hawk, Weird-Ohs, Killer McBash, 1964, assembled & mostly pnt, D9...$65.00

Hawk, Weird-Ohs, Sling Rave Curvette #637, 1960s, M (EX+ box), T2...$30.00

Hawk, Weird-Ohs Customizing Set, 3 kits in 1: Leaky Boat Louie, Davy & Digger, M (EX+ lg photo box), rare, T2...$795.00

Heller, Lunar Orbiter Apollo #021, 1/100, MIB, G5 ....$7.00

Horizon, Bat Version Dracula, 1992, vinyl, M (EX+ box), D9.$35.00

Horizon, Batman Returns, Penguin #033, 1992, 1/6, MIB, from $40 to...$45.00

Horizon, Bride of Frankenstein #003, 1988, MIB, G5 ......$50.00

Horizon, Creature From the Black Lagoon, 1993, 1/6, some glue but disassembled & complete, EX box, D9 ....$25.00

Horizon, Incredible Hulk, 1990, 1/6, MIB, D9/G5, from $25 to...$35.00

Horizon, Indiana Jones, Dr Jones #035, 1993, 1/6, MIB, D9/G5, from $35 to...$40.00

Horizon, Indiana Jones, 1993, MIB, D9/G5, from $35 to.$40.00

Horizon, Mole People, Mole Man #002, 1988, MIB, G5..$40.00

Horizon, Robocop, ED-209 Robot, 1989, M (EX+ 9½x14x5" box), D9...$35.00

Horizon, Terminator 2, T-800 Terminator #020, 1991, 1/5, MIB, G5 ....$55.00

Horizon, The Thing, 1991, 1/6, some gluing but disassembled & complete, EX+ box, D9 ....$18.00

Hubley, 1930 Packard Roadster #4800-500, metal, sealed contents, M (EX box), S15...$60.00

Huia, Robocop, 1987, vinyl, assembled & pnt, 12", lt pnt wear, D9...$27.00

Huia, Robocop, 1987, 1/6, vinyl, MIB, G5 ....$120.00

Icarus Designs, War of the Worlds, Cowering Martian, 1987, 7", MIB, G5...$90.00

Imai, Armored Knights, Kaiser Maximillian II #1395, 1/12, MIB, G5 ....$15.00

Imai, Batmobile, TV version, MIB, T2 ....$75.00

Imai, Captain Scarlet, Concerto Angel #1212, 1982, MIB, E3/G5...$6.00

Imai, Captain Scarlet, SPV & Patrol Car #1202, 1983, MIB, G5 ....$30.00

Imai, Macross, VF-1A Fighter Valkyrie #1365, 1/170, MIB, G5...$7.00

Imai, Speed Racer Mach 5, MIB, T2 ....$65.00

Imai, Thunderbirds, Jet Mole #061, MIB, G5 ....$30.00

Imai, UFO, Sky I #1241, 1983, MIB, G5 ....$45.00

IMC, 1964 Ford Mustang II Convertible #102-150, 1/25, wht, MIB, M19...$100.00

ITC, Bumble Bee, 1959, assembled, missing pcs & decal sheet (EX 12x5" box), D9 ....$25.00

ITC, Greyhound, late 1950s-60s, M (G box), D9.............$20.00

ITC, Marvel Metal Giraffe, 1960, M (EX+ 9x13" box), D9..$45.00

ITC, Star-Blazers, Cosmo Zero #36132, 1984, MIB, G5.....$7.00

ITC, US Coast Guard Rescue Boat, 1950s, M (EX+ box), T2...$60.00

Japan, Ultraman, 1980s, MIB (sealed), F8 ....$16.00

Jo-Han, Chrysler Turbine Car, NMIB, J2 ....$65.00

Jo-Han, Customizing Car Kit #2559:140, 1959 Oldsmobile Sport Sedan, assembled & pnt, orig box, S15 ....$75.00

K&B, Sopwith Tri-Plane WWI Aircraft, MIB (sealed), J2 ....$20.00

Kabaya, Batmobile, 1989, MIB, G5 ....$15.00

Kaiyodo, Aliens, Queen, MIB, E3 ....$275.00

Kaiyodo, Aliens, Warrior, MIB, E3 ....$200.00

Kenner, Major Roscoe Hawke's Amazing Flying Machine, 1971, styrofoam, plastic & wood w/rubber-band power, M (VG box), D9 ....$10.00

KMT, Talos Missile/Booster #B15, 1959, 1/24, MIB, G5 .$50.00

Lifelike, American Wildlife Mallard Duck, 1970s, MIB, from $15 to $20.00

Lifelike, Dutch Flintlock Pistol #09230, 1/1, MIB, G5 .....$35.00

Lifelike, The Diplomat, 1971, MIB, from $65 to $70.00

Lifelike, The General, 1971, M (EX box), D9 ....$72.00

Lindberg, Dune Tiger Motorized, 1969, MIB, J2 ....$25.00

Lindberg, Flintstones, Flintmobile #72411, 1994, 1/20, MIB, G5 ....$15.00

Lindberg, Flying Saucer, assembled, EX, J2 ....$30.00

Lindberg, Jurassic Park, Tyrannosaurus Rex #70271, 1993, 10", MIB, G5 ....$12.00

Lindberg, Lucky Loser, 1965, MIB, J6, $20.00.

Lindberg, Ryan Navion Airplane, 1956, MIB, J2 ....$35.00

Lindberg, Satellite w/3-Stage Launching Rocket, 1950s, MIB, J2 ....$130.00

Lindberg, Swedish Jet Dragon, NMIB, J2 ....$20.00

Lindberg, 13th-Century Clock #339, 1969, 16", MIB, G5 .$30.00

Lindberg, 1971 Ford Mustang Mach 1 #72151, 1/25, red, MIB, M19 ....$20.00

Lodela (Revell of Mexico), Agata (angel fink), MIB, E3 .$65.00

Lodela (Revell of Mexico), Lost in Space, Cyclops Diorama #FG20, MIB, G5 ....$135.00

Lodela (Revell of Mexico), Lost in Space, Penny Robinson #FG47, 1/8, MIB, G5 ....$68.00

Lunar, Famous UFOs, MIB, E3 ....$45.00

Lunar, 2001: Space Odyssey, Aries 1B, MIB, E3 ....$40.00

Lunar, 2001: Space Odyssey, Discovery, MIB, E3 ....$60.00

Mad Labs, Famous Monsters of Filmland Resin Plaque, 1990s, 11x5", NMIB, D9 ....$25.00

Mad Labs, Ren & Stimpy, MIB, E3 ....$25.00

Mad Labs, Tiny Terrors, Bride of Frankenstein, MIB, G5 ..$12.00

Maryland Toy Corp, Royal Bengal Tiger, 1958, M (NM box), D9 ....$85.00

Merit, 1949 Alfa Romeo Race Car #4601, 1/24, red, MIB, M19 ....$25.00

Monogram, Apollo-Saturn V Rocket #6051, 1983, 1/144, MIB, G5 ....$25.00

Monogram, Battlestar Galactica Cylon Raider, missing 1 pc, some sm pnt pcs, 1 pc glued, EX+ box, D9 ....$35.00

Monogram, Buck Rogers (TV), Marauder #6031, 1979, 1/48, MIB (sealed), G5 ....$55.00

Monogram, Classic 1930 Packard Boat-tail Speedster, 1975, MIB (sealed), J2 ....$25.00

Monogram, Elvira's Macabre Mobile, MIB, E3 ....$25.00

Monogram, Firecracker Fire Engine Show Rod, Tom Daniels, NMIB, J2 ....$80.00

Monogram, First Lunar Landing, 1970, NMIB, J2 ....$35.00

Monogram, First Lunar Landing 25th Anniversary 1969-1994, 1/48, MIB (sealed), P3 ....$16.00

Monogram, Flip Out! The Beachcomber, 1965, NMIB, J6, $155.00.

Monogram, Garbage Truck, reissue, 1/24, MIB (sealed), P3 ..$20.00

Monogram, Go-Bots, Cy-Kill, 1984, MIB (sealed), D9 ....$25.00

Monogram, Go-Bots, Leader-1, 1984, MIB (sealed), D9 ..$25.00

Monogram, Go-Bots, Trans Am Convertible, 1985, MIB (sealed), D9 ....$15.00

Monogram, Hawker Mk 1B Typhoon Aircraft, 1968, NMIB, J2 ....$30.00

Monogram, Invaders, UFO #6012, 1979, 1/72, MIB, G5 .$70.00

Monogram, Li'l Coffin, 1966, M (EX+ box), D9 ....$65.00

Monogram, Masters of the Universe, Attak Trak, 1983, MIB (sealed), D9 ....$25.00

Monogram, Masters of the Universe, Roton Assault Vehicle #6016, 1984, MIB (sealed), D9 ....$25.00

Monogram, Miami Vice, Ferrari Testarossa #2756, 1987, 1/24, MIB, G5/S15, from $20 to $25.00

Monogram, Paddy Wagon Show Car, 1991, reissue, 1/24, MIB (sealed), P3 ....$15.00

Monogram, PBY-5A Catalina, Old Dumbo, 1955, missing decals, EX+ box, D9 ....$25.00

Monogram, Shogun Warriors (TV), Mazinga #6021, 1977, 1/10, MIB (sealed), G5 ....$30.00

Monogram, Simon & Simon, Z/28 Camaro #1407, 1981, 1/24, MIB (sealed), G5 ....$45.00

Monogram, Space Buggy, 1969, NMIB, J2.....................$40.00

Monogram, Speed Shift, 1965, NMIB, J6, $155.00.

Monogram, Turbo-Teen Convertible, 1985, MIB (sealed), D9 ....$20.00

Monogram, Tyrannosaurus Rex, 1987, M (VG box), D9 ..$35.00

Monogram, US Army Eager Beaver 2½-Ton Military Truck, 1950s, M (NM box), T2 ....$80.00

Monogram, Vietnam Memorial (figure), assembled, EX, J2..$20.00

Monogram, Voyage to the Bottom of the Sea, Flying Sub #S6011, 1979, 1/60, MIB (sealed), G5 ....$95.00

Monogram, Wooly Mammoth #6075, 1987, 1/13, MIB (sealed), G5 ....$20.00

Monogram, Wright Brothers Plane, Kitty Hawk, 1958, M (EX+ box), D9 ....$25.00

Monogram, 1939 Chevy Delivery Panel Truck #2240, 1/24, gr, MIB, M19...$35.00

Monogram, 1957 Chevy Funny Car, assembled, EX, J2....$15.00

Monogram, 1957 Corvette, 1977, NMIB, J2.................$15.00

Monogram, 1963 Cobra Convertible #2764, 1/25, bl, MIB, M19 ....$10.00

Monogram, 1969 Street Camaro 2, assembled, EX, J2......$15.00

MPC, Advanced Dungeons & Dragons, Orc War #2101, 1982, MIB, G5 ....$30.00

MPC, Alien, 1979, EX (EX box), J2 ....$55.00

MPC, Alien, 1979, from 1st movie, MIB (sealed), C1, from $90 to...$125.00

MPC, Barnabas Vampire Van, 1969, partially assembled, w/coffin & instruction sheet (EX 9x6½" box), D9.............$35.00

MPC, Barris T-Buggy Show Rod, EX+ (EX box), J2 ....$50.00

MPC, Beverly Hillbillies TV Truck, 1968, NMIB, D9...$100.00

MPC, Bionic Woman Repair Lab #0610, 1976, 1/12, MIB (sealed), G5 ....$40.00

MPC, Black Hole, Maximillian Robot #1982, 1979, 1/12, MIB, D9/G5, from $30 to $35.00

MPC, Bruce Larsen, USA-1 Funny Car, EX+ (EX box), J2.$110.00

MPC, Cannonball Run, Countach #0682, 1981, 1/25, MIB, G5 ....$40.00

MPC, Columbia Space Shuttle, 1982, missing 4 clear pcs & decals, EX box, D9 ....$10.00

MPC, Condemned to Chains Forever, 1974, assembled, D9 ....$35.00

MPC, Disney's Haunted Mansion, Vampires Midnight Madness #5051, 1974, 1/12, MIB, G5.................................$170.00

MPC, Disney's Pirates of the Caribbean, Dead Men Tell No Tales, MIB, $120.00.

MPC, Disney's Pirates of the Caribbean, Fate of the Mutineers, 1974, assembled, D9 ....$32.00

MPC, Disney's Pirates of the Caribbean, Hoist High the Jolly Roger, 1972, M (EX+ box), D9 ....$35.00

MPC, Dukes of Hazzard, Daisy's Jeep CJ #0662, 1980, 1/25, MIB, G5 ....$50.00

MPC, Dukes of Hazzard, General Lee Dodge Charger MIB (sealed), from $45 to.......................................$60.00

MPC, Dukes of Hazzard Cooter's Tow Truck, 1/25, complete, NMIB, P4 ....$35.00

MPC, Engine Company #13, NMIB, J2 ....$45.00

MPC, Hardcastle & McCormick, Coyote Super Sportscar #0684, 1983, 1/25, MIB, G5 ....$35.00

MPC, Hot Rodder Tall T, NMIB (sealed), J2................$180.00

MPC, Knight Rider, Knight 2000-KITT #6377, 1988, 1/25, MIB, G5 ....$50.00

MPC, Laser Warriors, Phantom Intruder #2306, 1984, MIB, G5...$5.00

MPC, Mannix, Roadster #609, 1968, MIB, G5 ....$170.00

MPC, Millennium Falcon, Star Wars, 1978, missing instructions o/w M (EX+ 10x14" box), D9 ....$35.00

MPC, Pilgrim Observer Space Station, Nuclear-Powered Interplanetary Spacecraft, 1970s, MIB (sealed), D9 ....$40.00

MPC, Pilgrim Space Station #9001, 1970, MIB (sealed), P3 ....$20.00

MPC, Play It Again Sam, 1974, assembled & pnt, D9 .....$55.00

MPC, Six Million Dollar Man Bionic Bustout, MIB (sealed), J2 ....$35.00

MPC, Star Wars, C-3PO, 1977, MIB, D9/G5, from $25 to...$30.00

MPC, Star Wars, Darth Vader, 1979, MIB (sealed), from $30 to $35.00

MPC, Star Wars, Darth Vader Bust Action Model, 1978, MIB (sealed), D9..$55.00

MPC, Star Wars, Darth Vader's TIE Fighter, 1978, MIB (sealed), D9...$35.00

MPC, Star Wars, R2-D2 #1912, 1977, MIB (sealed), G5, from $30 to...$50.00

MPC, Star Wars, Skywalker's X-Wing Fighter #1914, 1/48, MIB, from $15 to...$20.00

MPC, Star Wars (ESB), Battle on Ice Planet Hoth #1922, 1981, 1/75, MIB (sealed), from $25 to.................................$35.00

MPC, Star Wars (ESB), Rebel Base #1924, 1981, 1/75, MIB, G5..$20.00

MPC, Star Wars (ROTJ), A-Wing Fighter, 1983, MIB (sealed), D9...$8.00

MPC, Star Wars (ROTJ), AT-AT, 1980s, MIB, from $15 to...$20.00

MPC, Star Wars (ROTJ), C-3PO, 1983, MIB (sealed), D9...$25.00

MPC, Star Wars (ROTJ), Jabba the Hut Throne Room Action Scene, 1983, MIB (sealed), D9.................................$27.00

MPC, Star Wars (ROTJ), Shuttle Tydirium #1920, 1983, 1/100, MIB, D9/G5, from $20 to.................................$30.00

MPC, Star Wars (ROTJ), Speeder Bike, 1983, MIB (sealed), D9...$25.00

MPC, Star Wars (ROTJ), TIE Interceptor, 1983, MIB (sealed), D9...$10.00

MPC, Superman, 1984, reissue of 1965 Aurora model, MIB, D9/T2, from $20 to...$25.00

MPC, Surfer's Idol Hot Curl, 1960s, MIB (sealed), D9 ....$55.00

MPC, V-Rod Street Buggy Show Rod, NMIB, J2.............$20.00

MPC, Wacky Races, Mean Machine, 1969, M (VG box), D9...$35.00

MPC, Wacky Races, Penelope's Pussycat #901, 1969, MIB (sealed), G5 ....$140.00

MPC, Welcome Back Kotter, Sweathog Car & Figures #641, 1976, 1/25, MIB, G5...$40.00

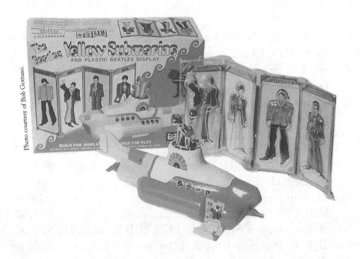

Photo courtesy of Bob Gottuso.

MPC, Yellow Submarine, complete, EX+ (EX+ box), $200.00.

MPC, 1970 Chevy Pick-Up Truck, NMIB, J2..................$65.00

MPC, 1976 AMC Pacer Stock Car #1-7601, 1/25, wht, MIB, M19..$22.00

MPC, 1976 Chevette, NMIB, J2...................................$28.00

MPC, 1984 Dodge Daytona 2-Door #1-0823, 1/25, red, MIB, M19..$16.00

MRC, Stargate, Anubis #01, 1994, 1/9, MIB, G5.............$30.00

Multiple, Rube Goldberg's Automatic Baby Feeder, 1965, missing sm pcs, 2 pcs glued, w/used cb signs, VG+ box, D9......$20.00

Multiple, Rube Goldberg's Painless False Teeth Extractor, 1965, MIB (sealed), from $90 to..$125.00

Multiple, Rube Goldberg's Signal for Shipwrecked Sailor #957, 1965, MIB, from $65 to...$75.00

Nikken, Eagle Apollo Lunar Module #001, 1969, 1/80, MIB, G5..$15.00

Nitto, SF3D, Armored Fighting Suit #23072, 1980s, 1/20, MIB, From $15 to..$20.00

Nitto, SF3D, Fireball, MIB, E3...................................$15.00

Nitto, SF3D, Hornisse, MIB, E3..................................$30.00

Oz Shop, Child's Play, Chucky, resin, MIB, G5 ....$60.00

Palmer, Animals of the World, Atlantic Sailfish, 1950s, M (EX+ box), D9...$25.00

Palmer, Animals of the World, Kodiak Bear #22, 1950s, MIB, D9/G5, from $20 to..$25.00

Palmer, Animals of the World, Shoveler Duck #24, 1950s, M (EX box), D9...$20.00

Palmer, Animals of the World, Timber Wolf, 1950s, M (EX+ box), D9...$26.00

Palmer, Animals of the World, White-Tail Deer, 1950s, M (EX+ box), D9...$26.00

Palmer, Civil War Cannon, late 1950s, M (EX+ box), D9..$12.00

Palmer, Gatling Gun, MIB, J2....................................$15.00

Palmer, Scout Award Trophies, Kodiak Bear #22, 1950s, MIB, G5..$22.00

Palmer, Spanish Conquistador #32, 1950s, 1/5, MIB, G5.$75.00

Palmer, Visible Dissecting Frog, 1950s, M (EX+ 12x8" box), D9..$45.00

Parks, Born Losers, Fidel Castro, MIB, H4.....................$100.00

Parks, Born Losers, Napoleon, 1965, assembled & pnt, orig issue, D9..$27.00

Parks, Born Losers, Napoleon, 1965, MIB, E3 ....$75.00

Precision, Cap'n Kidd the Pirate #402, 1959, 1/10, MIB, G5.$110.00

Precision, Fighting Blue Marlin, 1958, MIB, D9/G5, from $25 to..$30.00

Precision, Mighty American Buffalo #202, 1958, MIB, G5 .$25.00

Premiere, Star Trek, Phaser II, 1993, 1/1, MIB, G5..........$22.00

Pyro, Ankylosaurus #D277, 1968, 1/24, MIB, G5.............$25.00

Pyro, Corythosaurus #280, 1968, 1/50, MIB, D9/G5, from $20 to..$25.00

Pyro, Der Baron & His Harley #166, 1970, 1/16, MIB, G5..$80.00

Pyro, Figian Outrigger, 1960s, M (EX+ 10x7" box), D9 ...$20.00

Pyro, Gladiator Three-Wheeled Motorcycle, #175, 1970, M (EX box), D9...$35.00

Pyro, Gladiator Three-Wheeled Motorcycle #175, 1970, 1/16, MIB (sealed), G5 ....$70.00

Pyro, Moorish Miquelet Pistol #227, 1960, 1/1, MIB, G5...$35.00

Pyro, Peacemaker .45, M (VG box), I2 ....$30.00

Pyro, Protoceratops #D279, 1968, 1/8, MIB (sealed), G5 ..$30.00

Pyro, Restless Gun, Deputy Sheriff Vint Bonner #227, 1958, 1/8, MIB, G5..$100.00

Pyro, Ring-Necked Pheasant, 1948, Mark Trail Series, M (EX+ box), D9...$35.00

Pyro, Surf's Up Trailer Bike, 1970, M (P 12x9" box), D9.......$25.00

Pyro, Surf's Up Trailer Bike w/Figure #176, 1970, 1/8, MIB, from $40 to...$65.00

Pyro, Texas Cowboy #284, 1960s, 1/8, MIB, G5.............$80.00

Pyro, Thunder Lizard, MIB, J2............................$30.00

Pyro, Western Series, Cowboy, 1950s, paint-by-numbers, MIB, H4..$30.00

Raven Hood, Vampirella (Jim Fawkes) #JF, 1/6, MIB, G5...$145.00

Realspace, Gemini/Titan, 1/144, MIB, G5 ....$22.00

Renwal, Botany Science, 1964, MIB (sealed), D9 ....$45.00

Renwal, Busy Mechanic Construction Kit #375, 1950s, complete w/5 plastic vehicles to build, unused, NM (EX box), A $280.00

Renwal, Human Skeleton #803, 1950s-early '60s, MIB....$45.00

Renwal, LaCrosse Missile #560, 1974, 1/32, MIB, G5 ...$80.00

Renwal, The Thinker, 1950s-early '60s, MIB (sealed), D9..$70.00

Renwal, Visible Dog, #806, 1960s, 2 sm broken pcs (could rpr), o/w complete (G+ box), D9 ....$55.00

Renwal, Visible Dog #806, 1960s, 1/3, MIB, G5.............$85.00

Renwal, Visible Horse #807, 1960s, 1/3, MIB, G5 ....$145.00

Renwal, Visible Man #800, early 1960s, partially assembled & pnt, missing 1 eye pc (EX 13x16" box), D9 ....$12.00

Revell, Apollo Astronaut on Moon #R1860, 1995, 1/10, MIB, G5 ....$30.00

Revell, Apollo Lunar Module #1861, 1975, 1/48, MIB (sealed), G5 ....$60.00

Revell, Apollo 11-Columbia & Eagle, 1969, MIB (sealed), from $65 to...$85.00

Revell, Apollo 11-Hornet+3 #354, 1969, 1/490, MIB, G5 ..$45.00

Revell, Apollo-Soyuz Link-Up #1800, 1975, 1/96, MIB (sealed), G5 ....$135.00

Revell, Baa Baa Black Sheep, Pappy Boyington's Corsair #580, 1976, 1/32, MIB, G5.......................................$35.00

Revell, Batman Forever, Batmobile #6720, 1995, 1/25, MIB, G5 ....$20.00

Revell, Beatles, Ringo, unused, M (sealed VG+ box), B3..$200.00

Revell, Billy Carter's Redneck-Power Pick-Up, 1978, MIB (sealed), D9...$16.00

Revell, Blunderbus, 1955, 1st issue, M (EX+ box), D9.....$38.00

Revell, Bonanza, 1966, missing 3 pcs o/w complete, w/base & instructions, no box, D9 ....$50.00

Revell, CD-7 Mainliner United Flight 707 Airport Scene, S Kit, 1955, NMIB, J2 ....$190.00

Revell, Challenger Spacecraft, 1982, MIB (sealed), J6.....$28.00

Revell, Chicken Little, Miracle of Life in an Eggshell, 1976, M (EX box), D9...$60.00

Revell, CHiPs Kawasaki #7800, 1980, 1/12, MIB (sealed), G5 ....$35.00

Revell, Corvair B-24, Liberato, 1969, MIB (sealed), J2....$38.00

Revell, Deal's Wheels, Glitter Bug #1352, 1970, MIB (sealed), G5 ....$75.00

Revell, Deal's Wheels, Swine Hut #1356, 1970, MIB (sealed), G5 ....$75.00

Revell, Douglas X-3 Stiletto, 1969, NMIB, J2 ....$15.00

Revell, Dr Seuss' Game of the Yertle #2100, 1960, missing 3 pcs o/w complete, orig box, G5 ....$125.00

Revell, Drag Nut, 1963, MIB, J6, $120.00.

Revell, Dr Seuss' Horton the Elephant, 1960, complete, NM (EX+ box), F8.....................................$170.00

Revell, Dune, Ornithopter #1775, 1985, 1/50, MIB, G5 ..$45.00

Revell, Dune, Sand Crawler #1776, 1985, 1/25, MIB, G5 ..$60.00

Revell, Ed 'Big Daddy' Roth, Beatnik Bandit #R1282, 1994, 1/25, MIB, G5.....................................$20.00

Revell, Ed 'Big Daddy' Roth, Brother Rat Fink on Bike #1304, 1960s, MIB, T2.....................................$115.00

Revell, Ed 'Big Daddy' Roth, Drag Nut, reissue, 1990s, MIB (sealed), T2..$25.00

Revell, Ed 'Big Daddy' Roth, Drag Nut #1303, 1960s, MIB (sealed inside), T2...................................$100.00

Revell, Ed 'Big Daddy' Roth, Fink Eliminator, 1990, MIB (sealed), T2...$45.00

Revell, Ed 'Big Daddy' Roth, Mother's Worry #1302, 1963, MIB, G5/T2, (watch for recent reissue) from $155 to $175.00

Revell, Ed 'Big Daddy' Roth, Mr Gasser, 1964, missing 4 pcs, 3 pnt pcs o/w complete & unassembled, VG+ box, D9...$70.00

Revell, Ed 'Big Daddy' Roth, Mr Gasser #1301, 1964, MIB ..$150.00

Revell, Ed 'Big Daddy' Roth, Mr Gasser #6197, 1990, MIB (sealed), G5/T2......................................$40.00

Revell, Ed 'Big Daddy' Roth, Rat Fink, 1960s, signed by Ed Roth, MIB, E3...$150.00

Revell, Ed 'Big Daddy' Roth, Rat Fink #6199, 1990, MIB (sealed), G5/T2......................................$45.00

Revell, Ed 'Big Daddy' Roth, Scuzz Fink #1309, 1960s, M (EX box), T2..$750.00

Revell, Ed 'Big Daddy' Roth, Super Fink #1308, 1960s, M (NM box), from $350 to...................................$500.00

Revell, Ed 'Big Daddy' Roth, Surf Fink #6198, 1990, MIB (sealed), G5/T2......................................$40.00

Revell, Endangered Species, California Condor #702, 1974, MIB, D9/G5, from $30 to.................................$35.00

Revell, Enterprise & Space Lab, 1978, MIB (sealed), D9.$28.00

Revell, F-4C Phantom II, 1970, MIB (sealed), J2.............$20.00

Revell, Fly w/Mini Hangar Aviation Nostalgia Show, 1976, NMIB, J2..$40.00

Revell, Gemini Astronaut, 1967, MIB (sealed), D9 ....$70.00

Revell, Go Mad Nomad, Dave Deal Show Rod, 1971, MIB (sealed), J2...$45.00

Revell, Goodyear Blimp #999, 1977, 1/169, MIB (sealed), G5 ....$16.00

Revell, Great Waldo Pepper Sopwith Camel, 1975, partially assembled, decals 70% used o/w complete, VG+ box, D9..$12.00

Revell, Grummen F4F-4 Wildcat, 1971, MIB (sealed), J2..$25.00

Revell, Hardy Boys Van #1398, 1977, 1/25, MIB, G5 ......$55.00

Revell, Highway Pioneers, 1900 Packard, 1950s, NMIB, J2..$15.00

Revell, Highway Pioneers, 1915 Model T Ford Sedan, 1950s, NMIB, J2..$15.00

Revell, Huey Attack Helicopter, 1969, NMIB, J2 ....$35.00

Revell, Huey Cobra Helicopter, 1969, NMIB, J2 ....$15.00

Revell, John Travolta's Firebird Fever, 1979, MIB (sealed), J6, $42.00.

Revell, LTV-7D Corsair II Aircraft, 1969, NMIB, J2 ....$15.00

Revell, Magnum PI, TC's Helicopter #4416, 1981, 1/32, MIB, G5 ....$50.00

Revell, Magnum PI 308 GTS Ferrari, 1982, MIB (sealed), C1 ....$36.00

Revell, Master Cheater Kookie Kab Show Rod, 1970, MIB (sealed), J2 ....$65.00

Revell, Messerschmitt BF109F, 1971, NMIB, J2..............$30.00

Revell, Midnight Cowboy Custom Chevy Wrecker Truck, 1978, M (EX box), H4..$20.00

Revell, Moon Ship #1825, 1957, 1/96, MIB, G5 ....$240.00

Revell, Moonraker James Bond Space Shuttle #4306, 1979, 1/144, MIB (sealed), G5...$20.00

Revell, Mother's Worry, Roth Monster, 1963, MIB, J6, $95.00.

Revell, Mutiny on the Bounty, HMS Bounty #326, 1961, 1/110, MIB, G5 ....$55.00

Revell, NASA/USAF B-52 & X-15, 1964, MIB, J2 ....$35.00

Revell, Nike Hercules, S Kit, 1948, MIB, J2 ....$60.00

Revell, Pepperbox/Six-Barrel Revolving Pistol, 1954, M (EX+ box), D9...$45.00

Revell, Perri the Squirrel #1900, Disney, 1956, 1/1, MIB, G5 ....$100.00

Revell, Polaris Nuclear Submarine #437, 1975, 1/261, MIB, G5 ....$16.00

Revell, Robotech, Gartan, 1984, MIB (sealed), D9..........$25.00

Revell, Robotech, Ziyon, 1984, MIB (sealed), D9 ....$25.00

Revell, Russian T-34 Tank, S Kit, 1948, EX (EX box), J2..$50.00

Revell, S Kit, Northrup Shark SM, 62 Intercontinental Guided Missile, 1957, MIB, J2...$70.00

Revell, Shuttle Challenger #4526, 1982, 1/144, MIB, G5 ..$16.00

Revell, Sopwith Camel, 1969, NMIB, J2 ....$30.00

Revell, Suzuki TM-400 Dirt Racer #1512, 1976, 1/12, MIB, G5 ....$15.00

Revell, Talos Anti-Aircraft Missile, S Kit, 1957, MIB, J2 .$60.00

Revell, The Phantom, MIB (sealed), C10 ....$295.00

Revell, US Army Nike Hercules, S Kit, 1958, MIB, J2 ..$140.00

Revell, US Army Tactical Missile Set, S Kit, 1958, NMIB, J2 ....$60.00

Revell, US Frigate Constitution Old Ironsides, 1966, M (EX+ 13x9" box), D9..$15.00

Revell, US Navy Hospital Ship, Haven, S Kit, 1955, MIB, J2 ....$85.00

Revell, 1959 Ford Galaxie Skyliner #H-1227, 1/25, gr, MIB, M19..$125.00

Revell, 1963 Jaguar XKE, missing instructions o/w NMIB, J2 ....$25.00

Revell, 1965 Ford Mustang Fastback #H-1286, 1/16, yel, MIB, M19..$65.00

Scoop, Alien, Egg, 1980s, 4", MIB, G5 ....$55.00

Screamin', Betty Page in Orbit, 1990s, MIB, E3 ....$12.00

Screamin', Chatterer Cenobite #800, 1991, 1/4, MIB, G5 .$70.00

Screamin', Flash Gordon, 1993, 1/4, NM (EX+ box), D9..$35.00

Screamin', London After Midnight Vampire, 1990, M (EX+ box), D9..$45.00

Screamin', Star Wars, Han Solo #3500, 1993, 1/4, MIB, G5..$65.00

Screamin', Star Wars, Yoda #3300, 1992, 1/4, MIB, G5...$48.00

Screamin', Tales From the Crypt, Cryptkeeper #1300, 1994, 1/4, MIB, G5 ....$50.00

Sector One, Battlestar Galactica #6028, 1979, Monogram recast, MIB, G5 ....$85.00

Sevans, Dr Who, Dalek #1, 1987, 1/5, MIB, G5 ....$46.00

Strombecker, China Clipper #D31, 1950s, 1/130, MIB, G5..$100.00

Strombecker, Disneyland Stagecoach #D28, MIB, G5...$250.00

Superior Plastics, Deep Sea Lobster, 1962, M (G box), D9..$40.00

Superior Plastics, World-Wide Wonders Taj Mahal, 1963, M (G box), rare, D9...$58.00

Tamiya, German Artillery Officer, MIB (sealed), J2 ....$25.00

Tamiya, Triceratops #6901, 1982, 1/35, MIB, G5...............$6.00

Testors, Grodies, Davey #531, 1983, MIB, G5..................$10.00

Testors, Grodies, Digger #530, 1983, MIB, G5 ....$10.00

Testors, Grodies, Flameout Freddie #533, 1983, MIB, G5 .$20.00

Testors, Grodies, Killer McBash #539, MIB, from $15 to.$30.00

Testors, Grodies, Steel Pluckers #547, MIB, from $15 to .$30.00

Testors, Silly Surfers, Beach Bunny Catchin' Rays, 1990s, MIB (sealed), T2 ....$15.00

Testors, Silly Surfers, Hot Dogger Hangin' Ten, 1990s, MIB (sealed), T2 ....$15.00

Testors, Weird-Ohs, Digger the Way-Out Dragster #730, 1993, MIB, G5 ....$10.00

Testors, Weird-Ohs, Freddie Flameout #733, 1990s, MIB (sealed), T2 ....$15.00

Testors, Weird-Ohs, Leaky Boat Louie, 1990s, MIB (sealed), T2 ....$15.00

Testors, 1971 Toyota Supra 2-Door #373, 1/25, wht, MIB, M19 ....$12.00

Tsukuda, Alien #02, 1984, 1/5, 18", MIB, G5 ....$215.00

Tsukuda, Batman Returns, Penguin #07, 1992, 1/6, vinyl, MIB, G5 ....$85.00

Tsukuda, Captain America #06, 1984, 1/6, resin, MIB, G5 ..$55.00

Tsukuda, Ghostbusters, Stay Puft Man #15, 1984, 1/90, vinyl, MIB, G5 ....$125.00

Tsukuda, Terminator 2, T800 Endoskeleton #13, 1991, 1/9, MIB, G5 ....$30.00

Tsukuda, This Island Earth, Metalunan Mutant #20, 1985, 1/5, partially assembled, orig box, G5 ....$60.00

Union, Shuttle Challenger #15, 1980s, 1/288, MIB, G5 ..$20.00

Union, Space Shuttle Columbia #14, 1981, 1/288, MIB, G5 ....$15.00

Miscellaneous

Box, Pyro, Wyatt Earp, Hugh O'Brian photo, VG, J5 ......$35.00

Box, Revell, The Ghost Who Walks/The Phantom, 1965, w/instructions, EX+, F8 ....$30.00

Instructions, Aurora Lone Ranger & Tonto Comic Scenes, 1970s, comic style, NM, J5, pr.............................$15.00

Revell-O-Rama Clouds Above the Coast, 1964, 3-D display for 1/72 scale planes, unused, orig envelope, D9 ....$35.00

Revell-O-Rama Hidden Airstrip, 1964, mc 3-D display for 1/72 scale planes, unused, orig 11x15" envelope, D9 ....$35.00

Movie Posters and Lobby Cards

This field is a natural extension of the interest in character collectibles, and one where there is a great deal of activity. There are tradepapers that deal exclusively with movie memorabilia, and some of the larger auction galleries hold cataloged sales on a regular basis. The hottest genre right now is the monster movies, but westerns and Disney films are close behind.

Advisors: John and Sheri Pavone (P3).

Absent Minded Professor, 1961, 1-sheet, Disney, Fred MacMurray, VG, M17...$75.00

Addams Family, 1991, 1-sheet, 27x41", rolled, NM+, P3.$12.00

Alien 3, 1992, 1-sheet, Sigourney Weaver, 27x41", rolled, NM+, P3 ....$15.00

Allan Rocky Lane, lobby card set, El Paso Stampede, 1953, set of 8, J5 ....$65.00

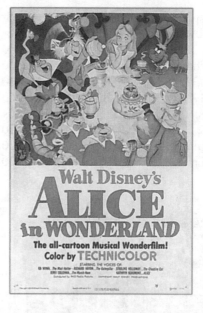

Alice in Wonderland, 1951, 1-sheet, linen backed, 41x27", NM, $975.00.

Amityville Horror, 1979, lobby card set, 11x14", NM, P3..$22.00

Andy Hardy Comes Home, 1958, 1-sheet, Mickey Rooney, 27x41", EX, A3 ....$85.00

Barefoot Executive, 1971, 1-sheet, Disney, Kurt Russell, 27x41", EX, M17 ....$30.00

Battle for the Planet of the Apes, 1973, 1-sheet, 27x41", EX+, P3 ....$45.00

Beast of the Yellow Night/Creature With the Blue Hand, 1971, 1-sheet combo, EX+, P3 ....$40.00

Because They're Young, 1960, lobby card #3, Dick Clark & Tuesday Weld, VG+, I2...$35.00

Ben, 1972, ½-sheet, 22x28", EX, P3...$22.00

Beneath the Planet of the Apes, 1970, 1-sheet, EX, P3 ....$50.00

Beverly Hillbillies, 1993, 1-sheet, 27x41", rolled, NM+, P3 ....$10.00

Blondie's Hero, 1-sheet, Columbia, 1949, Penny Singleton, EX, A3 ....$95.00

Burnt Offerings, 1976, 1-sheet, style B, Bette Davis w/lg cast, 27x41", EX, P3...$17.00

Cold Turkey, 1971, 1-sheet, Dick Van Dyke & Bob Newhart, 27x41", EX-, P3...$12.00

Die Monster Die!, 1965, lobby card set, NM, $65.00.

Conquest of the Planet of the Apes, 1972, 1-sheet, 27x41", EX, P3 ....$45.00

Day Mars Invaded Earth, 1963, 1-sheet, 27x41", NM, P3 ..$25.00

Death Ship, 1960, 1-sheet, George Kennedy, 27x41", EX+, P3 ....$12.00

Dick Tracy Vs Phantom Empire, 1952 reissue of 1941 serial, 1-sheet, NM, D11...$100.00

Dick Tracy's G-Men, lobby card, 1955, 11x14", M, D11..$40.00

Dr Blood's Coffin, 1961, 1-sheet, 27x41", EX, P3.............$45.00

Dr Phibes Rises Again, 1972, 1-sheet, 27x41", EX+, P3...$35.00

Dracula, 1976, 1-sheet, reprint from movie, 21x29", M, J2...$30.00

Empire of the Ants, 1977, 1-sheet, Joan Collins, 27x41", EX, P3 ....$18.00

Farewell to Arms, 1948, 1-sheet, Rock Hudson & Jennifer Jones, 27x41", EX+, P3 ....$25.00

Fog, 1980, ½-sheet, 22x28", EX, P3 ....$25.00

For Your Eyes Only, James Bond, 1981, 1-sheet, Roger Moore, 27x41", EX, P3 ....$45.00

From Russia with Love, James Bond, 1-sheet, NM, D8..$125.00

Gamma People, 1956, insert, 14x36", EX, P3 ....$45.00

Godzilla, 1985, 1-sheet, M, J2 ....$10.00

Goodbye Mr. Chips, MGM, 1939, 1-sheet, linen backed, 41x27", NM, $650.00.

Gorgon, 1964, 1-sheet, linen-bk, Hammer Film, 27x41", EX, P3 ....$125.00

Green Hornet, Bruce Lee as Kato, EX, D8.........................$55.00

Gremlins, 1985, 1-sheet, rerelease, We're Back, 27x41", NM+, P3 ....$15.00

Halloween II, 1981, 1-sheet, 27x41", EX+, P3.................$45.00

Hard Day's Night, 1960s Spanish release, 1-sheet, 30x40", minor edge stains o/w EX, J5...$245.00

Help!, lobby card set, Girosign Ltd/UK, 8x10", EX+, B3 ....$460.00

Here Comes the Nelsons, 1951, lobby card #2, VG+, I2..$35.00

Hitcher, 1986, 1-sheet, 27x41", EX+, P3 ....$18.00

Invasion of the Body Snatchers, 1978, advance 1-sheet, 27x41", NM, P3...$20.00

Iron Mountain Trail, 1953, lobby card #4, Rex Allen, VG+, I2 ....$35.00

Island of Terror/Projected Man, 1966, 1-sheet combo, EX, P3 ....$35.00

It's a Wonderful Life, 1946, lobby card set, professionally restored and mounted to linen-type paper, 11x14", EX, estimated from $4,000.00 to $6,000.00.

It's Alive, 1974, 1-sheet, 27x41", EX, P3 ....$20.00

Jewel of the Nile, 1985, 1-sheet, Michael Douglas, 27x41", EX+, P3 ....$15.00

Jiggs & Maggie Out West, Monogram, 1950, 1-sheet, 27x41", EX, A3 ....$175.00

Last Action Hero, 1983, 1-sheet, Schwarzenagger, 27x41", rolled, NM+, P3...$10.00

Lion King, Happy Holidays w/cast, ½-sheet, 22x17", NM+, P3 ....$8.00

Lion King, 1-sheet, 27x41", rolled, M, P3 ....$45.00

Llanero Solitario, Spanish Lone Ranger, NM, S18...........$55.00

Macabre, 1958, 1-sheet, William Castle, linen-bk, 27x41", EX+, P3 ....$115.00

Mary Poppins, 1954, insert card, 14x35", NM, M17........$30.00

Murders in the Rue Morgue, 1971, lobby card set, 11x14", NM, P3 ....$25.00

Murders in the Rue Morgue, 1971, 1-sheet, EX, P3 ....$40.00

Never Say Never Again, James Bond, 1983, 1-sheet, 27x41", rolled, NM+, P3...$40.00

Night of the Blood Monster, 1972, lobby card set, 11x14", NM, P3 ....$45.00

Nightmare, 1964, 1-sheet, Hammer Prod, 27x41", EX, P3 .$40.00

Nightmare Before Christmas, 1-sheet, 40x45", M, J6.......$40.00

Nightmare on Elm Street Part 3, 1987, 1-sheet, 27x41", EX, P3 ....$15.00

Octopussy, James Bond, 1983, 1-sheet, Roger Moore & Maude Adams, 27x41", EX+, P3 ....$35.00

Painted Hills, MGM, 1951, 1-sheet, Lassie, 27x41", EX, A3 .$80.00

Return From Witch Mountain, Disney, 1978, 1-sheet, 27x41", EX+, P3 ....$25.00

Return of Count Yorga, 1971, 1-sheet, 27x41", EX+, P3..$35.00
Robin Hood, window card, 1952, 14x22", EX, J5 ....$45.00
Russians Are Coming, 1966, insert, 14x36", VG+, P3 .....$25.00
Scream & Scream Again, 1970, 1-sheet, Price, Lee & Cushing, 27x41", EX+, P3 ....$35.00
Standing Tall, 1989, poster, Campbell/Public TV Exclusive, John Wayne, 26x30", rolled, NM+, P3 ....$10.00
Tarzan the Fearless, Chapter 12, Jungle Justice, Buster Crabbe, EX+, A3...$150.00
Terror in the Wax Museum, 1973, lobby card set, 11x14", NM, P3 ....$40.00

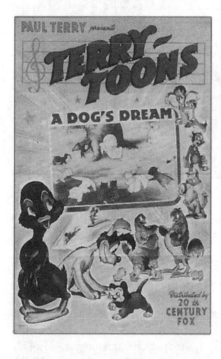

Terry-Toons, A Dog's Dream, 1940, 1-sheet, 41x27", EX, $250.00.

The Last Round-Up, Columbia, 1947, 1-sheet, Gene Autry, 27x41", EX, A3...$250.00
Vampire & the Ballerina, 1962, 1-sheet, 27x41", EX, P3.$30.00
Who Slew Auntie Roo?, 1971, 1-sheet, Shelley Winters, 27x41", EX, P3...$28.00
Who's Harry Crumb?, 1988, 1-sheet, John Candy, 27x41", NM, P3 ....$10.00
Witchcraft, 1964, 1-sheet, Lon Chaney, 27x41", NM, P3 ....$25.00
Wizard of Oz, lobby card, 1985, colorized Bolger dance scene from That's Dancing, 11x14", NM, S6 ....$72.00
101 Dalmatians, lobby card set, 1969, 1st release, set of 9, scarce, MIP, M8 ....$125.00

Musical Toys

Whether meant to soothe, entertain or inspire, musical toys were part of our growing-up years. Some were as simple as a windup music box, others as elaborate as a lacquered French baby grand piano.

See also Disney; Character, TV and Movie Collectibles.

Accordion, Emenee, 1957, plastic w/18 keys & 52 tuned reeds, cb case, complete w/song book & harness strap, NM $50.00
Accordion, Everest, 1940s, 5x6", NMIB $40.00
Accordion, Hohner, 2-octave, leatherette case, 10", EX, A $230.00
Blippy-in-the-Music-Box, 1968, psychedelic litho tin, working, NM, I2 ....$175.00
Drum, Donaldson Bros, c 1894, paper litho depiction of 6 Brownies in band on wooden drum, EX, 8x10" dia, EX, A $965.00
Drum, mk Nonpariel, tin, images of Admiral's Flagship & Armored Aeroplane, 5¼" dia, VG, A....................$190.00
Drum, tin w/wood rims, Canadian flags w/crest on maple leaf background, metallic mc, 8" dia, VG, A.................$165.00
Drum, tin w/wood rims, children marching in patriotic parade, 8" dia, G, A...$550.00
Drum, tin w/wood rims, Converse/USA, portrait of Admiral Dewey flanked by Am flags, 11" dia, VG, A...........$715.00
Drum, tin w/wood rims, Indians on horseback, 7" dia, G, A $210.00
Drum, tin w/wood rims, litho paper inserts of Washington crossing the Delaware, 13" dia, G, A $910.00
Drum, tin w/wood rims, mounted soldiers alternating w/soldiers at attention, 13", G, A $120.00
Drum, tin w/wood rims, Santa leading an animal orchestra, gold on red, 6" dia, VG, A...$255.00
Drum, tin w/wood rims, Uncle Sam w/eagles on bunting, 9" dia, VG, A $255.00
Drum, tin w/wood rims, Union soldiers in battle, 13" dia, VG, A $500.00
Drum, wood veneer shell w/wood rims, images of various battleships, 10" dia, VG, A..$550.00
Drum, wood veneer shell w/wood rims, oval images of cavalry officer, artillery, battleship, etc, 13" dia, EX, A $580.00
Drum, wood veneer w/metal rims, when side knob is pulled internal mechanism beats drum, 8", EX, A $75.00

Photo courtesy of June Moon.

Farmer in the Dell Music Maker, Mattel, 1950s, lithographed tin, crank operated, EX, J6, $125.00.

Guitar, Mattel, Mother Goose graphics, NM...................$55.00
Piano, unmk (Bliss ?), wood & metal, 14x17", EX, A........$55.00

Noah's Ark

What Bible story is more delightful to children than Noah's? In the late 1800s, Bliss produced arks of various sizes along with animal pairs made of wood with applied paper lithographed details. Others imported from Germany had hand-carved or composition animals, some rather primitive, others wonderfully detailed. They're seldom found today at all, and when they are, the set is seldom complete.

German, painted wood on flat boat-shaped base, 29 realistic hide-covered animals and 6 detailed figures, 29", G, A, $3,200.00.

German, late 1800s, pnt wood w/hinged roof on flat boat-shaped base, 32 simplistic animals & 2 figures, 14½", EX, A...$800.00
German (?), pnt wood house on flat boat-shaped base, 39 primitive animals w/3 human figures, 14", EX, A $825.00
Marx/England, plastic, complete, NM (EX box), A.......$175.00
Three-Story, pnt wood w/stalls on main & lower decks, 8 hide-covered animals w/1 human figure, 17", VG, A $415.00

Nodders

Nodders representing comic characters of the day were made in Germany in the 1930s. These were small doll-like figures approximately 3" to 4" tall, and the popular ones often came in boxed sets. But the lesser-known characters were sold separately, making them rarer and harder to find today. While the more common nodders go for $125.00 and under, Ambrose Potts, The Old Timer, Widow Zander and Ma and Pa Winkle often bring about $350.00 — Happy Holligan even more, about $600.00. (We've listed the more valuable ones here; any German bisque nodder not listed is worth $125.00 or under.)

Advisor: Doug Dezso (D6).

See also Character Bobbin' Heads; Sports Collectibles.

Ambrose Potts, German, pnt bsk, NM...........................$350.00
Auntie Blossom, German, pnt bsk, NM...........................$150.00
Auntie Mamie or Uncle Willie, German, pnt bsk, NM, ea...$350.00
Bill, Dock, Avery, Max or Pop Jenks, German, pnt bsk, NM, ea...$200.00

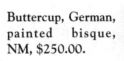

Buttercup, German, painted bisque, NM, $250.00.

Chubby Chaney, German, pnt bsk, NM $200.00
Corky, German, pnt bsk, NM..$475.00
Fanny Nebbs, German, pnt bsk, NM $250.00
Ferina, German, pnt bsk, NM $350.00
Grandpa Teen, German, pnt bsk, NM $350.00
Happy Hooligan, German, pnt bsk, NM.........................$600.00
Harold Teen, German, pnt bsk, NM..............................$150.00

Jeff Regus, German, painted bisque, small, NM, $175.00; medium or large, NM, $250.00 each.

Junior Nebbs, German, pnt bsk, NM $525.00
Lillums, German, pnt bsk, NM......................................$150.00
Little Annie Rooney, German, pnt bsk, movable arms, NM..$250.00
Little Egypt, German, pnt bsk, NM................................$350.00
Lord Plushbottom, German, pnt bsk, NM $150.00
Ma or Pa Winkle, German, pnt bsk, NM, ea $350.00

Majorie, Patsy, Lilacs or Josie, German, pnt bsk, NM, ea..$425.00
Mary Ann Jackson, German, pnt bsk, NM $250.00
Min Gump, German, pnt bsk, NM $150.00
Mr Bailey, German, pnt bsk, NM...............................$150.00
Mr Bibb, German, pnt bsk, NM $400.00
Mr Wicker, German, pnt bsk, NM $250.00
Mushmouth, German, pnt bsk, NM $200.00
Mutt or Jeff, German, pnt bsk, NM, ea $250.00
Nicodemus, German, pnt bsk, NM $350.00
Old Timer, German, pnt bsk, NM $350.00
Our Gang Set, German, pnt bsk, 6-pc, MIB...............$1,200.00
Pat Finnegan, German, pnt bsk, NM $400.00

Patsy, German, painted bisque, NM, $400.00.

Photo courtesy of Doug Dezso.

Pete the Dog, German, pnt bsk, NM $150.00
Rudy, German, pnt bsk, NM $250.00
Scraps, German, pnt bsk, NM $250.00
Uncle Willie, German, pnt bsk, NM $350.00
Widow Zander, German, pnt bsk, NM $400.00
Winnie Winkle, German, pnt bsk, NM.........................$150.00

Optical Toys

Compared to the bulky viewers of years ago, contrary to the usual course of advancement, optical toys of more recent years have tended to become more simplified in concept.
See also View-Master and Tru-View.

Anamorphoses, Julien/France, 1850s, 24 mc cards w/distorted images transform under viewing glass, EX+ (orig case), B12 ....$4,500.00
Cinderella Pixie Viewer, Stori-Views, 1950s, plastic viewer w/6 3-D slides, NM (EX+ box), T2...................................$15.00
Give-A-Show Projector, Kenner, 1963, NMIB, J2 ....$45.00
Jeu de Thaumatrope, Academie Arts Graphiques, 1890s, complete set of 12 disks, spin to merge images, EX+ (orig box), B12 ....$2,850.00

Kaleidoscope, CC Bush, cb & brass cylinder on turned walnut base, 13¼", EX, A...$690.00
Kaleidoscope, Pixie, MIB, T1.....................................$45.00
Kaleidoscope, Walt Disney Epcot Center/Figment, 1980s, 7¼", EX+, M8...$25.00

Kaleidoscope Wonder Wheel, Steven Manufacturing, 1975, NM, $15.00.

Kiddie Kamera, 1930s, w/12 filmstrips, NMIB, L4..........$275.00
Lantern Slide, The Elephant's Revenge, England, 1890s, set of 8, 3¼x3¼", EX+ (orig box), B12 ....$165.00
Magic Lantern, Bing, electric, w/few slides, 11x10", EX+, M5..$100.00
Magic Lantern #7, Plank, w/12 slides, G (orig litho paper-covered box w/hinged lid), A...................................$120.00

Magic Lantern, Plank/Germany, painted tin, contains 11 slides, complete with lamp and glass chimney, 6", VG (VG wood box), A, $230.00.

Panorama of the Visit of Santa Claus..., Milton Bradley, knobs revolve film showing happy children, EX (fragile box), A $250.00
Praxinoscope Theater, France, optical theater in wooden box w/stage presentation, candle holder w/shade, VG, A..$600.00
Promenade de Longchamp (Walk to Longchamp), France, 1830s-40, peep show w/3 holes, 5 levels, EX+ (cover forms box), B12..$2,250.00
See-A-Show Stereo Viewer Set, Kenner, 1962, NMOC, J2 ..$40.00
Telescopic View of the Great Exhibition, C Moody, Holborn (London), 1851, peep show, 10-level litho on cb, EX, B12 ....$850.00

Tunnel Views, Germany, 1830s-40s, peep show, 7 levels showing Thames Tunnel interior scenes, EX (orig cb case), B12 ....$1,050.00

Paper Dolls

Turn-of-the-century paper dolls are seldom found today and when they are, they're very expensive. Advertising companies used them to promote their products, and some were printed on the pages of leading ladies' magazines. By the late 1920s most paper dolls were being made in book form — the doll on the cover, the clothes on the inside pages. Because they were so inexpensive, paper dolls survived the Depression and went on to peak in the 1940s. Though the advent of television caused sales to decline, paper doll companies were able to hang on by making paper dolls representing Hollywood celebrities and TV stars. These are some of the most collectible today. Even celebrity dolls from more recent years like the Brady Bunch or the Waltons are popular. Remember, condition is very important; if they've been cut out, even when they're still in fine condition and have all their original accessories, they're worth only about half as much as an uncut book or box set.

For more information, refer to *Price Guide to Lowe and Whitman Paper Dolls* by Mary Young, *Collecting Toys* by Richard O'Brien, and *Toys, Antique and Collectible* by David Longest.

Advisor: Mary Young (Y2).

Adventures of Henry Theatre Book, English, 1810, cutouts of Henry in various poses, storybook included, EX, A .$360.00
Annette Funicello, Walt Disney, 1950s, uncut, M, H12 ..$55.00
Archies, #1987 Whitman, 1969, 5 dolls, uncut, M (EX folder), D9/J7/F8, from $25 to $30.00
Babes in Toyland, 1961, uncut, M, J7 ....$35.00
Baby Sparkle Plenty Paper Dolls, Saalfield, 1948, 10½x13", NM, D11 ....$50.00
Barbie, Ken & Midge, #1976 Whitman, 1963, near complete, B10 ....$16.00
Barbie Quick Curl, #1984 Whitman, 1973, near complete, B10 ....$10.00
Barbie's Jewel Secrets, #1537 Whitman, 1987, B10...........$5.00

Circus Paper Dolls, #2610 Saalfield, 1952, uncut, $35.00.

Belles of the Civil War, Costume Dolls #226A Platt & Munk, 1962, cut, EX (VG+ box), P3...................................$12.00
Beverly Hillbillies, #1955 Whitman, 1964, 4 dolls, partially punched out & cut, nearly complete, EX+.................$38.00
Blondie (TV show), #4434 Sallfield, 1968, uncut, M, V1 .$38.00
Book of Plays, J&S Fuller/London, 1811, by Shakespeare & other authors w/hand-colored cut-out characters, EX, A...$550.00
Bozo the Clown Circus, 1966, unused, M, V1 ....$23.00
Buster Brown & Tige, ca 1910, 2 dolls, heavy cb w/easel back, 4 outfits & hats, uncut, EX+ (orig envelope), A3 ......$325.00
Cabbage Patch Deluxe Paper Dolls, Avalon, 1983, NM, B10 ..$10.00
Chuck & Di Have a Baby, Simon & Schuster, 1982, uncut, M, M15..$15.00
Debbie Reynolds Cut-Outs, #1956 Whitman, 1960, cut, NM (NM folder) $35.00
Dinah Shore & George Montgomery Cut-Outs, #1970 Whitman, 1959, cut, EX $30.00
Dodie, #6044 Saalfield, 1971, unused, MIB, V1 ....$32.00

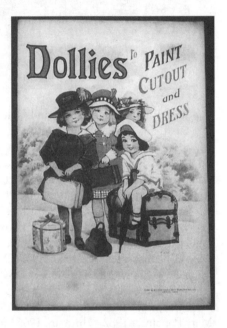

Dollies To Paint, Cut Out and Dress, #5218 Saalfield, 1918, complete and uncut, EX, $85.00.

Dolls w/Williamsburg Colonial Dress, Samuel Gabriel, 1940, 6 dolls, complete w/booklet, cut, EX+ (orig box) $80.00
Dolly Darlings, #1963 Whitman, 6 dolls w/41 pcs of clothing, cut, G (orig folder), M15 ....$20.00
Dolly Dingle Celebrates Halloween, Oct 1918, uncut sheet w/2 dolls & various Halloween designs, framed, 16x10", EX, A $40.00
Donny & Marie Osmond, #1991 Whitman, 1977, uncut, M, V1...$22.00
Family Affair's Buffy, #1985 Whitman, 1968, uncut, M...$25.00
Family Affair's Mrs Beasley Paper Doll Fashions, #1986 Whitman, 1972, NM (NM folder)......................................$25.00
Faye Emerson, #2722 Saalfield, 1952, uncut, NM, J5 ....$85.00
Finger Ding Paper Dolls, #1993 Whitman, 1971, uncut, M..$15.00
Flying Nun, #5121 Saalfield, 1968, M, C1 ....$40.00
Gentleman & Lady, ca 1895, 2 uncut dolls & 1 lady's outfit in center, matted & framed, 15x19", EX, A $60.00
Grace Kelly Cut-Out Dolls, #2069 Whitman, 1956, 2 dolls, uncut, NM $110.00

Green Acres, #1979 Whitman, 1967, 2 dolls & 25 outfits, punched out, complete, EX+ (EX+ folder) $30.00

Green Acres Magic Stay-On Dolls, #4773 Whitman, 1968, 2 dolls & 29 outfits, missing stand & scissors, EX (EX box), F8 ....$25.00

Happy Days, Fonzie, #105 Toy Factory, 1976, MIP (sealed), J7.$25.00

Hayley Mills Summer Magic Cutouts, #1966 Whitman, 1963, uncut, M, V1 ....$35.00

Howdy Doody Puppet Show, 1952, cut, VG, J7 ....$25.00

Jaclyn Smith, Charlie's Angels Kelly, #112 Toy Factory, 1977, NRFB, M15...$45.00

Photo courtesy of Mary Young.

Jane Russell Paper Dolls and Coloring Book, #4328 Saalfield, 1955, uncut, $95.00.

Julia, #6055 Saalfield, 1968, MIB, H12 ....$45.00

Katy Keene, doll w/colored outfits, VG+ (orig mailer), A3 ..$75.00

Kiddle Kolognes, #1992 Whitman, 1969, uncut, flocked cover, M...$25.00

Laugh-In Paper Doll & Punch-Out Book, #1325 Saalfield, 1969, NM, C1 ....$45.00

Little Ballerina, #1963 Whitman, 1961, EX (orig folder), I2 .$25.00

Margie TV Show Cynthia Pepper Cut-Out Doll Book, #1818-A WS, 1963, M, C1 ....$32.00

Mary Poppins, #1967 Whitman, 1973, uncut, M, V1.......$25.00

Mary Poppins, #1982 Whitman, 1966, uncut, M, J7 ....$40.00

Mary Poppins, Jane & Michael, #1892 W/Strathmore, 1964, uncut, M, J7 ....$35.00

Mickey & Minnie Steppin' Out, #1979 Whitman, WDP, 1977, complete, cut, 10x13", A6..$15.00

My Fair Lady, Columbia Broadcasting, 1965, uncut, M, V1 .$35.00

Nanny & the Professor, #4213 Artcraft, 1970, complete, unused, M (NM folder), F8...$35.00

National Velvet, #1958 Whitman, 1961, cut but appears complete, EX+ (EX folder), F8.....................................$25.00

Oklahoma! A Golden Paper Doll Story Book, Simon & Schuster, 1956, uncut, M $85.00

Partridge Family, #5137 Artcraft, 1971, uncut, M (NM folder), F8 ....$40.00

Pat Boone Cutouts, #1968 Whitman, 1959, uncut, M, V1 ..$50.00

Petal People, #1980 Whitman, 1969, cut, near complete w/folder, P2 ....$10.00

Playhouse Kiddles, #1954 Whitman, 1971, uncut, M.......$30.00

Princess Di Paper Doll Book, #1985-50, 1985, uncut, M, M15.$15.00

Raggedy Ann & Andy, #1979 Whitman, 1966, uncut, M, V1...$26.00

Raggedy Ann & Andy, #7413-B Whitman, 1978, uncut, MIB, M15...$18.00

Ranch Family, #2584 Merrill, 1957, complete and uncut, NM, $35.00.

Ricky Nelson, #2081 Whitman, 1959, uncut, NM $65.00

Rock Hudson, #2087 Whitman, 1957, uncut, NM, J6 .....$65.00

Roy Rogers & Dale Evans, #1950 Whitman, 1954, cut, EX (EX folder)...$40.00

Shirley Temple, #4388 Whitman, 1976, MIB, $25.00.

Shirley Temple, Saalfield #1715, 1935, uncut, NM, H12..$195.00

Shirley Temple, Saalfield #290, uncut, 6 pgs of clothes, H12 ..$135.00

Sid & Marty Krofft's Kaleidoscope Puppets, Hemisphere/Coca-Cola, 1968, uncut, M, V1 ....$30.00

Snow White & the Seven Dwarfs, #970 Whitman, 1938, 8 dolls, ensembles & forest friends, 15" Snow White, uncut, EX, P6...$145.00

Storybook Kiddles Sweethearts, #1956 Whitman, 1969, uncut, M..$30.00

Tammy & Her Family, #1977 Whitman, 1964, 5 dolls, uncut...$30.00
That Girl, #4479 Saalfield, 1967, uncut, M, V1 ....$38.00
Twiggy, 1967, #1999 Whitman, NM, J7 ....$35.00

Welcome Back Kotter Sweathogs, #108 Toy Factory, 1976, MIB (sealed), J6, from $25.00 to $30.00.

Photo courtesy of June Moon.

Walter Lantz Cartoon Stars, #1344 Saalfield, 1963, uncut, M, V1 ....$30.00

Paper-Lithographed Toys

Following the development of color lithography, early toy makers soon recognized the possibility of using this technology in their own field. Both here and abroad, by the 1880s toys ranging from soldiers to involved dioramas of entire villages were being produced of wood with colorful and well-detailed paper lithographed surfaces. Some of the best known manufacturers were Crandall, Bliss, Reed, and McLoughlin. This style of toy remained popular until well after the turn of the century.

Advisors: Mark and Lynda Suozzi (S24).

See Also Black Americana; Boats; Circus Toys; Dollhouses; Games; Noah's Ark; Pull Toys; Puzzles

Alphabet Barrel Toy, ca 1890, litho oilcloth roll winds out of red wooden barrel w/blk ends, 3½", EX, A $440.00
Baby's Rattle Blocks, Germany, set of 4, 4" sq, EX (orig box), A $300.00

Band Chariot with Musicians and Driver, Reed, ca 1895, 27½" long, EX, $2,000.00.

Block Set, Bliss, colorful animal scenes w/the alphabet, set of 12, EX, A $285.00
Block Set, Bliss, paper litho wagon holds building blocks of various shapes, 7x10½", EX......................................$275.00
Block Set, Bliss, Read & Learn, 8 cylindrical blocks w/letters & other graphics, 4", G (G box), A $2,200.00
Block Set, Hill, Alphabet & Building Blocks, builds schoolhouse-type building, G (orig box), A......................$690.00
Block Set, Hill, Spelling Blocks, w/numbers on reverse, set of 20, G (box w/Victorian image of children at play), A.....$85.00
Block Set, Hill, 1870, Alphabet Blocks, set of 18, G (orig box), A $55.00
Block Set, McLoughlin, alphabet, numbers, animals & soldiers, set of 15, 1x2x3½", EX, A......................................$635.00
Block Set, McLoughlin, Play & Learn, 2-sided, complete set of 16, 7½" sq, EX (damaged box), A............................$715.00
Block Set, Reed, cut-out ABCs, VG+ (orig box), A...$2,200.00
Block Set, Strauss, 1904, Clock Blocks, learning clock reverses to months & seasons, 8½x8½", EX (EX cb box), A $165.00
Brownie Blocks, McLoughlin/Palmer Cox, 1891, shows Brownies in various activites, set of 20, 11x13", EX, S24......$1,050.00
Converse Circus Acrobatic Toy, ca 1885, stenciled paper & wood pull toy, 12", EX, S24.................................$825.00
Crandall's District School, ca 1876, pnt wood, 10 articulated students, teacher, desk & books, VG (orig hinged box), S24...$1,100.00
Crandall's Expression Blocks, ca 1895, 28 flat pictorial blocks w/alphabet on reverse, 4½x8", EX (orig wooden box), A $525.00
Crandall's Great Show Acrobats, 1867, EX (EX wooden box), S24...$750.00
Crandall's Jack Straws, wooden straws w/ends depicting alphabet letters, 6¼", EX (orig wood & cb cylinder), A $385.00
Crandall's Menagerie, 1875, pnt jtd wood pcs form 6 different figures, 7½x13", EX (EX wooden box), A.............$1,100.00
Crandall's Stacking Blocks, set of 8, 7½" sq, G-, A.........$95.00
Crandall's Ye Spirit of '76 George Washington, articulated figure on orig slotted base, 9", VG, A $385.00

Kitchen Set, Reed, ca 1880, set of bowls, dishes, pitchers, cups, etc., ready for assembly, EX (stenciled wood box), A $175.00

Military Fort, Reed, ca 1880, stenciled blocks form fort, w/soldiers & cannon, complete, 8½x18", EX, A $1,870.00

Nesting Blocks, German, 1920s, scenes of animals & children, set of 10, VG, A...$200.00

Nesting Blocks, McLoughlin, ABC blocks w/animals & birds, set of 7 (2 missing), paper damage, A............................$800.00

Nesting Blocks, McLoughlin, alphabet blocks w/animal scenes & nursery rhymes, set of 7, 3x3" to 7x7", EX, A......$245.00

Nesting Blocks, McLoughlin, ca 1890, alphabet letters w/pictorial nursery rhymes, stack to 36", EX, S24............$1,850.00

Nesting Blocks, scenes of children, animals, alphabet & multiplication tables, set of 10, 1½x1½" to 5x5", EX, A.$385.00

Old Guard Soldiers, Ives, set w/cannon, EX, S24........$1,100.00

Pony Circus, Gibbs, 1940s, EX, A, $175.00.

Pretty Village, McLoughlin, litho paper on cb, 17 buildings w/people & plat plan, G, A $100.00

Pretty Village, Milton Bradley, 1909, later issue, complete, MIB, S15 ....$350.00

Rocking Horse, Gibbs, metal rockers, 9", VG, A $200.00

Train, Bliss, Adirondack Railroad, engine w/1 passenger car & 1 baggage car, 16 alphabet blocks, 27", VG, A...........$935.00

Train, Bliss, ca 1885, 'US Grant' engine, tender & passenger coach, Columbian Expo Chicago Floor Train, 36", VG-EX, S24...$4,750.00

Train, Germany, early 1900s, litho paper & pnt wood, engine & tender w/6 passenger cars, 23", rstr, A $750.00

Train, Milton Bradley, ca 1880, Hercules engine, tender & Atlantic-Pacific coach, 34", VG+, S24 ....$3,750.00

Zoological Garden, Luxux Papier-Fabrik/Berlin, 1890s, cutouts, metal holders, instructions & base, EX (orig box), B12 .$575.00

Zoologischer Garten, Verlag Eigth/Germany, 1840-50, 47 cutouts w/wood stands, labels w/5 languages, EX+ (orig box), B12..$3,000.00

Pedal Cars and Other Wheeled Goods

Just like Daddy, all little boys (and girls as well) are thrilled and happy to drive a brand new shiny car. Today both genera-tions search through flea markets and auto swap meets for cars, boats, fire engines, tractors and trains that run not on gas but pedal power. Some of the largest manufacturers of wheeled goods were AMF (American Machine and Foundry Company), Murray, and Garton. Values depend to a very large extent on condition, and those that have been restored may sell for upwards of $500.00, depending on year and model.

Advisor: Nate Stoller (S7).

Atomic Missile, Murray, 1950s, white plane-type vehicle with blue and orange trim, chain drive, 2 levers, 44", restored, $2,500.00.

Baby Buggatti, 1930s, dk bl w/chrome spoked wheels & grille, upholstered seat, only 90 made, 73", rstr, A.......................$33,000.00

Buick, Murray, 1949, bright bl w/chrome trim, wht-walls w/bl wheels & chrome hubs, 39", professionally rstr, A ..$2,310.00

Buick Roadster, Steelcraft, tan & cream w/dk brn fenders & stripes, chrome trim, w/spare & horn, wht-walls, 46", rstr, A...$5,720.00

Cadillac, 1925, gr, orange striping, wht-walls w/gr hubs, blk fenders & running boards, battery-op lights, rstr..$3,500.00

Car, British, bl & wht w/blk rubber tires, opening door & trunk, 42", dents & rust, M5 ....$600.00

Chevrolet Bel Air Convertible, 1955, red and white with Indianapolis 500 Mile Race flag and lettering on sides, white-wall tires, EX, A, $4,500.00.

Dump Truck, BMC, red w/silver-pnt grille & headlights, wht windshield & steering wheel, chrome hubs, 41", EX, A $600.00

Fire Chief Car, simple designed red Stutz w/blk undercarriage, curved seat back, disk wheel, 36", needs rstr, A.......$660.00

Fire Chief Truck, Am National, red w/upholstered seat, chrome trim, wht-walls w/red spokes, 2 ladders, 66", rstr, A..$3,960.00

Fire Ladder Truck, 1950s, red w/wht-walls, Fire lettered on sides, back step w/blk side bars, 42", EX $350.00

Ford, Steelcraft, 1936, red w/yel striping, yel cut-out wheels w/chrome hubs & red trim, maroon steering wheel, rstr $1,750.00

Locomotive, 1930s, blk & red, electric headlight, 26", G, A $345.00

Locomotive No 68, Pioneer or Gendron, pressed steel & wood, rubber tires w/spoked wheels, blk & red, 57", EX, A......$1,100.00

Mack Dump Truck, yel open cab w/blk trim, heavily decaled, mk Playboy Trucking Co, 50", rstr, A $2,200.00

Mack Gasoline Truck, R Doan Custom, Gilmore ads on wht C-style cab & tank, blk chassis & nose, red hubs, 55", EX, A...$3,410.00

Mack 5-Ton Dump Truck, Steelcraft, red w/blk fenders, chassis & steering wheel, red hubs, 62", rstr, A................$3,300.00

Packard Convertible, Am National, 1923, yel & blk, yel hubs, blk-cushioned interior, pedals in front & back seat, VG, A..$7,370.00

Sportster, Gendron, pressed steel with rubber tires, green and black with gold striping, 41", VG, A, $3,960.00.

Toledo De Luxe, Toledo Metal Co, 1927, pressed steel & wood, maroon w/yel & blk trim, doors open, 54", rstr, A .$4,950.00

White Dump Truck, Toledo, gr w/red bed, fenders, hubs & radiator protector, chrome grille, wht-walls, 68", rare, G, A.$7,370.00

White Truck Line Dump Truck, Am National, 1927, red & blk w/yel striping, blk vinyl seat, wht-walls, rstr.........$2,800.00

Windy City GMC Tow Truck, dk bl w/bl & pk flame design on hood, chrome boom, trim & hubs, custom decals, 48", M, A..$1,760.00

Packard Convertible, American National, 1928, red steel body with black fenders and running board, white-wall tires with red hubs, restored, $4,500.00.

Packard Fire Chief Car, Am National, red w/blk fenders & running boards, yel & blk striping, bell on hood, 27", EX, A...$9,570.00

Patrol Plane, silver w/red & bl trim, blk steering wheel & prop, blk rubber tires w/red hubs, rstr, A............................$855.00

Racer, Eureka, sleek lt bl body w/latched hood, chrome steering wheel, radiator & lights, bl disk wheels, 56", rstr, A ..$2,200.00

Ride-'Em Steam Shovel, Keystone, VG+ $400.00

Roadster, Am National, 1920s, gray & blk w/red striping, rumble seat, rubber tires w/hubs, side spare, 70", rstr, A...$8,000.00

Roadster, simple design w/outlined hood & 3 pnt side vents, disk wheels, no ornamentation, 30", EX, A $200.00

Roadster, Toledo, orange & brn w/gr striping, blk trim, wht-walls w/orange hubs, rear tool box, 46", rstr, A $1,650.00

Sky Kar, Evans, red & wht, VG $525.00

Station Wagon, Garton, maroon w/simulated wood panels, bl trim, maroon disk wheels w/chrome hubs, 47", rstr, A.........$935.00

Sterns Pedal Car, Gendron, 1920, bl metal body w/wht stripes on steel & wood fr, wood dash & seat, spoke wheels, G..$2,500.00

White Truck Line Dump Truck, American National, 1927, red and black with yellow striping, black vinyl seat, white-wall tires, restored, $2,800.00.

Scooters

Buddy L, blk sturdy platform on 3 wheels, blk & red jtd derrick-type hdl w/wood grip, rubber tires w/red hubs, rstr, A........$2,310.00

Henley, rectangular platform on base w/4 metal spoked wheels, vertical hdl, 33", G, A $115.00

Wagons

Covered Wagon, wood, wrought-iron hoops, canvas cover, wood spoked wheels, water barrel, red lantern, 46x48", EX, A.$360.00

Express Wagon, orange-pnt tin w/wood bottom, metal spoked wheels, wood hdl & twisted wire pull rod, 32", VG+, A $165.00

Express Wagon, wood w/dovetailed corners, Express stenciled on sides, disk wheels (2 szs), w/hdl, 29", G, A.................$50.00

Fire Patrol, Paris Wagon, ca 1890, wood buckboard type w/side seats & brass rails, wood spoked wheels, 55", EX, A...........$3,410.00

Hercules, 1930s, pnt wood & pressed steel w/removable stake sides, rear dual rubber wheels, 48", EX, A................$175.00

Patrol, red wood fire wagon w/front bench seat, footrest & lantern, rear flanged side benches, spoked wheels, VG, A...$1,650.00

Pioneer, red tin w/wood bottom & pull hdl, metal spoked wheels, 25", EX, A..$550.00

Unknown Maker, red wood body & hdl w/speeding train & yel design pnt on sides, metal spoke wheels, EX, A.......$300.00

Penny Toys

Penny toys were around as early as the late 1800s and as late as the 1920s. Many were made in Germany, but some were made in France as well. With few exceptions, they ranged in size from 5" on down; some had moving parts, and a few had clockwork mechanisms. Though many were unmarked, you'll sometimes find them signed 'Kellermann,' 'Meier,' 'Fischer,' or 'Distler,' or carrying an embossed company logo such as the 'dog and cart' emblem. They were made of lithographed tin with exquisite detailing — imagine an entire carousel less than 2½" tall. Because of a recent surge in collector interest, many have been crossing the auction block of some of the country's large galleries. Our values are prices realized at several of these auctions. Advisor: Jane Anderson (A2).

Airplane, att Kellerman/Germany, pilot in open cockpit, single prop, 2 disk wheels, 3½", EX, A...............................$360.00

Airplanes on Rod, Germany, spring activated, 7", EX, A..$385.00

Bank, Germany, church w/high bell tower atop hinged roof w/slot, 2½", G, A..$145.00

Bank, sentry at guardhouse enters & exits as tab is pushed, slot on top, also stores candy, 3", EX, A $330.00

Battleship, Germany, pnt zinc, displays 6 cannons through portholes, colored flags strung from fore to aft, 4", EX, A .$360.00

Biplane, att Kellerman/Germany, pilot in open cockpit, single prop, 2 spoked wheels, 5", EX, A $715.00

Bird in Cage, Issmayer, bird in wht house-shaped cage on pole w/red rnd base, 8½", G, A...$135.00

Boy & Rabbit in Victorian Rocker, Meier, 3", rare, EX, A ..$365.00

Boy on Sled, Germany, 1915, litho tin, 2½", NM, A.....$420.00

Bus, early coach w/open rear entrance & seated driver, flywheel in undercarriage, 4 disk wheels, 4", EX, A...............$470.00

Butting Goat, att George Fischer, begins kicking at basket when spring slide is pushed, 3", EX, A $525.00

Camera, early type on tripod w/removable image of a pig, stained tin, 4", G-, A..$385.00

Cassion & Hot Stove Trailer, Germany, 1915, 2 soldiers in camouflage cart w/hot stove pulled by 2 wht horses, 7", EX, A...$165.00

Charabanc, Henri Avoiron/France, open coach w/6 passengers, ornate emb sides, 2 lg & 2 sm spoked wheels, 4", G, A..$440.00

Child in Stroller, marked Germany, ca 1910, 3", rare, EX, $275.00.

Climbing Monkey, pull string to lift monkey, litho tin, 7", EX, A..$385.00

Dirigible in Hanger, Meier/Germany, airship reveals itself when spring slide is pushed, 4", VG, A.............................$690.00

Dog Cart, Germany, gold dog pulling bl cart w/gold spoked wheels, stained & plated tin, 5¾", VG+, A $440.00

Donkey, IJF, coppery brn donkey on gr platform w/4 spoked wheels, 3", EX, A...$470.00

Duck on Wheels, Germany, opens mouth when moving, 2¾", EX, A $230.00

Equestrians, Meier/Germany, 3 riders mounted on platform, spring slide activates galloping motion, 4", G, A...$1,320.00

Fire Hose Truck, Meier, driver clanging bell, EX, H7 ....$285.00

Fireman w/Water Container, prewar Japan, litho tin, 3½", EX+, A $700.00

Galloping Bugler, Meier, green platform with red wheels, 3⅛", EX, A, $1,400.00.

Garage w/2 Cars, Kellermann, 3½", EX, A $635.00
Gas Station, Germany, w/gas pump in front, 4", NM (NM box), A $990.00
Gas Station & Car, JDN/Germany, litho tin, 4x2½" gas station, EX, A $450.00
Gas Station & Car, Distler, 4", EX, A $600.00
Goat on 4-Wheeled Platform, Germany, 3", EX, A $360.00
Golden Fly, France, on platform w/4 spoked wheels, name on wings, 4½" W, NM, A $250.00

Highchair, Meier, opens to form chair and table with lithographed farm scene, 3¾", EX, A, $225.00.

Horse, gray saddled horse trotting on platform w/4 sm disk wheels, 4", M, A $100.00
Horse, Henri Avoiron/France, gold-pnt prancing horse in red bridle on platform w/4 spoked wheels, 3¼", M, A... $330.00
Horse, reddish brn saddled horse w/blk mane & tail trotting on platform w/4 sm disk wheels, 4", M, A $110.00
Horse-Drawn Cart, driver w/whip in 2-wheeled cart, 3½", VG, A $300.00
Horse-Drawn Military Cart, Meier/Germany, mounted soldier & another horse pulling wagon w/4 spoked wheels, 4½", NM, A $220.00
Limousine, Distler/Germany, driver in open-sided front seat, litho passengers, spoked wheels, rack atop, 4½", EX, A $330.00
Limousine, Germany, gr w/blk roof, yel trim, 2", EX, A . $100.00
Limousine, KS/Japan, early auto w/open driver's seat, litho Japanese passenger in window, 2¾", VG, A $360.00
Military Set, Meier/Germany, includes 4 horse-drawn wagons: ammunition, medical, canteen & artillery, 4x11", NMIB, A $1,430.00
Passenger Boat, Fischer/Germany, wht w/2 yel stacks, red trim, 2 rows of cut-out windows, spoked wheels, 4¼", EX, A.. $660.00
Pool Player, Germany, player at end of pool table, hand-op, 4", EX, A $220.00
Porter w/Trunk, possibly Fischer/Germany, porter pushing 2-wheeled cart w/red trunk, 3", EX $300.00
Punch, Henri Avoiron/France, Punch in stride on platform w/4 spoked wheels, 4¼", NM, A $275.00

Punch & Judy, Germany, figures separately hand-op, litho tin, 2¾", VG+, A $660.00
Puppy, Distler/Germany, wide-eyed puppy in scarf w/front leg up on platform w/4 spoked wheels, 2½", G, A $300.00
Rifle, Japan, actually shoots (possibly candy pellets), 5", NM, A $150.00
Runabout, Germany, gold spoked wheels, w/driver, inertia mechanism, 4¼", VG+, A $330.00
Sailing Ship, Germany, hand-pnt zinc w/cast sails & smokestack, wht w/red trim, applied ring on bottom, 2¾", VG, A $195.00

Sedan, Fisher, 4", VG, $125.00.

Sedan, Germany, early auto w/cream top over bl body, red capped spoke wheels, 2½", EX, A $135.00
Sewing Machine, Fischer/Germany, 1920s, detailed treadle machine, hand crank activates needle, 3", G, A........ $55.00
Steamship, Distler/Germany, wht w/3 smokestacks & flag, red trim, spoked wheels, clockwork, 4¾", G, A............. $360.00
Stutz Bearcat, Gesch/Germany, figure in bl open car w/yel spoked wheels, 4½", EX, A $330.00
Toy Town Railroad, Parker Bros, 1907, complete w/cb village & penny toys made in Germany, EX+ (G box), A..$1,525.00
Two-Man Flying Hollander, att Kellerman/Germany, 2 young boys seated on flat vehicle w/4 spoked wheels, 4", G, A $470.00
Vis-A-Vis, Meier/Germany, driver in open car, lanterns & railing stamped on sides, spoked wheels, 3", EX, A $300.00
Whistle, blow whistle to move propeller atop red & bl auto-gyro airplane, EX, H7 .... $265.00
Whistle, Distler/Germany, monkey at grindstone spins, 4¼", VG, A $275.00
Whistle, EC/France, dancing poodle, wire-wrapped poodle plays organ for dancing dog that spins, 4", EX, A $275.00
Whistle, EC/France, wire-wrapped figure spins wheel of fortune, 3¼", EX, A $165.00
Whistle, Germany, dirgible, mk Los Angles, 4", EX, A..$415.00
Whistle, Kicko, carousel, 4 children spin on horses when whistle is blown, 4", EX, A $300.00

Pez Dispensers

Every few years a collecting phenomenon occurs, and none has been quite as intense in recent memory as the Pez craze. Pez was originally designed as a breath mint for smokers, but by the fifties kids were the target market, and the candies were packaged in the dispensers that we all know and love today. There is already more than three hundred variations to collect, and more arrive on the supermarket shelves every day. Though early on collectors seemed to prefer the dispensers without feet, that attitude has changed, and now it's the character head they concentrate on. Feet were added in 1987, so if you were to limit yourself to only 'feetless' dispensers, your collection would be far from complete. Some dispensers have variations in color and design that can influence their values. Don't buy any that are damaged, incomplete, or that have been tampered with in any way; those are nearly worthless. For more information refer to *A Pictorial Guide to Plastic Candy Dispensers Featuring Pez* by David Welch and *Collecting Toys #6* by Richard O'Brien. Values are for mint-condition dispensers unless noted otherwise.

Advisor: Richard Belyski (B1).

Other Sources: O1, T1

Angel, no ft, 1970s, B1	$25.00
Annie, no ft, B1	$55.00
Arlene, w/ft, pk, from $1 to	$3.00
Baloo, w/ft	$20.00
Bambi, no ft	$25.00
Barney Bear, no ft, H4	$35.00
Barney Bear, w/ft	$20.00
Baseball Glove, no ft	$150.00
Batgirl, w/ft, soft head, MIP (w/candy) H4	$65.00
Batman, no ft, H4	$12.00
Batman, no ft, w/cape, B9	$120.00
Batman, w/ft, bl or blk, ea, from $1 to	$3.00
Betsy Ross, no ft, J6	$100.00
Bouncer Beagle, w/ft, M, B1	$6.00
Boy, w/ft, brn hair, from $1 to	$3.00
Bozo, no ft, diecut, B9	$125.00

Bugs Bunny, w/ft, from $1 to	$3.00
Bullwinkle, no ft	$175.00
Candy Shooter, red & wht, w/candy & gun license, unused	$95.00
Captain America, no ft	$45.00
Captain Hook, no ft	$35.00
Casper, no ft	$70.00
Charlie Brown, w/ft, from $1 to	$3.00
Charlie Brown, w/ft & tongue	$6.00
Chick, w/ft, from $1 to	$3.00
Chick (no hat), B9	$50.00
Chick in Egg, no ft, H4	$12.00
Chick in Egg, no ft, w/hair	$50.00
Clown, w/ft, whistle head, P10	$6.00
Clown w/Collar, no ft	$65.00
Cockatoo, no ft, bl face, red beak	$35.00
Cool Cat, w/ft	$35.00
Cow (A), no ft, bl	$45.00
Cow (B), no ft, bl	$45.00
Creature From the Black Lagoon, no ft	$175.00
Crocodile, no ft	$65.00
Daffy Duck, no ft, H4	$10.00
Daffy Duck, w/ft, from $1 to	$3.00
Dalmatian Pup, w/ft, B1	$25.00
Daniel Boone, no ft	$110.00
Dino, w/ft, purple, from $1 to	$3.00
Dinosaur, w/ft, 4 different, ea, from $1 to	$3.00
Doctor, M	$70.00
Donald Duck, no ft	$15.00
Donald Duck, no ft, diecut	$115.00

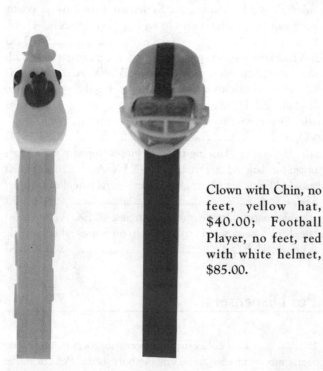

Clown with Chin, no feet, yellow hat, $40.00; Football Player, no feet, red with white helmet, $85.00.

Donald Duck's Nephew, no ft...............................$20.00
Donald Duck's Nephew, w/ft, gr or bl hat, ea, B1 ....$6.00
Donald Duck's Nephew, w/ft, red hat, B1 ....$10.00
Donkey, w/ft, whistle head, P10 ....$6.00
Droopy Dog (A), no ft, plastic swivel ears, MIP, B1 ....$15.00
Droopy Dog (B), w/ft, pnt ears, B1 ....$6.00
Dumbo, w/ft, bl head...$20.00
Elephant, no ft, orange & bl, flat hat $45.00
Erie Specters, no ft, 6 different, B1, ea, from $75 to $95.00
Fat-Ears Rabbit, no ft, pk head $15.00
Fat-Ears Rabbit, no ft, yel head.............................$10.00

Photo courtesy of June Moon.

Fireman, no feet, $25.00; Policeman, no feet, $25.00.

Fishman, no ft, gr...$125.00
Foghorn Leghorn, w/ft $50.00
Fozzie Bear, w/ft, from $1 to $3.00
Frankenstein, no ft.......................................$150.00
Fred Flintstone, w/ft, B1, from $1 to.........................$3.00
Frog, w/ft, whistle head, B1................................$30.00
Garfield, w/ft, orange w/gr hat, from $1 to $3.00
Garfield, w/ft, teeth, B1, from $1 to $10.00
Garfield, w/ft, visor, from $1 to............................$3.00
Girl, w/ft, blond hair, B1..................................$15.00
Gonzo, w/ft, from $1 to $3.00
Goofy, no ft, old..$10.00
Goofy, no ft, removable nose & teeth $30.00
Gorilla, no ft, blk head....................................$45.00
Green Hornet, 1960s, from $150 to.........................$250.00
Gyro Gearloose, w/ft, B1.....................................$6.00
Henry Hawk, no ft...$65.00
Hulk, no ft, dk gr..$20.00
Hulk, no ft, lt gr..$10.00
Hulk, w/ft, lt gr, remake, P10...............................$3.00
Indian, w/ft, whistle head, B1 ....$6.00
Indian Brave, no ft, reddish...............................$150.00
Indian Chief, no ft, marbleized............................$65.00

Indian Chief, no ft, yel headdress $45.00
Indian Maiden, no ft, w/headband $70.00
Jerry Mouse, w/ft, plastic face, B1........................$15.00
Jerry Mouse, w/ft, pnt face $6.00
Jiminy Cricket, no ft......................................$85.00
Joker (Batman), no ft, soft head............................$70.00
Kermit the Frog, w/ft, red, from $1 to $3.00
Knight, no ft..$150.00
Koala, w/ft, whistle head..................................$25.00
Lamb, no ft...$10.00
Lamb, w/ft, from $1 to......................................$3.00
Lamb, w/ft, whistle head, from $15 to $20.00
Li'l Bad Wolf, w/ft...$15.00
Lion w/Crown, no ft.......................................$55.00
Lion's Club Lion...$950.00
Lucy, w/ft, from $1 to......................................$3.00
Maharajah, no ft $30.00
Make-A-Face, works like Mr Potato Head, minimum value..$1,500.00
Mary Poppins, no ft, B1, minimum value.....................$500.00
Merlin Mouse, w/ft.......................................$15.00
Mexican, no ft, B9..$65.00
Mickey Mouse, no ft, removable nose or cast nose, ea, from $10
    to $15.00
Mickey Mouse, w/ft, from $1 to $3.00
Mimic Monkey (monkey w/ball cap), no ft, several colors, ea,
    from $25 to...$35.00
Miss Piggy, w/ft, ea, from $1 to $3.00
Miss Piggy, w/ft, eyelashes, B1............................$10.00
Monkey Sailor, no ft, w/wht cap, M, J2.....................$25.00
Mowgli, w/ft...$20.00
Mr Ugly, no ft...$20.00
Muscle Mouse (gray Jerry), w/ft, plastic nose $15.00
Nermal, w/ft, gray, from $1 to $3.00
Nurse, no ft, brn hair, B1.................................$75.00
Octopus, no ft, blk.......................................$45.00
Olive Oyl, no ft, B1, minimum value.......................$125.00
Olympic Wolf..$600.00
Orange, no ft..$75.00
Panda, no ft, diecut eyes $20.00
Panda, w/ft, remake, from $1 to $3.00
Panda, w/ft, whistle head $6.00
Papa Smurf, w/ft, red, P10..................................$5.00
Parrot, w/ft, whistle head, B1..............................$6.00
Pebbles Flintstone, w/ft, B1, from $1 to.....................$3.00
Penguin, w/ft, whistle head, P10............................$6.00
Penguin (Batman), no ft, soft head, NM.....................$75.00
Peter Pez (A), no ft......................................$65.00
Peter Pez (B), w/ft, from $1 to $3.00
Pilgrim, no ft, J6..$100.00
Pirate, no ft..$30.00
Pluto, no ft, red...$10.00
Pluto, w/ft, from $1 to.....................................$3.00
Popeye (B), no ft...$40.00
Popeye (C), no ft, w/removable pipe........................$45.00
Practical Pig (B), no ft...................................$30.00
Psychedelic Eye, no ft, from $350 to $450.00
Psychedelic Flower, no ft, B1, from $375 to................$400.00
Pumpkin (A), no ft, from $10 to $15.00

Pumpkin (B), w/ft, from $1 to................................$3.00
Raven, no ft, yel beak $30.00
Regular (looks like Bic lighter), no ft, many variations, ea .$100.00
Rhino, w/ft, whistle head, P10.........................$6.00
Ringmaster, no ft $125.00

Road Runner, no feet, $20.00; Uncle Sam, no feet, $65.00.

Road Runner, w/ft, B1 ....$6.00
Rooster, w/ft, whistle head, B1 ....$25.00
Rooster, w/ft, wht or yel head, ea $25.00
Rudolph, no ft..$25.00

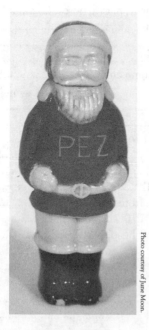

Santa Claus, full body, $125.00.

Santa Claus (A), no ft, steel pin, from $95 to $125.00
Santa Claus (B), no ft, B1 ....$85.00
Santa Claus (C), no ft, from $5 to....................$15.00
Santa Claus (C), w/ft, B1, from $1 to................$3.00
Scrooge McDuck (A), no ft, B1 ....$20.00
Scrooge McDuck (B), w/ft, B1...........................$6.00

Sheik, no ft...$30.00
Skull (A), no ft, from $5 to $10.00
Skull (B), w/ft, from $1 to................................$3.00
Smurf, w/ft...$5.00
Smurfette, w/ft, bl, P10....................................$5.00
Snoopy, w/ft, from $1 to...................................$5.00
Snowman (A), no ft, from $5 to.......................$10.00
Snowman (B), w/ft, from $1 to.........................$5.00
Space Gun Candy Shooter, orange, D8 ....$75.00
Space Trooper Robot, no ft, full body, from $250 to $325.00
Spaceman, no ft, bl..$100.00
Speedy Gonzales (A), w/ft.................................$10.00
Speedy Gonzolas (B), no ft, from $1 to $3.00
Spider-Man, no ft, from $10 to.........................$15.00
Spider-Man, w/ft, from $1 to $3.00
Spike, w/ft, B1...$6.00
Sylvester (A), w/ft, cream whiskers, B1 ....$5.00
Sylvester (A), w/ft, wht whiskers, B1 ....$2.00
Sylvester (B), w/ft...$1.00
Teenage Mutant Ninja Turtles, w/ft, 8 variations, ea, from $1 to $3.00
Thor, no ft...$150.00
Thumper, w/ft, no copyright, D8......................$30.00
Tiger, w/ft, whistle head, P10...........................$6.00
Tinkerbell, no ft...$100.00
Tom, no ft...$35.00
Tom, w/ft, plastic face $15.00
Tom, w/ft, pnt face $6.00
Tweety Bird, no ft, H4.......................................$10.00
Tweety Bird, w/ft, from $1 to $3.00
Tyke, w/ft, B1...$6.00
Whistle, w/ft, from $1 to $3.00
Wile E Coyote, w/ft, B1.....................................$25.00
Winnie the Pooh, w/ft, B1.................................$25.00

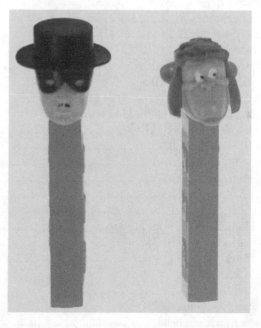

Zorro, no feet, with Zorro logo, $75.00, no logo, $45.00; King Louie, no feet, orange, $20.00.

Witch, 3-pc, no ft $10.00
Wolfman, no ft $185.00
Wonder Woman, no ft, soft head........................$75.00
Wonder Woman, w/ft, from $1 to $3.00
Woodstock, w/ft, from $1 to $3.00
Woodstock, w/ft, pnt feathers............................$10.00
Yappy Dog, no ft, orange or gr, ea $35.00
Yosemite Sam, w/ft...$1.00

Foreign

Barney Bear, w/ft, P10......................................$5.00
Daffy Duck, w/ft, P10 ....$5.00
Donald Duck, w/ft, P10 ....$5.00
Girl Duck (Webby), w/ft, P10 ....$6.00
Gonzo, w/ft, P10...$5.00
Huey, w/ft, P10...$6.00
Jerry Mouse, w/ft, lavender or bl, P10, ea $8.00
Kermit the Frog, w/ft, P10.................................$5.00
Louie, w/ft, P10 ....$6.00
Lucy, w/ft, P10...$5.00
Mickey Mouse, w/ft, P10....................................$5.00
Pluto, w/ft, P10..$5.00
Santa, w/ft, P10..$5.00
Scrooge McDuck, w/ft, P10.................................$8.00
Snoopy, w/ft, P10 ....$5.00
Snowman, w/ft, P10 ....$5.00
Spike, w/ft, P10..$8.00
Tom, w/ft, P10..$8.00
Tyke, w/ft, P10...$8.00

Miscellaneous

Bank, truck (1), metal $100.00
Bank, truck (2), metal......................................$40.00
Bracelet, pk, P10 ....$5.00

Clicker, US Zone Germany, 1950, lithographed tin, 3½",
NM, $300.00.

Mask, Spider-Man or Hulk, paper, ea................$15.00
Tin, 1930s, Pez Spezials, stars & lines on checked background,
    gold colors, 2½x4½", rare, EX, A $225.00
Watch, pk face w/yel band or yel face w/bl band, ea........$10.00

Pin-Back Buttons

Pin-back buttons produced up to the early 1920s were made
with a celluloid covering. After that time, a large number of buttons were lithographed on tin; these are referred to as tin 'lithos.'

Character and toy-related buttons represent a popular collecting field. There are countless categories to base a collection
on. Buttons were given out at stores and theatres, offered as premiums, attached to dolls or received with a club membership.

In the late forties and into the fifties, some cereal companies
packed one in boxes of their product. Quaker Puffed Oats
offered a series of movie star pin-backs, but probably the best
known are Kellogg's Pep Pins. There were eighty-six in all, so
theoretically if you wanted the whole series as Kellogg hoped
you would, you'd have to buy at least that many boxes of their
cereal. Pep pins came in five sets, the first in 1945, three more in
1946, and the last in 1947. They were printed with full-color
lithographs of comic characters licensed by King Features and
Famous Artists — Maggie and Jiggs, the Winkles, and Dagwood
and Blondie, for instance. Superman, the only D.C. Comics
character, was included in each set. Most Pep pins range in
value from $10.00 to $15.00 in NM/M condition; any not mentioned in our listings fall into this range. There are exceptions,
and we've made sure they're evaluated below.

Nearly all pin-backs are collectible today with these possible
exceptions: common buttons picturing flags of various nations,
general labor union buttons denoting the payment of dues, and
common buttons with clever sayings. Be sure that you buy only
buttons with well-centered designs, well-alligned colors, no fading or yellowing, no spots or stains, and no cracks, splits, or
dents. In the listings that follow, sizes are approximate.

Advisor: Doug Dezso (D6), Kellogg's Pep Pins only.
Other Sources: C10, D11, S20

'93 Disneyland Hotel w/Belle & Beast, 3", NM, M8..........$8.00
Alphonse & Gaston, Omaha Grocers Picnic of Aug 6, 1903,
    1¾", EX+, A3 ....$60.00
Andy Gump for Congress, Globe Democrat, blk & wht, ⅞",
    VG $12.00
Authorized Guide to Dick Tracy, Tracy & 50th Anniversary
    Strip, 2¼", M, D11 ....$25.00
Baby Gloria, RBL doll button, yel, bl & red, ⅞", EX........$18.00
Bart Simpson, Under Achiever & Proud of It Man, gr, 6", MIP,
    K1 ....$4.00
Batman & Robin Society, Button World Mfg, 1966, mc, 3½",
    MIP $22.50
Beatles, blk & wht photo under clear plastic w/gr plastic trim,
    3", B3...$25.00
Beatles, flashes to 4 head shots w/names, red on bl, 2½",
    B3 ....$25.00
Beatles, group photo, bl or pk plastic rim, 3", R2, ea $18.00
Bimbo a Paramount Star, blk & wht, ⅞", G $12.00
Buster Brown & Tige, Member Brown Bilt Club, mc, ⅞",
    EX...$18.00
Captain Frank Hawks, Flight Commander, 1936-37, VG,
    S20 ....$75.00

Casper the Friendly Ghost, Los Angeles Herald, S20.....$100.00

Chip & Dale Rescue Rangers, 1994, mc, 3", NM, M8........$3.00

Cisco Kid, I Eat Butter-Nut Bread, red & wht, 1", EX......$25.00

Cub Scouts, full face, mc on red, wht & bl, VG $10.00

Dad's Root Beer, Have You Had It?, logo & wht letters on bl, VG, S20 ....$10.00

Dale Evans, blk & wht photo on gr, 1950s, 1¼", VG, M16..$8.00

Davy Crockett, Indian Fighter, 1940s, yel & red, 1½", EX, M17..$18.00

Dick Tracy Detective, profile w/gun, mc w/beige face & hands (repros are pk), 1¼", EX...$45.00

Dorothy Hart, Sunbrite Junior Nurse Corps, blk, red & wht, 1", EX $25.00

Effanbee, Member Patsy Doll Club, blk, red & wht, 1", EX..$25.00

Elvis, Don't Be Cruel, broken heart & 2 guitars, red, wht & bl, ⅞", EX..$18.00

ET & Elliot, photo, 1982, 6", NM, D9.........................$3.00

Fonz Is Cool, Fonz w/thumbs up, 1976, 3½", EX $10.00

Gene Autry, mc face on wht, 1¼", VG..........................$15.00

Ginny Dolls, Hi I'm Ginny w/logo, 1950s, M, H12..........$25.00

Harold Teen Cap the Original, signed Carl Ed, blk & wht, 1¼", EX..$75.00

Hi-Yo Silver, Lone Ranger, blk, wht & red, 1¼", EX.......$85.00

Home of Dick Tracy, Woodstock, Illinois, Tracy in profile talking on wrist radio, 2¼", M, D11...............................$20.00

Homer Simpson, No Problemo!, Button-Up, 1¾", M, K1..$1.00

Honey I Blew Up the Baby, 1990s, rectangular, NM, M8 ..$3.00

Hopalong Cassidy Savings Club, 1950, 3", EX, $45.00.

Hoppy in the Boston Traveler, 1950s, blk & red on wht, 2", EX+, A3 ....$45.00

I Go Pogo, w/face, blk & wht on gold litho tin, mk 1956 Walt Kelly, ⅞", VG $15.00

I Love the Beatles, bl on wht in red circle, 3", B3.............$20.00

I Love the Beatles, Green Duck, Chicago, red, wht & bl litho tin, ⅞", B3 ....$10.00

I Was There, Pocahontas preview at Wang Center, 1995, NM, M8..$15.00

I'm a Beatle Fan, In Case of Emergency Call Paul or Ringo, red & blk on wht, 3", VG, B3...$35.00

I'm a Camper Scout, tent in background, mc, 1¼", VG, S20 ....$10.00

I'm a Dixie Racer/Excuse My Dust, boy in car, red, wht & bl, 1¼", EX...$75.00

I'm an Official Beatles Fan, blk, red & wht litho tin, sm dent o/w VG, R2...$12.00

I'm an Official Beatles Fan, blk & wht faces w/autographs on red & wht, Green Duck, VG+, B3 ....$25.00

Jackie Gleason, Joe the Bartender or The Bus Driver, 1950s, EX, P6, ea..$25.00

John Wayne, late 1940s, black, white and blue, 1¼", EX, $45.00.

Jetsons, Kool-Aid giveaway at movie theatres, oval, H4.....$5.00

Knott's Berry Farm, Friendliest Place in the West, wht & gold litho tin, 2", M, H11...$12.00

Land of Oz, Beech Mountain, Banner Elk, NC, stylized bl & yel Scarecrow w/logo, 2⅛", EX+, scarce, S6..................$120.00

Lionel Engineers Club, emb train front, brass, ⅝", EX $70.00

Lone Ranger, Sunday Herald, blk, wht & orange litho tin, 1", VG $45.00

Lone Ranger Bond Bread Safety Club Star, VG, S20.......$30.00

Lone Ranger Victory Corps, bl on gold-tone metal, 1942, VG, S20 ....$50.00

Mickey Mouse Globe Trotters Member, issued by various bread companies, 1930s, black, red and white, 1¼", EX, $75.00.

Lucy, Gal Friday, litho tin, 2", EX, H11 ....$3.00

Mary Hartline, Canada Dry Super Circus Club, mc litho tin, 1⅝", EX..............................$25.00

McNugget Mania, flasher w/jumping man, mc, 3", EX $15.00

Mickey Mouse, Follow My Adventures, Buy Cote's Master Loaf, image of Mickey on off-wht, 1¼", EX+, M5 ....$50.00

Mickey Mouse, red lettering arched above image of Mickey, 1¼", EX..............................$65.00

Mickey Mouse Boston Advertiser Comic Section, 1930s, red & blk on yel litho tin, 1¼", VG, A3 ....$40.00

Mickey Mouse Club, pie-eyed Mickey, 1928-30, blk, red & wht, 1¼", 1 spot w/lt foxing o/w VG..............................$60.00

Monkees, guitar logo, red on wht, 2½x1½", EX+, D9 ......$15.00

Moon Mullins, Los Angeles Evening Express, 1¼", VG $40.00

Official Baby Ruth-Katz Pinocchio Club, EX+, T1 ....$45.00

Official Green Hornet Agent, 1966, gr, bl & blk, 4", NM, M17..............................$40.00

Official Sky Observer Space Satellite, 1950s, 1½", M, P4 ..$6.00

Paul McCartney World Tour 89-90, 1½", B3 ....$2.00

Reel Music (Beatles), blk & silver, 1", B3 ....$9.00

Renfrew of the Mounted, red, blk & wht, 1¼", EX $18.00

Rocky Jones Space Ranger, Harvest Bread, blk, bl & wht litho tin, 1⅜", EX..............................$25.00

Roy Rogers, blk & wht photo on gray, w/name in lg letters at bottom, 1940s, 1¼", VG+, M16..............................$25.00

Roy Rogers, Nellybelle (car), Post Grape-Nuts, mc litho tin, 1953, ⅞", EX..............................$20.00

Roy Rogers, Post Grape-Nuts, mc litho tin, 1953, ⅞", EX..............................$25.00

Santa, bust portrait w/gray fur-trimmed hat, store advertisement, 1¼", EX..............................$100.00

Sgt Pepper, movie logo on wht, 3", B3 ....$5.00

Shirley Temple Club, Chicago Times, bl & wht litho tin, ⅞", VG $50.00

Skippy SSSS (Skippy Skinner's Secret Society), mc, ⅞", EX..............................$18.00

Smurfs, roller skater, soccer player or trumpet player, 1½", P10, ea $5.00

Snoopy, Happy Birthday, Hallmark, 1990, 1½", MOC, H11.$4.00

Snoopy & Woodstock, dancing, Get Met It Pays, Met Life, 1992, 3", M, H11..............................$8.00

Snoopy Astronaut, I'm on the Moon, litho tin, 1969, 2", EX, rare, H11 ....$25.00

Snoopy Fan Club, litho tin, 2¼", EX, H11 ....$6.00

Snoopy's Gallery Santa Rosa, litho tin, 2", M, H11..........$5.00

Superman Action Comics, 1939, mc litho, ⅞", EX+, rare, A3 ....$350.00

Superman Club, 1960s, 3", D8..............................$25.00

Tom & Jerry Go for Sunbeam Bread, red, wht & blk litho tin, 1⅛", EX..............................$20.00

Wha-Ramm, Stop Them Robin, orange, yel & gr, VG, S20 ....$10.00

Woodstock, Party Animal, Hallmark, 1990, MOC, H11....$4.00

Zorro, c Disney, 3", C10..............................$35.00

1st Disneyana Convention, Walt Disney World, 1992, NM, M8..............................$7.00

101 Dalmatians, puppies on red ground, 3", NM, M8........$3.00

Kellogg's Pep Pins

Bo Plenty, NM $30.00
Corky, NM $16.00
Dagwood, NM $30.00
Dick Tracy, NM $30.00
Fat Stuff, NM $15.00
Felix the Cat, NM..............................$75.00
Flash Gordon, NM..............................$30.00
Flat Top, NM $30.00
Goofy, NM $10.00
Gravel Gertie, NM $15.00
Harold Teen, NM $15.00
Inspector, NM..............................$12.50
Jiggs, NM..............................$25.00
Judy, NM..............................$10.00
Kayo, NM..............................$20.00
Little King, NM $15.00
Little Moose, NM $15.00
Maggie, NM $25.00
Mama De Stross, NM..............................$30.00
Mama Katzenjammer, NM $25.00
Mamie, NM..............................$15.00

Moon Mullins, $10.00.

Photo courtesy of Doug Dezso.

Navy Patrol, NM..............................$6.00
Olive Oyl, NM..............................$30.00
Orphan Annie, NM..............................$25.00
Pat Patton, NM..............................$10.00
Perry Winkle, NM..............................$15.00
Phantom, NM..............................$75.00
Pop Jenks, NM..............................$15.00
Popeye, NM $30.00
Rip Winkle, NM..............................$20.00
Skeezix, NM..............................$15.00
Superman, NM..............................$38.00
Toots, NM..............................$15.00
Uncle Walt, NM..............................$20.00
Uncle Willie, NM..............................$12.50
Winkles Twins, NM $75.00
Winnie Winkle, NM $15.00

Pipsqueaks

Pipsqueak toys were popular among the Pennsylvania Germans. Many featured animals made of painted papier-mache, some were on spring legs. All had bellows that produced a squeaking sound, hence the name. Early toys had bellows made from sheepskin. Cloth bellows followed, and on later examples, the bellows were made of paper.

Bird, blk & wht cloth-covered w/full feathered tail, coiled wire legs, squeaker in felt bag on wood hdl, EX, A..........$245.00

Bird w/Flapping Wings, pnt compo & wood w/crest, wings flap when squeaker base is pushed, 4", EX, A..............$1,210.00

Cat, American, late 1800s, painted composition, 7¾", EX, $600.00.

Chicken, mk Germany, pnt papier-mache w/coiled wire legs, squeaker base (non-working), 5", A........................$120.00

Clown, papier-mache & cloth figure, squeaks & sticks out tongue, 5", EX, A......................................$200.00

Clown & Donkey, papier-mache, wood & wire, clown seated backwards on donkey pulling his tail, oval base, 8½", VG, A...$545.00

Duck, pnt papier-mache w/coiled wire legs, squeaker base, 6½", EX, A..$190.00

Girl Holding Lamb, pnt papier-mache girl standing w/lamb in her arms, squeaker base (non-working), 4½", EX, A...$745.00

Girl on Goat, pnt papier-mache, girl seated on resting goat, squeaker base (non-working), 4¼", EX, A..............$580.00

Monkey, early 1900s, bsk head w/wood & wire body, cloth dressed, press base & he covers face w/clown mask, 7¼", EX, A...$490.00

Monkey, wood & wire body w/bsk head wearing cotton clown suit, w/bowl, sq base, 7⅜", EX, A........................$490.00

Plastic Figures

Plastic figures were made by many toy companies. They were first boxed with playsets, but in the early fifties, some became available individually. Marx was the first company to offer single figures (at 10¢ each), and even some cereal companies included one in boxes of their product. (Kellogg offered a series of 16 54mm Historic Warriors, and Nabisco had a line of ten dinosaurs in marbleized, primary colors.) Virtually every type of man and beast has been modeled in plastic; today some have become very collectible and expensive. There are lots of factors you'll need to be aware of to be a wise buyer. For instance, Marx made cowboys during the mid-sixties in a flat finish, and these are much harder to find and more valuable than the later figures with a waxy finish. Marvel Super Heroes in the fluorescent hues are worth about half as much as the earlier, light gray issue. Because of limited space, it isn't possible to evaluate more than a representative few of these plastic figures in a general price guide, so if you'd like to learn more about them, we recommend *Geppert's Guide* by Tim Geppert. See the Clubs and Newsletters section for information on how to order the *Plastic Figure & Playset Collector* magazine.

Advisors: Mike and Kurt Fredericks (F4).

See also Playsets.

Action and Adventure

Photo courtesy of June Moon.

Archer, Spacemen, 1950s, various colors and poses, 4", NM, J6, $45.00 each.

Ideal, Captain Action, 70mm, Action Boy's panther, missing tip of tail o/w M, F5......................................$30.00

Ideal, Captain Action, 70mm, Batman outfit w/10 accessory pcs, EX+, F5..$130.00

Ideal, Captain Action, 70mm, Phantom outfit w/7 accessory pcs, NM, F5...$100.00

Ideal, DC Villain, Keyman, 60mm, flourescent gr soft plastic, NM, from $35 to.....................................$50.00

Ideal (Portugal), Batman, 70mm, Batman w/bl cape, pnt soft plastic, NM, F5...$80.00

Marx, Aliens, 45mm, crawling, gray, P11 ....$22.00

Marx, Arctic, 54mm, explorer, various poses, flat lt gray soft plastic, M, ea, from $4 to.............................$5.00

Marx, Astronauts, 54mm, silver, P11, ea.........................$4.00

Marx, Ben Hur, 54mm, central building w/columns, complete, 8-pc set, gray hard plastic, M..................................$100.00

Marx, Ben Hur, 54mm, chariot driver, tan, M.................$10.00

Marx, Ben Hur, 54mm, chariot driver w/spear, dk brn soft plastic, EX+, F5..$4.00

Marx, Ben Hur, 54mm, chariot w/4 wht horses, soft plastic, orig issue, from $60 to.....................................$70.00

Marx, Ben Hur, 54mm, coliseum spectator, seated, tan soft plastic, M..$10.00

Marx, Ben Hur, 54mm, emperor or empress, purple soft plastic, M, ea..$40.00

Marx, Ben Hur, 54mm, fighting pose, cream or gray, P11, ea...$8.00

Marx, Ben Hur, 54mm, fighting pose, tan, P11, ea...........$10.00

Marx, Ben Hur, 54mm, horse, galloping or halting, flat brn soft plastic, M, ea..$10.00

Marx, Ben Hur, 54mm, merchant w/money box, gray soft plastic, M..$8.00

Marx, Ben Hur, 54mm, non-fighting pose, cream or gray, P11, ea...$4.00

Marx, Ben Hur, 54mm, Romans, full set of 16 different, matching cream soft plastic, M..........................$120.00

Marx, Ben Hur, 54mm, slave in chains, cream soft plastic, M..$10.00

Marx, Ben Hur, 54mm, woman walking w/vase, gray soft plastic, M..$10.00

Marx, Cave Man, 6", advancing w/club, stone knife in left hand, rust soft plastic, EX+, F5............................$7.50

Marx, Cave Man, 6", holding rock overhead, rust soft plastic, NM, F5..$12.50

Marx, Cavemen, 45mm, reddish brn, P11, ea.....................$2.00

Marx, Cavemen, 45mm, 6 poses, caramel, P11, ea..............$.50

Marx, Cavemen, 6", P11, ea................................$7.00

Marx, Cinema Monsters, 6", Creature From Black Lagoon, 2nd issue, flourescent orange soft plastic, VG+, F5............$9.50

Marx, Cinema Monsters, 6", Creature From the Black Lagoon, 1st issue, orange, NM, D9.............................$25.00

Marx, Cinema Monsters, 6", Hunchback of Notre Dame, c Universal Pictures, aqua soft plastic, M...................$35.00

Marx, Cinema Monsters, 6", Wolfman, c Universal Pictures, orig issue, aqua soft plastic, NM, F5....................$25.00

Marx, Eskimos, 54mm, igloo, translucent wht soft plastic, M..$30.00

Marx, Jungle Jim or Daktari, 54mm, Daktari w/stethoscope, P11..$15.00

Marx, Jungle Jim or Daktari, 54mm, jungle hut on posts, 7 pcs, brn & beige hard plastic, M.......................$35.00

Marx, Man From UNCLE, 6", Napoleon Solo, steel bl soft plastic, M..$32.00

Marx, Man From UNCLE, 6", THRUSH Officer, aiming pistol, steel bl soft plastic, M...............................$25.00

Marx, Marvel Super Heroes, 6", Iron Man, 1st issue, lt gray soft plastic, M..$40.00

Marx, Marvel Super Heroes, 6", Iron Man, 2nd issue, M, from $10 to..$15.00

Marx, Marvel Super Heroes, 6" Incredible Hulk, orange, P11..$10.00

Marx, Perils of Pauline, Sam Slick & Pauline, pnt hard plastic, MIP..$18.00

Marx, Pirates, 60mm, bl, M, ea................................$12.00

Marx, Pirates, 60mm, cream, P11, ea $12.00

Marx, Robin Hood, 54mm, Little John, silver, P11 ....$12.00

Marx, Robin Hood, 54mm, Robin Hood Merrymen, 5 pcs in 2 poses, mustard-tan soft plastic, M................................$15.00

Marx, Robin Hood, 54mm, Sheriff of Nottingham, P11 ..$14.00

Marx, Robin Hood, 60mm, Friar Tuck or Little John, matt lt gr soft plastic, M, ea $20.00

Marx, Robin Hood, 60mm, Merryman, various poses, brn soft plastic, M, ea, from $7 to $9.00

Marx, Robin Hood, 60mm, Sheriff of Nottingham, flat lt gr soft plastic, M $17.00

Marx, Space, 48mm, Rex Mars & Space Patrol figures, 10 different poses, bl & orange vinyl plastic, NM, F5 ....$32.50

Marx, Space, 54mm, Apollo astronauts, 5 pcs in 4 poses, wht soft plastic, M..$20.00

Marx, Space, 54mm, Apollo astronauts, 9 pcs in 5 poses, flourescent orange soft plastic, M...................................$32.50

Marx, Space Patrol, 45mm, female climbing ladder, tan or orange, P11, ea..$18.00

Marx, Space Patrol, 45mm, tan or orange, P11, ea $8.00

Marx, Spacemen, 45mm, bl, P11, ea $2.00

Marx, Spacemen, 45mm, yel, P11, ea $3.00

Marx, 6", Man From UNCLE, Napoleon Solo, scuffed, P11 ..$9.00

Campus Cuties and American Beauties

Marx, American Beauties, ballerina, 1955, NM $18.00

Marx, American Beauties, hula dancer, peach, NM $18.00

Marx, American Beauties, reclining nude, M $40.00

Marx, Campus Cuties, Lazy Afternoon, Lodge Party and Stormy Weather, 6", M, from $8.00 to $15.00 each.

Marx, Campus Cuties, Dinner for Two, M, from $8 to.....$15.00

Marx, Campus Cuties, Nighty Night, M, from $8 to $15.00

Marx, Campus Cuties, On the Beach, M, from $8 to $15.00

Marx, Campus Cuties, On the Town, M, from $8 to........$15.00

Marx, Campus Cuties, Shopping Anyone, M, from $8 to...$15.00

Circus and Animals

Marx, Animal Kingdom Series, gorilla, MIB....................$12.50

Marx, Animal Kingdom Series, leopard, MIB..................$12.50

Marx, Animal Kingdom Series, rhinoceros, MIB..............$12.50

Marx, Animal Kingdom Series, tiger, MIB $12.50

Marx, Dinosaur #PL-0750, set of 6 in different poses, gray soft plastic, 1950s, M $30.00

Marx, Dinosaur #PL-0750, set of 6 in different poses, waxy lt gr soft plastic, 1950s, M $12.50

Marx, Dinosaur #PL-0755, set of 7 in 5 poses, waxy lt gray soft plastic, M $12.50

Marx, Dinosaur #PL-7055, set of 7 in 5 poses, lt gr hard plastic, 1950s, M...$40.00

Marx, Dinosaurs, Hadrosaurus, sitting, duck-billed, matt gray soft plastic, M, from $10 to....................................$15.00

Marx, Dinosaurs, Kronosaurus, lt gr soft plastic, from $8 to $10.00

Marx, Dinosaurs, Moschops, tan soft plastic, M................$22.50

Marx, Dinosaurs, Stegosaurus, 1st issue, matt lt gray soft plastic, M, from $10 to $15.00

Marx, Dinosaurs, Trachodon, 1st issue, foreleg down, matt gray soft plastic, M, from $10 to...................................$15.00

Marx, Dinosours, Allosaurus, 1st issue, matt gray soft plastic, M, from $10 to..$15.00

Marx, Ice-Age Mammals, Smilodon (saber-toothed tiger), gray soft plastic, M $5.00

Marx, Ice-Age Mammals, Smilodon (saber-toothed tiger), red-brn soft plastic, M $10.00

Marx, Ice-Age Mammals, Woolly Mammoth, dk brn soft plastic, M $22.50

Marx, Prize Livestock, set of 10 in different poses, tan soft plastic, NM+, F5 ....$50.00

Marx, Super Circus, accessories set, 14 pcs, matching red hard plastic, w/trapeze & tightrope wires, M, F5 ....$85.00

Marx, Super Circus, animal set, 16 pcs in 13 poses, gray soft plastic, M, F5..$70.00

Marx, Super Circus, balloon vendor w/mc balloons, P11 .$10.00

Marx, Super Circus, Mary Hartline, M $12.00

Marx, Super Circus, Nicky Clown, M $10.00

Marx, Super Circus, performers, complete set of 17, salmon, M, F5 ....$75.00

Marx, Super Circus, Ringmaster Kirchner, M...................$12.00

Marx, Super Circus, Scampy Clown, M $10.00

Marx, Wild Animals, 60mm, Atlantic walrus, peach vinyl plastic, no copyright mk, M..$8.00

Marx, Wild Animals, 60mm, ostrich, flat tan soft plastic, M $8.00

Marx, Wild Animals, 60mm, seal, lt gray vinyl plastic, M..$2.50

Comic, Disney and Nursery Characters

Lido, Disney, 3¼", Zorro, P11...$5.00

Lido, Disney, 4½", Zorro, P11...$4.00

Marx, Comic Strip, Boltar, P11 ....$12.00

Marx, Comic Strip, Prince Valiant, P11 ....$22.00

Marx, Comic Strip, 2½", Dick Tracy, Jr, Gravel, BO & Sparkle Plenty, 1960s, NM, scarce, D11, set of 5................$125.00

Marx, Comic Strip, 60mm, Blondie or Dagwood, waxy lt bl soft plastic, M, ea, from $42 to $48.00

Marx, Disney, Sleeping Beauty & Prince Phillip on Samson, w/15 accessories, NM (facsimile color box) $185.00

Marx, Disney, Zorro on horseback, P11 ....$40.00

Marx, Disney, 35mm, Goofy, P11 ....$15.00

Marx, Disney, 35mm, Minnie Mouse, P11........................$15.00

Marx, Disney, 35mm, Professor Von Drake, P11 ....$15.00

Marx, Disney, 6", Donald Duck, bendable arms & legs, in cloth sailor suit, EX+, M8 ....$25.00

Marx, Disney, 6", Goofy, flourescent red soft plastic, M $6.00

Marx, Disney, 6", Mickey Mouse, flourescent orange soft plastic, M $7.50

Marx, Disney, 6", Peter Pan, cobalt bl soft plastic, feather in hat, M $12.50

Marx, Disney, 6", Snow White, cobalt bl soft plastic, M ..$10.00

Marx, Disney, 6", Tinker Bell, cobalt bl soft plastic, M $12.50

Marx, Disney, 60mm, Dumbo Singing Clown, beige soft plastic, M $8.00

Marx, Disney, 60mm, Goofy, pk soft plastic, M.................$22.00

Marx, Disney, 60mm, Huey, Louie or Dewey, beige soft plastic, M, ea..$7.50

Marx, Disney, 60mm, Monty/Morty Mouse, beige soft plastic, M $8.00

Marx, Disney, 8", Zorro on Tornado, complete w/accessories, M (facsimile box), from $150 to $170.00

Marx, Disney (Holland), 60mm, Happy Dwarf, pnt vinyl, NM, F5..$7.50

Marx, Disney (Holland), 60mm, Mickey Mouse, pnt vinyl, 1950s, NM, F5...$8.50

Marx, Disney (Holland), 60mm, Monty/Morty Mouse, pnt vinyl, 1950s, NM...$7.50

Marx, Disney (Holland), 60mm, Sneezy Dwarf, pnt vinyl, 1950s, NM, F5...$7.50

Marx, Disney Fun-Pal, 2", Colonel Haithi (Jungle Book), soft plastic, EX+, M8 ....$30.00

Marx, Disney Twistables, Goofy, complete, NM+, F5 ......$30.00

Marx, Disneyking Toyland Soldier, Private Galland, 1960s, w/trading card, NMIB, M8 ....$45.00

Marx, Disneykings, Blue Fairy, Peter Pan, Sleepy, Figaro or Thumper, 1st series, EX+, M8, ea...............................$10.00

Marx, Disneykings, Doc, 1960s, EX+ (orig box), M8 ....$20.00

Marx, Disneykings, Dumbo, NM+ (NM box), F5............$22.50

Marx, Disneykings, Geppetto, pnt hard plastic, NM (NM box), F5 ....$20.00

Marx, Disneykings, 1960s, Goofy and Donald, MIB, J6, from $15.00 to $20.00 each.

Marx, Disneykings, Jiminy Cricket, pnt hard plastic, NM+ (VG box), F5 ....$17.00

Marx, Disneykings, Joe Carioca, pnt hard plastic, M (NM box), F5 ....$22.50

Marx, Disneykings, Minnie Mouse, pnt hard plastic, M...$10.00

Marx, Disneykings, 15-pc set, 1960s, EX+ (EX+ box), M8 ....$250.00

Marx, Disneykings, 2nd series, Si (Lady & the Tramp cat), EX+, M8 ....$75.00

Marx, Fairytales, 60mm, Little Miss Muffet, wht hard plastic, EX $6.00

Marx, Fun-on-Wheels, 1950s, $35.00 each.

Marx, Fun-on-Wheels, 3", Lady, on 4 wheels, 1950s, NM..$35.00

Marx, Hanna-Barbera, Flintstones; 54mm, any town people, cream, P11, ea $1.00

Marx, Hanna-Barbera, Flintstones; 60mm, Baby Puss, P11..$4.00

Marx, Hanna-Barbera, Flintstones; 60mm, Barney Rubble, cream soft plastic, NM..$4.50

Marx, Hanna-Barbera, Flintstones; 60mm, Bedrock fireman or gas station attendant, cream soft plastic, EX, ea...........$1.00

Marx, Hanna-Barbera, Flintstones; 60mm, Dino, P11 ....$4.00

Marx, Hanna-Barbera, TV Tinykins; 35mm, Flintstones, Barney Rubble, MIB, from $15 to..$18.00

Marx, Hanna-Barbera, TV Tinykins; 35mm, Flintstones, Betty Rubble, MIB, from $15 to..$18.00

Marx, Hanna-Barbera, TV Tinykins; 35mm, Flintstones, Wilma, MIB, from, $15 to $18.00

Marx, Hanna-Barbera, TV Tinykins; 35mm, Huckleberry Hound, Dixie Mouse or Mr Jinx, pnt hard plastic, M, ea, from $18 to...$25.00

Marx, Hanna-Barbera, TV Tinykins; 35mm, Quick Draw McGraw's Sniffles, MIB, P6 ....$18.00

Marx, Hanna-Barbera, TV Tinykins; 35mm, Quick-Draw McGraw, Augie Doggie or Babba Louie, pnt hard plastic, M, ea...$22.00

Marx, Hanna-Barbera, TV Tinykins; 35mm, Top Cat's Officer Dibble, MIB, P6 ....$18.00

Marx, Hanna-Barbera, TV Tinykins; 35mm, Yogi Bear or Boo Boo Bear, pnt hard plastic, M, ea $15.00

Marx, Hanna-Barbera, TV Tinykins; 35mm, Yogi Bear's Ranger Smith, MIB, P6...$18.00

Marx, 6", Terrytoons, Tom & Jerry on motorcycle, EX, B10..$25.00

Famous People and Civilians

Marx, Business Tycoons, 60mm, Louis Marx, hard plastic, M, from $50 to...$75.00

Marx, Business Tycoons, 60mm, Louis Marx, missing cigar, from $15 to...$25.00

Marx, Civilians & Workmen, 1½", race car driver, head & torso, cream soft plastic, M $1.00

Marx, Civilians & Workmen, 3¼", fireman w/extinguisher, cream soft plastic, M...$10.00

Marx, Civilians & Workmen, 35mm, motorcycle cop, P11..$6.00

Marx, Civilians & Workmen, 45mm, construction worker w/hammer, gray, P11...$4.00

Marx, Civilians & Workmen, 45mm, railroad worker, P11, ea..$2.00

Marx, Civilians & Workmen, 54mm, chauffeur, movable arms, cream soft plastic, M...$5.00

Marx, Civilians & Workmen, 60mm, Schoolhouse People, set of 9 in 7 poses, cream soft plastic, NM+, F5..................$90.00

Marx, Entertainers, 60mm, Jackie Gleason/Ralph Kramden, wht hard plastic, M $50.00

Marx, Entertainers, 60mm, Pinky Lee, c NBC, wht hard plastic, M $50.00

Marx, Presidents & Politicals, 21mm, President Eisenhower, wht hard plastic w/sq base, M, from $8 to $15.00

Marx, Presidents & Politicals, 60mm, Adlai Stevenson, wht plastic w/sq base, M $22.00

Marx, Presidents & Politicals, 60mm, General MacArthur, wht plastic w/sq base, M $15.00

Marx, Presidents & Politicals, 60mm, General Vandefrift, wht hard plastic, M $60.00

Marx, Presidents & Politicals, 60mm, Jackie Kennedy, wht hard plastic, M $50.00

Marx, Presidents & Politicals, 60mm, Mammie Eisenhower, wht hard plastic, M, from $8 to $15.00

Marx, Presidents & Politicals, 60mm, President FD Roosevelt in Yalta cape, wht hard plastic w/sq base, M $12.50

Marx, Presidents & Politicals, 60mm, Winston Churchill, wht hard plastic, M, from $15 to $25.00

Marx, Presidents & Politicals, 60mm, 5-Star US General Arnold, pnt hard plastic, M, from $15 to...................$25.00

Marx, Queen Elizabeth II Coronation, 60mm, Princess Margaret, wht hard plastic, M...$20.00

Marx, Religious, 60mm, Andrew the Apostle, P11.............$5.00

Marx, Religious, 60mm, Cardinal Spellman, ivory hard plastic w/sq base, M..$20.00

Marx, Sports, 54mm, football team, set of 32 in various poses, gray soft plastic, MIP $150.00

Marx, Sports, 54mm, football team, set of 32 in various poses, ca 1966, red soft plastic, MIP......................................$80.00

Marx, Sports, 60mm, bowler, wht hard plastic, M $3.00

Marx, Sports, 60mm, long distance runner, wht hard plastic, M..$2.50

Marx, Sports, 60mm, World Cup soccer player, wht hard plastic, M $2.50

Military and Warriors

Airfix, British Infantry, P11, ea $1.00

Airfix, Medieval Foot Soldiers, P11, ea............................$1.50

Airfix, Waterloo French Infantry, P11, ea.........................$2.00

Airfix, WWII, British Commandos, P11, ea $1.00

Airfix, WWII, German Infantry, P11, ea $1.00

Airfix, WWII, German Mountain Troops, P11, ea............$1.00

Airfix, WWII, German Paratroopers, P11, ea $1.00

Airfix, WWII, Russian Infantry, P11, ea $1.00

Esci-Ertl, 1815 British Infantry, 1/72, 50-pc set, cream soft plastic, MIP, F5...$4.50

Esci-Ertl, 1815 French Imperial Guard, 1/72, 50-pc set, gray soft plastic, MIP, F5...$4.50

Esci-Ertl, 1815 Scots Greys British Cavalry, 1/72, 36-pc set, tan soft plastic, MIP, F5..$4.50

Marx, Air Force, various poses, gray, P11, ea $1.00

Marx, Alamo, 54mm, Shako Mexican, advancing, soft plastic, M, from $4 to $6.00

Marx, Alamo, 54mm, Shako Mexican, firing, soft plastic, M, from $4 to $6.00

Marx, Alamo, 54mm, Sombrero Mexican, firing, flat bl soft plastic, M, from $4 to $6.00

Marx, Civil War, Confederate; General Lee, P11...............$5.00

Marx, Civil War, Confederate; Jeff Davis, P11 ....$6.00

Marx, Civil War, Confederate; 1st issue, set of 8 includes 2 riders, dk gray, P11..$25.00

Marx, Civil War, Confederate; 54mm, Centennial series, set of 5 in various poses, P1...$20.00

Marx, Civil War, Union; Centennial series, set of 16 in 13 poses, dk waxy bl, P11...$62.00

Marx, Civil War, Union; General Grant, P11 ....$5.00

Marx, Foreign Legion & Arabs, 60mm, Legionaire, bl, P11..$9.00

Marx, Gallant Men, 60mm, Cuffy Sanders/Cullen Crabbe, saluting, lt bl soft plastic, M...$15.00

Marx, Goldmarx Ancient Warriors, 6", Egyptian, spear & shield, 1st version, pnt hard plastic, M, from $15 to $30.00

Marx, Goldmarx Ancient Warriors, 6", Egyptian pharaoh, raised spear & shield, M, from $15 to.................................$30.00

Marx, Goldmarx Ancient Warriors, 6", Egyptian w/raised sword & rnd shield, pnt hard plastic, M, from $15 to $30.00

Marx, Goldmarx Ancient Warriors, 6", knight guard w/plume crest, pnt hard plastic, M, from $10 to $20.00

Marx, Goldmarx Ancient Warriors, 6", Roman, standing w/sword & oval shield, pnt hard plastic, M, from $10 to..$20.00

Marx, Goldmarx Ancient Warriors, 6", Roman w/sword overhead & rectangular shield, pnt hard plastic, M, from $10 to..$20.00

Marx, Goldmarx Ancient Warriors, 6", Roman w/whip in left hand & sword in right hand, pnt hard plastic, M, from $10 to..$20.00

Marx, Goldmarx Ancient Warriors, 6", Roman/Maximus, w/raised sword & rectangular shield, pnt hard plastic, M..$35.00

Marx, Goldmarx Ancient Warriors, 6", Roman/Septimus Pius, w/spear & shield, M..$25.00

Marx, Goldmarx Ancient Warriors, 6", Viking, aiming bow & arrow, pnt hard plastic, M, from $15 to.....................$30.00

Marx, Goldmarx Ancient Warriors, 6", Viking, attacking w/axe & shield, horned helmet, pnt hard plastic, M, from $15 to..$30.00

Marx, Goldmarx Ancient Warriors, 6", Viking, winged helmet, holds mace & rnd shield, pnt hard plastic, M, from $15 to........$30.00

Marx, Johnny Tremain, 54mm, American soldier, marching w/shouldered rifle, cream soft plastic, M $12.50

Marx, Johnny Tremain, 54mm, Johnny Tremain/James Otis, c WDP, cream soft plastic, M.......................................$30.00

Marx, Johnny Tremain, 54mm, Paul Revere, soft plastic, M...$30.00

Marx, Johnny Tremain, 54mm, Redcoat officer or firing soldier, ea..$5.00

Marx, Johnny Tremain, 54mm, Redcoats, complete set of 12 in 6 poses, flat red soft plastic, M.............................$90.00

Marx, Medieval Knights, 6", on-guard pose w/sword & shield, silver soft plastic, M, from $6 to $10.00

Marx, Medieval Knights, 6", w/raised sword & swing-open visor, silver soft plastic, M, from $6 to..................$10.00

Marx, Medieval Knights, 60mm, P11, ea $5.00

Marx, Medieval Vikings, 6", w/raised battle axe & horned helmet, mint gr soft plastic, M, from $20 to.....................$30.00

Marx, Medieval Vikings, 6", w/raised knife & club in left hand, mint gr soft plastic, M, from $20 to...........................$30.00

Marx, Mexican War, 60mm, US soldier aiming rifle, metallic bl soft plastic, M, from $15 to...................................$20.00

Marx, Mexican War, 60mm, US soldier marching, metallic bl soft plastic, M, from $15 to...................................$20.00

Marx, Mexican War, 60mm, US soldier reading orders, metallic bl soft plastic, M, from $15 to...................................$20.00

Marx, Warriors of the World, Civil War Confederates; 60mm, Richard Travis III, standing w/rifle, MOC................$22.00

Marx, Warriors of the World, Civil War; 60mm, General US Grant, hand-pnt hard plastic w/sq base, M $20.00

Marx, Warriors of the World, Civil War; 60mm, John Brown w/bore swab, M, from $15 to $25.00

Marx, Warriors of the World, Indians; 60mm, Black Kettle, dancing w/2 rattles, M $12.50

Marx, Warriors of the World, Indians; 60mm, Strong Eagle, standing & aiming bow, M...$15.00

Marx, Warriors of the World, Mexican War; 60mm, Amador de Leon, wounded officer, M...$25.00

Marx, Warriors of the World, Mexican War; 60mm, Francisco Ruiz, marching w/rifle, MOC $25.00

Marx, Warriors of the World, Pirates; 60mm, Captain Cobham, hands on pistols in belt, MIB...$25.00

Marx, Warriors of the World, Pirates; 60mm, Captain Flood, lunging w/cutlass, MIB $22.50

Marx, Warriors of the World, Pirates; 60mm, Thomas Veale, digging w/shovel, M..$17.00

Marx, Warriors of the World, Revolutionary War; 60mm, D Dickson, advancing w/rifle at waist, M, from $15 to...$25.00

Marx, Warriors of the World, Revolutionary War; 60mm, E Bray, marching w/rifle, M, from $15 to $25.00

Marx, Warriors of the World, Revolutionary War; 60mm, Horace Swire, kneeling w/rifle, M, from $15 to.........$25.00

Marx, Warriors of the World, Revolutionary War; 60mm, James Black, officer, walking, M, from $15 to $25.00

Marx, Warriors of the World, Revolutionary War; 60mm, John Reeves, drummer, M, from $15 to.........................$25.00

Marx, Warriors of the World, Revolutionary War; 60mm, Johnny Wilson, playing fife, M, from $15 to.............$25.00

Marx, Warriors of the World, Revolutionary War; 60mm, Randall Jayes/minuteman, M, from $15 to $25.00

Marx, Warriors of the World, Revolutionary War; 60mm, Richard Travis, officer w/sword, M, from $15 to........$25.00

Marx, Warriors of the World, Revolutionary War; 60mm, Richard Ellis, British, w/tricorner hat & rifle, M, from $15 to $25.00

Marx, Warriors of the World, Revolutionary War; 60mm, Roger Medford, M, from $15 to $25.00

Marx, Warriors of the World, Romans; 60mm, Laelius, guard w/spear, M..$15.00

Marx, Warriors of the World, Romans; 60mm, Septimus Pius, w/spear & raised shield, M..$15.00

Marx, Warriors of the World, Vikings; 60mm, Eric the Red, advancing w/club & shield, hard plastic, M, from $15 to............$30.00

Marx, Warriors of the World, Vikings; 60mm, Haakon, aiming bow & arrow, hard plastic, M, from $15 to $30.00

Marx, Warriors of the World, Vikings; 60mm, Leif Ericsson, w/sword & shield, winged helmet, hard plastic, M, from $15 to $30.00

Marx, Warriors of the World, Vikings; 60mm, Olaf, standing w/spear, hard plastic, M, from $15 to $30.00

Marx, Warriors of the World, WWI Germans; 60mm, Friedrich Baden, goose-stepper, hard plastic, MIB $35.00

Marx, Warriors of the World, WWII Germans; 60mm, Martin Ferbach, standing & aiming rifle, hard plastic, M......$18.00

Marx, Warriors of the World, WWII Germans; 60mm, Walter Praum, standing at attention, hard plastic, M............$18.00

Marx, West Point Cadets, 54mm, w/plumes, P11, ea..........$5.00

Marx, WWII, Americans; 3¼", combat soldier, complete set of 6, olive drab soft plastic, MIP..................................$30.00

Marx, WWII, Americans; 48mm, Air Corps, set of 11 in various poses, MIP..$20.00

Marx, WWII, Americans; 48mm, Armed Forces, set of 11 in various poses, bl soft plastic, MIP...............................$20.00

Marx, WWII, Americans; 5", Army driver in helmet, for military vehicles, cream soft plastic, M...............................$7.00

Marx, WWII, Americans; 5", Army MP driver, for Army Command Car, wht soft plastic, M $10.00

Marx, WWII, Americans; 54mm, US paratrooper, airborne, olive drab soft plastic, M, from $12 to......................$15.00

Marx, WWII, Americans; 60mm, army band drum major, marching w/baton, olive drab vinyl plastic, M...........$20.00

Marx, WWII, Americans; 60mm, combat soldier, crouching or walking w/gas mask, olive drab soft plastic, M, ea, from $2 to $5.00

Marx, WWII, Americans; 60mm, General Gruenther, hand-pnt soft plastic, M, from $5 to...$10.00

Marx, WWII, Americans; 60mm, General Patton, hand-pnt soft plastic, M, from $10 to...$20.00

Marx, WWII, Americans; 60mm, Naval officer w/binoculars, wht soft plastic, M **$12.00**

Marx, WWII, Americans; 60mm, sailor pulling rope, wht soft plastic, M **$17.00**

Marx, WWII, Americans; 60mm, sailor standing at attention, lt bl soft plastic, M **$7.00**

Marx, WWII, Americans; 60mm, shore patrolman, flat royal bl soft plastic, M **$12.50**

Marx, WWII, British; cannon carriage, from Battleground Europe set, flat tan soft plastic, M **$12.50**

Marx, WWII, Germans; 54mm, set of 12 in 10 poses, dk gray soft plastic, M **$20.00**

Marx, WWII, Germans; 54mm, soldier on motorcycle, lt brn soft plastic, M, from $20 to......................................**$25.00**

Marx, WWII, Japanese; 54mm, flag bearer, running, flat tan soft plastic, M, from $2 to.......................................**$4.00**

Marx, WWII, Japanese; 54mm, radio man, kneeling, flat tan soft plastic, M, from $2 to.......................................**$4.00**

Marx, WWII, Japanese; 54mm, soldier, complete set of 16 in 12 poses, flat tan soft plastic, M, from $50 to..................**$65.00**

Marx, WWII, Japanese; 6", aiming & firing gun, M, from $2 to **$6.00**

Marx, WWII, Japanese; 6", officer holding binoculars & pointing, M, from $2 to **$6.00**

Marx, WWII, Japanese; 6", throwing grenade, M, from $2 to **$6.00**

Marx, WWII, Marines; 6", running w/machine gun or throwing grenade, olive drab soft plastic, M, ea, from $2 to........**$6.00**

Marx, WWII, Russians; 6", throwing grenade, dk mint gr soft plastic, M **$10.00**

Revell, Swedish Cavalry, 1/72, 30-Years War, 30-pc set, gray soft plastic, MIP, F5 ....**$4.50**

Nutty Mads

Photo courtesy of June Moon.

The Thinker, Suburban Sidney and Bullpen Boo-Boo, NM, from $20.00 to $35.00 each.

Marx, All-Heart Hogan, pk, 1960s, EX, D9.....................**$18.00**

Marx, All-Heart Hogan, 1st issue, flat dk gr soft plastic, NM, F5 ....**$24.00**

Marx, Blame It, I Didn't Push Him, EX, J2 ....**$60.00**

Marx, Dippy the Deep Diver, lime gr soft plastic, NM, F5 ....**$25.00**

Marx, Dippy the Deep Diver, lt gr, EX, D9 ....**$12.00**

Marx, Dippy the Deep Diver, lt gr, M, from $20 to **$35.00**

Marx, End Zone, 1st issue, flat maroon soft plastic, NM, F5 ....**$35.00**

Marx, End Zone, florescent orange, EX+, D9 ....**$15.00**

Marx, Lost Teepee, flat dk gr soft plastic, NM, F5 ....**$35.00**

Marx, Lost Teepee, flat maroon soft plastic, NM, F5........**$35.00**

Marx, Lost Teepee, pk soft plastic, EX+, F5.....................**$20.00**

Marx, Manny the Reckless Mariner, lime gr soft plastic, NM, F5 ....**$20.00**

Marx, Mudder, 3rd series, flourescent gr soft plastic, missing frying pan o/w NM, F5 ....**$30.00**

Marx, Rocko the Champ, bl, VG+, I2 ....**$14.00**

Marx, Roddy the Hod Rod, lime gr soft plastic, NM, F5 ..**$25.00**

Marx, Roddy the Hot Rod, pk, EX+, J2 ....**$20.00**

Marx, Waldo the Weightlifter, florescent gr, EX+, D9.....**$15.00**

Marx, Waldo the Weightlifter, purple, EX, B10 ....**$23.00**

Western and Frontier Heroes

Auburn, Cowboys, rubber, M, ea, from $2 to **$3.00**

Auburn, Cowboys, vinyl, M, ea, from $2 to **$3.00**

Auburn, GIs, rubber, M, ea, from $2 to **$3.00**

Auburn, GIs, vinyl, M, ea, from $2 to **$3.00**

Auburn, Horses, for Indian or w/military saddle, vinyl, M, ea, from $2 to..**$3.00**

Auburn, Indians, rubber, M, ea, from $2 to......................**$3.00**

Auburn, Indians, vinyl, ea, from $2 to.............................**$3.00**

Auburn, Pioneers, vinyl, M, ea, from $2 to **$3.00**

Marx, Cavalry, 45mm, various poses, tan, P11, ea **$5.00**

Marx, Cavalry, 6", aiming rifle, wide-brimmed hat, steel bl soft plastic, NM, F5..**$12.50**

Marx, Cavalry, 60mm, officer w/sword & pistol, metallic bl soft plastic, M **$17.00**

Marx, Cavalry, 60mm, soldier, kneeling & aiming pistol, metallic bl soft plastic, M..**$15.00**

Marx, Cavalry, 60mm, soldier w/raised sword, metallic bl soft plastic, M **$12.50**

Marx, Colonials, 60mm, wht, P11, ea **$10.00**

Marx, Cowboys, orange, from $2.00 to $8.00.

Marx, Cowboys, 54mm, Alaskan cowboy w/drawn pistol, flat gray soft plastic, M...**$10.00**

Marx, Cowboys, 54mm, red, P11, ea **$2.00**

Marx, Cowboys, 6", aiming rifle from waist, flat tan soft plastic, NM, F5 ....$7.50

Marx, Cowboys, 6", fanning pistol, rust soft plastic, NM, F5..$2.50

Marx, Cowboys, 6", wounded, w/hat & pistol, flat tan soft plastic, NM, F5..$12.50

Marx, Famous Frontier Americans, 35mm, Davy Crockett, ivory hard plastic, missing rifle tip, EX+, F5 ....$6.50

Marx, Famous Frontier Americans, 35mm, Davy Crockett w/rifle at side, brn hard plastic, M $25.00

Marx, Famous Frontier Americans, 35mm, Matt Dillon, P11...$15.00

Marx, Famous Frontier Americans, 4¾", Roy Rogers on Trigger, cream soft plastic w/brn vinyl accessories, M $60.00

Marx, Famous Frontier Americans, 50mm, Davy Crockett, mk WDP, cream, M..$25.00

Marx, Famous Frontier Americans, 54mm, Lone Ranger, P11 ....$20.00

Marx, Famous Frontier Americans, 60mm, Tonto, feather in headband, flat cream soft plastic, M........................$20.00

Marx, Frontiersman, 6", running w/long rifle in left hand, caramel soft plastic, NM, F5 ....$18.00

Marx, Frontiersman, 60mm, aiming pistol, revised pose w/new base, cream soft plastic, M $40.00

Marx, Horses, 3¾", for Davy Crockett, Indian or sheriff riders, blk soft plastic, M, ea, from $8 to...........................$10.00

Marx, Horses, 3¾", for Davy Crockett, Indian or sheriff riders, tan soft plastic, M, ea, from $8 to............................$10.00

Marx, Horses, 48mm, saddled western style, rearing, cream soft plastic, M, ea..$6.00

Marx, Horses, 54mm, saddled western style, rearing, beige or red-brn soft plastic, M, ea $6.00

Marx, Indian throwing spear, orange, NM, from $2.00 to $8.00.

Marx, Indians, 3¼", attack position w/raised tomahawk, flat yellow soft plastic, M...$27.00

Marx, Indians, 45mm, shooting, scalping or riding, P11, ea..$4.00

Marx, Indians, 54mm, butterscotch, P11 ....$.50

Marx, Indians, 6", brave w/war club & spear, pumpkin soft plastic, NM, F5..$6.00

Marx, Indians, 6", chief w/spear & shield, pumpkin soft plastic, NM, F5 ....$4.00

Marx, Indians, 6", dancing w/spear & club, NM, P3..........$9.00

Marx, Indians, 6", lg headdress, running w/tomahawk & knife, NM, P3...$9.00

Marx, Indians, 6", throwing spear or running w/tomahawk, NM, P3, ea...$9.00

Marx, Pioneers, 45mm, lt bl, P11, ea................................$4.00

Marx, Pioneers, 54mm, firing, silver, P11 ....$2.00

Marx, Pioneers, 54mm, firing, turq, P11.........................$2.00

Marx, Pioneers, 60mm, firing, M, ea $4.00

Plasticville

From the 1940s through the '60s, Bachmann Brothers produced plastic accessories for train layouts such as buildings, fences, trees, and animals. Buildings often included several smaller pieces — for instance, ladders, railings, windsocks, etc. — everything you could ever need to play out just about any scenario. Beware of reissues.

Advisor: Gary Mosholder, Gary's Trains (G1).

#AD-4 Airport Administration Building, wht sides, bl roof $45.00

#AP-1 Airport Hanger, G1...$25.00

#BB-9 Billboard, gr or wht, ea...$.50

#BK-1 Bank, gray sides, gr roof.....................................$30.00

#BL-2 Bridge & Pond, G1..$7.00

#BN-1 Barn, red sides, wht roof....................................$12.00

#BR-2 Trestle Bridge $18.00

#BY-4 Barnyard Animals..$12.00

#C-18 Cathedral, wht sides, dk gray roof.......................$25.00

#CC-7 Church, wht sides, gray roof...............................$12.00

#CC-8 Country Church, wht sides, gray roof, lg door $12.00

#CC-9 Church, wht sides, lt gray roof, G1......................$15.00

#CS-5 Chain Store/5 & 10¢..$18.00

#DE-7 Diner, gray sides, red roof...................................$18.00

#DH-2 Hardware/Pharmacy $18.00

#FB-1 Frosty Bar, yel sides, wht roof.............................$15.00

#FB-4 Fire House, wht sides, red roof, G1 ....$15.00

#FP-5 Fireplace, gray..$3.00

#FP-5 Flag Pole..$3.00

#GO-2 Gas Station (sm), wht sides, red roof, wht insert..$15.00

#GO-3 Gas Station (lg), w/Plasticville logo & pumps......$25.00

#HP-8 Cape Cod House, wht sides, red roof & trim $9.00

#HS-6 Hospital, no furniture...$18.00

#HS-6 Hospital, w/furniture $25.00

#LC-2 Log Cabin, w/fence..$15.00

#LH-4 Two-Story Colonial House, wht sides, gray roof & trim..$18.00

#LM-3 Station Platform...$8.00

#LP-9 Lamppost..$.50

#MH-2 New England Ranch House, tan sides, brn roof...$18.00

#ON-5 Outdoor Necessities..$15.00

#PB-5 Footbridge..$7.00
#PD-3 Police Station, dk gray....................................$25.00
#PD-3 Police Station, lt gray.....................................$20.00
#PF-4 Citizens, w/pnts...$15.00
#PH-1 Town Hall, tan sides, red roof.........................$25.00
#PO-1 Post Office, gray front & roof..........................$18.00
#RH-1 Ranch House, wht sides, bl roof & trim, G1.........$10.00
#RS-7 Suburban Station, gr roof & trim, brn platform.......$8.00
#SA-7 Outhouse, red sides, wht roof............................$4.00
#SC-4 School, red sides, gray roof, G1.......................$20.00
#SG-2 Signal Bridge, blk..$8.00
#SL-1 Boulevard Light..$1.00
#SM-6 Super Market, sm...$15.00
#SW-2 Switch Tower, brn sides, gray roof...................$6.00
#WG-2 Crossing Gate, blk & wht.................................$.50
#WW-3 Wishing Well, brn...$3.00
#YW-4 Yard Pump, brn..$3.00
#0012-A Railroad & Street Signs.................................$8.00
#1090 Telephone Booth, wht sides, bl roof.................$10.00
#1302 Farm Implement Set, yel vehicles w/red trim........$30.00
#1304 Crossing Signal..$10.00
#1305 Block Signal...$10.00
#1406 Playground Equipment, yel accessories & pool......$25.00
#1407 Watchman Shanty, brn sides, gray roof.............$11.00
#1408 Windmill, lt gray...$40.00
#1502 Cape Cod House, pk, G1..................................$35.00
#1503 Add-A-Floor...$30.00
#1504 Mobile Home, wht sides, turq roof & trim...........$55.00
#1603 Ranch House, G1..$27.00
#1608 School, G1...$20.00
#1615 Water Tower, gray sides, brn roof.....................$10.00
#1617 Farm Buildings & Animals.................................$25.00
#1618 TV Station, wht sides, red roof & antenna, G1.....$40.00
#1620 Loading Platform, brn shack, gray roof & platform..$8.00
#1621 Motel, w/3 autos, paper flowers.......................$18.00
#1622 Dairy Barn, wht sides, red roof, G1..................$22.00
#1623 Cattle Loading Pen...$45.00
#1624 House, under construction, lt gray....................$45.00
#1625 Railroad Work Car...$15.00
#1626 Corner Store...$45.00
#1627 Hobo Shack, gray sides, brn roof...................$135.00
#1629 Bungalow, wht sides, gray roof.........................$28.00
#1700 Two-Story Colonial House, G1..........................$22.00
#1703 Colonial Mansion, wht sides, red roof, G1..........$30.00
#1803 Colonial Church..$20.00
#1804 Greenhouse, w/flowers, G1..............................$75.00
#1805 Covered Bridge...$18.00
#1806 Roadside Stand, w/pnt......................................$30.00
#1853 Drug Store..$25.00
#1900 Turnpike...$45.00
#1901 Union Station..$25.00
#1906 Factory, tan sides, gray roof.............................$35.00
#1907 Apartment House..$65.00
#1908 Split-Level House, G1.......................................$25.00
#1912 New England Ranch, G1....................................$28.00
#1918 Park Assortment...$15.00
#1922 Two-Story house, G1...$20.00
#1957 Coaling Station...$35.00

Playsets

Louis Marx is given credit for developing the modern-age playset, and during the fifties and sixties produced hundreds of boxed sets, each with the buildings, figures and accessories that when combined with a child's imagination could bring any scenario alive, from the days of Ben Hur to medieval battles, through the cowboy and Indian era, and on up to Cape Canaveral. Marx's prices were kept low by mass marketing (through retail giants such as Sears and Montgomery Wards) and overseas production. But on today's market, playsets are anything but low-priced; some mint-in-box examples sell for upwards of $1,000.00. Just remember that a set that shows wear or has even a few minor pieces missing quickly drops in value.

Advisors: Bob Wilson, Phoenix Toy Soldier Co. (P11); Mike and Kurt Fredericks (F4).

American Civil War Artillery Set, Airfix, NMIB, T1......$15.00
American Civil War Confederate Infantry, Airfix, 66-pc, NMIB, T1..$15.00
American Civil War Union Infantry, Airfix, 33-pc, NMIB, T1...$15.00
American Militia, Accurate, 1/32, 19-pc, MIB...............$14.00
Armed Forces Training Center #4150, 90% complete (EX box)..$250.00
Army Combination #5560, Buddy L, incomplete, EX (EX+ box), A...$220.00
Battle Gear #775, Gay Toys, MOC..............................$20.00
Battleground, Lido, complete w/soldiers & vehicles, NM (EX box), A..$100.00
Battleground #4756, Marx, ca 1967, 54mm, WWII & German soldiers, 107-pc, NM (EX+ photo box), F5.............$135.00
Bavarian Figures, HK, 12-pc, NM+ (VG box), F5...........$90.00

Ben Hur Series 2000, box only, Marx, P11, $200.00.

Block City Playset, MIB, T1..$75.00
Bootcamp Carry-All Playset, Marx, EX+ (EX box), J2.....$90.00
Boys' Camp Cabin, Marx, complete, P11....................$115.00
Buffalo Bill, Atlantic, 1/32, 18-pc, MIB, P11..................$15.00
Casey's Car Wash, Remco, complete, NMIB, P11........$125.00
Cavalry & Indians, Multiple, 1972, 50-pc, MIB, P11......$12.00
Coastal Patrol, Atlantic, 1/32, 2 vehicles, MIB, P11......$10.00

Cape Canaveral #4521, box only, Marx, P11, $60.00.

Combat Attack Set, 1960s, soldiers & accessories, EX (VG box), T1 ....$65.00

Commandos #117, Atlantic, HO, complete, MIB, P11 ......$4.00

Confederate Infantry, Accurate, 1/32, 20-pc, MIB, P11 .....$7.00

Confederate Pioneers, Revell, 1/72, 55-pc, MIB, P11 ....$6.00

Cowboys & Indians, Payton, MIP (sealed), P11 ....$25.00

Davy Crockett Far West Story, Atlantic, 1/32, 17-pc, MIB, P11 ....$16.00

Davy Crockett Western Playset, Archer, missing 1 wagon wheel, VG (G+ box), T1 ....$100.00

Disney's Aladdin Final Battle, MIB, B10 ....$12.00

English Soldiers Put-To-Gether #T-152, 8-pc, NM+ (EX box), F5 ....$60.00

Farm Set #6050, Marx, 54mm, complete, orig bags, M (NM+ wht Sears box), F5 ....$260.00

Fighting Knights Carry-All Set #4635, Marx, 1968, 54mm, EX+ (EX+ metal case), F5 ....$120.00

Flintstones #4672, Marx/Hanna-Barbera, 1961, missing few pcs, F5 ....$390.00

Fort Apache, Heritage, Sears Exclusive, 80% complete (G- box), H4 ....$85.00

Fort Apache, Marx, 1992, M (Sears box), P11 ....$25.00

Fort Apache #3681, Marx, early 1970s, 54mm, 82 pcs, full stockade, NM (NM photo box), F5 ....$140.00

Fort Set w/Cavalry & Indians, Elastolin, includes cowboys, covered wagon, tents, fencing, etc, complete, EX, A $550.00

Freight Trucking Terminal #5420, Marx, complete & unused, NM (EX+ box), A $250.00

French Grenadiers Imperial Guard, Airfix, 29-pc, MIB, P11 .$35.00

French Imperial Guard #5505, Esci, 14-pc, MIB, P11.........$7.00

Frogmen, Atlantic, 1/32, 1-pc, MIB, P11 ....$6.00

Frogmen #110, Atlantic, HO scale, MIB, P11 ....$4.00

Galaxy Command, EX (orig box), H4 ....$75.00

Gallant Gladiator Warship, Remco, 85% complete, EX (orig box), P11 ....$235.00

German Infantry, Atlantic, 1/32, 11-pc, MIB, P11 ....$4.00

GMC Western Roundup Set, Buddy L, complete w/ranch scene, truck & figures, unused, EX+ (EX box), A $350.00

Happy Time Service Station, Marx, box only, EX+, J2 ..$25.00

Invaders, Remco, w/3 bugs, 3 vehicles & figures, NM $425.00

John Deere Dealership Playset, Ertl, MIB, T1 ....$40.00

Johnny Service Car Wash #6800, Topper/Deluxe-Reading, 1968, unassembled, w/10" bl car & instructions, NMIB, P4 .$60.00

Johnny Service Gas Station, Topper, VG (VG box)........$65.00

Johnny Seven Oma Helmet & Walkie-Talkie Playset, EX (VG box), T1 ....$225.00

Jungle Land, Lido, 1950s, complete w/vacuform plastic landscape & animals, NM (EX box), A $100.00

Knights, Multiple, 1972, 50-pc, MIB, P11 ....$25.00

Knights & Vikings, Marx, Sears & Roebuck, missing chains & flags (NM box w/inserts), H4 ....$190.00

Little Red Schoolhouse, Remco, 1967, NMIB, J6.............$55.00

Little Red Schoolhouse #3381, Marx, box only, EX, F5 ...$95.00

M*A*S*H Headquarters Mini Playset, MOC, J2 ....$20.00

McDonaldland Train Playset, Remco, 1976, complete, orig box, B10 ....$125.00

NATO Assault Troops #5508, Esci, 12-pc, MIB, P11 ....$6.00

Noah's Ark Miniature Playset, Marx, boxed, P11.............$45.00

Panama Canal #273, Renwal, 1950s, complete, NM (VG box), A $200.00

Pet Shop #4210, Marx, 75mm, 56-pc, w/dollhouse people, F5 ....$390.00

Pirate Mickey Mouse Ship, Ideal, w/6 figures, P11 ....$110.00

Pirate Ship, Ideal, 95% complete, NMIB, P11 ....$225.00

Prehistoric Playset #3398, Marx, 1971, cavemen, dinosaurs, rock formations & booklet, MIB, M17 ....$120.00

Presidents of US, Marx, 7-pc w/booklet, MIB, P11 ....$30.00

Ranch House, Marx, 1950s, snap-together assembly, incomplete, EX (NM box), K4 ....$35.00

Rifleman Ranch, Marx, 99% complete, P11, $750.00.

Road Construction #6000, Tootsietoy, dump truck, 2 road scrapers, 2-pc truck-hauler & 6 road signs, MIB, H12 .....$450.00

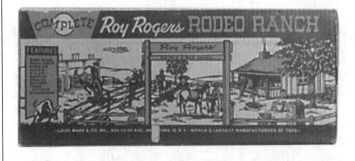

Roy Rogers Rodeo Ranch #3992, Marx, complete, NM (NM box), A, $265.00.

Robin Hood Castle #4720, Marx, EX (EX box), J2 ....$275.00

Roy Rogers Western Town #4258, Marx, complete, EX+ (EX box), A..$455.00

Sailors, Atlantic, 132, 10-pc, MIB, P11...................$6.00

Service Station Attendants #0899 MO, Marx, complete w/8 plastic vehicles & 5 figures, NM+ (NM box), A.....$100.00

Shop King, Marx, 99% complete, P11 ....$30.00

Special Forces Unit, Multiple, MIB (sealed), P11 ....$10.00

Suky Cinderella Playset #090234, NRFB (damaged box), P2..$20.00

Suky Picnic Playset #090230, Matchbox/Lesney, 1975, NRFB, P2 ....$25.00

Super Catapult Plane Carrier, Saunders, 1950s, complete w/5 planes to shoot from deck w/rubber bands, NM (EX box), A $60.00

Ten Commandments, Marx/Montgomery Wards, missing 2 pyramids 4 figures & 12 sm pcs, EX (orig box), S21 ....$375.00

Tom Corbett Space Academy #7010, Marx, complete, EX+ (EX box), A $375.00

Troll Village Mini Play Set #48-24396, Marx, 1969, complete, orig bags, M (NM+ box), F5 ....$420.00

Turnpike Service Center #5918, Marx, Sears Exclusive, complete, NM (VG box), A $200.00

Union Artillery, Revell, 1/72, 42-pc, MIB, P11 ....$6.00

US Army Training Center #4133, Marx, complete, NM (EX+ box), A, $155.00; Fort Dearborn #3514, Marx, complete, NM (EX+ box), A, $320.00.

US Paratroopers #5501, Esci, 1/35, 14-pc, MIB, P11 ....$7.00

USS Ferrestal Aircraft Carrier, Lido, ca 1960, gray w/bl, red & gr movable pcs, 22", w/12 scale planes, MIB, P4............$75.00

Viking Ship, Renwal, 95% complete, NMIB, P11..........$250.00

Walt Disney's Frontierland Logs Playset, w/instructions, EX (VG+ box), T1..$100.00

Waltons, cb, appears complete, NMIB, T1......................$85.00

Waterloo French Infantry, Airfix, 29-pc, MIB, P11 ....$35.00

Waterloo Highland Infantry, Airfix, 29-pc, MIB, P11 .....$35.00

Western Wagon, Marx, for 6" figures, appears complete, w/instructions, NMIB, V1................................$170.00

Westgate Auto Center, Marx, complete w/litho tin automotive center & plastic accessories, unused, NM+ (EX+ box), A $325.00

Westgate Auto Center, Marx, 1968, complete, MIB (sealed), A $400.00

Westward Ho Wild West, Miner Industries, MIB (sealed), P11 ....$10.00

White House, Marx, sealed bags & instructions, MIB, P11 ....$80.00

Wild West Playset, Toy Street, MIB, P11......................$12.00

Wild West Train Set #2873, Marx, complete, P11........$275.00

Photo courtesy of June Moon.

Wizard of Oz Munchkinland, Mego, 1976, complete, MIB, J6, $450.00.

WWII British Soldiers, Marx, 32-pc, recast, MIB, P11.....$32.00

1800 British Infantry, A-Toys/Esci, 50-pc, MIB, P11 ....$5.00

Political

As far back as the 19th century, children's toys with a political message were on the market. One of the most familiar was the 'Tammany Bank' patented by J. & E. Stevens in 1873. The message was obvious — a coin placed in the man's hand was deposited in his pocket, representing the kickbacks William Tweed was suspected of pocketing when he was the head of Tammany Hall in New York during the 1860s.

Advisors Michael and Polly McQuillen (M11).

Agnew, Spiro; wristwatch, All American Time Co, caricature face, non-working, M11................................$40.00

Anthony, Susan B; doll, Hallmark, cloth, MIB, from $15 to $20.00

Carter, Amy; Amy Peanut, 3" baby Amy in peanut-shell case, MOC, H4..$12.00

Carter, Jimmy; comic figure, Circus Toy Ent, 1977, soft plastic, depress head, peanut pops up under towel, 8", H4.......$8.00

Carter, Jimmy; mug, 1977, porcelain, MIB, N2 ....$15.00

Carter, Jimmy; wristwatch, 1977, From Peanuts to President w/caricature face, flexible metal band, working, M11..$35.00

Clinton, Bill; alarm clock, Whitewater William, alligator snapping at Clinton ea second, w/up, 7", NM, M11 ....$40.00

Clinton, Hilary; doll, Dr Hillcare Draft Dodger, caricature, 27", NRFB, M15..$20.00

Clinton & Gore, wristwatch, EX+ $30.00

Eisenhower, Dwight D; figure, half elephant/half donkey, rubber, I Am Republicrat I Like Ike on base, EX, I2 ....$25.00

Eisenhower, Dwight D; nodder, 1950s, pnt compo elephant w/I'm for Ike, 6½", NM, M11....................$100.00

Goldwater, Barry; board game, 1964 Presidential Election Game, MOC, M11 ....$30.00

Goldwater, Barry; figure, Remco, 1964, NMIB, $35.00.

Goldwater, Barry; sunglasses, blk cb, NM, M11...............$12.00

Henry, Patrick; figure, RT/Hong Kong, M (VG box), B3...$20.00

Johnson, Lyndon B; bubble gum cigar, 1964, MIP, M11 ....$6.00

Johnson, Lyndon B; doll, Remco, 1964, MIB (sealed)......$45.00

Johnson, Lyndon B; doll, Remco, 1964, 5", NM (VG box), B3 ....$35.00

Kennedy, Jackie; mask, 1960, thin plastic, EX+, M11 ......$40.00

Kennedy, John F; balloon, Vote Kennedy, wht on bl, unused, M11...$10.00

Kennedy, John F; board game, The Kennedys, Mt Rushmore caricatures on box, NM, M11 ....$55.00

Kennedy, John F; doll, Kramar, in orig wood rocker, no music box, 14", VG, M15.............................$100.00

Kennedy, John F; mask, 1960, thin plastic, EX+, M11 .....$40.00

Kennedy, John F; record, The First Family, Cadence Records, 1962, 33⅓ rpm, EX+ (M sleeve), T2 ....$12.00

Kennedy, Ted; doll, 1980, cloth caricature, 5½", M11.....$15.00

King, Martin Luther; figure, Olmec, 1992, w/podium, microphone & I Have a Dream tape, 6", NRFB, M15 ....$55.00

King, Martin Luther; flicker rings, H4, set of 2 ....$12.00

Landon, Alf; bank, Land of Roosevelt emb on gr CI elephant, 6", EX, M11 ....$500.00

Lindsay, John; comb, bl plastic gun form w/Aim for Lindsay, NM, M11 ....$20.00

MacArthur, General Douglas; doll, Freundlich Novelty of NYC, 1942, compo w/military outfit, 18", NM, M17 ....$350.00

MacArthur, General Douglas; writing pad & candy, EX+ (EX+ mc portrait tin), M11...............................$55.00

McGovern, George; bubble gum cigar, McGovern for President, MIP, M11..$5.00

Nixon, Richard; hand puppet, 1968, plastic head w/cloth body, NM, M11 ....$32.00

Nixon, Richard; mask, 1970s, mc rubber, NM, M11 ....$25.00

Nixon, Richard; music box, 1972, w/up dancer, plays Ta Ra Ra Boom De Yea, NM, M11...........................$175.00

Nixon, Richard; pin, Unknown Comic, metal, M, J6.......$24.00

Nixon, Richard; puzzle, Puzzle Factory, 1970, 500-pc jigsaw caricature, 22x15" assembled, EX+ (EX+ box), T2 ....$15.00

Nixon, Richard; wristwatch, Honest Time Co, I Am Not a Crook w/caricature face, working, M11 ....$75.00

Patton, figure, Excel Toy Corp, posable w/cloth clothes & accessories, 9", M (shipping box), H4................................$30.00

Quayle, Dan; wristwatch, Crazy Times Co, caricature face, hands run backwards, NM, M11 ....$20.00

Reagan, Ronald; mask, 1980s, over-the-head style, M, N2 ..$25.00

Reagan, Ronald; wristwatch, caricature in garbage can, digital, leather band, MOC, M11...........................$30.00

Revere, Paul; figure, RT/Hong Kong, 8", NM (VG box), B3 ..$20.00

Roosevelt, Franklin D; puzzle, FD Puzzle, World Famous Initials, 1930s, complete, VG+ (mc box), M11 ....$55.00

Roosevelt, Teddy; game, Germany, 1904, drop balls into Teddy's mouth, mirror back w/glass cover, 2¼" dia, VG, M11 ..$850.00

Roosevelt, Teddy; Rough Riders, board game, Parker Bros, 1900, EX (VG+ box), scarce, M11.....................................$125.00

Uncle Sam, bank, Roseville, ceramic with blue shading, 4½", EX, D10, from $100.00 to $175.00.

Photo courtesy of Dunbar Gallery.

Washington, George; doll, Effanbee, 1983, 16", MIB, M15 ..$60.00

Premiums

Those of us from the pre-boomer era remember waiting in anticipation for our silver bullet ring, secret membership kit, decoder pin, coloring book, or whatever other wonderful item we'd seen advertised in our favorite comic book or heard about on the Tom Mix show. Tom wasn't the only one to have these exciting premiums, though, just about any top character-oriented show from the 1930s through the '40s made similar offers, and even through the '50s some were still being distributed. Often they could be had free for a cereal boxtop or an Ovaltine inner seal, and if any money was involved, it was usually only a dime. Not especially durable and often made in somewhat limited amounts, few have survived to the present. Today some of these are bringing fantastic prices, but the market at present is very volatile.

Condition is very important in assessing value; items in pristine condition bring premium prices.

Advisor: Bill Campbell (C10).

See also Advertising; Pin-back Buttons.

Andy Pafko, ring, Baseball, C10.....................................$225.00
Bobby Benson, book, Lost Hero, EX, V1...........................$15.00
Bobby Benson, booklet, HO Co, 1934, photos, EX, J5 .....$25.00
Bobby Benson, transfer book, Heker-Ho Co, 1933, 59 of 60 pictures present, 5x8", C1...$60.00
Buck Rogers, badge, Solar Scouts, C10 ....$125.00
Buck Rogers, book, Buck Rogers in the 25th Century, Kellogg's, 1933, 32 pgs w/color photos, EX, A $175.00
Buck Rogers, mask, mk Sip's New Dairy, Manayunk, PA, mc cb, 9x8", NM, D9 ....$25.00
Buck Rogers, membership kit, Satellite Pioneer Badge, member card & 3 bullets, C10 ....$400.00
Buck Rogers, pin, Chief Explorer, Cream of Wheat, 1936, metal, inscr Awarded for Distinguished..., 1½", scarce, NM, A $310.00

Buck Rogers, popsicle premium catalog, 1939, C10 ....$125.00
Buck Rogers, Ring of Saturn, C10...................................$550.00
Buck Rogers, Solar Scouts Map, Cocomalt, 1930s, full-color w/information on the Solar System, 18x22", EX, A ..$625.00

Buck Rogers, Space Ranger Kit, Sylvania TV, 1952, complete, NM (original envelope), A, $150.00.

Buffalo Bill, puzzle, Cocomalt, 1930s, standing w/rifle, horses & pioneers at back, missing 3 sky pcs, orig mailer, M16 ..$25.00
Buffalo Bill Jr, ring, 1950s, VG, S20.................................$45.00
Buster Brown, wrist decoder, 1950s, Moon Mission Agent, w/secret compartment under compass for decoder book, NM, H4..$50.00
Buster Brown Club, ring, Buster Brown & Tige on front only, VG, S20 ....$30.00
Buster Brown Shoes, Secret Agent Periscope, NM, J2 .....$25.00
Capt Action, flicker ring, 6 different, C10, ea $50.00
Capt Frank Hawks, ring, Air Hawks, 1930, VG, S20 .....$150.00
Capt Hawk, badge, 1930s, Sky Patrol w/wings, EX, S15...$45.00
Capt Marvel, comic book, Bond Bread, 1950, The Boy Who Never Heard of Capt Marvel, 7x3½", VG+, A3 ....$75.00
Capt Marvel, comic book, 3 Famous Flying Marvels, Reed, 1945, makes 3 figures w/no cutting or pasting, unused, NM, C1...$45.00

Buck Rogers, pin, Space Ship Commander, Solar Scouts, metal, blue and silver, 1¾x1", EX, $125.00.

Capt. Midnight, decoder badge, Secret Squadron, 1948, brass, NM, from $150.00 to $175.00.

Capt Marvel, figure, Flying Captain Marvel, Fawcett, 1944, uncut paper, M (orig envelope), P6 ....$38.00
Capt Marvel, Magic Whistle, M, C10.................................$95.00
Capt Midnight, badge, Weather Flight Patrol, C10.........$52.00
Capt Midnight, book, Trick & Riddle, EX+, J2................$35.00
Capt Midnight, decoder, 1940, VG, S20 ....$65.00
Capt Midnight, decoder, 1946, VG, S20 ....$85.00
Capt Midnight, decoder, 1947, M, C10 ....$80.00
Capt Midnight, decoder, 1949, w/key, EX, J2................$195.00
Capt Midnight, decoder badge, 1949, no key o/w EX.......$50.00
Capt Midnight, manual, 1940-41, Secret Squadron, EX+ (VG+ mailer), A $140.00

Photo courtesy of June Moon.

Capt. Midnight, manual, Secret Squadron, 1948, NM, J6, $85.00.

Capt Midnight, manual, 1949, Secret Squadron, EX, A...$100.00
Capt Midnight, manual, 1955, w/orig mailer, C10.........$325.00
Capt Midnight, manual, 1957, Flight Commander, w/orig mailer, C10..$250.00
Capt Midnight, membership card, Flight Patrol, G, S20..$40.00
Capt Midnight, membership medal, Skelly Oil, 1940, gold-tone metal, 1¼", EX, A6 ....$15.00
Capt Midnight, pin, Flight Commander, T1 ....$185.00
Capt Midnight, ring, Flight Commander, C10..............$325.00
Capt Midnight, ring, Marine Corps, Ovaltine, 1942, scarce, EX, A $300.00
Capt Midnight, ring, seal w/instructions, C10...............$600.00
Capt Midnight, Spy Scope, MIP, C10 ....$150.00
Capt Midnight, token, VG, S20.....................................$20.00
Capt Midnight, wings, Flight Patrol, no pin, G, S20........$20.00
Capt Midnight, wings, Mystro-Magic Weather, NM, J2 ..$30.00
Capt Video, key chain, Spaceship Pendant, w/glow-in-the-dark photo, C10...$800.00
Capt Video, manual for movie serial, 4 pgs, EX, V1 ....$36.00
Capt Video, Mini Space Map, glows in the dark, C10 .....$30.00
Capt Video, ring, Flying Saucer, 1951, S20.....................$150.00
Capt Video, ring, plastic cover over photo image of Capt Video w/ray gun, VG, A $100.00
Capt Video, ring, 1950s, gray plastic rocket shape w/line drawing under yel plastic dome, 2", NM, A $630.00

Capt Video, Secret Ray Gun, candy bar premium, 1950s, red plastic, complete w/pamphlet & map, 4", NM (EX+ mailer), A $125.00
Chandu, Weather Indicator Medallion, C10.................$200.00
Charlie McCarthy, figure, Chase & Sanborn, diecut cb w/lever on back for eye & mouth movement, 18", NM (VG envelope), A...$135.00
Charlie McCarthy, spoon, 1940s, silverplate, teaspoon sz, EX+, C1 ....$22.00
Dan Dunn, book, 1938, Dan Dunn Meets Chang Loo, gas station premium, rare, VG+, A3 ....$275.00
Dick Darling, manual, 1934, New Bag of Tricks, EX, J2...$25.00
Dick Tracy, badge, Girls' Division, EX, J2 ....$45.00
Dick Tracy, badge, Inspector General, C10...................$800.00
Dick Tracy, badge, Secret Service Patrol Member, Quaker, 1930-39, bl & gold w/pin back, EX+, D11, ea $30.00
Dick Tracy, badge, Sergeant, w/orig mailer, C10............$135.00
Dick Tracy, book, Secret Detective Methods & Magic Tricks, Quaker, 1939, EX+, D11 ....$75.00
Dick Tracy, Crime Fighters Kit, 1960s, mail-in from Chicago Tribune, MIB, L4...$125.00
Dick Tracy, Decoder Card, Post Cereal, early 1950s, red, NM, D11 ....$40.00
Dick Tracy, Flagship Plane, Quaker, balsa, NM (orig unmk box), D11 ....$250.00
Dick Tracy, flashlight, Quaker, 1930s, red barrel, 2¾x½" dia, lt scratches, VG, D11 ....$25.00
Dick Tracy, flashlight, Secret Service, gr, pocket sz, VG.......$20.00
Dick Tracy, Jr Dick Tracy Crime Detection Folio, radio show offer, 1942, w/puzzle, decoder, etc, MIP, scarce, D11 ....$300.00
Dick Tracy, kit, Chicago Tribune, 1961, complete w/11 pcs, M (unopened & unmk box), D11 ....$25.00
Dick Tracy, letter, Secret Service Patrol Officer Dispatch, Quaker, 1939, EX, D11...$25.00

Photo courtesy of Dunbar Gallery.

Dick Tracy, tunic and mask, 1954, complete with comic book and Motorola TV brochure, EX, D11, $80.00.

Dick Tracy, magnifying glass, NM, J2 ....$40.00

Dick Tracy, postcards, Coca-Cola, 1942, 3 different, unused, NM, D11, ea $10.00

Dick Tracy, ring, Secret Compartment, 1940s, VG $200.00

Dick Tracy, Secret Code Book, Quaker, 1938, 12 pgs, 3x6", G, D11 ....$15.00

Don Winslow, Ensign Pin, C10 ....$65.00

Flash Gordon, comic book, Wheaties, C10 ....$575.00

Flash Gordon, photo, Dixie, Buster Crabbe, EX, V1 ....$65.00

Frank Buck, Adventurer's Club Handbook, Pepsodent, 1934, premium offers & secret codes w/map on cover, EX, J5 ....$75.00

G-Man, badge, Melvin Pervis Secret Operator, C10 ....$65.00

G-Man, badge, tin star, C10 ....$35.00

G-Man, Fingerprint Kit, C10 ....$80.00

G-Man, knife, NM, C10 ....$195.00

G-Man, ring, Melvin Purvis Secret Operator, 1936, VG, S20 ....$125.00

Gabby Hayes, ring, cannon, brass, MIB, J2 ....$300.00

Gabby Hayes, ring, cannon, silver, C10 ....$245.00

Gene Autry, postcard, Sturdiboy/Gene Autry shirts, real photo, M, V1 ....$17.50

Gene Autry, ring, face, file copy, M, C10 ....$100.00

Gene Autry, ring, flag, C10 ....$50.00

Gene Autry, ring, horseshoe nail, MOC $210.00

Green Lantern, ring, glows, C10 ....$25.00

Hopalong Cassidy, Lucky Coin, S20 ....$12.00

Hopalong Cassidy, ring, Bar-20, 1950s, VG, S20 ....$50.00

Howdy Doody, carrying case, Welch's Grape Juice, Doodyville Circus, images of Howdy & friends, w/4 bottles, EX, A $255.00

Howdy Doody, flicker ring, Poll Parrot, C10 ....$110.00

Howdy Doody, game, Comic Circus Animals, Poll-Parrot Shoes, 1954, EX+, A $150.00

Howdy Doody, Poll-Parrot Jumble Joy Book, Kagran, 1955, Poll Parrot Shoes, 16 pgs to fold & cut, unused, NM, A ...$95.00

Howdy Doody, Poll-Parrot Magic Eye Picture, litho cb, 7x5", EX, A $255.00

I-Spy Ranger, membership pin & card, 1940s, EX, V1 .....$40.00

Jack Armstrong, book, Treasure Hunt Stamp, EX (orig envelope), J2 ....$45.00

Jack Armstrong, flashlight, torpedo, EX, J2/S20 ....$50.00

Jack Armstrong, pedometer, C10 ....$50.00

Jack Armstrong, ring, Egyptian Whistle, 1940s, gold-tone, from $75 to $100.00

Jack Armstrong, ring, Siren, C10 ....$100.00

Jack Armstrong, Secret Whistle Code Card, VG, S20 .....$25.00

Jack Armstrong, Shooting Propeller Plane Gun, 1933, VG (worn mailer box), M17 ....$36.00

Jack Armstrong, telescope, EX, J2 ....$50.00

Jimmy Allen, badge, Skelly Oil, VG, T1 ....$35.00

Jimmy Allen, card, Flying Club Membership, unused, VG, S20 ....$25.00

Jimmy Allen, ring, Flying Club, 1930, VG, S20 ....$95.00

Jimmy Allen, wings, Duplex, Colonial or Fairmaid, VG, S20, ea $55.00

Jimmy Allen, wings, Richfield Hi-Octane, VG, S20 ....$50.00

Jimmy Allen, wings, Skelly II, 1934, VG, S20 ....$55.00

Jr G-Man, ring, C10 ....$80.00

Kit Carson, bolo tie & neckerchief, w/promotional flyer, NM (orig envelope), A $80.00

Little Orphan Annie, comic book, Popped Wheat, 1947, EX+, M14 ....$7.00

Little Orphan Annie, comic book, Quaker, 1941, Sparkies & Little Orphan Annie Rescue, VG, M14 ....$25.00

Little Orphan Annie, decoder, 1938, C10 ....$65.00

Little Orphan Annie, ID bracelet, C10 ....$80.00

Little Orphan Annie, manual, 1937, C10 ....$45.00

Little Orphan Annie, Secret Guard Official Handbook, C10 ....$265.00

Little Orphan Annie, see also Radio Orphan Annie

Little Orphan Annie, Slideomatic Radio Decoder, C10 .$225.00

Little Orphan Annie, Sun Watch, w/orig envelope, C10 ...$115.00

Lone Ranger, ad card, Silver Cup Bread, EX, D8 ....$28.00

Lone Ranger, badge, Chief Scout, C10 ....$265.00

Lone Ranger, badge, Lone Ranger Deputy, gray metal star, S20 ....$35.00

Lone Ranger, badge, Safety Club, C10 ....$55.00

Lone Ranger, badge, Secret Compartment, 1949, M, J6 ...$62.00

Lone Ranger, blotter, Bond Bread, 1940s, NM, M17/D8 .$20.00

Lone Ranger, booklet, How the Lone Ranger Captured Silver, Silvercup, 1936, 4 pgs, incomplete, VG, J5 ....$45.00

Lone Ranger, Deputy Kit, Cheerios, 1980, NM (orig mailer), J2 ....$40.00

Lone Ranger, Hunt Map, w/mailer, C10 ....$300.00

Lone Ranger, mask, Lone Ranger, neatly cut from cereal box, EX, J5 ....$35.00

Lone Ranger, pedometer, VG, S20 ....$20.00

Lone Ranger, pedometer, 1950s, w/strap, MIP, S18 ....$35.00

Lone Ranger, picture, Merita Bread, 1940, paper litho of Lone Ranger & Silver, 11x10", rare, NM, A $295.00

Lone Ranger, ring, Atom Bomb, 1940, G, S20 ....$85.00

Lone Ranger, ring, Atom Bomb, M, C10 ....$125.00

Lone Ranger, ring, Defender, 1940s, shiny gold-tone, EX+, A $110.00

Lone Ranger, ring, Filmstrip, C10 ....$65.00

Lone Ranger, ring, Filmstrip, w/film, instructions & orig mailer, C10 ....$225.00

Lone Ranger, ring, Filmstrip Saddle, silver-tone metal w/stirrup ea side, gold-tone metal saddle at top, NM $150.00

Lone Ranger, ring, Flashlight, C10 ....$65.00

Lone Ranger, ring, Movie Film, 1940, no film, EX, from $50 to $75.00

Lone Ranger, ring, secret compartment, w/both photos, C10 ....$600.00

Lone Ranger, ring, Six Shooter, Kix Cereal, 1950, NM ..$125.00

Lone Ranger, ring, Weather, w/instructions & litmus strip, orig mailer, C10 ....$185.00

Lum & Abner, badge, Walking Weather Prophet, 1936, C10/S20, from $25 to $30.00

Mary Marvel, toss bag, C10 ....$95.00

Maverick, token spinner, Kaiser, coin w/James Garner & Jack Kelly, 1½", J5 ....$25.00

Melvin Purvis, badge, Junior G-Man Corps, shield form, VG+, T1 ....$25.00

Melvin Purvis, badge, Roving Operative Jr G-Man, Post, EX, J2 ....$48.00

Melvin Purvis, badge, Secret Operator, EX, S15/T1 ....$35.00

Owl, comic book, 1940, early super hero, artist Frank Thomas, 16 pgs, 7½x5", EX+, A3 ....$100.00

Pancho (Cisco Kid), mask, Tip Top Bread, 1950s, paper, lg, NM, J5 ....$15.00

Radio Orphan Annie, badge, Secret Society, bronze w/emb bust portrait, ⅞", NM, A6 ....$15.00

Radio Orphan Annie, book, Radio Orphan Annie Book on Dogs, EX, J2 ....$45.00

Radio Orphan Annie, decoder, 1935, VG, S20 ....$30.00

Radio Orphan Annie, decoder, 1935, w/spinner, M, I2 ..$42.00

Radio Orphan Annie, decoder, 1937, VG, S20 ....$50.00

Radio Orphan Annie, decoder, 1938, C10 ....$50.00

Radio Orphan Annie, decoder badge, 1935, C10 ....$65.00

Radio Orphan Annie, decoder booklet, Secret Society, 1940, EX, S20 ....$120.00

Radio Orphan Annie, patch, cloth, w/Sandy, VG, S20 ...$25.00

Radio Orphan Annie, puzzle, Tucker County Race, NM, V1 ....$30.00

Radio Orphan Annie, ring, Magnifying Glass, missing magnifier, C10 ....$1,200.00

Radio Orphan Annie, ring, Post, MIP, S20 ....$50.00

Radio Orphan Annie, Shadowettes, 1938, diecut cardboard faces with names and rhymes, 5"-6", NM (EX mailer), $100.00.

Radio Orphan Annie, various premiums in orig mailer, Slidomatic Radio Decoder, Official Handbook, etc, EX+, A $255.00

Red Ryder, Lucky Coin, JC Penney, 1942-46, M..............$15.00

Rin-Tin-Tin, compass/mirror, VG, S20 ....$50.00

Rin-Tin-Tin, Official Cavalry Hat, Nabisco, 1950s, felt w/insignia, w/orig NM mail-in coupon, EX+, C1 ....$100.00

Rin-Tin-Tin, photo, Ken-L-Ration, 1931, w/Lee Duncan facsimile signature, 7x6", EX, M17 ....$20.00

Roy Rogers, playset, Roy's Ranch, Post, 1950s, NMIP, T1 .$65.00

Roy Rogers, Ranch Set, Post, plastic figures, animals, accessories & metal jeep, MIB, C10 ....$295.00

Roy Rogers, ring, Branding Iron, C10 ....$175.00

Roy Rogers, ring, Microscope, C10 ....$115.00

Secret Agent, ring, Code, Wheat Chex, C10 ....$75.00

Sgt Preston, Square-Inch Klondike Land Deed, Quaker, 1950s, M $10.00

Shadow, blotter, C10 ....$95.00

Shadow, photo, 1930s, masked version w/facsimile autograph, EX, scarce, A3 ....$300.00

Shadow, ring, Blue Coal, C10 ....$550.00

Shadow, ring, bust on silver, w/box, C10 ....$80.00

Shadow, ring, Secret Agent, w/box, C10 ....$125.00

Sky King, ring, Aztec, C10 ....$600.00

Sky King, ring, Magni-Glo, C10 ....$75.00

Sky King, ring, Navajo Treasure, C10 ....$125.00

Sky King, Teleblinker, Peter Pan Peanut Butter, P10 ....$150.00

Space Patrol, binoculars, Ralston Purina, gr plastic w/red & blk Space Patrol insignia, 5", M (EX mailer box), A.....$125.00

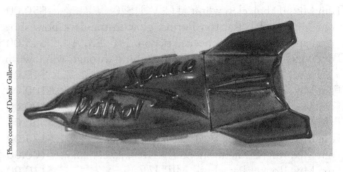

Photo courtesy of Dunbar Gallery.

Space Patrol, decoder belt buckle, Ralston Purina, 1950s, brass and aluminum, EX, J6, $185.00.

Straight Arrow, ring, Gold Nugget w/photo, 1940s, VG..$200.00

Straight Arrow, Rite-A-Lite Arrowhead, shell only, G, S20 ....$20.00

Superman, comic book, Superman Time Capsule, Sugar Smacks, 1955, 7x3½", EX, A3 ....$175.00

Superman, decoder card, 1940s, Superman of America Secret Code, G+, A3 ....$40.00

Superman, Krypton Rockets, Kellogg's, 1950, plastic, 1 red & 1 bl, NM+ (EX+ orig mailer), A $195.00

Superman, membership certificate, Supermen of America, 1940s, Clark Kent's facsimile signature, 8x11", EX, A3 ....$65.00

Superman, ring, Pep Airplane, blk or silver plane, C10, ea..$225.00

Superman, ring, S logo, C10 ....$50.00

Superman, ring, Signet, C10 ....$100.00

Superman, Supermen of America Membership Kit #Z3829, code book, button & letter, EX+ (VG+ mailer), A3 ....$750.00

Tarzan, flicker ring, figure shooting arrow, red letters, VG, S20 ....$35.00

Tarzan, Numa the Lion & Kala the Ape, figures, Gem Clay/Foulds Co premiums, wht plaster, w/paper ad, 2x5", M (1 box), A $85.00

Tarzan, pocketknife, Slesinger Inc, 1930s, blk image on wht, G, scarce, J5 ....$325.00

Terry & the Pirates, ring, Detection, gold, 1940s, VG, S20 ....$100.00

Tom Corbett, ring, Dress Uniform, plastic, EX, B10 ....$20.00

Tom Mix, badge, Ralston Purina, silver-tone metal, Tom on horse at top, 2", EX, A $80.00

Tom Mix, belt buckle, secret compartment, VG, S20 ......$65.00

Tom Mix, belt buckle, w/secret compartment & glow belt, EX, J2 ....$160.00

Tom Mix, Bird Call Telescope, w/instructions, orig mailer, C10 ....$150.00

Tom Mix, Coloring Book for Straight Shooters, Ralston, 1950s, unused, NM, J5 ....$25.00

Tom Mix, Compass Magnifier, w/glow-in-the-dark arrowhead, C10/S20, from $60 to $70.00

Tom Mix, decoder, 6-Shooter, VG, S20 ....$75.00

Tom Mix, decoder, 6-Shooter, 1941, gold-tone metal, NM, C1 ....$110.00

Tom Mix, decoder button, VG, S20 ....$15.00

Tom Mix, gun, Straight Shooter, Ralston, 1933, wood, 1st version w/revolving cylinder, M (orig mailer), P4 ....$285.00

Tom Mix, ID bracelet, w/initial C, VG, S20 ....$50.00

Tom Mix, medal, Ralston Purina, glow-in-the-dark horseshoe shape w/red & wht checked ribbon, 1½", EX, A $45.00

Tom Mix, picture, Ralston, Tom crashing through window on horse, VG+, M16 ....$10.00

Tom Mix, ring, Circus, 1930s, VG, S20 ....$100.00

Tom Mix, ring, Look Around, C10 ....$100.00

Tom Mix, ring, Magnet, C10 ....$60.00

Tom Mix, ring, Sliding Whistle, C10 ....$125.00

Tom Mix, ring, Straight Shooters, C10 ....$100.00

Tom Mix, Rocket Parachute, MIP, J2 ....$110.00

Tom Mix, Service Ribbon, w/mailer, C10 ....$100.00

Tom Mix, telephone, Ralston Purina, red & wht tin, 1¾" dia, NM (EX mailer), A $95.00

Tonto, poster, 1950s, 75", EX, A $180.00

Twigg, ring, Fireball Twigg Explorer, dial off but present, S20 ....$75.00

Wild Bill Hickok, badge, Post, litho tin, NM, J5 ....$15.00

Wild Bill Hickok & Jingles, Western Bunkhouse Kit, unused, M, M16 ....$28.00

Zorro, ring, Z logo, C10 ....$80.00

Pressed Steel

Many companies were involved in the manufacture of pressed steel automotive toys which were often faithfully modeled after actual vehicles in production at the time they were made. Because they were so sturdy, some from as early as the 1920s have survived to the present, and those that are still in good condition are bringing very respectable prices at toy auctions around the country. Some of the better-known manufacturers are listed in other sections.

See also Aeronautical; Buddy L; Keystone; Marx; Pedal Cars and Other Wheeled Goods; Structo; Tonka; Wyandotte.

Cars and Busses

Airflow Sedan, Cor-Cor, 1930s, brn 4-door w/blk rubber tires, 16", pnt pitted o/w EX, M5 ....$1,075.00

Airflow Sedan, Kingsbury, bl, VG $375.00

Airflow Sedan, Kingsbury, red, w/horn, EX $450.00

Golden Arrow Racer, Kingsbury, metallic bl sleek design w/wht rubber tires, w/up, 21", EX, A $1,320.00

Greyhound Bus, Kingsbury, bl flat-nose, wht greyhound logo, wht rubber tires, chrome hubs, cut-out windows, 18", rstr, A $230.00

Limousine, Turner, early, tan w/brn roof & visor, contour fenders, simulated headlights, 3 seats, G- pnt, A $2,860.00

MT Touring Car, Doepke, red, G $225.00

Mystery Sunbeam Racer, Kingsbury, red sleek design w/Am & British flag decals, w/driver, w/up, 19", EX, A $1,540.00

Passenger Bus, Kingsbury, bl long-nose w/red trim, wht tires w/red hubs, cut-out windows, w/seats, clockwork, 16", EX, A $770.00

Pierce Arrow Coupe, Girard, orange, wht & gr, 15", EX+ ..$325.00

Roadster, Kingsbury, bl, wht rubber tires w/red hubs, w/driver, w/up, 10½", G, A $400.00

Photo courtesy of Dunbar Gallery.

Roadster, Kingsbury, 1930s, gray with black tires and red hubs, 12", EX, D10, $625.00.

Roadster, Kingsbury, gr, red & tan, w/wide running boards & rumble seat, EX pnt $475.00

Roadster, Kingsbury, gr, rubber tires w/disk hubs, 12", G, A $450.00

Photo courtesy of Dunbar Gallery.

Roadster, Kingsbury, 1930s, tan and red, rubber tires with green hubs, electric, 12", EX, D10, from $700.00 to $1,200.00.

Roadster, Turner, red w/tan top & brass trim, simulated headlights, rear blk tool box, red hubs, friction, 26", G, A $850.00

Sedan, Cor-Cor (?), solid red w/long nose & sleek fenders, chrome grille & trim, blk rubber tires w/red hubs, 20", A $500.00

Yellow Taxi, Turner, blk w/orange sides & wheels, w/figures, friction, 9¼", EX, A $550.00

Zypher Coupe & Boat Trailer, Kingsbury, 1936, orange w/rubber wheels, 20½", no boat o/w EX, A $345.00

Firefighting

Aerial Ladder Truck, Kingsbury, red, gold trim, rear-mounted ladders, open center steering, driver, clockwork, 18", G, A $300.00

Aerial Ladder Truck, Kingsbury, red w/gold trim, yel spoked wheels, wooden ladders, seated figure, clockwork, 9", EX, A $440.00

Aerial Ladder Truck, Model Toys, red with black tires, aluminum-finish extension ladders on pedestal, 30", G, A, $200.00.

Aerial Ladder Truck, Nylint, 1970s, VG+ $40.00
Ahrens Fox Fire Engine, Turner, 1920, orig chartreuse & red pnt w/gold trim, 15", EX+ $300.00

Fire Chief Car, Kingsbury, 1930s, red with white rubber tires, 10", EX, D10, $950.00.

Fire Chief Siren Coupe, w/up, red w/yel lettering, battery-op lights, tin grille, NP bumpers & rubber tires, 14", EX, A $385.00
Fire Pumper, Wilkins, red w/open center steering, red spokes, brass-colored boiler w/silver bands, w/driver, 10", EX, A......$415.00
Fire Pumper, Wilkins, yel & red, open center steering, brass-look boiler w/silver bands, clockwork, driver, 11", VG, A..$880.00

Mack Ladder Truck, City Fire Dept., Steelcraft, red with black tires and red hubs, 25", EX, A, $1,155.00.

Ladder Truck, Master Metal, red, open cab, yel extension ladder mounted on side, electric lights, blk tires, 20", G, A ..$275.00

Ladder Truck, Republic, 1920s, red w/gold ladder, wheels & striping, gr running board, 18", missing 2 ladders, G, A $85.00
Ladder Truck, Schieble, 20", EX, from $600 to $650.00
Ladder Truck (City Fire Dept), Steelcraft, red w/open cab, ladders mounted to low sides w/railing, 26", EX, A...$1,540.00
Skyline Fire Dept Aerial Ladder Truck #6, Nylint, VG ..$120.00

Trucks and Vans

American Can Co Delivery Truck, Kelmet, open-sided cab w/name on sides of bed, rubber tires, spoked wheels, 25", VG, A..$3,750.00

American Railway Express Truck, Sturditoys, black C-style cab, green enclosed screen bed, red chassis and hubs, 26", EX, A, $1,650.00.

City Ice Cream Co Van, Steelcraft, red & cream, open cab, EX $375.00
Coal Truck, Sturditoy, blk doorless cab & dump bed, red chassis & hubs, w/attachable chute, ...Coal Co decal, 28", M, A..$3,300.00
Coal Truck, Sturditoy, orange w/blk fenders & running boards, orange hubs, doorless enclosed cab, tall bed, 25", VG, A..$2,310.00
Coronation Milk Delivery Truck, Banner, wht w/red trim & logo, 9½", EX...$250.00
Cream Crest Milk Truck, Steelcraft, red & wht, VG $400.00
CW Brand Coffee Dump Truck, Metalcraft, red & blk, VG $500.00
CW Brand Tow Truck, Metalcraft, blk cab w/open windows, orange bed & hook w/logo on side, EX $600.00
Dairy Tanker, Sturditoy, wht doorless cab & detachable tanker, chrome/brass trim, dual rear wheels, wht hubs, 34", EX, A..$2,090.00
Derrick Shovel Truck, Clark Equipment, Michigan, Model T24, Nylint, C10...$150.00
Dinty Moore 4x4 Explorer, Nylint, 1992, M (NM box), P3...$20.00
Dump Truck, Cor-Cor, 23½", VG, A $175.00
Dump Truck, Courtland, 5½", EX $100.00
Dump Truck, Girard, 1930s, side dump action, wht w/blk rubber tires, 11", EX, A..$155.00
Dump Truck, Steelcraft, red cab & chassis, gr dump bed, blk tires w/red hubs, electric lights, lever-op, 24", EX, A $525.00
Dump Truck, Sturditoy, blk doorless cab w/red chassis & hubs, gr bed w/Sturditoy Construction Co decals, 27", VG, A.$880.00
Dump Truck, Turner, blk & red, 20x8x7", G-, A...........$175.00

Photo courtesy of Dunbar Gallery.

Dump Truck, Turner, red & gr, C-style cab, 30", EX $700.00
Dump Truck, 1920s, blk cab & fr, orange dump, metal wheels w/orange hubs, 23", VG, H7 ....$950.00
Emergency Truck, Nylint, 1970s, 16", EX+, N2 ....$40.00
GMC 18-Wheeler Tractor & Trailer, Nylint, MIB $55.00
Gulf Gasoline Tanker, Sturditoy, bl cab & chassis w/orange tanker lettered GULF, orange spoked wheels, 27", rstr, A...$1,155.00
IH Livestock Truck, Tru-Scale, bl w/open cab & fender wells, G...$250.00
Jewel Tea Van, Banner, brn, G+ $135.00
Keebler Tractor & Trailer, G+, W5 ....$30.00
Kroger Delivery Truck, Metalcraft, orange, rpl tailgate, VG $350.00
Lincoln Construction Co Cement Truck, Lincoln/Canada, gr, yel & red w/blk tires, 13", VG, M5.............................$60.00
Lincoln Ice Delivery Truck, Lincoln/Canada, gr w/blk rubber tires, 14½", VG, A..$55.00
Mack Dump Truck, Boycraft, red enclosed cab & chassis, gr bed & hubs, blk rubber tires, 22", EX, A $605.00

Mack Dump Truck, Turner, orange cab and hubs, green bed, 26", M, D10, $850.00.

Mobile Crane, Nylint, bl & orange, EX $200.00
NAPA Automotive Parts Tractor & Trailer, Nylint, 1979, metallic silver cab, NM $800.00
NAPA Twin Boom Wrecker, Nylint, 1990, MIB.............$40.00
NAPA 18-Wheeler Tractor Trailer, Nylint, 1983, MIB ..$50.00
NAPA 4x4 Pickup Truck, Nylint, 1984, MIB................$125.00
Packard Dump Truck, Turner, red & blk, 27", G $500.00
Parts Plus City Delivery Truck, Nylint, MIB, W5 ....$30.00
Pure Oil Truck, Metalcraft, 1940s, wht lettering on navy bl, 14½", VG, A...$1,045.00

Shell Motor Oil Stake Truck, Metalcraft, red cab with yellow bed, black rubber tires with chrome hubs, 12", VG, $650.00.

Refuse Truck, Tri-ang Minic, bl & red, NM $90.00
Richfield Gasoline Tanker, Am National, blk w/lt yel chassis & hubs, 27", rstr, A $1,870.00
Sheffield Farms Co Select Dairy... Delivery Truck, Steelcraft, red, blk tires w/ yel hubs, electric lights, 21", EX, A......$1,155.00
Shell Motor Oil Stake Truck, Metalcraft, red cab w/yel stake bed, blk rubber tires w/chrome hubs, 8 barrels, 12", G, A...$580.00
Sunshine Stake Truck, Metalcraft, red & bl, VG...........$400.00
Tanker, Kelmite, blk w/red chassis, body support & spoked wheels, chrome straps, brass faucet, 26", EX, A....$4,400.00
Telephone Service Truck, Lincoln Toys/Canada, gr, 14", VG...$225.00
Telephone Truck, Lincoln Toys/Canada, gr w/Patricia Contractors Ltd decal on top, 11", EX, M5.........................$150.00
Traveling Store Van, Sturditoy, orange w/blk fenders & running boards, orange hubs, open cab w/extended roof, 26", VG, A...$3,850.00

U-Haul Truck and Trailers, Nylint, red and gray with black tires, VG, J6, $155.00.

U-Haul Ford Econoline Pickup Truck & Trailer, Nylint, EX.$125.00
Water Tower Truck (American La France), Sturditoy, red w/open cab, water tower & pump, lever action, 34", G, A .$1,375.00
We Move the Earth Truck, Courtland, yel, orange & red, VG $150.00
Wrecker, Metalcraft, blk cab & fr, orange body, 12", VG, A.$175.00
Wrecker, Sturditoy, red w/Sturditoy Trucking Co decal, black rubber tires w/red hubs, doorless cab, 30", EX, A .$2,310.00

Miscellaneous

Austin Western Telescoping Crane, Nylint, 1950, red and yellow with black rubber tires, EX, from $75.00 to $125.00.

Elgin Street Sweeper, Nylint, NMIB..............................$250.00

Ferris Wheel, Kelmar, 1940s, octagon-shaped wheel w/6 gondolas, 20½", VG, A $120.00

Michigan Shovel, Clark Model T-24, Nylint #2200, 1964, yel w/decals, oval headlights, complete, 28", minor wear, VG, P4 ....$110.00

Missile Launcher #2600, Nylint, MIB..........................$150.00

Mobile Home, Nylint, turq, NMIB $275.00

Pettibone Crane, Nylint, yel & red, G $65.00

Pullman Car, Cor-Cor, red & blk, 24", EX $200.00

Pullman Car, Turner, yel & red, 24", VG $140.00

Photo courtesy of June Moon.

Road Grader, Nylint, 1950s, red with black tires, NM, J6, $95.00.

Travel Loader, Nylint, orange, VG $110.00

Trolley Car, Schieble, Rapid Transit, red & bl, EX........$250.00

Turbo Roller, Nylint, rare, G+, W5 ....$65.00

Promotional Vehicles

Miniature Model T Fords were made by Tootsietoy during the 1920s, and though they were not actually licensed by Ford, a few of these were handed out by Ford dealers to promote the new models. In 1932 Tootsietoy was contacted by Graham-Paige to produce a model of their car. These 4" Grahams were sold in boxes as sales promotions by car dealerships, and some were sold through the toy company's catalog. But it wasn't until after WWII that distribution of 1/25 scale promotional models and kits became commonplace. Early models were of cast metal, but during the 1950s, manufacturers turned to plastic. Not only was the material less costly to use, but it could be molded in the color desired, thereby saving the time and expense previously involved in painting the metal. Though the early plastic cars were prone to warp easily when exposed to heat, by the mid-'50s, they had become more durable. Some were friction powered, and others held a battery-operated radio. Advertising extolling some of the model's features was often embossed on the underside. Among the toy manufacturers involved in making promotionals were National Products, Product Miniatures, AMT, MPC, and Jo-Han. Interest in '50s and '60s models is intense, and the muscle cars from the '60s and early '70s are especially collectible. The more popularity the life-size model attained, the more popular the promotional is with collectors.

Check the model for damage, warping, and amateur alterations. The original box can increase the value by as much as 30%. Jo-Han has reissued some of their 1950s and 1960s Mopar and Cadillac models as well as Chrysler's Turbine Car. These are usually priced between $20.00 and $30.00.

Advisor: Nancy and Jim Schaut (S15).

Key: u/c — undercarriage

1947 Studebaker, 1/32, 2-door, gr, rpt, M19 ....$225.00

1948 Hudson Sedan, 4-door, gr, 13", VG......................$750.00

1953 Buick Roadmaster, AMT, 1/25, 4-door, EX $135.00

1953 Chevy 150, PMC, 1/25, 2-door, gr, rpt, M19 ....$50.00

1953 Pontiac, 2-door hardtop, yel w/wht roof, friction, NMIB, S15 ....$95.00

1955 T-Bird, AMT, convertible, blk, friction, minor warp to right fender o/w NM, S15......................................$200.00

1956 Buick Century Convertible, AMT, 1/25, bl, rstr, M19...$155.00

1956 Chevy Belair, bank, PMC, 1/25, 4-door, gr, M $175.00

1956 Dodge Lancer, AMT, 1/25, 4-door, red & bl, M....$130.00

Photo courtesy of Continental Hobby House.

1957 T-Bird, red with black and white striped seat, EX, $75.00.

1958 Cadillac 60 S, 1/25, 4-door, wht, rstr, M19 ....$90.00

1958 Chevy Apache Pickup, 1/25, detailed u/c, yel, M..$225.00

1958 Chevy Belair, AMT, 1/25, 4-door, red & bl, rstr, M19...$150.00

1958 Chevy Belair, PMC, 1/25, 4-door, red, EX+ $100.00

1958 Edsel Ranger, AMT, 1/25, 2-door, salmon, M $240.00

1958 Rolls Royce, 1/25, silver, rpt, M19 ....$75.00

1959 Chrysler New Yorker, 1/25, 4-door, gr, EX+ $60.00

1959 Citroen, wht plastic, 13", VG $75.00

1959 Corvette Convertible, AMT, 1/25, wht, rstr, M19 ..$425.00

1959 Ford Wagon, red & wht litho tin, 11", VG............$135.00

1960 Chevy Fleetside Pickup, 1/25, rose, M $250.00

1960 Rambler Wagon, VG $75.00

1961 T-Bird, AMT, 1/25, 2-door, red, rpt, M19 ....$135.00

1962 Chevy Nova, AMT, 1/25, 2-door hardtop, silver, M..$250.00

1962 Ford Galaxie, AMT, 1/25, 2-door, yel, MIB, M19.$125.00

1962 Oldsmobile, MIB, T1 ....$35.00

1962 Rambler American Convertible, 1/25, gr, EX+........$55.00

1962 Rambler Classic Station Wagon, Johan, NMIB.......$75.00

1962 Studebaker Lark Convertible, 1/25, yel, EX+ $75.00

1962 T-Bird, w/orig trunk & ignition keys, VG, W5........$85.00

1963 Chevy Corvair Convertible, AMT, 1/25, bl, M.....$265.00

1963 Chevy Nova Station Wagon, AMT, 1/25, silver, M...$145.00
1964 Chevy Impala Convertible, AMT, 1/25, tan, M....$225.00
1964 Mustang, 2-door hardtop, wht, EX $75.00
1965 Chevy Malibu Station Wagon, AMT, 1/25, 4-door, brn, M...$95.00

1965 Mustang 2+2, red, M, from $125.00 to $150.00.

1966 Ford Fairlane GT, AMT/Ertl, 1/25, 2-door, blk, MIB, M19..$25.00
1966 Ford Hardtop, VG...$65.00
1966 Mustang Fastback, metallic sand, w/working radio in base, NM, S15..$125.00
1966 Pontiac GTO, MPC, 1/25, 2-door hardtop, blk, rstr, M19...$415.00
1966 Rambler Classic Station Wagon, NMIB.................$75.00
1967 Ambassador, VG...$85.00
1968 Cadillac, 1/25, 2-door, yel, MIB, M19....................$75.00
1968 Cadillac De Ville, 1/25, 2-door, bl, M.....................$75.00
1968 Chevrolet, plastic w/red-stripe tires, NM, J6............$85.00
1968 Corvette Convertible, AMT, 1/25, red, rstr, M19.$510.00
1968 Olds Cutlass, Johan, 1/25, 2-door, bl, MIB, M19...$125.00
1968 Olds Tornado, AMT, 1/25, 2-door, bl, MIB, M19.$100.00
1969 Chevy Impala, AMT, 1/25, 2-door hardtop, maroon, M19..$170.00

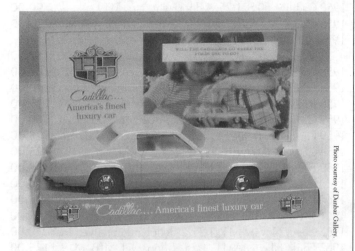

1970 Cadillac, yellow, MIB, $125.00.

1970 Chevrolet Fleetside Pickup, orange, NM, S15.......$125.00
1970 Pontiac GTO, MPC, 1/25, 2-door, red, rstr, M19..$135.00
1971 Chevelle, MPC, 1/25, 2-door, red, MIB, M19 ....$190.00
1975 AMC Racer, AMT, 1/25, 2-door, silver, MIB, M19 ..$40.00

1978 Chevette, MPC, 1/25, 2-door, camel, MIB, M19.....$15.00
1978 Chevy Monza, MPC, 1/25, 2-door, camel, MIB, M19..$15.00
1978 Corvette Coupe, MPC, 1/25, gray & silver, MIB, M19.$110.00
1979 Corvette Coupe, MPC, 1/25, red, MIB, M19.........$45.00
1981 Corvette, MPC, 1/25, 2-door, bl, MIB, M19............$65.00
1982 Chevy Camaro, MPC, 1/25, 2-door, bl, MIB, M19..$20.00
1984 Corvette Coupe, MPC, 1/25, silver, MIB, M19 ....$45.00
1989 Buick Reatta, 1/24, 2-door, red, MIB, M19 ....$45.00
1989 Chevy Silverado C-1500, Ertl, 1/25, red, MIB, M19..$25.00
1991 Chevy Storm, Ertl, 1/25, 2-door, teal, MIB, M19 ....$25.00
1991 Dodge Stealth, Ertl, 1/25, gr, MIB, M19 ....$30.00
1992 Corvette Convertible, Ertl, 1/25, red, MIB, M19.....$25.00
1993 Chevy Camaro, Ertl, 1/25, 2-door, bl, MIB, M19 ....$30.00
1993 Firebird, Ertl, 1/25, 2-door, yel, MIB, M19..............$30.00
1993 Ford Ranger Pickup STX 4x4, AMT/Ertl, 1/25, red, MIB, M19.......................................$25.00

Pull and Push Toys

Pull and push toys from the 1800s often were made of cast iron with bells that were activated as they moved along on wheeled platforms or frames. Hide and cloth animals with glass or shoe-button eyes were also popular, and some were made of wood.
See also specific companies such as Fisher-Price.

Bear on Bicycle, tin articulated bear in suit & glasses on bicycle w/support rod allowing travel on string, 7", VG, A .$275.00
Bear on Wheeled Bar w/Bells, Gong Bell, 1915, CI bear swings from side to side striking bells, spoked wheels, 6", G-, A $440.00

Borden's Farm Products Horse-Drawn Wagon, Rich Toys, 1920s, painted wood, 19", NM, D10, $1,250.00.

Boy Fishing on Platform, J&E Stevens, animated Black boy w/fishing pole over pond, 4 spoked wheels, 8", rpt, A $220.00
Boy in Sailboat on Platform w/Bell, Hull & Stafford (?), pnt tin, suspended by wire above platform, 11", G, A.......$1,650.00
Boy Pulling Round Revolving Platform w/3 Goats & Boy, Geo Brown (?), pnt tin, center flag, 3 spoked wheels, 9", VG, A $1,870.00
Boy Sawing Log on Platform, att Bergmann, pnt tin, blk-pnt figure & saw, red platform, spoked wheels, 7", G, A ..$3,190.00

Boy w/Butterfly Net on Platform, dressed wood & wire figure w/bsk head rings bell, paper-covered platform, 12", EX, A $990.00

Brake (3-Seat), litho paper on wood w/metal spoked wheels, yel w/gr trim, 15", VG, A...$360.00

Buffalo Bill Aiming at Buffalo, Fallows, ca 1880, painted tin, 9", EX, D10, from $6,000.00 to $9,000.00.

Butcher Boy w/Pig on Platform, clothed wood & wire figure w/bsk head, 4-wheeled platform, bell rings, 11", EX, A..$2,200.00

Cappy the Caterpillar, 1940s, jtd wood parts on wheels, MIB, H12 ....$35.00

Cinderella's Chariot, J&E Stevens, pnt CI, pony pulls ornate chariot on 2 heart-shaped spoke wheels, 9", EX, A.$770.00

Clown on Globe, clown straddling globe that revolves when pulled, litho tin, G, A $300.00

Clown on Pig, bell toy, Gong Bell, ca 1903, painted cast iron, 6½", scarce, EX, D10, from $900.00 to $1,500.00.

Clown on Wheeled Bar w/Bells, Gong Bell, CI clown swings from side to side striking bells, spoked wheels, 5¾", EX, A..$440.00

Clown w/Cymbals on Platform, seated clothed wood & wire figure w/bsk head, egg w/bells rotates, 9", VG+, A $660.00

Cow on Platform, cowhide over papier-mache, leather collar & bell, moos, wooden 4-wheeled platform, 11", EX, A...$470.00

Cow on Platform, hide-covered body w/horns & glass eyes, reddish brn w/wht nose, chest & inner side of legs, 8", EX, A $300.00

Cow on Platform, ruddy wht hide-covered body w/horns, glass eyes, leather collar, moos, inset iron wheels, 20", G, A $190.00

Cupid's Chariot, Kenton, pnt CI, cupid figure in blk shoe w/2 red spoked wheels pulled by blk horse, 10", VG, A .$360.00

Dog & Boy w/Flag on Platform, Francis, Field & Francis (?), pnt tin, boy on wht dog, spoked wheels, 4½", G+, A $500.00

Dog Cart, Harris, 1910, pnt CI, trotting dog pulling lady in blk 2-wheeled cart, reclining backrest, 11", rpt, A $145.00

Dog Cart, Wilkins, hand-pnt CI, 6", VG, A...................$425.00

Dog in House on Platform, Hustler, 1940s, wood & tin, 11", VG, A $275.00

Dog on Platform, pnt tin, realistic blk dog w/gold & red collar on gr platform, spoked wheels, 13", EX, A...............$935.00

Dog w/Basket on Platform, pnt tin, dog standing w/basket in mouth, spoked wheels, 6½", G, A...........................$440.00

Elephant on Platform, Fallows, 1880s, pnt gray w/bl & red blanket, rings bell w/trunk when pulled, 7", EX, A $440.00

Elephant on Platform, Kenton, CI, silver-tone elephant w/articulated head on 4-wheeled platform, 5½", G, A.......$210.00

Elephant on Platform, Stevens & Brown (?), pnt tin, gray w/tusks & red blanket, 4½", VG, A.........................$415.00

Elephant w/2 Riders on Platform, pnt CI, driver on head & rider on howdah w/umbrella, 4 spoked wheels, 4½", VG, A.....$255.00

Fox in Hunting Clothes on Wheels, ca 1914, celluloid figure w/human characteristics stands between 2 wheels, 5", G, A $345.00

Foxy Grandpa & Gloomy Gus in Horse-Drawn Cart, Wilkins, pnt CI, Gus drives w/Grandpa standing in stake bed, 13", rpt, A $250.00

Foxy Grandpa Rubber Neck Mule-Drawn Cart, Kenton, ca 1929, 9", EX, D10, from $400.00 to $700.00.

Girl Riding Sidesaddle on Wheeled Donkey, US Hardware, CI, red & yel figure, gray donkey, red spoked wheels, 6", G-, A.................$135.00

Girl w/Doll on Platform, wood & wire w/bsk head, 2-pc pants set, knit cap, head & arms move, wood platform, 12", VG, A.................$460.00

Girl w/Rod & Paddle on Platform, wood & wire figures dressed karate style, paper-covered platform, 12", EX, A.....$690.00

Goat Cart, pnt tin, goat w/red saddle pulling red box-type cart w/2 spoked wheels, 10", G-, A.................$230.00

Goat Cart w/Boy, Bergmann (?), 1870s, pnt tin, boy on platform standing next to goat pulling 2-wheeled cart, 8", EX, A..$800.00

Goat on Platform, blk goat hair w/glass eyes, neck ribbon & bell, baas when head moves, 21", EX, A.......................$1,700.00

Goat on Platform, pnt & stained tin, w/red saddle, spoked wheels, 9½", G-, A.................$220.00

Goat on Platform, pnt tin, yel-gold goat w/saddle in walking stance on wht platform (not orig), spoked wheels, 10", G, A.................$175.00

Goat w/Bell, European, pnt tin, goat attached to single-wheel rod pulling 2 lg spoked wheels w/bell, 14", G, A.....$550.00

Horse, Ives, CI articulated horse mounted on 3 spoked wheels, hair tail, 7½", EX, A.................$2,200.00

Horse & Rider on Platform, Fallows, 1870, pnt tin, mc jockey on blk horse, gr platform, 6½", VG, A.................$520.00

Horse & Rider on Platform, Fallows, 1880s, jockey in blk & red, brn horse, 9½", VG, A.................$1,650.00

Horse & Rider on Platform, Hull & Stafford, pnt tin, trotting horse, spoked wheels, 4½", G+, A.................$385.00

Horse & Rider on 2 Large Spoked Wheels, Wilkins, pnt CI, red rider on wht horse, 2 yel wheels, wood pull hdl, 35", EX, A.................$440.00

Horse & Rider w/Dog on Platform, Geo Brown (?), pnt tin, dog running along side of horse, spoked wheels, 6½", G-, A.....$690.00

Horse Balancing on Platform, Hull & Stafford, 1870, horse on half-circle wire mounted on 4-wheeled platform, 14", rst, A.................$1,265.00

Horse Galloping on Platform, Dexter, pnt tin, blk horse on gr platform, sm spoked wheels, 9½", G-, A.................$470.00

Horse on Platform, German, papier-mache, wht w/gray spots, blk hair mane & tail, wood platform, 14", EX, A.........$145.00

Horse on Platform, pnt & gessoed wood, metal eyes, horsehair mane & tail, leatherette tack, iron hdl, 24", G- pnt, A..........$635.00

Horse Trotting on Platform, Geo Brown (?), pnt tin, wht w/red saddle & blk reins, blk spoked wheels, 9", G, A......$440.00

Horse Walking, Ives, pnt CI, blk articulated horse on single spoked wheel, 6", missing rope tail, A.....................$385.00

Horse-Drawn American Dairy Wagon, wood, wht horse w/blk hair mane & tail on platform pulls yel & bl wagon, 30", EX, A.................$2,420.00

Horse-Drawn American Ice Co Wagon, A Jacrim Mfg, wood, yel wagon w/gr spoked wheels, brn & cream horse, 31", VG, A.................$825.00

Horse-Drawn Bell, Am, late 1800s, pnt tin horse pulling CI 2-wheeled cylinder, circle spokes, 10", G, A...............$690.00

Horse-Drawn Broadway & 10th Street Trolley, pnt & stenciled tin, 2 horses w/flags, w/conductor, spoked wheels, 14", G, A.................$3,190.00

Horse-Drawn Carousel w/American Flag, French (?), rider & horse pulling 2-wheeled carousel w/riders on horses, 8", VG, A.................$990.00

Horse-Drawn Carriage, pnt tin, wht trotting horse pulling red 2-wheeled carriage w/open wht interior, 8", G, A $300.00

Horse-Drawn Cart, Geo Brown (?), wht horse pulling bl box-type cart, 2 spoked wheels, 13½", G, A...................$285.00

Horse-Drawn Cart, Gibbs, litho paper on wood horse w/red-pnt wood cart, 2 metal spoked wheels, 14", VG, A........$175.00

Horse-Drawn Cart, pnt tin, wht trotting horse pulling red, yel & gr cart w/perforated rail, 2 spoked wheels, 10", G, A......$300.00

Horse-Drawn Chaise, Am, 1870s, pnt tin horse w/gilt-plated 2-wheeled chaise, 9", G, A.................$260.00

Horse-Drawn Chaise, Francis, Field & Francis, 1840s, pnt tin, horse w/barrel body & stick legs, iron wheels, 6", VG, A.................$2,990.00

Horse-Drawn Chariot in Form of Chicken, yel pnt horse w/red stained chariot, 2 spoked wheels, 5½", G, A...........$415.00

Horse-Drawn Coach w/Stable, French, single horse on platform pulling red & blk coach, 2-stall 5½" stable, VG, A.$500.00

Horse-Drawn Covered Wagon, Gibbs, litho paper-on-wood horses pulling wooden wagon w/cloth top, spoked wheels, 20", G, A.................$230.00

Horse-Drawn Covered Wagon, Gibbs, 2 litho paper-on-wood horses pulling red tin wagon w/cloth cover, 18½", G, A.................$70.00

Horse-Drawn Delivery Wagon, wood, brn horse on platform pulls flatbed wagon w/sm spoked wheels, w/cargo, 36", EX, A.................$635.00

Horse-Drawn Dump Cart, Merriam, 1870s, painted tin, 16", EX, D10, $2,600.00.

Horse-Drawn Fine Groceries Delivery Cart, Fallows, 1880s, pnt tin, brn horse pulls red & gr Amish-type wagon, 13", G, A.$865.00

Horse-Drawn Landau, Merriam, pnt & stenciled tin, 2 wht horses pull red & blk coach, 13", VG, A.............$4,070.00

Horse-Drawn Milk Wagon, Marklin, hide-covered horse on 4-wheeled wood platform, pnt tin wagon w/6 milk cans, 24", EX, A.................$1,100.00

Horse-Drawn Phaeton, Pratt & Letchworth, 1892, wht CI horse pulling tin open carriage w/rider, spoked wheels, 15", VG, A.................$470.00

Horse-Drawn Sheffield Farms Co Milk Wagon, wooden articulated horse pulling enclosed wagon, 21", EX, A $350.00

Horse-Drawn Surrey, mk France, pnt tin, 2 wht horses pulling lime gr surrey w/plain flat top, 4 spoked wheels, 9", VG, A.................$275.00

Horse-Drawn Trolley, Geo Brown, pnt yel & red tin trolley w/spoked wheels pulled by 2 wht horses, 12½", VG, A..............$1,320.00

Horse-Drawn Trolley, Lutz/Germany, 1870, pnt tin, horse on platform pulls red & blk Danzig-Langfuhr trolley, 17", NM, A..$6,600.00

Horse-Drawn Trolley, pnt tin, wht horse w/red saddle pulling sm scale yel trolley w/red roof, 2 spoked wheels, 6", G+, A .$385.00

Horse-Drawn Wagon, att Converse, 2 printed wood horses pulling wagon w/spoked wheels, 4 metal milk cans, 17", EX, A...$525.00

Horse-Drawn Wagon, Gibbs, 2 litho paper-on-wood horses pulling wooden wagon w/4 metal spoked wheels, 21", G, A...$190.00

Horse-Drawn Wagon, Ives, 1880s, horse w/hair mane on 4-wheeled platform pulling stake wagon w/spoked wheels, VG, A..$1,650.00

Horse-Drawn Water Trow, Am, 1870s, pnt tin, red 2-wheeled barrel-shape trow, 7½", G-, A..................................$290.00

Horse-Drawn Water Trow, French (?), pnt tin, trotting horse pulling horizontal red barrel on 2 spoked wheels, 9", VG, A...$415.00

Horses w/Boy on Platform, Geo Brown (?), 2 wht horses driven by oversized boy in red & brn, 8½", rstr, A..........$1,265.00

Krazy Kat w/2 Mice on Platform, Nifty, Krazy Kat printed on both sides of tail, 7½", NM, A $850.00

Lamb on Platform, pnt tin, wht w/gold neck bell, bl platform, spoked wheels, 9", G, A...$340.00

Lamb on Platform, wht cloth-covered body w/glass eyes, red neck ribbon & bell, red-pnt wood platform, 6¾", EX, A ..$330.00

Lamb on Platform, wool-covered body w/glass eyes, neck ribbon & bell, squeaks, stained wood platform, 7", EX, A.......$1,100.00

Lion on Platform, early 1900s, hide-covered w/glass eyes, sheepskin mane, grain-pnt platform, 8x12", G, A.............$115.00

Man in Wheeled Canoe, German, early, wood & wire body w/papier-mache head, papier-mache boat, cotton outfit, 11", VG, A...$175.00

Man on Bicycle, litho tin articulated figure on bicycle w/grooved wheels, support rod allows travel on string, 8", VG, A..$330.00

Men (2) Riding Handcar, Schieble/Am, flywheel allows articulated action when pulled, hand-pnt tin, 9", VG, A.$525.00

Pony Cart, Gibbs, litho paper-on-wood articulated pony pulling metal 2-wheeled cart, 7", VG, A...............................$90.00

Pony Chariot, Gibbs, red tin chariot on 2 gold spoked wheels pulled by litho paper-on-wood pony w/jtd legs, 8", G, A...$165.00

Rooster & Hen on Platform, German, papier-mache chickens & nest, squeaks when pulled, wooden platform, 6", G, A...$200.00

Snowflake & Swipes on Platform, c Oscar Hitt, jtd tin figures of Black boy & dog in running motion, 8", NM, A..$1,760.00

Steer on Platform, detailed rawhide cover, makes noise when head is turned, wood platform, 9", EX, A $415.00

Surfer Girl, Hubley, pnt CI, girl in yel suit w/red cap on Janzen surfboard, pull string w/ball end, 8", EX, A $9,020.00

Teddy Roosevelt & the Rough Riders w/Bell, 1900, 3 NP CI figures on steel fr w/heart-shaped spoke wheels, 10", VG, A..$575.00

Wild Mule Jack, bell toy, ca 1898, painted cast iron, 8½", EX, $650.00.

Mary and Her Lamb With Goat on Platform, Fallows, 1880s, 9", EX, D10, from $3,000.00 to $4,500.00.

Puppets

Though many collectible puppets and the smaller scale marionettes were made commercially, others were handmade and are today considered fine examples of folk art which sometimes sell for several hundred dollars. Some of the most collectible today are character-related puppets representing well-known television stars.

Advisor: Steven Meltzer (M9).

See also Advertising; Black Americana; Political.

Finger Puppets

Crypt Keeper, rubber, M, H4, set of 3 ....$12.00
Lamb Chop, 1960, VG+, N2...$35.00
Lucy (Peanuts), wearing bikini, EX, H11 ....$3.00

Monkees, Davy & Mickey, Clever Finger Dolls, MOC (sealed), B3 ....$90.00

Monkees, Davy & Mickey, Remco, 1960s, MOC, J2 .....$120.00

Pebbles & Bamm-Bamm, Knickerbocker, 1972, VG, C17, pr $10.00

Prince Charming, Mego, 1977, Puppet Love, MOC, C17 ..$25.00

Spider-Man, 1970s, NM, D8 ....$12.00

Hand Puppets

Archimedes the Owl (Sword & the Stone), EX, T1 ....$35.00

Bert & Ernie, 20", EX, J7, ea, minimum value $20.00

Bugs Bunny, early 1960s, vinyl head w/moving eyes, EX, C17 ....$35.00

Bugs Bunny, Mattel, talker, non-working o/w EX, B10 ....$30.00

Captain Hook, Gund, late 1950s-60s, pnt vinyl head w/checkered cloth body, 9", EX, minimum value $50.00

Casper the Friendly Ghost, EX+, T1 ....$45.00

Chairy (Pee-Wee's Playhouse), stuffed, 14", EX $20.00

Photo courtesy of Dunbar Gallery.

Charlie McCarthy, Ideal, 1930s, 10", NM, D10, $375.00.

Charlie McCarthy, Reliable Toy, compo head, EX+, T1...$125.00

Clarabell (Howdy Doody), 1953, rubber head w/cloth body, lt pnt wear, rpr at arm seam o/w EX.............................$50.00

Dennis the Menace, 1960, EX, J7.......................................$40.00

Dick Tracy, puppet, Ideal, 1961, rubber head w/cloth body, EX+, D11...$50.00

Dilly-Dally (Howdy Doody), 1953, pnt rubber head w/cloth body, worn pnt & stain on body o/w VG+.................$75.00

Dopey, Gund/Disney, EX+, T1/J2, from $25 to $35.00

Dr Dolittle, Mattel #5365, talker, 11½", NMIB, A7 ......$100.00

Dragon, 1960s, pnt vinyl head w/cloth body, EX, J5.........$25.00

Dumbo, Gund, 1950s, vinyl head w/squeaker, EX, C17 ..$45.00

Fauna the Fairy (Sleeping Beauty), Gund, 1950s, soft plastic head w/cloth body, EX+, M8......................................$18.00

Gnome, 1960s, pnt vinyl head w/cloth body, EX, J5 ....$25.00

Gomez (Addams Family), 1960s, vinyl head w/cloth body, EX, T1..$110.00

Grandpa Munster, Ideal/Kayro-Vue, 1964, fabric w/vinyl head & hand-pnt features, NMOC (sealed), A $150.00

Gumby, Hanna-Barbera, EX, T1 ....$25.00

Gumby & Pokey, 1960s, MIP, P12 ....$95.00

Herman Munster, 1960s, vinyl head w/cloth body, NM, T1 ..$145.00

Howdy Doody, 1950s, plastic head, cloth clothes, felt hands, 13", NM, J5...$195.00

Howdy Doody, Tee Vee Toy, 1950s, 4", NMIB, $85.00.

Huckleberry Hound, Knickerbocker, 1962, vinyl head w/cloth body, NM, C17 ....$45.00

Hush Puppy (Shari Lewis), 1962, lt bl soft plastic head w/bl cloth body, 9", EX+, T2...$25.00

Jerry Mahoney, 1966, rubber head w/vinyl body, EX+, rare, F8 ....$60.00

Joan Palooka, National Mask & Puppet/Ham Fisher, cloth w/vinyl head, complete w/blanket, 11", VG+ (VG+ box), A ..$55.00

King, 1960s, vinyl head w/cloth body, EX, J5 ....$25.00

Knucklehead, 1966, rubber head w/vinyl body, rare, EX+ ..$90.00

Lily Munster, Ideal/Kayro-Vue, 1964, fabric w/vinyl head & hand-pnt features, NMOC (sealed), A $170.00

Lone Ranger, vinyl, no hat o/w NM, P12 ....$40.00

Magilla Gorilla, Ideal, early 1960s, vinyl head, VG+, C17 ...$35.00

Man, 1960s, pnt vinyl head w/blk military cap, cloth body, EX J5 ....$25.00

Man, 1960s, pnt vinyl head w/red nightcap, cloth body, EX, J5 ....$25.00

Merlin, Gund/Disney, 1960s, w/working squeaker, lt pnt wear on hat o/w EX, orig tag, J5 ....$45.00

Miss Piggy (Muppets), Fisher-Price, lg vinyl head, EX $50.00

Monkees, Mattel/Raybert, 1966, features ea member, cloth w/vinyl heads, talker, NM (NM box), A $425.00

Morticia, 1960s, vinyl head, bl cloth body w/name across front, EX+, J5 ....$65.00

Mr Ed, Knickerbocker, 1960s, EX......................................$60.00

Mr Magoo, 1962, pnt vinyl w/cloth body, EX, J5.............$55.00

Mr Rogers' Neighbor Lady, EX+, T1.............................$75.00

Munchie Melon, Marx, 1968, vinyl head w/cloth body, EX, F8..$12.00

Mushmouth, Ideal, 1960s, pnt vinyl head w/gr cloth body, pnt wear & minor soiling o/w VG, J5............................$65.00

Papa Smurf, no tag o/w EX, B10...................................$18.00

Pinocchio, Disney, early 1930s, EX, J2.........................$115.00

Pixie Mouse, Hanna-Barbera, VG+, T1.........................$15.00

Pluto, Gund, 1950s, vinyl head w/squeaker, NM, C17.....$35.00

Porky Pig, 1964, talker, non-working o/w EX, J7/B10......$30.00

Princess Summer-Fall-Winter-Spring (Howdy Doody), 1953, rubber head w/cloth body, EX+..................................$50.00

Raggedy Ann & Andy, Knickerbocker, 1970s, MIP, H12..$15.00

Robin (Batman), 1960s, printed on thin sheet vinyl, slips over hand, NM, P12..$175.00

Rootie Kazootie, 1953, rubber head w/lt brn cloth body, EX+...$75.00

Snoopy, blk & wht plush w/collar, 10", VG, H11.............$10.00

Soupy Sales, Gund, 1965, w/yel body mk Soupy Sez Lets Do the Mouse, w/orig tie & tag, NM, J5/T1 ....$75.00

Spike (Tom & Jerry), Multitoy, 1989, MOC, B10 ....$16.00

Stingray, Aquaphibian, EX+, T1...................................$85.00

Sylvester, 1990, cloth, EX, B10....................................$12.00

Teddy Snow Crop, EX+, T1...$75.00

Three Stooges, vinyl heads w/cloth bodies, NM, T1, set of 3 ....$385.00

Three Stooges, vinyl heads w/cloth bodies, VG, H4, set of 3 ....$180.00

Tinkerbell, Disney, EX+, T1 ....$45.00

Toto (Wizard of Oz), 1960s, blk vinyl head w/thin plastic body, 10", NM..$45.00

Tweety Bird, vinyl, EX, B10..$15.00

Wonder Woman, Ideal, 1960s, MIP, scarce, P12 ....$195.00

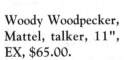

Woody Woodpecker, Mattel, talker, 11", EX, $65.00.

Yogi Bear, Huckleberry Hound Toy, 1961, EX+, B10 ......$25.00

Yogi Bear, Knickerbocker, 1962, vinyl head w/cloth body, EX $55.00

Yosemite Sam, Japan, vinyl, EX, B10 ....$15.00

Zero (Beetle Bailey), NM, T1.......................................$45.00

Marionettes

Alice, Hazelle's, talker, M, M9.....................................$125.00

Angel, Pelham, MIB, M9...$95.00

Bengo the Dog, Pelham, MIB, M9 ....$65.00

Bimbo the Clown, Hazelle's, 800 series, EX, M9 ....$75.00

Bimbo the Clown, Pelham, M, M9.................................$135.00

Boy, Pelham, talker, M9, MIB.......................................$85.00

Buckaroo Bill, Hazelle's, talker, EX, M9 ....$175.00

Clippo the Clown, Curtis Craft, MIB, M9......................$65.00

Clippo the Clown, Effanbee/WWII, MIB, M9 ....$250.00

Clown, Pelham, talker, MIB, M9 ....$95.00

Cop, Pelham, talker, MIB, M9......................................$125.00

Emily Ann (Clippo's Girlfriend), Effanbee, M, M9........$125.00

Father, Mother & Son, Effanbee, set of 3, EX, M9.........$425.00

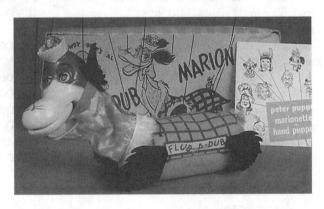

Flub-A-Dub (Howdy Doody's Pal), composition, 12", MIB, $375.00.

Freddy MC, Hazelle's, M, M9.......................................$125.00

Gepetto (Pinocchio), Pelham, MIB, M9 ....$125.00

Jim-Bob and Susy Pigtail, Curtis Crafts, 1950, M, M9, $525.00 for the pair.

Girl, Pelham, talker, MIB, M9.................................$85.00

Hansel & Gretel, Hazelle's, M, M9, pr.................$175.00

Hillbilly, Hazelle's, 800 series, M, M9 ....$95.00

Horse, Pelham, EX (EX box), M9.........................$75.00

Howdy Doody, Peter Puppet Playthings, 1950s, pnt compo face, NM, T1 ....$225.00

Little Boy Blue, Hazelle's, 800 series, compo, M, M9 .....$135.00

Marilyn, Hazelle's, talker, EX, M9.....................$155.00

Mickey Mouse, Mexico, bsk head & hands, balsa ft & ankles, wood body, pnt w/cloth clothes, tangled strings, VG, D9 ....$35.00

Minnie Mouse, Peter Puppet Playthings, compo, VG $150.00

Nurse, Pelham, M, M9..$75.00

Old Lady, Pelham, MIB, M9 ....$125.00

Pinocchio, Pelham, MIB, M9 ....$75.00

Planet Flyer, Hazelle's, 1950s, Tom Corbett look-alike, EX+ (EX+ box), J2.......................................$210.00

Pop Singer, Pelham, gray suit, M, M9 ....$250.00

Pop Singer, Pelham, Hawaiian shirt, M, M9 ....$145.00

Prince Charming, Pelham, MIB, M9 ....$125.00

Princess Summer-Fall-Winter-Spring (Howdy Doody), 1952, VG (orig box), J2 ....$190.00

Princess Summer-Fall-Winter-Spring (Howdy Doody), 1952, wood, compo & cloth, 13", NMIB..............$250.00

Sailor, Hazelle's, talker, EX, M9........................$125.00

Small Fry, Peter Puppet Playthings, 1949, EX, L4 ....$125.00

Wolf, Pelham, G, M9..$250.00

Wombles (Furry Creatures from English TV), Pelham, MIB, M9, ea...$55.00

Push-Button Puppets

Wonder Woman, Madison Ltd, vinyl head, painted-on top, 11½", EX, $95.00.

Atom Ant, Kohner, NM, C17.................................$40.00

Bamm-Bamm, Kohner, 1960s, missing club o/w VG, C17..$20.00

Bozo, Spinikin', EX, J2...$20.00

Cowboy, on wht horse, EX, O1.............................$50.00

Davy Crockett, Disney, 1950s, w/front label, EX+, T1...$225.00

Disney Pop Pals, Kohner/Hong Kong, WDP, Mickey, Donald, Pluto & Goofy, 3", EX+, D9.............................$35.00

Donald Duck Tricky Trapeze, MOC.......................$35.00

Felix the Cat, FTCP Inc, wood, 4", EX, B10/C10, from $22 to $30.00

Flub-a-Dub, EX, O1...$85.00

Photo courtesy of June Moon.

Fred and Wilma Flintstone, Kohner, 1960s, NM, J6, $35.00 each.

Giraffe, TM China, NM, I2 ....$6.00

Goofy, M, J6...$28.00

Goofy Tricky Trapeze, EX, J2 ....$20.00

Happy the Wonder Dog, Kohner, wood, VG+, I2 ....$22.00

Hit 'N Miss, EX, O1...$60.00

Hoppy the Hopparoo & Wilma Flintstone, Kohner, scarce, NM (NM box), A $380.00

Huckleberry Hound, w/sticker, EX, B10.....................$45.00

Incredible Hulk, Fleetwood, 1978, 2½", MOC, H4..........$30.00

Lone Ranger on Silver, Kohner, NM, T1 ....$100.00

Magilla Gorilla, EX, O1.......................................$35.00

McDonald's Mule, red, EX, O1.............................$10.00

Mickey Mouse, Kohner, 1970, 5", NRFB, M15................$45.00

Mickey Mouse Drummer, Kohner, 1948, NM, J6..........$225.00

Ossie Oyster, EX, O1 ....$125.00

Owl, w/jiggle eyes, no label o/w EX, O1 ....$40.00

Pluto, Kohner, 1970, 5", NRFB, M15......................$45.00

Richochet Rabbit, Kohner, early 1960s, sm ear chip o/w EX, C17..$35.00

Rocky Squirrel, 1960s, NM, C17..........................$45.00

Santa Claus, w/jingle bell, EX, O1 ....$30.00

Santa Mouse, EX, O1 ....$30.00

Spider-Man Tricky Trapeze, Kohner, 1960s, EX, H4 ....$30.00

Terry the Tiger, EX, O1..$30.00

Touche Turtle, Kohner, 1960s, NM, J6, $75.00.

Photo courtesy of June Moon.

Wakouwa Champ, EX, O1 ....$100.00

Ventriloquist Dolls

Boy, Pelham, M, M9...$125.00
Charlie McCarthy, Juros, NMIB, J2 ....$85.00
Girl, Pelham, M, M9...$125.00
Groucho Marx, Goldberger, 31", M (EX box), I2 ....$60.00
Jerry Mahoney, compo, 1950s, MIB, M9 ....$450.00
Jerry Mahoney, headstick w/moving eyes, 32", MIB, M9 ....$500.00
Knucklehead, 1950s, MIB, M9 ....$950.00
Monk, Pelham, M, M9 ....$225.00
Rover, Pelham, M, M9...$95.00

Puzzles and Picture Blocks

Jigsaw puzzles have been around almost as long as games. The first examples were handcrafted from wood, and they are extremely difficult to find. Most of the early examples featured moral subjects and offered insight into the social atmosphere of their time. By the 1890s jigsaw puzzles had become a major form of home entertainment. Cube puzzles or blocks were often made by the same companies as board games. Early examples display lithography of the finest quality. While all subjects are collectible, some (such as Santa blocks) often command prices higher than games of the same period.

Because TV and personality-related puzzles have become so popular, they're now regarded as a field all their own apart from character collectibles in general, and these are listed here as well, under the subtitle 'Character.'

Advisors: Bob Armstrong (A4); Norm Vigue (V1); character.
See also Advertising.

Adam & Eve, Richardson/Perplexit, ca 1909, solid wood, 118 push-to-fit pcs (2 rpl), 6½x8", EX (rpl box), A4 ....$30.00

After the Rain, Parker Bros, ca 1909, wood, 80 pcs (4 rpl) w/numbers on bk, 7½x7½", EX (rpl box), A4...........$15.00
Afterglow, Cape Cod Puzzle Co, 1930s, plywood, 215 interlocking pcs, 8x10", EX (orig box), A4 ....$40.00
Along America's Southern Route, Parker Bros/Pastime, 1932, plywood, 300 interlocking pcs, 14¾x10", EX (orig box), A4 ....$90.00
Ann Hathaway's Cottage, 1930s, artist Ray Stannait, plywood, 566 interlocking pcs, EX (orig box), A4 ....$75.00
Bern, Penelope, 1960s, artist photo, plywood, 150 interlocking pcs, EX (orig box), A4.......................................$12.00
Blossom Time, 1920-30, artist HC MacDonald, plywood, 556 interlocking pcs (2 rpl), 18x14", EX (orig box), A4 ..$100.00
Boulangerie, American Pub/Casse-Tete, 1985, cb, 100 diecut interlocking pcs, rnd curve strip, 29x23", EX (orig box), A..$6.00
Breaking High (boats on sea), Perfect, 1930s, cb, 325 interlocking pcs, 16x12", EX (orig box), A4..............................$5.00
Bringing Home the Bacon, Parker Bros/Pastime, 1927, plywood, 202 interlocking pcs (1 rpl), 10x13", EX (rpl box), A4 .$50.00
Catskill Mountains From Eastern Shore of Hudson, Russell, 1974, artist Currier & Ives, 336 pcs, 14x9", EX (orig box), A4 ....$50.00
Challenged (bears & Indians), Tuco/Deluxe, cb, 320 diecut pcs, cracked line strip, 19x15", EX (orig box), A4............$10.00
Child's Companion ABC Picture Blocks, W Peacock/London, shows children at play, 11x7", VG+ (orig wooden box), A $440.00
Ching-Fue, Southwestern Dist Co, 1927, solid wood, 14 blocks, 4½x4", EX (orig box), A4 ....$15.00

Cinderella Puzzle Blocks and Booklet, Germany, paper lithograph on wood, incomplete sliding lid, G, A, $175.00.

Circus Puzzle Box, Milton Bradley, boxed set of 3, complete, NM (EX+ box), A $400.00
Cowboys, Platt & Munk, 1940s, cb, 50 interlocking pcs, 9x11", EX (rpl box), A4...$15.00
Crandall's Masquerade Blocks, 8-pc set w/interchangeable images, 8¾", rare, VG+ (orig box), A $415.00
Dogs, 1930s, artist G Sperling, plywood, 222 push-to-fit & semi-interlocking pcs, EX (orig box), A4 ....$30.00
Ducks & Geese, Springbok/Puzzles in Rnd, 1966, 500 interlocking pcs, rnd curved semi-strip, 20x20", EX (orig box), A4...$5.00

Eiffel Tower, Condor Toys/Craftsman, 1950-60, plywood, 630 interlocking pcs (3 rpl), 19½x15½", EX (envelope), A4 ....$45.00

Equestrian Scene, jigsaw, Par Co Ltd, dtd 1925, artist Raoul Dufy, 21x28", EX, A $575.00

Face Puzzle, Ives, litho paper on wood, 4 different faces w/interchangeable parts, 5 pcs in wood fr, 9½x6½", G, A .$770.00

Fancy Footwork, jigsaw, Par Co Ltd, diecut border w/flamenco dancer, bullfighter, etc, 25x24", EX (orig box), A...$690.00

Fire Engine, jigsaw, McLoughlin, 1894, 3-horse-drawn steam engine w/front & back driver, complete, EX (G orig box)...$200.00

First Step, 1909, wood, 260 pieces, EX (orig box), A4, $45.00.

Fishermen's Return, Parker Bros/Pastime, 1934, plywood, 528 interlocking pcs, 24¼x17¼", EX (orig box), A4 .....$165.00

Fishing Fleet, 1930s, plywood, 172 interlocking pcs, 8x11½", EX (orig box), A4 ....$30.00

Fortune Teller, Parker Bros/Pastime, 1910s, plywood, 232 semi-interlocking pcs, 14½x10", EX (orig box), A4 ....$70.00

Glory of the Setting Sun, 1930s, plywood, 232 push-to-fit & semi-interlocking pcs, 12x10", EX (orig box), A4 .....$30.00

Guardian, Joseph Straus, 1950-60, plywood, 300 interlocking pcs (1 rpl), 12x16", EX (orig box), A4 ....$25.00

Harbor View, Parker Bros/Pastime, 1930s, plywood, 442 interlocking pcs (1 rpl), 21x16¾", EX (orig box), A4 ....$130.00

Haying Time — The Last Load, 1930s, artist Currier & Ives, plywood, 248 interlocking pcs, 13½x8½", EX (orig box), A4 ....$40.00

Hebrew Animal Puzzle, Israel, 1950s(?), 7 illus cards w/Hebrew letters to form names, EX+ (orig compartment box), B12 ....$575.00

Hex Sign: The Mighty Oak, Grameophiles/Pic-Me-Up, 1974, cb, 36 pcs, curved strip, 7½x7½", EX (orig box), A4 ..$2.00

Home Memories, Big Star, 1930s, cb, 250 interlocking pcs, 13½x10", EX (orig box), A4...$4.00

Hot Wheels, jigsaw, Whitman, 1970, 100 pcs, NMIB, T2...$20.00

House of Parliament & Westminster Bridge, Hayter/Victory Topical, 1950-60s, plywood, 288 pcs, 15x11", EX (orig box), A4 ....$35.00

Judenborg, Roland Chesley, 1973, artist E Niese, plywood, 206 interlocking pcs, EX (orig box), A4 ....$25.00

Lake Supreme, Ryther Novelty, 1940s, plywood, 14 curved interlocking pcs, 5x4¼", EX (orig box), A4.................$5.00

Last Ray, 1930s, plywood, 317 pieces, G (orig box), A4, $20.00.

Leaving the Inn, Joseph Straus, 1940s, artist TJ Slaughter, 300 interlocking pcs, 16x12", EX (orig box), A4.............$20.00

Little Gem ABC & Pretty Picture Blocks, McLoughlin Bros, set of 8, 6x7½", VG+ (orig box), A.........................$495.00

Locomotive, McLoughlin Bros, c 1901, litho paper on wood, VG (worn box), A..$345.00

M'm! M'm! Good!, Jaymar, 1960-70, cb, 100 diecut-interlocking pcs, 18x13", EX (orig box), A4...............................$10.00

Map of the United States, McLoughlin Bros, ca 1900, plywood, 59 interlocking pcs, 22x13¾", EX (orig box), A4 ...$100.00

Mediterranean Villa No 120, Perfect, ca 1940, cb, 375 interlocking pcs, EX (orig box), A4...$10.00

Morning Interlude, Par Co Ltd, artist Robert Brackman, 3 female nudes, dtd & monogrammed, 19x15", EX (orig box), A $520.00

North Atlantic Picture Puzzle, paper litho on cb, forms several navy ships, 32 blocks, 10x20", EX (EX box), A.......$550.00

Now for the Flush, Joseph Straus, 1930s, artist GM Arnold, plywood, 300 interlocking pcs, 12x16", EX (orig box), A4 ....$25.00

Old Homestead, Parker Bros/Pastime, 1929, plywood, 78 semi-interlocking pcs (1 rpl), 6½x8¼", EX (orig box), A4 ....$18.00

Old Venice, Gelco/Weekly Interlocking, 1933, cb, 150 interlocking pcs, 11¾x8¾", EX (orig box), A4.................$10.00

Old Windmill at Sunset, Parker Bros/Pastime, 1939, 302 interlocking pcs (1 rpl), 11½x16", EX (orig box), A4.......$85.00

On the Swing, JA Needham, 1930s, plywood, 173 semi-interlocking pcs, EX (orig box), A4................................$30.00

Our Battleship New York, McLoughlin Bros, 1895, 10½x12½", EX (EX box), A $525.00

Over Field & Fence, Tuco, 1930s, artist Metts, cb, 350 diecut pcs, crooked line strip, 15x19", EX (orig box), A4.......$6.00

Peaceful Retreat, Perfect, 1940-50, cb, 350 interlocking pcs, 13x18½", EX (orig box), A4...$6.00

Picture Blocks, Germany, blocks form 6 pictures of children, animals & village scenes, 16x19", VG (orig box), A....$385.00

Picture Puzzles of Famous Planes, Saalfield, 1941, boxed set of 6, NM (EX box), A $150.00

Pirate's Sweetheart, Tuco/Art Picture Puzzle, 1933, artist Frank Carbyn Price, 180 pcs, 15x11", EX (orig box), A4.......$6.00

Pretty Picture Blocks, paper lithograph on hollow wood, complete, minor paper loss otherwise VG (2 edges of lid missing), A, $450.00.

Pulling the Splinter, Stoughton Stud/Tiz-A-Teeze, 1930s, artist Emma King, plywood, 150 pcs, 10x8", EX (orig box), A4 ....$22.00

Recital, Joseph Straus, 1940-50, artist Sonoretti, plywood, 300 interlocking pcs (1 rpl), 12x16", EX (orig box), A4 ..$25.00

Return of the Bearwolf, Ceaco/Bialosky, 1988, cb, 60 interlocking pcs, curved strip, 2 sided, 11x15", EX (orig box), A4 .....$3.00

Return of the Soldier, Picture Puzzle Exchange, 1910s, wood, 178 push-to-fit pcs (2 rpl), 14½x9", EX (orig box), A4 ......$35.00

Riders Going on Hunt, Playtime House/Fine Arts, ca 1950, cb, 1,000 pcs (2 rpl), 27x21", EX (orig box), A4.............$10.00

Road at Louveciennes, C Pierson King, ca 1970, artist Sisley, 640 interlocking pcs (1 rpl), 23x15", EX (EX box), A4 ....$75.00

Rounding the Light Ship, Roland Chesley, 1971, artist Currier & Ives, plywood, 208 pcs, 13½x8½", EX (orig box), A4 ....$25.00

Scene in Venice, Norton/Jimig, 1930s, plywood, 436 interlocking pcs, 16x12", EX (orig box), A4 ....$60.00

Seaman's Joy & Sorrow, a Modern Cubic Game, Weigel/GW Faber, 1850s, 30 paper litho blocks w/3 languages, EX (box), B12 ....$1,350.00

Serie Mini 23001 (town), Conrad Armstrong, 1991, plywood, 108 interlocking pcs, 5½x11", EX (orig box), A4 .....$25.00

Serious Case, 1930s, artist Norman Rockwell, plywood, 360 interlocking pcs, 12x16", EX (rpl box), A4...............$60.00

Stay at Homes, Harter Pub/Jiggety Jig, 1933, artist Norman Rockwell, cb, 200 interlocking pcs, 11x15", EX (orig box), A4 ....$8.00

Thoroughbreds, Grinnell/Superior, ca 1909, plywood, 264 push-to-fit pcs, 15x10", EX (rpl box), A4 ....$50.00

Three O'Clock in the Morning, Perfect, ca 1950, cb, 375 interlocking pcs, 15½x19½", EX (orig box), A4 ....$8.00

United States, Parker Bros, ca 1915, pressboard, 32 edge-interlocking pcs, 20x12", EX (rpl box), A4...............$12.00

Vaches a L'Abrecvoir, Parker Bros/Pastime, 1910s, plywood, 400 semi-interlocking pcs (2 rpl), 19x15", EX (orig box), A4 ....$110.00

View of Harpers Ferry, Ronald Chesley, 1973, artist Currier & Ives, 231 interlocking pcs, 13x8½", EX (orig box), A4 ....$30.00

Village of Burbage, Leicestershire, England, Russell, 1977, plywood, 400 interlocking pcs, 13x10½", EX (orig box), A4 ....$55.00

Walk, Germany, 1850s, 30 picture blocks, paper litho on wood, 6 patterns w/5 separate picture sheets, EX (wood box), B12 ....$750.00

Washington at Mt Vernon, Jig of Week, 1932-33, cb, 300 push-to-fit pcs, semi-interlocking, 13x10", EX (orig box), A4 ....$5.00

White Squadron Picture Puzzles, McLoughlin Bros., 1892, shows US Cruiser New York, 10x13", EX (EX wood box), A, $525.00.

Windmill in Upminster, England, Charles Russell, 1976, plywood, 357 interlocking pcs, 13x11", EX (orig box), A4 ....$55.00

Yorkshire Cathedral, Charles Russell, 1977, artist photo, plywood, 406 interlocking pcs, 10½x13", EX (orig box), A4 ....$55.00

Yosemite Valley, Joseph Straus, 1930s, artist A Bierstadt, plywood, 175 interlocking pcs, 12x9", EX (orig box), A4 ....$15.00

Young Ship Builder's Picture Blocks, McLoughlin Bros, 1892, pictures ships, 12 blocks, 9x11", EX (EX wooden box), A $385.00

1948 Lincoln Continental/1940 Ford Station Wagon, fr-tray, American Pub, 1968, cb, 16 interlocking pcs, 5x7", EX, A4 ....$12.00

Character

American Bandstand #2, jigsaw, 400 pcs, MIB (sealed), J7 .... **$12.00**

Atom Ant, jigsaw, Whitman, 14x18", NMIB, F8 .... **$25.00**

Banana Splits, jigsaw, Whitman, 1970, 14x18", NM (EX box), F8 .... **$34.00**

Barney Google & Snuffy Smith, fr-tray, Jaymar, 1940s-50s, NM, C1 .... **$36.00**

Barney Google & Snuffy Smith, jigsaw, Jaymar, 1963, EX+ (EX+ box), T2 .... **$15.00**

Bat Masterson, jigsaw, Colorforms, 1960s, set of 2, NMIB, J5 .... **$35.00**

Batman, fr-tray, Western Pub/Whitman, 1979, cb, comic scene, 11 pcs, 8¼x11", EX, A4 .... **$4.00**

Beany & Cecil, fr-tray, Playskool, 1961, thick wood, Cecil in ocean, 11x13", EX+, F8 .... **$25.00**

Beatles, Meanies Invade Pepperland, jigsaw, 650+ pcs, VG+, B3 .... **$150.00**

Beatles, Yellow Submarine Blue Meanies Attack, jigsaw, 650+ pcs, VG+, B3 .... **$150.00**

Beatles in Pepperland, jigsaw, 100 pcs, MIB (sealed), B3...**$190.00**

Beatles in the Yellow Sub, jigsaw, 100 pcs, NM (VG box), B3 .... **$110.00**

Beatles Sgt Pepper Band, jigsaw, 100 pcs, MIB (sealed), B3 .... **$190.00**

Beverly Hillbillies, jigsaw, Lamar, 1963, group posing for family portrait, M (EX box), C1 .... **$27.00**

Black Hole, fr-tray, Whitman, 1979, astronaut & Maximillian, NM, D9 .... **$4.00**

Bonanza, jigsaw, Milton Bradley, On the Trail, 100 pcs, NM (EX+ box), T2 .... **$30.00**

Broken Arrow, fr-tray, Cochise & others in horse-drawn wagon, EX, M16 .... **$20.00**

Broken Arrow, jigsaw, Built-Rite, 1958, NMIB, F8 .... **$25.00**

Brownie Scroll Puzzle, 1891, litho paper-on-wood pcs forming 2 puzzles, 13x11", 3 pcs missing, G, A **$175.00**

Brownies & Cubbies, jigsaw, Jaymar, 1962, NM (EX+ box), T2 .... **$20.00**

Bullwinkle, jigsaw, Western Pub/Whitman, 1976, cb, 100 interlocking pcs, 14x18", EX (orig box), A4 .... **$3.00**

Capt America, fr-tray, Illco Toy/Marvel Super Hero, 1985, veneer, 11 pcs w/magnet tray, 7x11", EX (orig box), A4 .... **$3.00**

Capt Kangaroo, Mr Green Jeans & Teddy, jigsaw, Fairchild, 1971, M (NM box), C1 .... **$25.00**

Capt Marvel, jigsaw, L Miller & Son/Fawcett, over 200 pcs, complete, NM (EX box), A **$125.00**

Cheyenne, jigsaw, Milton Bradley, 1957, set of 3, 1 minor edge pc missing o/w NMIB, F8 .... **$48.00**

Cisco Kid, fr-tray, Doubleday, Cisco w/horse, 10x12", VG+, J5 .... **$25.00**

Cisco Kid, fr-tray, Saalfield, 1951, EX, F8 .... **$25.00**

Combat, fr-tray, Jaymar, 1950s, 11x14", EX+, T2 .... **$12.00**

Creature From the Black Lagoon, jigsaw, Golden, 1990, 200 pcs, MIB, B10 .... **$6.00**

Daktari, jigsaw, Whitman, 1967, 100 pcs, EX+ (rpr box), T2 .... **$12.00**

Davy Crockett, fr-tray, Disney, 1950s, cartoon graphics, 11x14", VG **$20.00**

Davy Crockett, fr-tray, fighting Indian, NM **$20.00**

Davy Crockett, Indian Attack, jigsaw, Jaymar, complete, EX+ (VG+ box), $30.00.

Deputy Dawg, jigsaw, Fairchild, 1977, M (NM box), C17..**$12.00**

Deputy Dawg, jigsaw, Milton Bradley, 1960, set of 4, NM (EX box), F8 .... **$40.00**

Dick Tracy, jigsaw, Jaymar, Dick Tracy at office party w/Crime Does Not Pay on wall, complete, EX+ (EX box), K4.**$40.00**

Dick Tracy & Manhunt for Mumbles, jigsaw, Jaymar, 1950s-60s, NM+ (EX box), C1 .... **$65.00**

Dr Dolittle, fr-tray, Whitman #4568, 1967, Dr testing horse's eye, NM **$12.00**

Dudley Do-Right, jigsaw, Whitman, 1975, Dudley takes Snydley's clothes, 100 pcs, M (EX sealed box) **$15.00**

Duel in the Sun, jigsaw, 1946, scene from movie, EX (damaged box), M16 .... **$35.00**

Farrah Fawcett, jigsaw, 1977, 405 pcs, wearing swimsuit, NM+ (EX photo box), C1 .... **$32.00**

Flintstones, fr-tray, Whitman, 1963, Pebbles on stuffed Dino toy, 11x14", EX+ **$20.00**

Flipper, jigsaw, Whitman, 1967, EX+ **$15.00**

Frankenstein, jigsaw, Golden, 1990, 200 pcs, MIB, B10 .....**$6.00**

Frankenstein, jigsaw, Jaymar, 1963, 60 pcs, NM (rpr box), T2 .... **$40.00**

Frankenstein Jr, jigsaw, MIB, H4 .... **$20.00**

Frankenstein's Revenge, jigsaw, Jaymar/Universal, 1963, complete, NM (VG box), K4 .... **$65.00**

Gumby, fr-tray, Whitman, 1968, 11x14", EX+, T2 .... **$15.00**

Gunsmoke, jigsaw, Jr Jigsaw, NM, D8 .... **$35.00**

Hair Bear Bunch, jigsaw, Western Pub/Whitman, 1974, 100 pcs, EX (orig box), A4 .... **$3.00**

Hair Bear Bunch, jigsaw, Whitman, 1972, Birthday for Hair Bear in cave, EX+ **$5.00**

Herman & Katnip, fr-tray, Warren, 1978, Katnip w/Herman in ice-cream cone, EX+, D9 .... **$4.00**

Hopalong Cassidy, jigsaw, Milton Bradley, complete w/3 film puzzles, NM (EX box), A **$125.00**

How the West Was Won, jigsaw, HG Toys, 1978, MIB (sealed)......$18.00

Howdy Doody, fr-tray, Whitman, 1950s, Howdy skiing w/Clarabell, 12x9", VG, J5......$35.00

Impossibles, fr-tray, Whitman, 1967, EX, F8......$18.00

James Bond Thunderball, jigsaw, MIB, J2/V1, from $30 to......$38.00

John Wayne, fr-tray, Saalfield #7336, John Wayne on fence w/prairie scene beyond, complete, scarce, EX, A......$45.00

King Leonardo, jigsaw, Jaymar, 1962, The Hunter Is Knighted, EX (VG+ box), T2......$15.00

KISS, jigsaw, APC, 1977, 200 pcs, EX (EX box)......$25.00

Lady & the Tramp, jigsaw, Jaymar, 1955, 11x14", EX, F8..$12.00

Land of the Giants, jigsaw, Whitman, 1969, 125 pcs, 20" dia, EX+ (EX box), F8......$45.00

Lariat Sam, jigsaw, Fairchild, 1977, EX+ (EX+ box), F8..$15.00

Lassie, jigsaw, Whitman, 1971, 100+ pcs, 14x18", NMIB, F8......$12.00

Little Lulu, jigsaw, Whitman, 1950s, EX+ (EX+ box), T2 .$20.00

Little Lulu, jigsaw, Whitman, 1973, set of 4, M (EX box), C1......$68.00

Little Orphan Annie, jigsaw, Famous Comics #1, early 1930s, missing 1 pc, EX (EX box), from $30 to......$35.00

Lone Ranger, jigsaw, Jaymar, 1947, Lone Ranger & Tonto leaving town, complete, EX+ (VG+ box)......$65.00

Lone Ranger, jigsaw, Parker Bros, 1938, set of 4, 1 pc missing, EX+ (EX+ box), F8......$140.00

Lone Ranger and Tonto, American Publishing Corp., 1970s, sealed in container, $15.00.

Love Bug, fr-tray, M (sealed), J6......$18.00

Major Matt Mason, jigsaw, Whitman, 1969, 125 pcs, NM (EX+ box)......$20.00

Man From UNCLE, jigsaw, Milton Bradley, 1965, Micro-Film Affair, 600+ pcs, NM (EX+ box), F8......$48.00

Marlin Perkins Wild Kingdom, jigsaw, 1971, MIB (sealed), J7......$20.00

Mary Poppins, fr-tray, Whitman, 1964, Mary w/Bambi characters, EX+......$15.00

Maverick, jigsaw, Jr Jigsaw, EX+, D8......$35.00

Mickey Mouse, jigsaw, Jaymar, 1940s, 300 pcs, EX (EX box), T2......$40.00

Mickey Mouse Club, fr-tray, Jaymar, 1950s, EX, T2......$10.00

Milton the Monster, fr-tray, 1966, NM, J2......$25.00

Milton the Monster, jigsaw, Whitman, 1967, NMIB, C1.$45.00

Mister Bug, fr-tray, Milton Bradley, 1955, EX, F8......$16.00

Monkees, jigsaw, Fairchild, 1967, Speed Boat, NMIB, F8/V1, frp, $35 to......$40.00

Mother Goose Comic Picture Puzzles, Parker Bros., 1950s, set of 4, MIB, J6, $45.00.

Mountie & a Friendly Visit, jigsaw, 1953, VG+, M16......$23.00

Munsters, jigsaw, Whitman, 1965, family in car or Lily playing organ, (EX box), H4, ea......$45.00

Oliver, jigsaw, Jaymar, 1968, 100 pcs, NM (EX+ box), T2..$25.00

Pinky Lee, fr-tray, Gabriel, 1955, set of 3, NMIB, C1......$55.00

Pinocchio, fr-tray, Whitman, 1973, 8x11", M (sealed), J6...$18.00

Popeye, jigsaw, Jaymar #82-8670, late 1950s-early '60s, Rough Waters, NMIB, C1......$24.00

Popeye, jigsaw, 1942, Sunday comic pg scene, 9x14", EX+, A3......$75.00

Raggedy Ann & Andy, fr-tray, Milton Bradley, 1955, EX+, F8......$18.00

Rin-Tin-Tin, jigsaw, Gabriel, 1956, set of 3, 9x11" ea, NMIB, F8......$70.00

Road Runner, jigsaw, Whitman, 1972, MIB (sealed), J7..$30.00

Robin Hood's Merry Men, jigsaw, Built-Rite, 1956, NMIB, F8......$20.00

Rocketeer, Golden Book #5151, 1991, 300 pcs, MIB, H10..$25.00

Rocketeer Movie Poster Puzzle, jigsaw, Golden & Golden, 1991, 300 pcs, MIB......$8.00

Rocky & Bullwinkle, fr-tray, Whitman, 1960, they pose as 2 Martians take photo, EX, H4......$25.00

Roger Ramjet, fr-tray, 1966, 18", EX, B10/H4, from $20 to ..$30.00

Rookies, jigsaw, 1975, EX (orig canister), C17......$10.00

Roy Rogers, fr-tray, Roy about to mount Trigger, 11x14", EX......$30.00

Roy Rogers, jigsaw, Frontiers, 1956, Roy between rocks w/gun drawn, 5x4", VG, M16......$25.00

Santa Claus, fr-tray, Whitman, 1966, 11x14", EX+, T2...$10.00

Shotgun Slade, jigsaw, Milton Bradley, 1960, 100 pcs, 10x18", NMIB, F8......$30.00

Simpson Family, jigsaw, Milton Bradley, 250 pcs, MIB......$3.00

Six Million Dollar Man, jigsaw, APC, 1975, Steve throwing oil drum at crooks, NM (EX+ can)......$15.00

Sky Hawks, fr-tray, Whitman, 1970, EX+......$8.00

Smokey Bear, fr-tray, Whitman, 1969, EX+ $15.00
Space Kidettes, jigsaw, Whitman, 1968, complete (VG box), H4 ....$18.00

Superman, jigsaw, Saalfield, 1940, set of 3, MIB, A, $330.00.

Superman, jigsaw, Whitman, 1965, 150 pcs, EX+, F8 ......$25.00
Superman, jigsaw, 1979, w/Christopher Reeve, NMIB.....$10.00
Tarzan, King of the Jungle, jigsaw, Movie Cut-Ups, 1930s, missing 3 pcs, EX (EX box), A3 ....$85.00
Tennessee Tuxedo, jigsaw, Fairchild, 1971, 100 pcs, MIB (sealed), J5 ....$25.00
The Deputy, jigsaw, Milton Bradley, 1960, set of 3, NMIB, F8 ....$75.00
Three Little Pigs, picture blocks, McLoughlin Bros, set of 9, 7½x7½", VG, A $55.00
Three Stooges, Hold Your Fire, jigsaw, Colorforms, complete, scarce, EX (VG box), A $460.00
Tom Mix & His New Horse Tony Jr in Universal Pictures, jigsaw, ca 1932, missing 3 pcs, VG+, M16.....................$45.00

Uncle Wiggily Picture Puzzles, jigsaw, Milton Bradley, 1900, set of 3, NM (EX box), A, $200.00.

Underdog, jigsaw, Whitman, 1973, steps on body of Simon & brings flowers to Sweet Polly, NM (EX+ box), F8.....$15.00
Weird-Ohs Daddy, The Swingin' Suburbanite, fr-tray, Fairchild, 1963, sm areas of missing paper o/w EX, D9 ....$25.00

Welcome Back Kotter, fr-tray, Whitman, 1977, EX+, D9 ..$3.00
Welcome Back Kotter, fr-tray, Whitman, 1977, MIP (sealed), V1 ....$12.50
Will Rogers, jigsaw, 1933, State Fair, EX (EX box), M16.$28.00
Wolfman, APC, 1974, EX (orig canister), H4 ....$20.00
Woody Woodpecker, jigsaw, Gaston, 1950s, 6 6-pc character sets mix to make combinations, missing 3 pcs, EX (EX box), F8 ....$30.00
Wyatt Earp, fr-tray, Whitman, 1958, Hugh O-Brien mc photo, NM, C1 ....$55.00
Zorro, jigsaw, Garcia & Diego, MIB, D8 ....$55.00

Radios, Novelty

Many novelty radios are made to resemble a commercial product box or can, and with the crossover interest into the advertising field, some of the more collectible, even though of recent vintage, are often seen carrying very respectible price tags. Some are likenesses of famous personalities such as Elvis or characters like Charlie Tuna house transistors in cases made of plastic that scarcely hint at their actual function. Others represent items ranging from baseball caps to Cadillacs. To learn more about this subject, we recommend *Collector's Guide to Tranistor Radios* by Sue and Marty Bunis and *Collecting Transistor Novelty Radios, A Value Guide* by Marty Bunis and Robert Breed.

Advisors: Sue and Marty Bunis (B11).

AMF Bowling Pin, NM, P12 ....$85.00
Avon Skin-So-Soft Bottle, NMIB, J2 ....$35.00
Big Bird, 2-dimensional figure, NM, T1 ....$15.00
Blabber Puppy, M, T1 ....$20.00
Bugs Bunny w/Carrot, working, EX, J7............................$25.00
Campbell's Cup of Soup Mix Box, M...............................$35.00
Campbell's Tomato Soup Can, NM, from $35 to $50.00
Camus Grand Cognac Bottle, AM, MIB, P12 ....$55.00
Champion Spark Plug, 14", M.......................................$100.00
Charlie McCarthy, Majestic, T1 ....$950.00

Coca-Cola Vending Machine, China, 1989, MIB, J6, $65.00.

Coca-Cola Bottle, MIB (sealed), J2 ....$45.00

Donny & Marie Osmond, LJN, 1977, bl plastic w/photo, name & AM Solid State, battery-op, working, EX, I2.........$35.00

F-1 Racer, MIB, T1 ....$25.00

Fred Flintstone, 1972, MIB..................................$75.00

Fudgie Wudgie, 1970s, chocolate ice cream bar, MIB $75.00

Gramophone, NMIB, J2.......................................$30.00

Gumby, Lewco, 1970s, NM..................................$150.00

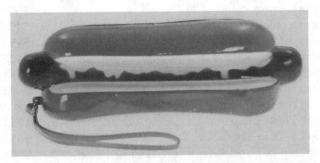

Hamburger and Hot Dog, Hong Kong, plastic, $65.00. each.

Hamburger Helper Helping Hand, EX, T1 ....$30.00

Heinz Ketchup Bottle, NM...................................$50.00

Hershey Syrup Bottle, MIB...................................$75.00

Hockey Puck, Flyer, MIB.....................................$40.00

Huckleberry Hound, Hanna-Barbera, 1972, transister, MIB, M17...$120.00

Joe Cool Wet Tunes, China, 1992, MIB, H11 ....$30.00

Jukebox, sm, MIB, T1 ....$25.00

KISS (rock group), transistor, M, from $50 to $60.00

Lemon, MIB, T1 ....$15.00

Lil' Sprout, M, P12..$50.00

Luv Me Bear, plush, NM, T1.................................$10.00

Male Chauvinist Pig, M, P12.................................$60.00

McDonald's Coast to Coast 1955-1985, can shape, EX, I2 ..$25.00

McDonald's French Fries, 1977, no battery cover, working, EX..$50.00

Mickey Mouse, Emerson tube radio, simulated wood w/emb images of Mickey playing different instruments, 8", VG...$2,000.00

Mork From Ork Eggship, 1978, working, EX+, N2...........$50.00

Mr Tom Candy Bar, British, M, P12 ....$85.00

Muralo Spackle Can, M, P12.................................$45.00

Nestle Nesquick, British, M, P12 ....$60.00

Oscar the Grouch, portable AM, Oscar in trash can, M (EX box), J6...$42.00

Pettable Sad Puppy, MIB, T1 ....$25.00

Planters Cocktail Nuts Can, MIB.............................$55.00

Polaroid 600 Filmpack, MIB, S15............................$25.00

Pound Puppy, unused, MIB, T1...............................$15.00

Racoon, plush, EX+, T1......................................$20.00

Raggedy Ann & Andy, EX+, T1 ....$22.50

Raid Bug, clock radio, M, P12..............................$225.00

Shell Super X-Motor Oil Can, NM, J2........................$45.00

Shell Super-X Motor Oil Can, MIB, P12......................$55.00

Sinclair Dino Gasoline, #1623, AM, red, $20.00.

Skittles, circular, M, P12 ....$75.00

Smurf Head, no battery cover, T1 ....$6.00

Snoopy, Determined #351, sitting on strap, blk & wht, EX, H11...$20.00

Snoopy, Radio Shack, sitting, plush, AM, 9", working, VG, H11...$15.00

Snoopy, Woodstock & Charlie Brown, Radio Concept 2000-4443, w/strap, 7", EX, H11 ....$25.00

Snoopy on Doghouse, Determined #354, 1970s, 7", EX ...$40.00

Snoopy's Hi Fi AM Radio, orange w/Snoopy earphones, EX ..$40.00

Spice Rack, EX, J2..$40.00

Starroid IM1 Star Command Leader Robot, 1977, EX, I2..$35.00

Starsky & Hutch Car, CB radio, w/booklet, MIB $50.00

Stereo Console, Panasonic, 1950, EX........................$25.00

Sunoco Gas Pump, yel & bl, 4", EX $25.00

Toot-A-Loop, Panasonic, yel, EX............................$15.00

Turtle, gold-tone metal, working, EX.........................$65.00

Welch's Grape Juice Can, M $50.00

Ramp Walkers

Ramp walkers date back to at least 1873 when Ives produced two versions of a cast-iron elephant walker. Wood and composition ramp walkers were made in Czechoslovakia and the U.S.A. from the 1930s through the 1950s. The most common were made by John Wilson of Pennsylvania and were sold worldwide. These became known as 'Wilson Walkies.' Most are two-legged and stand approximately 4½" tall. While some of the Wilson walkers were made of a composite material with wooden legs (for instance, Donald, Wimpy, Popeye and Olive Oyl), most were made with cardboard thread-cone bodies with wooden legs and head. The walkers made in Czechoslovakia were similar but they were generally made of wood.

Plastic ramp walkers were primarily manufactured by the Louis Marx Co. and were made from the early 1950s through the mid-1960s. The majority were produced in Hong Kong, but some were made in the United States and sold under the Marx logo or by the Charmore Co., which was a subsidiary of the Marx Co. Some walkers are still being produced today as fast-food premiums.

The three common sizes are: (1) small, about about 1½" x 2"; (2) medium, about 2¾" x 3"; and (3) large, about 4" x 5". Most of the small walkers are unpainted while the medium or large sizes were either spray painted or painted by hand. Several of the walking toys were sold with wooden plastic or colorful lithographed tin ramps.

Advisor: Randy Welch (W4).

Advertising

Captain Flint, Long John Silvers, 1989, w/plastic coin weight...$15.00
Choo-Choo Cherry, Funny Face Kool-Aid, w/plastic coin weight..$60.00
Flash Turtle, Long John Silvers, 1989, w/plastic coin weight ..$15.00
Goofy Grape, Funny Face Kool-Aid, w/plastic coin weight ..$60.00
Jolly Ollie Orange, Funny Face Kool-Aid, w/plastic coin weight..$60.00
Quinn Penguin, Long John Silvers, 1989, blk & wht, w/plastic coin weight $15.00
Root'n Toot'n Raspberry, Funny Face Kool-Aid, w/plastic coin weight..$60.00
Sydney Dinosaur, Long John Silvers, 1989, yel & purple, w/plastic coin weight $15.00
Sylvia Dinosaur, Long John Silvers, 1989, lavender & pk, w/plastic coin weight $15.00

Hanna-Barbera, King Features and Other Characters by Marx

Fred and Barney, $40.00.

Astro, Hanna-Barbera $150.00
Astro & George Jetson, Hanna-Barbera..........................$90.00
Astro & Rosey, Hanna-Barbera...................................$95.00
Chilly Willy, penguin on sled pulled by parent, Walter Lantz..$25.00
Fred & Wilma Flintstone on Dino, Hanna-Barbera $60.00
Fred Flintstone on Dino, Hanna-Barbera......................$70.00
Hap & Hop Soldiers $20.00
Little King & Guard, King Features $70.00
Pebbles on Dino, Hanna-Barbera $70.00
Popeye, Erwin, celluloid, lg.....................................$60.00
Popeye, pushing spinach can wheelbarrow, King Features..$40.00
Santa, w/open gold sack..$45.00
Santa, w/wht sack $40.00
Santa, w/yel sack $35.00
Santa & Mrs Claus, faces on both sides.........................$40.00
Santa & Snowman, faces on both sides.........................$40.00
Spark Plug..$175.00
Top Cat & Benny $65.00
Yogi Bear & Huckleberry Hound, Hanna-Barbera $50.00

Czechoslovakian

Dog $20.00
Man w/Carved Wood Hat $25.00
Monkey $30.00
Pig $20.00
Policeman...$40.00

Disney Characters by Marx

Big Bad Wolf & Mason Pig..$40.00
Big Bad Wolf & 3 Little Pigs $125.00
Donald Duck, pulling nephews in wagon.......................$35.00
Donald Duck, pushing wheelbarrow, all plastic $25.00
Donald Duck, pushing wheelbarrow, plastic w/metal legs, sm $30.00
Donald Duck & Goofy, riding go-cart............................$40.00

Mickey and Minnie Carrying Basket of Food, $40.00.

Fiddler & Fifer Pigs $40.00
Figaro the Cat, w/ball..$30.00
Goofy, riding hippo...$45.00
Jiminy Cricket, w/cello..$30.00
Mad Hatter & March Hare.......................................$50.00
Mickey Mouse, pushing lawn roller $35.00
Mickey Mouse & Donald Duck, riding alligator $40.00
Mickey Mouse & Minnie, plastic w/metal legs, sm..........$40.00
Mickey Mouse & Pluto, hunting $40.00
Minnie Mouse, pushing baby stroller $35.00
Pluto, all plastic..$20.00
Pluto, plastic w/metal legs, sm...............................$30.00

Marx Animals With Riders Series

Ankylosaurus w/Clown $25.00
Bison w/Native...$25.00
Brontosaurus w/Monkey $25.00
Hippo w/Native..$25.00
Lion w/Clown $25.00
Stegosaurus w/Black Caveman $25.00
Triceratops w/Native $25.00
Zebra w/Native...$25.00

Plastic

Baby Walk-A-Way, lg..$40.00
Cow, w/metal legs, sm...$15.00
Cowboy on horse, w/metal legs, sm $20.00
Dog, plastic Pluto look-alike w/metal legs, sm $15.00
Double Walking Doll, boy behind girl, lg $45.00
Elephant, w/metal legs, sm......................................$20.00
Horse, lg $30.00
Horse, yel w/rubber ears & string tail, lg $30.00
Horse w/English rider, lg...$40.00
Mexican Cowboy on Horse, w/metal legs, sm $20.00
Milking Cow, lg $40.00
Popeye & Wimpy, heads on springs, lg $65.00
Teeny Toddler, walking baby girl, Dolls Inc, lg $40.00
Walking Baby, in Canadian Mountie uniform, lg............$50.00
Walking Baby, w/moving eyes & cloth dress, lg.............$40.00
Wiz Walker Milking Cow, Charmore, lg $40.00

Wilson

Black Mammy $35.00
Donald Duck..$175.00
Eskimo $75.00
Indian Chief $45.00
Nurse $30.00
Olive Oyl $175.00
Penguin $25.00
Pinocchio..$175.00
Popeye $175.00
Rabbit $40.00
Sailor $30.00
Santa Claus $60.00
Soldier $25.00

Little Red Riding Hood, $40.00; Clown, $30.00; Nurse, $30.00.

Wimpy $175.00

Miscellaneous

Baseball Player w/Bat & Ball $40.00
Bear $15.00
Boy & Girl Dancing...$40.00
Bull $15.00
Bunnies Carrying Carrot...$30.00
Bunny Pushing Cart...$45.00
Camel w/2 Humps, head bobs..................................$20.00
Chicks Carrying Easter Egg.....................................$30.00
Chinese Men w/Duck in Basket $30.00
Chipmunks Carrying Acorns....................................$30.00
Chipmunks Marching Band w/Drum & Horn $30.00
Dachshund $15.00
Dairy Cow $15.00
Duck $15.00
Dutch Boy & Girl $30.00
Elephant...$20.00
Farmer Pushing Wheelbarrow $20.00

Firemen,
$30.00.

Frontiersman w/Dog....................................$95.00

Goat $20.00
Horse, circus style $15.00
Indian Woman Pulling Baby on Travois.........................$95.00
Kangaroo w/Baby in Pouch....................................$25.00
Mama Duck w/3 Ducklings......................................$25.00
Marty's Market Lady Pushing Shopping Cart $40.00
Monkeys Carrying Bananas $50.00
Nursemaid Pushing Baby Stroller $15.00
Pig $15.00
Pigs, 2 carrying pig in basket............................$40.00
Pumpkin Head Man & Woman, faces both sides $45.00
Reindeer..$35.00
Sailors SS Shoreleave $20.00
Sheriff Facing Outlaw $65.00
Tin Man Robot Pushing Cart................................$125.00

Records

Most of the records listed here are related to TV shows and movies, and all are specifically geared toward children. The more successful the show, the more collectible the record. But condition is critical as well, and unless the record is excellent or better, its value is lowered very dramatically.

Advisor: Peter Muldavin (M21).

33⅓ rpm Records

Addams Family, 1965, soundtrack w/12 songs, EX+ (EX+ sleeve), F8 ....$45.00
Alice in Wonderland & Show-&-Tell Picture Sound Program, 1969, 7", w/booklet, EX, J7.............................$8.00
Alvin & the Chipmunks Sing the Beatles, 1964, EX (EX sleeve), F8 ....$15.00
Amazing Spiderman, Peter Pan, 1974, w/comic book, EX, H4.$5.00
Amazing Spiderman #1, Marvel Comics/Golden Records, 1966, EX (EX sleeve), A3.................................$50.00
Batman & the Catwoman's Revenge, Power, 1975, 7", MIP (sealed), C1...$25.00
Beneath the Planet of the Apes, 1974, 7", w/booklet, EX, J7 .$15.00
Blackbeard's Ghost, Disney, 1967, movie soundtrack, EX (EX sleeve), J7...$10.00
Bob Dylan Song Book, Epic #BN26158, 1960s, NM (EX sleeve), J5 ....$45.00
Bonanza, Welcome to the Ponderosa, 1964, NM (photo sleeve), from $35 to...$50.00
Car 54, Allison, 1961, EX (illus 6x6" sleeve), M17 ....$40.00
Cinderella, Disney, 1965, movie soundtrack, EX (EX sleeve), J7 ....$10.00
Dark Shadows, NM, J6 ....$24.00
Dark Shadows, w/orig poster, NM, H4......................$45.00
Dick Tracy Original Radio Broadcast Case of Firebug Murders, mc illus sleeve, D11 ....$70.00
Flash Gordon Interplanetary Adventurers, Golden Age, 1977, orig radio broadcasts, M (M sleeve), A6 ....$15.00
Flintstones Flip Fables, Goldi Rocks & the Three Bearosauruses, #HLP-2021, 1965, M (sealed sleeve), J5 ....$85.00

Gene Autry, Rudolph...& Other Christmas Favorites, Stereo, 1960s, EX+ (EX sleeve), F8 ....$15.00
Hector Heathcote Show TV Soundtrack, 1964, EX+ (EX sleeve), F8 ....$28.00
Jetson's First Family on the Moon, 1977, EX (NM sleeve), J2.$20.00
Jimmy Nelson's Instant Ventriloquism, NM (NM sleeve), J6 ....$20.00
John Travolta, Midland International #BKL1-1563, 1976, promotional copy, NM (NM sleeve), J5.....................$25.00
Kids From the Brady Bunch, Paramount, 1972, VG+ (VG+ sleeve), T2...$6.00
KISS Alive II Album, w/Evolution of KISS booklet, EX+ (EX sleeve), H4..$30.00
Lady & the Tramp, Disney, 1962, EX (EX sleeve), J7 ......$10.00
Lady & the Tramp, Stereo, 1979, EX+, F8....................$8.00
Last Starfighter, Buena Vista, 7", w/24-pg booklet, M (sealed sleeve), D9...$5.00
Laugh-In, Stereo, 1968, EX+ (EX+ 2-part sleeve w/joke wall), F8 ....$20.00
Leonard Nimoy-Two Sides, Dot #DLP-25835, 1960s, NM (NM sleeve w/most orig cellophane), J5 ....$35.00
Lone Ranger Saves the Boonville Gold, Decca #K-77, VG (fair sleeve), S18...$22.00
Mary Poppins, Walt Disney/Buena Vista, 1964, NM (EX+ sleeve), P3...$10.00
Muhammad Ali Fights Mr Tooth Decay, 1976, M (Ali, Frank Sinatra & Howard Cossell photo on sealed sleeve), J5.........$25.00
Muppet Show, Artista, 1977, orig soundtrack, EX (EX sleeve), P3 ....$8.00

Muppets Take Manhattan, 1984, 7", w/booklet, EX, J7......$8.00

Pepe Orig Soundtrack, Colpix, 1960, EX+ (EX+ folding sleeve), T2 ....$12.00

Pete's Dragon, Disney, 1977, movie soundtrack, EX (EX sleeve), J7 ....$15.00

Pete's Dragon, Walt Disney/Capitol, 1977, NM (NM sleeve), P3 ....$8.00

Pixie & Dixie w/Mr Jinks & Story of Cinderella, #HLP-2025, 1965, M (sealed sleeve), J5 ....$85.00

Planet of the Apes & Mountain of Delphi, Power, 1974, 7", M (sealed sleeve), C1 ....$15.00

Popeye's Favorite Stories, 1960, 6 orig stories, NM (EX+ sleeve), F8 ....$20.00

Richie Rich Mysteries of the Deep, Parachute #811-1101-M-3, 1983, M (sealed sleeve), J5 ....$15.00

Shari (Lewis) in Storyland, RCA Victor, 1962, EX (EX folding sleeve w/8 photo pgs), F8 ....$18.00

Six Million Dollar Man Christmas Adventures, 1978, M (sealed sleeve), C1 ....$22.00

Snoopy & the Red Baron, Peter Pan, 1970s, VG (VG sleeve), P3 ....$5.00

Space: 1999, 1976, 7", w/booklet, EX, J7 ....$20.00

Spider-Man, diecut shape, 1960s, NM, D8 ....$35.00

Star Wars Soundtrack, 20th-Century Records, 1977, w/lg Death Star Battle poster, EX (EX sleeve), D9 ....$12.00

Superman: Three New Adventures, Power Records, 1975, M (M sealed sleeve), A6 ....$8.50

Terry & the Pirates, Mark 56 Records, 1973, M (M sealed sleeve), A6 ....$12.50

Tiny Tim Concert in Fairyland, NM (NM sleeve), J6......$25.00

Top Cat & the Story of Robin Hood, #HLP-2031, 1965, M (sealed sleeve), J5 ....$85.00

Touche Turtle & Dum-Dum the Reluctant Dragon, #HLP-2029, 1960s, M (sealed sleeve), J5 ....$85.00

Touche Turtle & the Reluctant Dragon, 1960s, G (VG+ sleeve), F8 ....$8.00

Virginian, Randy Boone & Roberta Shore, Deca #DL-4619, 1960s, M (sealed sleeve), J5 ....$45.00

Visit to Disneyland, 1960s, NM (EX sleeve), F8 ....$15.00

Yertle the Turtle (Dr Seuss), Stereo, 1960, EX (EX sleeve), F8 ....$25.00

Yogi Bear & Boo Boo Tell Stories & Sing, #HLP-2023, 1960s, M (sealed sleeve), J5 ....$85.00

45 rpm Records

Beatles, Yel Submarine, VG+ (VG+ picture sleeve), B3..$18.00

Bozo's Big Top/Anchor's Away, 1976, w/booklet, EX, J7 ...$6.00

Bugs Bunny in Storyland, Capitol #CBX3022, 1949, set of 2 w/mc 20+-pg booklet, EX (EX sleeve), J5 ....$25.00

Casey Jones/John Henry, 1959, EX (EX+ sleeve), F8 ....$7.00

CHiPs, 1979, EX (EX photo sleeve), J7 ....$20.00

Dr Who, TV series theme, NM, J6................................$20.00

Felix the Cat/The Cat's March, Cricket, 1958, EX (EX sleeve), F8 ....$12.00

Flash/Aquaman, 1975, M (sealed sleeve), J7 ....$10.00

Flying Nun, 1967, EX (EX sleeve), J7 ....$25.00

Frosty the Snowman, 1951, EX (EX sleeve), J7 ....$12.00

Gunsmoke, RCA Victor, 1960s, EX (EX sleeve), F8 ....$12.00

Heidi, Disney, 1972, extended play, 4 songs, EX, J7 ....$5.00

Here Come the Dukes of Hazzard, M (sealed illus sleeve), J7.$20.00

Howdy Doody Laughing Circus, RCA Victor #WY-414, 1950s, set of 2 w/4-pg booklet, EX (EX sleeve), J5 ....$45.00

Journey to the Center of the Earth, 1950s, NM (NM sleeve), V1 ....$14.00

Laurel & Hardy, Golden, 1963, theme to cartoon show, EX+ (EX sleeve), F8 ....$12.00

Loopy De Loop, Golden, 1960, NM (NM sleeve), F8 ......$15.00

Mary Poppins, 1960s, EX (EX sleeve w/Julie Andrews photo), J7 ....$7.00

Mickey Mouse Club March, 1955, VG+ (EX+ sleeve), F8 ..$12.00

Mighty Mouse in Toyland, Peter Pan, 1962, VG (EX+ sleeve), F8 ....$7.00

Partridge Family's Danny Sings Dreamland, 1972, EX+ (EX sleeve), F8 ....$15.00

Peter Pan, Disney, 1972, extended play, 4 songs, EX, J7.....$7.00

Pinocchio, 1961, EX (EX illus sleeve), J7................................$12.00

Quick Draw McGraw As El Kabong/Ooch, Ooch, Ouch!, Golden #593, 1960, VG (EX picture sleeve), J5 ....$25.00

Roy Rogers, Thank You God, EX+, D8................................$22.00

Superman Song/Tarzan Song, Golden #723, 1960s, NM (VG picture sleeve), J5 ....$25.00

Tex Ritter's Sunday School Songs, Capitol, 1960s, 2 record set w/6 songs, EX+ (EX+ sleeves), F8 ....$18.00

Woody Woodpecker March/Andy Panda Polka, Golden, 1962, EX+ (EX+ sleeve), F8 ....$12.00

78 rpm Picture and Non-Picture Records

Astro Boy/Cosmic Rangers, Golden #R776A, yel, EX (plain sleeve), I2 ....$6.00

Bugs Bunny, Rabbit Seasoning, Capitol, 1953, EX+ (EX+ sleeve), F8 ....$15.00

Captain Kangaroo, When a Bunny Wants a Carrot/Treasure House on Parade, 1962, EX (EX sleeve), C1.............$22.00

Howdy Doody and the Air-O-Doodle, RCA Victor, Little Nipper Series Y-397, 1949, EX+ (EX+ sleeve), from $45.00 to $50.00.

Carrot Seed Children's Record, Children's Record Guild, early 1950s, 10" dia, EX (EX sleeve), from $10 to $15.00

Davy Crockett, Indian Fighter, Columbia #C-516, set of 2, NM (EX Fess Parker & Buddy Ebsen photo sleeve), J5.....$45.00

Deputy Dawg, 1962, EX (mc illus paper sleeve), C1.........$22.00

Flash Gordon, City of Sea Caves, Record Guild of Am, 1949, picture disk, EX, from $45 to......................................$55.00

Flipper, Golden, 1960s, EX+ (EX sleeve), F8...................$12.00

Gene Autry's Rudolph the Red-Nosed Reindeer, Columbia, EX (EX sleeve), from $10 to..$15.00

I Saw Mommy Kissing Santa Claus, Peter Pan, 7", VG (VG sleeve), P3...$3.00

John Slaughter, Golden, 1958, theme from Disney show, EX+ (EX+ sleeve), F8 ....$15.00

Laurel & Hardy Chiller Diller Thriller, 1963, EX+ (NM sleeve mk 29¢), C1..$32.00

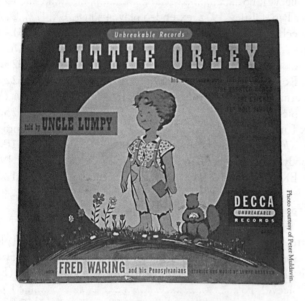

Little Orley Told by Uncle Lumpy, Decca, CUS-7, 1948, EX+ (EX+ sleeve), from $12.00 to $15.00.

Lone Ranger Theme, Hi-Yo Silver, Hi-Yo!, Golden #R521, 1958, yel, EX (EX picture sleeve), J5 ....$25.00

Peter & the Wolf, Disney, 1949, w/booklet, EX, J7.........$25.00

Popeye Launches His New Song Hit, Peter Pan, 1958, VG (EX+ sleeve), F8 ....$6.00

Rin-Tin-Tin Songs: A Dog's Best Friend/Cold Nose-Warm Heart, Golden #R370, 1950s, EX (EX sleeve), J5......$15.00

Roy Rogers Calling Cowboy Square Dances, Decca #226, 1950s, set of 3, EX (folding sleeve), P6.............................$55.00

Roy Rogers' Pecos Bill, 1949, set of 3, G (G sleeve).........$25.00

Saga of Andy Burnett, Golden #449/Walt Disney, 1950s, yel, EX (EX picture sleeve), J5...$15.00

Tom Terrific, Golden, 1960, EX+ (NM sleeve), F8..........$30.00

Tweety Bird, I Taut I Taw a Puddy Tat/Yosemite Sam, Capitol, 1950s, EX+ (EX+ 10x10" sleeve), F8 ....$15.00

Walt Disney's Pinocchio, Victor, 1940s, set of 3 w/illus 8-pg booklet, EX+, scarce version, M8..............................$75.00

We're the Mouseketeers, Disney, 1958, VG- (VG sleeve w/Annette photo), J7 ....$15.00

Singing Mother Goose Book, Magic Talking Books, T-1, 1955, EX+ (EX+ cover), from $10.00 to $15.00.

Kiddie Picture Disks

Listed here is a representative sampling of kiddie picture disks that were produced through the 1940s. Most are 6" to 7" in diameter and are made of cardboard with plastic-laminated grooves. They are very colorful and seldom came with original sleeves. Value ranges are for items in very good to near-mint condition. Ultimately, the value of any collectible is what a buyer is willing to pay, and prices tend to fluctuate. Our values are for records only (no sleeves) — note that unlike other records, the value of a picture disk is not diminished if there is no original sleeve.

Advisor: Peter Muldavin (M21).

Boy Who Cried Wolf/When the King Sneezes, Picture Records #11066/10966, 1948, from $10 to $17.00

Buffalo Gals/Waltzing Matilda, Picturetone Records #D 459/460, 78 rpm, from $8 to......................................$15.00

Cinderella, Playola Records #102, 1948, 78 rpm, set of 3 w/folder, from $40 to $50.00

Doggie in the Window/Play Activity, Record Guild of America #C 11, 1948-51, 78 rpm, from $15 to........................$20.00

Elephant Clown/Circus, Voco Records, 1946-49, 78 rpm, diecut shape, from $15 to $20.00

Erie Canal/Frere Jacques, Picturetone Records #S 573/574, 1948, from $7 to..$10.00

Favorite Mother Goose Songs, Magic Talking Books #T1, 1955, 78 rpm, from $15 to $25.00

Flash Gordon: City of Sea Caves, Record Guild of America #F 301, 1948-51, 78 rpm, from $40 to..........................$50.00

Humpty Dumpty, Dupli-Kut/Pix Records #PIX 102, 1941, 78 rpm, 1-sided, from $50 to..$60.00

Jack & Jill, Dupli-Kut/Pix Records #PIX 108, 1941, 78 rpm, 1-sided, from $50 to $60.00

Jesse James/Indians Lament, Playsong #WW 39/40, 1947-49, 78 rpm, from $7 to $12.00

Kiddy Prayer, Voco Records #522/622, 1946-49, 78 rpm, from $18 to $15.00

Me & My Teddy Bear/Teddy Bears' Picnic, Red Raven Movie Records, 78 rpm, 6¾" (picture record), from $25 to ..**$30.00**

Me & My Teddy Bear/Teddy Bears' Picnic, Red Raven Movie Records, 1956, 78 rpm, 8" (picture label), from $15 to ..**$20.00**

Old King Cole/Dickory-Dickory Dock, Playsong #MM 63/64, 1947-49, 78 rpm, from $9 to **$14.00**

Peter Pan/Sleeping Beauty, Record Guild of America #PR-5, 1948-51, 78 rpm, 10", from $60 to **$80.00**

Round the Village/Looby Loo, Record Guild of America #G4014, 1948-51, 78 rpm, from $8 to.......................**$12.00**

Superman, the Magic Ring; Musette, 1947, 78 rpm, set of 2 w/folder, from $80 to **$110.00**

Tales of Peter Rabbit, Magic Talking Books #T10, 78 rpm, from $15 to **$25.00**

The Lion, Talking Book Corp, 1919, 78 rpm, from $30 to **$40.00**

Winnie-The-Pooh Songs, RCA Victor, #221, #222 and #223, 1931-33, 78 rpm, with original folder, very rare, from $300.00 to $400.00.

Your Trip to Disneyland, Rainbow Re-Card, 1955, 78 rpm, 1-sided, set of 5 w/folder, from $70 to **$100.00**

Reynolds Toys

Reynolds Toys began production in 1964, at first making large copies of early tin toys for window displays, though some were sold to collectors as well. These toys included trains, horse-drawn vehicles, boats, a steam toy and several sizes of Toonerville trolleys. In the early 1970s, they designed and produced six animated cap guns. Finding the market limited, by 1971 they had switched to a line of banks they call 'New Original Limited Numbered Editions (10-50) of Mechanical Penny Banks.' Still banks were added to their line in 1980 and figural bottle openers in 1988. Each bank design is original; no reproductions are produced. Reynolds' banks are in the White House and the Smithsonian as well as many of the country's major private collections. *The Penny Bank Book* by Andy and Susan Moore (Schiffer Publishing, 1984) shows and describes the first twelve still banks Reynolds produced. Values are given for mint-condition banks.

Advisor: Charlie Reynolds (R5).

Mechanical Banks

1M, Train Man Bank, 1971, edition of 30 ....$350.00
2M, Trolley Bank, 1971, edition of 30 ....$350.00

3M, Drive-In Bank, 1971, edition of 10..........................$750.00
4M, Pirate Bank, 1972, edition of 10 ....$725.00
5M. Blackbeard Bank, 1972, edition of 10.....................$650.00
6M, Frog & Fly Bank, 1972, edition of 10 ....$1,200.00
7M, Toy Collector Bank, 1972, unlimited edition $550.00
8M, Balancing Bank, 1972, edition of 10........................$725.00
9M, Save the Girl Bank, 1972, edition of 10...............$1,400.00
10M, Father Christmas Bank, 1972, 1 made ea year at Christmas..$750.00
11M, Gump on a Stump Bank, 1973, edition of 10.....$1,100.00
12M, Trick Bank, 1973, edition of 10.........................$1,000.00
13M, Kid Savings Bank, 1973, edition of 10...............$1,200.00
14M, Christmas Tree Bank, 1973, edition of 10.............$725.00
15M, Foxy Grandpa Bank, 1974, edition of 10................$975.00
16M, Happy Hooligan Bank, 1974, edition of 10........$1,075.00
17M, Chester's Fishing Bank, 1974, edition of 10 ....$900.00
18M, Gloomy Gus Bank, 1974, edition of 10...............$1,200.00
19M, Kids Prank Bank, 1974, edition of 10..................$1,100.00
20M, Mary & the Little Lamb, 1974, edition of 20 ....$850.00
21M, Spook Bank, 1974, edition of 10............................$800.00
22M, Decoy Bank, 1974, edition of 10............................$600.00
23M, Decoy Hen Bank, 1974, edition of 10 ....$600.00
24M, Comedy Bank, 1974, edition of 10 ....$975.00
25M, Bozo Bank, 1974, edition of 10 ....$825.00
26M, Reynolds Foundry Bank, 1974, edition of 15 .....$2,000.00
27M, Toonerville Bank, 1974, edition of 10...................$950.00
28M, Bank of Reynolds Toys, 1974, edition of 10..........$425.00
29M, Simple Simon Bank, 1975, edition of 10...............$925.00
30M, Humpty Dumpty Bank, 1975, edition of 20.......$1,250.00
31M, Three Blind Mice Bank, 1975, edition of 15......$1,100.00
32M, Clubhouse Bank, 1975, edition 10 ....$1,100.00
33M, Boat Bank, 1975, edition of 10............................$1,500.00
34M, St Nicholas Bank, 1975, edition of 50...................$775.00
35M, Forging America, 1976, edition of 13.................$1,200.00
36M, Suitcase Bank, 1979, edition of 22 ....$725.00
37M, North Wind Bank, 1980, edition of 23 ....$675.00
40M, Columbia Bank, 1984, edition of 25....................$135.00
41M, Whirligig Bank, 1985, edition of 30 ....$800.00

46M, Hollywood, 1989, edition of 35, $750.00.

42M, Miss Liberty, 1986, edition of 36 ....$950.00
42M, Miss Liberty on a Pedestal, 1986, edition of 4....$1,400.00
43M, Auto Giant Bank, 1987, edition of 30 ....$1,900.00
45M, Campaign '88 Bank, 1988, edition of 50...........$2,600.00
47M, Buffalos Revenge, 1990, edition of 35 ....$900.00
48M, Williamsburg Bank, 1991, edition of 35 ....$725.00
49M, Duel at the Dome Bank, 1992, edition of 50.........$850.00
50M, '92 Voting Bank, 1992, edition of 50 ....$1,800.00
51M, Oregon Trail Bank, 1993, edition of 50...............$800.00
52M, Norway Bank (Lillehammer), 1994, edition of 50..$825.00
53M, Shoe House Bank, 1994, edition of 50 ....$950.00
54M, J&E Stevens Co Bank, 1995, edition of 50........$1,200.00

Still Banks

1S, Amish Man Bank, 1980, edition of 50....................$135.00
2S, Santa, 1980, edition of 50 ....$80.00
3S, Deco Dog, 1981, edition of 50................................$70.00
4S, Jelly Bean King, 1981, edition of 100 ....$250.00
5S, Hag Bank, 1981, edition of 50 ....$125.00
6S, Snowman, 1981, edition of 50.................................$90.00
7S, Mark Twain, 1982, edition of 50 ....$110.00
8S, Santa, 1982, edition of 50 ....$125.00
10S, Redskins Hog Bank, 1983, edition of 50.................$125.00
11S, Lock-up Savings Bank, 1983, edition of 50.............$45.00
12S, Miniature Bank Building, 1983, edition of 50 ....$110.00
13S, Santa in Chimney, 1983, edition of 50 ....$80.00
14S, Santa With Tree (bank & doorstop), 1983, edition of
    25 ....$325.00
15S, Redskins NFC Champs, 1983, edition of 35...........$185.00
16S, Chick Bank, 1984, edition of 50 ....$50.00
17S, Ty-Up Bank, 1984, edition of 35 ....$225.00
18S, Tiniest Elephant Bank, 1984, edition of 50.............$45.00
19S, Baltimore Town Crier, 1984, edition of 50..............$55.00
20S, Father Christmas Comes to America, July 4th, 1984, edi-
    tion of 25 ....$290.00
21S, Campaign '84 Bank, 1984, edition of 100...............$160.00
22S, Santa, 1984, edition of 50 ....$100.00
23S, Reagan '85 Bank, 1985, edition of 100 ....$275.00
24S, Columbus Ohio, 1985, edition of 50.........................$55.00
25S, Austrian Santa (bank & doorstop), 1985, edition of
    25 ....$280.00
26S, Halloween Bank, 1985, edition of 50........................$90.00
27S, 1893 Kriss Kringle Bank (w/tree & candle decorations),
    1985, edition of 20 ....$1,400.00
28S, Santa Coming to a Child, 1985, edition of 50........$165.00
29S, Halley's Comet, 1986, edition of 50.......................$190.00
30S, 20th Anniversary Bank, 1986, edition of 86...........$155.00
31S, Father Christmas (bank & doorstop), gr, 1986, edition of
    25 ....$280.00
32S, Santa & the Reindeer, 1986, edition of 50.............$160.00
33S, Charlie O'Conner Bank, 1987, edition of 50...........$65.00
34S, Chocolate Rabbit Bank, 1987, edition of 50............$85.00
35S, St Louis River Boat, 1987, edition of 60.................$55.00
36S, German Santa (bank & doorstop), 1987, edition of
    25 ....$255.00
38S, Old Stump Halloween, 1987, edition of 50 ....$75.00
39S, Santa in Racecar, 1987, edition of 100 ....$95.00

40S, Technology Education Bank, 1988, edition of 88.....$50.00
41S, Super Bowl XXII Redskins, 1988, edition of 50........$80.00
42S, Easter Rabbit Bank, 1988, edition of 50..................$45.00
43S, Florida Souvenir Bank, 1988, edition of 75 ....$90.00
44S, Father Christmas w/Lantern (bank & doorstop), 1988, edi-
    tion of 35 ....$260.00
45S, Halloween Spook, 1988, edition of 50 ....$70.00
46S, NCRPBC (National Capitol Region Club), 1988, edition
    of 20 ....$300.00
47S, Santa on Polar Bear, 1988, edition of 75 ....$90.00
48S, Bush-Quale, 1989, edition of 100 ....$200.00
49S, Shuffle Off to Buffalo, 1989, edition of 75 ....$65.00

50S, Pocket Pigs, 1989, edition of 75, $125.00.

51S, Regal Santa (bank & doorstop), 1989, edition of 35 ..$250.00
52S, Tiniest Snowman, 1989, edition of 75 ....$50.00
53S, Santa on Motorcycle, 1989, edition of 75................$85.00
54S, Rabbit w/Mammy, 1990, edition of 75....................$125.00
55S, Antique Row Sign Post, 1990, edition of 75............$65.00
56S, Duck w/Puppy & Bee Bank, 1990, edition of 75.......$90.00
57S, 1865 Santa w/Wreath, 1990, edition of 35 ....$250.00
58S, Santa Coming on a Pig, 1990, edition of 75 ....$65.00
59S, St Louis Sally Bank, 1991, edition of 55 ....$60.00
60S, Santa w/Wassail Bowl, 1991, edition of 35............$250.00
61S, Santa Express Bank, 1991, edition of 55................$125.00

64S, Jack-O'-Lantern, 1992, edition of 75, $65.00.

62S, Pig on Sled Bank, 1992, edition of 55 ....$65.00

63S, Santa About To Leave, 1992, edition of 25............$250.00

64S, Jack-O-Lantern Bank, 1992, edition of 75 ....$65.00

65S, Santa in Zeppelin Bank, 1992, edition of 60 ....$85.00

66S, Clinton Bank, 1993, edition of 100 ....$250.00

67S, Windy City Bank (Chicago Convention), 1993, edition of 60 ....$85.00

68S, Santa & the Bad Boy (Summer Santa), 1993, edition of 50 ....$225.00

69S, Arkansas President, 1994, edition of 100................$150.00

70S, Santa & the Good Kids, 1994, edition of 35 ....$200.00

71S, Penny Santa, 1994, edition of 60 ....$75.00

72S, School Days Bank, 1995, edition of 100 ....$75.00

Robots and Space Toys

Space is a genre that anyone who grew up in the sixties can relate to, but whether you're from that generation or not, chances are the fantastic robots, space vehicles and rocket launchers from that era are fascinating to you as well. Some emitted beams of colored light and eerie sounds and suggested technology the secrets of which were still locked away in the future. To a collector, the stranger, the better. Some were made of lithographed tin, but even plastic toys (Atom Robot, for example) are high on the want list of many serious buyers. Condition is extremely important, both in general appearance and internal workings. Mint-in-box examples may be worth twice as much as one mint-no-box, since the package art was often just as awesome as the toy itself.

Because of the high prices these toys now command, many have been reproduced. Beware!

Other Sources: 01

See also Marx; Guns, Miscellaneous.

Adventure Boy in Skymobile, Remco, 1970, finger puppet figure w/space vehicle, MIB, H4..$20.00

Airport Saucer, MT, battery-op, MIB, L4......................$125.00

Apollo II Eagle Lunar Module, DSK, battery-op, 10", MIB, L4..$400.00

Apollo Space Patrol With Satellite Ship, TPS, battery-op, EX (EX box), L4..$175.00

Apollo X Moon Challenger, TN, battery-op, EX, L4 .....$185.00

Area Radiation Tester, Sears/Japan, advances w/several actions, tin w/astronaut, battery-op, 20", rare, NM+ (EX box), A..$1,135.00

Astro Captain, Daiya, plastic astronaut w/NASA helmet, advances w/sparks in chest, w/up, 6", NM (VG box), A $235.00

Astro Dog, Yone, dog w/bubble helmet walks w/swinging arms, barks & wags tail, wht plush, battery-op, EX (EX box), A...$150.00

Astro Ray Flashlight/Dart Ray Gun Target, Ohio Art, ca 1969, litho tin w/Friendship 7, w/2 darts, VG, P4 ....$110.00

Astronaut, Y, advances w/engine noise & sparks, litho tin, w/up, 8½", rare, EX, A...$1,085.00

Atlas ICBM Missile Launcher w/Missiles & Flying Target, battery-op, NMIB, L4..$675.00

Atom Boat, China, 1960s, w/animated Oriental astronaut, friction, 12", VG+ (G box), A $250.00

Atom Robot, KO, bump-&-go action w/swinging arms, litho tin, crank action, 6½", EX+, from $325 to.....................$350.00

Atom Rocket #7, MT, 1950s, non-fall action w/spinning antenna & flashing lights, tin, battery-op, 9", EX (EX box), A $410.00

Atomic Jet Flying-O-Saucer, 1950s, w/instructions, M, J2 .$20.00

Atomic Robot Man, Japan, advances w/side-to-side action, litho tin w/pressed tin arms, w/up, 5", EX, H7................$850.00

Atomic Robot Man, litho tin, w/up, 13x4¾", G, A $850.00

Atomic Spaceship, TN, mk XX-2, rear attachment spins as spaceship advances, tin & plastic, friction, 13", EX (EX box), A..$210.00

Attacking Martian, SH, advances as chest guns fire, flashing lights & sound, tin & plastic, battery-op, 9", MIB, A..........$135.00

Attacking Martian, SH, advances w/swinging arms, stops, chest opens & gun fires, tin, battery-op, 11", EX (VG+ box), A..$250.00

Big Maxx Robot, Remco, battery-op, 8", NMIB, L4.......$200.00

Boy Astronaut, Yone, boy in primitive suit walks w/sparking action in neck area, claw-like hands, 8½", VG+, A..$350.00

Busy Robot, SH/Japan, litho tin, battery-op, 12", head slightly loose o/w EX, M5..$140.00

Cape Canaveral Mobile Satellite Tracking Station, missing antenna o/w EX, L4..$185.00

Capsule Mercury, SH, mk Friendship 7, advances w/sparks, sound & astronaut spinning inside, friction, 9", NM (EX box), A..$360.00

Captain Robot, MIB, L4..$150.00

Chief Robotman, KO, gray version, skirted bottom, walks, turns w/lighted head & spinning antennas, 12", EX+ (G box), A..$850.00

Chief Smoky, KO, bump-&-go w/swinging arms, head lights up & puffs smoke, tin, battery-op, 12", rare, M (EX+ box), A...$3,300.00

Chime Trooper Astronaut, Aoshin, advances with musical chimes, lithographed tin, windup, 9½", NMIB, A, $2,400.00.

Countdown Rocket Laucher, Ideal, EX+, J2 .... $65.00

Cragstan Astronaut, bl w/yel striping, holds ray gun, litho tin, battery-op, 11", EX, A $175.00

Cragstan Flying Saucer, KO, bump-&-go action, girl figure in clear plastic dome, lights & noise, 8" dia, EX (G+ box), A $150.00

Cragstan Mr Robot, Y, bump-&-go action, advances w/spinning devices, head lights up, litho tin, battery-op, 11", EX, A $385.00

Cragstan Mr Robot, Y, bump-&-go action w/flashing lights in dome, tin & plastic, 11", EX (EX box), A $600.00

Cragstan Satellite, mystery action w/flashing lights & diecut cb floating astronaut, litho tin, 9", NM, A $155.00

Cragstan Talking Robot, advances w/friction, push button in chest & he talks, 11", scarce, NM+, A $760.00

Ding-a-Ling Robot, Topper, 1971, regular-sz boxer or flying saucer, NRFB, H4, ea.. $45.00

Ding-A-Ling Super Return Space Skyway, Topper, w/robot, power pack & accessories, VG+ (VG box), T1 .... $100.00

Dino-Robot, SH, advances & stops as head splits open & dinosaur appears, w/sound, tin, battery-op, 11", NM, A $800.00

Dino-Robot, SH, battery-op, MIB, L4 .... $1,250.00

Dux Astroman, West Germany, advances, bends over and crushes rocks in his hands, flashing lights in chest, plastic, remote control, 14", NMIB, A, $2,200.00.

Earth Satellite, Alps, flies in different directions, litho tin, remote control, EX+ (EX+ box), A $580.00

Engine Robot, SH, battery-op, 9½", MIB, L4 .... $150.00

Fighting Robot, SH, advances w/swinging arms & antennas, w/chest gun, battery-op, tin, 12", EX (VG box), A .$375.00

Fighting Spaceman, SH, advances w/swinging arms & blinking helmet, chest fires w/sound, litho tin, 12", EX+ (EX box), A $400.00

Fighting Spaceman, SH, tin w/plastic chest cover, battery-op, 12", light not working on gun o/w EX, M5 .... $140.00

Fire Rocket X-007, Yonezawa, advances w/siren, pilot pops out when object is hit, litho tin, 14", EX+ (EX box), A .$235.00

Flying Saucer Space Patrol 3, KO, advances w/lights & sound, tin w/astronaut, battery-op, 7½" dia, NM (EX box), A $260.00

Flying Saucer w/Space Pilot, Japan, tin & plastic, battery-op, 7½" dia, EX (EX box), A, from $190 to $235.00

Flying Saucer 8, Haji, advances w/siren sound & sparking action, litho tin & plastic, friction, 7" dia, EX+ (EX box), A..$260.00

Forbidden Planet Spaceship, Childs/Smith, England, 1950s, tin, remote control, 5½" dia, rare, VG (EX box), A $500.00

Friendship Rocket #7, battery-op, NMIB, L4 .... $375.00

Friendship 7 Space Capsule, SH, 1960s, capsule rolls w/rocking action, revolving astronaut, friction, 10", VG+, A..$100.00

Getta-1 Robot, mostly metal, w/up, movable limbs, 7½", M, H12 .... $175.00

Giant Ding-A-Ling Bridge Set w/4 Ding Robots, EX (EX box), T1 .... $185.00

Gold Robot, Linemar, sq head w/facial features, litho knob panel on chest, walks, arms swing, remote control, 7", VG+, A $1,050.00

Golden Sonic Spaceship, Bizarre Toy, 19", NMIB, J2 ....$150.00

High Wheel Robot, KO, advances w/spinning chest gear & sparking action, blk & red tin, w/up, 10", NM+ (EX box), A $400.00

H2O Missile, Mattel, 1959, EX (EX box), T1 .... $125.00

Interplanetary Research Unit, Tri-ang Minic, complete w/plastic vehicles & rockets, friction, NM (EX box), A $240.00

Interplanetary Space Saucer, Merit, flies & makes siren sound when cord is pulled, plastic, 7" dia, EX (EX box), A ..$185.00

Johnny Astro Toy, w/launcher, launch pad & basket, EX (VG box), T1 .... $65.00

Jumping Rocket, SY, robot pilot in rocket, hopping & bucking motions, litho tin, w/up, 6", NM (EX box), A......... $275.00

Jumping Rocket, SY, robot pilot in rocket, hopping & bucking motions, litho tin, w/up, 6", VG+ (EX box), A $100.00

Jupiter Jyro Set, battery-op, MIB, L4.......................... $150.00

Jupiter Rocket, Masaya, advances, hits object & rises to upright position, litho tin, friction, 10", NM (M box), A....$135.00

Kiddy Rocket, Yonezawa, advances w/U-turn action, litho tin w/vinyl figure, w/up, 6", NM (EX box), A $100.00

King Ding Robot, battery-op, EX, L4 .... $325.00

Laughing Clown Robot, J, 14", NM, L4........................ $325.00

Lavender Robot, Modern Toys, rolls forward w/blinking eyes & mouth, battery-op, 15", EX (G box), A $6,500.00

Lighted Space Vehicle, MT, styrofoam ball suspended by stream of air above, lights flash, battery-op, 8", NM, A $270.00

Lighted Space Vehicle, MT, 1950s, bump-&-go w/ball floating overhead, lights & sound, battery-op, 8", NM (EX box), A $400.00

Looping Space Tank, Daiya, battery-op, NMIB, L4 .... $500.00

Looping Space Tank, Daiya, moves w/flashing lights & firing guns, clear plastic dome, tin, battery-op, EX (G- box), A $150.00

Lost in Space Robot, AHI, 1977, bump-&-go action w/flashing lights, plastic, battery-op, 10", NM (G box), A....... $190.00

Lost in Space Robot, Remco, EX+/NM, T1/L4, from $375 to $400.00

Luna Hovercraft, TPS, aluminized vehicle darts about, battery-op, remote control, 8", M (EX box), A $225.00

Lunar Explorer, battery-op, MIB, L4 .... $575.00

Lunar Explorer Delta 55, MIB, L4............................... $275.00

Lunar Loop, Daiya, capsule revolves around spinning loop, 13", NM (EX box), M5 .... $150.00

Magic Space Goggles, 1950s, unused, MIB, J2 .... $55.00

Man From Mars, Irwin, 1950s, walks & moves space guns, red plastic w/clear bubble helmet, w/up, 11", M (EX box), A...$350.00

Man in Space, Alps, lithographed tin with celluloid head and arms, EX (original box), A, $300.00.

Mars Explorer, SH, advances as face shield opens & chest fires w/light, litho tin, battery-op, 10", NM (G box), A...$410.00

Mars King, SH, advances, stops & screeches, chest lights up & shows Mars landscape, tin, battery-op, 10", VG+ (G box), A...$95.00

Mars King, SH, advances w/sound & light-up TV in chest, tin, battery-op, 10", MIB, A...$600.00

Mechanical Robot, Yonezawa, advances w/realistic motion, litho tin, remote control, 6", EX, A....................................$655.00

Meter Astronaut, Y, advances w/motor sound, scale in chest moves from 1 to 5, litho tin, w/up, 9", rare, EX+, A...........$1,355.00

Mini Robotank TR2, battery-op, MIB, L4......................$325.00

Mini-Martians Jet Car, Ideal, 1967, bright plastic spacecraft w/clear plastic dome & decal, 8", EX+ (EX box), A..$160.00

Missile Robot, TPS, advances w/chest issuing sparks, shoots missiles, chrome-plated plastic, w/up, 5", NM, (EX+ box), A...$140.00

Moon Astronaut, Daiya, advances & fires machine gun, litho tin, w/up, 9", EX (EX box), A $1,425.00

Moon City, Cragston, 1970, battery-op, MIB, J2............$260.00

Moon Explorer, KO, advances as his spin ray counter revolves, litho tin, w/up, 7", EX (EX box), A..........................$750.00

Moon Explorer, Yoshiya, flywheel bump-&-go action, red & blk, 7", NM, M5...$420.00

Moon Globe, w/record & stand, EX+, J2 ....$40.00

Moon Globe Orbiter, Mego, moon orbiter on track rotates & makes moon globe spin, plastic & tin, battery-op, 10", NMIB, A..$175.00

Moon Patroler, battery-op, MIB, L4..............................$375.00

Moon Spaceship, Nomura, lithographed tin with plastic dome and illuminated revolving radar mechanism, 13", NMIB (not shown), A, $2,800.00.

Moon Rocket, Masuya, hits object & rises to vertical position, astronaut appears, friction, 16", EX (EX box), A.....$295.00

Moon Rocket, Yone, bl litho tin upright rocket, video screen in cockpit, battery-op, 14½", G, A...............................$115.00

Moon Rocket Space Vehicle, battery-op, MIB, L4.........$325.00

Moon Tek, motorized flying rocket w/motorized prop, plastic, battery-op, 7", MIB, H12...$20.00

Mr Hustler, SH, advances w/engine noise & flashing lights in chest, tin, battery-op, 11½", scarce, MIB, from $575 to $675.00

Mr Machine, 1961, take-apart robot w/wrench & instruction sheets, EX+ (EX box), T1...$350.00

Mr Patrol, SH, advances as arrows on chest plate go up & down, stops, raises arm & screams, litho tin, battery-op, EX, A..$380.00

Mr Robot, Alps/Sonsco, remote control, 9", EX, A $3,080.00

Musical Space Scope, TN/Japan, 12", EX, J2....................$48.00

NASA Astronaut, Shudo, advances in swaying motion, litho tin, w/up, 6", EX, A $265.00

New Astronaut, SH, battery-op, 9½", MIB, L4 ....$130.00

New Space Capsule, SH/Japan, battery-op, NMIB, J2 ...$250.00

Nike Rocket, Masuya, advances, hits object & lifts to vertical position, litho tin, friction, 7", NM (EX+ box), A..$125.00

Pete the Spaceman, Bandai, battery-op, 5", MIB, L4 .....$200.00

Piston Robot, tin & plastic, 12", EX+, M5 ....$100.00

Planet Patrol Saucer, Park Plastics, 1950s, flies up to 40 ft when fired, EX+ (EX display box), A $100.00

Planet Robot, KO, tin body w/plastic head & hands, blk w/chrome trim, w/up, 9", EX (EX box), A $800.00

Planet-Y Space Station, TN, top spins w/lights & sound, lower part spins w/bump-&-go action, battery-op, NM (VG box), A..$200.00

Popcar Spacemobile, battery-op, child's riding toy, NM, L4..$475.00

Radar Robot, TN, advances w/light-up eyes, carries wrench, litho tin, battery-op, 8", scarce, EX+ (EX+ box), A.......$1,300.00

Radar Tank, TM/Japan, battery-op, 8", EX+, J2............$125.00

Remco Voice-Controlled Astronaut Base, 1969, EX+ (EX+ box), J2..$90.00

Robbie the Robot, Japan, bl w/red ft & hands, chrome trim, battery-op, 9", EX, A $290.00

Robby (Robot Bulldozer), Marusan, robot driver on yel dozer w/treads, litho tin, friction, 6", VG+ (G box), A $175.00

Robert the Robot, Ideal, red & gray plastic, battery-op, 14", G $100.00

Robot, Alps/Sonsco, remote control, 9", EX (orig box), A..$3,080.00

Robot & Son, battery-op, MIB, L4/T1 ....$550.00

Robot Bulldozer, KO, goes forward & backwards as robot works shovel, litho tin, remote control, 7", rare, NM (EX box), A...$525.00

Robot Hands, Kilgore, 1951, slide hands through wrist bands into spring-activated hands, complete w/mask, NM (NM box), A..$190.00

Robot Man, Kenner, 1985, plastic head w/stuffed body, plays music in chest, I2 ....$5.00

Robot Tractor, Showa/Japan, robot on treaded tractor moves back & forth w/lighted moving pistons, 9½", G, A.$150.00

Robot Tractor, Showa/Japan, w/lighted pistons, NMIB, L4 ..$575.00

Robot w/Spark, SY, advances w/sparking action in chest, litho tin, w/up, 7", NM+ (EX box), A $225.00

Robot w/Ultra Spark, metal & plastic, w/up, 6", MIB, H12.$20.00

Rocket Man, Rosko Toy, advances and fires rockets, tin and plastic, remote control, 12", NMIB, EX (original box), A, $2,860.00.

Rocket Racer #7, Modern Toys, red, yel & bl litho tin, w/driver, 7", G, A...$75.00

Rocket Ship, MT, 1950s, mk Sparkling Rocket Ship #3, advances w/sparks, litho tin, friction, 7", NM (EX+ box), A $355.00

Rocket Sock-it, England, 1950s, fires darts, plastic, 13", EX+ (EX+ box), A..$95.00

Rocket X-6, MT, 1950s, litho tin, friction, 4", scarce, NM (EX box), A...$350.00

Rocket XB-115, SH, advances w/sparks & space noise, nose cone spins, tin & plastic, friction, 11½", MIB, A....$150.00

Rotate-O-Matic Super Astronaut, litho tin, battery-op, 12", NM (EX box), M5..$165.00

Rotate-O-Matic Super Astronaut, silver version, battery-op, MIB, L4..$375.00

Rotate-O-Matic Super Giant Robot, SH, walks & rotates upper body, tin, plastic arms, battery-op, 16", EX+ (VG+ box), A...$150.00

Roto-Robot, SH, advances & body rotates as guns fire w/lights & sound, tin & plastic, battery-op, M (EX box), A.$300.00

Round Rocket Space Patrol, Asahitoy, litho tin, w/up, 5", NM (NM box), A...$255.00

R35 Robot, MT, battery-op, 7½", EX, L4 ....$575.00

S-61 Space Explorer Friction Vehicle, Japan, mc tin, 13", EX+, J2..$65.00

SAC Sonic Ear Space Age Communicater, Ohio Art, plastic & cb ray-gun listening device, battery-op, w/earphones, NMIB, P4...$90.00

Satellite Barometer, 1950s, EX+, J2 ....$40.00

Satellite Fleet, TPS, ship pulls 3 sm saucers as they turn, litho tin, w/up, 12", NM (EX+ box), A $350.00

Satellite in Orbit, Japan, satellite circles globe as it turns on axis, litho tin, battery-op, 10", EX (EX box), A...............$585.00

Satellite Launcher, Ideal, 1950s, 7x17", EX+ (EX+ 12x19x6" box), D9 ....$45.00

Satellite Launching Truck, Y, push button to launch disks, litho tin, friction, 12", NM (EX box), A $960.00

Satellite Rocket, Parles, 1950s, water-powered action, EX (EX box), J2..$35.00

Satellite X-107 w/Astronaut in Orbit, Modern Toys, pnt tin, 7½" dia, VG (orig box), A $120.00

Smoking Robot, Yonezowa, gray w/NP trim, stop & go, lighted eyes & sq dome atop head, smokes, etc, 12", EX+ (EX+ box), A...$980.00

Solar-X Rocket Ship, silver, red & yel, tin & plastic w/rubber wheels, battery-op, 15", EX, A $55.00

Sonicon Rocket, MT, litho tin w/astronaut under clear plastic dome, battery-op, 14", EX (EX box), A $500.00

Space Bus, Bandai, battery-op, NMIB, L4 ....$850.00

Space Capsule, bump-&-go, hatch opens to emit astronaut, silver & red, battery-op, 9½", NM (EX+ box), M5.....$220.00

Space Capsule, SH, advances w/engine noise & sparks, astronaut at controls, litho tin, friction, 6", NM (EX box), A ..$260.00

Space Capsule, SH, realistic NASA-style vehicle, astronaut inside, litho tin, friction, 9½", VG, A......................$90.00

Space Capsule w/Floating Astronaut, MT, mk Apollo, bump-&-go w/lights & sound, tin, battery-op, 10", M (EX box), A...$125.00

Space Capsules Merry-Go-Round, ATC, mercury capsules mk w/astronauts names spin around tower, tin, w/up, 7", NM, A $260.00

Space Car, MT, vinyl-headed driver in tin space car, non-fall action, blinking lights, battery-op, 10", EX (EX box), A...$175.00

Space City Rocket Launcher #221, 1940s, futuristic city w/movable launcher & darts, litho wood, NM (VG+ box), A...$390.00

Space Commando, TN, walks while swinging left arm, carries rifle in right hand, litho tin, w/up, 8", MIB, A $2,000.00

Space Dog, KO, advances w/flapping ears & opening & closing mouth, silver, w/up, 6", EX, A.................................$365.00

Space Dog, KO, wobbles w/sparking action, ears flap & mouth opens, litho tin, w/up, 6", NM (EX box), A, from $650 to...$750.00

Space Explorer, SH, advances & chest opens to show lighted space scenes, tin & plastic, battery-op, 11", M (EX box), A...$280.00

Space Fighter, SH, bounces, walks, stops & chest door opens w/guns, tin & plastic, battery-op, 10", NM (EX box), A...$150.00

Space Fleet of the Future Space Ships, Pyro, 1950s, plastic, set of 4, scarce, EX+ (EX box), A..$875.00

Space Frontier, battery-op, MIB, L4................................$325.00

Space Frontier Rocket, KY, tin & plastic rocket, hatch exposes astronaut w/camera, battery-op, 18", EX (G box), A..$100.00

Space Helmet with Radar Goggles, Banner Plastics, 1950s, NM (EX box), A, $400.00.

Space Model QX-2 Walkie-Talkies, Remco, 1950s, red & bl plastic, cardboard rocket-shaped instructions, NMIB, P4 ....$90.00

Space Monorail, Japan, litho tin, w/up, 7½", surface wear, G+, M5...$200.00

Space Navigator Pin & Compass Set, WSNY/Japan, ca 1955, brn cloth leather band holds tin compass & pin, MOC, P4 ....$45.00

Space Patrol, MT, dome-shaped saucer rolls forward w/satellite ball, litho astronauts, battery-op, 8", EX (EX box), A $175.00

Space Patrol Commander Helmet, plastic bubble w/decal & face cutouts, 11", rare, missing harness & hoses o/w EX, A...$185.00

Space Patrol Saucer 2019, battery-op, EX, L4...................$85.00

Space Patrol Walkie-Talkies, Randall/England, 1950s, plastic, unused, 5", MIB, A..$130.00

Space Patrol Walkie-Talkies, red plastic, EX (EX box), M5 .$50.00

Space Patrol XII (tank), battery-op, VG+, L4...............$185.00

Space Patrol 2019, battery-op, MIB, L4........................$225.00

Space Patrol 3 Saucer, KO, 7½" dia, EX, L4...................$125.00

Space Pilot Helmet, Tarrson, plastic, NM (orig box), A..$75.00

Space Raider X-21, Alps, 1950s, advances w/sparks, litho tin w/pilots in windows, friction, 9", scarce, VG, A......$500.00

Space Rocket, SY, rocket w/swinging-arm robot moves w/space noise, litho tin, friction, 6", VG+ (G box), A.........$150.00

Space Rocket Bank, Japan, place coin on rocket dish & it shoots into moon surface, litho tin, 7", rare, EX, A............$400.00

Space Rocket Blue Eagle, Masuya, battery-op, 15", EX, L4...$175.00

Space Rocket Blue Eagle, Masuya, battery-op, 15", MIB, L4...$375.00

Space Rocket Solar X7, TN, battery-op, 15½", MIB, L4..$200.00

Space Scooter, TM/Japan, tin, battery-op, 8", EX (EX box), J2..$225.00

Space Scout, 1960s, litho tin, battery-op, working, EX, I2..$190.00

Space Scout X-100 Ship, Pyro, 5", NM, J2 ....$35.00

Space Shooting Range, England, 1950s, spring action gun fires spaceships across ramp, litho tin, NM (EX box), A...$645.00

Space Station Morse Code Signaling Set, Hong Kong, 1960s, bright plastic w/2 Morse Code units, complete, EX (EX box), A..$115.00

Space Survey X-09, triangular space vehicle w/bump-&-go action, astronaut has animated arm, 9", EX (G box), A..$125.00

Space Tank M-18, battery-op, EX (EX box), L4............$125.00

Space Totes, So-Lo Marx, 1950s, soft latex boots w/lightning bolt across top, EX (VG box), A $95.00

Space Trip, MT, cars navigate track as space station spins, litho tin, battery-op, EX (VG+ box), A, from $325 to.....$350.00

Space Vehicle, MT, litho tin space tank w/bump-&-go action, ball floats above, battery-op, 8", EX (EX box), A....$150.00

Spaceman w/Light, Linemar, advances w/rifle, helmet glows, litho tin, remote control, 8", scarce, EX (VG+ box), A .$3,200.00

Spaceman Watch, store display card w/12 toy watches, Indian Head/Japan, NM (NM card), A $55.00

Spacemobile & Pilot, KO, advances as engine moves in & out, litho tin, friction, 7", rare version, M (EX+ box), A...........$2,150.00

Spaceship Bubble Pipe, Mattel, MIB, V1 ....$28.00

Sparking Robot, N, advances w/sparks, litho tin, w/up, 6½", NM (M box), A $210.00

Sparkling Spaceman Car, Usagaya, SP-1 futuristic vehicle w/coiled-head robot driver, friction, NM (NM box), A $935.00

Sparky Robot, advances w/sparks (not working), silver w/red ft & ears, tin, w/up, 8", EX+, M5 ....$240.00

Star Defender Playset, Woolworth/Woolco, 1970s, complete with plastic space rifle and fighter jet, EX (EX card), A, $100.00.

Sparky Robot, KO, advances w/sparking action, tin w/red plastic inserts on eyes, w/up, 7", EX+ (EX box), A, from $335 to..$400.00

Star Defender Playset, Woolworth/Woolco, 1970s, complete w/plastic space rifle & fighter jet, EX (EX card), A.$100.00

Star Strider Robot, SH, battery-op, 12", MIB, L4...........$225.00

Strange Explorer, DSK, tank moves & stops while gorilla flips over, lighted dome, battery-op, 8", EX (EX box), A..$150.00

Strenco Robot, Strenco, 1950s, silver & red tin, w/up, 7½", rare, H12...$375.00

Suction Cups Space Alien, 11", EX+, J2.........................$40.00

Super Robot, N, advances w/moving arms & legs & sparking action in chest, tin & plastic, w/up, 5", EX (VG box), A..$275.00

Super Sonic Space Rocket, battery-op, MIB, L4............$750.00

Super Space Commander, SH, advances w/lighted space scene in chest, plastic, battery-op, 9½", M (EX+ box), A...$65.00

Swinging Baby Robot, Yone, baby robot on swing, litho tin, w/up, 6", M (NM box), A...$885.00

Talking Robot, Y, talks & fires rockets from head, plastic, push-button action, battery-op, 12", rare, MIB, A $250.00

Television Spaceman, Alps, advances as space scenes revolve in chest, antenna rotates, tin, w/up, 6", MIB, A..........$575.00

Television Spaceman, Alps, advances w/screeching noise & light-up chest, eyes spin, litho tin, 13", EX+ (VG+ box), A..$615.00

Television Spaceman, Alps, plastic antenna version, TV screen in chest, walks w/moving eyes & arms, 11", EX+ (G box), A...$400.00

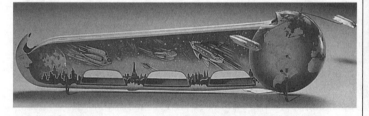

Terra Lune, Technofix, 1947, balancing spaceships fly around the Earth as car travels from the Earth to the moon and back, lithographed tin, windup, 18" long, EX, A, $1,050.00.

Turbo Jet Car, Ideal, EX, J2..$100.00

TV Space Patrol, Japan, advances w/sound as astronaut w/camera revolves, litho tin, friction, 9", scarce, NM (M box), A .$1,300.00

Two-Stage Rocket Launching Pad, TN, 1950s, technician sits in front of screen, many actions, tin, battery-op, 8", MIB, A...$500.00

UFO XO5, MT, bump-&-go w/flashing lights & sound, robot at controls, tin & plastic, w/up, 7" dia, M (EX box), A ..$85.00

USA-NASA Apollo, MT, piloted ship moves w/non-fall action, astronaut rotates above, tin, battery-op, 10", EX (EX box), L4...$185.00

Video Robot, Japan, tin & plastic, EX, J2.....................$110.00

Walking Robot, Linemar, walks w/swinging claw-like hands, rests on wire easel-back stand, w/up, 6", VG+, A $200.00

Walking Spaceman, Linemar, advances in high-stepping motion w/swinging arms, tin & plastic, w/up, 5", VG+ (VG+ box), A...$625.00

Wheel-A-Gear Robot, Taiyo, lg working gear box on chest, tin & plastic, battery-op, 14½", EX (EX box), A.......$1,750.00

Whistling Space Top Set, Linemar, insert 1 of 2 globes into activator & push lever for action, litho tin, M (EX box), A..$150.00

Whiz Bang Exploding Rocket Arrows, 1950s, MOC, J2...$25.00

Winner Space Rocket, Exelo/Japan, rocket moves along track, litho tin, battery-op, 5½", EX (EX box), A $250.00

Wonder L Rocket, battery-op, MIB, L4 ....$150.00

X-10 Space Vehicle, battery-op, EX, L4 ....$375.00

X-12 Moon Crawler, battery-op, M, L4 ....$100.00

X-15 Flying Saucer, 1950s, red, w/up, 6" dia, EX, J2.......$190.00

X-5 Spaceship, TM, bump-&-go action w/flashing lights, tin & plastic, battery-op, 8½", MIB, L4...........................$100.00

X-5 Spaceship, TM, bump-&-go action w/flashing lights, tin & plastic, battery-op, 8½", NM (VG box), M5 ....$85.00

X-70 Astronaut, Hong Kong, advances w/sound & moving arms w/walkie-talkie, plastic, w/up, 6", EX+ (EX box), A..$185.00

X-70 Space Robot, fold-down petals on head reveal TV camera and screen, lithographed tin and plastic, battery-operated, NMIB, A, $2,300.00.

X-80 Planet Explorer, Modern Toys, pnt tin, dome top, battery-op, 7½" dia, VG (orig box), A $95.00

X-950 Rocket Ship, Arnold/W Germany, 1955, advances w/sparks, litho tin, friction, 9", rare, NM (EX box), A $650.00

XX-2 Atomic Spaceship, TN, advances w/sparks, litho tin, friction, 13", NM (EX box), A $190.00

Zoomer Robot, Japan, bl tin w/diamond-shaped antenna & metal coiled hair atop head, holds wrench, battery-op, 9", EX, A $230.00

Zoomer Robot, tin, battery-op, missing ear cups & non-working o/w EX (VG+ box), M5 ....$295.00

Miscellaneous

Bank, Astro Mfg, silver diecast rocket w/rubber nose, fires coin into nose cone, 13", missing 2 rubber fin tips, NM, P4..........$90.00

Bank, Duro Strato Bank, ca 1955, diecast, mk Plainfield Savings, rocket ship fires coin into moon, missing key, VG, P4 ..$85.00

Bank, Mr Robot, Wolverine, 1950s, red, yel & clear plastic w/gold foil decal, lock & key, sorts change, 10½", NM, P4 ....$50.00

Bank, Space Shuttle Columbia, Leonard/Japan, 1980s, silver metal, 8", M, P4 ....$55.00

Bendee, Alpha-7 Man From Mars, Colorforms, w/helmet, no broken wires o/w NM, F5 ....$85.00

Bendee, Electron+ From Pluto, Colorforms, EX, F5 ....$80.00

Bendee, Xodiac From Saturn, Colorforms, no broken wires o/w EX, F5 ....$70.00

Boots, 1950s, astronaut-styled felt-like material w/soles, sm sz, NM, I2 ....$20.00

Bottle, Souvenir; Apollo 13, M, J6 ....$32.00

Cap, cloth w/Official Space Patrol insignia & silkscreened rockets, flip-down glasses attached, scarce, EX+, A........$180.00

Container, Clanky Chocolate Syrup, 1963, plastic, 10", NM, M17 ....$36.00

Game, Magic Robot, Merit, 1960s, NMIB, M17 ....$90.00

Game, Robot Sam the Answer Man, Jacmar, 1950, NMIB, M17 ....$70.00

Interplanetary Space Bank, box only, Regis Space Toys, rare, EX+, A..$385.00

Nodder, Space Boy, Norcrest, 1960s, silver & bl w/gold base, NM, M17 ....$110.00

Ornament, Hallmark, astronaut w/Neil Armstrong's voice, The Eagle Has Landed, MIB, I2 ....$48.00

Pencil Sharpener, Admiration Ray Gun, 1950s, plastic w/removable sharpener, grip holds shavings, 3⅜", M, P4........$65.00

Pin-back Button, Space Patrol, 1950s, plastic w/emb rocket ship mk USA & X-8, 1" dia, EX, A $60.00

Poster, Historic Moon Landing, Rand McNally, 24x18", MIP, H4...$5.00

Puzzle, Astronauts of Apollo 11, Milton Bradley, 1969, MIB (sealed), M17 ....$20.00

Shaker, Major Space Rocket Ship, 1950s, yel & translucent red plastic, M, P4 ....$55.00

Space Ranger Inter Planet Wallet & Space Money, 1950s, red cb w/diecast badge, code card & 20 pcs money, NM, P4 ....$65.00

Space Suit, Moon McDare, VG, H4 ....$10.00

Wristwatch, US Time, 1950, Space Patrol on face, NM, A $90.00

Rock 'n Roll

From the '50s on, Rock 'n Roll music has been an enjoyable part of many of our lives, and the performers themselves have often been venerated as icons. Today some of the all-time great artists such as Elvis, the Beatles, KISS, and the Monkees, for instance, have fans that not only continue to appreciate their music but actively search for the ticket stubs, concert posters, photographs, and autographs of their favorites. More easily found, through, are the items that sold through retail stores at the height of their careers — dolls, games, toys, books, maga-

zines, etc. In recent years, some of the larger auction galleries have sold personal items such as guitars, jewelry, costumes, automobiles, contracts, and other one-of-a-kind items that realized astronomical prices. If you're an Elvis fan, we recommend *Elvis Collectibles* and *Best of Elvis Collectibles* by Rosalind Cranor (Overmountain Press).

Advisors: Bob Gottuso (B3), Beatles, KISS, Monkees; Rosalind Cranor (C15), Elvis.

See also Action Figures; Bubble Bath Containers; Coloring, Activity and Paint Books; Dolls, Celebrity; Model Kits; Paper Dolls; Pin-Back Buttons; Puppets.

Andy Gibb, flip book, Shadow Dancing, EX, B3 ....$25.00

Beatles, bank, Paul, Pride Creations, pnt compo from Yellow Submarine, w/orig stickers & stopper, NM, B3........$430.00

Beatles, banks, 1980s but dtd 1964, yel or wht plastic drum w/blk heads, autographs & notes, top slot, 3", B3, ea $10.00

Beatles, beach bag, 1960s, cloth w/vinyl lining, heavy rope drawstring, EX, B3 ....$190.00

Beatles, beach hat, bl, VG+, R2 ....$95.00

Beatles, beach towel, Cannon, 1964, VG, R2 ....$90.00

Beatles, Beatlemaniac Fan Club Kit, complete w/photographs, cards, sticker & puzzle, EX (EX envelope), A..........$175.00

Beatles, bedspread, United Kingdom, ca 1964, mc appliques on wht chenille, EX, B3..$250.00

Beatles, binder, SPP, tan, 2-tone Starburst interior, 3-ring style, EX, rare color, B3 ....$150.00

Beatles, birth certificate, 1964, 5x11", set of 4, VG (orig envelope), R2 ....$65.00

Beatles, book, Beatles Quiz Book, United Kingdom, 1964, paperback, VG+, R2 ....$40.00

Beatles, book, Lennon: In His Own Write, 1968, hardbound, EX, R2 ....$65.00

Beatles, book, Love Letters to the Beatles, 1964, hardbound, w/dust jacket, EX $25.00

Beatles, book, Out of the Mouths of Beatles, Dell, 1964, EX..$25.00

Beatles, book, The Beatles Yesterday, Today & Tomorrow, Larkin, 1971, paperback, B3 ....$6.00

Beatles, book, We Love You Beatles, 1971, hardbound, w/dust jacket, VG, R2 ....$30.00

Beatles, book covers, set of 7 w/insert card, VG+ $65.00

Beatles, booklet, Official Fan Club, 1971, gr cover, 20 pgs, EX, B3 ....$18.00

Beatles, booklet, The Beatles, Pixerama, 1963, fold-out w/12 glossy photos, 3½x5", VG, B3 ....$15.00

Beatles, bookmarks, John, Ringo or Apple Bonker (Yellow Submarine), 9½x3", R2, ea..$8.00

Beatles, brooch, blk & wht photo pin on gold-tone metal, signatures on back, 2" dia, EX, B3 ....$65.00

Beatles, brooch, George's guitar, VG (orig card), R2........$35.00

Beatles, brooch, photo disk w/autograph, 2", VG, R2.......$50.00

Beatles, bulletin board, Yellow Submarine, group photo, 7½x23", NM (orig shrink wrap), B3 ....$140.00

Beatles, cap, blk leather w/Ringo lettered inside circle on side, VG+, B3 ....$140.00

Beatles, cap, brn corduroy w/Ringo image, VG+, R2 .....$100.00

Beatles, charms from gumball machine, blk plastic records w/faces & labels, ¾", set of 4, B3 ....$28.00

Beatles, coin purse, 1960s, red vinyl, 3x3", NM+, T2.......$25.00

Beatles, coloring set, Kit Fix, United Kingdom, 1964, includes 6 colored pencils & 5 pictures, rare, B3 ....$750.00

Beatles, diary booklet, 1965, vinyl w/blk & wht photos, 3x4", EX..$30.00

Beatles, Disk-Go-Case, record carrier, Charter/NEMS, 1966, plastic, rnd w/angled hdl, portraits & signatures, EX+, A.$110.00

Beatles, Disk-Go-Case, record carrier, pk (rarer color) plastic w/group photo, autographs & logo, VG+, B3 ....$125.00

Beatles, doll, George Harrison, Applause, 1988, 24", original tag, NM, J6, $85.00.

Photo courtesy of June Moon.

Beatles, dolls, inflatable cartoon image of ea member, set of 4, EX, R2/B3, from $100 to $125.00

Beatles, drum set, Ringo Starr, Selcol, complete w/stand & drumsticks, EX (orig box)...$625.00

Beatles, figure, Jeremy/The Nowhere Man, Yellow Submarine, 4", B3 ....$350.00

Beatles, figurines, Subuteo, United Kingdom, 1965, set of 4 , MIB, R2 ....$180.00

Beatles, flasher rings, bl, set of 4, S2 ....$65.00

Beatles, frisbee, 1976, Rock 'N Roll Music LP promo, 9" dia, VG, R2..$35.00

Beatles, greeting cards, Yellow Submarine, complete, M (VG box), B3 ....$190.00

Beatles, guitar, New Beat by Selcol, orange & maroon 4-string w/signatures, 33", EX (EX box) $600.00

Beatles, guitar, New Sound by Selcol, orange & cream 4-string w/facsimile portraits & signatures, 23", EX, A.........$380.00

Beatles, guitar strings, Hofner, M $75.00

Beatles, hairbrush, Genco, 1964, MIP, from $35 to $40.00

Beatles, handkerchief, United Kingdom, With Love From Me to You, 8½", VG, R2...$35.00

Beatles, headband, Better Wear, Love the Beatles, MIP, B3, from $55 to...$70.00

Beatles, headband, L&C Vincent/Australia, w/pictures & guitars, M (sealed pkg mk Official Headband), B3.......$230.00

Beatles, hummer, mc group photo, 11", VG, R2.............$100.00

Beatles, iron-ons, Star Trip, 1975, 3" dia, set of 4, MIP (sealed), R2...$25.00

Beatles, Kaboodle Kit, Standard Plastic Products, vinyl w/group portrait & fascimile signatures, 7x10", EX $800.00

Beatles, key chain, Come Together, M, V1 ....$15.00

Beatles, key chain, Yellow Submarine, 6x2½", VG, R2 ...$35.00

Beatles, key chains, Pride Creations, plastic, set of 4, B3..$80.00

Beatles, Licorice Record Candy, candy w/wrapper & photo insert, candy broken o/w VG $110.00

Beatles, locket, plastic over front photo, 11 blk & wht photos inside, brass ribbon & pin top, B3.........................$100.00

Beatles, magazine, Teen Talk, Sept 1965, EX, B3.............$10.00

Beatles, mobile, Sunshine Art Studios, Yellow Submarine, punch-out characters & string to hang, MIP (sealed), B3...$160.00

Beatles, mobile, Whitman, 4 punch-out portraits w/stage, 10x14" cb sheet, 1 punched out o/w complete, EX, B3...$150.00

Beatles, nesting dolls, Russian, hand-pnt wood, set of 5, B3...$40.00

Beatles, nodders, Carmascots, 1964, compo, facsimile signature on gold base, set of 4, 8", EX+ (EX+ box), minimum value $550.00

Beatles, notebook, group photo in Paladium doorway, top-bound, unused, EX, B3..$60.00

Beatles, nylons, Ballito, textured w/faces & guitars woven in, unused, MIP, from $100 to...................................$140.00

Beatles, paint-by-number set, set of 4 prints, Beatles Fan Club Membership card on header, MIP (sealed), B3..........$80.00

Beatles, pen, bl barrel w/4 metal heads at lapel holder, VG+ (orig card), B3..$145.00

Beatles, pencil case, yel vinyl w/group image & autographs, zip closure, EX, B3...$140.00

Beatles, pennant, Canadian, cartoon portraits playing instruments on blk & gold felt, 27", VG+, B3 ....$170.00

Beatles, pennant, I Love the Beatles w/hearts on red ground, 29", VG+, B3...$110.00

Beatles, pillow, House Pillows, full figures on red background EX, rare, B3...$350.00

Beatles, pillow, waist-up photos w/instruments on bl, VG+, B3...$250.00

Beatles, pin, Mastro, pk plastic guitar w/rubber band strings, brn printed faces, signatures & logo, 5½", B3 ....$170.00

Beatles, playing cards, Apple Records, wht border w/gold trim on gr, unused, M (hard plastic case), B3 ....$120.00

Beatles, Pop-Out Art Decorations, King Features, 1968, Yellow Submarine, M, H4..$35.00

Beatles, poster, Dell #2, 4 lg blk & wht photos on shades of red, 19x54", EX, B3..$32.00

Beatles, poster, John, Richard Avedon, 1968, psychedelic style, mail order from Look magazine, 22x31", EX, B3 ....$60.00

Beatles, punch-out portraits, Whitman, 1964, unused, VG, R2...$100.00

Beatles, purse, Dame, wht cloth clutch w/blk faces & autographs, leather strap w/orig hang tag, unused, NM, B3 ....$300.00

Beatles, puzzle, United Kingdom, waist-up portraits on stage, 340 pcs, complete, EX (VG+ box), B3 ....$300.00

Beatles, record box, Airflite, cb, gr w/plastic hdl, G-, R2..**$150.00**

Beatles, record box, Airflite, cb, red w/wht top & hdl, 8½x8x5", VG+, B3 ....**$380.00**

Beatles, record box, Apple Records, cb w/Apple logo, VG+, R2..**$30.00**

Beatles, record carrier, Seagull Ent/United Kingdom, standing pose under plastic on bl, 7½x7½", EX **$180.00**

Beatles, ring, gold metal w/group photo disk, EX.............**$45.00**

Beatles, rub-on sheets, 1968, cereal premium, Yellow Submarine litho on waxed paper, 2½x3½", M..........................**$35.00**

Beatles, scarf, Blackpool/United Kingdom, brn & pk photos & designs on wht, 26x26", NM, B3.............................**$230.00**

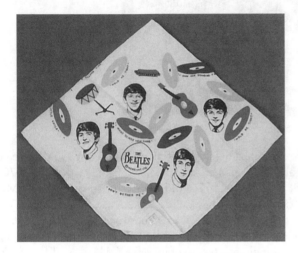

Beatles, scarf, multicolored designs and photos on white, 26x26", EX, $45.00.

Beatles, scrapbook, Whitman, stickers in corner, G, R2 ..**$35.00**

Beatles, sheet music, She Loves You, 1964, group photo on cover, EX...**$10.00**

Beatles, shirt, wht knit w/3 buttons & blk piping, orig hang tag w/wallet photo, unused, VG+, R2..........................**$185.00**

Beatles, stage, Applause, mc cb platform for 22" Sgt Pepper dolls, B3 ....**$50.00**

Beatles, stamps, Hallmark, set of 100 (20 of ea member & 20 of group), M (orig booklet), B3 ....**$45.00**

Beatles, stationery, Yellow Submarine, Flying Horseman, set of 20 w/matching envelopes, MIB (sealed), B3..............**$45.00**

Beatles, stationery, 1968, Yellow Submarine, 4 sheets & envelopes w/different member on ea, EX+, R2 ....**$12.00**

Beatles, stick pin, 1968, hand-pnt diecut Yellow Submarine, ⅞" w/1" pin, B3 ....**$35.00**

Beatles, sticker, gumball machine prize, gold & blk w/faces & names, 1x3"..**$20.00**

Beatles, switchplate, Yellow Submarine Snapping Turk, MIP (sealed), R2..**$25.00**

Beatles, talcum powder, Margo of Mayfair/United Kingdom, EX, B3...**$490.00**

Beatles, tote bag, Japan, 1966, heavy gauge plastic w/hdl, orig hang tag, 14x13", VG, R2 ....**$80.00**

Beatles, wallet, brn vinyl w/pictures under plastic, Florida on back, bi-fold, 3½x4½", B3 ....**$200.00**

Beatles, wallpaper, 1964, single panel, 21x21", VG+, R2.**$30.00**

Beatles, watercolor set, complete w/4 Yellow Submarine pictures & pnt, M (VG+ box), B3...**$135.00**

Beatles, wig, Lowell Toys, M (VG+ card), B3 ....**$110.00**

Beatles, Yellow Submarine, resin reproduction of the Corgi Yellow Submarine w/base, figures & octopus, EX, B3 .....**$70.00**

Bee Gees, guitar, 1979, plastic, 29½", EX **$60.00**

Bill Haley & the Comets, song book, 1954, photo cover, EX+, N2 ....**$20.00**

Black Sabbath, frisbee, 1979, promo for tour, B3 ....**$20.00**

Blondie, International Fan Club Book, 1981, #2, B3........**$10.00**

Bob Dylan, magazine, Hit Parade, Nov 1970, EX, J5........**$25.00**

Bruce Springsteen, book, Born To Run, 1976, w/photos, 176 pgs, 1979, EX..**$6.00**

Bruce Springsteen, poster, Cover Me, EX **$25.00**

Crosby, Stills & Nash, whistle, ABC Records, Whistling Down the Wire, B3 ....**$12.00**

Dave Clark Five, souvenir booklet, 1960s, 28 pgs, EX......**$25.00**

Dave Clark Five, tour book, 1964, lg format, B3..............**$38.00**

David Bowie, poster, Changes, EX **$4.00**

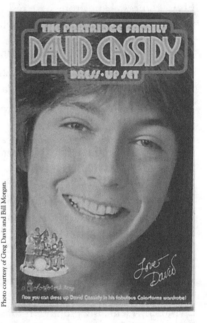

David Cassidy, Colorforms Dress-Up Set, 1972, from $25.00 to $35.00.

Photo courtesy of Greg Davis and Bill Morgan.

Def Leppard, pencil holder, Pyromania, 1984, metal, EX, B3 ....**$18.00**

Dick Clark, book, Twenty Years of Rock 'N Roll, Buddha Records Inc, 1953-73, 24 pgs, EX **$50.00**

Donny & Marie Osmond, amplifier, 1977, VG, M15.......**$25.00**

Donny & Marie Osmond, Dress-Up Kit, Colorforms, 1977, NMIB, J7...**$35.00**

Donny & Marie Osmond, record player, mk Sing Along Radio Record Player, MIB...**$60.00**

Donny & Marie Osmond, TV Show Playset, NRFB, H4..**$50.00**

Donny Osmond, Keepsake Photo & Activity Book, Artcraft, 1973, NM, C1...**$20.00**

Donny Osmond, nodder, NMIB...................................**$30.00**

Elvis, balloon, advertises Kid Galahad movie, unused, M...**$50.00**

Elvis, book, Meet Elvis Presley, Scholastic, 1971, softbound, EX..**$10.00**

Elvis, binder, Elvis Presley Enterprises, 1956, white leather with zipper closure, 14x10", NM, $1,000.00; Elvis, pillow, Elvis Presley Enterprises, 1956, pink with sketched image of Elvis, 10½x10½", NM, $365.00.

Elvis, charm bracelet, 1956, MOC, from $220 to $260.00

Elvis, figures, Hamilton, cast resin, 1950s w/guitar or 1970s Aloha jumpsuit, limited & numbered edition, 9", M, B3, ea $65.00

Elvis, guitar, Lapin Production, 1984, plastic, M (EX card), H4 ....$60.00

Elvis, hat, GI Blues, RCA Victor/Paramount, brn paper, 5x12", B3 ....$100.00

Elvis, key chain, flasher type w/full figure on yel background, M, B3 ....$18.00

Elvis, magazine, Photoplay, October 1958, Elvis in uniform on cover, NM, C1 ....$30.00

Elvis, menu, Las Vegas, 1972, 10¾" dia $40.00

Elvis, music box, Hamilton, cast resin figure plays Love Me Tender, limited & numbered edition, 10", M, B3 ....$80.00

Elvis, music box w/pull-out jewelry drawer, plays Hound Dog as Elvis dances, 8", scarce, NM, A $125.00

Elvis, ornament, Hallmark, 1992, brass-look figure, MIB, I2 ..$20.00

Elvis, paint-by-number set, Elvis Presley Enterprises, 1956, minimum value $1,800.00

Elvis, pen, Tickle Me promotion w/feathers at top, B3.....$18.00

Elvis, pencil sharpener, Elvis Presley Enterprises, 1956 ..$210.00

Elvis, photo album, 1956, concert souvenir (orig 50¢ price) $175.00

Elvis, picture, 1956, 5x7", w/molded gold & wht fr $330.00

Elvis, scrapbook, Solid Gold Memories, Ballantine Books, 1977, EX $16.00

Elvis, standee, Love Me Tender, 72" $1,000.00

Elvis, teddy bear, Elvis Presley Enterprises, 1957, 24", NM ..$450.00

Elvis, towels, Cannon, Sincerely Elvis Presley, 4-pc set, EX, I2 ....$15.00

Fabian, pillow, 1950s, blk & wht printed cloth w/bl back, 11x11", EX, J5 ....$75.00

Herman's Hermits, figure, Peter Noon, Show Biz, EX, H4 .$75.00

Jackson Five, pillow, VG $35.00

Jackson Five, sheet music, I'll Be There, 1970, group photo cover, EX $10.00

KISS, bracelet, gold chain & logo w/red inset, EX (orig card), B3 ....$35.00

KISS, Colorforms Set, 1979, EX (EX box), J6, $85.00.

KISS, combs, Lady Jane/Australia, 1980, set of 35, MIP (sealed), rare, B3 ....$170.00

KISS, lapel pin, 1977, gold & blk on sterling, 2¾", MOC, B3 ....$35.00

KISS, makeup kit, Remco, Kiss Your Face, MIB $95.00

KISS, music book, Rock 'N Roll Over, Almo Publications, 1978, 6 color photos, 64 pgs of music, EX, H4 ....$10.00

KISS, necklace, gold letters, gum machine item, B3..........$4.00

KISS, necklace, rnd pendant w/logo, NM, H4 ....$15.00

KISS, necklace, 1980, lightning bolt, silver logo, 1¾x½", w/chain, B3 ....$25.00

KISS, poster, Put-Ons, Bi-Rite Enterprises, 1976, 9½x9½", MOC, D9 ....$18.00

KISS, puffy stickers, Rockstics, set of 4, MOC $60.00

KISS, stickers, Live II, 8x10", B3 ....$10.00

KISS, tour program, Lick It Up, 1984 World Tour, 24 pgs, VG+, B3 ....$45.00

KISS, wastebasket, P&K Products, 1978, litho metal, 19x11" dia, NM, J6 ....$225.00

Led Zeppelin, patch, Song Remains the Same, 4x3½", NM $8.00

Madonna, notebook, Desperately Seeking Susan, 1985, EX, J7 ....$20.00

Madonna, removable tattoos, Just Toys, 1991, MOC, S2..$15.00

Michael Jackson, Colorforms, 1984, MIB (sealed), C1.....$25.00

Michael Jackson, sheet music, Ben, 1972, lg photo cover w/movie credits, EX+, P3 ....$20.00

Michael Jackson, slipper socks, Mfa, 1984, B3 ....$20.00

Monkees, book, Monkees Go Mod, 1967, illus, softbound, EX $8.00

Monkees, book, Who's Got the Button, Whitman, 1968, 208 pgs, NM $20.00

Monkees, bracelet, color head shots in brass-colored disk, MIB, B3 ....$30.00

Monkees, flasher ring, changes from 2 portraits to other 2 portraits, chrome, VG, B3 ....$20.00

Monkees, guitar, Mattel, 1966, plastic w/mod art, 19",
   EX+ $100.00
Monkees, playing cards, MIB, B3 ....$35.00
Monkees, Private Picture Book, Laufer, fan club offer, 32 pgs,
   NM $75.00
Monkees, record carrier, for 45rpm records, Mattel/Canadian,
   vinyl, EX+ $80.00
Monkees, tablet, photo cover, unused, M, B3 ....$40.00
Monkees, tambourine, EX, B3 ....$85.00
Monkees, tour program, summer 1987, B3 ....$8.00
New Kids on the Block, fashion plates, Hasbro, 1990, EX (EX
   box), I2 ....$5.00
New Kids on the Block, figures, Danny or Jordan, posable, 6",
   MIB, ea $6.50
Paul McCartney & Wings, book, Paul McCartney & Wings,
   Jeremy Pascall, hardbound, w/dust jacket, VG, R2 ....$15.00
Paul McCartney & Wings, card set, Back to the Egg, set of 5 blk
   & wht photos, EX $15.00
Police, puffy stickers, set of 5, EX, B3 ....$5.00
Prince, poster, Graffiti, dbl-sided, EX $10.00
Rolling Stones, fan club kit, EX $12.00
Rolling Stones, puffy stickers, 1983, MOC, J7 ....$8.00
U2, poster, Hamburg Germany Live Tour, EX...............$10.00
Van Halen, binoculars, w/logo, B3 ....$15.00
Van Halen, program, 1980 concert tour, ticket taped on back pg,
   H4 ....$35.00
Van Halen, puffy stickers, 3 different sets w/David Lee Roth, B3,
   ea $5.00
Van Halen, scarf, blk, EX, I2 ....$5.00

Rubber Toys

Toys listed here are made of rubber or a rubber-like vinyl.
Some of the largest producers of this type of toy were Auburn
Rubber (Indiana), Sun Rubber (Ohio), Rempel (also Ohio) and
Seiberling. Because of the very nature of the material, most rub-
ber toys soon cracked, collapsed or otherwise disintegrated, so
they're scarce today. Character-related rubber toys are listed in
Character, Movie and TV Collectibles.

See also Character, Movie and TV Collectibles; Soldiers.

Army Truck, Made in USA, gr rubber w/canvas-look top, 5½",
   EX, I2 ....$12.00
Bobtail Racer, Sun Rubber, gr & wht, 4", VG+, T1 ....$15.00
Bobtail Racer, Sun Rubber, 6", VG+, T1 ....$25.00
Boy on Tricycle, Auburn, NM, J6 ....$24.00
Bum Fred Greinert, Rempel, 1940s(?), EX, I2 ....$35.00
Calf, Auburn, sm, late version, scarce, A1 ....$10.00
Catcher, Auburn, in bl, scarce, A1........................$46.00
Chipper, Holland Hall Products, 1967, monkey, jtd arms, 12",
   EX, I2 ....$12.00
Collie, Auburn, lg, A1 ....$14.00
Cow, Auburn, blk & wht, slight warp to base, A1 ....$8.00
Cow, Rempel, missing valve o/w VG, T1 ....$10.00
Dog, Rempel, 5", EX, I2 ....$10.00
Farmer, Auburn, A1..$20.00

Fire Truck, Auburn, w/rubber tires, 8", VG, N2 ....$35.00
Froggy the Gremlin, Rempel, EX, T1....................$125.00

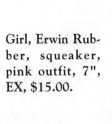
Girl, Erwin Rub-
ber, squeaker,
pink outfit, 7",
EX, $15.00.

Graham-Bradley w/Farmer, Auburn, upper & lower hooks work,
   A1 ....$48.00
Horse, Auburn, A1 ....$10.00
Indy Racer, Arcor Safe Toys/Auburn, red w/wht rubber tires,
   5¼", S15 ....$45.00
Jet Plane, Auburn, XR 577 on wings, red & silver mks, very
   scarce, A1..$65.00
JoJo the Trick Doll, squeeze & eyes, nose, ears & mouth pop out,
   1960s, MIB, T1 ....$20.00
Krazy Tow Set, Auburn, 1950s, 8" truck pulls 7" hot rod car,
   NM (EX+ box), A $75.00
Locomotive, Auburn Western, 7", VG, I2 ....$15.00
Marmon-Harrington Tank, Auburn, NM $38.00
Paneled Truck, Sun Rubber, silver, 5", EX, A...............$25.00
Peeper the Frog, Rempel, squeeze toy, 12", EX, V1.........$40.00
Pig, Auburn, sm, late version, A1 ....$9.00
Sedan, Auburn, red 4-door w/blk tires, scarce, A1..........$45.00
Sheep, Auburn, sm, late version, A1 ....$9.00
Telephone Truck, Auburn, 1960s, VG, N2 ....$25.00
Tractor, Auburn, 1950s, 4", G, A $35.00
Truck, Auburn, open back, VG+, T1 ....$25.00
Turkey, Auburn, M, A1 ....$8.00
1948 Lincoln Convertible, Arcor Safe Toys/Auburn, gr w/blk
   tires, S15 ....$45.00

Russian Toys

Many types of collectible toys continue to be made in Russia. Some are typical novelty windups such as walking turtles
and pecking birds, but they have also made robots, wooden puzzles, and trains. In addition they've produced cars, trucks and

military vehicles that are exact copies of those once used in Russia and its Republics, formerly known as the Soviet Union. These replicas were made prior to June 1991 and are marked Made in the USSR/CCCP. They're constructed of metal and are very detailed, often with doors, hoods and trunks that open.

Because of the terrific rate of inflation in Russia, production costs have risen to the point that some of these toys are no longer being made.

Advisors: Natural Way (N1); David Riddle (R6).
Other Sources: O1

Replicas of Civilian Vehicles

Aeroflot (Russian Airline) Service Station Wagon, 1/43 scale, MIB...$18.00

Belarus Farm Tractor, 1/43 scale, MIB, $20.00.

Gorbi Limo, 1/43 scale, metal, MIB, R6............................$25.00
Kamaz Model #53212 Cargo Truck, 1/43 scale, MIB, R6.$40.00
Kamaz Model #5511 Dump Truck, 1/43 scale, MIB, R6...$40.00
KamA3 Model #5320 Flat Bed Truck, cab tilts forward, 1/43 scale, MIB, R6...$35.00
KamA3 Model #53213 Airport Fire Truck, 1/43 scale, MIB, R6...$40.00
KamA3 Model #5410, Truck Cab, 1/43 scale, MIB, R6 ...$40.00
KamA3-53212 Oil Truck, 1/43 scale, MIB, R6.................$40.00
Lada #2121 4x4, trunk, doors & hood open, 1/43 scale, MIB, R6...$15.00
Lada #2121 4x4 w/Trailer, trunk, doors & hood opens, 1/43 scale, MIB, R6...$18.00
Lada Auto Service Station Wagon, trunk & hood opens, 1/43 scale, MIB, R6...$15.00
Lada Sedan, trunk & hood opens, 1/43 scale, MIB, R6 ....$15.00
Lada Station Wagon, trunk & hood opens, 1/43 scale, MIB, R6...$15.00
Moskvitch Aeroflot (Soviet Airline) Station Wagon, hood opens, 1/43 scale, MIB, R6 ....$15.00
Moskvitch Auto Service Station Wagon, hood opens, 1/43 scale, MIB, R6...$15.00
Moskvitch Medical Services Sedan, 1/43 scale, MIB, R6 .$15.00
Moskvitch Panel Station Wagon, hood opens, 1/43 scale, MIB, R6...$15.00
Moskvitch Sedan, hood opens, 1/43 scale, MIB, R6.........$15.00

Moskvitch Slant-Back Sedan, 1/43 scale, MIB, $15.00.

Moskvitch Soviet Traffic Sedan, hood opens, 1/43 scale, MIB, R6 ....$15.00
Moskvitch Station Wagon, hood opens, 1/43 scale, MIB, R6 ....$15.00
Moskvitch Taxi Sedan, hood opens, 1/43 scale, MIB, R6..$15.00
OMO 1937 Fire Truck, #1 in series of 6, 1/43 scale, MIB, R6 .$40.00
OMO 1937 Fire Truck, #2 in series of 6, 1/43 scale, MIB, R6 ....$40.00
RAF Ambulance Van, back & 3 doors open, 1/43 scale, MIB, R6 ....$20.00
RAF Traffic Police Van, 1/43 scale, MIB, R6 ....$20.00
Volga Ambulance Station Wagon, back & 3 doors open, 1/43 scale, MIB, R6...$22.00
Volga Sedan, trunk, hood & doors open, 1/43 scale, MIB, R6 ....$20.00
Volga Taxi Sedan, trunk, hood & doors open, 1/43 scale, MIB, R6 ....$20.00
Volga Taxi Station Wagon, trunk, hood & doors open, 1/43 scale, MIB, R6...$20.00
Volga Traffic Police Sedan, trunk, hood & doors open, 1/43 scale, MIB, R6...$22.00

Replicas of Military Vehicles

Armored Car, 1/43 scale, MIB, R6 ....$15.00
Armored Personnel Carrier, 1/43 scale, MIB, R6..............$15.00
Armored Troop Carrier, 1/86 scale, MIB, R6....................$15.00
Cannon, 1/86 scale, MIB, R6 ....$15.00
Command Car, 1/86 scale, MIB, R6..................................$15.00
N-153 Biplane Fighter, 1/72 scale, MIB, R6 ....$40.00
N-16 Fighter, 1/72 scale, MIB, R6....................................$40.00
Rocket Launcher Armored Truck, 1/86 scale, MIB, R6 ...$15.00
Self-Propelled Cannon, 1/86 scale, MIB, R6.....................$15.00

Tank, battery-operated, 1/72 scale, MIB, $45.00.

SU-100 Self-Propelled Cannon, 1/43 scale, MIB, R6.......$15.00
Tank, battery-op, 1/72 scale, MIB, R6 ....$45.00
Tank, 1/86 scale, MIB, R6 ....$12.00
Troop Truck, 1/86 scale, MIB, R6 ....$15.00
100mm Cannon, 1/43 scale, MIB, R6 ....$15.00
76mm Cannon, 1/43 scale, MIB, R6 ....$15.00

Miscellaneous

Cast metal, WWII Soldiers w/Rifles, set of 10, MIB, N1 ..$25.00
Metal, bird, w/up, MIB, N1 ....$5.00
Metal, car set, 6-pc set, MIB, N1 ....$12.00
Metal, car track, w/up, MIB, N1 ....$29.00
Metal, chicken, MIB, N1 ....$5.00
Metal, dancing snow girl, MIB, N1 ....$13.00
Metal, doll, Maytryoshki, w/up, MIB, N1 ....$18.00
Metal, hen, w/up, MIB, N1 ....$8.00
Metal, monster beetle, MIB, N1 ....$8.00
Metal, parking garage, MIB, N1 ....$29.00
Metal, rooster, w/up, MIB, N1 ....$8.00
Metal, train track, w/up, N1 ....$29.00
Plastic, car on garage lift, MIB, N1 ....$8.00
Plastic, chicken inside egg, w/up, MIB, N1 ....$5.00
Plastic, fighter jet, bl, MIB, N1 ....$5.00
Plastic, tank, MIB, N1 ....$5.00
Plastic & Metal, moon buggy w/2 cosmonauts, w/up, MIB, N1 .$15.00
Wood, doll set, Lenin, Stalin, Kruschev, Brezhnev & Gor-
bechev, Maytryoshki, made in China, MIB, N1 ....$30.00

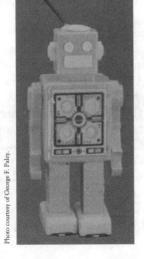

Plastic and tin, robot, w/up walker, 4-color panels in chest revolve, $29.00.

Wood, doll set, various sets of 5 or more, Matryoski, made in
Russia, MIB, N1, from $75 to................................$195.00

Sand Toys

In the Victorian era a sand toy was a boxed wooden or card-board scene with a glass front and a mechanism involving a hop-per and/or chute leading to a paddle, then to various rods and levers attached to cardboard or tin figures or animals with loosely jointed limbs at the front of the scene. When the sand was poured, the mechanism shifted and the figures went through a series of movements. These were imported mostly from Ger-many with a few coming from France and England.

By 1900, having seen the popularity of the European models, American companies were developing all sorts of sand toys, includ-ing free-standing models. The Sand Toy Company of Pittsburgh patented and made 'Sandy Andy' from 1909 onwards. The com-pany was later bought by the Wolverine Supply & Manufacturing Co. and continued to produce variations of the toy until the 1970s.

Today if you mention sand toys, people think of pails, spades, sifters, and molds, as the boxed scenes have all but disap-peared due to their being quite fragile and not surviving use.

We have a rich heritage of lithographed tin pails with such wonderful manufacturers as J. Chein & Co., T. Cohn Inc., Mor-ton Converse, Kirchoff Patent Co., Marx Toy Co., Ohio Art Co., etc., plus the small jobbing companies who neglected to sign their wares. Sand pails have really come into their own and are now recognized for their beautiful graphics and design. In fact, in April 1995 a 5" sand pail realized $770.00 at an auction in Pennsylvania. A new book, *Pails by Comparison, Sand Pails and Other Sand Toys, A Study and Price Guide* by Carole and Richard Smyth (our advisors for this category) is now available from the authors (S22 in Dealer Codes).

Capt Sandy Andy Loader, Wolverine, tower w/chute & sand car that
goes up & down, 13½", EX (orig box), minimum value..$300.00
Dutch Mill, McDowell Mfg Co, Pittsburgh PA, ca 1927, litho
tin, 12", EX, from $225 to $350.00
Leotard Acrobat, Brown, Blondin & Co/London, late 1800s,
8x10x3½", EX, minimum value...........................$1,000.00
Pail, Chein, fish in the sun, EX+, J2..................................$35.00
Pail, Chein, 4-sided w/nursery rhyme ea side, EX..........$185.00
Pail, emb tin, beach scenes w/children, images of birds & ani-
mals decorate sides, lobster on bottom, 5", VG, A ..$770.00
Pail, emb tin, before 1900, flowers & leaves fr rescue scene of
lifeboat w/American flag & ship in distress, 3", EX.$400.00
Pail, emb tin, boy & girl in boat, flock of geese on back, 3½", G,
A $120.00
Pail, emb tin, boy & girl w/teddy bear, children building castles
on back, 7", G, A..$635.00
Pail, emb tin, boy & girl w/teddy bear, children building castles
on back, 5", A...$415.00
Pail, emb tin, boy carries rope & walks w/girl, boy w/basket of
fish on back, floral trim, 5", VG, A........................$275.00
Pail, emb tin, boy carries rope & walks w/girl, boy w/basket of
fish on back, floral trim, 4½", VG..........................$300.00

Pail, emb tin, boy on horse & girl on goat, mc on red & bl w/gold trim, wood hdl grip, 5½", G+, A $470.00

Pail, emb tin, cats in uniform marching in band, red & gold on bl, wood hdl grip, 5¾", VG, A $385.00

Pail, emb tin, children & goat cart on the beach, floral border, emb lobster on bottom, 5", VG, A $385.00

Pail, emb tin, dog w/puppies, red w/gold, wood hdl grip, emb eagle on bottom, 6", VG, A $340.00

Pail, emb tin, girl on dog, gr w/bl & gold trim, dog & puppies on back, wood hdl grip, 6", VG, A $470.00

Pail, emb tin, Little Red Riding Hood w/the Big Bad Wolf, wood hdl grip, eagle on bottom, 6", VG, A $470.00

Pail, emb tin, 2 monkeys, 2 perched parrots on back, 3", VG, A..........................$145.00

Pail, Happynak #715, 1940s, features Mickey & Minnie Mouse, 4½", NM, minimum value $200.00

Pail, lithographed tin, children dressed as pirates, US Metal Toy Manufacturing Co., 7½", EX, from $45.00 to $75.00.

Photo courtesy of Carole and Richard Smyth.

Pail, litho tin, elephant, zebra & tiger safari scene, unsigned, 5¼", EX..........................$100.00

Pail, litho tin, nursery rhymes, w/matching sifter that fits inside, unsigned, 4", EX..........................$175.00

Pail, litho tin, Wright Bros-type plane & hot-air balloon, 4", rare, G, minimum value $300.00

Pail, litho tin, 1900-1920, fisher boy & girl walking by shore 1 side, boy w/basket of fish on other, 5¼", EX..........$300.00

Pail, litho tin, 1940s, dressed farm animals, 8", EX, G16.$110.00

Pail, Ohio Art #6F175, Lil' Red Riding Hood, 7½", EX $150.00

Pail, T Cohn, little pigs in Indian costume doing war dance, 4¾", EX..........................$125.00

Pail, US Metal Toy Mfg Co, Treasure Island, bottom of scrap tin, 7½", EX..........................$185.00

Pail & Shovel, litho tin, dressed cats, NM, G16..........$100.00

Pump, Ohio Art #77, children dressed as firemen, 10¼", EX $150.00

Sand Crane, Wolverine, 1916, mc litho, NM..........$375.00

Sand Lift, Ohio Art, M..........................$120.00

Sand Mill, Chein, sand causes cups to twirl, 11½", M (EX box), A..........................$175.00

Sand Set, Ohio Art, 1940s-50, litho tin shovel, sifter & 2 molds, M (orig card), from $80 to..........................$120.00

Sand Sifter, Ohio Art, 1930s, litho tin w/wire mesh bottom, Mickey & Minnie in beach scenes, 8" dia, EX, A ...$250.00

Sand Sifter, Ohio Art #187, litho tin, children playing in sea, artist signed by Elaine Ends Hileman, 7½" dia, EX ...$80.00

Sand Toy, Busy Mike, Chein, ca 1935, litho tin, boy & girl on seesaw, 7", EX..........................$275.00

Sand Toy, MAC, McDowell Mfg Co, Pittsburgh PA, ca 1927, Dutch windmill, man turns wheel to move paddles, EX..........................$350.00

Shovel, Chein, mc pirates, 14", EX $70.00

Soldiers in Battle, Imagerie Pellerind/France, paper litho wood, pour sand & soldiers attack, 9½", NM, minimum value..........................$1,000.00

Spade, mk RN Made in USA on hdl, 1920s, 2 girls at beach, 11½", EX..........................$150.00

Spade, Ohio Art #184, boy in lg sea waders shows girl his sm fish, wood hdl, 28", EX..........................$125.00

Sunny Andy Merry Miller, Wolverine, elf moves & wheel spins, comes w/can of sand, 12", NM (G- box), from $200 to..........................$325.00

Santa Claus

Christmas is a magical time for young children; visions of Santa and his sleigh are mirrored in their faces, and their eyes are wide with the wonder of the Santa fantasy. There are many who collect ornaments, bulbs, trees, etc., but the focus of our listings is Santa himself.

Among the more valuable Santas are the German-made papier-mache figures and candy containers, especially the larger examples and those wearing costumes in colors other than the traditional red.

See also Battery Operated; Books; Reynolds Toys; Windups, Friction and Other Mechanicals; and other specific categories.

Candy Container, 6", seated on snowball, papier-mache, red cloth jacket & bl pants, EX, A $330.00

Candy Container, 6½", on wooden sleigh full of gifts, compo head, crepe-paper suit, EX, A $80.00

Candy Container, 7", papier-mache & compo, orange suit, fur beard, wooden toy bag on back, EX, A $440.00

Candy Container, 8", papier-mache, red-pnt suit, wht trim, feather tree, cork stopper, EX, A $175.00

Candy Container, 8", papier-mache & compo, red cloth suit, wht trim, fur beard, feather tree, EX, A $155.00

Candy Container, 8½", papier-mache & compo, lt gr suit, fur beard, wicker toy bag, EX, A $825.00

Candy Container, 9", compo body w/snow-flecked lt gr suit, mauve pants, w/tree, wicker carrier, cb base, EX, A..$715.00

Candy Container, 10", cb & compo w/papier-mache boots, red & wht cloth robe-type suit, fur beard, w/tree, EX, A $800.00

Candy Container, 10", papier-mache, bl-pnt suit w/gold glitter, pnt beard, tree on arm, EX, A $825.00

Candy Container, 10", papier-mache, red & wht cloth suit, fur beard, felt bag, tree in hand, EX, A $440.00

Candy Container, 10", papier-mache, red-pnt suit covered w/wht dots, bl gloves, 10", EX, A $275.00

Candy Container, 10", papier-mache, wht terry hooded coat, gray pants, red felt satchel, 10", EX, A $880.00

Candy Container, 10", papier-mache & compo, flecked dk gr cloth suit, fur beard, wicker carrier, EX, A $990.00

Candy Container, 11", papier-mache, dk red felt suit, wht trim, fur beard, tree sprig in hand, EX, A $605.00

Candy Container, 11", papier-mache, red velvet jacket, bl cloth pants, wood rack w/bag, tree, EX, A $250.00

Candy Container, 11", papier-mache & compo, gr cloth suit, bl pants, fur beard, wooden carrier, EX, A $770.00

Candy Container, 12", papier-mache, flecked dk gr cloth suit, pk pants, fur beard, wicker carrier, w/tree, EX, A $1,375.00

Candy Container, 12", papier-mache, red felt jacket w/bl pants, wht fur trim, blk belt & boots, VG+, A $580.00

Candy Container, 12", papier-mache, red-pnt suit, wht cloth trim, pnt beard, w/tree, EX, A $140.00

Candy Container, 12", papier-mache & compo, red cloth suit, w/wooden crate, mk Chocolate Menier, EX, A $1,155.00

Candy Container, 13", papier-mache & compo, red cloth suit, bl trim, fur beard, gr cloth bag, EX, A $1,020.00

Candy Container, 14", papier-mache & compo, red felt suit, wht trim, twig in hand, wicker basket, EX, A $880.00

Candy Container, 16", papier-mache & compo, flecked lt red robe, cotton beard, switches & cloth bag, EX, A .$1,760.00

Candy Container, 22", papier-mache, red-pnt suit, wht trim, fur beard, sprig in hand, wooden base, EX, A $2,420.00

Doll, Steiff, hard rubber face & hands, red cloth suit & hat w/wht fur trim, orig tags, 9½", EX, A $155.00

Lantern, glass Santa on tin base, Japan, 1950s, battery-op, 6", NM (VG box), A $175.00

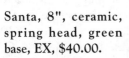

Santa, 8", ceramic, spring head, green base, EX, $40.00.

Roly Poly, papier-mache Santa in dbl-breasted suit w/wht trim, 4", VG, H7 ....$250.00

Santa, 4", bsk, on mica skis w/sack on back, 1930s, H12 ..$75.00

Santa, 4", papier-mache face, molded felt body, mica shoes, plush & pearl trim, blk belt, 1940s, H12 ....$25.00

Santa, 6", papier-mache, red felt suit, wht trim, 1920s, H12 ...$65.00

Santa, 7", papier-mache, fur beard, holds feather tree, H12 ...$95.00

Santa, 8", papier-mache & compo, red cloth suit, wht trim, fur beard, tree sprig in hand, 8", EX, A $250.00

Santa, 15", papier-mache & compo, red cloth suit, fur beard & trim, glass eyes, w/up, EX, A $1,870.00

Santa, 15", papier-mache & compo, red cloth suit, fur beard & trim, wooden back carrier, w/tree, EX, A $1,265.00

Santa, 15", red velvet 2-pc suit, wht plush trim, 1950s, H12.$165.00

Santa, 16", papier-mache & compo, gray fur suit, wht fur beard, w/bag, feather tree in hand, wood base, EX, A $2,860.00

Santa, 21", papier-mache, flecked bl suit w/glitter, cotton beard, glass eyes, w/tree, EX, A $1,375.00

Santa, 23", papier-mache & compo, red cloth suit, tree w/candles & bells, wicker carrier on belt, electric, 23", EX, A $1,100.00

Santa, 24", papier-mache & compo, flecked cloth suit w/cape collar, glass eyes, fur beard, tree in hand, EX, A ...$1,265.00

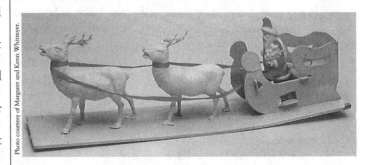

Santa in Sleigh, celluloid figures with cardboard sleigh, 10½", EX, from $65.00 to $75.00.

Santa in Sleigh, single flocked papier-mache reindeer on base, wicker-type sleigh w/tree, 46", rare, A $7,700.00

Santa on Sled, papier-mache Santa, cloth suit, cb sled, 5", EX, A $85.00

Santa Pulling Sled, German, papier-mache & compo w/flecked red cloth suit, wooded sled w/toys & tree, 12", EX, A $880.00

Schoenhut

Albert Schoenhut & Co. was located in Philadelphia, Pennsylvania. From as early as 1872 they produced toys of many types including dolls, pianos and other musical instruments, games and a good assortment of roly polys (which they called Rolly Dollys). Around the turn of the century, they designed a line they called the Humpty Dumpty Circus. It was made up of circus animals, ringmasters, acrobats, lion tamers and the like, and the concept proved to be so successful that it continued in production until the company closed in 1935. During the nearly thirty-five years they were made, the figures were continually altered either in size or by construction methods, and these variations can greatly affect their values today. Besides the figures themselves, many accessories were produced to go along with the circus theme — tents, cages, tubs, ladders and wagons, just to mention a few. Teddy Roosevelt's African hunting adventures inspired the company to design a line that included not only Teddy and the animals he was apt to encounter in Africa but native tribesmen as well. A third line featured comic characters of the day, all with the same type of jointed wood construction, many dressed in cotton and felt clothing. There were several, among them were Felix the Cat, Maggie and Jiggs, Barney Google and Spark Plug, and Happy Hooligan.

Several factors come into play when evaluating Schoenhut figures. Foremost is condition. Since most found on the market today show signs of heavy wear, anything above a very good rating commands a premium price. Missing parts and retouched paint sharply reduce a figure's value, though a well-done restoration is usually acceptable. The earlier examples had glass eyes; by 1920, eyes were painted on. Soon after that, the company began to make their animals in a reduced size. While some of the earlier figures had bisque heads or carved wooden heads, by the twenties, pressed wood heads were the norm. Full-size examples with glass eyes and bisque or carved heads are generally more desirable and more valuable, though rarity must be considered as well. As a general rule, a glass-eye version is worth 30% to 40% more than a painted-eye version in the same condition, but there are exceptions.

During the 1950s, some of the figures and animals were produced by the Delvan Company, who had purchased the manufacturing rights.

Consult the index for Schoenhut toys that may be listed in other categories.

Advisor: Keith and Donna Kaonis (K6).

Animals

Alligator, glass eyes, gr w/leather ft, 13", EX, from $400 to $650.00
Bear, pnt eyes, shades of brn, 7½", VG, from $125 to $200.00
Buffalo, pnt eyes, bk brn, 8", EX, from $450 to.............$600.00
Camel, dbl hump, pnt eyes, brn w/blk hoofs, rope tail, 7½", VG, from $235 to $400.00
Camel, single hump, glass eyes, brn w/blk hoofs, rope tail, 7", G, from $200 to $300.00
Cow, glass eyes, brn w/leather ears, horns & collar w/metal bell, rope tail, 8½", VG, from $635 to $800.00
Donkey, glass eyes, olive brn & blk stripes, rope tail & leather ears, 9½", VG, from $150 to $200.00
Donkey, glass eyes, olive brn & blk stripes, 9½", NMIB..$500.00
Donkey, pnt eyes, olive & blk, fabric mane, leather ears, rope tail, 8", G...$75.00
Donkey, pnt eyes, olive brn & blk stripes, fabric mane, leather ears, rope tail, 9½", G...$75.00
Elephant, glass eyes, gray w/wht tusks, rope tail, lg leather ears, 9", VG, from $210 to...$300.00
Elephant, pnt eyes, gray w/leather ears, rope tail & husks, felt headpiece, 9", G, from $75 to...............................$100.00

Giraffe, glass eyes, realistic colors, leather ears, short wooden horns, rope tail, 11", G, from $250 to $320.00
Giraffe, pnt eyes, realistic colors, pnt cloth ears, rope tail, 9½", VG, from $275 to $375.00
Goat, pnt eyes, blk & wht, leather ears, horns, beard & tail, 8", VG, from $195 to $240.00
Hippo, pnt eyes, deep brn, 10", MIB, A $910.00
Horse, pnt eyes, w/saddle & stirrups, 10", VG $240.00
Horse, pnt eyes, wht & blk w/leather ears & harness, string tail, red & gold wooden platform atop, 10", G...............$125.00

Lion, glass eyes, carved mane and ears, rope tail, 7½" long, VG, $550.00; Buffalo, glass eyes leather horns, tail missing otherwise VG, $575.00.

Lion, pnt eyes, cvd mane, lt to med brn, rope tail, 8", G, from $230 to...$260.00
Ostrich, glass eyes, blk & gray w/wht ribbed legs, 9½", VG, from $400 to...$480.00
Ostrich, glass eyes, gr w/blk ribbed legs, 9½", VG $525.00
Pig, pnt eyes, curled wire & rope tail, leather ears, 8", VG, from $250 to...$350.00
Polar Bear, glass eyes, 8", VG, from $1,300 to $1,800.00
Poodle, glass eyes, wht, rope tail, 7", EX (orig box), A....$500.00
Poodle, pnt eyes, wht, rope tail, 7", VG, from $150 to...$180.00
Rhino, pnt eyes, olive gr w/blk spots, 9", G, from $220 to ..$250.00
Tiger, glass eyes, rope tail, 8", VG, from $550 to............$750.00
Tiger, pnt eyes, rope tail, 8", G, from $190 to $250.00

People

Acrobat (Female), bsk head, blond hair, cloth costume, gr leotard w/red tights & shoes, 8", VG, from $350 to $500.00
Acrobat (Male), bsk head, brn hair, cloth costume, 8", G, from $250 to...$300.00
Bareback Rider (Female), bsk head, cloth costume, 8½", G, from $220 to...$250.00
Bareback Rider (Female), hand-pnt face, cloth costume, 6½", G.$100.00
Bareback Rider (Female), hand-pnt face, cloth costume, 8", G, from $135 to $200.00
Barney Google & Spark Plug, 1922-30, 8x9", EX, A......$980.00
Clown, hand-pnt face, cloth suit w/wooden hat, 7", G.....$75.00
Hobo, 1-part head, brn jacket, tan pants, orange scarf & tam, pnt face, leather ears, 8", G-, from $165 to.............$200.00
Maggie & Jiggs, hand-pnt faces, cloth clothing, Maggie holding rolling pin, Jiggs holding bucket, 7", VG, A...........$880.00

Maggie and Jiggs, hand-painted faces, cloth clothes, 9" and 7", with rolling pin and pail, EX, D10, pair, from $1,000.00 to $1,500.00.

Mary & Her Lamb, w/straw feeder, 7½", EX, A $1,045.00
Ringmaster, 1-part head, cloth clothing, top hat & whip, 8", VG, A $440.00
Teddy Roosevelt, cloth safari outfit w/rifle, 8", EX, A ..$1,925.00

Miscellaneous

Alderney Dairy Wagon, pnt wood, wht dappled horse on platform pulls wht wagon, w/bottles & figure, 25", G, A.......$1,430.00
Clothespin Doll, mk 1935 on ft, pnt features, yarn hair, orig pants & shirt, 12½", EX, A $65.00
Golf Game, long wooden hdl controls movement of golfer's swing, w/putting green, sand traps, etc, 36", MIB, A $2,145.00
Hollywood Home Builder, 1928, replica of President Jackson's home, complete, partly assembled, EX (EX box), A ..$85.00
Hollywood Home Builder, 1928, replica of President Jefferson's home, complete, partly assembled, EX (EX box), A ..$85.00

Rolly Dolly, clown, 15", VG, M5, $350.00.

Humpty-Dumpty Circus Cage Wagon, w/lion, 36", VG, A..$1,210.00
Humpty-Dumpty Circus Tent, ca 1914 to 1920, G+ ...$1,100.00
Piano, grained wood w/litho paper on front panel, 12", G, A .$30.00
Piano, upright, wood w/2 cast front support legs & candle holders, Schoenhut decal, rnd piano stool, EX, A $440.00
Rolly Dolly, Black clown, papier-mache, wht suit, felt hat, red trim, 9", EX, A...$855.00
Rolly Dolly, Santa, papier-mache, orig cloth label, 4", G-, A.$275.00
Rolly Dolly, Santa, papier-mache, 7½", G+, A...............$385.00
Store Display Clown, jtd wood w/blk & wht cloth costume & hat, blk, yel & red pnt features on wht face, 32", EX, A..$4,510.00

Schuco

A German company noted for mechanical toys as well as the teddy bears and stuffed animals we've listed here, Schuco operated from the 1930s well into the '50s. Items were either marked Germany or US Zone, Germany.

Advisor: Candace Gunther (Candelaine), (G16).

See also Battery-Operated; Windups, Friction and Other Mechanicals.

Bears, Schuco miniatures, 1920s-30s, left: brown mohair with felt paws; right: gold mohair with felt paws, 2⅜", EX, $325.00 each.

Bear, dk brn, orig ribbon, 3½", M, G16 ....$175.00
Bear, gold, 1930s, 17", NM....................................$550.00
Bear, gold, 2½", M, G16 ....$175.00
Bear, pk, 1930s, 5", M, G16....................................$1,200.00
Bear, tan, orig ribbon, 3½", M, G16............................$175.00
Bigo-Bello Dog, w/orig clothes, 14", NM, G16..............$175.00
Bigo-Bello Dumbo, w/orig tag, NM................................$225.00
Bigo-Bello Elephant, 1960s, 6", G, G16.........................$45.00
Bigo-Bello Elephant, 1960s, 8", G, G16.........................$55.00
Black Scotty, Noah's Ark, 3" L, MIB, G16....................$225.00
Blackbird, Noah's Ark, 3", MIB, G16 ....$225.00
Dog Mascot, wearing gr pants & hat, red tie & shoes, 3½", M, G16 ....$200.00
Elephant, Noah's Ark, 3" L, MIB, G16 ....$200.00

Fox, Noah's Ark, MIB, 3" L, rare, G16...........................$275.00
Hedgehog, Noah's Ark, 2" L, MIB, G16 ....$135.00
Janus Bear, 2-faced (googly & bear), cinnamon color, 3½", M, G16..$750.00
Jaq Mouse, 10", NM...$225.00
Ladybug, Noah's Ark, 3" L, MIB, G16 ....$200.00
Lion, Noah's Ark, 3" L, MIB, G16 ....$175.00
Monkey, cinnamon w/felt hands & ft, mk Germany on 1 ft, 2½", NM, G16...$200.00
Monkey, Noah's Ark, felt face, pipe-cleaner arms & legs, MIB, G16...$125.00
Monkey, Noah's Ark, w/metal tail, US Zone tag, 3" L, MIB, G16...$200.00
Monkey, wht w/felt paws & airbrushed metal face, stamped Germany, 1930s, 2", M $250.00
Orangutan, Noah's Ark, 3", very rare, MIB, G16 ....$275.00
Owl, Noah's Ark, 3", MIB, G16 ....$150.00
Panda, orig ribbon, paper label on leg, 3½", MIB, G16..$325.00
Panda, orig ribbon, 1950s, 3½", M, G16.....................$250.00
Penguin, Noah's Ark, 3", MIB, G16.............................$175.00
Perfume Bear, orange mohair, orig stopper, 1930s, 5", M..$950.00
Perfume Monkey, cinnamon color, 5", EX, G16 ....$250.00
Perfume Monkey, red, 5", rpl bottle o/w EX, G16...........$445.00
Pig, Noah's Ark, pk, orig ribbon, 3", MIB, G16 ....$300.00
Raccoon, Noah's Ark, 3", MIB, G16..............................$275.00
Squirrel, Noah's Ark, 3", M, G16..................................$225.00
Turtle, Noah's Ark, 3", MIB, G16 ....$175.00
Yes/No Bear, gray mohair, orig tag, 13", NM $1,200.00
Yes/No Bear, wht w/brn nose, 5", NM...........................$850.00
Yes/No Cat, 5", M..$650.00
Yes/No Monkey, 1950s, 5", M, G16 ....$450.00
Yes/No Rabbit, 5", M, G16.......................................$650.00
Yes/No Tricky Monkey, US Zone Tag & orig ribbon, 13", NM, G16...$450.00

Slot Cars

Slot cars first became popular in the early 1960s. Electric raceways set up in retail storefront windows were commonplace. Huge commercial tracks with eight and ten lanes were located in hobby store and raceways throughout the United States. Large corporations such as Aurora, Revell, Monogram, and Cox, many of which were already manufacturing toys and hobby items, jumped on the bandwagon to produce slot cars and race sets. By the end of the early 1970s, people were loosing interest in slot racing, and its popularity diminished. Today the same baby boomers that raced slot cars in earlier days are revitalizing the sport. Vintage slot cars are making a comeback as one of the hottest automobile collectibles of the 1990s. Want ads for slot cars appear more and more frequently in newspapers and publications geared toward the collector. As you would expect from their popularity, slot cars were generally well used, so finding vintage cars and race sets in like-new or mint condition is difficult. Slot cars replicating the 'muscle' cars from the sixties and seventies are extremely sought after, and clubs and organizations devoted to these collectibles are becoming more and more commonplace. Large toy

companies such as Tomy and Tyco still produce some slots today, but not in the quality, quantity or variety of years past.

Aurora produced several types of slots: Screachers (5700 and 5800 number series, valued at $5.00 to $20.00); the AC-powered Vibrators (1500 number series, valued at $20.00 to $150.00); DC-powered Thunderjets (1300 and 1400 number series, valued at $20.00 to $150.00); and the last-made AFX SP1000 (1900 number series, valued at $15.00 to $75.00.)

Advisor: Gary Pollastro (P5).

Complete Sets

AMT, Cobra Racing Set, 1/25 scale, NMIB, A $185.00
Aurora, Stirling Moss, #1313, Table Top Racing Set, 1968, NMIB...$125.00
Aurora, Stirling Moss, 4-Lane Racing Set, EX (EX box), J2 .$150.00
Aurora AFX, Jackie Stewart Challenger Raceway, NMIB.$75.00
Aurora AFX, Revamatic Slot Car Set, EX (EX box) $50.00
Eldon, Power 8 Road Racer Set, 1960s, EX+ (EX box) $70.00
Ideal, Alcan Highway Torture Track, 1968, w/extra car & motor, M (EX+ box), D9...$50.00

Ideal, Dukes of Hazzard Racing Set, complete, MIB, J6, $85.00.

Ideal, Motorific Giant Detroit Race Track, w/Corvette, EX+ (EX+ box), T1 ....$85.00
Monogram, Ferrari & Ford GT, 1/24 scale, NM (NM box w/header card) $185.00
Motorific, GTO Torture Track, lg, EX (EX box), J2 ....$100.00
Remco, Mighty Mike Action Track, NMIB, T1 ....$100.00
Strombecker, James Bond's 007 Aston Martin, #8630, 1/32 scale, 1966, NMIB, A...$220.00
Strombecker, Road Racing Set, 1960s, EX (EX box), from $75 to..$100.00

Slot Cars Only

AC Gilbert, Sulky, #1, blk horse, 1/32 scale, M, B10 ....$60.00
AC Gilbert, 1940 Ford, #19090, 1/32 scale, VG, B10 ......$75.00
AMT, Mercury Comet, 1/24 scale, EX, B10....................$150.00
Aurora, Batmobile, #1385, blk, slightly cut wheel well, rare, EX, B10...$50.00

Aurora, Javelin, red, wht & bl, NM, B10...........................$30.00

Aurora, Pickup Hot Rod, O scale, EX+, J2....................$100.00

Aurora, Thunderbird, Indy Racer, tan, NM, J2.................$25.00

Aurora, Thunderbird Roadster, O scale, EX+, J2............$100.00

Aurora AFX, Autoworld Beamer #5, wht w/bl stripes, NM, B10...$12.00

Aurora AFX, Autoworld McClaren XJR, #54, orange, NM, B10...$12.00

Aurora AFX, Autoworld Porsche Can Am, wht w/bl, yel & red stripes, EX, B10...$12.00

Aurora AFX, Baja Bug, lime, EX, B10............................$12.00

Aurora AFX, Camaro Z28 Trans Am, lt bl & purple, NMIB, B10...$25.00

Aurora AFX, Capri Trans Am, wht w/bl & lime stripes, NM, B10...$16.00

Aurora AFX, Chevelle Stockcar #17, wht & orange, EX (in BP) B10...$12.00

Aurora AFX, Conventional Cab, red & wht, EX, B10.....$20.00

Aurora AFX, Corvette #7, red, wht & bl, EX+, B10........$15.00

Aurora AFX, Corvette Funny Car, orange & purple, VG, B10...$10.00

Aurora AFX, Datsun Baja Pickup, #211, yel & bl, M, B10..$14.00

Aurora AFX, Datsun 510 Trans Am #35, bl & wht, EX, B10...$14.00

Aurora AFX, Dodge Charger, bl, NM, J2.......................$20.00

Aurora AFX, Dodge Charger Stock Car #11, wht w/blk hood, NMIB, B10...$22.00

Aurora AFX, Dodge Daytona Charger, bl, EX+, J2..........$25.00

Aurora AFX, Dodge Fever Dragster, wht & yel, NM, B10..$20.00

Aurora AFX, Dodge Police Van, wht w/blk stripes, EX, B10...$15.00

Aurora AFX, Dodge Street Van, yel w/orange stripe, EX, B10...$10.00

Aurora AFX, Dodge Van, orange, NM, B10....................$15.00

Aurora AFX, Dragster, red, NM, B10..............................$25.00

Aurora AFX, Ferrari 512, red, NM, B10.........................$12.00

Aurora AFX, Ford Baja Bronco, red, NM, B10................$14.00

Aurora AFX, Ford Escort #46, gold & bl w/red stripes, NM, B10...$14.00

Aurora AFX, Ford Van, wht & bl, EX, B10.....................$12.00

Aurora AFX, Grand Am Funny Car, red, wht & bl, NM, B10...$14.00

Aurora AFX, Javelin (Trans Am) #5, bl w/blk stripe, NM, B10...$15.00

Aurora AFX, Lola T260 Can-Am, NM, B10....................$14.00

Aurora AFX, Matador Taxi, wht, NM, B10.....................$16.00

Aurora AFX, Nissan 300ZX #33, red, wht & bl, NM, B10.$14.00

Aurora AFX, Peace Tank, olive, NM, B10.......................$18.00

Aurora AFX, Pinto Funny Car, orange & purple, EX, B10..$10.00

Aurora AFX, Plymouth Cuda Funny Car, wht & orange, no wheelie bars, NM, B10 ....$15.00

Aurora AFX, Plymouth Roadrunner #43, wht & bl, EX, B10.$14.00

Aurora AFX, Pontiac Grand Am, red, wht & bl, NM, B10...$15.00

Aurora AFX, Porsche Carrera, wht, maroon & blk, EX+, B10...$12.00

Aurora AFX, Porsche 510K Type B, #3002, MIB, T1.......$15.00

Aurora AFX, Porsche 917 #2, wht & purple, NM, B10....$14.00

Aurora AFX, Furious Fueler Dragster, HO scale, yellow and white, MOC, $20.00; Aurora AFX, Magna Traction Corvette GT, HO scale, white with red, yellow and orange front, MOC, $20.00.

Aurora AFX, Porsche 917-10 Type A, #3001, MIB, T1 ...$15.00

Aurora AFX, Rallye Ford Escort #28, lime, yel & bl, NM, B10...$12.00

Aurora AFX, RC Porsche 917-10, wht w/red & bl stripe, NMIB, B10...$20.00

Aurora AFX, Roarin' Rolls, wht & blk, NM, B10............$15.00

Aurora AFX, Shadow Can Am, blk, NMIB, B10.............$20.00

Aurora AFX, Speed Beamer #11, red, wht & bl, NM, B10..$15.00

Aurora AFX, Turbo Porsche #3, red, wht & bl, EX, B10..$10.00

Aurora AFX, Turbo Turnon, red, wht & bl, NM, B10......$15.00

Aurora AFX, Twi-Night Beamer, wht, red & bl stripes, EX, B10...$10.00

Aurora AFX, Ultra 5 Porsche 510K Type B, MIB, T1......$15.00

Aurora AFX, Ultra 5 Porsche 917-10 Type A, MIB, T1...$15.00

Aurora AFX, Vega Funny Car, NMIB, J2........................$25.00

Aurora AFX, Vega Van Gasser, wht w/flames, EX, B10....$12.00

Aurora AFX, 1929 Model A Woodie, MIB, B10.............$15.00

Aurora AFX, 1957 Chevy Nomad, bl, NM, B10.............$22.00

Aurora G-Plus, American Racing Can Am, yel w/blk & wht stripes, NM, B10...$14.00

Aurora G-Plus, Camaro (NASCAR) #76, wht, orange & gold, NM, B10 ....$12.00

Aurora G-Plus, Capri, wht w/gr & bl stripes, NM, B10....$12.00

Aurora G-Plus, Indy Car, blk w/wht, yel, orange & red stripes, EX, B10...$12.00

Aurora G-Plus, Lotus F-1, blk & yel, NM, B10...............$14.00

Aurora G-Plus, Monza GT #0, wht & gr stripe, NM, B10.$15.00

Aurora Thunderjet, Alpha Romeo Type 33, #1409, red, no fins, VG+, B1, from $35 to...$40.00

Aurora Thunderjet, Bushwakker Snowmobile, bl & blk, M, B10...$40.00

Aurora Thunderjet, Camaro, cracked window post, EX, B10...$30.00

Aurora Thunderjet, Chaparral 2F, Tuff One, #7, wht & blk, NM, B10...$25.00

Aurora Thunderjet, Cheetah, bl, VG, B10........................$7.00

Aurora Thunderjet, Chevy Baja Blazer, wht, bl, red flames, NM...$30.00

Aurora Thunderjet, Cobra Daytona GT, #1375, med bl w/wht stripes, EX, B10..$25.00

Aurora Thunderjet, Corvette, turq, NM, J2.....................$45.00

Aurora Thunderjet, Cougar, #1389, wht, M, B10.............$35.00

Aurora Thunderjet, Cougar, yel, EX (EX box), J2 ....$35.00

Aurora Thunderjet, Dino Ferrari, #1381, yel w/red stripes, NM, B10...$28.00

Aurora Thunderjet, Dino Ferrari, #5, NM, J2.................$28.00

Aurora Thunderjet, Dune Buggy, wht w/red striped roof, EX, B10...$30.00

Aurora Thunderjet, Ferrari GTO 250, #1368, candy w/silver stripes, EX+, B10.......................................$45.00

Aurora Thunderjet, Ford AC Cobra, #1370, wht, red & blk, M, B10...$60.00

Aurora Thunderjet, Ford GT 40, #1374, yel w/blk stripe, M, B10...$25.00

Aurora Thunderjet, Ford J Car, #1382, wht & bl, EX, B10..$20.00

Aurora Thunderjet, Ford Lola GT, yel cream w/blk & wht stripes, NM, B10.......................................$25.00

Aurora Thunderjet, Hot Rod Roadster, tan, NM, J2 ....$35.00

Aurora Thunderjet, Indy Racer #7, #1359, red, NM, B10.$25.00

Aurora Thunderjet, Jaguar XKE, #1358, olive drab, NM, B10...$37.00

Aurora Thunderjet, Lola GT, #1378, gr w/wht stripe, NM, B10...$20.00

Aurora Thunderjet, Mack Dump Truck, #1362, yel cream & gray, NM, B10.......................................$65.00

Aurora Thunderjet, Mangusta Mongoose, #1400, med bl, NM, B10...$33.00

Aurora Thunderjet, McLaren Elva, #1431, wht w/red stripe, NM, B10...$25.00

Aurora Thunderjet, Mustang 2+2 Fastback, #1373, yel w/blk & red stripes, EX+, B10.......................................$35.00

Aurora Thunderjet, Porsche 904, #1376, bl w/wht stripe, NM, B10...$24.00

Aurora Thunderjet, Porsche 906, red w/wht stripe, EX, B10...$22.00

Aurora Thunderjet, Snowmobile, #1485-400, M, B10 .....$35.00

Aurora Thunderjet, 1967 Thunderbird, #1379, EX, B10, from $35 to $40.00

Aurora Vibrator, Hot Rod Roadster, #1553, bl, yel or gr, VG, ea $75.00

Aurora Vibrator, International Pickup Truck, #1580, dk gray & blk, EX $150.00

Aurora Vibrator, Mercedes, #1542, yel, EX.....................$50.00

Aurora Vibrator, Mercedes-Benz 300SL, #1542, bl, NM ..$75.00

Aurora Vibrator, Van Body Trailer, #1586, dk gray, VG ...$15.00

Classic, Viper, burgundy, 1/24 scale, EX, B10..................$80.00

Eldon, 1966 Dodge Charger (from set #48), 1/32 scale, red, EX, $35.00.

Cox, Ford GT 40, 1/32 scale, EX, B10 ....$75.00

Eldon, Chevy Impala, 1/32 scale, NM, J2 ....$45.00

Eldon, Ford Thunderbird, orange, 1/32 scale, NM, J2 ......$50.00

Eldon, Pontiac Bonneville, wht, 1/32 scale, NM, J2.........$50.00

Motorific, Grand Prix, NMIB, J2 ....$35.00

Motorific, Mini Chaparral D2, unused, MIB, J2 ....$25.00

Strombecker, Cheetah, 1/32 scale, EX, B10.....................$35.00

Strombecker, Ford GT, 1/32 scale, EX, B10 ....$35.00

Strombecker, Pontiac Bonneville, 1/32 scale, EX, B10.....$40.00

TCR, Blazer, blk w/yel & orange flames, NM, B10...........$14.00

TCR, Jam Car, yel & blk, NM, B10 ....$14.00

TCR, Maintenance Van, wht & red, NM, B10...................$14.00

TCR, Mercury Stock Car, purple, w/chrome, NM, B10 ...$18.00

Tyco, A-Team Van, blk w/red stripe, NM, B10 ....$38.00

Tyco, Autoworld Carrera, wht w/red, wht & bl stripes, VG, B10 ....$10.00

Tyco, Bandit Pickup, blk & yel, NM, B10.........................$12.00

Tyco, Blackbird Firebird, #6914, blk & gold, NM, B10 ....$12.00

Tyco, Blazer, red & blk, EX, B10 ....$10.00

Tyco, Chaparral 2G #66, wht, EX, B10............................$14.00

Tyco, Corvette Cliffhanger, Glo-in-the-Dark, EX, B10....$10.00

Tyco, Ferrari, #8967, red, EX, B10..................................$12.00

Tyco, Fiero #23, yel, wht & orange stripe, NM, B10........$12.00

Tyco, Funny Mustang, orange w/yel flame, NM, B10 ....$25.00

Tyco, Ghostracer Corvette, blk w/pnt skull, NM, B10 .....$14.00

Tyco, Hardee's Car, orange & bl, NM, B10......................$14.00

Tyco, Indy Diehard, blk & gold, wing loose, NM, B10 ....$12.00

Tyco, Jam Car, yel & blk, w/lights, NM, B10 ....$10.00

Tyco, Javelin, red, wht & bl, EX+, B10............................$15.00

Tyco, Jeep CJ7, red & lt bl, EX, B10 ....$12.00

Tyco, Lamborghini, red, EX, B10.....................................$12.00

Tyco, Mack Truck, dk bl & blk, NM, B10........................$22.00

Tyco, McLaren M8F, #8503, blk w/red stripe, NM, B10...$25.00

Tyco, Mustang #1, orange w/yel flames, EX, B10.............$20.00

Tyco, Porsche #2, lighted, silver w/red nose, NM, B10.....$20.00

Tyco, Porsche Carrera, #8527, yel & blk, NM, B10..........$25.00

Tyco, Porsche 917, #3, gr & silver, NM, B10 ....$16.00

Tyco, Silverstreak Porsche 908 #3, lighted, silver w/gray, EX, B10 ....$15.00

Tyco, Silverstreak Porsche 917, lighted, silver w/bl & gr stripes, NM, B10 ....$16.00

Tyco, Super American, #8525, lighted, red, wht & bl, NM, B10 ....$20.00

Tyco, Turbo Firebird, blk & gold, NM, B10 ....$12.00

Tyco, Turbo Hopper #27, red, NM, B10..........................$12.00

Tyco, Van-Tastic, #8539, bl & wht, EX, B10 ....$20.00

Tyco, Z-28 Camaro #7, red, wht & bl, 5.0 Liter decal, NM, B10 ....$12.00

Tyco, 1940 Ford Coupe, #8534, blk w/flames, NM, B10...$20.00

Tyco, 1957 Chevy, red w/orange & yel stripes, NM, B10 .$18.00

Accessories

Aurora AFX, Speed Steer Breakout Wall, #6056, MIB, B10..$18.00

Aurora AFX, Speed Steer Intersection Overpass, #6055, 1979, MIB, B10..$20.00

Aurora Model Motoring, Auto Starter, #1507, 1960, EX (EX box), B10 ....$15.00

Aurora Model Motoring, Curved Roadway, #1519, 6 pcs, EX (EX box), B10, from $10 to $15.00
Aurora Model Motoring, Guard Rails & Posts, #1532, complete, EX (EX box), B10 ....$8.00
Aurora Model Motoring, Loop the Loop Track Set, #1504, EX (EX box), B10 ....$20.00
Aurora Model Motoring, Monza Banked Curve, #1467, EX (EX box), B10 ....$15.00
Aurora Model Motoring, Speed Control steering wheel, G, B10..............................$10.00
Aurora Model Motoring, Straight Roadway, #1517, 6 pcs, EX (EX box), B10, from $10 to $15.00
Gilbert Autorama, Automatic Lap Counter, #19339, MIB, B10..............................$35.00
Gilbert Autorama, Fly Over Chicane Kit, #19342, MIB, B10..............................$40.00
Strombecker, Avenger V6 Motor, MOC (sealed), J2........$15.00

Smith-Miller

Smith-Miller (Los Angeles, Calfiornia) made toy trucks from 1944 until 1955. During that time they used four basic cab designs, and most of their trucks sold for about $15.00 each. Over the past several years, these toys have become very popular, especially the Mack trucks which today sell at premium prices. The company made a few other types of toys as well, such as the train toy box and the 'Long, Long Trailer.'

Advisor: Doug Dezso (D6).

COE Semi Tractor, w/flat bed trailer, G $200.00
CS Army Overseas Supply Truck, M..............................$700.00
GMC Bank of America Truck, NM $300.00
GMC Kraft Van, G..............................$425.00
GMC Mobil Tow Truck, EX $350.00
GMC Super Cargo Truck, VG $350.00
Log Trailer, G..............................$150.00
Mack Custom Union 76 Tanker Truck, NM..................$585.00
Mobil Gas GMC Tow Truck, VG..............................$350.00
Silver Streak Trailer, VG..............................$200.00
SMFD Aerial Ladder Truck, red long-nose w/enclosed cab, aluminum extension ladders, blk tires, VG..................$500.00
SMFD Mack Aerial Ladder Truck, EX $600.00
Smith-Miller Tandem Box Van, NM $1,650.00
Transcontinental Freighter, EX $600.00

Snow Domes

Snow domes are water-filled paperweights that come in several different styles. The earliest type was made in two pieces and consisted of a glass globe on a separate base. First made in the middle of the 19th century, they were revived during the thirties and forties by companies in America, Italy and Germany. Similar weights are being imported into the country today from the Orient. The most common snow domes on today's market are the plastic half-moon shapes made as souvenirs or Christmas toys, a style that originated in West Germany during the 1950s. Other shapes were made as well, including round and square bottles, short and tall rectangles, cubes and other simple shapes.

During the 1970s, figural plastic snow domes were especially popular. There are two types — large animate shapes themselves containing the snow scene, or dome shapes that have figures draped over the top. Today's collectors buy them all, old or new. For further information we recommend *Collector's Guide to Snow Domes* by Helene Guarnaccia, published by Collector Books.

Advisor: Nancy McMichael (M18).

Advertising

Coca-Cola Mania, Santa w/bottle, music box in base, MIB, T1..............................$30.00
Days Inn, Catch Some Rays at Days, w/2 Flintstone characters, sm oval plastic dome, M18 ....$10.00
Days Inn, The Whole Family Stays at Days, yel & turq, plastic, sm oval plastic dome, M18 ....$10.00
Jubileum Vodka, Forget Vodka With a Twist..., bottle inside, blk base, bullet-shaped clear plastic dome, 3½", M18 .....$15.00
Michelin Man, Mr Bib in mountains, European issue, MIB, P12 ....$45.00

Figures

Bear, wearing Christmas hat & gr ribbon at neck, no plaque, M18..............................$9.00
Bear atop sm dome, Great Smokey Mountains on plaque, old, M18..............................$12.00

Photo courtesy of Helene Guarnaccia.

Bugs Bunny, wood with glass dome, VG, $95.00.

Boot, Santa in sled w/pine trees & red church inside, plastic, old, M18..............................$7.00

Cat Playing Drum, drum as water compartment, M18........$9.00

Christmas Tree, covered w/lights & balls, old, M18 ....$10.00

Coffeepot, clear plastic, girl & snowman inside, old, M18.$10.00

Creature From the Black Lagoon, MIB, J2 ....$15.00

Crucifiction, Montenero emb on flat panel, Madonna & Child before monastery, plastic ball, elongated base, M18 ..$25.00

Dog w/Chistmas Gift, gift is water compartment, M18.......$9.00

Fish, yel Florida or orange Canada, M18, ea $10.00

Frog, Puerto Rico, w/frog family inside, no seesaw, M18.....$7.00

Gift Box, w/lg red plastic bow at top, clear cube w/waving snow-man inside, old, rare, M18...$15.00

Ice Mountain, 2 deer inside, sm, M18 ....$7.00

Orange, no leaves or base, M18 ....$8.00

Santa, climbing out of chimney, plastic, M18 ....$8.00

Santa atop lg oval dome, holds wrapped gift, angel & deer inside, old, rare, M18..$12.00

Santa on Lamppost, M18 ....$8.00

Snowman, w/tall blk hat, red ear muffs & lg red smile, hole in face where carrot nose broke off, tall, old, M18 ....$8.00

Holidays and Special Occasions

Christmas Carol, Tiny Tim on Bob Cratchit's shoulder w/Scrooge nearby, no plaque, wood base, lg glass dome, M18 ....$15.00

Fantasia (at front), Mickey Mouse as Sorcerer's Apprentice w/brooms, glass dome, Disney, 5½x3", M18..............$25.00

Merry Christmas to All, Enesco, 1987, Santa in sleigh flying around roof, EX, I2..$6.00

Rabbit, full-scale model w/Easter eggs at front, stands next to pine tree, Austrian, glass dome, new, M18.................$10.00

Saturday Evening Post, Norman Rockwell Christmas, December 4, 1926, on brass plaque on dk wood base, lg glass dome, M18 ....$30.00

Souvenir and Commemoratives

Alaska Bear, lg wht bear bending over stream, sm oval plastic dome, M18 ....$6.00

Artis Zoo, Amsterdam, penguins marching in a row, sm oval plastic dome, M18..$10.00

Atlanta, blk skyine in front of puffy bl & wht clouds, orange sun & plane, M18 ....$4.00

Bahamas 500th Anniversary on Lucite panel, sailing ship w/1942-1992 on yel banner across sails, lg, M18 ....$10.00

Berlin Blelbt Doch Berlin (Berlin Will Always Be Berlin), West Germany, mc city scene, sm oval plastic dome, M18...$8.00

Big Merino Goulburn, NSW, Australia, huge sheep w/national flag at front, sm oval plastic dome, M18 ....$18.00

Blue Ridge Parkway, 2 blk bears on seesaw, gr hills & rainbow at back, sm oval plastic dome, M18 ....$9.00

Buffalo, New York, buffalo before Niagara Falls & rainbow, sm oval plastic dome, M18 ....$8.00

Cancun, Cozumel, Mexico, on outside at top, fish on string inside, lg plastic dome, M18 ....$8.00

Cancun, Mexico, in blk script on outside lip of lg dome, 2 pk dolphins inside, M18...$6.00

Cape Cod, 2 sailboats, sm oval plastic dome, old, M18 ......$7.00

Capri Grotta Azzurra, Blue Grotto in brilliant bl, lg plastic dome, M18..$10.00

Carcassonne, word on plaque, French town w/red roofs, sm oval plastic dome, M18..$8.00

Colorado's Native American, on lg plaque, Indian chief Lucite panel transforms to eagle, lg plastic dome, M18...........$8.00

Connoaut Lake Park, in Gothic letters on plaque, 2 Lucite panels of amusement park rides, sm plastic dome, M18.....$6.00

Cooper Union (NYC building), detailed replica, clear all around, broad blk base w/gold decal, rnd, lg, M18.....$18.00

Cozumel, Mexico, script letters on outside of base at bottom, fish on string inside, sm plastic dome, M18 ....$6.00

Devon, England, lg letters on plaque, Lucite panel w/mc elf, owl & mushrooms, rainbow panel at back, plastic dome, M18 ..$8.00

Enchanted Forest, lg fairy tale character w/forest & castle on back panel, sm plastic dome, late 1980s, M18.............$7.00

Florida Snowman, w/top hat, cane & pipe, plaque on ea side, all-clear oval plastic dome, orig version, ca 1980, M18.....$6.00

General Jackson, letters on lg plaque at base of lg bottle, panel w/drawing of paddle-wheeler, M18...............................$8.00

Gillette Castle, Hadlyme, Connecticut, w/castle & trees, low rectangle form, old, M18...$8.00

Gillette Castle State Park, Connecticut, w/castle inside, 3 peg-leg style, old, M18...$8.00

Hi Y'All From Georgia, wht script on blk plastic base, lg peach at front w/fields at back, Lucite dome, M18.................$5.00

Howe Caverns, New York, lg letters w/caverns & boat tour, lg plastic dome, M18..$8.00

I (a heart) Greece, Korinth Canal on front at base, 2 sailboats inside, water-filled & bl oil-filled cube, M18..............$8.00

Kansas City, written on wavy band over star & diamond on Lucite panel, flat rectangular dome, early, M18...........$6.00

Lake George, sailboat on lake scene, lg plastic dome, M18 .$6.00

Lake George, wht block letters at front, 2 sailboats, lg yel sun w/radiating spokes, lg blk dome, unusual, M18 ....$4.00

Library of Congress on Lucite panel w/building, mc panel of DC monuments, Washington DC at outside, lg blk dome, M18 ....$6.00

Louisville Zoo, wht letters on base, bears on Lucite panel, seals at front, turq, toaster-shaped dome, M18 ....$5.00

Maritime Lobster on plaque, fishing village & lobster, sm oval plastic dome, M18...$8.00

Mayflower II, emb in gold on base, ship scale model inside, cube dome, old, M18...$10.00

Mayflower II, lg blk letters on plaque, lg sailing ship inside, sm oval plastic dome, M18...$12.00

Melbourne, Australia, wht letters on back of base, trolley moves on groove, buildings inside, blk plastic dome, M18 .....$7.00

Minnesota Common Loon, State Bird, lg loon & rainbow inside, lg plastic dome, old, M18..$8.00

Myrtle Beach, South Carolina, blk letters on band at bottom, sailing scene inside, plastic dome, old, sm chip, M18 ..$8.00

Nashua, Iowa, Little Brown Church in Vale (not written) scene, flat-back plastic dome, old, M18 ....$9.00

Niagara Falls, Canada, lg red letters on plaque at bottle neck, sm boat w/shore at back, plastic dome, M18....................$5.00

Oberammergau Passion Theatre on curved band at base of detailed town w/red-domed church, Germany, plastic dome, M18 ....$12.00

Oregon Coast, fish inside, treasure-chest form, M18 ....$7.00

Outer Banks, North Carolina, fish on string w/seaweed, low flat rectangular dome, words slightly faded, M18 ....$5.00

Paris, w/Eiffel Tower, Notre Dame & Sacre Coeur at back, glitter, lg plastic dome, M18...$7.00

Pittsburgh Post Extra! Feeney & Hirsh Marry, written newspaper pg, wedding couple & May 15, 1993, lg plastic dome, M18...$12.00

Plymouth, Massachusetts, fish on string, seaweed w/sea horse & fish sculpted into back, low rectangular dome, old, M18...$7.00

Roman S Pietro, peasant woman & Swiss guard in front of St Peter's Cathedral, sm plastic dome, M18......................$7.00

San Francisco, California, red trolley moves on groove, city scene at back, sm plastic dome, old, M18.....................$6.00

San Gimignano (Italy), medieval town w/7 towers & red roofs, lg plastic dome, M18..$10.00

San Gimignano (Italy), medieval town w/7 towers & red roofs, sm plastic dome, M18 ....$8.00

Save the Earth, birds on Lucite, lg blk dome, M18 ....$5.00

Save the Earth, forest animals, sm oval plastic dome, M18 .$5.00

Sea World, San Diego, lg red letters on plaque at bottle neck, dolphin w/penguins against tree panel, old, M18 ......$10.00

Sears Tower, Chicago, lg blk letters, fat bullet-shaped dome, M18...$10.00

St Thomas, Virgin Islands, parrot inside, sm oval plastic dome, M18...$10.00

Ste Anne de Beaupre (Canada), church & Sainte Anne, lg plastic dome, late 1980s, M18....................................$8.00

Sunsphere, Knoxville, Tennessee, w/Tower from World's Fair, tall popsicle form, old, rare version, M18...................$13.00

Taronga Zoo, tigers inside w/1 on lg dome, Australia, M18..$10.00

United Nations, written on blk base, UN building inside, heart-shaped dome, M18...$10.00

US Constitution, open-work ship inside, plastic dome, old, M18...$12.00

USS Massachusetts, Fall River, Massachusetts, lg gray battleship, sky panel at back (lose), glitter, 1960s, G-, M18..........$7.00

Venice, Florida, script on outside of base, 2 arched pk dolphins & seaweed, sm oval plastic dome, M18 ....$6.00

Williamsburg, Virginia, scene w/house, carriage & church in front, bottle form, minor water loss, M18....................$9.00

Wisconsin, blk w/state name in wht script letters on outside, Lucite cow panel before barn scene, sm plastic dome, M18........$3.00

Wisconsin, deer in center of seesaw, pine trees on ends, barn & cows at back, sm oval plastic dome, M18 ....$5.00

Soldiers

'Dimestore soldiers' were made from the 1920s until sometime in the 1960s. Some of the better-known companies who made these small-scale figures and accessories were Barclay, Manoil, and Jones (hollow cast lead); Gray Iron (cast iron); and Auburn (rubber). They're about 3" to 3½" high. They were sold in Woolworth's and Kresge's 5 & 10 Stores (most for just five cents), hence the name 'Dimestore.' Marx made tin soldiers for use in target gun games; these sell for about $8.00. Condition is most important as these soldiers saw lots of action. They're most often found with much of the paint worn off and with some serious 'battle wounds' such as missing arms or legs. Nearly 2,000 different figures were made by the major manufacturers, plus a number of others by minor makers such as Tommy Toy and All-Nu. Serious collectors should refer to *Collecting Toys* (1993) or *Toy Soldiers* (1992), both by Richard O'Brien, Books Americana.

Another very popular line of toy soldiers has been made by Britains of England since 1893. They are smaller and usually more detailed than 'Dimestores,' and variants number in the thousands. O'Brien's book has over 200 pages devoted to Britains and other foreign makers.

You'll notice that in addition to the soldiers, many of our descriptions and values are for the vehicles, cannons, animals, and cowboys and Indians made and sold by the same manufacturers. Note: Percentages in the description lines refer to the amount of original paint remaining, a most important evaluation factor.

Advisors: Sally and Stan Alekna (A1).

See also Dinky (for accessory vehicles); Plastic Figures.

Key: ROAN — Regiments of All Nations

Six Flags Over Georgia and Six Flags Magic Mountain, calendar domes with seesaws, EX, $20.00 each.

Photo courtesy of Helene Guarnaccia.

Snowy Mountains, skier in orange suit, snow scene at back, Austrailia, M18 ....$10.00

Space Needle, Seattle, Washington, salt & pepper shakers, pk & bl plastic, tall popsicle shape, M18, pr $18.00

Squire Boone Caverns & Village, Squire Boone w/whiskey still & geological formation, flat rectangular dome, M18 ...$8.00

SS Admiral River Boat, on 2 plaques inside bottle, St Louis plaque at neck, Arch & Stadium at back, water loss, rare, M18...$18.00

St Augustine, Florida, fish on string, glitter, low rectangular dome w/blk rim, old, M18...$7.00

St Francis Indian Mission, Stone Lake, Wisconsin, Mission School building on panel, lg plastic dome, M18........$12.00

Auburn Rubber, soldier marching, port arms, early version, NM, A1 ....$19.00

Auburn Rubber, soldier w/binoculars, early version, pnt pouch, glasses, etc, 97%, A1 ....$20.00

Auburn Rubber, soldier wounded, 90%, A1 ....$18.00

Auburn Rubber, stretcher bearer, scarce, 94%, A1 ....$36.00

Barclay, AA gunner, brn, 97%, A1 ....$14.00

Barclay, AA gunner, cast hat, 99%, A1 ....$29.00

Barclay, aircraft carrier, w/both orig Tootsietoy airplanes, all 4 guns intact, scarce, A1 ....$150.00

Barclay, Army truck, 98%, A1 ....$25.00

Barclay, aviator, brn, 96%, A1 ....$20.00

Barclay, battleship, all 4 guns intact, #377, scarce, 99%, A1 ..$95.00

Barclay, Black porter, w/whisk broom, 99%, A1 ....$19.00

Barclay, Black Red Cap, w/bags, 99%, A1 ....$26.00

Barclay, boy, gray, 99%, A1 ....$15.00

Barclay, Boy Scout hiking, scarce, 99%, A1 ....$54.00

Barclay, boy skater, 98%, A1 ....$13.00

Barclay, brakeman, M, A1 ....$10.00

Barclay, bull, M, A1 ....$15.00

Barclay, cadet officer, in wht, short stride, 96%, A1 ....$26.00

Barclay, cannon, high barrel elevation, 97%, A1 ....$20.00

Barclay, cannon, silver w/red metal wheels, open hitch variation, 98%, A1 ....$25.00

Barclay, cannon car, khaki, 95%, A1 ....$20.00

Barclay, cavalryman, sm, 1930s, 97%, A1 ....$31.00

Barclay, conductor, HO scale, M, A1 ....$11.00

Barclay, convertible, w/couple, bl, 1960s, 99%, A1 ....$21.00

Barclay, convertible, w/vacationing family, bl w/wht tires, scarce, 97%, A1 ....$80.00

Barclay, cow, grazing, M, A1 ....$15.00

Barclay, cow, lying, M, A1 ....$15.00

Barclay, cowboy, no lasso, gray, 98%, A1 ....$20.00

Barclay, cowboy, w/tin hat brim, brn outfit, 93%, A1 ......$19.00

Barclay, delivery truck, mustard yel, no decals, 98%, A1 ..$14.00

Barclay, dining steward, 99%, A1 ....$10.00

Barclay, dirigible, silver body, red gondola, blk metal wheel, 1930s, scarce, 95%, A1 ....$150.00

Barclay, dump truck, red & bl, 1960s, M, A1 ....$15.00

Barclay, dump truck, yel & bl, side dump, 1960s, NM, A1 ..$15.00

Barclay, engineer, 99%, A1 ....$16.00

Barclay, girl, in rocker, red outfit, 99%, A1 ....$20.00

Barclay, girl, on red sled, gr outfit, 99%, A1 ....$21.00

Barclay, girl, red outfit, 99%, A1 ....$16.00

Barclay, girl skater, in bl, 99%, A1 ....$20.00

Barclay, girl skater, in red, 98%, A1 ....$13.00

Barclay, horse, grazing, blk, M, A1 ....$16.00

Barclay, horse-drawn milk wagon, scarce, 1930s, 97%, A1 ..$175.00

Barclay, Indian, on horse, 99%, A1 ....$36.00

Barclay, Indian, w/knife & spear, 97%, A1 ....$17.00

Barclay, Indian, w/rifle, scarce 65mm sz, 88%, A1 ....$29.00

Barclay, Indian, w/tomahawk & shield, 97%, A1 ....$13.00

Barclay, Indian Chief, w/tomahawk & shield, hex base, early 50mm, scarce, 94%, A1 ....$19.00

Barclay, jockey on gold horse, wearing red & silver silks, #2, 98%, A1 ....$26.00

Barclay, log truck, w/3 logs, 1960s, 99%, A1 ....$16.00

Barclay, machine gunner, brn, 98%, A1 ....$16.00

Barclay, machine gunner, gr, tiny dent in side of helmet, 97%, A1 ....$17.00

Barclay, mailman, HO scale, 99%, A1 ....$10.00

Barclay, mailman, 99%, A1 ....$18.00

Barclay, man, in bl, HO scale, M, A1 ....$10.00

Barclay, man, on yel sled, 98%, A1 ....$20.00

Barclay, man passenger, gray suit, 99%, A1 ....$15.00

Barclay, man pulling kids on sled, scarce, 99%, A1 ....$54.00

Barclay, marine, marching, short stride, 98%, A1 ....$34.00

Barclay, marine, 93%, A1 ....$14.00

Barclay, milk van, bottle on side, wht tires, 99%, A1 ......$40.00

Barclay, moving truck, red & silver, no decals, 1960s, 98%, A1 ....$13.00

Barclay, newsboy, in brn & orange, 99%, A1 ....$17.00

Barclay, newsboy, M, A1 ....$10.00

Barclay, nurse, blk hair, NM, A1 ....$37.00

Barclay, nurse, hands on hip, red hair, 97%, A1 ....$24.00

Barclay, officer, brn, 97%, A1 ....$16.00

Barclay, officer, gr, M, A1 ....$21.00

Barclay, officer, on brn horse, in khaki, 98%, A1 ....$37.00

Barclay, oil truck, bl & silver, Sunoco decals, 1960s, NM, A1 ..$16.00

Barclay, policeman, 97%, A1 ....$19.00

Barclay, ram, yel w/blk horns, M, A1 ....$15.00

Barclay, reindeer, extremely rare, from $90.00 to $125.00.

Barclay, sailor, in wht, brn hair, 99%, A1 ....$21.00

Barclay, Santa, no skis, poles or holes for poles, very scarce, 94%, A1 ....$120.00

Barclay, searchlight (#5), swivel base, lens is intact but not shiny, very scarce, 99%, A1 ....$95.00

Barclay, skier, in wht, w/machine gun, no skis, 95%, A1 ..$27.00

Barclay, soldier, bayonetting, tin hat, 96%, A1 ....$55.00

Barclay, soldier, bomb thrower, 95%, A1 ....$24.00

Barclay, soldier, charging, cast hat, gr helmet, 98%, A1 ..$28.00

Barclay, soldier, charging, gr, 98%, A1 ....$20.00

Barclay, soldier, charging, tin hat, short stride, 97%, A1 ..$27.00

Barclay, soldier, charging w/tommy gun, 93%, A1 ....$17.00

Barclay, soldier, crawling w/rifle, 95%, A1 ....$26.00

Barclay, soldier, in gas mask, w/rifle, rusty helmet, 95%, A1 ....$23.00

Barclay, soldier, marching, cast hat, NM, A1 .... $31.00

Barclay, soldier, marching w/rifle slung, brn, M, A1 .... $17.00

Barclay, soldier, marching w/rifle slung, gr helmet, 99%, A1 .... $21.00

Barclay, soldier, sniper kneeling, brn, 98%, A1 .... $16.00

Barclay, soldier, standing at searchlight, 95%, A1 .... $39.00

Barclay, soldier, telephone operator, 96%, A1 .... $26.00

Barclay, soldier, tommy gunner, gr helmet, 93%, A1 .... $20.00

Barclay, soldier, under marching orders, brn, 99%, A1 ..... $16.00

Barclay, soldier, w/shell, tin hat, 94%, A1 .... $17.00

Barclay, soldier, wireless operator, orig antenna, diecut in orig helmet, 98%, A1 .... $42.00

Barclay, soldier, wounded head & arm, brn, scarce, M, A1 ... $35.00

Barclay, soldier crew (2), at AA gun, bl barrel, 97%, A1 . $38.00

Barclay, soldier crew (2), at radar equipment, 98%, A1 .... $35.00

Barclay, soldier crew (3), at range finder, 98%, A1 .... $31.00

Barclay, stretcher bearer, 95%, A1 .... $23.00

Barclay, tank, khaki, wht tires, long, 94%, A1 .... $19.00

Barclay, tractor/trailer, Allied Van Lines decals, 1960s, 97%, A1 .... $24.00

Barclay, truck, open bed, yel, 1960s, 99%, A1 .... $14.00

Barclay, VW, gr, scarce, 99%, A1 .... $25.00

Barclay, woman, elderly, in lavender outfit, 99%, A1 .. $18.00

Barclay, woman, in red, no dog, HO scale, 99%, A1 .... $9.00

Britains, #1, Life Guards, mounted in review w/officer on cantering horse, few chips, 5-pc, EX (VG box), A $130.00

Britains, #2, Royal Horse Guards, mounted in review, officer on prancing horse, 5-pc, EX (G box), A $160.00

Britains, #8F, Farm Rake w/driver & horse, working model, 3-pc, EX (VG box), A $120.00

Britains, #11, Black Watch, charging in review order, ca 1940, 8-pc, VG (G Whisstock box), A $130.00

Britains, #11, 42nd Highlanders, prewar, 6-pc, VG (VG Whisstock box), A $155.00

Britains, #13, 3rd Hussars, 5-pc, VG, A $145.00

Britains, #17, Somerset Light Infantry, standing & kneeling w/officer w/binoculars, 8-pc, EX (VG box), A $190.00

Britains, #27, Band of the Line, 12-pc, EX (G+ Types of the World Armies box), A $495.00

Britains, #28, Royal Artillery Gun, gun, 6 gunners, 4 mules & mounted officer, EX (EX box), A $275.00

Britains, #30, Drums & Bugles of the Line, marching, w/drum major, 1940s, 7-pc, EX (VG box), A $225.00

Britains, #32, Royal Scots Greys, mounted on walking & trotting horses, 5-pc, VG (orig box), A $145.00

Britains, #33, 16th Lancers, mounted at the halt, 5-pc, G (G box), A $80.00

Britains, #37, Full Band of the Coldstream Guards, marching w/instruments, 21-pc, EX (Armies of the World box), A .. $490.00

Britains, #39, King's Troop Royal Horse Artillery, w/gun, limber, 6-horse team, outriders, & officer, NM (VG box), A $550.00

Britains, #44, Queen's Bay Dragoon Guards, 5-pc, VG, A .. $145.00

Britains, #47, Skinner's Horses, 5-pc, EX (EX Regiments of All Nations box), A $200.00

Britains, #69, Pipers of the Scots Guards, marching in review, ca 1935, 7-pc, EX (VG Whisstock box), A $400.00

Britains, #74, Royal Welch Fusiliers, marching at slope in review order, officer, goat mascot, 8-pc, G, A $140.00

Britains, #76, Middlesex Regiment, 8-pc, some hat spike missing, A $100.00

Britains, #82, Colours & Pioneers of the Scots Guards, w/axes, officer w/flag, ca 1925, G- (G Whisstock box), A ... $275.00

Britains, #92, Spanish Infantry, marching at slope in review order, ca 1930, 8-pc, VG, A $450.00

Britains, #111, Grenadier Guards at Attention, 6 guardsmen, mounted officer, ca 1920, 7-pc, G (G Whisstock box), A .. $550.00

Britains, #112, Seaforth Highlanders, 8-pc, EX (EX Regiments of All Nations box not orig to pcs), A $110.00

Britains, #114, Queen's Own Cameron Highlanders, marching in tropical dress, 8-pc, ca 1930, G (G Whisstock box), A .. $180.00

Britains, #117, Egyptian Infantry, standing at attention, 8-pc, EX (orig box lid), A $145.00

Britains, #123, Bikanir Camel Corps, mounted in review, ca 1935, 3-pc, VG (VG Types of the Indian Armies box), A ... $600.00

Britains, #128, 12th Lancers, 5-pc, VG (reproduction box), A .. $120.00

Britains, #133, Russian Infantry, marching at trail in review order w/officer, ca 1930, 8-pc, VG, A $100.00

Britains, #147, African Zulus, running w/spears, 8-pc, EX, A . $115.00

Britains, #152, North American Indians, mounted on galloping horses, 5-pc, VG, A $85.00

Britains, #153, Prussian Hussars, mounted in review w/lances, officer, ca 1930, some chips, 5-pc, VG, A $250.00

Britains, #154, Prussian Infantry, marching at slope in review order, 1908, 8-pc, chips, VG, A $275.00

Britains, #157, Gordon Highlanders, standing, kneeling & firing lying down, 9-pc, G (orig Whisstock box), A $85.00

Britains, #164 Arabs on Horses, 5-pc, EX (rstr Regiments of All Nations box), A $110.00

Britains, #167, Turkish Infantry, on guard position w/rifles, ca 1935, 8-pc, some chips, G (G Whisstock box), A ... $325.00

Britains, #172, Bulgarian Infantry, marching w/officer, 2 mismatched figures, 8-pc, G (G Armies of the World box), A $275.00

Britains, #179, Cowboys, mounted on galloping horses w/pistols & lariats, 5-pc, G, A $115.00

Britains, #189, Belgina Infantry, standing on guard, 8-pc, G (orig box lid), A $115.00

Britains, #197, 1st King George V's Own Gurka Rifles, 8-pc, EX (EX Regiments of All Nations box), A $120.00

Britains, #209, Cowboys Mounted & on Foot, w/rifles, pistols, lassos & wild horse, 1952-60, 11-pc, NM (VG box), A . $275.00

Britains, #212, Royal Scouts, marching slope arms w/piper, 5-pc, EX (Regiments of All Nations box), A $145.00

Britains, #213, Highland Light Infantry, marching at slope arms, 8-pc, G (orig Whisstock box), A $145.00

Britains, #218, Spanish Cavalry, mounted on walking horses, 5-pc, G, A $400.00

Britains, #225, King's African Rifles, 8-pc, EX (EX Regiments of All Nations box), A $210.00

Britains, #229, US Cavalry, mounted at the walk in service dress, 5-pc, G-, A $100.00

Britains, #267, US Army Cavalry & Infantry, mounted & walking, 12-pc (Regiments of All Nations box), A $115.00

Britains, #321, Drum & Fife Band of Line, 8 drummers (1 bass), 8 fifers & drum major, ca 1935, 17-pc, VG (G- box), A. $1,400.00

Britains, #429, Scots Guards & 1st Life Guards in Winter Dress, 13-pc, VG (VG Regiments of All Nations box), A.. $210.00

Britains, #432, 8-pc, EX (EX Regiments of All Nations box), A...$120.00

Britains, #1253, US Navy Whitejackets, marching at slope w/officer, 8-pc, VG (G box), A.............$180.00

Britains, #1257, Yeoman of the Guard, standing w/halberds, 9-pc, VG (orig Historical box), A..................$115.00

Britains, #1258, 13th Century Knights in Armor, 6-pc, NM, (EX Historical box), A.................................$400.00

Britains, #1318, British Machine Gunners, 6-pc, EX (EX Regiments of All Nations box), A $110.00

Britains, #1321, Armoured Car w/Swiveling Gun, olive drab, wht rubber tires, ca 1935, sm dents, VG (VG box), A...$300.00

Britains, #1323, Royal Fusiliers, Royal Sussex & Seaforth Highlanders, marching at slope arms, 23-pc, VG (orig box), A...$200.00

Britains, #1335, 6-Wheel Army Lorry, dk gr, w/driver, ca 1935, VG (VG box), A.......................................$225.00

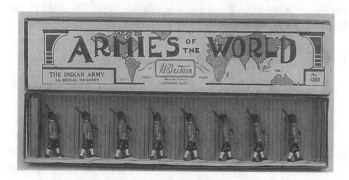

Britians, #1342, 7th Bengal Infantry (later 3rd Battalion, 7th Rajput Regiment), marching at slope in review order, ca 1935, EX (G Armies of the World box), A, $1,300.00.

Britains, #1349, Royal Canadian Mounted Police, on galloping horses, w/officer, 5-pc, G, A $80.00

Britains, #1349, Royal Canadian Mounted Police, 5-pc, VG, A $110.00

Britains, #1470, Coronation Coach, NM (EX box), M5 .$400.00

Britains, #1518, British Line Infantry, at attention w/muskets, officer w/sword, 1937-41, 8-pc, NM (G Historical box), A..$375.00

Britains, #1603, Irish Free State Infantry, marching at slope, gr dress & peak caps, w/officer, 1937-41, 8-pc, VG, A..$500.00

Britains, #1621, 12th Frontier Force Regiment, marching, 1940s, 8-pc, VG (G Armies of the World box), A $700.00

Britains, #1625, US Infantry, charging in battle dress w/gas masks, ca 1938, 7-pc, NM (EX Soldiers in Action box), A....$225.00

Britains, #1628, Infantry in Gas Masks, 15-pc, EX, A $105.00

Britains, #1631, Governor General's Horse Guard Canada, 2 officers & 3 troopers, EX (EX illus box), A............$155.00

Britains, #1634, Governor General's Foot Guards of Canada, marching at slope w/officer, few chips, 8-pc, EX, A..$110.00

Britains, #1711, Foreign Legion, 7-pc, EX (EX illus box), A..$155.00

Britains, #1717, 2-pounder AA gun on mobile chassis, brass breach cover & rubber wheels, 4½", H12.............$225.00

Britains, #1720, Band of the 2nd Dragoons, mounted on gray walking horses, 7-pc, VG (Regiments of All Nations box), A..$230.00

Britains, #1791, Royal Corps of Signals Motorcycle Dispatch Riders, khaki service dress, peak caps, 4-pc, VG (G box), A..$250.00

Britains, #1792, Mobile Traffic Police on Motorcycles, 4-pc, VG, A..$490.00

Britians, #1900, Regiment Louw Wepener, marching at slope in bluish-green uniforms with officer, 1948-1949, rare, EX (G box), A, $900.00.

Britains, #1901, Capetown Highlanders, 8-pc, NM (VG+ Regiments of All Nations box), A $120.00

Britains, #2019, Danish Life Guard, marching in full-dress uniforms, w/officer, 1955-59, 7-pc, EX (EX box), A $350.00

Britains, #2021, Snowdrops MP, 3 officers w/4 infantrymen, 7-pc, VG (Regiments of All Nations box), A...............$85.00

Britains, #2029, Life Guards, mounted & walking, 6-pc, EX (VG Regiments of All Nations box), A $145.00

Britains, #2030, Australian Infantry, marching at slope in 1948 Blue Ceremonial Dress, w/officer, 8-pc, VG, A.......$180.00

Britains, #2031, Australian Infantry, marching at slope in battle dress, w/officer in peak cap, 8-pc, chips, G-, A..........$90.00

Britains, #2035, Swedish Life Guards, marching at slope in review order, officer, EX (EX box), A $160.00

Britains, #2046, Arabs of the Desert, mounted & walking, 12-pc, G+ (G- box), A..$175.00

Britains, #2055, Confederate Cavalry, 5-pc, EX (EX Regiments of All Nations box), A $100.00

Britains, #2067, Sovereign's Standard, mounted on walking horses, 7-pc, VG (Regiments of All Nations box), A.............$200.00

Britains, #2071, Royal Marines, present arms w/officer holding sword at salute, 7-pc, EX (G box), A $180.00

Britains, #2073, Royal Air Force, marching at slope in RAF uniforms, w/officer, 8-pc, EX (VG+ box), A.................$130.00

Britains, #2076, 12th Lancers, mounted on cantering & trotting horses, 5-pc, VG (VG Regiments of All Nations box), A $115.00

Britains, #2078, Irish Guards, present arms w/officer saluting w/sword, 7-pc, EX (VG box), A...............................$170.00

Britains, #2079, Royal Company of Archers, some bows at rest, others firing, w/officer, 13-pc, VG, A......................$160.00

Britains, #2082, Coldstream Guards, 8-pc, EX (EX Regiments of All Nations box), A $110.00

Britains, #2087, 5th Royal Inniskilling Dragoons, at attention in #1 Dress, w/officer, 8-pc, minor mismatched colors, VG, A...$30.00

Britains, #2092, Royal Parachute Regiment, marching at the slope in #1 dress, w/officer, 8-pc, G (G- box), A $160.00

Britains, #2098, Venezuelan School Cadets, marching w/officer carrying national standard, 1955-59, 7-pc, NM (G- box), A $325.00

Courtenay, De Bohun Livery, Man-At-Arms, w/long bow in movable right arm, blk base, few chips, VG, A $500.00

Courtenay, Edward, The Black Prince, position 6, blk armor & gold crown, sword in right hand, signed, VG, A $400.00

Courtenay, King Edward III, position M2, mounted w/lance in movable right arm, great helm, blk base, EX, A $400.00

Courtenay, Lord John Mohun, position H12, mounted on charging horse, full trappings, sword, visor, signed, EX, A.................................$1,600.00

Courtenay, Oxford Livery, Man-At-Arms, crossbow in movable right arm, blk base, few chips, VG, A $350.00

Courtenay, Pembroke Livery, Man-At-Arms, crossbow in movable, right arm, blk base w/chips, VG, A $500.00

Courtenay, Robert De Bere, position 14, sword in right hand, w/kettle helmet, signed, few chips, VG, A $475.00

Courtenay, Simon De Montfort, mounted, rare version using King Richard I figure, G, A...........................$575.00

Courtenay, Sir Bartholomew Burghuren, position 20, signed, missing short sword handle otherwise EX, A, $240.00; Courtenay, John, King of France, position H6, gold and white tunic, signed, EX, A, $170.00.

Courtenay, Sir John Grey, KG, position H6B, mounted on rearing horse, axe in right arm, blk base, ca 1940, VG, A.......$550.00

Courtenay, Tournament Knight of Sir Henry Percy, position H12, mounted w/trappings, sword, visor, signed, EX, A $900.00

Courtenay, Tournament Knight of Thomas, Erle of Warwick, KG, mounted w/tournament trappings, lance, great helm, EX, A $800.00

Crescent, US & British Infantry, firing & throwing grenades, mounted officer, medical unit, 5 knights, 26-pc, G, A ..$60.00

Crescent, US Marines, 28-pc, EX (orig box), A $95.00

Dinky, #EBR panhard FL-10, w/insert & antenna in orig envelope, MIB, F2 ....$130.00

Dinky, #150B, private, seated, EX+, F2.....................$28.00

Dinky, #150C, private, standing, NM, F2 ....$28.00

Dinky, #150E, NCO, walking, EX, F2.......................$20.00

Dinky, #151A, med tank, EX, F2...............................$150.00

Dinky, #151C, cooker trailer, EX, F2........................$75.00

Dinky, #151D, water tanker trailer, M, F2.................$35.00

Dinky, #152A, lt tank, NM, F2..................................$140.00

Dinky, #152C, Austin Seven military, M, F2 ....$35.00

Dinky, #160A, officer w/binoculars, EX, F2 ....$22.00

Dinky, #160B, gunner, seated, VG, F2 ....$10.00

Dinky, #160D, gunner, standing, EX, F2....................$20.00

Dinky, #161B, antiaircraft gun, M, F2.......................$85.00

Dinky, #603, Army private, M, F2............................$14.00

Grey Iron, bandit, surrendering, red scarf, pnt chips on chin & cheeks, scarce, 92%, A1 ....$115.00

Grey Iron, bench, 99%, A1......................................$11.00

Grey Iron, Black porter, scarce, 98%, A1 ....$18.00

Grey Iron, cadet, bl jacket, early version, 96%, A1 ....$20.00

Grey Iron, calf, 99%, A1..$12.00

Grey Iron, cannon, #24, later version, 96%, A1 ....$29.00

Grey Iron, cannon, #48, early version, scarce, 95%, A1 ...$43.00

Grey Iron, colonial soldier, 98%, A1...........................$29.00

Grey Iron, conductor, 97%, A1 ....$11.00

Grey Iron, cow, blk & wht, NM, A1 ....$13.00

Grey Iron, cowboy, early version, 97%, A1 ....$27.00

Grey Iron, engineer, 98%, A1.....................................$11.00

Grey Iron, Ethiopian chief, stain on back, scarce, 96%, A1 ....$80.00

Grey Iron, farmer, 96%, A1 ....$14.00

Grey Iron, farmer's wife, 98%, A1 ....$16.00

Grey Iron, Foreign Legion, machine gunner, US Marine, scarce, 95%, A1 ....$47.00

Grey Iron, garage man, olive gr, postwar, 99%, A1 ....$19.00

Grey Iron, garage man, yel, prewar, 94%, A1.....................$17.00

Grey Iron, girl, 94%, A1 ....$15.00

Grey Iron, goat, 97%, A1 ....$11.00

Grey Iron, holdup man in blk, Hoppy, 97%, A1 ....$23.00

Grey Iron, horse, lt brn, 99%, A1..............................$12.00

Grey Iron, Indian, mounted on brn horse, early version, scarce, 98%, A1 ....$51.00

Grey Iron, knight in armor, 98%, A1 ....$20.00

Grey Iron, lady skater, 1920s, orig pnt, scarce, 95%, A1..$145.00

Grey Iron, Legion bugler, 96%, A1 ....$22.00

Grey Iron, Legion color bearer, 97%, A1 ....$30.00

Grey Iron, mailman, 99%, A1 ....$15.00

Grey Iron, milkman, scarce, 98%, A1 ....$22.00

Grey Iron, Naval officer, in wht, 96%, A1 ....$18.00

Grey Iron, nurse, helping wounded soldier, very scarce, 96%, A1 ....$245.00

Grey Iron, old man sitting, 99%, A1 ....$14.00

Grey Iron, old woman sitting, 98%, A1 ....$14.00

Grey Iron, pirate, w/dagger, 97%, A1 ....$35.00

Grey Iron, pirate, w/hook, brn outfit, 97%, A1.............$35.00

Grey Iron, pirate, w/sword, gr outfit, 98%, A1 ....$32.00

Grey Iron, pirate boy, few chips on face, 95%, A1 ....$33.00

Grey Iron, pirate chief, few chips on face, 97%, A1 ....$35.00

Grey Iron, policeman, 98%, A1 ....$14.00

Grey Iron, Red Cross doctor, scarce, 95%, A1 ....$38.00

Grey Iron, sailor, in bl, postwar, 97%, A1 ....$12.00

Grey Iron, sheep, 98%, A1 ....$11.00

Grey Iron, ski trooper, 1940s, rpl skis, 94%, A1 ....$41.00

Grey Iron, stretcher bearer, scarce, 97%, A1 ....$44.00

Grey Iron, US Doughboy, bomber crawling, brn pistol, 95%, A1 ....$27.00

Grey Iron, US Doughboy, charging, blk puttee & rifle, early version, 98%, A1 ....$22.00

Grey Iron, US Doughboy, combat trooper, 99%, A1 ....$35.00

Grey Iron, US Doughboy, port arms, blk puttees, rifle, early version, 97%, A1 ....$20.00

Grey Iron, US Doughboy, shoulder arms, 99%, A1 ....$22.00

Grey Iron, US Doughboy, w/bayonet, 96%, A1 ....$33.00

Grey Iron, US Infantry officer, blk trim, early version, 98%, A1 ....$19.00

Grey Iron, US machine gunner, early version, 96%, A1 ..$27.00

Grey Iron, US machine gunner, postwar, 96%, A1 ....$18.00

Grey Iron, US Marine, early version, 99%, A1 ....$28.00

Grey Iron, woman, w/basket, few chips on face, 96%, A1 .$14.00

Heyde, Mounted Band of the Prussian Dragoons, review order w/full band, ca 1920, 12-pc, G (G- box), A $400.00

Jones, British Marine of 1775, firing musket at angle, scarce, 98%, A1 ....$28.00

Jones, calf, #236, 93%, A1 ....$10.00

Jones, cow, lying, #221, M, A1 ....$11.00

Jones, cow, standing, 99%, A1 ....$10.00

Jones, dog, reddish brn, sm, scarce, 97%, A1 ....$18.00

Jones, donkey, #226, 98%, A1 ....$11.00

Jones, farmer, 99%, A1 ....$19.00

Jones, farmer's wife, 98%, A1 ....$18.00

Jones, fox, brn, scarce, 99%, A1 ....$28.00

Jones, fox, gray, scarce, 99%, A1 ....$28.00

Jones, German soldier, gray, kneeling w/rifle, scarce, 99%, A1 .$195.00

Jones, hen, M, A1 ....$10.00

Jones, Hessian soldier, at guard, bayonet intact, scarce, 90%, A1 ....$29.00

Jones, horse, gray, #228, 98%, A1 ....$11.00

Jones, mule, M, A1 ....$11.00

Jones, Scot Highlander of 1814, scarce, 98%, A1 ....$28.00

Jones, soldier, kneeling at searchlight, brn, scarce, 99%, A1 .$105.00

Jones, soldier, kneeling w/AA gun, brn, scarce, NM, A1 ..$115.00

Jones, US Marine, shoulder arms, scarce, 98%, A1 ....$21.00

Jones, Waynes Legion soldier, on guard w/bayonet, 54mm, scarce, M, A1 ....$32.00

Manoil, anti-aircraft searchlight, 94%, A1 ....$28.00

Manoil, aviator, carrying bomb sight, sm base variant, scarce, 97%, A1 ....$59.00

Manoil, bawling calf, 99%, A1 ....$16.00

Manoil, bench, 95%, A1 ....$12.00

Manoil, boy carrying wood, 98%, A1 ....$27.00

Manoil, bull, head turned, 97%, A1 ....$16.00

Manoil, cactus, lg, scarce, 97%, A1 ....$36.00

Manoil, caisson, w/soldier, solid stand, 98%, A1 ....$32.00

Manoil, carpenter, carrying door, scarce, 99%, A1 ....$68.00

Manoil, carpenter, sawing lumber, 99%, A1 ....$32.00

Manoil, coastal defense cannon, early version w/brace inside to hold halves together, 98%, A1 ....$35.00

Manoil, colt, brn, scarce, 98%, A1 ....$26.00

Manoil, cook's helper, w/ladle, 4 eggs on grill, 98%, A1 ...$48.00

Manoil, cow, grazing, 98%, A1 ....$15.00

Manoil, cowboy, bl pants & purple shirt, 95%, A1 ....$18.00

Manoil, cowboy, mounted, shooting short pistol, scarce, 98%, A1 ....$75.00

Manoil, cowboy, 2nd version, 93%, A1............................$15.00

Manoil, doctor, in wht, 97%, A1 ....$29.00

Manoil, farmer, at water pump, 96%, A1 ....$21.00

Manoil, farmer, cutting corn, 97%, A1 ....$24.00

Manoil, farmer, sharpening scythe, 97%, A1 ....$25.00

Manoil, fire engine, red & silver, scarce, 98%, A1............$42.00

Manoil, fuel truck, Gasoline decal, 99%, A1 ....$32.00

Manoil, girl, in wht dress, 96%, A1 ....$12.00

Manoil, girl, watering flowers, 97%, A1...........................$25.00

Manoil, Happy Farm Set, 1941, complete, rare, NM (EX box), A $225.00

Manoil, hound, 96%, A1 ....$22.00

Manoil, jet plane, red & yel, no wheels or axles, scarce, 80-85%, A1 ....$17.00

Manoil, lady, w/churn, 965, A1 ....$22.00

Manoil, lineman & rnd base telephone pole, scarce, 98%, A1 ....$115.00

Manoil, machine gunner, prone, grass on base, 98%, A1 .$29.00

Manoil, machine gunner, seated, 95%, A 1 ....$37.00

Manoil, man, chopping wood, tiny casting flaw, 96%, A1..$21.00

Manoil, man & woman, sitting on park bench, 97%, A1.$31.00

Manoil, marine, 2nd version, 96%, A1 ....$28.00

Manoil, motorcycle rider, 98%, A1 ....$48.00

Manoil, nurse, red bowl, 95%, A1 ....$17.00

Manoil, observer, 95%, A1 ....$42.00

Manoil, oil tanker, red & silver, scarce, 98%, A1 ....$42.00

Manoil, old man, fixing shoes, 97%, A1 ....$36.00

Manoil, policeman, 99%, A1..$29.00

Manoil, scarecrow, w/straw hat, 99%, A1 ....$26.00

Manoil, shell for truck, lg, 96%, A1 ....$29.00

Manoil, sniper, kneeling, thick rifle, 99%, A1 ....$30.00

Manoil, sniper, standing, short thin rifle, 97%, A1..........$28.00

Manoil, soldier, at anti-tank gun, sq shield, metal wheels, scarce, 98%, A1 ....$42.00

Manoil, soldier, at crutch w/carbine, 97%, A1.................$46.00

Manoil, soldier, firing carbine in air, 98%, A1 ....$38.00

Manoil, soldier, running w/cannon, wooden wheels, thin face, scarce, 99%, A1 ....$68.00

Manoil, soldier, tommy gunner, 2nd version, 94%, A1.....$25.00

Manoil, soldier, w/barbed wire, wide face version, scarce, 95%, A1 ....$46.00

Manoil, soldier, w/gas mask & flare pistol, 95%, A1........$31.00

Manoil, soldier, w/rifle & pack marching, 99%, A1..........$24.00

Manoil, water wagon, no number, NM, A1 ....$28.00

Manoil, woman, sweeping w/broom, 97%, A1 ....$28.00

Mignot, Ancient Franks, marching in mail armor & helmets w/spears & axes, ca 1955, 4-pc, VG (G box), A $110.00

Mignot, Ancient Greek Infantry, marching w/swords, spears & shields, ca 1950, 12-pc, EX (VG box), A $300.00

Mignot, Austrian Infantry, attacking w/bayonets, wht uniforms, w/officer, drummer & bearer, 12-pc, ca 1950, VG, A $275.00

Mignot, Cuirasseurs, bugler & 4 men, 1808, G, A.........$175.00

Mignot, Diorama #585, LaChambre, barracks scene w/3 men, NM, A $450.00

Mignot, Diorama #587, LaCuisine, kitchen scene w/5 figures, NM (box lid missing), A $550.00

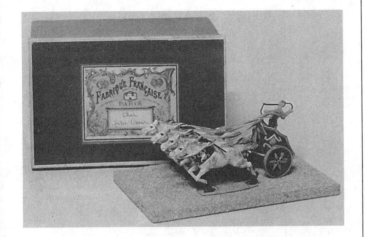

Mignot, Julius Caesar's Chariot, EX (VG box), A, $200.00.

Mignot, French Hussars, officer, bugler & 4 men, 1806, G, A .$160.00

Mignot, French Napoleonic Artillery Servants, 8-pc, G (G box), A $130.00

Mignot, French Napoleonic Dragoons, mounted w/sabres, gr & wht uniforms, trumpeter & bearer, 1810, 5-pc, minor rpt, VG, A $225.00

Mignot, Medieval Men-At-Arms, carrying bills, crossbows & axes, ca 1920, prewar, 7-pc, G, A $130.00

Mignot, Prussians, firing, 1808, 9-pc, VG+, A.................$80.00

Timpo, US Infantry in Action WWII GIs, 19-pc, VG, A .$85.00

Wollner, Emperor Franz Josef & Staff, Austro-Hungarian Army, mounted, in parade uniforms, ca 1920, 12-pc, VG, A .$325.00

Sporting Collectibles

Baseball — the great American pastime — has given us hundreds of real-life sports heroes plus a great amount of collectible memorabilia. Baseball gloves, bats, game-worn uniforms, ephemera of many types, games and character watches are among the many items being sought out today. And there are fans of basketball, football, and hockey that are just as avid in their collecting.

As you can see, many of our listings describe Kenner's Starting Lineup figures. These small plastic likenesses of famous sports greats were first produced in 1988. New they can be purchased for $5.00 to $8.00 (though some may go a little higher), but they have wonderful potential to appreciate. As the sports' stars fluctuate in popularity, so do their Starting Lineup figures, and some may occasionally sell for several hundred dollars, but on the average most from 1988 run from $25.00 to $50.00. Football and basketball series have been made as well, and in 1993 Kenner added hockey. If you're going to collect them, be critical of the condition of the packaging.

Bobbin' head dolls made of papier-mache were manufactured in Japan during the 1960s until about 1972 and were sold at ball parks, stadiums and through the mail for about $2.98. They were about 7" high or so, hand painted and then varnished. Some of them represent sports teams and their mascots. Depending on scarcity and condition, they'll run from as low as $35.00 up to $100.00, though there are some that sell for $300.00 or so. A few were modeled in the likeness of a particular sports star; these are rare and when they can be found sell in the $500.00 to $1,000.00 range. Base colors indicate when the doll was made. During 1961 and '62, white bases were used; today these are very scarce. Green bases are from 1962 until '66, and gold bases were used from 1967 until 1972. Mascot-heads are favored by collectors, and football figures are becoming very collectible as well. Our advisor has prepared a *Bobbin' Head Guide*, with a rarity scale and current values. See Dealer Codes for his address.

For further information, read *Value Guide to Baseball Collectibles* by Donald and Craig Raycroft (Collector Books).

Advisor: Tim Hunter (H13).

See also Cereal Boxes; Character Clocks and Watches; Games; Pin-Back Buttons.

Baltimore Orioles, compact, 1940s, MIB, scarce, V1 ....$65.00

Bo Jackson, autographed football, M...............................$175.00

Bob Feller, pen & pencil set, NMIB, C10 ....$195.00

Bobby Orr, skates, M (illus box), V1 ....$80.00

Cincinnati Reds, pennant, felt, 1940s, 28", EX.................$75.00

Detroit Tigers, doll, 1977, stuffed cloth, 12", EX..............$35.00

Ernie Banks, baseball glove, Wilson, pro-style, EX, J6......$65.00

Graig Nettles, baseball glove, Louisville Slugger, w/facsimile autograph, adult sz, EX, I2 ....$10.00

Harry Carey, book, Holy Cow!, 1989, EX $20.00

Houston Astros, doll, stuffed cloth, 12", EX, I2 ....$15.00

Ken Griffey Jr, pennant, 1992, M....................................$12.50

Los Angeles Dodgers, doll, 1960s, stuffed cloth, 12", VG, N2 ....$25.00

Los Angeles Dodgers, scarf, 1951, silk, illustrates scoreboard, Ebbets Field & map of Brooklyn, scarce, EX, from $900 to $1,200.00

Michael Jordan, autographed baseball, w/authenticity certificate, MIB $75.00

Michael Jordan, Chicago Bulls cap, signed on bill, M $120.00

Michael Jordan, Chicago White Sox jersey, signed, M...$300.00

Mickey Mantle, baseball glove, Rawlings, VG, I2 ....$40.00

Mickey Mantle, pen, 1960s, bat form, MIP (sealed), I2....$26.00

Robin Roberts Baseball Glove, McGregor, 1950s, VG (VG box), A, $100.00.

Mike Ditka, helmet, signed, authentic, M $350.00

Minnesota Fats, cue ball, MOC, T1 ....$5.00

Nebraska Cornhuskers, doll, cheerleader, Mattel, 1970, talker, 13", EX+, N2 ....$40.00

New York Knicks, bear, Good Stuff, 1991, stuffed plush w/uniform & ball, 6", NM, P3 ....$20.00

New York Yankees, pennant, blk felt, 1950s, EX $75.00

Oakland A's, program & score card, 1984, VG $5.00

Pete Rose, baseball bat, H&B Leaguer, #88, blk, VG+, I2 .$15.00

St Louis Cardinals, doll, 1960s, stuffed body w/vinyl head & hands, EX, T1 ....$65.00

Stan Musial, bat rack, 1964, MIP, V1.............................$60.00

Ted Williams, baseball bat, Sears, 1950s, EX....................$90.00

Ted Williams, figure, Hartland, 1960, from $225.00 to $275.00; Yogi Berra, figure, Hartland, 1960, from $200.00 to $225.00.

Vince Lombardi, game, Research Games, 1970, EX+ (EX+ box), T2...$25.00

Bobbin' Head Dolls

Atlanta Braves, team mascot, 1967-72, gold base, minimum value..$130.00

Atlanta Falcons, 1967, gold base $75.00

Baltimore Bullets, Little Dribblers...................................$125.00

Baltimore Colts, 1962, sq base...$60.00

Baltimore Orioles, team mascot, 1961-62, wht base, rare, minimum value $400.00

Boston Bruins, 1962, miniature $75.00

Chicago Bears, Black player, 1965, gold base...................$425.00

Chicago Blackhawks, 1962, sq base.................................$225.00

Chicago Bulls, Little Dribblers $75.00

Chicago Cubs, team mascot, 1962-62, wht base, minimum value $400.00

Chicago White Sox, Black player, 1962-66, gr base $700.00

Cincinnati Reds, Black player, 1962-66, gr base..........$1,100.00

Cleveland Indians, team mascot, 1962-66, gr base, minimum value..$200.00

Dallas Cowboys, 1965, rnd base $175.00

Denver Broncos, 1962, rnd base......................................$425.00

Detroit Tigers, team mascot, 1962-66, gr base, minimum value $200.00

Green Bay Packers, 1967, NM, $90.00.

Harlem Globetrotters, 1962 ....$250.00

Houston Astros, 1967-72, bl hat, gold base, minimum value $80.00

Kansas City Royals, 1967-72, gold base, minimum value .$110.00

Los Angeles Dodgers, Black player, 1962-66, gr base......$600.00

Los Angeles Lakers, Black player, 1967......................$400.00

Los Angeles Lakers, 1962 ....$325.00

Mickey Mantle, 1961-62, sq or rnd wht base, ea $700.00

Milwaukee Brewers, 1967-72, gold base, minimum value.$75.00

New York Giants, 1967, rnd gold base $90.00

New York Yankees, 1961-62, wht base, minimum value..$235.00

Oakland A's, 1967-72, gold base, yel uniform, minimum value $60.00

Roberto Clemente, 1961-62, rnd wht base, rare..........$1,300.00

Roger Maris, 1961-62, sq wht base $485.00

Seattle Sonics, 1967, yel uniform...................................$200.00

St Louis Blues, 1967, gold base.......................................$350.00

St Louis Cardinals, team mascot, 1961-62, wht base, minimum value...$400.00

Washington Senators, 1961-62, wht base, minimum value $325.00

Willie Mays, 1961-62, dk face, rnd wht base...................$475.00

Willie Mays, 1961-62, lt face, rnd wht base $300.00

Kenner Starting Lineup Figures

Babe Ruth & Lou Gehrig, 1989, MIP, D9 ....$35.00

Don Mattingly, 1988, MIP, B10.......................................$30.00

Don Mattingly, 1991, w/collector coin, MIP, I2 ....$15.00

Doug Jones, 1989, MIP, D9..$15.00

Eric Davis, 1988, MIP, D9..$12.00

Gale Sayers, MIP, B10...$25.00
George Bell, 1989, MIP, I2..$12.00
Jerry Rice, 1991, MIP, H4 ....$28.00
Jerry Rice, 1992, MIP, H4 ....$25.00
Joe Montana, 1990, MIP, H4 ....$45.00
Joe Montana, 1991, MIP, H4 ....$35.00
Joe Montana, 1992, MIP, H4 ....$25.00
John Taylor, 1990, MIP, H4 ....$24.00
Johnny Bench & Pete Rose, 1989, set of 2, MIP, D9 ....$45.00
Johnny Unitas, Legends, MIP, B10..........................$35.00
Jose Canesco, 1990, MIP, H4...................................$25.00
Jose Uribe, 1989, MIP, H4 ....$15.00
Julius Erving, Legends, MIP, B10 ....$30.00
Kevin Mitchell, 1990, MIP, H4 ....$18.00
Kevin Mitchell, 1991, w/collector coin, MIP, H4 ....$10.00
Mark McGwire, 1990, MIP, H4 ....$18.00
Matt Williams, 1991, w/collector coin, MIP, H4 ....$45.00
Mike Marshall, 1989, MIP, I2 ....$12.00
Mike Pagliarulo, 1989, MIP, I2 ....$12.00
Nolan Ryan, 1988, M (NM card), T1 ....$300.00
Patrick Ewing, 1988, MIP, B10 ....$35.00
Ricky Henderson, 1989, MIP, I2 ....$12.00
Roger Craig, 1990, MIP, H4......................................$12.00
Steve Bedrosian, 1990, MIP, H4 ....$10.00
Steve Young, 1992, MIP, H4.....................................$40.00
Steve Young, 1994, MIP, B10 ....$12.00
Tom Rathman, 1990, MIP, H4...................................$18.00

Wally Joyner, 1988, MIP, $14.00.

Will Clark, 1990, swinging bat, MIP, H4 ....$25.00
Will Clark, 1991, w/collector coin, MIP, H4.....................$20.00
Willie McCovey & Willie Mays, MIP, I2 ....$25.00
Wilt Chamberlin, Legends, MIP, B10................................$38.00

Star Trek

The Star Trek concept was introduced to the public in the mid-1960s via a TV series which continued for many years in syndication. The impact it had on American culture has spaned two generations of loyal fans through its animated TV cartoon series (1977), six major motion pictures, Fox network's 1987 TV show, 'Star Trek, The Next Generation,' and two other television series, 'Deep Space 9,' and 'Voyager.' As a result of its success, vast amounts of merchandise, both licensed and unlicensed, have been marketed including jewelry, clothing, calendars, collector plates, comics, costumes, games, greeting and gum cards, party goods, magazines, model kits, posters, puzzles, records and tapes, school supplies, and a wide assortment of toys. Packaging is very important; an item mint and in its original box is generally worth 75% to 100% more than one rated excellent.

Advisor: Craig Reid (R9).

Other Sources: B10, P3

See also Character and Promotional Drinking Glasses; Fast-Food Collectibles; Halloween Costumes; Lunch Boxes; Model Kits.

Figures

Ertl, Kirk, Star Trek III, Kirk, 3¾", MOC, H4.................$25.00
Ertl, Klingon Leader, Star Trek III, 3¾", MOC, H4 ....$30.00
Ertl, Scotty, Star Trek III, 3¾", MOC, H4.......................$25.00
Galoob, Capt Piccard, STNG, 3¾", MOC, from $12 to ..$15.00
Galoob, Commander Riker, STNG, 3¾", MOC, from $12 to..$15.00
Galoob, Geordi LaForge, STNG, 3¾", MOC, from $12 to..$15.00
Galoob, Lt Commander Data, STNG, 3¾", 2nd series, speckled
    face, MOC, from $25 to..$35.00
Galoob, Lt Commander Data, STNG, 3¾", 3rd series, flesh face,
    MOC, from $20 to $30.00
Galoob, Lt Commander Data, STNG, 3¾", 1st series, bl face,
    MOC, P12 ....$125.00
Galoob, Lt Tasha Yar, STNG, 1988, 3¾", MOC, D9/H4, from
    $20 to $30.00
Galoob, Lt Worf, STNG, 3¾", MOC, from $12 to $15.00
Mego, Captain Kirk, The Motion Picture, 3¾", MOC, from $28
    to $35.00
Mego, Captain Kirk, 12", NMIB, H4 ....$80.00
Mego, Captain Kirk, 1974, 8", MOC, D4/D9/H4, from $40 to.$50.00
Mego, Captain Kirk, 8", complete, EX, from $20 to $30.00

Mego, Ilia, 12½", MIB, from $65.00 to $85.00.

Mego, Decker, The Motion Picture, 3¾", MOC, from $30 to...$35.00

Mego, Dr McCoy, The Motion Picture, 3¾", MOC (unpunched), minimum value.................................$35.00

Mego, Dr McCoy, 8", no accessories, from $30 to............$35.00

Mego, Ilia, The Motion Picture, 3¾", MOC, from $25 to.$30.00

Mego, Klingon, 1974, 8", MOC, from $45 to..................$55.00

Mego, Klingon, 8", complete, EX, from $20 to................$25.00

Mego, Scotty, The Motion Picture, 3¾", NMOC, from $30 to...$35.00

Mego, Spock, The Motion Picture, 3¾", M (EX+ card), from $30 to...$35.00

Mego, Spock, 12", NMIB, H4....................................$75.00

Mego, Spock, 1974, 8", MOC $50.00

Mego, Spock, 8", complete, EX $25.00

Mego, Spock, 8", missing belt & weapons.......................$15.00

Playmates, Lt. Commander Deanna Troy, 5", MOC, from $20.00 to $25.00.

Playsets and Accessories

Mission to Gamma VI, Mego, complete, very rare, MIB, from $700 to...$950.00

Star Trek Command Communication Console, Mego, 1976, M (EX+ box), from $70 to $80.00

Star Trek USS Enterprise Bridge, Mego, 1975, vinyl fold-out, w/chair, control panel, cb views, VG $30.00

Star Trek USS Enterprise Bridge, Mego, 1975, vinyl fold-out, NRFB (sealed), from $150 to $175.00

Star Trek USS Enterprise Bridge, Mego, 1980, The Motion Picture, molded wht plastic, for 3¾" figures, NRFB, from $100 to .$135.00

Vehicles

Ferengi Fighter, Galoob, STNG, 1988, MIB, from $35 to .$50.00

Klingon Warship, Corgi #149, Star Trek II, M (NM card), from $18 to...$25.00

Klingon Warship, Dinky, MIB, from $75 to....................$85.00

Shuttlecraft Galileo, Galoob, STNG, NRFB, H4............$50.00

USS Enterprise, Corgi, 1982, Star Trek II, MOC, from $18 to.$25.00

USS Enterprise, Dinky #803, 1979, The Motion Picture, diecast, 4", MOC, P4...$30.00

USS Enterprise, Ertl, 1984, Star Trek III, MOC, from $18 to .$25.00

USS Enterprise, Galoob, 1988, STNG, 1988, NMOC, from $25 to...$35.00

Miscellaneous

Book, Mission to Horatius, Whitman, 1968, TV Authorized Edition, NM, C1 ....$27.00

Bookmark, Capt Kirk, Antioch, EX, E3 ....$1.00

Bowl, Cereal; 1975, plastic, EX, from $10 to...................$15.00

Calendar, Star Date 1977, EX, J7 ....$25.00

Calendar, Star Date 1979, EX, J7 ....$20.00

Coloring Book, Rescue at Raylo, Whitman, 1978, Kirk on cover, EX+, from $8 to...$10.00

Coloring Book, Star Trek Futuristic Fun, Whitman, 1978, NM, from $8 to...$10.00

Coloring Book, Star Trek Planet Ecnal's Dilemma, Whitman, 1979, NM, from $8 to...$10.00

Comic Book, Gold Key #2, 1968, Spock & Kirk on cover, EX, C1 ....$125.00

Comic Book, Gold Key #8, photo cover, G, F8...............$14.00

Comic Book, Gold Key #27, EX, C1 ....$24.00

Communicators, Mego, 1974, blue plastic, MIB, $150.00.

Costume, Captain Kirk, 1976, NM (Star Trek box) $40.00

Costume, Mr Spock, 1975, NM (Star Trek box)...............$40.00

Display Piece, Spaceshuttle Galileo, 1992, lights up & talks w/Spock's voice, M, from $125 to $175.00

Doll, Spock, Knickerbocker, 1972, vinyl head on plush body, poseable, 12", NM (EX box)................................$40.00

Eraser, Mr Spock, 1983, EX, from $8 to $10.00

Game, Star Trek, Ideal, 1967, complete, EX+ (EX+ box), from $50 to...$70.00

Game, Star Trek The Motion Picture, Milton Bradley, missing 5 pcs o/w EX (EX box), D9......................$20.00
Game, Star Trek The Motion Picture, Milton Bradley, 1979, NMIB, from $25 to $40.00
Greeting Cards, Captain Kirk, 6 different, M, ea, from $1 to .$2.00

Inter-Space Communicator, Lone Star, 1974, MIB, J6, $55.00.

Lunch Box, Star Trek The Next Generation, 1988, purple plastic, EX, I2 ....$10.00
Lunch Box, Star Trek The Next Generation, 1988, w/thermos, M, N2 ....$20.00
Model Kit, USS Enterprise Bridge, built up, EX+, T1 ......$20.00
Ornament, Galileo, Hallmark, NRFB, from $25 to $35.00
Ornament, USS Enterprise, Hallmark, M (NM box), T1 .$285.00
Patch, Starbase, EX, E3 ....$3.00
Phaser Water Gun, AHI, blk plastic, 5", MOC, from $40 to ..$50.00
Photo Mug, Mr Spock, MIB, T1 ....$17.50
Photo Mug, Sulu, MIB, T1 ....$17.50
Pin-Back Button, 1976, blk & wht photos of Kirk & Spock, 2¼", M, from $5 to $10.00
Plaque, Captain Picard, limited edition, T1 ....$125.00
Postcard Book, set of 48 cards, M, T1 ....$35.00
Puzzle, Whitman, 1978, fr-tray, 8x10", MIP (sealed), from $10 to..$12.00
Space Launching Gun, AHI, 1976, MOC $65.00
Star Trek Dart/Cap Pistol, Remco, 1966-67, bl plastic w/blk grips & muzzle, diecast works, 12½", worn o/w G $50.00
Star Trek The Motion Picture Water Pistol, Aviva/Taiwan, 1979, gray plastic, 7", MOC, from $35 to $40.00
T-Shirt, 1990, gold, adult, EX, from $15 to $25.00
USS Enterprise, inflatable, Kraft premium, 24", M, D4 ....$15.00
Utility Belt, Remco, 1975, w/phaser, tricorder & communicator, M (VG box)........................$150.00
Wristwatch, Bradley/20th Century-Paramount, 1980, Swiss movement, USS Enterprise on face, blk vinyl band, M, from $65 to $85.00

Star Wars

The original 'Star Wars' movie was a phenomenal box office hit of the late 1970s, no doubt due to its ever-popular space travel theme and fantastic special effects. A sequel called 'Empire Strikes Back' (1980) and a third hit called 'Return of the Jedi' (1983) did just as well. As a result, an enormous amount of related merchandise was released — most of which was made by the Kenner Company. Palitoy of London supplied England and other overseas countries with Kenner's products and also made some toys that were never distributed in America. Until 1980 the logo of the 20th Century Fox studios (under whom the toys were licensed) appeared on each item; just before the second movie, 'Star Wars' creator, George Lucas, regained control of the merchandise rights, and items inspired by the last two films can be identified by his own Lucasfilm logo. Since 1987 Lucasfilm, Ltd., has operated shops in conjunction with the Star Tours at Disneyland theme parks.

The first action figures to be introduced were Luke Skywalker, Princess Leia, R2-D2 and Chewbacca. Because of delays in production that prevented Kenner from getting them on the market in time for Christmas, the company issued 'early bird' certificates so that they could be ordered by mail when they became available. In all, more than ninety action figures were designed. The last figures to be issued were the 'Power of the Force' series (1985), which though of more recent vintage are steadily climbing in value. A collector coin was included on each 'Power of the Force' card.

Original packaging is very important in assessing a toy's worth. As each movie was released, packaging was updated, making approximate dating relatively simple. A figure on an original 'Star Wars' card is worth more than the same character on an 'Empire Strikes Back' card, etc.; and the same 'Star Wars' figure valued at $50.00 in mint-on-card condition might be worth as little as $5.00 'loose.'

Especially prized are the original 12-back Star Wars cards (meaning 12 figures were shown on the back). Second issue cards showed eight more, and so on. Unpunched cards tend to be valued at about 15% to 20% more than punched cards, and naturally if the proof of purchase has been removed, the value of the card is less. (These could be mailed in to receive newly introduced figures before they appeared on the market.) A figure in a factory (Kenner) bag is valued at $2.00 to $3.00 more than it is worth loose, and an original backing card adds about $1.00 to $2.00. In our listings, you'll find many of these variations noted. These have been included for the information of potential buyers; remember, pricing is not a science — it hinges on many factors. For more information we recommend *Modern Toys, American Toys, 1930 to 1980* by Linda Baker.

Advisor: George Downes (D8).

Other Sources: B10, D4, D9, J2, O1, P3

See also Character and Promotional Drinking Glasses; Coloring, Activity and Paint Books; Fast-Food Collectibles; Halloween Costumes; Model Kits; Trading Cards.

Key:	ESB — Empire Strikes Back
	POTF — Power of the Force
	ROTJ — Return of the Jedi
	* — proof of purchase removed

Figures

A-Wing Pilot, POTF, 3¾", MOC, D8 ....$115.00

Action Masters, 4-pack, MIP, scarce, J6 ....$60.00

Admiral Ackbar, ROTJ, 3¾", MOC, P11 ....$22.00

Admiral Ackbar, ROTJ, 3¾", MOC*, from, $14 to $18.00

Admiral Ackbar, ROTJ, 3¾", w/accessories, M, H4 ....$6.00

Amanaman, POTF, 3¾", MOC, D8 ....$175.00

Amanaman, POTF, 3¾", no accessories o/w M, H4 ....$40.00

Anakin Skywalker, POTF, 3¾", from $30 to...................$40.00

Anakin Skywalker, 3¾", w/accessories, M, H4 ....$29.00

Anakin Skywalker, Tri-Logo, 3¾", MOC, D4 ....$45.00

AT-AT Commander, ESB, 3¾", M (EX 48-back card w/Revenge of the Jedi offer), B3 ....$26.00

AT-AT Commander, ESB, 3¾", w/accessories, M, H4......$10.00

AT-AT Commander, ROTJ, 3¾", MOC, H4/D8, from $18 to...........$22.00

AT-AT Driver, ESB, 3¾", MOC, from $40 to...................$50.00

AT-AT Driver, ESB, 3¾", w/accessories, M.....................$10.00

AT-AT Driver, ROTJ, 3¾", MOC*, H4...............$32.00

AT-ST Driver, POTF, 3¾", MOC, from $40 to...............$50.00

AT-ST Driver, ROTJ, 3¾", MOC, from $16 to.............$20.00

AT-ST Driver, ROTJ, 3¾", w/accessories, M, H4............$10.00

AT-ST Driver, Tri-Logo, 3¾", MOC, H4.................$16.00

B-Wing Pilot, POTF, 3¾", MOC, from $15 to $20.00

B-Wing Pilot, ROTJ, 3¾", MOC*, H4.................$16.00

B-Wing Pilot, ROTJ, 3¾", w/accessories, M, H4 ....$5.00

Barada, POTF, 3¾", w/accessories & coin, M, H4 ....$39.00

Ben Obi-Wan Kenobi, ESB, 3¾", MOC, from $55 to......$60.00

Ben Obi-Wan Kenobi, POTF, MOC, from $85 to..........$100.00

Ben Obi-Wan Kenobi, SW, 3¾", gray hair, w/accessories, M, H4 ....$15.00

Ben Obi-Wan Kenobi, 12", EX, from $95 to...................$115.00

Ben Obi-Wan Kenobi, 12", MIB, from $350 to $375.00

Ben Obi-Wan Kenobi, 12", NM, from $100 to.............$125.00

Bespin Security Guard, ESB, 3¾", Blk or Caucassian, w/accessories, M, H4, ea........................$8.00

Bespin Security Guard, ESB, 3¾", Blk or Caucassian, MOC, from $40 to........................$45.00

Bespin Security Guard, ROTJ, 3¾", Blk or Caucassian, MOC, D8/H4, from $25 to $30.00

Bib Fortuna, ROTJ, 3¾", MOC*, D8 ....$22.00

Bib Fortuna, ROTJ, 3¾", w/accessories, M $12.00

Biker Scout, ROTJ, 3¾", MOC*, D8.............................$28.00

Biker Scout, ROTJ, 3¾", w/accessories, M, H4................$8.00

Boba Fett, ROTJ, 3¾", MOC*, H4................................$40.00

Boba Fett, SW, 3¾", w/accessories, M, H4......................$15.00

Boba Fett, 12", NMIB..$400.00

Boba Fett, 12", no accessories o/w NM, D8..................$55.00

Bossk, ESB, 3¾", bounty hunter, w/accessories, M, H4 ....$10.00

Bossk, ROTJ, 3¾", MOC $60.00

C-3PO, ESB, 3¾", removable limbs, MOC $45.00

C-3PO, ROTJ, 3¾", removable limbs, MOC, D8/H4 ......$28.00

C-3PO, ROTJ, 3¾", removable limbs, w/accessories, M, H4..$10.00

C-3PO, SW, 3¾", MOC (12-back), D8............................$135.00

C-3PO, SW, 3¾", w/accessories, H4, M...........................$8.00

C-3PO, 12", EX..$35.00

C-3PO, 12", M (NM box)..$145.00

Chewbacca, ESB, 3¾", MOC, from $75 to.....................$80.00

Chewbacca, POTF, 3¾", MOC, from $120 to $135.00

Chewbacca, ROTJ, 3¾", MOC*, D8...............................$28.00

Chewbacca, SW, 3¾", MOC (12-back, unpunched), D8..$175.00

Chewbacca, SW, 3¾", w/accessories, M, H4...................$10.00

Chewbacca, 12", EX, D8...$65.00

Chief Chirpa, ROTJ, 3¾", MOC, D8/H4, from $15 to $20.00

Chief Chirpa, ROTJ, 3¾", w/accessories, M, H4 ....$6.00

Cloud Car Pilot, ESB, 3¾", w/accessories, M, H4...............$8.00

Cloud Car Pilot, ROTJ, 3¾", MOC*, D8........................$35.00

Darth Vader, ESB, 3¾", M (NM 48-back card w/Revenge of the Jedi offer), B3..$50.00

Darth Vader, POTF, 3¾", MOC, from $65 to $80.00

Darth Vader, ROTJ, 3¾", MOC, D4...............................$35.00

Darth Vader, ROTJ, 3¾", MOC*, D8...............................$25.00

Darth Vader, SW, 3¾", MOC (12-back, unpunched), D8..$175.00

Darth Vader, SW, 3¾", w/accessories, M, H4...................$15.00

Darth Vader, 12", EX, D8...$85.00

Death Squad Commander, ESB, 3¾", MOC $75.00

Death Squad Commander, SW, 3¾", MOC (12-back, unpunched), D8...$175.00

Death Squad Commander, SW, 3¾", NM..........................$7.00

Death Star Droid, ESB, 3¾", MOC.................................$125.00

Death Star Droid, ROTJ, 3¾", MOC $80.00

Death Star Droid, SW, 3¾", MOC, from $125 to $150.00

Death Star Droid, SW, 3¾", w/accessories, M, H4..............$8.00

Dengar, ESB, 3¾", M (NM 41-back card), H4 ....$55.00

Dengar, ESB, 3¾", w/accessories, M, H4..........................$8.00

Dengar, ROTJ, 3¾", MOC*, D8/H4, from $30 to...........$35.00

Dulok Scout, Ewoks, 3¾", MOC, D8................................$15.00

Emperor, ROTJ, 3¾", M (in mail-order box).....................$18.00

Emperor, ROTJ, 3¾", MOC*, D8...................................$35.00

Emperor, Tri-Logo, 3¾", MOC..$25.00

Emperor's Royal Guard, ROTJ, 3¾", MOC, P11.............$30.00

Emperor's Royal Guard, ROTJ, 3¾", MOC*, from $15 to..$18.00

Emperor's Royal Guard, ROTJ, 3¾", w/accessories, M, H4 .$6.00

EV-9D9, POTF, 3¾", M (NM card), H4.........................$130.00

FX-7, ESB, 3¾", M (NM 48-back card w/Revenge of the Jedi offer), B3 ....$42.00

FX-7, ESB, 3¾", w/accessories, M, H4 ....$10.00

Boba Fett, Star Wars, 3¾", MOC (21-back), J6, $485.00.

Photo courtesy of June Moon.

Gammorean Guard, ROTJ, 3¾", MOC, from $15 to **$20.00**

Gammorean Guard, ROTJ, 3¾", w/accessories, M, H4 ......**$5.00**

General Madine, ROTJ, 3¾", MOC, D8/H4, from $12 to ..**$15.00**

General Madine, ROTJ, 3¾", w/accessories, M, H4 ....**$6.00**

Greedo, ESB, 3¾", MOC, from $85 to **$100.00**

Greedo, SW, 3¾", MOC (21-back), D8 ....**$150.00**

Greedo, SW, 3¾", w/accessories, M, H4 ....**$10.00**

Hammerhead, SW, 3¾", M (in Kenner bag).....................**$15.00**

Hammerhead, SW, 3¾", MOC **$125.00**

Hammerhead, Star Wars, 3¾", EX, $12.00

Imperial Dignitary, Power of the Force, 3¾", MOC, from $60.00 to $75.00.

Photo courtesy of June Moon.

Han Solo, ESB, 3¾", Bespin outfit, complete, M, H4 ......**$15.00**

Han Solo, ESB, 3¾", Hoth gear, complete, M, H4...........**$14.00**

Han Solo, ESB, 3¾", Hoth gear, MOC.............................**$65.00**

Han Solo, POTF, 3¾", Carbonite Chamber outfit, w/coin, complete, M, H4 ....**$90.00**

Han Solo, POTF, 3¾", M (VG card), H4, from $130 to ..**$150.00**

Han Solo, ROTJ, 3¾", Bespin outfit, MOC*, H4 ..**$50.00**

Han Solo, ROTJ, 3¾", lg head, MOC **$125.00**

Han Solo, ROTJ, 3¾", trench coat, MOC, D4.................**$30.00**

Han Solo, SW, 3¾", sm head, w/accessories, M, H4.........**$20.00**

Han Solo, 12", no gun or medal o/w EX, D8...................**$175.00**

IG-88, ESB, 3¾", MOC, from $40 to................................**$50.00**

IG-88, ESB, 3¾", w/accessories, M, H4 ....**$14.00**

IG-88, ROTJ, 3¾", M (EX unpunched card*), H4...........**$45.00**

IG-88, 12", no accessories o/w EX, D8 ....**$125.00**

IG-88, 12", w/bandolier, missing weapons o/w EX, H4...**$170.00**

IG-88, 15", M, complete...**$425.00**

Imperial Commander, ESB, M (EX 41-bk card), H4 ....**$55.00**

Imperial Commander, ESB, M (EX 47-bk card), H4 ....**$30.00**

Imperial Commander, ESB, 3¾", w/accessories, M, H4......**$8.00**

Imperial Commander, ROTJ, 3¾", MOC*, D8/H4 ....**$30.00**

Imperial Gunner, POTF, 3¾", w/accessories, M, H4.........**$45.00**

Imperial Stormtrooper, ESB, M (VG 41-back card), H4 ..**$30.00**

Imperial Stormtrooper, ESB, 3¾", w/accessories, M, H4 ..**$12.00**

Imperial Stormtrooper, ROTJ, 3¾", Hoth outfit, MOC (unpunched), H4...**$30.00**

Imperial TIE Fighter Pilot, ESB, 3¾", MOC, from $50 to.**$60.00**

Imperial TIE Fighter Pilot, ESB, 3¾", w/accessories, M, H4 ....**$12.00**

Imperial TIE Fighter Pilot, ROTJ, 3¾", M (NM unpunched card), H4/P11...**$48.00**

Jawa, ESB, 3¾", MOC, from $70 to................................**$80.00**

Jawa, POTF, 3¾", MOC, from $65 to **$75.00**

Jawa, ROTJ, 3¾", M (VG+ card*), H4 ....**$30.00**

Jawa, SW, 3¾", cloth cape & accessories, M, H4 ....**$14.00**

Jawa, SW, 3¾", MOC (12-back), D8.............................**$175.00**

Jawa, 12", MIB..**$225.00**

King Gorneesh, Ewoks, 3¾", MOC, D8..........................**$15.00**

Klaatu, ROTJ, 3¾", MOC, D4/D8.................................**$15.00**

Klaatu, ROTJ, 3¾", Skiff Guard outfit, MOC, H4/P11, from $15 to **$20.00**

Klaatu, ROTJ, 3¾", w/accessories, M, H4........................**$6.00**

Lando Calrissian, ESB, MOC (31-back), H4....................**$45.00**

Lando Calrissian, ESB, 3¾", wht eyes & teeth, w/accessories, M, H4 ....**$15.00**

Lando Calrissian, ROTJ, 3¾", Skiff Guard outfit, M, H4.**$10.00**

Lando Calrissian, ROTJ, 3¾", Skiff Guard outfit, MOC, H4/D4/D8 ....**$20.00**

Lando Calrissian, SW, 3¾", w/accessories, M, H4 ....**$12.00**

Lobot, ESB, 3¾", M (VG card w/Revenge of the Jedi offer), B3...**$22.00**

Lobot, ESB, 3¾", MOC, H4...**$28.00**

Lobot, ESB, 3¾", w/accessories, M, H4 ....**$6.00**

Lobot, ROTJ, 3¾", MOC*, D8.......................................**$35.00**

Logray, ROTJ, 3¾", MOC, D8..**$22.00**

Logray, ROTJ, 3¾", w/accessories, M, H4 ....**$6.00**

Luke Skywalker, ESB, 3¾", Bespin fatigues, complete, M, H4 ....**$15.00**

Luke Skywalker, ESB, 3¾", Hoth battle gear, complete, M, H4 ....**$15.00**

Luke Skywalker, ESB, 3¾", X-Wing Pilot outfit, MOC ...**$95.00**

Luke Skywalker, POTF, 3¾", Imperial Stormtrooper outfit, MOC, D8...**$275.00**

Luke Skywalker, POTF, 3¾", Jedi Knight outfit, MOC, from $150 to..$175.00

Luke Skywalker, ROTJ, 3¾", Bespin outfit, MOC (unpunched), H4...$60.00

Luke Skywalker, ROTJ, 3¾", Hoth battle gear, MOC (unpunched), H4...$48.00

Luke Skywalker, ROTJ, 3¾", Jedi Knight outfit (gr), MOC, P1..$65.00

Luke Skywalker, ROTJ, 3¾", X-Wing Pilot outfit, MOC .$50.00

Luke Skywalker, SW, 3¾", MOC (12-back, bubble opened, resealed), H4.......................................$60.00

Luke Skywalker, SW, 3¾", MOC (12-back), D8............$325.00

Luke Skywalker, SW, 3¾", w/accessories, M, H4..............$20.00

Luke Skywalker, SW, 3¾", X-Wing Pilot outfit & accessories, M, H4...$12.00

Luke Skywalker, 12", M (EX box)...................................$275.00

Luke Skywalker, 12", VG...$85.00

Lumat, POTF, 3¾", MOC, from $40 to $50.00

Lumat, ROTJ, 3¾", MOC*, D8...$22.00

Nein Numb, ROTJ, 3¾", MOC, P11...................................$25.00

Nien Numb, ROTJ, 3¾", w/accessories M, H4 ....$6.00

Nikto, ROTJ, 3¾", MOC, from $15 to $18.00

Nikto, ROTJ, 3¾", w/accessories, M, H4 ....$6.00

Paploo, POTF, 3¾", MOC...$45.00

Paploo, POTF, 3¾", w/accessories, M, H4.......................$18.00

Paploo, ROTJ, 3¾", MOC, from $20 to $28.00

Power Droid, ESB, M (G- 41-back card), H4 ....$25.00

Power Droid, ROTJ, 3¾", M (VG card*), H4 ....$34.00

Power Droid, SW, 3¾", MOC (21-back), D8 ....$95.00

Power Droid, SW, 3¾", w/accessories, M, H4 ....$8.00

Princess Leia Organa, ESB, 3¾", Bespin gown, MOC, from $85 to..$100.00

Princess Leia Organa, ESB, 3¾", Bespin gown w/regular collar, w/accessories, M, H4, from $18 to..............$25.00

Princess Leia Organa, ESB, 3¾", Hoth outfit, MOC........$70.00

Princess Leia Organa, ESB, 3¾", Hoth outfit, w/accessories, M, H4 ....$15.00

Princess Leia Organa, POTF, 3¾", combat poncho, MOC..$75.00

Princess Leia Organa, ROTJ, 3¾", Boushh disguise, complete, M, H4...$18.00

Princess Leia Organa, ROTJ, 3¾", Boushh disguise, MOC*, D8/H4, from $35 to $40.00

Princess Leia Organa, ROTJ, 3¾", combat poncho, MOC, from $30 to..$40.00

Princess Leia Organa, SW, 3¾", MOC (12-back), D8 ...$295.00

Princess Leia Organa, SW, 3¾", w/accessories, H4...........$25.00

Princess Leia Organa, 12", MIB, from $235 to................$275.00

Princess Leia Organa, 12", NM.....................................$100.00

Prune Face, ROTJ, MOC, 3¾", P11/H4 ....$18.00

Prune Face, ROTJ, 3¾", NM...$8.00

Rancor Keeper, ROTJ, 3¾", MOC, D4/D8/H4 ....$18.00

Rancor Keeper, ROTJ, 3¾", w/accessories, M, H4.............$5.00

Rancor Monster, ROTJ, arms & jaw move, 10x7", EX+, D9...$35.00

Rebel Commander, ESB, M (EX 48-back card w/Revenge of the Jedi offer), B3...$25.00

Rebel Commander, ESB, 3¾", w/accessories, M, H4 ....$6.00

Rebel Commander, ROTJ, 3¾", MOC, from $25 to $30.00

Rebel Commando, ESB, 3¾", w/accessories, M, H4...........$6.00

Rebel Commando, ROTJ, 3¾", MOC, H4/P11, from $18 to...$22.00

Rebel Commando, ROTJ, 3¾", w/accessories, M, H4........$6.00

Rebel Soldier, ESB, 3¾", Hoth gear, MOC....................$30.00

Rebel Soldier, ESB, 3¾", w/accessories, M, H4................$8.00

Rebel Soldier, ROTJ, 3¾", Hoth gear, MOC, H4............$28.00

Ree-Yees, ROTJ, 3¾", MOC, D8/H4...............................$15.00

Ree-Yees, ROTJ, 3¾", w/accessories, M, H4...................$6.00

Romba, POTF, 3¾", MOC (unpunched), D8.....................$30.00

R2-D2, ESB, 3¾", w/sensorscope, complete, M, H4........$10.00

R2-D2, radio controlled, EX...$60.00

R2-D2, ROTJ, 3¾", w/sensorscope, MOC (unpunched), H4...$45.00

R2-D2, ROTJ, 3¾", w/sensorscope, MOC*, H4..............$30.00

R2-D2, SW, 3¾", MOC (12-back), D8 ....$135.00

R2-D2, SW, 3¾", w/accessories, M, H4............................$8.00

R2-D2, 12", complete w/blueprints, EX+, H4................$50.00

R2-D2, 12", remote control, MIB, D8............................$125.00

R5-D4, SW, 3¾", MOC (21-back), D8 ....$125.00

R5-D4, SW, 3¾", w/accessories, M, H4............................$8.00

Sand People, ESB, 3¾", MOC, from $65 to $70.00

Sand People, SW, 3¾", MOC (12-back), D8 ....$185.00

Security Guard, ROTJ, 3¾", wht, MOC, P11..................$30.00

Snaggletooth, ESB, 3¾", MOC.......................................$80.00

Snaggletooth, ROTJ, 3¾", MOC, from $50 to................$60.00

Snaggletooth, SW, 3¾", MOC (21-back), D8................$125.00

Snaggletooth, SW, 3¾", w/accessories, M, H4.................$8.00

Squid Head, ROTJ, 3¾", MOC*, D8/H4..........................$15.00

Star Destroyer Commander, ROTJ, 3¾", MOC $40.00

Star Destroyer Commander, SW, 3¾", w/accessories, M, H4...$12.00

Stormtrooper, ESB, 3¾", MOC, from $70 to...................$80.00

Stormtrooper, ROTJ, 3¾", M (EX card), D8/H4, from $30 to...$35.00

Stormtrooper, SW, 3¾", w/accessories, M, H4................$10.00

Stormtrooper, 12", EX...$95.00

Sy Snootles and the Rebo Band, Return of the Jedi, 1983, MIB, J6, $125.00.

Stormtrooper, 12", VG, H4.................................$70.00
Teebo, ROTJ, 3¾", MOC, from $15 to.............$20.00
Teebo, ROTJ, 3¾", w/accessories, M, H4...........$6.00
Teebo, Tri-Logo, 3¾", MOC, H4 ....$10.00
Ugnaught, ESB, 3¾", MOC...............................$40.00
Ugnaught, ESB, 3¾", w/accessories, M, H4 ....$8.00
Ugnaught, ROTJ, 3¾", MOC, from $35 to..........$40.00
Walrus Man, ESB, 3¾", MOC $80.00
Walrus Man, SW, 3¾", MOC (21-back), D8 ....$125.00
Walrus Man, SW, 3¾", w/accessories, M, H4 ......$10.00
Warok, POTF, 3¾", MOC, from $30 to..............$35.00
Weequay, ROTJ, 3¾", MOC*, D8/H4..................$18.00
Weequay, ROTJ, 3¾", w/accessories, M, H4 ....$6.00
Wicket W Warrick, ROTJ, 3¾", MOC, D8/H4 ......$30.00
Wicket W Warrick, Tri-Logo, 3¾", MOC, P11 ....$14.00
Yak Face, POTF, 3¾", MOC, D8 ....$750.00
Yoda, ESB, 3¾", orange snake, MOC, P11 ....$50.00
Yoda, ROTJ, 3¾", MOC*, D8/H4 ....$45.00
Zuckuss, ESB, 3¾", w/accessories, M, H4............$8.00
Zuckuss, ROTJ, 3¾", MOC*, D8 ....$40.00
2-1B, ESB, 3¾", M (EX 41-back card), H4...........$55.00
2-1B, ESB, 3¾", M (NM 48-back card w/Revenge of the Jedi
      offer), B3 ....$45.00
2-1B, ESB, 3¾", w/accessories, M, H4 ....$10.00
2-1B, ROTJ, 3¾", M (VG card), H4...................$32.00
4-Lom, ROTJ, 3¾", MOC*, D8..........................$45.00
4-Lom, ROTJ, 3¾", w/accessories, M, H4 ....$6.00
8D8, ROTJ, 3¾", MOC, D8/H4, from $20 to........$25.00
8D8, SW, 3¾", w/accessories, M, H4....................$6.00

Playsets and Accessories

Photo courtesy of June Moon.

Bespin Control Room, Micro Collection, MIB, J6, $42.00.

Bespin Control Room, Micro Collection, NRFB, H4.......$55.00
Bespin Control Room, Micro Collection, w/4 figures, NM,
      D8 ....$28.00
Bespin Gantry, Micro Collection, w/4 figures, NM, D8....$28.00

Cantina Adventure, Sears promo, EX, D8 ....$195.00
Cloud City, EX (EX box), D8.............................$295.00
Creature Cantina, EX (EX box), D8 ....$75.00
Creature Cantina Adventure, SW, w/4 figures, EX (VG+ box),
      H4 ....$170.00

Photo courtesy of June Moon.

Death Star Compactor, Star Wars, Micro Collection, MIB, J6, from $70.00 to $85.00.

Droid Factory, SW, EX (VG box), from $70 to $95.00
Ewok Assult Catapult, ROTJ, MIB $25.00
Ewok Village, EX..$55.00
Hoth Generator Attack, Micro Collection, NRFB (minor wear),
      H4 ....$55.00
Hoth Ice Planet, EX, H4.....................................$30.00
Hoth Ion Cannon, Micro Collection, NRFB (minor wear),
      H4 ....$70.00
Hoth Turret Defense, Micro Collection, EX, H4 ....$25.00
Hoth Wampa Cave, Micro-Collection, MIB, from $25 to .$35.00
Imperial Attack Base, EX, H4 ....$32.00
Imperial Attack Base, EX (EX box), from $55 to.............$65.00
Jabba the Hutt, MIB, D8/B3/H4, from $45 to...................$50.00
Jabba the Hutt Dungeon, Sears, w/3 figures, NRFB, H4.$100.00
Land of the Jawas, EX $50.00
Radar Laser Cannon, ROTJ, w/instructions & insert, NM (EX
      box), H4..$20.00
Tauntaun, complete, EX, D8/H4 ....$20.00
Tauntaun, ESB, w/insert & instructions, M (NM box), H4...$40.00
Tripod Laser Cannon, ESB, no insert o/w M (EX+ box),
      H4 ....$20.00
Tripod Laser Cannon, w/instructions, EX, H4 ....$15.00
Turret & Probot, EX, H4 ....$30.00
Turret & Probot, EX (EX box), D8........................$80.00
Vehicle Maintenance Energizer, M (VG box), B3 ....$15.00

Vehicles

Armored Sentinel Transport (AST-5), ROTJ, w/insert &
      instructions, NM (EX box), H4................................$20.00
AT-AT, EX-, H4 ....$80.00

B-Wing Fighter, Return of the Jedi, 1983, MIB, J6, $185.00.

Boba Fett's Slave I, diecast, EX, H4.................................$25.00
Darth Vader TIE Fighter, diecast, MOC $60.00
Darth Vader TIE Fighter, SW, no insert o/w NM (EX+ box),
    H4 ....$75.00
Desert Sail Skiff, Mini-Rigs, EX (EX box), from $25 to ...$30.00
Ewok Combat Glider, MIB $22.00
Imperial Cruiser, diecast, NM, from $45 to $55.00
Imperial Shuttle, ROTJ, MIB, from $325 to $375.00
Imperial TIE Fighter, Battle Damaged; ROTJ, w/instructions &
    insert, NM (EX box), H4...$80.00
Imperial TIE Fighter, Micro Collection, no figure o/w NM,
    D8 ....$25.00
Imperial Troop Transport, EX (EX box), D8 ....$65.00
Imperial Troop Transport, SW, EX, H4 ....$35.00
Interceptor (INT-4), Mini-Rigs, EX, H4 ....$10.00
Jawa Sandcrawler, EX+, D8/J6, from $300 to.................$350.00
Landspeeder, diecast, NM, D8 ....$35.00
Landspeeder, SW, no insert o/w M (EX box), H4 ....$40.00
Millennium Falcon, diecast, EX $50.00
Millennium Falcon, diecast, M (NM box), H4...............$100.00
Millennium Falcon, SW, EX, H4 ....$65.00
Millennium Falcon, SW, EX (VG box), H4 ....$130.00

Millennium Falcon, Star Wars, Micro Collection, Sears Exclusive, 1982, scarce, MIB, J6, $600.00.

Mobile Laser Cannon (MLC-3), EX, H4 ....$10.00

Multi-Terrain (MTV-7), EX, H4 ....$10.00
Multi-Terrain (MTV-7), EX (EX box), D8 ....$18.00
One-Man Sand Skimmer, POTF, 1984, M (NM card), rare,
    H4 ....$80.00
Personnel Deployment Transport, EX, H4 ....$10.00
Rebel Armored Snow Speeder, ESB, no insert o/w M (EX box),
    H4 ....$70.00
Scout Walker, ROTJ, w/instructions, no insert o/w NM (EX
    box), H4 ....$50.00
Side-Gunner, Droids, M (EX+ box), H4 ....$40.00
Slave I, diecast, EX, from $35 to.....................................$50.00
Speeder Bike, ROTJ, NRFB, H4 ....$40.00
Speeder Bike, ROTJ, VG, H4, from $15 to.......................$25.00
Star Destroyer, diecast, missing shuttle o/w VG, H4.........$30.00
TIE Bomber, diecast, EX, H4 ....$250.00
TIE Bomber, diecast, MIB, J6 ....$795.00
TIE Interceptor, EX...$75.00
Twin Pod Cloud Car, diecast, EX, H4 ....$25.00
Twin Pod Cloud Car, EX, H4 ....$22.00
Twin Pod Cloud Car, NMIB, from $60 to $75.00
X-Wing Fighter, Battle Damaged; ROTJ, w/instructions &
    insert, NM (EX box), H4...$75.00
X-Wing Fighter, diecast, EX, from $30 to.........................$45.00
X-Wing Fighter, Micro Collection, w/1 figure, NM, D8...$55.00
X-Wing Fighter, SW, complete w/instructions & insert, M (EX
    box), H4 ....$75.00
Y-Wing Fighter, diecast, MOC, from $175 to $200.00
Y-Wing Fighter, NM $85.00

Miscellaneous

Ad Sheet, Topps, 1977, mc, M, M17.................................$35.00
Album, ROTJ, picture disk, 33 rpm, w/picture of Ewok,
    H4 ....$16.00
Bank, Chewbaca, Sigma, pnt ceramic, MIB, D4..............$25.00
Bank, Darth Vader, plastic, EX+, D8................................$18.00
Bank, Emperor's Royal Guard, ROTJ, Adam Joseph Ind, 1983,
    plastic, missing stopper, 9", EX+, D9 ....$5.00
Belt, ROTJ, elastic, w/Darth Vader buckle, EX, H4.........$12.00
Book, ESB, pop-up, EX $10.00
Book, Star Wars Book of Masks, Random House, hardback, M,
    H4 ....$12.00

Chewbacca Bandolier Strap, Return of the Jedi, 1983, MIB, J6, from $18.00 to $25.00.

Book & Cassette, SW ROTJ, EX, H4..........................$5.00

Boots, SW, Darth Vader pictured, EX, D8........................$75.00

Case, C-3PO, VG, H4 ....$15.00

Case, Darth Vader, 15x14", EX, D9........................$10.00

Case, ESB, no insert, H4......................................$12.00

Case, Laser Rifle, NM (EX box) $45.00

Case, SW, vinyl w/orig color, cb insert, EX, H4 ....$16.00

Chewbacca Bandolier Strap, NRFB, H4 ....$30.00

Cookie Jar, R2-D2, ceramic, MIB, J6 ....$175.00

Costume, R2-D2, Ben Cooper, NMIB.......................$12.00

Display Stand, for 12 orig figures, w/cb background scene, EX, H4 ....$45.00

Dixie Cups, SW, SW Saga, ESB, or ROTJ, MIB, J6, ea....$40.00

Figure, any character, Sigma, ceramic, NM, J6, ea...........$30.00

Figure, Yoda, Illusive Concepts, life sz, M, D4 ....$375.00

Game, Battle at Sarlacc's Pit, ROTJ, 3-D, EX (EX box)...$24.00

Game, Escape From Death Star, EX, D8 ....$18.00

Intergalactic Passport, Ballantine, 1983, H4...................$14.00

Iron-On Transfer Book, 1978, NM, D8 ....$30.00

Kite, Luke Skywalker, Spectra, MIP, H4......................$12.00

Lobby Cards, ESB, 11x14", 8 pcs, EX, D8....................$75.00

Lobby Cards, SW, 8 pcs, EX, D8 ....$135.00

Mask, Boba Fett, Don Post, full head, M, D4..................$75.00

Mask, Cantina Band Member, Don Post, full head, M, D4 ....$45.00

Mask, Chewbacca, Don Post, full head, M, D4................$75.00

Mask, Darth Vader, Don Post, full head, M, D4/D8, from $55 to...$65.00

Mask, Stormtrooper, Don Post, full head, M, D4 ....$75.00

Mask, Yoda, Don Post, full head, M, D4 ....$35.00

Movie, Star Wars, 1977, super 8mm blk & wht 200-ft film, NM (EX+ rpr box), F8.................................$25.00

Movie Poster, ESB, 1-sheet, 27x41", EX, D8...................$95.00

Movie Viewer, w/3 cartridges, EX, H4........................$22.00

Mug, Chewbacca figural, Rumph, California Originals, 1977, 7", J6..$225.00

Paint Kit, Craft Master, Luke or Han Solo, M (EX card), H4, ea..$9.00

Pendant, C-3PO, Darth Vader, Yoda or R2-D2, MOC, J6, ea...$24.00

Pendant, figural w/movable parts, 1978, M, D4, any $15.00

Pin, pnt metal figural, C-3PO or Darth Vader, NM, H4, ea...$3.00

Place Mats, R2-D2 & C-3PO, 2-pc set, NM (NM pkg) ...$25.00

Plate, Han Solo, Hamilton, limited edition, 8½", MIB, J6 ..$125.00

Plush Toy, Ewok, 15", NM, J6.................................$24.00

Plush Toy, Ewok, 8", NM, J6...................................$18.00

Portfolio, ROTJ, EX, D8..$85.00

Poster, Procter & Gamble premium, 1978, EX, H4, any.....$6.00

Puppet, Yoda, Kenner, 1981, hollow vinyl, 7½x5", EX+ ..$25.00

Puzzle, Darth Vader, frame-tray, EX, D8.....................$15.00

Puzzle, Sandpeople, MIB (sealed), D8.........................$18.00

Racing Set, Duel at Death Star, Lionel, 1978, M (NM sealed wht box), C1...$295.00

Record, Story of Star Wars, dialogue & music from orig movie, 33⅓ rpm, H4..$12.00

Speaker Phone, Darth Vader, MIB, D8 ....$125.00

Stamp Collectors Kit, HE Harris, 1977, MIB (sealed), M17..$25.00

Photo courtesy of June Moon.

Running Shoes, Clark's Jet Fighter, 1977, blue and yellow, original tags, NM, J6, $125.00.

Stickers, ESB, puffy, 1980, MIP, J7 ....$10.00

Toothbrush, Oral B, NRFB, H4, ea............................$8.00

Tote Bag, ROTJ, canvas, w/hang tag, NM, B3 ....$14.00

Waste Can, ROTJ, Cheinco, litho tin, VG+, I2...............$22.00

Wristwatch, Bradley/20th Century Fox, 1979, Swiss movement, Darth Vader on dial, chrome case, blk vinyl band, M, P4 .$90.00

Wristwatch, Bradley/20th Century Fox, 1981, Yoda on dial, planets for numbers, Swiss movement, blk vinyl band, M, P4...$75.00

Wristwatch, Fantasm, Darth Vader or Millennium Falcon, MIP, ea...$40.00

Yoda Fortune Teller, turn him upside down & look at your fortune, 5", M (VG+ box), H4 ....$70.00

Steam Powered

During the early part of the century until about 1930, though not employed to any great extent, live steam power was used to activate toys such as large boats, novelty toys and model engines.

See also Boats.

Accessory, butcher, Carette, articulated figure standing at rnd butcher's block, rectangular base, mc tin, 5", VG, A.$190.00

Accessory, lady at sewing machine, German, pnt tin, 5", G, A ..$935.00

Accessory, swing ride, Doll, compo figures in 2 swings attached to rnd carousel, pnt tin, 6½", VG, A $470.00

Automobile, Bing, open auto w/center steering, 2-seater, spoked wheels, steam plant at rear, 11¼", VG+, A..........$8,500.00

Boiler, Weeden #3/Germany, ca 1910, stamped metal, 8½x10" dia, VG, A $250.00

Ferris Wheel, Doll, 1900s, 3 of 6 gondolas on wheel w/roof & flag, beveled base, steam or hand powered, 15", VG, A $980.00

Ferris Wheels, Doll, tin, 6 gondolas w/4 seated compo figures on wheels between 2 towers w/flags, 22", rstr, A $1,100.00

Fire Pumper, Buckman, Pat 1872, copper boiler on tin firebox, pnt CI fr, 10½", EX, A $2,640.00

Fire Pumper, Marklin, ca 1900, tinplate and cast iron, hand-painted chassis and wheels, ornate brass steam dome, complete with fire hose and original burner, 9½x11", EX, A, $11,000.00.

Fire Pumper, Weeden, Pat 1885, pnt CI w/brass boiler, engine w/dbl cylinders on wrist pins, 17¼", EX, A $1,980.00

Log Splitter, rustic hand-pnt tin building w/conveyor & log ready to simulate splitting operation, 15", EX, A $300.00

Mining Plant, tin coal mine w/chain drive tower & conveyor belt, bulk house, see-through scene w/workers, 10x15", EX, A $880.00

Pickup Truck, Doll, blk & yel tin, rubber tires w/red spokes, chain-driven live steam mechanism, 19", rpt, EX, A $3,300.00

Photo courtesy of Dunbar Gallery.

Sausage Maker, German, ca 1910, EX, D10, $275.00.

Ship's Engine, Marklin, blk tin horizontal boiler w/copper bands, stairs, catwalk & rail, beveled base, 21x15", rstr, A .$1,485.00

Steam Engine, Frisbee/Am, Pat Aug 15, 1871, pnt CI water tank w/flywheel & other mechanisms, 3-legged, 8", EX, A..$1,595.00

Steam Engine, Linemar, complete, EX (EX box), T1 .....$245.00

Steam Engine, single-cylinder engine w/upright boiler, spoked flywheel, metal base, 14x6½", EX, A....................$1,100.00

Steam Engine, Weeden, 1890, brass boiler, single cylinder upright engine w/glass fill line, 9x5", EX (orig wood box), A...$330.00

Steam Engine w/5 Operative Accessories, Linemar, red & blk metal, MIB, A...$145.00

Steam Plant, Bing, horizontal single-cylinder engine w/flywheel, boiler & stack, on simulated brick, 11x7", EX, A $200.00

Steam Plant, Bing, single-cylinder engine w/flywheel, brass boiler, brick-like stack on blk burner, 14x14", VG, A...........$525.00

Steam Plant, Doll, horizontal single-cylinder engine w/flywheel, brass dynamo light, etc, beveled base, 15x11", VG, A.$300.00

Steam Plant, Doll, oscillating cylinder engine w/2 flywheels, horizontal boiler, stairs, catwalk, 7½", G, A $300.00

Steam Plant, Marklin, single-cylinder engine, horizontal boiler, simulated stack & burner, 13x17", EX (orig box), A ..$660.00

Steam Plant, Marklin, single-cylinder engine w/flywheel, brass boiler w/gauges on simulated brick burner, 16x11", M, A $550.00

Tractor, Mamod, brass boiler, tall front stack, spoked wheels, 9", VG, A $225.00

Tractor, Mamod, early tractor w/aluminum spoked wheels & canopy, burner, whistle & lever, 10½", EX (torn box), A $55.00

Steiff

Margaret Steiff made the first of her felt toys in 1880, stuffing them with lamb's wool. Later followed toys of velvet, plush and wool, and in addition to the lamb's wool stuffing, she used felt scraps, excelsior and kapok as well. In 1897 and '98 her trademark was a paper label printed with an elephant; from 1900 to 1905 her toys carried a circular tag with an elephant logo that was different than the one she had previously used. The most famous 'button in ear' trademark was registered on December 20th, 1904. 1904 and '05 saw the use of the button with an elephant (extremely rare) and the blank button (which is also rare). The button with Steiff and the underscored or trailing 'F' was used until 1948, and the raised script button is from the 1950s.

Steiff Teddy bears, perhaps the favorite of collectors everywhere, are characterized by their long thin arms with curved wrists and paws that extend below their hips. Buyer beware: the Steiff company is now making many replicas of their old bears. For more information about Steiff's buttons, chest tags and stock tags as well as the inspirational life of Margaret Steiff and the fascinating history of Steiff toys we recommend *Button in Ear Book* and *The Steiff Book of Teddy Bears*, both by Jurgen and Marianne Cieslik; *Teddy Bears and Steiff Animals* 2nd and 3rd series by Margaret Fox Mandel; *4th Teddy Bear and Friends Price Guide* by Linda Mullins; and *Collectible German Animals Value Guide* by Dee Hockenberry. See also Clubs, Newsletters and Other Publications under Cynthia's Country Store.

Advisor: Cynthia's Country Store, Cynthia Brintnall (C14). **See also Disney; Santa.**

Arco German Shepherd, mohair, standing w/mouth closed, orig collar & chest tag, 4", rare, M $350.00

Baby Boar, velvet, raised script button, stock tag, 4", M, G16..$100.00

Bazi Dog, standing, raised script button, remnant stock tag, watermelon chest tag, orig collar, 4", NM, G16 ......$125.00

Bendy Bear, caramel, 1960s, 2½", M, G16......................$55.00

Bendy Bear, honey, all ID, 3½", M, G16..........................$75.00
Bendy Bear, wht, all ID, 3½", M, G16 ....$100.00
Bengal, seated, w/chest tag, sm, M $275.00
Bessy Cow, wht w/brn spots, all ID, 6", M......................$325.00

Camel, mohair and felt, glass eyes, all ID, M, $165.00.

Camel on Wheels, lt brn fur w/2 humps, red felt seat blanket, 17", EX, A..........................$880.00
Cat, blk & wht striped, crouching, not jtd, 7", G, G16 ....$65.00
Cat, brn & wht striped, raised script button, orig ribbon w/bell, 5", NM, G16 ....$100.00
Chow Dog, raised script button, 4½", rare, EX, G16......$185.00
Cockie, red-lettered chest tag, raised script button, stock & US Zone tags, w/orig ribbon, 1948, 5", M, G16 ....$250.00
Coco Baboon, walking on 4 limbs, all ID, 8", M.............$400.00
Collie Dog, seated, no ID, 4", rare, EX, G16...................$150.00
Dachshund, blk & brn wool w/blk shoe-button eyes, embroidered features & claws, jtd, 1930, 18", fiber loss & rprs, A..........................$345.00
Dachshund on Eccentric Wheels, felt, FF underscored button, 1920s-30, 10", NM, G16 ....$585.00
Donkey, tag in ear & front, 1950s, 5½", MIB, H12 ....$155.00
Dormouse, no ID, 1960s, NM, G16..................................$65.00
Elephant, raised script button, stock tag, red felt collar, 3½", NM, G16..........................$85.00

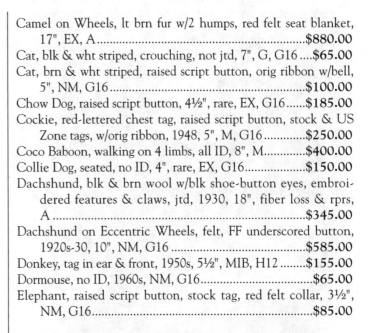

Eric Bat, mohair with cloth wings, 1960s, rare, minimum value, $675.00.

Fawn, in resting position w/legs fully extended, ear tag, 16", EX, A..........................$450.00
Floppy Hansi, all ID, orig ribbon, 1970s, 9" $65.00
Floppy Zotty, all ID, 1960s, 7", M (orig box)....................$95.00
Fox, brn, button in ear, VG, 7", A...................................$95.00
Fox, seated, no ID, 3½", EX, G16 ....$65.00
Giraffe, velvet, all ID, 1950s, 6", VG, G16 ....$60.00
Hedgehog, raised script button, stock tag, 1950s, 6", NM, G16 .$75.00
Hexie Dog, raised script button, stock & chest tags, orig collar, 5½", M, G16..........................$100.00
Hucky Raven, blk w/red beak, all ID, 4", M...................$150.00
Jocko, wht, fully jtd, 1950s, 4½", NM, from $145 to......$165.00
Joggi Hedgehog, standing, w/chest tag, 5", M $100.00
Jolanthe Pig, mohair, all ID, 4", M..................................$150.00
Lamb, incised button, 1960s, 10", VG, G16 ....$65.00
Lamb on Wheels, curly wool w/felt face, ears & legs, glass eyes, ear button, ca 1913, 11x12½", VG, A..................$1,610.00
Llama, all ID, 6", M $225.00
Lobster, felt, raised script button & stock tag, 1950s, 4", M, G16..........................$225.00
Mallard Duck, all ID, 4", M..$125.00
Manni Rabbit, begging, raised script button & chest tag, w/orig ribbon & bell, 4", M..........................$135.00

Micki and Mecki, 10", EX, from $145.00 to $165.00 each.

Monkey, plush, jtd, no ID, 4½", EX $95.00
Monkey, wht, fully jtd, all ID, 1950s, 4", NM, from $145 to..$165.00
Moosy Moose, stuffed felt antlers, raised script button & chest
    tag, 10", NM $475.00
Mopsy, dog w/glass eyes, no ID, 1950s, 4½", EX $55.00
Mouse, wht, no ID, 1960s, 3", M, G16 ....$50.00
Navy Goat, chest tag, 1950s, 6½", NM, G16 ....$185.00
Navy Goat, chest tag, 6", NM, G16 ....$325.00
Orangutan, mk King Louie/Walt Disney, orig tag, 11", EX, A .$165.00
Original Teddy, brn, raised script button & chest tag, 16", scarce,
    NM $1,500.00
Original Teddy, caramel, inscribed button & stock tag, 10", NM ..$140.00
Original Teddy, gold, raised script button, chest tag, 20", NM,
    G16...$1,200.00
Original Teddy, wht w/glass eyes, straw stuffing, chest tag, 1950s,
    13", NM, G16 ....$950.00
Peky Dog, chest tag & orig ribbon, 1950s, 4", M, G16 .....$75.00
Perri Squirrel, all ID, 1950s, 5", M, G16 ....$100.00
Piccy Pelican, wht w/yel bill, chest tag, 6½", M $350.00
Pieps Mouse, brn, chest tag, 3½", NM, G16 ....$85.00
Rabbit, sitting, blond mohair w/pk glass eyes, excelsior stuffing,
    jtd, ca 1913, 12", lt moth damage, A $800.00
Rabbit, sitting, cream velveteen w/rust markings, blk bead eyes,
    ear button, 1908, 5", lt pile loss, A..........................$345.00
Rabbit, stands upright, velour pants & jacket, glass eyes, jtd, 13",
    EX, A...$1,320.00
Renny Reindeer, raised script button, chest & stock tags, 9", M,
    G16 ....$300.00
Robby Seal, all ID, 1950s, 11", M, G16 ....$165.00
Rooster, raised script button, chest tag, 6", NM, G16.....$100.00
Rooster, raised script button, remnant stock tag, 1950s, 7", EX.$155.00
Sarras Boxer, w/collar & US Zone chest tag, 7", M $325.00
Skunk, velvet & mohair, chest tag, 1950s, 4", M, from $195 to .$210.00
Sonny Rabbit, jtd, all ID, 1960s, 6", M $145.00

Sonny Rabbit, jtd, all ID, 1960s, 8", M $225.00
Squirrel, blond mohair, blk steel eyes w/felt backing, embroi-
    dered nose, mouth & claws, jtd, 1920, 7½", EX, A .$400.00
Squirrel, velvet & mohair, 4", NM, G16.........................$85.00

**Susi, tan mohair,
no button or tag,
4", EX, $50.00.**

Tabby, chest tag, w/orig ribbon & bell, 2½", M $125.00
Teddy Baby, blond, raised script button, sweater not orig, 9",
    EX $950.00
Teddy Bear, all ID, 1960s, 12", M, G16..........................$165.00
Teddy Bear, apricot w/shoe-button eyes, embroidered snout, jtd,
    blank button, 12", EX...$1,500.00
Teddy Bear, beige mohair w/glass eyes, embroidered features,
    plush pads, jtd, ear button, 1970s, 9½", EX, A $115.00
Teddy Bear, blond mohair w/blk bead eyes, embroidered nose &
    mouth, jtd, 4", fiber loss, damage at neck, A $230.00
Teddy Bear, blond mohair w/blk button eyes, blk embroidered
    snout & pads, ear button, 15", VG, A $1,265.00
Teddy Bear, blond mohair w/blk shoe-button eyes, embroi-
    dered snout & claws, felt pads & red felt shoes, 1906,
    15", VG, A $980.00
Teddy Bear, blond mohair w/embroidered features & claws,
    felt pads, jtd, excelsior stuffing, no button, 12½", VG,
    A...$1,380.00
Teddy Bear, blond mohair w/shoe-button eyes, emroidered
    features, excelsior stuffed, ear button, 1906, 11", rpr,
    VG..$1,000.00
Teddy Bear, caramel w/orig ribbon, no ID, 1950s, 5", M,
    G16..$200.00
Teddy Bear, champagne w/orig ribbon, incised button & stock
    tag, 1960s, 7", NM, G16...$85.00
Teddy Bear, dk brn w/glass eyes, straw stuffed, raised script but-
    ton, remnant stock tag, 1950s, 13", EX, G16...........$750.00
Teddy Bear, gold, fully jtd, no ID, 1950s, 3½", EX, G16..$250.00
Teddy Bear, gold mohair w/orig ribbon, 1950s, 5½", NM,
    G16..$195.00
Teddy Bear, gold w/glass eyes, straw stuffed, no ID, 1950s, 9", EX,
    G16 ....$225.00

Teddy Bear, honey-colored mohair, black button eyes, embroidered nose, mouth and claws, fully jointed, 1906-10, 27", from $10,000.00 to $12,000.00.

Teddy Bear, honey mohair w/blk button eyes, embroidered snout & claws, whip-stiched felt pads, 1906-10, 27", VG, from $10,000 to $12,000.00

Teddy Bear, lt apricot w/shoe-button eyes & embroidered nose, mouth & claws, jtd, blank ear button, 1903-04, 15", VG...$3,000.00

Teddy Bear, tan, raised script button, fully jtd, 3½", NM, G16 ....$285.00

Teddy Bear, tan w/orig ribbon, no ID, 1950s, 5½", M, G16 ....$200.00

Teddy Bear on Wheels, tan mohair w/shoe-button eyes, iron fr, ca 1908, 19", VG, A $175.00

Terry Airdale, all ID w/US Zone tag, orig collar, 7", NM....$125.00

Tiger, running, chest tag, 6", M, G16 ....$145.00

Tiger Cub, seated, 4", EX, G16 ....$65.00

Vario Rabbit, jtd rear legs, all ID, 5", M.........................$275.00

Turtle, tan mohair with glass eyes, 5½", EX, $65.00.

Waldi Dog, lt brn w/blk nose, all ID, early US Zone chest tag, M...$220.00

Woolie Bird, 1960s, M, 1" to 2", ea $40.00

Woolie Mouse, gray, inscribed button, stock tag, 1½", M, G16..$45.00

Woolie Owl, inscribed button, stock tag, plastic feet, 2½", M, G16 ....$45.00

Woolie Rabbit, apricot & wht, 1960s, M, G16 ....$40.00

Woolie Raven, metal ft, 2½", EX, G16 ....$45.00

Zebra, mohair, incised button, 8", M..............................$175.00

Zebra, velvet, raised script button, chest tag & partial stock tag, 1950s, 5" or 7", EX, ea $135.00

Zotty Bear, reddish, rpl ribbon, 8", EX, G16 ....$165.00

Strauss

Imaginative, high-quality tin windup toys were made by Ferdinand Strauss (New York, later New Jersey) from the onset of World War I until the 1940s. For about fifteen years prior to his becoming a toymaker, he was a distributor of toys he imported from Germany. Though hard to find in good working order, his toys are highly prized by today's collectors, and when found in even very good to excellent condition, many are in the $500.00 and up range.

Advisor: Scott Smiles (S10).

Air Devil, airplane w/pilot, 1926, 8½", EX, from $500 to ..$600.00

Alabama Coon Jigger (Tombo), 1910, Black man does jig on stage, blk & yel-checked pants, rare version, VG (VG box), from $700 to $750.00

Boob McNutt, man in red polka-dot pants & blk jacket, rnd flat hat, 8¾", VG, A...$450.00

Bus de Lux, lt bl long-nose w/visor, dk bl & wht stripe trim, curtained windows, aluminum tires w/dk bl hubs, 14", G, A $600.00

Dandy Jim Clown Dancer, 1921, does the jig and plays cymbals atop circus tent, lithographed tin, 10", EX, $600.00.

Chek-A-Cab #69, yel & blk w/checked trim, yel hubs, 8½", VG $650.00

Dandy Jim Clown Dancer, 1921, does jig & plays cymbals atop circus tent, 10", NM...$700.00

Flying Zeppelin, 1920, hung from string, propelled by spinning prop, aluminum, mk Graf...GZ-2017, 16", NM (EX box) $1,100.00

Ford Fliver Sedan, figures in blk-pnt tin sedan w/simulated tread-mk tires, 8½", VG, A...............................$385.00

Ham & Sam, 1921, Black banjo player standing by piano player, litho tin, 5½", EX, from $850 to $950.00

Ham & Sam, 1921, 5½", G, from $600 to $650.00

Handcar, workmen pump yel handcar w/2 yel wheels, EX+, from $250 to..$300.00

Inter-State Double-Decker Bus, gr w/yel trim, rear steps lead to open deck, aluminum tires, 11", EX, from $800 to ..$900.00

Inter-State Double-Decker Bus, 11", VG, from $700 to .$800.00

Jackie the Hornpipe Dancer, ca 1930, boat moves forward as sailor dances on deck, EX, from $900 to...............$1,000.00

Jazzbo Jim, 1920s, Jazzbo plays banjo & dances atop cabin roof, 10", G, from $350 to....................................$400.00

Jitney Bus #66, 1920s, gr w/yel name & trim, metal tires w/gr hubs, w/driver, 9¼", EX.......................................$600.00

Leaping Lena Car, 1930, blk w/allover wht wording, w/driver, 8", VG, from $400 to $450.00

Man Pushing Wheelbarrow, man in red cap, bl coat & yel pants pushes yel & bl wheelbarrow w/Tip Top decal, 5½", VG $175.00

Play Golf, articulated golfer hits ball into scoring holes on gr beveled base, MB, from $750 to $850.00

Racer #21, w/driver, yel & red w/gr tires, bullet-shaped back, pnt side louvers, raised side trim, 9", VG+, from $350 to..$400.00

Rollo-Chair, G, from $650 to $750.00

Santee Claus, 1923, Santa bounces up and down as sleigh advances, lithographed tin, 11", EX, from $1,000.00 to $1,100.00.

Speedboat Ferdinand, red tin floor toy w/driver, 10", G, from $200 to..$250.00

Spirit of St Louis Airplane, silver-tone w/pilot in open cockpit, litho tin, 8", EX $450.00

Tom Twist the Funny Clown, 8½", EX (orig box), from $1,100 to...$1,200.00

Tourist Car, 33 on front grille, full-figure chauffer, raised designs on doors & louvers, 10", VG+...............................$580.00

Travelchiks, 4 chicks atop railroad car bend & peck for food, litho tin chick passengers, 8", VG+ (G box), from $400 to...$450.00

Trik Auto, early tin auto w/driver travels forward & reverse, circles w/cracy-car action, 7½", NM (G box).............$575.00

Wildfire Trotter, driver jumps up & down in seat as donkey cart advances, 8½", EX...$250.00

Photo courtesy of Dunbar Gallery.

Yell-O-Taxi, #59, with driver, lithographed tin, 8", VG, from $500.00 to $600.00.

Structo

Pressed steel vehicles were made by Structo (Illinois) as early as 1920. They continued in business well into the 1960s, producing several army toys, trucks of all types, and firefighting and construction equipment.

Ballantine Beer & Ale Tractor & Trailer, dk bl, 24", EX+, A ..$375.00

Cattle Truck #708, red & wht, MIB................................$225.00

Deluxe Roadster, orange w/blk convertible top, running boards & fenders, wht tin tires w/spoke wheels, 14", EX, A.....$825.00

End Loader, 1950s, orange, 15½", VG, A......................$110.00

Ladder Truck, red, w/hose reel, bell & overhead ladders, hub wheels, 18", G, A..$200.00

Lumber Truck #77, red w/blk rubber tires, carries 5 wooden logs on bed, 10", NM (partial box), A..............................$80.00

Mobile Crane #810, gr & yel w/blk plastic tires, 19", NM (EX box)..$225.00

Mobile Steam Shovel, #2/2, baked-on metallic enamel w/blk rubber tires, 20", NM+ (NM box), A $175.00

Motor Dispatch Tow Truck, bl, 24", VG $525.00

Ready Mix Cement Mixer #700, metallic enamel w/blk tires, NM (EX box)..$230.00

Road Grader, orange, 17½", 1 wheel rpl, G, A...........$1,600.00

Scout Wrecker, red & wht, NMIB $160.00

Steam Shovel, orange, battery-op, EX $150.00

Structo Excavating Co Dump Truck, silver cab w/red dump, VG+ $75.00

Taxicab, early 2-tone 4-door w/spoke wheels, w/driver, 11", G, A $250.00

Steam Shovel, 1950s, green with yellow decals, 16", EX, from $75.00 to $125.00.

Transport Tractor-Trailer, bl pnt cast aluminum cab pulls red
    pressed-steel trailer, rubber tires, 22", G.....................$35.00
Truck Fleet Set #725, NMIB $550.00
US Army Troop Carrier, M $115.00
66 Tanker Truck, red, VG..$150.00

Teddy Bears

    Early bears have long snouts, jointed limbs, large feet and
felt paws, long curving arms, and glass or shoe-button eyes. Most
have a humped back and are made of mohair stuffed with straw
or excelsior. Some of the most desirable were made early in the
century by the Steiff company (see Steiff), but they don't neces-
sarily have to be old to be collectible. Buyer beware! The Steiff
company is producing replicas of their early bears, and 'old'
Bings are being distributed as well.

    Note: Teddies with short stubby feet and bodies are general-
ly not as valuable as the early styles, whose long thin arms are
curved at the wrist with paws that hang below their hips.

    Advisor: Cynthia's Country Store, Cynthia Brintnall (C14).
See also Schuco; Steiff.

7", golden-yel fur w/glass eyes, bell on neck ribbon, M, H2....$75.00
8½", mohair w/shoe-button eyes, jtd at shoulders & hips, excel-
    sior stuffing, long thin arms, Steiff-like, 1905, VG ..$900.00
12", English, ca 1929, brn fur w/tan snout, dressed in
    sweater & gray suit w/checked cap, stitched claws, jtd,
    VG, A $270.00
12", Mr Robeling, blond mohair w/glass eyes, embroidered
    features & claws, felt pads, jtd, soft stuffed, 1920s, VG,
    A $230.00
12½", gold mohair w/glass eyes & embroidered nose, long
    arms, felt pads, Steiff-like, 1920s, 50% fur loss, from
    $950 to..$1,150.00

13", early 1920s, blond mohair w/shoe-button eyes, gr overalls
    w/checked shirt, jtd, rpl pads, fiber & fur loss, A.....$230.00
14½", cinnamon mohair, glass eyes, embroidered snout,
    cloth pads, straight arms & legs, excelsior & kapok, '20s,
    G, A..$115.00
15", blond mohair, triangular face w/long snout, shoe-button eyes,
    floss nose & claws, long arms, soft, Ideal (?), VG.....**$1,000.00**

**16", burnished gold long pile mohair, straw
stuffed, embroidered nose and mouth, music box in
tummy, VG, minimum value, $325.00.**

16", yel mohair w/blk shoe-button eyes, embroidered snout,
    curved arms & straight legs, checked clown suit, 1920s, VG,
    A $145.00
16", yel plush mohair w/shoe-button eyes, appliqued nose,
    embroidered mouth, short arms & legs, jtd, Am (?), 1920s,
    G, A...$200.00
16½", early 1900s, orange mohair Roosevelt type w/glass eyes,
    mouth opens to expose teeth, oval body, jtd, VG, A ..$460.00
17", yel mohair w/glass eyes, embroidered snout, felt pads, jtd,
    kapok stuffing, England, 1930s, VG, A...................$210.00
17", yel mohair w/long oval body, short curved arms, long
    straight legs, bl & wht knitted overalls, Am (?), 1920s, VG,
    A $145.00
18½", beige curly mohair w/glass eyes, embroidered snout & printed
    claws, fat body w/short fat limbs, 1940s, VG, A $145.00
18½", gold short-hair fur in wht sleeveless shirt & bl pants,
    embroidered snout, glass eyes, fully jtd, VG+, A $75.00
19", yel mohair w/glass eyes, embroidered snout, curved
    arms w/straight legs, excelsior stuffing, jtd, Am, 1920s,
    VG, A...$315.00
20", long dark blond fur w/cloth nose & pads, frowning mouth,
    glass eyes, full jtd, G, A $75.00
20½", blond mohair w/glass eyes, embroidered long snout & claws,
    curved arms & straight legs, lg ft, 1920s, rprs, A..........$115.00

20½", deep honey gold short-hair fur w/embroidered snout, pk pads, fully jtd, wearing watch, Am, early, EX, A $200.00

22½", honey gold short-hair fur w/embroidered snout, thick plush ears, fully jtd, stitched paws, Am, early, EX, A $220.00

22½", gold plush mohair w/glass eyes, fabric nose, straight limbs w/flannel pads, excelsior stuffing, Am, 1920s, G, A .$316.00

24", Am 1910, lt gold short-hair fur w/embroidered snout, fully jtd, lg padded paws, VG+, A $275.00

Tekno

The Tekno company was formed in Denmark during the late 1920s. The toy vehicles they made were of the highest quality, fully able to compete with the German-made Marklin toys then dominating the market. The earliest Tekno vehicles were made of tinplate, and though some were not marked at all, others were stamped with a number. The factory continued to expand until WWII broke out and restrictions made further building impossible. In 1940 the government prohibited the use of tinplate for toy production, and the company began instead to manufacture diecast vehicles in a smaller (1/43) scale. These were exported worldwide in great volume. Collectors regard them as the finest diecasts ever made. Due to climbing production costs and the resulting increases in retail prices that inevitably hurt their sales, the company closed in 1972. Tekno dies were purchased by Mercury Kirk Joal who used them to produce toys identical to the originals except for the mark.

Photo courtesy of Continental Hobby House.

Junior Assembly Set, MIB, $300.00.

#0 ASG Transport-Spedition, dk bl & yel, 1 headlight missing & front license plate detached o/w NMIB, C6 ....$30.00

#00 Transport-Spedition Truck, wht w/bl cover, MIB, C6..$40.00

#000 Scania Truck & Trailer, MIB, C6 ....$70.00

#142 Scania Truck & Long Wheel Base Trailer, bl & red w/silver trailer cover, NM, C6..$50.00

#356 Porsche, metallic bl w/wht rubber tires, NM, A $150.00

#434 Volvo BP Tanker, wht & gr, M, L1.......................$150.00

#451 Scania Truck & Trailer, red w/wht trailer covers, separate boxes, M (VG boxes), C6 ....$100.00

#452W Transport Trailer, wht w/bl cover, M, C6............$14.00

#452Y Covered Trailer, Tekno Transport, yel w/bl cover, M (G box), C6...$14.00

#775 Small Utility Trailer, MIB, C6 ....$30.00

#814K US Army Cannon, MIB, C6.................................$30.00

#832 MG 1100, wht, MIB, C6..$55.00

#833 Ford Mustang, 1967, wht & blk w/Rallye Monte Carlo #169 decals, EX, C6...$70.00

#834BH Ford Mustang, 1967, bl w/blk hardtop, M (M box), C6...$70.00

#834GBH Ford Mustang, 1967, metallic gold w/blk hardtop, M (M box), C6..$70.00

#834GCB Ford Mustang Convertible, metallic gold w/blk interior, M (M box), C6...$70.00

#834K Ford Mustang Kit, 1967, contents sealed, MIB, C6...$30.00

#834WC Ford Mustang Convertible, 1967, wht, M (M box), C6...$70.00

#834WH Ford Mustang Hardtop, 1967, wht w/blk top, M (M box), C6...$70.00

#837 SAAB 99, wht, MIB, C6 ....$40.00

#851 Scania CR 76 Bus, dk red, MIB, C6 ....$40.00

#864RH Ford Mustang, 1967, red w/blk hardtop & interior, M (M box), C6..$70.00

#915 Ford D-Truck, red & silver, M (EX box), A.............$85.00

#930 Monza GT, silver, MIB, C6 ....$65.00

#931 Monza Spyder, wht, MIB, C6 ....$65.00

#934S Toyota 2000 GT, silver body, M (M box), C6.......$40.00

#934TM Toyota 2000 GT, mustard body, M (M box), C6 .$40.00

#950 Mercedes Benz 0302 Bus, Osterreische Post, MIB, C6.$40.00

RSK Volvo Truck, red w/wht cab roof, M (M box), C6 ...$40.00

Telephones

Novelty phones representing a well-known advertising or cartoon character are proving to be the focus of lots of collector activity — the more recognizable the character the better. Telephones modeled after a product container are collectible too, and with the intense interest currently being shown in anything advertising related, competition is sometimes stiff and values are rising.

Advisor: Jon Thurmond (T1).

Bart Simpson, MIB, T1...$35.00

Beetle Bailey, 1983, MIB..$95.00

Bozo the Clown, Telemania, MIB, T1 ....$75.00

Cabbage Patch Girl, 1980s, EX+, T1 ....$85.00

Charlie the Tuna Triumphs!, MIB, from $45 to $60.00

Crest Sparkle, MIB, from $45 to.......................................$55.00

Inspector Gadget, 1984, MIB $60.00

Joe Cool, Seika, 1992, M, H11 ....$60.00

Keebler Elf, NM, T1 ....$100.00

Kermit the Frog, EX+, T1, $225.00.

Express Wagon, Althof-Bergmann, 1870s, 18", EX, D10, $4,500.00.

Horse-Drawn Trolley, George Brown/Am, yel w/blk roof & spoked wheels, mk Grand Central Depot, 2 wht horses, 14", EX, A $1,210.00

Little Green Sprout, EX+, T1 .... $75.00
Little Orphan Annie, 1983, unused, M, P12 .... $85.00
Mario Brothers, 1980s, MIB, T1 .... $45.00
Mickey Mouse, ATC, NM, I2 .... $100.00
Pizza Hut Pete, 1980s, NM $55.00
Raid Bug, EX+, P12 .... $125.00
Snoopy, Determined #4987, reclining figure w/push buttons, wall-mount, M, H11 .... $30.00
Snoopy & Woodstock, Am Telephone, rotary dial, EX, from $100 to $125.00
Snoopy & Woodstock, Am Telephone, 1970s, touch-tone, EX, from $75 to $100.00
Snoopy as Joe Cool, 1980s, MIB, T1 .... $55.00
Star Trek Enterprise Spaceship, MIB, T1 .... $75.00
Tang, #1, MIB, P12 .... $95.00
Tetley Tea, man on rnd base inscribed Tetley, Canadian premium, M, P12 .... $195.00
Winnie the Pooh, sq base, M, from $225 to $250.00
Ziggy, 1989, MIB, T1 .... $75.00

Horse and Jockey on Rocker, Fallows, 1880s, 7", EX, D10, $2,100.00.

Lamb on Rocking Base, wht w/red neck ribbon & bell, gr half-disk base, 4½", G, A $525.00
Lion & Elephant on Bell Rocker, att Bergmann, pnt tin, yel lion facing silver elephant w/red blanket, 7½", G-, A $935.00
Orion Engine, Fallows, ca 1880, red & blk hand-pnt tin w/bl & gold trim, heart-shaped spoke wheels, 9", rare, VG, A $1,320.00
Red Cross Ambulance, WWI British model w/open cab, spoke wheels, Red Cross symbols, litho driver & nurse, 8", EX, A $500.00
Water Truck, Marklin, early open truck w/water tank, gr w/blk trim, brass faucet, red spoke wheels, 15", rpt, A ... $1,980.00
Watermill, European, water buckets on pulley chain empty into tank that operates mill on table saw, 12", VG+, A . $910.00

Tin Toys

Toys listed here are from the last decade of the 1800s up through the early years of this century.

See also Pull and Push Toys; Windups, Friction and Other Mechanicals.

Double-Decker Bus, Smith-Cavey/England, 1920s, red w/yel roof, Eat More Fruit on yel panel, litho passengers, 8", VG, A $525.00
Happy Hooligan in Cart, Ingae/Italy, figure in 2-wheeled cart pulled by donkey, VG, A $250.00
Horse & Carriage, wht horse w/leather harness, blk carriage w/yel trim, bsk driver, tufted cloth seat, 29", EX, A $4,510.00
Horse & Jockey on Rocker, Fallows (?), pnt tin, scrolled rocker w/repeated embossed knob decoration, 4¼", G, A .. $525.00
Horse w/Circus Acrobat on Bell Rocker, Bergmann, pnt tin, figure posed to jump on back of horse, 7", G-, A $770.00

Tonka

Since the mid-forties, the Tonka Company (Minnesota) has produced an extensive variety of high-quality painted metal trucks, heavy equipment, tractors and vans.

Advisor: Doug Dezso (D6).

AAA Wrecker, 1956, w/boom, rpt, VG+ $300.00
Aerial Ladder Fire Truck, 1958, NM $250.00
Aerial Sand Loader, EX $200.00
Airport Service Tractor & Trailer, 1962, bl, NM...........$200.00
Allied Van Lines Truck, 1956, NM $300.00
Army Jeep, 1964, EX $140.00
Big Mike Dump Truck, 1957, 'V' plow accessory, G+ $450.00
Cattle Semi Tractor & Trailer, 1955, G+ $225.00
Cement Mixer, 1958, EX+ $185.00
Cement Mixer #620, 1965, red & wht cab, wht plastic drum
    rotates, 14", minor pnt chip o/w VG, P4....................$75.00
Changeable Stake Bed Truck, 1955, VG $285.00
COE Allied Van Lines Truck, G- $95.00
COE Low Boy & Shovel, M..$300.00
COE Utility Truck, orange & gr, G- $75.00
Cross Country Freight Semi, 1955, VG $300.00
Deluxe Fisherman Truck w/Trailer & Boat, 1960, VG+ .$250.00
Dump Truck, bronze w/open cab, G...............................$125.00
Dump Truck, red cab & yel dump, 13½", EX $150.00
Farm Set, 1960, NMIB $485.00
Farm Truck #B204, 1961, w/4 horses, M......................$300.00
Fire Jeep Pumper, 1963, EX $160.00
Fire Jeep Pumper, 1963, M $215.00
Flamer Custom Pickup Truck, 1956, blk, M $175.00
Gambles Pickup, 1955, EX $190.00
Gambles Semi, 1955, EX $325.00
Gambles Semi, 1958, EX $250.00
Grain Truck, 1954, VG $160.00
Green Giant Semi, 1954, G+ $200.00
Hi-Way Custom Mixer, 1957, VG+ $185.00
Hi-Way Dually Pickup Truck, 1959, VG+ $140.00
Hi-Way Dump Truck #975, G $140.00
Hi-Way Side Dump Truck, 1956, EX.............................$250.00
Jeep Surrey, blk & wht, NMIB......................................$200.00
Jeep Surrey, pk, NMIB...$125.00
Jeep Wrecker, blk & wht, w/plow, NMIB......................$175.00
Jeepster, late version, 13", VG+ $30.00
Livestock Truck, 1952, NM $250.00
Low Boy & Shovel, 1955, red & bl, EX $300.00
Low Boy Carry-All Truck, 1952, G.................................$55.00
Lumber Changeable Flatbed Truck, 1955, EX $325.00
Marine Boat Service Truck, 1961, G $130.00
Minute Maid Delivery Truck, 1956, EX.........................$450.00
Mobil Dragline #135, 1960, EX (EX box) $200.00
Mobile Clam #942, orange, VG+...................................$100.00
Motor Transport Car Hauler, 1963 ....$125.00
Pickup Truck, 1955, red, EX...$200.00
Pickup Truck #2, 1958, bl, EX (EX box).........................$250.00
Pickup Truck w/Horse Trailer, 1961, VG $125.00
Pickup Truck w/Stake Trailer, 1957, w/blk sheep, VG+ .$250.00
Ramp Hoist Truck, 1963, red w/wht trim, EX $375.00
Rescue Truck, 1960, VG $175.00
Road Grader, 1959, orange, G.......................................$60.00
Ser-Vi-Car, 1963, VG $125.00
Service Truck, 1959, bl, EX...$185.00
Sportsman Pickup Truck, 1958, G $130.00

Road Grader, 1960, marked State Hi-Way Dept on door, yellow, 17", VG, $35.00.

Sand Loader, 1961, red, 11½", EX, $45.00.

Sportsman Pickup w/Trailer & Boat, 1958, VG $275.00
Stake Truck, 1963, VG+ $100.00
Standard Oil Tanker Semi, 1961, G $200.00
StarKist Utility Truck, 1955, EX...................................$300.00
Suburban Pumper #46, 1958, NMIB..............................$275.00
Sunkist Orange Tanker Truck, 1981, plastic, 10", EX,
    N2..$30.00
Terminix Van, 1961, EX $400.00
TFD Tanker Fire Truck, 1958, wht, NM $600.00
Tow Truck, 1959, VG $140.00
Transport Truck #140, ca 1950, w/trailer, EX+ $360.00
Truck Camper, 1963, turq & wht, EX+ (EX box) $200.00
USAF Jeep, 1964-65, bl w/wht interior, MIB $175.00
Wheaton Van Lines Truck, 1956, G...............................$450.00
White Thunder Bird Express Truck, 1959, VG+............$250.00

Toothbrush Holders

Figural ceramic toothbrush holders have become very popular collectibles, especially those modeled after well-known cartoon characters. Disney's Mickey Mouse, Donald Duck, and the Three Little Pigs are among the most desirable, and some of the harder-to-find examples in mint condition sell for upwards of $200.00. Many were made in Japan before WWII. Because the paint was not fired on, it is often beginning to flake off. Be sure to consider the condition of the paint as well as the bisque when evaluating your holdings. For more information we recommend *Pictorial Guide to Toothbrush Holders* by Marilyn Cooper. Plate numbers in the following listings refer to her book.

Advisor Marilyn Cooper (C9).

Andy Gump & Min, Japan, pnt bsk, standing arm-in-arm, mk
  FAS, 4x3¼", plate #221, NM........................$85.00
Baby Bunting, Germany, arm holds brush, 6¾", plate #1, NM..$365.00
Bellhop, Japan, lustre glaze, head cocked to side, pockets hold
  brushes, 6½", plate #169, NM....................$60.00
Bonzo w/Sidetray, Germany, lustre, mouth holds brush, 3⅝",
  plate #23, M...............................$135.00
Boy Brushing Teeth, Japan, standing on stool at bl sink, 2 holes,
  6½", plate #24, NM........................$90.00
Boy in Nickers Next to Mailbox, Japan, 4¼", EX.............$60.00
Boy in Top Hat, Japan, w/spotted dog at side, glossy red, blk &
  wht pnt, 2 holes, 5½", plate #29, M...................$75.00
Boy w/Violin, Goldcastle/Japan, sm dog on base, 2 holes, 5½",
  plate #30, M...............................$80.00
Calico Cat, Japan, 2 holes, 5½", plate #37, NM.............$90.00
Cat w/Bass Fiddle, Japan, 6", plate #38, EX..................$150.00
Chef, Japan, lustre w/pnt details, arms on hips, 2 holes, 5¼",
  plate #39, EX..............................$65.00
Children in Auto, Japan, gr, gray, brn & tan lustre, 2 holes, 5",
  plate #40, NM.............................$80.00
Clown Holding Mask, Japan, 5½", plate #62, EX..........$100.00
Cowboy w/Cactus, Japan, folded arms, holsters hold brushes, 5",
  plate #70, EX.............................$75.00
Doctor w/Satchel, Japan, 1 hole, 5¾", plate #206, NM....$90.00
Donald Duck, prewar Japan, 2 long-billed Donalds w/arms
  entwined, 4½", plate #247, NM.............................$400.00
Frog w/Mandolin, Goldcastle/Japan, 6", plate #209, EX...$85.00
Jiminy Cricket, DuPont, 1960s, plastic figure holds brush in
  hand, MOC, M5.........................$30.00
Little Orphan Annie & Sandy, prewar Japan, pnt bsk, standing
  version, plate #241, NM..........................$100.00
Mickey Mouse, pnt bisque w/gr pants & brn shoes, movable arm
  & string tail, 5", plate #232, NM, from $400 to $425.00

Mickey Mouse & Minnie Mouse, Japan/WDE, pnt bsk, pie-eyed,
  standing arm-in-arm, 4½", plate #234, EX+............$275.00

Photo courtesy of Marilyn Cooper.

Mickey and Minnie with Pluto, Japan, painted bisque, 4½", EX, $300.00.

Mickey Mouse & Pluto, prewar Japan, pnt bsk, Mickey helping
  Pluto blow his nose, 3½x4½", plate #122, M..........$250.00
Minnie Mouse, Japan/WDE, pnt bsk, jtd arm, other arm holds
  brush, 5", plate #233, NM, from $400 to.................$425.00
Moon Mullins & Kayo, Japan, pnt bsk, 4", EX.................$85.00
Teacher w/Book & Cane, Japan, glossy bl, blk & brn ceramic,
  5½", NM.................................$90.00
Three Little Pigs, prewar Japan/WDE, playing flute, violin &
  drums, 2 holes, 5", NM, from $200 to......................$225.00
Three Little Pigs, prewar Japan/WDE, pnt bsk, center pig at
  brick piano, 4x3½", plate #250, NM, from $200 to.$225.00

Tootsietoys

The first diecast Tootsietoys were made by the Samuel Dowst company in 1906 when they reproduced the Model T Ford in miniature. Dowst merged with Cosmo Manufacturing in 1926 to form the Dowst Manufacturing Company and continued to turn out replicas of the full-scale vehicles in actual use at the time. After another merger in 1961, the company became known as the Stombecker Corporation. Over the years, many types of wheels and hubs were utilized, varying in both style and material. The last all-metal car was made in 1969; recent Tootsietoys mix plastic components with the metal and have soft plastic wheels. Early prewar mint-in-box toys are scarce and command high prices on today's market. For more information we recommend *Collector's Guide to Tootsietoys*, Volumes I and II, by our advisor, David E. Richter. The recently released second edition features Tootsietoys from 1910-79 and contains nearly seven hundred color photos.

Advisor: David E. Richter (R1).

American LaFrance Fire Engine, 1970-79, red & wht, M...**$8.00**
Army Jeep #2935, 1960s, w/cannon & 3 men, MIP **$65.00**
Army Supply Truck #4634, 1939, M...........................**$75.00**
Austin Healy, 1956, red w/blk tires, 6", EX.................**$35.00**
Boat-Tail Roadster #233, 1940-41, lt gr w/wht tires, NM..**$32.00**
Buck Rogers Attack Ship, 1937, red & wht, MIB **$350.00**
Buck Rogers Battle Cruiser #1031, 1937s, 5", MIB, A ...**$350.00**

Fire Watertower Truck #4653, 1927-33, red, yellow and orange, NM, $95.00.

Buick Estate Wagon, 1948, wine and cream, closed grille, 6", rare, M, $100.00.

Buick Roadster #6001, NM **$60.00**
Cadillac #62, 1954, 4-door, bl w/wht top & blk tires, 6", NM...**$45.00**
Can Am Racer, 1974-77, M......................................**$6.00**
Cat Bulldozer #1910, yel w/blade, 6", M **$60.00**
Chevy Coupe #231, 1947-1952, lt gr, NM.......................**$35.00**
Chevy El Camino Camper & Boat, 1962-64, red, wht & bl, NM **$100.00**
Chevy Fastback Coupe, 1947-49, red w/blk tires, M.........**$45.00**
Chrysler Convertible, 1960, lt bl w/blk tires, 4", M **$25.00**
Chrysler New Yorker, 1953, dk bl w/blk tires, 6", NM **$40.00**
CJ3 Army Jeep, 1950, no cast steering wheel on dashboard, M...**$25.00**
CJ3 Civilian Jeep, red w/blk rubber tires, 4", M...............**$25.00**
CJ5 Jeep, 1956, bl w/blk tires & windshield down, 6", M.**$35.00**
Deluxe Trucks Set #05310, 1933, set of 8, NM (NM box), A...**$2,350.00**
Doodle Bug, 1935-37, gr, 4", G, A................................**$80.00**
Dune Buggy, Motorcycle & Trailer Set, Little Toughs, 1971, MIP **$15.00**
Exxon Oil Tanker Truck #1295, 1977-79, MIP..............**$10.00**
Farm Tractor & Spreader #2535, 1970-73, gr w/wht trim, blk tires w/wht hubs, M **$25.00**
Ferrari #8, 1974-77, M **$6.00**
Fire Station, MIB...**$50.00**
Fleet #5700, 1941, w/aircraft carriers, battleships, submarine, ocean liner, etc, set of 12, NMIB **$750.00**
Ford, 1928, gr, 2½", M (rare box missing end flaps) **$200.00**
Ford Fairlane 500 Convertible, 1957, red, M....................**$25.00**
Ford Mainliner, 1952, 4-door, red, 3", EX **$25.00**
Ford Station Wagon, 1960, dk bl w/blk tires, 3", M.........**$25.00**
Ford Tractor, 2-tone w/detailed motor, M **$75.00**
Ford Tractor & Disc Harrow, red w/blk tires, 7", NM (NM box), A...**$185.00**
Ford Wrecker #0133, 1934, 3", NM **$90.00**
Ford 8-N Tractor w/Loader, 1959, 6¼", G........................**$65.00**
Freighter #1038, red, wht & bl, NM............................**$28.00**

Funnies Set #5091, 1932, set of 6 comic characters in vehicles, NM (G box) **$3,200.00**
GMC Scenicruiser, 1955, bl & silver w/blk tires & solid bottom, 7", M...**$45.00**
Graham 6-Wheel Roadster #0611, 1934, red w/blk fenders, 3¾", VG, A...**$145.00**
Graham 6-Wheel Sedan #0613, M **$150.00**
Graham 6-Wheel Town Car #0616, 1933, 2-tone gr, 4", G+, A...**$85.00**
Hitch-Ups #1745, 1971, diecast, contains 6 of 7 vehicles, 2"-4", EX (EX+ box), A.......................................**$45.00**
Horse Trailer, 1961-65, red & wht w/blk tires, M............**$25.00**
Interchangeable Truck Set #170, 1925-1931, NMIB **$200.00**
Jumbo Wrecker #1027, 1940s, red & silver w/blk tires, 6", NM...**$55.00**
Jumpin' Jeeper, 1970-79, metallic gr w/decal, M **$6.00**
Lancia Racer, 1956, red w/wht driver & blk wheels, 6", NM.**$40.00**
LaSalle Coupe, 1930s, brn w/tan top, wht rubber tires, VG+...**$250.00**
LaSalle Coupe, 1930s, orange w/tan body, wht rubber tires, 4¼", VG+...**$250.00**
LaSalle Sedan #230, 1947-52, red w/blk rubber tires, EX .**$35.00**
Lincoln Zephyr & Roamer Trailer, 1936, red, 8½", rear bumper & w/up mechanism missing o/w EX, A....................**$375.00**
Mack L-Line Van Trailer, 1954-59, blk & orange, NM ...**$90.00**
Mack Van Trailer #0803, 1930s, gr w/red trailer roof, Long Distance Hauling in raised letters on side, wht tires, NM...**$125.00**
Mercedes 190 SL Coupe, 1956, lt bl w/blk tires, 6", M.....**$45.00**
MG TF Roadster, 1954, dk gr, 6", M..............................**$45.00**
Off-Road Pickup, 1977-79, M......................................**$4.00**
Open Touring Car #232, 1940-41, lt bl, M.....................**$55.00**
Packard Sedan, 1956, 4-door w/tow hook, 6", M **$50.00**
Pontiac Safari Wagon #895, 1956-58, bl & wht w/blk tires, 7", rare, M **$300.00**
Pontiac Sedan, 1950, 2-tone, 4", rare, M **$40.00**
Porsche Roadster, 1956, red w/blk wheels, 6", M..............**$45.00**
Rambler Wagon, 1960, bl w/blk tires, 4", M **$25.00**
School Bus #2490, 1960s, yel & blk w/silver grille, HO series, scarce, NM...**$40.00**
Scorpion Chopper #2220, 1976, gr & yel, MOC.............**$10.00**
Scorpion Helicopter #2220, 1977-79, gr & yel, M.............**$8.00**
Smitty on Motorcycle w/Sidecar #5013, 1932-33, yel, 3", EX, A...**$690.00**

Spearhead Set #1732, 1973, MIP $25.00
Speedway Set #5081, 1932, complete w/8 racers, spinner & litho paper racetrack, NM (EX box), A $1,900.00
Station Wagon #1046, 1940-41, brn & cream w/wht tires, M $75.00
Station Wagon #239, 1947-52, orange w/blk tires, EX $35.00
Swedish Saab J35 Dragon (plane), 1970-75, red, M $10.00
Tow Truck #2485, HO series, 1960s, wht w/red trim, M..$45.00

Twin Coach Bus, 1949, orange with black tires, 3", NM, $45.00.

USN Los Angeles Zeppelin #1030, 1930s, silver w/emb letters, 5", M (EX box), A $350.00
Waco Dive Bomber #718, 1937, 3⅛", G- $65.00
Wrigley's Box Van #1010, 1940-41, red w/decal, wht rubber tires, NM $100.00
Wrigley's Spearmint Gum Express Truck #0810, 4", G, A .$100.00
Zephyr Railcar #117, 1935, gr, 4", rare, NM $100.00

Tops and Other Spinning Toys

Tops are among the oldest toys in human history. Homer in *The Iliad*, Plato in the *Republic* and Virgil in *The Aeneid* mention tops. They are found in nearly all cultures, ancient and modern.

There are seven major categories: 1) The twirler — spun by the twisting action of the fingers upon the axis. Examples are Teetotums, Dreidels, advertising spinners, and Tippe Tops. 2) The supported top — started by a string while the top is supported upright. These include 'recuperative,' having a string that automatically rewinds (Namurs); 'separative,' with a top that detaches from the launcher; 'spring launched,' which is spun using a wound spring; 'pump' or 'helix,' whereby a twisted rod is pumped to spin the top; and 'flywheel,' or 'inertia wheel powered.' 3) The peg top — spun by winding a string around the peg of the top which is then thrown. 4) The whip top — which is kept spinning by the use of a whip. 5) The Yo-Yo or return top. 6) The gyroscope. 7) The Diavuolo or Diablo.

Advisor: Bruce Middleton.
See also Yo-Yos.

Air Powered, Cracker Jack, Dowsy, Chicago, red, wht & bl, M, M20 ....$12.00
Air Powered, Poll Parrot Shoes, yel, NM, M20 ....$12.00
Aladdin Ball & Top, early 1900s, helix rod powered, EX (EX box), M20 ....$550.00

Autogyro Horse Race, Britians, lead & wire, flywheel mechanism, w/4 jockeys on horses, 11" L, EX, A............**$1,210.00**
Disk, maroon & red wood flat-top w/natural wood holder, 3½" dia, EX, A...$45.00
Disk, red & natural wood w/gr stripes, w/hdl, 4" dia, EX, A..$75.00
Electric Top, Am, spinner on base w/dry-cell battery, w/2 spinners & instruction sheet, 4", EX (orig dovetailed box), A...$690.00
Game, Big Top, Marx, plastic, battery-op, MIB, M20 ......$35.00
Game, Brownie Kick-In, MH Miller, litho tin w/Brownies, top kicks balls into indentations for score, VG (G box), M20...$50.00
Game, Double Diabolos, Parker Bros, 1930s, w/instructions, EX (orig box), M20.......................................$60.00

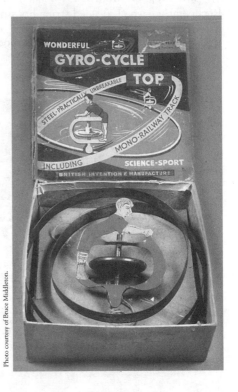

Gyro-Cycle Top, British Invention and Manufacture, boy rides circular track, EX (EX box), M20, $600.00.

Gyroscope, German, red-pnt tin ball-shaped clown w/outstretched arms & legs, wht head & hat, yel trim, 4½", EX, A $600.00
Hummer, German, mc litho tin, clown-head knob w/wooden hat, 8", VG+, A..$580.00
Hummer, inverted wood beehive-shape w/mc stripes, 2½" dia, VG, A $415.00
Hummer, Marklin, emb silver-tone metal w/plunger, 2-pc, 4" dia, EX, A..$135.00
Hummer, mc & natural wooden ball w/geometric design, 6", EX, A $85.00
Hummer, natural wood ball w/holder, 1¾" dia, EX, A...$415.00
Hummer, wht celluloid ball w/mc stripes, tall hdl, 7", EX, A .$415.00
Hummer, wood dome shape w/red, bl & gr stripes, natural wood hdl, 7", VG, A..$360.00
Multiform Combination Top, FH Lovell, ca 1894, wood & glass, w/instruction sheet, 2½", very rare, EX, A $715.00
Musical Top, Chein, 1948, tin w/litho Disney characters, 7" dia, M (EX+ box), A......................................$225.00

Namur, MIB, M20 ....$80.00

Namur, wooden ball w/brass string housing, EX, M20 .....$20.00

Peg Top, Duncan Chicago Twister #329, wood, MIP (wear), M20 ....$20.00

Peg Top, Duncan Tournament #349, wood, MIP (wear), M20 ....$20.00

Peg Top, Duncan Twin Spin #310, wood, MIP (wear), M20 ....$20.00

Peg Top, Duncan Whistler #320, wood, MIP (wear), M20 .$20.00

Peg Top, Helix Rod Launcher, advertising Kinney Shoes, VG, M20 ....$15.00

Ratchet Ballerina, German, litho tin figure in gr dress, hands on hips, w/ratchet, 5½", EX (orig box), A $175.00

Recuperative, natural wood w/pnt stripes, wood string housing w/flat top, EX, from $50 to $100.00

Recuperative, wood, 6-sided string housing over ovoid body, G, M20 ....$85.00

Reversible Pan Am Expo 1901, Pat 1899, natural wood, 3½", VG, A $275.00

Spinners, Robin Hood Shoes; Derby Petroleum Products; Cracker Jack, Tastykake Cakes and Pies; M, M20, from $20.00 to $75.00 each.

Spinner, Alemite Motor Oil, Bakelite, 'Keeps Your Car Humming Like a Top,' NM+, M20 ....$15.00

Spinner, Betsy Ross Bread, 1½" dia, NM, A $20.00

Spinner, Brown-Bilt Shoes, Buster Brown, blk & red letters on yel background w/red rim, EX, M20 ....$45.00

Spinner, Cracker Jack, wht background, spinner through center of Cracker Jack box, EX, M20 ....$45.00

Spinner, litho man w/mug of beer, 'Hvem Betaler' on hat, metal, foreign, spin to see who pays, NM, M20 ....$85.00

Spinner, Marklin, set of 4 litho tin spinners w/plunger, EX (EX box), A $440.00

Spinner, Monarch Paint, tin, 1½", NM, A $35.00

Spinner, Nolde's American Maid Bread & Cakes, red & wht, NM, M20 ....$30.00

Spinner, OTC Trenton Oyster Crackers, bl letters on wht, M, M20 ....$50.00

Spinner, Peters Weatherbird Shoes, tin, shaped like a 4-leaf clover, 1½" dia, NM, A $25.00

Spinner, Poll Parrot Shoes, red parrot w/blk shoes on yel ground, M, M20 ....$30.00

Spinner, shaped like pointing spaniel, flat, 'Heads I Win, Tails You Lose,' NM, M20 ....$25.00

Spinner, Tasty Kake, T in shape of girl, red, wht & bl, M, M20 ....$30.00

Spinner, Tip Top Bread, plastic, NM, M20 ....$10.00

Spinner w/Flying Saucers, wood w/red, wht & blk stripes, when spun 5 saucers fly out & spin, 3¾", EX, A $600.00

Supported, pressed board disk w/graphics of a boy shooting a toy gun, M, M20 ....$60.00

Supported, Rainbow, Seneca, pnt metal 4-tooth colored disks inside lg disk rotating around shaft, changes color, NM, M20 ....$65.00

Tip Tray, Canada Dry, red, gr, wht & yel, dimple in center to spin on, G, M20 ....$20.00

Tip Tray, SS Pierce, Wine & Spirit Merchants..., dimple in center to spin on, M, M20 ....$60.00

Trading Cards

Modern collector cards are really just an extension of a hobby that began well before the turn of the century. Advertising cards put out by the food and tobacco companies of that era sometimes featured cute children, their pets, stage stars, battle scenes, presidential candidates, and so forth. Collectors gathered them up and pasted them in scrapbooks.

In the twentieth century, candy and bubble gum companies came to the forefront. The cards they issue with their products carry the likenesses of sports figures, fictional heroes, TV and movie stars, Disney characters, Barbie dolls and country singers!

Distinguishing a collectible trading card from other cards may be a bit confusing. Remember, trading cards are released in only two ways: 1) in a wax or foil pack, generally in multiples of 12 — 24, 36, or 48; or 2) as a premium with another product. The only exception to this rule are sets issued as limited editions, with each set individually numbered. Cards issued as factory sets are not trading cards and have no collector value unless they cross over into another collecting area, for example, the Tuff Stuff Norma Jean (Marilyn Monroe) series. In general, from 1980 to the present, wrappers tend to fall into the 50¢ to $2.00 range, though there are some exceptions. For more information we recommend *Collector's Guide to Trading Cards* by Robert Reed.

Advisors: Mark and Val Macaluso (M1).

Other Sources: C1, C10, D11, F8, H4, H11, H12, J6, J7, M8, M17, T2

Akira, Cornerstone, 1994, set of 100 ....$18.00

Alf, Topps, 1988, 2nd series, set of 44 w/11 stickers $12.00

Alien, Topps, 1979, set of 84 w/22 stickers $35.00

Alien Vs Predator, Topps, 1995, set of 72 w/15 stickers ...$18.00

Alien 3, Star Pics, 1992, set of 80 ....$16.00

All My Children, Star Pics, 1991, set of 72......................$20.00
All Pro Skateboard, Donruss, 1977, set of 44 ....$9.50
American Bandstand, Collect-a-Card, 1993, set of 100 ...$15.00
American Transfer Pictures, MP & Co, 1940s, set of 6 ......$4.00
Americana, Starline, 1992, set of 250 ....$30.00
Andretti Racing, Collect-a-Card, 1992, set of 100 ....$15.00

Andy Gibb, Donruss, 1978, with full-color 15x10⅜" poster, unopened, $10.00.

Around the World With Walt Disney, Mexico, unopened box of 100 pkgs $80.00
Astounding Sci-Fi, 21st Arch, 1994, set of 50 ....$14.00
Back to the Future II, Topps, 1989, set of 88 w/11 stickers.$11.00
Bad Channels, Full Moon, 1991, set of 5.............................$2.50
Barbie, Dart/Panani, 1991, 1st series, set of 196...............$30.00
Batman (from movie), Topps, 1989, 2nd series, set of 132 w/22 stickers $15.00
Batman Animated, Topps, 1993, set of 100 w/6 vinyl stickers...$30.00
Batman Candy Cigarette Boxes, British, 1989, set of 12 ..$18.00
Batman Returns, Zellers, 1992, set of 24 ....$7.50
Batman Returns Stadium Club, Topps, 1992, set of 100 ..$30.00
Battlestar Galactica, Topps, 1978, set of 132 w/22 stickers.$45.00
Beatles, River Group, 1993, set of 220 ....$25.00
Beetlejuice, Dart, 1990, set of 100 w/20 stickers $18.00
Bernard & Bianca, Panini, set of 360 ....$35.00
Best of Cracked Magazine, Fleer, 1978, set of 55 ....$18.00
Beverly Hills 90210, Topps, 1991, set of 77 w/11 stickers..$17.50
Beyond Bizarre, Comic Image, 1993, set of 90 ....$12.00
Bill & Ted's Adventure, Pro Set, 1991, set of 140 ....$8.50
Bionic Woman, Donruss, 1976, set of 44 ....$20.00
Boris, Comic Image, 1991, science fiction & fantasy art, set of 90 ....$20.00
Bozo, Lime Rock, 1994, set of 54.....................................$10.00
Branson on Stage, Hit Cards, 1992, set of 100..................$18.00
Cabbage Patch Kids, Coleco, circus series, came 1 per doll, set of 6 ....$60.00
Captain America, Comic Image, 1990, set of 45 ....$25.00

Caterpillar (earthmovers), TGM Assoc, 1993, 1st series, set of 100 ....$18.00
CB Convoy Dode, Donruss, set of 44 ....$28.00
Charlie's Angels, Topps, 1977, 3rd series, set of 66 w/11 stickers..$18.00
Cinderella, Panini, 1987, set of 225 ....$40.00
Classic Pulps, Sperry, 1992, science fiction art, set of 90..$15.00
Coke, Collect-a-Card, 1994, 3rd series, set of 100 ....$16.00
Country Gold, Sterling, 1992, set of 100 ....$20.00
Creature Feature, Topps, 1980, set of 88 w/22 stickers $40.00
Cyndi Lauper, Topps, 1985, set of 33 w/33 stickers $9.50
Dallas Cowboy Cheerleaders, Topps, 1981, set of 30........$30.00
Dark Crystal, Donruss, 1982, set of 78 ....$10.00
Dark Horse, Topps, 1994, set of 100.................................$20.00
DC Bloodlines, Skybox, 1993, set of 81 ....$12.00
DC Comic 3 Pack Cards, DC Comic, 1988, set of 48, scarce...$60.00
DC Cosmic, Impel, 1992, set of 180.................................$18.00
Deathwatch 2000, Classic, 1993, set of 100 ....$12.00
Decision '92, Wild Card, 1992, set of 100 ....$15.00
Deep Space 9, Skybox, 1994, set of 100 ....$15.00
Demolition Man, Skybox, 1993, set of 100 ....$18.00
Desert Storm Victory, Topps, 1991, 2nd series, set of 88 w/11 stickers...$9.00
Dinamatian Dinosaurs, Star Pics, 1992, set of 80.............$16.00
Dinosaurs, Nu-Card, 1962, set of 80 ....$400.00
Disney Tattoos, Denmark, set of 6 different packs............$25.00
Disneyland Bubble Gum, Donruss/WDP, 1965, features Mickey, Donald & Daisy, scarce, unopened, NM, A $115.00
Dolly Show, Morris National, unopened box w/100 pkgs.$40.00
Dr Who, Cornerstone, 1995, 2nd series, set of 110...........$18.00
Elvis, River Group, 1992, 1st series, set of 220..................$35.00
Empire Strikes Back, Dixie, 1980, 1st series, set of 40 ......$25.00
Empire Strikes Back, Topps, 1980, 2nd series, set of 132..$38.00
Evil Ernie, Krome Pro, 1994, set of 100............................$30.00
Fangoria, Comic Image, 1992, set of 90 ....$12.00
Fantasy Girls, Imagine, 1994, 2nd series, set of 60............$12.00
Fievel-American Tail II, Impel, 1991, set of 90 ....$15.00
Flaming Carrot, Comic Image, 1988, set of 50..................$60.00
Flash Gordon, MV Jasinski, 1990, limited & numbered edition of 5,000 sets, set of 36..$30.00
Flintstones, Cardz, 1993, set of 100 ....$28.00
Flying Things, Taiwan, 1989, set of 12..............................$15.00
Garbage Pail Kids, Topps Trebor, set of 88 stickers $35.00
Garbage Pail Kids Posters, Topps, 1988, set of 18.............$12.00
Ghost Rider, Comic Image, 1990, set of 45 ....$30.00
Ghostbusters, Panini, 1987, set of 264 ....$35.00
GI Joe, Diamond, 1987, set of 225 ....$20.00
GI Joe, Impel, 1991, set of 200 ....$15.00
GI Joe, Milton Bradley, 1986, set of 192 w/12 stickers $55.00
Gong Show, Fleer, 1979, set of 66 ....$25.00
Growing Pains, Topps, 1988, set of 66 w/11 stickers $18.00
Happy Days, Topps, 1976, set of 44 w/11 stickers.............$25.00
Harley-Davidson, Collect-a-Card, 1992, 2nd series, set of 100 ....$15.00
Hellraisers, Eclipse, 1992, set of 110................................$20.00
Hildebrandt, Comic Image, 1993, 2nd series, set of 90.....$12.00
Hockey Freaks, Dart, 1992, set of 100 ....$15.00

Hollywood Walk of Fame, Starline, 1991, set of 250........$20.00

Howard the Duck, Topps, 1986, set of 77 w/22 stickers ...$18.00

I Love Lucy, Pacific, 1991, pk or silver border, set of 110.$18.00

Iditarod, Motor Art, 1992, set of 110 ....$20.00

In Living Color, Topps, 1992, set of 88 w/11 stickers.......$15.00

Indian Chiefs, unknown maker, 1930s, set of 24 ....$125.00

Indiana Jones & the Temple of Doom, Topps, 1984, set of 88 w/11 stickers...$17.00

James Dean, European, 1990, set of 8..............................$10.00

Jaws 3-D, Topps, 1983, set of 44......................................$9.50

John Kennedy, Rosan, set of 64..$60.00

Jurassic Park, Topps, 1993, 1st series, gold, set of 88 w/10 stickers..$45.00

Kelly (Ken), Freidlander, 1993, set of 90 ....$15.00

King Kong, Eclipse, 1993, set of 110 ....$20.00

KISS II, Donruss, 1978, set of 66......................................$60.00

Knight Rider, Donruss, 1985, set of 66 w/11 puzzle variations .$18.00

Kung Fu, Topps, set of 55 ....$100.00

Lady Death, Chads, 1994, set of 100 ....$50.00

Laffs, Impel, 1991, set of 80 ....$8.00

Legend of Big Foot, Leesley, 1989, set of 100.................$12.00

Lighthouses of Yesteryear, Total Graphics, 1994, 2nd series, set of 50 ....$30.00

Little Mermaid, Pro Set, 1991, set of 90...........................$10.00

Loaded Weapon, Eclipse, 1993, set of 110 ....$16.00

Lois & Clark, Skybox, 1995, set of 90 w/6 tattoos $20.00

Mad (Magazine) Stickers, Fleer, set of 128 w/64 stickers.$135.00

Marilyn Monroe, European, 1990, set of 8 ....$10.00

Marvel IV Heroic Origins, Comic Image, 1988, set of 90.$35.00

Marvel Masterpieces, Skybox, 1993, 1st series, set of 90 ..$40.00

Marvel Promo Cards, Marvel Comics, 1989, set of 6, comic store promotions $18.00

Marvel Super Heroes, Topps, 1975, set of 9 w/40 stickers .$75.00

Michael Jackson, Topps, 1984, 2nd series, set of 33 w/33 stickers...$10.00

Mickey Mouse, Americana, set of 360 ....$150.00

Mike Zeck, Comic Image, 1989, set of 45 ....$25.00

Miss USA, Star Co, 1993, set of 101 ....$22.00

Monster in My Pocket, Source Group, 1991, set of 48 w/24 stickers $22.00

Monster Laffs, Topps, 1966, set of 66..............................$75.00

Moon Mars, Space Ventures, 1991, emb, set of 36 ....$65.00

Moonraker, Topps, 1979, set of 99 w/22 stickers $24.00

Mortal Kombat, Topps, 1994, set of 100 ....$10.00

Nightmare Before Christmas, Skybox, 1993, set of 90......$18.00

Nightmare on Elm Street, Comic Image, 1988, set of 264 w/album...$16.00

Norman Rockwell, Comic Image, 1993, set of 90.............$18.00

Odder Odd Rods, Donruss, 1970, set of 66 ....$150.00

Pac-Man, Fleer, 1980, set of 28 w/54 stickers...................$45.00

Pagemaster, Skybox, 1994, set of 90.................................$15.00

Paul McCartney & Wings, Tour Set, scarce, set of 6........$18.00

Petty Girls, 21st Century, 1994, set of 50..........................$12.00

Planet of the Apes TV, Topps, 1975, set of 66 ....$55.00

Pop Stars, Panini, set of 100 ....$35.00

Popeye, Card Creations, 1995, set of 100..........................$15.00

Power Rangers, Collect-a-Card, 1944, 1st series, set of 72 w/10 stickers $18.00

Prince Valiant, Comic Image, 1995, set of 90...................$10.00

Pro Football Cheerleaders, Lime Rock, 1992, set of 156 ..$20.00

Punisher, Comic Image, 1st series, set of 50.....................$30.00

Rambo, Topps, 1985, set of 66 w/11 stickers....................$18.00

Ren & Stimpy, Topps, 1994, set of 50...............................$15.00

Return of Superman, Skybox, 1993, set of 100..................$23.00

Return of the Jedi, Topps, 1983, set of 180 w/album $25.00

Rhonda Shear, Imagine, 1993, set of 60............................$18.00

Robin Hood, Topps, 1991, set of 88 w/9 stickers $12.50

Robocop II, Topps, 1990, set of 88 w/11 stickers..............$11.00

Robotech Macross, FTCC, 1986, set of 60.........................$18.00

Rock Stars, Donruss, 1979, set of 66.................................$16.00

Rock Superstars, Pro Set, 1991, 2nd series, set of 340 ......$20.00

Rocketeer, Topps, 1991, set of 99 w/11 stickers................$10.00

Rocketship X-M, FTCC, 1979, set of 50............................$35.00

Roger Rabbit, Topps, 1988, set of 132 w/22 stickers.........$18.00

Royal Canadian Mounted Police, OPC, set of 55 ....$50.00

Royal Family, Press Pass, 1993, set of 110 ....$22.00

Santa Around the World, TCM, 1994, set of 72 ....$10.00

Saturday Night Live, Star Pics, 1992, set of 150 ....$16.00

Saturday Serials, Epic Cards, 1988, set of 40....................$25.00

Saved by the Bell, Pacific, 1994, College Years series, set of 110 ....$18.00

Seedpeople, Full Moon, 1991, set of 5...............................$2.50

Shadowhawk, Comic Image, 1992, set of 90......................$18.00

Silver Surfer, Comic Image, 1992, set of 72 ....$35.00

Six Million Dollar Man, Donruss, 1975, set of 66.............$75.00

Snow White, Skybox, 1993, set of 90................................$20.00

Sonic Hedgehog, Topps, 1993, set of 33 w/33 stickers........$9.50

Space 1999, Panini, 1976, set of 400.................................$65.00

Spaceshots, Space Ventures, 1991, 1st series, set of 110...$50.00

Spider-Man, French, set of 300 ....$35.00

Spider-Man/Team-Up, Comic Image, 1990, set of 45 ......$35.00

Spitting Image, Trebor, 1990, set of 66 ....$30.00

Star Trek I, Impel, 1987, 1st series, 25th Anniversary issue, set of 160 ....$20.00

Star Trek II, Monty Gum, set of 100.................................$125.00

Star Trek III, FTCC, 1984, set of 60 w/20 stickers $55.00

Star Wars, Topps, 1977, 1st series, set of 66, $50.00.

Star Trek IV, FTCC, 1987, set of 60 ....$24.00
Star Trek Masterpieces, Skybox, 1993, set of 90 ....$25.00
Star Trek Next Generation, Panini, 1989, set of 240 ....$55.00
Star Trek Next Generation, Skybox, 1992, set of 120 ......$20.00
Star Trek Next Generations Episodes, Skybox, 1994, 1st series,
     set of 108 ....$25.00
Star Trek The Motion Picture, Topps, 1976, set of 88 ...$32.00
Star Trek TV Cards, Topps, 1976, set of 88 ....$295.00
Star Wars, Panini, 1978, set of 256 ....$150.00
Star Wars, Topps, 1977, 2nd series, set of 66 ....$30.00
Star Wars, Topps, 1977, 3rd series, set of 66 ....$22.00
Star Wars, Wonder Bread, 1978, set of 16 ....$18.00
Star Wars Galaxy, Topps, 1994, 2nd series, set of 135.....$30.00
Stargate, Collect-a-Card, 1994, set of 100 w/12 stickers...$15.00
State Birds & Flowers, Bon Air, 1991, set of 50 ....$4.50
Stupid Smiles, Topps, 1990, set of 44 ....$15.00
Supergirl the Movie, Nabisco, 1985, set of 15 ....$70.00
Superman, Drakes, 1979, set of 24 ....$75.00
Superman, OPC, 1979, set of 132 ....$35.00
Superman II, Topps, 1981, set of 88 ....$12.00
Superman Man of Steel, Skybox, 1994, regular series, set of
     90 ....$18.00
Superman the Movie, Topps, 1978, 1st series, set of 77....$18.00
Surf Supercards, Topps, 1984, set of 55 ....$12.00
Tales From the Crypt, Cardz, 1993, set of 110 ....$30.00
Tank Girl, Comic Image, 1994, set of 90 ....$15.00
Teenage Mutant Ninja Turtles, OPC, 1990, set of 88 ....$8.50
Teenage Mutant Ninja Turtles Cartoon, Topps, 1990, 2nd
     series, set of 88 w/11 stickers......................................$10.00
Teenage Mutant Ninja Turtles Movie, Topps, 1990, set of 132
     w/11 stickers...$10.00
Terminator 2, Topps, 1991, set of 44................................$6.00
Terrorist Attacks, Piedmont Candy, 1987, set of 35.........$16.00
Three Stooges, FTCC, 1985, set of 60 ....$75.00
Thunder Motorcycles, Thunder, 1993, set of 100 ....$36.00
Thundercats, Panini, set of 264 ....$25.00
Tiny Toons, Cardz, 1994, set of 50 w/10 stickers $18.00
Tom & Jerry, Cardz, 1993, set of 60 ....$15.00
Toxic High, Topps, 1992, set of 88.....................................$8.00
Trading Card Treats, Impel, 1991, set of 36 ....$9.00
Traks '91, Traks, 1991, set of 200 ....$30.00
Trivia Battle, Topps, 1984, set of 132 w/11 stickers..........$18.00
Truckin', Donruss, 1970s, set of 44....................................$18.00
TV Smelly Awards, Fleer, 1970s, set of 64 ....$25.00
Ultraverse, Skybox, 1993, set of 100 ....$22.00
Unity, Comic Image, 1992, set of 90.................................$20.00
Universal Monsters, Topps, 1994, set of 100 ....$28.00
V (TV Show), Fleer, 1984, set of 66 ....$25.00
Valiant, Upper Deck, 1993, set of 120 ....$15.00
Vietnam War, Dart, 1988, set of 66 ....$34.00
Vroom (race cars), Protrac's, 1991, set of 150..................$12.00
Wacko-Saurs, Diamond, 1987, set of 48 ....$10.00
Web of Spider-Man, Comic Image, 1991, set of 75 w/album.$85.00
Weird Ball, Mel Appel, 1986, set of 42 ....$10.00
Where Are They?, Pacific, 1992, set of 110 ....$12.00
Where's Waldo?, Mattel, 1991, set of 128.........................$15.00
Wild CATS, Topps, 1993, set of 100 ....$20.00
Winston Cup, Pro Set, 1991, set of 200 ....$40.00

Wacky Packages Stickers, Topps, 1979, contains 36 unopened packs, J6, $85.00.

Photo courtesy of June Moon.

Wizard of Oz, Pacific, 1990, set of 110 ....$20.00
Women in Terror, 21st Century Archives, 1993, set of 50..$16.00
Wrestlemania III, Topps, 1987, set of 75 w/22 stickers.....$15.00
X-Force, Comic Image, 1991, set of 90..............................$25.00
X-Men, Comic Image, 1991, 2nd series, set of 45 ....$30.00
Yogi Bear, Barratt/England, 1964, set of 35.......................$65.00

Boxes

Aladdin, Panini, 1993 ....$4.00
Alf, Topps, 1987, 1st series $5.00
Andy Griffith, Pacific, 1991, 1st series $5.00
Babysitter's Club, Topps, 1992 ....$8.00
Barbie, Dart/Panini, 1992 ....$4.00
Battlestar Galactica, Topps, 1978.......................................$15.00
Beauty & the Beast, Upper Deck, 1993 ....$4.00
Betty Boop, Khrome, 1995...$5.00
BMX, Donruss, 1984 ....$6.00
Charlie's Angels, Topps, 1977, 1st series.............................$20.00
CHiPs, Donruss, 1979 ....$6.00
Coneheads, Topps, 1993 ....$4.00
Dark Crystal, Donruss, 1982 ....$4.00
Deep Space 9, Skybox, 1994 ....$4.00
Dune, Fleer, 1984 ....$5.00
Duran Duran, Topps, 1985 ....$6.00
Excalibur, Comic Image, 1990...$10.00
Flintstones the Movie, Topps, 1994 ....$4.00
Fright Flicks, Topps, 1988..$6.00
Ghostbusters II, Topps, 1989 ....$4.00
Grease II, Tops, 1978 ....$4.00
Heavy Metal, Comic Image, 1991 ....$4.00
Home Alone II, Topps, 1992 ....$4.00
Indy 500, Hi-Tech, 1993, 1st series $4.00
James Bond, Eclipse, 1993, 1st series $5.00
KISS I, Donruss, 1978...$12.00
Leave It to Beaver, Pacific, 1984 ....$10.00
Masters of the Universe, Topps, 1984 ....$6.00

Monster in My Pocket, Source Group, 1991 ....$4.00
Muppets, Cardz, 1994..$4.00
New Kids on the Block, Topps, 1990 ....$4.00
Pagemaster, Skybox, 1994...$4.00
Power Ranger, Collect-a-Card, 1994, 1st series................$5.00
Rambo, Topps, 1985 ....$5.00
Rocketship X-M, FTCC, 1979 ....$10.00
Scream Queen, Imagine, 1993, 3rd series........................$5.00
Snow White, Skybox, 1994, 2nd series $4.00
Spy Vs Spy, Lime Rock, 1993 ....$4.00
Star Trek Generations, Skybox, 1994 ....$5.00
Star Trek III, FTCC, 1984...$15.00
Star Trek TV Cards, Topps, 1976 ....$35.00
Superman III, Topps, 1983 ....$6.00
Superman the Movie, Topps, 1978 ....$10.00
Tom & Jerry, Cardz, 1993 ....$4.00
Transformers, Milton Bradley, 1985 ....$5.00
Trolls Force, Star Pics, 1992 ....$4.00
V (TV Show), Fleer, 1984...$6.00
Winnebago, TCM, 1994..$4.00
Wrestling, Topps, 1985, 1st series......................................$6.00
Yo Raps Series 2, Pro Set, 1991 ....$3.00
Young Indiana Jones Chronicles, Pro Set, 1992..................$3.00

Trains

Some of the earliest trains (from ca 1860) were made of tin or cast iron, smaller versions of the full-scale steam-powered trains that transversed America from the East to the West. Most were made to simply be pushed or pulled along, though some had clockwork motors. Electric trains were produced as early as the late 19th century. Three of the largest manufacturers were Lionel, Ives and American Flyer.

Lionel trains have been made since 1900. Until 1915 they produced only standard gauge models (measuring 2½" between the rails). The smaller O gauge (1¼") they introduced at that time proved to be highly successful, and the company grew until by 1955 it had become the largest producer of toys in the world. Until discontinued in 1940, standard gauge trains were produced on a limited scale, but O and 027 gauge models dominated the market. Production dwindled and nearly stopped in the mid-1960s, but the company was purchased by General Mills in 1969, and they continue to produce a very limited number of trains today.

The Ives company had been a major producer of toys since 1896. They were the first to initiate manufacture of the O gauge train and at first used only clockwork motors to propel them. Their first electric trains (in both O and #1 gauge) were made in 1910, but because electricity was not yet a common commodity in many areas, clockwork production continued for several years. By 1920, #1 gauge was phased out in favor of standard gauge. The company continued to prosper until the late 1920s when it floundered and was bought jointly by American Flyer and Lionel. American Flyer soon turned their interest over to Lionel, who continued to make Ives trains until 1933.

The American Flyer company had produced trains for several years, but it wasn't until it was bought by AC Gilbert in 1937 that it became successful enough to be considered a competitor of Lionel. They're best noted for their conversion from the standard (wide gauge) 3-rail system to the 2-rail S gauge (⅞") and the high-quality locomotives, passenger and freight cars they produced in the 1950s. Interest in toy trains waned during the space-age decade of the 1960s. As a result, sales declined, and in 1966 the company was purchased by Lionel. Today both American Flyer and Lionel trains are being made from the original dies by Lionel Trains Inc., privately owned.

Because of limited space, the only time we will use the number sign will be to indicate a set number. Numbers of individual pieces will not be preceded by the sign. For more information we recommend *Collecting Toy Trains, An Identification and Value Guide*, by Richard O'Brien.

Advisors: Bill Mekalian (M4) and Richard Trautwein (T3).

See also Buddy L (for that company's Outdoor Railroad); **Paper-Lithographed Toys.**

Key:

acces — accessories	obv/c — observation car
b/c — boxcar	pass — passenger
bg/c — baggage car	st/c — stock car
fl/c — flat bed car	tk/c — tank car
loco — locomotive	/c — car
OB — original box	

American Flyer

O ga, freight set, 2-4-2 loco, 8-wheeled tender & cars, crane, gondola, fl/c, b/c & caboose, 1930-35, G, A............$345.00
O ga, freight set, 2-6-4 loco, 8-wheel tender, fl/c (OB), b/c (OB), derrick/c, tk/c, gondola, caboose, 1930s, VG, A $435.00
O ga, pass set, Burlington Zephyr Streamliner, #9900 power/c (OB), coach, bg/c, #9900 tail/c (OB), VG, A $690.00

O Gauge, set, black engine #1218, pair of Chicago, Milwaukee & St. Paul Seattle boxcars #1206, mail car #1205, complete, VG (original box), from $800.00 to $1,200.00.

S ga, acces, #162 Mysto-Magic Factory, 3 roof sections need reglued, 1952, EX, A $140.00

S ga, acces, #168 hotel, missing 2 window inserts, roof reattached, dirty, 1953, EX, A $180.00

S ga, acces, #23780 Gabe the lamplighter, w/controller, decal flaking, 1958-59, EX+, A $575.00

S ga, acces, #795 station & terminal, complete w/inserts, 1954, EX+, A $390.00

S ga, car, #24047 GN Plugdoor b/c, K/C, EX, A $85.00

S ga, car, #24125 Bethelehem Steel gondola w/3 rails, 1960-64, EX+, A $30.00

S ga, car, #24191 Canadian National reefer, minor sticker wear, 1958, EX, A $230.00

S ga, car, #24323 Baker's Chocolate tk/c, gray ends, knuckle couplers, unrun, 1959-60, NM (worn box), A $290.00

S ga, car, #24409 NP reefer, orange & brn, Pikemaster coupler, lt scratches, 1958, EX-, A $220.00

S ga, car, #24569 crane/c, 1962-66, factory sealed, A $45.00

S ga, car, #24578 NH fl/c w/Corvette (teal), Pikemaster couplers, unrun, 1962-63, NM+ (sealed in plastic bag), A $160.00

S ga, car, #25049 operating cookie box b/c, wht, dirty, 1958-60, EX, A $200.00

S ga, car, #35515 rocket sled fl/c, VG, A $135.00

S ga, car, #752 Seaboard coaler, 3-button controller, 1946-50, EX+, A $470.00

S ga, car, #981 Central of Georgia b/c, minor oxidation on guide pins, 1956, EX, A $120.00

S ga, cars, #25058 Moe & Joe, Pikemaster couplers, w/controller, dusty, 1961-64, EX+ (OB), A $150.00

S ga, engine, #24812 T&P Baldwin loco, screw crack, EX, A $160.00

S ga, engine, #370 GP-7 Diesel, 1950-53, G, A $90.00

S ga, engine & tender, #21130 Hudson & tender (plastic), 1 cracked step, 1959-60, EX, A $160.00

S ga, pass set, #466, #960, #962, #963, 1954, G, A $290.00

S ga, pass set, engine #21927; cars #24773, #24813 & #24833, 1960-62, VG, A $435.00

S ga, set, #326 Hudson, w/tender (die-cast), #960 combine, #962 vista dome, #963 obv/c, 1953-57, EX, A $360.00

S ga, set, engines #360 & #364; cars #660, #661, #662 & #663, 1950-52, VG, A $260.00

S ga, set, Washington, #21089 loco & tender, #24055 b/c, #24565 fl/c w/rpl cannon, #24750 coach, EX+, A ...$600.00

S ga, set #20767, Eagle, #21920 MP Alco PA, #24856 combine, 24863 vista dome, 24866 obv/c, no track, 1963-64, NMIB, A $1,500.00

S ga, set #5003, #290 loco, cars #651, #650 (3), 1946-53, VG (OB), A $345.00

S ga, set #5525, #293 loco, cars #937, #912, #916 & #930, 1953-58, VG, A $405.00

Set, #3105 loco (no headlight), #3150 bg/c, #3151 coach, #3152 obv/c, 2-tone bl, gray fr & trucks, VG+, A $370.00

Set, Century, #9915 loco w/integral tender, #3178 coaches (2), #3179 obv/c, G-, A $825.00

Set, Illini, #3015 loco, #300 bg/c, #3001 pullman, #3001 obv/c, gr, EX-, A $310.00

Set, Minnie Ha-Ha, loco, 3 coaches, orange & gray, wear to rs & skirts, EX, A $275.00

Set, Nation Wide, #1093 loco, gr & blk w/brass trim, combine & coach, EX+, A $575.00

Set #7522, 425 loco, Vanderbilt tender, #406 log/c, #408 b/c, #409 dump/c, #411 caboose, EX (all OBs), A $100.00

Std ga, car, #4006 hopper, red, EX (OB), A $450.00

Std ga, set, #1218 loco (blk), #1205 bg/c, #1206 coach, #120 obv/c (orange & blk litho tin, blk roofs), VG+ (OBs), A $200.00

Std ga, set, Am Legion Ltd, #4019 loco, #4040 bg/c, Am pullman, Pleasant View obv/c, maroon litho & roofs, EX, A $600.00

Std ga, set, Statesman, #4654 loco, pullmans (2), obv/c, missing 5 journals & 1 airtank, dirty, VG, A $300.00

Std ga, set #6512 Warrior, #4692 loco, #4693 tender, #4331 pullmans (2), #4332 obv/c, EX+, A $2,200.00

Lionel Prewar

Acces, #155 freight station, early colors, dirty, 1930-42, EX-, A $550.00

Acces, #156 station platforms (2), 1939-42, EX, A $210.00

Acces, #164 log loader, gray w/vermillion roof, w/controller, needs rewiring, 1940-42, EX, A $450.00

Acces, #165 Magnetic Crane, w/controller, dirty, 1940-42, EX, A $525.00

Acces, #300 Hellsgate Bridge, late colors, lt rpt, 1928-42, EX+, A $1,000.00

Acces, #435 power station, mustard, terra cotta & gr, dirty, 1926-38, EX-, A $250.00

O ga, acces, #99N Block Signal, red base, 1932-42, M, A ..$200.00

O ga, car, #2814 b/c, yel & maroon, 1 brakewheel missing & 1 bent, 1938-42, EX (OB taped), A $130.00

O ga, car, #814 b/c, yel & brn, minor oxidation on catwalk, 1926-42, EX, A $400.00

O ga, freight set, #224 & #224W, cars #2758, #2660, #3461X (OB), #2757, log-loading bin, Q-transformer, 1939-41, VG, A $260.00

O ga, freight set, engine, #1666 (blk), #2666 (blk), cars #1679, #1680 & #1682, 1938-40, VG, A $140.00

O ga, freight set, engine #225E & #2235 tender (both blk), cars #2755 (2), #2758 & #2757, 1938-42, VG, A $490.00

O ga, pass set, #253 loco, cars #610 (2), #612, all dk gr w/maroon inserts, 1924-25, G, A $260.00

O ga, pass/freight set, #259E & #259T loco & tender, cars #804, #805, #806, #807, #1690 (2), #1691, 1930s, G, A ...$345.00

O ga, set, #1816W Silver Streak loco, clockwork (not working), #1817 coach, #1818 obv/c, orange/chrome, 1935-47, VG+, A $210.00

O ga, set, Blue Streak, #265, #265WX (no coach drawbar), #619, #618, #617, 1935-41, tender VG o/w EX, A ..$725.00

O ga, set, City of Denver, #636W loco, #637 coaches (2), #638 obv/c, 1936-39, VG+, A $525.00

O ga, set, Flying Yankee, #616 loco, #617 coaches (2), #618 obv/c, gunmetal front, back & skirts, 1935-41, EX (OBs), A $600.00

O ga, set, Flying Yankee, #616E loco, #617 coaches (3), #618obv/c, gunmetal & chrome, 1935-41, VG, A ..$260.00

O ga, set, Hiawatha, #250E loco, #250W tender, #782 coach, #783 coach, #784 obv/c, some fatigue, 1935-41, G-, A $1,200.00

O ga, set #140, #224 (blk, OB), #2224W (blk, OB), #2640 (2), #2641 (2-tone gr w/cream inserts), 1939-41, VG, A $350.00

O ga, set #141, #224E (blk), #2666W (blk), #3651 log/c, #2654 tk/c, #2757 caboose, 1939-41, VG, A $310.00

O ga, set #296, #252X loco (rewheeled), #607 coaches (2), #68 obv/c, peacock & orange, 1926-27, NMIBs, A **$1,200.00**

OO ga, engine & tender, #001E & #001T, spring latch, 1938-42, EX+, A.. $425.00

Std ga, acces, #115 station, late colors, dirty, 1935-42, EX-, A $250.00

Std ga, acces, #122 station, 1920-30, EX, A $325.00

Std ga, car, #214 b/c, yel & orange, 1926-40, EX+, A $350.00

Std ga, car, #215 tk/c, pea gr, 2" scratch, 1926-38, EX+, A.$400.00

Std ga, car, #219 crane, early colors, missing boom decal & 1 handrail, w/toolbox & 2 tools, 1926-40, VG+, A....$170.00

Std ga, car, #442 Tempel Blue Comet obv/c, nickel trim, 1930-40, EX, A $800.00

Std ga, car, #514R reefer, ivory & peacock, 1929-40, EX (OB worn), A $310.00

Std ga, car, #516 coal train hopper/c, brass plates, 1928-40, EX, A $280.00

Standard Gauge, #380 engine (maroon), #190 Mojave observation car (green), #18 Mojave parlor car (green), #19 Mojave baggage car (green), NM, D10, from $1,500.00 to $2,200.00.

Std ga, engine, #1912 loco, sq cab, 1910-12, EX, A $250.00

Std ga, freight set, #33, #35 & #36, all olive gr, 1920, VG, A $350.00

Std ga, freight set, #8E loco (olive w/OB), cars #511, #515 (terra cotta) & #517, 1927-40, VG, A $635.00

Std ga, pass set, #421 WestPhal Pullman Blue Comet coach, 1936-38, VG, A $800.00

Std ga, set, #1835E loco, #1835W tender, #513 st/c, #511 lumber/c, #517 caboose, 1934-39, EX (OBs), A $460.00

Std ga, set, #8 loco (olive), cars #337, #338 (olive w/maroon trim), #512, #513 & #517, 1925-32, G, A.............. $575.00

Std ga, set, State, #381E loco, #412 CA, #413 CO, #414 IL, #316 NY, 2-tone gr, 1929-35, EX-, A $8,000.00

Std ga, set, Stephen Girard, #392E, #392W, #424 Liberty Bell, #425 S Girard, #426 Coral Isle obv/c, 1931-40, EX, A $4,000.00

Std ga, set #352E, #10E loco, #332 bg/c, #339 coach, #341 obv/c, 1926-30, loco w/fatigue o/w EX (all OBs), A............ $500.00

Std ga, set #353E, #8E loco, #511 lumber/c, #512 gondola, #517 caboose, 1926-32, EX- (OBs), A................................ $500.00

Std ga, set #41, #38 loco, #114 b/c, #112 Lakeshore gondola, #113 st/c, #116 hopper, #117 caboose, 1913-24, VG+ (OB), A $320.00

Lionel Postwar

O ga, acces, #350 engine transfer table, w/#350-50 extension, complete, 1957-60, NM (OBs), A $800.00

O ga, acces, #415 diesel fueling station, 1955-57, NMIB (w/inserts), A $250.00

O ga, acces, #445 oil derrick, gr top, missing sign & drums, 1950-54, NM (OB & inserts), A................................ $250.00

O ga, car, #3330 f/c w/operating submarine kit, 1960-62, NMIB (sealed), A $375.00

O ga, car, #3360 Burro crane, missing trips, 1956-57, EX- (OB), A $230.00

O ga, car, #3413 Mercury Capsule Launching/c, no hole, unrun, 1962-64, NMIB, A $310.00

O ga, car, #3470 target launcher, dk bl bottom, red stack, 4 orig useable ballons, test run, 1962-64, NMIB, A........... $170.00

O ga, car, #3494-150 MoPac operating b/c, 1956, EX, A .$150.00

O ga, car, #3494-150 MoPac operating b/c, 1956, NMIB, A.$300.00

O ga, car, #3494-550 Monon operating b/c, unrun, 1957-58, NM+ (OB), A $450.00

O ga, car, #3540 radar/c, unrun, 1959-60, NMIB, A $225.00

O ga, car, #3820 USMC fl/c w/submarine, 1960-62, EX+, A $300.00

O ga, car, #460 Piggyback Transport, unrun, 1955-57, NM+ (OB & inserts), A $230.00

O ga, car, #6464-325 B&O Sentinel b/c, unrun, 1956, EX+ (OB), A $600.00

O ga, car, #6464-375 Central of Georgia b/c, Timkin trucks, test run, 1956-57, NMIB, A.. $150.00

O ga, car, #6464-400 B&O Timesaver b/c, 1 decal has sm chip, metal trucks, 1956-57, EX (OB), A $120.00

O ga, car, #6464-510 Pacemaker b/c, bl & yel, 1957-58, NM-, A $450.00

O ga, car, #6464-515 MKT b/c, yel & bl, 1957-58, NM-, A.$450.00

O ga, car, #6464-825 Alaska b/c, 1959-60, NM (G- box), A.$700.00

O ga, car, #6501 jet motor boat transport/c, unrun, 1962-63, NMIB (sealed), A $270.00

O ga, car, #6557 caboose, w/smoke fluid, box rub on cupola catwalk, 1958-59, NMIB, A $240.00

O ga, car, #6816 fl/c (red), w/bulldozer (dk orange, blk & wht letters), 1959-60, NMIB, A $450.00

O ga, car, #6828 fl/c w/P&H crane, 1 upright split, cab broke missing cones, 1960-63, EX, A.............................. $130.00

O ga, engine, #2023 UP Alco AA, anniversary colors, 1950-51, EX (OB), A $375.00

O Gauge, engine #624, Chesapeake & Ohio, 1953, minor decal wear otherwise EX, J6, $350.00.

O ga, engine, #2023 UP Alco AA, missing 1 coupler pickup, 1950-51, VG+, A $110.00

O ga, engine, #2322 Virginia FM, hairline screw crack on 1 side, test run, 1965-66, NM+, A $700.00

O ga, engine, #2322 Virginian FM, sm factory pnt spot on 1 end, unrun, 1954-56, NMIB, A...$850.00

O ga, engine, #2328 Burlington GP7, 1955-56, EX+ (OB), A $475.00

O ga, engine, #2338 Milwaukee Road GP7, blk-pnt version, 1955-56, NM, A $375.00

O ga, engine, #2339 Wabash GP7, 1957, EX+, A $450.00

O ga, engine, #2346 B&M GP9, box rub on top of vent, 1965-66, EX+, A..$350.00

O ga, engine, #2363 IC F3 AB, minor decal chip, 1955-56, EX-, A...$1,200.00

O ga, engine, #2367 Wabash F3 AB, minor decal chipping, 1955, EX, A..$1,200.00

O ga, engine, #611 Jersey Central NW2 switcher, 1957-58, EX, A..$250.00

O ga, engine, #614 Alaska NW2 switcher, w/dynamic brake unit, rub on cab roof, hairline screw crack, 1959-60, EX, A..$350.00

O ga, engine, #623 SF NW2 switcher, 3-handrail station version, strong decals, 1952-54, EX+ (OBs), A $375.00

O ga, engine, #624 C&O NW2 switcher, some decal chips, 1952-54, EX-, A..$350.00

O ga, engine, #625 Lehigh Valley 44 Tonner, blk & red, w/wht stripe, 1957-58, EX-, A...$230.00

O ga, engine, #626 B&O 44 Tonner, minor handrail chipping, 1959, EX+ (OB & inserts), A $500.00

O ga, engine & tender, #746 N&W & #746W, rpl nose cap, tender w/short stripe, 1957-60, VG+ (OB), A $1,300.00

O ga, engine & tender, #773 Hudson, #773W NY Central, test run, 1964 version, NMIB, A $1,600.00

O ga, engine #2332 GGI, blk w/weak stripes, 1947, VG, A..$1,000.00

O ga, pass set #1434WS, #2025 loco, #2466WX tender, #2440 cars (2, 2-tone gr), #2441 obv/c, 1946-47, G, A......$400.00

O ga, set, Super Chief, #2383 SF Alco AA, #2562 vista domes (2), 2563 coach, #2561 obv/c, 1959-61, NM- (OBs), A...$4,000.00

O ga, set #1402, #1666 loco, #2466T tender, #2440 pullmans (2),#2441 obv/c, w/flying shoe trucks, 1946-47, EX+ (OBs), A..$600.00

O ga, set #1425B, #1656 loco, #6043B tender, #6465 tk/c, #6465 LV hopper, #6257 SP caboose, 1948-49, EX (worn OBs), A...$1,000.00

027 ga, set #1612, General, #1862 loco, #1862T tender, #1866 bg/c, #1865 coach, 1959-62, NMIB (inserts), A......$800.00

027 ga, set #1800, Deluxe Gen, #1862, #1862T, #1866, #1865, #1877 f/c w/horses, 1959-62, NMIB (insert), A ...$1,200.00

Williams

O ga, engine, GGI loco, blk w/5 gold stripes, MIB, A $320.00

O ga, engine, Pennsylvania GG-7 loco, Brunswick gr w/gold stripe, MIB, A...$220.00

O ga, engine, Pennsylvania Sharknose Baldwin, M, A ..$290.00

O ga, engine, Pennsylvania Tuscan Trainmaster Diesel, MIB, A..$115.00

O ga, engine, Tuscan SD-45 Diesel, MIB, A $175.00

O ga, engine, Virginian Trainmaster Diesel, bl & yel, MIB, A..$130.00

O ga, engine & tender, Lackawanna 3-Rail Camelback, MIB, A..$405.00

O ga, engine & tender, PRR E6S 4-4-2, MIB, A $345.00

O ga, engines, Amtrak F-7 A-Units, 1 powered & 1 dummy, MIB, A..$230.00

O ga, pass set, Amtrak, 5 cars, MIB, A...........................$210.00

O ga, pass set, Amtrak Amfleet, 4 cars, MIB, A $210.00

O ga, pass set, Great Northern, Missouri, Michigan, Lincoln & Mississippi pullmans, pnt aluminum, MIB, A.........$230.00

O ga, pass set, Pennsylvania, 5 cars, pnt aluminum, MIB, A..$210.00

O ga, pass set, Pennsylvania Congressional GGI loco, 5 cars, MIBs, A...$635.00

O ga, pass set, Pennsylvania RR F-3-S Units (1 powered & 1 dummy diesel), 4 cars, MIB, A $375.00

O ga, pass set, Southern Pacific Madison #2519, 5 cars, MIB, A..$290.00

O ga, set, NASA Space Shuttle Transporter, MIB, A....$190.00

Miscellaneous Manufacturers

Am, Passenger Train, 1880s, pnt tin, red, gr & yel locomotive, 1 orange & 2 yel passenger cars, 5" ea, G-, A $315.00

Am, PRR Locomotive & Tender, ca 1875, pnt tin, blk, red & yel, open cab w/engineer figure, spoked wheels, 7¼", VG, A...$175.00

Beggs, #1 loco (livesteam), integral tender, hand-pnt blk cab & coal burner, w/burner, VG (G OB), A.....................$340.00

027 Gauge, set, Midnight Flyer, 1984, MIB (sealed), J6, $55.00.

Buddy L, engine and tender, 1930s, black with red decals, M, $1,350.00.

Bing, destination board, for Am market, hand-pnt tin, EX, A $190.00

Bing, 1 ga, Budweiser b/c, worn litho tin, brn roof, VG+, A .$270.00

Dorfan, std ga, bridge w/2 approaches, 1926-28, VG, A.$320.00

Eldon, Little Big Train, HO scale, tunnels, mountains, buildings, figures & accessories, VG (fair OB), T1...................$125.00

Eliot Weltz, O ga, pass set, 4 Amtrak Metroliner cars, 1 power car & 3 coaches, MIB, A......................................$230.00

Fallows, Flash Central Transportation Train, Pat 1883, pnt & stenciled tin, engine, tender & 2 cars, 12", G, A .$2,530.00

George Brown, Cuba Trike Locomotive, pnt & stenciled tin w/wood components & smokestack, 2 spoked wheels, 10½", G, A $770.00

Hafner, set, #1010 loco (clockwork, working), tender, coach & obv/c, red & yel litho, VG, A $180.00

Hafner, set #5120X, cast-aluminum loco (clockwork), #1190 tender, bg/c, UP coach, UP obv/c, w/acces (EX), NMIB, A...$850.00

Photo courtesy of Dunbar Gallery.

Hull and Stafford, passenger train, 1870s, locomotive: 9" long, each car: 9½" long, EX, $3,000.00.

Ives, #64 Canadian Pacific b/c, gray roof, 1 coupler imcomplete, EX, A $240.00

Ives, acces, #322 ringing signal (missing finial), #331 block signal, gr & cream, EX-, A...............................$325.00

Ives, engine & tender, United States, pnt & stenciled tin, blk & red, gold-tone disk wheels, 13", EX, A $2,750.00

Ives, std ga, #3235 loco, 1924-25, G, A $105.00

Ives, std ga, pass set, engine, #3242R, cars #184, #185 & #186, 1925-26, VG, A...$545.00

Marx, #05945 Happitime, #21 SF F9 AA, #3125 coaches (2), #3197 SF obv/c, GAEX b/c, SF caboose, EX (OB & inserts), A $140.00

Marx, #1829 SF loco & tender, plastic, electric, NM- (orig master carton), A...$130.00

Marx, Grade Crossing Signal Man, tin building on metal base, press signal & door opens to reveal figure, NM (VG+ box), A $95.00

Marx, set, #M10000 loco (clockwork, working), 3 coaches, obv/c, red & silver, EX-, A $210.00

Marx, set, Stream Line, UP on cars, #M10005 on engine, complete w/tracks & transformer, EX (EX box), A $235.00

Marx, set #M10000, loco, 4 coaches, obv/c, gr & yel, loco VG o/w VG+, A..$150.00

Marx, set #1500S, #3000 loco, CP tender, reel fl/c, log fl/c, derrick, NYC caboose, VG+ (OB & inserts), A $190.00

Marx, set #25249, #999 loco, NYC tender, Pacemaker b/c, NYC gondola, cattle/c, NYC caboose, EX (OBs), A $100.00

Marx, set #4923, Marline loco (electric), NYC tender, MS Oil tk/c, RI gondola, UP st/c, NYC caboose, NM (OBs), A $110.00

Marx, set #54742, Tales of the Wells Fargo TV Show, loco, tender, bg/c, coach, test run, NM+ (OB & inserts), A .$400.00

Mike's Train House, std ga, #444 Roundhouse section, MIB, A $405.00

Mike's Train House, std ga, Blue Comet, #400E & #400T loco & tender, 2-tone bl w/nickel trim, MIB, A..............$980.00

Randall, std ga, pullman kit, cast aluminum, missing doors, unpnt, 28", VG+, A $130.00

Scale Models Inc, loco & tender, brass, assembled in exacting detail, G- (OB), A $40.00

Schoenut, acces, #6 RR station, pnt wood, EX+ (OB worn), A $260.00

West Germany, 5" loco pulls coal/c & pass/c, tin w/plastic wheels, complete w/tracks, NM (EX OB), A...........$110.00

Transformers

Made by the Hasbro Company, Transformers were introduced in the United States in 1984. Originally there were twenty-eight figures — eighteen cars known as Autobots and ten Decepticons, evil robots capable of becoming such things as a jet or a handgun. Eventually the line was expanded to more than two hundred different models. Some were remakes of earlier Japanese robots that had been produced by Takara in the 1970s. (These can be identified through color differences and in the case of the Diaclone series, the absence of the small driver or pilot figures.)

The story of the Transformers and their epic adventures were told through several different comic books and animated series as well as a highly successful movie. Their popularity was reflected internationally and eventually made its way back to Japan. There the American Transformer animated series was translated into Japanese and soon inspired several parallel series of the toys which were again produced by Takara. These new Transformers were sold in the U.S. until the line was discontinued in 1990.

A few years ago, Hasbro announced their plans to reintroduce the line with Transformers: Generation 2. Transformers once again had their own comic book, and the old animated series was brought back in a revamped format. So far, several new Transformers as well as recolored versions of the older ones have been released by Hasbro, and the size of the series continues to grow. Sustained interest in them has spawned a number of fan clubs with chapters worldwide.

Because Transformers came in a number of sizes, you'll find a wide range of pricing. Our values are for Transformers in unopened original boxes. One that has been opened or used is worth much less — about 25% to 75%, depending on whether it has all its parts (weapons, instruction book, tech specks, etc., and what its condition is — whether decals are applied well or if it is worn.

Advisor: David Kolodny-Nagy (K2).

Other Sources: H4, O1, P3

Series 1, 1984

Autobot Car, #TF1021, Ironhide, red van, MIP..............$45.00

Autobot Car, #TF1023, Sunstreak, yel Countach, MIP ...$55.00
Autobot Car, #TF1025, Bluestreak, bl Datsun Z, MIP $90.00
Autobot Car, #TF1025, Bluestreak, silver Datsun Z, MIP .$55.00
Autobot Car, #TF1027, Jazz, Porsche, MIP......................$50.00
Autobot Car, #TF1029, Ratchet, ambulance, MIP...........$50.00
Autobot Car, #TF1031, Trailbreaker, camper, MIP $50.00
Autobot Car, #TF1033, Sideswipe, red Countach, MIP...$50.00
Autobot Car, #TF1035, Hound, jeep, MIP $50.00
Autobot Car, #TF1037, Mirage, Indy car, MIP................$50.00
Autobot Car, #TF1039, Prowl, police car, MIP $50.00
Autobot Car, #TF1041, Wheeljack, Mazzerati, MIP $50.00
Autobot Car, #TF1055, Camshaft, silver car, mail-in, MIP...$30.00
Autobot Car, #TF1057, Downshift, wht car, mail-in, MIP...$30.00
Autobot Car, #TF1059, Overdrive, red car, mail-in, MIP .$30.00
Autobot Car, #TF1061, Powerdasher #1, jet, mail-in, MIP.$15.00
Autobot Car, #TF1063, Powerdasher #2, car, mail-in, MIP...$15.00
Autobot Car, #TF1063, Powerdasher #3, drill, mail-in, MIP.$30.00
Autobot Commander, #TF1053, Optimus Prime w/Roller, trac-
    tor trailer, scout vehicle, MIP $150.00
Case, #TF1069, Collector's Case, briefcase, MIP.............$15.00
Case, #TF1071, Collector's Case, rnd 3-D version, MIP ..$25.00
Cassette, #TF1017, Ravage & Rumble, MIP....................$20.00
Cassette, #TF1019, Frenzy & Lazerbeak, MIP.................$20.00
Decepticon Communicator, #TF1049, Soundwave & Buzzsaw,
    tape player & gold condor, MIP $50.00
Decepticon Jet, #TF1043, Starscream, gray jet, MIP $75.00
Decepticon Jet, #TF1045, Thundercracker, bl jet, MIP ...$50.00
Decepticon Jet, #TF1047, Skywarp, blk jet, MIP.............$50.00
Decepticon Leader, #TF1051, Megatron, Walther P-38,
    MIP...$125.00
Minicar, #TF1000, Bumblejumper, M (Bumblebee card).$40.00
Minicar, #TF1000, Bumblejumper, M (Cliffjumper card) .$40.00
Minicar, #TF1001, Bumblebee, yel VW bug, MIP............$35.00
Minicar, #TF1003, Bumblebee, red VW bug, MIP $25.00
Minicar, #TF1005, Cliffjumper, red race car, MIP............$25.00
Minicar, #TF1007, Cliffjumper, yel race car, MIP $25.00
Minicar, #TF1009, Huffer, orange semi cab, MIP.............$20.00
Minicar, #TF1011, Windcharger, red Firebird, MIP.........$20.00
Minicar, #TF1013, Brawn, gr jeep, MIP.........................$20.00
Minicar, #TF1015, Gears, bl truck, MIP $20.00
Watch, #TF1067, Time Warrior, transforming watch w/Autobot
    insignia, mail-in, MIP....................................$80.00

Series 2, 1985

Autobot Air Guardian, #TF1201, Jetfire, F-14 jet, MIP.$125.00
Autobot Car, #TF1163, Skids, Le Car, MIP $50.00
Autobot Car, #TF1165, Red Alert, fire chief, MIP...........$40.00
Autobot Car, #TF1167, Grapple, crane, MIP $40.00
Autobot Car, #TF1169, Hoist, tow truck, MIP................$40.00
Autobot Car, #TF1171, Smokescreen, red, wht & bl Datsun Z,
    MIP $40.00
Autobot Car, #TF1173, Inferno, fire engine, MIP...........$40.00
Autobot Car, #TF1175, Tracks, Corvette, MIP................$50.00
Autobot Communicator, #TF1199, Blaster, radio/tape player,
    MIP $45.00
Autobot Scientist, #TF1197, Perceptor, microscope, MIP .$50.00
Constructicon, #TF1127, Bonecrusher (1), bulldozer, MIP .$20.00

Constructicon, #TF1129, Scavenger (2), steam shovel, MIP.$20.00
Constructicon, #TF1131, Scrapper (3), front-end loader,
    MIP $20.00
Constructicon, #TF1133, Hook (4), crane, MIP $20.00
Constructicon, #TF1135, Long Haul (5), dump truck, MIP .$20.00
Constructicon, #TF1137, Mixmaster (6), cement mixer,
    MIP $25.00
Constructicon, #TF1139, Devastator, construction gift set,
    MIP $100.00

Decepticon Jet, #TF1187, Ramjet, $35.00.

Decepticon Jet, #TF1189, Dirge, bl & yel jet, MIP...........$30.00
Decepticon Jet, #TF1191, Thrust, maroon jet, MIP $30.00
Decepticon Military Operations Commander, #TF1203, Shock-
    wave, lazer gun, MIP....................................$70.00

Deluxe Insecticon, #TF1157, Barrage, $50.00.

Deluxe Insecticon, #TF1155, Chop Shop, beetle, MIP $50.00

Deluxe Insecticon, #TF1159, Benom, bee, MIP $50.00

Deluxe Insecticon, #TF1161, Ransack, grasshopper, MIP .$50.00

Deluxe Vehicle, #TF1193, Whirl, lt bl helicopter, MIP...$70.00

Deluxe Vehicle, #TF1195, Roadster, off-road vehicle, MIP..$60.00

Dinobot, #TF1177, Grimlock, Tyrannosaurus, MIP.........$40.00

Dinobot, #TF1179, Slag, Triceratops, MIP $35.00

Dinobot, #TF1181, Sludge, Brontosaurus, MIP $35.00

Dinobot, #TF1183, Snarl, Stegosaurus, MIP....................$35.00

Insecticon, #TF1141, Kickback, grasshopper, MIP...........$20.00

Insecticon, #TF1143, Shrapnel, beetle, MIP.....................$20.00

Insecticon, #TF1145, Bombshell, boll weevil, MIP $20.00

Jumpstarter, #TF1147, Twin Twist, drill tank, MIP $15.00

Jumpstarter, #TF1149, Topspin, spaceship, MIP.............$15.00

Minicar, #TF1101, Bumblebee, yel VW bug, MIP............$25.00

Minicar, #TF1102, Bumblebee, yel w/minispy, MIP.........$35.00

Minicar, #TF1103, Bumblebee, red VW bug, MIP.........$15.00

Minicar, #TF1104, Bumblebee, red w/minispy, MIP $25.00

Minicar, #TF1105, Cliffjumper, red race car, MIP...........$15.00

Minicar, #TF1106, Cliffjumper, red w/minispy, MIP........$25.00

Minicar, #TF1107, Cliffjumper, yel race car, MIP $15.00

Minicar, #TF1108, Cliffjumper, yel w/minispy, MIP........$25.00

Minicar, #TF1109, Huffer, orange semi cab, MIP............$15.00

Minicar, #TF1110, Huffer, w/minispy, MIP $25.00

Minicar, #TF1111, Windcharger, red Firebird, MIP........$15.00

Minicar, #TF1112, Windcharger, w/minispy, MIP $25.00

Minicar, #TF1113, Brawn, gr jeep, MIP $15.00

Minicar, #TF1114, Brawn, w/minispy, MIP $25.00

Minicar, #TF1115, Gears, bl truck, MIP $15.00

Minicar, #TF1116, Gears, w/minispy, MIP $25.00

Minicar, #TF1117 Seaspray, hovercraft, MIP $10.00

Minicar, #TF1119, Powerglide, plane, MIP $15.00

Minicar, #TF1121, Warpath, tank, MIP $15.00

Minicar, #TF1123, Beachcomber, dune buggy, MIP........$15.00

Minicar, #TF1125, Cosmos, spaceship, MIP $15.00

Motorized Autobot Defense Base, #TF1205, Omega Supreme, rocket launcher base, MIP......................................$130.00

Triple Charger, #TF1151, Blitzwing, tank/plane, MIP $30.00

Triple Charger, #TF1153, Astrotrain, shuttle/train, MIP.$30.00

Watch, #TF1207, Autoceptor, Kronoform watch car, MIP $25.00

Watch, #TF1209, Deceptor, Kronoform watch jet, MIP ..$25.00

Watch, #TF1211, Listen 'n Fun, w/tape & yel Cliffjumper, MIP $35.00

Series 3, 1986

Aerial bot, #TF1271, Silverbolt (5), Concorde, MIP $35.00

Aerialbot, #TF1263, Air Raid (1), F-14 jet, MIP............$15.00

Aerialbot, #TF1265, Skydive (2), F-15 jet, MIP..............$15.00

Aerialbot, #TF1267, Fireflight (3), Phantom jet, MIP $15.00

Aerialbot, #TF1269, Slingshot (4), Harrier jet, MIP........$15.00

Aerialbot, #TF1273, Superion, Aerialbot gift set, MIP ..$180.00

Autobot Car, #TF1333, Blurr, futuristic car, MIP............$40.00

Autobot Car, #TF1335, Kup, pickup truck, MIP $40.00

Autobot Car, #TF1337, Hot Rod, red race car, MIP $70.00

Autobot City Commander, #TF1365, Ultra Magnus, car carrier, MIP $50.00

Autobot City Commander, #TF1367, Reflector, Spectro, Viewfinder & Spyglass into camera, mail-in, MIP.....$60.00

Autobot City Commander, #TF1369, STARS Control Center, action cb, mail-in, MIP..$60.00

Autobot City/Battle Station, #TF1359, Metroplex, robot city w/Scamper, blk minicar, Slammer, tank, Six-Gun, tower & guns $75.00

Battlecharger, #TF1311, Runamuch, Corvette, MIP........$15.00

Battlecharger, #TF1313, Runabout, Trans Am, MIP........$15.00

Cassette, #TF1315, Ratbat & Frenzy, bat & bl robot, MIP..$10.00

Cassette, #TF1317, Rewind & Steeljaw, gold weapons, blk robot & lion, MIP..$10.00

Cassette, #TF1318, Rewind & Steeljaw, silver weapons, blk robot & lion, MIP..$10.00

Cassette, #TF1319, Ramhorn & Eject, gold weapons, rhino & gray robot, MIP..$10.00

Cassette, #TF1320, Ramhorn & Eject, gold weapons, rhino & gray robot, MIP..$10.00

Combaticon, #TF1287, Brawl (1), tank, MIP................$15.00

Combaticon, #TF1289, Swindle (2), jeep, MIP...............$15.00

Combaticon, #TF1291, Blast Off (3), shuttle, MIP $15.00

Combaticon, #TF1293, Vortex (4), helicopter, MIP........$15.00

Combaticon, #TF1295, Onslaught (5), missile transport, MIP $30.00

Combaticon, #TF1297, Bruticus, Combaticon gift set, MIP.$300.00

Decepticon City Commander, #TF1363, Galvatron, laser cannon, MIP..$80.00

Heroes, #TF1131, Rodimus Prime, futuristic RV, MIP.....$45.00

Heroes, #TF1329, Wreck-Gar, futuristic motorcycle, MIP.$40.00

Jet, #TF1353, Scourge, hovercraft, MIP..........................$35.00

Jet, #TF1355, Cyclonus, space jet, MIP $45.00

Minicar, #TF1252, Wheelie, futuristic car, MIP..............$20.00

Minicar, #TF1253, Outback, brn jeep, MIP....................$15.00

Minicar, #TF1255, Tailgate, wht Firebird, MIP...............$15.00

Minicar, #TF1257, Hubcap, yel race car, MIP $15.00

Minicar, #TF1259, Pipes, bl semi cab, MIP....................$15.00

Minicar, #TF1261, Swerve, red truck, MIP.....................$15.00

Motorized Autobot Space Shuttle Robot, #TF1359, Sky Lynz, shuttle, MIP $90.00

Motorized Decepticon City/Battle Station, #TF1357, Trypticon, dinosaur w/Brunt, robot tank & Full-Tilt, buggy, MIP $130.00

Predacon, #TF1339, Razorclaw (1), lion, MIP..................$35.00

Predacon, #TF1341, Rampage (2), tiger, MIP $35.00

Predacon, #TF1343, Divebomb (3), vulture, MIP $35.00

Predacon, #TF1345, Tantrum (4), bull, MIP....................$35.00

Predacon, #TF1347, Headstrong (5), rhino, MIP $35.00

Predacon, #TF1348, Predaking, Predacon gift set (Japan only), MIP $350.00

Sharkticon, #TF1351, Gnaw, futuristic shark, MIP..........$40.00

Stunticon, #TF1275, Dead End (1), Porsche, MIP...........$10.00

Stunticon, #TF1277, Breakdown (2), Countach, MIP.....$10.00

Stunticon, #TF1279, Wildrider (3), Ferrari, MIP.............$10.00

Stunticon, #TF1281, Drag Strip (4), Indy car, MIP.........$10.00

Stunticon, #TF1283, Motormaster (5), tractor trailer, MIP.$30.00

Stunticon, #TF1285, Menasor, Stunticon gift set, MIP .$300.00

Triple Changer, #TF1321, Springer, armored car/helicopter, MIP $45.00

Triple Changer, #TF1323, Sandstorm, dune buggy/helicopter, MIP $30.00

Triple Changer, #TF1325, Broadside, aircraft carrier/plane, MIP $30.00

Triple Changer, #TF1327, Octane, tanker truck/jumbo jet, MIP $30.00

Series 4, 1987

Cassette, #TF1441, Slugfest & Overkill, Stegosaurus & Tyrannosaurus, MIP $10.00

Clone, #TF1443, Pounce & Wingspan, puma & eagle, MIP .$40.00

Clone, #TF1445, Fastlane & Cloudraker, dragster & spaceship, MIP $40.00

Double Spy, #TF1447, Punch-Counterpunch, Fiero, MIP.$40.00

Duocon, #TF1437, Battletrap, jeep/helicopter, MIP.........$20.00

Duocon, #TF1439, Flywheels, jet/tank, MIP.................$20.00

Headmaster Autobot, #TF1477, Chromedome w/Stylor, futuristic car, MIP $55.00

Headmaster Autobot, #TF1479, Hardhead w/Duros, tank, MIP $40.00

Headmaster Autobot, #TF1481, Highbrow w/Gort, helicopter, MIP $40.00

Headmaster Autobot, #TF1483, Brainstorm w/Arcana, jet, MIP $40.00

Headmaster Base, #TF1497, Scorponok w/Lord Zarak & Fasttrack, scorpion, mini-tank, MIP $80.00

Headmaster Base, #TF1499, Fortress Maximus w/Cerebros & Spike, Gasket, Grommet, battle station/city, MIP ..$300.00

Headmaster Decepticon, #TF1485, Skullcruncher w/Grax, alligator, MIP $35.00

Headmaster Decepticon, #TF1487, Mindwipe w/Vorath, bat, MIP $35.00

Headmaster Decepticon, #TF1489, Weirdwolf w/Monzo, wolf, MIP $35.00

Headmaster Horrorcon, #TF1491, Apeface w/Spasma, jet/ape, MIP $40.00

Headmaster Horrorcon, #TF1493, Snapdragon w/Krunk, jet/dinosaur, MIP $40.00

Monsterbot, #TF1461, Grotusque, tiger, MIP.................$30.00

Monsterbot, #TF1463, Doublecross, 2-headed dragon, MIP.$30.00

Monsterbot, #TF1465, Repugnus, insect, MIP.................$30.00

Sixchanger, #TF1495, Sixshot, starfighter jet, winged wolf, lazer pistol, armored carrier, tank, MIP $70.00

Targetmaster Autobot, #TF1449, Pointblank w/Peacemaker, race car & gun, MIP $30.00

Targetmaster Autobot, #TF1451, Sureshot w/Spoilsport, off-road buggy & gun, MIP..$30.00

Targetmaster Autobot, #TF1453, Crosshairs w/Pinpointer, truck & gun, MIP $30.00

Targetmaster Autobot, #TF1455, Hot Rod & Firebolt, race car & gun, MIP $45.00

Targetmaster Autobot, #TF1457, Kup & Recoil, pickup truck & gun, MIP $35.00

Targetmaster Autobot, #TF1459, Blurr w/Haywire, futuristic car & gun, MIP $45.00

Targetmaster Decepticon, #TF1467, Triggerhappy w/Blowpipe, dk bl jet w/gun, MIP $30.00

Targetmaster Decepticon, #TF1469, Misfire w/Aimless, spaceship & gun, MIP $30.00

Targetmaster Decepticon, #TF1471, Slugslinger w/Caliburst, twin jet & gun, MIP $30.00

Targetmaster Decepticon, #TF1475, Scourve w/Fracas, hovercraft & gun, MIP..$35.00

Technobot, #TF1425, Afterburner (1), motorcycle, MIP..$10.00

Technobot, #TF1426, Afterburner, w/decoy, MIP $15.00

Technobot, #TF1427, Nosecone (2), drill tank, MIP.......$10.00

Technobot, #TF1428, Nosecone, w/decoy, MIP.............$15.00

Technobot, #TF1429, Stafe (3), fighter plane, MIP.........$10.00

Technobot, #TF1430, Stafe, w/decoy, MIP....................$15.00

Technobot, #TF1431, Lightspeed (4), race car, MIP........$10.00

Technobot, #TF1432, Lightspeed, w/decoy, MIP............$15.00

Technobot, #TF1433, Scattershot (5), spaceship, MIP $30.00

Terrocon, #TF1413, Rippersnapper (1), lizard, MIP.........$10.00

Terrocon, #TF1414, Rippersnapper, w/decoy, MIP $15.00

Terrocon, #TF1415, Sinnertwin (2), 2-headed dog, MIP.$10.00

Terrocon, #TF1416, Sinnertwin, w/decoy, MIP.............$15.00

Terrocon, #TF1417, Cutthroat (3), vulture, MIP.............$10.00

Terrocon, #TF1418, Cutthroat, w/decoy, MIP $15.00

Terrocon, #TF1419, Blot (4), monster, MIP....................$10.00

Terrocon, #TF1420, Blot, w/decoy, MIP........................$15.00

Terrocon, #TF1421, Hun-grrr (5), 2-headed dragon, MIP..$30.00

Terrocon, #TF1423, Abominus, Terrocon gift set, MIP....$70.00

Throttlebot, #TF1401, Goldbug, VW bug, MIP $10.00

Throttlebot, #TF1402, Goldbug, w/decoy, MIP.............$15.00

Throttlebot, #TF1403, Freeway, Corvette, MIP $10.00

Throttlebot, #TF1404, Freeway, w/decoy, MIP.............$15.00

Throttlebot, #TF1405, Chase, Ferrari, MIP $10.00

Throttlebot, #TF1406, Chase, w/decoy, MIP..................$15.00

Throttlebot, #TF1407, Wideload, dump truck, MIP $10.00

Throttlebot, #TF1408, Wideload, w/decoy, MIP............$15.00

Throttlebot, #TF1409, Rollbar, jeep, MIP.....................$10.00

Throttlebot, #TF1410, Rollbar, w/decoy, MIP...............$15.00

Throttlebot, #TF1411, Searchlight, race car, MIP...........$10.00

Throttlebot, #TF1412, Searchlight, w/decoy, MIP...........$15.00

Series 5, 1988

Cassette, #TF1539, Squawkalk & Beastbox, hawk & gorilla, MIP $10.00

Cassette, #TF1541, Grand Slam & Raindance, tank & jet, MIP..$10.00

Firecon, #TF1507, Cindersaur, dinosaur, MIP $10.00

Firecon, #TF1509, Flamefeather, monster bird, MIP........$10.00

Firecon, #TF1561, Sparkstalker, monster, MIP................$10.00

Headmaster Autobot, #TF1555, Hosehead w/Lug, fire engine, MIP $30.00

Headmaster Autobot, #TF1557, Siren w/Quig, fire chief car, MIP $25.00

Headmaster Autobot, #TF1559, Nightbeat w/Muzzle, race car, MIP $25.00

Headmaster Decepticon, #TF1561, Horri-bull w/Kreb, bull, MIP $25.00

Headmaster Decepticon, #TF1563, Fangry w/Brisko, winged wolf, MIP $25.00

Headmaster Decepticon, #TF1565, Squeezeplay w/Lokos, crab, MIP $25.00

Powermaster Autobot, #TF1567, Getaway w/Rev, MR2, MIP..$35.00

Powermaster Autobot, #TF1569, Joyride w/Hotwire, off-road buggy, MIP..$35.00

Powermaster Autobot, #TF2571, Slapdash w/Lube, Indy car, MIP...$35.00

Powermaster Autobot Leader, #TF1617, Optimus Prime w/HiQ, tractor trailer, MIP.................................$80.00

Powermaster Decepticon, #TF1573, Darkwing w/Throttle, dk gray jet, MIP.......................................$40.00

Powermaster Decepticon, #TF1575, Dreadwind w/Hi-Test, lt gray jet, MIP.......................................$40.00

Powermaster Mercenary, #TF1613, Doubledealer w/Knok (robot) & Skar (bat), missile launcher, MIP.............$65.00

Pretender, #TF1577, Landmine, race car w/shell, MIP.....$25.00

Pretender, #TF1579, Cloudburst, jet w/shell, MIP...........$25.00

Pretender, #TF1581, Waverider, submarine w/shell, MIP .$25.00

Pretender, #TF1583, Skullgrin, tank w/shell, MIP...........$25.00

Pretender, #TF1585, Bomb-burst, spaceship w/shell, MIP.$25.00

Pretender, #TF1587, Submarauder, submarine w/shell, MIP .$25.00

Pretender, #TF1589, Groundbreaker, race car w/shell, MIP..$25.00

Pretender, #TF1591, Sky High, jet w/shell, MIP $25.00

Pretender, #TF1593, Splashdown, sea skimmer w/shell, MIP.$25.00

Pretender, #TF1595, Iguanus, motorcycle w/shell, MIP ...$25.00

Pretender, #TF1597, Bubly, plane w/shell, MIP..............$25.00

Pretender, #TF1599, Finback, sea skimmer w/shell, MIP .$25.00

Pretender Beast, #TF1601, Chainclaw, bear w/shell, MIP.$20.00

Pretender Beast, #TF1603, Catilla, sabertooth tiger w/shell, MIP...$20.00

Pretender Beast, #TF1605, Carnivac, wolf w/shell, MIP ..$20.00

Pretender Beast, #TF1607, Snarler, boar w/shell, MIP $20.00

Pretender Vehicle, #TF1609, Gunrunner, red jet w/vehicle shell, MIP..$40.00

Pretender Vehicle, #TF1611, Roadgrabber, purple jet w/vehicle shell, MIP.......................................$40.00

Seacon, #TF1513, Overbite (1), shark, MIP....................$15.00

Seacon, #TF1515, Seawing (2), manta ray, MIP $15.00

Seacon, #TF1517, Nautilator (3), lobster, MIP $15.00

Seacon, #TF1519, Skalor (4), fish, MIP...........................$15.00

Seacon, #TF1521, Tentakil (5), squid, MIP......................$15.00

Seacon, #TF1523, Snaptrap (6), turtle, MIP....................$35.00

Seacon, #TF1525, Piranacon, Seacon gift set, MIP........$150.00

Sparkbot, #TF1501, Fizzle, off-road buggy, MIP..............$10.00

Sparkbot, #TF1503, Sizzle, funny car, MIP......................$10.00

Sparkbot, #TF1505, Guzzle, tank, MIP $10.00

Targetmaster Autobot, #TF1543, Scoop w/Tracer & Holepunch, front-end loader & 2 guns, MIP $20.00

Targetmaster Autobot, #TF1545, Landfill w/Flintlock & Silencer, dump truck & 2 guns, MIP..................$20.00

Targetmaster Autobot, #TF1547, Quickmix w/Boomer & Ricochet, cement mixer & 2 guns, MIP $20.00

Targetmaster Decepticon, #TF1549, Quake w/Tiptop & Heater, tank & 2 guns, MIP.......................$20.00

Targetmaster Decepticon, #TF1551, Spinster w/Singe & Hairsplitter, helicopter & 2 guns, MIP..............$20.00

Targetmaster Decepticon, #TF1553, Needlenose w/Sunbeam & Zigzag, jet & 2 guns, MIP..........................$20.00

Tiggerbot, #TF1527, Backstreet, race car, MIP.................$15.00

Tiggerbot, #TF1529, Override, motorcycle, MIP.............$15.00

Tiggerbot, #TF1531, Dogfight, plane, MIP......................$15.00

Triggercon, #TF1533, Ruckus, dune buggy, MIP.............$15.00

Triggercon, #TF1535, Windsweeper, B-1 bomber, MIP ...$15.00

Triggercon, #TF1537, Crankcase, jeep, MIP....................$15.00

Series 6, 1989

Legends, K-Mart Exclusive, #TF1727, Bumblebee, VW bug, MIP...$30.00

Legends, K-Mart Exclusive, #TF1729, Jazz, Porsche, MIP .$40.00

Legends, K-Mart Exclusive, #TF1731, Grimlock, dinosaur, MIP...$40.00

Legends, K-Mart Exclusive, #TF1733, Starscream, jet, MIP...$45.00

Mega Pretender, #TF1717, Vroom, dragster w/shell, MIP .$35.00

Mega Pretender, #TF1719, Thunderwing, jet w/shell, MIP...$35.00

Mega Pretender, #TF1721, Crossblades, helicopter w/shell, MIP...$25.00

Micromaster Base, #TF1679, Skyhopper & Micromaster, helicopter & F-15, MIP....................................$35.00

Micromaster Base, #TF1681, Groundshaker & Micromaster, self-propelled cannon & stealth fighter, MIP............$35.00

Micromaster Base, #TF1735, Skystalker, Space Shuttle Base & Micromaster Porsche, MIP..........................$55.00

Micromaster Base, #TF1737, Countdown, Rocket Base & Micromaster Lunar Rover, MIP................................$60.00

Micromaster Patrol, #TF1651, Off-Road Patrol Series, 4 different, MIP, ea $10.00

Micromaster Patrol, #TF1653, Air Strike Patrol Series, 4 different, MIP, ea $10.00

Micromaster Patrol, #TF1655, Race Car Patrol Series, 4 different, MIP, ea $10.00

Micromaster Patrol, #TF1657, Sports Car Patrol Series, 4 different, MIP, ea $10.00

Micromaster Patrol, #TF1659, Rescue Patrol Series, 4 different, MIP, ea.................................$10.00

Micromaster Patrol, #TF1661, Battle Patrol Series, 4 different, MIP, ea.................................$10.00

Micromaster Station, #TF1671, Greasepit, pickup w/gas station, MIP $20.00

Micromaster Station, #TF1673, Hot House, plane w/fire station, MIP $20.00

Micromaster Station, #TF1675, Ironworks, semi w/construction site, MIP $20.00

Micromaster Station, #TF1677, Airwave, jet w/airport, MIP...$20.00

Micromaster Transport, #TF1663, Overload, car carrier, MIP...$15.00

Micromaster Transport, #TF1665, Flattop, aircraft carrier, MIP...$15.00

Micromaster Transport, #TF1667, Roughstuff, military transport, MIP..$15.00

Micromaster Transport, #TF1669, Erector, construction crane, MIP...$15.00

Pretender, #TF1697, Pincher, scorpion w/shell, MIP $20.00

Pretender, #TF1699, Longtooth, hovercraft w/shell, MIP .$20.00

Pretender, #TF1701, Stranglehold, rhino w/shell, MIP $20.00

Pretender, #TF1703, Octopunch, crab w/shell, MIP $20.00

Pretender, #TF1705, Bludgeon, tank w/shell, MIP $30.00

Pretender, #TF1707, Doubleheader, twin jet w/shell, MIP ...$20.00

Pretender Classic, #TF1709, Bumblebee, VW bug w/shell, MIP $30.00

Pretender Classic, #TF1711, Grimlock, dinosaur w/shell, MIP $30.00

Pretender Classic, #TF1713, Starscream, jet w/shell, MIP.$30.00

Pretender Classic, #TF1715, Jazz, Porsche w/shell, MIP ...$30.00

Pretender Monster, #TF1683, Icepick (1), MIP...............$12.00

Pretender Monster, #TF1685, Bristleback (2), MIP $12.00

Pretender Monster, #TF1687, Wildfly (3), MIP $12.00

Pretender Monster, #TF1691, Birdbrain (5), MIP $12.00

Pretender Monster, #TF1693, Slog (6), MIP $12.00

Pretender Monster, #TF1695, Monstructor, Pretender Monster gift set, not produced, MIP.......................................$1,000.00

Ultra Pretender, #TF1725, Roadblock, tank w/figure & vehicle, MIP $40.00

Ultra Pretender, #TF1727, Skyhammer, race car w/figure & vehicle, MIP..$40.00

Series 7, 1990

Action Master, #TF1781, Soundwave: Soundwave (bat), Wingthing, MIP..$15.00

Action Master, #TF1783, Treadshot: Treadshot, Catgut (panther), MIP...$15.00

Action Master, #TF1785, Grimlock: Grimlock, Anti-Tank Cannon (tank gun), MIP $15.00

Action Master, #TF1787, Jazz: Jazz, Turbo Board (skateboard), MIP $20.00

Action Master, #TF1789, Rad: Rad, Lionizer (lion), MIP $15.00

Action Master, #TF1791, Rollout: Rollout, Glitch (mini-robot), MIP $20.00

Action Master, #TF1793, Devastator: Devastator, Scorpulator (scorpion), MIP $15.00

Action Master, #TF1795, Krok: Krok, Gatoraider (alligator), MIP $10.00

Action Master, #TF1799, Blaster: Blaster, Flight-Pack (jet pack), MIP $15.00

Action Master, #TF1803, Mainframe: Mainframe, Push-Button (mini-robot), MIP......................................$15.00

Action Master, #TF1805, Shockwave: Shockwave, Fistfight (mini-robot), MIP $15.00

Action Master, #TF1807, Banzai-Tron: Banzai-Tron, Razor-Sharp (crab), MIP..$10.00

Action Master, #TF1809, Inferno: Inferno, Hydro-Pack (water laser backpack), MIP $15.00

Action Master, #TF1811, Snarl: Snarl, Tyrannitron, MIP ..$10.00

Action Master, #TF1813, Skyfall: Skyfall, Top-Heavy Rhino, MIP $10.00

Action Master, #TF1815, Kick-Off: Kick-Off, Turbo-Pack (rocket backpack), MIP..$10.00

Action Master, #TF1817, Prowl: Prowl, Turbo Cycle, MIP..$30.00

Action Master, #TF1819, Axer: Axer, Off-Road Cycle, MIP..$30.00

Action Master, #TF1821, Over-Run, Over-Run, Attack Copter, MIP $30.00

Action Master, #TF1823, Starscream: Starscream, Turbo Jet, MIP $35.00

Action Master, #TF1825, Wheeljack: Wheeljack, Turbo Racer, MIP $35.00

Action Master, #TF1827, Sprocket: Sprocket, Attack Cruiser, MIP $35.00

Action Master, #TF1829, Gutcruncher: Gutcruncher, Stratotronic Jet, MIP..$35.00

Action Master, #TF1831, Megatron: Megatron, Neutro-Fusion Tank, MIP..$60.00

Action Master, #TF1833, Optimus Prime: Optimus Prime, Armored Convoy, MIP.....................................$65.00

Micromaster Combiner, #TF1763, Battle Squad: Meltdown, Half-Track, Direct-Hit, Power Punch, Fireshot & Vanquish, MIP $15.00

Micromaster Combiner, #TF1765, Constructor Squad: Stonecruncher, Excavator, Sledge, Hammer, Grit & Knock-out, MIP...$15.00

Micromaster Combiner, #TF1767, Metro Squad: Wheel Blaze, Road Burner, Oiler, Slide, Power Run & Strike-down, MIP...$15.00

Micromaster Combiner, #TF1769, Astro Squad: Phaser, Blast Master, Moonrock, Missile Master, Barrage & Heave, MIP $15.00

Micromaster Combiner, #TF1771, Tanker Truck: Tanker Truck, Pipeline & Gusher, MIP...........................$15.00

Micromaster Combiner, #TF1773, Cannon Transport: Cannon Transport, Cement-Head & Terror-Tread, MIP........$15.00

Micromaster Combiner, #TF1775, Missile Launcher: Missile Launcher, Retro & Surge, MIP $15.00

Micromaster Combiner, #TF1777, Anti-Aircraft Base: Anti-Aircraft Base, Blackout & Spaceshot, MIP................$15.00

Micromaster Combiner, #TF1779, Battlefield Headquarters: Battlefield Headquarters, Full-Barrel & Overflow, MIP..$15.00

Micromaster Patrol, #TF1751, Race Track Patrol: Barricade, Roller Force, Ground Hog & Motorhead, MIP............$7.00

Micromaster Patrol, #TF1753, Construction Patrol: Takedown, Neutro, Groundpounder & Crumble, MIP $7.00

Micromaster Patrol, #TF1755, Air Patrol: Thread Bolt, Eagle Eye, Sky High & Blaze Master, MIP............................$7.00

Micromaster Patrol, #TF1757, Monster Truck Patrol, Hydraulic, Slow Poke, Big Hauler & Heavy Tread, MIP..............$7.00

Micromaster Patrol, #TF1759, Hot Rod Patrol, Big Daddy, Trip-Up, Greaser & Hubs, MIP $7.00

Micromaster Patrol, #TF1761, Military Patrol: Bombshock, Tracer, Dropshot & Growl, MIP $7.00

Generation 2, Series 1, 1992-93

Autobot Car, #TF1863, Jazz, Porsche, MIP.....................$25.00

Autobot Car, #TF1865, Sideswipe, blk Countach, MIP...$25.00

Autobot Car, #TF1867, Inferno, fire truck, MIP $25.00

Autobot Leader, #TF1879, Optimus Prime w/Roller, tractor trailer w/electronic sound-effect box, MIP................$35.00

Autobot Minicar, #TF1881, Bumblebee, metallic VW bug, MIP $10.00

Autobot Minicar, #TF1883, Hubcap, metallic minicar, MIP .**$10.00**

Autobot Minicar, #TF1885, Beachcomber, metallic dune buggy, MIP **$10.00**

Autobot Minicar, #TF1887, Seaspray, metallic hovercraft, MIP **$10.00**

Color Change Transformer, #TF1905, Deluge, MIP.........**$15.00**

Color Change Transformer, #TF1907, Jetstorm, MIP **$15.00**

Color Change Transformer, #TF1911, Gobots, MIP **$15.00**

Color Change Transformer, #1909, Drench, MIP **$15.00**

Constructicon (orange version), #TF1851, Bonecrusher (1), bulldozer, MIP..**$7.00**

Constructicon (orange version), #TF1853, Scavenger (2), steam shovel, MIP...**$7.00**

Constructicon (orange version), #TF1855, Scrapper (3), front-end loader, MIP..**$7.00**

Constructicon (orange version), #TF1857, Hook (4), crane, MIP...**$7.00**

Constructicon (orange version), #TF1859, Long Haul (5), dump truck, MIP...**$7.00**

Constructicon (orange version), #TF1861, Mixmaster (6), cement truck, MIP..**$7.00**

Constructicon (yel version), #TF1851, Bonecrusher (1), bulldozer, MIP...**$6.00**

Constructicon (yel version), #TF1853, Scavenger (2), steam shovel, MIP...**$6.00**

Constructicon (yel version), #TF1855, Scrapper (3), front-end loader, MIP..**$6.00**

Constructicon (yel version), #TF1857, Hook (4), crane, MIP .**$6.00**

Constructicon (yel version), #TF1859, Long Haul (5), dump truck, MIP...**$6.00**

Constructicon (yel version), #TF1861, Mixmaster (6), cement truck, MIP..**$6.00**

Decepticon Jet, #TF1875, Starscream, gray jet w/electronic light & sound-effect box, MIP **$30.00**

Decepticon Jet, #TF1877, Ramjet, purple jet w/electronic light & sound-effect box, MIP **$30.00**

Decepticon Leader, #TF1913, Megatron, gr tank w/electronic sound-effect treads, MIP...**$45.00**

Dinobot, #TF1869, Grimlock, bl Tyrannosaurus, MIP.....**$25.00**

Dinobot, #TF1869, Grimlock, orig gray Tyrannosaurus, MIP...**$30.00**

Dinobot, #TF1870, Grimlock, turq Tyrannosaurus, MIP .**$50.00**

Dinobot, #TF1871, Slag, gr Triceratops, MIP...................**$25.00**

Dinobot, #TF1871, Slag, orig gray Triceratops, MIP **$30.00**

Dinobot, #TF1873, Snarl, orig gray Stegosaurus, MIP......**$30.00**

Dinobot, #TF1873, Snarl, red Stegosaurus, MIP..............**$25.00**

Small Autobot Car, #TF1897, Rapido, MIP **$6.00**

Small Autobot Car, #TF1899, Skram, MIP.......................**$6.00**

Small Autobot Car, #TF1901, Windbreaker, MIP.............**$6.00**

Small Autobot Car, #TF1903, Turbofire, MIP..................**$6.00**

Small Decepticon Jet, #TF1889, Afterburner, MIP **$6.00**

Small Decepticon Jet, #TF1891, Eagle Eye, MIP **$6.00**

Small Decepticon Jet, #TF1893, Terradive, MIP...............**$6.00**

Small Decepticon Jet, #TF1895, Windrazor, MIP.............**$6.00**

Generation 2, Series 2, 1994

Aerialbot, #TF1915, Skydive (1), F-15, MIP **$7.00**

Aerialbot, #TF1917, Air Raid (2), F-14, MIP **$7.00**

Aerialbot, #TF1919, Firefight (3), Phantom, MIP.............**$7.00**

Aerialbot, #TF1921, Slingshot (4), Harrier, MIP **$7.00**

Aerialbot, #TF1923, Silverbolt (5), Concorde, MIP **$18.00**

Combaticon, #TF1927, Brawl (1), tank, MIP **$7.00**

Combaticon, #TF1929, Swindle (2), jeep, MIP.................**$7.00**

Combaticon, #TF1931, Blast Off (3), shuttle, MIP **$7.00**

Combaticon, #TF1933, Vortex (4), helicopter, MIP **$7.00**

Combaticon, #TF1935, Onslaught (5), missile transport, MIP.**$18.00**

Heroes, #TF1953, Autobot Hero Optimus Prime, MIP **$15.00**

Heroes, #TF1955, Decepticon Hero Magatron, MIP........**$15.00**

Laser Rod Transformer, #TF1937, Electro, 1993, MIP **$15.00**

Laser Rod Transformer, #TF1939, Volt, 1993, MIP **$15.00**

Laser Rod Transformer, #TF1941, Jolt, 1993, MIP **$15.00**

Laser Rod Transformer, #TF1943, Sizzle, 1993, MIP........**$15.00**

Rotor Force, #TF1945, Leadfoot, MIP..............................**$7.00**

Rotor Force, #TF1947, Manta Ray, MIP **$7.00**

Rotor Force, #TF1949, Powerdrive, MIP..........................**$7.00**

Rotor Force, #TF1951, Ransack, MIP **$7.00**

Stunticon, BotCon '94 Exclusive, #TF1925, Breakdown (2), Countach, MIP...**$100.00**

Watch, #TF1957, Superion, MIP **$12.00**

Watch, #TF1959, Galvatron, MIP **$12.00**

Watch, #TF1961, Ultra Magnus, MIP **$12.00**

Watch, #TF1963, Autobot, MIP......................................**$12.00**

Watch, #TF1965, Scorpia, MIP.......................................**$12.00**

Trolls

The first trolls to come to the United States were molded after a 1952 design by Marti and Helena Kuuskoski of Tampere, Finland. The first trolls to be mass produced in America were molded from wood carvings made by Thomas Dam of Denmark. As the demand for these trolls increased, several US manufacturers were licensed to produce them. The most noteworthy of these were Uneeda Doll Company's Wishnik line and Inga Scandia House True Trolls. Thomas Dam continued to import his Dam Things line. Today trolls are enjoying a renaissance as baby boomers try to recapture their childhood. As a result, values are rising.

The troll craze from the '60s spawned many items other than just dolls such as wall plaques, salt and pepper shakers, pins, squirt guns, rings, clay trolls, lamps, Halloween costumes, animals, lawn ornaments, coat racks, notebooks, folders and even a car.

In the '70s, '80s and '90s new trolls were produced. While these trolls are collectible to some, the avid troll collector still prefers those produced in the '60s. Remember, trolls must be in mint condition to receive top dollar.

For more information, we recommend *Collector's Guide to Trolls* by Pat Petersen.

Advisor: Roger Inouye (I1).

Bride-Nik, Uneeda, MOC, T1..**$20.00**

Christmas Stocking, Norfin, lg vinyl head, M, I2, pr..........**$6.00**

Clown, Dam, 1965, pnt-on clothes, yel eyes & red nose, 5½", I1, from $175 to **$250.00**

Ballerina, Dam, bright red mohair, green eyes, original outfit, MIP, I1, $55.00.

Photo courtesy of Roger Inouye.

Cow, Dam, 1964, sm, M, I1 ....$45.00
Elephant, Dam, 1964, wrinkled flesh-tone skin & orange hair, w/bell, 5½", I1 ....$175.00
Elephant, Japan, 1960s, bl hollow plastic w/fuzzy hair, 3", EX+, F8 ....$25.00
Giraffe, Dam, amber eyes, gray hair, 12", G, I1 ....$125.00
Giraffe, Japan, 1960s, hollow body w/hair, posable head, EX+, F8 ....$25.00
Horse, Dam, 1964, solid body w/long mane & tail, w/heart-decor felt saddle, EX+, F8 ....$48.00
Indian, 1960s, dk skin, Indian headband, outfit & shoes, 3½", EX+, F8 ....$15.00
Kool-Aid Troll, pk hair, 5", M, T1 ....$15.00
Leprechaun, 1969, w/jacket, EX, B10............................$25.00
Lion, Dam, lg, M, I1 ....$125.00

Viking, Dam, white mohair, brown eyes, blue felt dress, silver belt and helmet, NM, I1, from $150.00 to $200.00.

Photo courtesy of Roger Inouye.

Moonitik, Uneeda Wishnik, mohair body w/rubber ft & shake eyes, 18", extremely rare, I1......................................$100.00
Nodder, MIB, L4..$135.00
True Troll, Scandia House Ent, 1965, felt swimsuit w/heart tag around neck, orange hair, gr spiral eyes, 3", M, I2 .....$25.00
Voodoo Doll, 1960s, blk plastic w/cloth outfit, wht fuzzy hair, red ruby eyes, M, T2 ....$15.00
Weird Creature, 1960s, real animal hair, 3", MIB, I1 ....$30.00
Werewolf Monster, 1960s, 3", I1 ....$40.00

Miscellaneous

Carrying Case, Ideal, Wishnik, Niks & Naks labels inside, 4x7", w/5 trolls & outfits, EX, F8 ....$55.00
Paper Dolls, Wishnik, Whitman, 1966, 4 dolls w/24 outfits & accessories, cut, appears complete, EX, F8 ....$28.00
Playhouse, Wishnik Mini Trolls, Ideal, 1960s, EX, B10 ...$18.00

View-Master and Tru-Vue

View-Master, the invention of William Gruber, was introduced to the public at the 1939-1940 New York World's Fair and the Golden Gate Exposition in California. Since then, View-Master reels, packets and viewers have been produced by five different companies — the original Sawyers Company, G.A.F (1966), View-Master International (1981), Ideal Toys and Tyco Toys (the present owners). Because none of the non-cartoon single reels and three-reel packets have been made since 1980, these have become collectors' items. Also highly sought after are the 3-reel sets featuring popular TV and cartoon characters. The market is divided between those who simply collect View-Master as a field all its own and collectors of character-related memorabilia who will often pay much higher prices for reels about Barbie, Batman, The Addams Family, etc. Our values tend to follow the more conservative approach.

The first single reels were dark blue with a gold sticker and came in attractive gold-colored envelopes. They appeared to have handwritten letters. These were followed by tan reels with a blue circular stamp. Because these were produced for the most part after 1945 and paper supplies were short during WWII, they came in a variety of front and back color combinations, tan with blue, tan with white, and some were marbleized. Since print runs were low during the war, these early singles are much more desirable than the printed white ones that were produced by the millions from 1946 until 1957. Three-reel packets, many containing story books, were introduced in 1955, and single reels were phased out. Nearly all viewers are very common and have little value except for the very early ones, such as the Model A and Model B. Blue and brown versions of the Model B are especially rare. Another desirable viewer, unique in that it is the only focusing model ever made, is the Model D. For more information we recommend *View-Master Single Reels, Volume I*, by Roger Nazeley.

Advisor: Roger Nazeley (N4).
Other Source: M15

ABC Circus, B-411, MIP (sealed), B10...........................$18.00
Adam 12, B-593, 1972, MIP, C1..............................$30.00
Adventures of GI Joe, B-585, MIP (sealed), B10.............$40.00
Alice in Wonderland, B-360, MIP, B10.......................$15.00
America's Man in Space, B-657, MIP, B10....................$18.00
American Indian, B-725, 1958, MIP, N4......................$10.00
Apollo Moon Landing, B-663, MIP, B10.......................$15.00
Apple's Way, B-558, MIP (sealed), B10......................$25.00
Archies, B-574, MIP (sealed), B10/C1.......................$30.00
Aristocats, B-365, MIP, J5.................................$10.00
Babes in Toyland, B-375, 1961, NMIP, F8....................$36.00
Bambi, B-400, MIP (sealed), B10............................$18.00
Barbie Around the World Trip, 1965, EX+ (EX pkg), F8.$35.00
Batman, B-492, MIP (sealed), B10...........................$38.00
Beautiful Cypress Gardens Florida, A-959, EX+ (EX pkg),
    P3...$5.00
Bedknobs & Broomsticks, B-366, 1971, MIP, N4...............$20.00
Beep, Beep, the Roadrunner; B-538, MIP (sealed), B10...$20.00
Beverly Hillbillies, B-570, 1963, MIP, N4..................$45.00
Bible Heroes, B-852, 1967, MIP, N2.........................$10.00
Big Blue Marble, B-587, MIP (sealed), B10..................$26.00
Birth of Jesus, B-875, MIP, B10............................$12.00
Black Hole, K-35, 1979, MIP, N4............................$18.00
Blondie & Dagwood, B-537, 1966, MIP, N4....................$40.00
Bonanza, 1964, 3-reel set, EX+, F8.........................$15.00
Bonanza, 1971, NMIP, J7....................................$50.00
Brave Eagle, Chief of the Cheyennes, 1956, NM (EX+ pkg),
    F8..$45.00
Buck Rogers in the 25th Century, J-1, 1978, MIP, N4 ....$5.00
Buffalo Bill Jr, 1955, NMIP, from $25 to...................$35.00
Bugs Bunny, B-531, MIP, B10................................$15.00
Bugs Bunny in Big Top Bunny, B-549, MIP (sealed), B10..$22.00
Butterflies of North America, B-610, 1955, MIP, N4.......$12.00
Captain America, H-43, MIP (sealed), B10...................$26.00
Captain Kangaroo, B-560, 1957, MIP, N4.....................$30.00
Carlsbad Caverns Tour 1, A-376, MIP, B10...................$15.00
Casper the Friendly Ghost, B-533, MIP, B10.................$12.00
Casper's Ghostland, B-545, MIP (sealed), B10...............$25.00
Cat From Outer Space, 1978, NMIP, J7.......................$20.00
Charlie Brown's Summer Fun, B-548, 1972, MIP, N4......$15.00
Charlotte's Web, B-321, MIP, B10...........................$15.00
Children's Zoo, B-617, MIP (sealed), B10...................$18.00
CHiPs, L-14, 1980, MIP (sealed), C1........................$22.00
Christmas Carol, B-380, MIP (sealed), B10..................$22.00
Christmas Story, B-383, MIP (sealed), B10..................$18.00
Cinderella, B-318, MIP, B10................................$12.00
City Beneath the Sea, B-496, MIP, B10/T1, from $25 to.$35.00
Civil War, B-790, 1960s, NMIP, F8..........................$45.00
Close Encounters of the Third Kind, J-47, 1977, MIP, N4..$20.00
Colonial Williamsburg, A-813, MIP (sealed), B10...........$25.00
Daktari, B-498, MIP (sealed), B10..........................$45.00
Daniel Boone, B-479, 1965, MIP, N4.........................$35.00
Dark Shadows, 1968, missing booklet o/w NM (NM pkg),
    C1...$75.00
Dennis the Menace, B-539, MIP (sealed), from $22 to $28.00
Dinosaurs (TV Show), #4138, MIP (sealed), B10..............$8.00
Disney World Fantasyland, A-948, MIP (sealed), B10.....$22.00
Disney World Frontierland, A-951, MIP (sealed), B10....$18.00

Disney World Liberty Square, A-950, MIP (sealed), B10.$18.00
Donald Duck, B-525, MIP, B10...............................$15.00
Dr Shrinker & Wonderbug, H-2, 1977, MIP (sealed) $30.00
Dr Strange, K-22, 1979, MIP (sealed), C1 ....$18.00
Dracula, B-324, 1976, MIP (sealed), from $18 to $22.00
Dukes of Hazzard, L-17, 1980, MIP, N4 ....$20.00
Easter Story, B-880, MIP, N4 ....$10.00
Eight Is Enough, K-76, 1980, MIP (sealed), C1 ....$20.00
Emergency!, B-597, MIP (sealed), B10 ....$22.00
Expo '67, A-074, missing booklet, EX+ (EX+ pkg), F8 ....$25.00
Family Affair, B-571, 1969, MIP, N4 ....$38.00
Fangface, K-66, 1980, NMIP, J7 ....$15.00
Fantastic Four, K-36, 1979, MIP, T1 ....$15.00
Fantastic Voyage, B-546, 1968, MIP, N4 ....$8.00
Fat Albert & the Cosby Kids, B-554, 1974, MIP, N4 ....$4.00
Flash Gordon, B-583, MIP (sealed), B10 ....$22.00
Flintstones, B-514, 1964, MIP, N4..........................$10.00
Flintstones, Beasts of Bedrock, L-6, 1980, MIP, N4..........$8.00
Flintstones, Pebbles & Bamm-Bamm, B-520, 1964, MIP,
    N4...$12.00
Flipper, B-485, MIP, B10...................................$35.00
Flipper (TV Show), 1964, set of 3, EX, F8..................$12.00
For the Love of Benji, H-54, NMIP, B10.....................$12.00
Frankenstein, B-323, 1976, MIP (sealed), C1................$20.00
Germany, Now Series, B-193, no coin, MIP, B10.............$16.00
Golden Book Favorites, H-14, MIP (sealed), B10 ....$30.00
Goldilocks & the Three Bears, B-317, MIP (sealed), B10.$22.00
Green Hornet, B-488, 1966, MIP, N4.........................$75.00
Grizzly Adams, 1978, MIP (sealed), C1 ....$24.00
Hair Bear Bunch, B-552, MIP (sealed), B10..................$25.00
Happy Days, B-586, 1974, MIP, N4...........................$18.00
Happy Days, Requiem for a Malph, J-13, 1978, MIP, N4.$20.00
Hardy Boys, H-69, 1977, MIP, N4 ....$14.00
Hare & the Tortoise, B-309, MIP (sealed), B10 ....$20.00
Harlem Globetrotters, 1977, MIP (sealed), C1...............$25.00

KISS, Canadian issue, GAF, 1978, 3-reel set, MIP, J6, $85.00.

Photo courtesy of June Moon.

Hawaii Five-O, B-590, MIP (sealed), B10.........................$28.00
Hearst Castle, A-190, MIP, B10.....................................$18.00
Herbie Rides Again, B-578, MIP, B10 ....$15.00
Horses, H-5, 1977, MIP, N4 ....$25.00
Huckleberry Hound & Yogi Bear, B-512, NM (EX pkg), P3 .$15.00
Inspector Gadget, BD-232, MIP, N4 ....$8.00
It's a Bird, Charlie Brown, B-556, MIP, B10 ....$12.00
Jetsons, L-27, 1981, MIP, N4 ....$4.00
Joe Forrester, BB-454, MIP (sealed), B10 ....$25.00
Johnny Moccasin, 1957, complete w/booklet, NM (VG+ pkg),
     F8 ....$40.00
Julia, B-572, 1969, NMIP, J7 ....$35.00
Jungle Book, B-363, MIP, B10 ....$15.00
King Kong, B-392, MIP (sealed), B10 ....$35.00
Knight Rider, #4054, 1982, MIP, N4 ....$12.00
Land of the Giants, B-494, 1968, MIP, N4 ....$60.00
Land of the Lost No 2, H-1, NMIP, B10 ....$15.00
Lassie & Timmy, B-474, 1959, MIP, B10 ....$20.00
Lassie Look Homeward, B-480, 1965, MIP, N4 ....$20.00
Lassie Rides the Log Flume, B-489, 1968, MIP, B10........$15.00
Laverne & Shirley, J-20, 1978, MIP (sealed), J7.............$25.00
Legend of Indiana Jones, #4092, 1989, MIP, N4................$6.00
Legend of the Lone Ranger, L-26, 1981, MIP, T1 ....$12.00
Little Drummer Boy, B-871, MIP (sealed), B10................$18.00
Little Orphan Annie, J-21, 1978, MIP, C1 ....$25.00
Little Red Riding Hood, B-310, MIP (sealed), from $15 to ..$20.00
Lost in Space, B-482, 1967, NMIP, F8 ....$75.00
Love Bug, B-501, MIP (sealed), B10 ....$22.00
M*A*S*H, J-11, 1978, M (NM pkg), C1 ....$25.00
Man From UNCLE, B-484, MIP, from $35 to $40.00
Mannix & Enter Tami Okada, BB-450, MIP (sealed), C1 .$30.00
Marineland of Florida, A-964, MIP, B10 ....$15.00
Marineland of the Pacific, A-188, MIP, N4.....................$12.00
Mary Poppins, B-376, 1964, MIP, N4 ....$15.00

Mod Squad, B-478, MIP, B10.......................................$35.00
Monkees, B-493, 1967, MIP, N4 ....$30.00
Moon Rockets & Guided Missiles, B-656, MIP, B10........$20.00
Moonraker (James Bond), K-68, 1979, MIP, N2 ....$22.00
Mork & Mindy, K-67, 1979, MIP, N4 ....$18.00
Mount Vernon, A-812, MIP (sealed), B10 ....$25.00
Movieland Wax Museum, 1974, NMIP, J7 ....$20.00
Niagara Falls, A-655, MIP, B10.....................................$15.00
Night Before Christmas, B-382, MIP, B10 ....$15.00
One of Our Dinosaurs Is Missing!, 1975, NMIP, J7 ....$20.00
Partridge Family, B-592, 1973, MIP, J7..........................$75.00
Peanuts, B-536, MIP (sealed), B10................................$15.00
Pete's Dragon, 1977, NMIP, J7......................................$20.00
Pikes Peak & Colorado Springs, A-321, MIP, B10 ....$15.00
Pink Panther, J-12, 1978, MIP, B10...............................$15.00
Planet of the Apes, B-507, 1967, MIP, N4......................$30.00
Pluto, B-529, 1980, MIP (sealed), J7..............................$12.00
Pogo, 1980, MIP (sealed), F8...$20.00
Popeye, B-516, MIP, B10...$12.00
Poseidon Adventure, B-391, 1972, MIP, N4 ....$28.00
Prehistoric Animals, B-619, MIP, B10............................$22.00
Prehistoric Life Paleontology, B-676, MIP, B10 ....$22.00
Project Apollo, B-658, MIP, B10 ....$25.00
Quick Draw McGraw, B-534, 1961, MIP, N4...................$18.00
Raggedy Ann & Andy, B-406, 1971, MIP, N4 ....$15.00
Ren & Stimpy, #1084, MIP (sealed), B10.........................$7.00
Rescuers, H-26, 1978, MIP, N4 ....$14.00
Rin-Tin-Tin, B-467, 1976, MIP, N4 ....$12.00
Robin Hood, B-342, MIP (sealed), B10 ....$25.00
Rookies, BB-452, MIP (sealed), B10 ....$26.00
Rudolph the Red-Nosed Reindeer, B-870, MIP (sealed),
     B10..$18.00
Run, Joe, Run, B-594, MIP, B10 ....$16.00
San Diego Zoo Packet No 1, A-173, MIP, B10................$15.00
San Francisco Sight-Seeing, A-167, MIP, B10 ....$15.00
Scooby & Scrappy-Doo, B-553, 1980, MIP, N4 ....$18.00
Search (TV show), B-591, 1973, MIP, N4........................$30.00

Mighty Mouse, B-526, 1968, NMIP, $10.00.

Mickey Mouse, B-528, MIP, B10....................................$15.00
Mighty Thor, 1977, NMIP, J7..$25.00
Million Dollar Duck, B-506, 1971, MIP, N4 ....$20.00

Star Trek, B-499, 1968, MIP, $30.00.

Shaggy DA, B-368, MIP (sealed), B10 ....$20.00
Shazam!, Spanish version, 1976, MIP (sealed), J7 ....$30.00
Six Million Dollar Man, B-559, MIP (sealed), from $25 to ..$30.00
Sleeping Beauty, B-308, MIP, B10 ....$15.00
Smokey Bear, The True Story of View-Master Reels, GAF,
     1969, NMIP, J5 ....$25.00
Snoopy & the Red Baron, B-544, MIP (sealed), B10 ....$20.00
Snow White & the Seven Dwarfs, B-200, NMIP, P3 ....$15.00
Space 1999, BB-451, MIP, B10 ....$28.00
Spiderwoman, The Enforcer Strikes, L-7, 1980, MIP, N4 ..$5.00
Star Trek: Mr Spock's Time Trek; B-555, MIP (sealed),
     B10 ....$40.00
Star Trek: The Motion Picture; K-57, MIP, B10/J7 ....$25.00
Statue of Liberty, A-648, MIP, B10.....................................$18.00
Superman II, L-46, MIP, N4..$20.00
Superman Meets Computer Crook, B-584, MIP (sealed),
     B10..$28.00
SWAT, BB-453, MIP (sealed), B10 ....$22.00

Talking Viewmaster Gift Pak III, GAF, #2275, NM (EX canister), $30.00.

Tarzan of the Apes, B-580, 1950, MIP, N4.......................$32.00
Time Tunnel, B-491, 1966, MIP, N4.................................$50.00
UFO, B-417, 1969, MIP, N4 ....$40.00
Voltron, Defenders of the Universe, #1055, MIP (sealed),
     B10..$7.00
Westward Expansion, B-812, MIP (sealed), B10 ....$25.00
White House, A-793, MIP, B10...$20.00
Who Framed Roger Rabbit?, #4086, MIP, N4 ....$15.00
Winnie the Pooh & the Blustery Day, K-37, 1979, MIP,
     N4 ....$10.00
Winnie the Pooh & the Honey Tree, B-362, MIP, B10/P3 ..$15.00
Wizard of Oz, B-361, MIP, N4 ....$20.00
Wolfman, J-30, 1978, MIP, N4 ....$16.00
Wonders of the Deep, B-612, MIP, B10...............................$18.00
Woody Woodpecker, 1964, complete w/booklet, NMIP,
     F8 ....$25.00
World of Liddle Kiddles, B-577, 1970, MIP, N4 ....$75.00

X-Men, Captive Hearts, #1085, MIP (sealed), B10 ....$7.00
Yellowstone National Park, A-306, MIP, N4......................$8.00
Zorro, B-469, 1958, MIP, N4...$40.00
20,000 Leagues Under the Sea, NMIP, J7 ....$35.00

Western

No friend was ever more true, no brother more faithful, no acquaintance more real to us than our favorite cowboys of radio, TV, and the siver screen. They were upright, strictly moral, extrememly polite, and tireless in their pursuit of law and order in the American West. How unfortunate that such role models are practically extinct nowadays.

This is an area of strong collector interest right now, and prices are escalating. For more information and some wonderful pictures, we recommend *Character Toys and Collectibles, First* and *Second Series,* by David Longest and *Guide to Cowboy Character Collectibles* by Ted Hake.

Advisors: Donna and Ron Donnelly (D7).

See also Books; Cereal Boxes; Character and Promotional Drinking Glasses; Character Clocks and Watches; Coloring, Activity and Paint Books; Guns; Lunch Boxes; Premiums; Windups, Friction and Other Mechanicals; and other specific categories.

Annie Oakley, outfit, Pla-Master, 1950, red blouse & fringed skirt
     w/silkscreen of Annie on pockets, M (EX box), A......$150.00
Annie Oakley, soap, Shooting Gallery, Pure Castile Soap, 2
     rows of soap ducks, unused, 6½x19½" box, M16.....$100.00
Bat Masterson, cane, 1958, chromed plastic hdl w/emb name,
     plain plastic tip missing o/w EX+, F8 ....$25.00
Bat Masterson, holster set w/cane & vest, Carnell, 1960, unused,
     MIB, J2...$320.00
Brave Eagle, outfit, complete w/headdress, NM (EX box),
     M5 ....$120.00

Buck Jones, Rangers Cowboy Suit, Yankiboy, 1930s, complete, NMIB, A, $550.00.

Charles Starret, photo, Dixie, 1950s, mc w/gr border, 8x10", EX,
     J5 ....$25.00

Cochise, doll, Excel, w/outfit & accessories, 9½", NM, I2.**$30.00**

Dale Evans, fan, 1950s, cb, VG, N2 ....**$15.00**

Dale Evans, sheet music, I Dream of Jeanie, 1940s, photo cover, EX, J5 ....**$10.00**

Dale Evans, vest & skirt, red & tan skirt w/fringe, blk vest, EX, M5 ....**$95.00**

Daniel Boone, target set, Walt Disney, M, V1 ....**$78.00**

Daniel Boone, wallet, Fess Parker illus, 1964, EX, J7........**$35.00**

Davy Crockett, Arrow Kit, MIP, C10 ....**$60.00**

Davy Crockett, Auto-Magic Picture Gun, Stephens/WDP, Fess Parker as Davy on lid, complete w/gun & film, NM (NM box), A **$140.00**

Davy Crockett, belt, metal arrow-shaped buckle, NM, M5 ..**$25.00**

Davy Crockett, belt, metal buckle w/rifle between Davy Crockett & Old Betsy, NM, M5 ....**$45.00**

Davy Crockett, belt, vinyl w/image of Davy & frontier scenes, NM (EX photo card) **$85.00**

Davy Crockett, belt, 1950s, leather w/Frontierland illus & lg metal buckle, child's sz, EX, A3 ....**$25.00**

Davy Crockett, bolo tie, 1955, EX, J7 ....**$35.00**

Davy Crockett, charm bracelet, WDP, 1950s, 7 charms w/history of Davy Crockett, MOC, C1...............................**$80.00**

Davy Crockett, cuff links & tie clasp set, 1950s, EX (orig box), J5 ....**$25.00**

Davy Crockett, guitar, EC France, mk Walt Disney, circular decal picturing Davy on end, 24", EX (EX box) **$350.00**

Davy Crockett, lamp, Cactus Craft, 1950s, shaped like covered wagon w/western scenes, 8", EX, A..........................**$120.00**

Davy Crockett, material, flannel, 1 yard, NM, J2 ....**$22.00**

Davy Crockett, night light, Kupper Inc, 1950s, glass bust image, 2", M (EX box), A **$75.00**

Davy Crockett, patch, yel or red, 4½x6", NM, D8 ....**$12.00**

Davy Crockett, pin, long rifle form, EX+, T1 ....**$20.00**

Davy Crockett, Pioneer Scout outfit, Eddy, 1955, complete and unused, MIB, A, $245.00.

Davy Crockett, plate, Disney, paper, 8" sq, EX, J5............**$15.00**

Davy Crockett, scarf, NM, J6 ....**$65.00**

Davy Crockett, shirt, cotton flannel w/4½" sq patch, curled fringe o/w VG+, M16 ....**$75.00**

Davy Crockett, shoe holder, vinyl, hanging, M, V1 ....**$70.00**

Davy Crockett, suitcase, WDP, raised image of Davy on horse, mk King of the Wild Frontier, plastic hdl, 7", EX, A.**$85.00**

Davy Crockett, tablecloth, mk WDP, paper, various scenes of Davy in action poses, 28x86", EX, A........................**$85.00**

Davy Crockett, tool kit, Liberty Steel Chest Corp., contains generic tool set, EX+, A, $250.00.

Davy Crockett, transfers, 4 sheets, 3½x7½", EX, M16.....**$25.00**

Davy Crockett, TV chair, mk WDP, vinyl-covered seat w/frontier designs, raised lip mk Davy Crockett, 13" dia, VG+, A.**$350.00**

Davy Crockett, wastebasket, 1955, litho tin, pictures Davy & images of his life history, 11", EX+, A...................**$95.00**

Gabby Hayes, charm, C10 ....**$25.00**

Gene Autry, belt, leather, mk Gene Autry & Tooled Western Steerhide, complete w/extra leather pc, EX, A **$50.00**

Gene Autry, outfit, scarce, NMIB, $650.00.

Gene Autry, postcard, 1940s, blk & wht w/horse, NM, J5..**$10.00**

Gene Autry, poster, 1951, for personal appearance in Albany, NY area, 6x9", EX...**$35.00**

Gene Autry, sheet music, Goodbye Little Darlin', VG, J5..**$10.00**

Gene Autry, song book, Cowboy Songs & Mountain Ballads, EX, J5 ....**$15.00**

Gunsmoke, tablet, 1950s, James Arness cover, unused, EX, J5 ....**$10.00**

Gunsmoke/Matt Dillon, cowboy vest & badge, NMOC, T1.**$145.00**

Hopalong Cassidy, autograph book, 1950s, stylized photos of Hoppy & Topper w/raised western designs, 5x5", NM............**$165.00**

Hopalong Cassidy, bank, bronze-toned bust, NM, J2 ....$75.00

Hopalong Cassidy, bath towel, 20x38", faded, J5 ....$25.00

Hopalong Cassidy, belt, blk leather w/red & wht graphics, lt rust on buckle o/w VG+, J5 ....$25.00

Hopalong Cassidy, bicycle horn, w/orig box, C10 ....$350.00

Hopalong Cassidy, booklet, Hoppy Press Books, photos, articles & contest tie-ins, 10x14", EX, J5 ....$25.00

Hopalong Cassidy, cereal bowl & juice glass, Anchor Hocking, 1950s, milk glass w/images of Hoppy, M, A $125.00

Hopalong Cassidy, cowboy hat, blk felt, VG $85.00

Hopalong Cassidy, Dudin'-Up Kit, Fuller Brush, 1950, 2 bottles of hair trainer, shampoo & comb, scarce, NM (EX+ box), A......$800.00

Hopalong Cassidy, earmuffs, NMIB $225.00

Hopalong Cassidy, Field Glasses, EX (EX box), $295.00.

Hopalong Cassidy, film, Bar-20 Rides Again, Castle Films, EX (orig box w/out lid), J5 ....$15.00

Hopalong Cassidy, fork, NM, J6....................................$24.00

Hopalong Cassidy, greeting card, 1950s, mechanical w/spinner showing 4 different photos, unused, EX+ $45.00

Hopalong Cassidy, handkerchief, Hoppy & Topper on bl ground, C10 ....$50.00

Hopalong Cassidy, ice-cream cup, Sealright, 1950, waxed cb, 3" dia, EX+, A..$100.00

Hopalong Cassidy, flashlight, 1950s, tin with plastic cover, Morse Code decal on other side, 7", EX, A, $115.00; Roller Skates, Rollfast, scarce, NMIB, $1,000.00.

Hopalong Cassidy, jewelry, Anson, 1950, complete w/gold-tone key ring, chain & clip, rare, M (EX box), A $185.00

Hopalong Cassidy, neckerchief slide, w/steerhead, C10 ...$60.00

Hopalong Cassidy, night light, Aladdin/William Boyd, 1950, glass gun & holster w/decal, 10", EX+, A $345.00

Hopalong Cassidy, pencil, gold letters on gr, unused, VG, J5 ....$15.00

Hopalong Cassidy, pennant, 1950s, wht on blk felt, 27", EX ..$65.00

Hopalong Cassidy, picture fr, ca 1950, litho cb easel-back w/image of Hoppy on horse, 9x7", unused, NM, A....$75.00

Hopalong Cassidy, place mat, 1950, plastic, shows Hoppy on Topper in desert scene, 12x18", EX....................$95.00

Hopalong Cassidy, plate, paper, 6" sq, EX, J5....................$10.00

Hopalong Cassidy, pocketbook, 1946, mk Hopalong Cassidy Returns, M, P6...$18.00

Hopalong Cassidy, poster, Hopalong's Creed for American Boys & Girls, Cornet Magazine, 10x12", fr, sm water spots, J5 ....$25.00

Hopalong Cassidy, Shooting Gallery, w/orig shot pellets, EX+ (EX box) $350.00

Hopalong Cassidy, spurs, C10, pr $195.00

Hopalong Cassidy, store display, Langendorf Enriched Bread, NM..$45.00

Hopalong Cassidy, T-Shirt box, Morse & Morse Inc, 1951, mk Movieland Product From Hollywood, photo image, scarce, NM, A $285.00

Hopalong Cassidy, television set, box only, Automatic Toy #352, 5" sq, VG+, A...$170.00

Hopalong Cassidy, transfer, Hopalong Cassidy Deputy w/steer's head at center, 2½x7", EX, J5 ....$25.00

Hopalong Cassidy, Woodburning Set, Am Toy & Furniture, complete, EX+ (EX box mk Wm Boyd Ltd-1950), A.......$260.00

John Wayne, postcard, Italian, mc photo in sports coat, EX, J5 ....$10.00

Johnny Mack Brown, movie cards, Wild West Days, 1937, blk & wht, set of 12, 3¼x2½", unused, MIP (sealed), M16.$50.00

Johnny Mack Brown, photo, Dixie, 1950s, mc w/brn border, 8x10", EX, J5..$25.00

Lone Ranger, ad sheet, 1950s, Amazing Silver Bullet offer, lt stain o/w NM, S18...$15.00

Lone Ranger, Official First Aid Kit, dated 1938, tin, 4x4", EX, $95.00; Lone Ranger on Silver, dated 1938, plaster, name embossed on base, 4", EX, $40.00.

Lone Ranger, ballpoint pen, Everlast Pen Corp, 1950s, silver metal, EX (EX illus card).........................$165.00

Lone Ranger, belt, plastic w/blk & wht photos, silver buckle, VG+, M16.........................$86.00

Lone Ranger, bolo tie, Half a Century, M, S18 ....$22.00

Lone Ranger, counter display, Kix Branding Iron, M, V1 .$125.00

Lone Ranger, Electric Drawing Set, Lakeside, 1968, EX+ (VG+ box), T2.........................$15.00

Lone Ranger, harmonica, Harmonica Corp, 1950, inscr Lone Ranger, NM (EX display box w/header card), A $175.00

Lone Ranger, hat, C10.........................$130.00

Lone Ranger, key chain, Hamilton #P2875, 1990, silver bullet, MIB, S18 ....$15.00

Lone Ranger, Military Brush Set, TLR Inc, 1939, wood w/colorful decal, EX (VG box) $115.00

Lone Ranger, Official School Kit Pencil Box, Am Pencil, 1941, red & gold, EX, P6.........................$65.00

Lone Ranger, paperweight, Hamilton, Lucite silver bullet, M, S18 ....$15.00

Lone Ranger, pin, MOC, S18.........................$8.00

Lone Ranger, suspenders, MOC, C10 ....$105.00

Lone Ranger, tattoo transfers, Swell (bubble gum), 1960s, set of 4, NM, J5 ....$25.00

Lone Ranger & Tonto, plate, Hamilton, #3066B, MIP, S18 ....$100.00

Patsy Montana, song folio, 1941, 100 pgs, facsimile signature on cover, 9x12", VG, A3 ....$25.00

Red Foley, song book, Cowboy Songs & Mountain Ballads, MM Cole, 1940s, photo cover, EX, J5.........................$10.00

Red Ryder, gloves, brn, VG, S20.........................$30.00

Red Ryder, medallion, Lucky Coin, Penney's for Super Value on back, VG+, I2 ....$7.00

Photo courtesy of June Moon.

Restless Gun, cowboy hat, felt, EX, J6, $42.00.

Roy Rogers, Bunkhouse Boots, box only, 1950s, head shot photo & RR logo on front, 10x4", EX $135.00

Roy Rogers, display, Roy Rogers Straight Shooter Gun Puzzle, Plas-Trix, cb w/2 of 24 key chains, 14", NM (VG card), A $130.00

Roy Rogers, Fix-It Chuck Wagon & Jeep, Ideal, plastic, complete, NM (NM box), A.........................$310.00

Roy Rogers, Fix-It Stagecoach, Ideal, 1955, EX (VG box), H4.........................$240.00

Roy Rogers, Flash Camera, Herbert George, plastic w/metal plate picturing Roy on Trigger, complete, EX+ (EX box), A.........................$195.00

Roy Rogers, flashlight, Bantamlite, plastic w/attached string, photo of Roy & signature, 3", EX+ (EX+ rare card), A.........................$190.00

Roy Rogers, Give-A-Show Slide Strip, Kenner, 1962, Mark of the Big Cat, 7 35mm color slides, NM+, C1.........................$15.00

Red Ryder, salesman's case for gloves, EX, $225.00.

Restless Gun, cowboy hat, felt, EX, J6 ....$42.00

Rin-Tin-Tin, doll, Ideal, EX, J2.........................$70.00

Rin-Tin-Tin, flyer, 1956, for rodeo at Madison Square Garden, stiff paper, 4 pgs, 8½x11", EX, M16 ....$16.00

Rin-Tin-Tin, uniform, 1955, child sz, EX, J7 ....$75.00

Rin-Tin-Tin & Rusty, belt buckle, EX, J6 ....$65.00

Roy Rogers, Buckboard, Ideal, 1958, complete w/plastic figures & buckboard, MIB.........................$450.00

Roy Rogers, horseshoe set, Ohio Art, lithographed tin, complete, NMIB, $265.00.

Roy Rogers, horseshoe set, rubber w/litho bases, no wooden stakes, VG+, J6 ....$95.00

Roy Rogers, paint set, 1950s, unused, NMIB, V1 ....$125.00

Roy Rogers, pencil set, cb, pull-out drawer contains generic material, lid shows Roy on Trigger, 6x9", EX, A $55.00

Roy Rogers, postcard, 1950s, glossy blk & wht photo, NM, C1 ....$15.00

Roy Rogers, Ranch Lantern, Ohio Art, tin w/litho longhorns, NMIB.........................$195.00

Roy Rogers, Signal Siren Flashlight display, Usalite, 1950s, diecut cb w/slot for flashlight, 9", EX+, A $260.00

Roy Rogers, socks, 1950s, nylon, features RR logo & profile of Trigger at top, sz 9-11, unused, M, A $95.00

Roy Rogers, song book, 1943, G+, D8...........................$35.00

Roy Rogers, store display sign, 1950, Roy Rogers Wagon Train of Bargains, shows Roy on Trigger, 2-sided, 20x14", EX, A $350.00

Roy Rogers, sweatshirt, orange, unused, w/sticker, C10 .$155.00

Roy Rogers, Western Suit #4550, bright corduroy w/RR logo in rope design, complete, scarce, EX+ (EX box), A.....$275.00

Roy Rogers & Trigger, cowboy hat, Lancaster Hat, 1950, wool, pistol & spurs w/name on band, EX+, A....................$95.00

Roy Rogers & Trigger, outfit, Merit/England, complete, scarce, NM (EX box), A $485.00

Roy Rogers & Trigger, plate & bowl, Universal, 1950s, mc graphics & gold on ivory, 5¼" plate & 6" dia bowl, P6, pr...$95.00

Roy Rogers Riders, harmonica, Reed, 1955, 4", NMOC, A .$65.00

Seventh Cavalry, glove & neckerchief set, Reigel, 1950s, MIP, J2 ....$60.00

Tales of the Texas Rangers, badge, 1950s, Deputy, bright silver metal star, NM, C1 ....$22.00

Texas Pete, soap-on-a-rope, unused, NM, J2 ....$35.00

Texas Rangers, display card, Butterfingers, 1950s, tinted Jake Pearson, 5x9", NM, M17...$65.00

Tom Mix, blotter, Tom Mix Circus, 1930s, mc photo, 3x6", NM..$65.00

Tom Mix, card, Official Circus Route, early 1930s, lists towns in OH, PA & NY for July, 5½x3¼", EX $50.00

Tonto, Indian outfit, Esquire, 1955, complete with vest, Texan Jr. cap gun, holster and belt, NM (EX box), $345.00.

Wagon Train, pitcher, British, 1960s, Robert Horton/Flint McCullough, ceramic, 7", NM, J5.............................$45.00

Wagon Train, sign, Major Adams, Nabisco, early 1960s, EX, D8 ....$125.00

Wild Bill Hickok & Jingles, outfit, box only, Leslie-Henry, 14x11", EX, A...$85.00

Wyatt Earp, badge, Wyatt Earp Ent, 1957, diecast metal, 2", VG, P4 ....$20.00

Zorro, dominos, NMIB, C10 ....$195.00

Zorro, film, Unmasked, Super 8, w/box, C10 ....$50.00

Zorro, flashlight, 1950s, plastic w/push button, mask flips up, complete, 3¼", non-working o/w EX+, M8 ....$16.00

Zorro, gloves, 1958, EX, J7, pr $50.00

Photo courtesy of June Moon.

Zorro, Pencil by Number Coloring Set, NMIB, J6, $55.00.

Zorro, pinwheel, WDP, 1950s-60s, blk, red & silver w/Zorro graphics, 18", 1 fin torn o/w EX, D9.........................$30.00

Zorro, Secret Sight Scarf Mask, Westminster Products, 1950s, 1-way mirror lens set on blk scarf, EX+, scarce, M8..$75.00

Windups, Friction and Other Mechanicals

Windup toys represent a fun and exciting field of collecting — our fascination with them stems from their simplistic but exciting actions and brightly colored lithography, and especially the comic character or personality-related examples are greatly in demand by collectors today. Though most were made through the years of the thirties through the fifties, they carry their own weight against much earlier toys and are considered very worthwhile investments. Various types of mechanisms were used — some are key wound while others depend on lever action to tighten the mainspring and release the action of the toy. Tin and celluloid were used in their production, and although it is sometimes possible to repair a tin windup, experts advise against investing in a celluloid toy whose mechanism is not working, since the material is usually too fragile to withstand the repair.

Many of the boxes that these toys came in are almost as attractive as the toys themselves and can add considerably to their value.

Advisors: Richard Trautwein (T3); Scott Smiles (S10).

See also Aeronautical; Automobiles and Other Replica Vehicles; Boats; Chein; Lehmann; Marx; Robots and Space Toys; Strauss.

American

Acrobatic Monkeys, Wyandotte, 1930s, clown on cycle hits monkeys on rod and they spin, lithographed tin, 10" base, NM (EX box), from $400.00 to $425.00.

Acrobatic Monkeys, Wyandotte, 1930s, clown on cycle hits monkeys on rod & they spin, 10" dia, NM (EX box), from $400 to...$425.00

Acrobats, Ives, 1875, 2 pnt wooden figures w/papier-mache heads against shadow box, silk costumes, clockwork, 8", EX, A...$2,300.00

Action Clown Mobile, Mattel #463, 1952, plastic, friction, 7", NMIB, P4.....................................$85.00

Aero Zep, Buffalo Toys, 1925, 3 zeppelins circle tower w/spinning props, litho tin & celluloid, 14", NM (EX box), A.....................................$550.00

Alpine Cable Car Ride, Ohio Art, 2 cable cars travel up & down 3-level slope, litho tin, NM.....................................$125.00

American Railway Express w/Trailer, Lindstrom, tandem trailer w/hinged roof, litho tin, 16", EX, A.....................$675.00

Artie Car, Unique Art, smiling clown in dunce-type hat rides crazy car w/dog on hood, 7", VG, from $200 to.......$250.00

Auto-Laundry, Ranger Steel, crank action releases car down ramp, litho tin, 14", NM (EX box), A.....................$315.00

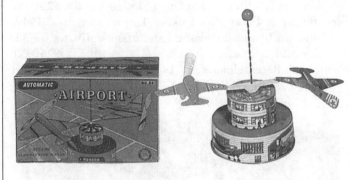

Automatic Airport, Ohio Art, 2 airplanes circle tower, lithographed tin with celluloid props, 9", EX+ (EX box), A, $350.00.

Baggage Cart w/Operator, Unique Art, operator on front platform guides 4-wheeled flat cart w/baggage, 14", VG+, A.....................................$175.00

Bear, Henry's Toy Warehouse, plush w/carved wooden hands & ft, red mouth w/simulated teeth, 9", M (orig wood box), A $600.00

Betty, Lindstrom, 1930s, litho tin girl in bib overalls vibrates around, 8", NM, A..................................$300.00

Billiard Players, Ranger Steel, 1930s, 2 men at pool table, ball is hit when activated, 14", EX (EX+ box), from $300 to $325.00

Bombo the Monk, Unique Art, monkey swings from palm tree, litho tin, 10", EX (orig box) from $150 to $250.00

Bugs Bunny & Porky Pig, Talking Toy/Warner Bros, 1949, litho tin figures on plastic base, crank activates sound, EX+ $250.00

Capitol Hill Racer, Unique Art, 1930, spring lever action, litho tin, 16", M (taped box) from $250 to......................$275.00

Carnival Shooting Gallery, Ohio Art, NMIB, $150.00.

Photo courtesy of Continental Hobby House.

Cinderella, Irwin Toys/WDP, 1950s, connected figures of Cinderella & the Prince dancing, MIB, P6....................$225.00

Climbing Monkey, Lindstrom, monkey goes up & down rope, G (G box) $55.00

Clown Dancer, Ives, 1880s, jtd wood figure w/papier-mache head & cotton costume atop wooden box, clockwork, 9", EX, A...$1,725.00

Commando Joe, Ohio Art, US soldier w/rifle crawls in realistic motion, litho tin, 9", EX+ (EX+ box).....................$150.00

Coney Island Giant Dip, H Katz, 1920, roller coaster w/8 litho figures on car, 4 planes on towers, 19", EX+ (G box) $2,500.00

Crying Boy, Lindstrom, 1930s, child w/litho tears vibrates around, tin, 5", EX, A.......................................$175.00

Dancing Dude & Music Box, Mattel, cowboy does the jig on stage, hand crank, NM (box rprs) $130.00

Dancing Dutch Boy, Lindstrom, 1930s, boy w/concertina vibrates around, litho tin, 8", NM (EX box)...........$300.00

Dancing Indian, Lindstrom, 1930s, Indian w/knife & axe vibrates around, litho tin, 5½", EX, A $100.00

Dancing Lassie, Lindstrom, girl in plaid vibrates around, litho tin, 8", EX+..$155.00

Dandy Jim, Unique Art, 1921, clown dances & plays cymbals atop building, 9½", NM (worn box) from $1,000 to $1,100.00

Daredevil Motor Cop, Unique Art, lithographed tin, 8½", NM (G box), from $850.00 to $900.00.

Doin' the Howdy Doody, Unique Art, Howdy dances while Buffalo Bob plays piano, litho tin, EX (G box), S10..$1,400.00

Donald Duck, see also Walking Donald Duck

Donald Duck Carousel, Borgfeldt, Donald balances open umbrella w/attached figures & balls on wheeled base, 4", EX, A..$3,000.00

Donald Duck Rail Car, Lionel #1107, Donald & Pluto on house car, tin w/compo figures, 9½", EX (EX+ box) $1,600.00

Donald Duck Rail Car, Pride Lines, Donald & Pluto on house car w/track, O gauge, pnt steel, electric, 10", NMIB $170.00

Doodle-Bug, Nosco, 1950, plastic w/full-figure driver, 10", MIB, A $230.00

Drum Major, Wolverine, 1930s, beats drum & plays marching tune, litho tin, 14", EX $225.00

Elgin Street Sweeper, Nylint, yel litho metal w/plastic driver, turning brushes, rubber wheels, 8½", EX, from $160 to.....$175.00

Finnegan, Unique Art, bump-&-go, cb figure on front of luggage cart w/uncut cb luggage pcs, 14", NM (EX box)......$250.00

Fire Pumper, DP Clark, tin body w/wood seats & boiler, open center steering w/driver, spoke wheels, friction, 10", G-, A $385.00

Fire Truck, Renwal, 1950s, wht plastic w/blk rubber tires, friction, complete w/ladder, hose & firemen, 11", NM, A.......$250.00

Flasho the Mechanical Grinder, Girard, 1920s, G, from $150 to..$175.00

Gertie the Galloping Goose, Unique Art, 1930s, pecks & bounces, litho tin, 9½", EX (G box), A...................$175.00

GI Joe & His Jouncing Jeep, Unique Art, 1941, forward & reverse action, litho tin, 7", MIB $300.00

GI Joe & His Jouncing Jeep, Unique Art, 1941, forward & reverse action, litho tin, 8", VG..............................$175.00

GI Joe & His K-9 Pups, Unique Art, walks while carrying litho pups in cages, 9", EX, from $200 to.........................$300.00

Giant Ride Ferris Wheel, Ohio Art, 1950s, spins w/bell noise, litho tin, 17", NM+ (EX+ box)..............................$350.00

Girl on Velocipede, Brown & Stevens, ca 1875, hand-pnt tin & CI, compo head & cloth dress, 10", EX, A .:..........$1,600.00

Greatest Show on Earth, Lindstrom, 1930, elephant pulls circus wagon, other animals trailing behind, EX $1,700.00

Hee Haw, Unique Art, 1930s, farmer drives donkey cart w/crazy action, litho tin, 10½", NM, from $225 to $250.00

Hoky Poky, Wyandotte, 2 clowns in polka-dot suits & cone hats work red & yel handcar, litho tin, 6", EX, from $275 to $325.00

Home Run King, Selrite, 1930s, batter swings at ball, gr rectangular base, VG (G box) from $850 to $950.00

Honeymooners, Jackie Gleason Bus, Wolverine, 1955, tin friction w/litho images of characters in bus windows, 12", VG, A..$300.00

Hoppo the Mechanical Rabbit, Automatic Toy, rabbit advances w/cart, litho tin & plastic, 9", NM (EX+ box), from $50 to...$85.00

Hott & Trott, Unique Art, Black banjo & piano players, 5½", EX...$1,000.00

Humphery Mobile, Wyandotte, 1950, 9", NM, from $500 to $650.00

Humphrey Mobile, Wyandotte, 1950, boy on tricycle pulling slant-roof house, litho tin, 9", NM (G+ box), A.....$750.00

Jazzbo Jim, Unique Art, 1920s, Jim dances & plays banjo atop cabin, litho tin, 10", VG (VG box) from $550 to ...$650.00

Jet Roller Coaster, Wolverine, car travels down ramp into Ferris wheel mechanism, tin, 12", EX (G- box) from $250 to .$275.00

Johnny the Clown, Lindstrom, 1930s, clown w/hands behind back vibrates around, red & yel litho tin, 8", EX+ ..$225.00

Kiddy Cyclist, Unique Art, child on tricycle w/bell, erratic action, litho tin, 9", NM from $300 to $375.00

Krazy Kar, Unique Art, 1920s, soapbox racer style w/balloon design, yel wheels, farmer driving, EX (G box), from $575 to..$700.00

Li'l Abner and His Dogpatch Band, Unique Art, 1945, lithographed tin, 7", NMIB, from $850.00 to $900.00.

Li'l Abner & His Dogpatch Band, Unique Art, 1945, characters around piano, 7", EX (VG box) from $725 to $750.00

Lincoln Tunnel, Unique Art, vehicles travel road w/tunnels at both ends, cop in center, litho tin, 24", NM, A $325.00

Little Red Hen, Baldwin, hen lays wooden eggs & cackles, litho tin, crank action, 5", EX (G box), A $175.00

Loop De Loop, Wolverine, 1930s, car performs loop-the-loop, litho carnival scenes on base, 19", MIB...................$400.00

Man on the Flying Trapeze, Wyandotte #516, man swings & turns on trapeze, litho tin, 9", NMIB.......................$250.00

Mechanical Playground, Lee Mfg, playground base w/6 magnetized kids, several actions, VG..................................$190.00

Mickey Mouse Hand Car, Lionel, 1930s, Mickey & Minnie work hdl, 8-pc track, 8", NM (EX box)...............$2,200.00

Mickey Mouse Washing Machine, Ohio Art, 1930s, shows Mickey & Minnie washing clothes, 7½", NM (VG rare box) $1,100.00

Mickey Mouse Circus Train, Lionel, 1930s, lithographed tin with composition figure, EX (G box), $3,500.00.

Midget Roller Coaster, Reeves Mfg, car (not included) navigates track from top to bottom, litho tin, 10", EX (G box), A $300.00

Monkey Shines, Emporium Specialties, 1950, monkey goes up & down palm tree, litho tin w/paper leaves, 18", MIB, A .$300.00

Mr Machine, Ideal, 1960s (later version), robot-type man w/lettered hat, plastic, 16", G..$100.00

Music Box Carousel, Mattel, 1953, riders & horses move up & down as they circle, crank action, 9", NM (NM box), A..$215.00

Musical Merry-Go-Round, Ohio Art, 1954, airplanes & horses spin, litho tin, 9", NM (EX+ box), A $525.00

Musical Merry-Go-Round, Wolverine, 1930s, rotates as planes fly out, litho tin, lever action, 13", NM $450.00

Musical Sail Away, Unique Art, kids in 3 plastic boats attached to canopy fly out & circle lighthouse, 9", EX (G box) $265.00

Mystery Alpine Express, Automatic Toy, train cars navigate track w/tunnel & station, litho tin, 20", EX+ (EX box) $230.00

Mystery Gas Station, Ideal, 1950s, cars travel around gas station, litho tin & plastic, complete, 18", EX, A................$275.00

Neck & Neck, Wolverine, turn crank & 4 horses w/jockeys race down track, litho tin, NM (G box) from $200 to....$225.00

No. 31 Merry-Go-Round, Wolverine, 1950s, plays music as it turns, lithographed tin, MIB, J6, $500.00.

Oreo Tailspin Pup, Orianna Metal Products, 1940s, spinning action, 5", MIB, S10, from $75 to $100.00

Peter Rabbit Chick-Mobile, Lionel, 1930s, Peter pumps handcar, painted composition and steel, 10", EX, from $600.00 to $625.00.

Rap & Tap in a Friendly Scrap, Unique Art, 1921, boxers jump around in boxing ring, litho tin, 6", NM (EX box), A..$1,600.00
Red Ranger Ride 'Em Cowboy, Wyandotte, 1930s, cowboy on horse mounted on rocking platform, litho tin, 7", EX.$175.00
Roadster, Kingsbury, driver in open car, disk wheels, litho tin, 11", rpt, G, A..$200.00
Rodeo Joe, Unique Art, jeep travels w/crazy action as figure bounces in seat, litho tin, 7", VG.............................$225.00
Rowboat Mary, Ives, Pat 1869, female figure in bl dress seated in tin boat w/wooden oars, 13", VG+, A $4,300.00
Runabout Auto, Fallows, blk w/gold trim, lady driver w/dog, spiked wheels, string-operated spool motor, 7", VG, A $2,860.00
Sandy Andy Full Back, Wolverine, football player on lettered base, litho tin, 8", NMIB......................................$1,000.00
Santa Car, Lionel, features Mickey Mouse in Santa's bag, MIB $1,500.00
Santa Hand Car, Pride Lines, Santa works car w/trees on trailers, w/track, O gauge, electric, 9½", EX (EX box) $170.00
Santa Walker, Ives, ca 1880, clothed in hooded jacket & pants, 9", EX, A $800.00
Scooter-Girl, Buffalo Toys, 1925, girl in swimsuit drives golf cart-type scooter in figure-8 pattern, 7", NM (EX box)......$515.00
See-Saw Circus, Lewco Products, 1940s, VG, from $150 to .$200.00
See-Saw Motion Toy, Gibbs, 2 pnt tin figures on rod that spins up & down pole, 14", EX (damaged box), from $250 to $300.00
Skeeter Duck #55, Lindstrom, advances in 'S' pattern, head moves, rubber bumper, 9½", NM (EX box)............$135.00
Ski Jumper, Wolverine, skier rolls down track & somersaults over obstacle, litho tin, MIB, A $400.00
Sky Rangers Tower, Unique Art, 1930s, plane & zeppelin circle tower, litho tin, EX, from $275 to $325.00
Spark Plug (Wa-Gee Walker), gold cloth & felt over tin, 9", VG, A $440.00
Spiral Speedway, Automatic Toy, 1950s, 2 buses travel on track that loops on overpass, MIB...................................$200.00

Stardust Racer #30, mk Made in USA New York, cream, orange & bl litho tin, 6½", minor rust & soiling, A............$160.00
Streetcar, Kingsbury, orange litho tin w/blk rubber disk-type tires, cut-out windows, w/seats, top crank, 14", VG, A........$440.00
Stutz Roadster, 1914, Gilbert, yel w/blk trim, spoked wheels, w/driver, 9", EX, A $850.00
Sunbeam Racer, Kingsbury, red-pnt pressed steel w/Am flag decal, 12 rear pipes, w/driver, 18½", EX (torn box), A $2,750.00
Sunny Andy Kiddie Kampers, Wolverine, 1930s, w/active semaphore scout, litho tin, 14", rare, EX+, from $350 to.................$400.00
Sunny Andy Tank, Wolverine, 1930s, advances w/sound, blk & yel litho tin, 15", EX (VG box).............................$350.00
Sweeping Mammy, Lindstrom, 1930s, vibrates around while sweeping, 8", NM (EX+ box), A..............................$400.00

Toe Joe, Ohio Art, MIB, from $150.00 to $175.00.

Transitional Phaeton, Hafner, 1902, gr-pnt sheet metal w/velvet upholstering, open 2-seater, spoke wheels, 10", VG, A.$2,530.00
US Mail/Parcel Post Auto Wagon, AC Gilbert, blk & yel litho tin w/red spoked wheels, driver, clockwork, 8", VG, A $550.00
Wa-Gee Walker, see Spark Plug
Walking Bear, Ives, 1882, fur-covered w/wire muzzle & chain leash, holds walking stick, 8", NM, A..................$1,380.00
Walking Donald Duck, Lewis & Scott/Borgfeldt, pnt compo, 1 arm behind back & 1 in front, 10½", EX (worn box), A..$1,150.00
Walking Man w/3 Faces, Unique Art, man standing in suit w/revolving head that reveals 3 different faces, 8½", VG, A....$1,870.00
Zilotone, Wolverine, figure plays tunes on xylophone w/3 interchangeable disks, litho tin, 8½", NMIB $1,000.00

English

Airplane Carousel, mk Made in England, 3 celluloid airplanes spin around on pressed-steel base, 6", EX, A $225.00

Broderick Crawford Highway Patrol Car, Welsotoy, shows Dan Mathews on box, friction, 11", scarce, NM (NM box) .$350.00

Clown on Motorcycle, Mettoy, tin clown w/compo head on red, wht & bl cycle, wht-wall tin tires, 7¼", G, A..........$600.00

Crazy Bumper Car, mk Codeg, advances in erratic motion as driver turns head, tin w/rubber bumper, 10", EX $125.00

Double-Decker Bus, Tri-ang Minic, advertising on sides, 7½", MIB, from $200 to...$250.00

Express Delivery Truck, Whittance, early red tin wagon-type auto w/gray spoked wheels, open driver's seat, 5", VG, A $2,300.00

Ford Saloon, Minic, bl, 3½", NM (EX+ box) $150.00

Inverted Clown, Wells, stars & crescent moons on pants, litho tin, EX (EX box), S10 ....$200.00

Jab & Gus on Handcar, celluloid figures on litho tin handcar w/image of blk cat, 8", NM....................................$600.00

Mickey Mouse Circus Train, Wells, Silver Link engine, Mickey in tender, VG (orig box), A.................................$2,100.00

Mickey Mouse Handcar, Wells, 1948, Mickey & Donald work car, Pluto & Horace shown on sides, MIB, from $1,500 to...$1,750.00

Mr Porter & His Truck, elderly man drives baggage cart w/bump-&-go action, litho tin, 12", EX (EX box), A...$450.00

Nautilus Submarine, 20,000 Leagues Under the Sea, Sutcliffe, MIB, S10, from $450 to..................................$500.00

Police Car, Tri-ang Minic, No 2, red plastic w/blk rubber tires, dual roof airhorns, w/foldout catalog, NM (NM box), A..$145.00

Royal Mail Van, Minic, red tin w/decals, 3½", EX.........$110.00

Santa Claus, Brimtoy, 1940s, 4", EX (original box), from $350.00 to $375.00.

Photo courtesy of Dunbar Gallery.

Searchlight Lorry, Minic, electric searchlight, Shell gas can, blk tin w/rpl rubber tires, NM (EX box) $585.00

Taxi, Minic, blk tin, complete w/meter & spare tire on rear, 4", NM (EX box)..$275.00

Tractor, Mettoy, litho tin, 7½", NM (EX box), M5 ....$100.00

Transport Express Van, Minic, bl tin w/decals, 3½", NM, from $80 to..$125.00

Vauxhall Cabriolet, Minic, lt bl tin, rpl wht rubber tires, 5", EX, from $130 to $160.00

Vauxhall Tourer Convertible, Minic, gr & blk tin, 5", NM (EX box)..$180.00

French

Alpha Romeo Racer #2, CIJ, bright bl pressed steel w/red trim, blk rubber tires, working steering wheel, 21", EX, A...$2,420.00

Bellvue, 2 cars travel through tunnels & stations on 3-D base w/litho country scenes, 13" base, NM (EX box) $230.00

Boy on Velocipede, cloth-dressed figure w/bsk head on red wire trike, 7", NM, A $2,970.00

Bugatti Racer #2, JEP, red litho tin w/yel & blk stripes, disk wheels, w/driver, 9", EX, A.....................................$600.00

Bugatti Racer #3, JEP, red w/circular spoked wheels, silver grille w/emb Bugatti logo, w/driver, 14", G, A...............$1,650.00

Bugatti Racer #4, JEP, bl boat-tail w/blk trim, spoked wheels, w/driver, 17", EX, A...$3,250.00

Circus Boy, Joustra, clown boy turns head as he rings bell & waves, litho tin, 6", EX+, A $350.00

Citroen Fire Engine, red open style w/ladders & hose reels, blk rubber tires w/red hubs, 2 firemen, EX, A.............$1,320.00

Citroen Wagon, Joustra, 1960s style, tailgate opens, pnt & litho tin, friction, 8", VG (orig box)................................$120.00

Civilian Motorcycle, JML, 1930s, litho tin w/full-figure driver, balloon tires, 12", EX, A...$935.00

Climbing Fireman, Martin, ca 1910, articulated tin figure climbs & descends triangular ladder, 8", G, from $575 to ..$625.00

Compagnie General Des Omnibus (Double-Decker Bus), yel pnt tin w/red trim, spoked wheels, 4 compo figures, 10", G, A..$580.00

Dancing Couple, Martin, hand-pnt tin, she in pk cloth dress & he in red & blk cloth suit, 7½", some rpt, A $635.00

Delahaye Hose Truck, red w/blk & gold trim, rubber tires, Boucher fireman doll, battery-op lights, 16", G, A..$935.00

Horse-Drawn Cart, early 1900s, galloping horse on single wheel pulls 2-wheeled cart w/driver, flywheel, 8½", G, A.$200.00

Le Clown Orchestre, VB&C, clown sits atop piano & plays w/his feet, rings bells w/hands, tin w/cloth suit, 11", VG, A...$990.00

Le Pochard, Martin, ca 1900, walking drunk, hand-pnt tin, orig clothes, 8", EX+ (orig box).......................................$975.00

Melon Boy, Martin, Black boy pulling melon wagon in zigzag motion, G (orig box), A...$1,650.00

Military Motorcycle w/Sidecar, SFA, driver w/armed passenger, litho tin, 4", VG $250.00

Miracle Car, stop-&-go, hood & driver's door open showing chauffer attached to door, 6", EX (EX box), from $175 to...$210.00

Moto-Police, SFA, 1930s, policeman in sidecar w/sparking machine gun, balloon tires, 4", EX (EX box), S10...$450.00

Mysterious Ball Toy, Martin, 1906, string clockwork activates figure in ball, tin, 12", VG, from $800 to................$900.00

Performing Clowns, 1 performs on parallel bars & 1 on 2 wooden chairs, tin & compo w/cloth suits, 11", VG, A..$440.00

Perpetual Motion Acrobat, P&F, compo clown, interconnecting metal rods allow endless motion, 16", VG (orig box), A $220.00

Rabbit in Cage, Martin, rabbit in exercise wheel attached to rabbit house, hand-pnt tin, 8", G, A.................................$140.00

Renault Limousine, CR, tan & brn tin, open driver's seat, blk spoke wheels, scrolled luggage rack atop, 10", VG, A.$825.00

Roadster, Pintel, 1920s, brn open boat-tail w/blk running boards, front crank, 7", very rare, VG, A $770.00

Ruban Bleu Speedboat, JEP, wht tin boat w/compo driver, prop spins, lever-activated steering, 13", NM (EX+ box) .$600.00

Streamline Sedan, Rosinol, brn & yel litho tin w/full running boards, wht tin tires, 14", EX, A.................................$580.00

Street Bus, Chas Rossignol, litho tin long-nose w/extended roof, destinations listed, 8½", EX $750.00

Street Bus, JEP, litho tin 6-wheeled long-nose w/extended roof, destinations listed, 10½", EX, A $800.00

Swimming Fish, CIJ, tail moves, pnt & stenciled tin fish on wooden base, crank on mouth, 17", EX (EX box) .$1,400.00

Touring Car, JEP, open car, windshield divider, rear spare & luggage trunk, disk wheels, w/driver, 21", EX, A.......$5,500.00

Trained Bear, Martin, walks w/tin bar on shoulders, hand-pnt tin w/fabric body, chained mouth & neck, 7", EX, A...$1,100.00

German

Airship, M&K Mueller, man seated between propeller & airship attached to revolving rod on center pole, EX, A..$4,750.00

Amusement Park Airplane, WK, litho tin w/celluloid props, battery-op lights, 12", EX.................................$1,000.00

Andy Sparkler (Amos 'n Andy), tin face in derby hat w/glass eyes smoking cigar, still sparks, 7", EX $750.00

Angel, Schuco, tin w/pk cloth robe & yel wings, 5", some moth damage o/w VG+ $1,485.00

Arabian Trotter, 1950s, travels in circles, tin & compo w/full-figure jockey, 6", NM (EX box), from $150 to.........$200.00

Army Transport Truck, Tipp & Co, 1938, open bed w/soldiers on bench seats, wht tires, 12", EX, A......................$660.00

Bagpipe Player, Gunthermann, standing on rnd base, hand-pnt tin, 10½", EX, A...$465.00

Ball Chute Toy, Gely, ball travels down chute to boy in soccer uniform, litho tin, 10", EX (orig box), A.................$660.00

Balloon Vendor, 1940s, holding Mickey Mouse & animals on string in 1 hand & balloons in the other, gr base, EX, from $750 to...$1,000.00

Bandit Chase, Gunthermann, cop on motorcycle circles car, litho tin & plastic, 14", EX+ (VG+ box), A............$175.00

Barney Google & Spark Plug, Nifty, 1920s, Barney riding Spark Plug, 7", VG, from $900 to $1,200.00

Barrel Clown, Erco/US Zone, clown balances on barrel as it rolls, 8", rare, EX (EX box).....................................$825.00

Beetle, Gunthermann, 1911, advances in erratic motion, tin, 8", VG $150.00

Bicycle Clown, Technofix/US Zone, clown peddles bicycle as head bobs, 5½", EX+, A...$940.00

Black Native on Alligator, mk Made in Germany, advances w/flapping jaw, native holds onto rope, 15", EX, from $200 to...$250.00

BOBY, US Zone, circus monkey peddles tricycle in circular motion, litho tin, 4", VG+ $175.00

Boy on Sled, Hess, boy on belly w/jtd arms steers sled w/cast wheels, litho tin, 7", VG $450.00

Boy Riding Dog, dog is mounted on rockers, hand-pnt tin, 6½", G-, A...$145.00

Cable Car, Technofix #303, cars travel from station house up mountain as 2 others travel road, 18", NMIB, from $250 to..$300.00

Canvas-Covered Truck, Orobr, 1920, litho tin, bl body w/arched simulated gray canvas top, open cab, w/driver, 6", VG, A...$300.00

Capt Campbell's Blue Bird Racer, Gunthermann, litho tin w/Am & British flag decals, w/driver, 20", EX (orig box), A $2,750.00

Carnival Airplane Carousel, 1950s, 4 litho tin airplanes w/celluloid props circle tower, 9", NM (EX box) $450.00

Cat Chasing Mouse, 1930s, cat & mouse on wires attached to rnd base chase each other, litho tin, 10", EX+ (EX box) $365.00

Charlie Chaplin, Schuco, tin w/cloth outfit, 6½", EX (EX box) $1,500.00

Charlie Chaplin, Schuco, tin w/cloth outfit, 6½", G $900.00

Charlie Chaplin, see also Happy Jack

Charlie Chaplin Walker, Schuco, litho tin w/CI shoes, 8½", EX (orig box)...$1,000.00

Chinaman Playing Banjo, Gunthermann, figure seated on rock playing mandolin, hand-pnt tin, 8½", G-, A...........$320.00

Civilian Motorcycle, Arnold, advances w/sparks, litho tin w/full-figure driver, 8", NM (EX box), from $900 to $1,200.00

Clarinet Player & Dancer, clown w/clarinet seated on drum playing to dancer in cloth dress on platform, tin, 9", rpr, A...$935.00

Clown Circus Cart, G&K, 1930, travels in erratic motion as clown holds steering wheel, litho tin, 6", VG+, A ..$350.00

Coney Island Carnival Ride, Technofix, 2 cars navigate track, vacuform plastic and tin, 20", NM (EX+ box), from $275.00 to $325.00.

Clown Musicians, EHN, 1940s, 2 seated clowns on base playing drums & cymbals, litho tin, 8½", EX, from $600 to .$750.00

Clown Musicians, Gunthermann, 1890s, 2 seated clowns w/violin & bells, musical, pnt tin, gr beveled base, VG+, A.....................................$1,380.00

Clown Riding Donkey, clown in yel costume on donkey, hand-pnt tin, 5½", EX $725.00

Clown w/Running Dogs, Tipp, 2 dogs & clown on wheels, litho tin, 8¼", EX, A $1,200.00

Clown w/Trick Dog, clown w/wand seated on wheeled platform, upright dog at other end, hand-pnt tin, 6", EX, A...$825.00

Club Sedan (1933), Tipp, orange & gray tin sedan w/electric lights, simulated spoke wheels, running boards, 17", EX, A.....................................$1,045.00

Comical Conductor, Kellerman, hand-activated figure w/lg animated head, litho tin, 5½", EX, A $300.00

Cowboy on Horse, GNK/US Zone, tin, MIB, S10, from $175 to $200.00

Crawling Baby Buttercup, articulated baby w/single curl atop head, litho tin, 7½", G, A.....................................$100.00

Cyclist & Stunt Man, Arnold, cyclist & stunt man hold spoked wheels & revolve in unison, 11½", VG, from $525 to $675.00

Dalli Car, Schuco, driver w/glasses & hat in cream convertible sports car, NMIB, from $350 to.....................................$450.00

Dancers, Schuco, mother rabbit holds & swings plastic baby w/floppy ears & pipe-stem legs, 4¼", EX, from $150 to.$200.00

Donald Duck, Schuco, 1930s version, vibrates around while opening and closing bill, tin, 6", rare, EX (VG box), from $750.00 to $850.00.

Double-Decker Bus, Orobr, advances w/full-figure chauffer in driver's seat, litho tin, 6", VG+, A..........................$300.00

Double-Decker Streetcar, Orobr, cream litho tin w/brn striped trim, cut-out windows, w/guide rod, 10", EX $600.00

Drinking Mouse, Schuco, raises ceramic beer mug, tin w/cloth clothes, 4", EX, from $175 to $200.00

Drummer Boy, early, beats drum w/sticks when activated, pnt tin w/pointed hat, 7", G, A $275.00

Express Boy Porter, US Zone, porter pushes trunk, stops & kicks his legs, compo & tin, 3", NM (EX scarce box), A..$350.00

Express Delivery Truck, Orobr, 1920, gr litho tin, enclosed body w/roof extending over open cab, w/driver, 6", VG ..$325.00

Ferry, Nifty, 1920s, forward & reverse action, pump assembly goes up & down, tin, 8", rare, from $275 to.............$400.00

Fishing Fred, US Zone, man holding metal pole w/attached fish on simulated pond, litho tin, 6", NMIB.................$400.00

Flamenco Dancer, Gunthermann, hand-pnt tin female figure, 8", G, A.....................................$415.00

Flying Trapeze Artist, Gunthermann, articulated figure on wire trapeze w/rear prop, 8", EX.....................................$1,100.00

Flying Trapeze Artist, Gunthermann, articulated figure on wire trapeze w/rear prop, 8", G.....................................$650.00

Ford Model T Sedan, Bing, ca 1925, blk tin w/metal spoke wheels, w/driver, 6½", EX $425.00

Format Coupe 2900, Arnold, lt gauge steel, 2 compo figures, 10", NM (damaged box) $300.00

Friendly Cycle, Technofix, litho tin w/male driver & female passenger, friction, 8", EX, from $350 to.......................$500.00

Gardener, woman holding watering can & rake over her shoulder, hand-pnt tin, 7", rstr, A $220.00

George Washington Bridge, Bueschel/Borgfeldt, 1930s, Greyhound bus travels bridge, tin, 25", scarce, NM (partial box), A.....................................$1,400.00

German Military Motorcycle, Kellerman, German soldier on camouflage cycle w/headlight, tin, 7½", EX, from $475 to.....................................$600.00

German Submarine, Arnold, advances w/spinning prop, red & gr tin w/swivel deck gun, fences, tower & Nazi flag, EX .$500.00

Girl on Potty, mk Yellowstone Park, litho tin, hand action, 5", EX, A $330.00

Girl w/Baby, Schuco, cloth clothing & hat, NM, from $145 to.....................................$185.00

Gordon Bennet Car, Gunthermann, open 2-seater w/driver, wht w/shamrock decal, flywheel mechanism, 6", VG, A .$2,300.00

Go-Kart, Schuco #1055, advances with sound, 6", NM (NM box), from $375.00 to $400.00.

Hand-Standing Clown, US Zone, balances on hands & moves back & forth, 5", NM, S10 ....$350.00

Happy Jack (Charlie Chaplin), Kraus, diecut Charlie dances on base, litho tin, lever action, scarce, EX, A $900.00

Hessmobile, Hess Matthews, 1918, gr convertible w/red trim, spoked wheels, w/driver, 9", EX, A $1,700.00

Hi-Way Henry, c Oscar Hitt, crazy car with dog-house hood, stove pipe on rear and clothesline on roof, 10", NM, from $2,250.00 to $2,500.00.

Hopsa Monkey w/Mouse, Schuco, plush monkey twirls & lifts mouse up & down, 5", NM (EX box), from $300 to.$400.00

Horse-Drawn Coach, Orobr, 1910, red & yel tin coach w/red spoked wheels, 2 horses & driver, 8½", VG, A $600.00

Howdy Doody the Live Acrobat, Arnold/Kagran, Howdy Doody performs tricks on trapeze, lever action, 15", NM (EX box) $1,200.00

Jack Sprat, Gunthermann, early 1900s, Jack & his wife dance, pnt tin, 6½", rpt, EX..$460.00

Jackie, Gundka & Kelpert, articulated ostrich pulling boy in 4-wheeled cart, litho tin, 9½", EX, A $1,155.00

Jalopy, Orobr, 1920s, blk 4-door w/gold lettering, doors open, wht tires w/spoked wheels, 6", missing door, EX finish, A..$115.00

Jazzman, Black musician holding saxophone & cymbal on both ankles on sq platform, lever action, 7", VG, from $250 to..........$300.00

Jubilating Singing Bird, GNK, moves mouth & sings, wings & tail flap, litho tin w/plastic legs, 7", NM (EX box), A $195.00

Jumbo the Elephant, US Zone, olive gr, orange & yel, working, VG, S10 ....$150.00

Katrinka Lifting Jimmie, Nifty, 1923, Katrinka advances as she lifts Jimmy in wheelbarrow, 6½", EX....................$2,000.00

Krazy Kat on Skooter, Nifty, 1920s, tin, EX $1,200.00

Lasso Cowboy, US Zone, cowboy spins lasso overhead as horse spins around base, litho tin, 6", EX+ (EX box).......$225.00

Laughing Black Man, figure in top hat peers through podium & laughs, litho tin, 7", EX, A $275.00

Limousine, Bing, bl litho tin w/blk roof, disk hubs, rear doors open, w/driver, 12", EX, A $2,100.00

Limousine, Bing, 1908, maroon w/yel trim, beige top, rubber tires w/spoked wheels, lady driver, 14", EX, A......$4,400.00

Limousine, Bub, brn w/yel & red trim, fold-out glass windshield, rubber tires w/spoked wheels, w/driver, 14", EX, A..$1,700.00

Limousine, Bub, red open cab w/blk extended roof, fenders & trim, spoked wheels, 8", EX, A $440.00

Limousine, Carette, 1910, beige w/red & bl trim, barge glass windows, luggage rack atop, w/driver, 13", VG, A $2,200.00

Limousine, Fischer, brn, open-sided driver's cab, 2 side lamps, rear folding canopy, w/driver, 8½", VG+, A $2,600.00

Limousine, Fischer, ca 1910, maroon w/blk vertical stripe, luggage rack atop, spoked wheels, w/driver, 13", VG, A.......$3,400.00

Limousine, Hess, 1910, gr w/blk roof, red trim & interior, orange spoke wheels, front crank, no driver, 10", VG, A..$1,045.00

Limousine, Moko, gr litho tin w/2 opening doors & lift-up hood that reveals working engine, w/driver, 10", EX, A...$770.00

Limousine, Rissman, orange & tan litho tin, chauffer exits car to let out lady passenger, 9½", EX, A........................$4,070.00

London General Bus, Distler, conductor moves about collecting tickets, litho tin dbl-decker w/rear stairs, 9", VG+, A $1,200.00

Mac 700 Motorcycle, Arnold/US Zone, driver dismounts when activated, litho tin, red, 7½", EX, from $850 to $950.00

Maggie & Jiggs, Nifty, figures fighting on 4-wheeled platform joined by spring, litho tin, 7", G, A6 ....$990.00

Maggie & Jiggs, Nifty, 7", EX, A................................$1,550.00

Major Seagrave's Golden Racer, Gunthermann, gold salt-flat-type racer showing British flag, w/driver, 21", EX (EX box) $2,000.00

Man Carrying Bananas, dapper Black man carrying bananas in both hands, litho tin, 7½", EX, A......................$2,860.00

Mercedes Phaeton, Huki, 1912, open w/V-radiator, gr, beige, bl & red litho tin, w/driver, 3", VG, A $440.00

Mercedes Racer, Marklin, silver, limited edition, 12", M (orig box w/clasp closure), from $200 to..........................$350.00

Merry-Go-Round, Gunthermann, red, wht & bl w/attendant & children on horses & pigs, serrated band around top, 8", EX..$725.00

Micey Maus (Mickey Mouse) Twisti Dancer, Schuco #941, waddles, plastic w/cloth clothes, 4", NM (EX box), from $450 to..$550.00

Mickey Mouse, S&S, plays cymbals attached to shoes, arms spread & saxophone moves, flat tin, squeeze action, 6", EX, A..$600.00

Mickey Mouse Hurdy-Gurdy, Nifty, ca 1931, Mickey operates wheeled cart while Minnie Mouse dances atop, 8", G..$1,400.00

Mickey Mouse Jazz Drummer (Closed Mouth), Nifty, plunger activated, litho tin w/jtd arms, 6½", EX, A..........$2,200.00

Mickey Mouse Jazz Drummer (Open Mouth), Nifty, plunger activated, litho tin w/jtd arms, 6½", NM $2,750.00

Minstrel, plays banjo, pnt tin figure in top hat & tails, 8", G, A $500.00

Minstrel, plays tambourine & holds umbrella, tin w/cloth clothes, 9", G, A $330.00

Mirako Peter Cycle, Schuco #1013, 1950s, full-figure driver w/wild blond hair, litho tin, 5", scarce, EX $825.00

Miraocar 1001, Schuco, non-fall action, red tin streamlined body, 4½", EX+ (EX box) $180.00

Mobile Racer, Hess, olive gr w/orange trim, front hand crank, diecut tin driver, 8", NM, A.....................................$770.00

Monkey Drummer, Distler, realistic figure in red fez & jacket marching w/drum on gr platform, 8", EX, A $650.00

Photo courtesy of Dunbar Gallery.

Monkey on Trike, Arnold/US Zone, highly detailed monkey pedals and steers tricycle, 3½", VG, from $200.00 to $250.00.

Motorcycle w/Driver, Gunthermann, red w/full splash guards & detailed engine, spoked wheels, 7", NM, A.........$3,520.00

Motorcycle w/Driver, Schuco, orange w/silver tank, litho tin, 5", NM $450.00

Motorcycle w/Driver, Technofix/US Zone, red, 7", VG.$280.00

Motorcycle w/Sidecar, orange w/wht striping, Dunlop tires, driver w/lady passenger, 10", VG, A $1,300.00

Motorcycle w/Sidecoach, Gundka, driver & lady passenger w/umbrella, litho tin, 6½", EX, A.........................$2,420.00

Mountain Express, Technofix/US Zone, bus travels along tracks & through Alpine mountains, 45", NM (VG box), from $200 to..$250.00

Mouse in Convertible, Schuco, Sonny 2005, bl car w/gray fabric mouse, tin, 6", G, from $220 to................................$260.00

Musical Carousel, prewar, circles as music plays, 2 motorcycles w/drivers & 2 fore trucks, tin, rare, VG, from $450 to $600.00

Mystery Car & Garage, PN #900, enters & exits garage in circular motion, litho tin, EX+ (EX+ box) $390.00

Old Lady, Bing, woman wearing scarf & glasses holding basket & folded umbrella, hand-pnt tin, 7", G, A $200.00

Old Sailor, Gama, advances in waddling motion, litho tin, 7", EX, A $430.00

Organ Grinder & Monkey, Gunthermann, ca 1900, pnt tin, musical, 9", VG $3,500.00

Peacock, Eberl, 10", EX, M5.....................................$250.00

Performing Circus Elephant, balances object on nose, separate tin lever moves ball in see-saw motion, 8", NM (EX box), A...$185.00

Phaeton, Carette, ca 1905, figures in 2-seater sedan, glass windshield, luggage rack atop, spoke wheels, 9", VG, A...$2,300.00

Phaeton, Gunthermann, 1908, figure in wht car w/red trim, wht tires w/red spokes, 7", EX, A $1,430.00

Phaeton, Orobr, 1915, red open-seater w/2 folding jump seats & 2 bench seats, gray running boards, 8", VG, A $800.00

Pigmyphone, Bing, gr litho tin, 3x6x6", EX, M5 ....$390.00

Police Car, Arnold, blk & wht litho tin, chrome trim, wht-walls, w/driver, friction, 10", EX, A $440.00

Police Motorcycle, TCO/West Germany, gr, w/driver, 11", EX $550.00

Police Patrol Motorcycles, PN, 2 drivers on cycles in slanted position on wheeled platform, 6½", NM, from $650 to..$800.00

Police Varianto 3040, Fernlenk Auto, Schuco, 2-tone VW w/adjustable gearing for speed, litho tin, 4", MIB, from $300 to $400.00

Pool Player, Kico, 1912, single player w/cue at table, litho tin, 6", G...$300.00

Pot Ball Clown, George Levy, 1935, clown w/parasol & duck atop chute, several actions, litho tin, 9½", EX+ ..$1,025.00

Rabbit w/Cymbals, Gunthermann, 9½", EX..................$375.00

Race Car Loop, Arnold, car shoots around loop & automatically stops, litho tin, M (EX box) $200.00

Racer, Hess, gr litho tin open racer w/2 red side-by-side front seats, spoke wheels, tailgate & hood opens, 9", VG, A $1,320.00

Racer #3, Schuco, red, 5½", EX $175.00

Racer #6, AS, 1908, beige litho tin w/gold trim, slanted back, center steering wheel, spoke wheels, w/driver, 7", VG, A $855.00

Radio Man, Kellermann, articulated litho tin figure atop domed crank base, 8", G, A...$385.00

Rallye 66 Racing Set, Technofix, complete with 2 cars and track, EX (orig box), from $300.00 to $350.00.

Riding Cowboy, US Zone, horse vibrates while cowboy twirls lasso, litho tin, 6", EX (EX box), from $175 to........$200.00

Roadster, Karl Bub, wht w/red trim & 2 simulated upholstered front seats, w/driver, 9", VG, A $1,650.00

Roundabout Carnival Ride, Muller & Kadeder, 3 figures in canoes w/paper propellers spin around base, tin, 13", G, A.$1,100.00

Roundabout Carnival Ride, W&K, 4 figures in swings that spin around on base w/flags atop pole, tin, 13", EX, A..$1,375.00

Rowboat Carnival Ride, US Zone, 4 rowboats w/child passengers swing as melody plays, striped canopy overhead, 9", NM $400.00

Santa Driving Roadster, Tipp, tin car w/assorted litho toys, balloons & animals, clockwork w/battery-op tree, VG, A..$7,150.00

Scottie Dog, Schuco, advances w/moving legs, tin & plush, 4½", NM, from $160 to...$185.00

Seal, DRGM, litho tin, 7½", VG, from $100 to $130.00

Ship Ahoy, Distler, several actions, lithographed tin, 10" base, rare, EX (EX box), A, $2,000.00.

Silver Arrow Racer, Marklin, limited edition, 11", M (orig box w/clasp), from $250 to $400.00

Silver Mine Express, Technofix #314, engine car travels from station house to ramp & returns, litho tin, 23", MIB, A...$275.00

Skidoodle Car, Nifty, back-to-back characters on car, litho tin, 10½", EX, A $2,860.00

Slugger Champions, Biller/US Zone, 2 boxers in ring, 3½x3½", VG+..$250.00

Smitty Scooter, Nifty, 1920s, 8", G...............................$675.00

Solisto Clown Drummer, Schuco, vibrates while beating snare drum, tin w/cloth clothes, 4½", NM (EX box)........$500.00

Solisto Clown Juggler, Schuco, vibrates while juggling, tin w/cloth clothes, 5", scarce, NM+ $500.00

Solisto Monkey Violinist, Schuco, vibrates while playing, tin w/cloth clothes, 4½", MIB, from $325 to $350.00

Solisto Monkey Violinist, Schuco, 4½", EX+.................$275.00

Sonny 2005, Schuco, mouse drives convertible & swings balloon, red tin w/gray felt mouse, 5", NM (EX box), from $750 to..$850.00

Spark Plug, Sunshine & Barney Google Scooter Race, Nifty, articulated action on wheeled platform, litho tin, EX, A...$2,530.00

Sparking Choo Choo, Kraemer, 1950s, litho tin, friction, complete w/tracks, 17", M (VG box), A.........................$160.00

Strawbridge & Clothier Van, Tipp, litho tin, rear door opens, w/driver, 8", VG+..$1,980.00

Taxi, Fischer, red & blk tin coach w/open driver's seat, 2 upper side lamps, spoked wheels, w/driver, 9", EX, A.....$1,595.00

Taxi, Gunthermann, 1912, red tin w/blk trim & running boards, open passenger seat, wht tires w/red spokes, 10", EX, A..$2,640.00

Taxi (1922), Orobr, orange & blk litho tin sedan w/2 opening side doors, w/driver, 6", VG, A $200.00

Tick-Tack Express, US Zone, 2 buses travel track into tunnels & station house, 18", EX (G box) $225.00

Tipping Hat Clown, 1950s, advances in vibrating motion while tipping hat, litho tin, 6", scarce, EX........................$540.00

Toonerville Trolley, Nifty, 1922, red & yel litho tin, 6¾", NM $1,000.00

Topsy Turvy Car, Rissman, mc litho tin crazy car w/roll bars, chrome hubs, clown driver, 10", EX, A $1,100.00

Touchdown Chimp, Technofix, holds ball & moves legs rapidly, litho tin w/celluloid ball, 3", EX.............................$250.00

Touring Car, Fischer, tan litho tin 4-door convertible w/red trim, spoked wheels, driver & 2 lady passsengers, 9", EX, A $910.00

Touring Car, Hess, red tin w/2 side-by-side seats, center steering wheel, red spoke wheels, curved hood, EX, A $1,320.00

Towing Car, Gunthermann, 1920, red w/blk fenders, blk & wht striping, spoked wheels, w/driver, 10", VG+, A.......$290.00

Toy Vendor, 1930s, man raises toys on string & eyes shift as monkeys swing under box, litho tin, 6½", EX, A $500.00

Track & Engine, Technofix, engine pulls coal car along 2-tiered building site, litho tin, 23" track, NM (EX+ box), A..$175.00

Tractor, Distler, silver tin w/red spoke wheels, full-figure driver, 7", EX, M5 ....$325.00

Traffic Crossing w/Police Control, Technofix, vehicles navigate track, litho tin, 19" track, NM (EX box), A $300.00

Traffic Policeman, Gosco, trolley car & automobile travel in & out of garages, litho tin, 9½", EX, A $400.00

Tramp, waddles back & forth while swinging bag & umbrella, tin w/cloth outfit, 5", rare, EX, A...............................$165.00

Transworld Flyer, plane circles above base & lands on different countries, litho tin, NM (VG box) $200.00

Triumphator, horse & rider on gyroscope, flat tin figures, 4", EX (VG box) $180.00

Trolley Car, Gunthermann, red & yel litho tin w/sliding doors, interior bench seats, cable conductors, 15", EX, A .$1,540.00

Tumbling Mouse, Schuco, tumbles in continuous motion, felt over tin, 4", EX+, from $450 to...............................$600.00

Uncle Wiggily Car, crazy-quilt pattern, arm w/cane & ears rpl by Joe Freeman's Tin Toy Works, EX........................$1,000.00

Vis-A-Vis, Gunthermann, figure in pnt & litho tin open car, spoke wheels, 5", NMIB, A....................................$2,640.00

Vis-A-Vis, Gunthermann, figure in pnt & litho tin open car, spoke wheels, 10", EX, A $3,300.00

Walking Bear, Schuco, free-standing, golden mohair w/red felt jacket & hat, 10", EX, A $1,700.00

Walking Goose, fur over tin w/cloth outfit, carries wicker basket on back, 6½", EX, A...$165.00

Walking Hobo, Gama, advances in waddling motion, litho tin, 7", EX, A $430.00

Water-Driven Mill, early 1900s, pnt tin, 11", EX, A......$400.00

XK 120 Jaguar, Prameta/British Zone, travels w/3 speeds, chrome-plated, rubber wht-walls, 6", EX+ $350.00

Yellow Cab, Bing, blk & yel litho tin w/yel hubs, 8½", EX, A..$1,000.00

Zeppelin Go Round, Mueller Kadeder, pnt tin, 10½", VG..$770.00

Japanese

Acrocycle, Alps, cycle advances as clown flips over handlebars, litho tin, 6", EX+ (EX+ box), A $410.00

Agajanian Special Racer #98, Yonezawa, cream w/tan flame design on nose, chrome side pipes, bl hubs, driver, 18", G, A $3,080.00

Air Carousel, ATC, 3 planes w/child riders swing away from tower, lever action, celluloid & litho tin, 6", EX.....$120.00

Air Command Jeep, KKS, WWII jeep w/driver & rear gunner, 6", EX+ (torn flaps on box), A $85.00

American Circus, M, advances as 2 monkeys rock & 2 go up & down, litho tin, 7", EX, A $610.00

Amusement Park Rocket Ride, Yone, 2 rockets circle tower w/bell, litho tin, 8" base, EX (VG box)....................$200.00

Animal Barber Shop, mouse barber's head & arms move back & forth as if to shave rabbit customer, EX+ (VG box), A .$300.00

Animal's Playland, TPS, treehouse w/rotating animals, others on seesaw & swinging, litho tin, NMIB $325.00

Apache Rider, Haji, litho tin, 7", horse missing right ear, o/w VG, A $40.00

Army Jeep Set, Sanshin, tin, friction, complete w/jeep, driver & 3 trailers, 5", NM (EX box), A $200.00

Arty the Trapeze Artist, Toyland Toys, tumbles & somersaults on trapeze, celluloid, 12", scarce, MIB $150.00

Atom Motorcycle, TN, rider dismounts, litho tin, 11½", VG .$250.00

Atom Racer, box only, Marusan, full-color paper label featuring #9 racer, 8", EX, A $75.00

Atomic Race Car X-8, M, 1950s, w/driver, litho tin, friction, 6", EX (EX box), A $550.00

Automatic Racing Game, Haji, 3 cars advance from garage, plunger action, litho tin, EX (EX box), from $165 to .$225.00

Ball-Playing Giraffe, TPS, seated giraffe catches ball on wire, litho tin, 8½", NMIB, from $350 to..........................$400.00

Banjo Bunny, Alps, bunny sits on red tree trunk & plays banjo, celluloid bunny, 8", NM (G box)............................$225.00

Bar-B-Que Bear, Alps, plush bear pours sauce on hamburger & takes a bite, 7", EX+ (EX box) $145.00

Bar-X Cowboy, Alps, twirls lariat on horse, 6", EX (orig box) $225.00

Barney on Dino, advances in waddling motion w/sound, litho tin & vinyl, 8½", EX+ (EX+ box) $535.00

Baseball Catcher, celluloid, advances & circles w/realistic action, celluloid, 5½", M..$200.00

Batman, Billiken, 1989, advances w/swinging arms, litho tin w/vinyl cape, 9", MIB..$100.00

Batman Car, ASC, 1959, tin w/vinyl figure, blk rubber tires, friction, 8½", rare, NM (EX box), A $1,600.00

Bear, Occupied Japan, fur-covered tin, brn, 5", NM, M5 .$45.00

Bear Golfer, TPS, hits ball across ramp into net, litho tin, 4½", 1 ear missing o/w NM (EX box), from $225 to $250.00

Ben-Hur Trotter, Mikuni, litho tin chariot w/driver, 7½", rare, EX (NM box), A $210.00

Bestmaid Marionette Theatre, 2 celluloid figures on tin stage w/paper tent awning, 12x10", MIB, A $690.00

Big League Hockey Player, TPS, advances in erratic motion, kicks leg & shoots hockey puck, litho tin, 6", EX (EX box), A $375.00

Bird Cage, KS, 2 birds in cage fly upwards, 1 bird pecking at food & 1 rotates, litho tin, 10", NMIB, A........................$340.00

Black Boy on Mule, prewar, boy's legs move as mule advances, wood & celluloid, 8", NM, A $225.00

Boardwalk Delight, umbrella spins above girl & duck w/many other actions, litho tin & celluloid, 6" base, NM, A .$295.00

Bobby's Crazy Car, KO, early 1950s, clown in bumper car, litho tin & vinyl, 8", NM (EX box) $350.00

Bobo the Magician, TN, lifts hat & egg & chick appear, litho tin, 9", EX (G box mk Happy-Go-Lucky), A...........$500.00

Bobo the Magician, TN, lifts hat & egg & chick appear, litho tin, 9", NM $400.00

Bobo the Strong Man, TPS, bounces ball from hand to hand, 6", EX $350.00

Boxing Dog, Y, staggers side to side & boxes in erratic motion, litho tin & plush, 6", MIB $85.00

Bozo the Drumming Clown, Alps, 1950s, moves side to side while drumming, litho tin, 8", scarce, EX (EX+ box), A...$1,015.00

Bucking Bronco, 1950s, cowboy bounces up & down on bucking horse, celluloid & litho tin, 5½", MIB....................$115.00

Bump Car w/Pop-Up Clown, clown pops up when car hits solid object, litho tin, friction, 7", EX (EX box), from $135 to $200.00

Bumpety-Bump Convertible, GW, goes from convertible to coupe, 6", EX (EX box), A $95.00

Bunny Family Parade, TPS, 3 connected bunnies swivel behind mama as she advances, litho tin, 12", EX (EX+ box), A $95.00

Busy Mouse, TPS, mouse on base, several actions, litho tin, 6x9", NMIB, A $175.00

Butterfield Stagecoach, Alps, horses gallop & driver moves up & down, litho tin, 13", NM, A....................................$100.00

Calypso Joe, Linemar, native in grass skirt beats tune on tom tom, rocking platform, 6", EX $125.00

Camera Shooting (Cine) Bear, Linemar, bear lifts camera to lighted eyes, worms shoot out of camera, 11", MIB..............................$1,100.00

Carnival Ride, Yone, lithographed tin, 5½", EX, J6, $95.00.

Photo courtesy of June Moon.

Candy Loving Canine, TPS, flips candy in mouth, litho tin, 6", MIB...$250.00

Car Set, 1950s, Taxi, US Mail, G-Men, Red Cross, etc, litho tin, set of 12, ea 4", EX (orig box missing lid), A...........$525.00

Carnival Man, Alps, clown holding cane, litho tin w/cloth outfit, 9", MIB, A..$210.00

Casper the Ghost, Linemar, walking & bobbing movement, litho tin, 5", MIB, A...$550.00

Casper the Ghost Tank, Linemar, Casper forces tank to flip over, litho tin, 4", NM (NM box)............................$725.00

Champion Racer #98, ETC, Indianapolis-style racer w/driver, friction, 19", G-, A...$500.00

Circus Boat, KO, clown driver rocks as boat moves, litho tin & vinyl, friction, 7", NM (EX box), from $150 to.......$200.00

Circus Clown, TPS, advances in erratic motion on unicycle, litho tin, 6", NM (EX box), A.....................................$450.00

Circus Clown Robot in Mercedes, ATC/Cragstan, mk Circus 8, driver catapults from seat, siren sound, 8", NM (NM box)......$2,300.00

Circus Elephant, M, advances & turns as bell in trunk rings, litho tin w/full-figure rider, 7", rare, NM (EX box), A......$350.00

Circus Parade, TPS, elephant pulls 3 performing clowns, litho tin, 11", NM (EX+ box), from $300 to.....................$375.00

Circus Seal, TPS, shifts side to side while balancing ball on nose, 6", EX (VG box), from $175 to.................................$200.00

Circus Trailer, K, cab pulls cage w/tiger & 1 w/elephant, mk American Circus, litho tin, friction, 18", EX, A......$350.00

Circus Train, KKK, advances as tiger's body spins, clown faces at both ends, friction, 15", NM (EX box).....................$100.00

Clever Monkey Circus, Haji, monkey holds sign, peddles drum & turns, litho tin, 7", EX (EX box), A.....................$175.00

Clever Quacky, Alps, advances smoothly & shakes head w/frog in her mouth, litho tin, 6", EX (EX box), A..............$90.00

Climbing Pirate, TPS, climbs up & down rope pulled by finger loops, litho tin, 5½", NM+ (EX box).....................$225.00

Clown Jalopy Cycle, TPS, clown seated on cycle, litho tin, friction, 9", NMIB...$700.00

Cowboy on Rocking Horse, K, 1950s, lithographed tin, 6½", EX, from $150.00 to $175.00.

Clown on Hands, prewar, rocks back & forth while balancing on his hands, tin, cloth & celluloid, 10", NM+ (EX box), A...$200.00

Clown on Roller Skates, TPS, swings leg, leans forward & skates, litho tin w/bl cloth pants, 7", MIB..............$325.00

Clown w/Lion, TPS, lion jumps through red felt hoop, litho tin, 6", NM (EX+ box), S10...$350.00

College Bear, MT, advances in waddling motion, plush over tin w/litho hands & feet, 6", EX+ (EX+ box), A..........$100.00

Comet Racer #37, Y, litho tin w/vinyl-headed driver, blk rubber tires, friction, 9", NM (EX box), A.............................$95.00

Comical Driver, M, monkey sits in car & flips backwards causing front to raise & spin, tin, 5½", rare, NM (EX box), A.$210.00

Continental Super Special, Cragstan, convertible w/working windshield wipers, w/driver, friction, 13¾", NMIB, A...$650.00

Cragstan Sky Bolt, trigger action propels spinning prop, litho tin w/2 plastic rockets to fire, 7", EX (EX box), A...........$75.00

Crazy Car, Yone, clown's head spins as car advances, gr w/red plastic spoke wheels, 5", MIB, from $100 to...........$125.00

Dancing Couple (George & Martha Washington), celluloid, 5", rare, M, from $400 to..$425.00

Dancing Couple (Sailor & Girl), prewar, celluloid, 4", scarce, MIB, A..$200.00

Dandy, Mikuni, advances while tipping his hat, eyes roll, litho tin, 6", EX+ (EX box)...$225.00

Disney Express Bus, MT, mk Disney Electric Line, litho tin, friction, 10", scarce, NM (NM box), A........................$600.00

Dizzy Clown w/Musical Balls, CK, prewar, clown spins w/2 balls that play music, celluloid, 12", NM (EX box), A....$360.00

Dog Chasing Puppy, Mikuni, mother hops along w/flapping ears trying to get puppy, tin, 8", EX (EX box), from $150 to...$175.00

Donald Duck Dipsy Car, Linemar, advances w/erratic action, litho tin w/plastic figure, 6", EX+ (NM box), from $825 to...$850.00

Donald Duck Dipsy Doodle, Linemar, 1950s, Donald Duck on tractor-type vehicle, metal body, 6", EX.................$675.00

Donald Duck Drummer, Linemar, advances & rocks while beating drum, litho tin, 6", NM, from $650 to.............$675.00

Donald Duck Flivver, Linemar, push down on Donald's head for movement, 5", NM (NM box).............................$750.00

Donald Duck on Rocking Horse, mk Made in Japan, early, celluloid on pressed steel base, 4½", EX+.....................$1,400.00

Donald Duck Race Car, MT, mk OJ, bl & red open wheel racer w/celluloid figure, 3", NM (EX box), A..................$600.00

Donald Duck the Acrobat, Linemar, Donald performs on wire, mk Gym Toys on flag, celluloid figure, 13", MIB, from $500 to...$525.00

Donald Duck the Fireman, Linemar, Donald climbs extension ladder, 13" (extended), EX (orig box), A...............$525.00

Donald Duck w/Huey & Voice, Linemar, Donald pulls Huey as he quacks, litho tin, 5", NM+ (EX+ box), A.......$1,300.00

Donald Duck Waddler, K, advances side to side, celluloid, 3", EX+ (EX box)...$650.00

Drummer Boy, sailor boy sways & plays drum, papier-mache body w/celluloid head & hands, cloth suit, MIB, from $225 to...$250.00

Drinking Sam, Alps, tin with cloth clothes, 8", NM (NM box), from $125.00 to $150.00.

Photo courtesy of Mike's General Store.

Duckmobile, duck pops in & out of car, litho tin w/celluloid figure, friction, 6½", scarce, M (VG box)....................$390.00

Dump Truck, Yonezawa, red & wht w/GMC plate & JTY plate on door, blk tires w/yel hubs, friction, 14", NM (VG box), A..$225.00

Photo courtesy of Mike's General Store.

Easter on Parade, MM, celluloid and pressed steel, 8", M (worn box), from $200.00 to $225.00.

Family Giraffe Loco, TPS, train advances as 3 giraffe riders bob their heads, litho tin, 11", EX+ (EX box), A..........$335.00

Ferdinand the Bull, Linemar, 1950s, advances w/twirling tail & head movement, litho tin, 5½", scarce, EX (VG box), A..$500.00

Fire Car, SSS, mk Josteele FD above rear plate, litho tin, friction, 6", NM (NM box), A.......................................$225.00

Fire Chief Car, Ichiko, advances w/warning light, red litho tin, friction, 6", NM (EX box), M5..................................$75.00

Fishing Bear, TPS, fish bounces in & out of bear's net, litho tin, 7", NM (EX box), from $200 to $300.00

Fishing Boy, Linemar, boy spins & fish wraps around pole, litho tin, 4", MIB, from $225 to.......................................$275.00

Fishing Monkey on Whale, TPS, moves back & forth w/flapping fins, litho tin, 9", NM (EX box), from $375 to........$400.00

Flappy Duck, TT, litho tin, friction, 5½", NMIB, A........$45.00

Flintstone Turnover Tank, Linemar, 1961, Fred forces tank to turn over, litho tin, 4", NM (EX scarce box), A ..$1,000.00

Flying Birds, TPS, 2 birds fly & chirp above base w/farmhouse, litho tin, 4½" dia base, NM (EX box)......................$200.00

Flying Car, Masuya, futuristic style car advances w/spinning blades overhead, friction, 8", scarce, NM (NM box), A........$275.00

Flying Fish Boat, Asahi, litho tin, 11", VG.....................$50.00

Gay Cabellero, Alps, Mexican in sombrero on vibrating donkey w/spinning tail, celluloid, 6", NM (EX box)............$200.00

Gerry the Juggler, GW, clown juggles 4 balls, litho tin w/hand-pnt celluloid face, cloth clothes, 6", NM (EX+ box), A..$300.00

Girl Skipping Rope, TPS, boy & girl swing rope & girl jumps, litho tin, girls have vinyl faces, 12", NM (EX box), A.........$300.00

Girl w/Chickens, TPS, girl simulates throwing feed to chickens as she nods her head, tin, 5", EX (EX box), from $400 to $425.00

Golden Racer #3, SN, litho tin w/full-figure driver, friction, 11", NM (EX box), A...$210.00

Good Time Charlie, Alps, clown moves up & down while twirling cane & blowing party horn, 10", NM (EX box), from $400 to $450.00

Goofy the Unicyclist, Linemar, litho tin w/rubber ears, cloth pants, MIB..$1,500.00

Goofy Whirling Tail w/Turtle, Linemar, vibrates w/turtle on whirling tail, litho tin, 5", NM (NM box), from $650 to..............$850.00

Grasshopper, TN, advances & turns w/moving legs, litho tin w/plastic wings, 6", MIB...$125.00

Grasshopper, TN, advances & turns w/moving legs, litho tin w/plastic wings, 6", EX, G16.......................................$75.00

Great Magician Fox, TN, lifts hat from stand & chick, egg & rabbit appear, litho tin & plush, 9", rare, EX (EX box)....$500.00

Ham 'N Sam, Linemar, Sam dances as Ham plays the piano, 5½", NMIB..$2,000.00

Hand-Standing Clown, MT, balances on hands & rocks to & fro as bells jingle, celluloid, 9", EX+ (EX box), A.........$200.00

Happy Birthday To You, Yonezawa, spins w/ringing bell sound as bird flies overhead, litho tin, 6" dia, NM (EX+ box), A..$175.00

Happy Grandpa, farm scene w/man reading a book, 2 chickens & spinning umbrella atop barn, EX (EX box), from $100 to..$125.00

Happy Hippo, TPS, moves erratically while trying to catch bananas held by native, tin, 6", EX (VG+ box), from $450 to..$600.00

Happy Life, Alps, girl rocks in beach chair as umbrella spins & goose rotates, tin & celluloid, 9", NM (EX+ box)...$350.00

Happy Life, Alps, 9", EX, L4..$275.00

Happy Mr Penguin, SAN, advances in waddling motion w/quacking sound, litho tin, 6", MIB......................$175.00

Happy Skaters, TPS/Cragstan, rabbit skates in realistic motion, 6", NM (EX+ box)..$650.00

Happy the Violinist, TPS, clown on stilts playing violin, litho tin, cloth costume, 8½", MIB, from $300 to...........$350.00

Happy-Go-Lucky, see Bobo the Magician

Henry & His Brother, 2 figures on separated wheeled platforms, MIB, A..$1,540.00

Henry & His Friends, prewar, figures perform acrobats on high-bar, celluloid, scarce, EX, from $650 to....................$850.00

Henry Eating Ice-Cream Cone, Linemar, vibrates while head moves as if eating cone, tin, 5½", NM, from $750 to...$850.00

Henry on Elephant, Borgfeldt, Henry rides on trunk & boy rides on back, celluloid & litho tin, 8", EX (orig box)..$1,350.00

Highway Patrol Cycle, ATC, litho tin, w/policeman driver, friction, 10", MIB, A...$360.00

Highway Patrol Helicopter, TN, tin, 16", EX, J2...........$100.00

Hobby Horse with Bear, MM, rocks back and forth as horse advances, lithographed tin and plush, 6", NM (EX+ box), $100.00.

Honey Bear, Alps, plush bear licks bees' nest while bee flies overhead, 7", EX+ (EX box), from $200 to............$250.00

Honeymoon Cottage, Linemar, train circles under 3 tunnels, gate raises & lowers, 7x7", NM $200.00

Honk-Along Children Bus, Kanto Toys, music plays as bus advances, litho tin, friction, 8½", EX+ (EX box) $130.00

Hopping Cary the Crow, tin crow w/blk suit, checked vest, red bow tie & hat, MIB $125.00

Hot Rod, TN, red w/visible pistons, jutting headlights, trunk mk Century, friction, 7", EX (VG box) $150.00

Housekeeper Cat, MM, changes direction as she vacuums, plush & tin w/fabric clothes, rubber sweeper, 6", EX (EX box) $100.00

Howdy Doody's Pal Clarabell, Linemar, 1950s, cable control, 7", NM (EX box)...$650.00

Huckleberry Aeroplane, Linemar, 1961, litho tin w/vinyl figure, friction, 10", NMIB $675.00

Huckleberry Hound Go-Mobile, Linemar, litho tin w/blk rubber tires, friction, 6½", NM (EX box), A....................$500.00

Hula Girl, prewar, performs the hula, celluloid w/silk grass skirt, 8½", EX, A..$75.00

Hula-Hoop Monkey, Plaything, 1950s, monkey stands on barrel & hula-hoops, litho tin, 10", NM (EX box) $100.00

Hungry Cub, TN, pours milk from bottle to cup & drinks it, base mk Farm Milk, tin & plush, 6", NM (EX+ box) $100.00

Hunting Grandpa, TN, fires rifle w/moving hands & head, emits gun sound, litho tin, 7", NM (VG+ box).................$125.00

Ice Cream Monkey, Alps, vibrates & licks ice-cream cone, plush over tin, 6", NM (EX box) $125.00

Indian Big Chief, Indian w/tomahawk walks, turns head & moves arms, tin w/cloth clothes, 7", NM (G box), A $100.00

Ironing Monkey, TN, moves her iron across cloth on ironing board, tin & plush, 6½", NM (EX box), A.............$100.00

Jalopy Stock Car #10, NGS/Cragstan, mk 32 HP on hood, litho tin w/blk rubber tires, friction, 6", NM (EX+ box), A $120.00

Japanese Military Motorcycle, TYDY, celluloid soldier on litho tin cycle, VG $200.00

Jocko the Climbing Monkey, Linemar, jockey climbs up & down string, litho tin, 6½", NM (EX box) $125.00

Joe the Acrobat, TPS, clown w/cloth pants rolls forward on ball, litho tin, 6", scarce, EX (EX box)...........................$800.00

Joe the Xylophone Player, Linemar, clown plays xylophone & sways, litho tin w/cloth outfit, 5", EX+ (VG+ box), A...........$545.00

John the Naughty, toddler tries to run as dog bites his behind, celluloid, 6", scarce, NM (EX box) $455.00

Joker (Batman), Billiken, 1989, advances w/swinging arms, litho tin, 9", MIB...$100.00

Jolly Pig, advances w/clown pulling his tail, celluloid, 7", MIB, from $125 to $150.00

Jolly Snake, TPS, wiggles as head turns from side to side, litho tin, 7½", NM (EX box) $125.00

JTY Y53 Racer, Yonezawa, red & bl litho tin w/blk rubber tires, driver in wht helmet, 12", EX, A $600.00

JTY Y54 Racer, Hadson, red & gray litho tin w/blk rubber tires, driver in wht helmet, 12", EX, A $660.00

Juke Box Bank, NY, 1950s, insert coin & push lever for several actions, litho tin, 5", EX, A.......................................$160.00

Jumping Dog, TTT, shaggy dog jumps & shakes shoe in his mouth, plush over tin, 5", NM (NM box) $75.00

Jungle Constructor Elephant, KO, pulls drum & bell rings, head nods & ears flap, litho tin, 7½", MIB.....................$200.00

Knitting Cat, TN, wht plush cat realistically knits, litho tin base, 6", NM (EX box) $100.00

KO-KO Sandwich Man, TN, moves up & down, tips hat & waves cane, tin & vinyl w/cloth clothes, 7", MIB, from $175 to...$250.00

Lady Bug Family, TPS, mother bug pulls 3 kids behind her as they turn & zigzag, litho tin, 12", M (EX box) $100.00

Liberty Ferry, boat travels on river from Manhattan Island to Statue of Liberty, litho tin, 21" base, EX+ (EX box), A $365.00

Little Shoemaker, Alps, shoemaker hammers nail in shoe, litho tin w/cloth shirt & orig hat, 6", EX+ (EX+ box).....$175.00

Loop Hoop Bear, Alps, clothed plush bear spins in hoop, 8" dia, MIB, A..$210.00

Louie in His Dream Car, Linemar, litho tin w/celluloid figure, friction, 5", NM (EX+ box)...................................$575.00

Lucky Baby Sewing Machine, girl at sewing machine, several actions, celluloid & tin, 5", EX (EX box) $350.00

Magic Circus, TPS, monkey & seal dance & shake w/magnetic action on platform, litho tin & plastic, 6", NM (NM box)..$195.00

Magic Tunnel & Dream Land Bus, TPS, bus travels around carnival base, litho tin, NM (EX box) $175.00

Mad Hatter's Sky-View Taxi, Linemar/WDP, marked Disneyland Taxi Service, lithographed tin, friction, 5", scarce, NM (EX+ box), from $500.00 to $550.00.

Magician Bank, Yonezawa, place coin on stage & mouse pushes it into magician hat, litho tin, 4" dia, NM (EX+ box), A $90.00

Mammal of the Sea, Cragstan, whale opens his mouth & gobbles up fish, tin, 6", NM (EX box), from $200 to............$250.00

Marching Soldier, Fukuda, advances & swings rifle, wheeled cylinders, litho tin & celluloid, 9", EX+ (EX+ box), A $300.00

Marionette Theatre, prewar, 2 clowns dance on stage, bell rings, tin w/celluloid figures, 10½", scarce, NM, A $485.00

Mary & Her Little Lamb, 1920s, Mary pulls nodding lamb, celluloid, 7", NM (EX box), A..$300.00

Photo courtesy of Ju ne Moon.

Merry Ball Blower Circus Car, KO, advances and balances ball in stream of air above, lithographed tin, 5", NM (EX box), $125.00.

Merry-Go-Round Circus, TN, 4 seals bob heads in openings as elephant balances parasol, clown atop, 9", NM (EX box)..$275.00

Merry-Go-Round Truck, TN, carousel circles w/bell noise as truck advances, litho tin, friction, 8", EX $175.00

Mickey & Minnie Acrobats, Borgfeldt, celluloid figures on swinging wires w/wire base, 11½", EX......................$725.00

Mickey & Minnie Trapeze, Borgfeldt, Mickey & Minnie perform on highbar, celluloid, 7", NM (EX+ box), A........$1,200.00

Mickey Mouse, see also Rocking Mickey Mouse on Pluto and Walt Disney's Mechanical Tricycle

Mickey Mouse Dipsy Car, Linemar, advances w/erratic action, litho tin w/plastic figure, 6", EX (NM box) $725.00

Mickey Mouse Motorcyclist, Linemar/WDP, litho tin, friction, 3½", EX, from $250 to....................................$400.00

Mickey Mouse on Horse, prewar, Mickey as cowboy on horse, celluloid w/wooden horse, 7½", NM, A $2,750.00

Mickey Mouse on Scooter, Linemar/WDP, Mickey on 3-wheeled scooter, litho tin & rubber, 4", VG, A.......$525.00

Mickey Mouse Roller Skater, Linemar, litho tin body w/rubber ears, cloth pants, 7", MIB, from $1,750 to............$1,850.00

Mickey Mouse the Unicyclist, Linemar, litho tin body w/rubber ears, cloth pants, 5½", MIB, from $1,650 to.........$1,750.00

Mickey Mouse Walker, Borgfeldt, 1934, celluloid with hand-painted features, 8", non-working otherwise EX (VG+ box), A, $4,000.00.

Mickey Mouse Whirligig, STS/Borgfeldt, Mickey spins on ball under umbrella, 10", rare, EX (orig box), A $5,000.00

Mickey Mouse Xylophone Player, Linemar, rocks & plays xylophone, litho tin w/rubber nose & tail, 7", EX $850.00

Military Motorcycle w/Sidecar, TN, soldier w/passenger on camouflage cycle, litho tin, 8", EX................................$300.00

Millionaire's World Bank, Bandai, open latch & plate shows kids depositing money at booth, litho tin, 5", NM (EX box), A $250.00

Minnie Mouse Knitting in Rocking Chair, Linemar, 1950s, litho tin, 7", NM, from $600 to...$650.00

Monkee Mobile, ASC, red tin w/plastic figures holding instruments, press button for music, friction, 12", M (VG box), A $455.00

Monkey & Seal, K, monkey rides unicycle & pulls seal w/many actions, tin w/cloth outfit, 7", EX+ (EX box), from $150 to...........$175.00

Monkey Basketball Player, TPS, monkey shoots ball into net, litho tin, 8", EX (NM box), from $350 to...............$375.00

Monkey Batter, Cragstan, bat raises, head turns & tail spins while moving about, litho tin, 7", NMIB, from $450 to $475.00

Monkey Cycle, Bandai, monkey peddles motorcycle as eyes pop in & out, litho tin, 5", rare, NM (EX box), from $325 to...$350.00

Motorcycle Cable Rider, MT, 1950s, motorcycle w/driver rides on wire cable, 5", MIB.............................$275.00

Mountain Climber, TPS, man goes up & down rope, pull-string action, litho tin w/cloth outfit, 7", scarce, MIB, A..$300.00

Mr Dan Coffee-Drinking Man, TN, 1960s, litho tin, MIB, S10, from $125 to $150.00

Mr Dan Hot Dog Eating Man, TN, lifts hot dog to mouth, chews & wipes mouth, 7", M (NM box), S10, from $150 to......$175.00

Mule & Elephant Rocking Horse, animals on rocking base w/litho stars & angels, 7", VG.................................$150.00

Musical Bunny, TN, plays cymbals w/animated arms, litho tin w/vinyl face & fabric jacket, 7", NM (EX box), A.....$80.00

NBC Television Car, Asahitoy, mk Cragstan Broadcasting Co Inc, cameras on roof, friction, 6", EX (EX box), from $200 to...$250.00

Obstinate Donkey, KT, clown holds donkey's tail as they advance, celluloid, 6", NM (EX+ box) $150.00

Old Jalopy, Linemar, litho tin w/printed slogans, celluloid driver & passenger, friction, 9", VG $150.00

Old Timer Locomotive, K, litho tin w/full-figure driver, friction, 7", NM (VG+ box), M5 ....$45.00

Olive Oyl Ballet Dancer, Linemar, put blade in slot and pull base for action, friction, 6", NMIB, A, $450.00.

Olive Oyl Mechanical Tricycle w/Revolving Bell, Linemar, 1950s, litho tin, MIB, from $1,500 to..................$1,800.00

Over the Field Fox Hunt, Alps, rider & 2 hounds chase fox on attached rods, celluloid & tin, 8", EX (orig box), A.$300.00

Pango-Pango African Dancer, TPS, vibrates around w/shield & spear, head moves, litho tin, 6", NM (EX box), from $325 to...$350.00

Pango-Pango African Dancer, TPS, 6", NM, from $250 to.$275.00

Pat the Pup, TPS, twirls his tail & barks, pat nose for action, litho tin, 5", EX+ (EX+ box)..................................$150.00

Patrol Wagon, litho tin, friction, 10½", NM (EX box), M5 .$85.00

Pecking Rooster, prewar, man w/bowl & rooster on base, 7", EX+, M5 ....$325.00

Percy Penguin, TN, advances on skis w/flapping arms, litho tin, friction, 5", NM (EX box) $200.00

Pinocchio, see also Walking Pinocchio

Pinocchio the Acrobat, Linemar, Pinocchio rocks on illus base, litho tin, 11" base, VG, A $275.00

Playful Pluto & Goofy, Linemar, figures vibrate around w/spinning tails, 5¼", EX+ (EX box)...........................$1,350.00

Playful Puppy, TPS, puppy on rectangular base chases butterfly, non-fall action, litho tin, 9" base, M......................$175.00

Playland Express, Yone, train & trolley circle track as airplane flies overhead, litho tin & plastic, EX+ (EX box), A $125.00

Pluto, see also Walt Disney's Mechanical Tricycle; Rock 'N Roll Pluto and Walking Pluto

Pluto Convertible, Linemar/WDP, litho tin w/vinyl Pluto, blk rubber tires, friction, 6", scarce, EX+ $500.00

Pluto Delivery Wagon, Linemar, Pluto pedals 'Mickey's Delivery Cart,' friction, 6", EX+ $390.00

Pluto on Motorcycle, Linemar, litho tin, friction, 3½", EX+..$450.00

Pluto the Drum Major, Linemar, rocks while tooting horn & shaking bell, litho tin, 6½", M (VG box), from $600 to.....$625.00

Police Sidecar Motorcycle, Modern Toys, litho tin w/driver & passenger, friction, 7", NMIB, from $300 to $350.00

Poor Pete, Black toddler w/melon tries to run as dog bites his behind, celluloid, 6", scarce, M, from $550 to $700.00

Popeye, see also Skating Popeye

Popeye & Olive Oyl (In Chair), Linemar, 1950s, Popeye spins Olive Oyl in chair on his head, litho tin, 9", MIB.$3,000.00

Popeye & Olive Oyl Ball Toss, Linemar, Popeye & Olive Oyl flip ball back & forth, litho tin, VG, from $600 to..$650.00

Popeye Basketball Player, Linemar, Popeye stands below basket & manipulates ball on string, 9", NM, A $1,250.00

Popeye in Roadster, Linemar, Popeye in realistic sports car w/wht-wall tires, friction, 8", EX, A $650.00

Popeye on Tricycle, Linemar, bell rings as Popeye peddles trike, litho tin, 4", EX, from $900 to.................................$950.00

Popeye Pilot, Linemar, moves in circles, Popeye in 3-wheeled single-prop airplane, litho tin, 6", NM, A $1,850.00

Popeye Transit Co Hauler & Trailer, Linemar, litho tin, friction, 13", NM (EX box), A...$3,350.00

Popeye Transit Co Moving Van, Linemar, 1950s, litho tin, friction, 14", NM $750.00

Power Shovel, Linemar, tin, friction, 8", EX, J2 ....$100.00

Professor Ludwig Von Drake, see also Walking Professor Ludwig Von Drake

Professor Ludwig Von Drake Go-Mobile, Linemar, 1961, litho tin w/vinyl head, friction, 6", NM+ (EX box) $250.00

Quick Draw McGraw Go-Mobile, Linemar, litho tin w/blk rubber tires, friction, 6½", NM (EX box), A.................$350.00

Rabbit & Bear Playing Ball, TPS, rabbit & bear toss ball back & forth on base, litho tin, 19" base, EX (EX+ box) $250.00

Rabbit Drummer, mk CC Made in Japan, pre-war, plays drum & moves head, celluloid, 9", EX (EX scarce paper label box), A $500.00

Racer #8, YM, yel litho tin, w/driver, 8½", G, A............$180.00

Reading Santa Claus, Alps, Santa flips pgs in book as his head moves, cloth over tin, 7", EX (VG box) $225.00

Red Hot Rhythm Band, Alps, 3 felt-covered monkeys on base playing cymbals, drum & trumpet, litho tin, 11", MIB, A $220.00

Rock 'N Roll Monkey, Cragstan, vinyl face, NM, J2......$225.00

Rock 'N Roll Pluto, Cragstan/WDP, 1969, advances w/gyro-powered swaying motion, plastic, 5", EX+ (EX box), A $100.00

Rocking Mickey Mouse on Pluto, Linemar, 1950s, litho tin, 6", MIB, A $5,190.00

Rodeo Cowboy, Alps, twirls lasso as upper body moves, celluloid, tin & cloth, 9", NM (EX box), from $175 to...$200.00

Roly Poly Circus Clown, SK, rolls in hoop while bell on foot jingles, litho tin w/cloth clothes, 6" dia, EX (EX box), A $200.00

Rowing Boat, Acorn, fisherman rows boat, litho tin, 8", EX+ (EX box), A $175.00

Royal Guard, prewar, vibrates & moves side to side, celluloid w/tin legs, 8", EX+ (EX+ box)................................$250.00

Rubber Neck Willie, vibrates around & spins cane, celluloid, 6½", NM, A $200.00

Sam the Strolling Skeleton, Mikuni, advances as body shifts side to side, litho tin, 5", NM (VG box), A....................$225.00

Sandwitch (sic) Man, clown advances, rings bell & swings sign, Eat At Joe's Diner, litho tin, 6", rare, NM (EX+ box)........$450.00

Santa Claus, TN, Santa rings bell & waves Merry Christmas sign, litho tin, 6", NM (EX+ box), from $225 to.....$250.00

Santa Claus Cycle, 1950s, advances in circular motion w/ringing bell, litho tin & celluloid, 4½", M............................$200.00

Savings Bank, drop toy in back, put coin in & it comes out slot between litho boy & girl, number changes, 6", EX, A.$250.00

School Line Bonnet Bus, Marusan, litho tin w/greyhound on both sides, friction, 7", EX+, A $500.00

Skating Popeye, Linemar, lithographed tin with cloth pants, 7", EX, from $750.00 to $850.00.

Sea Wolf, Alps, peg-legged pirate circles while eyes open & close, litho tin, 7", EX+, from $175 to $200.00

Shuttle Zoo Train, TPS, train travels track w/giraffe in ea car, heads move, litho tin, 12" base, M (EX box), A......$130.00

Skater Bunny, Cragstan, bobs up & down on skis using pole for balance, plush & tin w/cloth clothes, 9", NM (EX box)...$75.00

Skating Chef, TPS, chef w/plate of food kicks leg back & skates around, litho tin w/cloth pants, 7", MIB.................$350.00

Skating Hobo Clown, TPS, realistic skating motion w/push-off leg action, litho tin, 6", EX................................$250.00

Skier, Occupied Japan, litho tin w/hand-pnt celluloid face, 5", scarce, NM (EX+ box), A $590.00

Skip Rope Animals, TPS, bear & squirrel twirl rope as baby bear jumps, litho tin, 8", MIB, A $250.00

Skipping Couple, Occupied Japan, celluloid couple molded together skip rope on pressed steel fr, 5", NM (EX box) $225.00

Skipping Puppy, TN, dog dressed as young boy skips rope & nods head, litho tin, 6", NM (NM box)...................$110.00

Skippy the Tricky Cyclist, TPS, rides cycle w/animated leg action, litho tin w/cloth outfit, 6", EX (EX box) $300.00

Sled Boy, Occupied Japan, sled advances & spins, tin & celluloid, 4", MIB, A..$125.00

Slim the Seal & His Friends, TPS, circus seal w/parasol pulls 3 squirrels on leaf, litho tin, 10", rare, NM (EX box), A.$750.00

Smiling Sam the Carnival Man, Alps, vibrates, twirls cane & head shakes, litho tin w/cloth clothes, 9", EX (VG box).....$200.00

Snapping Alligator, S&E, twists & snaps jaws as he tries to catch bee in front of him, tin, 12", NM (EX box), J2............$200.00

Soldier on Motorcycle, KT, full-figure soldier on camouflage motorcycle, 5½", G, A $175.00

Space Whale, KO, mk Pioneer, advances w/opening & closing mouth, rolling eyeballs & flapping ears, 9½", EX....$350.00

Speed Ship, MT, mk X125, advances on wheels w/clicking sound, litho tin, 7", NM (EX+ box), A....................$195.00

Starfire #52 Racer, Marusan, silver, yel & red tin w/tin driver, blk rubber tires w/red hubs, friction, 12", EX............$165.00

Strato Flap Wing Sports Car, ASC, travels w/engine noise, bl litho tin w/driver, friction, 11", NM (VG box), A ..$170.00

Strutting Sam, Linemar, Black man performs tap dance atop drum-like stage, litho tin, 13", NM (VG box), from $500 to .$550.00

Super Duck Car, advances w/quacking sound, litho tin, friction, 8", EX, A..$120.00

Super Racer #42, Gem, wht racer w/bl flame design, chrome side pipes, red hubs, w/driver, friction, 18", EX, A $4,620.00

Super Rocket Ride, Yone, 2 rockets w/riders perform loop-de-loop, litho tin & vinyl, 9", EX (EX box)...................$235.00

Superman Rollover Tank, Linemar, advances as Superman figure forces tank to flip over, litho tin, 4", VG..........$450.00

Swan, Marusan, waddles & cackles, litho tin, 7", NM (EX box), A $75.00

Swimming Tarzan, SAN, moves arms in swimming motion, knife in mouth, celluloid & tin, 6", rare, NM (M box), A $860.00

Tabby the Cat & Her Pet Canary, Alps, advances & shakes cage while trying to catch her bird, 10½", EX (VG box) .$275.00

Talking Parrot, parrot sitting atop pole flaps wings & moves beak, 8", EX (EX+ box), A......................................$295.00

Tambourine Clown, NGT, litho tin w/cloth costume, 7", EX+ (EX+ box), A..$385.00

Tap Dancer, Black man tap dances on sidewalk in front of sign, tin w/cloth outfit, 8½", EX......................$350.00

Tarzan, see Swimming Tarzan

Teddy's Cycle, Occupied Japan, 1950s, tin w/celluloid figure, 4½", MIB...$125.00

Televi Jeep, Usagaya, mk Crown Television Jeep, advances & shows boxing scene, litho tin, friction, 6", NM (EX+ box), A..$65.00

Texas Ranger Horse Carrier, YH, advances as horses bob their heads up & down, litho tin, friction, 9", EX (EX box), A.......$140.00

Three Little Pigs & Big Bad Wolf, Linemar, hoppers, ea has box that converts into house, EX (NM boxes)............$2,000.00

Tom Tom Canoe, MS, 2 Indian chiefs in canoe that moves along as 1 rows & 1 beats drum, 9½", NM (EX box), from $275 to..$300.00

Touchdown Pete, TPS, 1950s, advances w/football, stoops down & charges forward, litho tin, 6", NM (EX box), from $450 to...$550.00

Tricky Tricycle, Yonezawa, bulldog rocks on seat as tricycle advances, litho tin, friction, 7", rare, EX+ (EX box), A..$165.00

Triksie the Magician Dog, plush dog barks & drops hat over chick then lifts it to reveal an egg, 8", EX.............$435.00

Tumbling Clown, SK, tumbles forward, celluloid w/hand-pnt features, 7", EX+ (EX box), A....................$80.00

Upsy Down Clown, Alps, clown on motorcycle, litho tin, friction, 6½", NM (EX box), from $775 to..................$875.00

US Marine Corps Flying Jeep, Indian Head Logo, advances w/visible spinning engine, litho tin, 6", NM (NM box), A..$185.00

Venus Auto Cycle, TN, litho tin, no driver, simulated piston action, friction, 9", MIB, A....................................$525.00

Wagon Fantasy Land, TPS, 2 twirling squirrels & rocking monkey on leaf pulled by snail, litho tin, 12", NM (EX box), A...$300.00

Walking Panda, 1950s, plush over tin, 8", EX, $75.00.

Walking Pinocchio, Linemar/WDP, advances w/moving arms, litho tin w/rubber nose, 6", NM (NM box), from $450 to $475.00

Walking Pluto, Linemar/WDP, advances in realistic walking motion, tin & plush, 5", 1 ear missing o/w VG+, A .$245.00

Walking Professor Ludwig Von Drake, Linemar, litho tin, 6", MIB, A..$525.00

Walt Disney's Mechanical Tricycle, Linemar, Donald Duck on tricycle, tin & celluloid, 4", EX+ (EX box), from $450 to $500.00

Walt Disney's Mechanical Tricycle, Linemar, Mickey Mouse on tricycle, tin & celluloid, 4", EX (EX box), from $475 to .$525.00

Walt Disney's Mechanical Tricycle, Linemar, Pluto on tricycle, tin & celluloid, 4", NM (VG box), from $375 to $425.00

Walt Disney's Television Bank, Linemar, 1956, screen rotates as Mickey and friends perform, lithographed tin, 4", rare, EX+ (EX+ box), $1,000.00.

Wild Roaring Bull & Boy, Mikuni, bull raises up on hind legs as boy holds tail, litho tin, 9", EX (EX box), from $200 to..$225.00

Wimpy (unauthorized), vibrates around & leans forward & backward, head moves, celluloid, 6½", scarce, M, A..........$900.00

Wonder MG Car, Marusan, car w/2 passengers travels track & turns w/twirling umbrella above, NM (NM box), from $325 to...$375.00

Yogi Bear Go-Mobile, Linemar, litho tin w/blk rubber tires, friction, 6½", NM (EX box), A...................................$425.00

Yogi Bear Plane, litho tin w/rubber figure, friction, 10", G, A $250.00
101 Dalmatians Bus, MT/WDP, Dalmatians in windows, litho tin, friction, 16", NM (EX box) $575.00

Spanish

Bugatti 1-970 Racer, Paya, bl litho tin w/red, yel & blk trim, wht spoke wheels, w/goggled driver, 19½", M $300.00
Charlie Chaplin on 3-Wheeler, Paya, Charlie in seat on trike w/hanging lanterns, tin, 5", EX, A $1,870.00
Donald Duck Walking Car, Geyper, 1965, bl w/Donald's nephew & Ludwig Von Drake on sides, 6", NM (NM box), from $175 to $250.00
Hoop Clown, Clan, 1950s, clown performs tricks as hoop advances, litho tin & cloth, 6" dia, scarce, EX+ (NM box), A $450.00
Minnie Mouse Carrying Felix in Cages, RS, 1930, litho tin, 7", EX $6,000.00
Rodeo Joe, Rico, 1950s, jeep travels in circular motion as vaquero jumps up & down, 5", EX+ (EX+ box), from $425 to $475.00
Rodeo Joe, Rico, 1950s, 4½", EX, S10, from $375 to $400.00

Wyandotte

Though the Wyandotte Company (Michigan) produced toys of all types, included here are only the heavy-gauge pressed-steel cars, trucks, and other vehicles they made through the 1930s and '40s.

See also Aeronautical; Boats; Character, TV and Movie Collectibles; Windups, Friction, and Other Mechanicals.

Ambulance, wht w/chrome grille, Red Cross decal on side, rear door opens, 11", EX, A $230.00
Cabriolet Sedan, red & wht w/NP grille, wooden wheels, 6", NM $165.00
Car & Trailer, gr w/wht rubber tires, 26", VG+, M5 ......$360.00
Car Carrier, orange w/yel wheels, no cars, 21¼", EX, A..$200.00
Cattle Truck, red, yel & bl, 23", VG, A $95.00
Circus Trailer, 1930s, cage w/Greatest Show on Earth on backplate, 7", EX, A $300.00
Circus Truck, red cab w/rear caged bed mk Wyandotte Circus, wooden wheels, 10¾", G, A $95.00
Circus Truck & Trailer, red cab w/2 cages containing paper animals, 19", EX, A $800.00
Circus Truck & Trailer, 1930s, Greatest Show on Earth on backplate, 11", EX, A $500.00
Coal Truck, bl cab & fr w/red bed, w/coal chute, 15¾", VG, A $110.00
Coupe, red w/chrome grille, electric lights, rubber tires, 8¾", G, A $145.00
Coupe, 1930s, gr w/blk fenders, wht rubber tires, 6½", NM, A $145.00
Coupe & Trailer, 1930s, orange w/wooden wheels, 11½", EX, A $290.00

Photo courtesy of Jeff Bub.

Construction Truck and Steam Shovel, 1940s, white, blue and yellow with black tires, NM, $400.00.

Dump Truck, gr w/chrome grille & headlights, bed w/slanted back gate, electric lights, 10", EX, A $190.00
Dump Truck, red & gr, 14", EX $125.00
Express Delivery Truck, bl & yel, EX $175.00
Fire Truck w/Water Pump & Hose, #127, mk #5, complete w/extension ladder, 10", NM (EX box), A $200.00
Flash Strat-O-Wagon, 1940, red, wht & bl futuristic wagon w/fins, litho rocket ship, 6", NM (VG box) $175.00
La Salle Sedan w/House Trailer, solid red sleek design w/chrome grille, wht rubber tires, 26", G, A $440.00
Metropolitan Garbage Truck, NMIB $475.00
Moto-Fix Tow Truck, NM $170.00
Moving Van, Wyandotte Van Lines Coast To Coast... on sides, red, wht & bl w/blk rubber tires, 8", NM (G- box), A $170.00
Nationwide Air Rail Service Truck, red & cream w/blk rubber tires, 12", EX $200.00
Official Service Car, red cab, bright yel & gr bed w/red winch, blk rubber tires w/chrome hubs, 21", EX, A $315.00
Painter's Truck, #126, red, wht & bl w/Jiffy's Painting & Decorating decal, 10", NM (EX box), A $325.00
Roadster, yel w/red simulated convertible top & hubs, 13", EX, A $415.00
Sedan, red & blk 4-door w/wht rubber tires, 6½", VG $65.00
Sinclair Tanker Truck, 1930s, gr w/yel & blk decal, 17", G, A $200.00
Stake Truck, red & blk w/yel wheels, yel dolly, 15", VG, A $470.00
Stake Truck, red sleek cab & gr stake bed, 1-pc floor & chassis, litho front grille, blk metal wheels, 20", EX, A........$145.00
Stake Truck, 1930s, red & gr w/bl grille, wooden wheels, 12½", EX $165.00
Stratocruiser, bl & red, 13", NMIB $165.00
Tank Truck, 1935, red w/rubber wheels, rear door, 10½", VG+, A $115.00
Toytown Estate Ice Truck, yel & bl, NM......................$185.00
Toytown Estate Wagon, simulated wood side panels, features opening passenger doors, 21", VG..........................$150.00
Truck, bl & wht w/Igloo Ice decal, blk balloon tires w/wht hubcaps, 2 plastic ice cubes in truck bed, EX.................$225.00

Yo-Yos

Yo-Yos are starting to attract toy collectors, especially those with special features such as Hasbro's 'Glow-Action' and Duncan's 'Whistler.'

Advisor: Lucky Meisenheimer (M3).

Avon, Garfield, plastic, MIP, M20 ....$10.00
Avon, Teenage Mutant Ninja Turtles, MIP, M20...........$10.00
Champion, Style #44, return top, red, VG, M20 ....$12.00
Cheerio, Pro 99, bright gr, gold foil sticker label, NM......$35.00
Duncan, Beginner, Bosco Bear advertising, sm, G, M20 ....$7.00
Duncan, Beginner, wooden, #1044, MIP, M20................$25.00
Duncan, Beginner, wooden, #44, MIP, M20....................$25.00
Duncan, blk & red, VG $15.00
Duncan, Glow Imperial, wht, EX, I2 ....$5.00
Duncan, Imperial, Kool-Aid premium, MIP, M20...........$10.00

Photo courtesy of Lucky Meisenheimer.

Duncan Jeweled, M, $50.00.

Duncan, Magic Motion, 1975, Hulk, MIP, M20..............$20.00

Duncan, Shrieking, Sonic Satellite, #500, MIP, M20 ......$35.00
Duncan, Sir Duncan Spin Top, 1960s, MOC, T1.............$7.00
Duncan, Super Yo-Yo, tournament, natural wood w/gr stripe, VG, M20..$15.00
Duncan, Wheels, plastic, 1978, MIP, M20 ....$10.00
Knott's, Snoopy & Woodstock on house tangled w/yo-yo string, 2½", M, H11...$8.00
Spectra Star, Bart Simpson, MOC, K1 ....$8.00
Spectra Star, Radical Curve Ball Model #1502, 1988, MIP, M20...$10.00
Spirello, heavy pressed cb, red & wht spiral, 1 side stained o/w VG, M20...$15.00

Photo courtesy of Lucky Meisenheimer.

Trick Books, *The Art of Yo-Yo Playing,* **Cheerio and Duncan, EX, $25.00 each; Post, EX, $15.00.**

Twin Twirler, plastic, blk, NM, M20 ....$12.00
Whirl King, top standard model, G, M20 ....$10.00

Dealer Codes

Most of our description lines contain a letter/number code just before the suggested price. They correspond with the names of the following collectors and dealers who sent us their current selling list to be included in this addition. If you're interested in buying an item in question, don't hesitate to call or write them. We only ask that you consider the differences in time zones, and try to call at a convenient time. If you're corresponding, please send a self-addressed, stamped envelope for their repy. **Because our data was entered several months ago, many of the coded items will have already sold,** but our dealers tell us that they are often able to restock some of the same merchandise over and over. Some said that they had connections with other dealers around the country and might be able to locate a particular toy for you. But please bear in mind that because they may have had to pay more to restock their shelves, they may also have to charge a little more than the price quoted in their original sales list.

If you have lists of toys for sale that you would like for us to use in the next edition, please send them to us at the address as soon as possible. We will process incoming lists as they arrive and because our space is limited, the earlier you send it, the better. Please do not ask us to include you in our Categories of Special Interest unless you contribute useable information. Not only are we limited on available space, it isn't fair to those who do. If you would like to advertise with us but cannot contribute listings, display ads are available (see page 477 for rates). We will hold a previously assigned dealer code over for you who are our contributors/advisors from year to year as long as we know you are interested in keeping it, but if we haven't heard from you by February 1, we will reassign that code to someone else. Because the post office prefers your complete 9-digit zip code, please send us that information for our files.

Direct your correspondence to:

Huxford Enterprises, Inc.
1202 7th St.
Covington, IN 47932

(A1)
Stan and Sally Alekna
4724 Kernan Mill Lane East
Jacksonville, FL 32224
904-992-9525

(A2)
Jane Anderson
R.R. 5, Box 5525
Saylorsburg, PA 18353

(A3)
Avalon Comics
Larry Curcio
P.O. Box 821
Medford, MA 02155
617-391-5614

(A4)
Bob Armstrong
15 Monadnock Rd.
Worcester, MA 01609

(A5)
Geneva Addy
P.O. Box 124
Winterset, IA 50273

(A6)
Jerry Alingh
505 5th Ave. #302
Des Moines, Iowa 50309

(A7)
Matt and Lisa Adams
1234 Harbor Cove
Woodstock, GA 30189
770-516-6874

(B1)
Richard Belyski
P.O. Box 124
Sea Cliff, NY 11579
516-676-1183

(B2)
Larry Blodget
Box 753
Rancho Mirage, CA 92270

(B3)
Bojo
Bob Gottuso
P.O. Box 1403
Cranberry Twp., PA 16066
Phone or FAX 412-776-0621

(B4)
Dick Borgerding
RJB Toys
720 E Main
Flushing, MI 48433
810-659-9859

(B6)
Jim Buskirk
3009 Oleander Ave.
San Marcos, CA 92069
619-599-1054

(B7)
Danny Bynum
P.O. Box 440818
Houston, TX 77244-0818
713-531-5711

(B8)
Stanley A. and Robert S. Block
P.O. Box 51
Trumbull, CT 06611
203-261-3223 or 203-775-0138

(B10)
Tom Bremer
P.O. Box 49
Newark, NY 14513
Phone or FAX 315-331-8146

(B11)
Sue and Marty Bunis
RR 1, Box 36
Bradford, NH 03221-9102

(B12)
Bromer Booksellers, Inc.
607 Boylston St.
Boston, MA 02116
617-247-2818 or FAX 617-247-2975

(C1)
Casey's Collectible Corner
HCR Box 31, Rt. 3
N Blenheim, NY 12131
607-588-6464

(C2)
Mark E. Chase and Michael Kelley
Collector Glass News
P.O. Box 308
Slippery Rock, PA 16057
412-946-2838

(C3)
Ken Clee
Box 11412
Philadelphia, PA 19111
215-722-1979

(C4)
Arlan Coffman
1223 Wilshire Blvd., Ste. 275
Santa Monica, CA 90403
310-453-2507

(C5)
Joe Corea
New Jersey Nostalgia Hobby
401 Park Ave.
Scotch Plains, NJ 07076
908-322-2676 or FAX 908-322-4079

(C6)
Cotswold Collectibles
P.O. Box 249
Clinton, WA 98236
360-579-1223; FAX 360-579-1287

(C9)
Marilyn Cooper
8408 Lofland Dr.
Houston, TX 77055; 713-465-7773
Author of *The Pictorial Guide to Tooth-brush Holders*

(C10)
Bill Campbell
1221 Littlebrook Lane
Birmingham, AL 35235
205-853-8227; FAX 405-658-6986

(C11)
Jim Christoffel
409 Maple
Elburn, IL 60119
708-365-2914

(C12)
Joel J. Cohen
Cohen Books and Collectibles
P.O. Box 810310
Boca Raton, FL 33481
407-487-7888; FAX 407-487-3117

(C13)
Brad Cassidy
1350 Stanwix
Toledo, OH 43614
419-385-9910

(C14)
Cynthia's Country Store
12794 W Forest Hill Blvd.
Commerce Park - Wellington
West Palm Beach, FL 33414
407-793-0554; FAX 407-795-4222
(24 hours)

(C15)
Rosalind Cranor
P.O. Box 859
Blacksburg, VA 24063

(C17)
John and Michele Casino
633 Franklin Ave., Suite #169
Nutley, NJ 07110
201-759-2520

(C18)
Classic Golf & Collectibles
P.O. Box 8
Lake Havasu City, AZ 86406-0008
520-855-9623

(D1)
Allen Day
Yesterday's Toys
P.O. Box 525
Monroe, NC 28810

(D2)
Marl Davidson
(Marl & B)
10301 Braden Run
Bradenton, FL 34202
941-751-6275; FAX 941-751-5463

(D3)
Larry DeAngelo
516 King Arthur Dr.
Virginia Beach, VA 23464
804-424-1691

(D4)
John DeCicco
57 Bay View Dr.
Shrewsbury, MA 01545
508-797-0023

(D6)
Doug Dezso
864 Patterson Ave.
Maywood, NJ 07607
201-488-1311

(D7)
Ron and Donna Donnelly
Saturday Heroes
P.O. Box 7047
Panama City Beach, FL 32413
904-234-7944

(D8)
George Downes
Box 572
Nutley, NJ 07110
201-935-3388

(D9)
Gordy Dutt
P.O. Box 201
Sharon Center, OH 44274-0201
330-239-1657 or FAX 330-239-2991

(D10)
Dunbar's Gallery
Leila and Howard Dunbar
76 Haven St.
Milford, MA 01757
508-634-8697; FAX 508-634-8696

(D11)
Larry Doucet
2351 Sultana Dr.
Yorktown Heights, NY 10598
914-245-1320

(D12)
Doris' Dolls & Collectibles
325 E. 10th St.
Mt. Vernon, IN 47620
Phone or FAX 812-838-5290

(D13)
Dr. Doors Miniatures
3111 S. Valley View, Suite O-104
Las Vegas, NV 89102
702-362-2722

(E3)
Alan Edwards
Toys From the Crypt
P.O. Box 3294
Shawnee, KS 66203
913-383-1242

(F1)
Figures
Anthony Balasco
P.O. Box 19482
Johnston, RI 02919
401-946-5720; FAX 401-942-7980

(F2)
Paul Fideler
20 Shadow Oak Dr., Apt. #18
Sudbury, MA 01776
617-386-0228 (24 hours)

(F3)
Paul Fink's Fun and Games
P.O. Box 488
59 S Kent Rd.
Kent, CT 06757
203-927-4001

(F4)
Mike and Kurt Fredericks
145 Bayline Cir.
Folsom, CA 95630
916-985-7986

(F5)
Fun House Toy Co.
G.F. Ridenour
P.O. Box 343
Bradfordwoods, PA 15015-0343
412-935-1392 (FAX capable)

(F7)
Finisher's Touch Antiques
Steve Fisch, proprietor
10 W Main St.
Wappingers Falls, NY 12590
914-298-8882; FAX 914-298-8945

(F8)
52 Girls Collectibles
P.O. Box 36
Morral, OH 43337
614-465-6062

(F9)
Donald Friedman
660 W Grand Ave.
Chicago, IL 60610
708-656-3700 (day)
or 312-226-4741
(evening & weekends)
FAX 708-656-6292

(G1)
Gary's Trains
R.D. #2, Box 147
Boswell, PA 15531
814-629-9277

(G2)
Mark Giles
510 E Third St.
Ogalala, NE 69153
308-284-4360

(G5)
John F. Green Inc.
1821 W. Jacaranda Pl.
Fullerton, CA 92633-USA
714-526-5467; 800-807-4759

(G6)
Carol Karbowiak Gilbert
2193 14 Mile Rd. 206
Sterling Height, MI 48310

(G16)
Candelaine
(Candace Gunther)
Pasadena, CA 91103-2320
818-796-4568; FAX 818-796-7172

(H1)
The Hamburgs
Happy Memories Antique Toy Co.
P.O. Box 1305
Woodland Hills, CA 91365
818-346-9884 or 818-346-1269
FAX 818-346-0215

(H3)
George Hardy
1670 Hawkwood Ct.
Charlottesville, VA 22901
804-295-4863; FAX 804-295-4898

(H4)
Jerry and Ellen L. Harnish
110 Main St.
Bellville, OH 44813
Phone or FAX 419-886-4782

(H6)
Phil Helley
Old Kilbourne Antiques
629 Indiana Ave.
Wisconsin Dells, WI 53965
608-254-8770

(H7)
Jacquie and Bob Henry
Antique Treasures and Toys
Box 17
Walworth, NY 14568
315-986-1424

(H8)
Homestead Collectibles
Art and Judy Turner
R.D. 2, Rte. 150
P.O. Box 173-E
Mill Hall, PA 17751
717-726-3597; FAX 717-726-4488

(H9)
Pamela E. Apkarian-Russell
The Halloween Queen
C.J. Russell & The Halloween Queen
    Antiques
P.O. Box 499
Winchester, NH 03470
603-239-8875

(H10)
Don Hamm
712 N. Townsend St.
Syracuse, NY 13203
315-478-7035

(H11)
M.R. Huber, the SNO-PEA Trader
Norman and Marilyn Huber, Buyers
931 Emerson St.
Thousand Oaks, CA 91362
805-497-0119; FAX 1-800-SNO-OPY-2

(H12)
Roslyn L. Herman
124-16 84th Rd.
Kew Gardens, New York 11415
718-846-3496 or 718-846-8491

(H13)
Tim Hunter
1668 Golddust
Sparks, NV 89436
702-626-5029

(I1)
Roger Inouye
765 E Franklin
Pomona, CA 91766

(I2)
Terri Ivers
Terri's Toys and Nostalgia
419 S 1st St.
Ponca City, OK 74601
405-762-8697; FAX 405-765-5101

(I3)
Dan Iannotti
212 W. Hickory Grove Rd.
Bloomfield Hills, MI 48302-1127
810-335-5042

(J1)
Bill Jackameit
200 Victoria Dr.
Bridgewater, VA 22812
703-828-4359
(Monday-Thursday, 7 pm-9 pm EST)

(J2)
Ed Janey
2920 Meadowbrook Dr. SE
Cedar Rapids, IA 52403
319-362-5213

(J3)
Dana Johnson Enterprises
1347 NW Albany Ave.
Bend, OR 97701-3160
503-382-8410

(J5)
Just Kids Nostalgia
310 New York Avenue
Huntington, NY 11743
516-423-8449
FAX 516-423-4326

(J6)
June Moon
245 N Northwest Hwy.
Park Ridge, IL 60068
847-825-1411
(24-hr phone)
FAX 847-825-6090

(J7)
Jim's TV Collectibles
P.O. Box 4767
San Diego, CA 92164
Phone/FAX 619-462-1953

(J8)
Jeff and Bob's Fun Stuff
7324 Reseda Blvd #168
Reseda, CA 91335
818-705-3368

(K1)
K-3 Inc.
Bendees Only; Simpson Mania
2335 NW Thurman
Portland, OR 97210
503-222-2713

(K2)
David Kolodny-Nagy
May through Jan:
3701 Connecticut Ave. NW #500
Washington, DC 20008
Jan through May:
MB 845 Brandeis University
P.O. Box 9110
Waltham, MA 02251-9110
202-364-8753

(K3)
Ilene Kayne
1308 S Charles St.
Baltimore, MD 21230
410-685-3923

(K4)
Debby and Marty Krim
P.O. Box 2273
W Peabody, MA 01960
508-535-3140
or FAX 508-535-7522

(K5)
Kerry and Judy's Toys
7370 Eggleston Rd.
Memphis, TN 38125-2112
901-757-1722

(K6)
Keith and Donna Kaonis
60 Cherry Ln.
Huntington, NY 11743
516-261-8337
or FAX 516-261-8235

(L1)
Jean-Claude H. Lanau
740 Thicket Ln.
Houston, TX 77079
713-497-6034
(after 7:00 pm, CST)

(L2)
John and Eleanor Larsen
523 Third St.
Colusa, CA 95932
916-458-4769 (after 4 pm)

(L4)
Tom Lastrapes
P.O. Box 2444
Pinellas Park, FL 34664
813-545-2586

(L5)
Stephen Leonard
Box 127
Albertson, LI, NY 11507
516-742-0979

(L6)
Kathy Lewis
187 N Marcello Ave
Thousand Oaks, CA 91360
805-499-8101

(L7)
Terry and Joyce Losonsky
7506 Summer Leave Ln.
Columbia, MD 21046-2455
301-381-3358

(M1)
Mark and Val Macaluso
3603 Newark Rd.
Marion, NY 14505
315-926-4349; FAX 315-926-4853

(M2)
John McKenna
801-803 W Cucharres
Colorado Springs, CO 80905
719-630-8732

(M3)
Lucky Meisenheimer
7300 Sand Lake Commons Blvd.
Orlando, FL 32819
407-354-0478

(M4)
Bill Mekalian
550 E Chesapeake Cir.
Fresno, CA 93720
209-434-3247

(M5)
Mike's General Store
52 St. Annes Rd.
Winnipeg, Manitoba, Canada R2M-2Y3
204-255-3463; FAX 204-253-4124

(M6)
Paul David Morrow
13550 Foothill Blvd. #28
Sylmar, CA 91342
818-898-9592

(M7)
Judith A. Mosholder
R.D. #2, Box 147
Boswell, PA 15531
814-629-9277

(M8)
The Mouse Man Ink
P.O. Box 3195
Wakefield, MA 01880
Phone or FAX 617-246-3876

(M9)
Steven Meltzer
670 San Juan Ave. #B
Venice, CA 90291
310-396-6007

(M10)
Gary Metz
263 Key Lakewood Dr.
Moneta, VA 24121
540-721-2091; FAX 504-721-1782

(M11)
Michael and Polly McQuillen
McQuillen's Collectibles
P.O. Box 11141
Indianapolis, IN 46201-0141
317-322-8518

(M13)
Helen McCale
P.O. Box 397
Butler, MO 64730-0397
816-679-3690

(M14)
Ken Mitchell
710 Conacher Dr.
Willowdale, Ontario
Canada M2M 3N6
416-222-5808 anytime

(M15)
Marcia's Fantasy
Marcia Fanta
R.R.#1, Box 107
Tappen, ND 58487-9635
701-327-4441

(M16)
Gene Mack
408 Yorkshire Blvd.
Syracuse, NY 13219
315-487-9023

(M17)
Mrs. Miller's Memorabilia
70a Greenwich Ave., Box #116
New York, NY 10011
212-614-9774
(leave message)

(M18)
Nancy McMichael
P.O. Box 53262
Washington DC 20009

(M19)
Model Auto
P.O. Box 79253
Houston, TX 77279
Phone or FAX 713-468-4461
(phone evenings; FAX anytime)

(M20)
Bruce Middleton
5 Lloyd Rd.
Newburgh, NY 12550
914-564-2556

(M21)
Peter Muldavin
173 W 78th St., Apt. 5-F
New York, NY 10024
212-362-9606

(N1)
Natural Way/dba Russian Toy Co.
820 Massachusetts
Lawrence, KS 66044
913-841-0100

(N2)
Norman's Olde & New Store
Philip Norman
126 W Main St.
Washington, NC 27889-4944
919-946-3448

(N3)
Neil's Wheels, Inc.
Box 354
Old Bethpage, NY 11804
516-293-9659
FAX 516-420-0483

(N4)
Roger Nazeley
4921 Castor Ave.
Philadelphia, PA 19124
FAX 215-288-8030

(O1)
Olde Tyme Toy Shop
120 S Main St.
Fairmount, IN 46928
317-948-3150
FAX 317-948-4257

(P2)
Dawn Parrish
9931 Gaynor Ave.
Granada Hills, CA 91343-1604
818-894-8964

(P3)
American Pie Collectibles
John and Sheri Pavone
29 Sullivan Rd.
Peru, NY 12972
518-643-0993; Internet
http://www.invis.com/collectiblescastle/americanpie/

(P4)
Plymouth Rock Toy Co.
P.O. Box 1202
Plymouth, MA 02362
508-746-2842 or 508-830-1880 (noon to 11 pm EDT); FAX 508-830-1880

(P5)
Gary Pollastro
5047 84th Ave. SE
Mercer, WA 98040
206-232-3199

(P6)
Judy Posner
R.D. 1, Box 273
Effort, PA 18330
717-629-6583
(or winter) 4195 South Tamiami Trail
Suite #183
Venice, FL 34293
941-497-7149

(P8)
Diane Patalano
P.O. Box 144
Saddle River, NJ 07458
201-327-2499

(P10)
Bill and Pat Poe
220 Dominica Circle E
Niceville, FL 32578-4068
904-897-4163; FAX 904-897-2606

(P11)
The Phoenix Toy Soldier Co.
Bob Wilson
P.O. Box 26365
Phoenix, AZ 85068
602-863-2891

(P12)
Michael Paquin, That Toy Guy
72 Penn Blvd.
E Lansdowne, PA 19050
610-394-8697 (10 am - 10 pm EST)
FAX 610-259-8626 (24 hr)

(P13)
Lorraine Punchard
8201 Pleasant Ave. South
Bloomington, MN 55420
612-888-1079

(R1)
David Richter
6817 Sutherland Dr.
Mentor, OH 44060-3917

(R2)
Rick Rann, Beatlelist
P.O. Box 877
Oak Park, IL 60303
708-442-7907

(R3)
Jim Rash
135 Alder Ave.
Egg Harbor Twp., NJ 08234-9302
609-646-4125 (evenings)

(R4)
Robert Reeves
104 Azalea Dr.
St. Mathews, SC 29135
803-578-5939 (leave message)

(R5)
Reynolds Toys
Charlie Reynolds
2836 Monroe St.
Falls Church, VA 22042
703-533-1322

(R6)
David E. Riddle
P.O. Box 13141
Tallahassee, FL 32308
904-877-7207

(R7)
Leo E. Rishty, Toy Doctor
77 Alan Loop
Staten Island, NY 10304

(R9)
Craig Reid
1911 E Sprague Ave.
Spokane, WA 99202
509-536-8489

(S1)
Sam Samuelian, Jr.
700 Llanfair Rd.
Upper Darby, PA 19082
215-566-7248

(S3)
Irwin Stern
407-483-1440 or 908-561-4880

(S5)
Son's a Poppin' Ranch
John Rammacher
1610 Park Ave.
Orange City, FL 32763-8869
904-775-2891

(S6)
Bill Stillman
Scarfone & Stillman Vintage Oz
P.O. Box 167
Hummelstown, PA 17036
717-566-5538

(S7)
Nate Stoller
960 Reynolds Ave.
Ripon, CA 95366
209-599-5933

(S8)
Steve Santi
19626 Ricardo Ave.
Hayward, CA 94541
510-481-2586

(S10)
Scott Smiles
848 SE Atlantic Dr.
Lantana, FL 33462-4702
407-582-4947

(S12)
Nancy Stewart Books
1188 NW Weybridge Way
Beaverton, OR 97006
503-645-9779

(S14)
Cindy Sabulis
P.O. Box 642
Shelton, CT 06484
203-926-0176

(S15)
Jim and Nancy Schaut
P.O. Box 10781
Glendale AZ 85318-0781
602-878-4293

(S16)
Bill Smith
56 Locust ST.
Douglas, MA 01516
508-476-2015

(S18)
The Silver Bullet
Terry and Kay Klepey
P.O. Box 553
Forks, WA 98331
360-327-3726

(S19)
Craig and Donna Stifter
P.O. Box 6514
Naperville, IL 60540
708-717-7949

(S20)
Pat and Kris Secor
P.O. Box 3367
Rock Island, IL 61204-3367
309-786-4870

(S21)
Stad's
815 N 12th St.
Allentown, PA 18102
610-770-1140 (days)
or FAX 610-770-1740

(S22)
Carole & Richard Smyth
Carole Smyth Antiques
P.O. Box 2068
Huntington, NY 11743

(S24)
Mark & Lynda Suozzi
P.O. Box 102
Ashfield, MA 01330
Phone or FAX 413-628-3241
(9am to 5pm)

(S25)
Steve Stevenson
11117 NE 164th Pl.
Bothell, WA 98011-4003
206-488-6265
FAX 206-488-2841

(T1)
Jon Thurmond
Collector Holics
15006 Fuller
Grandview, MO 64030
816-322-0906

(T2)
Toy Scouts, Inc.
Bill Bruegman
137 Casterton Ave.
Akron, OH 44303
216-836-0668
FAX 216-869-8668

(T3)
Richard Trautwein
Toys N Such
437 Dawson St.
Sault Ste. Marie, MI 49783
906-635-0356

(T4)
Toy Talk
2509 Brookside Drive
Lancaster, PA 17601
717-898-2932

(T5)
Bob and Marcie Tubbs
31 Westwood Rd.
Fairfield, CT 06432-1658
203-367-7499

(T6)
TV Collector
P.O. Box 1088
Easton, MA 02334
508-238-1179
or FAX by pre-set agreement

(V1)
Norm Vigue
62 Bailey St.
Stoughton, MA 02072
617-344-5441

(V2)
Marci Van Ausdall
P.O. Box 946
Quincy, CA 95971

(W1)
Dan Wells Antique Toys
P.O. Box 6751
Louisville, KY 40206
FAX 502-897-1598

(W4)
Randy Welch
1100 Hambrooks Blvd.
Cambridge, MD 21613
410-228-5390

(W5)
Linda and Paul Woodward
14 Argo Drive
Sewell, NJ 08080-1908
609-582-1253

(W6)
John D. Weatherhead
5224 S. Guerin Pass
New Berlin, WI 53151
414-425-4481

(Y1)
Henri Yunes
971 Main St., Apt. 2
Hackensack, NJ 07601
201-488-2236

(Y2)
Mary Young
1040 Greenridge Dr.
Kettering, OH 45429

Categories of Special Interest

If you would like to be included in this section, send us a list of your 'for sale' merchandise. These listings are complimentary to those who participate in the preparation of this guide by doing so. Read the paragraph under the title Dealer Codes for more information. If you have no catalogs or lists but would like to advertise with us, see the display ad rate sheet on page 477.

Action Figures
Also GI Joe, Star Wars and Super Heroes
John DiCicco
57 Bay View Dr.
Shrewsbury, MA 01545
508-797-0023

Captain Action, Star Wars, Secret Wars and other character-related Western, TV, movie, comic or paperback tie-ins
George Downes
Box 572
Nutley, NJ 07110
201-935-3388

Figures
Anthony Balasco
P.O. Box 19482
Johnston, RI 02919
401-946-5720
FAX 401-942-7980

GI Joe, Captain Action and other character-related TV, advertising, Marx and Mego figures; send $2 for sales catalog
Jerry and Ellen Harnish
110 Main St.
Bellville, OH 44813
Phone or FAX 419-886-4782

Advertising
Gary Metz
263 Key Lakewood Dr.
Moneta, VA 24121
540-721-2091
FAX 504-721-1782

Also general line
Mike's General Store
52 St. Annes Rd.
Winnipeg, Manitoba, Canada R2M 2Y3
204-255-3463
FAX 204-253-4124

Advertising figures, novelty radios, Barbies, promotional watches, character toys and more
Michael Paquin, That Toy Guy
72 Penn Blvd.
E Lansdowne, PA 19050
610-394-8697 (10 am - 10 pm EST) or
FAX 610-259-8626 (24 hrs)

Coca-Cola and Pepsi-Cola toys
Craig and Donna Stifter
P.O. Box 6514
Naperville, IL 60540
708-717-7949

Automobilia
Especially model kits, promotional model cars, books and literature
Model Auto
P.O. Box 79253
Houston, TX 77279
Phone or FAX 713-468-4461
(phone evenings; FAX anytime)

Banks
Ertl; sales lists available
Homestead Collectibles
Art and Judy Turner
R.D. 2, Rte. 150
P.O. Box 173-E
Mill Hall, PA 17751
717-726-3597
FAX 717-726-4488

Modern mechanical banks: Reynolds, John Wright, James Capron, Book of Knowledge, Richards, Wilton; sales lists available
Dan Iannotti
212 W. Hickory Grove Rd.
Bloomfield Hills, MI 48302-1127
810-335-5042

Also children's sadirons, Black Americana dolls and memorabilia
Diane Patalano
Country Girls Appraisal and Liquidation Service
P.O. Box 144
Saddle River, NJ 07458
201-327-2499

Penny banks (limited editions): new, original, mechanical, still or figural; also bottle openers
Reynolds Toys
Charlie Reynolds
2836 Monroe St.
Falls Church, VA 22042
703-533-1322

Ertl; First Gear
Toy Talk
2509 Brookside Dr.
Lancaster, PA 17601
717-898-2932

Barbie and Friends
Wanted: Mackies, holiday and porcelain as well as vintage Barbies; buying and selling ca 1959 dolls to present issues
Marl Davidson (Marl & B)
10301 Braden Run
Bradenton, FL 34202
941-751-6275
FAX 941-751-5463

Especially NRFB dolls ca 1980 to present, also Barbie Hallmark ornaments
Doris Gerton (Doris' Dolls & Collectibles)
325 E 10th St.
Mt. Vernon, IN 47620
Phone or FAX 812-835-5290

Battery-Operated
Tom Lastrapes
P.O. Box 2444
Pinellas Park, FL 34664
813-545-2586

Also Windups, Friction, Japan, Marx, etc.; broken is OK. Buy or trade
Leo E. Rishty
Toy Doctor
77 Alan Loop
Staten Island, NY 10304

Also general line
Mike Roscoe
3351 Lagrange
Toledo, OH 43608
419-244-6935

Boats and Toy Motors
Also Japanese wood toys
Dick Borgerding
RJB Toys
720 E Main St.
Flushing, MI 48433
810-659-9859

Books
Little Golden Books, Wonder Books, many others; 20-page list available
Ilene Kayne
1308 S Charles St.
Baltimore, MD 21230
410-685-3923

Specializing in Little Golden Books and look-alikes
Steve Santi
19626 Ricardo Ave.
Hayward, CA 94541
510-481-2586
Author of *Collecting Little Golden Books, Volumes I and II.* Also publishes newsletter, *Poky Gazette,* primarily for Little Golden Book collectors

Children's Books
Nancy Stewart Books
1188 NW Weybridge Way
Beaverton, OR 97006
503-645-9779

Breyer
Carol Karbowiak Gilbert
2193 14 Mile Rd. 206
Sterling Height, MI 48310
Author of *Breyer Value List*; available by sending $6.50 (includes shipping and handling) with information on models made through 1995 with their catalog numbers and colors

Bubble Bath Containers
Including foreign issues; also character collectibles, character bobbin' head nodders, and Dr. Dolittle; write for information or send SASE for Bubble Bath Bulletin
Matt and Lisa Adams
1234 Harbor Cove
Woodstock, GA 30189
770-516-6874

Building Blocks and Construction Toys
Arlan Coffman
1223 Wilshire Blvd., Ste. 275
Santa Monica, CA 90403
310-453-2507

Richter's Anchor (Union) Stone Building Blocks
George Hardy
1670 Hawkwood Ct.
Charlottesville, VA 22901
804-295-4863; FAX 804-295-4898

California Raisins
Ken Clee
Box 11412
Philadelphia, PA 19111
215-722-1979

California Raisins (PVC); buying collections, old store stock and closeouts
Larry DeAngelo
516 King Arthur Dr.
Virginia Beach, VA 23464
804-424-1691

John D. Weatherhead
5224 S. Guerin Pass
New Berlin, WI 53151
414-425-4481

Candy Containers
Jeff Bradfield
Corner of Rt. 42 and Rt. 257
Dayton, VA 22821
703-879-9961

Also Tonka, Smith-Miller, Shafford black cats, German nodders
Doug Dezso
864 Patterson Ave.
Maywood, NJ 07607
201-488-1311

Cast Iron
Pre-war, large-scale cast-iron toys and early American tinplate toys
John McKenna
801-803 W Cucharres
Colorado Springs, CO 80905
719-630-8732

Character and Promotional Glasses
Especially fast-foods and sports glasses; publishers of Collector Glass News
Mark Chase and Michael Kelly
P.O. Box 308
Slippery Rock, PA 16057
412-946-2838

Character Clocks and Watches
Also radio premiums and decoders, P-38 airplane-related items from World War II, Captain Marvel and Hoppy items, Lone Ranger books with jackets, selected old comic books, toys and cap guns; buys and sells Hoppy and Roy items
Bill Campbell
Kirschner Medical Corp.
1221 Littlebrook Ln.
Birmingham, AL 35235
205-853-8227; FAX 405-658-6986

Character Collectibles
All characters, TV stuff, monsters, Toy Story, Disney, etc. Extensive lists available
Jerry Alingh
505 5th Ave #302
Des Moines, IA 50309

Dolls, rock 'n roll personalities (especially the Beatles), related character items and miscellaneous toys
BOJO
Bob Gottuso
P.O. Box 1403
Cranberry Twp., PA 16066
Phone or FAX 412-776-0621

Children's plastic character cups by F&F, Deka, etc.; also related advertising and catalogs; SASE required when requesting information
Cheryl and Lee Brown
7377 Badger Ct.
Indianapolis, IN 46260

1940s-'60s character items such as super heroes, TV and cartoon items, games, playsets, lunch boxes, model kits, comic books and premium rings
Bill Bruegman
Toy Scouts, Inc.
137 Casterton Ave.
Akron, OH 44303
216-836-0668; FAX 216-869-8668

Hanna-Barbera, Warner Bros, Disney, vintage TV and 'toons; also collectible dolls of the '60s and '70s
John and Michele Casino
633 Franklin Ave., Suite #169
Nutley, NJ 07110
201-759-2520

TV, radio and comic collectibles; sports and non-sports cards; silver and golden age comics
Casey's Collectible Corner
HCR Box 31, Rt. 3
N Blenheim, NY 12131
607-588-6464

Disney, especially books and animation art
Cohen Books and Collectibles
Joel J. Cohen
P.O. Box 810310
Boca Raton, FL 33481
407-487-7888
FAX 407-487-3117

Early Disney, Western heroes, premiums and other related collectibles
Ron and Donna Donnelly
Saturday Heroes
P.O. Box 7047
Panama City Beach, FL 32413
904-234-7944

Dick Tracy collectibles; free appraisals of DT items with SASE and photo or detailed description
Larry Doucet
2351 Sultana Dr.
Yorktown Heights, NY 10598
914-245-1320

Large comprehensive catalog available by subscription ($2 for sample copy, $10 per yr for 4 issues, 1st class); 100% satisfaction guaranteed
52 Girls Collectibles
P.O. Box 36
Morral, OH 43337
614-465-6062

Rocketeer memorabilia
Don Hamm
712 N. Townsend St.
Syracuse, NY 13203
315-478-7035

Snoopy/Peanuts classics, new and old
M.R. Huber, The SNO-PEA Trader
931 Emerson St.
1000 Oaks, CA 91362
805-497-0119
FAX 1-800-SNO-OPY-2

Any and all, also Hartland figures
Terry-Mardis Ivers
Terri's Toys
419 S 1st St.
Ponca City, OK 74601
405-762-8697
FAX 405-765-5101

Characters from comic strips/comic books, related memorabilia
Jeff and Bob's Fun Stuff
7324 Reseda Blvd #168
Reseda, CA 91335
818-705-3368

TV characters and shows, original network stills from 1955-85, soundtrack albums from 1950-90
Jim's TV Collectibles
P.O. Box 4767
San Diego, CA 92764
Phone or FAX 619-462-1953

Games, models, action figures, dolls, general line; especially Nightmare Before Christmas
June Moon
245 N Northwest Hwy
Park Ridge, IL 60068
847-825-1411 (24-hour phone)
FAX 847-825-6090
Open 2 to 6 PM Tues - Sat

TV, Western, space, Beatles; auction as well as set-price catalogs available
Just Kids Nostalgia
310 New York Ave.
Huntington, NY 11743
516-423-8449; FAX 516-423-4326

Especially bendy figures and the Simpsons
K-3 Inc.
Bendees Only; Simpson Mania
2335 NW Thurman
Portland, OR 97210
503-222-2713

Auction house with consignments welcomed; specializing in western Hartlands and 1920s-60s toys
Kerry and Judy's Toys
7370 Eggleston Rd.
Memphis, TN 31825-2112
901-575-1722

Western stars of radio, movies and TV
Gene Mack
408 Yorkshire Blvd.
Syracuse, NY 13219
315-487-9023 (anytime)

Disney and other character collectibles
Kathy and Skip Matthews
Second Childhood Antiques & Collectibles
1154 Grand Ave.
Astoria, OR 97103
503-325-6543

Any and all, also gum cards, sports, movie posters, etc.
Mrs. Miller's Memorabilia
70a Greenwich Ave., Box 116
New York, NY 10011
212-614-9774 (leave message)

Especially Disney; send $5 for annual subscription (6 issues) for sale catalogs
The Mouse Man Ink
P.O. Box 3195
Wakefield, MA 01880
Phone or FAX 617-246-3876

General line, especially Raggedy Ann, Disneyana, Star Wars, GI Joe
Olde Tyme Toy Shop
Jim May and Debra Coleman
120 S Main St.
Fairmount, IN 46928
317-948-3150 or FAX 317-948-4257
Also tin windups, cast iron, old toy stock, cap pistols and trains

Especially pottery, china, ceramics, salt and pepper shakers, cookie jars, tea sets and children's china; with special interest in Black Americana and Disneyana; illustrated sale lists available
Judy Posner
R.D. #1, Box 273
Effort, PA 18330
717-629-6583
(or winter):
4195 South Tamiami Trail
Suite #183
Venice, FL 34293
941-497-7149

Buying, selling and trading original Beatles memorabilia
Rick Rann, Beatlelist
P.O. Box 877
Oak Park, IL 60303
708-442-7907

Special interest in Star Trek and Aurora slot cars
Craig Reid
1911 E Sprague Ave.
Spokane, WA 99202
509-536-8489

Also battery-ops, character clocks and novelties
Sam Samuelian, Jr.
700 Llanfair Rd.
Upper Darby, PA 19082
215-566-7248

Lone Ranger collector, buy and sell; publisher of Silver Bullet Newsletter (see Clubs, Newsletters and Other Publications)
The Silver Bullet
Terry and Kay Klepey
P.O. Box 553
Forks, WA 98331
360-327-3726

Wizard of Oz memorabilia; quarterly mail/phone bid auctions available for $2; always buying Oz
Bill Stillman
Scarfone and Stillman Vintage Oz
P.O. Box 167
Hummelstown, PA 17036
717-566-5538

General line; extensive inventory. Anything and everything
Jon Thurmond
Collector Holics
15006 Fuller
Grandview, MO 64030
816-322-0906

Especially tinplate toys and cars, battery-op toys and toy trains
Richard Trautwein
Toys N Such
437 Dawson St.
Sault Ste. Marie, MI 49783
906-635-0356

TV, movie, rock 'n roll, comic character, commercials, radio, theater, etc., memorabilia of all kinds; Send $4 for sale catalog. We are not interested in buying items. All inquiries must include SASE for reply unless ordering catalog
TV Collector
P.O. Box 1088
Easton, MA 02334
508-238-1179 or FAX by pre-set agreement

Games, premiums, cartoon personalities, Dick Tracy, Popeye, Buck Rogers, Flash Gordon, Tarzan, Lone Ranger and others
Norm Vigue
62 Bailey St.
Stoughton, MA 02072
617-344-5441

Especially Garfield, Smurfs, comic/character collectibles, dolls, monsters, premiums, etc. Lists available.
Adrienne Warren
1032 Feather Bed Lane
Edison, NJ 08820
908-381-7083 (EST)

Especially Disneyana and Roger Rabbit
Yesterday's Toys
Allen Day
P.O. Box 525
Monroe, NC 28810

Children's Play Dishes
Author of book
Lorraine Punchard
8201 Pleasant Ave. South
Bloomington, MN 55420
612-888-1079

Chinese Tin Toys
Also buying and selling antiques, old toys and collectibles; custom refinishing and quality repairing
Finisher's Touch Antiques
Steve Fisch, proprietor
10 W Main St.
Wappingers Falls, NY 12590
914-298-8882; FAX 914-298-8945

Comic Books
Also Western pulps, Big Little Books, magazines, Mad and other humor publications; large catalog available
Avalon Comics
Larry Curcio
P.O. Box 821
Medford, MA 02155
617-391-5614

Also Sunday comics, books, pulp magazines, premiums, character collectibles, non-sports cards and more
Ken Mitchell
710 Conacher Dr.
Wilowdale, Ontario
Canada M2M 3N6
416-222-5808 (anytime)

Dakins
Jim Rash
135 Alder Ave.
Egg Harbor Twp., NJ 08234-9302

Diecast
Matchbox, extensive lists available
Classic Golf & Collectibles
P.O. Box 8
Lake Havasu City, AZ 86406-0008
520-855-9623

Buying complete or partial collections of diecast banks, promos, and any Nascar products
Dr. Doors Miniatures
3111 S. Valley View, Suite O-104
Las Vegas, NV 89102
702-362-2722

Especially Dinky; also selling inexpensive restorable diecast as well as reproduction parts and decals for many diecast brands
Paul Fideler
20 Shadow Oak Dr., Apt. #18
Sudbury, MA 01776
617-386-0228 (24 hours)
FAX 617-386-0159 (24 hours)

Especially English-made toy vehicles
Mark Giles
510 E Third St.
Ogalala, NE 69153
308-284-4360

Especially Matchbox and other small-scale cars and trucks
Bill Jackameit
200 Victoria Dr.
Bridgewater, VA 22812
703-828-4359 (Mon. – Thurs., 7 – 9 pm EST)

Especially Matchbox, Hot Wheels, Majorette
Dana Johnson Enterprises
1347 NW Albany Ave.
Bend, OR 97701-3160
503-382-8410
Author/publisher of *Matchbox Blue Book, Hot Wheels Blue Book* and *Collecting Majorette Toys* (prices updated yearly)

Especially Dinky; also obsolete French, German, Italian and English-made vehicles
Jean-Claude Lanau
740 Thicket Ln.
Houston, TX 77079
713-4971-6034

Matchbox of all types including Dinky, Commando, Convoys, Harley-Davidson, Indy/Formula 1, and Looney Tunes; also Corgi, Hartoy, Hot Wheels, Tomica, and Tyco slot cars
Neil's Wheels, Inc.
Box 354
Old Bethpage, NY 11804
516-293-9659
FAX 516-420-0483

Also pressed steel trucks and comic character toys
Jim and Nancy Schaut
P.O. Box 10781
Glendale, AZ 85318-0781
602-878-4293

Ertl, banks, farm, trucks and construction
Son's a Poppin' Ranch
John Rammacher
1610 Park Ave.
Orange City, FL 32763-8869
904-775-2891

All types; also action figures such as GI Joe, Johnny West, Matt Mason and others
Robert Reeves
104 Azalea Dr.
St. Mathews, SC 29135
803-578-5939 (leave message)

Especially Soviet-made toys (marked USSR or CCCP)
David E. Riddle
P.O. Box 13141
Tallahassee, FL 32308
905-877-7207

Hot Wheels
Steve Stevenson
11117 NE 164th Pl.
Bothell, WA 98011-4003
206-488-6265 or FAX 206-488-2841

Especially Corgi and Dinky
Irwin Stern
407-483-1440 or 908-561-4880

Hot Wheels, Matchbox and all obsolete toy cars, trucks and airplanes
Dan Wells Antiques Toys
P.O. Box 6751
Louisville, KY 40206
502-896-0740

Dolls
Strawberry Shortcake dolls, accessories and related items
Geneva Addy
P.O. Box 124
Winterset, IA 50273
515-462-3027

Hard plastic and composition, Ginny and accessories, pincushion dolls, doll dishes; catalogs available
Roslyn L. Herman
124-16 84th Rd.
Kew Gardens, NY 11415
718-846-3496 or 718-846-8491

Chatty Cathy and Mattel
Kathy Lewis
187 N Marcello Ave.
Thousand Oaks, CA 91360
805-499-8101
Author of book: *Chatty Cathy Dolls, An Identification and Value Guide*

Ad dolls, Barbies and other Mattel dolls, premiums, character memorabilia, modern dolls, related items
Marcia Fanta
Marcia's Fantasy
RR 1, Box 107
Tappen, ND 58487-9635
701-327-4441

Holly Hobbie dolls and collectibles
Helen McCale
P.O. Box 397
Butler, MO 64730-0397
816-679-3690

Liddle Kiddles and other small dolls from the late '60s and early '70s
Dawn Parrish
9931 Gaynor Ave.
Granada Hills, CA 91343-1604
818-894-8964

Dolls from the 1960s-70s, including Liddle Kiddles, Barbie, Tammy, Tressy, etc. Co-author of The Collector's Guide to Tammy, the Ideal Teen (Collector Books)
Cindy Sabulis
P.O. Box 642
Shelton, CT 06484
203-926-0176

Betsy McCall
Marci Van Ausdall
P.O. Box 946
Quincy, CA 95971

Celebrity and character dolls
Henri Yunes
971 Main St., Apt. 2
Hackensack, NJ 07601
201-488-2236

Dollhouse Furniture
Renwal, Ideal, Marx, etc.
Judith A. Mosholder
R.D. #2, Box 147
Boswell, PA 15531
814-629-9277

Dollhouses
Tin and fiberboard dollhouses and plastic furniture from all eras
Bob and Marcie Tubbs
31 Westwood Rd.
Fairfield, CT 06432-1658
203-367-7499

Elvis Presley Collectibles
Rosalind Cranor
P.O. Box 859
Blacksburg, VA 24063
Author of books: *Elvis Collectibles, Best of Elvis Collectibles*

Ertl
Also Tonka, construction and logging toys, pressed steel, diecast toy trucks, Smokey Bear items
Glen Brady
P.O. Box 3933
Central Point, OR 97502
503-772-0350

Fast Food
All restaurants
Jim Christoffel
409 Maple
Elburn, IL 60119
708-365-2914

All restaurants and California Raisins
Ken Clee
Box 11412
Philadelphia, PA 19111
215-722-1979

McDonald's® only, especially older or unusual items
John and Eleanor Larsen
523 Third St.
Colusa, CA 95932
916-458-4769

McDonald's®
Terry and Joyce Losonsky
7506 Summer Leave Lane
Columbia, MD 21046-2455
410-381-3358
Authors of Illustrated *Collector's Guide to McDonald's® Happy Meals® Boxes, Premiums, and Promotionals* ($9 plus $2 postage), *McDonald's® Happy Meal® Toys in the USA* and *McDonald's® Happy Meal® Toys Around the World* (both full color, $24.95 each plus $3 postage), and Illustrated *Collector's Guide to McDonald's® McCAPS®* ($4 plus $2 postage)

Source for catalog: McDonald's® Collectibles and Other Fast-Food Toys and Memorabilia
Bill and Pat Poe
220 Dominica Circle E
Niceville, FL 32578-4068
904-897-4163; FAX 904-897-2606; Prodigy #ANEM34A
Send $3.00 for catalog; see Clubs, Newsletters and Other Publications for information on McDonald's club

Fisher-Price
Brad Cassidy
1350 Stanwix
Toledo, OH 43614
419-385-9910

Games
Victorian, cartoon, comic, TV and nostalgic themes
Paul Fink's Fun & Games
P.O. Box 488
59 S Kent Rd.
Kent, CT 06757
203-927-4001

Paul David Morrow
13550 Foothill Blvd. #28
Sylmar, CA 91342
818-898-9592

Circa 1900 to modern
Bill Smith
56 Locust St.
Douglas, MA 01516
508-476-2015

Gas-Powered Toys
Airplanes, cars and boats; publishes Gas Toy Collector newsletter
Danny Bynum
P.O. Box 440818
Houston, TX 77244-0818
713-531-5711

GI Joe
Also diecast and Star Wars
Cotswold Collectibles
P.O. Box 249
Clinton, WA 98236
360-579-1223
FAX 360-579-1287

Guns
Pre-WWII American spring-air BB guns, all Red Ryder BB guns, cap guns with emphasis on Western six-shooters; especially wanted are pre-WWII cast iron six-guns
Jim Buskirk
3009 Oleander Ave.
San Marcos, CA 92069
619-599-1054

Parts for 1940 cast-iron and 1950 diecast guns: steer-head grips, 2-pc silver or silver and brass bullets for Nicholas paint 6-shooter and spitfire rifle
ED Drew
7530 146th Ave. NE
Redmond, WA 98052
206-885-7378

Specializing in cap guns
Happy Memories Antique Toy Co.
The Hamburgs
P.O. Box 1305
Woodland Hills, CA 91365
818-346-9884 or 818-346-1269
FAX 818-346-0215

Also model kits, toy soldiers and character toys and watches; character watch service available
Plymouth Rock Toy Co.
P.O. Box 1202
Plymouth, MA 02362
508-746-2842 or 508-830-1880 (noon to 11 pm EDT); FAX 508-830-0364

Hartland Plastics, Inc.
Issues price guide
Gail Fitch
1733 N. Cambridge Ave.
Milwaukee, WI 53202

Specializing in Western Hartlands
Kerry and Judy's Toys
7370 Eggleston Rd.
Memphis, TN 38125-2112
901-757-1722

Halloween Collectibles
Also postcards
Pamela E. Apkarian-Russell
C.J. Russell and The Halloween Queen Antiques
P.O. Box 499
Winchester, NH 03470
603-239-8875

Lunch Boxes
Norman's Olde and New Store
Philip Norman
126 W Main St.
Washington, NC 27889-4944
919-946-3448

Also characters such as cowboys, TV shows, cartoons and more
Terri's Toys
Terri Ivers
1104 Shirlee Ave.
Ponca City, OK 74601
405-762-8697 or 405-762-5174
FAX 405-765-5101

M&M Toppers
Ken Clee
P.O. Box 11412
Phil., PA 19111
215-722-1979

Marionettes and Puppets
Steven Meltzer
670 San Juan Ave. #B
Venice, CA 90281
310-396-6007

Marx
Figures, playsets and character toys
G.F. Ridenour
Fun House Toy Co.
P.O. Box 343
Bradfordwoods, PA 15015-0343
412-935-1392 (FAX capable)

Model Kits
Specializing in figures and science fiction
Gordy Dutt
P.O. Box 201
Sharon Center, OH 44274-0201
330-239-1657
or 330-239-2991

Also action figures, monsters (especially Godzilla and Japan automated toys), Star Trek and non-sports cards
Alan Edwards
Toys From the Crypt
P.O. Box 3294
Shawnee, KS 66203
913-383-1242

From and of science fiction, TV, movies, figures, space, missiles, comics, etc.
John F. Green Inc.
1821 W. Jacaranda Pl
Fullerton, CA 92633
714-526-5467; 800-807-4759

Character, space, monster, Western, radio and cereal premiums and toys; GI Joe, Captain Action, tin toys and windups
Ed Janey
2920 Meadowbrook Dr. SE
Cedar Rapids, IA 52403
319-362-5213

Also plastic toys and radio, movie or TV tie-ins, movie posters
John and Sheri Pavone
29 Sullivan Rd.
Peru, NY 12972
518-643-0993; Internet http://www.invis.com/collectiblescastle/americanpie/

Non-Sport Trading Cards
Send $1 for our 40-page catalog of non-sport cards ca 1970 to date; dealers send large SASE for our 10-page wholesale and closeout list
Mark and Val Macaluso
3603 Newark Rd.
Marion, NY 14505
315-926-4349; FAX 315-926-4853

Paper Dolls
Author of books
Mary Young
1040 Greenridge Dr.
Kettering, OH 45429

Paper Lithographed Toys
Rare 18th-, 19th- and 20th-century games, paper dolls, books, etc.
Bromer Booksellers, Inc.
607 Boylston St.
Boston, MA 02116
617-247-2818; FAX 617-247-2975

Mark and Linda Suozzi
P.O. Box 102
Ashfield, MA 01330
Phone/FAX 413-628-3241 (9am to 5pm)

Pedal Cars
Also specializing in Maytag collectibles
Nate Stoller
960 Reynolds Ave.
Ripon, CA 95366
510-481-2586

Penny Toys
Jane Anderson
R.R. 5, Box 5525
Saylorsburg, PA 18353

Pez Candy Dispensers
Richard Belyski
P.O. Box 124
Sea Cliff, NY 11579

Plastic Figures
Also Dakins, cartoon and advertising figures, and character squeeze toys
Jim Rash
135 Alder Ave.
Egg Harbor Twp., NJ 08234-9302
609-649-4125

Stad's
815 N 12th St.
Allentown, PA 18102
610-770-1140 (days)
FAX 610-770-1740

Playsets
Also GI Joe, Star Trek and dinosaurs
Mike and Kurt Fredericks
145 Bayline Circle
Folsom, CA 95630-8077

Political Toys
Michael and Polly McQuillen
McQuillen's Collectibles
P.O. Box 11141
Indianapolis, IN 46201
317-322-8518

Promotional Vehicles
'50s and '60s models (especially Ford); also F&F Post Cereal cars; author of 2 books on promotional model cars, both available directly from him
Larry Blodget
Box 753
Rancho Mirage, CA 92270
619-862-1979

Puzzles
Wood jigsaw type, from before 1950
Bob Armstrong
15 Monadnock Rd.
Worcester, MA 01609

Specializing in advertising puzzles
Donald Friedman
660 W Grand Ave
Chicago, IL 60610
Day phone: 708-656-3700
Evenings and weekends: 312-226-4741
FAX 708-656-6292

Radio Premiums
Also Fisher-Price; lists available
Pat and Kris Secor
P.O. Box 3367
Rock Island, IL 61204-3367
309-786-4870

Radios
Authors of several books on antique, novelty, and transistor radios
Sue and Marty Bunis
RR 1, Box 36
Bradford, NH 03221-9102

Ramp Walkers
Specializing in walkers, ramp-walking figures, and tin windups
Randy Welch
1100 Hambrooks Blvd.
Cambridge, MD 20783
410-228-5390

Records
78 rpm children's records and picture disks; buys, sells, and trades records as well as makes cassette recordings for a small fee
Peter Muldavin
173 W 78th St., Apt. 5-F
New York, NY 10024
212-362-9606

Russian and East European Toys
Wooden Matrioskha dolls, toys of tin, plastic, diecast metal; military theme and windups
Natural Way/DBA Russian Toy Co.
820 Massachusetts
Lawrence, KS 66044
913-841-0100

Specializing in Russian toys
David E. Riddle
P.O. Box 13141
Tallahassee, FL 32308
904-877-7207

Sand Toys
Jane Anderson
Rt. 1, Box 1030
Saylorsburg, PA 18353

Authors of book; send $25 plus $3 for postage for a signed copy. New York residents please add 8¼% sales tax.
Carole and Richard Smyth
Carole Smyth Antiques
P.O. Box 2068
Huntington, NY 11743

Schoenhut
Publishers of Inside Collector and Antique Doll World
Keith and Donna Kaonis
60 Cherry Ln.
Huntington, NY 11743
516-261-8337 or FAX 516-261-8235

Slot Cars
Especially HO scale from the 1960s to the present; also vintage diecast
Joe Corea
New Jersey Nostalgia Hobby
401 Park Ave.
Scotch Plains, NJ 07076
908-322-2676; FAX 908-322-4079

Specializing in slots and model racing from the '60s-'70s; especially complete race sets in original boxes
Gary Pollastro
5047 84th Ave. SE
Mercer, WA, 98040
206-232-3199

Snow Domes

Broad assortment from states, cities, tourist attractions, novelties, also glass domes; list available
Nancy McMichael
P.O. Box 53262
Washington DC 20009
Editor of *Snow Biz*, quarterly newsletter, see Clubs, Newsletters and Other Publications

Soldiers

Barclay, Manoil, Grey Iron, Jones, dimestore types and others; also Syrocco figures
Stan and Sally Alekna
4724 Kernan Mill Lane E
Jacksonville, FL 32224
904-992-9525

Recasts, conversions, diorama work; price list available
Bryan and Val Davis
3132 E. Prince Rd.
Tucson, AZ 85716
502-323-2598 (9 am - 7 pm, Mountain Standard)

Auburn, Airfix, Atlantic, etc; also Marx plastic figures, playsets and accessories; lists available with SASE
Phoenix Toy Soldier Co.
Bob Wilson
P.O. Box 26365
Phoenix, AZ 85068
602-863-2891

Sports Bobbin' Head Dolls

Tim Hunter
1668 Golddust
Sparks, NV 89436
702-626-5029

Star Wars

Also vehicles, model kits, GI Joes, games, ad figures, View-Master, non-sports cards, Star Trek, advertising, antiques, fine art and much more
June Moon
Jim and Nancy Frugoli
245 N Northwest Hwy
Park Ridge, IL 60068
847-825-1411 (24-hr phone)
FAX 847-825-6090
Open 2 to 6 PM Tues - Sat

Steiff

Also Schucos and children's things
Candelaine (Candice Gunther)
Pasadena, CA 91103-2320
818-796-4586; FAX 818-796-7172

Especially limited editions
Cynthia's Country Store
12794 W Forest Hill Blvd
West Palm Beach, FL 33414
407-793-0554 or FAX 407-795-4222

Particularly bears; also Schucos and dolls
Bunny Walker
Box 502
Bucyrus, OH 44820; 419-562-8355

Tonka

Also candy containers and German nodders
Doug Dezso
864 Patterson Ave.
Maywood, NJ 07607
201-488-1311

Toothbrush Holders

Also Pez
Marilyn Cooper
8408 Lofland Dr.
Houston, TX 77055

Tootsietoys

David Richter
6817 Sutherland Dr.
Mentor, OH 44060-3917
Author of *Collector's Guide to Tootsietoys*

Tops and Other Spinning Toys

Yo-yos, advertising spinners, gyroscopes, spinning games, Victorian figural tops; any unique spinning toy. Buy, sell, trade
Bruce Middleton
5 Lloyd Rd.
Newburgh, NY 12550
914-564-2556

Trains

Lionel, American Flyer and Plasticville
Gary's Trains
R.D. #2, Box 147
Boswell, PA 15531
814-629-9277

Also Fisher-Price, Tonka toys and diecast vehicles
Bill Mekalian
550 E Chesapeake Cir.
Fresno, CA 93720
209-434-3247

Buying American Flyer S gauge. Toys of all types for sale. Satisfaction guaranteed; color photos with SASE; shipping extra. No return calls on sold items; phone until midnight
Linda and Paul Woodward
14 Argo Drive
Sewell, NJ 08080-1908
609-582-1253

Toy mall; general line (toys on 2nd floor)
Bo-Jo's Antique Mall
3400 Summer Avenue
Memphis, TN 38122
901-323-2050

Transformers

Specializing in Transformers, Robotech, Shogun Warriors, Gadaikins, and any other robot; want to buy these MIP — also selling
David Kolodny-Nagy
May – Jan:
3701 Connecticut Ave. NW #500
Washington, DC 20008

Jan – May:
MB 845 Brandeis University
P.O. Box 9110
Waltham, MA 02251-9110
202-364-8753
For copy of *BotCon Transformer Comic Book, Comic Smorgasbord Special*, send $3 + $1.50 for single issues, $2.50 each for 10 or more + $2. Also available: *Transformers: BotCon '94 Ten-Year Retrospective* (130+ pages) at $15 + $2

Trolls

Roger Inouye
765 E. Franklin Ave.
Pomona, CA 91766

View-Master

Also games, slot cars, Pez, lunch boxes, Halloween costumes, dolls, premiums, TV Guides, Mad magazines
Tom Bremer
P.O. Box 49
Newark, NY 14513
Phone or FAX 315-331-8146

Roger Nazeley
4921 Castor Ave.
Phil., PA 19124
FAX 215-288-8030

Windups

Especially German and Japan tin toys, Cracker Jack, toothbrush holders, radio premiums, pencil sharpeners and comic strip toys
Phil Helley
Old Kilbourne Antiques
629 Indiana Ave.
Wisconsin Dells, WI 53965
608-254-8770

Also pressed steel toys, battery-ops, candy containers, dolls and children's things, games, soldiers, Noah's ark, space, robots, etc.
Jacquie and Bob Henry
Antique Treasures and Toys
Box 17
Walworth, NY 14568-0017
315-986-1424

Fine character windups; also Black Americana
Stephen Leonard
Box 127
Albertson, LI, NY 11507
516-742-0979

Also friction and battery operated; fast-food toys, displays
Scott Smiles
848 SE Atlantic Dr.
Lantana, FL 33462-4702
407-582-4947

Yo-Yos

Lucky Meisenheimer
7300 Sand Lake Commons Blvd.
Orlando, FL 32819
407-354-0478

Clubs, Newsletters and Other Publications

There are hundreds of clubs, newsletters and magazines available to toy collectors today. Listed here are some devoted to specific areas of interest. You can obtain a copy of many newsletters simply by requesting a sample.

Action Figure News & Toy Review
James Tomlinson, Editor
556 Monroe Turnpike
Monroe, CT 06458
203-452-7286
FAX 203-452-0410

Action Toys Newsletter
P.O. Box 31551, Billings, MT 59107
406-248-4121

The Antique Trader Weekly
Kyle D. Husfloen, Editor
P.O. Box 1050
Dubuque, IA 52004

American Game Collectors Assn.
49 Brooks Ave.
Lewiston, MA 04240

American International Matchbox Collectors & Exchange Club News-Monthly
Dottie Colpitts
532 Chestnut St.
Lynn, MA 01904
617-595-4135

Anchor Block Foundation
908 Plymouth St.
Pelham, NY 10303; 914-738-2935

Antique Advertising Association
P.O. Box 1121
Morton Grove, IL 60053
708-446-0904

Antique & Collectors Reproduction News
Mark Cherenka
Circulation Department
P.O. Box 71174
Des Moines, IA 50325; 800-227-5531
Monthly newsletter showing differences between old originals and new reproductions; subscription: $32 per year

Antique Trader Weekly
Kyle D. Husfloen, Editor
P.O. Box 1050
Dubuque, IA 52004
Subscription $32 (52 issues) per year

The Autograph Review (newsletter)
Jeffrey Morey
305 Carlton Rd.
Syracuse, NY 13207; 315-474-3516

Autographs & Memorabilia
P.O. Box 224
Coffeyville, KS 67337; 316-251-5308
6 issues per year on movie and sports memorabilia

Barbie Bazaar (magazine)
5617 Sixth Ave., Dept NY593
Kenosha, WI 53140; 414-658-1004; FAX 414-658-0433. 6 issues for $25.95

Barbie Talks Some More!
Jacqueline Horning
7501 School Rd.
Cincinnati, OH 45249

The Baum Bugle
The International Wizard of Oz Club
Fred M. Meyer
220 N 11th St.
Escanaba, MI 49829

Berry-Bits
Strawberry Shortcake Collectors' Club
Peggy Jimenez
1409 72nd St.
N Bergen, NJ 07047

Beyond the Rainbow Collector's Exchange
P.O. Box 31672
St. Louis, MO 63131

Big Little Times
Big Little Book Collectors Club of America
Larry Lowery
P.O. Box 1242
Danville, CA 94526; 415-837-2086

Bojo
P.O. Box 1203
Cranberry Township, PA 16033-2203; 412-776-0621 (9 am to 9 pm EST). Issues fixed-price catalog containing Beatles and Rock 'n' Roll memorabilia

Buckeye Marble Collectors Club
Betty Barnard
472 Meadowbrook Dr.
Newark, Oh 43055; 614-366-7002

Bulletin
Doll Collectors of America
14 Chestnut Rd.
Westford, MA 01886; 617-692-8392

Canadian Toy Collectors Society
Gary A. Fry
P.O. Box 636
Maple, Ontario, Canada L6A 1S5

Candy Container Collectors of America
P.O. Box 352
Chelmsford, MA 01824-0352
or Jeff Bradfield
90 Main St.
Dayton, VA 22821

The Candy Gram newsletter
Candy Container Collectors of America
Douglas Dezso
864 Paterson, Ave.
Maywood, NJ 07607; 201-845-7707

Captain Action Collectors Club
P.O. Box 2095
Halesite, NY 11743; 516-423-1801
Send SASE for newsletter information

Cast Iron Toy Collectors of America
Paul McGinnis
1340 Market St.
Long Beach, CA 90805

Cat Collectors Club
33161 Wendy Dr.
Sterling Heights, MI 48310
Subscription: $18 per year

Cat Talk
Marilyn Dipboye
31311 Blair Dr.
Warren, MI 48092; 313-264-0285

Century Limited
Toy Train Collectors Society
160 Dexter Terrace
Tonawanda, NY 14150; 716-694-3771

Children's Cups America
Cheryl and Lee Brown
7377 Badger Ct.
Indianapolis, IN 46260; newsletter, information share, free ad space; send SASE

Coca-Cola Collectors Club International
P.O. Box 49166
Atlanta, GA 30359. Annual dues: $25

Collecting Tips Newsletter
% Meredith Williams
P.O. Box 633
Joplin, MO 64802; 417-781-3855 or 417-624-2518. 12 issues per year focusing on fast-food collectibles

Collector Glass News
P.O. Box 308
Slippery Rock, PA 16057; 412-946-9012; FAX 412-946-2838. 6 issues per year focusing on character glasses, $15 per year

The Cookie Jar Collector's Club News
Louise Messina Daking
595 Cross River Rd.
Katonah, NY 10536
914-232-0383
FAX 914-232-0384

Cookie Jarrin' With Joyce: The Cookie Jar Newsletter
R.R. 2, Box 504
Walterboro, SC 29488

Cynthia's Country Store
Wellington Mall #15A
12794 West Forest Hill Blvd.
West Palm Beach, FL 33414
FAX or Phone 407-793-0554
Specializing in Steiff new, discontinued and antique. Publishes quarterly Steiff and bear-related newsletter and limited edition yearly price guide. $15 per year for both. Call or FAX for information or if you have any questions. Also specializes in pieces by R. John Wright, other bear manufacturers, toy soldiers and some old toys. Many Steiff color catalogs and books available.

Dark Shadows Collectibles Classified
Sue Ellen Wilson
6173 Iroquois Trail
Mentor, OH 44060
216-946-6348
For collectors of both old and new series

Dionne Quint Collectors Club (see also *Quint News*)
Jimmy Rodolfos
P.O. Box 2527
Woburn, MA 01888
617-933-2219

Doll Castle News Magazine
P.O. Box 247
Washington, NJ 07882; 908-689-7042 or FAX 908-689-6320; Subscription: $16.95 per year or $31.95 for 2 years; issued 6 times a year, serves general interests of doll and miniature collectors as well as dollmaking

Doll Investment Newsletter
P.O. Box 1982
Centerville, MA 02632

Doll News
United Federation of Doll Clubs
P.O. Box 14146
Parkville, MO 64152

Dollhouse & Miniature Collectors Quarterly
Sharon Unger, Editor
P.O. Box 16
Bellaire, MI 49615; $20.00 for 4 issues per year, 45-50 pages of information, buy & sell ads, pricing information.

Dunbar's Gallery
76 Haven St.
Milford, MA 01757
508-634-8697; FAX 508-634-8698
Specializing in quality advertising, Halloween, toys, coin-operated machines; holding cataloged auctions occasionally, lists available

Ephemera News
The Ephemera Society of America, Inc.
P.O. Box 37, Schoharie, NY 12157
518-295-7978

The Ertl Replica
Ertl Collectors Club
Mike Meyer, Editor
Hwys 136 & 20
Dyersville, IA 52040; 319-875-2000

The Fisher-Price Collector's Club
This club issues a quarterly newsletter packed with information and ads for toys. For more information write to:
Fisher-Price Club, CC Jeanne Kennedy
1442 N. Ogden
Mesa, AZ 85205

FLAKE, The Breakfast Nostalgia Magazine
P.O. Box 481
Cambridge, MA 02140; 617-492-5004. Bimonthly illustrated issue devoted to one hot collecting area such as Disney, etc., with letters, discoveries, new releases, and ads; single issue: $4 ($6 foreign); annual: $20 ($28 foreign); free 25-word ad with new subscription

Friends of Hoppy Club and Newsletter
Laura Bates
6310 Friendship Dr.
New Concord, OH 43762-9708
614-826-4850

Game Times
American Game Collectors Assn.
Joe Angiolillo, Pres.
4628 Barlow Dr.
Bartlesville, OK 74006

Garfield Collectors Society Newsletter
% David L. Abrams, Editor
744 Foster Ridge Rd.
Germantown, TN 38138-7036
901-753-1026

Gas Toy Collector
P.O. Box 440818
Houston, TX 77244-0818; Membership: $15 per year; sample issue $1.00

Gene Autry Star Telegram
Gene Autry Development Assn.
Chamber of Commerce
P.O. Box 158
Gene Autry, OK 73436

Ginny Doll Club News
Jeanne Niswonger
305 W Beacon Rd.
Lakeland, FL 33803; 813-687-8015

Gone With the Wind Collectors Club Newsletter
8105 Woodview Rd.
Ellicot City, MD 21043; 301-465-4632

Good Bears of the World
Terri Stong
P.O. Box 13097
Toledo, OH 43613

Grandma's Trunk
P.O. Box 404
Northport, MI 49670
Subscription: $8 per year for 1st class or $5 per year for bulk rate

Hartland Newsletter
Gail Fitch
1733 N. Cambridge Ave., #109
Milwaukee, WI 53202
Subscription: $8 for 6 issues or $4.50 for 3 issues. Classified ads are $2 for 50 words.

Headquarters Quarterly, for GI Joe Collectors
Joe Bodnarchuk
62 McKinley Ave.
Kenmore, NY 14217-2414

Hello Again, Old-Time Radio Show Collector
Jay A. Hickerson
P.O. Box 4321
Hamden, CT 06514
203-248-2887
FAX 203-281-1322
Sample copy upon request with SASE

Highballer for Toy Train collectors
% Lou Bohn
109 Howedale Dr.
Rochester, NY 14616-1543

Hobby News
J.L.C. Publications
Box 258
Ozone Park, NY 11416

Holly Hobbie Collectibles of America
c/o Helen McCale
P.O. Box 397
Butler, MO 64730-0397
Send SASE for membership application and information regarding bimonthly newsletter, ads, and conventions; appraisals may be obtained by sending $5 per item to cover expenses; sample newsletters available by sending 55¢-SASE

Hopalong Cassidy Fan Club International
Laura Bates
6310 Friendship Dr.
New Concord, OH 43762
614-826-4850
Subscription: $15 (USA) or $20 (Canada and overseas); includes quarterly newsletter and information on annual Cambridge, Ohio, festival

Hopalong Cassidy Newsletter
Hopalong Cassidy Fan Club
P.O. Box 1361
Boyes Hot Springs, CA 95416

Ideal Doll & Toy Collectors Club
P.O. Box 623
Lexington, MA 02173; 617-862-2994

International Figure Kit Club
Gordy's
P.O. Box 201
Sharon Center, OH 44274-0201; 216-239-1657; FAX 216-239-2991

International Wizard of Oz Club Inc.
P.O. Box 95
Kinderhook, IL 62345

Kit Builders Magazine
Gordy's
P.O. Box 201
Sharon Center, OH 44274-0201; 216-239-1657; FAX 216-239-2991

Madame Alexander Fan Club Newsletter
Earl Meisinger
11 S 767 Book Rd.
Naperville, IL 60564

Marble Mania
Marble Collectors Society of America
Stanley Block
P.O. Box 222
Trumbull, CT 06611; 203-261-3223

Martha's Kidlit Newsletter
Box 1488A
Ames, IA 50010. A bimonthly publication for children's books collectors. Subscription: $25 per year

Matchbox USA
Charles Mack
62 Saw Mill Rd.
Durham, CT 06422; 203-349-1655

McDonald's® Collecting Tips
Meredith Williams
Box 633
Joplin, MO 64802. Send SASE for information

McDonald's® Collector Club
Joyce and Terry Losonsky
7506 Summer Leave Ln.
Columbia, MD 21046-2455; 301-381-3358. Authors of *Illustrated Collector's Guide to McDonald's® Happy Meal® Boxes, Premiums, & Promotions®* ($9 plus $2 postage), *McDonald's® Happy Meal® Toys in the USA* and *McDonald's® Happy Meal® Toys Around the World* (both full color, $24.95 plus $3 postage), and *Illustrated Collector's Guide to McDonald's® McCAPS®* ($4 plus $2), both available from the authors.

McDonald's® Collector Club 'Sunshine Chapter'
Bill and Pat Poe, founders
c/o Dominica Circle. E.
Niceville, FL 32578-4068; 904-897-4163; FAX 904-897-2606

McDonald's® Collector Club Newsletter
% Tenna Greenberg
5400 Waterbury Rd.
Des Moines, IA 50312
515-279-0741

Model & Toy Collector Magazine
Toy Scouts, Inc.
137 Casterton Ave.
Akron, OH 44303
216-836-0668; FAX 216-869-8668

Modern Doll Club Journal
Jeanne Niswonger
305 W Beacon Rd.
Lakeland, FL 33803

The Mouse Club East (Disney collectors)
P.O. Box 3195
Wakefield, MA 01880. Family membership: $25 (includes newsletters and 2 shows per year)

The Mouse Club (newsletter)
Kim and Julie McEuen
2056 Cirone Way
San Jose, CA 95124
408-377-2590; FAX 408-379-6903

Movie Advertising Collector (magazine)
George Reed
P.O. Box 28587
Phil., PA 19149

NAOLH Newsletter
National Assn. for Outlaw & Lawman History
Hank Clark
P.O. Box 812
Waterford, CA 95386; 209-874-2640

NAPAC Newsletter
National Assn. of Paper and Advertising Collectors
P.O. Box 500
Mt. Joy, PA 17552
717-653-4300

National Fantasy Fan Club
(for Disney collectors)
Dept. AC, Box 19212
Irvine, CA 92713
Membership: $20 per year, includes newsletters, free ads, chapters, conventions, etc.

National Headquarters News
Train Collectors Assn.
300 Paradise Ln.
Strasburg, PA 17579

Novelty Salt and Pepper Club
% Irene Thornburg, Membership Coordinator
581 Joy Rd.
Battle Creek, MI 49017
Publishes quarterly newsletter & annual roster. Annual dues: $20 in USA, Canada and Mexico; $25 for all other countries

Old Toy Soldier
The Journal for Collectors
209 N Lombard Ave.
Oak Park, IL 60302; 708-383-6525 or FAX 708-383-2182. Subscription: $35 per year for 6 issues (1st class U.S. mail); current sample copy available by sending $3. Written for collectors by collectors, this magazine shares useful information on military and civilian toy figures and the companies that produced them

On Line With Betsy McCall
Marci Van Ausdall
P.O. Box 946
Quincy, CA 95971. Subscription: $10 per year for 4 issues

Paper Collectors' Marketplace
470 Main St., P.O. Box 128
Scandinavia, WI 54977; 715-467-2379. Subscription: $17.95 (12 issues) per year in USA; Canada and Mexico add $15 per year

Paper Doll News
Emma Terry
P.O. Box 807
Vivian, LA 71082

Paper Pile Quarterly
P.O. Box 337
San Anselmo, CA 94979-0337; 415-454-5552. Subscription: $12.50 per year in USA and Canada

Peanuts Collector Club Newsletter
Peanuts Collector Club
Andrea C. Podley
P.O. Box 94
N Hollywood, CA 91603

The Pencil Collector
American Pencil Collectors Soc.
Robert J. Romey, Pres.
2222 S Millwood
Wichita, KS 67213; 316-263-8419

Pepsi-Cola Collectors Club Newsletter
Pepsi-Cola Collectors Club
Bob Stoddard
P.O. Box 1275
Covina, CA 91722; 714-593-8750
Membership: $15

Pez Collector's News
Richard and Marianne Belyski, Editors
P.O. Box 124
Sea Cliff, NY 11579; 516-676-1183
First issue due to be released October 1995; call for information

Piece by Piece
Frances Main, Editor
P.O. Box 12823
Kansas City, KS 66112-9998; for Springbok puzzle collectors; subscription: $8 per year

Plastic Figure & Playset Collector
5894 Lakeview Ct. E
Onalaska, WI 54650

The Pokey Gazette, A Little Golden Book collector newsletter
Steve Santi
19626 Ricardo Ave.
Hayward, CA 94541
510-481-2586

The Prehistoric Times
Mike and Kurt Fredericks
145 Bayline Circle
Folsom, CA 95630
916-985-7986
For collectors of dinosaur toys; 6 issues (1 yr), $19

The Puppet Collector's Newsletter
Steven Meltzer
670 San Juan Ave. #B
310-396-6007

Quint News (see also Dionne Quint Collectors Club)
Dionne Quint Collectors
P.O. Box 2527
Woburn, MA 01888
617-933-2219

Record Collectors Monthly (newspaper)
P.O. Box 75
Mendham, NJ 07945
201-543-9520
FAX 201-543-6033

Roy Rogers-Dale Evans Collectors Assn.
Nancy Horsley
P.O. Box 1166
Portsmouth, OH 45662

Schoenhut Collectors Club
For membership information:
Patricia J. Girbach
1003 W Huron St.
Ann Arbor, MI 48103-4217

The Shirley Temple Collectors News
8811 Colonial Rd.
Brooklyn, NY 11209
Dues: $20 per year; checks payable to Rita Dubas

The Silent Film Newsletter
Gene Vazzana
140 7th Ave.
New York, NY 10011
Subscription $18, send $2.50 for sample copy

The Silver Bullet
Terry and Kay Klepey
P.O. Box 553
Forks, WA 98331; 206-327-3726. Subscription $10 per year, sample issue $4; also licensed mail-order seller of memorabilia and appraiser

Smurf Collectors Club
24ACH, Cabot Rd. W
Massapequa, NY 11758. Membership includes newsletters. LSASE for information

Snow Biz
c/o Nancy McMichael
P.O. Box 53262
Washington, DC 20009. Quarterly newsletter (subscription $10 per year) and collector's club, annual meeting/swap meet

Steiff Life
Steiff Collectors Club
Beth Savino
% The Toy Store
7856 Hill Ave.
Holland, OH 43528
419-865-3899 or 800-862-8697

The Television History Magazine
William J. Flechner
700 E Macoupin St.
Staunton, IL 62088; 618-635-2712

Toy Collector Club of America (for Ertl toys)
P.O. Box 302
Dyersdille, IA 52040; 800-452-3303

Toy Dish Collectors
Abbie Kelly
P.O. Box 351
Camillus, NY 13031
315-487-7415

Toy Gun Collectors of America Newsletter
Jim Buskirk, Editor and Publisher
3009 Oleander Ave.
San Marcos, CA 92069; 619-599-1054;
Published quarterly, covers cap guns, spring air BB guns and other toy guns. Dues: $15 per year; SASE for information

Toy Shop
700 E State St.
Iola, WI 54990
715-445-2214
Subscription (3rd class) $23.95 for 26 issues

Toy Trader
100 Bryant St.
Dubuque, Iowa 52003
1-800-364-5593; subscription in US $24 for 12 issues

Toychest
Antique Toy Collectors of America, Inc.
2 Wall St., 13th Floor
New York, NY 10005
212-238-8803

Toys & Prices (magazine)
700 E State St.
Iola, WI 54990-0001
715-445-2214; FAX 715-445-4087
Subscription: $14.95 per year

Transformer Club
Liane Elliot
6202 34th St., NW
Gig Harbor, WA 98335

The Trick or Treat Trader
CJ Russell and the Halloween Queen Antiques
P.O. Box 499, 4 Lawrence St. and Rt. 10
Winchester, NH, 03470
Subscription is $15 a year for 4 issues or $4 for a sample.

Trainmaster (newsletter)
P.O. Box 1499
Gainesville, FL 32602
904-377-7439 or 904-373-4908
FAX 904-374-6616

Troll Monthly
5858 Washington St.
Whitman, MA 02382
800-858-7655 or 800-85-Troll

Turtle River Farm Toys
Rt. 1, Box 44
Manvel, ND 58256-9763

The TV Collector
Diane L. Albert
P.O. Box 1088
Easton, MA 02334-1088
508-238-1179; Send $4 for sample copy

View-Master Reel Collector
Roger Nazeley
4921 Castor Ave.
Phil., PA 19124
215-743-8999

Western & Serials Club
Rt. 1, Box 103
Vernon Center, NM 56090
507-549-3677

The Working Class Hero (Beatles newsletter)
3311 Niagara St.
Pittsburgh, PA 15213-4223
Published 3 times per year; send SASE for information

The Wrapper
Bubble Gum & Candy Wrapper Collectors
P.O. Box 573
St. Charles, IL 60174
708-377-7921

The Yellow Brick Road Fantasy Museum & Gift Shop
Rt. 49 and Yellow Brick Rd.
Chesterton, IN 46304
219-926-7048

Yo-Yo Times
P.O. Box 1519-SCT
Herndon, VA 22070

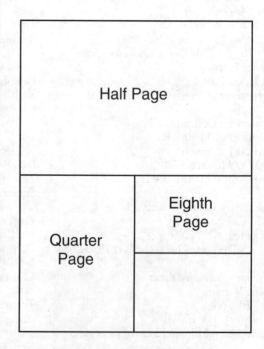

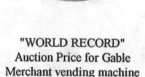

Antique Toys and Collectibles

Auctions held in our galleries at Christie's East,
219 East 67th Street, New York, New York 10021.
For further information, please contact the Collectibles
Department at 212 606 0543. For auction catalogues,
please telephone Christie's Publications at
800 395 6300.

A rare tinplate Marklin Ferris Wheel, circa 1890s, 21 in. high.
Sold at Christie's New York, June 1994, for $55,200.

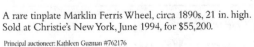
Principal auctioneer: Kathleen Guzman #762176

CHRISTIE'S
EAST

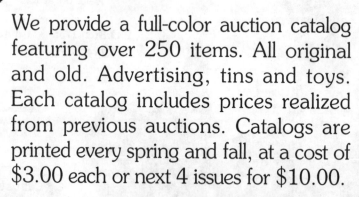
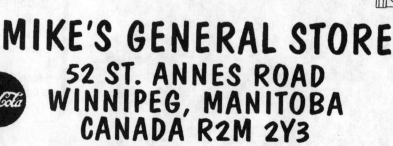

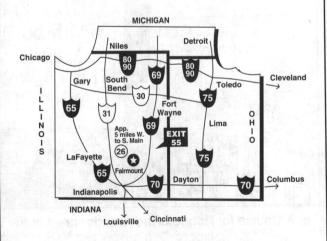

Index to Advertisers